PRIMA Official Game Guide

Written by:

David S.J. Hodgson

Prima Games

An Imprint of Random House, Inc.

3000 Lava Ridge Court, Suite 100

Roseville, CA 95661

www.primagames.com

Senior Product Manager: Mario De Govia

Product Manager: Shaida Boroumand

Interior Design: Jamie Bryson and Jody Seltzer

Layout: Jody Seltzer

Technical & Screenshot Editor: Tracy Erickson

Maps: 99 Lives Design

Copy Editor: Asha Johnson

Manufacturing: Stephanie Sanchez

ISBN: 978-0-307-46994-6

Library of Congress Catalog Card Number: 2010936884

Printed in the United States of America

10 11 12 13 LL 10 9 8 7 6 5 4 3 2 1

Bethesda Softworks Credits

Written By:
David S.J. Hodgson

Concept Artist:
Brian Menze

Additional Editing:
Sam Bernstein, Regi Jacob, Michael McGinn, Joe Mueller, Ian Rogers, Dan Ross, Greg Ruddick, Andrew Scharf, Jen Tonon

Editors-in-Chief:
Willam Noble
Pete Hines

Fallout New Vegas Executive Producer:
Jason Bergman

Special Thanks to:
J.E. Sawyer, Chris Avellone, Lawrence Liberty, Charlie Staples, John Gonzalez, Jesse Farrell, Eric Fenstermaker, Akil Hooper, Jeff Husges, Rob Lee, Jorge Salgado, Matt Singh, Travis Stout, J.R. Vosovic, Eric Beaumont, Jessica Johnson, Matt Maclean, Stephanie Newland, Tess Treadwell, Denise McMurry, Sydney Wolfram, Casey Kwock, Anthony Rogers, and Ashley Betters

About the Author

Originally hailing from the English city of Manchester, David began his career in 1995, writing for numerous classic British gaming magazines from a rusting, condemned, bohemian dry-docked German fishing trawler floating on the River Thames. Fleeing the United Kingdom, he joined the crew at the part-fraternity, part-sanitarium known as *GameFan* magazine. David helped launch GameFan Books and form Gamers' Republic, was partly responsible for the wildly unsuccessful *incite* Video Gaming and Gamers.com. He began authoring guides for Prima in 2000. He has written over 60 strategy guides, including: *The Legend of Zelda: Twilight Princess*, *Half-Life: Orange Box*, *Fallout 3*, and *Fallout 3: Game of the Year*. He lives in the Pacific Northwest with his wife Melanie, and an eight-foot statue of Great Cthulhu.

Special Thanks:

To my wonderful and loving wife Melanie; Mum, Dad & Ian; John and Liz; Bryn, Rachel, Samuel and Ben; The Moon Wiring Club, Boards of Canada, Ulrich Schnauss, Laibach and Kraftwerk; Ron & Fez, Special Delivery; and "M" for Miskatonic University, An Ivy League School over 200 years old, Housing the largest occult collection in the western world, And the most varied alumni, I'm told.

Extra special thanks to Jody Seltzer, Shaida Boroumand, Tracy Erickson, and the cartographers at 99 Lives for their dedication, help, and support. Thanks also to all at Prima.

One thousand and two thanks to everyone at Bethesda Softworks, especially Pete Hines and Will Noble, for their help, generosity, and knowledge throughout this project. The book would not have been possible without you.

We want to hear from you! E-mail comments and feedback to dhodgson@primagames.com.

New Vegas Navigation

This Navigation indexes all the essential information contained in this guide so you can easily find what you're looking for. For all those wandering the wastes who want an even deeper breakdown, we provide an expanded (and searchable) Navigation. Download it for free at [www.primagames.com/features/fallout].

Training

WELCOME TO THE MOJAVE WASTELAND

You've narrowly escaped almost certain death and suffocation in a shallow grave: Welcome to the Mojave Wasteland, survivor! The following few chapters details how to spend your Statistics, Skill, and Perk points; choose traits; and learn the key survival skills for Crafting and Upgrading armaments. It also includes the following: tips on the inhospitable Hardcore mode and how to interact with the Factions and your Reputation; character archetypes to help you streamline your advancement; more involved training; and a showcase of all the weapons, armor, and aid you should look for during your adventure.

The *Fallout: New Vegas* game manual that came with your copy of the game must be read from cover to cover so you're familiar with the basics of this adventure. Come back here when you're done....

> **Tip** For those with experience adventuring on the East Coast, look for this icon, which introduces any major changes between *Fallout 3* and *Fallout: New Vegas*, so you know what's different.

PRIMARY ATTRIBUTES

SPECIAL Effects

Also known as Primary Statistics, *SPECIAL* is an acronym that stands for your seven primary attributes (which are Strength, Perception, Endurance, Charisma, Intelligence, Agility, and Luck). Think of these as the foundation of not only your character, but those you encounter in the Mojave as well, including creatures. Each attribute can range from 1 (wretched) to 10 (astounding). Remember that in general terms, the higher a primary attribute, the more impressive the associated ability and skill bonuses are, as the following table indicates:

SPECIAL Associations Table I

SPECIAL	ASSOCIATED ABILITY	SKILLS MODIFIED
Strength	Carry Weight	Melee Weapons, Guns (heavier weapons)
Perception	Compass Range, Accuracy	Explosives, Lockpick, Energy Weapons
Endurance	Heath, Resistance	Survival, Unarmed
Charisma	Companion Nerve, Disposition	Barter, Speech
Intelligence	Skill Points per level	Medicine, Repair, Science
Agility	Action Points (APs) in VATS, Speed (Weapon Draw, Weapon Reload, Maximum Run)	Guns, Sneak
Luck	Critical Chance (all weapons), Enemy mishaps	All skills (a little)

When a SPECIAL attribute affects a skill, it does so by the amount shown in the next table, with the exception of Luck (which affects all skills, but at a much lower rate).

SPECIAL Associations Table II

SPECIAL	SKILL MODIFIER (%)	LUCK MODIFIER (%)	SPECIAL	SKILL MODIFIER (%)	LUCK MODIFIER (%)
1	Skill + 2	Skill + 1	6	Skill + 12	Skill + 3
2	Skill + 4	Skill + 1	7	Skill + 14	Skill + 4
3	Skill + 6	Skill + 2	8	Skill + 16	Skill + 4
4	Skill + 8	Skill + 2	9	Skill + 18	Skill + 5
5	Skill + 10	Skill + 3	10	Skill + 20	Skill + 5

FUN! ACCURATE! SCIENTIFIC! TRY IT NOW!

You allocate SPECIAL points during your time of convalescence at Doc Mitchell's House, before you venture out into Goodsprings for the first time since the "premature burial." Test your attributes out at the Vit-o-matic Vigor Tester (as shown), where you can redistribute points manually to lay the foundation for exactly the type of Courier you want to be. Once you leave Goodsprings for the first time, you have the option to "Rebuild your Character," if you want to make changes since you left Doc Mitchell's recuperation room.

You have a grand total of 40 points to spend across the seven primary attributes; however seven of those points are automatically allotted, as you must have a minimum of 1 point in every attribute. However, the rest can be freely distributed as you wish. Before you do, be sure to check the following information on which associated skills and perks are affected by each attribute.

> **Tip** Flip forward a few pages, read up on the skills and perks that you're interested in, and then check back here to figure out which primary attribute affects them; then bump up the attribute to get the biggest bonus you can (without crippling your character in other ways, of course!).

> **Tip** It appears Vault-Tec ran out of Bobbleheads to distribute to Western Vaults: Attributes can only be augmented with special, and highly expensive Implants, which is the only way to improve your statistics.

Associated Skills, Perks, and Derived Statistics

Perk: Intense Training

With 10 ranks, and each allowing you to add 1 point to any attribute, this allows you to add 10 additional points, instead of accessing other perks.

Strength

Strength will tell you how easily a cowboy totes his saddle and those bigger firearms, or how much help he's gonna be for ya in the saloon brawl.

STRENGTH	CARRY WEIGHT (LB)*	UNARMED DAMAGE (HP)†	SKILL MODIFIERS (%)‡
1 Wet Noodle	160	0.5	Melee Weapons +2
2 Beached Jellyfish	170	1	Melee Weapons +4
3 Doughy Baby	180	1.5	Melee Weapons +6
4 Lightweight	190	2	Melee Weapons +8
5 Average Joe	200	2.5	Melee Weapons +10
6 Barrel Chested	210	3	Melee Weapons +12
7 Beach Bully	220	3.5	Melee Weapons +14
8 Circus Strongman	230	4	Melee Weapons +16
9 Doomsday Pecs	240	4.5	Melee Weapons +18
10 Hercules' Bigger Cousin	250	5	Melee Weapons +20

* Carry Weight: Every item you scavenge has a weight associated with it. The stronger you are, the more you can carry without being over-encumbered (which stops you running and slows your normal speed).

† Unarmed Damage: If you're planning to use your fists, or Unarmed Weapons (such as the Zap Glove), expect to add this amount of damage to every strike.

‡ Skill Modifiers: You permanently add this percentage to your Melee Weapons skill.

Associated Skills, Perks, and Derived Statistics

Skill: Melee Weapons

Skill: Unarmed

Statistic: Carry Weight

PERK	STR REQUIRED	LEVEL
Heave, Ho!	STR 5	2
Stonewall	STR 6	8
Strong Back	STR 5	8
Super Slam	STR 6	8

PERK	STR REQUIRED	LEVEL
Unstoppable Force	STR 7	12
Weapon Handling	STR < 10	16
Strength Implant	STR < 10	N/A

Perception

A perceptive cowboy always knows when there's a lit stick of dynamite nearby… or when a varmint's sneakin' up on him.

PERCEPTION	SKILL MODIFIERS (%)*
1 Deaf Bat	Energy Weapons +2, Explosives +2, Lockpick +2
2 Senile Mole	Energy Weapons +4, Explosives +4, Lockpick +4
3 Squinting Newt	Energy Weapons +6, Explosives +6, Lockpick +6
4 Unsuspecting Trout	Energy Weapons +8, Explosives +8, Lockpick +8
5 Wary Trout	Energy Weapons +10, Explosives +10, Lockpick +10
6 Alert Coyote	Energy Weapons +12, Explosives +12, Lockpick +12
7 Big-eyed Tiger	Energy Weapons +14, Explosives +14, Lockpick +14
8 Monocled Falcon	Energy Weapons +16, Explosives +16, Lockpick +16
9 Sniper Hawk	Energy Weapons +18, Explosives +18, Lockpick +18
10 Eagle with Telescope	Energy Weapons +20, Explosives +20, Lockpick +20

** Skill Modifiers: You instantly (and permanently) add this percentage to these skills.*

Associated Skills, Perks, and Derived Statistics

Skill: Energy Weapons

Skill: Explosives

Skill: Lockpick

Statistic: Easier to detect enemies on Compass

Statistic: Increased accuracy to your attacks

PERK	PER REQUIRED	LEVEL
Four Eyes (Trait)	PER < 10	N/A
Friend of the Night	PER 6	2
Sniper	PER 6	12
Light Step	PER 6	14

PERK	PER REQUIRED	LEVEL
Better Criticals	PER 6	16
Infiltrator	PER 7	18
Perception Implant	REP <10	N/A

Endurance

You can't keep a good cowboy down, not if he's the endurin' type…and not if he's got a six-shooter the size of all tarnation.

ENDURANCE	INITIAL HEALTH*	SKILL MODIFIERS (%)†	
1 Basically Dead	120	20 + (Level x10)	Survival +2, Unarmed +2
2 Crumbly	140	40 + (Level x10)	Survival +4, Unarmed +4
3 Do Not Bend	160	60 + (Level x10)	Survival +6, Unarmed +6
4 Handle with Care	180	80 + (Level x10)	Survival +8, Unarmed +8
5 Stain-resistant	200	100 + (Level x10)	Survival +10, Unarmed +10
6 Hardy	220	120 + (Level x10)	Survival +12, Unarmed +12
7 Tough-as-nails	240	140 + (Level x10)	Survival +14, Unarmed +14
8 Flame Retardant	260	160 + (Level x10)	Survival +16, Unarmed +16
9 Bulletproof	280	180 + (Level x10)	Survival +18, Unarmed +18
10 Unstoppable	300	200 + (Level x10)	Survival +20, Unarmed +20

** Initial Health: Because this is the amount of damage you can take before dying, figure out what type of combat you're planning: You need more health if you're going to wade into hand-to-hand combat, and less if you're sniping from long range.*

† Skill Modifiers: You instantly (and permanently) add this percentage to these skills.

Note Fatigue: Fatigue is nonfatal damage. If enough Fatigue damage is sustained, a character will simply become unconscious. This is a invisible stat that determines when you get knocked down/stunned—hand to hand weapons like the boxing gloves or some poisons deal damage to fatigue rather than HP. The higher your END, the longer you last before becoming Fatigued.

Associated Skills, Perks, and Derived Statistics

Skill: Survival

Statistic: Poison Resistance

PERK	END REQUIRED	LEVEL
Lead Belly	END 5	6
Rad Resistance	END 5	8
Stonewall	END 6	8
Strong Back	END 5	8
Life Giver	END 6	12

Skill: Unarmed

Statistic: Radiation Resistance

PERK	END REQUIRED	LEVEL
Long Haul	END 6	12
Solar Powered	END 7	20
Rad Absorption	END 7	28
Endurance Implant	END < 10	N/A

Charisma

You'll find there are some smooth-talkin' cowboys out there that got themselves a voice sounds like an angel's harmonica.

CHARISMA	COMPANION NERVE (%)*	SKILL MODIFIERS (%)†
1 Misanthrope	Armor and Damage +5	Barter +2, Speech +2
2 Old Hermit	Armor and Damage + 10	Barter +4, Speech +4
3 Creepy Undertaker	Armor and Damage + 15	Barter +6, Speech +6
4 Peevish Librarian	Armor and Damage + 20	Barter +8, Speech +8
5 Substitute Teacher	Armor and Damage + 25	Barter +10, Speech +10
6 Cheery Salesman	Armor and Damage + 30	Barter +12, Speech +12
7 Diplomat	Armor and Damage + 35	Barter +14, Speech +14
8 Movie Star	Armor and Damage + 40	Barter +16, Speech +16
9 Casanova	Armor and Damage + 45	Barter +18, Speech +18
10 Cult Leader	Armor and Damage + 50	Barter +20, Speech +20

** Companion Nerve: This is the percentage bonus to Armor and Damage inflicted by a Follower.*

† Skill Modifiers: You instantly (and permanently) add this percentage to these skills.

Associated Skills, Perks, and Derived Statistics

Skill: Barter

Statistic: Companion Nerve

PERK	CHR REQUIRED	LEVEL
Ferocious Loyalty	CHR 6	6
Animal Friend	CHR 6	10

Skill: Speech

Statistic: Disposition of Others

PERK	CHR REQUIRED	LEVEL
Charisma Implant	< 10	N/A

Intelligence

A smart cowboy's good at most anything, from suckin' the poison out of your rattler bite to fixin' your broken wagon axle.

INTELLIGENCE	SKILL POINTS*	SKILL MODIFIERS (%)†
1 Sub-brick	10.5	Medicine +2, Repair +2, Science +2
2 Vegetable	11	Medicine +4, Repair +4, Science +4
3 Cretin	11.5	Medicine +6, Repair +6, Science +6
4 Knucklehead	12	Medicine +8, Repair +8, Science +8
5 Knowledgeable	12.5	Medicine +10, Repair +10, Science +10
6 Gifted	13	Medicine +12, Repair +12, Science +12
7 Smartypants	13.5	Medicine +14, Repair +14, Science +14
8 Know-it-all	14	Medicine +16, Repair +16, Science +16
9 Genius	14.5	Medicine +18, Repair +18, Science +18
10 Omniscient	15	Medicine +20, Repair +20, Science +20

** Skill Points: The number of points you can allocate to skills each time you level up. Any "half-points" are carried over to an even level number. So an adventurer with 9 Intelligence gains 14 Skill Points at Level 3, 15 Skill Points at Level 4, and so on.*

† Skill Modifiers: You instantly (and permanently) add this percentage to these skills.

At Levels 10 and 20, this is what a 1, 5, and 10 Intelligence adventurers' Skill Points total look like:

INTELLIGENCE	SKILL POINTS (LEVEL 10)	SKILL POINTS (LEVEL 20)
1	105	210
5	125	250
10	150	300

Associated Skills, Perks, and Derived Statistics

 **Skill: Medicine**

 **Skill: Repair**

Skill: Speech

Statistic: Skill Points

PERK	INT REQUIRED	LEVEL
Retention	INT 5	2
Swift Learner	INT 4	2
Comprehension	INT 4	4
Educated	INT 4	4
Entomologist	INT 4	4

PERK	INT REQUIRED	LEVEL
Pack Rat	INT 5	8
Nerd Rage!	INT 5	10
Computer Whiz	INT 7	18
Intelligence Implant	INT < 10	N/A

Monosyllabic Grunting, or Polite Discourse?

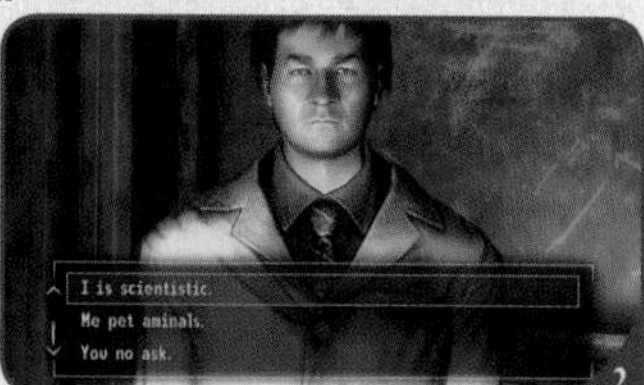

Intelligence affects occasional conversations you can have with Mojave Wasteland folk, as these pictures demonstrate. One picture **(1)** is a conversation dialogue you can have if you're gifted in the arts of brain power. The other **(2)** shows that basic grasping of sentences can be difficult for less Intelligent adventurers.

 Agility

When a fella's in a gunfight and shoots the other guy six times before they can get off a shot, it's 'cause that fella is agile.

AGILITY	ACTION POINTS (AP)*	SKILL MODIFIERS (%)†
1 Walking Disaster	68	Guns +2, Sneak +2
2 Accident Prone	71	Guns +4, Sneak +4
3 Oaf	74	Guns +6, Sneak +6
4 Butterfingers	77	Guns +8, Sneak +8
5 Under Control	80	Guns +10, Sneak +10
6 Catlike	83	Guns +12, Sneak +12
7 Knife Thrower	86	Guns +14, Sneak +14
8 Knife Catcher	89	Guns +16, Sneak +16
9 Acrobatic Marvel	92	Guns +18, Sneak +18
10 Walks on Water	95	Guns +20, Sneak +20

* Action Points: These are used up during VATS attacks each time you fire or hit a foe. They regenerate faster depending on your Agility too.

† Skill Modifiers: You instantly (and permanently) add this percentage to these skills.

Associated Skills, Perks, and Derived Statistics

 **Skill: Guns**

 **Skill: Sneak**

Statistic: Speed (Weapon Draw, Weapon Reload, Maximum Run Speed)

Statistic: Action Points

Statistic: Action Points Regeneration

PERK	AGL REQUIRED	LEVEL
Small Frame (Trait)	AGL < 10	N/A
Rapid Reload	AGL 5	2
Quick Draw	AGL 5	8
Silent Running	AGL 6	12
Sniper	AGL 6	12

PERK	AGL REQUIRED	LEVEL
Light Step	AGL 6	14
Action Boy/Action Girl	AGL 6	16
Slayer	AGL 7	24
Nerves of Steel	AGL 7	26
Agility Implant	< 10	N/A

The Need for Speed

1

2

Speed isn't something you can easily quantify, but Agility has an effect on three different aspects of your speed:

- Weapon Draw (1): The time it takes to grab a weapon from its holster, and point it forwards.
- Weapon Reload (2): The time it takes to shove in another clip or slug into a ranged weapon.
- Maximum Run Speed (3): How quickly you traverse the landscape, whether encumbered or not.

Tip Even without an amazing Agility, you can increase your Run Speed by putting away any two-handed weapon you'd otherwise be using.

 Luck

Some folks claim not to believe in luck, but when they lose in a duel you'll hear them say "That lucky son-of-a-gun!"

LUCK	SKILL MODIFIERS (%)*
1 13 Pitch-black Cats	Critical Chance +1, All Skills +1
2 Broken Gypsy Mirror	Critical Chance +2, All Skills +1
3 Sickly Albatross	Critical Chance +3, All Skills +2
4 Spilled Salt	Critical Chance +4, All Skills +2
5 Coin Flip	Critical Chance +5, All Skills +3
6 Stacked Deck	Critical Chance +6, All Skills +3
7 Lucky 7	Critical Chance +7, All Skills +4
8 Leprechaun's Foot	Critical Chance +8, All Skills +4
9 21-Leaf Clover	Critical Chance +9, All Skills +5
10 Two-headed Coin Flip	Critical Chance +10, All Skills +5

* *Skill Modifiers: This affects Critical Chance and raises every skill value by a small amount.*

Associated Skills, Perks, and Derived Statistics

 **Skill: All**

Statistic: Critical Chance

Statistic: Enemy Mishaps

Statistic: Gambling

PERK	LCK REQUIRED	LEVEL
Fortune Finder	LCK 5	6
Scrounger	LCK 5	8
Miss Fortune	LCK 6	10

PERK	LCK REQUIRED	LEVEL
Mysterious Stranger	LCK 6	10
Better Criticals	LCK 6	16
Luck Implant	LCK < 10	N/A

All the Luck in the World

1

2

Statistically speaking, Luck plays a role that's difficult to properly spot. However, expect a greater chance of the following occurring if you have a high Luck:

- Critical Chance (1): A higher possibility of scoring a Critical Hit in VATS which (depending on the weapon) causing additional damage with a single shot, or a host of other effects (such as Crippling, killing, or passing through the armor of a target).
- Enemy Mishaps (2): If you have a high Luck, expect enemy grenades to detonate a little earlier, they may fire slightly later, aim slightly wider, or hit their brethren slightly more frequently.
- Gambling (3): If you're playing Blackjack, Roulette, or the Slots, and you "feel lucky" during a win, that's a direct result of your Luck score.

DERIVED STATISTICS

Derived Statistics are a second, related set of values determined automatically, based on the primary attributes (SPECIAL) and skills that you can allocate points to, or certain perks. There are different ways to increase (and decrease) these Derived Statistics; they aren't just affected by your attributes.

Tip Imagine you want to modify your Carry Weight. This is affected by the following:
You could increase or decrease your Strength,
Or, you could take the Strong Back perk.

Action Points

As the name suggests, the higher the number, the more actions you can accomplish before another entity (whether friend or foe) reacts back. Your total number of Action Points (AP) is visible only on your Pip-Boy's Stats screen. Otherwise, AP are represented by a bar on your HUD. Your AP bar is constantly in motion, retracting as you shoot weapons or access your inventory, and filling back up when not engaged in these types of moves. Don't worry about running out of AP unless you are engaged in VATS mode combat.

So, why not act in "real time" and ignore VATS mode? Because VATS allows easier takedowns, focused combat, and more pronounced effects. That Fiend in the distance may be difficult to manually decapitate, but expend some Action Points in VATS, and you're playing at your full potential; you're as proficient as your points allocations allow. Most of all, VATS gives you an additional +15% chance of a critical hit: That's a four times improvement for a character with a Luck of 5.

AGILITY	ACTION POINTS (AP)
1 Walking Disaster	68
2 Accident Prone	71
3 Oaf	74
4 Butterfingers	77
5 Under Control	80

AGILITY	ACTION POINTS (AP)
6 Catlike	83
7 Knife Thrower	86
8 Knife Catcher	89
9 Acrobatic Marvel	92
10 Walks on Water	95

Action Point Modifiers

MODIFIER TYPE	NAME	BONUS/PENALTY	TIME-FRAME
Perk	Math Wrath	AP Costs -10%	Permanent
Perk	Plasma Spaz	AP Costs -10%	Permanent
Perk (Challenge)	Beautiful Beatdown	AP Costs Reduced (Unarmed)	Permanent
Food	Irradiated Sugar Bombs	AP +15	Temporary
Food	Mississippi Quantum Pie	AP +20	Temporary
Food	Mushroom Cloud	AP +9	Temporary
Food	NukaLurk Meat	AP +30	Temporary
Food	Nuka-Cola Quantum	AP +20	Temporary
Food	Nuka-Cola Victory	AP +30	Temporary
Food	Sugar Bombs	AP +15	Temporary
Food	Trail Mix	AP +15	Temporary
Chem	Jet	AP +15	Temporary
Chem	Dixon's Jet	AP +10	Temporary
Chem	Rocket	AP +30	Temporary
Chem	Ultrajet	AP +40	Temporary
Radiation	400 Rads	AP -2	Temporary
Radiation	600 Rads	AP -4	Temporary
Radiation	800 Rads	AP -4	Temporary

Note You can perform a number of actions in both regular "run and gun" and VATS modes. These actions consume Action Points. Attack with any kind of weapon except a Rifle or Big Gun and it takes 10 AP. Crouching or standing takes 10 AP. Firing a Rifle takes 25 AP. Firing a Big Gun with a projectile takes 75 AP.

Carry Weight (aka Inventory Weight)

Your Carry Weight, shown on your Pip-Boy's Inventory menu, determines how much you can carry before you become over-encumbered, slow down, and eventually stop. It is determined by your Strength.

STRENGTH	CARRY WEIGHT (LB)
1 Wet Noodle	160
2 Beached Jellyfish	170
3 Doughy Baby	180
4 Lightweight	190
5 Average Joe	200

STRENGTH	CARRY WEIGHT (LB)
6 Barrel Chested	210
7 Beach Bully	220
8 Circus Strongman	230
9 Doomsday Pecs	240
10 Hercules' Bigger Cousin	250

Carry Weight Modifiers

MODIFIER TYPE	NAME	BONUS/PENALTY	TIME-FRAME
Perk	Strong Back	CW +50	Permanent
Food	Bighorner Steak	STR +3 (CW +30)	Temporary
Food	Brahmin Steak	STR +3 (CW +30)	Temporary
Food	Cook-Cook's Fiend Stew	STR +3 (CW +30)	Temporary
Food	Gecko Meat	STR -3 (CW -30)	Temporary
Food	Mississippi Quantum Pie	STR +1 (CW +10)	Temporary
Food	Mole Rat Stew	STR +3 (CW +30)	Temporary
Drink	Rum & Nuka	STR +1 (CW +10)	Temporary
Drink	Beer	STR +3 (CW +30)	Temporary
Drink	Jake Juice	STR +3 (CW +30)	Temporary
Drink	Moonshine	STR +2 (CW +20)	Temporary
Drink	Scotch	STR +3 (CW +30)	Temporary
Drink	Whiskey	STR +3 (CW +30)	Temporary
Drink	Dixon's Whiskey	STR +3 (CW +30)	Temporary
Drink	Wine	STR +2 (CW +20)	Temporary
Chem	Ant Nectar	STR +4 (CW +40)	Temporary
Chem	Buffout	STR +2 (CW +20)	Temporary
Chem	Silver Sting	STR -2 (CW -20)	Temporary
Radiation	600 Rads	STR -1, CW -20	Temporary
Radiation	800 Rads	STR -2, CW -20	Temporary
Addiction	Nectar Withdrawal	STR -2 (CW -20)	Temporary
Addiction	Buffout Withdrawal	STR -1 (CW -10)	Temporary
Addiction	Steady Withdrawal	STR -1 (CW -10)	Temporary

Critical Chance

Every time you strike an opponent (or receive a hit yourself) there's a chance that hit will inflict Critical Damage. The exact amount of Critical Damage varies depending on the weapon, whether or not it's a Sneak attack, and whether or not you are in VATS In most cases Critical Damage is double normal damage and the chance of a critical hit is simply your Luck as a percentage. However, with certain weapons, such as the Laser Rifle, additional effects occur when a critical is successful, such as the enemy being immolated into a pile of dust!

LUCK	CRITICAL CHANCE (%)
1 13 Pitch-black Cats	Critical Chance +1
2 Broken Gypsy Mirror	Critical Chance +2
3 Sickly Albatross	Critical Chance +3
4 Spilled Salt	Critical Chance +4
5 Coin Flip	Critical Chance +5

LUCK	CRITICAL CHANCE (%)
6 Stacked Deck	Critical Chance +6
7 Lucky 7	Critical Chance +7
8 Leprechaun's Foot	Critical Chance +8
9 21-Leaf Clover	Critical Chance +9
10 Two-headed Coin Flip	Critical Chance +10

Critical Chance Modifiers

MODIFIER TYPE	NAME	BONUS/PENALTY	TIME-FRAME
Perk	Finesse	Crit. Chan +5%	Permanent
Perk	Finesse	Crit. Chan +15% (Melee and Unarmed only)	Permanent
Perk	Ninja	Crit. Chan +15%	Permanent
Trait	Built to Destroy	Crit. Chan +3%	Permanent
Magazine	True Police Stories	Crit. Chan +20%	Temporary

Damage Threshold

When you attack a foe, you may notice a small shield icon pop up to the left of his health. This indicates the foe is wearing Armor which is absorbing some of the damage your weapon is inflicting on him. This is called "Damage Threshold" (DT). DT is the amount of damage subtracted from every instance of DAM hitting a target. For practical purposes, this means that heavier armor requires higher DAM weapons to overcome the armor's toughness.

For example, if a foe has a total DT of 7, and is hit by three bullets each inflicting 12 points of damage (DAM), the foe takes 5 damage per bullet (12 - 7) for a total of 15.

Another example: The Anti-Material Rifle is one of the most powerful weapons in the Mojave; not because of the DPS it inflicts, but because there is no armor that resists it. However, no armor is completely bullet-proof; weapons always inflict damage equal to their Minimum DAM multiplier. Exact statistical evidence for this isn't available to you, but this multiplier kicks in where a foe's DT is obliterating more of your weapon's DAM. Practically; this means that weapons still inflict marginal damage, even when seriously outclassed. How can you tell? When you fire off a burst, and your enemy only loses a tiny bit of health, and the "shield" icon flashes near their Hit Points.

Sneak Attacks and "Ignoring Armor": Weapons that ignore armor and Sneak attacks now technically don't actually ignore a foe's protection. Instead, weapons may have a property known as "Armor Piercing." This lowers a foe's DT by -15.

Stealth attacks negate DT equal to 25 percent of the weapon's DAM. But don't fret; these type of attacks are still devastating: Leather armor may be completely ignored, Metal Armor is only as strong as an Armored Vault Jumpsuit, and even the mighty T51-b Power Armor can become as weak as standard leather.

Tip Having trouble taking down a foe due to their DT? Then switch weapons and try out others that may be more effective. Or swap your ammunition type to armor-piercing. When the "shield" is no longer seen when you inflict damage on a foe, you're striking with full damage. Many ammo types can be converting to armor-piercing variants at a Reloading Bench.

Damage Threshold Modifiers

MODIFIER TYPE	NAME	BONUS/PENALTY	TIME-FRAME
Perk	Toughness 1	DT +3%	Permanent
Perk	Toughness 2	DT +6%	Permanent
Perk	Nerd Rage!	DT +15% (when Health = 20% or lower)	Permanent
Drink	Nuka-Cola Quartz	DT +6%	Temporary
Drink	Whiskey	DT +6%	Temporary
Chem	Med-X	DAM RES +25%	Temporary
Chem	Slasher	DAM RES +25%	Temporary

Hit Points

Your Hit Points (Health) is shown both in your Pip-Boy and onscreen. When you reach 0 Hit Points, you are dead. Your Endurance statistic determines your starting Hit Points, and you gain 10 more each time you level up. Naturally, the more Hit Points you have, the better your chances at survival are.

Your enemies also have a finite amount of Hit Points, and the same rules apply. In addition, your Hit Points represent the total health of your entire body: each body part accounts for a percentage of total Hit Points. This means, for example, that shooting a 100 Hit Point Fiend in the torso requires you to damage her for 46 points before the body part is crippled. Remember that the Fiend's armor also stops some of the incoming damage. The following table shows every entity's body part health as a percentage of the total Hit Points. Creatures all have unique body part Hit Points distributions. Notice that you have very high body part Hit Points. You are the hero. You're a pretty tough guy.

BODY PART	ENTITY HIT POINTS (HUMAN-SHAPED)	YOUR HIT POINTS
Head	20%	75%
Torso	60%	255%
Left Arm	25%	100%
Right Arm	25%	100%
Left Leg	25%	150%
Right Leg	25%	150%

Tip This is one reason why limb shots are favored by professional Wasteland killers. As long as your aim is good, you only need pare down a percentage of a foe's total Health to cripple that limb. In most cases you inflict double damage if you aim at the head too; make cranial destruction an essential part of your combat repertoire!

If you fall a great distance, or you're shot or wounded in a specific area, you may lose the use of that body part. For example, a fall from the rocky outcrops above Goodsprings can cripple a leg. Seek a doctor, or inject yourself with a Stimpak to heal yourself.

Hit Points Modifiers

MODIFIER TYPE	NAME	BONUS/PENALTY	TIME-FRAME
Perk	Life Giver	HP +30	Permanent
Perk	Solar Powered	HP +1(10s)	Permanent
Perk	Better Healing	HP bonus	Permanent (with Arcade Gannon)
Perk	Calm Heart	HP +50 (Cass)	Permanent (with Cass)
Implant	Monocycle Breeder	HP +1(3s)	Permanent
Chem	Buffout	HP +60	Temporary

Note Note: There are a large number of Food and associated ingestible items giving an HP bonus. Consult the "Ingestibles" table in the "Guns and Gear" chapter for more information.

Melee and Unarmed Damage

These two types of "close quarter" damage are sometimes difficult to distinguish, so follow this rule: If you're inflicting Melee Damage, you are using a weapon in one or both hands that is designed to directly strike a foe, such as a 9 Iron golf club. Unarmed Damage is punishment inflicted by just your fists, and by specialized Unarmed weapons such as Brass Knuckles. Unarmed Damage is determined by your Unarmed skill. Your Unarmed Damage is 25% of your Unarmed skill. So if you have a skill of 60, you do 15 points of damage. Any Unarmed Weapon Damage is added to this. You can do additional Melee damage if you increase your strength, and Unarmed damage if you increase your Endurance.

STRENGTH	UNARMED DAMAGE (HP)	MELEE WEAPON SKILL BONUS
1 Wet Noodle	+0.5	Melee Weapons +2
2 Beached Jellyfish	+1	Melee Weapons +4
3 Doughy Baby	+1.5	Melee Weapons +6
4 Lightweight	+2	Melee Weapons +8
5 Average Joe	+2.5	Melee Weapons +10
6 Barrel Chested	+3	Melee Weapons +12
7 Beach Bully	+3.5	Melee Weapons +14
8 Circus Strongman	+4	Melee Weapons +16
9 Doomsday Pecs	+4.5	Melee Weapons +18
10 Hercules' Bigger Cousin	+5	Melee Weapons +20

ENDURANCE	UNARMED SKILL BONUS
1 Basically Dead	Unarmed +2
2 Crumbly	Unarmed +4
3 Do Not Bend	Unarmed +6
4 Handle with Care	Unarmed +8
5 Stain-resistant	Unarmed +10

ENDURANCE	UNARMED SKILL BONUS
6 Hardy	Unarmed +12
7 Tough-as-nails	Unarmed +14
8 Flame Retardant	Unarmed +16
9 Bulletproof	Unarmed +18
10 Unstoppable	Unarmed +20

Melee and Unarmed Damage Modifiers

MODIFIER TYPE	NAME	BONUS/PENALTY	TIME-FRAME
Trait	Good Natured	-5 Melee Dam., -5 Unarmed Dam.	Permanent
Perk	Intense Training -10	+1-10 STR (Unarmed Dam. +0.5-5)	Permanent
Perk	Intense Training -10	+1-10 END (Melee Dam. +2-20)	Permanent
Perk	Piercing Strike	Ignores 15 DT Points (Melee and Unarmed)	Permanent
Perk	Unstoppable Force	Increased Melee and Unarmed Damage through enemy blocking	Permanent
Perk	Strength Implant	+1 STR (Unarmed Dam. +0.5)	Permanent
Implant	Endurance Implant	+1 END (Melee Dam. +2	Permanent
Food	Barrel Cactus Fruit	END -3 (-6 Melee. Dam)	Temporary
Food	Bighorner Steak	STR +3 (Unarmed Dam. +1.5)	Temporary
Food	Brahmin Steak	STR +3 (Unarmed Dam. +1.5)	Temporary
Food	Cook-Cook's Fiend Stew	STR +3 (Unarmed Dam. +1.5)	Temporary
Food	Gecko Meat	STR -3 (Unarmed Dam. -1.5)	Temporary
Food	Mississippi Quantum Pie	STR +1 (Unarmed Dam. +0.5)	Temporary
Food	Mole Rat Stew	STR +3 (Unarmed Dam. +1.5)	Temporary
Food	White Horsenettle	END -3 (-6 Melee. Dam)	Temporary
Drink	Rum & Nuka	STR +1 (Unarmed Dam. +0.5)	Temporary
Drink	Beer	STR +3 (Unarmed Dam. +1.5)	Temporary
Drink	Jake Juice	STR +3 (Unarmed Dam. +1.5)	Temporary
Drink	Moonshine	STR +2 (Unarmed Dam. +1.0)	Temporary
Drink	Scotch	STR +3 (Unarmed Dam. +1.5)	Temporary

MODIFIER TYPE	NAME	BONUS/PENALTY	TIME-FRAME
Drink	Whiskey	STR +3 (Unarmed Dam. +1.5)	Temporary
Drink	Dixon's Whiskey	STR +3 (Unarmed Dam. +1.5)	Temporary
Drink	Wine	STR +2 (Unarmed Dam. +1.0)	Temporary
Chem	Ant Nectar	STR +4 (Unarmed Dam. +2.0)	Temporary
Chem	Buffout	STR +2 (Unarmed Dam. +1.0), END +3 (+6 Melee. Dam)	Temporary
Chem	Silver Sting	STR -2 (Unarmed Dam. +1.0)	Temporary
Radiation	600 Rads	STR -1 (Melee Dam. -0.5)	Temporary
Radiation	800 Rads	STR -2 (Melee Dam. -1)	Temporary
Addiction	Nectar Withdrawal	STR -2 (Melee Dam. -1)	Temporary
Addiction	Buffout Withdrawal	STR -1 (Melee Dam. -0.5)	Temporary
Addiction	Steady Withdrawal	STR -1 (Melee Dam. -0.5)	Temporary

Poison and Radiation Resistance

Certain foes and weapons inflict a poisonous attack on you, and Poison Resistance reduces how much the poison hurts you. If you have a Poison Resistance of 20%, you take that much less damage. Because poison ignores your armor and Damage Resistance, this is the only defense you have against poison. Certain areas of the Wasteland are irradiated; this includes all water sources, muddy pools, and areas where bombs were dropped long ago. Your Radiation Resistance indicates how adept your body is at ignoring exposure.

ENDURANCE	POISON RESISTANCE	RADIATION RESISTANCE
1 Basically Dead	0%	0%
2 Crumbly	5%	2%
3 Do Not Bend	10%	4%
4 Handle with Care	15%	6%
5 Stain-resistant	20%	8%

ENDURANCE	POISON RESISTANCE	RADIATION RESISTANCE
6 Hardy	25%	10%
7 Tough-as-nails	30%	12%
8 Flame Retardant	35%	14%
9 Bulletproof	40%	16%
10 Unstoppable	45%	18%

Take precaution by wearing specialized armor, a Radiation Suit, consuming Rad-X, or choosing the Rad Resistance perk. Your Endurance helps you tough out poison or radiation. Although you can't see it in your Pip-Boy, you can calculate it. Exposure to radiation is calculated in "Rads" on your Pip-Boy, and the exposure you receive (without visiting a doctor or taking the Chem RadAway) results in appalling poisoning that is detrimental to your well being. Specifically, the following effects occur:

APPROX. RAD EXPOSURE	EFFECTS
0	No effect
200	-1 END
400	-2 END, -1 AGL

APPROX. RAD EXPOSURE	EFFECTS
600	-3 END, -2 AGL, -1 STR
800	-3 END, -2 AGL, -2 STR
1,000	Death

Poison or Radiation Modifiers

MODIFIER TYPE	NAME	BONUS/PENALTY	TIME-FRAME
Perk	Rad Child	Radiation = HP Regeneration	Permanent
Perk	Rad Resistance	Rad. Res. +25	Permanent
Perk	Rad Absorption	Radiation -1(20s)	Permanent (if not in Rad Zone)
Food	Spore Plant Pods	Poison Res. +75	Temporary
Chem	Antivenom	Cures Animal Poison	Temporary
Chem	Rad-X	Rad. Res. +75	Temporary
Armor	T-45d Power Armor	Rad. Res. +10	Permanent (item equipped)
Armor	T-51b Armor	Rad. Res. +25	Permanent (item equipped)
Armor	T-51b Armor Helmet	Rad. Res. +8	Permanent (item equipped)
Armor	Remnants Power Armor	Rad. Res. +15	Permanent (item equipped)
Armor	Remnants Power Helmet	Rad. Res. +5	Permanent (item equipped)
Armor	Radiation Suit	Rad. Res. +30 / Rad. Res. +100	Permanent (item equipped)
Armor	Advanced Radiation Suit	Rad. Res. +40 / Rad. Res. +100	Permanent (item equipped)

Speed

How quickly you move around the Mojave is governed by a three factors:

1. How much you are carrying: If your inventory weighs more than your Carry Weight, you become over-encumbered. Discard items so you can move more quickly, or live with it.
2. The armor you are wearing: Heavy Power Armor slows you down, but provides excellent protection. Dirty Pre-War Business Suits provide quick mobility, and no protection whatsoever. Switch your outfits according to your situation. There's no penalty for carrying both types of outfits (or more) as long as your Carry Weight allows it.
3. Remaining unarmed: Flick between carrying a two-handed weapon and stowing it, and you'll see a difference in your speed. There's no difference if your weapon is one-handed.

SKILLS OVERVIEW

The backbone of your character, skills determine whether you're a brute, genius, sharpshooter, melee-combat master, or any combination of those. Remember that certain skills serve as a prerequisite for certain perks. Skills are rated from 0-100, although your starting value is always 7.

Learning the Basics

Each skill is affected by a single SPECIAL attribute (except for Strength) and Luck. The higher that is, the larger your starting bonus in the related skill. Each point in the attribute gives you two points in the skill. This chart shows the starting values of all skills, based on an Attribute score of 5, and a minimum statistic rank of 1.

SKILL	LOWEST STARTING VALUE	STARTING VALUE (ATTRIBUTE = 5)	RELATED SPECIAL
Barter	7	15	Charisma
Energy Weapons	7	15	Perception
Explosives	7	15	Perception
Guns	7	15	Agility, Strength (weapon weight)
Lockpick	7	15	Perception
Medicine	7	15	Intelligence
Melee Weapons	7	15	Strength
Repair	7	15	Intelligence
Science	7	15	Intelligence
Sneak	7	15	Agility
Speech	7	15	Charisma
Survival	7	15	Endurance
Unarmed	7	15	Endurance

Notice that most attributes influence more than one skill? This means it can be beneficial to increase an attribute, and then focus on associated skills more than others. For example, if you want to specialize in Explosives and Energy Weapons, you might want to also put points into Lockpick first, and not Science (as Lockpick is affected by Perception, like Explosives).

Tip Remember that Tag skills (of which you begin with three) receive a +15 higher points score than your others. These should be the skills you want to specialize in. Remember you can also receive a +3 (or +4 with the Comprehension perk) increase to a specific skill if you find and read the Skill Book associated with it. Also remember that increasing attributes (such as with the use of Implants or Intense Training perks) gives you skill increases too.

Skill Points Awarded

When you receive enough Experience Points (XP) to level up, you receive Skill Points you can "spend" to increase the exact skills you want to advance, one point at a time (if you have an odd-numbered Intelligence score, the half-points are carried over to the next level). The number you're given is dictated by Intelligence, as this table indicates:

INTELLIGENCE	SKILL POINTS PER LEVEL
1 Sub-brick	10.5
2 Vegetable	11
3 Cretin	11.5
4 Knucklehead	12
5 Knowledgeable	12.5

INTELLIGENCE	SKILL POINTS PER LEVEL
6 Gifted	13
7 Smartypants	13.5
8 Know-it-all	14
9 Genius	14.5
10 Omniscient	15

AVAILABLE SKILLS

Barter

The Barter skill affects the prices you get for buying and selling items. In general, the higher your Barter skill, the lower your prices on purchased items. You use this automatically when you encounter a Vendor (you're given the best price related to your skill). In addition, there are many conversation choices, and additional Caps you can negotiate, by using this skill in conversation, where flagged.

Attribute: Charisma

Charisma has effects in dialogue, opening new conversation choices, and it also affects Companions' Nerve, which is a your companions' percentile bonus to armor and damage inflicted. Each point of Charisma grants a +5% bonus to both.

PERK	SKILL LEVEL	CHARACTER LEVEL
Good-Natured (Trait)	+5	N/A
Pack Rat	70	8
Long Haul	70	12

Energy Weapons

The Energy Weapons skill determines your effectiveness with any weapon that uses Small Energy Cells, Micro Fusion Cells, EC Packs, or Flamer Fuel as ammunition. As this skill increases, so does your accuracy and damage with all weapons referenced by the Energy Weapons icon (shown), both in and out of VATS mode.

Laser and Plasma weapons are more distinct. Laser weapons fire very quickly when compared to conventional weapons, are more accurate, and do less damage. Plasma weapons have slow moving projectiles, slow rates of fire, and do enormous damage. Consult the "Guns and Gear" chapter as there are pulse weapons which are, of course, devastating against Robots and Turrets.

Attribute: Perception

PERK	SKILL LEVEL	CHARACTER LEVEL
Fast Shot (Trait)	+20% speed, -20% accuracy	N/A
Good Natured (Trait)	-5	N/A
Trigger Discipline (Trait)	-20% Speed, +20% accuracy	N/A
Run 'n Gun	45	4
Plasma Spaz	70	10
Meltdown	90	16
Concentrated Fire	60	18
Laser Commander	90	22

Explosives

The Explosives skill determines the ease of disarming any hostile mines and the effectiveness of any explosive weapon (all mines, all grenades, Missile Launcher, Fat Man, etc). The higher your skill, the more you automatically "overload" the explosive and increase its damage output. For disarming purposes, when you approach a Mine, a "countdown beep" increases until the Mine explodes. The higher your skill, the more time you have to disarm it. Explosives covers the accuracy you have when throwing a Grenade as well as the damage. A well-aimed Grenade will land right at an enemy's feet, won't roll away, and usually explodes immediately.

Attribute: Perception

PERK	SKILL LEVEL	CHARACTER LEVEL
Good Natured (Trait)	-5	N/A
Heave, Ho!	30	2
Demolition Expert	50	6
Hit the Deck	70	12
Pyromaniac	60	12
Splash Damage	70	12

Guns

Guns determines your effectiveness with any weapon that uses convention ammunition (.22 LR, .357 Magnum, 5mm, 10mm, 5.56mm, .308, 45-70 Gov't, etc.). Simply reference the ammunition of the weapon you pick up, or check the Icon on the Pip-Boy to ensure you know which firearms are which. As your skill increases, so does your accuracy and damage with all of these weapons, both in and out of VATS mode. Also note that the larger and more cumbersome weapons (such as the Sniper Rifle) require a higher Strength than smaller, or one-handed Guns. Check your Weapon stats for the exact Strength needed to fire a weapon without encumbrance.

Attribute: Strength (weapon wt.)

Attribute: Agility

PERK	SKILL LEVEL	CHARACTER LEVEL
Fast Shot (Trait)	+20% speed, -20% accuracy	N/A
Good Natured (Trait)	-5	N/A
Trigger Discipline (Trait)	-20% Speed, +20% accuracy	N/A
Rapid Reload	30	2
Run 'n Gun	45	4
Shotgun Surgeon	45	6
Cowboy	45	8
Center of Mass	70	14
Concentrated Fire	60	18
Hand of Vengeance	+15%	Cass only

Lockpick

The Lockpick skill is used to open locked doors and containers. If you don't have a high enough skill, you won't even be allowed to try. The higher your Lockpick skill, the easier it is to pick the lock, because the "sweet spot" where the tumblers fall into place is larger. Or, if you choose the locking minigame's "auto attempt" function, your Lockpick skill largely determines your chance of success.

The number of damage (or Hit Points) a Bobby Pin has, is in direct proportion to your skill. For example, Lockpick 50 means that a Bobby Pin has 150% of its normal (base) Hit Points.

Tip Attempt a Lockpick with gentle touches. Line the Bobby Pin up anywhere in the 180 degree arc. Try the lock If there's give, move it slightly in one direction. If there's more give, you're moving the Bobby Pin in the correct direction. if there's less give, move it in the opposite direction. Let the lock reset after each try. On the third turn, the lock should open. If not, the Bobby Pin usually snaps. Prevent this by stopping the Lockpick entirely, and then starting again, to save on Bobby Pins. Try again, remembering where there was most give, and place the Bobby Pin there to start with. Patiently continue with this until the lock opens.

Attribute: Perception

PERK	SKILL LEVEL	CHARACTER LEVEL
Infiltrator	70	18

Medicine

The Medicine skill determines how many Hit Points you'll replenish upon using a Stimpak, and the effectiveness of Rad-X and RadAway. If you maximize your Medicine skill at 100, your Stimpak effectiveness is doubled.

In Hardcore mode, Stimpaks do not heal crippled limbs. Instead, you must use a Doctor's Bag, which are much rarer than Stimpaks. In less difficult modes, Doctor's Bags heal both limbs and base Hit Points damage. Also in Hardcore Mode, when you use any Stimpak, Doctor's Bag or RadAway, the effects on you are metered out over time. Half of the total effect will be given within the first 2-3 seconds, with the remainder trickling in over the following 10 seconds. In less difficult modes, these effects are still instantaneous.

Attribute: Intelligence

PERK	SKILL LEVEL	CHARACTER LEVEL
Good Natured	+5	N/A
Living Anatomy	70	8
Fast Metabolism	N/A	12
Chemist	60	14
Chem Resistant	60	16

Melee Weapons

The Melee Weapons skill determines your effectiveness with any melee weapon, from the simple lead pipe all the way up to the high-tech Super Sledge. As this skill increases, so does your damage inflicted with associated weapons, both in and out of VATS mode. This also enables you to use a melee weapon to block an attack; the higher the skill, the more damage is absorbed.

The amount of damage blocked while using a Melee Weapon directly correlates as a Damage Threshold. In additional, as your Melee Weapon skill increases, you can unlock special moves in VATS (or as a forward power attack) for many melee weapons, with many being unique. Consult the "Guns and Gear" chapter for a list of all the available moves; some of which inflict heavy damage, have a large hit area, slices through a foe, or can hit multiple foes.

Attribute: Strength

PERK	SKILL LEVEL	CHARACTER LEVEL
Good Natured (Trait)	-5	N/A
Cowboy	45	8
Super Slam	45	8
Unstoppable Force	90	12
Ninja	80	20

Repair

The Repair skill allows you to maintain any weapons and apparel. In addition, Repair allows you to create items and Guns ammunition at Reloading Benches. This makes it one of the most useful skills. Any Repair skill level can get an item to 100%, higher skill just modifies the amount repaired for each repair job done to the item. Before attempting, look at how much extra CND you get. If the amount is low, don't bother; you're probably wasting the repair, so wait for the item to wear out a little more before attempting a repair.

When you repair an item, you essentially destroy one just like it. So always Repair your highest condition item using the lowest condition one in your inventory. The only exception is with Modded Weapons; you must repair these, and not use them to repair other weapons, or the upgrades are lost!

Attribute: Intelligence

PERK	SKILL LEVEL	CHARACTER LEVEL
Good Natured	+5	N/A
Hand Loader	70	6
Jury Rigging	90	14

Science

The Science skill represents your combined scientific knowledge, and is primarily used to hack restricted computer terminals. It can also be used to recycle Energy Weapon ammunition at Workbenches. There are also a fair number of conversations you can affect with this skill, making it highly effective, and it affects a large number of perks, too.

Attribute: Intelligence

PERK	SKILL LEVEL	CHARACTER LEVEL
Good Natured	+5	N/A
Vigilant Recycler	70	6
Math Wrath	70	10
Nerd Rage!	50	10
Robotics Expert	50	12
Computer Whiz	70	18
Nuka Chemist	90	22

Tip Hacking is delightfully simple, as long as you understand look for proper words within the "garbled code," select the word with your cursor, and try it. The computer indicates how many letters in the word were correctly placed. Use that as a clue, and search for a second word that incorporates the number of correct letters, to gradually reveal the correct password before the terminal locks up. Of course, you can stop before you're locked out, but if you hack again immediately, you must wait 10 seconds as the terminal to boot up. But if you back up a few feet, wait a few seconds, and then hack, the reboot doesn't occur.

Sneak

The higher your Sneak skill, the easier it is to remain undetected, steal an item, or pick someone's pocket. Successfully attacking while undetected grants an automatic Critical Hit. When you're Crouched and stationary or moving slowly, you're even harder to spot. Sneak is used to successfully steal items or Pickpocket entities, and the skill is incredibly useful in combat as any attack made while you are Hidden is a Sneak attack critical, which can do more than twice the damage as a regular critical.

Lower-level entities are now easier to Sneak by, even if you have a low Sneak skill. As you progress through levels, the advantages of Sneak begin to balance out.

Attribute: Agility

PERK	SKILL LEVEL	CHARACTER LEVEL
Friend of the Night	30	2
Cannibal	N/A	4
The Professional	70	6
Mister Sandman	60	10
Ghastly Scavenger	N/A	12
Silent Running	50	12
Ninja	80	20
Stealth Girl	N/A	Lily as a Follower

Speech

The Speech skill governs how much you can influence someone through dialogue, and gain access to information they might otherwise not want to share. Generally, the higher your Speech, the more likely you are to succeed at a Speech Check (aka Challenge), or extract information from someone who has a low disposition toward you. Don't let the lack of related perks fool you; Speech is the most-used conversation skill of all, and incredibly useful for circumventing or calming situations, and getting what you want out of a situation.

Attribute: Charisma

PERK	SKILL LEVEL	CHARACTER LEVEL
Good Natured	+5	N/A
Terrifying Presence	70	8

Survival

The Survival skill increases the Hit Points you receive from food and drink. It also helps you create consumable items at Campfires. Survival is used primarily to increase the healing benefits of Food and Drink (in the same way that Medicine does to Stimpaks). Survival is also vital for Crafting Recipes at Campfires, allowing you to collect ingredients and cook them to make a much more potent item, ranging from Tanned Gecko Hides to sell for profit, to poisons you can coat Melee Weapons, or nutritious cuisine. This is one skill to seriously consider if you're hoping to survive in Hardcore Mode.

Attribute: Endurance

PERK	SKILL LEVEL	CHARACTER LEVEL
Hunter	30	2
Entomologist	45	4
Rad Child	70	4
Travel Light	45	4
Lead Belly	40	6
Rad Resistance	40	8
Animal Friend	45	10

Unarmed

The Unarmed skill is used for fighting without a weapon, or with weapons designed for hand-to-hand combat, like Brass Knuckles, Power Fists, and Displacer Gloves. As a rule, if you're close enough to a foe, you'll always hit them; your Unarmed skill and weapon combined determines how much Unarmed damage you inflict. Unarmed also allows you to use your hands to block an attack; the higher the skill, the more damage is blocked.

At Unarmed 25, the you may randomly begin to strike with Uppercuts in addition to Left Jab and Right Jab. These do more damage. At Unarmed 50, you may randomly start to do Crosses in addition to Left Jab, Right Jab, and Uppercuts. These do large damage and are very fast. You then have access to these attacks for every battle. Finally, you can also unlock three special moves from characters in the Wasteland: Legion Assault, Scribe Counter, and Ranger Takedown. They are listed in the "Unarmed Perks" section of this chapter, below.

Attribute: Endurance

PERK	SKILL LEVEL	CHARACTER LEVEL
Good Natured	-5	N/A
Heavy Handed	More DAM, Less CRIT	N/A
Piercing Strike	70	12
Paralyzing Palm	70	18
Slayer	90	24
Legion Assault	N/A	N/A
Ranger Takedown	N/A	N/A
Scribe Counter	N/A	N/A

TRAITS OVERVIEW

At the end of your evaluation with Doctor Mitchell, just after you've chosen your Tag skill, you're given the option to pick one, two, or zero traits, which are permanent eccentricities tied to your character. These usually have both positive and counterbalancing negative qualities. You only get to choose up to two, and can't choose any more afterward.

Built to Destroy

Req: — | **Ranks: 1**

The Flamer that burns twice as bright burns half as long. All weapons have +3% chance to Critically Hit, but equipment condition decays 15% faster. Is this worth it? Only if you are skilled in repairing your own gear, or you have someone like Raul the Ghoul Follower to constantly Repair your weapons. You can always hope to find Weapon Repair Kits, or merchants specialized in Repair, so you don't need to rely on cannibalizing the same weapon type over and over.

Fast Shot

Req: — | **Ranks: 1**

While using Guns and Energy Weapons, you fire 20% more quickly but your shots are 20% less accurate. This is a toss-up, and usually reserved for Weapons you attack with at closer range, where you have more chance to hit. It's a good idea to pair this trait with the Rapid Reload perk, to off-set the speed at which you'll empty your guns' ammo. Remember not to choose Fast Shot combined with Trigger Discipline, as they cancel each other out!

Four Eyes

Req: PER < 10 | **Ranks: 1**

While wearing any type of glasses, you have +1 PER. Without glasses, you have -1 PER. This is worth taking, not only because there's a pair of Reading Glasses on the table in front of you when you wake up in Doctor Mitchell's House, but also because glasses don't break easily, either. Note that glasses cannot be worn with some types of headgear, so plan carefully.

Good Natured

Req: — | **Ranks: 1**

You're Good Natured at heart, more prone to solving problems with your mind than violence. You gain +5 to Barter, Medicine, Repair, Science, and Speech, but have -5 to Energy Weapons, Explosives, Guns, Melee Weapons, and Unarmed. If you're not combat-centric, this is thoroughly recommended. If you are combat-centric, this is also recommended; mainly because you usually only focus on one or two Combat skills but tend to use all four cerebral skills, and the net gain is well worth it. However, this does not apply to characters that just want one thing: to blow everything to smithereens.

Heavy Handed

Req: — | **Ranks: 1**

Your melee and unarmed attacks do more damage, but less critical hit damage. This is worth considering, especially if you're using such weapons and want to rely on good, old-fashioned bludgeoning. A good choice for fighters especially if you also improve critical hit damage chances with the appropriate perks, bringing further finesse to your mighty brawn. This trait can also help with overcoming enemy Damage Threshold early in the game, especially if you reduced your Luck attribute and have a lowered chance to critically hit anyway.

Kamikaze

Req: — | **Ranks: 1**

You have +10 Action Points but your reckless nature causes you to have -2 Damage Threshold. This is actually very tempting, as although you're less well-armored, if you're fighting at a distance, or apt to stay away from most fights, or can inflict more attacks thanks to your increased AP, you won't need to worry about your DT. Or choose heavier armor. This is also a viable trait for high Endurance/low Agility melee characters who already have a lot of Hit Points but low AP.

Loose Cannon

Req: — | **Ranks: 1**

From Frag Grenades to Throwing Spears, you can throw weapons 30% faster at the cost of 25% less range. Pick this, and you'll take enemies down faster, but at the expense of long-range combat (so employ a Follower there), and you'll use up more projectiles, of course. This a good pick for characters that plan on building an arsenal of explosives with which to rain destruction upon groups of foes. If your style is more subtle, and precise, skip this one. Also combines well with Heave Ho! perk.

Small Frame

Req: AGL < 10 | **Ranks: 1**

Due to your small size, you have +1 AGL but your limbs are more easily crippled. This is worth considering if you want the extra speed, reload times, and you're using a number of AGL-related skills and perks. However, you'll do best to avoid situations where crippling can easily occur (traps, and certain types of combat, and enemies). Also, you'll have to be extra careful on Hardcore Mode, because healing your limbs will be trickier than in regular difficulty mode. Take the Adamantium Skeleton perk to lessen the negative effects of this trait, or take Intense Training: Agility at Level 2 and skip the trait altogether.

Trigger Discipline

Req: — | **Ranks: 1**

While using Guns and Energy Weapons, you fire 20% more slowly, but are 20% more accurate. This is a toss-up, and usually reserved for Weapons you attack with at far range, where you have more time to line up a shot, or you like to face fewer enemies, or have Followers with you. Of course, this may not matter if you're gonna put bullets right between their eyes! Remember not to choose Fast Shot combined with Trigger Discipline, as they cancel each other out.

Wild Wasteland

Req: — | **Ranks: 1**

Wild Wasteland unleashes the most bizarre and silly elements of post-apocalyptic America. Not for the faint of heart or the serious of temperament. If you take your Fallout adventuring extremely seriously, don't take this trait. If you're after some humorous Easter Eggs, go for it! All of the Wild Wasteland Easter Eggs are in the Appendices.

PERKS OVERVIEW

These are benefits that are specific to your character's development, and help your specialization. They have wildly different benefits (and possible minor hindrances), and are added every two levels, as well as a substitute perk called Intense Training (see below). In many cases, you need a particular minimum attribute or skill level to access a perk. You can also choose a previously available perk when you level up, too. Finally, some perks have one (or more) additional "ranks", for even more potency.

Tip Look down this list before your adventure begins and learn the perks with the some prerequisites. For example, Fortune Finder (Level 6) and Better Criticals (Level 16) both require a Luck 5+ and 6+ respectively, so seriously look at both of them. Be forward-thinking, so you can obtain associated perks as early as possible.

Level 2 Perks

Confirmed Bachelor
Cherchez La Femme

Req: Level 2, Male/Female | **Ranks: 1**

In combat, you do +10% damage against opponents of the same sex. Outside of combat, you'll sometimes have access to unique dialogue options when dealing with the same sex. There are generally more male characters to interact with than female ones, so Confirmed Bachelor is slightly more useful.

Intense Training

Req: Level 2 | **Ranks: 10**

With the Intense Training perk, you can put a single point into any of your SPECIAL attributes. This perk is unique due to the number of ranks. Figure out the "knock on" effects. Recommended attributes to raise include Luck (increased Criticals and sometimes Skill Points), Intelligence (extra Skill Points during level-ups), and Strength (extra Carry Weight). However, raised an attribute may not be as profoundly helpful as other perks; unless you're doing so to make a particular perk available to you.

Lady Killer
Black Widow

Req: Level 2, Male/Female | **Ranks: 1**

In combat, you do +10% damage against opponents of the opposite sex. Outside of combat, you'll sometimes have access to unique dialogue options when dealing with the opposite sex. There are usually more male characters to speak or shoot, so Black Widow is slightly more useful compared to Lady Killer.

Rapid Reload

Req: Level 2, Guns 30, AGL 5 | Ranks: 1

Rapid Reload makes all of your weapon reloads 25% faster than normal. This is particularly helpful with Shotguns, or more cumbersome weapons. This perk applies to ALL weapons that have a "reload" – so basically anything that's not a melee, thrown or unarmed weapon.

Retention

Req: Level 2, INT 5 | Ranks: 1

With the Retention perk, the bonuses granted by Skill Magazines last three times as long. This has advantages depending on the Skill Magazine itself. Is it worth being able to master Lockpick for thrice as long? Probably not; but for combat skills (such as Melee, Unarmed, Energy Weapons, and Guns), and a protracted battle, this can be very useful; especially when combined with Comprehension.

Swift Learner

Req: Level 2, INT 4 | Ranks: 3

With each rank in the Swift Learner perk, you gain an additional 10% to total Experience Points (XP) whenever Experience Points are earned. Obviously, take this as early as possible. This sounds great, but the downside is that the other perks grant you much more exciting abilities.

- Rank 1: Modify experience +10%
- Rank 2: Modify experience +20%
- Rank 3: Modify experience +30%

Friend of the Night

Req: Level 2, PER 6, Sneak 30 | Ranks: 1

You are a true friend of the night. Your eyes adapt quickly to low-light conditions indoors and when darkness falls across the Wasteland. If you want a Chem-induced approximation of this perk, take Cateye. This is handy as you do see better, but you can simply Wait for the sun to rise instead.

Heave, Ho!

Req: Level 2, Explosives 30, STR 5 | Ranks: 1

Quite an arm you've got there. All thrown weapons fly farther and faster for you. This is advantageous for the adventurer who is stocking up on Frag Grenades, and other projectiles such as Throwing Spears. If you're specializing in this manner, take this perk.

Hunter

Req: Level 2, Survival 30 | Ranks: 1

In combat, you do +75% Critical Damage against animals and mutated animals. This is excellent when you're wanting to take out Coyotes, Geckos, and even Nightstalkers. A quick way to make some Caps is to slaughter Geckos, and tan their hides on a Campfire, and selling them for good profit.

Level 4 Perks

Cannibal

Req: Level 4 | Ranks: 1

With the Cannibal perk, when you're in Sneak mode, you gain the option to eat a corpse to regain Health. But every time you feed, you lose Karma, and if the act is witnessed, it is considered a crime against nature. This certainly helps you in Hardcore Mode, and allows you to take Ghastly Scavenger at Level 12. If you aren't bothered about Karma, and can feast away from those you're wanting to gain Reputation with, chow down!

Comprehension

Req: Level 4, INT 4 | Ranks: 1

With the Comprehension perk, you gain double the bonus from reading magazines and one additional point from Skill Books. This is thoroughly recommended if you plan to search for required reading. Take this as early as you can, and don't read any Skill Books or Magazines until you claim this perk! Be sure you have Retention too; Skill Magazines have just become incredibly useful!

Educated

Req: Level 4, INT 4 | Ranks: 1

With the Educated perk, you gain two more Skill Points every time you advance in level. This perk is best taken early on, to maximize its effectiveness. You might wish to spend these points on skills you normally wouldn't choose. Pick this at Level 4, because there are diminishing returns the longer you leave it. Although +2 Skill Points may not seem a lot, by Level 30 you'd have 52 additional points.

Entomologist

Req: Level 4, Survival 45, INT 4 | Ranks: 1

With the Entomologist perk, you do an additional +50% damage every time you attack a mutated insect, like the Radroach, Giant Mantis, or Radscorpion. Also affected are Giant Ants, and Spore Plants and Carriers. If you plan to explore the lairs of these creatures, or undertake Quests where these critters are commonplace, this a perk to consider.

Rad Child

Req: Level 4, Survival 70 | Ranks: 1

You truly are a rad child. As you go through the increasingly devastating stages of radiation sickness, you will regenerate more and more health. An excellent perk to choose in Hardcore Mode, this allows you to explore every radiation hot-spot in the Mojave. However, this isn't a great deal of territory, and there's no large-scale, heavily irradiated areas. It makes wandering through Camp Searchlight and Vault 34 a breeze, though.

Run 'n Gun

Req: Level 4, Guns 45 OR Energy Weapons 45 | Ranks: 1

The Run 'n Gun perk reduces accuracy penalties with one-handed Guns and Energy Weapons while walking or running. This is a must-have for those focusing on either of these skills (and especially both), who favor manual aiming rather than the help of VATS to take enemies down. It isn't necessary if you're using two-handed Rifles, for example.

Travel Light

Req: Level 4, Survival 45 | Ranks: 1

While wearing light armor or no armor, you run 10% faster. If you have somewhere to go, and no time to get there, this is a perk to take. However, the lack of protection may not be worth the slight improvement in speed. Fast Travel also hinders this, making it more useful in Hardcore Mode, where you might need to reach a destination before you become too hungry or thirsty. Remember that you can carry more than one outfit as long as you've got the spare Carry Weight to do so. Hot key some heavy armor to put on in a pinch and switch back to your traveling clothes when you're done.

Level 6 Perks

Bloody Mess

Req: Level 6 | Ranks: 1

With the Bloody Mess perk, characters and creatures you kill will often explode into a red, gut-ridden, eyeball-strewn paste. Fun! Oh, and you'll do 5% extra damage with all weapons. The hilarious and disgusting explosions are certainly a sight to see, but they can prove problematic during Side Quest: Three Card Bounty, where you're asked to defeat targets and leave the head intact. Don't take this before that Quest is complete.

Demolition Expert

Req: Level 6, Explosives 50 | Ranks: 3

With each rank of this perk, all of your Explosive weapons do an additional 20% damage. This is an obvious perk to take if you're spending your time killing foes with Mines, Grenades, and the various two-handed grenade weapons, Missile Launchers, and fabled Fat Man. A true expert can place a series of Bottlecap Mines in the path of an Alpha Male Deathclaw and bring it down single-handedly! This is a great way to clear out Quarry Junction [4.04].

Ferocious Loyalty

Req: Level 6, CHR 6 | Ranks: 1

The power of your personality inspires die-hard loyalty from your Followers. When you drop below 50% Health, your companions temporarily gain much greater resistance to damage. Naturally, this is helpful if you're relying on your Followers to fight your battles for you. In fact, you might want to purposefully keep your health low, then put armor on, to keep your Followers battle-tough. Make sure you have two Followers, and they are at the front of every battle!

Fortune Finder

Req: Level 6, LCK 5 | Ranks: 1

With the Fortune Finder perk, you'll find considerably more bottle caps in containers than you normally would. Although tempting (to find around twice the normal number of Caps in containers), you may wish to wait until you can take Scrounger; netting ammunition instead nets you more Caps when you sell it (and you can use ammo in combat as well as break it down at Reloading Benches).

Gunslinger

Req: Level 6 | Ranks: 1

While using a pistol (or similar one-handed weapon), your accuracy in VATS is significantly increased. This includes any weapon flagged as "one-handed ranged" in the "Guns and Gear" chapter. View the stats for some of the powerful weapons of this type, and then use them. You can drop foes easily and reliably, without wasting ammunition. Great if you're going to rely on this weapon type.

Hand Loader

Req: Level 6, Repair 70 | Ranks: 1

You know your way around a Reloading Bench and don't let good brass and hulls go to waste. When you use Guns, you are more likely to recover cases and hulls. You also have all hand load Recipes unlocked at the Reloading Bench. This is obviously beneficial to those who use Guns, and a Reloading Bench; it makes it even more appealing to search for components and then strip them down and build up your collection of ammo types.

Lead Belly

Req: Level 6, Survival 40 OR END 5 | Ranks: 1

With the Lead Belly perk, you take 50% less radiation when consuming irradiated food and drink. These include sinks, toilets, valves under water towers, and lakes. If you're playing Hardcore Mode, and you're out in the desert (and at lesser difficulty, you didn't bring Stimpaks with you), this is most helpful; although many of the areas aren't particularly radioactive.

Shotgun Surgeon

Req: Level 6, Guns 45 | Ranks: 1

Your precision with a scattergun is something to behold. When using shotguns, regardless of ammunition used, you ignore an additional 10 points of a target's Damage Threshold. This is for those who are using Guns skill and shotguns exclusively. But it does help you take down armored foes, and allow you a wider array of ammunition types to use.

The Professional

Req: Level 6, Sneak 70 | Ranks: 1

Up close and personal, that's how you like it. Your Sneak Attack Criticals with pistols, revolvers, and submachine guns, whether Guns or Energy Weapons, all inflict an additional 20% damage. This is a must for those who are constantly Sneaking and surprising an enemy. Choose the weapon that delivers the most damage that you own, and employ it.

Toughness

Req: Level 6, END5 | Ranks: 2

With the Toughness perk, you gain +3 to overall Damage Threshold. This perk may be taken twice, with the second rank granting an additional +3. Extra Damage Threshold? A total of 6 DT is like having free armor! There's no reason not to immediately take this perk.

Vigilant Recycler

Req: Level 6, Science 70 | Ranks: 1

Waste not, want not. When you use Energy Weapons, you are more likely to recover drained ammunition. You also have more efficient Recycling recipes available at the Workbench. You must be primarily focused and using Energy Weapons, and be knowledgeable of Crafting and use it regularly to get the most out of this perk.

Level 8 Perks

Commando

Req: Level 8 | Ranks: 1

While using a rifle (or similar two-handed weapon), your accuracy in VATS is significantly increased. You gain a 25% better chance to hit in VATS: For example, a 40% chance becomes a 50% chance. This includes Unique Rifles and two-handed Guns. This is arguably advantageous over Gunslinger if you're using rifles and other two-handed weaponry. Later in the adventure, two-handed weapons tend to be much more powerful, and this perk becomes even more advantageous. Are you using VATS and guns? Then take this perk!

Cowboy

Req: Level 8, Guns 45, Melee Weapons 45 | Ranks: 1

You do 25% more damage when using any revolver, lever-action firearm, dynamite, knife, or hatchet. Similar to the Commando and Gunslinger, apart from the type of weapon you employ, and the fact this straddles the Guns and Melee Weapon skills. Check the type of weapon, and pick this perk if you use them as a primary armament.

Living Anatomy

Req: Level 8, Medicine 70 | Ranks: 1

Living Anatomy allows you to see the Health and Damage Threshold of any target. It also gives you a +5% bonus to damage against Human and nonferal Ghouls. If you're stats-driven, and want to see precisely the Hit Points you're taking off each individual foe, these appear under their health bar. This is handy, and as there's more human-sized foes than any other entity, gaining additional advantage is an excellent idea.

Pack Rat

Req: Level 8, INT 5, Barter 70 | Ranks: 1

You have learned the value of careful packing. Items with a weight of 2 or less weigh half as much for you. If you're apt for collecting Recipe Ingredients, playing on Hardcore Mode, like to be a loner without a Follower helping you carry items, lack Strength, or simply want to grab loads of ammunition to break down, take this helpful perk.

Quick Draw

Req: Level 8, AGL 5 | Ranks: 1

Quick Draw makes all of your weapon equipping and holstering 50% faster. Getting the draw on the enemy is always important, and although it is suited to a style of play that involves a lot of rearranging your armaments, every advantage helps. Also, consider that running around with heavy weapons already drawn slows your speed down—holstering, and drawing weapons quickly, suits characters that like speed, and precise fighting. This perk is useful for melee focused players as well. Run fast to close the distance and then draw your two-handed weapon at the last second.

Rad Resistance

Req: Level 8, Survival 40, END 5 | Ranks: 1

Rad Resistance allows you to resist radiation. This perk grants an additional 25% to Radiation Resistance. Sell any Rad-X you find, and wander off into the irradiated areas of the Wasteland. You can get by without this, but it is helpful in Hardcore Mode.

Scrounger

Req: Level 8, LCK 5 | Ranks: 1

With the Scrounger perk, you'll find considerably more ammunition in containers than you normally would. When you check safes, cabinets, and lockers, expect the perk to pay dividends; it is arguably better than Fortune Finder, as you have the flexibility of finding more ammunition, which you can sell, break down, or use in fights, instead of just finding Caps.

Stonewall

Req: Level 8, END 6, STR 6 | Ranks: 1

You gain +5 Damage Threshold against all Melee Weapons and Unarmed attacks and cannot be knocked down in combat. For those who favor combat up close and personal, and you're allied with a Faction (such as the NCR) that is battling another (Caesar's Legion) that has a number of enemies that use Melee Weapons and Unarmed attacks, then take this perk. It's also good against Deathclaws and Bighorners which have a knockdown attack. As well as anyone who has ever fought Legate Lanius and his frequent knockdown hits.

Strong Back

Req: Level 8, STR 5, END 5 | Ranks: 1

With the Strong Back perk, you can carry 50 more pounds of equipment. If you simply want to carry more, or wish to use heavier items, it stands to reason to take this. Or, employ a Follower to carry the brunt of your belongings and choose a different perk. This is another handy perk to have in Hardcore Mode.

Super Slam

Req: Level 8, STR 6, Melee Weapons 45 | Ranks: 1

All Melee Weapons (except thrown) and Unarmed attacks have a chance of knocking your target down. This is great news if you employ these two types of Combat skill, as a downed enemy is prone for a second and it's easy to keep piling on the punishment, or flee the fracas.

Terrifying Presence

Req: Level 8, Speech 70 | Ranks: 1

In some conversations, you gain the ability to initiate combat while terrifying a mob of opponents, sending them fleeing away for safety. This intimidation certainly gets you noticed, and sometimes the fleeing occurs, but other times this is just something ruthlessly cool to say to someone you're about to eviscerate! Look for the major conversations with this perk throughout the Main and Side Quest Walkthrough.

Level 10 Perks

Animal Friend

Req: Level 10, CHR 6, Survival 45 | Ranks: 2

At the first rank of this perk, animals simply won't attack unless attacked first. At the second rank, they will actually come to your aid in combat, but never against another animal. This includes Bighorners, Brahmin, Dogs, Coyotes, Nightstalkers and other animals. This does forfeit the XP you gain from killing them, however. Or perhaps you want to coax a Viper Gang into a Coyote Den! In Hardcore Mode, this can help you out, and even provide a buffer zone between the animal fighting for you, and a Deathclaw that would otherwise savage you.

Finesse

Req: Level 10 | Ranks: 1

With the Finesse perk, you have a higher chance to score a critical hit on an opponent in combat, equivalent to 5 extra points of Luck. This increases your critical hit chance as if your Luck were five points higher, usually doubling the base chance of a Critical. If you enjoy inflicting critical hits, then take this and combine it with Better Criticals (and a high Luck).

Here and Now

Req: Level 10 | Ranks: 1

The Here and Now perk immediately grants an additional experience level, complete with all the advantages that brings. This is useful if you're only two levels away from a perk you really must have, or you're simply impatient. The downside is that by the time this is available, there are many incredible perks to choose from instead. Note you have to be lower than Level 20 to take this perk.

Math Wrath

Req: Level 10, Science 70 | Ranks: 1

You are able to optimize your Pip-Boy's VATS logic, reducing all AP costs by 10%. This has numerous benefits relating to all the weapons you use, but only when you're not fighting manually. If you use VATS for most of your attacks, this is an excellent way to use AP more efficiently, and therefore extra attacks.

Miss Fortune

Req: Level 10, LCK 6 | Ranks: 1

Just when your enemies think they have the upper hand, Miss Fortune appears to turn their world upside down. Appearing only in VATS, she has the ability to snatch defeat from the jaws of victory. More of an entertainment than a necessity. Clad in fancy feathers, once she turns up (there is a 10% chance) and hits, Miss Fortune's particular attacks occur as follows:

- 35% = Knockdown
- 30% = Weapon flies out of enemy hand (if no weapon, results are chosen again)
- 35% = Random limb is crippled (if the limb is already crippled, results are chosen again)

10% Head	15% Left leg
15% Left arm	15% Right leg
15% Right arm	30% Torso

Mister Sandman

Req: Level 10, Sneak 60 | Ranks: 1

With the Mister Sandman perk, when you're in Sneak mode, you gain the option to silently kill any human or Ghoul while they're sleeping. And, all Mister Sandman kills earn bonus XP. Can't seem to fathom why anyone would take this perk? Then you haven't heard the legends of a stealthy man who killed an entire city of sleeping inhabitants in a single night. That man had a Mister Sandman perk. If you're attacking a settlement at night, this is incredibly useful, especially as it keeps your Reputation intact (unless you're spotted!). Slit the throats of the leaders of Camp McCarran, but still keep your Reputation with the NCR!

Mysterious Stranger

Req: Level 10, LCK 6 | Ranks: 1

You've gained your own personal guardian angel... armed with a fully loaded .44 Magnum. With this perk, the Mysterious Stranger will appear occasionally in VATS mode to lend a hand, with deadly efficiency. If at the end of a VATS attack, your opponent has less than 150 points of health, there is a 10% chance the Mysterious Stranger will show up and finish him off. This perk is most useful if your game is set to a higher difficulty. This is also a perk to take for sheer entertainment value, but it's useful in battle nevertheless; you save on ammo and APs, and he takes the head-shot for you.

Nerd Rage!

Req: Level 10, Science 50, INT 5 | Ranks: 1

You've been pushed around long enough! With the Nerd Rage! perk, your Strength is raised to 10 and you gain +15 Damage Threshold whenever your Health drops to 20% or below. This is an impressive amount, so don't just think of this perk being for those skilled in noncombative abilities. It can get you out of an otherwise tight jam. If you have a high Endurance, you naturally have a fair amount of Health, so this perk lasts a lot longer. This is good if you're playing this adventure on a higher difficulty.

Night Person

Req: Level 10 | Ranks: 1

When the sun is down, a Night Person gains +2 to both Intelligence and Perception (up to a maximum of 10). This perk directly affects your "internal clock," and remains active both inside and outside. This benefit (which occurs between 6 PM and 6 AM) continues into areas that aren't outside. Check your Pip-Boy's Clock for the correct time.

Plasma Spaz

Req: Level 10, Energy Weapons 70 | Ranks: 1

You're just so excited about plasma that you can't (magnetically) contain yourself! The AP costs for all plasma weapons (including Plasma Grenades) are reduced by 10%. If you're focusing on Energy Weapons (and to a much lesser extent, Explosives), this is incredibly handy if you're constantly utilizing Plasma weapons in VATS. Note that this benefit does not extend to Laser weapons!

Level 12 Perks

Fast Metabolism

Req: Level 12 | Ranks: 1

With the Fast Metabolism perk, you gain a 20% Health bonus when using Stimpaks. When used with the Medicine skill, you can increase your Health by a spectacular amount. If you're focusing on Unarmed or Melee skills, or you're busy creating Stimpaks as Recipes, this perk is especially useful.

Ghastly Scavenger

Req: Level 12, Cannibal | Ranks: 1

With Ghastly Scavenger, when you're in Sneak mode, you gain the option to eat a Super Mutant or Feral Ghoul corpse to regain Health. Every time you fee, you lose Karma, and if the act is witnessed, it is considered a crime against nature. This is essentially free food, and if you're not concerned with Karma, and have utilized the guide maps to locate the concentrations of Ghouls and Super Mutants (the REPCONN Test Site is a veritable banquet!), chow down! Combine this with Cannibal for an even wider menu, but don't munch on corpses near a Faction you're trying to up your Reputation with.

Hit the Deck

Req: Level 12, Explosives 70 | Ranks: 1

Your extensive familiarity with Explosives allows you to ignore a portion of their damage. Your Damage Threshold is increased by 50% against any and all Explosives—even your own. This is helpful if you set off traps, and you're facing enemies that like to use Explosives, such as Powder Gangers. It is an obvious choice if you're specializing in the Explosives skill, but as there are far more enemies that employ other weapons compared to Explosives, think twice before choosing this.

Life Giver

Req: Level 12, END 6 | Ranks: 1

With the Life Giver perk, you gain an additional 30 Hit Points. Do you want or need these Hit Points? Then this is an easy decision to make!

Long Haul

Req: Level 12, Barter 70, END 6 | Ranks: 1

You have learned how to pack mountains of gear for the Long Haul. Being over-encumbered no longer prevents you from using Fast Travel. Obviously, if you travel light, have Followers who carry your belongings, or like wandering around, there's no need to take this perk. But if you're in Hardcore Mode, have a smaller Carry Weight due to a low Strength, or you're desperate to be weighed down, and able to teleport, then this is for you.

Piercing Strike

Req: Level 12, Unarmed 70 | Ranks: 1

Piercing Strike makes all of your Unarmed and Melee Weapons (including thrown) negate 15 points of Damage Threshold on the target. A no-brainer for those focusing on these specific weapons, this can really take down foes if you combine it with (for example) poisons you've Crafted. If you're going down this specialization path, take this.

Pyromaniac

Req: Level 12, Explosives 60 | Ranks: 1

With the Pyromaniac perk, you do +50% damage with fire-based weapons, like the Flamer and Shishkebab. This is another perk that is chosen depending entirely on your play-style. Do you use these weapons more often than not, or exclusively? Then this is a must-have. Otherwise, pass on this.

Robotics Expert

Req: Level 12, Science 50 | Ranks: 1

With the Robotics Expert perk, you do an additional 25% damage to any robot. But, even better, sneaking up on a hostile robot undetected and activating it will put that robot into a permanent shutdown state. Employ this if you have a very high Sneak skill, so you can easily disrupt any robots. Remember to destroy the robot afterwards for the XP and loot. There are a few additional conversation and general Quest options, too.

Silent Running

Req: Level 12, AGL 6, Sneak 50 | Ranks: 1

With the Silent Running perk, running no longer factors into a successful sneak attempt. Before this perk, moving quickly while crouching made more noise than moving slowly while crouching. Afterwards, crouch and move in for the kill with much less noise problems. Remember you must be crouched for this to be effective! You must take this if you're focuing on Unarmed, Sneak, or Melee Weapons and want to inflict Sneak attacks.

Sniper

Req: Level 12, AGL 6, PER 6 | Ranks: 1

With the Sniper perk, your chance to hit an opponent's head in VATS is significantly increased. This is around 25%, and is excellent if headshots are your preferred method of foe disposal. Combine this with Commando or Gunslinger to turn yourself into a ruthless killing machine.

Splash Damage

Req: Level 12, Explosives 70 | Ranks: 1

When you're deep in enemy territory, you just start chucking grenades and hope for the best. All Explosives have a 25% larger area of effect. Remember that you'll now want to be 25% further away if you're prone to lobbing grenades at closer quarters. But for those focusing on Explosives, and wanting to attack settlements where foes are close together, or inside corridors or enclosed structures, this is worth it.

Unstoppable Force

Req: Level 12, STR 7, Melee Weapons 90 | Ranks: 1

Your martial might is truly legendary. You do a large amount of additional damage through enemy blocks with all Melee Weapons and Unarmed attacks. This allows you to negate the mainly real-time annoyance of swiping at a foe and watching them block. It takes foes down quicker, removes their defenses admirably, and is a must for those who are becoming close-combat monsters.

Level 14 Perks

Adamantium Skeleton

Req: Level 14 | Ranks: 1

With the Adamantium Skeleton perk, your limbs only receive 50% of the damage they normally would. Your overall Hit Points aren't effected. It allows you to heal with Stimpaks for longer before you need to find a bed, and is helpful during Hardcore Mode, but not as much as it first appears, because most adventurers aren't constantly crippling themselves.

Center of Mass

Req: Level 14, Guns 70 | Ranks: 1

You don't fool around with fancy trick shots. Straight to the midsection and down they go. In VATS, you do an additional 15% damage with attacks targeting the torso. This is handy if you're not exclusively (and psychotically) only aiming at heads, and for overall damage, this is more than acceptable, although armor plays a major preventative over this body part.

Chemist

Req: Level 14, Medicine 60 | Ranks: 1

With the Chemist perk, any Chems you take last twice as long. If you're using and abusing Chems, you must take this perk. Be sure to mix your Chems up; taking (for example) Jet, Psycho, and Med-X before battling the tougher foes; your combat is much improved until the Chems wear off.

Jury Rigging

Req: Level 14, Repair 90 | Ranks: 1

You possess the amazing ability to Repair any item using a roughly similar item. Fix a Trail Carbine with a Hunting Rifle, a Plasma Defender with a Laser Pistol, or even Power Armor with Metal Armor. How does it work? Nobody knows... except you. Increasing the number of useful items to scavenge is never a bad plan, although this may weigh you down unduly, and there are other ways (Followers and Weapon Repair Kits) to keep some of your favorite armaments working properly. It certainly helps when you're wearing something incredibly rare, and you can fix it with something easily found.

Light Step

Req: Level 14, PER 6, AGL 6 | Ranks: 1

With the Light Step perk, you'll never set off an enemy's mines or floor-based traps. If Mines, Bear Traps, or Tripwires annoy you, take this perk. It is useful if you're Sneaking in Trap-laced areas, too. Or, you can just take the extra care, consult the "Tour" chapter that flags where all the major traps are, and slow down when you get there!

Purifier

Req: Level 14 | Ranks: 1

As a purifier of the wasteland, you do +50% damage with Melee and Unarmed weapons against Centaurs, Nightstalkers, Spore Plants, Spore Carriers, Deathclaws, Super Mutants, and Feral Ghouls. Abominations must die! Check the tour for the "Faction" present in every location, and if any of these creatures are listed, you'll know this perk is going to help you. As always, this is a perk for those focusing on a particular skill set.

Level 16 Perks

Action Boy

Action Girl

Req: Level 16, AGL 6 | Ranks: 2

With the Action Boy perk, you gain an additional 15 Action Points to use in VATS. This is a sizable increase, and can often mean an extra attack with your favorite weapon. If you use VATS in combat, consider this.

Better Criticals

Req: Level 16, PER 6, LCK 6 | Ranks: 1

With the Better Criticals perk, you gain a 50% damage bonus every time a critical hit is scored on an opponent. This doesn't mean you score critical hits more frequently. Use this if your attacks are prone to deliver critical hits, adept at killing blows, you have a high Luck, or you've taken the Finesse perk.

Chem Resistant

Req: Level 16, Medicine 60 | Ranks: 1

Having the Chem Resistant perk means you're 50% less likely to develop an addiction to Chems, like Psycho or Jet. Much like Chemist, this is an essential perk for you if you're always using and abusing Jet, Mentats, Cateye, Buffout, and the other Chems. Pair it with Chemist to really enhance your attacks!

Meltdown

Req: Level 16, Energy Weapons 90 | Ranks: 1

Meltdown causes foes killed by your Energy Weapons to give off a corona of harmful energy. Note: this can cause a chain reaction. This is vaguely similar to "Bloody Mess', but with the added benefit of causing splash damage as the target explodes. This helps clear out rooms where foes are close together, and there's no downsides to this, unless you're only wanting to kill one entity, and a target you're wanting to help is caught in the ensuing plasma storm.

Tag!

Req: Level 16 | Ranks: 1

The Tag! perk allows you to select a fourth skill to be a Tag skill, which instantly raises it by 15 points. If you've ignored a skill for too long that you really want to try, or you're wanting to raise a skill to the next tier (such as Science, so you can unlock hard terminals instead of average ones), then take this.

Weapon Handling

Req: Level 16, STR < 10 | Ranks: 1

Weapon Strength Requirements are now 2 points lower than normal for you. If you're weedy, but like carrying larger, weightier firearms, then choose this. As larger weapons tend to be more powerful, this is a great alternative to shaking off the weight penalties without expensive Implant perks, or if you want a change of armaments and put points into other attributes. This diminishes the usefulness of Strength, so remember this during Character creation.

Level 18 Perks

Computer Whiz

Req: Level 18, Science 70, INT 7 | Ranks: 1

Fail a hack attempt and get locked out of a computer? Not if you're a Computer Whiz! With this perk, you can attempt to re-hack any computer you were previously locked out of. Because you can quit out of any terminal, and wait 10 seconds for it to reboot, this is of limited value.

Concentrated Fire

Req: Level 18, Energy Weapons 60, Guns 60 | Ranks: 1

With Concentrated Fire, your accuracy to hit any body part in VATS increases slightly with each subsequent hit on that body part. Take this is you have a large number of Action Points, and the weapon you're using has a low AP. If you've taken Commando, Gunslinger, and/or the Sniper perks, you're already a killing machine, and this becomes less useful (as the foe won't likely survive to the point where this becomes useful).

- Targeting first time: Normal %
- Targeting second time: +5%
- Targeting third time: +10%, and so on

Infiltrator

Req: Level 18, Lockpick 70, PER 7 | Ranks: 1

With Infiltrator, if a lock is broken, and can't normally be picked again, you can attempt to pick it again one more time. This includes locks previously broken by a "Force Lock" attempt. You can't do this a third time. Simply perfect the Lockpick minigame (which you should already be good at with Lockpick 70) instead. Force the lock once, then pick it.

Paralyzing Palm

Req: Level 18, Unarmed 70 | Ranks: 1

With Paralyzing Palm, you will sometimes perform a special VATS palm strike that paralyzes your opponent for 30 seconds. Note that in order to perform the Paralyzing Palm, you must be completely unarmed. "Completely unarmed" actually means "with an Unarmed Weapon, or using your fists," and this is a death sentence for a foe, freezing them so you can re-equip, and drop your enemy at your leisure. Unarmed characters must take this.

Level 20 Perks

Explorer

Req: Level 20 | Ranks: 1

When you choose the Explorer perk, every location in the world is revealed on your map. So get out there and explore! Not necessary due to the maps this guide contains, but for those who want everything revealed as quickly as possible, this is a great reference.

Grim Reaper's Sprint

Req: Level 20 | Ranks: 1

If you kill a target in VATS, 20 Action Points are restored upon exiting VATS. If you have a large number of Action Points, this can increase the duration of a fight, and allow many more foes to fall.

Ninja

Req: Level 20, Melee Weapons 80, Sneak 80 | Ranks: 1

The Ninja perk grants you the power of the fabled shadow warriors. When attacking with either Melee or Unarmed, you gain a +15% Critical Chance on every strike. Sneak attack criticals do 25% more damage than normal. For the ultimate warrior specializing in Melee or Unarmed combat, this is the ultimate perk.

Solar Powered

Req: Level 20, END 7 | Ranks: 1

With the Solar Powered perk, you gain an additional 2 points to Strength when in direct sunlight, and slowly regenerate lost Health. Getting back Hit Points is incredibly useful, especially in Hardcore Mode, as you regenerate 1 point every 10 seconds you're in sunlight, but doesn't heal limbs. Combine this with Adamantium Skeleton, and wander the Mojave during the day, and sleep during the night. Or combine with Night Person and get bonuses day and night.

Level 22 Perks

Laser Commander

Req: Level 22, Energy Weapons 90 | Ranks: 1

From the humble Laser Pistol to the mighty Gatling laser, you do +15% damage and have +10% chance to critically hit with any laser weapons. As Laser weapons fire quickly, but are less powerful than plasma weapons, this evens the score, and makes any type of laser weapon even more potent. This is great news if you have cultivated a large collection of powerful, unique, or modded Laser Pistols, Rifles, and the like.

Nuka Chemist

Req: Level 22, Science 90 | Ranks: 1

You have unraveled some of the greatest mysteries of Pre-War masters; formulas for developing special Nuka-Colas! This perk unlocks special Nuka-Cola recipes at the Workbench. If the stat increases of Nuka-Cola interest you, take this as it allows you to concoct Ice Cola, Quartz, and Victory variants of the infamous soda. Which can be handy since the Atomic Cocktail recipe calls for 2 Victory colas.

Spray and Pray

Req: Level 22 | Ranks: 1

Your attacks do much less damage to companions, allowing you to liberally spray an area with reckless abandon. Or you could just stand in front of your Followers and not hit them. However, if you like using more "area-effect" weapons such as a Minigun, or you have melee companions (like Rex, Lilly, and Veronica) and you're worried about mowing them down, this perk lets you worry less.

Level 24 Perk

Slayer

Req: Level 24, Unarmed 90, AGL 7 | Ranks: 1

The slayer walks the earth! The speed of all melee weapons and unarmed attacks is increased by 30%. Prepare to beat, bludgeon, cut, slice, and tear apart anything that dares cross your path. This is an obvious, and extremely exciting perk for the Courier with close-combat prowess.

Level 26 Perk

Nerves of Steel

Req: Level 26, AGL 7 | Ranks: 1

With the Nerves of Steel perk, you regenerate Action Points much more quickly than you normally would. Consider this if your ill-conceived earlier decisions left you with less Action Points than you wanted, and don't take this with the Grim Reaper's Sprint, which is arguably a better bet. Naturally the upshot of this perk is your ability to tackle more opponents before they have their turn. Or you can or take all the AP perks, plus all the VATS perks like commando, sniper or center of mass and spend all your time in VATS

Level 28 Perk

Rad Absorption

Req: Level 28, END 7 | Ranks: 1

With the Rad Absorbtion perk, your radiation level slowly decreases on its own over time. This is assuming you're not in an irradiated area, and you lose one Rad Point every 20 seconds, which allows you to function without Rad-X or RadAway. This is perfect for the ultimate Hardcore Mode adventurer, who wants to trek to the furthest (irradiated) areas the Mojave has to offer.

CHALLENGE, FOLLOWER, UNARMED, AND OTHER PERKS

The following perks are available only after certain obligations, or vast sums of Cap transactions, are completed. Also listed are perks that are available from a Follower, but only during the time they are with you.

Power Armor Training

Req: Learn the subtleties of Power Armor from a trained individual.

Ranks: 1

Available: Side Quest—For Auld Lang Syne and/or Still in the Dark

You have received the specialized training needed to move in any form of Power Armor. Complete either Quest to request this perk, which allows you to wear any type of Power Armor. These are flagged in the Guns and Gear section of this guide.

Challenge-Related Perks

The perks, which are primarily reward you with an increased statistic, are awarded after you've performed the same action numerous times, and are skilled enough to eke extra benefits from this experience. The complete list of Challenges, and how these perks, and some associated Achievements/Trophies are unlocked, is listed in the Appendices of this book. As you know the Challenge you've completed by looking at your Pip-Boy, the bonus you're given should be self-explanatory.

Follower-Related Perks

Each of the Followers (aka Companions) you can come across in the Mojave Wasteland brings a unique perk with them, which helps you out until you part ways. Note that once you complete a Free or Side Quest related specifically to that Follower, in some cases an additional perk (one of two you choose) becomes available.

Better Healing

Req: Have Arcade Gannon as a Follower

Ranks: 1

When Arcade is a companion, the player regains 20% more health from all sources. This includes Stimpaks, Doctor's Bags, Food, Recipes, and anything that grants you more Hit Points. Having your own portable Doctor has copious benefits, and favors the adventurer who leaves the healing to others, and focuses on the killing themselves.

Calm Heart

Req: Have Cass as a Follower, complete Side Quest: Heartache by the Number

Ranks: 1

Cass has +50 Hit Points. This helps her survive longer in combat. If Cass is constantly near death, or falling unconscious during fights, this can help her have a more aggressive stance.

Enhanced Sensors

Req: Have ED-E as a Follower

Ranks: 1

While ED-E is a companion, the player can detect enemies at an increased range. Additionally, enemies will appear on the player's compass and can be targeted in VATS even when cloaked. This is obviously helpful when you're attacking Nightkin (who use Stealthboys) or Nightstalkers, and when combined with Boone's Spotter perk, allow you never to be ambushed again!

Full Maintenance

Req: Have Rose as a Follower and get him to upgrade through his freeform quest

Ranks: 1

While Raul is a companion, the Condition of weapons and armor decays 75% slower. This helps remove the negative effects of the Built to Destroy trait, and generally keeps your armaments and outfits in excellent condition. Raul can Repair items in his Shack too, so you can take full advantage of his considerable tinkering prowess.

Hand of Vengeance

Req: Have Cass as a Follower, complete Side Quest: Heartache by the Number

Ranks: 1

Cass does 15% more damage with all Guns. Cass is a great shot normally, and making her better with Guns (and giving her a powerful Gun for her to use, complete with Mods or a Unique variant, and Crafted ammunition) makes this all the sweeter.

Old Vaquero

Req: Have Raul as a Follower, complete Free Quest: Old School Ghoul

Ranks: 1

Raul's rate of fire with revolvers and lever-action firearms is 33% faster than normal. Choose this perk for him, and he keeps his Regular Maintenance perk too, but becomes more proficient in combat. Select this over Full Maintenance if you want more firepower in battles, and are happy with the current state of your weapons and armor, and don't need to worry about them even less than you do now.

Regular Maintenance

Req: Have Raul as a Follower

Ranks: 1

While Raul is a companion, the Condition of weapons and armor decays more slowly. This can counteract the negative effects of the Built to Destroy trait. It simply lengthens the amount of time you have with a weapon or armor in the condition you want it to be in. Which is almost universally handy.

Scribe Assistant

Req: Have Veronica as a Follower

Ranks: 1

While Veronica is a companion, the player can craft Workbench items through Veronica's dialogue. Having a portable Workbench has considerable benefit, as you can create Weapon Repair Kits (keeping Unique and Modded Weapons in tip-top shape), and you have the added benefits of Veronica's impressive close combat skills to rely on, too. This is less impressive if you have full knowledge of every Workbench and enjoy Fast-Travel, though.

Search and Mark

Req: Have Rex as a Follower

Ranks: 1

While Rex is a companion, unequipped Chems, firearms, and ammunition within a short distance and any and all containers, including bodies, hidden safes, and hollow rocks within visible range are highlighted when you zoom the camera. This aids considerably when you're scavenging, and if this is a big part of your adventuring (if you're in Hardcore Mode, or you're trying to find ammo to break down, for example), then this becomes most helpful. However, careful inspection of areas is almost as easy.

Spotter

Req: Have Boone as a Follower

Ranks: 1

While Boone is a companion, hostile targets are highlighted whenever you are actively aiming with iron sights. Combine this with ED-E's scanning perk to see every enemy before they spot you! This perk highlights foes in a red outline, which is great because it helps to differentiate between friends and foes. Plus it's especially effective at night, causing enemies to stand out in the dark.

Stealth Girl

Req: Have Lily as a Follower

Ranks: 1

While Lily is your companion, the duration of Stealth Boys is increased by 200% and all Sneak Attack Critical Hits do an additional 10% damage. If you're focusing on Sneak and use Stealth Boys regularly, this is of great benefit. Otherwise, Lily's psychotic episodes and great strength are the reasons to keep her around.

Whiskey Rose

Req: Have Cass as a Follower

Ranks: 1

While Cass is a companion, you and her gain Damage Threshold when you both drink Whiskey. Additionally, you don't suffer Intelligence loss from consuming alcohol, and ignore the negative effects of alcohol addiction. This increases your DT, leaves you without a drawback when swigging Alcohol, and gives you the positive aspects of it.

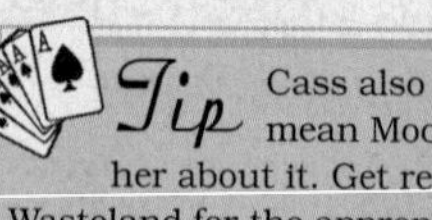

Tip Cass also makes some mean Moonshine, if you ask her about it. Get ready to scour the Wasteland for the appropriate items, though!

Implant-Related Perks

Implants are able to be purchased from Doctor Usanagi over at the New Vegas Medical Center [2.10], and only there. This is a Followers of the Apocalypse location, so be sure you haven't ruined your Reputation with them (at least, until you've acquired the Implants you want!). If you have the (huge amount of) Caps necessary to pay for the operation, and the Endurance to handle one or more Implants, you can increase any of your attributes, add armor, or even regenerate!

Caution The cost of Implants is astronomical; even with a huge Barter skill, you need Caps in the thousands (or tens of thousands). They are not tailored to low-level players but help the experienced character take a final step in increasing skills to be just a bit more super-specialized.

Agility Implant

Req: Necessary funds and END, AGL < 10

Ranks: 1

Your central nervous node has been enhanced with the Reflex Booster, increasing your Agility by 1.

Charisma Implant

Req: Necessary funds and END, CHR < 10

Ranks: 1

Your prefrontal cortex has been enhanced with the Empathy Synthesizer, increasing your Charisma by 1.

Sub-Dermal Armor

Req: Necessary funds and END

Ranks: 1

Your skin has been toughened by the NEMEAN Sub-Dermal Armor, increasing your total Damage Threshold by 4.

Endurance Implant

Req: Necessary funds and END, END < 10

Ranks: 1

Your nervous system has been enhanced with the Nociception Regulator, increasing your Endurance by 1.

Intelligence Implant

Req: Necessary funds and END, INT < 10

Ranks: 1

Your cerebral cortex has been enhanced with the Logic Co-Processor, increasing your Intelligence by 1.

Luck Implant

Req: Necessary funds and END, LCK < 10

Ranks: 1

Your frontal lobe has been enhanced with the Probability Calculator, increasing your Luck by 1.

Perception Implant

Req: Necessary funds and END, PER < 10

Ranks: 1

Your optic nerve has been enhanced with the Optics Enhancer, increasing your Perception by 1.

Monocyte Breeder

Req: Necessary funds and END

Ranks: 1

Your regenerative ability has been enhanced by the PHOENIX Monocyte Breeder Implant, causing you to slowly regenerate lost Hit Points at a rate of 1HP for every 10 seconds. This is a permanent effect.

Strength Implant

Req: Necessary funds and END, STR < 10

Ranks: 1

Your muscle mass has been enhanced with the Hypertrophy Accelerator, increasing your Strength by 1.

Unarmed-Related Perks

These perks are specialized moves taught by those highly skilled in the arts of hand-to-hand combat. You must seek the individual out, and learn from them. Then the move can be attempted in Unarmed Combat only.

Khan Trick

Teacher: Jack

Req: Complete Side Quest: Aba Daba Honeymoon, teach Jack about Chems

Ranks: 1

By relying on the dirty unarmed fighting tricks of the great Khans, you can throw dust into the eyes of your enemies, temporarily stunning them. Perform a Power Attack while moving left or right to execute the Khan Trick.

Legion Assault

Teacher: Lucius

Location: The Fort [3.28]

Req: Speak to him with Unarmed 50+ and Positive Legion Reputation.

Ranks: 1

Caesar's elite cadre of bodyguards, the legendary Praetorians, use an aggressive Legion Assault to brutalize enemies. Perform a Power Attack while running forward to execute the Legion Assault.

Ranger Takedown

Teacher: Ranger Andy

Location: Novac [5.18]

Ranks: 1

Req: Meet Ranger Andy, befriend him, and ask about his leg.

When caught without their weapons, NCR's rangers rely on the Ranger Takedown to quickly incapacitate opponents. Perform a Power Attack while moving backwards to execute a Ranger Takedown. This has the added benefit of stunning (and incapacitating) an enemy, if attempted properly.

Scribe Counter

Teacher: Veronica

Location: Anywhere

Req: Present Veronica with a White Glove Society dress (stolen from the Ultra-Luxe Casino)

Ranks: 1

Scribes in the Brotherhood of Steel are often not well-trained in the combat use of the high-tech gear employed by Paladins. They rely on unarmed defensive moves like the Scribe Counter to keep enemies at bay. Perform a standard attack out of a block hit reaction to execute a Scribe Counter.

SUCCESSFUL CHARACTER DEVELOPMENT

Now you've learned the attributes, skills, traits, and perks you can use; it is time to finish building the most proficient character ideally suited to your play style. Do so by following the advice in this section.

Tip Stop! In the time it takes you to leave Doc Mitchell's house, and leave Goodsprings, make an important Game Save. Then, when you're ready to try a new character, simply begin at this point without the need to replay your convalescence and recovery with Doc Mitchell. You can change all your stats (even your appearance) as you exit Goodsprings.

Plan 1: Cross-Referencing

Check all your SPECIAL attributes against the skills you are primarily wanting to use, so you're not wasting any points: Be sure to place points in the correct attribute. For example, are you interested in using Guns? Then bump up your Agility to 7 or higher. But do you want to use guns that are extremely weighty, such as the Heavy Incinerator? Then you'll also need to increase your Strength to 8, too! And if you're more apt to rely on Medicine, Repair or Science; Intelligence is the attribute to bump up.

Every point you add to a SPECIAL attribute raises the associated skill by two points, with the exception of Luck. It affects all your skills, but at half its value. For example, a Luck of 7 adds +4 to all skills, but so does a Luck of 8. That extra point is less useful (specifically to Skill Point allocation), so keep your Luck at an odd number to maximize Skill Point allocation.

Plan 1A: Lowering Attributes

Lower attributes you don't care about, and use the extra points on the ones you're focusing on, as long as you're willing to live with the consequences! For each attribute, look at the associated skills and derived statistics. Don't care about them? Then consider lowering that attribute to 3, or even to 1!

There are exceptions though; don't lower your Strength by too much, as the amount you can carry is critical (especially on Hardcore mode), and although you can increase your carrying capacity by using Followers, you'll always find you need more inventory spots for important items.

Think long and hard before dropping Endurance, as it controls Health, and your ability to withstand Implants. Simply put; you die more easily with a low Endurance.

Intelligence governs how many Skill Points you receive each time you level up, so expect to advance much more slowly if you lack higher brain functionality. Although this leads to some humorous (and unique) dialogue choices, this usually isn't worth the fewer skills and their lower values.

Plan 1B: Raising Attributes

Wouldn't it be great to throw all your available points into a single attribute such as Strength or Endurance, and create a completely lopsided character? No, it wouldn't; there are too many general benefits from having reasonable across-the-board statistics for this to work unless you want to be severely specialized.

It is less important to pick attributes based on their associated skills. Instead, pick them based on their Derived Statistics, or perks you may want in the future. Yes; your Unarmed skill goes up by two points for each Attribute Point you give Endurance, but that's nothing compared to your Hit Points increasing by 20 points with that same Endurance Attribute Point allocated.

If you're considering Attribute Points for your very first character, or don't want to figure out the type of character you want to play yet, consider the "big three" attributes are usually seen as Strength, Endurance, and Intelligence. Although the others are almost as important, the big three have benefits for every character; so consider raising them to at least 7. With any left-over points, Agility and Luck are good if you're wanting a combat-based Courier.

Plan 2: Primary Combat Skill Choices

At the most basic level, your Guns skill is the usual (and recommended) choice when choosing a Combat-related skill. However, whatever choice you make, ensure that your Primary Combat skill is the usual method you use to defeat enemies, make it one of your three Tag skills, and raise it as much as possible, as early as possible. Usually it is wise to also choose a Secondary Combat skill that you're adding lesser amounts to, which you can rely on later into your adventure (in case you run out of ammunition, or you're facing an especially tough opponent). Energy Weapons, Unarmed, and Melee Weapons are also viable, but beware of a lack of Melee Weapons that pack a real punch at higher levels. Unarmed and Melee Weapons have their advantages those; Unarmed allows different combat moves (including ones you learn) when using VATS, and both don't need ammunition, so you can ignore ammo (especially in Hardcore mode where your Inventory Weight is a factor), or sell them, or break them down into component parts. The following chart helps you make these initial choices:

COMBAT SKILL	PRACTICALITY*	ADVANTAGES	DISADVANTAGES
Energy Weapons	●●●●○	Highly accurate (laser) or damaging (plasma)	Sometimes guns and ammo are hard to find, and expensive
Explosives	●●○○○	C-4, Heavy damage to multiple foes	Dangerous to the user up-close, or in confined spaces
Guns	●●●●●	One and two-handed, light and heavy; plentiful weapons and ammo	Heavy weapons are heavy (STR = 8 to avoid movement penalties), heavy weapon ammo may be hard to find
Melee Weapons	●●●●○	Weapons are numerous, no ammo needed	Obviously, combat must be up close, and attacks can be blocked
Unarmed	●●●○○	Additional VATS attack types, no ammo needed	Just your fists aren't as devastating as Brass Knuckles, Boxing Gloves, or other Unarmed weapons

** The higher the score, the more useful*

Plan 3: Combat Skill Combos

A secondary Combat skill is always useful to pair with another skill (whether overly violent like Guns, or more stealthy, such as Sneak). The following combinations are good to build up as you progress:

Guns and Explosives

- If you can soften up Deathclaws with thrown grenades, and follow that up with a Carbine Rifle, you might just survive the infamous Quarry Junction.
- You can also place mines along patrol paths, or around corners, wait for a target to detonate one, then finish them with gunfire.
- Sneaking, Melee Weapons, Unarmed, and/or Explosives
- More involved and tactical, crouching and then Sneaking (and using the Stealth-Boy), before attempting to strike with a powerful attack.
- Lay plenty of Mines along the route you're going to take to escape, allowing you to flee if you're overwhelmed, and keeping the enemy occupied to ensure a safe escape.
- Remember to return and pick up unused Mines when the coast is clear.
- Guns/Energy Weapons and Unarmed
- Energy Weapons are more expensive, but laser guns have a faster rate of fire and lower AP cost than many Guns.
- High Agility in combination with Energy Weapons and Unarmed is a good choice, as you can land four punches (or laser blasts) in VATS.
- Try punching weaker foes, and collect the ammunition they drop so you can Craft, or afford to purchase Energy Weapon ammunition and armor suited to Unarmed skirmishes. Save Energy Weapons for larger foes.

Plan 4: The Third Tag Skill—Repair

Construction and cannibalizing weapons is still one of the most fundamentally useful abilities you can learn. The construction of better quality weapons and armor at Workbenches enables you to withstand more attacks, and spend less time (and Caps) on Stimpaks, or searching for Recipes to remedy your maladies. Enemies in groups tend to use the same types of weapon, allowing you to manage your loot. Are the NCR Troopers you just butchered all carrying Service Rifles? Then gather them all up, and Repair them to create one or two Service Rifles in great condition.

Furthermore, Repair is used at Reloading Benches to create special types of ammunition for your weapon from spent casings, powder, primers, and lead. Creating the ammo you most need by breaking down the elements of ammo you don't? That's another incredible reason to pick Repair.

First Time in the Mojave: Recommended Tag Skills

If you're entering the Mojave Wasteland with no previous adventuring experience, heed the above advice and make your three Tag skills a Primary Combat, Secondary Combat, and Repair. Or to sum up:

THIRD TAG SKILL	MOST USEFUL WITH	REMARKS
Repair	Guns, Melee Weapons, Energy Weapons	Weapons in good repair inflict more damage, and can be sold for more Caps.
Sneak	All Combat Skills	Inflicting bonus damage when close to a foe, or avoiding them without being spotted, is always advantageous.
Medicine/Survival	Melee Weapons, Unarmed	If you have to be struck by foes to kill a foe, becoming adept at healing or Recipes becomes crucial.
Explosives	Melee Weapons, Unarmed (or all Combat Skills)	Attack at a distance with projectiles, or plant mines, and run in to finish the job.

Plan 5: Noncombat Skills—Survival in the Mojave

New to the Mojave Wasteland is the Survival skill, familiar to outdoorsmen everywhere. As its primary use is to increase the healing benefits of Food and Drink (in the same way that Medicine does to Stimpaks), if you're planning to keep your Caps and scavenge for Plant life and Recipes, you may not ever need a Stimpak again. Survival also allows you to make a variety of items not only at Campfires, but at Reloading Benches and Workbenches too. This is one to definitely take, perhaps at the expense of Medicine, if you're planning on being Hardcore, wanting a few unique dialogue choices and perks, or if you like hiking for plants and scavenging for Recipe items as much as fighting.

Plan 6: What About the Other Skills?

The other skills are certainly of no less importance, and the flexibility of them means there are no wrong skills to pick (although you can overspecialize, or pick skills that aren't in synch with your attributes).

Tip As a general rule, it is never good to increase a skill to 100 due to the vast number of Skill Magazines available. In a (rare) occasion calls for a 100 skill, bolster your 90 skill with a quick read.

Tip Many skills that appear to be poor choices compared to others actually have hidden benefits; such as great perks associated with them (which usually balance out the poor choice in the first place). For example, a higher Barter allows you to pick Pack Rat or Long Haul; so you could lower your Strength and related skills and obtain these perks to balance out Inventory issues. Be sure to read all the variations and advantages each skill and perk has.

Barter

Although Bartering yields you better prices with Vendors (and sometimes more ammunition and weapons), and has a large number of unique dialogue choices during Quests, many of the same conversations can be completed using Speech (of which there are far more dialogue choices for obvious reasons). If Caps are all you crave, you can always clean out everything in a cave and drag it to a merchant to sell it, or Pickpocket (or Steal) items you need.

Lockpick

One of the more advantageous of the noncombat skills, this allows you to wrestle open every storage room and scavenge the treasures within. Of course, you can consult the "Tour" chapter of this guide closely to find this out too! As this guide flags every major lock on safes, doors, footlockers, and Ammo Boxes, you can easily tell how much to increase this skill. A good rule is to keep your Lockpick at around 55. Most locks are Average, requiring 50 Lockpick to easily open. If you find a Hard lock (75 Lockpick usually required), simply read a Skill Magazine for that lock. Magazines only increase by +10 so having the skill around 55 won't help with Hard locks without the Comprehension perk.

Medicine

If you're living off the scientific discoveries of man instead of Recipes, Medicine is definitely the way to go. Increasing the effectiveness of Stimpaks, Super Stimpaks, Doctor's Bags, Rad-X, and RadAway, if you only need to use half the regular number of Stimpaks to fully heal, you can spend your Caps on other items. Medicine is also slightly more useful than Survival during Quests if you're wanting dialogue choices or need to heal a wounded character you encounter. There are some fine perks to unlock, too.

Science

If controlling turrets, and turning them on those they used to guard is appealing to you, or you need to unlock doors or safes with a connecting terminal? Then this is your skill. You have a few dialogue options unique to Science, too. As there are fewer terminals to hack than there are locks to pick, and with rewards for hacking a terminal being less immediate or tangible, many adventurers rely on either Lockpick or Science (and tend toward Lockpick), but not both.

Sneak

Crouching so you're hidden, and then moving slowly around a settlement of hardy foes is a real thrill, and Sneak is responsible for keeping you alive in these circumstances. A highly useful combat support skill, attacking unsuspecting targets yield greater damage (and safety for you). If you lack subtlety in your combat, this isn't for you. Otherwise, it is a fine choice. However, Unarmed and Melee attacks while using Sneak are difficult to land; but the Sneak Critical Hit bonus is huge. Be sure to Sneak up on a foe who is unaware (rather than alert), and be sure you enter VATS to "line up" Sneak attacks on numerous foes.

Tip Is Sneak still not on your skill shortlist? Then note that a headshot from a Riot Shotgun is likely to kill a Deathclaw if your skill is high enough, and you're close enough to that horned head.

Speech

Like to chat? Enjoy fast-talking your way out of situations? Then succeeding in Speech challenges when speaking to others becomes not only rewarding but incredibly useful. You can calm down a hostile situation (or occasionally create them!), but unlike Barter, there are no real other benefits than a host of unique dialogue choices. Even a cursory glance at the Main, Side, and Free Quests of this guide show that Speech is used in almost every conversation, and can sometimes grant you better items, and save hours of wandering, or even your life! This is one skill you must consider seriously.

Plan 7: Skill Point Allocation

For those with limited previous exploration experience, it is recommended that you increase your Primary Combat, and your Repair skills up to around 55, and then 75 points as soon as possible. Then add to your Secondary Combat skill, and your preferred other skills as needed. Generally, a good rule is to spend around 60-75% of your Skill Points allotment on your Primary and Repair skills until they reach 75.

A common mistake is to raise your skills up to 100 as soon as possible. Because certain Collectibles (Skill Books) and perks can permanently raise your skills, and Magazines temporarily up a specific skill by 10 points, the extra points are negated due to your over-eagerness to max out. Consult this guide to learn the location of every Skill Book and Skill Magazine that are related to your preferred skills, so you can take them as early as possible to further develop your best skills.

Plan 8: Dressing for Success

Simply wearing an outfit or piece of armor because it looks cool or is a pretty color isn't the best way to maximize your wardrobe. Along with the skills you are concentrating on, look for Armor and Clothing that add related benefits. The "Guns and Gear" chapter of this Guide showcases the bonuses of every single important wearable item and weapon in the Mojave Wasteland, allowing you to peruse and locate at your leisure. Then ensure you take at least a couple of changes of clothing with you; for example, a set for combat **(1)**, a set for Speech checks **(2)**, and attire for Repairs **(3)**.

It is important to view the items you pick up on your Pip-Boy to work out their abilities. If you're heading into combat, and you're sure you won't get shot, replace heavy armor with something lightweight that gives you bonuses to skills such as Guns. Carrying around some extra outfits can be an immense help, especially as many items weigh next to nothing but have excellent extra effects, such as Vault Utility Jumpsuits.

Example #1: Raise your Lockpick skill to 45. Then put on apparel that gives you +5 to Lockpick (like the Vault 3 Utility Jumpsuit), and you can now Pick Average locks.

Example #2: Before you go adventuring, raise your Perception by two points, and your Luck by one point, which cumulatively adds +5 to your Lockpick. Now raise your Lockpick skill to 45, but with five additional points to spend on other skills.

It is wise to go back over your attributes and ensure you've placed enough points to help enhance associated skills.

 Faction Armor

Putting on an NCR Ranger's outfit and hat **(4)**, and wandering into a Caesar's Legion stronghold—even if you're allied with the Legion—is a foolhardy idea, as you're clad in the threads of a sworn enemy. This is because Faction Armor; the clothing worn specifically by a known Faction or tribe, such as the Legion **(5)** or the Great Khans **(6)** causes you to be treated as one upon superficial (or distant) inspection. Be careful where you're wandering. Or, use the outfit to your advantage and walk into the camp of an enemy faction wearing their attire! But beware of Guard Dogs that can sniff out an intruder!

Plan 9: Good Reading (and Eating)

Until items disintegrate out of use, they can be considered permanent modifiers to your skills. But there are items that give a temporary boost to all manner of your statistics, including skills. The most obvious of these are Skill Books (giving a permanent +3 to a skill) and Skill Magazines (giving a temporary +10 to a skill). Are these useful? Exceptionally; as you can read the guide, know the difficult locations where you need a skill boost, and bring some required reading with you.

Example #3: Raise your Lockpick skill to 37. Then locate a copy of Tumblers Today (Skill Book) to permanently boost your skill to 40 (+3). Now locate an Average lock, and read a copy of Locksmith's Reader (+10, Skill Magazine). This temporarily boosts your skill to 50; enabling you to open the lock without much Skill point expenditure at all!

Example #4: Raise your Lockpick skill to 51. Reach Level 4, and take the Comprehension perk. Now read a copy of Tumblers Today (Skill Book) to permanently boost your skill to 55 (+4, +1 because of the perk). Now locate a Hard lock, and read a copy of Locksmith's Reader (+20, +20 because of the perk). This temporarily boosts your skill to 75, enabling you to open this even-more difficult lock!

Also note that certain items you can eat, or make in a Recipe also help you out too; you are wise to check the skills, perks, and Recipes section of this guide forthwith!

Now take this a stage further, and read up on all the perks that affect your favored skills, so you know which ones to pick as you level up.

Plan 10: Character Growth

With an average of 12 to 13 Skill Points to spend when you level up, you can easily make a change to your character's preferred skill set (if you do this early enough) with minimal penalties. Think about the actions you tried since the last time you leveled up, and those you wanted to do but couldn't. Then place points into the skills that help you succeed in those actions.

For first-timers, split your points evenly between your three Tag skills until around Level 6; you chose Tag skills because you wanted to use them; so ensure they're above 50 as soon as possible. Two important skills to raise to specific levels are Lockpick and Science, as they have threshold values. Every 25 points opens up a new level of difficulty of locks and terminals. Set your Lockpick and/or Science to 25 early, then bump one or both to 50 in as few steps as possible. A Science skill of 49 is annoyingly close to being able to Hack into Average terminals, but only with item augmentations. One more point, and no items are needed.

Between Levels 5 through 10, keep the focus on the Tag skills, raising them to 70. Place some points into secondary skills like Lockpick (for Average locks), Medicine (for extra benefits from Stimpaks and the like), and Survival (for an increased number of Recipes).

Above Level 10, stop raising skills when they reach above the mid-80s, and rely instead on clothing, armor, Skill Books, and Skill Magazines for the hardest skill checks (which only occur occasionally anyway). Why have a skill of 100, and 10 Skill Magazines you can't use? Don't waste points!

CHARACTER ARCHETYPES

Whatever the environment, and however you want to approach your adventure, there is a character archetype for you! The following sample characters show which attributes, skills, perks, traits, Weapons, Armor, and Followers that complement that particular character's style of play. Behold the rogues' gallery....

Although these archetypes have been extensively bench-tested to be the very best at their specific role, you may ignore any aspect of these characters if you don't agree with them. They are simply here to aid you in making specific character styles.

Basil "The Sniper" Crowcross

S: 6 (8)*
P: 8
E: 5
C: 2 (1)*
I: 2 (1)*
A: 8
L: 9

A sneaky ranged specialist with maxed critical chance but minimal social graces.

* Optionally, drop CHA and INT to 1 and increase STR to 8 for Minigun/Heavy Weapons prowess.

Skills

Guns, Sneak, Repair

Traits

Four Eyes, Small Frame (Stealthy Sniper) or Trigger Discipline, Built to Destroy (Critical Hit Specialist/Sharpshooter)

Perks

Sniper, Commando, Finesse, Center of Mass, Better Criticals, Rapid Reload, Weapon Handling, Silent Running, Hand Loader, Confirmed Bachelor, Bloody Mess, Hunter, Entomologist, Robotics Expert, Travel Light, Living Anatomy

Weapons

All rifles, especially: Varmint Rifle (Night Scope, Silencer, Ext Mags, 5.56mm AP and HP) Hunting Rifle (Custom Action, Scope, Ext Mags .308, all types) Sniper Rifle (Carbon Fiber Parts, Suppressor, .308, all types)/Gobi Campaign Scout Rifle, Anti-Materiel Rifle with Match (hand load) ammo

Other Equipment

1st Recon Beret, Stealth Boys for losing hostiles if spotted, Weapon Repair Kits, Reinforced Leather armor for Travel Light perk, Sunglasses for Four Eyes trait

Implants

Perception, Agility, Luck

Followers

Boone, ED-E, (or no one)

Wyatt Pinkerton: The Gunslinger

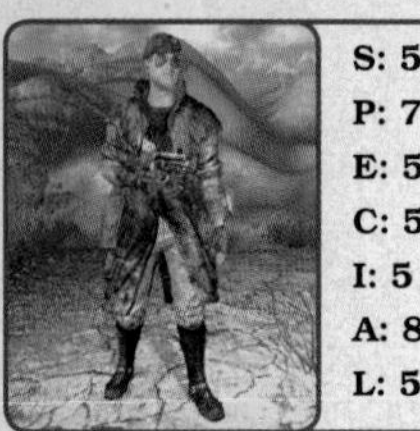

S: 5
P: 7
E: 5
C: 5
I: 5
A: 8
L: 5

A one-handed guns specialist; fast, light, generally well-rounded but crumples against heavily armored enemies.

Skills
Guns (For perks: Science [70], Medicine [70], Sneak [70], Repair [70], Survival [45], Melee [45]), Energy Weapons (Optional)

Traits
Fast Shot (Optional), Built to Destroy (Optional), Wild Wasteland (Optional)

Perks
Cowboy, Quick Draw or Educated, Rapid Reload, Gunslinger, Run 'n Gun, Travel Light, Shotgun Surgeon or Confirmed Bachelor, The Professional, Living Anatomy, Hand Loader, Toughness (2), Action Boy (2), Math Wrath, Nerves of Steel

Weapons
All one-handed guns, especially Maria, 10mm Pistol, Alien Blaster, That Gun (5.56mm AP and HP), Ranger Sequoia (.45-70 Govt Hand load)

Other Equipment
Desperado Cowboy Hat or 1st Recon Beret, with Shotgun Surgeon: Lever Action Shotgun (20ga Magnum or Slug) or Sawed-off Shotgun (12ga Magnum or Slug).

Implants
Armor, Regeneration, Perception, Agility, Intelligence

Followers
Raul, Rex (or Lily, or any)

Elizabeth Fortunate-Bradley: The Cat Burglar

S: 5
P: 5
E: 5
C: 5
I: 5
A: 9
L: 6

A stealthy thief, focused on lithe looting and lapping up the Caps.

Skills
Sneak, Lockpick, Science, Barter, Guns

Traits
Good Natured, Small Frame

Perks
Light Step, Infiltrator, Educated, Fortune Finder, Strong Back, Pack Rat, Scrounger, The Professional, Silent Running, Long Haul, Computer Whiz

Weapons
Anything silenced, especially holdout weapons. Good choices include: Silenced .22 Pistol, Silenced .22 SMG (Exp. Drums), 10mm Pistol (Laser Sight, Ext. Mags, Silencer), 12.7mm Pistol (Silencer), 12.7mm SMG (Silencer), Varmint Rifle (Silencer, Nightscope, Ext. Mags), Sniper Rifle (Carbon Fiber Parts, Suppressor)

Other Equipment
Scout Armor, Chinese Stealth Armor, Faction clothing for disguises: NCR uniforms, Powder Ganger outfits, Caesar's Legion armor, White Glove Society Mask, Great Khans armor

Implants
Agility, Intelligence, Luck

Followers
Lily, ED-E (or Rex, or none)

Eulogy Smith: The Smooth Talker

S: 5
P: 6
E: 4
C: 9
I: 6
A: 4
L: 6

A diplomatic pacifist type, with the ability to talk the hind legs off a Bighorner.

Skills
Speech, Barter, Medicine, Science, Repair, Survival, [optional] Unarmed or any combat skill of choice

Traits
Good Natured

Perks
Confirmed Bachelor/Lady Killer or Black Widow/Cherchez la Femme, Ferocious Loyalty, Educated, Retention, Comprehension, Terrifying Presence, Nerd Rage!, Mysterious Stranger, Miss Fortune, Animal Friend (2)

Weapons
This depends on combat skill chosen; see other lists for specialist types.

Other Equipment
Skill Magazines (any and all), outfits with skill/attribute bonuses and a few skill/attribute-enhancing Chems like Mentats or Alcohol.

Implants
Intelligence, Perception, Luck, Charisma

Followers
Arcade, Boone, Cass (Whiskey Rose perk)

Gary 666: The Incandescent Death

S: 7
P: 5
E: 8
C: 3
I: 6
A: 6
L: 5

An implacable Energy Weapons heavy trooper; melting minds into piles of ash and goo.

Skills
Energy Weapons, Medicine, Repair, Science, Guns (70 for perks)

Traits
Fast Shot, Built to Destroy

Perks
Center of Mass, Rapid Reload, Plasma Spaz, Laser Commander, Meltdown, Lifegiver, Toughness, Improved Criticals, Vigilant Recycler, Jury Rigging, Stonewall, Commando, Action Boy or Math Wrath, Grim Reaper Sprint, Spray 'n Pray (if taking companions), Power Armor Training

Weapons
Any Energy Weapon, especially Gauss Rifle, Gatling Laser(Carbon Fiber Frame, Focus Optics), Flamer(Expanded tanks), Plasma Caster (HS Electrode) and as many Max or Over charged cells you can get your hands on

Other Equipment
Weapon repair kits (and lots of them), heaviest armor you can find (Metal, Reinforced Metal, Power Armor), Steady, Psycho, Jet, Fixer

Implants
Endurance, Armor, Regeneration

Followers
Raul (Full Maintenance, Repair service), Arcade (Tesla/Power Armor path), Veronica (Workbench, Power Armor path)

Edgar "Space Ventura" Wellington III

S: 6
P: 8
E: 5
C: 3
I: 5
A: 8
L: 5

A Master Blaster man with an Energy Weapons plan.

Skills
Energy Weapons, Science, Explosives

Traits
Trigger Discipline

Perks
Rapid Reload, Run 'n Gun, Commando, Vigilant Recycler, Plasma Spaz, Center of Mass, Meltdown, Concentrated Fire, Laser Commander,

Weapons
Q-35 Modulator, Laser RCW, Alien Blaster (Wild Wasteland encounter), Euclid's C Finder, Recharger Pistol, Recharger Rifle

Other Equipment
Power Armor, Chinese Stealth Armor, Space Suit, Reinforced Combat Armor Mk 2

Implants
Endurance, Armor, Regeneration

Followers
Arcade Gannon, Veronica

Samuel "Red" McDonald: The Midnight Wanderer

S: 8
P: 5
E: 6
C: 4
I: 7
A: 6
L: 4

A Melee specialist perfect for Hardcore mode. Why buy Stimpaks when you can skin and eat your lunch?

Skills
Survival, Melee, Unarmed, Sneak (Science, Repair, Medicine for Crafting), Barter (70) for perks

Traits
Good Natured, Four Eyes, Heavy Handed or Wild Wasteland

Perks
Strong Back, Pack Rat, Travel Light, Hunter, Long Haul, Intense Training: Strength/Endurance/Agility, Super Slam, Stone Wall, Slayer, Unstoppable Force, Purifier, Rad Resistance, Rad Absorption and/or Rad Child, Solar Powered, Ninja or Grim Reaper Sprint

Weapons
Any melee or hand to hand, like the Power Fist, Paladin Toaster, Ballistic Fist, Spiked Knuckles, Machete Gladius, and especially the Super Sledge/Oh Baby!

Other Equipment
Eyeglasses (for Four Eyes trait), Combat Armor, Reinforced Combat Armor Mk 2, any and all Crafting items

Implants
Armor, Regeneration, Endurance, Intelligence, Luck, Agility

Followers
Rex, Cass

Anthea "The Trailblazer" Littlehorn

S: 5
P: 8
E: 8
C: 2
I: 5
A: 8
L: 4

A Hardcore mode explorer with one goal; to uncover all 213 Primary Locations!

Skills
Survival, Lockpick, Barter

Traits
Four Eyes

Perks
Hunter, Rad Child, Travel Light, Lead Belly, Strong Back, Long Haul, Pack Rat, Explorer, Solar Powered, Night Person, Rad Absorption

Weapons
Rifles (preferably scoped): Varmint Rifle (Scope, Silencer, Ext Mags), Cowboy Repeater (Maple Stock, Custom Action, Long Tube) Hunting Rifle (Custom Action, Ext Mags, Scope), Trail Carbine (Scope), Brush Gun(Forged Receiver), Sniper Rifle(Carbon Fiber Parts, Suppressor), Anti-Materiel Rifle, Lever-Action Shotgun (for close encounters), Hunting Shotgun (Choke, Long Tube)

Other Equipment
Eyeglasses (for Four Eyes trait), Leather Armor, Reinforced Leather Armor, Scout Armor, Merc Grunt Outfit

Implants
Perception, Armor, Regeneration

Followers
ED-E, Boone, Cass

Opie "Knuckle Sandwich" Moriarty

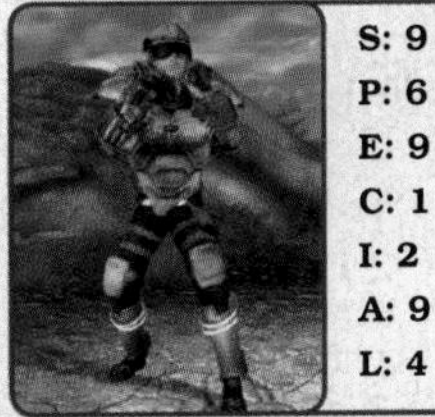

S: 9
P: 6
E: 9
C: 1
I: 2
A: 9
L: 4

A proud pugilist, escaping from a place back east; Unarmed attacks come with a real wallop.

Skills
Unarmed, Medicine, Explosives

Traits
Heavy Handed, Kamikaze

Perks
Piercing Strike, Slayer, Purifier, Unstoppable Force, Stonewall, Super Slam

Weapons
Brass Knuckles, Spiked Knuckles, Power Fist, Ballistic Fist, Recompense of the Fallen, Pushy, Grenades, Dynamite, Grenade Rifle (Long Barrel), Thump Thump, Grenade Machinegun.

Other Equipment
Combat Armor, Reinforced Combat Armor, Reinforced Combat Armor Mk 2, Reinforced Metal Armor, Reinforced Metal Helmet

Implants
Strength, Armor, Regeneration, Endurance

Followers
Boone, Cass

Michael Falin

S: 6
P: 6
E: 6
C: 5
I: 6
A: 6
L: 5

Michael fell out of the incompetent tree, and hit every branch on the way down.

Skills
Repair, Barter, Medicine

Traits
None

Perks
Retention, Comprehension, Animal Friend, Here and Now, Math Wrath, Nerd Rage!, Chemist

Weapons
Straight Razor, Boxing Tape, BB Gun

Other Equipment
Sexy Sleepwear, Sunglasses, Chems, Alcohol, and Skill Magazines of all types

Implants
None

Followers
None

Gordon Cram-say

S: 4
P: 4
E: 8
C: 4
I: 9
A: 3
L: 8

Specializing in highly crafted Recipes, delicious Brahmin steaks, and a hair-trigger temper.

Skills
Survival, Repair, Science, Medicine, Barter (70)

Traits
Good Natured

Perks
Hunter, Entomologist, Hand Loader, Vigilant Recycler, Chemist, Jury Rigging, Nuka Chemist, Chem Resistant, Chemist, Long Haul, Pack Rat

Weapons
Hunting Rifle, Hunting Shotgun, Knife, Cleaver (or find the Chopper at Wolfhorn Ranch)

Other Equipment
Leather Armor, Reinforced Leather Armor, any and all Crafting supplies

Implants
Endurance, Luck, Armor

Followers
Veronica, Raul

Billie "Pin Holder" DeLoria

S: 9
P: 8
E: 8
C: 1
I: 2
A: 5
L: 7

A fanatic for grenades, mines, and a variety of highly polished projectile-lobbing rifles.

Skills
Explosives, Medicine, Barter (70) for perk

Traits
Loose Cannon (Optional)

Perks
Heave, Ho!, Demolition Expert (3), Pack Rat, Hit the Deck, Splash Damage, Adamantium Skeleton, Light Step, Better Criticals, Nuka Chemist, Spray 'n Pray

Weapons
Grenades, Grenade Rifle (Long Tube), Grenade Launcher, Grenade Machinegun (High Speed Kit), Missile Launcher (Guidance System, HE Missiles, HV Missiles) Fat Man (Little Boy kit), Mercy, Thump Thump, Annabelle

Other Equipment
Metal Armor, Reinforced Metal Armor, Combat Armor, Reinforced Combat Armor, Reinforced Combat Armor Mk2, Power Armor

Implants
Armor, Regeneration, Perception, Endurance

Followers
Cass, Boone, Arcade—generally avoid melee-centric companions because Spray 'n Pray can only do so much.

Albert "Penny Pincher" Tenpenny

S: 3
P: 4
E: 4
C: 8
I: 8
A: 4
L: 9

Having been banned from New Reno's casinos, this gambler is ready to break the banks on and off The Strip.

Skills
Barter, Speech, Unarmed

Traits
Good Natured

Perks
Fortune Finder, Miss Fortune, Pack Rat, Scrounger, Mysterious Stranger, Long Haul, Travel Light

Weapons
Brass Knuckles, Spiked Knuckles, Golden Boxing Gloves, Ballistic Fist, Power Fist

Other Equipment
Benny's Suit, Sunglasses, Pimp Boy 3 Billion

Implants
Luck, Armor, Regeneration, Intelligence

Followers
Rex and Boone or Lily

GENERAL TRAINING AND ADVICE

You now have all the advice you need to nurture the ultimate Courier of the Mojave Wasteland, so let's move on to the major challenges you'll face regarding interactions with others, all of which is details on your Pip-Boy. Read the Game Manual to gain basic familiarity with your Pip-Boy before continuing.

Game Difficulty

Settings > Difficulty of your Main game menu: You can choose to increase or decrease this aspect of the game (which defaults to Normal, and has some Hardcore mode exceptions; see below). Generally, the higher the difficulty, the more damage enemies inflict on you, and the less damage you inflict on them. This is balanced out by you sometimes receiving slightly higher Experience Points (XP) for kills at higher difficulty levels.

DIFFICULTY	ENEMY'S DMG. ON YOU	YOUR DMG. ON THEM
Very Easy	50%	200%
Easy	75%	150%
Normal	100%	100%

DIFFICULTY	ENEMY'S DMG. ON YOU	YOUR DMG. ON THEM
Hard	150%	75%
Very Hard	200%	50%

 Hardship in the Desert: Hardcore Mode

Settings > Hardcore mode of your Main game menu: As you're about to leave the warmth and comfort of Doc Mitchell's house, you're asked if you'd like some extra hardship with your adventure, and an option for Hardcore mode presents itself. You have an important decision to make; you can leave Hardcore mode at any time, and choose a less difficult, "normal" adventure. But you cannot access Hardcore mode once you decline to play in this mode!

Differences in Difficulty

There are a number of aspects to Hardcore mode that you must understand:

1. A special reward (Achievement of Trophy) is given for completing the adventure entirely in Hardcore mode.
2. Stimpaks do not heal instantly, but rather over time.
3. Crippled limbs cannot be healed with Stimpaks or by resting. They require Doctor's Bags or a Healer who can fix the problem.
4. All ammunition has weight, forcing you to pick and focus on weapons, and upgrades much more closely.
5. Companions can die, rather than just going unconscious like in Normal mode.
6. Dehydration, Starvation, and Sleep Deprivation. These are described in the following section.

Food, Water, and a Warm Bed

1

2

Lack of these three basic elements is a constant problem in Hardcore mode. Your Pip-Boy monitors your current Dehydration (H2O), Starvation (FOD), and Sleep Deprivation (SLP) levels constantly, so be sure to keep checking the Status menu for updated information. These levels build up over time at varied rates (Dehydration is fastest, then Starvation, and then Sleep Deprivation). Watch for a jump in these levels if you attempt a large amount of Fast Travel! Leave any of these unchecked, and your previously healthy visage **(1)** begins to suffer as deleterious effects are inflicted on you **(2)**. Here's what to watch out for:

Dehydration Break Points

H20	STATUS	EFFECT	WARNING
0-199	NORMAL/NONE	NO EFFECT	NONE
200-399	Minor Dehydration	-1 END	Dark HUD
400-599	Advanced Dehydration	-1 PER, -2 END	Light HUD
600-799	Critical Dehydration	-1 PER, -3 END, -1 INT	Red
800-999	Deadly Dehydration	-2 PER, -3 END, -1 AGL, -1 INT	Pulse Red
1000+	Lethal Dehydration	Death	No HUD

Starvation Break Points

H20	STATUS	EFFECT	WARNING
0-199	NORMAL/NONE	NO EFFECT	NONE
200-399	Minor Starvation	-1 STR	Dark HUD
400-599	Advanced Starvation	-2 STR, -1 CHR	Light HUD
600-799	Critical Starvation	-3 STR, -2 CHR, -1 PER	Red
800-999	Deadly Starvation	-3 STR, -2 CHR, -2 PER	Pulse Red
1000+	Lethal Starvation	Death	No HUD

Sleep Deprivation Break Points

H20	STATUS	EFFECT	WARNING
0-199	NORMAL/NONE	NO EFFECT	NONE
200-399	Minor Sleep Deprivation	-1 AGL	Dark HUD
400-599	Advanced Sleep Deprivation	-2 AGL, -1 INT	Light HUD
600-799	Critical Sleep Deprivation	-3 AGL, -2 INT, -1 END	Red
800-999	Deadly Sleep Deprivation	-3 AGL, -2 INT, -2 END	Pulse Red
1000+	Lethal Sleep Deprivation	Death	No HUD

When you reach one of these break points, you receive a warning, and there's a permanent reminder on your HUD. Solve the problems of these three issues by drinking water, eating food, and using a bed.

Living off the Land: Hardcore Tactics for Surviving and Thriving

If you're having difficulty acclimatizing to a Hardcore Mojave Wasteland, follow these tried-and-tested plans for survival.

A Place to Camp

Simply wandering into the countryside may get you killed. Between Quests, you need to establish a base camp where you can rest. Here are three great examples:

3

Goodsprings Source [4.11] is a little out of the way from the bright lights and big city, but it features everything you need; Food, Water, and a place to Sleep. Geckos spawn here every three days **(3)**, and they provide delicious Gecko Meat (which it is advisable to turn into Gecko Steaks at any of the nearby Campfires [Survival 25]). The wells provide unlimited supplies of Rad-free water, and the bed is in the small trailer. Should you require Crafting, a Reloading Bench and Workbench are next to the General Store in nearby Goodsprings [4.05].

4

Wolfhorn Ranch [6.14] is a little more wild, and there's Viper Gunslingers marauding about, but this is another good place to camp. Look for the bed inside the shack, an irradiated well (which offers unclean, but not overly toxic water, which you can augment with RadAway. The garden may have some harvestable crops (or there's Bighorner meat nearby), and there's a campfire up on the ridge **(4)**, near the grave.

5

Safehouses **(5)**, of which there are four (this example shows a concrete structure owned by a Faction called the Followers of the Apocalypse) also make fantastic camping spots; there's a Faction member there two days out of every week, a place to store items permanently, usually a full-stocked fridge, purified water from a fountain, and a comfy bed. To gain the keys to these castles you need to be at least Liked and sometimes Idolized by the faction. Some will also ask you to complete other pre-requisites.

A Place to Survive

The following locations provide one or two key elements for survival in Hardcore mode, and are handy if you're suffering from one or more ailments.

Water, Water Everywhere

Choose Lake Las Vegas [3.22], Lake Mead, the Colorado River, Goodsprings, and The Strip [Zone 2D] for limitless supplies of clean, radiation-free water.

Crafty Crafting

Harper's Shack **(6)** [5.21] has an excellent stash of crafting supplies, as well as a Reloading Bench and Workbench. There's even a bed and a Campfire right outside!

188 Trading Post [5.02] has a few beds where you can safely rest, along with a Reloading Bench and some Vendors to trade with.

Novac [5.18] is worth visiting for more than just Dinky the dinosaur; you can stay at the motel, and use the Workbench in town, as well as trading with vendors that wander down Highway 95 to reach here.

Primm [4.17] is initially in a desperate state, but once you find them a new Sheriff, all of their services return to normal, including Ruby Nash's delicious Radscorpion Casseroles!

Camp McCarran [2.19] has a supply shack at the southern end of the Concourse where Sergeant Contreras is happy to trade with you. He even sells NCR uniforms which is useful for blending in or using the Monorail if you don't have enough Fame with the NCR, and want to quickly reach the Strip. There's a Reloading and Workbench in the shack, too, as well as clean water in the drinking fountains, and beds in the barracks.

Sloan [4.08] may be suffering as its workers fend off Deathclaw incursions from their place of work, but there's a large stash of supplies and a Workbench if you check out the Machine Shop in the shack settlement.

Black Mountain [5.07] is a terrifying place, not least for an imprisoned Ghoul named Raul, who you can rescue as part of Side Quest: Crazy, Crazy, Crazy. Save him, and he shows you the map marker for his shack [3.05]. Journey there for a good amount of supplies, a bed, and Workbench.

Hardcore Tenets to Thrive By

Attributes and Skills for the Mountain Man

It is advisable to invest some Skill Points in Survival as soon as possible; cooked or prepared items are generally much more effective than their raw counterparts; but a higher Survival skill allows better results even from raw items.

With a Campfire, some common Food and Plants, and 30 Survival, you can get by on Cactus Water and Gecko Steaks **(7)**.

You should ideally be Crafting during Hardcore mode, and if you do, make sure you're constantly looking out (and have enough free Inventory space) for "junk" items as most of them are useful in Recipes. Basically, if a location in the "Tour" chapter of this guide mentions "Scrap Metal," there's likely to be other useful junk nearby.

One early advantage to take is the Good Natured trait. This takes five points from each combat skill, and places them into noncombat skills. For a Hardcore survivalist, the noncombat skills are used frequently. Fortunately, you only really need to choose one combat skill. Why waste points that you'd never use on three pointless combat skills? Make efficient use of everything, as early and often as possible. It's the only way to survive!

Upping your Intelligence attribute is an obvious and excellent choice for the Hardcore adventurer. Intelligence allows more Skill Points over the long term, and directly boosts the four Crafting skills: Medicine, Repair, Science, and Survival.

An obvious perk choice for the Hardcore Courier is the Leady Belly perk. But have you tried Cannibal and/or Ghastly Scavenger? This increases your available cuisine considerably....

Another two excellent perks to obtain is Strong Back to generally help with your inventory. But for the survivalist, the Pack Rat perk is vital, as almost all Crafting and Food materials end up weighing 2lbs or less.

During the latter stages of your adventure, pick Rad Absorption as you're probably having a hard time locating more RadAway.

Hunger, Thirst, and Tiredness Begone!

Sleep Deprivation may be of constant concern, but don't worry; it accrues very slowly and doesn't increase if you're Waiting. However, hunger and thirst do, so ensure sure you have Food and Water before stopping to wait for a while.

Keep more Water around than Food; although the rate at which you gain thirst decreases during the night, it always increases at a faster rate than hunger or sleep deprivation.

Coyote Tobacco Chew, made from the plant of the same name, can be obtained in numerous wilderness areas around the Mojave Wasteland, and it allows you to go without sleep for quite some time (even if your Survival skill is low). As it's extremely lightweight, stock up whenever you spot the plant, and you may never need a bed!

Have you sampled the Gecko Kabob or the Bloatfly Slider? You should; as they reduce both hunger and thirst! This not only satiates you in half the time, but these take up less space (and weight) in your Inventory. Keep this in mind if you need to reduce what you're carrying.

Conversely, some Foods (and even a few drinks) actually increase your thirst! The simple plan here is to avoid using them if you don't have a ready supply of water (and perhaps some RadAway) to hand.

Health and Human Interaction

Solve your own Crippling injuries by locating the ingredients for a Doctor's Bag, as you can Craft them at Workbenches with a Medicine skill of 40.

Consulting the "Tour" chapter of this guide, which has the location of every Healer (aka Doctor) in the Mojave Wasteland is crucial, as you'll need to make regular use of them (especially if you have a crippled limb). Of course, when in doubt, hobble back to Doc Mitchell, and the safety of Goodsprings.

See a doctor frequently: beds do not heal crippled limbs in Hardcore mode, and Doctor's Bags (or Hydra) can be expensive (or hard to find), and should be saved for emergencies where a doctor is unavailable.

Beware: The Death of a Follower

Followers can (and often do) die during fights in Hardcore mode. This should prompt you into being extremely careful; not only of where and who you're shooting, but the orders you're giving your companions. Be sure to upgrade a companion's armor as soon as and whenever possible, and keep them well-supplied with Stimpaks while you heal using Recipes and Food types.

Proper Weapon and Ammo Usage

If you find a Unique Weapon, remember that you must stock up on Weapon Repair Kits if you want to keep it working.

Being brash in combat and taking unnecessary damage results in a quicker death. Even so, you should begin to gather a number of healing items that start to clog your inventory; remember to check their effectiveness, and use them all.

Ammunition fills up your inventory like no other item, so traveling as lean as possible is the order of the day. Invest in the Hand Loader perk at Level 6; this is essential because regular ammo has weight, but component parts (such as Lead and primers) do not.

With or without Hand Loader, cannibalizing cartridges you never use to make more of what you're firing helps you lose the dead weight that ammo was becoming.

Special rounds of a weapon all have a function, as it is important to select the ammo types that suit how often you use a weapon, and what it is used for. Take the 12/20ga ammunition: If a Shotgun is your main weapon, the standard buckshot is what you need. However, if you only use it as an emergency back-up weapon, then the Magnum loads are the better plan as the increased wear on the gun doesn't matter as much.

Slugs are useful if you don't use rifles, or you're fine with a loss in performance for the sake of not carrying the weight of an extra weapon and its ammo.

Similarly, while it isn't usually a great idea to use guns with different roles but of the same caliber—such as the Cowboy Repeater and the .357 Magnum Revolver—using different special ammo types in each prevents one from eating into the other's ammo.

Tip The Character Archetypes section earlier in this chapter has a couple of example characters created just for Hardcore mode. Be sure to check them out!

Experience Points (XP)

Stats > top-right corner of your Pip-Boy: The only way to level up your character and access more Skill Points and perks is to obtain Experience Points (XP). Generally, XP is received after you kill a foe (the Bestiary section has a general value for each enemy type you slay), and finish a Quest (see the Quests in this guide for the XP rewards) and Challenge. You also receive a small XP reward for unlocking a door or safe, hacking a terminal, and completing Speech check, which depends on the Difficulty of the activity: 20 XP = Very Easy (1–24 skill), 30 XP = Easy (25–49 skill), 40 XP = Average (50–74 skill), 50 XP = Hard (75–99 skill), 60 XP = Very Hard (100 skill). Note that your skill level vs the difficulty of the task can prevent you from gaining XP on very easy tasks. A Very Easy lock will give 20 XP for skill 1–74, but 75+ it gives 0 XP. This scale is for all challenges from locks and terminals to speech/skill challenges in dialogue.

As your HUD reveals when this occurs **(1)**, you'll always be able to keep track of your current total, and the total needed for the next level (which is in the Experience Points and Karma chart in the next section). When you reach Level 30, your XP reads "Maxed."

As you're likely to reach around Level 13 or 14 if you're close to finishing the Main Quest, you should augment your XP by attempting all the 70+ Side Quests (and some Free Quests). Side Quests are usually worth 100-500 XP depending on the complexity. And searching out world map markers (Data > world map) also nets you 10 XP per location.

Are You Experienced?

- You receive +10% XP when you are Well Rested, and the bonus lasts for 12 game hours. You can only obtain this by sleeping in a bed you own or rent; from the Novac Motel, Safehouses, and any comped suite at the Lucky 38, The Tops, or the Atomic Wrangler.
- If you take the Swift Learner perk, you obtain +10% additional XP for each rank (up to three) that you take. This includes Quests, unlocking safes, and every other aspect of gaining XP; not just killing enemies.
- XP does not scale with your level; all enemies and challenges you encounter offer roughly the same degree of challenge no matter when you attempt them, although you're at an advantage with better equipment and a Follower by your side.

Tip Double-shot XP time! When you encounter a door that is locked with a terminal, and a regular lock, hack the terminal (Science), but don't disengage the lock. Then pick the lock (Lockpick) and get a second shot of XP for completing both tasks!

Mapping the Mojave

Data > Local Map; Data > World Map of your Pip-Boy: Assuming you're already familiar with Fast Travel, and you've noticed the maps that came with this guide—which reveal every single location on both your local **(1)** and world **(2)** maps—there are some tactical plans to ensure investigating new areas is as safe as possible:

- Use a place you've previously cleared out, or a location you know is safe (such as Goodsprings, or Camp McCarran if you're allied with the NCR) as a base until you know your immediate surroundings. Figure out how far a new location is from (for example) Goodsprings, as this is the safest place to return to.
- Utilize landmarks; every time you stop, you should be able to spin 360 degrees around and see at least two recognizable structures. Notice the large skyscraper tower to the north? That's the Lucky 38 tower [Location 2D.02]. Now you know this, learn what the adjacent locations there are, and if any interest you.
- Use smaller visual cues to figure out specifically where you are. See that bright white memorial cross known as the Yangtze Memorial [4.07]? That's just southwest of the much-larger Quarry Junction [4.04]. Begin to fill in the topography of the area so you don't get lost.
- Utilize the compass, the location of the sun in the sky, as well as roads and railroads to situate yourself. If you know, for example, that the "Long 15" runs all the way from the Searchlight Airport [6.26] to the south, all the way to Freeside's East Gate [2.15] at the edge of The Strip to the north, you can keep to the roads, exploring along the way. Also flag interesting locations with your Pip-Boy's Route Marker on the World Map screen, too.
- When you discover a single location in an unexplored area, check it out before backtracking to a safer environment, and when you want to return, Fast Travel to the location and explore in a concentric circle out from this secondary base.
- This guide has flagged every Primary Location (which appear on your Pip-Boy's world map), and Secondary Location (which appear on the local map, or not at all) with a special, unique number. For example, Goodsprings is labeled "[4.05]." The first number refers to the Zone [4] and the second to the number of the settlement in that Zone [05]. These don't appear in the game; they are referenced so you can keep track of the hundreds of locations on the guide map.

Mapping the New Vegas Conurbation

When you enter the glittering metropolis of New Vegas, and its outlying areas, mapping matters get a little more complicated. Certain locations, such as the Lucky 38 Casino, can't be seen (or Fast Traveled to) via your world map. This is because they are within an "Interior Zone" unique to New Vegas (Zone 2). There are six of these Interior Zones (which are known in the guide as Zones 2A, 2B, 2C, 2D, 2E, and an Underground Sewer system flagged as "U2" that allows you to access different areas within Zone 2 from), which are usually accessed via a gate **(3)**. The "Tour" chapter separates these into Interior Zones so you know which areas are accessible from the outside Wasteland (or world map), and which you need to enter a gate to access.

Tip You might want to check the Challenges section of this guide (an Overview in the Training, and a complete list at the end of the Quest section), as there's a Challenge that rewards you for finding a set number of Primary Locations.

Miscellaneous Data: Notes

Data > Misc > Show Active Quest Notes: When you pick up either a scrap of paper, such as the note this corpse is carrying **(4)**, or a Holotape (aka Holodisk), this part of your Pip-Boy updates to reveal the contents, which can be either in audio or written form. Many of these are journals or thoughts that give you a better understanding of your surroundings, but don't affect your adventure. But some give hints on certain Quests that don't appear on your Pip-Boy; known as Freeform (or Free) Quests. A complete list and strategies on all of those (90+) Quests is contained later in this book.

Miscellaneous Data: Challenges

Data > Misc > Challenges: Access this part of your Pip-Boy to keep track of the (100+) Challenges that you are engaged in. You Pip-Boy logs almost every aspect of your adventure, and when you attempt an action a multiple number of times, this is recorded. When you hit a predetermined total, you receive a reward. Challenges can range from "I Can Stop Any Time I Want": Take 25 Chems, but not all at once) to "Click": Inflict 20,000 points of damage with a Minigun **(5)**. The rewards take the form of usually one of the following:

- Experience Points
- Caps
- Perks
- Achievements
- Another related Challenge

For a complete list of Challenges, consult the Appendices.

Radio Waves

Data > Radio: Whether it's the syrupy tones of Mr. Vegas, or the insanity of Tabitha and Rhonda, there's radio chatter to listen to as you traverse the Mojave Wasteland. Select the Radio station you want to listen to (or turn off) on your Pip-Boy.

Black Mountain Radio

Twenty-five-thousand-meter radius. Centered on the summit of Black Mountain, listen as Super Mutant Tabitha, and her gal-pal Rhonda put the world to rights, and sentence their Ghoul engineer to a thousand deaths.

Camp Guardian Radio

Three-thousand-meter radius. An NCR post deep in the wilderness just north of Lake Mead hasn't been heard from in a while. Should you hear this, prepare for an emergency broadcast with instructions to follow.

NCR Emergency Radio Station

Three-thousand-meter radius. Should Caesar's Legion attempt another Hoover Dam assault, the NCR will begin broadcasting on this emergency frequency, with tactical advice and troop orders.

Mojave Music Radio

Entire Wasteland. Whether you're sitting by a campfire, gazing at your Gecko Steaks a-cooking, or wandering the lonely trails near Wolfhorn Ranch, the finest music New Vegas has can be pumped straight to your wrist.

Radio New Vegas

Entire Wasteland. The voice of New Vegas brings you a mixture of dulcet tones, news reports from the Wasteland (which change as you progress through your adventure) and the best sounds around. Classy.

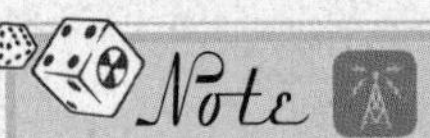

Note: Certain Casinos, like the Ultra-Luxe, have their own piped music which you can tune in as well.

Flashlight

Press and hold Pip-Boy button: Switching your Pip-Boy's Flashlight on or off is dependant on your style of play and knowledge of the area: If you're employing stealth, don't want to be seen, or know an area very well, keep the light off. If you're searching for items, want to see the ground and walls around you **(6)**, and need illumination to stop you stumbling, switch it on.

Karma: Beyond Good and Evil

General > Stats > General: Karma measures how pleasant or unkind you're being, based on your past actions. Karma is implicitly tied to Reputation, which in turn affects how you're treated by others, the Followers who agree to join you, and even the settlements in the Wasteland you can visit **(7)**. You begin with a Karmic value of zero, and this value fluctuates depending on your evil or good actions. Karma ranges from -1,000 (pure evil) to +1,000 (a true saint). Below the Values table, is a second table showing what common actions to choose to easily effect your Karma:

ICON	KARMA VALUE	TYPE
	-1,000 to -750	Very Evil
	-749 to -250	Evil
	-249 to 249	Neutral
	250 to 749	Good
	750 to 1,000	Very Good

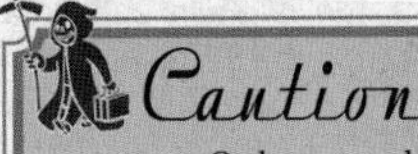

Caution: These values aren't visible to you, so you can't check specifically on the precise number you are: Only your character's type and icon are shown.

ACTION	KARMIC EFFECT
Killing an Evil character or creature	None
Killing a Very Evil character or creature	+100
Murdering (unprovoked) a Neutral or Good creature	-25
Murdering (unprovoked) a Neutral or Good character (07)	-100
Stealing from a Neutral or Good character, or non-evil Faction	-5 (per item)
Donating Caps	Dependent on the number
Performing a "good" action in a Free Quest	> +50
Performing an "evil" action in a Free Quest	> -50

Karma has much less of an impact on your adventure, as Reputation is the much more vital component to keep in check. However, Karmic actions usually have Reputation benefits or pitfalls that are awarded too, so be sure you know what you can get away with!

Raise and lower your Karma in Quests by undertaking certain actions, the most major of which are flagged in the Main and Side Quest chapters of this guide. Karma also influences the type of ending you receive when your expedition is over.

Experience Points and Karmic Title

This shows your character's level, XP required for the next level, and Karma depending on their alignment. This title also appears to Friends who can see you playing.

LEVEL	XP REQUIRED	EVIL TITLE (-250 OR LESS)	NEUTRAL TITLE (-249 – +249)	GOOD TITLE (+250 OR MORE)
1	0	Grifter	Drifter	Samaritan
2	200	Outlaw	Renegade	Martyr
3	550	Opportunist	Seeker	Sentinel
4	1,050	Plunderer	Wanderer	Defender
5	1,700	Fat Cat	Citizen	Dignitary
6	2,500	Marauder	Adventurer	Peacekeeper
7	3,450	Pirate of the Wastes	Vagabond of the Wastes	Ranger of the Wastes
8	4,550	Betrayer	Mercenary	Protector
9	5,800	Desert Terror	Desert Scavenger	Desert Avenger
10	7,200	Ne'er-do-well	Observer	Exemplar
11	8,750	Vegas Crimelord	Vegas Councillor	Vegas Crusader
12	10,450	Defiler	Keeper	Paladin
13	12,300	Mojave Boogeyman	Mojave Myth	Mojave Legend
14	14,300	Sword of Despair	Pinnacle of Survival	Shield of Hope
15	16,450	Vegas Boogeyman	Vegas Myth	Vegas Legend
16	18,750	Villain of the Wastes	Strider of the Wastes	Hero of the Wastes
17	21,200	Fiend	Beholder	Paragon
18	23,800	Wasteland Destroyer	Wasteland Watcher	Wasteland Savior
19	26,550	Evil Incarnate	Super-Human	Saint
20	29,450	Scourge of the Wastes	Renegade of the Wastes	Guardian of the Wastes
21	32,500	Architect of Doom	Soldier of Fortune	Restorer of Faith
22	35,700	Bringer of Sorrow	Profiteer	Model of Selflessness
23	39,050	Deceiver	Egocentric	Shepherd
24	42,550	Consort of Discord	Loner	Friend of the People
25	46,200	Stuff of Nightmares	Hero for Hire	Champion of Justice
26	50,000	Agent of Chaos	Model of Apathy	Symbol of Order
27	53,950	Instrument of Ruin	Person of Refinement	Herald of Tranquility
28	58,050	Soultaker	Moneygrubber	Last, Best Hope of Humanity
29	62,300	Demon Spawn	Gray Stranger	Savior of the Damned
30	66,700	Devil	True Mortal	Messiah

Reputation: Who Loves You, Baby?

General > Stats > Reputation (and) Data > World Map: The first signs that the residents of the Mojave Wasteland are judging your actions much more closely than before is seen on your Pip-Boy's world map. Notice how some of the locations have "(Neutral)" underneath them? This refers to your Reputation to that particular settlement, and more generally, the Faction that lives there. You change your Reputation based on deeds that the Faction is pleased with (known as "Fame"), or antics that the Faction is furious about (known as "Infamy"). This has a knock-on effect of giving the same Reputation at every location a Faction owns, as shown in the Faction Reputation Map.

For example: You head into Ranger Outpost Bravo **(8)**, and kill everyone in there (as they were looking at your twitchy eye). You're instantly awarded an "Infamy" gain, and Vilified by the NCR, who own the Outpost. But you're also Vilified (and attacked on sight) by every other NCR location, too! Think very carefully before you begin to assert a particular Reputation!

Tip The Reputation you have for each of the main Factions is shown on your Pip-Boy too, so you can keep an eye open for possible problems. As inter-Faction animosity is already a problem in the Mojave (the NCR and Caesar's Legion hate each other, and the Great Khans hate the NCR, for example), it is worth knowing any "knock-on" effects for gaining too much Fame with opposing Factions. The Factions part of this guide has more detailed information on this.

Fame and Infamy in Action

What constitutes an Action that can get you Fame (or Infamy) within a Faction? The following tables show very general examples of Fame and Infamy-based Actions that yield a variety of points.

FAME-BASED ACTION	SEVERITY	VALUE
Giving a few caps to a kid	Very Minor	1
Declining a minor reward	Minor	2
Helping someone with a nonvital task	Average	4
Saving someone's life	Major	7
Saving many lives at great risk/sacrifice	Very Major	12

INFAMY-BASED ACTION	SEVERITY	VALUE
Saying something mean-spirited to an innocent	Very Minor	1
Brusquely demanding an excessive reward	Minor	2
Beating someone severely/screwing them over	Average	4
Killing someone who didn't deserve it	Major	7
Screwing over/killing groups that didn't deserve it	Very Major	12

Like Karma, these points are never explicitly shown; but they are used to calculate your ongoing Reputation with all Factions. Your current Reputation is calculated by comparing these different Fame and Infamy values to an overall scale, and you're given a title based on the percentage values.

For example, if you were rude to a Follower of the Apocalypse (Very Minor Infamy), but then thought better of it, and completed some Quests and saved two characters associated with the Followers, and established a trade beneficial to the Followers (multiple Very Major Fame), your Negative Range with the Followers would be low (0 to 15%), but your Positive Range would be huge (>100%). This calculation would be seen in-game as the title "Idolized"; the best Positive Reputation you can get!

Infamy! Infamy! They've All Got It in for Me!

The following chart shows the different titles you are given, based on the Fame or Infamy you've caused.

Note The size of the faction is also calculated into your Reputation; so annoying the Great Khans or the Omertas is much less of a threat than going into Caesar's Fort and starting a ruckus...unless they are allied to a bigger Faction, like the Crimson Caravan Company and the NCR!

REPUTATION TITLE	FAME (POSITIVE) RANGE	INFAMY (NEGATIVE) RANGE
OVERALL REPUTATION INTERACTION: Unknown (contact not made, or Reputation not tested greatly)		
Neutral	0 to 15%	0 to 15%
OVERALL REPUTATION INTERACTION: Unsure: The Faction member whether you will act in helpful or harmful way.		
Mixed	>15% to 50%	>15% to 50%
Unpredictable	>50% to 100%	>50% to 100%
Wild Child	>100%	>100%
Smiling Troublemaker	>50% to 100%	>15% to 50%
Dark Hero	>100%	>50% to 100%
Sneering Punk	>15% to 50%	>50% to 100%
Soft-Hearted Devil	>50% to 100%	>100%
OVERALL REPUTATION INTERACTION: Good: The Faction member should interact with you as though you can be counted on to behave in a benevolent way.		
Accepted	<15% to 50%	0 to 15%
Liked	>50% to 100%	0 to 15%
Idolized	>100%	0 to 15%
Good-Natured Rascal	>100%	>15% to 50%
OVERALL REPUTATION INTERACTION: Evil: The Faction member should assume you are a destructive force or presence.		
Shunned	0 to 15%	>15% to 50%
Hated	0 to 15%	>50 to 100%
Vilified	0 to 15%	>100%
Merciful Thug	>15% to 50%	>100%

Reputation on a Sliding Scale

The following Reputation titles show the exact standing you are within a given Faction, and what to expect next depending on your actions. It also attributes a number to your title, which is handy to remember when trying to become Liked or Hated when starting a Quest: A score of 4 or more on the Evil scale indicates Hated, and 4 or more on the Good scale indicates Liked. Now you know how many Fame or Infamy Gains you need to reach your preferred standing with any Faction!

PTS.	REPUTATION TITLE	PTS.	REPUTATION TITLE	PTS.	REPUTATION TITLE
	Evil Scale:		**Good Scale:**		**Mixed Scale:**
1	Neutral	1	Neutral	1	Neutral
2	Sneering Punk	2	Smiling Trouble Maker	2	Soft-hearted Devil
3	Merciful Thug	3	Good Natured Rascal	3	Dark Hero
4	Shunned	4	Accepted	4	Mixed
5	Hated	5	Liked	5	Unpredictable
6	Vilified	6	Idolized	6	Wild Child

If you're Liked, expect beneficial Trading arrangements, free Food or Drink on occasion, and for the largest Factions, the use of a Safehouse and even equipment drops!

If you're Unpredictable, the Faction won't usually attack, but you can't rely on the Faction to help you, but you can start to earn their trust by completing tasks that give you Fame, if you need them.

If you're Hated, expect the Faction to attack you on sight. Unless you're Sneaking, or dressed as a Faction member (and even then, forces like the NCR have Military Police and Guard Dogs to sniff out undesirables), expect combat.

Keep in mind that Reputation is assessed per location and Faction and are not moral absolutes. You might be Hated by the New California Republic because, in part, you helped the residents of Freeside get better access to water; Idolized by Caesar's Legion for committing atrocities; seen as a Smiling Troublemaker in Primm; Shunned in Novac; and Liked in Goodsprings. You are liked or disliked based on the values of the Faction or location, not on the basis of universal moral law, as is the case with Karma.

Tip So how do you choose which Factions you want to suck up to, and which you want to slaughter? Consult the Main and Side Quest Walkthroughs (which has all the major Reputation choices you can make) and the Factions section of this guide; and choose an allegiance that allows you to increase Reputation with the Factions you most identify with. Or no-one at all, if you're a maniac!

Or to sum it all up: Create Fame by doing helpful tasks. Create Infamy by shooting people. Then live with the consequences!

THE BATTLE FOR WASTELAND SUPREMACY

Learn the rudiments of combat, both with and without computerized aiming help, and learn the basic facets of the different offensive weapons to scavenge.

Running and Gunning

There are now three ways to deliver a blow to your enemies in the combat zone. You can:

Crosshairs: Strike at them with manual aiming, using the crosshairs on the screen's HUD **(1)**. The benefits are a real-time and fast-paced combat, where your reaction time saves you.

Iron Sights: Aim a ranged firearm down the sights manually, with just your eyesight and trigger finger between you and your victim **(2)**. The benefits are true accuracy and a sense of reality to your firing. Try crouching (or increasing your Strength) to aid in diminishing the sway your weapons have due to inertia and weight. A Chem called Steady also helps with this, too.

VATS: Or pause the action, take in your surroundings without penalty, locate most of your threats; and then kill them in slow, methodical ballets of bullets or battering **(3)**. This offers the most help.

The damage reduction in VATS you may have experienced in the Capital Wasteland is no longer active; you are hurt just as much in VATS as outside it, so be cautious when using it to fight a group of enemies; and prioritize your targets accordingly.

Tip A Follower named Boone has a Spotter perk, and zooming in (either with a scope, or using Iron Sights) allows you to see the enemy with an easily visible red outline, in real-time. This aids locating foes in combat considerably. Use Iron Sights in combination with VATS: Employ VATS to target precisely where you wish to strike a foe, then exit and the crosshairs are left there, and an immediate shot almost guarantees a hit every time!

VATS Entertainment

Before attempting large-scale battles, perfect the art of VATS Learn to flick between enemies and enemy parts, learn when to enter VATS (as soon as you see an opening, and usually when a head is available to target), and what benefits there are for tagging the various appendages. Best of all, there is a +15% chance of a critical hit with VATS.

Head: Damage is usually doubled. If the chance to hit the head is more than half that of other limbs, aim there, unless the foe is extra-tough. Otherwise, you are better off aiming for the arms or legs.

Weapon: If your foe is damaging you with a nasty weapon, remove it from play. With an Unarmed Attack in return, you can shrug this off as you rain in the free hits.

Arms: If an opponent needs two hands to hold a dangerous weapon, such as a Minigun, cripple one of them. He will drop the weapon. Even if he picks it up again, his aim will be horrible.

Legs: Strike the legs of foes that are apt to flee, and remain quicker than they are. Dispose of them as you wish. This is a great tactic for Super Mutants, Geckos, LakeLurks, and Deathclaws.

Control Boxes and Antennae: Robots, Turrets, and Giant Ants have these. Once destroyed, they will frenzy and attack anything nearby, even their friends. This is excellent when shooting Turrets, and a single foe within a group, but pointless in one-on-one confrontations.

Melee and Unarmed Antics

There's never been a better time to get up close and personal with an enemy, thanks to the additional attacks you receive in VATS with certain Melee Weapons, and every Unarmed Weapon.

Unique Attacks (Melee): All Melee Weapons have an additional, heavy strike attack listed in the top-right corner of your VATS screen. It takes approximately double the Action Points to attempt (compared to your regular attack), but the results are often more than twice as damaging! For example, after a visit to Camp Golf, the Courier located a 9 Iron, and then took this enemy down with a heavy strike attack called "Fore!" **(4)**, unique to that weapon.

Poison Attacks (Melee): Learning to Craft at a Campfire is extremely important to those training in Melee Weapons, as you can make a variety of poisons, coat your chosen Melee Weapon with it, and inflict additional debilitating damage to a foe.

Uppercut and Cross (Unarmed): These become available as your skill increases. All Unarmed weapons allow two different attacks **(5)**, which inflict the same amount of damage, but are useful if a foe is constantly blocking one of these attacks (simply switch to another or randomize them until your Action Points are used up). Be sure you're using both attack types!

Blocking (Unarmed): All well as real-time (non-VATS) blocking, which is useful if you're fighting a foe armed with Melee or Unarmed Weapons. This allows you to predict, and shake off an attack. It isn't nearly as useful when you're trying to block bullets though!

Weapon Condition

The effect that condition has on the functionality of a weapon has been tweaked slightly, based on the following range:

CONDITION	WEAPON EFFECT	CONDITION	WEAPON EFFECT
75–100	100% listed Stats	1–74	-0.67% DAM per point

Check your Items > Weapons (or > Apparel) Pip-Boy screen. Notice the tick mark on your weapon's (or armor's) CND bar? That's the 75% (50%) mark, and once the CND is less than that, the condition deteriorates based on the table, and weapons misfire and jam when reloading. You should maintain your Weapons and Apparel once they hit this mark; using your Repair skill, Follower, or Vendor.

Weapons Detail

- Some weapons are easier to employ in real-time, such as the Flamer. You can also circle-strafe an enemy, make quick evasive maneuvers in and out of cover, and use your dexterity more easily. However, it is sometimes more difficult to precisely aim, especially at range.
- If you're out of Action Points, you can still use VATS to excellent effect. Use it to center your aim on a target, even if you have no APs left. Then, without firing, exit VATS Your run-and-gun manual aim is now dead-center on your foe. Fire away!
- If you're quick at entering VATS, you can often target an adversary before they throw a Grenade. Shoot the Grenade, either when it's in the air or in the enemy's hand. Detonation in the air causes no harm to you. Detonating in the enemy's hand causes it to explode.
- Are you trying to avoid confrontation with a foe, and don't want to kill it? Target the legs in VATS, cripple them both, then out-run the foe. If you are running away, try closing any doors between you and your foes; this slows them down, and prevents them from shooting you.

Note Hot Key: This allows you to place one of eight objects for quick access. It's an incredible benefit. Stick your three or four favorite weapons, a variety of Chems, Stimpaks, and Rad-X, and you'll cut down on the time spent fiddling with your Pip-Boy.

Note  The "up" location in your Hot Key layout is reserved for Ammo Type. Simply hit it, and you reload ammo based on the types you've collected or made; the exact type is shown next to the CND under your AP bar in the lower-right area of your in-game HUD.

Weapon Types

1

In New Vegas, there are no "big guns"; weapons are separated by the type of ammunition they use. They now all have a STR rating (which you can see in the Items > Weapons section of your Pip-Boy). The icon next to the Vault Boy icon shows the type of weapon, and the associated skill needed to fire it without penalty.

For example, the 12.7mm Pistol **(1)** is a Gun (and therefore requires that skill to operate). The "75" next to the Gun icon indicates you need a Gun skill of 75+ to properly operate it.

Tip Some weapons require two hands to use, and all have a STR value. Two-handed weapons slow you down when you run, so holster them if you want to move faster.

Attack from higher ground; it's always easier to slink back behind ground cover than flee with foes descending after you.

Energy Weapons

 Flamers and Incinerators are now known as Energy Weapons. Some Energy Weapons can be modified.

The technology of tomorrow, here today! Energy Weapons allow you to dispatch your foes into Ash or Goo Piles (which fortunately still yields the same loot). These are more expensive to keep in ammunition. Aside from the Unique variants, Plasma-based weapons tend to be slower to fire, but more damaging. Laser-based weapons are faster at hitting, but leave less of a mark. Most Energy Weapons are more accurate than old-fashioned guns.

Explosives

Grenade Launchers, Grenade Rifles, Missile Launchers, and the infamous Fat Man are all Explosives weapons now. C-4 Explosives can be shot at, but ideally need a Detonator for an explosion where you want (and this can be on the body of a target if you "reverse Pickpocket" them).

Lobbing Grenades as a back-up for your Gun fire is an effective combat strategy, and judging distance by checking the hit chances in VATS first is always a good plan. Don't forget to pack Pulse varieties, because they dispatch robot adversaries in seconds. Setting up ambushes using mines (of any kind) is always entertaining. In interior locations, look for a doorway and set a couple there, then provoke an enemy (usually with a 10mm Pistol) and run back past the doorway. You don't set off your own Mines, but your enemy does! A similar trick is available in the city by setting Mines around corners. Finally, for the ultimate kill, place a Mine with Grenades around it; when the Mine detonates the Grenades also explode.

Tip Remember when manually aiming Explosives weapons to judge where your foe will be when the projectile arrives, not where he is at the moment.

Guns

Any weapon that uses bullets, clips, slugs, or otherwise lead-based projectiles are in this category. So a Minigun and a Magnum are both classified as a Gun now. Many Guns can be modified.

This is the weapon choice for the initial explorer, and it's good to figure out the type of Gun you want based on your style of play. Use the "Guns and Gear" chapter to compare the statistics of each weapon: For example, Sniper Rifles are fantastic for long-distance takedowns from a (usually high) vantage point. Powerful Magnums and other Revolvers are great for headshots. Shotguns are great for close-range blasting. Guns also have the widest number of modifications, so be sure to Upgrade your weapons as often as possible, select two or three stalwart Guns you want to keep and collect, and then break down the ammo and sell the rest.

Tip If you are using long distance weapons like the Sniper Rifle, it's sometimes better to aim manually rather than using VATS The VATS chance to hit will be lower than what you can probably do manually. However, you will be giving up the +15% bonus chance for a critical that VATS provides. Also, for all long-range attacks, you should be stealthed to get the stealth attack critical bonus as well as help steady your aim.

Melee Weapons

 Remember that many Melee Weapons have a unique heavy strike in VATS that costs more APs, but is more devastating.

Take your pick, and test them out on Geckos as some of these hand-carried weapons and blades have a slower swing than others. Practice until you can churn body parts with the Chainsaw, or graduate to something heavy like the Super Sledge or Thermic Lance. Don't bother with Rolling Pins, Police Batons, or Nailboards. They just aren't tough enough. As stated previously, you should be attempting the element of surprise using these weapons, not wading in from a distance into a barrage of fire.

Unarmed

There is a wider variety of Unarmed Weapons, and some (like the Zap Glove and Boxing Gloves) are tailored to a particular enemy (in this case, Robots and enemies you want to knock out but not kill). You can also find four instructors in the Mojave that can teach you an additional Unarmed perk; a move you can try in combat along with the Uppercut and Cross, which are unlocked as your skill increases.

Due to the small variety of Unarmed Weapons, using Unarmed combat can be challenging. You'll get Spiked Knuckles pretty easily. If you find a Ballistic Fist (taken from one of Caesar's guards), you're set for a while. Do what you must to keep it repaired. At higher levels, attempt to use the Displacer Glove as soon as you can. VATS is entertaining when you use these weapons, because it is easier to hit, providing you can wade through enemy gunfire. Sneak to ensure that your attacks land with additional (and critical) force.

 Weapon Modification

New to the Mojave Wasteland is the ability to Modify some of the Guns, Energy Weapons, and a few firearm-based Explosive devices you may have collected on your travels. You don't need a Bench, or indeed any type of Repair skill to modify, or "mod," a weapon; you just need the necessary Upgrade Part or Parts. Modify a weapon to increase its combat effectiveness; it is incredibly useful, and should be done as soon as possible; in fact, while you're still in Goodsprings!

- Some weapons have one, two, or three Upgrade Parts, and you can upgrade in stages, or all at once. The former is recommended.
- When a weapon is modded, it has a "+" next to its name in your Pip Boy's Items > Weapons menu. You should also see the Mods you've added underneath the Stats for that weapon.
- Upgrade parts are mainly found at Vendors, such as Chet in Goodsprings, the Gun Runners' Vendertron, and Gloria Van Graff in the Silver Rush Casino. It is important you keep a pleasant rapport with these Vendors; killing them means you can't purchase any of the Upgrades, and they are lost forever.
- You can Upgrade more than one of the same weapon, but there's little point; simply Repair the current modded weapon and use that exclusively.
- Unique variants of a particular weapon cannot be modified.
- Be monumentally careful when you Repair a modded weapon. You want to *select the modded weapon*, and not a regular version of that weapon you're cannibalizing from. If you select a regular weapon, and then Repair it with a modded version, *you will lose all modifications*! You have been warned!
- A complete list of Vendors who sell Modification Upgrades is listed in the "Tour" chapter and Appendices.

Modification Example: 9mm Pistol+

1

With a Barter skill of 100 (which increases the VAL of the item more than it may appear on your Pip Boy), the Courier returned to Goodsprings with a 9mm Pistol, and Repaired it to Perfect condition. This is what it looked like **(1)**. After Trading with Chet (at the General Store in Goodsprings), the Courier purchased the two available Modifications for the 9mm Pistol:

9mm Pistol Extended Mags

9mm Pistol Scope

2

3

4

With no need for a Workbench or a Repair skill, the Courier simply slotted the Extended Mags into place. The 9mm Pistol now looked like this **(2)**. Then the Scope was added, and the fully modded 9mm Pistol looked like this **(3)**. Later in his adventure, a man named Benny was kind enough to give him a Unique 9mm Pistol called "Maria" **(4)**. The difference in stats between the 9mm Pistols was noticeable:

WEAPON	SKILL	LEVEL	STR	DAM	DPS	WG	VAL	CLIP	NOTES
9mm Pistol	Guns	0	0	20	78	0.75	100	9mm (13)	Basic 9mm Pistol, in 100% CND
9mm Pistol+	Guns	0	0	20	78	0.75	375	9mm (20)	Note the extra value, and seven shots in the mag.
9mm Pistol+	Guns	0	0	20	78	0.75	500	9mm (20)	The scope allows more accurate manual aiming. Note the large increase in Value.
Maria	Guns	0	0	24	141	0.75	998	9mm (13)	Maria is more powerful (and valuable), but can't be modded for that extended mag.

GOING ON MANEUVERS

The places you'll go, and how you act when you get there is all-too important. This has a look at some environmental hazards, and how to live off both the grid and the land without using violence.

Clandestine Activities

Sneaking and the Stealth-Boy

1

Don't want to attack foes due to disposition, lack of ammunition, low Health, or as part of a Quest? Then Sneak! Begin by practicing around the Settlers of Goodsprings: Crouch and learn when you're spotted, and when you're Hidden. Then try it out on more hostile foes, like the Ghouls outside the REPCONN Test Site **(1)**. The key to staying Hidden is to be 180 degrees to a target's rear, or behind cover (and not seen by anyone else). If the Caution warning occurs, combat is likely, so you should switch to an aggressive posture. If the target is further away, sit tight and don't move; the warning will return to Hidden if you aren't spotted, and you can resume moving.

Low-level Sneaking is much more useful, as you receive a bonus based on your level, and you're given bonuses when dealing with characters and enemies that are a lower level than you (which you can't see in the game). Low-level foes are now easier to Sneak by (even if you have a low Sneak skill). As you increase in levels, this bonus lessens, as shown in the following tables:

CHARACTER LEVEL	BONUS TO SNEAK
1	+50
2	+35
3	+20
4	+5
5+	—

LEVEL DIFFERENCE*	BONUS/PENALTY TO SNEAK
>4	+45
+3 to +4	+30
+1 to +2	+15
0	—
-1 to -2	-15
-3 to -4	-30
<-4	-45

** Positive values are in your favor.*

Consult the Bestiary of this guide to learn the level of all the entities in the Mojave Wasteland.

Tip Encourage an enemy to move or turn around so you can Sneak past an enemy or light source by tossing a Grenade or shooting your gun at a distant wall: They investigate that area. Silenced weapons work perfectly for this, because they doesn't give your position away. Remember; shoot the wall, not the foe!

Tip The Stealth Boy, a device you pick up then activate via your Pip-Boy, turns you almost invisible for a limited amount of time. It's the perfect companion to Sneaking, as it allows temporary invisibility. However, you're still audible!

Tip Lights off, please! Don't expect much success if your Pip-Boy's Flashlight is on.

Stealing

2

The Karma losses are small, and Stealing items is excellent to add to your inventory. But it's also a great way to lose a carefully built-up Reputation, and for previously friendly denizens to turn hostile on you! For this reason, combine Stealing with Sneaking (and a Stealth Boy for important items). Items you steal are marked with red text **(2)**. Usually you can get away with checking a cabinet while being watched, as long as you don't take anything. Otherwise, Steal only if no one is looking: So long as the HUD reads "Hidden," you are safe.

Hostile Settlements

3

Have matters taken a turn for the violent while you were Stealing, or did you commit violent acts in an otherwise peaceful settlement? Then expect a full-on battle **(3)**, Karma loss, and a huge dent in your Reputation. Unless you're trying to kill everyone in the entire Wasteland, there will be some Factions you should ally with, and therefore others you can attack (usually as part of your Quest objectives from an omnipresent Faction leader). This makes Stealing simple in certain locations (where you don't care about annoying anyone), and very problematic in others (where you're trying to maintain your trust and Fame).

Pickpocketing

4

The basics of Pickpocketing remain unchanged; if you want to take a valuable item (such as a key) without talking to or killing an individual, use your Sneak skill, and Crouch, silently moving up from behind. The value of the item affects the chances of discovery; prized items shouldn't be grabbed unless you're highly skilled. If you're in doubt, employ a Stealth Boy. You can't Pickpocket items such as carried weapons or clothes that are being worn, or certain items that an individual has to give you; only by killing someone can you access everything they have.

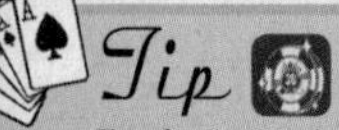

Tip Be sure you attempt the Reverse Pickpocket. Silently step up to a foe, and place a Grenade, or C-4 Explosive onto them. Then back away, and wait for the explosion (or better yet, wait for them with a C-4 Detonator **(4)**, watch as they walk into an area with a large population, and trigger the unknown bomber!).

Environmental Hazards

Vehicular Manslaughter

Destroy cars and trucks with engines to witness a large and satisfying explosion, and a chain-reaction if a subsequent vehicle catches fire. This can catch foes in the splash damage, but you may move an important item that was in the blast radius. Attract enemies with this technique, or destroy each vehicle you come across, leaving your mark so you know where you've been.

Danger! Hazards Ahead!

Taken a rigged shotgun blast to the midriff? Stepped on a Bear Trap? Trot near a traffic cone, only to find a Frag Mine was hidden under it? Then you've experienced the many Traps of this Wasteland. Placed by the more enterprising (and deranged) of entities, most can be disarmed or ignored if you have a particular perk or a reasonable Repair skill.

Traps

There are a variety of Traps to trigger. Here are some of the more troublesome:

Chain Traps: Simply find the trip wire (sometimes difficult if you're being attacked) to deactivate them.

Rigged Shotguns: Almost always activated by trip wire. Duck in locations you suspect of having these Traps. Or, move around the plate or trip wire, and disarm from the side. You receive shotgun ammo for your troubles.

Grenade Bouquets: These take a few seconds to detonate, giving you time to flee (usually into a second Trap!). Either disarm the trip wire, or look up and reach the Grenade cluster to bag three Frag Grenades. Or, shoot them from a safe distance.

Rigged Terminals: Always take extra time to inspect terminals, especially ones with a small antenna on the back, used to detonate a Frag Grenade hidden on the unit itself. This only happens when you try to use the terminal, so approach from the side or rear to disarm it and pocket a Frag Grenade.

Rigged Mailboxes: Certain Fiends in the southwest of New Vegas use these as a deterrent and ambush spot. Simply (and carefully) move to the Mailbox and disarm the trap. Rig it to explode if you want to ambush Fiends yourself.

Bear Traps: An ancient form of crippling, Bear Traps are nasty and quick to snap, although you can disarm them relatively easily too. There's little point in rearming them; either avoid them completely or risk the injury.

Gas Leaks: Occasionally encountered in subterranean Vaults, these are triggered by a muzzle flash, so no live firing! Either step around the corner and lob in a Grenade to clear the path, or drop a Grenade, and sprint to a door and close it before it detonates.

Radiation

Take a Rad-X before you go wading into any water, or investigating any craters, and you'll shrug off the light radiation. Visiting a wider radiation zone? Then pack a Radiation Suit, or Advanced Radiation Suit. Or simply avoid the area; there's a lot less radiation in the Mojave Wasteland than back East.

Mines

Tread slowly and lightly, looking down and rotating until you find your Mine, then disarm it. The Mine is added to your inventory. Beware of more cunning foes, such as the Viper Gang, placing Mines under objects such as traffic cones. If you are crouched in the Sneak mode, you can grab them from slightly farther away. If you're happy Sneaking, place Mines in a foe's path, then hide and fire at them to attract their attention. The results are messily effective.

AIDING AND ABETTING THE MOJAVE COURIER

How to use the residents, and even the flora and fauna of the Mojave Wasteland to your advantage.

Scavenging

1

The Mojave Wasteland, and the twisted ruins circling the shining spire of New Vegas, are filled with objects and bric-a-brac that may be useless to many, but helpful to some. The most valuable items are known as Collectibles (and are listed later in this chapter). The more common items vary in their usefulness. But many of them have a use; and it is important to know which to collect, and which to discard. But first, some rules to follow:

Any item that appears visibly in the world stays there until you pick it up. Any Ammunition, Health, Chems, and rare items are flagged for collecting during the "Tour" chapter.

Any items that appears inside another storage device, unless they are flagged in the "Tour" chapter, are almost always randomly generated. This means that if you open the same desk during two different scavenger hunts, you won't find the same items. However, the items you do find are likely to be what you need, such as Ammo, Health, or Crafting parts **(1)**.

Always check the VAL (Value) of the item you're grabbing, as well as its weight. A Carton of Cigarettes, for example, is worth 50 Caps, and well worth stuffing into your pockets.

Check every desk, filing cabinet, footlocker, shelf, bookcase, safe (on desks, floors, in walls, or floors) or corpse; peer into bathtubs and behind cabinets; and conduct a thorough sweep of your location.

If you're having a hard time finding Ammunition, take the Scrounger or Fortune Finder perks.

The main objects to locate are Ammo Boxes and First Aid Boxes. They always contain what they say on the tin! In fact, First Aid Boxes are likely to contain Chems and Bobby Pins too. Remember that some of these boxes are locked.

Plant Life of the Mojave Wasteland

2

3

Dotting throughout the desert are hundreds of naturally occurring plants that you can pick. The NCR, and certain settlers are also attempting the cultivation of crops, too. These are (literally) ripe for the picking. The general rule to follow is to explore the less populated and irradiated areas to find the plants you're looking for. Plants serve three purposes:

1. You can eat most of them (always check the Effects first!), giving you a (usually small) boost to your Health. For example, Banana Yucca Fruit **(2)** adds +3 to your HP (7s). However, the Barrel Cactus Fruit **(3)** gives relatively similar results, but also temporarily reduces your Endurance, too!
2. The health benefits that plants give you can best be described as "miniscule." What you must do is utilize your Survival skill, and combine and cook them as part of a Recipe at a Campfire (see below).
3. The third plan is to make a bit of money collecting fruit and then selling them to a Vendor. The Value is around 5 Caps per fruit, which isn't too bad if there's a cluster of Fruit in a relatively compact area. But there are more lucrative ways to use the land to make Caps (see Crafting, below).

Cooking, Tinkering, and Creating: Crafting Time

4

5

6

Dotted across the Mojave are three different types of helpful objects that allow you to Craft. These are the Campfire **(4)**, Reloading Bench **(5)**, and the Workbench **(6)**.

Campfires

These allow you to Craft Recipes, depending on the availability of ingredients collected, and your Survival skill. You can Craft:

- Recipes for Antivenom (to cure poisons).
- Poisons (to coat on a Melee Weapon before a difficult fight).
- Food (to use—particularly in Hardcore mode—instead of Stimpaks).
- Chems (more potent versions of some already available).
- Gecko Hides (which you can sell for an impressive sum of Caps).

Reloading Benches

These enable you to Craft Recipes related to ammunition instead of aid. Depending on the ammo you've collected, and your Repair skill, you can:

- Craft ammunition for many types of Gun, so you don't have to purchase or scavenge for ammo. Simply locate the raw ingredients, and recycle ammo parts to create new (or preferred) ammunition types.
- Break down ammunition you don't want or need to their component parts. This is incredibly useful, as it allows you to use those parts to Craft other ammo types. Make sure you do this, and you'll never need to pay or hunt down Gun ammo again! Create different types of ammo for different situations, such as armor-piercing bullets for armored foes.
- Although you can break down Scrap Metal into Lead (as Lead is the component used the most during ammo creation), this isn't a great idea, as you require Scrap Metal for Free Quests, and the amount of Lead created (200) is only worth a few rounds of ammunition.

Workbenches

These allow you to work on a variety of Crafted items, ranging from Energy Weapon ammunition to new flavors of Nuka-Cola:

- Aid: You can create Stimpaks, Super Stimpaks, Doctor's Bags, and a Weapon Repair Kit (all are incredibly potent and useful).
- Ammo: If you're a fan of future weapons that go "zap," you can change the ammunition types and craft more potent Energy and Microfusion Cells, and more.
- Food: Three types of Nuka-Cola (Ice Cold, Quartz, and Victory) can be used to quench your thirst, and in some cases, temporarily increase your low-light vision.
- Scrape together the components for a couple of nasty explosive devices; the Bottlecap Mine and the Time Bomb; perfect for ambushing foes.

A Taste of the Mojave

The following is a dozen of the very best, most useful Recipes that you should survive off. Make sure you Craft all of the following items, which are numbered in order of usefulness.

1. Weapon Repair Kit

A great way to save Caps on Repairing high-level and Unique weapons, and to keep your overall weight down for Repairing on-the-fly, using common materials:

Duct Tape (1) | Scrap Metal (3) | Wrench (2)
Scrap Electronics (1) | Wonderglue (2)

2. Doctor Bag

Useful in Normal difficulty mode because it instantly restores all limbs, but vital in Hardcore mode when Stimpaks and beds won't cut it.

Forceps (1) | Scalpel (1) | Surgical Tubing (1)
Medical Brace (1)

3. Hydra

Regenerates limb condition over time and can be made with the Survival skill. Just be careful gathering the supplies.

Cave Fungus (5) | Night Stalker Blood (3) | Radscorpion Poison Gland (2)

4. Super Stimpak

Better than a regular Stimpak, with added temporary HP boost. Improve all of your Stimpaks today!

Leather Belt (1) | Nuka Cola (1) | Stimpak (1)
Mutfruit (1)

5. Slasher

When you're outgunned and overexposed, Slasher can help even the odds.

Banana Yucca (2) | Psycho (1) | Stimpak (2)

6. Rocket

Need a little more AP to clear that room than only Jet usually provides? Try new and improved Rocket!

Box of Detergent (1) | Jet (1) | Nuka Cola (1)

7. Party Time Mentats

Like Mentats, only with more Charisma. Great for Skill Checks or Speech challenges.

Honey Mesquite Pod (1) | Mentats (1) | Whiskey (1)

8. Bleak Venom

Gives your Melee Weapon that extra kick when you really need it.

Bark Scorpion Venom (3) | Cazador Poison Gland (1) | White Horsenettle Berry (5)

9. .50 MG Match Hand Load

Custom-made for increased accuracy and damage, this round is a must-have for snipers using the Anti-Materiel Rifle.

.50 MG Case (1) | Rifle Powder (25) | .50 MG Primer (1)
Lead (75)

10. Gecko Kebab

Handy for healing, and it keeps down the weight in Hardcore mode because it doubles as Food and Drink. Recipe makes 2 Kebabs!

Banana Yucca (1) | Gecko Meat (1) | Jalapeno Pepper (1)
Buffalo Gourd Seed (1)

11. Bloatfly Slider

Easy-to-find ingredients across the entire Wasteland, hydrates and provides sustenance without any Rads taken.

Bloatfly Meat (1) | Prickly Pear (2)

12. Cactus Water

When you're parched and thirsting for some Purified Water; make it using scavenged items for a simple, but handy Drink.

Prickly Pear (3) | Empty Soda Bottle (1)

Crafting Recipes

The table on the following page shows all the different Recipes you can make.

Note The VAL (Value) of a crafted item is per individual item; multiples are obviously worth more. Note that your Barter skill affects the value you can sell items for, and your Medicine and Survival skills boost the effects of a Recipe; for example, a Stimpak gives you more health if you have Medicine 100 instead of 20.

RECIPE	MADE AT...	SKILL REQ.	INGREDIENTS	WG	VAL*	EFFECTS
			RECIPES: AID			
Antivenom (2)	Campfire	Survival (40)	Night Stalker Blood (1), Radscorpion Poison Gland (4)	—	25	Cure Animal Poison
Bleak Venom (3)	Campfire	Survival (50)	Bark Scorpion Poison Gland (3), Cazador Poison Gland (1), White Horsenettle (5)	0.5	1	HP -15(10s)
Mass Purified Water (30)	Campfire	Survival (50)	Dirty Water (30), Glass Pitcher (3), Pressure Cooker (1), RadAway (1), Surgical Tubing (3)	1	20	HP +7(5s)
Mother Darkness (3)	Campfire	Survival (75)	Bark Scorpion Poison Gland (3), Cazador Poison Gland (1), White Horsenettle (5)	0.5	3	AGL -3(1m), PER -3(1m), HP -8(10s)
Rocket	Campfire	Survival (50)	Box of Detergent (1), Jet (1), Nuka-Cola (1)	—	20	AP +30
Silver Sting (3)	Campfire	Survival (30)	Bark Scorpion Poison Gland (3), Cazador Poison Gland (1), White Horsenettle (5)	0.5	2	STR -2(1m), HP -8(10s)
Tremble (3)	Campfire	Survival (90)	Bark Scorpion Poison Gland (3), Cazador Poison Gland (1), White Horsenettle (5)	0.5	5	Guns -50(20s), Explos. -50(20s), Melee Weap. -50(20s), Ener. Weap. -50(20s), HP -2(20s)
			RECIPES: CHEMS			
Atomic Cocktail (4)	Campfire	Science (25)	Mentats (1), Nuka-Cola Victory (2), Vodka (2), Wine (1)	1	25	Ener. Resis +75, Fire Resis. +75, Rads +9
Healing Powder	Campfire	None	Broc Flower (1), Xander Root (1)	0	5	PER -3, HP +3(18s)
Hydra (2)	Campfire	Survival (75)	Cave Fungus (5), Night Stalker Blood (3), Radscorpion Poison Gland (2)		55	Restore Limb Condition (60s)
Party Time Mentats	Campfire	Survival (50)	Honey Mesquite Pod (1), Mentats (1), Whiskey (1)	—	20	CHR +5, PER +2, INT +2
Slasher	Campfire	Survival (50)	Banana Yucca Fruit (2), Psycho (1), Stimpak (2)	—	20	Damage +25%, Dam. Res. +25
			RECIPES: FOOD			
Bighorner Steak	Campfire	Survival (50)	Bighorner Meat (1)	0.8	5	STR +3, Rads +1, HP +7(10s)
Bloatfly Slider	Campfire	Survival (20)	Bloatfly Meat (1), Prickly Pear Fruit (2)	0.5	4	Rads +1, HP +10(15s)
Brahmin Steak (2)	Campfire	Survival (35)	Brahmin Meat (2), Wine (1)	0.8	5	STR +3, Rads +1, HP +7(15s)
Cactus Water	Campfire	Survival (30)	Empty Soda Bottle (1), Prickly Pear Fruit (3)	1	20	HP +7(5s)
Caravan Lunch	Campfire	Survival (30)	Cram (1), InstaMash (1), Lunchbox (1), Pork N' Beans (1), RadAway (1)	—	5	HP +3(15s), Rads -4 (10s)
Coyote Steak	Campfire	Survival (50)	Coyote Meat (1)	1	4	Rads +1(3s), HP +7(12s)
Desert Salad	Campfire	Survival (55)	Barrel Cactus Fruit (2), Brahmin Steak (1), Pinyon Nuts (2)	0.2	5	HP +25(15s)
Dog Steak	Campfire	Survival (40)	Dog Meat (1)	1	4	Rads +1, HP +7(10s)
Fire Ant Fricassée	Campfire	Survival (75)	Cazador Egg (1), Cram (1), Fire Ant Meat (2), Flour (1)	1	30	HP +3(1m)
Gecko Kebab (2)	Campfire	Survival (60)	Banana Yucca Fruit (1), Buffalo Gourd Seed (1), Gecko Meat (1), Jalape o Pepper (1)	0.3	4	Rads +1, HP +3(40s)
Gecko Steak	Campfire	Survival (25)	Gecko Meat (1)	1	5	Rads +1, HP +7(15s)
Grilled Mantis Leg	Campfire	Survival (30)	Honey Mesquite Pod (2), Mantis Foreleg (1), Wine (1)	1	8	Rads +1, HP +3(30s)
Mole Rat Stew	Campfire	Survival (65)	Beer (1), Honey Mesquite Pod (2), Maize (1), Mole Rat Meat (1), Pinto Bean Pod (1)	0.1	25	HP +3(3s)
Mushroom Cloud	Campfire	Survival (35)	Gum Drops (1), Night Stalker Eggs (2), Sugar Bombs (1)	1	50	AP +9, HP +10(20s)
Trail Mix	Campfire	Survival (25)	Fresh Apple (1), Fresh Pear (1), Pinyon Nuts (5), Sugar Bombs (1)	3	5	Rads +1, AP +15, HP +18(15s)
			RECIPES: MISC			
Tanned Fire Gecko Hide	Campfire	Survival (50)	Fire Gecko Hide (1), Turpentine (2), White Horsenettle (7)	1	125	—
Tanned Gecko Hide	Campfire	Survival (25)	Gecko Hide (1), Turpentine (1), White Horsenettle (5)	1	50	—
Tanned Golden Gecko Hide	Campfire	Survival (65)	Golden Gecko Hide (1), RadAway (1), Turpentine (2), White Horsenettle (10)	1	250	—
			RECIPES: UNIQUE			
Brahmin Wellington	Campfire	Survival (80)	Ant Egg (2), Blamo Mac & Cheese (1), Brahmin Meat (1), Flour (1)	1	5	Rads +1, HP +3(15s)
Cook-Cook's Fiend Stew	Campfire	Survival (75)	Beer (2), Brahmin Meat (2), Fresh Carrot (1), Fresh Potato (2), Jalapeño Pepper (2)	0	0	HP +3(5s)
Rose's Wasteland Omelet	Campfire	Survival (65)	Blamo Mac & Cheese (2), Crunchy Mutfruit (1), Deathclaw Egg (1), Lakelurk Meat (2), Tin Can (1)	1	0.1	HP +14(1m)
			RECIPES: AMMO			
.308 Round	Reloading Bench	Repair (25)	Case, .308 (1), Lead (0/17), Powder, Rifle (5), Primer, Large Rifle (1)	—	3	—
.308 JSP Hand Load	Reloading Bench	Repair (50)	Case, .308 (1), Lead (19), Powder, Rifle (6), Primer, Large Rifle (1)	—	6	—
.357 Magnum Round	Reloading Bench	Repair (25)	Case, .357 Magnum (1), Lead (16), Powder, Pistol (8), Primer, Small Pistol (1)	—	1	—
.357 Magnum , JFP Hand Load	Reloading Bench	Repair (50)	Case, .357 Magnum (1), Lead (20), Powder, Pistol (10), Primer, Small Pistol (1)	—	2	—
.44 Magnum Round	Reloading Bench	Repair (50)	Case, .44 Magnum (1), Lead (30), Powder, Pistol (10), Primer, Large Pistol (1)	—	2	—
.45-70 Gov't Round	Reloading Bench	Repair (65)	Case, .45-70 Gov't (1), Lead (30), Powder, Rifle (4), Primer, Large Rifle (1)	—	3	—
.45-70 Gov't, SWC Hand Load	Reloading Bench	Repair (90)	Case, .45-70 Gov't (1), Lead (40), Powder, Rifle (5), Primer, Large Rifle (1)	—	7	—
.50 MG Round	Reloading Bench	Repair (75)	Case, .50 MG (1), Lead (70), Powder, Rifle (22), Primer, .50 MG (1)	—	6	—
.50 MG Match Hand Load	Reloading Bench	Repair (100)	Case, .50 MG (1), Lead (75), Powder, Rifle (25), Primer, .50 MG (1)	—	8	—
10mm Round	Reloading Bench	Repair (25)	Case, 10mm (1), Lead (17), Powder, Pistol (9), Primer, Large Pistol (1)	—	1	—
10mm, JHP Hand Load	Reloading Bench	Repair (50)	Case, 10mm (1), Lead (21), Powder, Pistol (12), Primer, Large Pistol (1)	—	1	—
12 Ga. Buckshot	Reloading Bench	Repair (10)	Hull, 12 Gauge (1), Lead (40), Powder, Pistol (30), Primer, Shotshell (1)	—	1	—
12 Ga. Buckshot, Magnum	Reloading Bench	Repair (25)	Hull, 12 Gauge (1), Lead (40), Powder, Pistol (40), Primer, Shotshell (1)	—	3	—
12 Ga. Coin Shot	Reloading Bench	Repair (25)	Hull, 12 Gauge (1), Legion Denarius (8), Powder, Pistol (30), Primer, Shotshell (1)	—	40	—
12 Ga. Slug	Reloading Bench	Repair (25)	Hull, 12 Gauge (1), Lead (45), Powder, Pistol (30), Primer, Shotshell (1)	—	2	—
20 Ga. Buckshot	Reloading Bench	Repair (10)	Hull, 20 Gauge (1), Lead (30), Powder, Pistol (20), Primer, Shotshell (1)	—	1	—
20 Ga. Buckshot, Magnum	Reloading Bench	Repair (25)	Hull, 20 Gauge (1), Lead (30), Powder, Pistol (28), Primer, Shotshell (1)	—	3	—
20 Ga. Slug	Reloading Bench	Repair (25)	Hull, 20 Gauge (1), Lead (33), Powder, Pistol (20), Primer, Shotshell (1)	—	2	—
5.56mm Round	Reloading Bench	Repair (25)	Case, 5.56mm (1), Lead (12), Powder, Rifle (4), Primer, Small Rifle (1)	—	1	—
5mm Round	Reloading Bench	Repair (25)	Case, 5mm (1), Lead (13), Powder, Rifle (5), Primer, Small Rifle (1)	—	1	—

RECIPE	MADE AT...	SKILL REQ.	INGREDIENTS	WG	VAL*	EFFECTS
9mm Round	Reloading Bench	Repair (25)	Case, 9mm (1), Lead (13), Powder, Pistol (6), Primer, Small Pistol (1)	—	1	—
RECIPES: BREAKDOWN						
Breakdown .22 LR (3)	Reloading Bench	Repair (10)	Lead (2), Powder, Pistol (3)	—	—	—
Breakdown .308	Reloading Bench	Repair (25)	Case, .308, Lead (15), Powder, Rifle (4), Primer, Large Rifle (1)	—	—	—
Breakdown .357 Magnum	Reloading Bench	Repair (25)	Case, .357 Magnum, Lead (14), Powder, Pistol (6), Primer, Small Pistol (1)	—	—	—
Breakdown .44 Magnum	Reloading Bench	Repair (50)	Case, .44 Magnum, Lead (27), Powder, Pistol (8), Primer, Large Pistol (1)	—	—	—
Breakdown .45-70 Gov't	Reloading Bench	Repair (65)	Case, .45-70 Gov't (1), Lead (27), Powder, Rifle (3), Primer, Large Rifle (1)	—	—	—
Breakdown .50 MG (20)	Reloading Bench	Repair (75)	Case, .50 MG(1), Lead (64), Powder, Rifle (20), Primer, .50 MG (1)	—	—	—
Breakdown 10mm	Reloading Bench	Repair (25)	Case, 10mm (1), Lead (15), Powder, Pistol (7), Primer, Large Pistol (1)	—	—	—
Breakdown 12 Ga. (26)	Reloading Bench	Repair (10)	Hull, 12 Gauge (1), Lead (37), Powder, Pistol (26), Primer, Shotshell (1)	—	—	—
Breakdown 20 Ga. (18)	Reloading Bench	Repair (10)	Hull, 20 Gauge (1), Lead (26), Powder, Pistol (18), Primer, Shotshell (1)	—	—	—
Breakdown 5.56mm (3)	Reloading Bench	Repair (25)	Case, 5.56mm (1), Lead (10), Powder, Rifle (3), Primer, Small Rifle (1)	—	—	—
Breakdown 5mm (4)	Reloading Bench	Repair (25)	Case, 5mm (1), Lead (11), Powder, Rifle (4), Primer, Small Rifle (1)	—	—	—
Breakdown 9mm (3)	Reloading Bench	Repair (25)	Case, 9mm (1), Lead (11), Powder, Pistol (5), Primer, Small Pistol (1)	—	—	—
Breakdown Scrap Metal to Lead (200)	Reloading Bench	Repair (10)	Scrap Metal (1)	—	—	—
RECIPES: AID						
Doctor's Bag	Workbench	Medicine (40)	Forceps (1), Medical Brace (1), Scalpel (1), Surgical Tubing (1)	1	55	Restore All Body Parts
Stimpak	Workbench	Medicine (70)	Broc Flower (1), Empty Syringe (1), Xander Root (1)	—	25	HP +129
Super Stimpak	Workbench	Medicine (90)	Leather Belt (1), Mutfruit (1), Nuka-Cola (1), Stimpak (1)	—	100	Super Stimpak Debuff, HP +259
Weapon Repair Kit	Workbench	Repair (50)	Duct Tape (1), Scrap Electronics (1), Scrap Metal (3), Wonderglue (2), Wrench (2)	1	20	Restores currently equipped weapon condition
RECIPES: AMMO						
Conversion, ECP to MFC	Workbench	Science (45)	Electron Charge Pack (3)	—	3	—
Conversion, ECP to SEC	Workbench	Science (25)	Electron Charge Pack (2)	—	2	—
Conversion, MFC to ECP (3)	Workbench	Science (40)	Microfusion Cell (1)	—	1	—
Conversion, MFC to SEC (3)	Workbench	Science (20)	Microfusion Cell (2)	—	2	—
Conversion, SEC to ECP (2)	Workbench	Science (50)	Energy Cell (1)	—	1	—
Conversion, SEC to MFC (2)	Workbench	Science (30)	Energy Cell (3)	—	3	—
Efficient Recycling, Electron Charge Pack	Workbench	Science (65)	Drained Electron Charge Pack (3)	—	1	—
Efficient Recycling, Energy Cell	Workbench	Science (35)	Drained Small Energy Cell (3)	—	2	—
Efficient Recycling, Flamer Fuel	Workbench	Science (40)	Drained Flamer Fuel Tank (3)	—	1	—
Efficient Recycling, Microfusion Cell	Workbench	Science (50)	Drained Microfusion Cell (3)	—	3	—
Electron Charge Pack, Max Charge (2)	Workbench	Science (85)	Electron Charge Pack (5)	—	1	—
Electron Charge Pack, Over Charge (2)	Workbench	Science (55)	Electron Charge Pack (3)	—	1	—
Energy Cell, Max Charge (2)	Workbench	Science (70)	Energy Cell (5)	—	3	—
Energy Cell, Over Charge (2)	Workbench	Science (30)	Energy Cell (3)	—	2	—
Flamer Fuel, Homemade (20)	Workbench	Science (50)	Box of Detergent (1), Maize (2), Sugar Bombs (1)	—	0	—
Microfusion Cell, Max Charge (2)	Workbench	Science (75)	Microfusion Cell (5)	—	8	—
Microfusion Cell, Over Charge (2)	Workbench	Science (45)	Microfusion Cell (3)	—	5	—
RECIPES: FOOD						
Ice Cold Nuka-Cola (2)	Workbench	Science (90)	Nuka-Cola (3)	1	20	Rads +1, HP +4(20s)
Nuka-Cola Quartz	Workbench	Science (90)	Nuka-Cola (3)	1	40	Low-Light Vision, DT +6, HP +10(20s), Rads +2
Nuka-Cola Victory	Workbench	Science (90)	Nuka-Cola (3)	1	75	HP +10(20s), AP +30, PER -3, Rads +2
RECIPES: WEAPONS						
Bottlecap Mine	Workbench	Explosives (75)	Bottle Cap (10), Cherry Bomb (5), Lunchbox (1), Sensor Module (1)	0.5	150	DPS 96
Time Bomb	Workbench	Explosives (50)	Duct Tape (1), Dynamite (5), Egg Timer (1), Scrap Electronics (2)	0.5	750	STR 1, DPS 75

Vendors: Healing, Repairing, and Trading

1

As you've discovered, many items that you can collect on your travels can be combined into much more useful Ammunition and Aid. But for purchasing everything from Radiation curing and Caravan Cards to new Guns, high-priced Upgrades and incredibly expensive Implants, you'll need to meet a Vendor. Certain Vendors have rare or unique items you can purchase, too. They are usually stationary in a specific location, but occasionally you'll encounter them wandering as a Caravan **(1)**, sometimes down Highway 95 to Novac.

Your Barter skill reduces the number of Caps an item costs, and increases the Caps an item sells for. If Trading is a major facet of your Wasteland plan, bump up this skill. Because prices fluctuate due to your skill and Condition, if they are referenced in this guide, they listed for the highest Value (Barter = 100, CND = 100%). When you meet a Trader, talk to them to see their wares, and then purchase (or Trade using your Inventory) with them.

Most of a Vendor's inventory is random, although the type of items sold usually remain the same. The "Tour" chapter lists the type of Items a Vendor is selling, along with "Highlights"; the specific, most important items you might (but aren't guaranteed to) see.

Certain Traders (and a Companion Ghoul named Raul) have a Repair skill, and taking an item to them initially sounds like an excellent plan. However, you should be doing this yourself, or using Raul to help your items from wearing out as fast.

Or, you can make your own Weapon Repair Kits at Workbenches. This is far more advantageous than trudging to a Repairer each time you need something fixed. However, these don't fix damaged armor (especially the Unique varieties, where spare parts are not as commonly available). For this, you must visit a Repairer.

If you're crippled, unhealthy, suffering from radiation poisoning, or addicted to Chems, it's time to seek a doctor. Almost every large settlement has one, and they'll help you out, for the correct (Bartered) price. Or you can do it yourself: in non-Hardcore mode, any bed heals your crippled limbs and missing Health, and RadAway fixes radiation poison. Unfortunately, only a doctor can cure your addiction to Chems.

If you're wanting to acquire the very best Upgrades and Weapons, don't go killing the merchants you meet! For example, if you slaughter Chet in Goodsprings General Store, you can't buy his Upgrades, and they are lost forever. However, there's always an exception....

Although best done to the wandering Caravaneers on Highway 95 when no one else is around, killing these Vendors is most lucrative, as long as their inventory doesn't contain something Unique you don't want to purchase again. You'll take a Karma hit, but the amount of supplies you get from the vendor, his Brahmin, and his guard will make it worthwhile. Wandering Merchants sometimes wear Outfits that bolster your Barter skill, which you can then wear when you're dealing with other vendors you don't plan on killing...just yet.

Healers/Dealers: Purchase Medical Supplies (Aid, Implants), and request Healing, Radiation curing, and limb-healing (which usually costs between 50-100 Caps per consultation).

Repairers: Mend a weapon of your choice, without you needing to have the necessary spare parts.

Traders: Purchase any type of item from them (Upgrades, Weapons, Armor, Aid, Misc. Items, Ammo, Caravan Cards).

Find the location of every Vendor in the "Tour" chapter.

More Money, More Problems

Throughout your travels, you can collect more than just Caps: The NCR pay their soldiers in NCR Dollars, while Caesar's Legion have developed the Legion Denarius and Aureus. Meanwhile, each Casino has developed their own style of Chip, which is used as currently within that particular building when you're gambling. Both the NCR and Caesar's Legion denominations are less widely used than the almighty Cap; but most Vendors seem happy to accept them.

New Vegas Currency Conversion Table

DENOMINATION	FACTION	CONVERSION (IN CAPS)
\$5	NCR	2 caps
\$20	NCR	8 caps
\$100	NCR	40 caps
Denarius	Caesar's Legion	4 caps
Aureus	Caesar's Legion	100 caps
Poker Chip	Casino	1 Cap

Sleeping and Waiting

Why sleep? Because you gain Health and heal limb damage, and you can quickly add hours to your day. This is important if you want to travel across the Wasteland during daylight hours, or you're waiting 12 hours for a crazy robot to update you with hidden recordings. Note that if you pay for a night's rest (at Novac), or you're using a bed in a residence you own (in the Lucky 38, or a Safehouse), you receive a "well-rested" bonus, which gives you an additional +10% XP for 12 hours. Finally, remember there are numerous types of beds: from a blood-soaked mattress to a bedding roll.

Why wait? Well, if there are no enemies nearby, and you're not being damaged by radiation (which is the same when sleeping), you can wait around in a location and choose how long (in hours). While you don't gain the Health you would for a sleep, you can skip time, which is useful if you want to travel during daylight (or night) hours, or you want to enter a store or meet someone who keeps specific hours.

Limbs are not healed in Hardcore mode, and Waiting (as well as Fast Travel) makes you hungry, thirsty, and sleepy. Check the Hardcore tips earlier in this chapter for the best ways to avoid these problems.

Tip The best place to quickly heal up is Novac. There is a room to rent (or Barter about) approximately 20 steps from where you land when you Fast Travel there. You can Fast Travel in, rest for a hour, and Fast Travel back.

Health and Chems

Broaden your palate spectrum with this brave new choice, a particularly gamey taste known as Strange Meat....

By now, you've probably used a Stimpak once or twice, and are wondering what kind of other ingestible items can benefit you. The "Aid" table in the "Guns and Gear" chapter shows the statistics for all food, liquor and Chems available in the Wasteland. From here, you can see which of them are best-suited to your style of play, which you can Craft yourself, and which cause addiction.

Addiction

Chems caused addiction, and you must seek a doctor to cure you of your dependency, or use a Chem called Fixer. If you don't, you'll suffer attribute penalties from withdrawal unless you take more of that Chem. Each time you ingest a Chem, it increases the chance of addiction; you can get away with taking it twice. After that, you need to wait 30 hours for the Chem to be flushed from your system. Then you can take it again safely. This only becomes a problem if you don't have a large supply of that particular Chem, so you might wish to figure out your closest doctor, and have enough Chems, using them only when the situation arises.

Alcohol works differently. Each time you swig beer or wine, there is a 5% chance of addiction, regardless of how many times you drank or how long you waited between drinks. Scotch, whiskey and vodka have a 10% chance of addiction.

Stacking

Although addiction may put you off employing Chems, the stacking nature of Chems should let you see the benefits. If you take two Buffouts, for example, the effects last twice as long. Chems don't stack with each other, but they do stack with other items. With this in mind, cross-reference the chart, and you should begin to experiment with different concoctions of Chems, alcohol, and food (such as taking Psycho and Buffout, and then bludgeoning a Deathclaw with a Melee Weapon in the ensuing Chem rage).

Home Sweet Home

Finding a place to call home allows you to furnish your place with items of your choosing. The only available apartment is the one inside Mr. House's Lucky 38 Casino, and it's a Penthouse Suite! Check the "Tour" chapter for the furnishings on offer. Otherwise, you'll be roughing it in crummy motels, such as the one in Novac, gaining a comped room at less desirable locations like the Atomic Wrangler (which offer services other than furniture placement), or gaining Reputation with the Followers of the Apocalypse, NCR, Caesar's Legion or Brotherhood of Steel, and utilizing their Safehouses as place you can always return to.

GAMBLING

This wouldn't be a trip to New Vegas, or its seedy, outlying areas, without a visit to a gambling hall. The rules are more or less the same in each gambling establishment: Once your weapons have been removed, you head to the Bank **(1)**, where your NCR, Legion, or Cap money is exchanged for Casino Chips. You're then able to choose a table or slot machine, and begin a game.

Note that every Casino keeps a watchful eye on you, comping you with gifts if you're on a particularly thrilling winning streak. The Tops even offers you a complimentary suite, which is good of them. However, take too much of the Casino's money, and you're quietly asked to stop playing, and banned from the Casino. To learn the prizes you can win (not including the Chips you can gather, and exchange back into Caps before you leave), consult the "Big Winner" Free Quests later in this book. If you're wanting to gamble, locate these Casinos, some of which may not be open for business until certain Quest objectives are met.

LOCATION	GAMES AVAILABLE
Primm (Vikki & Vance Casino)	Blackjack, Roulette, Slots
Atomic Wrangler	Blackjack, Roulette, Slots
Gomorrah	Blackjack, Roulette, Slots
The Tops	Blackjack, Roulette, Slots

LOCATION	GAMES AVAILABLE
Ultra-Luxe	Blackjack, Roulette
Sunset Sarsaparilla Headquarters	Lucky Horseshoes
Caravan Player (various locations)	Caravan

Blackjack

All of the swankiest New Vegas Casinos (and the Atomic Wrangler) offer Blackjack. The rules are straightforward, and are posted on the Help menu of your game. Take a look at the actual table in each casino, as the felt has the dealer's rules (which are slightly different) emblazoned on it. If you're attempting to take a Casino for all their Chips, the following five tactics can help your progress:

- If the dealer is showing a set of cards that are likely to result in them busting (such as a 5), maximize your bet, and attempt to double-down, or split your hand as the hand favors you.
- Conversely, if the dealer shows a strong hand (20, 19, or 18), hit with a hand worth 16 or lower, even though you might be fearful of busting: You've lost anyway, so hope for a low card to equal or beat the dealer.
- Do not split a pair of tens or picture cards. You're on 20—mathematically hard for the dealer to beat—and you're more likely to lose one or both hands instead.
- Complex mathematics state that if you have a pair of eights, or a pair of Aces, you should split these cards, as this gives you a better chance to win than hitting with these hands.
- Double-down when if your hand is an 11. There is a strong possibility of receiving a high card afterwards, and beating the dealer. Naturally, this becomes much more common if you've a high Luck, through attribute allocation or an Implant.

Roulette

Spin the wheel and take your chance! Learn the rules of Roulette from the Help menu of your game, and understand that whatever you win is completely down to chance (and augmented slightly by your luck). Roulette is to be played for entertainment primarily, as the odds don't usually favor you. But if you want to quickly lose Chips, head on over and become seduced by the flush velvet. Or frayed velvet if you're playing at the Atomic Wrangler.

Slots

Slots is an entertaining game, involving gazing as three sets of mechanical symbols spin, and come to a rest in a random order. Certain machines have different symbols, depending on the casino. Each machine shows the order the symbols need to be in for you to win any Chips. Win, and you collect your Chips from the coin hopper. If your Luck attribute is high, prepare to win more often than not. Otherwise, approach this as a fun pastime, and move to the Blackjack table when you want to win your Chips using actual strategy.

Lucky Horseshoes

An entity known only as "Festus" sits in the Sunset Sarsaparilla Headquarters [2.17], and (among other utterances) asks if you want to play a game of Lucky Horseshoes: Cards are numbered two through ten, along with aces which count as one. You and Festus take turns drawing cards (the blue button). Each card is added to your totals. The totals need to add up as close to 21 without going over. You should hold the red button once you get up close to 21. If either of you draws a card that brings both totals to the same number, the other player's total goes up by one. The winner is the player who is closer to 21, after they hold at 21 or below, or if the other player's total is 22 or higher, and they "bust." Remember you can still lose, even if you're on 21! Or to put it another way, this is Blackjack without being able to know your cards. Naturally, it is geared towards a Festus victory.

Caravan

Finding a Caravan Player to Challenge

With many Vendors not having the standing, money, or inclination to visit The Strip's casinos, a more down-to-earth game was developed, using whatever cards could be scavenged. Currently, there are 15 characters across the Mojave Wasteland, that have their own Caravan Decks you can challenge. Find locations in the Tour. Ringo (just outside Goodsprings) actually gives you a deck to start with, so visit him first.

Locating Cards to Build Your Deck With

Naturally, collecting additional cards to augment your deck is the other part of the strategy of Caravan. Cards are distributed at random throughout the Mojave Wasteland, so finding a card you want is a matter of chance. Most cards are on sale at various Vendors, and may also be found on dead bodies too. The major locations where Caravan Cards are found can be seen in the "Tour" chapter of this guide.

Sample Decks

Caravan is a highly strategic game that you can play during your adventure, and away from your game as well! If you're having trouble beating a Caravan Player, consult the following sample decks that cater to different play styles:

The Five, Six, Seven, Eight

This 30 card build can be made out of a regular deck of cards with no extras added in. It consists of all the 5s, 6s, 7s, 8s, Jacks, Queens, and Kings from one deck, along with two Jokers. The strategy for this deck is for a medium game, with the game ending when you have approximately 5-10 cards left in your draw pile. This is great for learning the ropes, and using against early opponents, but may give you trouble with smarter players.

Pros

- Smaller range of numbers with most combinations of cards adding up to 21-26 within 3-4 cards.
- Jacks and Kings can be used offensively and defensively as needed.
- Great starting deck, since you start with all the necessary cards.

Cons

- Might be less effective against better opponents.
- Not intended for long games, as you can run out of cards quickly.
- Jokers, while not a major concern, can still cause problems if you have too many of one number on the table.

Note A variation on this build is Hi-Lo, where 3s, 4s, 9s, and 10s are used (instead of using 5s, 6s, 7s, and 8s). The principles are the same, just a different way of going about playing your cards.

The Two Suit

The idea behind the two suit deck is to use Aces and Jokers to destroy your opponent's Caravans. It consists of all but the Aces of two suits from one deck, multiple Aces of the other suits from other decks (for example, the 2-10 of Clubs and Spades and multiple Aces of Diamonds and Hearts), with a smattering of Jacks, Queens, Kings, and Jokers; fill with as many cards as needed to feel comfortable. This deck is all about suit control. The direction of your cards (ascending or descending) is going to be less of a problem, as you'll usually have a card of the same suit to play. Using Jokers on the opposing suit Aces causes problems for your opponent but leaves you in the clear, just make sure any Aces your opponent puts down of your suits get hit with a Jack before they can use a Joker. Nothing smarts more than losing half of your Caravans.

Pros

- Less of a worry about keeping cards the same suit, as you'll only have 2 you're working with.
- Using Jokers offensively can really screw up your opponent.
- Jokers are less of an issue coming from your opponent as long as you have a Jack handy.
- Can be tailored to add more cards to your deck if you need to play a longer game.

Cons

- Can take longer to build up your caravans.
- Opponents playing Queens on your cards can be a hassle to deal with if played correctly.
- An Ace of your suit that you don't play a Jack on can be devastating if the opponent manages to get a Joker on it.

The Sixes and a Whole Lotta Kings

This deck is a high risk, high reward set of cards. The object is to stack your deck with 6s and a whole lot of Kings (you can have up to 20 in game). Since Kings stack, you can play two Kings on a 6 and have it at 24, right in the safe zone for having a caravan. The object is to start with 6s across your three caravans, and play Kings on each of them until they hit 24. If your opponent can't counter you, the game can end in four to six turns. While this can be a fast deck, it can also turn sour extremely quickly.

Pros

- If not countered, can win the game very quickly.

Cons

- If countered, could cause you to lose very quickly.
- Once you are at 24, nothing is stopping your opponent from playing a King on one of your Caravans, busting you.
- Jokers played on a 6 can wipe your board.
- Relies on a good bit of luck.

The Single Suit

This is a variation on the "Two Suit" deck. The idea behind this deck is to cut out the threat of Queens almost entirely. It consists of numbered cards (*sans* Aces) from one suit only with a handful of Jacks and Kings. Since you are only playing with a single suit, you no longer need to worry about the direction of your caravans, unless your opponent plays a Queen of a different suit on one of your cards. Even then, after playing one card, you'll be back on track. Like the Two Suit deck, keep a Jack handy in case your opponent plays an Ace of your suit. The stakes are higher if they manage to get a Joker played on the Ace, as it'll wipe all your cards.

Pros

- The only time you'll need to worry about card direction is if your opponent plays a Queen on your cards.
- Can be tailored to add Jokers and Aces of the suits your not using to mess up your opponent.
- Can be tailored to add more cards to your deck if you need to play a longer game.

Cons

- Can take longer to build up your caravans.
- A Joker on an Ace of your suit can absolutely destroy your game if not hit with a Jack immediately.

FOLLOWERS (AKA COMPANIONS)

Tip: There are two references to "Followers" in this adventure. There are the Follower companions you can partner with (detailed here). Then there is a Faction called the Followers of the Apocalypse. The two are unrelated (except for the fact that Arcade Gannon is loyal to them, effectively making him a Follower, *and* a Follower!).

There are eight individuals scattered across this land, that you can pair up with. Karma is usually less important than your Reputation with Factions they may be aligned with, or seek to defeat when they are by your side. You can find out about their past by simply speaking to them (indeed, this is the key to unlocking their more potent upgrades). Use the Companion Wheel (detailed in the Game Manual) to give orders, heal, and speak.

Each Follower automatically grants you a unique perk when they join you, which disappears when they die (in Hardcore mode) or are dismissed (and return to the place where you found them, or a dwelling they want to stay in). Complete an associated Side Quest (or in certain cases, an unmarked Free Quest) and the Follower receives an Upgrade (usually a choice of two). Note that you can have more than one Follower at a time, as the following pictures reveal:

The Gruesome Twosome

When you find your first Follower, you can explore the Wasteland together.

The Terrible Trio

If you partner with a Robotic Follower, you can choose a Humanoid Follower as well.

The Awesome Foursome

If you've won favor with the NCR (Reputation = Liked), you can call upon either a Trooper or Ranger to help during fights, until they fall in battle (after which you can radio for another after waiting a day). This is in addition to your main Followers.

The Tiresome Fivesome

If you're in Freeside, you can hire a Bodyguard for 100 Caps at the North or East Gate. If you've brought two main Followers, plus an NCR Ranger or Trooper with you, you can technically swell your ranks to five (but only in Freeside)!

Robotic Companions

ED-E

The Prototype Eyebot with Repressed Memories.

Location: Primm [4.17]

Associated perk: Enhanced Sensors

Associated Side Quest: ED-E My Love

Upgrade (upon Quest completion): Enhanced Armor or Enhanced Weapon

Notes: Due to his sensor, ED-E is excellent at detecting enemies early, and fits perfectly into a ranged support role.

Combos: ED-E complements Boone well, but can also provide extra damage when supporting a Melee Weapons-centric character, and/or Follower.

Rex

The King's Best Friend. Fiercely loyal, but a broken brain.

Location: The King's School for Impersonation [2C.05]

Associated perk: Search and Mark

Associated Side Quest: Nothin' But a Hound Dog

Upgrade (upon Quest completion): New brain (enhanced Strength, Toughness, or Speed)

Notes: Rex is great at inflicting quick, melee damage, with a knockdown effect.

Combos: Rex works very well with any fundamentally ranged Follower (like Boone) by keeping foes busy in melee for them.

Humanoid Companions

Arcade Israel Gannon

A Follower of peace from a tribe devastated by war.

Location: Old Mormon Fort [2C.01]

Associated perk: Better Healing

Associated Side Quest: For Auld Lang Syne

Upgrade (upon Quest completion): Hoover Dam help, or Tesla Armor (gift)

Notes: Physically the weakest humanoid companion; Arcade is best used in a ranged support role with Energy Weapons. Obtain better armor for him as soon as possible.

Combos: Provides good support for combat characters with his perk, and ranged supplemental damage.

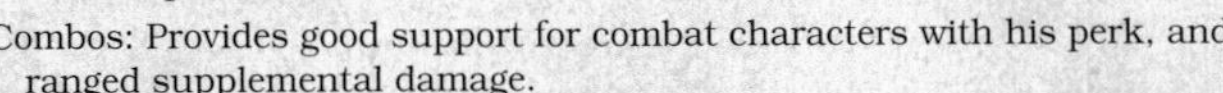

Craig Boone

He's lost his wife, but not his repressed rage and guilt.

Location: Novac [5.18]

Associated perk: Spotter

Associated Side Quest: One for My Baby and I Forgot to Remember to Forget

Upgrade (upon 1st Quest completion): 1st Recon Beret (+1 PER, +5% Critical Chance)

Upgrade (upon 2nd Quest completion): 1st Recon Survival Armor, or 1st Recon Assault Armor (cosmetic differences only)

Notes: A ranged specialist, Boone deals a high amount of damage as long as enemies aren't too close or numerous. Especially proficient against tough Melee enemies like Cazadors and RadScorpions; they usually die before they reach him. Try sniping at night; Boone's Spotter perk makes enemies visible even in the dark.

Combos: Partner with ED-E so you can detect enemies even earlier.

Rose of Sharon Cassidy (aka Cass)

A chip on her shoulder, and a thorn in her side.

Location: Mojave Outpost [4.27]

Associated perk: Whiskey Rose

Associated Side Quest: Heartache by the Number

Upgrade (upon Quest completion): Hand of Vengeance (bonus to Guns) or Calm Heart (bonus to Health)

Notes: Well-rounded, but lacks armor-piercing damage without upgrades to her weapons or ammo. Best used at range, but reasonable as a Melee fighter.

Combos: Partner her with another Melee character or Rex, or hang her back and both fire from range.

Lily

The Super Mutant Grandmother, overprotective of Little Jimmy.

Location: Jacobstown [1.10]

Associated perk: Stealthgirl

Associated Side Quest: Guess Who I Saw Today

Upgrade (upon Quest completion): Dialogue about Medicine (after psychotic breaks). Administer Medicine in varying amounts to affect the frequency of psychotic breaks and combat damage.

Notes: A tanklike giant adept at crushing Melee attacks, but also good at ranged firing.

Combos: The perfect bruiser supporting a weaker character who normally relies on Speech, Sneak, or Science. Bring Rex along, too.

Raul Tejada

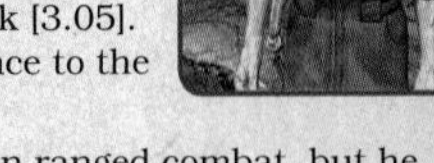

Dry humor, drier skin, but a flood of old memories.

Location: Black Mountain [5.07]

Associated perk: Regular Maintenance

Associated Free Quest: Old School Ghoul

Upgrade (upon Quest completion): Vaquero (increased combat ability), or Full Maintenance (perk upgrade)

Notes: Raul offers a Repair service at his Shack [3.05]. His perk provides exceptional counter-balance to the Built to Destroy trait.

Combos: When not repairing, he is best used in ranged combat, but he won't wear heavy armor.

Veronica

Inquisitive but battle-hardy; happy to be out of her bunker.

Location: 188 Trading Post [5.02]

Associated perk: Scribe Assistant

Associated Side Quest: I Could Make You Care

Upgrade (upon Quest completion): Power Armor, or increased damage with her Power Fist

Notes: She teaches you the Scribe Counter (an Unarmed Special Move) when you give her a White Glove Society dress.

Combos: She packs a lot of punch against armored foes; which is especially useful if you partner with her early on; she can take down foes like Legionaries.

Hardcore Assist: An excellent companion for Energy Weapons characters (especially those using the Gatling Laser or Laser RCW) as with the Vigilant Recycler perk you can convert zero-weight spent Energy Cells into ammo on the fly with her Repair Bench ability.

General Tips for Crucial Companionship

- Companions have their weapons removed when entering Casinos too, so don't count on them as much if you plan on starting a fight (unless you swap out their favored weapon and try to smuggle it in with a big enough Sneak score).
- Companions will grab available weapons off the ground when they need them, like in a Casino fight after disarming at the door.* Upgrade your human companion's armor as soon as possible. It doesn't wear out or slow them down, but it *will* keep them alive much longer.
- Companions do not die in Normal mode; instead they will regain consciousness as soon as combat ends. The same cannot be said for Hardcore mode, so keep those Stimpaks handy, and don't rush into combat that may overwhelm you.
- Companions automatically heal when combat ends, but you can heal them during a fight with Stimpaks from your own inventory.
- Companions will use Stimpaks to heal themselves in combat, so be sure to keep them well-stocked.
- Companions' default weapons have unlimited ammo but don't always deal a lot of damage to every enemy. They also know what type of weapon they'd prefer to use, and may be vocal if you swap it for something they aren't used to, or trained in!
- Companions can be given better weapons, and they won't degrade. Make sure to keep them supplied with ammo though or they will switch back to default. Try giving Boone an Anti-Materiel Rifle or Gauss Rifle for extra fun!
- Companions can't use modded weapons, but they *can* use ammo subtypes. Give Arcade overcharged or max-charged cells for his Energy Weapons since they won't degrade anyway.
- Companions can carry items and equipment for you, limited only by their Strength. Most can carry at least 200 pounds of gear. Be sure you're using all that extra Inventory space!
- If a Companion falls unconscious during battle, flee to the nearest door, that "loads" you into the next area. Your Follower magically springs to life by your side, once you appear! Now finish that fight!

MONEY IN THE MOJAVE: CHARACTERS, CRAFTING, & COLLECTIBLES

Searching for powerful or valuable Items, finding areas to Craft, or speaking to a Character with a particularly important set of items to sell you, is of paramount importance as you venture into the Mojave. The following section lists the collectibles this guide deems the most important to you (so you can look for the items in question before you even find the person who needs them, if that person isn't you), and where appropriate, indicates how many of a particular collectible is available.

Note Note that there may be the odd Vendor that can increase the number of Collectible objects to higher than the amount listed here. The "Number Available" refers to the actual number waiting to be found, not occasionally in a Vendor inventory. If the guide has specifically flagged the items, and the location of each is in the "Tour" chapter and maps, the name is followed by this symbol: (+)

Services and Vendors

Character: Caravan Players (+)

Number Available: 15

Certain individuals, including many Vendors, carry packs of Caravan Cards on them; the only way to play the game.

Character: Healer/Dealers (+)

Number Available: 31

The number of individuals that offer healing services, such as general medicine, radiation and Chem dependency treatment, the healing of crippled limbs (and sometimes medical supplies you can buy), as well as others offering Food or Drink.

Character: Repairers (+)

Number Available: 9

The quality of the Repairer is important, as many Vendors (and other individuals) offer a Repair service, exchanging Caps for improving the Condition of your chosen item.

Character: Traders (+)

Number Available: 33

Barter and obtain items ranging from the primitive to the amazing. Some Traders have spectacular goods on offer, but some don't. This is also the place to buy Caravan Cards, Implants, and Upgrades.

Crafting

Crafting: Campfires (+)

Number Available: 109

The locations of every Campfire (and thus, where you can brew Recipes, or make Tanned Gecko hides for fun and profit) are pinpointed.

Crafting: Reloading Benches (+)

Number Available: 36

The Benches that allow you to strip ammunition and create new ordnance are also listed, so you're never far from a tinkering spot.

Crafting: Workbenches (+)

Number Available: 41

Whether you're making new Nuka, Explosive bombs, Doctor's Bags, or the hugely useful Weapon Repair Kits, you need to know where every Workbench is.

Collectibles: Weapon Upgrades (+)

Number Available: 10

The exact Weapon Modification Upgrades that particularly well-equipped Vendors sell is random, so the locations of such Vendors are flagged for you.

Main Collectibles

Collectibles: Snow Globes (+)

Number Available: 7

Character: Jane at the Lucky 38 Casino [2D.02]

Speak to Jane, of Mr. House's personal assistants, and she mentions he is a keen collector of these otherwise pretty, but pretty useless items. You can display them in your Penthouse Suite at the Lucky 38 Casino, or hand them over to Mr. House for cold, hard Caps. 2,000 Caps per Snow Globe, in fact.

Collectibles: Caravan Cards (+)

Number Available: 30

Finding individual playing cards for Caravan is a matter of chance. In addition, there are entities that either sell, or have Caravan Cards on their person.

Collectibles: Hollowed-Out Rocks (+)

Number Available: 42

The sun might be killing you, so always look out for rocks with graffiti daubed on it; these contains random items. The locations of every Rock is shown.

Collectibles: Skill Books (+)

Number Available: 51

As each grants you +3 (or +4 with the Comprehension perk) permanently to a chosen skill, which is essentially a free augmentation to your character, you owe it to yourself to track down every last one.

Collectibles: Skill Magazines (+)

Number Available: 213

These provide a huge amount of initial knowledge on a skill-based subject, but this only lasts for a short while. Designed to be read once (ideally immediately before you're using the skill), gather as many as you wish for a temporary +10 (or +20 with the Comprehension perk) bonus to a chosen skill.

Collectibles: Star Bottle Caps (+)

Number Available: 100

Character: Festus at the Sunset Sarsaparilla Headquarters [2.17]

Side Quest: The Legend of the Star: Your plastic pal over at Sunset Sarsaparilla regales you with a story about a fabulous treasure that's awarded to anyone who can find 50 Star Bottle Caps. Fortunately, this guide shows you where 100 of them are!

Collectibles: Unique Items (+)

Number Available: 95

This includes outfits, headgear, and items that are Unique, or extremely rare (in which case, every nonrandom instance of finding them is shown). Look at this list for Recipes, and Schematics, too.

Collectibles: Unique Weapons (+)

Number Available: 42

Although they can't be modded, these are enhanced versions of regular weapons, and employed as the primary version of your weapon when found. Repair it using Weapon Repair Kits or Repairers.

Secondary Collectibles

Collectibles: Legion Ears

Number Available: N/A

Character: Private James Sexton at Camp Forlorn Hope [6.02]

Free Quest—An Ear to the Ground: Private James Sexton will pay (you a compliment) for every Legion's Ear you bring back to him. Agree to the task if you wish. For every Ear (whether on a Legionary or Caesar himself), you receive a small Fame gain.

Collectibles: Missiles

Number Available: N/A

Character: Raquel at Nellis Air Force Base [3.01]

Free Quest: Missing a Few Missiles. Raquel tells you the Boomers are low on missiles, and she'll take any that you have. Return with quantities of Missiles for her. Your Fame with the Boomers increases for Missiles you give.

Collectibles: NCR Dogtags (The Legion)

Number Available: N/A

Character: Aurelius of Phoenix at Cottonwood Cove [6.20]

Free Quest—Arizona Scavenger: Aurelius pays a bounty for NCR troops that you kill. You're rewarded 10 Caps per Dog Tag, but Irradiated Dog Tags from the Ghouls in Camp Searchlight do not count.

Collectibles: NCR Dogtags (NCR)

Number Available: N/A

Character: Quartermaster Mayes at Cam p Forlorn Hope [6.02]

Free Quest: Tags of Our Fallen. Mayes requests you locate any Dogtags you find from NCR soldiers found dead on your travels. For every Dogtag (not Irradiated), you receive a small Caps and Fame reward.

Collectibles: NCR Dogtags (Irradiated)

Number Available: 10

Character: First Sergeant Astor at Astor's Recon Camp [5.S23] and Camp Searchlight [6.16]

First Sergeant Astor patrolling near the Recon Camp requires Irradiated Dogtags from the fallen and Feral over in Camp Searchlight, as part of Side Quest: We Will All Go Together.

Collectibles: Radscorpion Glands

Number Available: N/A

Character: Ruby Nash at the Vikki & Vance Casino, in Primm [4.17]

Free Quest—Gland for Some Home Cooking: Ruby makes a mean casserole from the glands of Radscorpions. She gives a single Casserole for every Gland you have. Corporal William Farber at Camp McCarran, is also interested in sampling some as part of Free Quest: Not Worth a Hill of Corn and Beans.

Collectibles: Scrap

Number Available: N/A

Character: Isaac at Gun Runners [2.14]

Free Quest: Dealing with Contreras. Sergeant Contreras at Camp McCarran [2.19] has you visit the Gun Runners and speak with Isaac, who requires massive amounts of Scrap for a weapons shipment. Search for Scrap Metal, and Tin Cans.

Collectibles: Scrap Metal

Number Available: N/A

Character: Jack at the Nellis Hangar [3.02]

Free Quest—Iron and Stealing: Jack tells you he's looking for some Scrap Metal, if you can spare any. Return with quantities; your Fame with the Boomers increases for Scrap Metal you give.

Collectibles: Vault Jumpsuits (+)

Number Available: N/A

Character: Sarah Weintraub at Vault 21 [2D.06]

Free Quest—Suits You, Sarah: Mention Boomer Suits, and she pays for them, too! Explore the Vaults; Jumpsuits are almost always found in Dressers, some Lockers, and occasionally folded up on shelves, then return to her with them for a Caps reward.

Factions & Bestiary

This chapter reveals the major Factions across the Mojave Wasteland, and their goals, thirst for power, or antics they're likely to undertake. Then there's a Bestiary with statistics for all the adversaries lurking behind well-defended encampments, charging out of caverns, or ambushing you down dark corridors.

PART 1: MAJOR FACTIONS

Caesar's Legion

Base of Operations: The Fort [3.28]

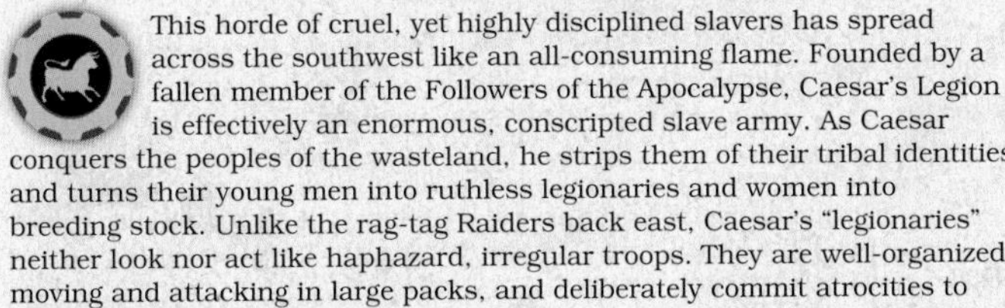

This horde of cruel, yet highly disciplined slavers has spread across the southwest like an all-consuming flame. Founded by a fallen member of the Followers of the Apocalypse, Caesar's Legion is effectively an enormous, conscripted slave army. As Caesar conquers the peoples of the wasteland, he strips them of their tribal identities and turns their young men into ruthless legionaries and women into breeding stock. Unlike the rag-tag Raiders back east, Caesar's "legionaries" neither look nor act like haphazard, irregular troops. They are well-organized, moving and attacking in large packs, and deliberately commit atrocities to terrorize those who might dare to oppose them.

True, Caesar is the perfect man. But he is not just a man: he is the Son of Mars, ordained by the god of war to conquer all of Earth. To prepare the way, Mars razed the Earth, cleansed it with fire, and brought the weak and the wicked low; and now his son has come to deliver the wasteland from chaos and barbarism. To follow Caesar is to obey the will of Mars; to disobey is to condemn oneself to death. As the Son of Mars, Caesar has the divine right to demand servitude from all he encounters. Not everyone believes that Caesar is the product of a god's loins, of course. The most recently captured slaves tend to be pretty skeptical. But they aren't very vocal in their criticisms, and their children are raised not by skeptical parents but by priestesses appointed to that task by virtue of their knowledge of and adherence to the state religion.

Nearly all physically capable, compliant males are compelled to serve in its armed forces. The primary value of pre-menopausal females is to serve as breeding stock (with Caesar or a legate governing how they are assigned to males), though they, like older females and less physically-capable men, are also used to perform a variety of other tasks. The largest unit of organization in Caesar's Legion is the Cohort, numbering about 480 infantrymen. Cohorts are further divided into Centuriae, which contrary to their name numbers about 80 men, and each Centuriae is divided into ten "tent groups" (Contubernia), making this the squad level of organization. Raiding parties are of this size (about eight men) and will be led by a Decanus (a squad leader, basically).

Caesar desires two things: a Carthage, and a Rome. In the NCR he has at last found a grand adversary, against which he can wage a military campaign worthy of history books. And in Vegas, powered and watered by its great dam, he has found a capital worthy of, well, a Caesar. Contrary to the old saw, Rome will be built in a day. All it takes is plentiful slave labor, and Caesar has that in spades.

New California Republic

Base of Operations: Camp McCarran [2.19], Hoover Dam [3.33]

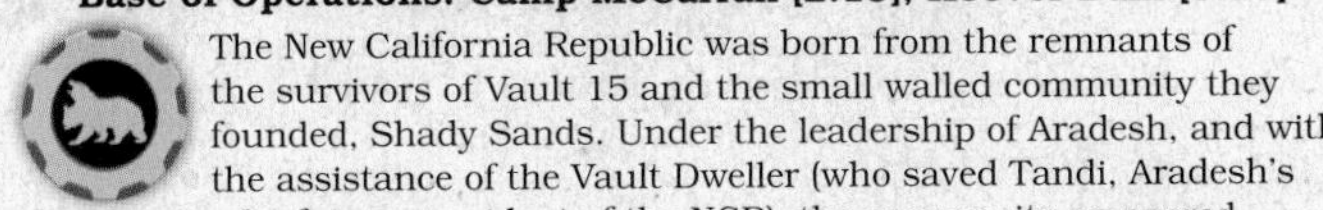

The New California Republic was born from the remnants of the survivors of Vault 15 and the small walled community they founded, Shady Sands. Under the leadership of Aradesh, and with the assistance of the Vault Dweller (who saved Tandi, Aradesh's daughter and a future president of the NCR), the community prospered. Trade routes with other settlements allowed cultural exchange, and a movement to form a national entity gradually took root and won popular acceptance. In 2186, the town of Shady Sands changed its name to "New California Republic" and formed a trial council government to draft a constitution. Four more settlements joined the council, and in 2189 the NCR was voted into existence as a sprawling federation of five states: Shady Sands, Los Angeles, Maxson, Hub, and Dayglow.

By post-apocalyptic standards, the NCR is a paragon of economic success and good ethical character: political enfranchisement, rule of law, a reasonable degree of physical security, and a standard of living better than mere subsistence are daily realities for its 700,000+ citizens. Currently, the NCR in a state of transition, with rapid economic growth and a sea change in political leadership endangering its grand humanitarian ideals. Nowhere is this more evident than in the Mojave, where the occupation of Hoover Dam has improved access to electricity and water, but at the cost of straining its budget and embroiling its armed forces in a morally corrosive imperialist project.

The NCR government's aim is to annex New Vegas as the republic's sixth state. While it already controls Hoover Dam, its treaty with Mr. House and the three families compels it to allot one-fifth of the dam's electrical and water production to local use free of charge. Adding injury to insult, the NCR is locked into protecting New Vegas from invasion by Caesar's Legion even as it receives not one cap in tax revenue from the Strip's highly lucrative resort operations. NCR citizens in the Mojave have largely come here for economic reasons, whether as paid citizen soldiers or as prospectors and fortune-seekers.

The Strip

Base of Operations: Lucky 38 Casino [2D.02]

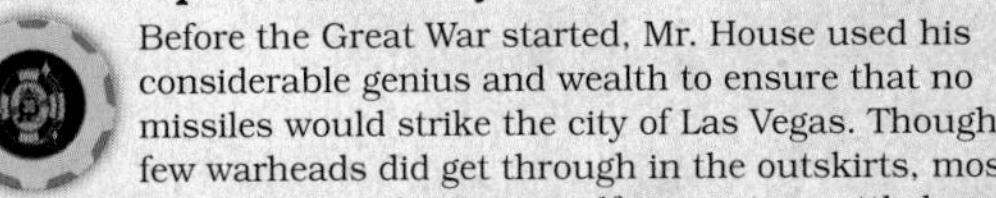

Before the Great War started, Mr. House used his considerable genius and wealth to ensure that no missiles would strike the city of Las Vegas. Though a few warheads did get through in the outskirts, most of the city was spared. Despite this, the Strip itself was not re-settled, and after close to two hundred years, Mr. House immediately began searching for a mysterious Platinum Chip, and rebuilding the glory of Las Vegas. Sending out Securitron scouts, Mr. House started negotiating with local tribes to exchange his considerable resource stockpiles for their help. Some of the tribes resisted, but three tribes eventually gained Mr. House's favor. They became the Omertas, Chairmen, and White Glove Society, running the Gomorrah, Tops, and Ultra-Luxe casinos, respectively. Because Mr. House was dedicated to restoring Las Vegas, he insisted on transforming the tribes into families with cultures that harkened back to Vegas' glory days.

In the process of rebuilding the Strip, Mr. House also effectively "bought out" the residents of Vault 21. After they evacuated, he had the Vault stripped of useful technology, most of its actual volume filled with concrete, and the entrance turned into a gift shop and small hotel. While the families were rebuilding the casinos, the rest of the locals were hard at work erecting an enormous wall around the Strip. When NCR traders and explorers arrived on the scene, they were amazed at the Strip and returned back to California with tales of opulence and great wealth awaiting travelers.

Eventually, the NCR military itself arrived and were surprised to find the Strip so well-protected and heavily policed. Though they struck a deal with Mr. House to establish a base in the area (along with control of Hoover Dam), the NCR has never had control of The Strip. After the Battle of Hoover Dam, the NCR negotiated an MP (military police) presence on The Strip, but their influence remains small.

Though the tribes that became The Strip's families were once hatefully opposed to each other, the demands of Mr. House have forced the families to play nice. They continue to hold long-standing grudges, but do not act openly against each other for fear of angering Mr. House.

The Chairmen

Base of Operations: The Tops Casino [2D.04]

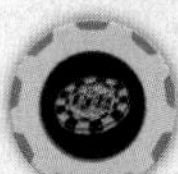

The Chairmen and their casino, The Tops, embody an ancient "cool" aesthetic of Vegas, plucked from Mr. House's historical data banks. Before The Strip's renovation in 2274, the Chairmen were a warrior tribe, and their traditions of honor continue to inform how they select their leadership and interact with each other and outsiders. Unbeknownst to the rest of the tribe, its current chief, Benny, has for months been scheming to seize control of Mr. House's technology and The Strip itself, violating the tribe's deeply-held values against duplicity and treachery.

The Omertas

Base of Operations: Gomorrah [2D.01]

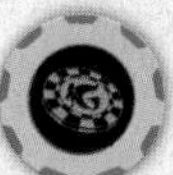

A highly organized and deadly tribe of Raiders, the Omertas murdered and looted all they encountered, sometimes holing up in a stronghold for years, other times leading a nomadic existence in restless pursuit of their next big score. The Omertas have just one rule: never betray the family. Everything else is permitted. Their casino, Gomorrah, is a sleazy vice den on a grand scale, and as such embodies the ruthless exploitation beneath the glitz and glamour of the Strip's neon signs. While by outside appearances the Omertas seem content with their lot, the family's penchant for treachery and murder is alive and well, and the tribe's leadership is collaborating with Caesar's Legion to bring about the Strip's downfall.

The White Glove Society

Base of Operations: The Ultra-Luxe Casino [2D.05]

The Ultra-Luxe is an establishment of incredible refinement that delicately conceals its operators' terrible past; a past which the tribe has been at pains to remove from public record or knowledge to the point of fanaticism. Run by the White Glove Society, the Ultra-Luxe pampers its clients and provides the Strip's most elite casino experience. A dress code is strictly enforced. All of the staff and family members are well-dressed, well-spoken, and well-behaved. The casino's prime attractions are its meat-oriented restaurant, The Gourmand, its cocktail lounge, Top Shelf, and its art gallery. Roulette and blackjack are the only games offered. But the real draw to the place are the steaks. Succulent and delicious, a variety of meat treats are available; but only to the most discerning (and sponsored) Society member.

PART 2: OTHER FACTIONS: FREESIDE AND GREATER NEW VEGAS

Freeside

Base of Operations: Outer and Inner Freeside [Zone 2C]

Las Vegas wasn't heavily damaged during the Great War, but people didn't immediately "settle" into the remnants of the old city. The various Vault tribes that emerged years later, hunted and fought among the ruins, but it was not until the "return" of Mr. House that they ceased (most) of their hostilities. Mr. House directed the tribes to use his sizable quantities of pre-war construction materials to build the crude (but effective) outer walls that separate The Strip and Freeside from the rest of New Vegas. While Mr. House valued the area around Fremont Street, he ultimately viewed it as secondary in importance to the Strip itself and had a second, inner wall that separated the two areas. When NCR prospectors (and eventually the army) arrived in the region, people typically went straight for The Strip, leaving Freeside (as it had become known by locals) as an informal stopping point. Eventually Mr. House recognized that he could use Freeside as a filter for undesireables, and pulled his favored tribes and all Securitrons into the Strip, leaving Freeside to fend for itself.

In the two years that followed, Freeside has slowly degenerated into a hostile, lawless den of ne'er-do-wells. For a while, it was completely without order, but two power groups managed to come to an understanding about how the area needed to be maintained. The Kings, formed from the dispossessed remnants of unfortunate tribes, prevent all-out chaos from erupting, but do little to deal with the day-to-day nastiness that Freesiders inflict on each other. The Followers of the Apocalypse, no longer associated with NCR, settled in the Old Mormon Fort. They receive some protection from the Kings in exchange for help with the community's basic needs (food, water, health services, and some education). Despite the oversight from the Kings and help from the Followers, the people in Freeside live in daily peril... from each other as well as outside forces.

Followers of the Apocalypse

Base of Operations: Old Mormon Fort [2C.01]

Originally, the Followers of the Apocalypse (also known simply as "The Followers") were a secular tribe formed in the Boneyard, with a purpose of educating humanity about the horrors of the Great War, and never to repeat those atrocities again. Forgoing preaching in favor of medical treatment and charity. When the Master died, they controlled the Boneyard with the help of the then-embryonic New California Republic, and accompanied a contingent of the NCR into Nevada, settling in an Old Mormon Fort, close to Freeside where they can save the wretched, and tend to those down on their luck. They take in stragglers of many creeds and colors, including the last few Enclave remnants. Despite the historic name of the place, there are no serious fortifications—just fences and gates with a few armed Followers inside.

The Kings

Base of Operations: The King's School of Impersonation [2C.05]

After unearthing some strange paraphernalia belonging to a tribe who worshipped some kind of ancient, black-coiffed deity (and as it transpired, a deity with some considerable style and singing talent) a tribe dedicated to him was formed by the scavenger himself, who took on the persona and visage as if divinely inspired. Known as The King, he dresses in a special suit crafted to look like the originator of the look, while his subordinates scavenge denim and leather jackets for their attire. The King is charming, rebellious, and well-dressed. His forces are almost always found in small packs, and have a lot of attitude, bravery, and members. They typically carry small guns, brass knuckles, and melee weapons. The King, and his robotic dog Rex, are currently facing a challenge as the NCR appears to be threatening their territory. The King is hoping they aren't the devil in disguise.

The Van Graffs

Base of Operations: Silver Rush Gambling Hall [2C.07]

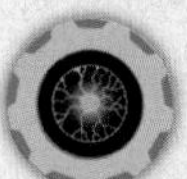

The Van Graff family has a history of ruthless behavior when it comes to rivals muscling in on their territory, and it seems old habits die hard; two of the Van Graffs have set up shop in a bedraggled old casino called the Silver Rush, where they specialize in Energy Weapons, and the maximizing of profits. Run by Gloria Van Graff and her elder half-brother Jean-Baptiste Cutting, their stronghold is heavily-defended with their Thugs armed with the latest in weapons technology. Gloria is in charge of general operations at the Silver Rush. She is the person responsible for the New Vegas Van Graffs' general strategy, including possible under-the-counter deals to wipe out the competition. The muscle of the van Graff operation, Jean-Baptiste personally handles all of Gloria's dirty work. He is a nasty, mean-spirited son-of-a-bitch. Despite the family's tendency to deal in energy weapons, Jean-Baptiste is a connoisseur of big guns and explosives. He threatens people for looking at him the wrong way and is far from all talk; he will go from zero-to-murder in the twitch of an eye.

Westside Cooperative

Base of Operations: Westside [Zone 2A]

The residents of the fortified Westside Zone have a small, but tight-knit community based around growing crops for themselves, and to sell to travellers and larger Factions. Currently embroiled in tense negotiations with the NCR regarding the siphoning of their water supplies, the Westside Co-op features a motley band of folk, including an escapee from New Reno named Clayton Etienne, and a Follower of the Apocalypse called Tom Anderson, who is single-minded in his defense of this operation.

The Crimson Caravan Company

Base of Operations: Crimson Caravan Headquarters [2.09]

A well-known trading company with a number of Caravaneers in their employ, the Crimson Caravan Company originally plied their wares in the Hub, historically famous for plying their trade across the most inhospitable areas, the Crimson Caravans now contract out much of their deliveries to wandering merchants across the Mojave. Recently, the Company has been hit hard by the instability along their trading routes. Deathclaw incursions at Quarry Junction have impeded trade south of New Vegas, and three sub-contractors have had their Caravans destroyed; possibly by Raiders, although Ash Piles at the scene of the massacre suggests otherwise. A hard-nosed, no-nonsense Alice McLafferty has been recently drafted in to aid in the recovery of the Company, to look for any openings in trade or rival companies to undercut, and to keep the trade flowing with the NCR and other favored clients.

The Gun Runners

Base of Operations: Gun Runners [2.14]

A loosely-knit band of Boneyard dwellers, the Gun Runners have had a long past in the business that bears their name. They take pride in constructing only the finest, and highest-quality weapons. After historic trade disputes between the Gun Runners and other groups were settled, many of the gunsmiths decided to move north, expanding their operations to a location where both Caps and supplies are plentiful. Their informal leader, Isaac, sees himself as part of a collective with no established hierarchy. They're just hard-working, meticulous craftsmen and women working to deliver armaments of the highest quality. Arriving in New Vegas, the Gun Runners established a base of operations that takes advantage of The Strip's outer wall defenses, as well as the high traffic of traders, explorers, and NCR passing to and from Freeside. All business is conducted from outside their highly-fortified stronghold.

PART 3: OTHER FACTIONS: MOJAVE WASTELAND

Boomers

Base of Operations: Nellis Air Force Base [3.01]

At the beginning of the war, Nellis Air Force Base scrambled an enormous number of fighters and bombers to respond to the missile launch. None of those planes ever returned. Additionally, despite the best efforts of a man named Mr. House, some of the missiles that struck the greater Las Vegas area impacted Nellis. As a result, Nellis was not an attractive site for salvagers for over a hundred years after the war.

Fifty years ago, a group of Vault 34's dissidents struck out on their own and started using Nellis as a base. Over a long period of time, they eventually decided to call Nellis their home. They learned a great deal of information from the records at Nellis and used that information to open the weapons storehouses at (currently unknown locations called) Area 2 and the Hawthorne Army Depot. The result of their efforts was an enormous stockpile of heavy ordnance, artillery, and small nuclear weapons.

Due to the tribe's paranoia, hostility, and excessive reverence for explosives, the New Vegas locals started calling them "Boomers". The Boomers didn't mind the name as long as it meant people kept their distance. No matter who approaches them (Mr. House, the Vegas families, NCR, or Caesar), the Boomers have the same response: artillery. While the Boomers' attitude has kept away trouble, all of the major players around New Vegas want to get on the tribe's good side. People simply have no idea how to accomplish that. As far as all intelligence indicates, the Boomers have a clean water supply from Lake Mead, power from solar panels inside the base, and thriving farms that they've learned to develop "the hard way" over the decades they've been in the base. Once, the NCR attempted to shut off the Boomers' water supply. The Boomers' response was to shell sections of the NCR's water pipeline in eastern New Vegas. The NCR promptly restored the flow.

In the months that followed that experiment, no one has tried to approach the Boomers, which is just how they like it.

Brotherhood of Steel

Base of Operations: Hidden Valley [5.11]

The Brotherhood of Steel is a militant organization devoted to the preservation of pre-war technology and human knowledge. Their professed mission is to preserve pre-war technology and human knowledge for the benefit of future generations. In practice, its definition of technology is strangely selective, ignoring basic but potentially useful technologies (genetic modification of crops and civil engineering, for example) in favor of combat technology such as energy weapons and power armor; and even now, nearly two centuries after the Great War, the Brotherhood zealously restricts the use and knowledge of such technologies to its own membership.

The Mojave Brotherhood operated freely amid the Vegas wastes for several years, carrying out many reclamation missions without serious opposition. The balance of power shifted in 2251, when a large contingent of NCR troops entered the region and occupied Hoover Dam. Conflict was inevitable. Nearly two years of guerilla skirmishes culminated in a pitched battle at HELIOS One, a solar energy plant the Brotherhood had been refurbishing for several months with the goals of bringing it back online and activating its hidden offensive capabilities (the ARCHIMEDES II death ray). The battle for HELIOS One (Operation: Sunburst) proved a disaster for the Mojave Brotherhood. More than half its Paladins and Knights were killed. The chapter's leader, Elder Elijah, disappeared without a trace. The Brotherhood was driven from the facility, which suffered extensive damage. Survivors retreated to Hidden Valley.

Since that defeat, the chapter's leader, Elder McNamara, has restricted activity outside the bunker to occasional reconnaissance missions and high-value raids. All operations take place at night, and engagement of NCR forces is strictly forbidden. Though the Brotherhood's ascetic lifestyle has prepared its members for a sequestered existence better than most, the passivity of their current situation has proved highly stressful.

Goodsprings

Base of Operations: Goodsprings [4.05]

Goodsprings is a small, barely active town that has been a mining community since the early days of Nevada. Most recently, it was settled under a grant from NCR to develop a low-risk mining environment near a reliable source of potable water. Even so, there are only a dozen or so people in the town due to trade along the Long 15 drying up. Signs along the highway direct people to Goodsprings, but they do the town no good if no one is on the highway to read them.

The residents of the town come to your aid after a Securitron named Victor witnessed your shooting and burial over by the Cemetery. There are few people in Goodsprings. It has never been that populous, and the troubles with Deathclaws, Raiders, and Powder Gangers hasn't made it any more appealing. A few folks have holed up here to wait things out, but overall it is quite "sleepy"; almost a Ghost Town if there weren't the odd settler, attempting to eke out an existence among the ruined ranch homes. Local activities include going to the spring (Goodsprings Source), hunting Geckos, Mole Rats, and Coyotes, and loafing around in the Prospector Saloon.

Great Khans

Base of Operations: Red Rock Canyon [1.15]

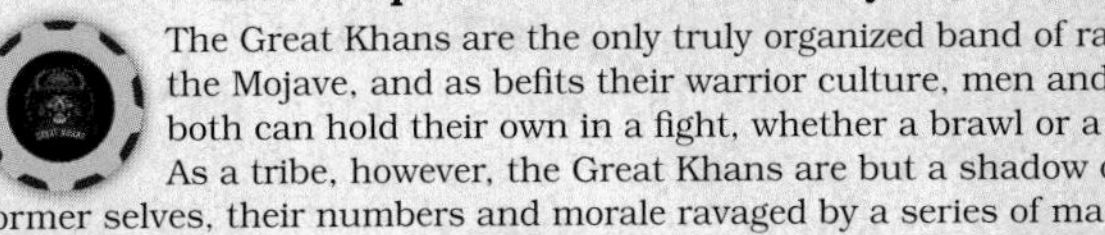

The Great Khans are the only truly organized band of raiders in the Mojave, and as befits their warrior culture, men and women both can hold their own in a fight, whether a brawl or a shootout. As a tribe, however, the Great Khans are but a shadow of their former selves, their numbers and morale ravaged by a series of massacres and displacements. From their rocky stronghold at Red Rock Canyon, they eke out a living by drug-trafficking and the occasional raid or salvage find.

Since the Bitter Springs massacre, the tribe has aspired to little more than survival and isolated, petty acts of vengeance on the occasional NCR citizen or deserter. The arrival of a Legion emissary, Karl, has changed this. Papa Khan, the tribe's leader, wants to believe Karl's assurances that the Great Khans will be absorbed intact by the Legion, assuming an honored place as one of its elite cohorts. To lead the assaults on Hoover Dam and the Vegas Strip would make for fine acts of vengeance. The rest of the Great Khans are not so entirely convinced.

Much as they want to exact revenge on the NCR and Mr. House's Three Families, they know that they lack the strength to do so. Indeed, they believe it is only a matter of time before their enemies track them down, and that the Great Khans would be unlikely to survive such a confrontation. The looming conflict between Caesar's Legion and the NCR and the message from Karl offers the possibility of a new way forward.

Novac

Base of Operations: Novac [5.18]

The faded and cracked concrete and peeling buildings give the impression of depression; and indeed, Novac is little more than a lonely desert highway motel with multiple buildings that have been fortified for the post-apocalyptic protection of its inhabitants. Watching over them is the landmark of the area: a giant fabricated tyrannosaurus rex biting off the top of "The World's 2nd Largest Thermometer". The interior of "Dinky" also serves as the city center (a converted gift shop from pre-war times, with a sniper's nest in Dinky's mouth). Dinky is the "attraction" that drew in tourists. Some of the locals are friendly folk, though most aren't trusting of outsiders. They appreciate the protection of NCR, but are afraid of what's going on at the REPCONN Test Site rocket plant up the road. The local law, Ranger Andy, is unable to investigate due to an injury.

Powder Gangers

Base of Operations: The NCR Correctional Facility [5.15]

The NCR Correctional Facility is the dominant location of the central Mojave Wasteland. In the distant past, it was the Jean Conservancy, a low-security all-female prison. Under recent NCR control, it was used to house prisoners on work release. The prisoners worked the railroad parallel to the Long 15 under NCR trooper supervision, maintaining the vital land link between the Boneyard and New Vegas. Eventually, prison guards (NCR troopers) were pulled away to run Colorado River border patrol. When the guard staff was low, the prisoners executed a daring and violent escape.

Because the rail crews often used explosives (typically dynamite) to blast through rock or get rid of train cars that were locked/fixed on the line, the prisoners inevitably acquired small amounts that they hid in their cells. When they made their break, they blasted their way out. The interior of the prison was clearly the scene of a large riot where the prisoners used explosives, improvised weapons, and stolen NCR trooper equipment to break through multiple walls and scatter through the desert. A lot of the prisoners weren't in on the escape plan formally; they just got caught up in the moment. Consequently, a lot of them didn't really know where to go when the dust settled. A large contingent of Powder Gangers can be found in Vault 19 though many squatted in the prison and have been informally raiding since then.

Primm

Base of Operations: The Vikki & Vance Casino, in Primm [4.17]

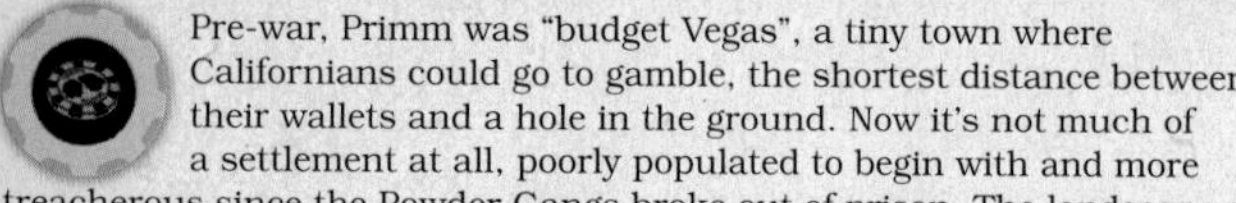

Pre-war, Primm was "budget Vegas", a tiny town where Californians could go to gamble, the shortest distance between their wallets and a hole in the ground. Now it's not much of a settlement at all, poorly populated to begin with and more treacherous since the Powder Gangs broke out of prison. The landscape of Primm is dominated by a few empty ranch homes, the rubble of the town's main streets and store-fronts, and a small NCR camp set up southwest of town to prevent Convicts from pushing further south to the NCR's Mojave Outpost. The townsfolk, now without a sheriff after he was murdered by Gangers, are holed up across the road from the Mojave Express Couriers, in the down-trodden old Vikki & Vance Casino. Low on supplies, the townsfolk can't hold out much longer, and the Convicts' presence continues to build as they've recently commandeered the larger, Bison Steve Casino and Hotel, patrolling the unstable El Diablo rollercoaster and wrecking the remaining grandeur this place once had. Primm faces a grim reality; there are few people here to keep order.

Ghouls: Bright Brotherhood

Base of Operations: REPCONN Test Site [5.17]

A strange cult of Ghouls, and a single human fully believing himself to be a Ghoul, are lead by a charismatic and prophetic Glowing One named Jason Bright. Thanks to a probable (and extremely rare) mutation, Bright never turned Feral, and has instead built up a small following of like-minded Ghouls, clad in the vestments of a tribe in the final stages of preparation to leave for a "new world"; a promised land foretold by Bright, that is the ghoul's ultimate goal. Jason Bright wasn't his birth name, it is the name that his flock started calling him when he began his cult. Shunned by frightened outsiders, and murdered by Nightkin convinced the Brotherhood are sitting on a mythical shipment of Stealthboys, the Brotherhood have long come to realize that they are not bound to, or long for this earth.

Super Mutants

Base of Operations: Jacobstown [1.10]

Jacobstown sits at the same general location as the pre-war settlement of Mount Charleston, a small alpine community high in the mountains west of the Las Vegas Valley. Post-war, the area was of little interest to travelers and scavengers due to its remote location and lack of salvageable material. It was not until the past twenty years that it became a permanent settlement for any group. Marcus, the mild-mannered Super Mutant sheriff of a settlement named Broken Hills, took it upon himself to find a refuge for the "broken-minded" of his kind—low-intelligence Super Mutants and schizophrenic Nightkin. It proved to be more difficult than holding on to Broken Hills, but he eventually discovered Mount Charleston and decided it was a good spot to set up a community.

Unfortunately for Marcus, not all of the Nightkin were content to live under his rules. Davison (who currently talks to a Brahmin Skull named Antler in the bowels of the REPCONN Test Site) and Tabitha (who broadcasts her particular brand of insanity from Black Mountain) broke off on their own, eventually winding up with their own dysfunctional Super Mutant communities. Though Marcus is disappointed at how things turned out, he does the best he can to take care of Lily and the other Super Mutants and Nightkin at Jacobstown.

Super Mutants: Nightkin

Base of Operations: Black Mountain [5.07]

Black Mountain, the dominant feature of the area, was unoccupied for over a century after the war. The victim of a direct strike, most of Black Mountain's radar arrays were knocked out immediately. Even though valuable materials were in the buildings that surrounded the arrays, the area was so irradiated that no one survived in it for more than an hour or so. After the fall of the Master, many of the first generation Super Mutants headed east. In Black Mountain, they were able to find a place to set up a camp where they could avoid most of the rest of the world. It took a long time for the Super Mutants to settle in and repair the equipment in the array, but they were finally able to enlist the help of some Ghouls to make the array operational.

Over time, Nightkin—more psychotic and temperamental Super Mutants thanks to their predisposition and eventual addiction to Stealth technology—and the more thuggish second generation Super Mutants trickled into Black Mountain, which eventually caused problems. The de-facto leader of the community was Marcus, from Broken Hills. Unfortunately, the influx of less-mentally stable super mutants proved to be more than he could handle. Eventually, he was pushed out of the group at Black Mountain. He left with a small group of (mostly first generation) super mutants, ghouls, and friendly humans to found Jacobstown. This left the Nightkin and second generation Super Mutants to fend for themselves. Within weeks, a paranoid schizophrenic NIghtkin named Tabitha (and Rhonda) progressively turned the satellite array into a fortress against any and all outsiders. She hallucinates regularly, and has convinced the other super mutants (especially the idiotic second-gen ones) that only she can see the threats against them, due to her "magic eyes" (actually a pair of oversized child sunglasses which—of course—she won't let anyone else touch).

Raider: Fiends

Base of Operations: Zone 2E: South Vegas Ruins

Vault 3 was once an ordinary, happy vault. Unfortunately, it—and the entire southwestern part of the New Vegas conurbation—has been taken over by a large force of Raiders calling themselves the Fiends. They are unexceptional in every way, but there are a slew of them. The vault itself is wide-open, practically being a feral den for the Fiends and their huge packs of dogs. Whether it is murder, rape, or shooting innocents for sport, the Fiends are more than happy to bring their anarchy to this area, which has become a source of growing concern for the NCR. The Fiends are erratic and dangerous; their mental stability isn't helped by the fact that they are almost constantly high on chems, most of which are provided by the Great Khans.

Raider: Greaser Gang
Raider: Jackal Gang
Raider: Scorpion Gang
Raider: Viper Gang

Base of Operations: North New Vegas Sewers [U2.N], Mojave Wasteland south of Goodsprings [4.05], Monte Carlo Suites [2.12], and Novac [5.18]

The Joshua Tree-speckled mountains provide a surprising amount of cover, especially the rock-strewn washes that run east-west just south of Nelson. This is the perfect location for packs of anarchic hunters, grifters, and psychotics to wait for an opportunity to steal, kidnap, or kill. These loosely-knit Raider gangs revel in chaos and anarchy. The Jackals are no more than a handful of scarred and tattooed reprobates, scraping out a living by preying on anything weaker than them. The (slightly) more organized Viper Gang consist of a slightly more skilled collection of ne'er-do-wells, dug in close to major roads to rob and plunder travellers and Merchant Caravans. Further north, are two much more pitiful gangs, who have lost their brethren (both in violence, or by recruitment) to the Fiends; the stinking Greaser Gang who terrorize the North Vegas Sewers, and the Scorpion Gang, who fight intermittent skirmishes with Westside residents. All these Raiders have no driving purpose or goal, other than to live to see tomorrow and raise as much hell as possible today.

Wastelanders: Prospectors and Scavengers

Base of Operations: Across the Mojave Wasteland

Wastelander is a catch-all term for anyone living in the Mojave Wasteland who is not affiliated with some other group. They make a subsistence living off the land, trade with local settlements, and try not to be ravaged by the abundant, and usually hostile wildlife, or bands of roaming Raider gangs. Most are not aggressive but will defend themselves if attacked. When that happens, they usually die. Quickly.

PART 4: THE BESTIARY

This Bestiary is separated into two main sections; entities that are human-sized in form and interaction, and larger, or more animalistic entities. Depending on your level, and the entity you're facing, expect to obtain between 10–50 Experience Points (XP) from defeating each of the following entities.

Human-Sized Entities with Higher Functions

Humans have different statistics from creatures, and it is important to understand what each note entails:

Name: The name your Pip-Boy gives to the human in question.

Level: Although these foes can appear at any time, they are commonly encountered when you reach this level; this also references their experience level.

Perception: This is measured from 1 to 10, the same as your Perception attribute. The higher the Perception, the quicker you're spotted, or reacted to.

Health: The full Hit Points of the human, prior to combat.

Guns: The entity's Guns skill (0–100), measured in the same way as yours.

Energy Weapons: The entity's Energy Weapons skill (0–100), measured in the same way as yours.

Melee Weapons: The entity's Melee Weapons skill (0–100), measured in the same way as yours.

Armor: The type of armor predominantly worn by the entity, and what to expect to find when looting the corpse. There may be other (random) items, but these are always present.

Possible Primary Weapons: The preferred weapon the adversary attacks with, usually accompanied by a back-up weapon, when listed.

CASINO PERSONNEL (The Strip and Freeside)

Although none of these entities present any great threats to your well-being (aside from, perhaps, the Zoara Bouncer), handing in your weapons within the casinos may put you at a disadvantage. Remember that Guards, Greeters, and Bouncers are reasonably adept gunslingers.

NAME	LEVEL	PERCEPTION	HEALTH	GUNS	ENERGY WEAPONS	MELEE WEAPONS	ARMOR	POSSIBLE PRIMARY WEAPONS
Atomic Wrangler Crier	1	5	70	5	5	5	Clothing	Knife
Atomic Wrangler Guard	5	5	85	46	15	15	Leather Armor	Cowboy Repeater/Police Baton
Bartender	1	5	35	15	15	26	Gambler Suit	Sawed Off Shotgun
Blackjack Dealer	1	5	35	15	15	26	Gambler Suit	None
Card Dealer	1	5	70	5	5	5	Gambler Suit	None
Chairman	12	5	80	74	70	72	Business Suit	9mm Pistol, Switchblade
Chairman Bodyguard	6-14†	5	75	65	15	67	Business Suit	Silenced 22 SMG, Grenade
Chairman Greeter	6-14†	5	75	65	15	67	Business Suit	Combat Knife, Grenade
Escort	5	5	85	46	15	15	Prewar Negligee	None
Gambler	1	5	70	5	5	5	Gambler Suit	None
Gomorrah Prostitute	2	5	70	18	14	12	Prostitute Outfit	None
Gunderson Hired Hand	4	5	140	43	14	41	Republican Outfit	Caravan Shotgun
Hooker	5	6	45	11	17	45	Prostitute Outfit	None
Omerta Thug	7	4	105	17	13	58	Business Suit	Sawed Off Shotgun, Combat Knife
Roulette Dealer	1	5	70	5	5	5	Gambler Suit	None
White Glove	4	5	140	43	14	41	White Glove Society Attire, White Glove Mask	Dress Cane
White Glove Bouncer	4	5	140	43	14	41	White Glove Society Attire, White Glove Mask	Dress Cane
Zoara Bouncer	16	5	140	89	85	87	Business Suit	Combat Knife/44 Magnum, 10mm Submachine Gun

(† Level 10 Statistics Shown)

Chairman Bodyguard

Omerta Thug

White Glove Bouncer

FREESIDE INHABITANTS (Streets)

Residents of the Interior Zones of New Vegas aren't usually a threat, but the Bodyguards, Gun Runner Gunsmiths, and Van Graff Thugs are all hardened individuals who aren't pushovers. The Van Graff Thugs have extreme competence with Energy Weapons, too.

NAME	LEVEL	PERCEPTION	HEALTH	GUNS	ENERGY WEAPONS	MELEE WEAPONS	ARMOR	POSSIBLE PRIMARY WEAPONS
Beggar	1	5	70	5	5	5	Wasteland Outfit	None
Bodyguard	15	8	255	85	85	85	Combat Armor, Leather Armor, Metal Armor, Merc Outfit	Hunting Rifle, 10mm Submachine Gun
Bodyguard for Hire	16	6	150	94	17	75	Leather Armor	Sawed Off Shotgun
Chem Addict	1	4	20	12	12	12	Wasteland Outfit	Knife
Followers Doctor	12	6	120	14	16	12	Followers Doctor Outfit	None
Followers Guard	14	6	140	86	17	15	Merc Outfit	Sawed Off Shotgun, 9mm Pistol, Lever Action Shotgun, Hunting Rifle
Followers Medical Student	10	6	90	14	16	12	Followers Doctor Outfit	None
Freeside Thug	5	10	150	5	5	45	Wasteland Outfit	None

Bodyguard for Hire

NAME	LEVEL	PERCEPTION	HEALTH	GUNS	ENERGY WEAPONS	MELEE WEAPONS	ARMOR	POSSIBLE PRIMARY WEAPONS
Greaser	3	5	70	39	15	41	Wasteland Outfit	Baseball Bat/Powerfist, Frag Grenade
Guard	9	5	120	63	14	63	Merc Outfit	Hunting Rifle
Gun Runner Guard	1	3	80	32	26	21	Merc Outfit	Caravan Shotgun
Gun Runner Gunsmith	5	5	240	45	14	45	Merc Outfit	9mm Pistol
King Groupie	1	5	30	30	15	30	Prewar Negligee	None
Kings Gang Member	1	5	70	5	5	5	Kings Outfit	357 Revolver/10mm Pistol/10mm Submachine Gun
New Vegas Citizen	3	5	75	39	14	39	Wasteland Outfit/Merc Outfit	9mm Pistol/Single Shotgun/Knife/Baseball Bat/Tire Iron/Sledgehammer/Caravan Shotgun
New Vegas Resident	1	5	70	5	5	5	Wasteland Outfit	None
North Vegas Resident	1	5	70	5	5	5	Wasteland Outfit	None
Scavenger	6	5	140	50	15	15	Wasteland Merchant Outfit	10mm Pistol/Hunting Rifle/Sawed Off Shotgun/10mm SMG
Sharecropper	1	6	80	14	16	33	Republican Outfit	None
Squatter	1	5	70	5	5	5	Wasteland Outfit	None
Thug	6	4	120	37	13	54	Wasteland Outfit	10mm Pistol
Underpass Citizen	1	5	70	5	5	5	Wasteland Outfit	357 Revolver
Van Graff Thug	17	7	215	5	95	5	Combat Armor Black	Plasma Rifle
Westside Citizen	1	5	70	5	5	5	Wasteland Outfit	None
Westside Militia	1	5	65	31	14	31	Leather Armor	Single Shotgun
Westside Resident	1	5	70	5	5	5	Wasteland Outfit	None
Westside Thug	5	5	85	47	14	47	Wasteland Outfit	Baseball Bat

Followers Guard

Gun Runner Gunsmith

Kings Gang Member

BOOMERS

Boomers are highly skilled in Guns and their devastating weaponry causes splash damage. Most Boomers also have a Knife or Sledgehammer for close-quarter fighting, and the wide-open Air Force Base means fewer chances to seek cover.

NAME	LEVEL	PERCEPTION	HEALTH	GUNS	ENERGY WEAPONS	MELEE WEAPONS	ARMOR	POSSIBLE PRIMARY WEAPONS
Boomer	16	6	145	90	17	17	Boomer Outfit	Grenade Launcher, Grenade, Sledgehammer/Combat Knife/Lead Pipe
Boomer Chef	16	6	145	90	17	17	Boomer Outfit	Sledgehammer/Combat Knife/Lead Pipe
Boomer Guard	14	6	95	82	17	17	Boomer Outfit, Combat Helmet	Missile Launcher, Knife
Boomer Munitions Manager	1	5	70	5	5	5	Boomer Outfit	None
Boomer Teacher	16	6	145	90	17	17	Boomer Outfit	None
Mini Boomer								

Boomer Guard

BROTHERHOOD OF STEEL

Brotherhood of Steel forces have imposing Power Armor, which greatly affects the amount of damage your weapons actually inflict, and they use Energy Weapons. Fortunately they're rarely seen, unless you're assaulting their hidden base.

NAME	LEVEL	PERCEPTION	HEALTH	GUNS	ENERGY WEAPONS	MELEE WEAPONS	ARMOR	POSSIBLE PRIMARY WEAPONS
Brotherhood of Steel Initiate	4	7	70	42	44	14	Recon Armor	Laser Pistol
Brotherhood of Steel Knight	7	7	95	53	55	14	Recon Armor	Laser Pistol/Tri-Beam Laser/Laser Rifle/Gauss Rifle
Brotherhood of Steel Paladin	11	6	120	73	16	69	T45d Power Armor/Helmet	Gauss Rifle, Tri-Beam Laser
Brotherhood of Steel Scribe	1	5	21	5	5	5	Brotherhood Scribe Robe	Laser RCW, Zap Gloves
Brotherhood Scout	1	5	70	5	5	5	Recon Armor/Helmet	Laser Rifle

Brotherhood of Steel Paladin

MOJAVE WASTELAND INHABITANTS

A wide variety of humans eke out an existence across the Mojave. Most are of little threat (and aren't initially hostile), although the Crimson Caravan guards are more handy than most in a combat situation.

NAME	LEVEL	PERCEPTION	HEALTH	GUNS	ENERGY WEAPONS	MELEE WEAPONS	ARMOR	POSSIBLE PRIMARY WEAPONS
Caravaneer	1	4	20	12	12	12	Wastelander Outfit	Silenced 22 Pistol/Varmint Rifle/9mm Pistol/357 Revolver/Single Shotgun/Straight Razor/Cleaver/Pool Cue/Police Baton/Knife
Convict	3	2	20	46	15	15	Merc Outfit	Cleaver/Tire Iron, 9mm Pistol/Varmint Rifle, Dynamite
Crazed Chem Addict	1	4	20	12	12	12	Wastelander Outfit	Knife
Crimson Caravan Guard	11	5	110	67	14	67	Leather Armor	Lever Action Shotgun, Grenade

Goodsprings Settler

NAME	LEVEL	PERCEPTION	HEALTH	GUNS	ENERGY WEAPONS	MELEE WEAPONS	ARMOR	POSSIBLE PRIMARY WEAPONS
Crimson Caravan Trader	11	5	110	67	14	67	Metal Armor	Caravan Shotgun, Knife
Destitute Traveler	1	5	65	30	15	15	Wastelander Outfit	Knife, 9mm Pistol
Goodsprings Settler	1	5	45	31	14	29	Republican Outfit	357 Revolver, Knife
Local	1	5	70	5	5	5	Wastelander Outfit	None
Mercenary	8	7	115	55	34	51	Merc Outfit/Leather Armor/Metal Armor	Grenade, 10mm Pistol/9mm Pistol/Laser Pistol, Machete/Knife/Combat Knife,
Mojave Inhabitant	3	6	80	39	14	39	Merc Outfit/Wasteland Outfit	
Novac Settler	6	5	70	51	14	16	Wastelander Outfit	Knife
Prospector	6	6	105	55	20	51	Wastelander Outfit/Merc Outfit/Leather Armor	10mm Pistol/10mm SMG/9mm Pistol/Caravan Shotgun/Single Shotgun/Silenced Pistol, Switchblade/Police Baton/Machete/Knife/Hatchet/9 Iron/Cleaver/Nail Board
Prospector Merchant	1	6	75	28	17	17	Wastelander Outfit	10mm Pistol/10mm SMG/9mm Pistol/Caravan Shotgun/Single Shotgun/Silenced Pistol, Switchblade/Police Baton/Machete/Knife/Hatchet/9 Iron/Cleaver/Nail Board
Quarry Worker	3	5	85	39	14	37	Republican Outfit	Varmint Rifle/9mm Pistol/357 Revolver/Single Shotgun/Knife/Lead Pipe
Refugee	1	5	70	5	5	5	Wasteland Outfit	None
Traveler	5	5	60	47	14	14	Gambler Outfit	None
Traveling Merchant	7	6	105	54	17	17	Leather Armor	Knife, 10mm Pistol
Wastelander	1	5	25	31	14	31	Republican Outfit/Wasteland Outfit	Baseball Bat/Combat Knife/Police Baton/Pool Cue/Knife/Lead Pipe/Tire Iron/Sledgehammer/9mm Pistol

Prospector

Novac Settler

Quarry Worker

NCR PERSONNEL

NCR forces run the gamut from the greenhorn with a modicum of Guns training to the NCR Rangers and more dangerous Veterans, clad in excellent-quality armor, and armed with potent weaponry. There's even a Heavy Trooper variant that uses "non-powered" Power Armor salvaged from previous battles with the Brotherhood of Steel.

NAME	LEVEL	PERCEPTION	HEALTH	GUNS	ENERGY WEAPONS	MELEE WEAPONS	ARMOR	POSSIBLE PRIMARY WEAPONS
Engineer	2	6	70	17	17	34	Jumpsuit Outfit	None
NCR Heavy Trooper	33	5	190	100	15	100	NRC Trooper Armor/Combat Helmet	Grenade, Combat Knife, Sniper Rifle/127mm Pistol/Marksman Carbine/Riot Shotgun
NCR Mercenary	8	7	115	55	34	51	Merc Outfit/Leather Armor/Metal Armor	10mm Pistol/Laser Pistol/9mm Pistol, Machete/Knife/Combat Knife, Frag Grenade/Frag Mine
NCR Military Police	8	6	85	57	16	56	NCR Trooper Armor MP/MP Helmet	Cattle Prod
NCR MP	5	5	50	46	15	46	NCR Trooper Armor MP/MP Helmet	Cattle Prod/10mm Pistol
NCR Prospector	6	6	105	55	34	51	Wastelander Outfit/Merc Outfit/Leather Armor	10mm Pistol/10mm SMG/9mm Pistol/Caravan Shotgun/Cowboy Repeater/Single Shotgun/Silenced 22 Pistol, Switchblade/Tire Iron/Police Baton/Machete/Knife/Hatchet/9 Iron/Cleaver/Nail Board
NCR Ranger	15	6	195	88	17	15	Ranger Patrol Armor	357 Revolver
NCR Ranger Veteran	1	6	100	32	17	15	Combat Ranger Armor/Helmet	Combat Knife, Brush Gun
NCR Ranger Veteran Commander	15	6	105	88	17	15	Combat Ranger Armor/Helmet	Combat Knife, Brush Gun, Hunting Revolver
NCR Recruit	5	5	50	46	15	46	Merc Outfit	Combat Knife, Hunting Rifle
NCR Sergeant	5	5	45	46	15	15	NCR Trooper Armor/Helmet	Service Rifle, Knife
NCR Sniper	5	5	85	46	15	15	Ranger Patrol Armor/Helmet	Sniper Rifle
NCR Trooper	5	5	50	46	15	46	Trooper Armor/Helmet	Service Rifle, Knife
NCR Trooper MP	8	6	85	57	16	56	MP Trooper Armor/Helmet	Cattle Prod
NCR Veteran Ranger	21	6	225	100	17	15	Ranger Combat Armor/Helmet	Hunting Revolver/Trail Carbine/Assault Carbine/Ranger Sequoia/Brush Gun/Anti-Material Rifle

NCR Heavy Trooper

NCR Military Police

NCR Trooper

NCR Veteran Ranger

POWDER GANGERS AND CONVICTS

Powder Gangers congregating around the NCR Correctional Facility are lightly armored and display a callous regard for humanity, but they aren't particularly a threat. You can eradicate this Faction without any major problems with other Factions. The biggest problem you face against these foes are the thrown explosives.

NAME	LEVEL	PERCEPTION	HEALTH	GUNS	ENERGY WEAPONS	MELEE WEAPONS	ARMOR	POSSIBLE PRIMARY WEAPONS
Escaped Convict	3	5	75	38	15	15	Merc Outfit	9mm Pistol/Varmint Rifle, Dynamite, Cleaver/Tire Iron
Escaped Convict Leader	4	5	50	42	15	15	Leather Armor	Incinerator, Cleaver/Tire Iron
Powder Ganger	1	6	60	29	16	29	Powder Ganger Guard Armor	Silenced 22 Pistol/Varmint Rifle/9mm Pistol/357 Revolver/Single Shotgun, Straight Razor/Cleaver/Pool Cue/Police Baton/Knife
Powder Ganger Bodyguard	4	6	85	40	16	40	Powder Ganger Guard Armor	9mm SMG, Brass Knuckles/Knife
Powder Ganger Deputy	5	5	85	46	15	15	Leather Armor	Varmint Rifle, Dynamite

Powder Ganger Bodyguard

RAIDERS

These thugs are always hostile, and are the least-troubling enemy for the combat specialist, unless encountered in large groups (such as the Fiends). You can quickly build up your Experience Points by hunting these dregs of humanity.

NAME	LEVEL	PERCEPTION	HEALTH	GUNS	ENERGY WEAPONS	MELEE WEAPONS	ARMOR	POSSIBLE PRIMARY WEAPONS
Fiend	3	5	65	41	37	39	Raider Armor, Fiend Helmet	Caravan Shotgun/Laser Rifle/Plasma Rifle/Laser RCW
Jackal Gang Leader	5	6	60	45	16	45	Merc Outfit/Leather Armor/Metal Armor	Knife/Lead Pipe, 10mm Pistol/Cowboy Repeater
Jackal Gang Member	4	6	50	41	16	41	Merc Outfit/Leather Armor/Metal Armor/Wastelander outfit	Knife/Lead Pipe
Scorpions Gang Member	10	5	110	65	15	65	Merc Outfit	10mm Pistol/Sawed Off Shotgun/Combat Knife
Viper Gunslinger	7	6	60	53	16	53	Merc Outfit/Metal Armor	Knife/Tire Iron/10mm Pistol/Combat Knife/Ripper/Lever Action Shotgun/44 Magnum/10mm SMG
Viper Leader	9	6	80	61	16	61	Leather Armor/Metal Armor/Combat Armor	Baseball Bat/Caravan Shotgun/Cowboy Repeater/Grenade Rifle/Sledgehammer/Hunting Rifle/10mm SMG/44 Magnum/Shiskebab/127mm Pistol/Hunting Shotgun/Hunting Revolver/Trail Carbine

Fiend

Viper Gunslinger

GREAT KHANS

Great Khans number in the few dozen, but their Warriors are still a force to be reckoned with due to their armor and helmet protection. Otherwise, this tribe can be allied with or culled for XP, because they react like slightly more competent Raiders when provoked.

NAME	LEVEL	PERCEPTION	HEALTH	GUNS	ENERGY WEAPONS	MELEE WEAPONS	ARMOR	POSSIBLE PRIMARY WEAPONS
Great Khan	8	5	100	57	15	57	Simple Khan Armor	Brass Knuckles
Great Khan Armorer	8	5	100	57	15	57	Simple Khan Armor	Combat Knife, Trail Carbine/Hunting Shotgun/Hunting Revolver/127mm Pistol
Great Khan Warrior	10	5	70	67	63	65	Great Khan Armor/Spiked Helmet	Lever Action Shotgun

Great Khan Warrior

CAESAR'S LEGION PERSONNEL

Skilled in both Guns and Melee Weapons, the Legion's shock troops employ a wide variety of (sometimes highly damaging) weaponry that can't be found anywhere else. The legionaries however, are much less of a threat. Look down the lists of armaments to see if any interest you; then attack those likely to be carrying such an implement.

NAME	LEVEL	PERCEPTION	HEALTH	GUNS	ENERGY WEAPONS	MELEE WEAPONS	ARMOR	POSSIBLE PRIMARY WEAPONS
Legion Centurion	12	5	130	74	15	76	Centurion Armor/Helmet	Chainsaw, Hunting Shotgun
Legion Explorer	10	5	120	66	15	68	Explorer Armor/Helmet	Machete, Hunting Rifle
Legion Vexillarius	12	5	180	74	15	76	Vexillarius Armor/Helmet	Machete, Service Rifle
Legionary Assassin	20	5	220	100	15	100	Vexillarius Armor/Helmet	Hunting Rifle
Legionary Blacksmith	10	5	145	66	15	68	Legion Veteran Armor/Helmet	Machete/Chainsaw
Legionary Instructor	5	5	95	46	15	46	Legion Veteran Armor	Machete

Legion Centurion

NAME	LEVEL	PERCEPTION	HEALTH	GUNS	ENERGY WEAPONS	MELEE WEAPONS	ARMOR	POSSIBLE PRIMARY WEAPONS
Legionary Main Gate Guard	10	5	145	66	15	68	Legion Armor Prime	Throwing Spear, Machete, 10mm Pistol/9mm Pistol/Cowboy Repeater/Single Shotgun/357 Revolver/Varmint Rifle
Praetorian Guard	15	5	195	86	15	88	Legion Armor Praetorian	Ballistic Fist
Prime Decanus	20	5	215	100	15	100	Legion Armor Prime/ Helmet	Machete
Prime Legionary	10	5	145	66	15	68	Legion Armor Prime/ Helmet	44 Magnum/Lever Action Shotgun/Hunting Rifle/Sawed Off Shotgun
Recruit Decanus	7	5	95	54	15	15	Legion Armor Recruit/ Helmet	Machete, 10mm SMG
Recruit Legionary	5	5	95	46	15	48	Legion Armor Recruit/ Helmet	Throwing Spear, Machete, 10mm Pistol/9mm Pistol/Cowboy Repeater/Single Shotgun/357 Revolver/Varmint Rifle
Veteran Decanus	15	5	170	90	15	88	Legion Armor Veteran/ Helmet	Machete, 127mm SMG
Veteran Legionary	10	5	145	66	15	68	Legion Armor Veteran/ Helmet	Police Baton

Legion Vexillarius

Praetorian Guard

Mutated Animals and Wild Abominations

Creatures with a more animalistic tendency to battle—including Super Mutants and other more grotesque atrocities—haunt the Mojave Wasteland. They have a slightly different set of statistics:

Name: The name your Pip-Boy gives to the creature in question.

Type: Whether the entity is wildlife, mutated wildlife (Mutated Animal or Insect), mechanical in nature (Robot), or some kind of freak of nature (Abomination).

Level: Although they can appear at any time, these critters are commonly encountered when you reach this level; this also references their experience level.

Inventory: What the creature's corpse usually contains when inspected. There may be other (random) items, but the noted ones are always present.

Perception: This is measured from 1 to 10, the same as your Perception attribute. The higher the Perception, the quicker you're spotted, or reacted to.

Health: The full Hit Points of the creature, prior to combat.

Damage: What damage it inflicts with its usual, regular weapon.

Special Weapon and Notes: Whether the entity has a special or unique attack, such as a Centaur's spittle, and any pertinent data regarding damage, or special damage caused, or abilities the creature has.

ALIENS, BIGHORNERS, BLOATFLIES, BRAHMIN, CAZADORS, CENTAURS, COYOTES

Bighorners are docile until you attack; then expect a nasty knockback, making close assault weapons trickier to connect with. Cazadors and disgusting Centaurs infect you with poison, so attack from range and aim at the heads!

NAME	TYPE	LEVEL	INVENTORY	PERCEPTION	HEALTH	DAMAGE	SPECIAL WEAPON AND NOTES
ALIENS							
Alien	Abomination	1	Laser Pistol	5	50		Laser Pistol. Wild Wasteland trait active.
Alien Captain	Abomination	1	Alien Blaster and Ammo	5	50		Alien Blaster. Wild Wasteland trait active.
BIGHORNERS							
Bighorner Calf	Mutated Animal	5	Bighorner Meat	2	50	15	Knockback Ram
Young Bighorner	Mutated Animal	1	Bighorner Meat	3	60	40	Knockback Ram
Bighorner	Mutated Animal	9	Bighorner Meat	3	100	35	Knockback Ram
Bighorner Bull	Mutated Animal	11	Bighorner Meat	4	120	45	Knockback Ram
Malnourished Bighorner Calf	Mutated Animal	5	Bighorner Meat	2	40	15	Knockback Ram
Malnourished Bighorner	Mutated Animal	9	Bighorner Meat	3	50	35	Knockback Ram
BLOATFLIES							
Bloatfly	Mutated Insect	1	Bloatfly Darts, Bloatfly Meat	6	15		Larva Spit. Flying enemy.
BRAHMIN							
Brahmin	Mutated Animal	1	Brahmin Meat	3	40		Heads take 50% damage.
Malnourished Brahmin Calf	Mutated Animal	1	Brahmin Meat	3	40		Heads take 50% damage.
Malnourished Brahmin	Mutated Animal	1	Brahmin Meat	3	40		Heads take 50% damage.
Water Brahmin	Mutated Animal	1	Brahmin Meat	3	40		Heads take 50% damage.
CAZADORS							
Young Cazador	Mutated Insect	12	None	7	100	45	Cazador Poison
Cazador	Mutated Insect	18	None	9	200	70	Cazador Poison
Legendary Cazador	Mutated Insect	25	None	10	400	120	Cazador Poison

Bighorner

Cazador

Evolved Centaur

NAME	TYPE	LEVEL	INVENTORY	PERCEPTION	HEALTH	DAMAGE	SPECIAL WEAPON AND NOTES
CENTAURS							
Centaur	Abomination	9	None	6	100		Radioactive Spit; legs take 75% damage, tongues take 25% damage.
Evolved Centaur	Abomination	14	None	7	150	50	Evolved Radioactive Spit; legs take 75% damage, tongues take 25% damage.
Giant Evolved Centaur	Abomination	18	None	8	220	70	Evolved Radioactive Spit; legs take 75% damage, tongues take 25% damage.
COYOTES							
Coyote Pup	Animal	1	Coyote Meat	6	10	7	
Coyote	Animal	3	Coyote Meat	8	30	15	
Coyote Den Mother	Animal	4	Coyote Meat	8	40	17	

Coyote Den Mother

DEATHCLAWS

Deathclaws have a tough hides, overwhelming quickness, and massive clawing damage. Attack them at range, in a position from which they can't reach you. Switch to close-combat weapons as they close. Rig the area with Mines, and be wary of entering a domain with numerous warning signs!

NAME	TYPE	LEVEL	INVENTORY	PERCEPTION	HEALTH	DAMAGE	SPECIAL WEAPON AND NOTES
Deathclaw Baby	Abomination	10	Deathclaw Hand	6	100	40	
Young Deathclaw	Abomination	10	Deathclaw Hand	6	100	40	
Blind Deathclaw	Abomination	20	Deathclaw Hand	8	250	100	
Deathclaw	Abomination	20	Deathclaw Hand	8	250	100	
Deathclaw Alpha	Abomination	12	Deathclaw Hand	8	500	200	
Deathclaw Alpha Male	Abomination	18	Deathclaw Hand	9	750	200	Knockback
Deathclaw Mother	Abomination	12	Deathclaw Hand	8	750	100	Knockback
Legendary Deathclaw	Abomination	30	Deathclaw Hand	10	850	250	Knockback

Deathclaw Alpha Male

DOGS, GECKOS

Geckos race forward and attack, so aim at their legs to slow them down. Remember to skin and tan a Gecko hide at a campfire to sell for many Caps.

NAME	TYPE	LEVEL	INVENTORY	PERCEPTION	HEALTH	DAMAGE	SPECIAL WEAPON AND NOTES
DOGS							
Dog	Animal	2	Dog Meat	6	20	12	Fast
Fiend Guard Dog	Animal	5	Dog Meat	7	55	25	Fast
Large Dog	Animal	4	Dog Meat	7	45	25	Fast
Large Wild Dog	Animal	5	Dog Meat	7	55	32	Fast
Legion Mongrel	Animal	1	Dog Meat	8	80	5	Fast, Legion Mongrel Hamstring
NCR Guard Dog	Animal	5	Dog Meat	7	55	25	Fast
Prospector's Dog	Animal	2	Dog Meat	6	20	12	Fast
Wild Dog	Animal	3	Dog Meat	6	30	18	Fast
GECKOS							
Young Fire Gecko	Mutated Animal	11	Fire Gecko Meat, Fire Gecko Hide	5	95	45	Fire Gecko Flame, immune to fire
Fire Gecko	Mutated Animal	16	Fire Gecko Meat, Fire Gecko Hide	7	165	60	Fire Gecko Flame, immune to fire
Fire Gecko Hunter	Mutated Animal	14	Fire Gecko Meat, Fire Gecko Hide	7	165	50	Fire Gecko Flame, immune to fire
Legendary Fire Gecko	Mutated Animal	25	Fire Gecko Meat, Fire Gecko Hide	8	385	115	Fire Gecko Flame, immune to fire
Young Gecko	Mutated Animal	3	Gecko Meat, Gecko Hide	4	40	15	
Young Gecko Hunter	Animal	1	Gecko Meat, Gecko Hide	5	50	5	
Gecko	Mutated Animal	3	Gecko Meat, Gecko Hide	3	20	5	
Gecko Hunter	Mutated Animal	3	Gecko Meat, Gecko Hide	3	20	15	
Golden Gecko	Mutated Animal	12	Golden Gecko Meat, Golden Gecko Hide	5	125	50	Fire Gecko Flame, radiation attack
Young Golden Gecko	Mutated Animal	7	Golden Gecko Meat, Golden Gecko Hide	4	60	35	Fire Gecko Flame, radiation attack

Prospector's Dog

Fire Gecko Hunter

Golden Gecko

GHOULS

Feral Ghouls are humans who slowly turned into Ghouls and were driven mad during the process. Tackle Glowing Ones first, because they are most dangerous, ideally laying Mines in the paths, and coaxing foes toward you. Some Ghouls have mutated from original vault dwellers.

NAME	TYPE	LEVEL	INVENTORY	PERCEPTION	HEALTH	DAMAGE	SPECIAL WEAPON AND NOTES
Feral Ghoul	Feral Ghoul	3	None	2	25	5	
Feral Ghoul Reaver	Feral Ghoul	12	None	7	180	40	
Feral Ghoul Roamer	Feral Ghoul	10	None	4	110	30	

NAME	TYPE	LEVEL	INVENTORY	PERCEPTION	HEALTH	DAMAGE	SPECIAL WEAPON AND NOTES
Feral Trooper Ghoul	Feral Ghoul	8	None	1	100	20	
Glowing One	Feral Ghoul	9	None	5	240	32	Radiation Burst, healed by radiation
Glowing Trooper Ghoul	Feral Ghoul	8	None	1	150	30	
Vault Dweller	Feral Ghoul	6	10mm Ammo	2	100	16	
Vault Security Guard	Feral Ghoul	8	10mm Ammo	2	200	25	
Vault Security Officer	Feral Ghoul	10	10mm Ammo	2	400	50	
Overseer	Feral Ghoul	9	10mm Ammo	2	900	100	

Vault Security Guard

GIANT ANTS, GIANT MANTISES, GIANT RATS, LAKELURKS

Beware of these scaly critters near large bodies of water or dank caverns. Sidestep their debilitating sonic attack as you press forward.

NAME	TYPE	LEVEL	INVENTORY	PERCEPTION	HEALTH	DAMAGE	SPECIAL WEAPON AND NOTES
GIANT ANTS							
Giant Ant Soldier	Mutated Insect	6	Ant Meat	4	100	16/sec.	Frenzies if antennae are destroyed. Legs take 50% damage.
Giant Ant Worker	Mutated Insect	6	Ant Meat	2	55	32/sec.	Frenzies if antennae are destroyed. Legs take 50% damage.
Giant Ant Queen	Mutated Insect	7	Ant Meat	5	450	55	Legs take 50% damage.
GIANT MANTISES							
Giant Mantis Nymph	Mutated Insect	1	None	2	15	25	
Giant Mantis	Mutated Insect	6	None	3	40	45	
Giant Mantis Female	Mutated Insect	9	Egg Clutch	6	50	40	
GIANT RATS							
Giant Rat Pup	Mutated Animal	1	None	2	12	7	
Giant Rat	Mutated Animal	2	None	3	40	15	
Rodent of Unusual Size	Mutated Animal	12	None	5	125	50	Wild Wasteland trait active.
Unnaturally Large Sized Rodent	Mutated Animal	6	None	6	70	35	
LAKELURKS							
Lakelurk	Mutated Animal	12	Lakelurk Meat	7	200	55	Sonic Ranged Attack
Lakelurk King	Mutated Animal	18	Lakelurk Meat	8	300	70	Sonic Ranged Attack

Giant Mantis

Lakelurk

MOLE RATS, NIGHTSTALKERS, RADROACHES

Nightstalkers are a crime against nature. They infect their victims with poison, making them dangerous during close-combat attacks. Some strains are almost invisible, so be wary during cavern exploration, and listen for their rattle.

NAME	TYPE	LEVEL	INVENTORY	PERCEPTION	HEALTH	DAMAGE	SPECIAL WEAPON AND NOTES
MOLE RATS							
Mole Rat Pup	Mutated Animal	2	Mole Rat Meat	1	18		
Mole Rat	Mutated Animal	4	Mole Rat Meat	3	60		
NIGHTSTALKERS							
Nightstalker	Abomination	15	None	9	120	70	Nightstalker Poison
Legendary Nightstalker	Abomination	15	None	10	250	100	Nightstalker Poison
Young Nightstalker	Abomination	9	None	8	70	45	Nightstalker Poison
Den Mother	Abomination	15	None	9	170	85	Nightstalker Poison
RADROACHES							
Radroach	Mutated Insect	1	Radroach Meat	3	12		Flees easily.

Nightstalker

ROBOTS, ROBOTS: TURRETS

Robots don't generally take bonus damage from headshots, so try targeting their weapons, and check the type before you attack; if a Mister Gutsy is armed with a flamethrower, for example, back off and attack. If Robots are seen with other enemies, shoot the control unit, turning the robot into a killing machine to both ally and adversary.

NAME	TYPE	LEVEL	INVENTORY	PERCEPTION	HEALTH	DAMAGE	SPECIAL WEAPON AND NOTES
ROBOTS							
Maintenance Robot	Robot	8	Flamer Fuel	5	50		Frenzies if control unit destroyed.
Mister Gutsy	Robot	9	Flamer Fuel, Energy Cells	6	75		Frenzies if control unit destroyed.
Mister Gutsy Prototype	Robot	4	Flamer Fuel, Energy Cells	6	50		Frenzies if control unit destroyed.
Mister Handy	Robot	3	Flamer Fuel	5	50		Frenzies if control unit destroyed.
Mobile Facial Recognition Scanner	Robot	8	Flamer Fuel	8	30		Frenzies if control unit destroyed.
Mr Steel	Robot	9	Flamer Fuel, Energy Cells	6	100		Frenzies if control unit destroyed.
Mr. Janitor	Robot	3	Flamer Fuel	5	50		Frenzies if control unit destroyed.
Hardened Mister Gutsy	Robot	9	Flamer Fuel, Energy Cells	6	125		Frenzies if control unit destroyed.

Mister Gutsy

NAME	TYPE	LEVEL	INVENTORY	PERCEPTION	HEALTH	DAMAGE	SPECIAL WEAPON AND NOTES
Hardened Sentry Bot	Robot	16	Electron Charge Pack	8	500		Armored head takes 50% damage, armored legs take 75% damage, frenzies if control unit destroyed.
NCR Sentry Bot	Robot	12	Electron Charge Pack	7	300		Armored head takes 50% damage, armored legs take 75% damage, frenzies if control unit destroyed.
Protectron	Robot		None	4	45		Frenzies if control unit destroyed.
Robobrain	Robot	6	Energy Cells	5	125		Frenzies if control unit destroyed.
Securitron Gatekeeper	Robot	7	Grenade Launcher Ammo	6	120	20	Sub Machine Gun, Grenade Launcher, frenzies if control unit destroyed.
Securitron Mk I	Robot	7	Grenade Launcher Ammo	6	120	20	Sub Machine Gun, Grenade Launcher, frenzies if control unit destroyed.
Securitron Mk II	Robot	15	Missiles	6	175	20	Laser Weaponry, Shoulder Missiles, frenzies if control unit destroyed.
Sentry Bot	Robot	12	Electron Charge Pack	7	300		Armored head takes 50% damage, armored legs take 75% damage, frenzies if control unit destroyed.
Sunset Sarsaparilla Eyebot	Robot	0	None	5	30	1	Flies, explodes on death.
Sunset Sarsaparilla Security	Robot	10	None	4	65	2	Frenzies if control unit destroyed.
				ROBOTS: TURRETS			
Vault-Tec Turret	Robot	2	None	10	40		5.56mm Gun or Laser Gun; frenzies if control unit destroyed.
Mark III Turret	Robot	5	None	10	200		5.56mm Gun or Laser Gun; frenzies if control unit destroyed.
Mark VI Turret	Robot	5	None	10	750		5.56mm Gun or Laser Gun; frenzies if control unit destroyed.
Mark VI Turret	Robot	7	None	10	100		5.56mm Gun or Laser Gun; frenzies if control unit destroyed.
Helios Turret	Robot	7	None	10	100		5.56mm Gun or Laser Gun; frenzies if control unit destroyed.

NCR Sentry Bot

Securitron Mk I

Securitron Mk II

SCORPIONS, SPORE PLANTS

Both Bark Scorpions and Spore creatures have additional poison attacks that can cause serious shortfalls to your combat game. Try shooting them from range, staying away from their stinger or burst respectively.

NAME	TYPE	LEVEL	INVENTORY	PERCEPTION	HEALTH	DAMAGE	SPECIAL WEAPON AND NOTES
				SCORPIONS			
Bark Scorpion	Mutated Insect	5	Poison Gland	3	20	25	Bark Scorpion Poison Stinger. Legs take 50% damage. Victim vision impaired.
Bark Scorpion Hunter	Mutated Insect	5	Poison Gland	3	20	30	Bark Scorpion Poison Stinger. Legs take 50% damage. Victim vision impaired.
Small Radscorpion	Mutated Insect	3	Poison Gland	3	20	20	RadScorpion Poison Stinger. Legs Take 50% damage.
Radscorpion	Mutated Insect	8	Poison Gland	4	75	35	RadScorpion Poison Stinger. Legs Take 50% damage.
Giant Radscorpion	Mutated Insect	15	Poison Gland	6	150	60	RadScorpion Poison Stinger. Legs Take 50% damage.
Radscorpion Queen	Mutated Insect	9	Poison Gland	6	200	60	RadScorpion Poison Stinger. Legs Take 50% damage. Radiation.
				SPORE PLANTS			
Spore Carrier Runt	Abomination	3	None	3	50	10	Spore Carrier Burst
Spore Carrier	Abomination	6	None	4	75	20	Spore Carrier Burst
Spore Carrier Brute	Abomination	9	None	5	125	32	Spore Carrier Burst
Spore Carrier Savage	Abomination	12	None	6	175	50	Spore Carrier Burst, regenerates
Spore Plant	Abomination	2	None	10	50	1	Spore Carrier Burst

Bark Scorpion

Spore Carrier Brute

SUPER MUTANTS

Super Mutants include the blue Nightkin, who are usually instantly aggressive (except in Jacobstown), and green Super Mutants (first and second generation) who can be friendly or hostile (at Black Mountain, for example). Use arm shots so they drop their weapons (because their aim becomes terrible). Super Mutants never flee.

NAME	TYPE	LEVEL	INVENTORY	PERCEPTION	HEALTH	DAMAGE	SPECIAL WEAPON AND NOTES
Nightkin	Super Mutant	6	Rebar Club, Frag Grenades	3	175	20	May not be initially hostile, depending on location.
Nightkin Master	Super Mutant	12	Super Sledge, Frag Grenades	6	360	6	May not be initially hostile, depending on location.
Nightkin Sniper	Super Mutant	14	Missile Launcher and Ammo	5	360	20	May not be initially hostile, depending on location.
Super Mutant	Super Mutant	6	Hunting Rifle, Rebar Club, Nail Board, Sledgehammer	3	100	5	May not be initially hostile, depending on location.
Super Mutant Brute	Super Mutant	9	Assault Carbine, Incinerator, Minigun, Sledgehammer	5	250	5	May not be initially hostile, depending on location.
Super Mutant Master	Super Mutant	12	Super Sledge, Light Machine Gun, Minigun, Heavy Incinerator, Missile Launcher	6	360	6	May not be initially hostile, depending on location.

Nightkin Master

Wasteland Guns and Gear

The following pages list every single weapon available in the Mojave Wasteland, whether a gun, melee weapon, or unarmed gauntlet. Next comes every single item of gear you can attach to yourself, whether a suit of armor, a hat, or even a head-wrap or glasses. Finally, all of the available ingestibles are shown, so you can see which items bump up the attributes or skills you need.

Note: The information is provided in a highly detailed table, so that you can easily compare statistics, learn the strengths and weaknesses of each, and know which to use.

PART I: WEAPONS

The following portions of the first table are segmented based on the skill required to use them. In each section, the following information is displayed. Here's how it all breaks down:

Name: The name of the weapon, as it appears on your Pip-Boy. Unique weapons have the prefix, so you can easily compare it to the "base" model.

Type: This indicates whether the weapon takes one or two hands to operate, and how the weapon is held. This is helpful because two-handed weapons slow you down; stow them to quicken your pace. One-handed weapons don't cause this encumbrance.

STR Needed: This is the minimum Strength attribute required to operate this weapon without penalties caused by the armament being too heavy. Choose the weapons you want to use, and compare the STR.

Skill Needed: This is the minimum skill (Energy Weapons, Explosives, Guns, Melee Weapons, or Unarmed) required to use the item without penalty. Some weapons need great skill, while others don't. Check this!

Weight: How heavy the weapon is. Add this to your overall Carry Weight.

Health: This is the "Hit Points" of the weapon when in full Condition (CND). It shows how tough the weapon is.

Value: This is what you'd expect a Trader to purchase the weapon for, before any Barter skill improvements are added.

Clip Count: This is how many bullets, slugs, or ammunition the weapon has in its "chamber" before it needs to be reloaded.

Ammo: This is the ammunition type that the weapon uses. Collect or Breakdown and then make more of this type (or a variant of this type) so you don't run out.

Attack Damage (DAM): How much damage the weapon inflicts, on average, each time you shoot or strike with it, using normal ammunition. This is an important statistic, so you know how damaging the weapon is.

Automatic: Whether you have to manually squeeze the trigger for each shot (like a Magnum), or whether you can hold down the trigger and fire constantly (like a Minigun).

Min. Spread: The minimum angle, in degrees, at which projectiles will radiate out of the gun's barrel. A sniper's bullet, for example, has a very low spread. But a blast of Shotgun pellets fans out, creating a wide spread. Notice the amazingly low spread of the Cowboy Repeater: La Longue Carabine, for example.

Rate of Fire: This is the number of shots, per second, that the weapon shoots. A rapid-fire Machine Gun has many more bullets leaving the weapon than a Shotgun, for example.

Crit % Mult: A weapon's Critical Chance is augmented by this statistic. This is how much the weapon multiplies to the chance of scoring a Critical Hit. The higher score, the better.

Uses Sight: "Yes" means the weapon uses a sight to zoom in on an enemy, and "no" means it doesn't.

Critical Damage: This is how much extra damage is usually called if a Critical Hit is successful. This value does not take the target's DR into account, effectively bypassing armor.

Action Points: This is how many Action Points it takes you to fire the weapon.

Unique Weapon: Whether there's only one of this weapon. If this is the case, the location of the weapon is listed in the Notes section.

Modifiable: Whether this weapon can be upgraded. The number indicates how many upgrades are available.

Note and Upgrade Modifications: This details any additional weapon effects, lists and describes what each upgrade modification does, and in the case of Unique Weapons, details where the weapon can be found.

Name	Type	STR Needed	Skill Needed	Weight	Health	Value	Clip Count	Ammo	Attack Damage (DAM)	Critical Damage	Crit % Mult	Automatic	Min. Spread	Rate of Fire	Uses Sight	Action Points	Unique Weapon	Modifiable	Note and Upgrade Modifications
ENERGY WEAPONS																			
Alien Blaster	One-Handed Pistol (Energy)	1	75	2	500	4,000	10	Alien Power Cell	100	100	100	No	0	1	No	20	Yes	No	Found at Hovering Anomaly [1.S02]. Wild Wasteland trait must be taken.
Euclid's C-Finder	One-Handed Pistol (Energy)	1	0	15	1,000	1	1	ARCHII Charge	0	0	50	No	0.5	0.1	No	50	Yes	No	Carried by Max, in Freeside [Zone 2C]
Flamer	Two-Handed (Handle)	5–7	50	15	200	2,350	60	Fuel	16	1	4	Yes	0.5	8	No	50	No	Yes (1)	1: Flamer Expanded Tanks: Increases ammunition capacity (+60)
Gatling Laser	Two-Handed (Handle)	6–8	100	18	1,500	6,800	240	EC Pack	7	7	1	Yes	0.6	30	No	30	No	Yes (2)	1: Gat. Laser CF Frame: Lowers weight. 2: Gat. Laser Focus Optics: Increases damage (+3)
Gauss Rifle	Two-Handed (Automatic)	3–5	75	7	80	3,000	5	MF Cell	120	60	2	No	0.03	1	Yes	40	No	No	
Gauss Rifle: YCS/186	Two-Handed (Automatic)	3–5	75	8	100	3,000	4	MF Cell	140	70	2	No	0.03	1	Yes	40	Yes	No	Found on a Mercenary at the small camp north of Brooks Tumbleweed Ranch [1.01]. Wild Wasteland trait must NOT be taken.
Heavy Incinerator	Two-Handed (Handle)	6–8	100	15	200	7,200	24	Fuel	15	5	4	Yes	0.5	4	No	50	No	No	
Incinerator	Two-Handed (Handle)	4–6	25	12	200	1,300	30	Fuel	1	1	4	Yes	0.1	2	No	50	No	No	
Laser Pistol	One-Handed Pistol (Energy)	1	0	3	200	175	30	E Cell	12	12	1.5	No	0.1	1	No	15	No	No	
Laser Pistol: Pew Pew	One-Handed Pistol (Energy)	1	0	3	80	2,500	30	E Cell	75	50	2.5	No	0.1	8	No	35	Yes	No	Found on the body of Allen Marks, after Side Quest: The Legend of the Star is completed: Sunset Sarsaparilla Headquarters [2.17].
Laser RCW	Two-Handed (Automatic)	2–4	50	4	400	2,150	60	EC Pack	15	15	0.5	Yes	0.08	9	No	20	No	Yes (1)	1: Laser RCW Recycler: Replenishes ammunition (1/4 shots).
Laser Rifle	Two-Handed Rifle (Energy)	1–3	25	8	125	800	24	MF Cell	15	15	1.5	No	0.03	1	Yes	18	No	Yes (3)	1: Laser Rifle Beam Splitter: Creates two beams that together do increased damage (+30%). 2: Laser Rifle Focus Optics: Increases damage (+3). 3: Laser Rifle Scope: Adds long-range scope.
Laser Rifle: AER14 Prototype	Two-Handed Rifle (Energy)	1–3	25	8.5	100	2,200	24	MF Cell	22	22	2	No	0.02	1	Yes	20	Yes	No	Found inside Vault 22 [1.09] Common Area, on the blocked stairwell only accessible from the Food Production level.
Multiplas Rifle	Two-Handed (Automatic)	2–4	50	7	50	2,500	60	MF Cell	105	105	1	No	1.5	1	No	35	No	No	
Plasma Caster	Two-Handed (Handle)	6–8	100	20	80	7,000	10	MF Cell	65	65	1	No	0.7	1	No	25	No	Yes (1)	1: Plasma Caster HS Electrode: Increases rate of fire.
Plasma Defender	One-Handed Pistol (Energy)	2	50	2	100	3,000	48	E Cell	36	36	1	No	0.3	1	No	20	No	No	
Plasma Pistol	One-Handed Pistol (Energy)	2	0	3	150	200	32	E Cell	22	22	1.5	No	0.5	1	No	30	No	No	
Plasma Rifle	Two-Handed (Automatic)	1–2	25	8	75	1,300	24	MF Cell	32	32	2	No	0.2	1	No	30	No	Yes (1)	1: Plasma Rifle Mag. Accelerator: Increases speed of plasma projectile.
Plasma Rifle: Q-35 Matter Modulator	Two-Handed (Automatic)	2	25	7	250	3,000	12	MF Cell	32	62	2	No	0.2	1	No	28	Yes	No	Found in a pod casement, in the locked shipping room of the REPCONN Headquarters [2.35].
Pulse Gun	One-Handed Pistol (Energy)	2	25	2	100	1,800	25	E Cell	5	5	1	No	0.1	12	No	20	Yes	No	EMP—Bonus Damage vs. Robots, Power Armor. Found in the Armory Cache; Vault 34 [3.12].
Recharger Pistol	One-Handed Pistol (Energy)	2	50	7	300	2,700	20	MF Breeder	12	12	1.2	No	0	1	No	13	No	Yes (1)	1: Laser RCW Recycler: Replenishes ammunition (1/4 shots).
Recharger Rifle	Two-Handed (Automatic)	3–5	0	15	200	250	7	MF Breeder	9	9	1.5	No	0.02	1	No	19	No	No	
Tesla Cannon	Two-Handed (Launcher)	6–8	100	8	80	8,700	40	EC Pack	40	30	2	No	0	1	No	37	No	No	
Tesla Cannon: Tesla-Beaton Prototype	Two-Handed (Launcher)	6–8	100	8	40	12,525	45	EC Pack	55	55	2	No	0	1	No	37	Yes	No	On the ground near the Crashed Vertibird [6.24].
Tri-beam Laser Rifle	Two-Handed (Energy Rifle)	2–4	75	9	50	4,800	24	MF Cell	52	15	1.5	No	0.5	1	No	23	No	No	
EXPLOSIVES																			
Bottlecap Mine	One-Handed (Mine)	1	0	0.5	5	150			1	0	1	No	1	0	No	35	No	No	
C-4 Plastic Explosive	One-Handed (Mine)	1	50	0.5	10,000	1,000			1	0	1	No	0	1	No	24	No	No	Detonator needed, unless you shoot or explode by shooting or splash damage.
Detonator	One-Handed (Pistol)	0	0	0.5	10,000	25	1		0	0	1	No	0	1	No	24	No	No	C-4 needed to be laid first.
Dynamite	One-Handed (Grenade)	1	0	0.3	5	25			1	0	1	No	0	1	No	24	No	No	
Dynamite: Long Fuse Dynamite	One-Handed (Grenade)	1	0	0.3	5	25			1	0	1	No	0	1	No	24	No	No	
Fat Man	Two-Handed (Launcher)	6–8	100	30	100	6,000	1	Mini Nuke	10	0	0	No	2	1	No	65	No	Yes (1)	1: Fat Man Little Boy Kit: Decreases weight (50%).

Name	Type	STR Needed	Skill Needed	Weight	Health	Value	Clip Count	Ammo	Attack Damage (DAM)	Critical Damage	Crit % Mult	Automatic	Min. Spread	Rate of Fire	Uses Sight	Action Points	Unique Weapon	Modifiable	Note and Upgrade Modifications
Frag Grenade	One-Handed (Grenade)	2	25	0.5	5	150			1	0	1	No	0	1	No	24	No	No	
Frag Grenade: Holy Frag Grenade	One-Handed (Grenade)	2	0	0.5	5	500			1	0	1	No	0	1	No	24	Yes	No	Found in the basement of the eastern church, Camp Searchlight [6.16]. Wild Wasteland trait must be taken.
Frag Mine	One-Handed (Mine)	1	25	0.5	5	75			1	0	1	No	1	1	No	35	No	No	
Grenade Launcher	Two-Handed (Rifle)	3–5	75	12	100	4,200	4	40mm Grenade	30	0	1	No	1	1	No	35	No	No	
Grenade Machinegun	Two-Handed (Handle)	6–8	100	15	200	5,200	30	25mm Grenade	0	0	1	Yes	1	3	No	50	No	Yes (1)	1: Grenade MG High-Speed Kit: Increases rate of fire.
Grenade Machinegun: Mercy	Two-Handed (Handle)	6–8	100	15	200	5,200	18	40mm Grenade	0	0	50	Yes	1	3.1	No	50	Yes	No	On the floor of the cavern, near the body of a dead Brotherhood of Steel Paladin; Dead Wind Cavern [5.22].
Grenade Rifle	Two-Handed (Rifle)	1–3	25	6	100	300	1	40mm Grenade	2	1	1	No	1	1	No	35	No	No	Long Barrel mod—doubles range
Grenade Rifle: Thump-Thump	Two-Handed (Rifle)	1–3	25	5.5	125	800	1	40mm Grenade	2	1	1	No	0.5	1	No	35	Yes	No	Lying on the floor, near the Ant mound; Nellis Array [3.03].
Incendiary Grenade	One-Handed (Grenade)	2	50	0.5	5	200			1	0	1	No	1	1	No	24	No	No	
Missile Launcher	Two-Handed (Launcher)	4–6	75	20	50	3,900	1	Missile	20	0	0	No	0.5	1	No	55	No	Yes (1)	1: Miss. Launcher Guidance Sys.: Decreases spread.
Missile Launcher: Annabelle	Two-Handed (Launcher)	4–6	75	20	100	5,200	1	Missile	20	0	0	No	0.2	1	No	47	Yes	No	Carried by the Nightkin Sniper on Black Mountain summit: Black Mountain [5.07].
Plasma Grenade	One-Handed (Grenade)	2	75	0.5	5	300			1	0	1	No	1	1	No	24	No	No	
Plasma Mine	One-Handed (Mine)	2	75	0.5	5	300			1	0	1	No	1	0	No	35	No	No	
Powder Charge	One-Handed (Mine)	1	0	0.5	5	25			1	0	1	No	1	1	No	35	No	No	
Pulse Grenade	One-Handed (Grenade)	2	50	0.5	5	40			1	0	1	No	1	3	No	24	No	No	EMP—Bonus Damage vs. Robots, Power Armor.
Pulse Mine	One-Handed (Mine)	2	50	0.5	5	40			1	0	1	No	1	0	No	35	No	No	EMP—Bonus Damage vs. Robots, Power Armor
Time Bomb	One-Handed (Mine)	1	50	0.5	50	750			1	0	1	No	0	1	No	24	No	No	
GUNS																			
.357 Magnum Revolver	One-Handed (Pistol)	1–3	0	2	200	110	6	.357 Mag.	26	26	1	No	0.5	1	No	20	No	Yes (2)	1: .357 Revolver HD Cylinder: Increases condition (+50%). 2: .357 Revolver Long Barrel: Increase damage (+3).
.357 Magnum Revolver: Lucky	One-Handed (Pistol)	1–3	0	2.5	225	1,500	6	.357 Mag.	30	30	2.5	No	0.3	1	No	17	Yes	No	In the floor safe inside the cashier's area of the Vikki & Vance Casino, in Primm [4.17].
.44 Magnum Revolver	One-Handed (Pistol)	3–5	50	3.5	250	2,500	6	.44 Mag.	36	36	1	No	0.7	1	Yes	28	No	Yes (2)	1: .44 Revolver Heavy Frame: Increases condition (+50). 2: .44 Revolver Scope: Adds short-range scope.
.44 Magnum Revolver: Mysterious Magnum	One-Handed (Pistol)	4–6	50	4	150	3,200	6	.44 Mag.	42	42	1	No	0.5	1	No	25	Yes	No	Owned by the Lonesome Drifter; Sunset Sarsaparilla Billboard [3.S21].
10mm Pistol	One-Handed (Pistol)	2–4	25	3	80	750	12	10mm	22	22	1	No	0.8	1	No	17	No	Yes (3)	1: 10mm Pistol Extended Mags: Increases ammunition capacity (+4). 2: 10mm Pistol Laser Sight: Decreases spread, adds laser sight effect. 3: 10mm Pistol Silencer: Silences weapon.
10mm Submachine Gun	One-Handed (Pistol)	3–5	50	5	250	2,375	30	10mm	19	19	1	Yes	4	9	No	20	No	Yes (2)	1: 10mm SMG Extended Mags: Increases ammunition capacity (+10). 2: 10mm SMG Recoil Comp.: Decreases spread.
12.7mm Pistol	One-Handed (Pistol)	5–7	75	3.5	80	4,000	7	12.7mm	40	33	1	No	1.1	1	No	17	No	Yes (1)	1: 12.7mm Pistol Silencer: Silences the weapon.
12.7mm Submachine Gun	Two-Handed (Automatic)	4–6	100	5	250	5,100	15	12.7mm	36	36	1	Yes	4	8	No	20	No	Yes (1)	1: 12.7mm Submachine Gun Silencer: Silences the weapon.
9mm Pistol	One-Handed (Pistol)	2	0	1.5	150	100	13	9mm	16	16	1	No	0.7	1	Yes	17	No	Yes (2)	1: 9mm Pistol Extended Mags: Increases ammunition capacity (+7). 2: 9mm Pistol Scope: Adds short-range scope.
9mm Pistol: Maria	One-Handed (Pistol)	2	0	1.5	200	1,000	13	9mm	20	20	2	No	0.2	1	No	15	Yes	No	On Benny, when you kill him.
9mm Submachine Gun	One-Handed (Pistol)	1–3	25	4	450	850	30	9mm	11	11	1	Yes	2.2	11	No	0	No	Yes (2)	1: 9mm SMG Drums: Increases ammunition capacity (+30). 2: 9mm SMG Light Bolt: Increases rate of fire.

Name	Type	STR Needed	Skill Needed	Weight	Health	Value	Clip Count	Ammo	Attack Damage (DAM)	Critical Damage	Crit % Mult	Automatic	Min. Spread	Rate of Fire	Uses Sight	Action Points	Unique Weapon	Modifiable	Note and Upgrade Modifications
9mm Submachine Gun: Vance's Submachine Gun	One-Handed (Pistol)	1–3	25	4	600	1,500	60	9mm	13	13	1	Yes	1.5	13	No	0	Yes	No	Inside the safe, inside the Wins Hideout [1.S05].
Anti-Materiel Rifle	Two-Handed (Rifle)	6–8	100	20	95	5,600	8	.50MG	110	80	1	No	0.03	5	Yes	65	No	No	
Assault Carbine	Two-Handed (Automatic)	1–3	75	6	400	3,950	24	5mm	12	12	0.5	Yes	1.5	12	No	20	No	Yes (1)	1: Assault Carbine Extended Magazines: Increases ammunition capacity (+6).
BB Gun	Two-Handed (Rifle)	1	0	2	50	36	100	BB	4	4	1	No	0.5	3	No	28	No	No	
BB Gun: Abilene Kid LE BB Gun	Two-Handed (Rifle)	1	0	2	100	500	100	BB	4	70	1.5	No	0.5	3	No	28	Yes	No	Bonus Critical Damage, Bonus Critical Chance. Found lying on a shelf inside the Fields' Shack [3.04]. With Wild Wasteland Perk, this is found in Jimmy's Well. Speak with Rex to make the well appear.
Brush Gun	Two-Handed (Rifle)	4–6	100	5	150	4,900	6	.45-70G	75	75	1	No	0.03	1	No	23	No	Yes (1)	1: Brush Gun Forged Receiver: Increases condition (+50).
Caravan Shotgun	Two-Handed (Rifle)	1–3	25	3	140	675	2	20ga	45	6	1	No	4	2	No	27	No	No	
Cowboy Repeater	Two-Handed (Rifle)	2–4	25	5	120	800	7	.357 Mag.	32	32	1.25	No	0.04	1	No	20	No	Yes (3)	1: Cby. Rep. Custom Action: Increases rate of fire. 2: Cby. Rep. Long Tube: Increases ammunition capacity (+4). 3: Cby. Rep. Maple Stock: Decreases weight.
Cowboy Repeater: La Longue Carabine	Two-Handed (Rifle)	3–5	25	5	150	1,500	11	.357 Mag.	35	35	1.5	No	0.2	1	Yes	18	Yes	No	Carried by Corporal Sterling, member of the 1st Recon; Camp McCarran [2.19].
Hunting Revolver	One-Handed (Pistol)	4–6	75	4	110	3,500	5	.45-70G	58	58	1	No	0.35	0	Yes	32	No	No	
Hunting Rifle	Two-Handed (Rifle)	4–6	50	6	300	2,200	5	.308	45	45	1	No	0.03	1	Yes	60	No	Yes (3)	1: Hunting Rifle Custom Action: Increases rate of fire. 2: Hunting Rifle Extended Mag: Increases ammunition capacity (+5). 3: Hunting Rifle Scope: Adds long-range scope.
Hunting Shotgun	Two-Handed (Rifle)	3–5	75	7.5	125	3,800	5	12ga	70	10	1	No	1.5	1	No	32	No	Yes (2)	1: Hunting Shotgun Choke: Decreases spread. 2: Hunting Shotgun Long Tube: Increases ammunition capacity (+3).
Hunting Shotgun: Dinner Bell	Two-Handed (Rifle)	3–5	75	7.5	150	4,800	5	12ga	75	11	1	No	1.2	1	No	0	Yes	No	Inside the shack, at the Old Nuclear Test Site [6.23].
Lever-Action Shotgun	Two-Handed (Rifle)	2–4	50	3	100	2,000	5	20ga	48	7	1	No	1.9	5	No	30	No	No	
Light Machine Gun	Two-Handed (Automatic)	6–8	100	15	400	5,200	90	5.56mm	21	21	0	Yes	3.2	12	No	30	No	Yes (1)	1: Light MG Expanded Drums: Increases ammunition capacity (+110).
Marksman Carbine	Two-Handed (Automatic)	2–4	100	6	400	5,200	20	5.56mm	24	24	1	No	0.04	1	Yes	20	No	No	
Marksman Carbine: All-American	Two-Handed (Automatic)	2–4	100	6	400	5,900	24	5.56mm	26	26	1	No	0.04	1	Yes	20	Yes	No	Found in Armory of Vault 34 [3.12].
Minigun	Two-Handed (Handle)	8–10	100	25	800	5,500	240	5mm	12	12	0.5	Yes	2.3	20	No	30	No	Yes (2)	1: Minigun Damped Subframe: Reduces spread. 2: Minigun High-Speed Motor: Increases spread.
Minigun: CZ57 Avenger	Two-Handed (Handle)	8–10	100	18	700	8,500	120	5mm	14	12	0.5	Yes	1.1	30	No	30	Yes	No	Inside, at the back of the container trailer, by the dead body; in the Devil's Throat [3.10].
Ranger Sequoia	One-Handed (Pistol)	4–6	75	4	150	1,200	5	.45-70G	62	62	1.5	No	0.1	0	No	30	No	No	
Riot Shotgun	Two-Handed (Automatic)	5–7	100	5	150	5,500	12	12ga	67	10	1	No	3.5	3	No	30	No	No	
Sawed-Off Shotgun	One-Handed (Pistol)	2–4	50	4	80	1,950	2	12ga	100	7	0	No	7	1	No	37	No	No	
Sawed-Off Shotgun: Big Boomer	One-Handed (Pistol)	2–4	50	4	80	2,500	2	12ga	120	9	0	No	6	1	No	35	Yes	No	Carried by Old Lady Gibson; in Gibson Scrap Yard [5.14].
Service Rifle	Two-Handed (Automatic)	2	25	8.5	400	540	20	5.56mm	20	20	1	No	0.55	1	No	22	No	Yes (2)	1: Svc. Rifle Forged Receiver: Increases condition (+50%). 2: Svc. Rifle Upgraded Springs: Increases rate of fire.
Silenced .22 Pistol	One-Handed (Pistol)	1	0	3	100	80	16	22LR	9	9	1	No	0.5	1	No	17	No	No	
Silenced .22 SMG	Two-Handed (Automatic)	2	50	8	500	1,850	180	22LR	10	6	1	Yes	2	11	No	18	No	Yes (1)	1: Sil. SMG Exp. Drums: Increases ammunition capacity (+60).
Single Shotgun	Two-Handed (Rifle)	3–5	0	7	200	175	1	20ga	50	7	1	No	1.4	1	No	45	No	No	
Sniper Rifle	Two-Handed (Automatic)	4–6	75	8	80	4,100	5	.308	62	62	5	No	0.02	1	Yes	38	No	Yes (2)	1: Sniper Rifle Carbon Fiber Parts: Decreases weight (-5). 2: Sniper Rifle Suppressor: Reduces weapon noise.
Sniper Rifle: Gobi Campaign Scout Rifle	Two-Handed (Automatic)	4–6	75	4.5	160	6,200	6	.308	60	60	5	No	0.02	1	Yes	33	Yes	No	In the footlocker of the Sniper's Nest [6.18], overlooking Cottonwood Cove [6.20].

Name	Type	STR Needed	Skill Needed	Weight	Health	Value	Clip Count	Ammo	Attack Damage (DAM)	Critical Damage	Crit % Mult	Automatic	Min. Spread	Rate of Fire	Uses Sight	Action Points	Unique Weapon	Modifiable	Note and Upgrade Modifications
That Gun	One-Handed (Pistol)	4–6	50	5	225	1,750	5	5.56mm	18	18	2.5	No	0.5	1	Yes	19	Yes	No	On a shelf in the locked storage room inside the Dino Bite Gift Shop, in Novac [5.18].
This Machine	Two-Handed (Rifle)	4–6	75	9.5	600	2,800	8	.308	65	65	1	No	0.5	1	No	22	Yes	No	Rewarded by Contreras if you don't turn him in, at the end of Free Quest: Dealing with Contreras, Camp McCarran [2.19].
Trail Carbine	Two-Handed (Rifle)	3–5	75	5.5	500	3,900	8	.44 Mag.	45	45	1	No	0.04	1	Yes	21	No	Yes (1)	1: Trail Carbine Scope: Adds mid-range scope.
Varmint Rifle	Two-Handed (Rifle)	1–3	0	5.5	120	75	5	5.56mm	18	18	1	No	0.02	1	Yes	22	No	Yes (3)	1: Varmint Rifle Extended Mags: Increases ammunition capacity (+3). 2: Varmint Rifle Night Scope: Adds long-range night scope. 3: Varmint Rifle Silencer: Silences the weapon.
Varmint Rifle: Ratslayer	Two-Handed (Rifle)	1–3	0	4.5	200	2,000	8	5.56mm	23	23	5	No	0.02	1	Yes	45	Yes	No	Propped up against the desk, inside the Broc Flower Cave [5.30].
MELEE WEAPONS																			
9 Iron	Two-Handed (Melee)	2	25	3	60	55			17	17	1	No	0	0	No	22	No	No	Special V.A.T.S. Attack: Fore!
9 Iron: Nephi's Golf Driver	Two-Handed (Melee)	2	25	1	50	500			30	30	1.2	No	0	5	No	21	Yes	No	Special V.A.T.S. Attack: Fore! Carried by a Fiend named Driver Nephi, in his territory [2.S22].
Baseball Bat	Two-Handed (Melee)	2–4	25	3	400	250			22	22	1	No	0	0	No	25	No	No	Special V.A.T.S. Attack: Grand Slam.
Binoculars	One-Handed (Melee)	0	0	1.5	250	50			0	0	0	Yes	0	1	Yes	20	No	No	Scoped sight. You cannot attack when holding or using this.
Bumper Sword	Two-Handed (Melee)	6–8	50	12	300	2,500			32	32	1	No	0	1	No	38	No	No	Special V.A.T.S. Attack: Mauler.
Bumper Sword: Blade of the East	Two-Handed (Melee)	7–9	100	12	800	45			65	35	1	No	0	0	No	35	Yes	No	Special V.A.T.S. Attack: Mauler. HP -2(10s). Carried by Legate Lanius, in the Legate's Camp [3.34].
Cattle Prod	One-Handed (Melee)	2–4	75	3	500	450			5	5	2	No	0	1	No	28	No	No	Special V.A.T.S. Attack: Lights Out. Inflicts Fatigue Damage (KO).
Chainsaw	Two-Handed (Melee)	5–7	75	20	800	2,800			100	0	0	Yes	0	1	No	65	No	No	Special V.A.T.S. Attack: Scrap Heap.
Cleaver	One-Handed (Melee)	2	0	2	250	20			7	7	1	No	0	0	No	22	No	No	Special V.A.T.S. Attack: Back Slash. Bonus Limb Damage.
Cleaver: Chopper	One-Handed (Melee)	2	0	2	250	800			14	14	2	No	0	0	No	22	Yes	No	Special V.A.T.S. Attack: Back Slash. Bonus Limb Damage. Found on the stove of the Wolfhorn Ranch [6.14].
Combat Knife	One-Handed (Melee)	1–3	50	1	90	500			15	15	2	No	0	1	No	17	No	No	Special V.A.T.S. Attack: Back Slash. Bonus Critical Chance.
Combat Knife: Chance's Knife	One-Handed (Melee)	1–3	50	1	90	900			22	22	2	No	0	1	No	17	Yes	No	Special V.A.T.S. Attack: Back Slash. Bonus Critical Chance. Found in Chance's Grave [4.S01].
Dress Cane	One-Handed (Melee)	2	50	3	50	40			22	35	1	No	0	5	No	27	No	No	Special V.A.T.S. Attack: Lights Out.
Fire Axe	Two-Handed (Melee)	3–5	75	8	200	2,500			55	27	1	No	0	0	No	22	No	No	Special V.A.T.S. Attack: Mauler.
Fire Axe: Knock Knock	Two-Handed (Melee)	3–5	75	8	110	3,200			66	33	1	No	0	0	No	21	Yes	No	Special V.A.T.S. Attack: Mauler. Found in the restrooms on the upper floor of the Fire Station, in Camp Searchlight [6.16].
Hatchet	One-Handed (Melee)	2	25	2	300	75			16	16	1	No	0	0	No	22	No	No	Special V.A.T.S. Attack: Back Slash. Bonus Limb Damage.
Knife	One-Handed (Melee)	1	0	1	150	20			8	8	1	No	0	0	No	20	No	No	Special V.A.T.S. Attack: Back Slash.
Lead Pipe	One-Handed (Melee)	3–5	50	3	50	75			22	22	1	No	0	5	No	24	No	No	Special V.A.T.S. Attack: Lights Out.
Lead Pipe: The Humble Cudgel	One-Handed (Melee)	3–5	50	3	75	350			26	26	1	No	0	5	No	21	Yes	No	Special V.A.T.S. Attack: Lights Out. Found near the Prospector Corpse inside the Sealed Sewers [U2.?]
Machete	One-Handed (Melee)	1–3	25	2	50	50			11	11	1.5	No	0	0	No	20	No	No	Special V.A.T.S. Attack: Back Slash. Bonus Limb Damage.
Machete Gladius	One-Handed (Melee)	2–4	25	2	75	1,000			28	28	1.5	No	0	0	No	20	No	No	Special V.A.T.S. Attack: Back Slash. Bonus Limb Damage.
Machete: Liberator	One-Handed (Melee)	1–3	25	2	75	1,000			18	18	3	No	0	0	No	18	Yes	No	Special V.A.T.S. Attack: Back Slash. Bonus Limb Damage. Carried by Dead Sea, in Nelson [6.06].
Nail Board	Two-Handed (Melee)	5–7	25	4	60	250			25	25	0	No	0	1	No	27	No	No	Special V.A.T.S. Attack: Grand Slam.
Police Baton	One-Handed (Melee)	1	0	2	250	70			10	10	1	No	0	5	No	23	No	No	Special V.A.T.S. Attack: Lights Out.
Pool Cue	Two-Handed (Melee)	2	0	1	50	15			15	15	0	No	0	5	No	27	No	No	Special V.A.T.S. Attack: Grand Slam.
Rebar Club	Two-Handed (Melee)	7–9	50	9	250	500			42	24	0.5	No	0	1	No	40	No	No	Special V.A.T.S. Attack: Mauler.
Ripper	One-Handed (Melee)	1–3	75	6	600	1,200			30	0	0	Yes	0	1	No	65	No	No	Special V.A.T.S. Attack: Long Cut.
Rolling Pin	One-Handed (Melee)	2	0	1	100	10			3	8	0	No	0	1	No	24	No	No	Special V.A.T.S. Attack: Lights Out.

Name	Type	STR Needed	Skill Needed	Weight	Health	Value	Clip Count	Ammo	Attack Damage (DAM)	Critical Damage	Crit % Mult	Automatic	Min. Spread	Rate of Fire	Uses Sight	Action Points	Unique Weapon	Modifiable	Note and Upgrade Modifications
Shishkebab	One-Handed (Melee)	4–6	75	3	500	2,500			40	20	2	No	0	5	No	28	No	No	Special V.A.T.S. Attack: Back Slash. HP -2(5s).
Shovel	Two-Handed (Melee)	1–3	0	3	300	55			12	20	3	No	0	0	No	28	No	No	Special V.A.T.S. Attack: Grand Slam. Used to exhume graves.
Sledgehammer	Two-Handed (Melee)	5–7	50	12	150	130			24	24	1	No	0	1	No	38	No	No	Special V.A.T.S. Attack: Mauler.
Straight Razor	One-Handed (Melee)	1	0	1	75	35			5	10	2	No	0	1	No	18	No	No	Special V.A.T.S. Attack: Back Slash. Bonus Critical Damage, Bonus Critical Chance.
Straight Razor: Figaro	One-Handed (Melee)	1	0	1	90	400			8	16	4	No	0	1	No	17	Yes	No	Special V.A.T.S. Attack: Back Slash. Bonus Critical Damage, Bonus Critical Chance. Owned by Sergio, in the back of King's School of Impersonation [2C.05].
Super Sledge	Two-Handed (Melee)	6–8	100	20	100	5,800			70	35	1	No	0	0	No	38	No	No	Special V.A.T.S. Attack: Mauler.
Super Sledge: Oh, Baby!	Two-Handed (Melee)	6–8	100	20	100	6,200			80	40	1	No	0	0	No	35	Yes	No	Special V.A.T.S. Attack: Mauler. Found near a Chewed Stealth Boy in the deepest part of Charleston Cave [1.07].
Switchblade	One-Handed (Melee)	1	25	1	100	35			7	11	2	No	0	1	No	18	No	No	Special V.A.T.S. Attack: Back Slash.
Thermic Lance	Two-Handed (Melee)	5–7	100	20	800	5,500			100	0	0	Yes	0	1	No	65	No	No	Special V.A.T.S. Attack: Scrap Heap.
Throwing Hatchet	One-Handed (Thrown)	1	25	2	1,000	20			20	20	1	No	0	0	No	22	No	No	Ranged Weapon.
Throwing Knife	One-Handed (Thrown)	1	0	0.5	1,000	20			15	7	1	No	0	0	No	20	No	No	Ranged Weapon.
Throwing Spear	One-Handed (Thrown)	1	25	0.5	1,000	25			35	7	1	No	0	1	No	24	No	No	Ranged Weapon.
Tire Iron	One-Handed (Melee)	3	0	3	200	40			15	15	1	No	0	5	No	27	No	No	Special V.A.T.S. Attack: Lights Out.
UNARMED WEAPONS																			
Ballistic Fist	Hand-to-Hand (Melee)	7–9	100	6	80	7,800			80	80	1	No	0	5	No	28	No	No	Special V.A.T.S. Attack: Cross and Uppercut.
Bladed Gauntlet	Hand-to-Hand (Melee)	3–5	25	10	60	200			25	40	2	No	0	2	No	26	No	No	Special V.A.T.S. Attack: Cross and Uppercut. Bonus Critical Damage, Bonus Critical Chance.
Bladed Gauntlet: Cram Opener	Hand-to-Hand (Melee)	3–5	25	10	75	800			28	44	2	No	0	2	No	26	Yes	No	Special V.A.T.S. Attack: Cross and Uppercut. Owned by Little Buster, in Camp McCarran [2.19].
Boxing Gloves	Hand-to-Hand (Melee)	1	0	6	200	100			1	1	1	No	0	5	No	28	No	No	Special V.A.T.S. Attack: Cross and Uppercut. Inflicts Fatigue Damage (KO).
Boxing Gloves: Golden Gloves	Hand-to-Hand (Melee)	1	0	6	250	100			1	1	2	No	0	5	No	28	Yes	No	Special V.A.T.S. Attack: Cross and Uppercut. Inflicts Fatigue Damage (KO). On the upper bar of the Casino floor, inside the Lucky 38 Casino [2D.02].
Boxing Tape	Hand-to-Hand (Melee)	1	0	0.25	500	100			4	4	1	No	0	5	No	28	No	No	Special V.A.T.S. Attack: Cross and Uppercut. Inflicts Fatigue Damage (KO).
Brass Knuckles	Hand-to-Hand (Melee)	2	25	1	200	120			18	18	1	No	0	5	No	18	No	No	Special V.A.T.S. Attack: Cross and Uppercut.
Displacer Glove	Hand-to-Hand (Melee)	2–4	100	6	100	3,500			50	50	1	No	0	5	No	28	No	No	Special V.A.T.S. Attack: Cross and Uppercut.
Displacer Glove: Pushy	Hand-to-Hand (Melee)	2	100	6	120	4,200			60	60	1	No	0	5	No	28	Yes	No	Special V.A.T.S. Attack: Cross and Uppercut. On the body of a Jackal Gang member inside the Ruby Hill Mine [1.03].
DogTag Fist	Hand-to-Hand (Melee)	1	0	3	100	50			20	20	1	No	0	5	No	35	No	No	Special V.A.T.S. Attack: Cross and Uppercut.
DogTag Fist: Recompense of the Fallen	Hand-to-Hand (Melee)	1	0	3	150	250			25	25	1	No	0	5	No	35	Yes	No	Special V.A.T.S. Attack: Cross and Uppercut. Found in Aurelius' desk, on the upper floor of the main building in Cottonwood Cove [6.20].
Mantis Gauntlet	Hand-to-Hand (Melee)	2–4	75	10	50	150			30	30	3	No	0	2	No	22	No	No	Special V.A.T.S. Attack: Cross and Uppercut. Bonus Critical Chance.
Power Fist	Hand-to-Hand (Melee)	3–5	50	6	80	800			40	40	1	No	0	5	No	28	No	No	Special V.A.T.S. Attack: Cross and Uppercut.
Spiked Knuckles	Hand-to-Hand (Melee)	1–3	50	1	300	500			25	25	1	No	0	5	No	19	No	No	Special V.A.T.S. Attack: Cross and Uppercut.
Spiked Knuckles: Love and Hate	Hand-to-Hand (Melee)	1–3	50	1	300	750			30	30	1	No	0	5	No	19	Yes	No	Special V.A.T.S. Attack: Cross and Uppercut. Found on the Viper Gang Leader in Bonnie Springs [1.20].
Zap Glove	Hand-to-Hand (Melee)	2–4	75	6	100	5,200			35	35	1	No	0	5	No	28	No	No	Special V.A.T.S. Attack: Cross and Uppercut. EMP—Bonus Damage vs. Robots, Power Armor.
Zap Glove: Paladin Toaster	Hand-to-Hand (Melee)	2–4	75	6	80	6,800			41	41	1	No	0	5	No	28	Yes	No	Special V.A.T.S. Attack: Cross and Uppercut. EMP—Bonus Damage vs. Robots, Power Armor. Found near the body of the dead Prospector in Black Rock Cave [5.08].

PART II: AMMUNITION BREAK DOWN

Knowledge about the different ammunition types, and the variants of each type, is vital to your adventure. The following represents advanced know-how about the basic and craftable ammo you should attempt to construct, and recommendations on use. Your opinions may differ.

Ammunition for Guns

Ammo: .22 Long Rifle

Basic: Low damage but easily silenced. Best for soft targets, especially with a Sneak attack.

Hollow Point: Damage increased 75 percent, but triples target DT. Best ammo for Silenced .22 weapons, since you shouldn't be attacking armored targets with a .22 anyway!

Plinking: Damage decreased 15 percent, but cheap and available in bulk.

Advice: Completely useless if you have access to ANY OTHER GUN in the Mojave Wasteland.

Ammo: 5.56mm

Basic: Accurate at range, but still the lowest-damage Rifle round per shot until you get to late-adventure weapons such as the Marksman Carbine or Light Machine Gun.

Armor Piercing: Reduces damage by 5 percent overall but cuts target DT by 15.

Hollow Point: Increases damage by 75 percent but triples target DT.

(Military) Surplus: Triples weapon decay but gives 15 percent damage increase. Give these to Boone or Raul with the Marksman Carbine and they won't wear out. Otherwise they should be avoided.

.223: Reduces wear by 20 percent, decreases damage by 10 percent and reduces target DT by 8. Good for lightly-armored or unarmored targets with low HP, especially in rapid-fire 5.56mm weapons like the Light Machine Gun.

Advice: A good choice early or late in your adventure, but suffers midway through (when not all variants can be crafted). It is cheap and readily available if you have nothing better.

Ammo: 9mm

Basic: Low damage but commonly available. Weak against anything more than a lightly armored target.

Hollow Point: Increased damage by 75 percent, but triples target DT. Only really useful against soft targets.

+P: Damage increased 10 percent and reduces target DT by 2 at the cost of 20 percent more wear on the weapon.

Advice: +P is the saving grace here, especially used with the Unique Weapon Maria. Otherwise ditch this ammo type as soon as you can get a 10mm.

Ammo: 20ga

Basic: Larger spread, effective on soft targets at close range, but damage is split between 7 pellets, making armor penetration difficult.

Magnum: Damage increased 15 percent at the cost of 15 percent more wear on the weapon.

Slug: Reduces spread 35 percent, making it better for long range in a pinch, but still not as accurate as a Rifle or Pistol shot.

Advice: Pretty good as a close-quarters weapon early in your adventure, but after that it becomes less effective, unless you have the Shotgun Surgeon perk. Even then, the Hunting Rifle rapidly overtakes Shotguns for all-around effectiveness and utility.

Ammo: 10mm

Basic: Fast rate of fire with superior damage and similar accuracy to the 9mm. Good for light-medium armored targets.

Hollow Point: Damage increased 75 percent but triples target DT.

JHP Handload: Hybrid of basic and hollow point. Damage increased 65 percent but doubles target DT.

Advice: Load this ammo up for the best early- to mid-adventure backup weapons bar none.

Ammo: .357 Magnum

Basic: Good damage and accuracy at medium to long range.

Armor Piercing: Reduces damage by 5 percent overall but cuts target DT by 15.

Hollow Point: Increases damage by 75 percent but triples target DT.

.38 Special: Damage and wear decreased by 25 percent. Best for rapid-fire .357 weapons against lightly armored targets.

.357 JFP Handload: Damage increased 25 percent, target DT reduced by 3, and spread reduced by 20 percent. Best for sniping armored targets at range.

Advice: Good early on, but slower than the 10mm. The Pistol has limited usefulness once you have the Cowboy Repeater.

Ammo: 12 Gauge

Basic: Similar to 20 Gauge, but damage is increased across the board.

Magnum: Damage increased 15 percent at the cost of 15 percent more wear on the weapon.

Slug: Reduces spread 35 percent, making it better for long range in a pinch, but still not as accurate as a Rifle or Pistol shot.

Coin Shot: Identical to Basic, but cheaper to craft.

Bean Bag: Damages target fatigue by 250 but at 95 percent less HP damage. Good for stunning high-damage targets to buy yourself some time.

Advice: A good replacement for the 20ga mid-way through your adventure, but it suffers later, even with Shotgun Surgeon and a modded Shotgun.

Ammo: 5mm

Basic: Low damage, but associated with high-rate-of-fire weapons; best used for lightly armored targets with high HP or multiple light-armored targets.

Armor Piercing: Reduces damage by 5 percent overall but cuts target DT by 15.

Hollow Point: Increases damage by 75 percent but triples target DT.

Advice: This type works well with a modded Carbine for the added ammo capacity, but generally weak in the later adventure without a modded Minigun, which really requires a specific Character Archetype to use effectively.

Ammo: .44 Magnum

Basic: Good damage against all but the tougher targets, but generally more expensive and harder to come by.

Hollow Point: Increases damage by 75 percent but triples target DT.

SWC Hand Load: Damage increased by 20 percent and reduces target DT by 6; best ammo to use for this type if you can craft it.

Advice: Excellent if you can find a Trail Carbine early on, otherwise it gets eclipsed by the .308 and 10mm/That Gun.

Ammo: .308

Basic: Best all-around Rifle ammo type. Accurate at range and damage scales up quite well.

Armor Piercing: Reduces damage by 5 percent overall but cuts target DT by 15.

Hollow Point: Increases damage by 75 percent but triples target DT.

JSP Hand Load: Increases damage by 50 percent; best ammo to use if you can craft it.

Advice: The most versatile ammo type available, effective against the bulk of enemies you'll encounter. The Hunting Rifle is exceptional, and the Sniper Rifle is even better.

 Ammo: 12.7mm

Basic: Highest-damage Pistol ammo type available. This has a slower rate of fire but packs a serious punch; effective against almost any target.

Hollow Point: Increases damage by 75 percent but triples target DT. Good against light or medium armored targets with higher HP.

Advice: The low rate of fire hurts this ammo type and it doesn't deal as much damage as the 45-70. Weapons using this type are stuck in a sort of limbo between heavy Pistol and rapid-fire room clearer. Other guns do the job better by filling more roles.

 Ammo: .45-70 Government

Basic: Excellent damage against even the toughest targets, but ammo is more expensive and can be harder to find than almost any other type.

Hollow Point: Increases damage by 75 percent but triples target DT. Damage output is high enough to remain effective against all but the most heavily armored targets.

SWC Hand Load: Damage increased by 20 percent and DT reduced by 6 but weapon decay is tripled. Useful for sniping heavily armored targets.

Advice: This is a great ammo type; this is the end-game goal for any Gun specialist.

 Ammo: .50MG

Basic: Highest damage and most expensive ammo type of all, used only by the Anti-Materiel Rifle. Most effective against single targets with lots of HP, and all but the heaviest armor.

Armor Piercing: Reduces damage by 5 percent overall but cuts target DT by 15. Effective against the heaviest armors available.

Incendiary: Add a damage over time effect identical to the flamer, affected by the Pyromaniac perk. Otherwise deals damage like the Basic shot.

Match Hand Load: Increases damage by 15 percent and reduces weapon spread by 35 percent. Best ammo to use for this weapon if you can craft it.

Advice: Awesome if you have the patience for sniping, otherwise the 45-70 fills out the high-damage utility role. This ammo type is super heavy in Hardcore mode.

Other Ammunition Types

 Energy: All Types

Basic: Normal damage, normal wear on the weapon; best for general usage.

Bulk: Reduces wear and damage by 15 percent. Best for rapid fire weapons (RCW/ Gatling Laser, Laser Rifle, Laser Pistol) or for weak targets with plasma.

Over charge: Increased damage 25 percent at the cost of 50 percent extra wear on the weapon. Good in a pinch when regular laser weapons can't beat the target's DT or for light-armored targets with a plasma weapon.

Max charge: Increases damage 75 percent but wears out the weapon nearly 2.5 times as fast. Best in slow-firing weapons that pack a lot of punch where you generally can't afford to miss anyway.

 Ammo: Flamer

Basic: Low direct damage, but good damage over time. Best against lightly armored opponents but can be effective against hard targets given enough time.

Homemade: More readily available than basic fuel, but triples the wear on the weapon.

 Explosives: 25mm Grenade

Basic: Smaller area effect damage overall but generally effective against most targets due to the high rate of fire.

High Explosive: Increases damage by 35 percent; best ammo for this type.

 Explosives: 40mm Grenade

Basic: Moderate area effect damage and generally more effective against all targets but suffers from a lower rate of fire.

Incendiary: Adds the flamer damage-over-time effect. Best used as an opening shot to put enemies at an early disadvantage.

 Explosives: Missile

Basic: Good direct plus area-effect damage. Dangerous to the user in close quarters and suffers from a lower rate of fire.

High Explosive: Increases area of effect damage by 35 percent. Generally the best option when you have enough range to use it.

High Velocity: Increased speed on the Missile makes it easier to use on moving targets at range. Also allows you to drop two Missiles on a stationary target at once by firing a HE or Basic Missile and then quickly swapping in a HV Missile and immediately firing at the same target.

PART III: GEAR (ARMOR AND OUTFITS)

The next table profiles all of the different pieces of armor, clothing, hats, protective clothing, and glasses available from scavenging, on the corpses of those you kill, or bought from vendors. Here's what each table column displays:

Name: The name of the gear in question; usually what appears on your Pip-Boy.

Power Armor: Whether the item is Power Armor or not; and therefore whether it requires the Power Armor Training perk to wear.

DR/DT: This is the value of the Damage Resistance/Damage Threshold of the gear. As only DT has a number, it is the amount of damage you can expect the armor to absorb before the user suffers Hit Point loss.

Weight: How heavy the item is, adding to your Carry Weight.

Weight Class: A quick check to see how heavy the gear is, so you can see at a glance how encumbered you're likely to be (both wearing and/or carrying the gear).

Value: How much you can expect to sell the gear for, before any Barter bonuses are added.

Health: This is the "Hit Points" of the gear when in full Condition (CND). It shows how tough it is.

Size: This indicates how bulky the item is, which is strictly a visual cue so you can gauge how much your character is likely to change, looks-wise.

Quest: Whether the gear is a crucial part of a Main or Side Quest.

Unique: Whether there's only one, or in a few cases, very few of this particular item. If this is the case, the tasks needed to find it is listed in the Notes and Location sections.

Notes: Additional protection, Stat increases (or decreases), and information for Unique Items are noted here.

Location: Notes on where the Gear is predominantly found.

Name	Power Armor	DT/DR	Weight	Weight Class	Value	Health	Size	Quest	Unique	Notes	Location
ARMOR											
Gladiator Armor	No	19	15	Light	160	150	0	Yes	No	AGL -1	
Advanced Radiation Suit	No	6	7	Light	100	25	26	No	No	Rad. Res. +40	In the Inventory of the Enclave Scientist at Hoover Dam.
Brotherhood T-45d Power Armor	Yes	22	45	Heavy	4,500	1,000	32	No	No	STR +2, AGL -2, Rad. Res. +10	Hidden Valley
Brotherhood T-51b Power Armor	Yes	25	40	Heavy	5,200	2,000	0	No	No	STR +1, Rad. Res. +25	Hidden Valley
Caesar's Armor	No	5	3	Light	1,500	450	0	No	Yes	Survival +5, Speech +5	Worn by Caesar, at The Fort.
Chinese Stealth Armor	No	12	20	Light	500	100	0	No	Yes	Sneak +5	In the Toxic Waste Room of Hoover Dam Offices.
Combat Armor	No	15	25	Medium	6,500	400	27	No	No		
Combat Armor	No	15	25	Medium	6,500	400	27	No	No		
Combat Armor, Reinforced	No	17	25	Medium	8,000	650	0	No	No		
Combat Armor, Reinforced Mark 2	No	20	25	Medium	8,000	650	0	No	No		
Explorer's Gear	No	8	3	Light	50	100	25	No	Yes	Melee Weap. +2, Guns +2	Available from Orion Moreno south of Gun Runners.
Gannon Family Tesla Armor	Yes	26	45	Medium	8,200	400	30	No	Yes	Ener. Weap. +10, Rad. Res. +20	Available from Arcade Gannon.
Great Khan Armored Leather	No	8	7	Light	100	100	23	No	No		
Great Khan Simple Armor	No	5	7	Light	100	100	0	No	No		
Great Khan Soldier Armor	No	5	7	Light	100	100	0	No	No		
Great Khan Suit Armor	No	5	7	Light	100	100	0	No	No		
Legion Centurion Armor	No	18	35	Medium	800	450	0	No	No		
Legion Explorer Armor	No	4	10	Light	120	150	0	No	No		
Legion Praetorian Armor	No	12	12	Light	300	150	0	No	No		
Legion Prime Armor	No	8	15	Light	220	200	0	No	No		
Legion Recruit Armor	No	6	12	Light	200	180	26	No	No		
Legion Veteran Armor	No	10	16	Light	300	250	0	No	No		
Legion Vexillarius Armor	No	14	26	Medium	600	350	0	No	No		
Metal Armor	No	12	30	Heavy	1,100	100	25	No	No	AGL -1	
Metal Armor, Reinforced	No	16	30	Heavy	3,500	250	25	No	No	AGL -1	
NCR Bandoleer Armor	No	10	26	Medium	300	400	0	No	No		
NCR Face Wrap Armor	No	10	26	Medium	300	400	0	No	No		
NCR Mantle Armor	No	10	26	Medium	300	400	0	No	No		
NCR Military Police Armor	No	10	26	Medium	300	400	0	No	No		
NCR Ranger Combat Armor	No	20	30	Medium	7,500	600	0	No	No		
NCR Ranger Patrol Armor	No	15	25	Medium	390	500	27	No	No		
NCR Salvaged Power Armor	No	20	40	Heavy	3,000	1,000	31	No	No	No Power Armor Training Required, AGL -2	
NCR Trooper Armor	No	10	26	Medium	300	400	23	No	No		
Powder Gang Guard Armor	No	5	8	Light	100	100	0	No	No		
Raider Badlands Armor	No	4	15	Light	180	100	24	No	No		
Raider Blastmaster Armor	No	4	15	Light	180	100	26	No	No		
Raider Painspike Armor	No	4	15	Light	180	100	27	No	No		
Raider Psycho-Tic Helmet	No	1	3	Light	20	15	17	No	No		
Raider Sadist Armor	No	4	15	Light	180	100	25	No	No		
Recon Armor	No	17	20	Medium	7,200	400	0	No	No	Sneak +5	
Remnants Power Armor	Yes	28	45	Heavy	6,500	400	30	No	No	STR +1, Rad. Res. +15	Given from Daisy after completing Side Quest: For Auld Lang Syne.
Space Suit	No	10	7	Light	800	100	0	No	Yes	Rad. Res. +40	Found at the REPCONN Test Site.
T-45d Power Armor	Yes	22	45	Heavy	4,500	1,000	0	No	No	STR +2, AGL -2, Rad. Res. +10	
T-51b Power Armor	Yes	25	40	Heavy	5,200	2,000	27	No	No	STR +1, Rad. Res. +25	
Van Graff Combat Armor	No	16	25	Medium	6,500	400	0	Yes	Yes		Given by Gloria Van Graff during Side Quest: Birds of a Feather.
Vault 34 Security Armor	No	16	15	Light	70	100	0	No	No		
CLOTHING											
Ambassador Crocker's Suit	No	1	1	Light	6	100	0	No	Yes		Worn by Ambassador Crocker
Benny's Suit	No	1	3	Light	390	100	0	No	Yes	Barter +5, Speech +5	Worn by Benny
Boomer Flightsuit	No	4	1	Light	6	100	0	No	No		
Boomer Jumpsuit	No	4	1	Light	6	100	0	No	No		
Bounty Hunter Duster	No	6	3	Light	70	150	26	No	No	CHR +1, Guns +5	
Brahmin-Skin Outfit	No	/	2	Light	6	100	26	No	No	AGL +1, END +1	
Bright Brotherhood Robe	No	2	2	Light	6	100	0	No	No		
Brotherhood Elder's Robe	No	1	2	Light	8	100	0	No	Yes		Worn by Elder McNamara
Brotherhood Scribe Robe	No	2	2	Light	6	100	25	No	No		

Name	Power Armor	DT/DR	Weight	Weight Class	Value	Health	Size	Quest	Unique	Notes	Location
Caravaneer Outfit	No	2	15	Light	180	100	75	No	No		
Chained Prostitute Outfit	No	/	2	Light	390	400	0	No	No		
Civilian Engineer Jumpsuit	No	/	1	Light	6	100	0	No	No	Repair +5	
Dapper Gambler Suit	No	/	1	Light	6	100	0	No	No		
Dirty Pre-War Businesswear	No	/	2	Light	8	100	25	No	No	Speech +5	
Dirty Pre-War Casualwear	No	/	2	Light	6	100	25	No	No	AGL +1	
Dirty Pre-War Parkstroller Outfit	No	/	10	Light	5	100	23	No	No	AGL +1	
Dirty Pre-War Relaxedwear	No	/	5	Light	6	100	25	No	No	AGL +1	
Dirty Pre-War Spring Outfit	No	/	2	Light	5	100	23	No	No	AGL +1	
Exposed Prostitute Outfit	No	/	2	Light	390	400	0	No	No		
Fancy Gambler Suit	No	/	1	Light	6	100	0	No	No		
Field Hand Outfit	No	2	15	Light	180	100	0	No	No		
Followers Doctor Coat	No	/	2	Light	8	100	0	No	No	Science +5	
Followers Lab Coat	No	/	2	Light	16	95	0	No	Yes	Med. +10, Science +10	Worn by Julie Farkas.
Formal Wear	No	/	1	Light	120	25	0	No	No		
General Oliver's Uniform	No	/	1	Light	0	100	26	No	Yes	CHR +2, AP +20	Worn by General Lee Oliver.
Grimy Pre-War Businesswear	No	/	2	Light	6	100	25	No	No	Speech +5	
Handyman Jumpsuit	No	/	1	Light	6	100	26	No	No	Repair +5	
Jailhouse Rocker	No	2	1	Light	50	100	0	No	No		
Kings Outfit	No	1	1	Light	6	100	0	No	No		
Lab Technician Outfit	No	/	2	Light	8	100	27	No	No	Science +5	
Leather Armor	No	6	15	Light	160	150	26	No	No		
Leather Armor, Reinforced	No	10	15	Light	1,200	250	0	No	No		
Memphis Kid Outfit	No	/	1	Light	6	100	0	No	No		
Merc Adventurer Outfit	No	1	8	Light	50	100	24	No	No	Melee Weap. +2, Guns +2	
Merc Adventurer Outfit	No	3	8	Light	50	100	24	No	No	Melee Weap. +2, Guns +2	
Merc Charmer Outfit	No	1	8	Light	50	100	25	No	No	Melee Weap. +2, Guns +2	
Merc Charmer Outfit	No	3	8	Light	50	100	25	No	No	Melee Weap. +2, Guns +2	
Merc Grunt Outfit	No	1	8	Light	50	100	28	No	No	Melee Weap. +2, Guns +2	
Merc Grunt Outfit	No	3	8	Light	50	100	28	No	No	Melee Weap. +2, Guns +2	
Merc Troublemaker Outfit	No	1	8	Light	50	100	25	No	No	Melee Weap. +2, Guns +2	
Merc Troublemaker Outfit	No	3	8	Light	50	100	25	No	No	Melee Weap. +2, Guns +2	
Merc Veteran Outfit	No	1	8	Light	50	100	24	No	No	Melee Weap. +2, Guns +2	
NCR Engineer Jumpsuit	No	/	1	Light	6	100	26	No	No	Repair +5	
NCR Trooper Fatigues	No	2	26	Light	300	400	0	No	No		
Naughty Nightwear	No	/	1	Light	200	100	22	No	Yes	Speech +10, LCK +1	Purchased as a special item from Mick of Mick & Ralph's [2C.02].
Powder Gang Plain Outfit	No	/	3	Light	15	100	23	No	No		
Powder Gang Simple Outfit	No	/	3	Light	15	100	0	No	No		
Powder Gang Soldier Outfit	No	/	3	Light	15	100	0	No	No		
Pre-War Casualwear	No	/	2	Light	8	100	25	No	No		
Pre-War Parkstroller Outfit	No	/	2	Light	6	100	23	No	No	AGL +1	
Pre-War Relaxedwear	No	/	2	Light	8	100	25	No	No	AGL +1	
Pre-War Spring Outfit	No	/	2	Light	8	100	23	No	No	AGL +1	
President Kimball's Suit	No	/	2	Light	6	100	25	No	Yes	Speech +5	Worn by President Aaron Kimball.
Prospector Outfit	No	2	15	Light	180	100	0	No	No		
Prostitute Outfit	No	/	2	Light	390	400	0	No	No		
Radiation Suit	No	4	5	Light	60	15	26	No	No	Rad. Res. +30	
Ranger Casual Outfit	No	/	1	Light	6	100	0	No	No		
Ranger Red Scarf Outfit	No	/	1	Light	6	100	0	No	No		
Ranger Vest Outfit	No	/	1	Light	6	100	0	No	No		
Regulator Duster	No	/	3	Light	70	150	26	No	Yes	CHR +1, Guns +5	Worn by the Lonesome Drifter, at the Sunset Sarsaparilla Billboard [3.S21]
RobCo Jumpsuit	No	/	1	Light	6	100	26	No	No	Repair +5	
Roving Trader Outfit	No	/	2	Light	6	100	24	No	No	Barter +5	
Scientist Outfit	No	3	2	Light	8	100	27	No	No	Science +5	
Settler Outfit	No	2	15	Light	180	100	0	No	No		
Sexy Sleepwear	No	/	1	Light	6	100	22	No	No	CHR +1	
Shabby Gambler Suit	No	/	1	Light	6	100	0	No	No		
Sheriff's Duster	No	/	3	Light	35	150	0	No	No	CHR +1, Guns +5	
Slave Rags	No	/	1	Light	6	100	0	No	No		
Sleepwear	No	/	1	Light	10	100	22	No	No	CHR +1	

Name	Power Armor	DT/DR	Weight	Weight Class	Value	Health	Size	Quest	Unique	Notes	Location
Vault 11 Jumpsuit	No	1	1	Light	6	100	33	No	No	Melee Weap. +2, Speech +2	
Vault 19 Jumpsuit	No	/	1	Light	6	100	0	No	No	Melee Weap. +2, Speech +2	
Vault 21 Jumpsuit	No	/	1	Light	6	100	33	No	No	Melee Weap. +2, Speech +2	
Vault 22 Jumpsuit	No	/	1	Light	6	100	0	No	No	Melee Weap. +2, Speech +2	
Vault 24 Jumpsuit	No	/	1	Light	6	100	0	No	No	Melee Weap. +2, Speech +2	
Vault 3 Jumpsuit	No	/	1	Light	6	100	0	No	No	Melee Weap. +2, Speech +2	
Vault 3 Utility Jumpsuit	No	/	1	Light	10	100	0	No	No	Lockpick +5, Repair +5	
Vault 34 Jumpsuit	No	/	1	Light	6	100	0	No	No	Melee Weap. +2, Speech +2	
Vault Lab Uniform	No	/	1	Light	6	100	29	No	No	Science +5	
Viva Las Vegas	No	5	1	Light	6	100	0	No	Yes		Worn by the King.
Wasteland Doctor Fatigues	No	/	2	Light	6	100	28	No	No	Med. +5	
Wasteland Settler Outfit	No	2	2	Light	6	100	23	No	No	AGL +1, END +1	
Wasteland Surgeon Outfit	No	/	2	Light	6	100	28	No	No	Med. +5	
Wasteland Wanderer Outfit	No	2	2	Light	6	100	34	No	No	AGL +1, END +1	
Well-Heeled Gambler Suit	No	/	1	Light	6	100	0	No	No		
White Glove Society Attire	No	/	1	Light	120	25	0	No	No		
HEADGEAR											
Authority Glasses	No	/	0	Light	6	100	0	No	No	PER +2	
1st Recon Beret	No	/	1	Light	40	50	0	No	Yes	PER +1, Crit. Chan. +5	Given to you by Craig Boone, in Novac [5.18].
Apocalypse Gladiator Helmet	No	5	3	Light	70	75	15	No	No		
Ballcap with Glasses	No	/	1	Light	30	100	0	No	No	PER +1	
Boomers Cap	No	/	1	Light	8	15	11	No	No	PER +1	
Boomers Hat	No	/	1	Light	8	15	12	No	No	PER +1	
Boomers Helmet	No	1	1	Light	8	15	11	No	No	PER +1	
Bandana	No	/	1	Light	6	10	11	No	No	PER +1	
Beret	No	/	0.1	Light	25	100	0	No	No		
Biker Goggles	No	/	1	Light	6	10	9	No	No		
Boone's Beret	No	/	0.1	Light	40	50	0	Yes	Yes		Worn by Craig Boone.
Caleb McCaffery's Hat	No	/	0	Light	0	100	17	Yes	Yes		Worn by Caleb McCaffery.
Cattleman Cowboy Hat	No	/	1	Light	8	15	17	No	No	PER +1	
Centurion Helmet	No	5	3	Light	70	50	0	No	No		
Combat Helmet	No	3	3	Light	800	50	12	No	No		
Combat Helmet, Reinforced	No	4	3	Light	1,000	50	0	No	No		
Combat Helmet, Reinforced Mark 2	No	5	2.5	Light	1,500	100	0	No	No		
Construction Hat	No	2	3	Light	50	50	0	No	No		
Dapper Gambler Hat	No	/	1	Light	8	15	0	No	No	PER +1	
Desperado Cowboy Hat	No	/	1	Light	8	15	20	No	No	PER +1	
Destroyed Collar	No	/	5	Light	1	1	0	Yes	Yes		Found on a dead man in Freeside.
Destroyed Party Hat	No	/	1	Light	5	10	10	No	No		
Enclave Officer Hat	No	/	1	Light	6	15	13	No	No	Ener. Weap +5	
Explorer Hood	No	1	2	Light	15	50	0	No	No		
Eyeglasses	No	/	0	Light	8	150	6	No	No	PER +2	
Fancy Gambler Hat	No	/	1	Light	8	15	0	No	No	PER +1	
Fiend Battle Helmet	No	1	1	Light	6	15	20	No	No	PER +1	
Fiend Helmet	No	1	1	Light	6	15	0	No	No	PER +1	
Fiend Warrior Helmet	No	1	1	Light	6	15	21	No	No	PER +1	
Fire Helmet	No	2	1	Light	10	100	0	No	No		
Gannon Family Tesla Helmet	Yes	6	5	Light	120	100	19	No	Yes	CHR -1, Rad. Res. +5	Available from Arcade Gannon.
General Oliver's Cap	No	/	1	Light	8	15	12	No	Yes	PER +1	Worn by General Lee Oliver.
Goggles Helmet	No	2	3	Light	50	50	0	No	No		
Great Khan Spike Helmet	No	2	1	Light	8	15	11	No	No		
Head Wrap	No	/	0	Light	0	10	16	No	No		
Hockey Mask	No	1	1	Light	10	15	11	No	No	Unarmed +5	
Jessup's Bandana	No	/	1	Light	6	10	0	No	Yes	Unique Item. PER +1	Worn by Jessup the Great Khan.
Legate Helmet	No	4	2	Light	250	100	0	No	Yes		Worn by Legate Lanius, the Beast from the East.
MP Trooper Helmet	No	2	3	Light	50	50	0	No	No		
Metal Helmet	No	3	3	Light	200	50	15	No	No		

Name	Power Armor	DT/DR	Weight	Weight Class	Value	Health	Size	Quest	Unique	Notes	Location
Metal Helmet, Reinforced	No	4	3	Light	280	150	20	No	No		
Motor-Runner's Helmet	No	2	1	Light	8	15	0	Yes	No	Melee Weap. +5, PER +1	
Motorcycle Helmet	No	2	1	Light	6	10	14	No	No		
Old Cowboy Hat	No	/	1	Light	8	15	16	No	No	PER +1	
Papa Khan Helmet	No	/	0	Light	0	100	0	No	Yes		Worn by Papa Khan.
Party Hat	No	/	1	Light	5	10	10	No	Yes		Find 10 in a storage room, inside REPCONN Headquarters top-floor Research laboratory.
Police Hat	No	/	1	Light	8	150	15	No	No		
Pre-War Baseball Cap	No	/	1	Light	8	15	12	No	No	PER +1	
Pre-War Bonnet	No	/	1	Light	8	15	26	No	No	PER +1	
Pre-War Hat	No	/	1	Light	8	15	14	No	No	PER +1	
Prime Decanus Helmet	No	2	3	Light	110	50	0	No	No		
Prime Helmet	No	2	3	Light	80	50	0	No	No		
Raider Arclight Helmet	No	1	3	Light	20	15	13	No	No		
Raider Blastmaster Helmet	No	1	3	Light	20	15	20	No	No	Guns +5, Explos. +5	
Raider Wastehound Helmet	No	1	3	Light	20	15	21	No	No		
Ranger Battle Helmet	No	3	5	Light	60	50	12	No	No		
Ranger Brown Hat	No	/	1	Light	30	100	17	No	No		
Ranger Grey Hat	No	/	1	Light	30	100	17	No	No		
Ranger Hat	No	/	0	Light	0	100	15	No	No		
Ranger Helmet	No	4	0	Light	0	100	0	No	No		
Ranger Tan Hat	No	/	1	Light	30	100	15	No	No		
Rattan Cowboy Hat	No	/	1	Light	8	15	16	No	No	PER +1	
Rawhide Cowboy Hat	No	/	1	Light	8	15	0	No	No	PER +1	
Reading Glasses	No	/	0	Light	12	150	5	No	No	PER +2	
Rebreather	No	3	0	Light	50	50	14	Yes	Yes	Water Breathing	Given to you by Loyal, the Boomer.
Recon Armor Helmet	No	2	3	Light	40	40	14	No	No		
Recruit Decanus Helmet	No	2	3	Light	90	50	0	No	No		
Recruit Helmet	No	2	3	Light	70	50	0	No	No		
Remnants Power Helmet	Yes	8	5	Light	2,800	75	19	No	No	CHR -1, Rad. Res. +5	
Roving Trader Hat	No	/	1	Light	6	10	13	No	No	Barter +5	
Salvaged Power Helmet	No	4	5	Light	1,200	75	0	No	No		
Shady Hat	No	/	1	Light	40	50	14	No	No	Sneak +5, PER +1	
Sheriff's Hat	No	/	1	Light	35	40	0	No	No	PER +1	
Slave Scarf	No	/	1	Light	8	15	0	No	No	PER +1	
Space Suit Helmet	No	4	0	Light	200	10	0	No	Yes		Found at the REPCONN Test Site.
Stormchaser Hat	No	/	1	Light	6	10	16	No	No	PER +1	
Stylish Gambler Hat	No	/	1	Light	8	15	0	No	No	PER +1	
Suave Gambler Hat	No	/	1	Light	8	15	0	No	No	PER +1	
Sunglasses	No	/	0	Light	8	150	6	No	No	PER +2	
T-45d Power Helmet	Yes	5	5	Light	1,300	75	19	No	No	Rad. Res. +3	
T-51b Power Helmet	Yes	/	4	Light	2,000	100	19	No	No	CHR +1, Rad. Res. +8	
Tinted Reading Glasses	No	/	0	Light	12	150	5	No	No	PER +2	
Tortoiseshell Glasses	No	/	0	Light	8	150	6	No	No	PER +2	
Trooper Helmet	No	2	3	Light	50	50	0	No	No		
Tuxedo Hat	No	/	1	Light	8	15	15	No	No	PER +1	
Vance's Lucky Hat	No	/	1	Light	8	15	0	No	Yes	PER +1	Found at the Wins Hideout.
Vault 34 Security Helmet	No	3	3	Light	30	25	13	No	No		
Veteran Decanus Helmet	No	3	3	Light	150	50	0	No	No		
Veteran Helmet	No	3	3	Light	100	50	0	No	No		
Vexillarius Helmet	No	1	3	Light	250	30	0	No	No		
Vikki's Bonnet	No	/	1	Light	8	15	0	No	Yes	PER +1	Found at the Wins Hideout.
Welding Helmet	No	2	3	Light	20	15	0	No	No		
Well-Heeled Gambler Hat	No	/	1	Light	8	15	14	No	No	PER +1	
White Glove Society Mask	No	/	1	Light	10	15	0	No	No		

PART IV: AID (INGESTIBLES)

The last table details all of the different items that appear in your Pip-Boy's Aid Menu. They are known as "ingestibles" (you eat or drink them). Here's what the following information all means:

Name: The item's name. Note the chart is separated into Food and Drink, Alcohol, Chems, and Magazines and More.

Weight (Wt.): How much the item adds to your Carry Weight.

Value (Val.): How much you can expect to sell the item for, before any Barter bonuses are added.

Quest Item (Q.I.): Whether this item is important (and usually critical) for a Main or Side Quest.

Poison (Poi.): Whether this is actually a poison, and should be applied to a Melee or Unarmed Weapon. Don't eat it!

Addictive (Ad.): Whether this causes a chance of addiction each time you consume it.

Craftable: Whether this item can be created on a campfire (or bench).

Harvestable (Har.): Whether this item can be plucked from a dead animal, or a plant dotted around the Mojave Wasteland.

Notes and Effects: This lists was initial benefits or problems the item causes when consumed.

Name	Wt.	Val.	Q.I.	Poi.	Ad.	Craftable	Har.	Effects
				FOOD AND DRINK				
Ant Egg	1	4	No	No	No		Yes	Rads +1, HP +3 (5s)
Ant Meat	1	4	No	No	No		Yes	Rads +1, HP +3 (5s)
Atomic Cocktail	1	25	No	No	No	Recipe	No	Ener. Resis. +75, Fire Resis. +75, Rads +2
Banana Yucca Fruit	0.5	6	No	No	No	Ingredient	Yes	HP +3 (7s)
Barrel Cactus Fruit	0.2	5	No	No	No	Ingredient	Yes	END -3, HP +3 (5s)
Bighorner Meat	1	5	No	No	No	Ingredient	Yes	Rads +1, HP +3 (15s)
Bighorner Steak	0.8	5	No	No	No	Recipe	No	STR +3, Rads +1, HP +7 (10s)
Blamco Mac & Cheese	1	5	No	No	No		No	Rads +1, HP +3 (5s)
Bloatfly Meat	0.25	4	No	No	No	Ingredient	Yes	Rads +1, HP +3 (5s)
Bloatfly Slider	0.5	4	No	No	No	Recipe	No	Rads +1, HP +10 (15s)
Blood Pack	1	5	No	No	No		No	HP +5 (5s)
Brahmin Meat	1	5	No	No	No		Yes	Rads +1, HP +3 (15s)
Brahmin Steak	0.8	5	No	No	No	Recipe	No	STR +3, Rads +1, HP +7 (15s)
Brahmin Wellington	0.8	5	No	No	No		No	HP +18 (10s)
Broc Flower	0.01	3	No	No	No	Ingredient	Yes	HP +3 (4s)
Bubblegum	1	1	No	No	No		No	Rads +1, HP +1
Buffalo Gourd Seed	0.02	2	No	No	No	Ingredient	Yes	HP +3 (2s)
Cactus Water	1	3	No	No	No	Recipe	No	HP +7 (5s)
Caravan Lunch	2.5	5	No	No	No	Recipe	No	Rads -2 (10s), HP +10 (15s)
Cave Fungus	1	50	No	No	No	Ingredient	Yes	Rads -5, HP +3 (4s)
Cazador Egg	1	4	No	No	No	Ingredient	Yes	Rads +1, HP +3 (4s)
Cook-Cook's Fiend Stew	1	25	No	No	No		No	STR +3, HP +7 (1m)
Coyote Meat	1	4	No	No	No	Ingredient	Yes	Rads +1 (3s), HP +3 (8s)
Coyote Steak	1	4	No	No	No	Recipe	No	Rads +1 (3s), HP +7 (12s)
Cram	1	5	No	No	No	Ingredient	No	Rads +1, HP +3 (5s)
Dandy Boy Apples	1	5	No	No	No		No	Rads +1, HP +3 (5s)
Desert Salad	0.2	5	No	No	No	Recipe	No	HP +25 (15s)
Dog Meat	1	4	No	No	No	Ingredient	Yes	Rads +1, HP +3 (8s)
Dog Steak	1	4	No	No	No	Recipe	No	Rads +1, HP +7 (10s)
Fancy Lads Snacks	1	5	No	No	No		No	Rads +1, HP +3 (5s)
Fire Ant Egg	1	4	No	No	No		Yes	Rads +1, HP +3 (5s)
Fire Ant Fricassée	1	30	No	No	No	Recipe	No	HP +3 (1m)
Fire Ant Meat	1	6	No	No	No	Ingredient	Yes	Rads +1, HP +3 (5s)
Fresh Apple	1	5	No	No	No	Ingredient	No	HP +3 (7s)
Fresh Carrot	1	5	No	No	No		No	HP +3 (7s)
Fresh Pear	1	5	No	No	No	Ingredient	No	HP +3 (7s)
Fresh Potato	1	5	No	No	No		No	HP +3 (9s)
Gecko Kabob	0.25	4	No	No	No	Recipe	No	Rads +1, HP +3 (40s)
Gecko Meat	1	4	No	No	No	Ingredient	Yes	STR -3, Rads +1, HP +3 (5s)
Gecko Steak	1	5	No	No	No	Recipe	No	Rads +1, HP +7 (15s)
Giant Rat Meat	1	4	No	No	No		Yes	Rads +1, HP +3 (5s)
Grilled Mantis Leg	1	8	No	No	No	Recipe	No	Rads +1, HP +3 (30s)
Gum Drops	1	2	No	No	No	Ingredient	No	Rads +1, HP +3
Honey Mesquite Pod	0.1	5	No	No	No	Ingredient	Yes	HP +3 (4s)
Human Flesh	1	1	No	No	No		No	Rads +2, HP +3 (5s)
Iguana Bits	1	5	No	No	No		No	Rads +1, HP +3 (5s)
Iguana on a Stick	1	5	No	No	No		No	Rads +1, HP +3 (12s)
InstaMash	1	5	No	No	No	Ingredient	No	Rads +1, HP +3 (5s)
Irradiated Banana Yucca	1	3	No	No	No		No	Rads +2, HP +3 (7s)
Irradiated Barrel Cactus	1	2	No	No	No		No	END -3, Rads +2, HP +3 (5s)
Irradiated Cram	1	2	No	No	No		No	Rads +2, HP +3 (5s)
Irradiated Crunchy Mutfruit	1	2	No	No	No		No	Rads +2, HP +3 (5s)
Irradiated Dandy Boy Apples	1	2	No	No	No		No	Rads +2, HP +3 (5s)
Irradiated Fancy Lads	1	2	No	No	No		No	Rads +2, HP +3 (5s)
Irradiated Gecko Meat	1	2	No	No	No		No	Rads +2, HP +3 (5s)
Irradiated InstaMash	1	2	No	No	No		No	Rads +2, HP +3 (5s)
Irradiated Mac & Cheese	1	2	No	No	No		No	Rads +2, HP +3 (5s)
Irradiated Mutfruit	1	2	No	No	No		No	Rads +2, HP +3 (5s)
Irradiated Pork N' Beans	1	2	No	No	No		No	Rads +2, HP +3 (5s)
Irradiated Potato	1	2	No	No	No		No	Rads +2, HP +7 (5s)
Irradiated Potato Crisps	1	2	No	No	No		No	Rads +2, HP +3 (5s)
Irradiated Salisbury Steak	1	2	No	No	No		No	Rads +2, HP +3 (5s)
Irradiated Sunset Sarsaparilla	1	0	No	No	No		No	HP +2 (25s), Rads +4
Irradiated Sugar Bombs	1	2	No	No	No		No	AP +15, Rads +2, HP +3 (7s)
Irradiated Water	1	5	No	No	No		No	H20 -171, Rads +3, HP +7 (5s)
Irradiated YumYum Devil Eggs	1	2	No	No	No		No	Rads +2, HP +3 (5s)
Jalapeño Pepper	0.02	5	No	No	No	Ingredient	Yes	HP +3 (5s)
Junk Food	1	5	No	No	No		No	Rads +1, HP +3 (5s)
Lakelurk Egg	1	4	No	No	No		Yes	Rads +1, HP +3 (5s)
Lakelurk Meat	1	12	No	No	No		No	Rads +1, HP +7 (10s)
Maize	0.25	5	No	No	No	Ingredient	Yes	HP +3 (9s)
Mole Rat Meat	1	4	No	No	No	Ingredient	Yes	Rads +1, HP +3 (5s)
Mole Rat Stew	1	25	No	No	No	Recipe	No	STR +3, HP +7 (30s)
Mole Rat Wonder Meat	1	20	No	No	No		No	Rads +1, HP +7 (10s)
Mushroom Cloud	1	50	No	No	No	Recipe	No	AP +9, HP +10 (20s)
Mutfruit	1	5	No	No	No	Ingredient	No	Rads +1, HP +3 (5s)
Crunchy Mutfruit	1	5	No	No	No		No	Rads +1, HP +3 (5s)
Nevada Agave Fruit	0.2	3	No	No	No		Yes	HP +3 (8s)
Nightstalker Tail	1	18	No	No	No		Yes	Rads +1, HP +3 (5s)
Noodles	1	5	No	No	No		No	Rads +1, HP +3 (5s)
Nuka-Cola	1	20	No	No	No	Ingredient	No	Rads +1, HP +2 (20s)
Nuka-Cola (Ice Cold)	1	20	No	No	No		No	Rads +1, HP +4 (20s)
Nuka-Cola Quartz	1	40	No	No	No		No	Low-Light Vision, DT +6, HP +10 (20s), Rads +2
Nuka-Cola Victory	1	75	No	No	No	Ingredient	No	HP +10 (20s), AP +30, PER -3, Rads +2
Pinto Bean Pod	0.05	0	No	No	No	Ingredient	Yes	HP +3 (3s)
Pinyon Nuts	0.03	5	No	No	No	Ingredient	No	HP +3 (5s)
Pork N' Beans	1	5	No	No	No	Ingredient	No	Rads +1, HP +3 (5s)
Potato Crisps	1	5	No	No	No		No	Rads +1, HP +3 (5s)
Prickly Pear Fruit	0.07	1	No	No	No	Ingredient	Yes	HP +3 (10s)
Ruby's Casserole	1	5	No	No	No		No	Rads +1, HP +3 (30s)
Radroach Meat	1	2	No	No	No		Yes	Rads +2, HP +3 (5s)
Radroach Meat	1	4	No	No	No		Yes	Rads +3, HP +3 (5s)
Rat Meat	1	2	No	No	No		Yes	Rads +1, HP +3 (5s)
Rum & Nuka	1	20	No	No	No		No	STR +1, Rads +1
Salisbury Steak	1	5	No	No	No		No	Rads +1, HP +3 (5s)

Name	Wt.	Val.	Q.I.	Poi.	Ad.	Craftable	Har.	Effects
Spore Plant Pods	1	0	No	No	No		Yes	Pois. Res. +75, HP +14 (6s)
Crispy Squirrel Bits	1	5	No	No	No		No	Rads +1, HP +3 (5s)
Squirrel Stew	1	5	No	No	No		No	Rads +1, HP +3 (5s)
Squirrel on a Stick	1	5	No	No	No		No	Rads +1, HP +3 (5s)
Strange Meat	1	2	No	No	No		No	Rads +1, HP +3 (5s), only eaten by Cannibals
Strange Meat Pie	1	2	No	No	No		No	Rads +1, HP +1 (5s)
Strange Meat Pie (Imitation)	1	2	No	No	No		No	Rads +1, HP +1 (5s)
Sugar Bombs	1	5	No	No	No	Ingredient	No	AP +15, Rads +1, HP +3 (7s)
Sunset Sarsaparilla	1	0	No	No	No		No	HP +2 (25s)
Trail Mix	3	5	No	No	No	Recipe	No	Rads +1, AP +15, HP +18 (15s)
Purified Water	1	20	No	No	No	Recipe	No	HP +7 (5s)
Dirty Water	1	10	No	No	No	Ingredient	No	Rads +1, HP +7 (5s)
Wasteland Omelet	1	100	No	No	No		No	HP +14 (1m)
White Horsenettle	0.02	2	No	No	No	Ingredient	Yes	END -3, HP +3 (5s), AGL -3
Xander Root	0.02	0	No	No	No	Ingredient	Yes	HP +3 (4s)
YumYum Deviled Eggs	1	5	No	No	No		No	Rads +1, HP +3 (5s)
ALCOHOL								
Absinthe	1	20	No	No	Yes		No	CHR +3, PER +3
Beer	1	2	No	No	Yes	Ingredient	No	CHR +3, STR +3
Irradiated Beer	1	1	No	No	Yes		No	Rads +2, CHR +3, STR +3
Irradiated Scotch	1	5	No	No	Yes		No	Rads +2, CHR +3, STR +3
Irradiated Whiskey	1	5	No	No	Yes		No	Rads +2, CHR +3, STR +3
Jake Juice	1	10	No	No	Yes		No	CHR +3, STR +3
Moonshine	1	20	No	No	Yes		No	CHR +2, STR +2
Scotch	1	10	No	No	Yes		No	CHR +3, STR +3
Vodka	1	20	No	No	Yes	Ingredient	No	CHR +3, STR +3
Whiskey	1	10	No	No	Yes	Ingredient	No	DT +6, HR +3, STR +3
Dixon's Whiskey	1	10	No	No	Yes		No	STR +3
Wine	1	10	No	No	Yes	Ingredient	No	CHR +2, STR +2
Drugged Wine	1	10	Yes	No	Yes		No	CHR +3, INT -3, STR +3, Quest Item in Side Quest: Beyond the Beef.
CHEMS								
Ant Nectar	0.25	20	No	No	Yes		Yes	STR +4, CHR -2, INT -2
Ant Queen Pheromones	1	75	No	No	No		Yes	PER -3, INT -3, CHR +3
Antivenom	0	25	No	No	No	Recipe	No	Cures Animal Poison
Bitter Drink	0	0	No	No	No		No	HP +7 (18s)
Bleak Venom	0.5	0	No	Yes	No	Recipe	No	HP -15 (10s)
Buffout	0	20	No	No	Yes		No	HP +60, END +3, STR +2
Cateye	0	20	No	No	No		No	Low-Light Vision
Coyote Tobacco Chew	0.01	1	No	No	Yes		Yes	PER +1, AGL +1
Doctor's Bag	1	55	No	No	No	Recipe	No	Restore All Body Parts
Fixer	0	20	No	No	No		No	Temporary Addiction Removal
Healing Powder	0.03	5	No	No	No	Recipe	No	PER -3, HP +3 (18s)
Leg. Healing Powder	0	0	No	No	No		No	PER -3, HP +10 (27s)
Jet	0	20	No	No	Yes	Ingredient	No	AP +15
Dixon's Jet	0	5	No	No	Yes		No	AP +10
Human Remains	1	0	No	No	No		No	HP +7 (5s)
Hydra	0	55	No	No	Yes	Recipe	No	Restore Limb Condition
Mentats	0	20	No	No	Yes	Ingredient	No	CHR +1, PER +2, INT +2
Med-X	0	20	No	No	Yes		No	Dam. Res. +25
Medical Supplies	10	55	Yes (SQ)	No	No		No	Restore All Body Parts. Only used during Main Quest: Et Tumor, Brute?
Mother Darkness	0.5	0	No	Yes	No	Recipe	No	AGL -3 (1m), PER -3 (1m), HP -8 (10s)
Party Time Mentats	0	20	No	No	Yes	Recipe	No	CHR +5, PER +2, INT +2
Psycho	0	20	No	No	Yes	Ingredient	No	Damage +25%
Rad-X	0	20	No	No	No		No	Rad. Res. +75
RadAway	0	20	No	No	No	Ingredient	No	Rads -180
Rebound	0	20	No	No	Yes		No	Regenerate AP
Rocket	0	20	No	No	Yes	Recipe	No	AP +30
Silver Sting	0.5	0	No	Yes	No	Recipe	No	STR -2 (1m), HP -8 (10s)
Slasher	0	20	No	No	Yes	Recipe	No	Damage +25%, Dam. Res. +25
Steady	0	20	No	No	Yes		No	Weapon Spread Reduced
Stealth Boy	1	100	No	No	No		No	Stealth Field +75, Sneak +100
Stimpak	0	25	No	No	No	Ingredient/ Recipe	No	HP +129
Super Stimpak	0	100	No	No	No	Recipe	No	Super Stimpak Debuff, HP +259
Tremble	0.5	0	No	Yes	No	Recipe	No	Guns -50 (20s), Explos. -50 (20s), Melee Weap. -50 (20s), Ener. Weap. -50 (20s), HP -2 (20s)
Turbo	0	20	No	No	Yes		No	Turbo +2
Ultrajet	0	50	No	No	Yes		No	AP +40
MAGAZINES AND MORE								
Boxing Times	0	20	No	No	No		No	Unarmed +20
Fixin' Things	0	20	No	No	No		No	Repair +20
Future Weapons Today	0	20	No	No	No		No	Ener. Weap. +20
Lad's Life	0	20	No	No	No		No	Survival +20
Locksmith's Reader	0	20	No	No	No		No	Lockpick +20
Meeting People	0	20	No	No	No		No	Speech +20
Milsurp Review	0	20	No	No	No		No	Guns +20
Patriot's Cookbook	0	20	No	No	No		No	Explos. +20
Programmer's Digest	0	20	No	No	No		No	Science +20
Salesman Weekly	0	20	No	No	No		No	Barter +20
Tæles of Chivalrie	0	20	No	No	No		No	Melee Weap. +20
Today's Physician	0	20	No	No	No		No	Med. +20
True Police Stories	0	20	No	No	No		No	Crit. Chan. +20
¡La Fantoma!	0	20	No	No	No		No	Sneak +20
NCR Emergency Radio	0	0	Yes	No	No		No	Unique Item, awarded by NCR: Free Quest: Emergency Radio Waves.
Weapon Repair Kit	1	20	No	No	No	Recipe	No	Repairs Current Weapon

Plant Life

Here are some locations where multiple plants have been spotted clumped together (bear in mind there are plenty more areas to search):

Plant Name	General Locations
Banana Yucca	[1.03] Ruby Hill Mine; along the road.
	[3.05] Around Raul's Shack.
Barrel Cactus	[1.05] Griffin Wares Sacked Caravan; surrounding terrain.
	[3.15] Coyote Tail Ridge; surrounding terrain.
Broc Flower	[3.08] Bitter Springs; rocky terrain to the northeast.
	[5.30] Broc Flower Cave; exterior surroundings.
Buffalo Gourd Seed	The cracks in the major roads throughout the Wasteland.
Cave Fungus	Very rare; try vendors or [1.09] Vault 22.
Coyote Tobacco	[3.08] Bitter Springs; rocky terrain to the northeast.
Honey Mesquite Pod	[1.20] Bonnie Springs; the area to the north.
	[3.09] Ranger Station; area to the east.
Jalapeño Pepper	[1.16] Chance's Map; area to the northeast
	[3.09] Ranger Station; area to the east.
Maize	[2.20] NCR Sharecropper Farms has a massive amount.
	[2.11] Mole Rat Ranch; the area to the west.
Nevada Agave	[1.05] Griffin Wares Sacked Caravan; surrounding terrain.
	[3.17] Fisherman's Pride Shack; area surrounding to the north.
Prickly Pear	[3.04] Fields' Shack; area south and west.
	[3.14] Cap Counterfeiting Shack; surrounding area.
White Horse Nettle	[3.12] Vault 34; area to the southeast
	[3.17] Fisherman's Pride Shack; area surrounding to the north.
Xander Root	[1.08] Silver Peak Mine; surrounding area.
	[3.07] Bloodborne Cave; area to the southwest.

Main Quest: Introduction

PREPARATION: AIN'T THAT A HOLE IN YOUR HEAD?

This chapter details the courier's journey from a half-buried corpse to a trek around the Mojave, into and out of New Vegas where alliances are both favored and broken, past a brief meeting with an NCR president, and a final attack or defense. This is broken down into three Acts. The following table shows the Quests within these Acts.

Caution Spoiler Alert! Remember that the optimal path to complete every Main Quest is shown, along with pretty much every possible conversation and combat choice. The farther you read, the more is revealed. Don't venture into pages unknown unless you're ready to read the consequences!

Act I: The Journey to New Vegas

NEUTRAL

Act I is straightforward: You regain consciousness, learn the basics of survival, and track the men who tried to kill you, all the way into the New Vegas Strip. You are considered "neutral" during this time, and the Quest has the preceding icon to show that you don't need to pick a side.

Act II: Alliances Are Made (to be Broken)

Act II is where your alliances are formed and Reputations are made. You cannot please all sides forever, and although you can meet every Faction leader, and even agree to their demands, sometime during Act II you'll need to take a stand! The Quest splits into four separate paths, depending on who you decide to align with:

INDEPENDENT

Should you attempt an "independent" New Vegas, and ignore all coaxing and offers from the three major Factions, your Quest progression occurs through Quests flagged with this icon.

MR. HOUSE

If you decide to ally with Mr. House, you receive instructions from him—and shrug off the threats of violence (and actual violence) from the NCR and Legion—and continue along the Quests marked with this icon.

NEW CA. REPUBLIC

The New California Republic wants you! If you want them back, and you can stall Mr. House and deal with periodic Legion incursions, you have a number of multiple-objective Quests to perform, all flagged with this icon.

CAESAR'S LEGION

If the Slavers swarming in from Arizona are your kind of people, you must gain an audience with Caesar himself, tackle the periodic assassination attempts by NCR Rangers, ignore the threats of Mr. House, and finish one gigantic, and one tiny (but vitally important) Quest, marked with this icon.

All the way through Act II, some of your major tasks involve shoring up support for your chosen ally. Secondary alliances, such as those with the Great Khans, Boomers, or Brotherhood of Steel, are investigated or tested; and these affect the forces you see during Act III. All of the secondary alliance Quests are "Side Quests," and are covered in the next chapter, although all the information you need appears here, too.

Then, at the very end of Act II, President Kimball decides to fly in and visit Hoover Dam. Depending on your alliances, you're also there to observe, defend, or assassinate him.

Act III: The Second Battle for Hoover Dam

Before you begin Act III, it is usually wise to complete all your other exploration plans (including Side and Free Quests). The side you've picked, and the secondary Factions you've allied with, all come into play for this final push. There are four separate ways to leave a mark on the Mojave, and all are detailed. As for the endings? Consult the Appendices, but only if you want Spoilers to sear into your eyeballs.

Main Quests: An Epic Adventure in Three Acts

The following table shows the names of every Quest, the major locations they take place in, and the associated Factions you're working for.

QUEST NAME	LOCATIONS
MAIN QUEST: ACT I	
Ain't That a Kick in the Head	[4.05] Goodsprings
Back in the Saddle	[4.11] Goodsprings Source
By a Campfire on the Trail	[4.06] Goodsprings Cemetery, [4.11] Goodsprings Source
They Went That-a-Way	[3.32] Boulder City, [4.05] Goodsprings, [4.17] Primm, [4.30] Nipton, [5.18] Novac
Ring-a-Ding Ding!	[2D.04] The Tops Casino
MAIN QUESTS: ACT II	
Wild Card: Change in Management	[2D.04] The Tops Casino, [2D.02] Lucky 38 Casino
Wild Card: You and What Army?	[6.20] Cottonwood Cove, [3.28] The Fort
Wild Card: Side Bets	[3.01] Nellis Air Force Base, [1.15] Red Rock Canyon, [2D.01] Gomorrah, [2D.05] Ultra-Luxe Casino, [5.11] Hidden Valley
Wild Card: Finishing Touches	[3.33] Hoover Dam, [5.04] El Dorado Substation, [2C.01] Old Mormon Fort, [2D.02] Lucky 38 Casino
The House Always Wins, I	[2D.02] Lucky 38 Casino, [2D.04] The Tops Casino
The House Always Wins, II	[6.20] Cottonwood Cove, [3.28] The Fort
The House Always Wins, III	[2D.02] Lucky 38 Casino, [3.01] Nellis Air Force Base
The House Always Wins, IV	[2D.02] Lucky 38 Casino, [2D.01] Gomorrah
The House Always Wins, V	[2D.02] Lucky 38 Casino, [5.11] Hidden Valley
The House Always Wins, VI	[2D.02] Lucky 38 Casino, [3.33] Hoover Dam
The House Always Wins, VII	[5.04] El Dorado Substation, [2D.02] Lucky 38 Casino
Render Unto Caesar	[6.20] Cottonwood Cove, [3.28] The Fort, [2D.02] Lucky 38 Casino, [3.01] Nellis Air Force Base, [2D.05] Ultra-Luxe Casino, [5.11] Hidden Valley
Et Tumor, Brute?	[3.28] The Fort, [2.10] New Vegas Medical Clinic, [3.12] Vault 34
Things That Go Boom	[2D.07] NCR Embassy, [3.01] Nellis Air Force Base
King's Gambit	[2D.07] NCR Embassy, [Zone 2C] Freeside, [2C.05] King's School of Impersonation, [2C.07] Silver Rush, [2C.01] Old Mormon Fort, [2.19] Camp McCarran, [3.33] Hoover Dam
For the Republic, Part 2	[3.33] Hoover Dam, [1.15] Red Rock Canyon, [2D.01] Gomorrah, [2D.02] Lucky 38 Casino, [5.11] Hidden Valley
You'll Know it When it Happens	[3.33] Hoover Dam
Arizona Killer	[3.33] Hoover Dam
MAIN QUESTS: ACT III	
No Gods, No Masters	[3.33] Hoover Dam, [3.34] Legate's Camp
All or Nothing	[3.33] Hoover Dam, [3.34] Legate's Camp
Veni, Vidi, Vici	[3.34] Legate's Camp, [3.33] Hoover Dam
Eureka!	[3.33] Hoover Dam, [3.34] Legate's Camp

Act 1

AIN'T THAT A KICK IN THE HEAD

ALLIED FACTION

NEUTRAL

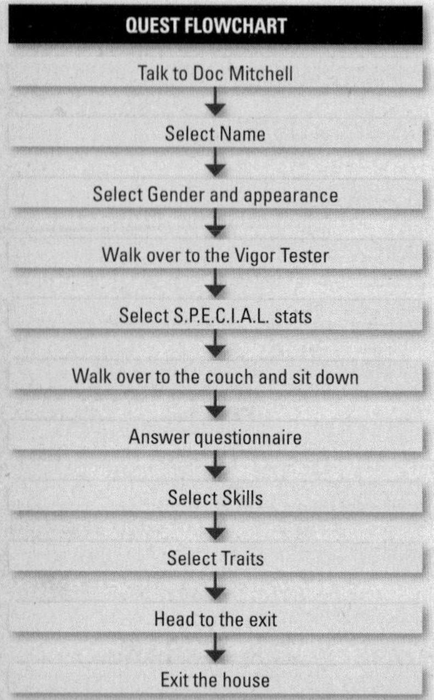

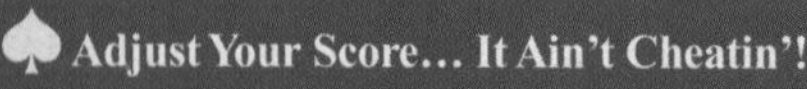

Adjust Your Score... It Ain't Cheatin'!

Walk to the Vit-o-matic Vigor Tester.

Use the Vit-o-matic Vigor Tester.

1

2

After a particularly bad evening, and rescue by Victor the Securitron, you awake inside Doc Mitchell's medical shack in the settlement of Goodsprings [4.05]. Choose your name, check your appearance, and then follow the doc and Activate the Vit-o-matic Vigor Tester **(1)**. Follow the on-screen prompts and adjust your S.P.E.C.I.A.L. attribute values, spending five additional points.

Sit down on the couch in Doc Mitchell's living room.

Follow Doc Mitchell to the exit.

Follow the doctor **(2)** to his comfy couch, and learn to use your body again. That shot to the head played havoc with your motor skills, so make sure you learn how to Jump, Pick Up Items (and put them down again). Pick up the Brahmin Skull above Doc Mitchell's fireplace, and put it down again. Then sit on the couch, and begin a series of word-association and Rorschach tests. Relax! There's no wrong answer, although your comments influence how your trio of Tag skills are chosen. Simply Reset and choose three new Tag skills if you don't like what you get. Next fill in a final form regarding your past medical history. Check up to two traits that best apply to your play style. Then simply follow Doc Mitchell to the Door to Goodsprings, where the Delivery Order you were carrying is presented to you, along with some Bobby Pins, a Pip-Boy, and a gift (see below). Doc suggests you talk to Sunny Smiles before leaving town; she can help teach you how to fend for yourself in the desert. When you're ready to leave, open the door. This prompts you into choosing Hardcore mode or not. Once go through the door, Main Quest: They Went That-A-Way begins.

As you leave, you're presented with a gift from the good doctor. The item in question all depends on which combat skill you tagged:

You receive a 9mm Pistol.

You receive a Laser Pistol.

You are handed some Dynamite.

If you tagged none of these, you receive a 9mm Pistol.

You also receive a Straight Razor, as well as the 9mm Pistol.

You also receive Boxing Gloves, as well as the 9mm Pistol.

Delivery Order

Bobby Pins x6

Stimpaks x4

Straight Razor

Boxing Gloves

9mm Pistol

Laser Pistol

Vault 21 Jumpsuit

Pip-Boy 3000

Note The Training chapter of this book has all the information you need regarding Attributes, Skills, Traits, and Hardcore mode.

Tip For more items and weapons, search all the rooms in Doc Mitchell's house to uncover ammunition, Antivenom, Stimpaks, Rad-X, a Gun Case with a Laser Pistol, a Chemistry Set, a Magazine, some Glasses, and a Broken 9mm Submachine Gun. This sets you up reasonably well for your initial explorations.

Note The first Quests (Back in the Saddle, followed by By a Campfire on the Trail, with the option to continue with Side Quest: Ghost Town Gunfight/Run Goodsprings Run) are now available, and the first two are detailed below (the third is in the Side Quests chapter). These are optional, but it's recommended that you complete all three before you start Main Quest: They Went That-A-Way.

BACK IN THE SADDLE

ALLIED FACTION

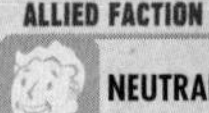

NEUTRAL

QUEST FLOWCHART

Speak with Sunny Smiles
↓
Get training behind the saloon
↓
Agree to go hunt Geckos
↓
Kill the Geckos at the first well
↓
Talk to Sunny
↓
Kill the Geckos at the second and third wells
↓
Talk to Sunny again

A Smashing Time at the Prospector Saloon

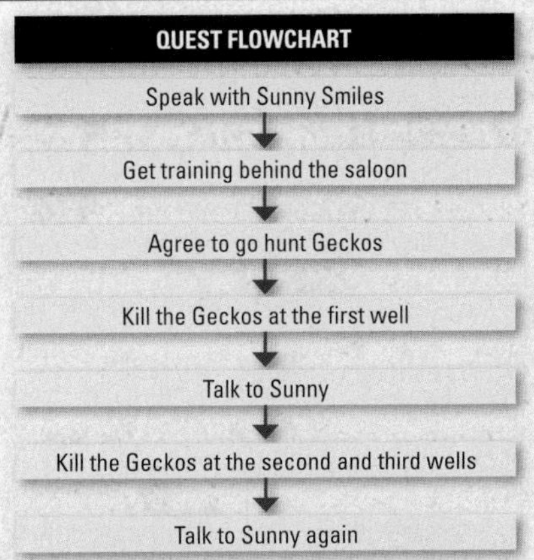

Take your first tentative steps into Goodsprings and locate Sunny Smiles to begin this Quest, ideally before beginning Main Quest: They Went That-A-Way. Simply head east from Doc's house along the main street until you reach the Prospector Saloon **(1)**. That old man by the door is Easy Pete **(2)**, a scavenger who prefers the term "prospector." Mine him for information on the NCR, Legion, Bighorners, Hoover Dam, and Victor, then open the Door to Prospector Saloon.

Inside the saloon, you're stopped by Sunny Smiles **(3)** and her dog Cheyenne. Aside from a wealth of background information, Sunny Smiles provides some useful additional items:

Ask her if there's any work available, and she says no, but suggests you look around inside the Goodsprings Schoolhouse for a safe, and gives you a relevant Skill Magazine!

 **Locksmith Reader**

 **Bobby Pins x3**

Tell Sunny that Doc Mitchell said she could teach you to survive in the desert. She agrees, and tells you to meet her outside, behind the saloon.

  Or, you can rampage through the town, killing everyone. This isn't terribly wise. If you're this way inclined, try siding with the Powder Gangers during Side Quest: Run Goodsprings Run, first.

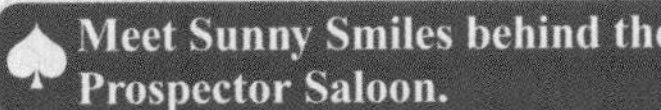

Meet Sunny Smiles behind the Prospector Saloon.

Shoot 3 sarsaparilla bottles outside the Prospector Saloon.

Note The Tour chapter of this guide details all scavenging. Simply read the entry on Goodsprings to find out what the Schoolhouse (and every other accessible building) contains.

Follow Sunny out the rear exit to the rocky scrub behind the saloon. Sunny hands you a Varmint Rifle, which you can use (or another firearm you've collected already). Stand next to Sunny, and aim at one of the bottles balanced on the fence **(4)**. Target each bottle, and fire. The bottles aren't alive, so V.A.T.S. is unavailable. Increase the chances of hitting each bottle by using Iron Sights, and looking down the barrel of your weapon. Also, try crouching.

With three bottles struck, Sunny congratulates you, and reckons you'd have more fun tagging some troublesome Geckos lurking near the Goodsprings water supply. Agree to follow Sunny to continue this Quest.

 **Varmint Rifle**

 **Follow Sunny.**

 **Kill the geckos at the well.**

Tip Is Sunny Smiles outrunning you? Sunny has her weapon stowed; you run more slowly if you're carrying a two-handed armament. So sheathe your firearm, blade, or fist to increase your pace.

Leapin' Lizards

Sunny dashes off to the south, then edges southwest toward Goodsprings Source [4.11], and waits behind a large rock formation. The Geckos are on the ridge behind her. You can:

 Crouch and sneak around, and blast them with a surprise attack.

Or, you can run in and fire, using any weapon you wish. Try out V.A.T.S., as well as manual aiming, looking down the barrel of your weapon, and crouch-firing **(5)**.

When combat is over, return to Sunny Smiles. She gives you some ammunition for your Varmint Rifle, and asks you to accompany her to a second well. There's Caps in it for you!

Talk to Sunny Smiles.

Kill the geckos at the other wells.

Talk to Sunny about your reward.

Agree (or the Quest ends), and continue along the rocky bluffs to a second well with more Geckos. Just over the ridge is a third and final well, located at Goodsprings Source **(6)** itself. There may be more Geckos there, along with a Goodsprings Settler (who rewards you with Purified Water if you save her). Be sure not to hit her, or face Sunny's wrath! Find Sunny on the rocky outcrop nearby, and ask about your reward, which she gives you, along with a chance to figure out how to live off the land. Interested? If so, By a Campfire on the Trail begins.

 **50 Caps**

 **Purified Water x3**

 **Goodsprings Fame Gained! (If the settler wasn't killed)**

Caution During the fights with the Geckos, Cheyenne enthusiastically bounds into the fray. Don't hit her, or any innocents! You may wish to use V.A.T.S. so you can count on every shot hitting its intended target.

BY A CAMPFIRE ON THE TRAIL

ALLIED FACTION

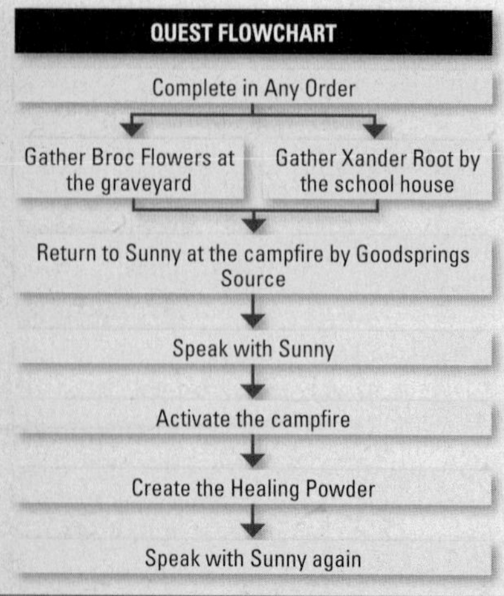

Find a Broc Flower and a Xander Root.

Cooking Something Up

If you agree to let Sunny Smiles teach you how to live off the land at the end of Back in the Saddle, you get instructions on where to search for two indigenous plants: the Broc Flower and Xander Root. At this point, you can:

Produce both plants, if you've already collected them on your travels, and move to the campfire.

Or you can search for the Broc Flower **(1)**. The nearest one is up at the Goodsprings Cemetery [4.06] **(2)**, close to the cliff edge and water tower, at the foot of a plant.

Or you can search for the Xander Root **(3)**. It is nestled by a tree-stump, near the Schoolhouse **(4)**.

Collect the two plants in any order. If you want to minimize backtracking, grab the Xander Root first.

Bring the Broc Flower and Xander Root to Sunny at the campfire.

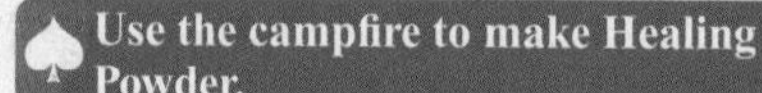

Use the campfire to make Healing Powder.

Return to Sunny Smiles. She's waiting for you at a prospector's campfire **(5)** just below Goodsprings Source [4.11]. You're going to make some Healing Powder. Move over and Activate the Campfire.

Scroll down your Recipes until you reach the one labeled Healing Powder, and click on it to make one Healing Powder.

Simple! Now you've been given step-by-step instructions on foraging for a wide variety of items to combine to make helpful elixirs. Sunny bids you farewell, asking you to stop back at the Prospector's Saloon to speak with Trudy, the proprietor. The Quest completes.

Healing Powder

Goodsprings Fame Gained!

Go and meet Trudy at the Prospector Saloon.

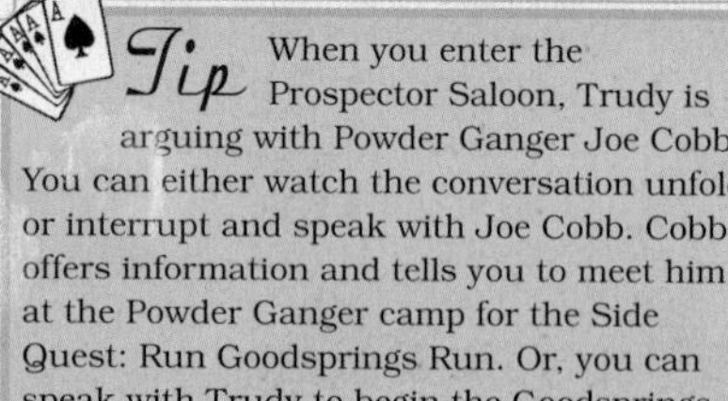

Tip When you enter the Prospector Saloon, Trudy is arguing with Powder Ganger Joe Cobb. You can either watch the conversation unfold or interrupt and speak with Joe Cobb. Cobb offers information and tells you to meet him at the Powder Ganger camp for the Side Quest: Run Goodsprings Run. Or, you can speak with Trudy to begin the Goodsprings side of this Quest: Ghost Town Gunfight.

Note If you have a greater Survival skill and a variety of other items, you can try a wide range of other Recipes. You can also subdivide the Recipes into Food, Aid, Chems, and Misc while at a campfire. Remember you can Upgrade and Repair Weapons using the same principle, but at a Workbench, or after purchasing weapon parts from vendors, or finding them. For more information, consult the Training chapter.

Tip Want evidence of your killer's identity? Then pick up the Cigarette Butts in the Graveyard; they might come in handy as proof later into your adventuring.

THEY WENT THAT-A-WAY

ALLIED FACTION

See flowchart on the following page

Victor, Vikki, and Vance

Inquire about your delivery assignment with the administrator of the Mojave Express in Primm.

(Optional) Talk to Victor in Goodsprings about your rescue.

Find the men who tried to kill you.

You have your marching orders. Primm [4.17] is south of Goodsprings [4.05], so finding Victor is the closest Objective. If you can't locate him outside Doc Mitchell's house, then he's wheeled himself to his shack to the southwest **(1)**. You can speak to him at any time following the completion of Main Quest 1: Ain't That a Kick in the Head. Either of the following comments completes the Objective:

Thanks for digging me out of that grave.

Do you know who those men were who attacked me?

Note This chapter covers the major choices and routes to take during your Main Quest. For combat and recipe help, consult the Training chapter and the previous Main Quest. To rummage around for weapons and equipment, check the Goodsprings location in the Tour of Mojave Wasteland chapter.

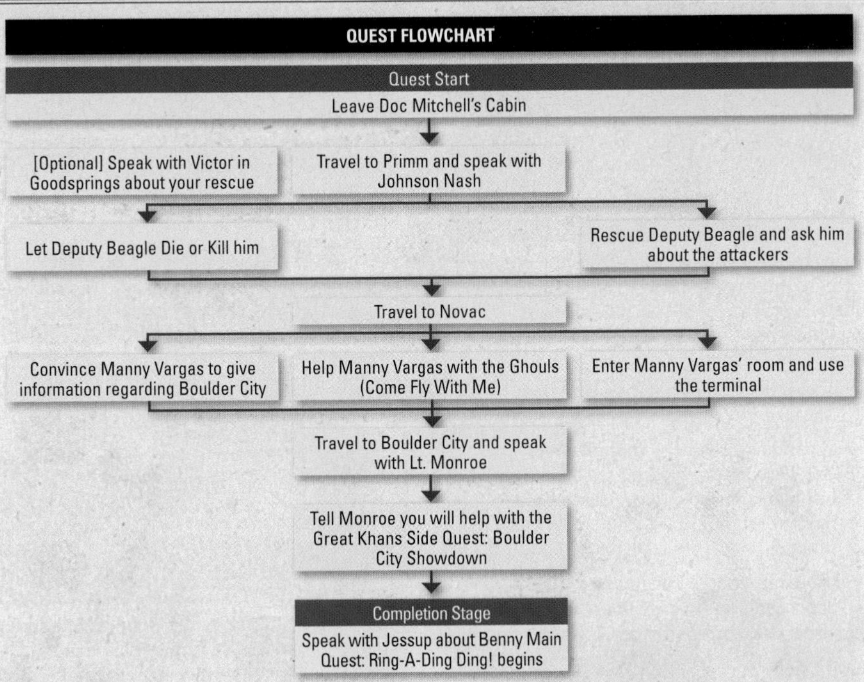

Tip While you can ignore much of the following investigation, it's wise to thoroughly explore the areas mentioned below. This furthers your knowledge of the area and Factions, and allows you to gather items and equipment to help your cause.

2

All evidence points to Primm as your next port of call. Trek southward and skirt around to the right, so you can cross the bridge by the small NCR camp holed up in the ruined buildings. The "administrator of the Mojave Express" is currently inside the Vikki & Vance Casino **(2)**, the smaller of the two giant buildings here. The area is dotted with Escaped Convicts (who are not affiliated with the Powder Gangers, and can therefore be executed without risking a Reputation loss with that Faction). Enter the Vikki & Vance Casino using one of the following techniques:

Fight through the Convicts to the main street between the casinos, and enter.

Using a Stealth Boy, Sneak around and enter the casino.

If you're currently on less than civil terms with the NCR, fight them first, ransack the camp, then deal with the Powder Gangers.

POWDER GANGERS If you've procured a Powder Ganger outfit, you can usually put it on and walk around this Faction without being seen as an imposter. But remember, these Convicts aren't part of the Powder Gangers, so wearing an outfit has no effect.

3

4

Upon entering the Vikki & Vance Casino **(3)**, you scarcely have time to speak to Primm Slim about the history of the place, when you're greeted by the proprietor, Johnson Nash **(4)**. Aside from challenging him to a game of Caravan, or meeting his wife, Ruby (and her interesting cooking skills), you can ask about the town, and the Factions he interacts with.

Be sure to ask about the men who stole the chip from you, and show him the Delivery Order you're carrying. He suggests you speak with Deputy Beagle, who's holed up inside the Bison Steve Casino.

Note Your chat with Johnson Nash triggers Side Quest: My Kind of Town. Additional Quests appear periodically during the Main Quest, and most of the Quests are purely optional, depending on your actions. Simply look up the Quest that's been added on your Pip-Boy, and check the appropriate page in this book for more information.

Betting Against the Renegades

Talk to Primm's Deputy to get information on where your attackers went.

5

6

The Bison Steve Casino **(5)**, across the main drag, is difficult to miss. Step through the double-doors, and Sneak or fight through to the small kitchen area in the southeast corner of the ground floor. All other exploration inside this building is optional. Expect resistance from around seven Convicts and a Leader armed with an Incinerator between the entrance and the kitchen, where Deputy Beagle is trussed up **(6)**. Plan your chat with Beagle accordingly:

- If Powder Gangers are still about, you may wish to leave him tied up, so he isn't caught in the crossfire.
- If you want him to sweat a little longer, you can set him free without extracting any information from him.
- Or, more cleverly, you should mention that he has "information on some Khans that came through here with a guy in a checkered suit." He tells you he'll talk after being released. The choices are:

"You can tell me or you can rot in here." Succeed, and he imparts the information. You can then choose to leave or release him.

Or you can simply release him. Whenever he's freed, he flees the building; you'll find him back at the Vikki & Vance Casino, where he imparts the information you need.

"If you try to run away instead of fighting at my side, I'll kill you myself." Succeed, and he stays with you. You may end up having to protect him if Convicts still roam the vicinity. Or you can arm him (see the adjacent Tip for more information).

You can forget any conversation with Beagle, and Pickpocket him to uncover his Journal, and listen to it.

You can execute Beagle, and find the Journal on his corpse, and listen to it.

Deputy Beagle's Journal

Tip If you decide to free Beagle, and escort him by threatening his life with the Speech check, you can arm him with a gun. This also allows access to his Journal. A more cunning plan is to offer the gun, then when his Inventory appears, take his Leather Armor and his 9mm Pistol! Hoodwinked by the cunning courier!

Into the Jaws of Dinky

Head to Novac through Nipton to look for signs of your attackers.

7

Nipton [4.30] and Novac [5.18] have appeared on your Pip-Boy's World Map. Head south-southeast, passing Jack Rabbit Springs [4.26] and Ivanpah Race Track [4.25] along the way. Use the remains of the road for safest (but not quickest) travel. When you eventually arrive at Nipton, you spot various tire bonfires belching smoke (and other, more unspeakable burnt offerings) skyward. Dotted about town are Powder Gangers, crucified by a heartless and vicious Faction known as Caesar's Legion.

CAESAR'S LEGION Move toward the Town Hall **(7)** and you're greeted by Vulpes Inculta (Side Quest: Cold, Cold Heart). Choose to listen, fight, or flee. You're actively encouraged to speak of these atrocities!

Or you can simply ignore Nipton completely, and make a bee-line for Novac.

Or you can thoroughly search this settlement. For a complete run-down of the items, dangers, and areas of interest, consult the Nipton entry in the Tour chapter of this guide.

8

Depart Nipton heading northeast. Following the remains of I164 east and north allows you to circumvent the more mountainous (and treacherous) terrain. Expect brief skirmishes with Viper Gunslingers if you stick to the road, which leads northeast past Ranger Station Charlie [5.23], and finally to Novac itself, whose skyline is dominated by a giant (and thankfully immobile) Dino Dee-lite dinosaur named Dinky **(8)**. Behind the metal monstrosity is a run-down motel connected to the landmark. Enter the main office and chat with Jeannie May Crawford for some local gossip. She points you toward Dinky.

> **Note** It sure looks like Victor is following you, pardner! You may spot this Securitron and chat with him, gaining further background information as you progress through Nipton. This is one of the four Free Quests: We Must Stop Meeting Like This. Free Quests don't appear on your Pip-Boy and are usually short. The Tour chapter lists them all, so check there each time you reach a new settlement.

9

Move around Dinky's tail and up the steps, entering the door to Dino Bite Gift Shop. Inside, you're greeted by Cliff Briscoe, hawking some T-rex figurines. Try one or more of the following:

You can purchase from him and chat with him.

You can ask about the man in the checkered coat. Briscoe hasn't a clue, but Manny (who's up in the dino's mouth) might know). The Quest Objective updates.

Or you can choose to ignore or kill Briscoe, depending on your disposition.

Find out from Manny Vargas where the Khans were headed.

Find Manny **(9)** at the top of the interior steps, technically outside, but enclosed in Dinky's mouth. This sniping point has surprisingly impressive views of the highway and surrounding area. Ask him who he protects the town from, and he mentions Ghouls from the road to REPCONN, out to the west. But the big threat is the Legion coming in from the east.

Move the conversation onto your search for the man in the checkered coat. Manny knows who you mean, but he needs your help. At this point:

Answer "You've had your needs neglected for far too long, haven't you. I can tell." With this perk, Manny tells you everything you need to know, and the Quest updates.

With any other answer, Manny's information comes at a price. He needs you to head over to the REPCONN test site and remove the Ghoul threat. This starts Side Quest: Come Fly With Me. Return to Manny after finishing this Quest to his satisfaction, and he gives you the information you seek.

Or you can venture back to the Novac Motel (before or after you speak to Manny), and open the door to Manny Vargas' Room. Activate the terminal in the far corner and read the entry marked "Message: Khan Hospitality," written by a Khan named McMurphy. This sheds light on Vargas' allegiances. This now appears in the Misc > Quest Notes section of your Pip-Boy.

SNEAK Crouching and Pickpocketing Manny Vargas allows you to swipe a Holotape and some ammunition from him. The Holotape contains the same "Message: Khan Hospitality" note. Listen to it for the Quest to update.

Killing Manny Vargas doesn't really help your cause, but you will find a Holotape on his corpse, along with that impressive-looking Sniper Rifle.

Message: Khan Hospitality

> **Note** Is a man named Boone waiting inside Dinky's mouth? That's due to the time of day. Either sleep, wait, or enter Manny Vargas' room to find Manny, if he's not up inside Dinky.

A Khan-Do Attitude

Intercept the Great Khans at Boulder City.

10

11

The checkered suited man now has a name (Benny) and accomplices, the Khans. Head roughly north-northeast, ideally using the remains of I95 to guide you toward your World Map marker, passing the El Dorado Gas & Service Station [6.01], and the El Dorado Dry Lake [5.09]. Boulder City [3.32] is just off I95, near the welcome signs, although it's more of a "Rubble City" currently **(10)**. Head around the mass of detritus, looking for the flaming barrel and NCR Lieutenant Monroe **(11)**. He's got a situation with some Great Khans that needs your attention. NCR hostages need to be rescued from the Boulder City Ruins (or killed, depending on your point of view). Side Quest: Boulder City Showdown now begins. Try one or more of the following:

If you're fighting against the NCR, bring your finest armaments and fight through the NCR troops to Jessup. You don't get a chance to speak to Monroe.

If you've been taking pot-shots at the Great Khans, the stealthy approach is your only option.

You have two main conversation options to help out Monroe:

"Negotiate a deal" allows you to enter the ruins without the Khans becoming aggressive.

"Sneak in there" enables you to enter the ruins with the Khans' weapons drawn. This is unnecessary to choose, as you can elect to begin the fight anyway. Monroe advises you wait until it's darker to pull this off.

Go in with a weapon drawn, and you fight the Khans.

Go in at night, crouched, and using a Stealth Boy to avoid the Khans' gaze.

Tip If you've found Benny's cigarette butts from your grave in Goodsprings, be sure to collect more evidence to implicate him from Jessup; the Lighter and Chairmen Job Offer.

Inside the ruins, you're either heading to the ruined building in the southwest corner with all guns blazing, or no guns blazing. Either way, you need to find the Khan's leader, Jessup **(12)**. You may recognize him from your recent burial. Find Jessup (if you're not fighting, he's inside the ruined building to the southwest, accessed via the Door to Great Khan Hideout). Enter the hideout, and you may spot McMurphy, the other Great Khan who helped try to end your life; it looks like he's at the end of his. Confront Jessup, and the following options are available to you:

Jessup is understandably surprised to see you. If you choose the fourth answer "When I kill you, however, the job will get done right," Jessup becomes hostile. Otherwise the conversation continues.

Additional chatter relates to Side Quest: Boulder City Showdown (including Speech checks). Consult that Quest for further information.

Choose "Where's the Platinum Chip?" and he tells you that Benny made off with it. You can ask more about both the Chip and Benny, but the Quest updates at this point.

If violence is your way, pick through the corpses until you find Jessup's. Search it to find a "Chairmen Job Offer" note. Read it in the Misc > Quest Notes section of your Pip-Boy to conclude this part of the Quest.

Benny's Lighter

Chairmen Job Offer

1,000 XP

Tip You can move directly from Goodsprings to Boulder City, and confront Jessup. Or, you can head out from Goodsprings and walk straight toward the New Vegas Strip itself, circumventing these detours, and finding Benny in record time.

RING-A-DING DING!

ALLIED FACTION: NEUTRAL

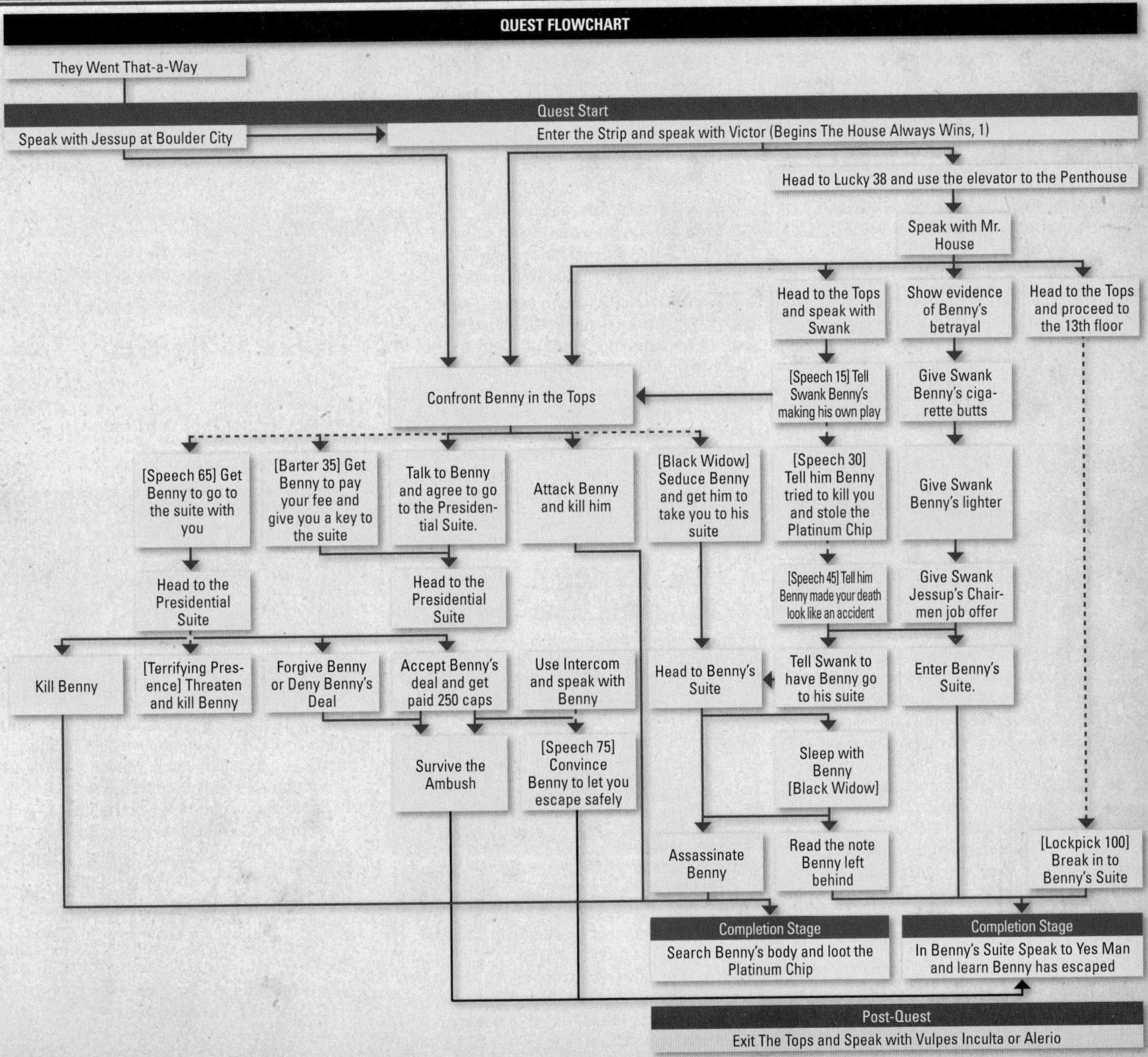

QUEST FLOWCHART

- They Went That-a-Way
- **Quest Start**
  - Speak with Jessup at Boulder City → Enter the Strip and speak with Victor (Begins The House Always Wins, 1)
- Head to Lucky 38 and use the elevator to the Penthouse
- Speak with Mr. House
  - Head to the Tops and speak with Swank → [Speech 15] Tell Swank Benny's making his own play → [Speech 30] Tell him Benny tried to kill you and stole the Platinum Chip → [Speech 45] Tell him Benny made your death look like an accident → Tell Swank to have Benny go to his suite
  - Show evidence of Benny's betrayal → Give Swank Benny's cigarette butts → Give Swank Benny's lighter → Give Swank Jessup's Chairmen job offer → Enter Benny's Suite.
  - Head to the Tops and proceed to the 13th floor → [Lockpick 100] Break in to Benny's Suite
- Confront Benny in the Tops
  - [Speech 65] Get Benny to go to the suite with you → Head to the Presidential Suite
  - [Barter 35] Get Benny to pay your fee and give you a key to the suite → Head to the Presidential Suite
  - Talk to Benny and agree to go to the Presidential Suite. → Head to the Presidential Suite
  - Attack Benny and kill him
  - [Black Widow] Seduce Benny and get him to take you to his suite → Head to Benny's Suite
- Head to the Presidential Suite → Kill Benny / [Terrifying Presence] Threaten and kill Benny / Forgive Benny or Deny Benny's Deal / Accept Benny's deal and get paid 250 caps / Use Intercom and speak with Benny
  - Survive the Ambush
  - [Speech 75] Convince Benny to let you escape safely
- Head to Benny's Suite → Assassinate Benny / Sleep with Benny [Black Widow] → Read the note Benny left behind
- **Completion Stage**: Search Benny's body and loot the Platinum Chip
- **Completion Stage**: In Benny's Suite Speak to Yes Man and learn Benny has escaped
- **Post-Quest**: Exit The Tops and Speak with Vulpes Inculta or Alerio

A Passport to Paradise

♠ Confront Benny at The Tops casino.

This Quest commences in one of two ways. You can ignore the tracking evidence you collected during Main Quest: They Went That-A-Way, and stumble across Victor in the Vegas Strip. Or, more likely, you've pried the information on Benny's whereabouts from Jessup at Boulder City, and you're following the trail.

From Boulder City, head roughly northwest, passing the Barstow Express in the rusting train yard. Deathclaws may be prowling the Mountain Shadows Campground [3.24]. You might spot Victor again outside Boulder City near the Barstow Express. We must stop meeting like this! Eventually, you'll trek into the built-up outer areas of New Vegas. As you reach the towering and shiny casino buildings, realize that there are multiple gated entrances. The quickest route to The Strip is to pass through the Freeside East Gate [2.15] (marked on your Pip-Boy, which leads into an interior perimeter of Vegas, known as Freeside **(1)**. For the full neon effect, wait until sundown, pass the Kings Gang members, and open the gate.

> **Note** This leads to Outer Freeside [Zone 2C]. You can seek the Northern Gate into Freeside [2.08], but this route is the quickest.

Enter the mean streets of Outer Freeside, passing the drunks and Mick and Ralph's emporium [2C.02], and heading northwest to the first street junction. Turn right, then left at the Bakery sign, passing the Old Mormon Fort on your right [2C.01]. At the next junction, various vehicle parts and concrete rubble have been fashioned into an effective barricade **(2)**. Shoot any Freeside thugs you wish, but don't target Kings Gang members unless you want to ruin your Reputation with them. Turn left (southwest) and open the Door to Freeside.

You're in the inner Freeside area, where The King has his School of Impersonation [2C.05]. Head southwest, following the road all the way to the heavily guarded entrance to The Strip **(3)**. Note the most famous New Vegas landmark—the Lucky 38 Casino

Tower—behind the heavily fortified gate, and pause at the Securitron Gatekeeper **(4)**. A passport or credit check is needed. You can:

Hand over 2,000 Caps; the "credit check" to prove you're not a "less-reputable person." The bad news? You'll need to scrounge together the necessary Caps. The good news? The check is just to see that you're good for the money, and you get to keep the Caps!

Answer "1C 3C R34 M," verbally hacking and confusing the Gatekeeper into letting you in.

Or you can attack the toughened Gatekeepers. Prepare for a protracted battle before forcing your way in.

Or, you can complete Side Quest: G.I. Blues, and request a passport from The King, as a reward.

Or, you can visit Mick & Ralph's [2C.02], speak to Ralph, and have him craft a passport for you. This is Free Quest: Papers, Please (which is detailed in the Tour chapter).

NEW CA. REPUBLIC Finally, if you're wearing NCR armor (Faction Clothing), you can journey to Camp McCarran [2.19] instead of The Strip, enter the Terminal Building, and board the Monorail. You can also do this without issue if Boone is your Companion.Or, you can wait (without being seen) until 9 AM or 6 PM, when the guards change shift. Board the monorail, and ride it to the Vegas Boulevard Station [2D.03]. Exit, and you're greeted by Victor. This method is dangerous and can severely impede your standing with the NCR.

Welcome to Fabulous New Vegas!

♠ "Search the Strip for the man who shot you" begins.

Entering the spectacular main Strip **(5)** [Zone 2D], you spot the friendly screen of Victor, who pops up at just the right moment. Talk with him to learn that the head honcho of New Vegas—Mr. House—is itching to make your acquaintance. This begins Main Quest: The House Always Wins, I. Now consider Plan 1A or 1B:

Plan 1A: Building a Foundation with Mr. House

Enter the Lucky 38 Casino **(6)** [2D.02] , and begin The House Always Wins, I. Once you meet Mr. House, he tells you a great deal about Benny, plus a host of other information and his plans for you. You can learn the additional information from Mr. House, which you can use to your advantage:

Benny is surrounded by at least four bodyguards except when he's in his private suite on the 13th floor of The Tops hotel.

If you approach him in a public place, it could be possible to leverage his fear of exposure to allow a private meeting.

Or, you could Sneak up onto the 13th floor, and pick the sturdy lock to his suite. That's a difficult task.

Finally, Benny's second-in-command, Swank, might be swayed to your side if you explain Benny's crimes.

> **Note** For complete conversations, and the entire Main Quest, consult Main Quest: The House Always Wins, I.

Plan 1B: To The Tops

Or, you can simply ignore (or delay) Victor's request for you to meet Mr. House, and head straight for The Tops Casino [2D.04].

Back on Track

With either path, if you mosey too close to the Gomorrah [2D.01], you're waylaid by a scruffy man in a suspicious coat: Mister Holdout **(7)**. He's selling a stash of concealed weapons. These weapons can help you remain armed while inside the casinos. You can:

Inform him that you're more than capable of sneaking a preferred weapon inside.

Or you can see what he has for sale.

Or refuse his frankly lackluster collection of blades and knuckle-dusters.

You Dirty Rat!

8

As soon as you enter the lavish and groovy main foyer of The Tops, you're met by a Chairman greeter **(8)**, who insists on confiscating all of your sharp implements and firepower. You can:

Oblige him. This isn't recommended (in case a fight breaks out accidentally, or otherwise, later in your stay here).

Oblige him, but secretly keep a hold-out weapon. The higher the Sneak, the better the weapon.

Refuse, which always starts combat, and shoot the place up. Unless you're extremely competent at combat, you may be overwhelmed, and your fracas remains etched in the memories of those on The Strip during future Quests.

Assuming you followed Tops Casino protocol, you have four main plans:

Plan 2A: Breaking, and Entering

Move east along the ground floor of the casino to the first bank of four elevators, and take the second one on your right, riding it up to the 13th floor.

Head along the corridor to the doors flanked by Chairman guards, and use your considerable Lockpicking prowess to open the door. Then step inside, circumventing all combat or even talking to Benny. Benny remains on the ground floor, and if you've spoken to Mr. House, or Yes Man, he is aware of it. He wants you to talk to him up in the casino's Presidential Suite, and the plan changes to 2C: Smooth Moves. Smooth.... Benny still carries the Platinum Chip, so you need to return to him to obtain it. But you can rummage around Benny's suite first, and speak to Yes Man (see Post-Quest activities).

Plan 2B: Getting Swank to Pull Rank

9

Follow the advice of Mr. House (although you don't need to visit him to execute this plan), and locate Swank **(9)**, who's standing at the front desk, next to the Chairman greeter. Aside from giving you a verbal tour of the major and minor Factions (including the White Glove Society and the Omertas), and letting you know that Tommy Torini might have work for you, he's pliable if you tell him "I think you should know something about Benny." You'll need a fast-talking mouth to succeed, however:

You tell Swank Benny's been making his own play.

Then he tried to kill you and stole Mr. House's Platinum Chip.

And the dirty rat tried to make it look like an accident.

Eventually, you persuade Benny that the chip will allow him to kill House and seize control!

Tip Or, present Swank with items you've gathered as evidence on your travels: Benny's cigarettes from your grave, and his Lighter and Chairmen Job Offer from Jessup; instead of a Speech check.

If you succeed in convincing him, Swank gives you Benny's Suite Key, and tells you he'll keep Benny away while you search the place.

If you don't succeed in all the Speech tests, Swank is suspicious of Benny, but doesn't have enough evidence to act. You need to face Benny without Swank's help. Plan 2C begins at this point.

"Search Benny's suite" begins.

Agree to this plan, and you're given all your weapons back, and are free to roam the hotel, but with the express intention of searching Benny's suite. You can:

Follow Swank's plan, take the elevator the 13th floor, and open the suite using the key. This circumvents all combat or even talking to Benny. Completion Consequence: Benny Escapes.

Disagree with Swank's plan, and say "we need to take him out right now." Swank agrees, and arranges to have Benny go to his suite, where you can wait for him. Agree to this and meet Benny in his suite. Completion Consequence: Dealing with Benny.

"Search for Benny in his suite" begins.

Or, wait until you get all your weapons back, and then go see Benny on the upper hotel floor. Plan 2C begins.

Plan 2C: Smooth Moves. Smooth...

10

At some point, you'll have to confront Benny and his goons on the ground floor, at the back of the tables, to the right of the front desk **(10)**.

The checkered suit and quartet of bodyguards (and the mark on your Pip-Boy's Local Map) make him difficult to miss. Conversation begins in one of a few ways:

Tell him "when you shot me, you ran off so fast I never got your name." This begins a flirtatious and slightly sickening conversation. See "One Sick Pussycat," below.

Or, you can tell him "Seems you need to work on your marksmanship," "I want the Platinum Chip and I want it now," or "Give me one reason not to kill you." All these prompt Benny to try to make amends, and continue the conversation up at the Presidential Suite.

Or offer threats of violence from yourself, or Mr. House.

You can attack, ideally with a concealed weapon (or better yet, with a full arsenal, assuming you spoke with Swank and completed Plan 2B).

With initial pleasantries out of the way, Benny begins to fast-talk his way out of his predicament. He tells you he wants to meet somewhere private. Keep talking, and he offers to comp you the Presidential Suite for a taste of the VIP lifestyle. This prompts the following possible actions:

You can agree to a meeting up at the suite, and reply with "Fine, but don't keep me waiting." You must head to the Presidential Suite without Benny.

Agree, but without Benny's bodyguards. Head to the Presidential Suite with Benny accompanying you. Completion Consequence: Dealing with Benny begins.

Agree, but insist that Benny pay off your contract. Benny agrees, and immediately hands you 500 Caps. You must head to the Presidential Suite without Benny.

500 Caps

Forcing Benny to talk right now results in a fight. You can also fight Benny at any point during the conversation.

The Tops Presidential Suite Key

Whether Benny accompanies you or not, head down the steps by Benny's table, and locate the nearby elevator bank (not the one allowing access to the 13th floor). Take the Elevator to Presidential Suite. If Benny isn't coming with you, Plan 2E is now in effect!

"Go to the Presidential Suite" begins.

Plan 2D: One Sick Pussycat

11

If you began your initial conversation during Plan 2C by flirting, Benny replies that you're out of his league.

2

you gain access to Benny's 13th floor suite **(2)**. To get to the 13th floor, head to the bank of four elevators (NOT the single one that leads to the Presidential Suite), and take the far right one. To enter Benny's suite, you can:

Speak to Swank, and through a number of Speech checks about Benny's alarming activities, get him to give you Benny's Suite Key.

Obtain the key by Pickpocketing Benny or any of his Chairmen bodyguards.

Or you can seduce Benny into taking you to bed.

Or you can open the door using skill and Bobby Pins.

All these options are extrapolated during Main Quest: Ring-a-Ding Ding.

I'm Just a Guy Who Can't Say No

3

4

When you're inside Benny's suite, head into the bedroom, and make sure you open the door in the far right. This leads to Benny's workshop **(3)** where a PDQ-88b Securitron with a happy face waits to greet you. Begin to speak, and Yes Man **(4)** spills the beans immediately; he's been reprogrammed to monitor Mr. House's data network and decode encrypted transmissions! He also tells you what the Platinum Chip is for (a data chip for upgrading Mr. House's defenses). Quiz him more to learn that Benny wanted to kill Mr. House to control his Securitrons.

Ask about taking over New Vegas yourself, and Yes Man suggests eliminating Mr. House, and installing his neuro-computational matrix on the Lucky 38's mainframe. Now ask how to commit such an act. This begins the Quest (assuming you have the Platinum Chip). You can also ask about the couriers; Yes Man was overseeing your tracking and execution, but this was due to Benny's programming. You can attack Yes Man at this point, but a better plan would be to ask about other tribes you could possibly ally with, ignore, or destroy. This begins Main Quest: Wild Card: Side Bets (and is also one way to begin the Omertas-related Side Quest: How Little We Know).

You can start a third Quest during your initial banter with Yes Man. Continue the line of questioning about Benny and Mr. House, and be sure to ask "you said something about a bunker at the Fort?" Yes Man tells you it is a place under Fortification Hill (AKA The Fort) [3.28] with a Platinum Chip reader. It should have some strategic significance; perhaps it contains a huge robot army. Tell Yes Man you'll check it out or think about it, and Main Quest: Wild Card: You and What Army? begins.

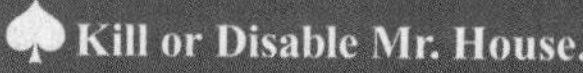
Kill or Disable Mr. House.

Recover the Platinum Chip from Benny at the Fort.

Recover the Platinum Chip from Benny.

Note Your conversation with Yes Man should have yielded three Quests: Wild Card: Change in Management (this Quest), Wild Card: Side Bets, and Wild Card: You and What Army? Make sure all three appear in your Pip-Boy's Data menu. You can attempt any you like, or head off and speak to another main Faction leader (Mr. House, Caesar, or Ambassador Crocker) to see what they want. The "Wild Card" Quests in this guide are listed in the order you receive them in.

Preparation: The Keys to Success

Gaining entry to "off-limits" areas of the Lucky 38 Casino can be tricky. To reach them, be sure you have one (or more) of the following before attempting the next part of this Quest:

The Platinum Chip that Benny "gave" you. Make sure you take this from him. If Benny has fled and has been captured by Caesar's Legion, another option is easier.

You can visit the H&H Tools Factory [2.06], and locate the Lucky 38 VIP Keycard inside the booby-trapped office. Find advice on exploring the factory in the Tour chapter.

Visit Camp Golf [3.23], and enter the intriguingly named House Resort. Inside, you can find a Lucky 38 VIP Keycard. Get advice on finding and exploring this location in the Tour chapter.

Or, you can trust your high-level Science skill, and manually hack the terminals necessary to reach Mr. House's inner sanctum!

Mr. House Goes Bust

5

6

Assuming you want Mr. House out of the picture, head over to the Lucky 38 Casino, where you're greeted by Victor, who opens the doors for you and also appears once you enter the casino floor **(5)**. Move to the elevator flanked by two Securitrons, and ask Victor to send you up to the penthouse. This is Mr. House's private quarters, and he's particularly keen on obtaining the Platinum Chip. You can engage Mr. House **(6)** in conversation (Main Quest: The House Always Wins, I), but it isn't necessary if you're on a mission to disable or kill this New Vegas stalwart.

Note If you already upgraded the Securitrons at Fortification Hill, you can complete Main Quest: The House Always Wins I, and II (and continue down this path with Mr. House). Give him the Platinum Chip, head to the bunker under Fortification Hill, upgrade the Securitrons, and return before choosing to end your servitude with Mr. House permanently.

7

8

Pass Jane, the Securitrons, and Mr. House himself, and inspect a terminal on the north wall, under the staircase, next to the bookcase. Access the terminal **(7)**, and select "Open Antechamber" from the menu. You're an unauthorized user, and the Securitrons go hostile if you confirm this.

A section of wall detaches, allowing you access into the antechamber. You can:

Fight the Securitron guard defenses in a highly dangerous and protracted battle **(8)**.

Or better yet, access the security terminal on the windowed side of the room, and override Mr. House's robots. They stop any aggressive behavior.

Or, you can simply run over to the elevator, head into Mr. House's chamber and kill him, and return. All of the Securitrons in the Lucky 38 revert to a non-combative threat indicator, and need not be fought.

Connection Lost...

With robot threats abated, access the terminal next to the control room elevator. Unlock it, and ride the elevator down to the control room. This vast, cool chamber contains Mr. House's Life Support (LS) Chamber **(9)**. You can:

Leave Mr. House, although this halts the Quest.

Access the terminal, and "Unseal LS Chamber." There's a microbial infection risk to Mr. House, but that's the least of his worries. Select "Yes."

At this point, you can:

Sterilize LS Chamber. This kills Mr. House, which is an unnecessarily thorough option to remove Mr. House from play.

Disable Cerebral Interface, which allows you to see the "real" Mr. House. He's not quite as dapper as his monitor image may have led you to believe. You can speak to him, kill him, let him live, or suffer pangs of guilt.

Once the deed is done, this Main Quest is over.

♠ The House Has Gone Bust!

You have irrevocably disconnected Mr. House from the Lucky 38's mainframe computers, forever trapping him in the prison of his own mind, or killing him outright. His grand dreams for New Vegas will never be realized.

♠ Return to Yes Man.

Retrace your steps. The monitors should now show a message indicating you've been successful. Over at The Tops 13th floor workshop, tell Yes Man that Mr. House is out of the picture. Depending on the almost infinite number of ways you can time this Quest, in some cases, Yes Man may appear on The Strip itself, near The Tops Casino.

♠ Meet Yes Man at the Lucky 38.

♠ Install Yes Man's A.I. in the Lucky 38's mainframe.

As long as you have the Platinum Chip, you can ask Yes Man to meet you back to the Lucky 38 Casino. Then backtrack to Mr. House's penthouse suite, where Yes Man awaits. Yes Man quickly accesses the Lucky 38 mainframe, and transfers his A.I. there **(10)**. You now have access to every Securitron on the network! Mr. House was readying a demonstration of the power of his Securitrons down in the basement. Yes Man encourages you to have a look. He also encourages you to go to The Fort, because Mr. House stashed an entire Securitron army there! That is, of course, only if you want your own private robot army!

♠ Go the basement of the Lucky 38.

♠ Observe upgrading of Securitrons.

You're automatically whisked down to a dimly lit and grimy basement. Move toward a small sunken area **(11)** where two Securitrons are going through combat programming. The true power of the Platinum Chip is then revealed, as Yes Man upgrades them from Mk I **(12)** to Mk II Securitrons **(13)**, with additional firepower and a more militaristic temperament. When prompted, return to the penthouse. Yes Man tells you that every Securitron on the network is now upgraded! In fact, the only ones not on the network are too far away, in The Fort bunker. This Quest concludes.

XP 500 XP

WILD CARD: YOU AND WHAT ARMY?

ALLIED FACTION
INDEPENDENT

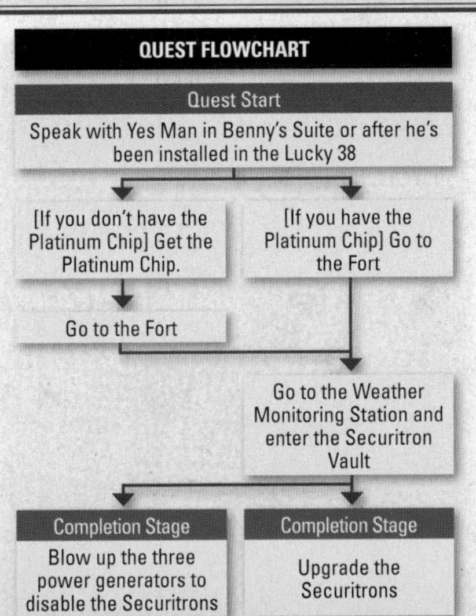

Tip Start this quest by either talking to Yes Man in The Tops Casino [2D.04], or heading to meet Caesar at The Fort first, although you won't know you're working independently (and this Quest won't trigger) until you speak with Yes Man. You can change allegiances to and from Mr. House, Caesar, and Yes Man during this Quest. You also must have the Platinum Chip (found on Benny during Main Quest: Ring-a-Ding Ding!, or during your visit to The Fort), and received The Mark of Caesar from Vulpes Inculta after exiting The Tops during Ring-a-Ding Ding! For this Quest's purposes, either conclusion is fine; you're independent, remember?

Suffering Through Pomposity

♠ [Optional] Go to the Fort and enter Mr. House's hidden bunker.

2

Leave The Strip and journey south to Cottonwood Cove [6.20]. For a detailed account of interacting with the Legion at this point, consult Main Quest: Render Unto Caesar. But generally, you must head to the wharf, speak to Cursor Lucullus, and agree to take his boat along the Colorado River to The Fort **(1)** [3.28]. Upon arrival, leave all (but your hold-out) weapons, and search out Caesar's Tent. Speak with Caesar **(2)** (and Benny if he's here) and claim the Platinum Chip. Caesar orders you to destroy whatever is inside the old bunker building. But you know better. Agree anyway.

Platinum Chip

3

4

Exit Caesar's Tent and head west, down the steps and into a flat promontory of tents, a radio mast, and a Weather Monitoring Station **(3)**. Enter, and your weapons are returned. Remember to rearm yourself before continuing! Activate the console next to the floor flap doors using the Platinum Chip. Open the Elevator Door to Securitron Vault, and step through into a connecting chamber with a large monitor on your right **(4)**. This has the visage of:

- Yes Man, if you've teamed up with him, and taken Mr. House out of the picture.
- Mr. House, if he is still alive.
- A "lost connection," if Mr. House has been taken offline.

Explore the Bunker.

Me, and This Army

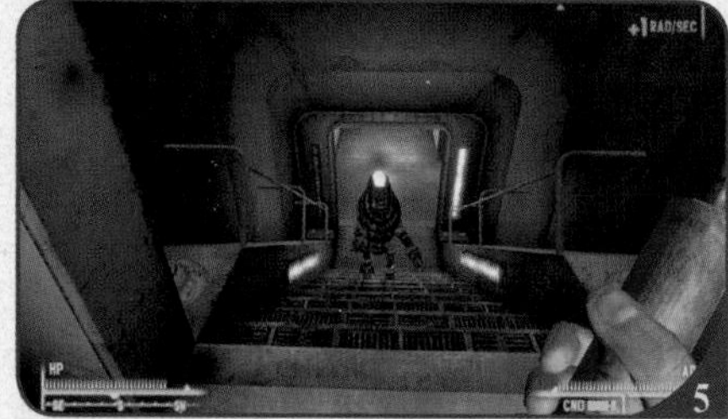

5

6

7

The Vault Status Terminal by the door informs you that turrets and Protectrons are active, and Sentry Bots are standing by. So you'll face the two former robotic foes throughout your exploration. Defeat the Protectron at the bottom of the steps **(5)**, then access the security room or turn right. The security room contains a Plasma Rifle and ammunition (perfect for taking out robotic foes), and three monitors.

The Protectron Operations Terminal can be hacked, and the alert turned off, effectively shutting down all Protectron attacks.

The Turret Operations Terminal can be hacked, and the turrets disarmed.

The Sentry Bot Operations Terminal is currently offline.

Whatever your choice, head down the corridor, past a door to the Sentry Bot chamber (which is locked, but can be sealed to prevent Sentry Bots from attacking you on the way out), and into a long, windowed hallway with two Protectrons and a turret ahead of you, and a huge army of deactivated Securitrons to your left and right, behind the reinforced windows. Shoot or avoid the robots, exit via the door, watch for another turret on the stairs, and head into the large generator room **(6)**. Face down around five Protectrons as you scout around the large generators, and you'll find three conduit chambers **(7)**. Each contains a Power Regulator. These control the flow of power throughout the vault, and without them, the power buildup could reach dangerous—and explosive— levels.

[Optional] Upgrade the Securitron army to use later for your own purposes.

[Optional] Destroy the Securitron army.

8

Power up the Securitrons: The "commotion" fools Caesar into thinking you've destroyed the base. Or, simply leave the Securitrons alone, because you don't need to return to Caesar (but this is a mistake, because a giant robot army is always useful).

Open the door in the west wall, and head up the stairs (watch out for turrets) to the door marked "Systems Room," taking out two more turrets before accessing the Securitron Operations Console. Insert the Platinum Chip and upgrade the Securitron army **(8)**; you now have a massive robotic force at your command for the upcoming final battle! Then (optionally) return to Caesar.

Caution If you destroy the Securitrons instead of upgrading them, then you're either making the final battle a lot more difficult for yourself, or you're readying an alliance with Caesar (or the NCR, but not Mr. House). If you want to be a Wild Card though, Securitron destruction is a terrible idea.

The Quest concludes once you've made this decision. You don't need to return to Yes Man if you've already spoken to him about the other "tribes" (Factions) you need to make contact with. Begin Main Quest: Wild Card: Side Bets right now.

500 XP

WILD CARD: SIDE BETS

ALLIED FACTION

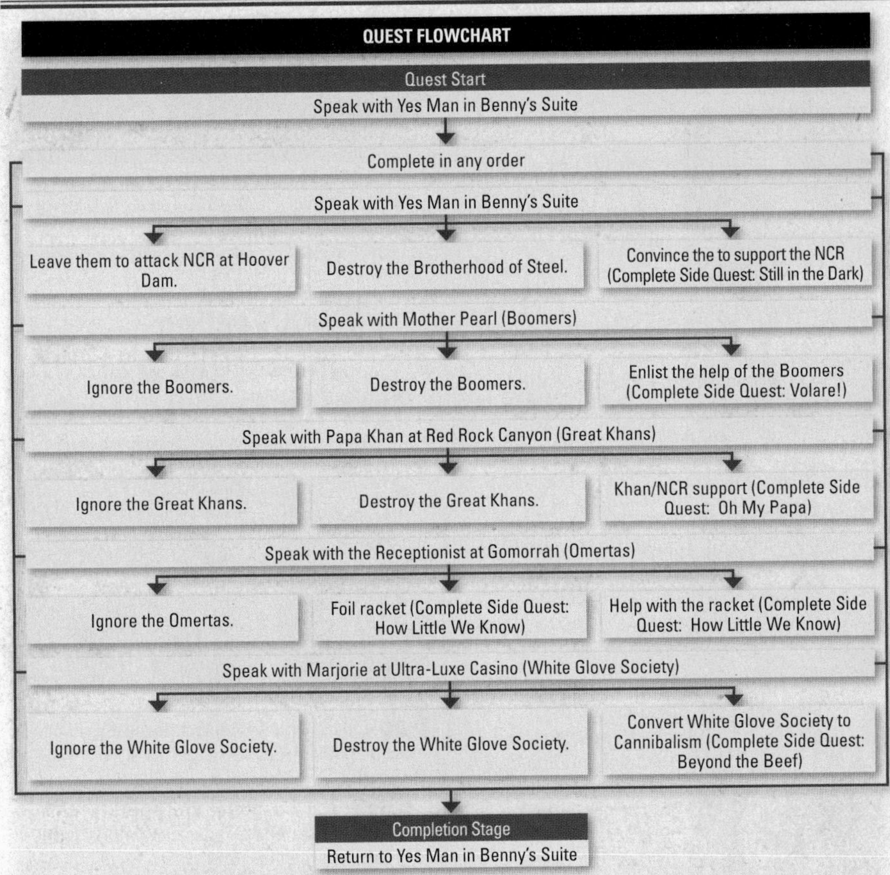

Tip To start this quest, just talk to Yes Man in The Tops Casino [2D.04], ideally during Main Quest: Ring-a-Ding Ding! You also begin the previous two Wild Card Quests during this Yes Man conversation, but make sure you ask about the other "tribes" that Yes Man suggests you contact. Optionally ask for even more detail on each of them, and ensure that your Pip-Boy's Data menu has this Quest active, with the following Objectives listed:

- **Make contact with the Boomers at Nellis AFB.**
- **Go to Red Rock Canyon and make contact with Great Khans.**
- **Observe the Omertas at their casino, Gomorrah.**
- **Visit the White Glove Society at the Ultra-Luxe casino.**
- **Make contact with the Brotherhood of Steel.**

Overview: Contact!

With Yes Man giving you free rein to figure out who you want to ally with or destroy, and complete freedom to approach each Faction in any order, this is the most flexible Main Quest of all. For every one of the five "tribes" Yes Man has information on, the bare minimum requirement is to make contact with a representative of each Faction. Then, after your initial conversation, you have the following options:

You can ignore their pleas, help requests, or orders. You've made contact, and that's enough. Return to Yes Man and tell him you don't need to work with this Faction. With the exception of the Brotherhood of Steel, the Faction plays no part in the final battle.

You can help the Faction out. This means completing the Side Quest associated with that particular Faction. This information is listed, and a truncated plan of action, is shown below. For a more detailed account, read the appropriate Side Quest (shown in the nearby flow chart). The Faction then may aid you in the final battle or affect the ending, depending on your interactions.

You can destroy the Faction. This sometimes means killing the leaders. Other times it means destroying their location. As with the first option, the Faction plays no part in the final battle, but this does affect the ending.

Faction 1: Shaking Up the Boomers

You can visit the Boomers, and complete any of their Quest-related tasks before or after Yes Man mentions it. Other Faction leaders have their own plans for the Boomers too; consult Side Quest: Volare! for all your options.

1

2

The nearest (and safest) spot to Boomer territory is the Fields' Shack **(1)** [3.04]. Take the road, and you'll run into George **(2)**, who offers information on how to safely navigate the howitzer barrages to reach the Boomer's Nellis Air Force Base [3.01].

Tip To navigate through the howitzer barrages, ignore George's deal unless you want to part with Caps. Run straight into the rubble of the first house you see, and hide in the corner. After the wave of shells, while the Boomers reload, either run to the next (mostly) intact house, or make a bee-line for the fence. When you're close enough to the perimeter fence, the Boomers stop firing (for fear of injuring their own people). Or, you can simply run along the rock wall to the left when you reach the top of the road; you might be struck by the outer splash damage once or twice, but you won't take a direct hit.

BOOMERS Faction Interaction #1A: From the Sea to the Skies

3

Now you begin Side Quest: Volare! Please refer to that specific Quest for details on how to safely enter the base **(3)**, and convince the Boomers to support you. But briefly, you need to:

- Reach the front gate, meet Raquel, and begin a cordial conversation with Mother Pearl.

BOOMERS You must then raise your Boomer Reputation Rank to "Idolized." Achieve this by completing any of the following tasks (some of which are their own Side Quests) until your Fame improves. Use your Pip-Boy to check the status. You don't have to perform all the tasks.

(Side Quest: Volare!) Visit Pete and learn all about Boomer history.

(Side Quest: Volare!) Speak to Argyle and treat all his patients.

(Side Quest: Volare! / Sunshine Boogie) Talk to Loyal, and repair the Solar Array Station.

(Side Quest: Volare! / Ant Misbehavin') Speak to Rachel about (and purge) the Ant infestation.

(Side Quest: Volare! / Young Hearts) Help Jack meet the love for whom he pines.

(Side Quest: Volare!) Speak to Mother Pearl, and agree to dredge a old bomber from Lake Mead [3.26].

(Free Quest: Malleable Mini Boomer Minds and Bear Necessities) Speak to the children playing in the Boomer's base.

(Free Quest: Iron and Stealing) Collect Scrap Metal to sell to Jack.

(Free Quest: Missing a Few Missiles) Collect Missiles to sell to Raquel.

- Once you've completed Side Quest: Volare!, you can speak with Mother Pearl. When she calls you "a trusted friend of us all," ask if they can offer you assistance if there's a battle at the Hoover Dam in the near future.
- Have you already done all of this before Yes Man mentioned it? Then this Quest is considerably shorter. Just reacquaint yourself with Mother Pearl, and ask for her assistance.

Boomers Fame Gained!

Tip Unless you have a dual-personality and want to destroy the Boomers halfway through helping them, completing the above list of tasks is more than enough to gain an Idolized Reputation!

BOOMERS Faction Interaction #1B: Boomer Death Cries

Yes Man is completely happy whatever your choice is regarding the Boomers. You can ignore all of Mother Pearl's tasks completely, and kill everyone at the Nellis Air Force Base **(4)**! Begin Side Quest: Volare! as normal, until you've spoken to Mother Pearl and received your Objectives. You're then free to shed blood, but from a closer range. Killing everyone is one option, but for the Boomer Tribe to fall into disarray and decline, a more tactical series of strikes is called for: Kill their leaders.

Mother Pearl **(5)**, the matriarch, is inside or near her barracks, or wandering outside. She is a critical kill.

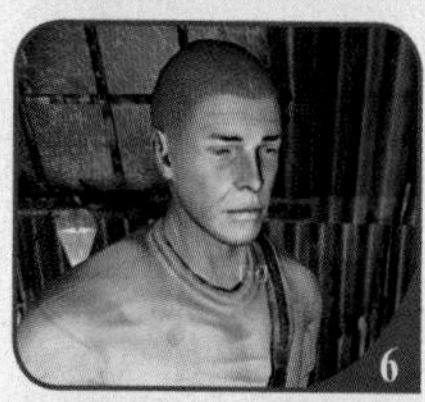

Argyll **(6)**, the doctor, is in the medical station. He is an optional kill.

Loyal **(7)**, the patriarch, is inside one of the two hangars, or wandering outside. He is a critical kill.

Jack **(8)** is usually inside one of the hangars, close to Loyal. He is an optional kill.

Raquel **(9)**, the master-at-arms, is usually standing on her viewing platform (in the center of the base, on the runway), or near the barracks. She is an optional kill.

Boomers Infamy Gained!

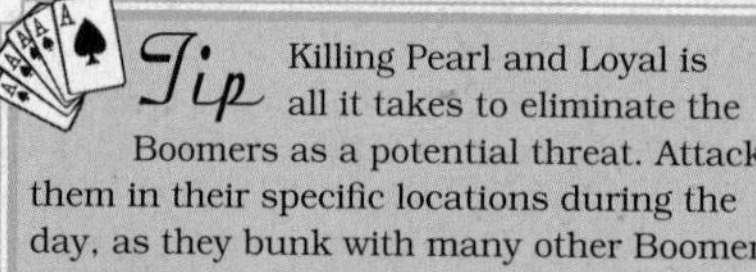

Tip Killing Pearl and Loyal is all it takes to eliminate the Boomers as a potential threat. Attack them in their specific locations during the day, as they bunk with many other Boomers at night.

Once you've completed these horrific acts, the Boomers won't be firing their guns at anyone, ever!

BOOMERS Faction Interaction #1C: Bye, Bye, Boomers

Finally, you can reach the base, speak to Mother Pearl, begin Side Quest: Volare!, and then never finish the Quest, choosing to ignore the Boomers. Tell Yes Man your decision at any time.

Faction 2: The Great Khans

Tip You can visit the Great Khans, and complete any of their Quest-related tasks before or after Yes Man mentions it. Other Faction leaders have their own plans for the Great Khans too. Consult Side Quest: Oh My Papa for every possibility.

Journey to the home of the Great Khans in the northwest mountains; the Red Rock Canyon **(10)** [1.15]. Choose your preferred method of dealing with Papa Khan and his minions.

GREAT KHANS Faction Interaction #2A: Severing Caesar's Control

Now you begin Side Quest: Oh My Papa. Check that Quest for the full run-down of how to get the Great Khans on your side. But briefly, you need to:

- Enter the longhouse and speak with Papa Khan **(11)**, who is currently allied with Caesar's Legion. You could have learned of this alliance during Main Quest: Render Unto Caesar, by sneaking around The Fort, or by finding Karl's Journal in Papa Khan's longhouse. You have to know about this alliance before you can ask Papa Khan break it and begin this side quest.
- Exit the longhouse, and then speak with Regis, who is thinking about a change in this alliance.

If you've been before, go to The Fort [3.28], take the Ledger from Caesar's Tent, and bring it to Regis to convince him.

Or, rummage round in the longhouse until you find Karl's Journal, and show this around.

- Travel to the Great Khan Encampment [4.03] and convince Melissa to switch her allegiance.
- Head to the Red Rock Drug Lab [1.14] and convince either Jack or Diane to switch:

Jack requires a Speech check to be convinced.

Diane requires her colleague Anders to be rescued from a crucifix near Cottonwood Cove [6.20].

- Caesar's enforcer—Karl—can optionally be removed from the picture:

You can succeed in Speech checks until Karl offends Papa Khan and is executed.

You can find Karl's journal inside the longhouse, and show it to Papa Khan.

Once Papa Khan agrees to go against the Legion, he requires an appropriate legacy for his tribe. You can solve this with some Speech checks. Otherwise visit Julie Farkas among at the Followers of the Apocalypse in the Old Mormon Fort [2C.01]. She knows someone who has studied Great Khan history and tribal cultures. Visit the 188 Trading Post [5.02] and locate Ezekiel, who gives you a book about the Mongols. Bring this book back to Papa Khan. This allows the Great Khans to pack up and exit the Mojave Wasteland under cover of the Hoover Dam battle.

Great Khan's Fame Gained!

GREAT KHANS Faction Interaction #2B: Death to Papa

12

NEW CA. REPUBLIC Another way to bring the Great Khans to your side is to remove Papa Khan as leader, which is only available if you're also working with the NCR, and have been sent here by Colonel Moore, during Main Quest: For the Republic, Part 2.

Wait until night-time, and creep around to the rear of the longhouse, and pry open the door with a Lockpick.

Locate the bed where Papa Khan is sleeping. Sneak around and attempt a murder **(12)**.

Sneak out, talk to Regis, and he follows your advice. You can utilize the Khans in the final battle.

Great Khan's Fame Gained!

GREAT KHANS Faction Interaction #2C: Death to the Horde

13

The other option is to kill everyone in Red Rock Canyon **(13)**, paying special attention to the Khans with a first name, including:

14

Papa Khan **(14)** the patriarch, found inside or near his longhouse, sitting in his outhouse, or wandering outside.

15

Regis **(15)** is the younger Khan, and Papa's successor. Slay him in near or inside the tents close to the longhouse.

Jack and Diane are in the Red Rock Drug Lab. Everyone else wearing a black Brahmin-skin jacket is fair game, too.

Great Khan's Infamy Gained!

GREAT KHANS Faction Interaction #2D: Goodbye, Great Khans

Finally, you can head to the canyon, speak to Papa Khan, begin Side Quest: Oh My Papa, and then never finish the Quest, choosing to ignore the Great Khans. Tell Yes Man your decision at any time.

Faction 3: The Omertas

> **Tip** As soon as Yes Man informs you that the Omertas are an interesting bunch to check out, you can begin Side Quest: How Little We Know. Note that the Omertas do not actually help you during the final battle, but getting them on your side aids in the aftermath of stabilizing The Strip, and placating the Families running the casinos there. You can begin Side Quest: How Little We Know in one of four ways:
>
> Successfully finishing Side Quest: Bye Bye Love
>
> Successfully starting Main Quest: The House Always Wins, IV.
>
> Dealing with the Great Khans during Main Quest: For The Republic, Part 2.
>
> Starting Main Quest: Wild Card: Side Bets (this Quest)

16

Now enter the Gomorrah Casino **(16)** [2D.01], and choose whether to help with the racket the Omerta bosses are planning, or foil it with the help of rogue lieutenant Cachino, or ignore the Omertas.

OMERTAS Faction Interaction #3A: Cachino's Colleague

17

Once you enter the Gomorrah Casino, to investigate the Omertas, you must begin Side Quest: How Little We Know. Briefly, you need to:

- Ask the receptionist or other casino workers about Cachino, then ask him about his side businesses.
- Confront Cachino **(17)** after obtaining details of his deeds against the other Omertas.
- Hand him the evidence, and then begin investigating two Omerta operatives:

Investigate Troike and obtain the blackmail note from Big Sal's Safe, OR

Investigate Troike and use his Thermite to destroy the Omertas' weapons storage.

Investigate Clanden and steal the Snuff Tapes from his safe. Then confront Clanden and either kill him or convince him to leave New Vegas.

- Kill Big Sal and Nero.

The Strip Fame Gained!

> **Caution** Warning! Excessive killing doesn't affect your Strip Reputation, but it gets you barred from the casino!

OMERTAS Faction Interaction #3B: Cachino's Reaper

18

Side Quest: How Little We Know can be completed in another way, which benefits the Omertas, but still keeps them loyal to you. Briefly, you need to:

- Ask the receptionist or other casino workers about Cachino, then ask him about his side businesses.
- Confront Cachino after obtaining details of his deeds against the other Omertas.
- Keep the evidence, and convince an Omerta thug that you need to speak to Big Sal or Nero.

Speak with Big Sal or Nero and give Cachino's evidence over. Then "help" Big Sal or Nero during Cachino's business meeting **(18)**. Then offer to help the boss with rackets they're planning.

Speak with Troike and retrieve a stolen weapons shipment from Fiends.

Speak with Clanden, and agree to find chlorine at the Ultra-Luxe, or at the Freeside supplier.

- Let Big Sal or Nero know that their rackets have been helped.

The Strip Infamy Gained!

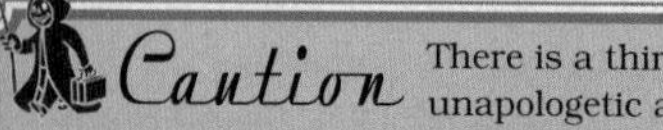

Caution There is a third, unapologetic and highly dangerous way to minimize the Omertas' presence, and that's to simply find the three bosses (Big Sal, Nero, and Cachino) and murder them all, and anyone else you spot with a first name and a sharp suit. The Omertas become hostile, and there is instability on The Strip. It doesn't help you in this Quest, either.

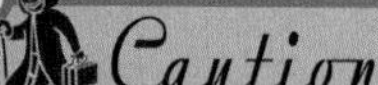

Caution If you haven't already completed the Free Quests "Big Winner" (detailed in the Tour section devoted to Gomorrah), you risk being unable to gain an Achievement or Trophy devoted to gambling. You have been warned!

OMERTAS Faction Interaction: Wise Guys' Mug Shots

19

This is Cachino **(19)**. You'll usually find him in the main level (he seeks out you). Then he moves to the bar near the stage on the main level.

20

This is Big Sal **(20)**. You'll find him on the balcony or pool table and offices area of the main level, or sleeping in the Gomorrah suites.

21

This is Nero **(21)**. You'll find him on the balcony or pool table and offices area of the main level, or sleeping in the Gomorrah suites.

22

This is Troike **(22)**. You'll find him in the Gomorrah lower lobby area, in the Zoara Club.

23

This is Clanden **(23)**. You'll find him sleeping or wandering the Gomorrah suites.

OMERTAS Faction Interaction #3D: Addio, Omertas

Finally, you can enter Gomorrah, speak to the receptionist (and optionally Cachino), to begin Side Quest: How Little We Know, and then never finish the Quest, choosing to ignore the Omertas. Tell Yes Man your decision whenever you wish.

Faction 4: The White Glove Society

Tip Once Yes Man mentions the White Glove Society, you can begin Side Quest: Beyond the Beef, although it starts any time you speak to Heck Gunderson or Mortimer inside the Ultra-Luxe Casino. Note that the White Glove Society doesn't actually help during the final battle, but allying with them aids in the aftermath of stabilizing The Strip, and placating the Families running the casinos there.

24

When you're ready, visit the Ultra-Luxe Casino **(24)** [2D.05], and choose whether you wish to expose (and destroy) the White Glove Society's more...*antisocial* behavior, or ally with them, and bring their meat up to a more *humane* standard. Or, you can simply ignore them once you've spoken to them. The ins and outs of this are detailed in Side Quest: Beyond the Beef.

WHITE GLOVE SOCIETY Faction Interaction #4A: A High Steaks Game

25

Although you can overlap and change your mind during the Quest, Beyond the Beef's "Exposure" option involves the following:

- Enter the Ultra-Luxe and speak with Heck Gunderson **(25)**, and learn about his missing son, Ted.
- Speak to Marjorie **(26)**, who directs you to Mortimer **(27)**. He reveals information about an investigator.
- Locate the investigator in his room, and uncover a Matchbook. Watch out for some over-eager staff.
- Examine the Matchbook to uncover a time and a place to meet Chauncey: in the Steam Room at 4 PM.
- Chauncey explains the reasons behind the guest disappearances, before disappearing himself.

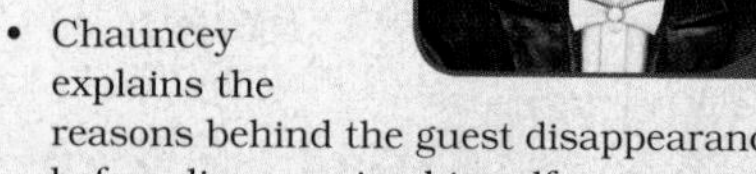

- Gain access to the kitchens, via the members-only sections of the White Glove Society. You can:

Open the door to the kitchen with a Bobby Pin.

Increase your Fame with the White Glove Society and The Strip.

Convince Mortimer or Marjorie to sponsor you.

Speak to Mortimer about your craving for a particular type of meat.

Obtain the Kitchen Keys by killing Mortimer.

Obtain a number of keys by siding with Mortimer (you can switch to "ally" or double-cross and expose him).

- Now in the kitchen, you can:

28

Remove Philippe **(28)** the chef and cook for the banquet before exposing the society:

Improvise a recipe while Philippe isn't in the kitchen.

Purchase the recipes from Philippe.

Ask for the recipes for a cookbook.

Kill Philippe and take the recipes.

Cook the meal of an approximation of human flesh.

Drug the wine with Med-X.

- Wait until 7 PM, then use the intercom to call the waiter to take the meal (or wine) to the banquet.
- Enter the freezer and rescue Ted. Kill him if you want to switch to "ally."
- Take Ted back to Heck, via the banquet and expose or kill Mortimer at the end of his speech. Then speak with Marjorie.
- Take Ted back to Heck, via the banquet while the patrons are drugged.
- Return Ted to Heck. You can:

Blame only Mortimer and keep the White Gloves Society intact.

The Strip Fame Gained!

White Glove Society Fame Gained!

If you tell Heck Gunderson that either Mortimer or the White Glove Society as a whole are responsible, he threatens to launch a food embargo on them.

You can calm him down, telling him "That's just what they'd want. You'd be driving the city to eat each other."

The Strip Infamy Gained!

White Glove Society Infamy Gained!

WHITE GLOVE SOCIETY Faction Interaction #4B: The Offal Truth

This path allows you to change your mind until around the mid-way point of the Quest. Beyond the Beef's "Alliance" option involves attempting the following:

- Enter the Ultra-Luxe Casino and speak with Mortimer **(27)**. Agree to help and receive his keys.
- Unlock the kitchens door, and locate Ted in the freezer.

Kill Ted, obtain his blood, and spread it around Heck Gunderson's penthouse suite. Find a Securitron and report the bloodshed, framing Heck.

Bring Ted back to Heck, but tell him you don't know who kidnapped him.

- Locate Carlyle St. Clair III **(29)** at his shack north of New Vegas, then:

Incapacitate him. Drop his body in the nearby dumpster.

Or convince him to join the White Glove Society.

- Rendezvous with Mortimer after the 7 PM feast, and his plans have come to fruition; there's a new meat on the menu!

WHITE GLOVE SOCIETY Faction Interaction #4C: Goodbye, White Gloves

You can enter the Ultra-Luxe, speak to either Marjorie or Mortimer, and then choose to ignore their strange ceremonial ways and stiff upper lips. Halt your progress during Side Quest: Beyond the Beef at any time, and inform Yes Man of your decision at your earliest convenience.

Faction 5: The Brotherhood of Steel

> *Tip* The Hidden Bunker, and the four Side Quests related to the Brotherhood of Steel (including Veronica's, a Follower) can occur before or after you speak with Yes Man. Consult Side Quest: Still in the Dark for all your options.

Journey to the strange, desolate, and windswept Hidden Valley [5.11], and enter the western bunker **(30)**. From this point on, you have three choices; to kill the Brotherhood of Steel, initially ally with them, or ignore them.

> *Note* You cannot ally with the Brotherhood of Steel if you're Independent. The only reason to ally is to be trained in Power Armor, or if you want to change your alliance to the NCR, which then allows you to ally with the Brotherhood.

BROTHERHOOD OF STEEL Faction Interaction #5A: Tick, Tick, Boom!

The Brotherhood of Steel's bunker can be destroyed, and there are cunning, and brutish ways to accomplish this. You can:

Enter the facility, and when Paladin Ramos stops you, kill him and then every single Brotherhood of Steel member **(31)**. This is long, highly dangerous, and ultimately pointless, because you have a better option.

Agree to see Elder McNamara, and once you're free to move about the bunker, head to the VR chamber in the southern quadrant of the bunker L2. When no one is looking, surreptitiously inspect the two terminals on the western wall; the Self-Destruct Authorization Terminal, and a link terminal to activate the self-destruct command. You can:

Hack the red terminal, and start the bunker self-destruct sequence. Or,

- You can locate the three senior Brotherhood of Steel members with keycard access to the authorization terminal, which is needed otherwise. The three targets are:

Head Scribe Taggart **(32)**, who is usually in his bed, or wandering this VR chamber.

Head Paladin Hardin **(33)**, who is at the entrance between bunkers L1 and L2.

Elder McNamara **(34)**, who is usually in his bed, or sitting in the command room.

Head Scribe's Keycard

Head Paladin's Keycard

Elder's Keycard

Obtain the keycards through Pickpocketing or shooting (which turns the entire bunker hostile).

Back at the authorization terminal, the keycards generate a password for the red terminal. Then access that, and choose the self-destruct sequence launch. Now flee to the surface.

Brotherhood of Steel Infamy Gained!

> *Tip* Your mass-slaying of the Brotherhood of Steel isn't for naught, as there's a hefty haul inside this bunker, although buying items from them nets much more potent weaponry. Check the Tour chapter for the stash, and remember to pillage the bunker before you start the self-destruct sequence!

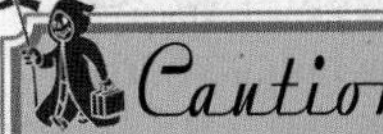

> *Caution* Beware: Activating the self-destruct sequence causes instant Vilification with the Brotherhood! You are marked, and may encounter patrols gunning for you later in your Questing!

Faction Interaction #5B: Into the Light

The second main plan is to complete Side Quest: Still in the Dark, and then forge an alliance with the elder, before eventually turning on them (you cannot be allied with them as an Independent). Consult that Quest for thorough information. But in brief, you need to:

- Speak with Elder McNamara, and agree to the test (if Veronica isn't with you) regarding the NCR Ranger.
- Speak with the elder, and begin the first task: retrieve Holotape Mission Data from three downed patrols **(35)**.
- Return to McNamara, and collect three reports from Brotherhood Scouts in the field **(36)**.
- Return to McNamara, and meet up with Senior Knight Lorenzo, who gives you a list of air filtration components to gather.
- Enter Vault 3 [2.24] and obtain a Reverse Pulse Cleaner from Motor-Runner's chamber.
- Enter Vault 11 [5.05], and locate a Differential Pressure Controller in the water-filled lower level.
- Enter Vault 22 [1.09], and wind down, then up into the oxygen recycling level to gather the HEPA Cartridge Filters.

With all this concluded, ask the head of the Brotherhood of Steel to help in your fight. They duly agree. This can only be achieved if you are also running a parallel Quest with the NCR (For the Republic, Part 2), and you flip your Wild Card and align with the NCR later.

Brotherhood of Steel Fame Gained!

Faction Interaction #5C: See You Later, Brotherhood of Steel

Or, you can visit the bunker door that isn't filled with rubble, and gain access to the Brotherhood of Steel (Veronica, who can be found at the 188 Trading Post [5.02] is a great help here). Then, simply ignore all the tasks Elder McNamara sets for you, and report to Yes Man that you aren't interested in forging an alliance with these paranoid technology cravers.

Now you must return to Yes Man and conclude this Quest.

WILD CARD: FINISHING TOUCHES

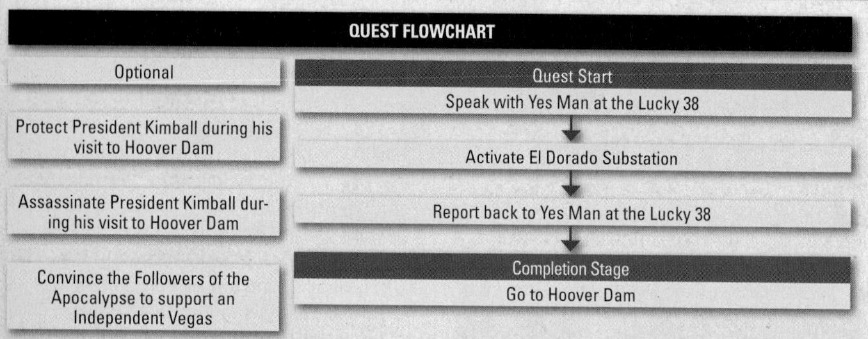

Final Preparations for Power

With any combination of the five lesser Factions either ignored, allied, or killed, you return to the penthouse suite in the Lucky 38 Casino. Yes Man **(1)** tells you that:

- The Securitrons at The Fort are on standby, and upgraded (if you completed Main Quest: Wild Card: You and What Army?).
- Or the Securitrons aren't part of the hardware that Yes Man controls.

With the tribes taken care of, Main Quest: Wild Card: Side Bets concludes. Yes Man has only a few more matters to contend with. Main Quest: Wild Card: Finishing Touches now begins.

Decoded military radio transmissions have revealed that NCR President Aaron Kimball is going to visit the Hoover Dam to increase the NCR's morale. Yes Man notes that Mr. House wanted Kimball to be kept alive and not assassinated, to avoid instability on The Strip. You can attempt Main Quest: You'll Know It When It Happens.

Your standing with the NCR matters greatly when obtaining Main Quest: You'll Know It When It Happens. You must be "Accepted" (or better) in your NCR Reputation to attend President Kimball's speech. The easiest way to know this is to check your Reputation on your Pip-Boy, or see how you're treated when you visit Hoover Dam [3.33].

Once you've stopped, or helped assassinate, or ignored Kimball, you have an imperative task. Yes Man hands you an Override Chip. You're to take it to the El Dorado Substation and attach it to the power control terminal. Yes Man will use the jolt of electricity to jump-start the Lucky 38's reactor, and boost the transmission strength of the network, allowing control over the Securitrons at Hoover Dam.

Override Chip

- **[Optional] Protect President Kimball during his official visit to Hoover Dam before powering up El Dorado Substation.**
- **Report to Ranger Grant.**
- **Go to the El Dorado power station and install the Override Chip.**

[Optional] Presidential Cordon

2

If you care about New Vegas stability, you'd do well to save President Aaron Kimball **(2)**. If you don't, you can kill him yourself, or ignore the visit altogether. The first (and second) options are detailed in Main Quest: You'll Know It When It Happens. Consult that section before continuing this Quest.

El Dorado Override

3

Between Vault 11 [5.05] to the east, and Black Mountain [5.07] to the west, lies the El Dorado Substation [5.04], which siphons power from HELIOS One [5.13] to the south. Once you reach the substation, a patrol of NCR grunts **(3)** stops your progress, and tells you that there's going to be trouble if you enter the control room. You can:

Assault the substation with all guns blazing (or Melee Weapons bludgeoning), which doesn't win you any favors (or Reputation) with the NCR.

NCR Infamy Gained!

Or, you can Sneak (ideally with a Stealth Boy) into the substation without being spotted, or the alarm raised.

Or, if you've procured an NCR uniform or armor, you can fool these grunts into thinking you're one of them, and enter the substation.

4

Once inside the substation, activate this terminal **(4)**, and power up the substation with the Override Chip. Yes Man's network tentacles now reach far and wide, and include the ability to control the massive Securitron army in the bunker under The Fort [3.28] that you (hopefully) brought online and upgraded. Now head outside, and prepare to tie up any remaining loose ends.

Report back to Yes Man at the Lucky 38.

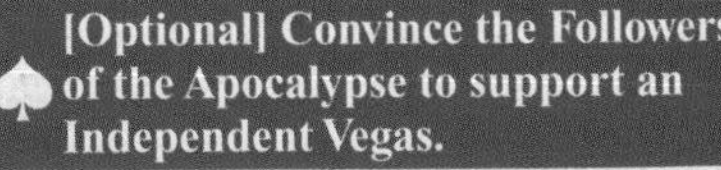
[Optional] Convince the Followers of the Apocalypse to support an Independent Vegas.

Ready to Roll!

Now that all those pesky loose ends have been tidied up, you can return to the Lucky 38 and Yes Man. He has some exciting news; the Legion is massing troops in a staging area east of the dam! Yes Man asks if you want to head for the dam straight away, or whether you'd rather keep the folks of New Vegas calm by requesting that the Followers of the Apocalypse provide medical aid. You can:

Agree to meet with the Followers over at the Old Mormon Fort [2C.01]. Those do-gooders can be convinced through a chat with their leader Julie Farkas to support an Independent New Vegas. This affects your ending, but little else.

Ignore the Followers and suffer the instability after the looming battle.

Tell Yes Man you have other matters to attend to. This stalls Act III until you are ready.

Or, let Yes Man know you're ready to head to the dam. Yes Man tells you his research has yielded two possible victory scenarios; both of which are detailed in the finale of Act III; Main Quest: No Gods, No Masters. Which begins now!

Go to Hoover Dam.

THE HOUSE ALWAYS WINS, I

ALLIED FACTION
MR. HOUSE

See flowchart on the following page

Before You Begin: Strip Search

The Securitron Guards at The Strip North Gate [2.13] require proof of your high-rolling status. You can:

Hand over 2,000 Caps; the "credit check" to prove you're not a "less-reputable person." The bad news? You'll need to scrounge together the necessary Caps. The good news? The check is just to see that you're good for the money, and you get to keep the Caps!

Answer "1C 3C R34 M," verbally hacking and confusing the Gatekeeper into letting you in.

Attack the toughened Gatekeepers. Prepare for a protracted battle before forcing your way in.

Complete Side Quest: G.I. Blues, and request a Passport from the King as a reward.

Visit Mick & Ralph's [2C.02], speak to Ralph, and have him craft a Passport for you. This is Free Quest: Papers, Please (which is detailed in the Tour chapter).

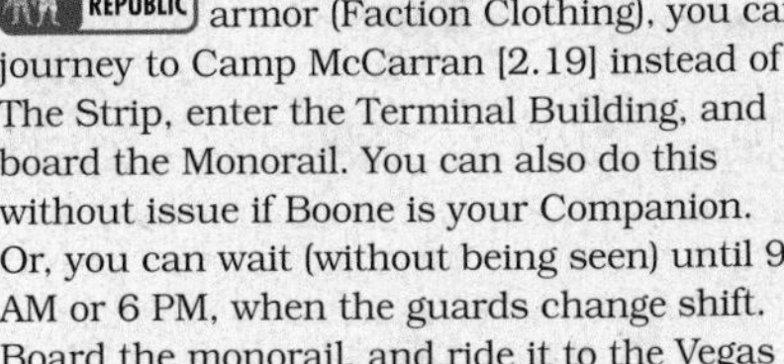
Finally, if you're wearing NCR armor (Faction Clothing), you can journey to Camp McCarran [2.19] instead of The Strip, enter the Terminal Building, and board the Monorail. You can also do this without issue if Boone is your Companion. Or, you can wait (without being seen) until 9 AM or 6 PM, when the guards change shift. Board the monorail, and ride it to the Vegas Boulevard Station [2D.03]. Exit, and Victor greets you. This method is dangerous and can severely impede your standing with the NCR.

Meeting Mr. House: From Outhouse to Penthouse

1

Once you're gazing up at the neon, concrete, and shockingly well preserved New Vegas Strip **(1)** [Zone 2D], you're greeted by Victor **(2)**. He tells you that the head honcho of New Vegas, Mr. House, is itching you make your acquaintance. You're free to answer however you like. The Quest begins now, and can be completed before, during, or after Main Quest: Ring-a-Ding Ding!

2

It is better to see Mr. House, and Barter for the maximum Caps in exchange for returning with the Platinum Chip, before you meet Benny during Main Quest: Ring-a-Ding Ding! You want more Caps, right?

Note

Securitrons such as Victor can "bounce" personalities to and from their robotic hosts. Therefore, it is impossible to kill Victor (unless you try killing every single Securitron in Nevada). In addition, if you choose to ignore Mr. House now, he greets you in the entrance to the Securitron Bunker, inside The Fort [3.28].

Talk to Mr. House at the Lucky 38.

QUEST FLOWCHART

Complete Main Quest: They Went That-A-Way and travel to Freeside

- Have 2000 caps.
- Hack the Securitrons into giving the player access [Science 80+]
- Complete Side Quest: G.I. Blues to gain a favor from the King

Get fake passport from Mick and Ralph's for 500 caps

Use the favor to get a passport to gain access to the Strip. Must also have 2000 caps in the player's inventory

Quest Start

After the player is force-greeted by Victor, head to the Lucky 38

Speak with Victor to enter the Lucky 38

Proceed forward and speak with Victor again to take the elevator to the Penthouse

Go down the stairs to the terminal with Mr. House's image on the monitor

Speak with House

- Ask him about his proposal
- Give him the Platinum Chip (obtained through Main Quest: Ring-A-Ding-Ding!)

- Ask for more caps [Barter 50+]
- Accept the terms as-is (1000 caps)

Travel to the Tops casino

Complete Main Quest: Ring-A-Ding-Ding! to get the Platinum Chip from Benny

- Be force-greeted by Vulpes Inculta outside of the Tops (Begins Main Quest: Render Unto Caesar)
- Be force-greeted by NCR trooper outside Tops if you haven't spoken to Mr. House already

Return to Mr. House and give him the Chip

Speak with Victor near the elevators and be taken to the to the basement

Walk forward and observe the two Securitrons firing missiles

Speak with Victor again to return to the Penthouse

Completion Stage

Speak with Mr. House

In a forest of gaudy illumination, the Lucky 38 Casino [2D.02] is the most ostentatious **(3)**. When you're ready to begin (there's no rush), meet Victor at the diamond-motif front doors. He tells you the boss is waiting upstairs. The outer doors slide open. Enter the Lucky 38 Casino floor. After an optional look around, head to the elevator bank **(4)** and speak with Victor once again. He summons the elevator; request "Penthouse."

At the penthouse floor, step out and you're met by "Jane." You can ask Jane some questions, ranging from her role ("special assistant") to the odd little Snow Globe collection that Mr. House keeps (and Jane looks after). Then head into an expansive mezzanine and great room **(5)** offering the best views of the Mojave Wasteland you've ever seen! Flanked by two Securitron guards

is a large cluster of monitors and advanced equipment. Mr. House's image appears on the largest screen **(6)**.

Mr. House is a keen collector of these tchotchkies; in fact, he's one of the world's biggest collectors of antique Snow Globes! If you happen to find any out in the Wasteland (or even inside the Lucky 38 Casino), bring them to Jane and you can add them to Mr. House's collection. You'll receive a reward, too! Consult the Appendices, or Free Quest: Useless Baubles or Fancy Trinkets? in the Tour chapter for more information.

Mr. House's Proposal: Retrieving the Platinum Chip

Speak with Mr. House **(7)**, or at least, the image on the screen, and you can talk about The Strip, the various Factions, and other interesting tidbits to help make sense of the complex societal interactions at play. Eventually ask to "get down to business, then." Mr. House replies that one of his employees has stolen an item of extraordinary value to him, and he wants it recovered. At this point, you can:

Hand over the Platinum Chip if you have it. You must have taken it from Benny during Main Quest: Ring-a-Ding Ding!

1,000 Caps

- Or, you can ask about Mr. House's proposal. You can then ask about (and gain valuable information on) Benny, the Platinum Chip, who exactly Mr. House is, and most importantly, what he's going to pay for your services.

You can lay on the charm after asking about Mr. House, telling him Jane makes sure his life always has beauty in it.

After a charming retort, you can tell Mr. House he's making you blush. Mr. House continues to gush before composing himself.

- You can also surmise that Mr. House appears to be a computer, not a man. Mr. House assures you he's all flesh and blood.

Respond that his lifespan is impossible, unless he's a Ghoul or Super Mutant. He tells you he's spent considerably in the pursuit of extending his lifespan.

Ask how he's stayed alive all this time. It was a costly sacrifice.

- Asking about the Platinum Chip reveals it to be "a very special item." Mr. House says little more. You can:

Tell him the more you know, the easier it will be to find it. He tells you to keep a lookout for any computers (or a laboratory) that Benny may have used.

The conversation then continues with Mr. House offering you intriguing, but not altogether revealing answers about the chip and its background.

- The proposal Mr. House is offering is four times the delivery bonus stipulated in your original courier contract. You can:

Increase the price to five times: 1,250 Caps. You won't get more than that!

Agree to accept the terms of 1,000 Caps.

Or refuse, and leave.

- Or you can leave (and "suspend" the Quest). In the future, this might not be such an easy task.

For information on Mr. House's knowledge of Benny, consult Main Quest: Ring-a-Ding Ding!

Deliver the Platinum Chip to Mr. House.

8

Exit the penthouse, ask Victor to take you down to the casino level, and leave the Lucky 38. You're stopped on the steps by a member of the NCR military police **(8)**. He hands you a message from Ambassador Crocker, and deems it "very important." Access the Data > Misc menu, and read it. It requests your presence at the NCR Embassy [2D.07] on the south side of The Strip.

Visit the Embassy, and you begin Main Quest: Things That Go Boom.

Ambassador Crocker's Note

Decisions, Decisions...

> *Note* You must now complete Main Quest: Ring-a-Ding Ding! Consult that Quest for all the possible outcomes. Whether Benny gave you the Platinum Chip in the "Completion Consequences" of that Quest has a direct effect on this one.

After Main Quest: Ring-a-Ding Ding! concludes, you have the following options (which you can select more than one of):

MR. HOUSE

Option #1: House Cleaning

9

If you took the Platinum Chip from Benny's dead body **(9)**, or he gave it you, you can conclude this Quest. You can return to Mr. House immediately (see below).

WILD CARD CAESAR'S LEGION

Option #2: Gone, Baby, Gone

10

If Benny has escaped, he's still carrying the Platinum Chip and you cannot finish Main Quest: The House Always Wins, I. Don't despair; simply agree to see Caesar **(10)** after meeting Vulpes Inculta (Option #4), and start Main Quest: The House Always Wins, II. You can also visit Yes Man in Benny's suite inside The Tops Casino (Option #3).

> *Tip* If Benny escapes, you get the Platinum Chip by speaking to Mr. House and starting Main Quest: The House Always Wins, II, and then seeking Caesar at The Fort [3.28]. Then accept Caesar's first task, and enter the weather station, where you do Mr. House's bidding.

WILD CARD

Option #3: The Independent Contractor

11

Whether or not Benny escaped, you should have visited Yes Man **(11)** up in the hidden computer room inside Benny's suite. Speak to Yes Man and you are given some mainly independent tasks: Main Quest: Wild Card: Change in Management; Wild Card: Side Bets; and Side Quest: How Little We Know.

CAESAR'S LEGION

Option #4: Propugnaculum Tumulosus Sermo

12

You automatically meet Vulpes Inculta **(12)** outside The Tops Casino after finishing Main Quest: Ring-a-Ding Ding! You can begin Main Quest: Render Unto Caesar at this point, or any other option.

NEW CA. REPUBLIC

Option #5: For the New California Republic

13

Finally, you can investigate the Note you received from the NCR military police **(13)** earlier in this Quest, and begin Main Quest: Things That Go Boom with Ambassador Crocker.

Cashing In the Chip

14

So, you've handled Benny and recovered the Platinum Chip, right? Then return to the Lucky 38, ask Victor to take you up to the penthouse level again **(14)**, and speak with Mr. House. You can ask questions to gain further understanding of the situation, but at some point, you need to give the Platinum Chip over, or refuse.

Give up the chip, and Mr. House instructs you to take the elevator down to the basement.

If you refuse, you're attacked by Mr. House's Securitrons, including Jane and Victor. You cannot complete any further Main Quests involving Mr. House.

You are transported to the basement of the Lucky 38.

Observe as Mr. House upgrades Securitrons.

Step out into the dimly lit and grimy basement chamber. Move toward a small sunken area **(15)** where two Securitrons are going through combat

programming. The true power of the Platinum Chip is then revealed, as Mr. House upgrades them from Mk I **(16)** to Mk II Securitrons **(17)**, with additional firepower and a more militaristic temperament. When the upgrade is complete you are taken back to the penthouse.

As you might expect, attacking the Securitrons turns the entire robotic population of the Lucky 38 against you and impedes your activities with Mr. House.

Return to Mr. House.

500 XP

Since broadcasting the upgrade, every Securitron within range has received an upgrade. But this Securitron re-programming into a private army has only just begun! Speak to Mr. House about the next step in his domination of The Strip, and beyond: Main Quest: The House Always Wins, II.

THE HOUSE ALWAYS WINS, II

ALLIED FACTION
Lucky 38 MR. HOUSE

QUEST FLOWCHART

Quest Start
Complete Main Quest: The House Always Wins, I
↓
Speak with Victor to leave the Lucky 38
↓
Perform Main Quest: Render Unto Caesar far enough to enter the securitron Vault
↓
Go down the stairs to the terminal with Mr. House's image on the monitor
↓
Speak with House
↓
Agree to upgrade his Securitrons.
↓
Fight through the bunker to the Securitron Operations Console.
↓
Activate the console to upload the data.
↓
Return to Mr. House after speaking with Caesar and leaving the Fort
↓
Completion Stage
Speak with House

This Quest starts in one of two ways:

- Either automatically, after a successful completion of Main Quest: The House Always Wins, I.
- Or if Benny escapes and you complete the first few Objectives of Main Quest: Render Unto Caesar.

We Aren't Legion

After completing the first of Mr. House's tasks, agree to listen to his next plan for you **(1)**. You must infiltrate Caesar's camp at Fortification Hill, also known as The Fort [3.28]. Mr. House wants you to open a hatch in the basement of the derelict weather station in the camp, which bears the same insignia as the Lucky 38 logo. Only the Platinum Chip opens this door, so Mr. House gives it back.

Platinum Chip

Use the Platinum Chip to open the secret bunker at Fortification Hill.

Tip

CAESAR'S LEGION

Caesar has set up camp on the eastern side of the Colorado River. To infiltrate the place, you need to achieve the following (all of which is detailed much more thoroughly in Main Quest: Render Unto Caesar, which also flags where options favorable to Mr. House can be chosen. But briefly, you need to:

Travel to Cottonwood Cove [6.20] and meet Cursor Lucullus on the dock, and ask him to escort you to the Legion's camp at Fortification Hill.

Disarm, walk to the fort drawbridge and navigate to Caesar's Tent. Agree to demolish Mr. House's bunker under the weather station.

If Benny escaped, Caesar gives you the Platinum Chip, which is the only way to enter this facility.

Another option appears, which is the one you must complete to continue this Quest:

Awakening the Securitron Army

At the far western end of The Fort is a drab concrete building with a radio mast **(2)**. Enter the door on the side wall to the Weather Monitoring Station, and receive your weapons from the Weather Station Guard **(3)**. Activate the console next to the floor flap doors using the Platinum Chip, and descend the steps. Open the Elevator Door to the Securitron Vault.

The Legion hasn't gained access to this place. It's still the domain of Mr. House, who greets you from the bank of computer monitors **(4)**. You can:

Agree to Mr. House's demands, and plan to upgrade the Securitrons.

Refuse (after which, all robotic security becomes hostile), or remain noncommittal. You don't have to keep your word though.

Upgrade Mr. House's secret Securitron army.

The Vault Status Terminal by the door informs you that turrets and Protectrons are active, and Sentry Bots are standing by. So you'll face the two former robotic foes throughout your exploration. Defeat the Protectron at the bottom of the steps **(5)**, after which you can access the security room, or turn right. The security room contains a Plasma Rifle and ammunition (perfect for taking out robotic foes), and three monitors.

The Protectron Operations Terminal can be hacked, and the alert turned off, effectively shutting down all Protectron attacks.

The Turret Operations Terminal can be hacked, and the turrets disarmed.

The Sentry Bot Operations Terminal is currently offline.

Whatever your choice, head down the corridor, past a door to the Sentry Bot chamber (which is locked, but can be sealed to prevent Sentry Bots from attacking you on the way out), and into a long, windowed hallway with two Protectrons and a turret ahead of you, and a huge army of deactivated Securitrons to your left and right, behind the reinforced windows. Shoot or avoid the robots, exit via the door, watch for another turret on the stairs, and head into the large generator room **(6)**. Face down around five Protectrons as you scout around the large generators, and you'll find three conduit chambers **(7)**. Each contains a Power Regulator. These control the flow of power throughout the vault, and without them, the power buildup could reach dangerous—and explosive—levels.

Lucky 38 MR. HOUSE Power up the Securitrons. The "commotion" fools Caesar into thinking you've destroyed the base. Leaving the Securitrons alone simply stalls this Quest.

Open the door in the west wall, and head up the stairs (watch out for turrets) to the door marked "Systems Room," taking out two more turrets before accessing the Securitron Operations Console. Insert the Platinum Chip, and upgrade the Securitron army **(8)**; you now have a massive robotic force at your command for the incoming final battle! Then return to Caesar.

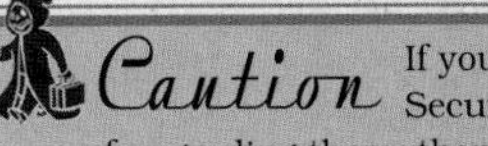

Caution If you destroy the Securitrons instead of upgrading them, then you're either making the final battle a lot more difficult for yourself, or you're readying an alliance with Caesar (or the NCR, but not Mr. House). The Quest fails if you destroy the Power Regulators.

Now return to Mr. House (as you exit the bunker), who tells you to report back to the Lucky 38 Casino to discuss "the next steps." Exit The Fort (either before or after telling Caesar you were victorious), and head back to The Strip [Zone 2D]. After you've met Victor and returned to the penthouse, speak to Mr. House. If this is the first time you've met Mr. House with the Platinum Chip, he asks you for it and tells you to head to the basement, where you watch as another Securitron upgrade take place (this is the conclusion of Main Quest: The House Always Wins, I).

Assuming you don't wish to annoy Mr. House, you can:

- Request the reward you Bartered for at the Securitron Vault.
- Ask what plans he has for his Securitron army.
- Or ask what happens next, and begin Main Quest: The House Always Wins, III.

THE HOUSE ALWAYS WINS, III

ALLIED FACTION
Lucky 38 MR. HOUSE

QUEST FLOWCHART

Quest Start
Complete Main Quest: The House Always Wins, II and accept House's next task.
↓
Speak with Victor to leave the Lucky 38
↓
Travel to Nellis AFB.
↓
Neutralize the Boomers by killing their leaders. / Convince the Boomers to join Mr. House [Side Quest: Volare!]
↓
Completion Stage
Return to Mr. House and inform him that the Boomers have been persuaded or neutralized.

This Quest begins as soon as you finish Main Quest: The House Always Wins, II, and agree to help with Mr. House's next task. It is also getting extremely important to pick a Faction to align with!

You can visit the Boomers and complete any of their Quest-related tasks before or after Mr. House requests it.

Shaking Up the Boomers

Mr. House's Securitrons on The Strip [Zone 2D] are upgraded, and those under The Fort [3.28] are ready for action. It is now simply a matter of adjusting the attitudes of some of the "lesser" Factions while you wait for Caesar's Legion to attack Hoover Dam. You can:

Continue these specific Quests, and ask about the next step.

- Or, you can ask further questions throughout your chat, and gain yet more background knowledge.
- Or, you can kill Mr. House, and fail his remaining Quests.

Assuming you're here to help Mr. House **(1)**, he tells you that outside New Vegas is an area once known as Nellis Air Force Base [3.01], which is now the home to an unusual tribe known as the Boomers. This "aggressively reclusive" clan has several howitzers, which they fire at intruders. Mr. House is interested in these big guns; they can fire on the Hoover Dam, and more specifically, any targets of his choosing. He wants the Boomers' support, or if that's not possible, he doesn't want them to sign treaties with the NCR or Caesar's Legion.

Reply that you'll make sure the Boomers support the correct side. Mr. House warns you of the sheer force of their bombardments, and that his Securitrons recently spotted a man near the base studying the patterns of these projectiles. Perhaps he can help?

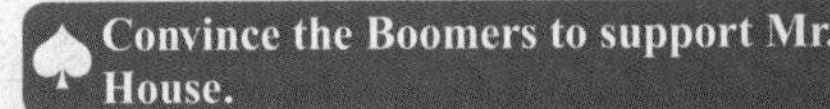

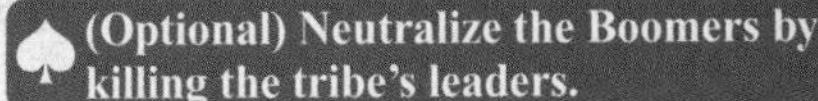

Leave the Lucky 38 and travel northeast. The nearest (and safest) spot to the Boomers' territory is the Fields' Shack **(2)** [3.04]. Take the road and you'll run into George **(3)**, who offers information on how to safely navigate the howitzer barrages to reach the Boomer's Nellis Air Force Base [3.01].

> **Tip** To navigate through the howitzer barrages, ignore George's deal unless you want to part with Caps. Run straight into the rubble of the first house you see, and hide in the corner. After the wave of shells, while the Boomers reload, either run to the next (mostly) intact house, or make a bee-line for the fence. When you're close enough to the perimeter fence, the Boomers stop firing (for fear of injuring their own people). Or, you can simply run along the rock wall to the left when you reach the top of the road; you might be struck by the outer splash damage once or twice, but you won't take a direct hit.

BOOMERS Faction Interaction #1A: Admired from Afar

Now you begin Side Quest: Volare! Please refer to that specific Quest for details on how to safely enter the base **(4)**, and convince the Boomers to support Mr. House. But briefly, you need to:

- Reach the front gate, meet Raquel, and begin a cordial conversation with Mother Pearl.

BOOMERS You must then raise your Boomer Reputation Rank to "Idolized." Achieve this by completing any of the following tasks (some of which are their own Side Quests) until your Rank improves. Use your Pip-Boy to check the status. You don't have to perform all the tasks.

(Side Quest: Volare!) Visit Pete and learn all about Boomer history.

(Side Quest: Volare!) Speak to Argyll and treat all his patients.

(Side Quest: Volare! / Sunshine Boogie) Talk to Loyal, and repair the Solar Array Station.

(Side Quest: Volare! / Ant Misbehavin') Speak to Rachel about (and purge) the Ant infestation.

(Side Quest: Volare! / Young Hearts) Help Jack meet the love for whom he pines.

(Side Quest: Volare!) Speak to Mother Pearl, and agree to dredge an old bomber from Lake Mead [3.26].

(Free Quest: Malleable Mini Boomer Minds and Bear Necessities) Speak to the children playing in the Boomer's base.

(Free Quest: Iron and Stealing) Collect Scrap Metal to sell to Jack.

(Free Quest: Missing a Few Missiles) Collect Missiles to sell to Raquel.

- Once you've completed Side Quest: Volare!, you can speak with Mother Pearl. When she calls you "a trusted friend of us all," ask if they can offer you assistance if there's a battle at the Hoover Dam in the near future.
- Have you already done all of this before Mr. House requested it? Then this Quest is considerably shorter. Just reacquaint yourself with Mother Pearl, and ask for her assistance.

Boomers Fame Gained!

> **Tip** Unless you're exhibiting symptoms of dual-personality and want to destroy the Boomers halfway through helping them, completing the above list of tasks is more than enough to gain an Idolized Reputation!

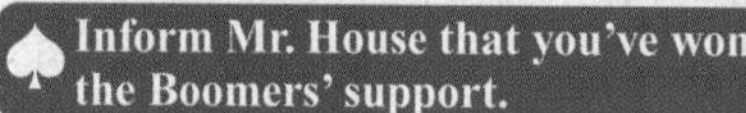

Inform Mr. House that you've won the Boomers' support.

BOOMERS Faction Interaction #1B: Killed at Close Range

Mr. House has a ruthless streak, which he's gradually revealing to you. He's given you a second option when it comes to treating the Boomers: execution! Begin Side Quest: Volare! as normal, until you've spoken to Mother Pearl and received your Objectives. You're then free to unleash hell, but from a closer range. Killing everyone **(5)** is one option, but for the Boomer Tribe to fall into disarray and decline, a more tactical series of strikes is called for: Kill their leaders.

Mother Pearl **(6)**, the matriarch, is inside or near her barracks, or wandering outside. She is a critical kill.

Argyll **(7)**, the doctor, is in the medical station. He is an optional kill.

Loyal **(8)**, the patriarch, is inside one of the two hangars, or wandering outside. He is a critical kill.

Jack **(9)** is usually inside one of the hangars, close to Loyal. He is an optional kill.

Raquel **(10)**, the master-at-arms, is usually standing on her viewing platform (in the center of the base, on the runway), or near the barracks. She is an optional kill.

Boomers Infamy Gained!

> **Tip** Killing Pearl and Loyal is all it takes to eliminate the Boomers as a potential threat. Attack them in their specific locations during the day, because they bunk with many other Boomers at night.

Once you've completed these horrific acts, the Boomers won't be making any deals with the NCR or Caesar's Legion ever!

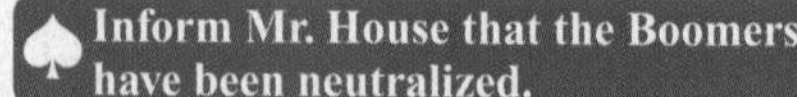

Inform Mr. House that the Boomers have been neutralized.

Faction Interaction: Complete

Back at the penthouse level of the Lucky 38, Mr. House asks for a progress report. You can:

Tell him you're still working on it (which is only advisable if you haven't secured their loyalty or murdered their leaders).

Inform Mr. House that the Boomers have had their loyalty secured, or they've been taken out of the equation. Mr. House is pleased, and immediately informs you of your next assignment.

THE HOUSE ALWAYS WINS, IV

ALLIED FACTION
Lucky 38 MR. HOUSE

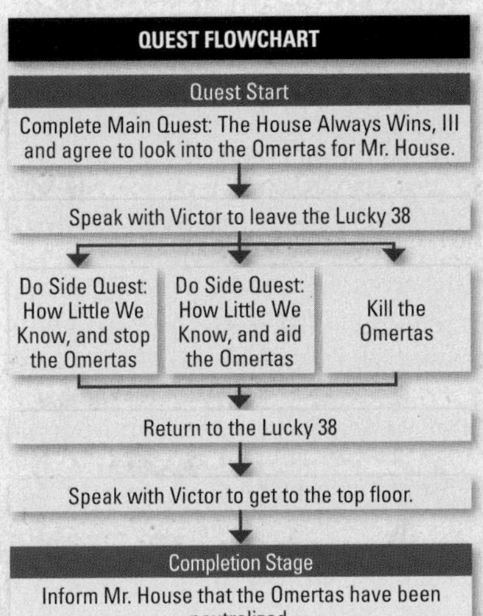

Tip To start this Quest, finish Main Quest: The House Always Wins, III, and your infiltration into the Omertas begins. You're likely to be Vilified by Caesar's Legion by the end of this Quest, so make sure you're happy working under the phosphorescent gaze of Mr. House! Remember too, that you can enter Gomorrah and complete any of the Omerta Quest-related tasks before or after Mr. House asks you.

Three Families. One House.

1

2

For your next task, you're to enter the den of vice known as Gomorrah Casino [2D.01]. Mr. House **(1)** is concerned about the Faction that runs this adult playground, the Omertas. He knows that the Omertas are underhanded, but the current cooperative silence is almost deafening. They're up to something, and you're going in to find out what it is!

You can also flirt with Mr. House.

Or ask about the backgrounds of the "Three Families" of The Strip, or the Omertas themselves.

Speak to Victor, travel down to the casino level, and leave the Lucky 38, then cross The Strip and enter Gomorrah **(2)**.

Investigate the Omertas and stop them if their plans oppose Mr. House's interests.

Caesar's Legion Infamy Gained!

[FAILED!] Render Unto Caesar: Beware the Wrath of Caesar!

The Legion has spies everywhere. If you continue to work against its interests, you will be marked an enemy.

OMERTAS Faction Interaction #2A: Cachino's Colleague

3

Once you enter Gomorrah Casino **(3)**, to investigate the Omertas, you must begin Side Quest: How Little We Know. Completing this Side Quest, ideally after minimizing the threat of the Omertas, completes the Main Quest, too. Please refer to that specific Side Quest for details on achieving this. But briefly, you need to:

- Ask the receptionist or other casino workers about Cachino, then ask him about his side businesses.
- Confront Cachino after obtaining details of his deeds against the other Omertas.
- Hand him the evidence, and then begin investigating two Omerta operatives:
- Investigate EITHER Troike OR Clanden (only one is necessary):

  Investigate Troike and obtain the blackmail note from Big Sal's Safe, OR

  Investigate Troike and use his Thermite to destroy the Omertas' weapons storage.

  Investigate Clanden and steal the Snuff Tapes from his safe. Then confront Clanden and either kill him or convince him to leave New Vegas.
- Kill Big Sal and Nero.

The Strip Fame Gained!

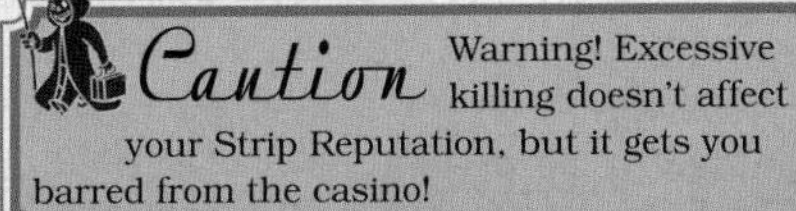
Caution Warning! Excessive killing doesn't affect your Strip Reputation, but it gets you barred from the casino!

OMERTAS Faction Interaction #2B: Cachino's Reaper

4

Side Quest: How Little We Know can also be completed in a way that benefits the Omertas but still keeps them loyal to you, and therefore Mr. House. Briefly, you need to:

- Ask the receptionist or other casino workers about Cachino, then ask him about his side businesses.
- Confront Cachino after obtaining details of his deeds against the other Omertas.
- Keep the evidence, and convince an Omerta thug that you need to speak to Big Sal or Nero.
- Speak with Big Sal or Nero and give them Cachino's evidence. Then "help" Big Sal or Nero during Cachino's business meeting **(4)**, and offer to help the boss with rackets they're planning.

  Speak with Troike and retrieve a stolen weapons shipment from Fiends.

  Speak with Clanden, and agree to find chlorine at the Ultra-Luxe or at the Freeside supplier.
- Let Big Sal or Nero know that their rackets have been helped.

The Strip Infamy Gained!

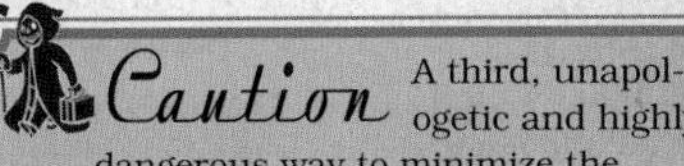
Caution A third, unapologetic and highly dangerous way to minimize the Omertas' presence is to simply find the three bosses (Big Sal, Nero, and Cachino) and murder them all, and anyone else you spot with a first name and a sharp suit. The Omertas become hostile, and there is instability on The Strip.

Caution If you haven't already completed the Free Quest "Big Winner" (detailed in the Tour section devoted to Gomorrah), you risk being unable to gain an Achievement or Trophy devoted to gambling. You have been warned!

(Optional) Inform Mr. House of the Omertas' treachery.

Tip For more information, look up the Side Quest in the next chapter. Begin Side Quest: How Little We Know in one of four ways:

Finish Side Quest: Bye Bye Love

Start Main Quest: The House Always Wins, IV (this Quest).

Deal with the Great Khans during Main Quest: For the Republic, Part 2.

Ask Yes Man about Side Bets.

Wise Guys' Mug Shots

This is Cachino **(5)**. You'll usually find him in the main level (he seeks you out). Then he moves to the bar near the stage on the main level.

Find Big Sal **(6)** on the balcony or pool table and offices area of the main level, or sleeping in the Gomorrah suites.

Find Nero **(7)** on the balcony or pool table and offices area of the main level, or sleeping in the Gomorrah suites.

Find Troike **(8)** in the Gomorrah lower lobby area, in the Zoara Club.

Find Clanden **(9)** sleeping or wandering the Gomorrah suites.

Note Already an enemy of the Omertas? Become a foe without offing all three bosses? Then this appears:

Inform Mr. House that the Omertas are hostile to you.

Inform Mr. House that the Omerta threat has been neutralized.

Faction Interaction: Complete

When you return to the penthouse level of the Lucky 38, Mr. House wants a progress report and isn't interested in half measures. You can:

Tell him you're still looking into it, or you found evidence. Mr. House doesn't care; he needs you to finish this!

If you sided with Cachino, Mr. House is less than pleased but will give you a new assignment.

If you sided with the bosses, the Omertas are likely to massacre everyone on The Strip when the Legion attacks, and Mr. House needs to divert more resources, which means fewer Securitrons for the final push, making this the less positive outcome.

Nevertheless, you're ordered to complete your next task at once.

THE HOUSE ALWAYS WINS, V

ALLIED FACTION: MR. HOUSE

QUEST FLOWCHART

Quest Start: Complete Main Quest: The House Always Wins, IV and agree to deal with the Brotherhood of Steel.

↓ Speak with Victor to leave the Lucky 38

↓ Kill off the Brotherhood of Steel.

↓ Return to the Lucky 38

↓ Speak with Victor to get to the top floor.

↓ Completion Stage: Inform Mr. House that you've negotiated peace with the Brotherhood of Steel, or have destroyed their bunker.

Tip Once you finish Main Quest: The House Always Wins, IV, you're asked to kill the Brotherhood of Steel because they're likely to oppose Mr. House's new regime due to their fanatical views on technology. The four Side Quests related to the Brotherhood of Steel (including Veronica's, a Follower) can occur before or after you speak with Mr. House. Consult Side Quest: Still in the Dark for all your options.

Find the Brotherhood of Steel and destroy them.

Journey to the strange, desolate, and windswept Hidden Valley [5.11], and enter the western bunker **(1)**. You can kill the Brotherhood of Steel (as Mr. House wants) or ally with them. The Brotherhood of Steel would make a fine fighting force for the battle to come...if you can convince them!

Faction Interaction #3: Tick, Tick, Boom!

The Brotherhood of Steel's bunker can be destroyed in cunning and brutish ways.

GUNS MELEE UNARMED: Enter the facility, and when Paladin Ramos stops you, kill him and every single Brotherhood of Steel member **(2)**. This is long, highly dangerous, and ultimately pointless, because you have a better option.

Agree to see Elder McNamara, and once you're free to move about the bunker, head to the VR chamber in the southern quadrant of the bunker L2. When no one is looking, surreptitiously inspect the two terminals on the western wall: the Self-Destruct Authorization Terminal, and a link terminal to activate the self-destruct command. You can:

Hack the red terminal, and start the bunker self-destruct sequence. Or,

- You can locate the three senior Brotherhood members with keycard access to the authorization terminal. The three targets are:

Head Scribe Taggart **(3)**, who is usually in his bed, or wandering this VR chamber.

Head Paladin Hardin **(4)**, who is at the entrance between bunkers L1 and L2.

Elder McNamara **(5)**, who is usually in his bed, or sitting in the command room.

Head Scribe's Keycard

Head Paladin's Keycard

Elder's Keycard

Obtain the keycards through Pickpocketing, or shooting (which turns the entire bunker hostile).

Back at the authorization terminal, the keycards generate a password for the red terminal. Access that, and choose the self-destruct sequence launch. Now flee to the surface.

Tip Your mass-slaying of the Brotherhood of Steel isn't for naught, as there's a hefty haul inside this bunker, although buying items from them nets much more potent weaponry. Check the Tour chapter for the stash, and remember to pillage the bunker before you start the self-destruct sequence!

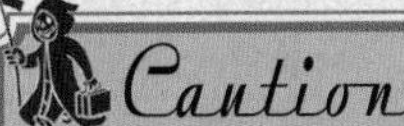

Caution Beware: Activating the self-destruct sequence causes instant Vilification with the Brotherhood! You are marked and may encounter patrols gunning for you later in your Questing!

Inform Mr. House that the Brotherhood's bunker has been destroyed.

Tip Should you wish to ally with the Brotherhood of Steel against Mr. House's wishes, consult Side Quest: Still in the Dark. If you're allied with Mr. House, the only reason to do this is to get Power Armor training, purchase goods from the store inside the Hidden Valley Bunker, or steal items. Afterward, kill everyone.

THE HOUSE ALWAYS WINS, VI

ALLIED FACTION
Lucky 38 MR. HOUSE

Out, Dam Plot

Back at Mr. House's penthouse, your news from the field has come just in time, as Aaron Kimball, the president of the New California Republic, is visiting the Hoover Dam **(1)** [3.33] to "boost morale."

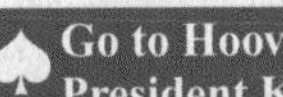

NEW CA. REPUBLIC Your standing with the NCR matters greatly when obtaining Main Quest: You'll Know It When It Happens. You must be "Accepted" (or better) in your NCR Reputation to attend President Kimball's speech (Mr. House sends a Securitron to smooth matters over, allowing you to work with the NCR). The easiest way to know this is to check your Reputation on your Pip-Boy, or see how you're treated when you visit Hoover Dam.

Go to Hoover Dam and protect President Kimball during his visit.

Presidential Cordon

Mr. House wants you to foil a Legion assassination plot. Ranger Grant is ready to brief you. This begins Main Quest: You'll Know It When It Happens. This is a Main (and not a Side) Quest, so consult it for all the possible options. If you care about New Vegas stability, be sure to save President Aaron Kimball during his visit **(2)** to Hoover Dam. Once Kimball is saved, or dies, return to Mr. House to conclude this Quest.

QUEST FLOWCHART

Quest Failed	Quest Start
NCR reputation not high enough; President Kimball dies, proceed to Main Quest: The House Always Wins, VII	Complete Main Quest: The House Always Wins, V and agree to protect President Kimball if NCR reputation high enough.

Speak with Victor to leave the Lucky 38
↓
Perform Main Quest: You'll Know It When It Happens
↓
Return to the Lucky 38
↓
Speak with Victor to get to the top floor.
↓
Completion Stage
Inform Mr. House that you've protected President Kimball, or that he's dead.

Inform Mr. House that President Kimball survived the assassination attempt.

Inform Mr. House that President Kimball is dead.

THE HOUSE ALWAYS WINS, VII

ALLIED FACTION
Lucky 38 MR. HOUSE

See flowchart on the following page

Final Preparations for Power

Once you've stopped, (or fled after the assassination of) President Kimball, Mr. House gives you an imperative task. With the Legion's assault imminent, you must journey to the El Dorado Substation [5.04], and attach an Override Chip to the power control terminal. Mr. House will use the jolt of electricity to jump-start the Lucky 38's reactor and boost the transmission strength of the network, allowing control over the Securitrons at Hoover Dam.

Override Chip

El Dorado Override

Between Vault 11 [5.05] to the east, and Black Mountain [5.07] to the west, lies the El Dorado Substation **(1)**, which siphons power

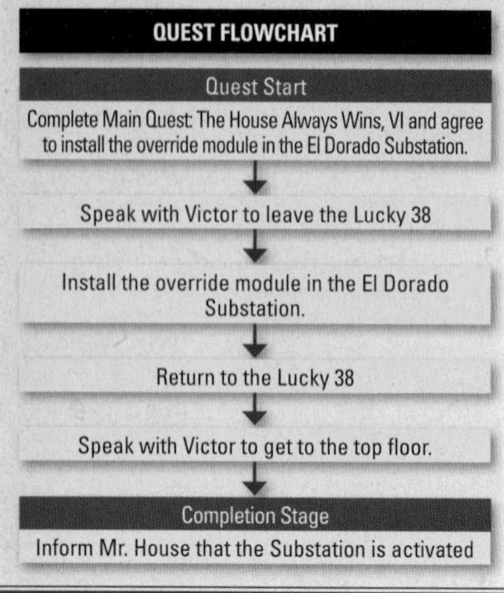
QUEST FLOWCHART

Quest Start

Complete Main Quest: The House Always Wins, VI and agree to install the override module in the El Dorado Substation.

Speak with Victor to leave the Lucky 38

Install the override module in the El Dorado Substation.

Return to the Lucky 38

Speak with Victor to get to the top floor.

Completion Stage

Inform Mr. House that the Substation is activated

from HELIOS One [5.13] to the south. Once you reach the substation, a patrol of NCR grunts **(2)** stops your progress, and tells you that there's going to be trouble if you enter the control room. You can:

Assault the substation with all guns blazing (or Melee Weapons bludgeoning), which doesn't win you any favors (or Reputation) with the NCR.

NCR Infamy Gained!

Or Sneak (ideally with a Stealth Boy) into the substation without being spotted, or the alarm raised.

Or, if you've procured an NCR uniform or armor, you can fool these grunts into thinking you're one of them, and enter the substation.

3

Once inside the substation, deal with any threats, activate this terminal **(3)**, and power up the substation with the Override Chip. Mr. House's network tentacles now reach far and wide; including the ability to control the massive Securitron army in the bunker under The Fort [3.28] that you (hopefully) brought online and upgraded. Now head outside, and prepare to tie up any remaining loose threads.

♠ Report back to Mr. House at the Lucky 38.

A Prelude to Complete Control

Mr. House is pleased with this new bolt of energy that has successfully jump-started the Lucky 38's reactor. Vegas is humming along, and Mr. House has been testing his c3i broadcasting arrays. Everything is in order. Which is great timing, because Caesar's forces are establishing a staging area east of the dam! Mr. House asks whether you want to head to the dam, or tie up any loose ends before the ultimate battle.

Since you successfully powered up the Securitrons under The Fort during The House Always Wins, II, they will be waiting to turn the tide of battle!

Otherwise, you're in for a tougher struggle.

Mr. House has a plan for ultimate victory, and the fate of New Vegas for decades to come lies in your hands. Act III: Main Quest: All or Nothing begins now!

RENDER UNTO CAESAR

ALLIED FACTION

See flowchart on the following page

Before You Begin

1

2

The first indication of Caesar's interest in you comes when a sharp-suited man with a steely glare accosts you on The Strip [Zone 2D] as you leave The Tops Casino [2D.04] after finishing Main Quest: Ring-a-Ding-Ding! He introduces himself as Vulpes Inculta **(1)**, or Alerio **(2)** if you killed Inculta in Nipton [4.30]. His master wishes your presence at his camp at Fortification Hill [3.28]; also known simply as "The Fort." You are handed the Mark of Caesar, and given instructions on reaching the place via boat.

You can complete some of this Quest even if you've already decided to ally with another Faction; whether it be Mr. House, the NCR, or yourself as an independent free-thinker. However, you must start this Quest if:

Benny escaped during Main Quest: Ring-a-Ding-Ding!, and you don't have the Platinum Chip.

If you're allying with Mr. House, and want to upgrade his secret army of Securitrons, but don't want to fight through a heavily guarded Fort.

Otherwise, this Quest is required if you wish to ally with Caesar, becoming impossible if you sway to the NCR.

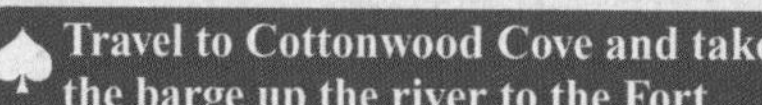
♠ Speak with Caesar.

♠ Travel to Cottonwood Cove and take the barge up the river to the Fort.

Initium: Finding The Fort

3

4

Leave the bright lights, and travel south to Cottonwood Cove [6.20], where your transport awaits. As you near this Legion staging camp **(3)**, a Legion Explorer stops you and asks your business. You can:

Inform him that you're "just a humble trader passing through." You're let past.

Any option (aside from attacking) also allows you to pass freely into the camp.

Move to the wharf, and speak to Cursor Lucullus **(4)** standing by the pontoon at the end of it. You may speak to him about the "honor" Caesar bestowed upon you, before deciding to leave.

5

6

After a long trip, you arrive on the western shores of the Colorado River overlooking Lake Mead, inside The Fort. A Legionary guard orders you to disarm and relinquish "all banned items." You can:

Agree.

Disagree, but you won't progress any further.

Whine a bit, then agree.

Ask what is considered a banned item. He states alcohol, Chems, and other stims. You can:

Inform him of your congenital heart defect, and smuggle in your Chems.

Or agree to disarm, or disarm with hold-out weapons.

Or agree, but keep your hold-out weapons.

Follow the dirt trail right, passing the crucifixion, and enter the ground drawbridge before making a steep, semicircular climb past a couple of Slaves, running children, and

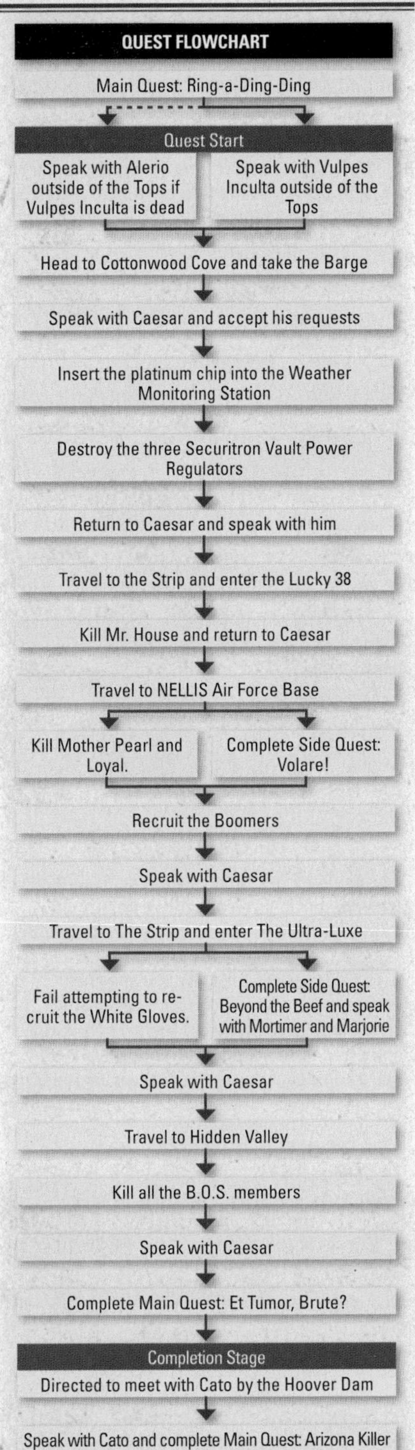

a Legionary Instructor. Open the drawbridge, and enter the inner fortification atop the hill. Pass the small arena, and climb the rocky summit to Caesar's Tent **(5)**. Once inside, you gain an audience with the man himself **(6)**. Hail, Caesar!

Accept Caesar's first task.

Caesar speaks to you, regaling you with knowledge of your past triumphs and transgressions (all of which are entirely dependant on your Main Quest choices up until this point, as well as your general Fame or Infamy with other Factions). When Caesar's finished, you can:

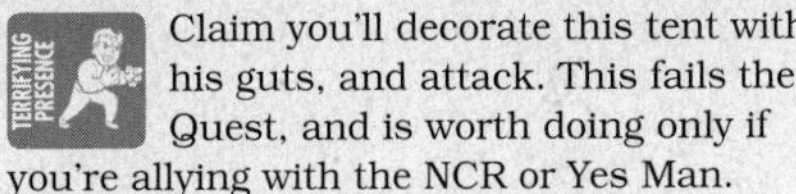

Claim you'll decorate this tent with his guts, and attack. This fails the Quest, and is worth doing only if you're allying with the NCR or Yes Man.

If Benny escaped, you may already have spotted him trussed up in a side tent (see below). You can ask about him, too.

You can ask about the Platinum Chip, or what employment Caesar wishes to tender you.

The invasion into the west is about to begin, but before this happens, Caesar wants you to remove Mr. House from the game with a quick one-two knockout. Ask what you must do, and Caesar describes an old building, here when The Fort was taken in 2277. The doors to that structure sport the same sigil as on the Platinum Chip you (or Benny) was carrying. You're to infiltrate the structure, destroy whatever is inside, and then return. Caesar gives you the Platinum Chip.

Platinum Chip

Demolish Mr. House's bunker under the weather station.

Intentio: House Shows His Hand

Exit Caesar's Tent and head west, down the steps and into a flat promontory of tents, a radio mast, and a Weather Monitoring Station **(8)**. Open the door, and once inside, you're given your weapons back. Remember to rearm yourself before continuing! Ahead is a floor grating that is activated by accessing the Weather Station Console. Slot the Platinum Chip into the console, and the floor door flaps retract. Open the Elevator Door to Securitron Vault, and step through into a connecting chamber with a large monitor on your right **(9)**. This displays the visage of:

Mr. House, if he is still alive.

Yes Man, if you've teamed up and taken Mr. House out of the picture (as part of Main Quest: Wild Card: A Change in Management).

A "lost connection" if Mr. House has been taken offline (through various means, detailed in appropriate Main Quests).

Assuming Mr. House is available to speak to, you can:

Agree to Mr. House's demands, and plan to upgrade the Securitrons.

Refuse (all robotic security becomes hostile), or remain noncommittal. You don't have to keep your word in any of the choices, though.

Enter the secret bunker.

Upgrade Mr. House's secret Securitron army.

Tip Lucky 38 MR. HOUSE Siding with Mr. House and only pretending to carry out Caesar's bidding is your second possible plan, which can take place during this Quest, and also Main Quest: The House Always Wins, II. But briefly, you need to:

Enter the operations room and access the console, and install the Mk II upgrade software for the Securitrons.

Return to Caesar, and tell him you were victorious, and then leave The Fort.

Then return to Mr. House to discuss "the next steps."

The Vault Status Terminal by the door informs you that turrets and Protectrons are active, and Sentry Bots are standing by. So you'll face the two former robotic foes throughout your exploration into the vault. Defeat the Protectron at the bottom of the steps **(10)**, after which you can access the security room or turn right.The security room contains a Plasma Rifle and ammunition (perfect for taking out robotic foes), and three monitors.

The Protectron Operations Terminal can be hacked, and the alert turned off, effectively shutting down all Protectron attacks.

The Turret Operations Terminal can be hacked, and the turrets disarmed.

The Sentry Bot Operations Terminal is currently offline.

Whatever your choice, head down the corridor, past a door to the Sentry Bot chamber (which is locked, but can be sealed to prevent Sentry Bots attacking you on the way out),and into a long, windowed hallway with two Protectrons and a turret ahead of you, and a huge army of deactivated Securitrons to your left and right, behind the reinforced windows. Shoot or avoid the robots, exit via the door, watch for another turret on the stairs, and head into the large generator room **(11)**. Face down around five Protectrons as you scout around the large generators, and you'll find three conduit chambers **(12)**. Each contains a Power Regulator. These control the flow of power throughout the vault and without them, the power buildup could reach dangerous—and explosive—levels. You have two choices.

Bicallis I: Waking Up the Robot Army

13

38 MR. HOUSE Open the door in the west wall, and head up the stairs (watch out for turrets) to the door marked "Systems Room," taking out two more turrets before accessing the Securitron Operations Console. Insert the Platinum Chip, and upgrade the Securitron army **(13)**, per Mr. House's instructions. The upgrade sequence fools Caesar into thinking you've destroyed the base. Then return to Caesar, and then Mr. House to complete Main Quest: The House Always Wins, II.

Tell Caesar the Securitron army is no longer a threat.

Tip If you upgrade the Securitrons instead of destroying them, Caesar still believes you've done the job he asked, because the ground shakes when the Securitrons are fired up, which he interprets as an explosion. This allows you to complete the Main Quests relating to Mr. House (The House Always Wins), or Yes Man (Wild Card: You and What Army?) without needing to fight your way out of The Fort.

Bicallis II: Blowing Up the Robot Army

CAESAR'S LEGION Destroy all three of the Power Regulators in each conduit chamber. The vault begins to shudder violently as the Securitrons explode, and the entire area begins to shut down. Optionally head up the stairs to the west, and enter the systems room to witness the destruction of the Securitron army **(14)**, per Caesar's

14

instructions. Then return to Caesar, optionally listening to Mr. House rant from his linked monitor before you exit. Beware: Sentry Bots have been released in the final corridor, so flee or stay and fight as you wish. Give your weapons (or all but your hold-out weapons) to the Weather Station Guard on your way out.

Caesar's Legion Fame Gained!

Peractio: The Chief Is Chuffed

Speak with Caesar, and he tells you he wants Mr. House out of the picture. You can agree (to advance this Quest, or ask him a variety of questions, including what that machine is in his tent). When you're done, depart from the Fort. Speak to his commanders flanking him. Both Lucius and Vulpes Inculta have Quests for you to complete. Start Side Quest: The Finger of Suspicion with Inculta now to minimize backtracking.

Kill Mr. House.

All About the Benjamin

7

Benny knows his game is over, but he's trying his hardest to slither out of an inevitable death. If you ask him, he tells you how to sabotage the bunker, but without destroying Mr. House's technology, and then you can return to Vegas to find Yes Man to plan your own destiny, not somebody else's. He also pleads for his life. You can:

- Free him, and he flees the Fort.
- Kill him in an un-sporting manner.
- Or challenge him to a duel in the arena, a prospect that the Legion find most entertaining **(7)**. Then kill him, and obtain his fancy gun.

Maria

Preparation: The Keys to Success

Gaining entry into "off-limits" areas of the Lucky 38 Casino can be tricky. Be sure you have one (or more) of the following:

The Platinum Chip that Benny "gave" you. Make sure you take this from him. If Benny fled and was captured by Caesar's Legion, another option is easier.

You can visit the H&H Tools Factory [2.06], and locate the Lucky 38 VIP Keycard inside the booby-trapped office. Dangers and advice on exploring the factory are in the Tour chapter.

Or, you can visit Camp Golf [3.23], and enter the intriguingly named House Resort building. Inside, you can find a Lucky 38 VIP Keycard. Find advice on this location in the Tour chapter.

Or, you can trust your high-level Science skill, and manually hack the terminals necessary to reach Mr. House's inner sanctum!

Bicallis: Unlucky 38

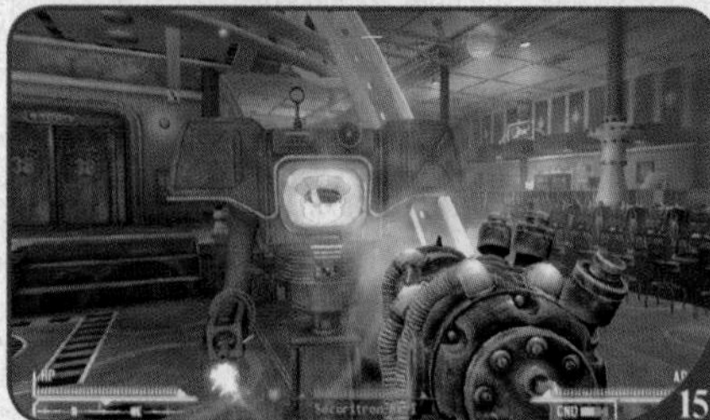
15

16

Travel back to Cursor Lucullus at The Fort gates, obtain (and re-equip) your inventory, and begin the trek back to The Strip from Cottonwood Cove. When you've entered The Strip, head for the front of the Lucky 38 Casino. Your first victim is Victor. Enter the casino level, and destroy the two Securitron Mk Is by the elevator **(15)**. Access the elevator, and ride it up to the penthouse. Once at the top, engage Jane and the other Securitron Mk Is in combat **(16)**, until all have exploded. Ignore the threats or pleading from Mr. House on the monitor, and head to the terminal on the north wall. Access it, and open the antechamber, hitting "Yes."

17

Inside is a hidden server room with a variety of complex equipment and two more Securitrons you can destroy, or

Override them without further destruction by accessing security on the windowed side of the room.

You can dash here through the previous Securitrons and achieve the same result, although this is more dangerous. With robot threats abated, access the terminal next to the control room elevator. Unlock it, and ride the elevator down to the control room. This vast, cool chamber contains Mr. House's Life Support (LS) chamber **(17)**. You can:

Leave Mr. House, although this halts the Quest.

Access the terminal and "Unseal LS Chamber." There's a microbial infection risk to Mr. House, but that's the least of his worries. Select "Yes."

Now attempt the following:

Sterilize LS Chamber. This kills Mr. House, which is exactly what Caesar wants (although he's fine with him being disabled). For any other Faction, this is an unnecessarily thorough removal of Mr. House from play.

Disable Cerebral Interface, which allows you to see the "real" Mr. House. He's not quite as chipper as his monitor image may have led you to believe. You can speak to him, kill him, let him live, or have pangs of guilt.

Once the deed is done, leave the Lucky 38 Casino, and Fast Travel back to The Fort.

Caution The instant you open the door to his antechamber, you forfeit any chance of staying friends with Mr. House. The reason? Germs.

The House Has Gone Bust!

You have irrevocably disconnected Mr. House from the Lucky 38's mainframe computers, forever trapping him in the prison of his own mind. His grand dreams for New Vegas will never be realized.

Return to Caesar and report that Mr. House has been neutralized.

Caesar is pleased with your actions (or reasonably happy if House is disabled). With him out of the way, Caesar can smooth a few lingering complications elsewhere in the Mojave. Caesar wishes to offer the Boomers their freedom; they can simply aim their guns at the NCR side of the dam when the Legion assaults it. Afterward, they stay free. If they aren't amenable to this offer, you're to destroy them. Agree to this mission.

Caesar's Legion Fame Gained!

Earn the trust of the Boomers and forge an alliance between them and the Legion.

[Optional] Kill the Boomer leadership to neutralize the Boomers as a threat to the Legion.

Tip Stop! Before you leave The Fort, speak to Lucius. He has a problem with a howitzer, which requires a part you'll find only inside the Nellis Air Force Base. Begin Side Quest: I Hear You Knocking before you go. Consult that Quest in this guide for the location of the howitzer part.

Tip You can visit the Boomers, and complete any of their Quest-related tasks before or after Caesar wishes you to visit. Other Faction leaders have their own plans for the Boomers too; consult Side Quest: Volare! for all your options.

Shaking Up the Boomers

18

19

Depart from The Fort, and head to the nearest (and safest) spot to the Boomers' territory: the Fields' Shack **(18)** [3.04]. Take the road, and you'll run into George **(19)**, who offers information on how to safely navigate the howitzer barrages to reach the Boomer's Nellis Air Force Base [3.01].

Tip To navigate through the howitzer barrages, ignore George's deal unless you want to part with Caps. Run straight into the rubble of the first house you see, and hide in the corner. After the wave of shells, while the Boomers reload, either run to the next (mostly) intact house, or make a bee-line for the fence. When you're close enough to the perimeter fence, the Boomers stop firing (for fear of injuring their own people). Or, you can simply run along the rock wall to the left when you reach the top of the road; you might be struck by the outer splash damage once or twice, but not a direct hit.

BOOMERS Faction Interaction #1A: All the Right Noises

20

Now you begin Side Quest: Volare! Please refer to that specific Quest for details on how to safely enter the base **(20)**, and convince the Boomers to support Caesar's Legion. But briefly, you need to:

Reach the front gate, meet Raquel, and begin a cordial conversation with Mother Pearl.

You must then raise your Boomer Reputation Rank to "Idolized." Achieve this by completing any of the following tasks (some of which are their own Side Quests) until your Fame improves. Use your Pip-Boy to check the status. You don't have to perform all the tasks.

(Side Quest: Volare!) Visit Pete and learn all about Boomer history.

(Side Quest: Volare!) Speak to Argyll and treat all his patients.

(Side Quest: Volare! / Sunshine Boogie) Talk to Loyal, and repair the Solar Array Station.

(Side Quest: Volare! / Ant Misbehavin') Speak to Rachel about (and purge) the Ant infestation.

(Side Quest: Volare! / Young Hearts) Help Jack meet the love for whom he pines.

(Side Quest: Volare!) Speak to Mother Pearl, and agree to dredge a old bomber from Lake Mead [3.26].

(Free Quest: Malleable Mini Boomer Minds and Bear Necessities) Speak to the children playing in the Boomer's base.

(Free Quest: Iron and Stealing) Collect Scrap Metal to sell to Jack.

(Free Quest: Missing a Few Missiles) Collect Missiles to sell to Raquel.

Once you've completed Side Quest: Volare!, you can speak with Mother Pearl. When she calls you "a trusted friend of us all," respond by asking if they can offer you assistance if there's a battle at the Hoover Dam in the near future.

Have you already done all of this before Caesar demanded it? Then this Quest is considerably shorter. Just reacquaint yourself with Mother Pearl, and ask for her assistance.

Boomers Fame Gained!

Tip Unless you have the beginnings of a split-personality and want to destroy the Boomers halfway through helping them, completing the above list of tasks is more than enough to gain an Idolized Reputation!

Inform Caesar that the Boomers will support the Legion against the NCR.

Tip For a lengthy tactical explanation of all these tasks, simply look up the appropriate Side (or Free) Quest in the Side Quests or Tour chapters of this book. It's wise to begin with Side Quest: Volare! because all the other Boomer-related Quests are offshoots from this.

BOOMERS Faction Interaction #1B: Boom and Bust

21

Caesar leaves it completely up to you whether you bring the Boomers over to his side or butcher them **(21)**. Choose violence, and there are two other ways to finish this Quest:

- You can speak to Mother Pearl about her agreeing to use her howitzers in the forthcoming battle prior to having enough Boomer Fame to justify this request. She refuses to help, and you can:

Return to Caesar and tell him,

Or gain enough Fame and talk to her again after completing Side Quest: Volare!

Or, you can ignore all of Mother Pearl's tasks completely, and kill everyone at the Nellis Air Force Base! Begin Side Quest: Volare! as normal, until you've spoken to Mother Pearl and received your Objectives. You're then free to unleash hell, but from a closer range. Killing everyone is one option, but for the Boomer Tribe to fall into disarray and decline, a more tactical series of strikes is called for: Kill their leaders.

22

Mother Pearl **(22)**, the matriarch, is inside or near her barracks, or wandering outside. She is a critical kill.

23

Argyll **(23)**, the doctor, is in the medical station. He is an optional kill.

24

Loyal **(24)**, the patriarch, is inside one of the two hangars, or wandering outside. He is a critical kill.

25

Jack **(25)** is usually inside one of the hangars, close to Loyal. He is an optional kill.

26

Raquel **(26)**, the master-at-arms, is usually standing on her viewing platform (in the center of the base, on the runway), or near the barracks. She is an optional kill.

Boomers Infamy Gained!

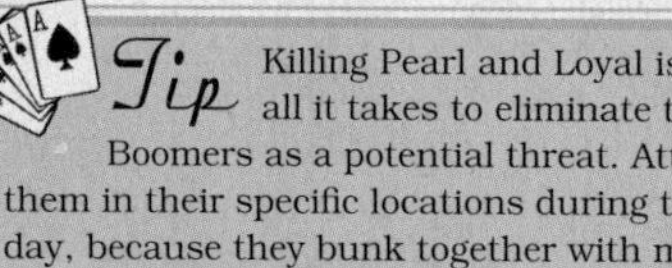

Tip Killing Pearl and Loyal is all it takes to eliminate the Boomers as a potential threat. Attack them in their specific locations during the day, because they bunk together with many other Boomers at night.

Once you've completed these horrific acts, the Boomers won't be firing their guns at anyone, ever!

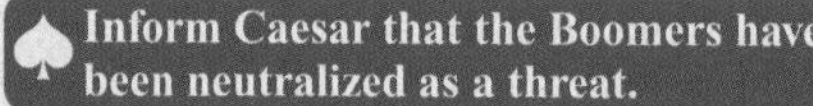

Inform Caesar that the Boomers have been neutralized as a threat.

BOOMERS Faction Interaction: Complete

Return to Caesar. You can:

Tell him that the Boomers are firm allies, and they're willing to help at the battle of the Hoover Dam. You will have slightly fewer foes to face during the final battle with the Boomers on your side.

Or tell him that you haven't secured this alliance, which troubles Caesar, and he tells you to complete it.

Or inform him that the Boomers are defeated. Caesar is disappointed that the guns won't be used, but you're allowed to continue in his service.

You are immediately given your next assignment.

Caesar's Legion Fame Gained!

Bicallis: Meat and Greet the White Glove Society

27

A second Faction—known as the White Glove Society—requires your attention. Caesar orders you to form an alliance with them, and tells you that they used to be cannibals. That information is key, and a useful manipulation tool. Caesar stops speaking and lets out a shout of anguish **(27)**. You can:

MEDICINE 40 Ask if it's the first time he's experienced sudden onset headaches. He responds that it has never been this bad before.

Or ask him if he's okay, or to speak again. Caesar shrugs off the pain, and goes off for a lie down.

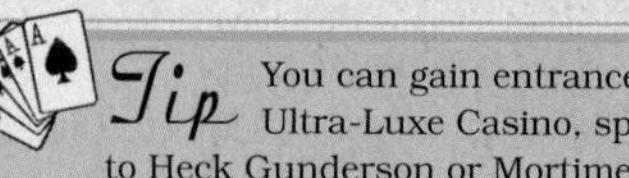

Bring the Legion's offer of alliance to Marjorie of the White Glove Society.

Tip You can gain entrance to the Ultra-Luxe Casino, speak to Heck Gunderson or Mortimer, and complete Side Quest: Beyond the Beef before or after Caesar decrees it. Other Faction leaders have their own plans for the White Glove Society. Consult the Side Quest chapter for all your options.

28

29

Head to The Strip, and move south past the Lucky 38 and The Tops to the imposing Ultra-Luxe Casino **(28)**. The White Glove greeter (very politely) asks you to remove your weapons **(29)**. You can:

Refuse, and be removed from the casino or begin to fight.

Or you can agree.

SNEAK Or you can keep hold-out weapons.

This can play out in two main ways: by following Caesar's orders, or by figuring out other means to finish Side Quest: Beyond the Beef. Expanded tactics are covered in the Side Quest chapter. Caesar's ideal tactics are listed below.

WHITE GLOVE SOCIETY Faction Interaction: Salutations from the Slaver

30

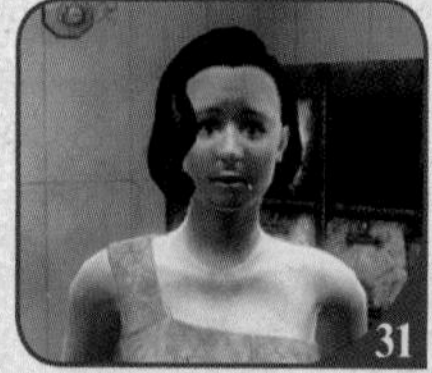
31

Ignore Heck Gunderson and enter the Ultra-Luxe Casino floor **(30)**, and head through the casino, turning left at the front desk, and looking for the door marked "The Gourmand at the Ultra-Luxe," and enter. Marjorie **(31)** welcomes you, but refuses Caesar's offer. You must:

Bring the Legion's offer of alliance to Mortimer of the White Glove Society.

32

Back in the casino floor area, head to the elevated desk with the dandy man scribbling away on his notepad. This is Mortimer **(32)**. Tell him of Caesar's request. Once you ask about cannibals, Mortimer tells you of a meal preparation that is going disastrously wrong. You can:

Discuss the situation at length.

Or lie, and tell Mortimer that you too, "know what it is to feel the Craving. How can I support your cause?" This accelerates the conversation considerably.

There's a problem with main course: Ted has a powerful father (a rancher named Heck Gunderson). Mortimer has two tasks for you: locate and bring back their original choice for a main course—Carlyle St. Clair—using coaxing or a Cattle Prod, and get rid of Ted.

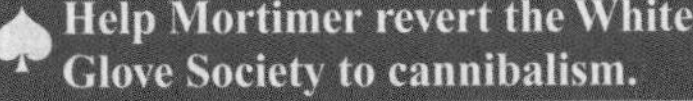

Help Mortimer revert the White Glove Society to cannibalism.

33

34

Get Ted first; head into The Gourmand, unlock the door to the Ultra-Luxe kitchen using the key Mortimer gave to you. When the White Glove asks what you're doing:

Simply tell him Mortimer sent you.

Another option is to lie, and tell him a water main has burst.

Head through the kitchens **(33)**, into the freezer (fourth door on the right, adjacent to the pantry), opening that with the second key Mortimer gave you. Ted **(34)** is in here. You can:

Kill him, head to Heck's penthouse room (opened with the third key Mortimer gave you), and smear Ted's blood around. Then locate a Securitron and frame Heck.

The Strip Fame Gained!

White Glove Society Fame Gained!

Or calm him down so he follows you to the circular front desk in the main casino area where his pappy Heck awaits.

When you speak to Heck, be sure to lie to him, telling Heck you don't know who took Ted. You'll get a nice chunk of Caps no matter what!

If you tell Heck Gunderson that either Mortimer or the White Glove Society as a whole are responsible, he threatens to launch a food embargo on them.

You can calm him down, telling him "That's just what they'd want. You'd be driving the city to eat each other."

The Strip Fame Gained!

White Glove Society Fame Gained!

Caps (500)

WHITE GLOVE SOCIETY Faction Interaction: The Steaks Are Nigh

35

36

If Ted has been returned to Heck, get Carlyle next; he's moping about at his shack north of New Vegas. The nearest Primary Location is the Mole Rat Ranch [2.11], although you can leave via the Freeside North Gate [2.08] and head toward the ramshackle building **(35)**. Meet up with Carlyle **(36)** and you can:

Talk to him for a while, until you can convince him to join the White Glove, and he runs off to the casino (you don't need to follow him).

Or prod him into unconsciousness; various ways are listed in Side Quest: Beyond the Beef.

One of the easiest is to shout "Look out, behind you!", and then pistol-whip him.

Then drag his body to the dumpster Mortimer marked on your map. Various ways are described in the Side Quest. Back at the Ultra-Luxe, Mortimer is happy with either outcome.

White Glove Society Fame Gained!

Speak to Mortimer after both tasks are done, and ask if he succeeded in turning the White Glove Society back to cannibalism. He won't know until 7 PM when the banquet occurs. Wait or sleep until after that time, and return to Mortimer (avoid entering The Gourmand, as the assembled guests don't want a nonmember seeing them tucking into their Carlyle amuse bouche), and ask how the dinner is going. He's ecstatic. Now for Marjorie.

Persuade Marjorie to shift her stance and join with Caesar.

Wait until the morning, when Marjorie returns to her desk at The Gourmand, and visit her then (and not at the banquet, unless you've already become a member during this Side Quest). Although she's unhappy with the hodgepodge of sporting equipment that passes for fashion with them, she agrees. You can return to Caesar with the result he ordered.

> **Tip** Side Quest: Beyond the Beef has three main outcomes: the preferred one for Caesar's Legion (above), as well as ones where you're acting against the White Glove Society, and eventually siding with Heck Gunderson, telling him some or all of the horrific cannibal secrets the Society has kept hidden. Naturally, if you try to ally with the White Glove Society and haven't helped them, you're refused an alliance.

Inform Caesar that the White Glove Society won't support the Legion.

Inform Caesar that the White Glove Society is now an ally of the Legion.

WHITE GLOVE SOCIETY Faction Interaction: Complete

Return to Caesar. You can:

Tell him your concerns about his headaches.

Or offer a less informed opinion: that his head might be ready to explode. Both options bring the conversation around to your last task, though.

Or forge ahead with the results of your interaction with the society.

If the White Glove Society wasn't persuaded, Caesar is less than pleased.

If the White Glove Society was persuaded, Caesar thinks they'll be valuable allies once the dam is taken.

Caesar's Legion Fame Gained!

For your next mission, the Mojave Chapter of the Brotherhood of Steel must be destroyed. He gives you a Hidden Bunker Key to enter the structure, and then pauses, in a temporal stupor. You can:

Tell him he just experienced an absence seizure, then warn him that he has a serious neurological condition.

Tell him he blanked out. Caesar waves off either comment, and heads to bed.

Or ask where the Brotherhood is, so you can kill them.

Hidden Bunker Key

Destroy the Brotherhood of Steel's bunker.

Tip The Hidden Bunker, and the two Side Quests related to the Brotherhood of Steel (and Veronica, a Follower) can occur before or after Caesar's order. Other Faction leaders have their own ideas about the value of the Brotherhood of Steel as allies or smoking husks. Consult Side Quest: Still in the Dark for all your options.

37

Journey to the strange, desolate, and windswept Hidden Valley [5.11], and enter the eastern bunker **(37)**. Caesar's plans are detailed:

Faction Interaction: Molten Steel

 Caesar wants the Brotherhood of Steel's bunker destroyed.

38

You could enter the facility, and when Paladin Ramos stops you, kill him, and then kill every single Brotherhood of Steel member **(38)**. This is long, highly dangerous, and ultimately pointless because you have a better option.

Agree to see Elder McNamara, and once you're free to move about the bunker, head to the VR chamber in the southern quadrant of the bunker L2. When no one is looking, surreptitiously inspect the two terminals on the western wall: the Self-Destruct Authorization Terminal, and a link terminal to activate the self-destruct command. You can:

 Hack the red terminal, and start the bunker self-destruct sequence. Or,

Locate the three senior Brotherhood members with keycard access to the authorization terminal, which is needed otherwise. The three targets are:

39

Head Scribe Taggart **(39)**, who is usually in his bed, or wandering this VR chamber.

40

Head Paladin Hardin **(40)**, who is at the entrance between bunkers L1 and L2.

41

Elder McNamara **(41)**, who is usually in his bed, or sitting in the command room.

 **Head Scribe's Keycard**

 **Head Paladin's Keycard**

 **Elder's Keycard**

 Obtain the keycards through Pickpocketing, or shooting them (which turns the entire bunker hostile).

Back at the authorization terminal, the keycards generate a password for the red terminal. Access that, and choose the self-destruct sequence launch. Now flee to the surface.

Tip Your mass-slaying of the Brotherhood of Steel isn't for naught, as there's a hefty haul inside this bunker, although buying items from them nets much more potent weaponry. Check the Tour chapter for the stash, and remember to pillage the bunker before you start the self-destruct sequence!

Caution Beware: Activating the self-destruct sequence causes instant Vilification with the Brotherhood! You are marked and may encounter patrols gunning for you later in your Questing!

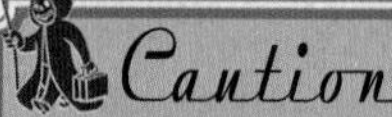
Tell Caesar that the Brotherhood of Steel threat has been neutralized.

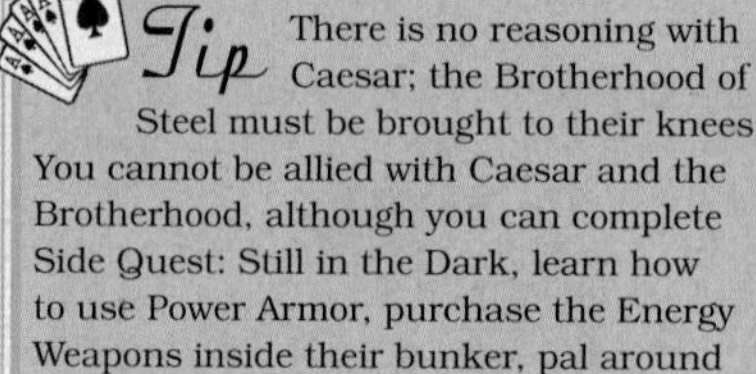
Tip There is no reasoning with Caesar; the Brotherhood of Steel must be brought to their knees. You cannot be allied with Caesar and the Brotherhood, although you can complete Side Quest: Still in the Dark, learn how to use Power Armor, purchase the Energy Weapons inside their bunker, pal around with them completing another related quest (Eyesight for the Blind or Tend to Your Business), and then kill them all!

Faction Interaction: Complete

Return to Caesar and inform him the bunker was destroyed.

Your actions advance Caesar's efforts to reshape the power balance of the Mojave. Join Caesar in his tent and he finally admits that something's seriously wrong with him.

 **Caesar's Legion Fame Gained!**

Meet with Caesar for a private conversation.

Peractio: Trepidatious Trepanning

Your meeting with Caesar brings a shocking revelation out in the open, and one you'd only previously suspected. Main Quest: Et Tumor, Brute? now begins. During that Quest, Lucius usually orders you to complete Side Quest: I Hear You Knocking, involving the location of a howitzer part over at the Nellis Air Force Base. Decide the fate of Caesar by reading up on this Quest (it is just after this one). There are two conclusions:

42

- A newly healed Caesar **(42)** tells you that the time for battle is almost upon us, and Lanius draws nigh! But as of now, the president of the NCR is paying Hoover Dam a visit. Caesar wishes it to be a permanent one.

43

- Lanius is now the de facto leader of the Legion. Lucius **(43)** informs you, after you've calmed him down, that his scouts have reported NCR President Kimball is en route to the Hoover Dam. This is an excellent opportunity to assassinate him. Cato Hostilius has the information you need.

Main Quest: Arizona Killer now begins. Once you complete that, return to Caesar (or Lucius), and prepare for your final battle! Only then does this Quest complete.

 **Caesar's Legion Fame Gained!**

 **1,000 XP**

ET TUMOR, BRUTE?

ALLIED FACTION

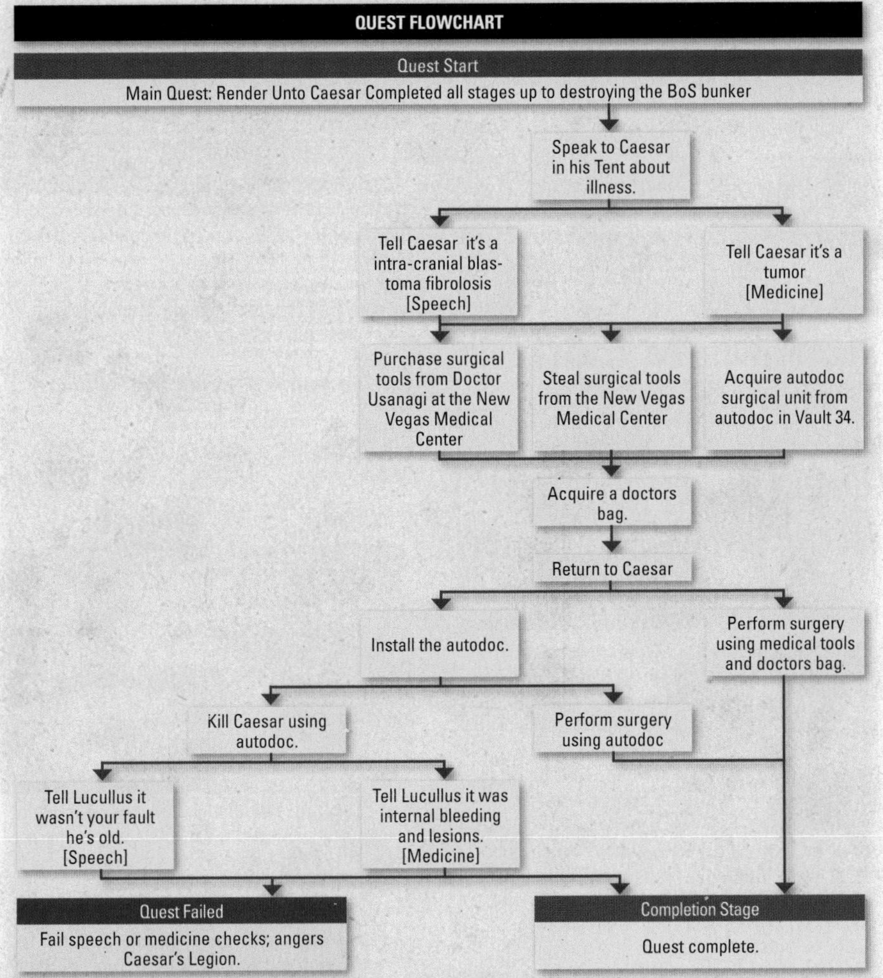

Initium: It's All in His Head

Over at The Fort [3.28], Caesar's conversations have been becoming increasingly erratic since you first talked to him, and once you've ransacked the Brotherhood of Steel during Main Quest: Render Unto Caesar, you're asked to have a private conversation inside Caesar's Tent **(1)**. The Legion's leader **(2)** tells you of his frequent, debilitating headaches, blanking out, and his left leg dragging. He wants to know the diagnosis:

Tell him he should be talking to someone else. This doesn't help matters.

Tell him it's likely he has a brain lesion, most likely a tumor.

Blurt out that it's a case of intra-cranial blastoma fibrolosis.

With a successful Medicine or Speech check, you become Caesar's personal physician, and he needs treatment. What do you suggest?

Explain that you can perform the surgery, but you need Surgical Tools and supplies from a Doctor's Bag. You can leave and find the items, or you can try another solution.

Ask about the Auto-Doc in his tent, and he says it's missing a diagnostic scanning module. He gives you some idea where to look for one. This option occurs if you don't have the necessary skills.

Tell him it's a simple procedure, relatively speaking. Caesar tasks you with finding Surgical Tools and a Doctor's Bag. If you chose this line of answers, you do NOT need to search the vaults for a scanning module.

Acquire a set of surgical tools.

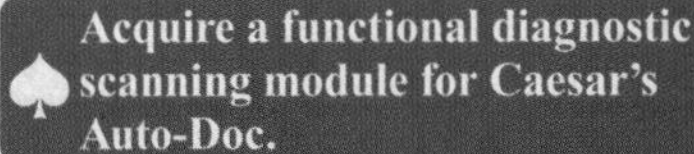

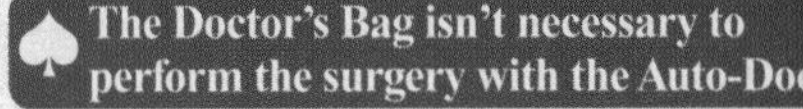

Intentio #1A: Surgical Tools

You must find these only if you don't locate the Auto-Doc parts. Caesar suggested you look in the New Vegas Medical Clinic [2.10]. Head there **(3)**, and enter the place, speaking to Doctor Usanagi **(4)**. She has an interesting line in Implants, but you're here for Surgical Tools. Ask what she has for sale, and search the inventory for the tools. They aren't cheap (around 1,000 Caps, depending on your Barter skill), but they're necessary.

If you've had a run-in with Doctor Usanagi (or you're about to!) that ended in her death, don't fret! The Surgical Tools can be removed from a First Aid Box in the first operating room of the clinic.

 **Surgical Tools**

They can also be stolen if you don't wish to pay the princely sum, but be prepared to disappoint the Followers of the Apocalypse considerably.

 **Followers of the Apocalypse Infamy Gained!**

 **Surgical Tools**

Intentio #1B: Doctor's Bag

This is mandatory to find (if you're not prepared to search for Auto-Doc parts). Either roam the Mojave Wasteland (consulting the Tour chapter for possible locations) searching for the Doctor's Bags, or simply visit Doctor Usanagi, bring up her inventory, and purchase one of her two Doctor's Bags for 60 Caps (each). Blake over at the Crimson Caravan Company [2.09] usually has some, too. This Doctor's Bag **(5)** was stolen from Violet's Caravan Compound, close to the Poseidon Gas Station [1.17]. Or, if you haven't used it already, a Doctor's Bag was next to the bed in Doc Mitchell's place when you first woke up.

Doctor's Bag

Intentio #2: Diagnostic Scanning Module

6

This is mandatory to find only if you failed the Medicine or Speech checks. Head across the desert to Vault 34 [3.12], dealing with a group of unruly Golden Geckos close to the surface by the entrance door **(6)**. You can also enter this vault via the hole at the top of the hill the vault is buried under, dropping down through a hole into the cave below. Take the following route to find the scanning module:

7

Head into the caves killing, or Sneaking by the Golden Geckos until you reach the vault door.

Begin takedowns of the Ghoul population **(7)**. Head down the steps to the cafeteria, down again to the lower corridors, cutting through more Ghouls. Alternately, you can use a hole in the southwest corner of the cafeteria to drop into the systems room. Exit, then turn left down the hallway to reach the clinic. Continue through the clinic to reach hallway with leaking pipe, beyond which is the utility room.

Locate the leaky pipe close to a submerged staircase, swim down, and search a drowned Vault Technician for his Utility Terminal Password.

8

Head to the door in the winding corridor close to the reactor room, and open it.

Battle through to the corridor with the second leaky pipe, and utility room and armory in it. Enter the utility room.

Access the Terminal (using the password or Science [100]) and system menu, and Activate Pump Station.

This drains the water from a nearby area accessed via the corridor with the second leaky pipe. Enter the 1st floor, and descend the steps, turn right and open the door marked Security Station A.

The room with the furniture crammed together as cover has a Broken Mk III Auto-Doc **(8)**. Activate the Auto-Doc and take the diagnostic scanning module. Then leave the way you came.

Diagnostic Scanning Module

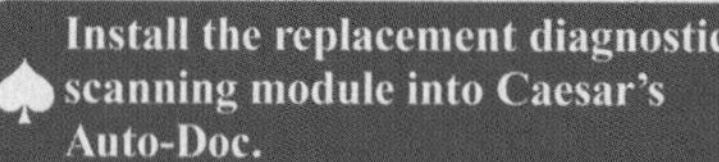
Install the replacement diagnostic scanning module into Caesar's Auto-Doc.

Reconcilio: The Brain Drain

9

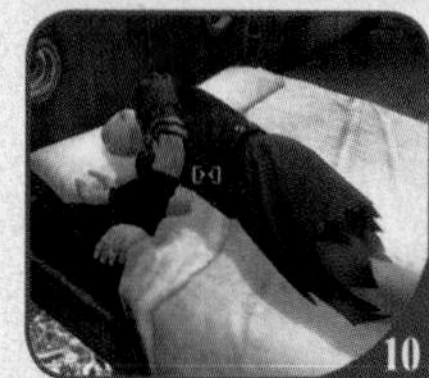
10

Upon your return to The Fort, you discover that Lucius **(9)** has taken command of the gravely ill Caesar. You can ask him a number of questions, and if you haven't yet completed Side Quest: I Hear You Knocking, now is the time. Once you have the necessary implements for the operation, Lucius lets you past and into Caesar's chamber. The leader is comatose **(10)**. It is up to you to save (or kill) him. You can:

Leave Caesar alone, postponing this Quest.

Perform the operation with the Surgical Tools and Doctor's Bag. The operation is a success if your Medicine skill is up to par. If it isn't? Then Caesar dies.

Perform the operation, and arrange for Caesar to die, if he's been annoying you in some way. This is only a choice if you're skilled enough.

You can trust in your luck and perform the operation. If your Luck is 9 or more, the operation is successful. If it isn't, Lucius accosts you and demands an answer (see below).

If you've obtained the scanning module, insert it into the Auto-Doc, and then start the operation. You can:

Arrange for the operation to succeed.

Arrange for the operation to fail.

Peractio: Regained Faculties

11

The operation was a success! Caesar regains his faculties fully, and rewards you with some of his own monies. He then presses on, telling you that Legatus Lanius approaches, as well as the NCR president. Main Quest: Arizona Killer now begins.

Caesar's Legion Fame Gained!

Legion Aureus (11)

Peractio: Et Tu, Courier?

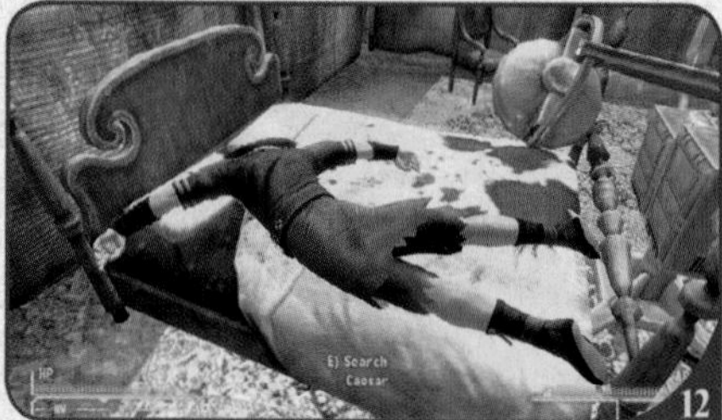
12

The operation failed! Caesar never regains consciousness, and a furious Lucius accuses you of murder! You can:

Ask why this one failure condemns you, or lie. Lucius doesn't buy it, the Quest fails, and the Legion attacks! On the off-chance that you survive, you're likely to be finishing the Main Quest as an Independent. Seek out Yes Man, or follow the Independent Quest choices from this point on.

Caesar's Legion Infamy Gained!

Indignantly berate Lucius for blaming you. He actually agrees!

Inform Lucius that the cranial bleeding was too much. He calms down.

Assuming you passed one of the two skill checks, Lucius informs you that NCR President Kimball will be visiting the dam. But he won't be leaving it if the Legion has its way. Main Quest: Arizona Killer now begins.

Caesar's Legion Fame Gained!

1,000 XP

THINGS THAT GO BOOM

ALLIED FACTION

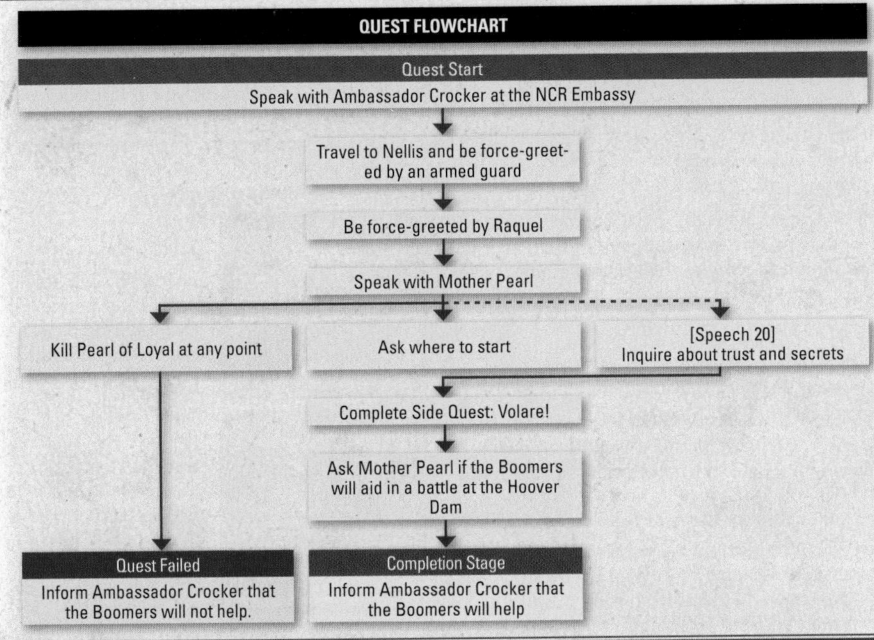

Before You Begin: Strip Search

The Securitron Guards at The Strip North Gate [2.13] require proof of your high-rolling status. You can:

Hand over 2,000 Caps; the "credit check" to prove you're not a "less-reputable person." The bad news? You'll need to scrounge together the necessary Caps. The good news? The check is just to see that you're good for the money, and you get to keep the Caps!

Answer "1C 3C R34 M," verbally hacking and confusing the Gatekeeper into letting you in.

Attack the toughened Gatekeepers. Prepare for a protracted battle before forcing your way in.

Complete Side Quest: G.I. Blues, and request a Passport from the King as a reward.

Visit Mick & Ralph's [2C.02], speak to Ralph, and have him craft a Passport for you. This is Free Quest: Papers, Please (which is detailed in the Tour chapter).

NEW CA. REPUBLIC Finally, if you're wearing NCR armor (Faction Clothing), you can journey to Camp McCarran [2.19] instead of The Strip, enter the Terminal Building, and board the Monorail. You can also do this without issue if Boone is your Companion.

Or, you can wait (without being seen) until 9 AM or 6 PM, when the guards change shift. Board the monorail, and ride it to the Vegas Boulevard Station [2D.03]. Exit, and Victor greets you. This method is dangerous and can severely impede your standing with the NCR.

Meeting Ambassador Crocker: Dealing with Dennis

1

2

When you finally reach the neon, concrete, and well-preserved facade of the New Vegas Strip [Zone 2D], Victor greets you and requests that you meet with the head honcho of New Vegas: Mr. House. Main Quest: The House Always Wins, I now begins. It can be completed before, during, or after Main Quest: Ring-a-Ding Ding!

Upon exiting the Lucky 38 Casino **(1)** [2D.02] or The Tops Casino [2D.04] for the first time, you're halfway down the steps when an NCR military police officer **(2)** flags you down with a "very important" message from Ambassador Crocker. Read the note; Crocker wants to discuss matters over at the NCR Embassy [2D.07] farther down (south) The Strip.

Note: Ambassador Crocker's Note

3

4

Stay on The Strip but journey south past The Tops, Vault 21 [2D.06], and the Ultra-Luxe [2D.05], and open the gates to the NCR Embassy **(3)**. Two buildings comprise this compound. The one to the right (south) is the NCR Military Police HQ, which you don't need to visit. Instead, head left (north) into the Embassy. You can look round, but then check in at the front desk with Liza O'Malley **(4)**. You can ask her about the Embassy, herself, and where Crocker is. Go down the L-shaped hallway to your left and Crocker's office is at the far end.

If you arrive and no one is at the front desk, or Crocker isn't in his office, the NCR staff are likely to be sleeping. Simply wake up Crocker from his bedroom on the eastern side of this building.

5

Begin to speak with Ambassador Dennis Crocker **(5)**. Tell him you're interested in the matters he wants to discuss, and he says that you're sure to have noticed the tension between the NCR, the Legion, and Mr. House. Something big is going to happen soon, and the NCR is in a tight spot. Continue to affirm your interest, and Crocker tells you of a settlement to the northeast. The inhabitants—known colloquially as "Boomers"—are sitting on a munitions stockpile invaluable to the NCR. You're to visit them and convince them to ally with the NCR. To sweeten the deal, Crocker says you have complete amnesty for any past crimes against the NCR. Agree to this mission, and the Quest starts. Then play a hand of Caravan with him, or quiz Crocker about the Boomers, himself, what's happening around the Strip, and request a long history about the NCR.

Convince the Boomers to aid you in the upcoming battle.

> **Tip** It is now extremely important that you pick a Faction to align with so you can start this Quest! You can visit fhe Boomers, and complete any of their Quest-related tasks before or after Ambassador Crocker requests it. Other Faction leaders have their own plans for the Boomers too; consult Side Quest: Volare! for all your options.

Shaking Up the Boomers

Depart from the NCR Embassy, and head northeast. The nearest (and safest) spot to the Boomers' territory is the Fields' Shack **(6)** [3.04]. At this point, take the road, and you'll run into George **(7)**, who offers information on how to safely navigate the howitzer barrages to reach the Boomer's Nellis Air Force Base [3.01].

Tip To navigate through the howitzer barrages, ignore George's deal unless you want to part with Caps. Run straight into the rubble of the first house you see, and hide in the corner. After the wave of shells, while the Boomers reload, either run to the next (mostly) intact house, or make a bee-line for the fence. When you're close enough to the perimeter fence, the Boomers stop firing (for fear of injuring their own people). Or, you can simply run along the rock wall to the left when you reach the top of the road; you might be struck by the outer splash damage once or twice, but won't take a direct hit.

BOOMERS Faction Interaction #1A: Things That Go Well

Now you begin Side Quest: Volare! Please refer to that specific Quest for details on how to safely enter the base **(8)**, and convince the Boomers to support the NCR. But briefly, you need to:

Reach the front gate, meet Raquel, and begin a cordial conversation with Mother Pearl.

BOOMERS You must then raise your Boomer Reputation Rank to "Idolized." Achieve this by completing any of the following tasks (some of which are their own Side Quests) until your Fame improves. Use your Pip-Boy to check the status. You don't need to perform all the tasks.

(Side Quest: Volare!) Visit Pete and learn all about Boomer history.

(Side Quest: Volare!) Speak to Argyll and treat all his patients.

(Side Quest: Volare! / Sunshine Boogie) Talk to Loyal, and repair the Solar Array Station.

(Side Quest: Volare! / Ant Misbehavin') Speak to Rachel about (and purge) the Ant infestation.

(Side Quest: Volare! / Young Hearts) Help Jack meet the love for whom he pines.

(Side Quest: Volare!) Speak to Mother Pearl, and agree to dredge an old bomber from Lake Mead [3.26].

(Free Quest: Malleable Mini Boomer Minds and Bear Necessities) Speak to the children playing in the Boomer's base.

(Free Quest: Iron and Stealing) Collect Scrap Metal to sell to Jack.

(Free Quest : Missing a Few Missiles) Collect Missiles to sell to Raquel.

Once Side Quest: Volare! Has been completed, you can speak with Mother Pearl. When she calls you "a trusted friend of us all," ask if they can offer you assistance if there's a battle at the Hoover Dam in the near future.

Have you already done all of this before Ambassador Crocker requested it? Then this Quest is considerably shorter. Just reacquaint yourself with Mother Pearl, and ask for her assistance.

Boomers Fame Gained!

Tip Unless you're barking mad, and want to destroy the Boomers halfway through helping them, completing the above list of tasks is more than enough to gain an Idolized Reputation!

Return to Ambassador Crocker and let him know the Boomers will help you.

BOOMERS Faction Interaction #1B: Things That Go "Phut"

Ambassador Crocker wants the Boomers alive and allied, not dead. But there are other ways to finish this Quest:

- You can kill the Boomers before beginning this Main Quest. If this has occurred, mentioning it to Crocker fails this Quest, but not the overall alliance with the NCR. Simply continue to Main Quest: King's Gambit.
- Or, you can speak to Mother Pearl about the forthcoming battle before having enough Boomer Fame to justify this request. She refuses to help, and you can:

Return to Crocker and tell him.

Or gain enough Fame and talk to her again after completing Side Quest: Volare!.

Or, you can ignore all of Mother Pearl's tasks completely, and kill everyone at the Nellis Air Force Base **(9)**! Begin Side Quest: Volare! as normal, until you've spoken to Mother Pearl and received your Objectives. You're then free to unleash hell, but from a closer range. Killing everyone is one option, but for the Boomer Tribe to fall into disarray and decline, a more tactical series of strikes is called for: Kill their leaders.

Mother Pearl **(10)**, the matriarch, is inside or near her barracks, or wandering outside. She is a critical kill.

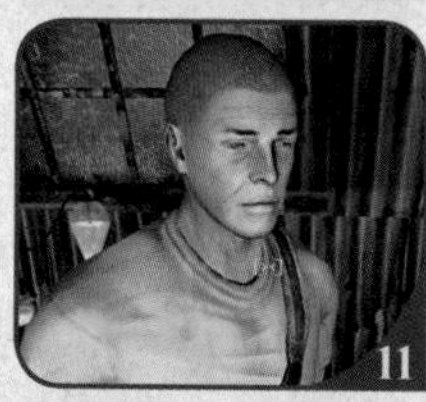

Argyll **(11)**, the doctor, is in the medical station. He is an optional kill.

Loyal **(12)**, the patriarch, is inside one of the two hangars, or wandering outside. He is a critical kill.

Jack **(13)** is usually inside one of the hangars, close to Loyal. He is an optional kill.

Raquel **(14)**, the master-at-arms, is usually standing on her viewing platform (in the center of the base, on the runway), or near the barracks. She is an optional kill.

Boomers Infamy Gained!

Killing Pearl or Loyal is all it takes to eliminate the Boomers as a potential threat. Attack them in their specific locations during the day, because they bunk with many other Boomers at night.

Once you've completed these horrific acts, the Boomers won't be making any deals with anyone ever!

Return to Ambassador Crocker and let him know the Boomers will not help you.

Faction Interaction: Complete

Back at the NCR Embassy, meet with Ambassador Crocker. You can:

Tell him that the Boomers are firm allies, and they're willing to help at the Battle of the Hoover Dam. Expect slightly fewer enemies after the Boomers join in the battle.

Or tell him that you didn't quite manage to secure this alliance, which annoys Crocker and fails the Quest, but still allows you to continue.

You are immediately informed of your next assignment.

200 XP (if the Boomers will help)

KING'S GAMBIT

ALLIED FACTION

QUEST FLOWCHART

- (Optional) Talk to Rotface and find out about Pacer and the VanGraffs or Pacer's Jet addiction → Complete Main Quest: Things That Go Boom
- Complete Main Quest: Things That Go Boom → Quest Start

Quest Start
Talk to Ambassador Crocker at the NCR embassy in The Strip

- Kill Pacer → **Quest Failed**: Assassinated Pacer leading suspicion back to the NCR
- Talk to The King at the Kings' School of Impersonation
  - Tell Ambassador Crocker that the King refuses to curb the violence
    - Speak with Colonel Moore at the Hoover Dam → Return to the King and offer him an ultimatum → King refuses the ultimatum → **Completion Stage**: Wiped out the Kings in the battle following refusal
    - (Optional) Speak with Colonel Hsu at Camp McCarran → Speak with The King and offer him NCR support
      - King rejects offer → **Completion Stage**: Wiped out the Kings in the battle following refusal
      - King accepts offer → **Completion Stage**: Sided with the King after accepting NCR's proposal
  - Complete Main Quest: GI Blues → **Completion Stage**: Convinced the King to curb violence against NCR
- Find Pacer's medical records in the Old Mormon Fort → Speak with Ambassador Crocker about Pacer's Jet addiction
  - (Optional) Spike Pacer's Jet with Psycho → [Medicine 60] Examine Pacer's Jet stash underneath his bed
  - [Medicine 60] Examine Pacer's Jet stash underneath his bed → **Completion Stage**: Assassinated Pacer through using drugs
- Talk to Rotface → (Optional) Kill Pacer and pin it on the VanGraffs → Speak with Ambassador Crocker about Pacer and the VanGraffs
  - Get Ralph to forge a note from Jean-Baptiste to Pacer → Take Jet from Pacer's stash and leave forged note → **Completion Stage**: Assassinated Pacer by pinning murder on the VanGraffs
  - Kill Pacer with an energy weapon → **Completion Stage**: Assassinated Pacer by pinning murder on the VanGraffs

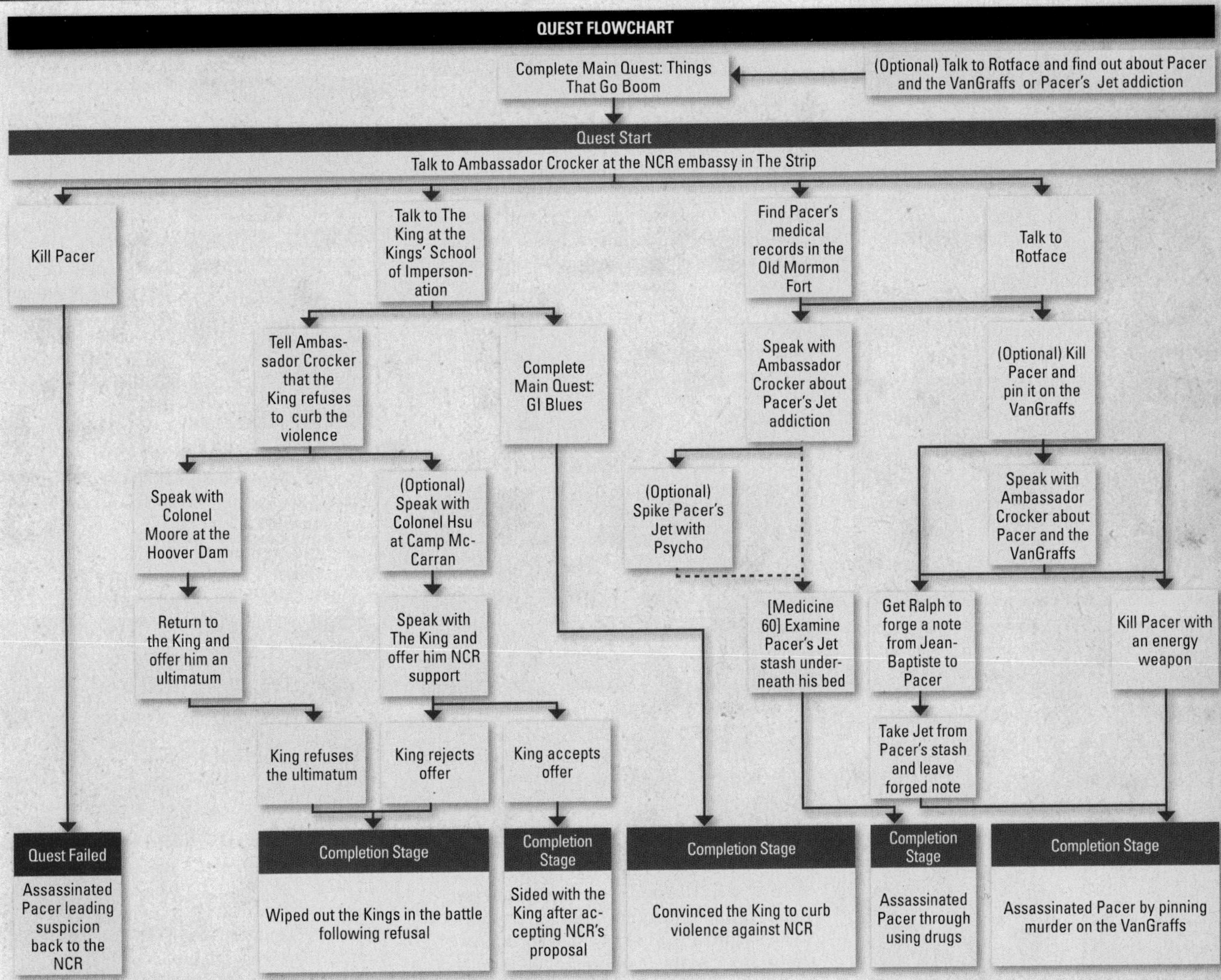

Before You Begin: Gossip Ghoul

Kill Pacer in a way that implicates someone other than the NCR, or talk the King into ceasing hostilities with the NCR.

1

This Quest begins once Main Quest: Things That Go Boom has been completed (or failed). However, you can gain some pertinent information about this Quest by entering Freeside, and locating one of the drunks scattered around Mick & Ralph's **(1)** [2C.02]. This non-feral fellow is called Rotface **(2)**, and if you spare him a few Caps, he'll dish out some gossip. These nuggets of information come to him at random, but two of them are particularly interesting:

2

Drugs are plentiful in Freeside, and even folks you don't expect become addicts. He mentions Jacob Hoff, a brilliant chemist, and now just another junkie. This refers to Side Quest: High Times. Another fan of the Chem Jet is Pacer; one of the King's crew. The Followers of the Apocalypse mentioned it was dangerous because Pacer has a heart condition.

At the northwest end of Fremont Street, you'll find the Silver Rush [2C.07], run by the "rather scary" Van Graff family. But if you're after energy weapons, the quality of goods they sell are second-to-none.

You may need up to 30 Caps to finally hear both these stories. For a complete list of Rotface's utterances, consult Free Quest: Rotface's Loose Lips in the Tour chapter.

[Optional] Kill Pacer by adding Psycho to his Jet.

[Optional] Kill Pacer in a way that implicates the Van Graff family.

Before You Begin: How the Web Was Woven

3

4

Now that Rotface has revealed a couple of additional possibilities, you have various paths to reach an acceptable conclusion to this Quest. All of them involve a visit to the King's School of Impersonation **(3)** [2C.05], and a run-in with Pacer **(4)**.

5

6

Your taskmaster for this Quest is in the NCR Embassy **(5)** [2D.07] on The Strip. Locate Ambassador Crocker **(6)** when you need to relate evidence or report back during any of the following paths.

7

8

If you decide to locate Pacer's room during Paths #1 or #2 (detailed below), here's how:

There's no need to speak to Pacer. Quietly enter the King's School of Impersonation, head to the door in the south corner **(7)**, and enter the corridors. Climb the stairs to Floor 2 (from the door, turn right, take the first left, head down to the end of the corridor, and turn right), and find more stairs to Floor 3 (by turning right at the top of the first stairs, then right and immediately left at the corridor junction, then down this corridor to the stairs on the right). Once on Floor 3, head to Pacer's room (left at the top of the stairs, and first door on your left) and step inside **(8)**. Examine Pacer's Jet Stash under the bed

Path #1: There's No Tomorrow

Implicating the Van Graffs in Pacer's death requires planning. Your first option is to return to Crocker and inform him of your discovery that Pacer and the Van Graffs have had a troubled history. Crocker suggests that getting the Van Graffs to kill Pacer would be ideal. However, if Pacer were found dead and a Laser or Plasma-based weapon was used, everyone would assume the Van Graffs did it. But snuffing out Pacer yourself would be incredibly hard, because he's almost always with other Kings gang members. But Crocker offers a more subtle way to infuriate Pacer, too, which involves using Pacer's debts against the Van Graffs against him.

Path #1A: All Shook Up

10

9

Planting evidence is the easier path, and involves a visit to Mick & Ralph's after speaking with Crocker. Locate the store in Freeside, and speak to Ralph **(9)**, inquiring about forging a handwritten note. Say it's written to Pacer from Jean-Baptiste Cutting (one of the two Van Graff bosses). Perhaps look through the huge variety of items Ralph (or Mick) has on offer, then take the Note and leave.

Note: Forged Jet Theft Note

Return to King's School of Impersonation; ignore Pacer, and plant the note in his Jet Stash under his bed. He wanders up to his bedroom almost immediately. You can follow silently, or wait in the King's bar for Pacer to rush back outside brandishing a gun! He sprints across the street, heading for the Silver Rush, and starts firing at Simon, a Van Graff security guard. He soon succumbs to Simon's superior firepower **(10)**.

Path #1B: Hard Knocks

11

12

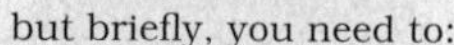
13

The second option is to kill Pacer yourself, ideally with an energy weapon. This is actually reasonably straightforward to accomplish, but involves joining the Van Graffs as door security, during the first part of Side Quest: Birds of a Feather. Consult that Quest for more detailed information, but briefly, you need to:

Enter the Silver Rush **(11)** and speak with Gloria **(12)**. Ask her for work, and she tells you to meet Simon outside.

Guard the entrance to Silver Rush with Simon **(13)**, ensuring that drunks are stopped, and everyone is patted down.

14

When Pacer arrives and speaks with Simon, tell him to get out of here before he gets hurt. This makes him mad; shoot him with your Laser or Plasma weapon **(14)**. You can do this even if Pacer isn't hostile.

You can still continue with the Side Quest, despite Simon's reservations.

Path #1C: Fool, Fool, Fool

15

An alternate way to dispatch Pacer is a lot more dangerous. Speak to him at the door to the audition room where the King is sitting, and optionally speak to the King himself. But focus on Pacer; waiting until he moves from the door he was guarding. Follow him up to his room, and plant a (ideally) silenced bullet into the back of his head (15). The

16

"dangerous" part of this plan comes soon afterward, as the entire King's Gang turns hostile, usually failing this Quest (which infuriates Crocker, although he allows you to continue working with the NCR), and leading to an un-winnable battle **(16)**!

Instead, you can try Pickpocketing Pacer, and placing C-4 on him, before backing away to another room, and detonating it. This is better than using an energy weapon, as you're easily revealed as the shooter.

Path #2: Wooden Heart

17

18

Another plan is to take advantage of Pacer's love of Jet, and dislike of following doctor's orders. Aside from Rotface, there's a second way of revealing Pacer's heart defect. Head to the Old Mormon Fort [2C.01] and enter the front gates **(17)**, but refrain from speaking to anyone. Head to the western tower section, and locate the doctor's surgery room atop the stairs **(18)**. Open the Filing Cabinet to find files on Pacer and Jacob Hoff (Side Quest: High Times). Take Pacer's file, and read it in your Pip-Boy's Data > Misc Menu. This gives you all the information you need.

Note: Pacer's Patient Record

Return to Crocker and inform him that Pacer has a heart condition, although Crocker doesn't know how to take advantage of this.

You do though: mixing Chems might cause the ticker to blow.

Don't forget to press Crocker on this subject!

19

20

Enter King's School of Impersonation, and proceed to Pacer's bedroom. Locate his stash of Chems under his bed **(19)**, and attempt one of the following:

Spike the Jet with a dose of Psycho (which you can purchase from a dealer named Dixon **(20)** close to Mick & Ralph's).

Or taint the Jet to make it overly potent, which doesn't require any Psycho.

21

Now wait for Pacer to move from his post. He walks up to his room, takes a Jet, and doesn't survive the high **(21)**. You don't need to observe the body, but you can take (or Pickpocket) a key. This opens the door inside the King's School of Impersonation that leads to the audition stage area, and the King himself. Ah-thank you very much!

Pacer's Key

Return to Ambassador Crocker with news of Pacer's death.

Path #3: A Little More Conversation

22

You can always speak to the organ grinder instead of the monkey. Enter the King's School of Impersonation, and locate the locked door, guarded by Pacer. He wants to know how much it's worth to meet the big man. You can:

Shoot the place up, and fail Side Quest: G.I. Blues, which is also what happens if you try opening the door without Pacer's say-so.

You can tell him you want to pay your respects. Pacer likes that, and lets you in.

Or, you can offer 5 Caps (you're turned away in disgust), 50 Caps (Pacer lets you in), or 500 Caps (Pacer lets you in while you remember not to give away all your Caps).

Once through the guarded door, step into the audition stage area and speak with the King **(22)**, who seems an affable sort. You can ask about working for him and the conditions in Freeside, but what you're really here for is to get him to stop the violence against NCR citizens. He's not about to change the situation just because "some random stranger" is asking. But there are ways of getting the King to curb the violence. You can:

Path #3A: Promised Land

Speak to the King and agree to work for him. This begins Side Quest: G.I. Blues; consult that Quest for detailed information.

(Optional) Perform tasks for the King in order to get on his good side.

But briefly, you need to:

23

Speak to Orris the bodyguard **(23)**, and expose his scam.

Speak to the King, then go to the Old Mormon Fort and talk to Wayne and Roy about their fight.

Inform the King of your findings, and optionally talk to Julie Farkas inside the Old Mormon Fort.

24

Then inquire at any of the squatter camps **(24)**, talking to an NCR "Man," and learn a password to a food distribution center.

25

Speak with Major Elizabeth Kieran **(25)** and ask why the locals aren't getting any food, then speak to the King about it.

Patch things up with Kieran and the NCR on behalf of the Kings, so that violence is curtailed in Freeside.

Once all of this is completed, return to the King, and request that he cease all hostilities with the NCR. He agrees, allowing you to return to Crocker.

Return to Ambassador Crocker with the news that the King has agreed to cease hostilities.

Path #3B: Trouble

Return to Ambassador Crocker with the news that the King will not curb the violence in Freeside.

Once the King rebuffs your initial request, return to Crocker, and tell him you want to speak about Freeside. Tell him the King won't deal with the NCR. Crocker deems this most unfortunate. He's been instructed to send you to Colonel Moore over at Hoover Dam [3.33] for further orders. This isn't really diplomacy; it's a show of force. You can agree to this, or not, but Crocker has another possible option, because he knows that solution would further destabilize the area. He suggests you speak with Colonel Hsu over at Camp McCarran [2.19]. He's the more level-headed option; especially as he can offer water and power distribution.

Speak with Colonel Moore at Hoover Dam for further instructions regarding the situation in Freeside.

[Optional] Speak with Colonel Hsu in Camp McCarran for further instruction regarding the situation in Freeside.

This path now splits into two possible outcomes. You can:

26

27

A. Meet Colonel Cassandra Moore: Journey to the east, and enter the Hoover Dam Visitor Center **(26)**, and locate Moore's chambers. Enter the visitor center and take the elevator down to Power Plant 01. Exit to the balcony and find the blast door to Hoover Dam Offices. Colonel Moore is in first office on the right. Tell Moore **(27)** that Ambassador Crocker sent you to receive instructions about Freeside. She isn't going to blink like the ambassador. She wants you to order the King and his gang to stand down or face annihilation. Your personal feelings don't enter into her decision, so head back to the King, or speak to Colonel Hsu.

Go to the Kings' School of Impersonation and deliver an ultimatum to the King, backed by a squad of NCR Troopers.

28

Inside the King's School of Impersonation, the NCR is exhibiting a show of force in the audition room, and the King is incensed. He's about five seconds away from massacring these NCR thugs. Respond with:

- An ultimatum from the NCR to cease hostilities or perish.
- An order to curb violence in Freeside or else.
- A request to stop the violence because NCR citizens are dying in Freeside.

The first two choices lead to all-out violence. To further this Quest, help with the mop up. The third choice also ends in a massacre. The Kings are out-gunned, and military weaponry prevails **(28)**.

Help the NCR Troopers kill all the Kings.

Return to Ambassador Crocker and report that the Kings have been wiped out.

29

30

B. Meet Colonel James Hsu: Go to the Terminal Building **(29)** inside Camp McCarran, and seek out Hsu's office on the east side. Tell Hsu **(30)** that Ambassador Crocker sent you and ask if he has a plan for Freeside. Hsu says you can tell the King that Hsu will personally guarantee that Freeside gets more water, power, and food as long as the violence stops.

Go to the Kings' School of Impersonation and offer the King official NCR support if he ceases hostilities.

31

Head back to the King. The NCR has made itself at home in the audition room, infuriating the King. He's about five seconds away from all-out warfare. Respond by letting him know that:

- There are more resources if the violence stops.
- Or, that you're sorry for the rudeness, and the NCR is offering peace and supplies.
- Or, that the soldiers would wipe the floor with his men.

The first two choices lead to a peaceful solution **(31)**. In both these options, Pacer attempts to sour the deal by opening fire. Put him down with help from the NCR and Kings to preserve the newly arranged deal. The third choice ends in mayhem and countless deaths.

Return to Ambassador Crocker and report that the King has accepted Colonel Hsu's pledge of NCR support.

Return to Ambassador Crocker and report that the Kings have been wiped out.

Conclusion: Farther Along

Once you've achieved a satisfactory conclusion to this Quest, return to Ambassador Crocker, who's most pleased with the results (unless Pacer died and it was traced back to the NCR). Assuming a positive conclusion, Crocker hands over a substantial number of Caps. You can:

Thank him.

Or request more, which he delves into his own pocket for.

Crocker has received a message from Colonel Moore over at Hoover Dam; she has requested that you meet with her. Although you're not an employee of the NCR, Crocker thinks you should visit her as soon as possible. This leads you farther along the path to cementing NCR as your Faction ally of choice, and begins Main Quest: For the Republic, Part 2.

1,200 XP (if Pacer's death had no connection to the NCR)

FOR THE REPUBLIC, PART 2

ALLIED FACTION
NEW CA. REPUBLIC

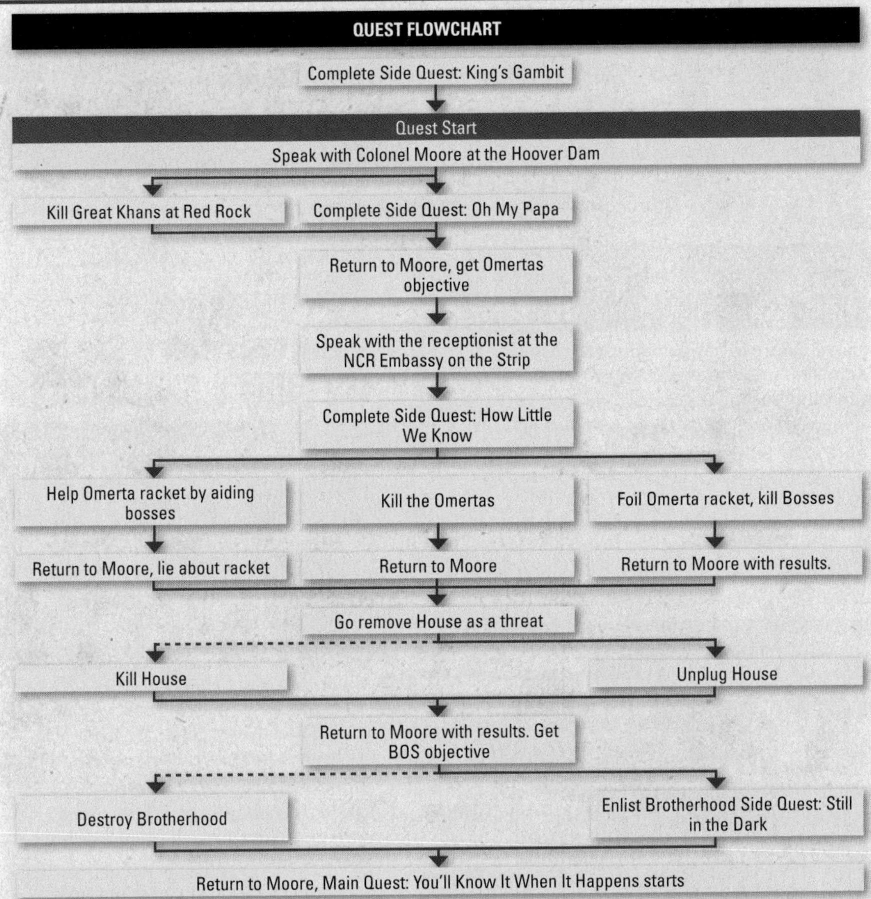

Moore's Law: More Dam Assignments

See Colonel Moore at Hoover Dam for further assignments.

1

2

3

Ambassador Crocker requests that you visit Colonel Moore at Hoover Dam [3.33]. She's been following your exploits with interest. Oblige, and set off to the east, taking the winding southern road to the Hoover Dam Visitor Center **(1)**, across from the winged statues. Enter the dome-like building, and locate the Elevator to Hoover Dam Power Plant 01. Step out of the elevator, turn right (east), and move onto the balcony overlooking the gigantic centrifuges **(2)**. Open the blast door in the north wall, and enter the Hoover Dam Offices area. A corridor leads to Colonel Moore's quarters on the right (east). Colonel Cassandra Moore **(3)** is either here, or walking the nearby corridors. She notes that you've proven yourself capable. She asks if you're up for a "real mission." If you want to continue this Quest, say you are.

GREAT KHANS Faction Interaction #1: The Great Khans

Moore wants some "loose ends" tied up, and she asks if you know of the Great Khans. Reply, and she mentions there's been "a rather sordid" history with them. She thinks they'll aid the enemy during the Legion battle. You're to make sure they're not in a fit state to fight against the NCR. This means killing them; Moore doesn't believe they'll ally with an organization like the NCR, which massacred them in the past. Perhaps you can prove her wrong?

Visit the Great Khans in Red Rock Canyon and either enlist their aid or destroy them.

Tip You can visit The Great Khans, and complete any of their Quest-related tasks before or after Colonel Moore commands it. Other Faction leaders have their own plans for the Great Khans too; consult Side Quest: Oh My Papa for every possibility.

4

Journey to the home of the Great Khans in the northwest mountains; the Red Rock Canyon **(4)** [1.15]. Choose your preferred method of dealing with Papa Khan and his minions.

GREAT KHANS Faction Interaction #1A: Severing Caesar's and Papa's Control

5

This begins the long, arduous process of getting the Great Khans to fight with the NCR. Check that Quest for the full run-down of how to get the Great Khans on your side. But briefly, you need to:

Enter the longhouse and speak with Papa Khan **(5)**, who is currently allied with Caesar's Legion.

Exit the longhouse, and then speak with Regis, who is thinking about a change in this alliance.

After this conversation, you can optionally return to Colonel Moore and inform her. She's interested in an alliance, if only to get more cannon fodder in front of NCR troops to soak up Legion attacks. She gives you a Locksmith's Reader to allow easier access into Papa Khan's bedroom. Consult Interaction #2B at this point.

Locksmith's Reader

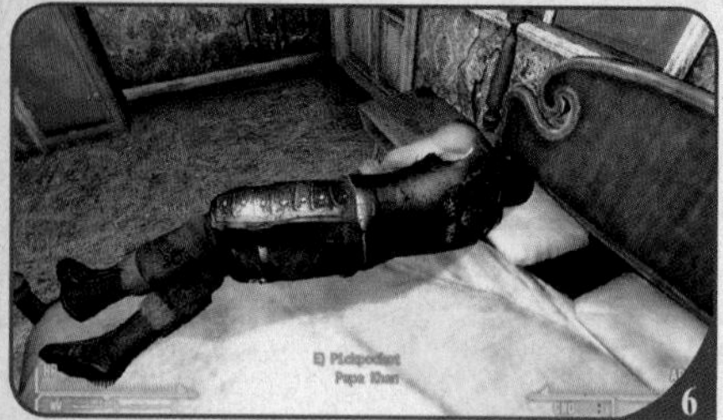
6

Return to Red Rock Canyon, and remove Papa Khan as leader:

Wait until night, and creep around to the rear of the longhouse, and pry open the door with a Lockpick, optionally reading the Locksmith's Reader if you need to boost your Lockpick.

Locate the bed with Papa Khan sleeping on it. Sneak around and attempt a Pickpocket; then murder him **(6)**. You can kill him, too for some Great Khan Infamy.

Sneak out, talk to Regis, and he follows your advice. You can utilize the Khans in the final battle.

Great Khan's Fame Gained!

Return to Colonel Moore with news that the Great Khans will help fight the Legion.

Tip Dealing with Caesar's envoy Karl, switching the other Khan leaders' alliances, and finding out Great Khan history is an interesting diversion (which can net you some additional XP and a meeting with Ezekiel), but this plan is ultimately pointless: Papa Khan's memory of past atrocities that the NCR perpetrated on his people means he will not—*ever*—ally with the NCR. Regis is your only option, and he won't switch sides until Papa is dead.

GREAT KHANS Faction Interaction #1B: Death to Papa's Horde

7

The other option is to kill everyone in Red Rock Canyon **(7)**, paying special attention to the Khans with a first name, including:

8

Papa Khan **(8)** the patriarch, found inside or near his longhouse, sitting in his outhouse, or wandering outside.

9

Regis **(9)** is the younger Khan, and Papa's successor. Slay him in near or inside the tents close to the longhouse.

Jack and Diane are in the Red Rock Drug Lab. Everyone else wearing a black Brahmin-skin jacket is fair game, too.

Great Khan's Infamy Gained!

Return to Colonel Moore with news that the Great Khans have been destroyed.

Colonel Moore is happy about your Great Khan solution, and wants you to apply your abilities in solving a problem the NCR are having with one of the three Families on The Strip. Apparently some of the high-ranking Omertas are having clandestine meetings, and Moore wants you to stop them if they threaten the NCR.

NCR Fame Gained!

Investigate the Omertas, and stop them if their plans oppose the NCR.

Speak to Liza O'Malley at the NCR Embassy on the Strip for a lead on the Omertas.

Render Unto Caesar: Beware! The Legion has spies everywhere. If you continue to work against its interests, you will be marked as an enemy.

OMERTAS Faction Interaction #2: The Omertas

10

Liza O'Malley over at the NCR Embassy has some knowledge about the Omertas when you return there and ask her **(10)**. She tells you that the receptionist at the Gomorrah owes the NCR some information. You can collect on it.

Tip As soon as Moore gives you your orders, begin Side Quest: How Little We Know. Note that the Omertas do not actually help you during the final battle; but getting them on your side aids in the aftermath of stabilizing The Strip, and placating the Families running the casinos there. Remember that you can begin Side Quest: How Little We Know in one of four ways:

Successfully finishing Side Quest: Bye Bye Love

Successfully starting Main Quest: The House Always Wins, IV.

Successfully starting Main Quest: Wild Card: Side Bets.

Dealing with the Great Khans during Main Quest: For The Republic, Part 2 (this Quest).

11

Now enter the Gomorrah Casino **(11)** [2D.01], and choose whether to help with the racket the Omerta bosses are planning, or foil it with the help of rogue lieutenant Cachino.

OMERTAS Faction Interaction #2A: Cachino's Colleague

12

Once you enter the Gomorrah Casino to investigate the Omertas, you must begin Side Quest: How Little We Know. Helping foil the bosses' rackets is Colonel Moore's preference. Briefly, you need to:

- Ask the receptionist or other casino workers about Cachino, then ask him about his side businesses.
- Confront Cachino **(12)** after obtaining details of his deeds against the other Omertas.
- Hand him the evidence, and then begin investigating two Omerta operatives:

Investigate Troike and obtain the blackmail note from Big Sal's Safe, OR

Investigate Troike and use his Thermite to destroy the Omertas' weapons storage.

Investigate Clanden and steal the Snuff Tapes from his safe. Then confront Clandon and either kill him or convince him to leave New Vegas.

- Kill Big Sal and Nero.

The Strip Fame Gained!

Caution Warning! Excessive killing doesn't affect your Strip Reputation, but it gets you barred from the casino!

Return to Colonel Moore and report that the Omertas' plans have been foiled.

OMERTAS Faction Interaction #2B: Cachino's Reaper

Side Quest: How Little We Know can be completed in another way, which

benefits the Omertas but still keeps them loyal to you. Briefly, you need to:

- Ask the receptionist or other casino workers about Cachino, then ask him about his side businesses.
- Confront Cachino after obtaining details of his deeds against the other Omertas.
- Keep the evidence, and convince an Omerta thug that you need to speak to Big Sal or Nero.
- Speak with Big Sal or Nero and give Cachino's evidence over. Then "help" Big Sal or Nero during Cachino's business meeting **(13)**. Then offer to help the boss with rackets they're planning.

Speak with Troike and retrieve a stolen weapons shipment from Fiends.

Speak with Clanden, and agree to find chlorine at the Ultra-Luxe, or at the Freeside supplier.

- Let Big Sal or Nero know that their rackets have been helped.

The Strip Infamy Gained!

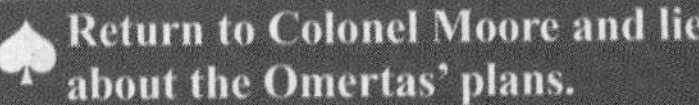

Return to Colonel Moore and lie about the Omertas' plans.

Caution A third, unapologetic, and highly dangerous way to minimize the Omertas' presence is to simply find the three bosses (Big Sal, Nero, and Cachino) and murder them all, and anyone else you spot with a first name and a sharp suit. The Omertas become hostile and there is instability on The Strip. It doesn't help you in this Quest, either.

OMERTAS Faction Interaction: Wise Guys' Mug Shots

This is Cachino **(14)**. You'll usually find him in the main level (he seeks out you). Then he moves to the bar near the stage on the main level.

Find Big Sal **(15)** on the balcony or pool table and offices area of the main level, or sleeping in the Gomorrah suites.

Find Nero **(16)** on the balcony or pool table and offices area of the Main Level, or sleeping in the Gomorrah suites.

Find Troike **(17)** in the Gomorrah lower lobby area, in the Zoara Club.

Find Clanden **(18)** sleeping or wandering the Gomorrah suites.

Caution If you haven't already completed the Free Quests "Big Winner" (detailed in the Tour section devoted to Gomorrah), you risk being unable to gain an Achievement or Trophy devoted to gambling. You have been warned!

Once you've completed this Side Quest, return to Colonel Moore, and inform her that:

You've foiled the racket and killed Big Sal and Nero (if this occurred). She is pleased with the results.

Or lie, and inform her the Omertas are planning to attack New Reno, and this isn't a concern. Although she doesn't agree, she is placated and the Quest continues.

NCR Fame Gained!

Any other blustering nonsense from your mouth fails to impress Colonel Moore, and this part of the Quest fails, although you can progress to the next Faction, with Moore's suspicions raised.

NCR Infamy Gained!

Moore quickly requests that you investigate Mr. House, because he isn't allied with the NCR and is likely to make a move when the battle breaks out. You can quiz Moore on why Mr. House is a problem, but there's only one solution; to take care of him. Leave Hoover Dam, and head toward the biggest landmark around: the Lucky 38 Casino [2D.02].

Remove Mr. House as a threat to the NCR.

Render Unto Caesar: For aiding and abetting the Legion's enemies, you have been declared "in damnatio memoraie"—an enemy of the Legion in perpetuity. Many will seek your head as a trophy.

Lucky 38 MR. HOUSE Faction Interaction #3: Mr. House

Gaining entry to "off-limits" areas of the Lucky 38 Casino can be tricky. To reach them, be sure you have one (or more) of the following before attempting the next part of this Quest:

The Platinum Chip that Benny "gave" you. Make sure you take this from him. If Benny has fled and has been captured by Caesar's Legion, another option is easier.

You can visit the H&H Tools Factory [2.06], and locate the Lucky 38 VIP Keycard inside the booby-trapped office. Find advice on exploring the factory in the Tour chapter.

Visit Camp Golf [3.23], and enter the intriguingly named House Resort. Inside, you can find a Lucky 38 VIP Keycard. Get advice on finding and exploring this location in the Tour chapter.

Or, you can trust your high-level Science skill, and manually hack the terminals necessary to reach Mr. House's inner sanctum!

Lucky 38 MR. HOUSE Faction Interaction: Mr. House Goes Bust

At the Lucky 38 Casino, you're greeted by Victor, who opens the doors for you, and also appears once you enter the casino floor **(19)**. Move to the elevator flanked by two Securitrons, and ask Victor to send you up to the penthouse. You can engage Mr. House **(20)** in conversation (Main Quest: The House Always Wins, I), but it isn't necessary.

Pass by Jane, the Securitrons, and Mr. House himself, and inspect a terminal on the north wall, under the staircase, next to the bookcase. You can access the terminal, and select "Open Antechamber" from the menu. You're an unauthorized user, and the Securitrons go hostile if you confirm this.

A section of wall detaches, allowing access into the antechamber **(21)**. You can:

Fight the Securitron guard defenses in a highly dangerous and protracted battle.

Or better yet, access the security terminal on the windowed side of the room, and override Mr. House's robots. They stop any aggressive behavior.

Or, you can simply run over to the elevator, head into Mr. House's chamber and kill him, and return. All of the Securitrons in the Lucky 38 revert to a non-combative threat indicator, and don't need to be fought.

Connection Lost...

22

23

With robot threats abated, access the terminal next to the control room elevator. Unlock it, and ride the elevator down to the control room. This vast, cool chamber contains Mr. House's Life Support (LS) Chamber **(22)**. You can:

Leave Mr. House, although this halts the Quest.

Access the terminal, and "Unseal LS Chamber." There's a microbial infection risk to Mr. House, but that's the least of his worries. Select "Yes."

At this point, you can:

Sterilize LS Chamber. This kills Mr. House, which is Moore's preferred plan. Unless you really want to kill him, this is an unnecessarily thorough option to remove Mr. House from play.

Disable Cerebral Interface, which allows you to see the "real" Mr. House. He's not quite as buff as his monitor image may have led you to believe. You can speak to him, kill him, let him live, or suffer pangs of guilt.

Once the deed is done, this Main Quest is over.

The House Has Gone Bust!

You have irrevocably disconnected Mr. House from the Lucky 38's mainframe computers, forever trapping him in the prison of his own mind, or killing him outright. His grand dreams for New Vegas will never be realized.

Return to Colonel Moore and report that Mr. House is no longer a threat.

Return to Hoover Dam. The monitors should now show this message **(23)**, indicating that you've been successful. When you meet Moore, you can inform her of how you dealt with Mr. House. She's pleased and mentions your efforts haven't gone unnoticed, and a presidential visit is being planned to re-energize the troops. While this is being organized, you're to destroy the remains of the Brotherhood of Steel chapter that was forced from the HELIOS One solar array several years ago. They've gone to ground, and you're tasked with digging them up. Moore reckons their bunker has a working reactor, and that's their vulnerability.

Find the Brotherhood of Steel chapter in this area and deal with them.

Faction Interaction #4: The Brotherhood of Steel

The Hidden Bunker, and the four Side Quests related to the Brotherhood of Steel (including Veronica's, a Follower) can occur before or after you speak with Colonel Moore. Consult Side Quest: Still in the Dark for all your options.

24

Journey to the strange, desolate, and windswept Hidden Valley [5.11], and enter the western bunker **(24)**. From this point on, you have two choices; to kill the Brotherhood of Steel, or (and this is surprising, given their history with the NCR) ally with them: Remember; the Brotherhood of Steel would make a fine fighting force for the battle to come.

Faction Interaction #4A: Tick, Tick, Boom!

The Brotherhood of Steel's bunker can be destroyed in cunning and brutish ways. You can:

25

Enter the facility, and when Paladin Ramos stops you, kill him and every single Brotherhood of Steel member **(25)**. This is long, highly dangerous, and ultimately pointless, because you have a better option.

Agree to see Elder McNamara, and once you're free to move about the bunker, head to the VR chamber in the southern quadrant of the bunker L2. When no one is looking, surreptitiously inspect the two terminals on the western wall: the Self-Destruct Authorization Terminal, and a link terminal to activate the self-destruct command. You can:

Hack the red terminal, and start the bunker self-destruct sequence. Or,

- You can locate the three senior Brotherhood members with keycard access to the authorization terminal. The three targets are:

26

Head Scribe Taggart **(26)**, who is usually in his bed, or wandering this VR chamber.

27

Head Paladin Hardin **(27)**, who is at the entrance between bunkers L1 and L2.

28

Elder McNamara **(28)**, who is usually in his bed or sitting in the command room.

Head Scribe's Keycard

Head Paladin's Keycard

Elder's Keycard

Obtain the keycards through Pickpocketing or shooting (which turns the entire bunker hostile).

Back at the authorization terminal, the keycards generate a password for the red terminal. Access that and choose the self-destruct sequence launch. Now flee to the surface.

Brotherhood of Steel Infamy Gained!

Return to Colonel Moore and report that the Brotherhood of Steel chapter in this area has been destroyed.

Tip Your mass-slaying of the Brotherhood of Steel isn't for naught, as there's a hefty haul inside this bunker, although buying items from them nets much more potent weaponry. Check the Tour chapter for the stash, and remember to pillage the bunker before you start the self-destruct sequence!

BROTHERHOOD OF STEEL Faction Interaction #4B: Into the Light

The second main plan is to complete Side Quest: Still in the Dark, and then forge an alliance with Elder McNamara. Consult that Quest for thorough information. But briefly, you need to:

Speak with Elder McNamara, and agree to the test (if Veronica isn't with you) regarding the NCR Ranger.

Speak with the elder, and begin the first task: retrieve Holotape Mission Data from three downed patrols **(29)**.

Optionally, you can keep Head Paladin Hardin informed of all your actions, but do not gain support from the other senior members of the Brotherhood: McNamara must remain in charge!

Return to McNamara, and collect three reports from Brotherhood scouts in the field **(30)**.

Return to McNamara, and meet up with Senior Knight Lorenzo, who gives you of a list of air filtration components to gather.

Enter Vault 3 [2.24] and obtain a Reverse Pulse Cleaner from Motor-Runner's chamber.

Enter Vault 11 [5.05], and locate a Differential Pressure Controller in the water-filled lower level.

Enter Vault 22 [1.09], and wind down, then up into the oxygen recycling level to gather the HEPA Cartridge Filters.

Then keep Elder McNamara at the helm. Do not replace him with Head Paladin Hardin.

With all this concluded, ask the head of the Brotherhood of Steel to help in your fight. Despite the past grievances, he actually agrees, supporting the NCR against a common enemy. If Hardin has been helped, he will not, for any reason, ally with the NCR.

Brotherhood of Steel Fame Gained!

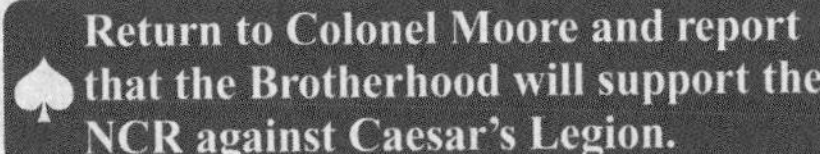

Return to Colonel Moore and report that the Brotherhood will support the NCR against Caesar's Legion.

Here Comes the Rain Again

Inform Colonel Moore of the outcome of your workings with the Brotherhood, and she appears preoccupied with the arrival of the president. You're to assist with the security detail; Kimball's safety is critical to maintaining the men's fighting spirit! Ranger Grant at the Visitor Center is in charge of security; report to him. This begins Main Quest: You'll Know It When It Happens. As this is a Main (and not a Side) Quest, consult it for all the possible options.

Talk to Ranger Grant about protecting President Kimball during his visit.

Return to Colonel Moore and report that President Kimball has safely left.

Return to Colonel Moore and report that President Kimball is dead.

Once the visit is over, and President Kimball is safely away, or in small pieces scattered across the Hoover Dam, report back to Moore. She's suitably happy (or fuming) depending on the results. But either way, the Legion is heading for the dam! As soon as you agree to it, you're to report to General Oliver. Act III: Eureka! begins now!

Go see General Oliver.

XP 1,500 XP (when you speak to General Oliver)

YOU'LL KNOW IT WHEN IT HAPPENS

ALLIED FACTIONS

Lucky 38 MR. HOUSE | NEW CA. REPUBLIC | INDEPENDENT

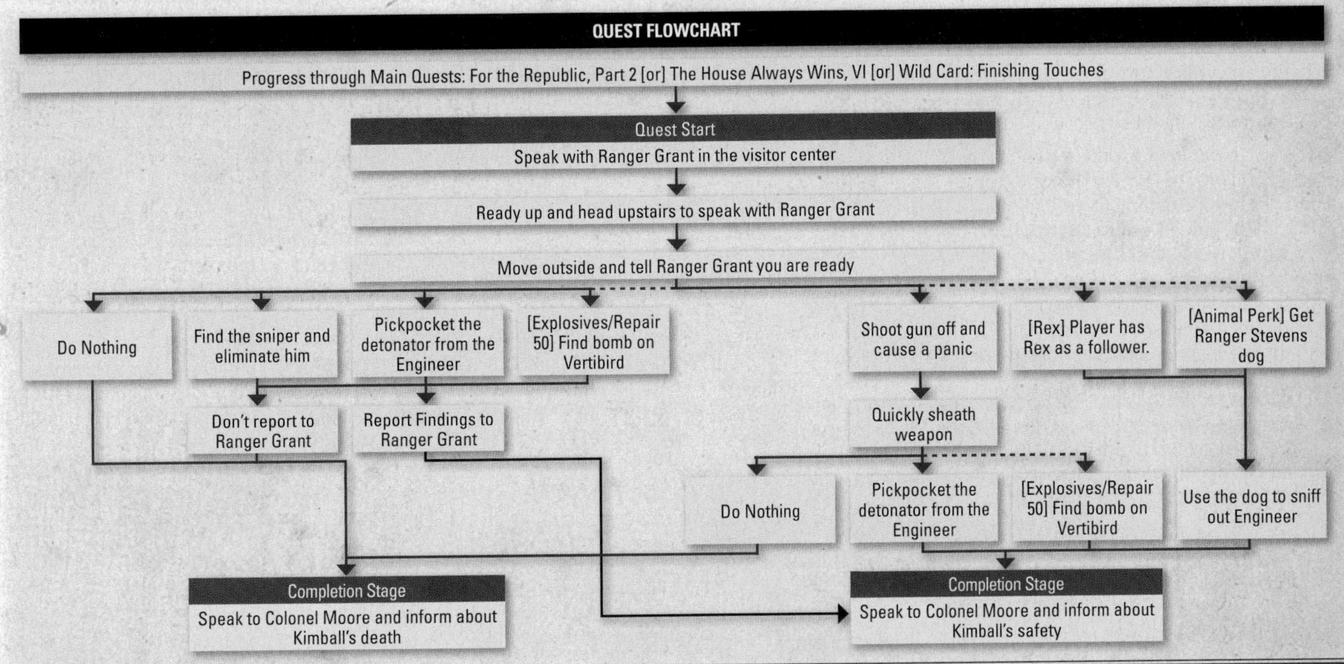

Before You Begin...

CAESAR'S LEGION This is a sister Quest to Main Quest: Arizona Killer, as the events depicted in both Quests are the same. However, this Quest is accessible only to those allied with the NCR, and is optional if you're doing the bidding of Mr. House or being your own boss with Yes Man. Whether or not you're here on NCR duty or as an outsider, your tasks are the same:

Report to Ranger Grant.

It's Quiet...Too Damn Quiet

1

2

Head to the Hoover Dam [3.33] if you're not here already, and locate the Visitor Center topped with the Vertibird landing pad **(1)**. You're here to rendezvous with Ranger Grant **(2)**. Read the remainder of this Quest, and figure out which method of protecting the NCR president will be easiest for you, depending on your armaments and skills. Then speak with Ranger Grant:

NEW CA. REPUBLIC If you have a Reputation of less than "Liked" with the NCR, Grant is none-too-happy having a last-minute and un-vetted addition to his security detail (you). You receive a limited amount of knowledge about the president's forthcoming visit, and you're grudgingly given access to Hoover Dam. However, expect to be taken down if you make any swift and violent movements (discharging a gun, for example). This makes the Quest more difficult to accomplish.

NEW CA. REPUBLIC If you have a Reputation of "Liked" or better with the NCR, Grant is happy for the help, and has no qualms giving you access to all restricted areas, a full presidential itinerary, and allows you to have your weapon drawn. You can even fire without any retribution, as long as you don't kill anyone you shouldn't.

Meet Ranger Grant on the observation deck.

[Optional] Investigate the area for clues.

3

4

Open the Doors to Hoover Dam and step out into the open. You're quite welcome to jog around, checking out the Hoover Dam pathway itself, the first tall guard tower on the dam (with the ranger atop it), the observation deck, stage, and assembled NCR troops. Nothing seems out of the ordinary. Either there's no threat, or the enemy is waiting until the president arrives. Report to Ranger Grant. The president arrives immediately afterward by Bear Force One; his personal Vertibird **(3)**. Several plans ensure that President Aaron Kimball **(4)** survives his pep-talk.

Protect President Kimball.

Plan #1: Nervous Rex

5

6

Ranger Stevens is patrolling the main road between the visitor center and gun emplacement, along with his Guard Dog **(5)**. You can:

Exclaim what a nice dog he has, and ask if you can borrow him to check out the area. He isn't sure.

You can tell him you're good with animals, and he lets you borrow the hound.

Ignore Ranger Stevens, and bring Rex, the companion (and ex-best friend of The King, a possible reward at the end of Side Quest: G.I. Blues).

Once you're with your animal, start to sniff out the Engineers within the crowd. Keep your eyes peeled for one who follows Kimball and his bodyguards in. The dog smells traces of explosives on the Engineer **(6)**. When you hear the dog growl, return to Grant and tell him.

> *Caution* Beware! If you speak to this Engineer, don't tell him anything is wrong, or he attempts to blow himself up then and there, causing the NCR to think you executed him, and they go hostile!

NCR Fame Gained!

Preparation for Plans #2 and #3

7

8

The Vertibird is a likely location for some kind of explosive device. But getting to the Vertipad is tricky. However, you can:

GUNS Fire off a gun when you're Hidden **(7)**. Make certain no one's looking or you're branded an assassin! In the ensuing panic, you can access the Vertipad.

SPEECH 50 Or head to the ladder leading up to the Vertipad, where you're stopped by a guard **(8)**. Tell him you really want to check out the craft. He agrees!

NEW CA. REPUBLIC Or earn permission to access the Vertibird landing pad from Ranger Grant, while chatting to him inside the Visitor Center, before the president's arrival. You can simply access the landing pad directly at this point.

Plan #2: Bomb on the 'Bird

9

Once Bear Force One lands and you've accessed the Vertipad, inspect the Vertibird **(9)**. It appears that the assassins could have fiddled with part of this craft.

You search the Vertibird and notice a bomb, skillfully disabling it and removing it from the craft.

Report the find to Ranger Grant immediately, so he can close down the event and prevent one of the other assassination attempts from occurring.

NCR Fame Gained!

Plan #3: Explosive on the Engineer

When the Vertibird lands, locate the Engineer who arrived with the craft. He's either on the roof or following the president at a careful distance. There's something suspicious about this fellow **(10)**.

Pickpocket him, and you'll uncover a Redundant Failsafe Detonator. This is obviously a device the Engineer was going to use.

> **Caution** Beware! Don't get detected, or be aggressive when speaking to him, or he blows himself up, which turns the NCR hostile because they think you killed him. Grab the detonator first!

If you don't speak to Ranger Grant afterward, another assassin makes the hit.

NCR Fame Gained!

♠ **Keep an eye on sniper locations.**

Plan #4: Sniper on the Roof

If you're playing nicely with the NCR, hack the terminal near Grant when he first gives you this assignment. There's mention of a possible sniper attempt on a guard tower, allowing you to prepare for it.

Or, you can simply prepare by training your eyes on the first guard tower itself.

Be sure you're also covering the first guard tower with the Ranger sniper already on the roof. During the speech, you'll see a second figure (dressed in Ranger garb) execute the sniper, and then put a sniper bullet through the president's head, while everyone watches agog.

Prevent that from happening by:

Standing guard with a high-powered weapon. Make sure you fire after the Ranger is executed, but before the president is shot. Otherwise it looks like you're aiming at a Ranger, and the NCR turn hostile!

Or, climb the tower, and wait for the assassin to appear through the sealed manhole cover. You can play around and annoy Grant over the radio prior to this. But when the time comes, wait for the assassin to take down the sniper, and then quickly finish him **(11)** with a high-powered weapon, or he shrugs off your attacks to focus on killing the president. Afterward, radio to Grant, so he can lock down the event and prevent further attempts.

NCR Fame Gained!

Plan #5: Fracas on the Floor

Time to panic! Not you; the assembled NCR troops! Just before Bear Force One touches down, fire some rounds into the air, forcing the NCR to turn on you **(12)**. Back away, but don't leave Hoover Dam until you witness the Vertibird turn tail and leave. Flee the vicinity (don't kill anyone!), and then wait a few hours. The NCR aren't best pleased by your actions, but the president did get away safely!

NCR Infamy Gained!

Plan #6: Speech on the Stage

Ranger Grant has a lot on his plate, so why not let him relax? If you remove both the bomb and the sniper as threats, but neglect to inform Grant, the president gets to finish his speech, congratulate that NCR halfwit **(13)**, and fly off in an intact Vertibird. Everything goes off without a hitch!

Plan #7: It Happens

The last plan is the least dangerous, but really puts a damper on NCR morale; simply let the assassination occur. Give the engineer away and he rushes the stage **(14)**. Remove that threat, but don't tell Grant, (or do nothing) and Kimball is executed by the sniper **(15)**. Remove that threat, and Kimball's Vertibird explodes once it takes off after the speech **(16)**. Avoid all three possibilities if you're allied with the NCR!

When you're done, head back to Colonel Moore, and prepare for the final push. Act III begins now!

♠ **Report your findings to Ranger Grant.**

♠ **Kimball saved, report back to Ranger Grant.**

♠ **Kimball killed, report back to Ranger Grant.**

NCR Fame Gained!

1,000 XP

ARIZONA KILLER

ALLIED FACTION

QUEST FLOWCHART

Progress through Main Quest: Render Unto Caesar finishing the BoS objective

Quest Start

Locate Cato Hostilius and speak with him

- Inquire about what he can do → [Explosives 50] Acquire the Vertibird Bomb → Tell him you are ready
- Tell him you are ready → Travel Hoover Dam
  - Examine Watson's Helmet → Plant C4 in the helmet and give it back to Private Watson → Ask Cato when the President is arriving → Detonate Watson when he is next to Kimball → Completion Stage: Report to Caesar of your Success
  - Examine the AA console on the observation deck → [Repair 50] Short the circuit to cause the stage to explode / [Science 50] Set the AA console to shoot the Vertibird / Hack Visitor Center terminal to send Vertibird into mountain → Ask Cato when the President is arriving → Watch the President explode → Completion Stage: Report to Caesar of your Success
  - Ask Cato when the President is arriving
    - [Speech 50] Gain access to the launch pad → [Explosives 50] Place bomb on the Vertibird → Wait for Kimball to leave...BOOM → Completion Stage: Report to Caesar of your Success
    - Shoot the President → Completion Stage: Report to Caesar of your Success
    - Do nothing → Completion Stage: Report to Caesar of your Failure
- Kill Cato → Completion Stage: Report to Caesar of your Failure

Completion Stage

Report to Caesar of your Success

Completion Stage

Report to Caesar of your Failure

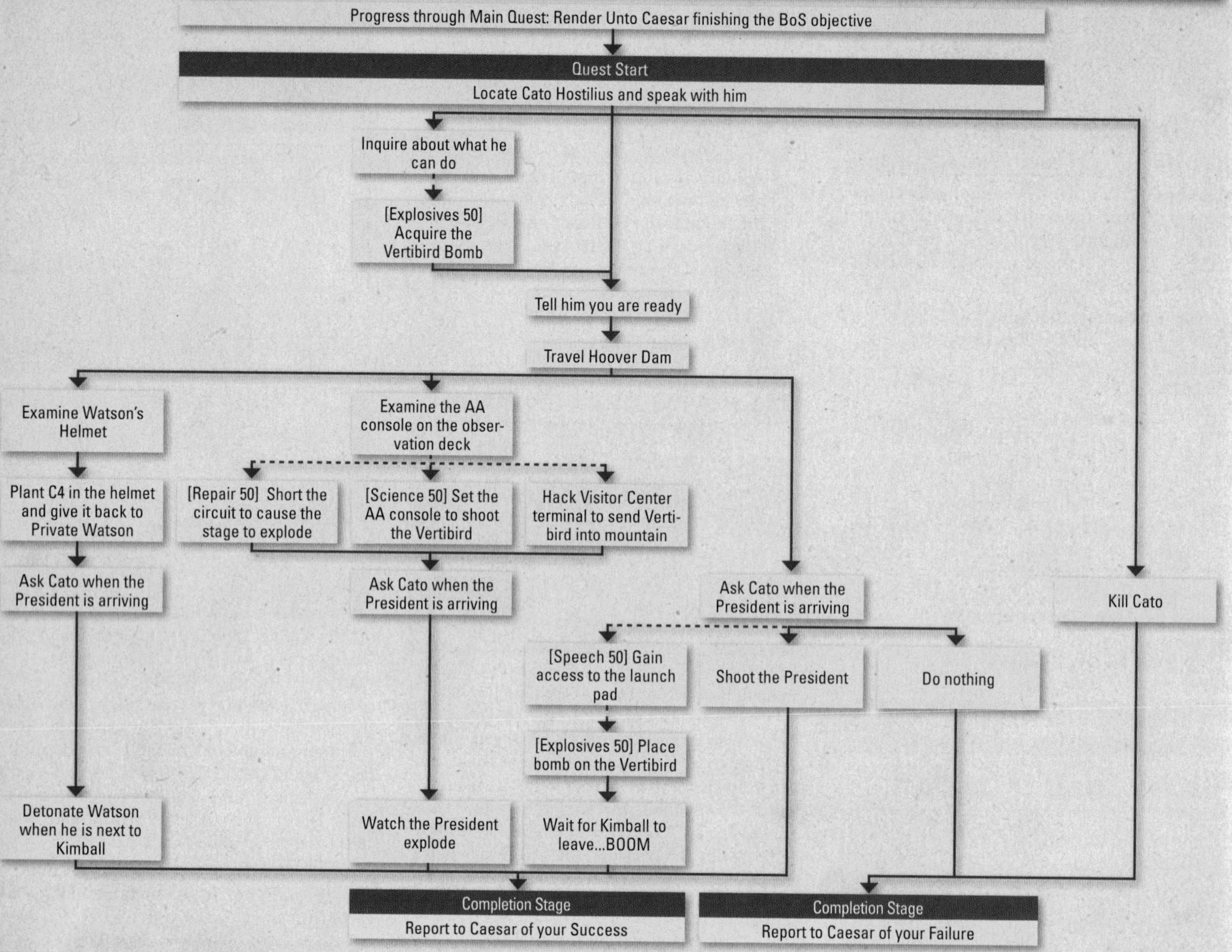

Before You Begin...

CAESAR'S LEGION This is a sister Quest to Main Quest: You'll Know It When It Happens, as the events depicted in both Quests are the same. However, this Quest is accessible only to those who have thrown in their lot with Caesar's Legion. You can only access this Quest if you've completed all of Main Quest: Render Unto Caesar. Once done, Caesar (or Lucius) informs you that NCR President Kimball is scheduled to land at the Hoover Dam [3.33], and you're to assassinate him. To help with this task, you're to rendezvous with a field operative named Cato Hostilius.

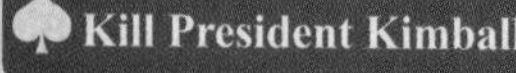

Kill President Kimball

Rendezvous with Cato Hostilius

Initium: Catching Up With Cato

Cato Hostilius has been roughing it while preparing for your arrival, in a rocky thicket **(1)** on the southeast outskirts of Boulder City [3.32], close to both Ranger Station Delta [3.36] and a dreaded Cazador Nest [3.35]. Be extremely careful, as you'll be Vilified by the NCR (so don't venture too close to their strongholds), and you don't want the Cazadors devouring Cato before you've had chance to speak with him. After some pleasantries, Cato **(2)** asks if you're ready to act. At this point, you begin this Quest, which is time-sensitive, so only agree to the Quest if you have all the equipment you want to carry out your goals.

Time passes. It is dawn, and Cato has changed into more appropriate civilian attire **(3)**. He asks what sort of plan you've thought up. You can tell him whatever you wish, and optionally gain a wealth of his suggestions; all of which are covered below.

You're given an NCR trooper uniform. Put it on now; you don't want to wade into Hoover Dam looking out of place! Ask "is there anything you can do to help?" during the conversation, and Cato reveals he's carrying a bomb that can be placed on the president's Vertibird.

Respond that you're familiar with explosives, and take the bomb.

Otherwise, Cato keeps it.

Although not part of the conversation, one of the assassination options involves a Detonator and C-4 Explosives. Make sure you're carrying these BEFORE you agree to start this Quest with Cato. An easy place to find some is over at the NCR checkpoint, on the road west of Nelson [6.06], which is part of Side Quest: Back in Your Own Backyard.

Report to Cato when you are prepared.

Then follow Cato along the road (holster your weapon if you fall behind). Cross the remains of the bridge and run into the Hoover Dam entrance road **(4)**. Stay clear of the Ranger patrols; if you come within about 15 feet of them, they realize you're in disguise, and the whole place erupts in hostile fire, failing the Quest. You now have a variety of ways to dispatch the president **(5)**, before or after you speak to Cato again (he tells you the president's Vertibird is descending).

Bicallis I and II: Big Guns. Bigger Explosions

Before speaking with Cato, move around the circular observation deck, and up the steps between the Ranger patrols. Locate the console by the radio, and examine the gun controls. You can:

Reactivate the gun and set it to shoot down the president's Vertibird, Bear Force One **(6)**.

Short the circuit board and cause the gun to explode during the president's speech **(7)**.

Choose either option if you have the skill. Then head to Cato, find a viewing spot, and watch the fireworks. Then listen to the shouts of dismay. Then get the hell out of there.

Caesar's Legion Fame Gained!

Bicallis III: Bear Farce One

Prior to speaking with Cato, head inside to the bottom floor of the Visitor Center. Locate the terminal next to the Snowglobe.

Hack the terminal and update the Vertibird Flight Control Settings.

Return to Cato and speak with him; the president will be arriving at any minute! Now sit back and relax as the president strides in with his armed guard **(8)** gives his speech, returns to Bear Force One, and takes off. Unfortunately for President Kimball, the Vertibird isn't going back to the great state of California, but instead loses control and plummets into the mountains **(9)**, to the dismay of the onlookers. From here, you can gawk with the other onlookers or casually make your way back to The Fort, with no one suspecting you as the culprit.

Caesar's Legion Fame Gained!

Bicallis IV: Telemetry, My Dear Watson

Prior to the Vertibird landing, head to the left side of the stage and sidle over to Private Jeremy Watson **(10)**. He's here to receive an award from the president, but he's having trouble locating his helmet. The helmet is sitting on a table at the foot of the observation deck steps, near the sandbags. Inspect it.

Assuming you have C-4 and a Detonator, cram some of the Explosives into the helmet. Return to Watson, and tell him where his hat is. Then speak to Cato, wait for the president to arrive and step on stage, and bring out your Detonator. This instantly turns everyone hostile, so detonate Private Watson immediately **(11)**. Then fight or flee.

NCR Infamy Gained!

Caesar's Legion Fame Gained!

Bicallis V: A Can-Do Altitude

Speak to Cato and watch the president's Vertibird land. Once Kimball has landed and is heading to the stage, move around the observation deck to the ladder. There's likely to be a guard here. Avoid the Ranger at all costs, because he's much more attuned to look for infiltrators. To reach the Vertipad on the roof, you can:

Attack the soldier, or sprint past him, causing an alert. Then quickly complete this plan and fight or flee.

Leap from the roadside of the observation deck onto the perimeter wall, and creep around behind the solder, and up the ladder. Or use a Stealth Boy.

Or step over to Private Jensen **(12)**, and ask to go upstairs. Tell him you've always wanted to see the president's Vertibird.

Then ask nicely. He lets you through.

Once on the Vertipad, look over the Vertibird and plant the bomb Cato gave you during your initial conversation. Then get off the roof, pretend to be an innocent bystander, and watch the Vertibird take off, and develop a severe malfunction **(13)**. Step away without incident if you wish.

Caesar's Legion Fame Gained!

Bicallis VI: Arizona Assassin

14

15

Do you have a particularly lethal aim with a Sniper Rifle **(14)** or want to surprise the president with an up-close and personal melee savaging? Then throw caution (and common sense) to the wind, wait for the president to begin his speech (so he has longer to run when he tries to escape), and then:

 Execute him with a headshot **(15)**.

 Execute him with a fierce pummeling or melee strike. Don't get cut down trying to reach the president; use a Stealth Boy.

 **NCR Infamy Gained!**

 **Caesar's Legion Fame Gained!**

Bicallis VII: A Cannon-Do Attitude

16

Do you have a particularly gigantic piece of technology—such as a Tesla Cannon—you want to test on a Vertibird? Then speak with Cato, head to a relatively safe position (such as the Vertipad atop the observation deck), and launch a barrage of shots **(16)** before the Vertibird lands or as it takes off. Shrug off the NCR ground attacks (no mean feat), and then flee, or stand and fire if you're bullet-proof.

Or, disable the Vertibird, and finish off President Kimball and his highly proficient guards in a thrilling and incredibly dangerous battle.

 **NCR Infamy Gained!**

 **Caesar's Legion Fame Gained!**

Bicallis VIII: Arizona Quitter

The last plan is by far the most pathetic. It involves failing the Quest in a truly incompetent manner. You can:

Attack Cato as soon as you meet him **(17)**.

17

18

Or head to the Hoover Dam, speak with Cato, remain unseen, watch the president's speech **(18)**, watch the Vertibird leave, and remember you were supposed to do something.... Oh well, too late now.

 **Return to Caesar to answer for your failure.**

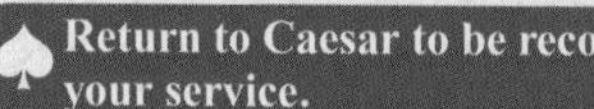 **Return to Caesar to be recognized for your service.**

The last part of this Quest is actually the very final part of Main Quest: Render Unto Caesar. Return to Caesar (or Lucius), and answer for your failure (choose the first conversation option to avoid being hacked to pieces).

Or, assuming you actually did as you were instructed, Caesar (or Lucius) rewards you.

The time for the final battle has begun! Main Quest: Veni, Vidi, Vici is upon you!

 **Caesar's Legion Fame Gained!**

 **1,000 XP (If the president dies)**

Act 3

NO GODS, NO MASTERS

ALLIED FACTION

INDEPENDENT

See flowchart on the following page

Preparation: Yes Man, We Can!

1

Yes Man is excited to let you know that the final battle for Hoover Dam [3.33] is now upon you! When you're speaking to Yes Man in the Lucky 38 Casino [2D.02], he describes two possible scenarios:

The first option is to route the dam's power output to the facility under The Fort (the vault bunker), which will restart its reactor and the Securitron army you left on standby and hopefully upgraded during Main Quest: Wild Card: You and What Army? This should give you enough troops to push the NCR and Legion right out of the Mojave Wasteland!

The second option is to destroy the dam's generators. Without those, the dam becomes just a giant block of concrete, and the NCR will leave because the area has no significant importance now. Of course, it'll get a lot darker and scarier around these parts. Obviously, if you never upgraded the Securitrons under The Fort, or made a tactical blunder and destroyed them, this is your only option.

Good news! Yes Man tells you that you don't have to decide yet. Simply take the Override Chip and install it on the terminal inside Hoover Dam's power control room. Now head for Hoover Dam **(1)**.

 **Override Chip**

 **NCR Emergency Radio**

 **Go to the Control Room in Hoover Dam and install the override chip.**

Note Tune in to NCR Emergency Radio to listen to a variety of background information about the conflicts occurring elsewhere in the Wasteland, as well as the dam.

You can hear broadcasts from Camp Golf (which change depending on your actions during Side Quest: Flags of Our Foul-Ups).

There's chatter about Fiends near Camp McCarran (which is affected by the Fiend leaders you culled during Side Quest: Three-Card Bounty).

There are skirmishes over at Camp Forlorn Hope and Nelson (which are affected by decisions you made during Side Quests: Restoring Hope and We Are Legion respectively).

There's also noise from The Strip, as the Omertas may make a move, depending on what you did during Side Quest: I Put a Spell on You.

Maybe we could build a fire, sing a couple of songs, huh? Why don't we try that? Listen for special chatter from the dam.

Caution Although you can complete this final battle without killing anyone, it requires considerable talents and skill. Therefore, if you haven't placed plenty of points into your Speech (and related) skills, "tool up" with all your finest hard-hitting projectiles and other favored weaponry before the Quest begins.

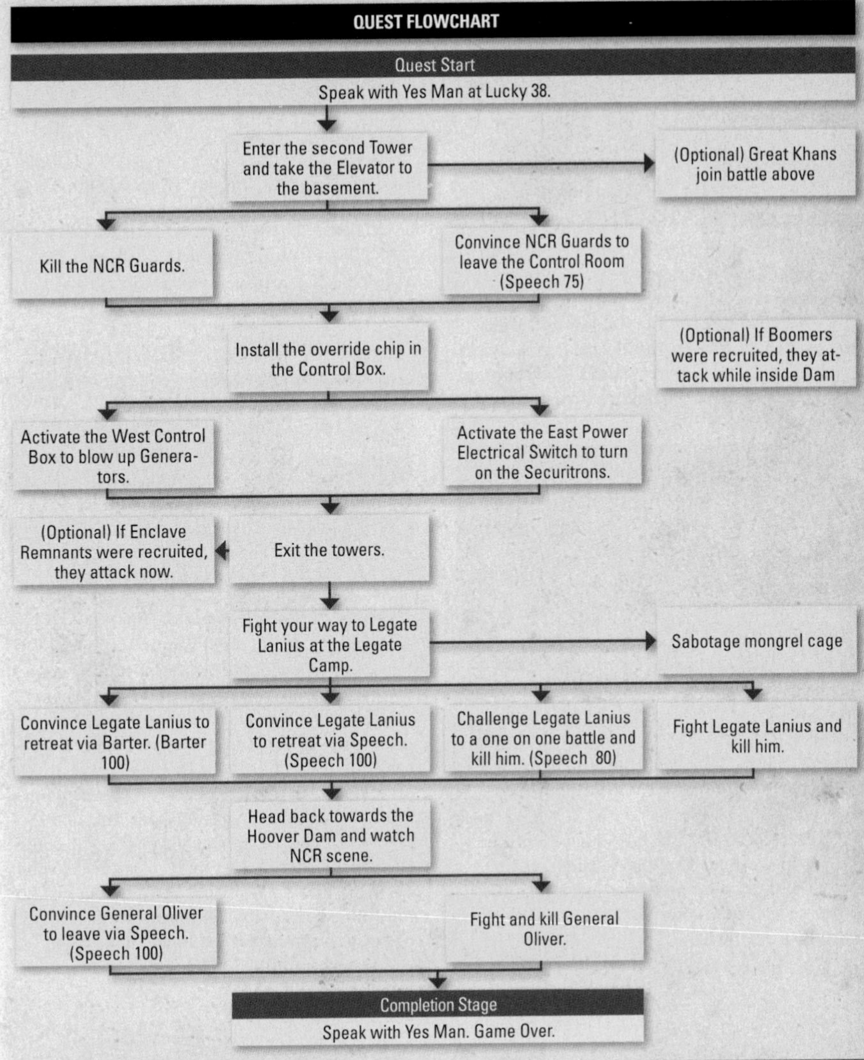

Dam Nuisances

You begin with your Securitron escort close to the Hoover Dam Visitor Center **(2)**, which is on fire and under heavy Legion attack. Leave your Securitron to tackle some of the Legion, and push forward.

GREAT KHANS If you severed the Great Khan alliance with the Legion and allied with them yourself, a team of warriors breaks out of the center, and provides some cannon fodder (and protection for you). They lob projectiles and attack the Legion on the curved dam bridge before succumbing to superior firepower and numbers.

Note To obtain Great Khan support here, you must have brokered a deal between the Great Khans and the NCR during Main Quest: For the Republic, Part 2, and then switched to the Wild Card path. So you'll rarely see the Khans.

If you have high Infamy with the NCR, you'll be fighting both them and the Legion!

You need to get into the Hoover Dam somehow, but the elevator and doors to the power plant in the Visitor Center are blocked. Instead, battle along the dam bridge **(3)**.

Employ a Stealth Boy if you want to reach the second guard tower unscathed and leave the fighting to the NCR and Legion.

As you continue across the curved structure, you may see a large steel bird in the sky. What demonry is this?

BOOMERS If you allied with the Boomers earlier, Loyal lives up to his word (and name) and flies over the troops, dropping bombs and coating the Legion troops in fire **(4)**. Watch the bomber fly by before you head into the dam.

Without a Boomer alliance, continue to battle across the sandbags, cutting down NCR forces if they are currently hostile, and then enter the dam.

Pass the first guard tower (where Kimball's sniper shot from, if you witnessed it during Main Quest: You'll Know It When It Happens), and then push through the fearsome Legion army toward the second guard tower **(5)**, and enter the double doors (or climb the ladder and enter from the roof hatch). Locate the

Elevator to Hoover Dam Offices, and access it. You appear in the northwest corridors adjacent to the huge power plant chamber itself. Exit through the blast door, and then head east along the corridors, until you reach the entrance to the control room. You'll know when you're nearing it—bodies are strewn everywhere **(6)**.

Two NCR Heavy Troopers guard the control room door **(7)**, and they're refusing you entrance. They yell a warning to you and open fire if you venture into the room. You can:

SPEECH 75 Lie, and tell them Colonel Moore is in trouble. They leave their post to help, which gives you access to the control room and allows you to keep your standing with the NCR.

Or gun them down where they stand, which causes your standing with the NCR to suffer.

NCR Infamy Gained!

Locate the bank of monitors; the control box connected to the main computer banks at Hoover Dam. You must install the Override Chip to continue. This instantly brings up a friendly face **(8)**, who asks what you'd like to do:

Activate the eastern power plant to power the Securitron Army.

Destroy the dam generators.

Caution Did you forget to power up the Securitrons during Wild Card: You and What Army? That's a real shame, buddy! Yes Man can only offer you the thrill of destroying the dam generators, and effectively pushing the NCR away from Hoover Dam, creating a much more lawless society in the long run.

Once you've chosen, Yes Man obliges. To complete the process, you must activate a manual switch.

Plan #1: Standby for Action!

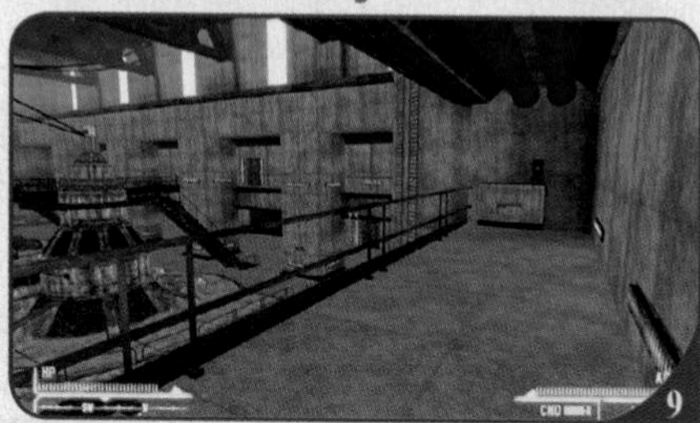

Head out of the control room, and turn left (east), then head east, south, and east again, cutting down any opponents (these are usually Legion unless you start firing on everyone), or Sneaking down the corridors and into side chambers to avoid combat. Yes Man's friendly face appears on all the wall monitors to cheer you on. Open the blast door that leads to Power Plant 01, step onto the small balcony **(9)**, turn right, and locate the East Power Electrical Switch. Flick it on and the east side of the plant powers up, re-routing power to The Fort. Backtrack to the second guard tower exit, and head topside.

Plan #2: Action on Standby

Exit the control room, and turn right (west), then head west, south, and west again, cutting down any opponents (these are usually Legion unless you start firing on everyone), or Sneaking into side rooms to avoid combat before progressing without killing anyone. Yes Man's friendly face appears on all the wall monitors to cheer you on. Open the blast door that leads to Power Plant 01, step onto the small balcony, turn left, and find the West Power Plant Control Box. Overload it, and spin around to watch the dam generators blow **(10)**! Backtrack to the second guard tower exit, and head topside. If the NCR haven't been attacking you, they certainly begin to after the generators explode!

Exit out to the east side of the Dam.

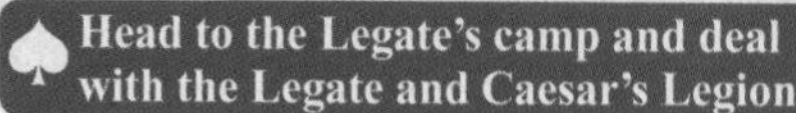

Head to the Legate's camp and deal with the Legate and Caesar's Legion.

Battle on the Bridge

Back on the dam bridge, continue to cross the curved structure as Legion foes descend on your position. They're especially angry if you upgraded the Securitron Army at The Fort, then powered them on at the generator just now; The Fort has gone up in a blaze of fire and explosions! Continue to face severe opposition as you thrust through to the opposite side of the dam, toward Legate's Camp. You're attacked by Legionaries plus the more powerful Centurions. Stand back and let your Securitrons do the fighting **(11)**, or face these ferocious foes, perhaps picking up and using their favored melee weapon **(12)**: the Chainsaw!

If you recruited the Enclave Remnants, a Vertibird drops in near the fourth guard tower **(13)** and drops off Power-Armored veterans, who fight by your side as you push into Legate Lanius' territory.

Whether the Remnants (or Securitrons) are with you or not, continue to push to the southeast, then east onto the remains of the overpass and road that winds through a small rocky enclave to a gate that leads into the Legate's Camp.

Courier from the City of Cowards

15

Give the Praetorian Guard a taste of your vengeance **(14)** as you enter the inner gates, or Sneak by him using your impressively stealthy abilities. Enter the camp, and deal with any Legion soldiers that may be about, before checking the Mongrel Cage **(15)** to your right. The place is currently closed up, and there's usually no reason to check this area, but if there are hounds inside, you can:

Remove the mechanism's springs to seal the gate shut.

Or ignore them, and cut through these frothing canines (if any are prowling the area) during the last desperate times for the Legion.

The Great Legate Debate

16

17

18

But now you face a more fearsome foe. Move to the steps cut into the earth, and follow them around and up toward the Legate's Tent. A mountain of a man approaches, wielding a blade as tall as a Super Mutant. Legate Lanius **(16)** has been waiting for you. You can:

GUNS: Immediately engage him in combat. Large, chunky, highly explosive, and incredibly damaging weapons are obviously the key to whittling down his considerable constitution.

You can engage him in conversation too, although anything but the most deferential talk turns him violent. However, if you state "maybe you're willing to listen to reason," he notes that you fight with words, "like all beneath the flag of the bear." You can:

SPEECH 55: Tell him this battle is decided. He asks if you're here to surrender, and then goes on about killing people. Lots of people. You can try to Barter (see below), or tell him anything else so he turns violent, or:

SPEECH 65: Tell him this advancing he's so proud of took the Legion years. Lanius responds that the dam has never see the massed strength of the East, only legates such as Graham, the burning man. You can tell him anything else to begin a fight, or:

SPEECH 75: Ask about what the East will become. Lanius says you're talking in circles, as HE is the personification of the might of the East! Respond with other words for a fight, or:

SPEECH 85: That if the Legion needs all the East to crush the West.... Lanius interrupts you, telling you victory here will be swift. The East will hold! Respond with fighting talk, or:

SPEECH 100: Say the weakness of the West will slow the Legion. Lanius is confused. Start verbal fisticuffs, or:

SPEECH 100: Note that the NCR's huge size means the Legion's whole army will be needed to hold the West. Lanius tells you that doesn't mean defeat. Once again, respond with fighting talk, or:

SPEECH 100: Tell him that moving the Legion's whole army West means losing the East. They can't hold both. Lanius verbally falters, blaming Caesar for drawing too much blood during the Eastern campaigns. But Lanius will not have Hoover Dam be the Legion's gravestone! He prepares to retreat!

There are several possible outcomes to this conversation. You can:

Legate's Conclusion #1:

Tell him there is wisdom in victory, or that you don't believe you've seen the last of the Legion. When he responds, you can speak again with a final Speech check or other final utterances. And then he is gone.

Or you can ask if he's retreating. This infuriates Lanius; you know nothing of who he is! You can fight him and his troops (Legate's Conclusion #5), or:

Legate's Conclusion #2:

SPEECH 80: You can bluff him, and face him in combat one-on-one. He agrees to the duel **(17)**.

BARTER 55: Tell him he could take the West, but not hold it. Lanius responds that anything the West sends against them will be broken. Respond with verbal threats, and combat begins. Or:

BARTER 75: Tell him an army to fight them isn't necessary because the Legion's supply lines will kill them first. Lanius replies that they have The Fort and Hoover Dam, and that other communities will fall. Verbally attack, or:

BARTER 95: Note that there are no communities to support them; the Legion has seen to that. He says there are many towns to harvest slaves from. Again, combat is but an offensive comment away, or:

BARTER 100: Argue that the West settlements are not self-sufficient, they need the NCR and caravans. He tells you that you rely too much on the trappings of civilization. You can:

Ask him if he really believes that, or if he is taking a chance. This leads to Legate's Conclusion #3.

Tell him the taming of the West is defeating the Legion; the NCR's weakness is their defense, OR that the Legion can't supply all the West any better than the NCR. He tells you about Denver. This leads to Legate's Conclusion #3, #4, or #5 (below).

BARTER 75: Or ask about Nipton, Searchlight, and Nelson. Lanius says Vulpes was responsible, and it was worth weakening the West. Ask if as a legate he really believes that, or if he's taking a chance. He tells you about Denver and a protracted battle. The West is a trap, and the bear is already caught in it. Respond with:

Legate's Conclusion #3:

BARTER 100: Your faith; that trade has helped man survive the Great War, and will do so again. When he returns, he will put this to the test with his blades. Respond that you grant him that time, or await the day. Then he retreats!

Legate's Conclusion #4:

SPEECH 100: You seeing death as change and a strength. He talks about what war would have brought, the bullet scars you possess, and that you're more than a match for Vulpes. With that, he retreats!

Or, ask if he's retreating. This leads to Legate's Conclusion #2.

Legate's Conclusion #5:

Tell him anything else, and he turns violent, and attacks you with his men **(18)**. Pick the choicest blade and helmet from the appendages you've sliced!

Blade of the East

Legate's Helmet

Tip Either fight this massive man at range—concentrating on his legs to cripple and slow him down so you can easily outrun him—by retreating and firing off powerful weaponry. Or use your very best armor-piercing weapons. Legate Lanius is a monster, so expect a tricky fight!

- Healing items are imperative, because Legate Lanius can inflict critical wounds in seconds, and he usually has Legion back-up.
- Armor-piercing (or similar) ammunition types are helpful if you're using Guns.
- If you're using Melee Weapons, remember to coat them with any of the Poisons you crafted at a campfire earlier. You did prepare for this fight, right?
- Crippling his legs or shooting his weapon are excellent ways to hold him back, as is scoring a knockdown or KO on him.
- Legate Lanius attacks with two bodyguards, who deliver massive damage with their Ballistic Fists but aren't too hardy. Take them out first (especially if you specialized in Melee or Unarmed combat) so you're only attacked from one direction.

Deal with General Oliver and the NCR.

Caesar on the Cross

19

20

Either battle back to the Legate Camp's inner gate, using ranged weaponry to tag the Legion snipers from the upper rocky outcrops you can't reach, and then slaughter the remaining troops (and Mongrel Dogs if you didn't secure their pen); or walk there after successfully preventing bloodshed. As you approach the gate, an explosion rocks the entrance, and General Lee Oliver, flanked by NCR Rangers, strides into view. He's tickled pink by the screams of those Legion bastards. At this point, you can introduce him to your Securitron friends **(19)**. Oliver isn't too keen to be menaced by 10-foot-tall robots, and asks you to tell them to stand down. You can:

- Get into all kinds of unpleasant and downright offensive back-and-forth chatter with the General, before ordering your Securitrons to kill the general and his bodyguards. Help out if you want **(20)**.
- Or, you can mention that you were hoping both sides could be pleasant about this. He tells you he's not going anywhere. You can:

Bluff him and say he's talking and not attacking.

Or ask whether he thinks these are all the forces you have, and then tell him you just stood down (or killed) Caesar's toughest general.

Oliver backs down, asking whether you've thought through this whole "nation building" plan. Respond with any comment you wish, before Oliver high-tails it out of here.

- Or, you can order Yes Man to eject General Oliver from the premises. This highly satisfying conclusion allows you to watch as Yes Man grabs Oliver and flings him off one of the Hoover Dam towers!

Return to Yes Man with news of your victory.

21

As the general leaves (or plummets), or you step through his remains, the Securitron with a happy face trundles up to meet you **(21)**. Yes Man says you just did a super job, and then lets you know he's going to use some code snippets he found to make his personality a little more assertive. Does that sound like a good idea...? Yes Man will be offline for a while. However, the Securitrons will ensure that New Vegas is protected. Take care now! The Main Quest concludes.

XP **4,000 XP**

Note "My only friend the end." You cannot explore after the ending. When you watch the ending, it may gradually dawn on you that the multitude of actions you took during your adventure directly affected the ending. These decisions are broken down in the Appendices.

ALL OR NOTHING

ALLIED FACTION: MR. HOUSE

Preparation: Keep Your Eyes on the Prize

1

Mr. House informs you that the ultimate battle for Hoover Dam [3.33], and the crescendo to his take-over plans for New Vegas and beyond, are about to come to fruition. During your last talk in the Lucky 38 Casino Penthouse [2D.02], he informs you of a single, overriding plan:

See flowchart on the following page

When you arrive at the dam, you must gain entrance to the dam's interior, and route the dam's power output to the facility under The Fort (the vault bunker), which restarts its reactor and the Securitron army you left on standby and upgraded during Main Quest: The House Always Wins, II. This should give you enough troops to push the NCR and Legion right out of the Mojave Wasteland! Mr. House orders you to take the Override Chip and install it on the terminal inside Hoover Dam's power control room. You appear at Hoover Dam **(1)**.

Override Chip

NCR Emergency Radio

Go to the Control Room in Hoover Dam and install the override chip.

Note Tune in to NCR Emergency Radio to listen to a variety of background information about the conflicts occurring elsewhere in the Wasteland, as well as the dam.

You can hear broadcasts from Camp Golf (which change depending on your actions during Side Quest: Flags of Our Foul-Ups).

There's chatter about Fiends near Camp McCarran (which is affected by the Fiend leaders you culled during Side Quest: Three-Card Bounty).

There are skirmishes over at Camp Forlorn Hope and Nelson (which are affected by decisions you made during Side Quests: Restoring Hope and We Are Legion respectively).

There's also noise from The Strip, as the Omertas may make a move, depending on what you did during Side Quest: I Put a Spell on You.

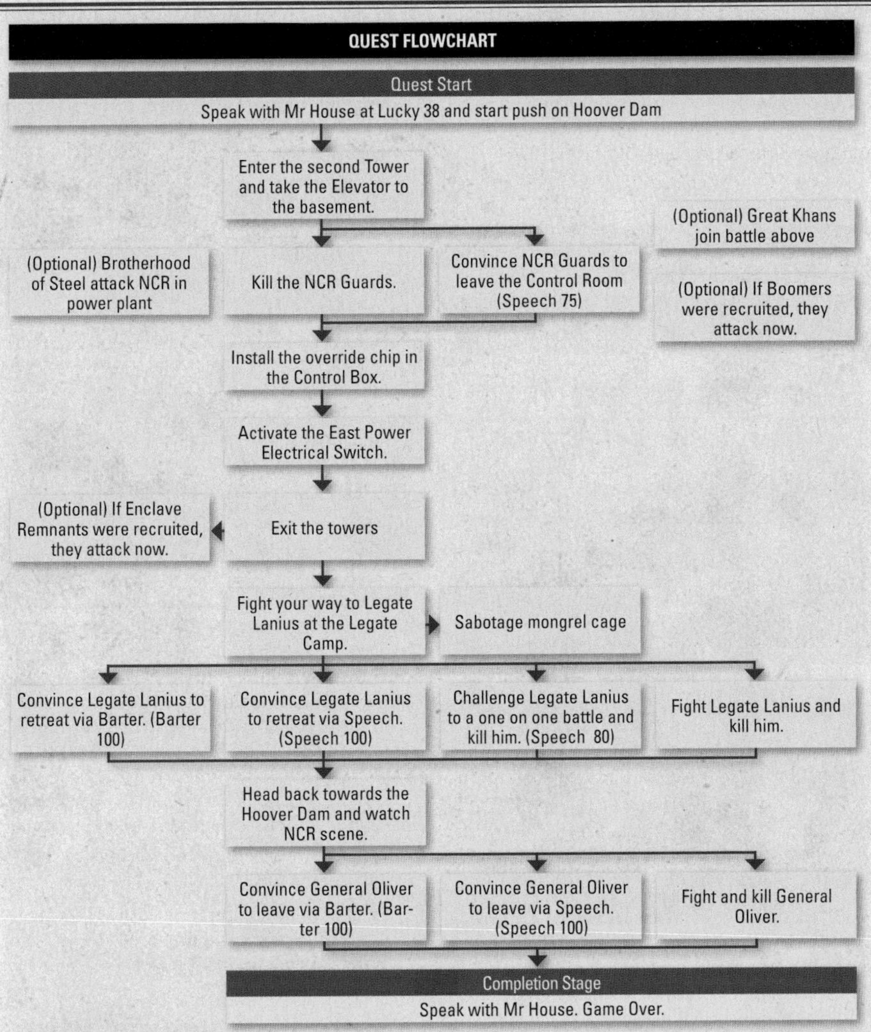

Note *(continued)*

WILD WASTELAND: Hold on one second. This installation has a substantial dollar value attached to it: Listen for special chatter from the dam.

Caution Although you can complete this final battle without killing anyone, it requires considerable talents and skill. Therefore, if you haven't placed an impressive number of points into your Speech (and related) skills, "tool up" with all your finest hard-hitting projectiles and other favored weaponry before the Quest begins.

Destroy Them, My Robots!

2

3

You commence with your Securitron escort close to the Hoover Dam Visitor Center **(2)**, which is on fire and under heavy Legion attack. Leave your Securitron to tackle some of the Legion, and push forward.

GREAT KHANS: If you severed the alliance between the Great Khans and the Legion, a team of warriors crashes out of the center. You can sidestep the fracas or join in. They lob projectiles and attack the Legion on the curved dam bridge before succumbing to superior firepower and numbers.

Note To obtain Great Khan support here, you must have brokered a deal between the Great Khans and the NCR during Main Quest: For the Republic, Part 2, and then switched to helping Mr. House afterward. So you'll rarely see the Khans.

If you have high Infamy with the NCR, you'll be fighting both them and the Legion!

You need to get into the Hoover Dam somehow, but the elevator and doors to the power plant in the Visitor Center is blocked. Instead, battle along the dam bridge **(3)**.

SNEAK: Employ a Stealth Boy at this point, if you want to reach the second guard tower unscathed and leave the fighting to the NCR and Legion.

4

As you continue across the curved structure, you may see a large steel bird in the sky. It looks like the old coot Loyal got his wish!

BOOMERS: If you allied with the Boomers earlier in your Quest, Loyal lives up to his word (and name) and flies over the troops, dropping bombs and coating the Legion troops in fire **(4)**. Watch the bomber fly by before you head into the dam.

With no Boomer alliance, continue to battle across the sandbags, cutting down NCR forces if they are currently hostile, and then enter the dam.

5

6

Pass the first guard tower (where Kimball's sniper shot from, if you witnessed it during Main Quest: You'll Know It When It Happens), and then continue your push through the fearsome Legion army toward the second guard tower **(5)**, and push open the double doors (or climb the ladder and enter from the roof hatch). Locate the Elevator to Hoover Dam Offices, and access it. You appear in the northwest corridors adjacent to the huge power plant chamber itself. Exit through the blast door, and then head east along the corridors, until you reach the entrance to the control room. You'll know when you're nearing it; Legion corpses are strewn about **(6)**.

7

Two NCR Heavy Troopers guard the control room door **(7)**, and they're certainly not going to step aside for you. They open fire if you venture into the room, leaving you with two options. You can:

SPEECH 75 Lie, and tell them that Colonel Moore needs their help, and they race off to help her. This allows you to keep your standing with the NCR and enter the control room.

Or gun them down where they stand, which causes your standing with the NCR to suffer.

NCR Infamy Gained!

8

Locate the bank of monitors; the control box connected to the main computer banks at Hoover Dam. You must install the Override Chip to continue this quest. This instantly brings up a familiar face **(8)**, who knew a resourceful type like you would make it. You install the override, which is functioning properly. Power re-routes to the Securitron bunker vault at The Fort. All Mr. House requires is that you head to the east power plant and manually activate the switch to complete the circuit.

Activate the eastern power plant to power the Securitron Army.

Standby for Action!

9

Head out of the control room, turn left (east), then head east, south, and east again, cutting down any opponents (these are usually Legion unless you start firing on everyone), or Sneaking down the corridors and into side chambers to avoid combat. Mr. House's painted smile and moustache flickers on every wall monitor you pass, gazing at you like a strange painting. Open the blast door, step onto the small balcony **(9)**, turn right and locate the East Power Electrical Switch. Flick it on and the east side of the plant powers up, re-routing power to The Fort. Backtrack to the second guard tower exit, and head topside. If the NCR haven't been attacking you, they certainly begin to after the generators explode!

Exit out to the east side of the Dam.

Head to the Legate's camp and deal with the Legate and Caesar's Legion.

Dam Busters

10

11

Back on the dam bridge, look up at The Fort, and you'll see it has gone up in a blaze of fiery explosions! Continue to face troublesome Centurions and Legionaries as you thrust through to the opposite side of the dam, toward Legate's Camp. Stand back and let your Securitrons do the fighting **(10)**, or face these ferocious foes, perhaps picking up and using their favored melee weapon **(11)**: the Thermic Lance!

12

If you recruited the Enclave Remnants, a Vertibird drops in near the fourth guard tower **(12)** and drops off Power-Armored veterans, who fight by your side as you push into Legate Lanius' territory.

Whether the Remnants are with you or not, continue to push to the southeast, then east onto the remains of the overpass and road that winds through a small rocky enclave to a gate that leads into the Legate's Camp.

A Little Too Late for the Legate

13

14

Give the Praetorian Guard a taste of your vengeance **(13)** as you enter the inner gates, or Sneak by him using your impressively stealthy abilities. Enter the camp, and deal with any Legion soldiers that may be about, before checking the Mongrel Cage **(14)** to your right. The place is currently closed up, and there's usually no reason to check this area, but if there are hounds inside, you can:

Remove the mechanism's springs to seal the gate shut.

Or, ignore them, and cut through these frothing canines (if any are prowling the area) during the last desperate times for the Legion.

A Battle of Weapons (or Wits)

15

16

17

But now you face a more fearsome foe. Move to the steps cut into the earth, and follow them around and up toward the Legate's Tent. A mountain of a man approaches, wielding a blade just as tall and twice as sharp as a Deathclaw. Legate Lanius **(15)** has been waiting for you. You can:

Immediately engage him in combat. Large, chunky, highly explosive, and incredibly damaging weapons are obviously the key to whittling down his considerable constitution.

You can engage him in conversation too, although anything but the most deferential talk turns him violent. However, if you state "maybe you're willing to listen to reason," he notes that you fight with words, "like all beneath the flag of the bear." You can:

Tell him this battle is decided. He asks if you're here to surrender, and then goes on about killing people. Lots of people. You can try to Barter (see below), or tell him anything else so he turns violent, or:

Tell him this advancing he's so proud of took the Legion years. Lanius responds that the dam has never see the massed strength of the East, only legates such as Graham, the burning man. You can tell him anything else to begin a fight, or:

Ask about what the East will become. Lanius tells you you're talking in circles, as HE is the personification of the might of the East! Respond with other words for a fight, or:

That if the Legion needs all the East to crush the West.... Lanius interrupts you, telling you victory here will be swift. The East will hold! Respond with fighting talk, or:

Say the weakness of the West will slow the Legion. Lanius is confused. Start verbal fisticuffs, or:

Note that the NCR's huge size means the Legion's whole army will be needed to hold the West. Lanius tells you that doesn't mean defeat. Once again, respond with fighting talk, or:

Tell him that moving the Legion's whole army West means losing the East. They can't hold both. Lanius verbally falters, blaming Caesar for drawing too much blood during the Eastern campaigns. But Lanius will not have Hoover Dam be the Legion's gravestone! He prepares to retreat!

Depending on how your conversation plays out, you can:

Legate's Conclusion #1:

Tell him there is wisdom in victory, or that you don't believe you've seen the last of the Legion. When he responds, you can speak again with a final Speech check or other final utterances. And then he is gone.

Or you can ask if he's retreating. This infuriates Lanius; you know nothing of who he is! You can fight him and his troops (Legate's Conclusion #5), or:

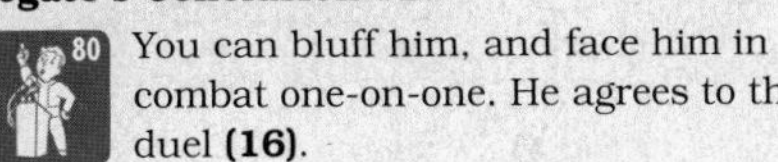

Legate's Conclusion #2:

You can bluff him, and face him in combat one-on-one. He agrees to the duel **(16)**.

Tell him he could take the West, but not hold it. Lanius responds that anything the West sends against them will be broken. Respond with verbal threats, and combat begins. Or:

Tell him an army to fight them isn't necessary because the Legion's supply lines will kill them first. Lanius replies that they have The Fort and Hoover Dam, and that other communities will fall. Verbally attack, or:

Note that there are no communities to support them; the Legion has seen to that. He says there are many towns to harvest slaves from. Again, combat is but an offensive comment away, or:

Argue that the West settlements are not self-sufficient, they need the NCR and caravans. He tells you that you rely too much on the trappings of civilization. You can:

Ask him if he really believes that, or if he is taking a chance. This leads to Legate's Conclusion #3.

Tell him the taming of the West is defeating the Legion; the NCR's weakness is their defense, OR that the Legion can't supply all the West any better than the NCR. He tells you about Denver. This leads to Legate's Conclusion #3, #4, or #5 (below).

Or ask about Nipton, Searchlight, and Nelson. Lanius says Vulpes was responsible, and it was worth weakening the West. Ask if as a legate he really believes that, or if he's taking a chance. He tells you about Denver and a protracted battle. The West is a trap, and the bear is already caught in it. Respond with:

Legate's Conclusion #3:

Your faith; that trade has helped man survive the Great War, and will do so again. When he returns, he will put this to the test with his blades. Respond that you grant him that time, or await the day. Then he retreats!

Legate's Conclusion #4:

You seeing death as change and a strength. He talks about what war would have brought, the bullet scars you possess, and that you're more than a match for Vulpes. With that, he retreats!

Or, ask if he's retreating. This leads to Legate's Conclusion #2.

Legate's Conclusion #5:

Tell him anything else, and he turns violent, and attacks you with his men **(17)**. Pick the choicest blade and helmet from the appendages you've sliced!

Blade of the East

Legate's Helmet

Tip Either fight this massive man at range—concentrating on his legs to cripple and slow him down so you can easily outrun him—by retreating and firing off powerful weaponry. Or use your very best armor-piercing weapons. Legate Lanius is a monster, so expect a tricky fight

- Healing items are imperative, because Legate Lanius can inflict critical wounds in seconds, and he usually has Legion back-up.
- Armor-piercing (or similar) ammunition types are helpful if you're using Guns.
- If you're using Melee Weapons, remember to coat them with any of the Poisons you crafted at a campfire earlier. You did prepare for this fight, right?
- Crippling his legs or shooting his weapon are excellent ways to hold him back, as is scoring a knockdown or KO on him.
- The Legate attacks with two bodyguards, who deliver massive damage with their Ballistic Fists but aren't too hardy. Take them out first (especially if you specialized in Melee or Unarmed combat) so you're only attacked from one direction.

Deal with General Oliver and the NCR.

We're Not Singing Koombahyah Here

18

19

Either battle back to the Legate Camp's inner gate, using ranged weaponry to tag the Legion snipers from the upper rocky outcrops you can't reach, and then slaughter the remaining troops (and Mongrel Dogs if you didn't secure their pen); or walk there after successfully preventing bloodshed. As you approach the gate, an explosion rocks the entrance, and General Lee Oliver, flanked by NCR Rangers, strides into view. He's tickled pink by the screams of those Legion bastards. Introduce him to your Securitron friends **(18)** that won the war for Vegas. Oliver isn't too keen to be menaced by these giant tin cans, and orders you to tell them to stand down. You can:

- Get into all kinds of unpleasant and downright offensive back-and-forth chatter with the general, before ordering your Securitrons to kill the general and his bodyguards. Help out if you want **(19)**.
- Or, you can mention that you were hoping both sides could be pleasant about this. He tells you he's not going anywhere. You can:

Bluff him and say he's talking and not attacking.

Or ask whether he thinks these are all the forces you have, and then tell him you just stood down (or killed) Caesar's toughest general.

Oliver backs down, telling you that the NCR may have its problems, but it is still a force to be reckoned with. Respond with any comment you wish, before Oliver high-tails it out of here.

Return to Mr. House with news of your victory.

20

As the general leaves, or you step through his remains, a Securitron with Mr. House's face on it rolls up to meet you **(20)**. He tells you that he's had thousands of employees; few have met his expectations, and fewer still surpassed them. But you're among the latter. He asks you back to New Vegas, where he'll begin to use his new resources to get the monorail running on time. The NCR's top brass are figuratively crippled, Vegas is once again the shining jewel in the Mojave desert, and this is where it starts, where it begins again. The Main Quest concludes.

4,000 XP

Note "Of our elaborate plans, the end?" You cannot explore after the ending. When you watch the ending, it may gradually dawn on you that the multitude of actions you exhibited during your adventure directly affected the ending. These decisions are broken down in the Appendices.

VENI, VIDI, VICI

ALLIED FACTION

CAESAR'S LEGION

See flowchart on the following page

Preparation: In Hoc Signo Taurus Vinces!

1

2

Caesar (or Lucius if Caesar is dead) wishes you victory, and the final battle for Hoover Dam [3.33] now begins! You automatically arrive at the Legate's Camp [3.34]. Enter the settlement **(1)**, passing the Legionaries in their final training, and climb the steps to the Legate's War Tent. A mountain of a man, Legate Lanius **(2)** greets and congratulates you on your exploits. When prompted, Lanius tells you that the NCR follow a strict chain of command, and you are to strike at a weakness in that link. You are to find General Oliver, and kill him or his resolve for fighting. You can ask Lanius further questions, but this simply delays the slaughter!

Caesar's Legion Fame Gained!

Caution Although you can complete this final battle without killing anyone, it requires considerable talents and skill. Therefore, if you haven't placed a prodigious number of points into your Speech (and related) skills, "tool up" with all your finest hard-hitting projectiles and other favored weaponry before the Quest begins.

Cross the dam and make your way to the western power plant.

NCR Emergency Radio

Note Tune in to NCR Emergency Radio to listen to a variety of background information about the conflicts occurring elsewhere in the Wasteland, as well as the dam.

You can hear broadcasts from Camp Golf (which change depending on your actions during Side Quest: Flags of Our Foul-Ups).

There's chatter about Fiends near Camp McCarran (which is affected by the Fiend leaders you culled during Side Quest: Three-Card Bounty).

There are skirmishes over at Camp Forlorn Hope and Nelson (which are affected by decisions you made during Side Quests: Restoring Hope and We Are Legion respectively).

There's also noise from The Strip, as the Omertas may make a move, depending on what you did during Side Quest: I Put a Spell on You.

I don't wanna rain on your parade, but those things are gonna come in here just like they did before. And they're gonna come in here... AND THEY'RE GONNA GET US! Listen for special chatter from the dam.

To Order Pontus: The Wolf Is at Your Door

3

The battle cry has been sounded! Race forth among the sprinting Legionaries (commanded by the decanus) and race to the Gate to Hoover Dam. Open it, and continue unchecked along the road to the edge of the dam **(3)**. At this point, the Legion comes under fire from NCR troops. Prepare to engage! For the emperor!

Secutus: Among the Throng

4

Attack the NCR vermin and push the wave of red toward the first dam bridge tower, cutting down foes with your preferred weapons. Employ bloodlust and all your collected firepower during this slog, but save most of your harder-hitting attacks for later. Continue to blast the enemy **(4)** behind their sandbags (Grenades work well here, as does area-of-effect ordnance) until you reach the Hoover Dam Checkpoint.

To Order Pontus: Incoming!

5

As you're moving across the bridge toward the checkpoint, you may spot something in the sky:

QUEST FLOWCHART

Quest Start

Speak with Legate Lanius inside his tent at the Legate Camp.

→ Proceed to Hoover Dam

→ Begin Crossing the Bridge (1)

→ (Optional) If Boomers were recruited, they attack now. (3)

→ Enter checkpoint building. (4)

→ Continue crossing the bridge. (5)

→ (If Great Khans are allied) Great Khans come in from rear flank.

→ Enter the visitor's center. (7)

→ Player takes elevator down. / Player takes staircase down.

→ Enter the first power plant area. (8)

→ Enter the second power plant area.

→ Enter the third power plant area. / Exit to the lower exterior section of the dam. (9)

→ Enter the fourth power plant area.

→ Enter General Oliver's compound. (10)

→ Confront Oliver.

→ [Speech 50] Convince Oliver to consider leaving. / Kill Oliver.

→ [Speech 100] Convince Oliver to stand down and flee. / Kill Oliver.

→ Speak with Legate Lanius

→ Quest Completes, Game Over.

Optional

- Release the Legion reinforcements inside the intake tower.
- Take out the snipers in the western portion of the dam.

BOOMERS If you allied with the Boomers earlier in your Quest, Loyal lives up to his word (and name) and flies over the troops, dropping bombs and coating the NCR troops in fire **(5)**. Wait until the firestorm subsides, and continue to cross.

With no Boomer alliance, continue to battle across the heavily fortified sandbags, cutting down NCR troops with the remains of your initial Legionaries **(6)**.

NCR Infamy Gained!

To Order Pontus: Mars Favors the Bold

There is a small respite inside the checkpoint **(7)** halfway across the dam bridge, where the Legion decanus **(8)** briefs you. He warns you that the area ahead is much more fortified, with snipers set up to keep his men pinned down. In another setback, the NCR managed to defend one of the intake towers and prevent the Legion from emerging. Can you help?

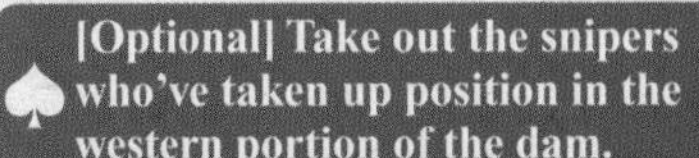

[Optional] Take out the snipers who've taken up position in the western portion of the dam.

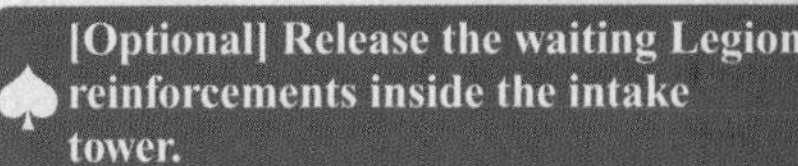

[Optional] Release the waiting Legion reinforcements inside the intake tower.

Lectio I: Rallying the Reinforcements

To the right (north) is a side bridge leading to the other two intake towers **(9)**. You can optionally peel off from the main bridge, deal with a couple of troublesome NCR Rangers guarding Intake Tower 01, and then enter this domed structure. At the terminal inside the tower, unlock the maintenance hatch, and allow the Legion reinforcements through. A lead Centurion appears, and you should inform him of your plans. You can:

Instruct him to keep his forces undivided, focusing their attack here to secure the dam surface.

Or, to send all his troops to attack the power plant while you finish up here.

This simply gives you more Legionaries in different parts of the dam.

Lectio II: Silencing the Snipers

The decanus also asked you to remove the sniper threat across the western dam. Start by removing the two Rangers guarding Intake Tower 01 **(9)**. Back on the main bridge, when you're pushing across (ideally with the reinforcements you just freed), the remaining snipers are hidden behind sandbags, and on top of the Visitor Center **(10)**.

GUNS: If you're having trouble defeating them all, and a group of hairy allies don't jump into the fray, climb the guard tower overlooking the main artillery gun, and engage in some sniping yourself from the safety of cover.

If your optional Objective hasn't completed yet, head to the observation deck and use the ladder to reach the Vertipad roof, where the remaining snipers are likely to be. You have a commanding view of the area too; scoped weaponry and good eyesight should be enough to find any remaining stragglers.

GREAT KHANS: If you kept the Great Khan alliance strong with the Legion, a team of warriors breaks through the barricade to the south of the visitor center **(11)**, and provides some cannon fodder (and protection for you). They lob projectiles and attack the remaining snipers dug in on the Vertipad roof.

Iuxta Victoria: Dam Breach

You and your Legion troops should now be inside the maze of corridors and rooms leading to the first of four giant power plant chambers. You can reach these locations various ways:

- Access through the stairwell in the circular chamber of the main visitor center area **(12)**.
- Ride the elevator down and push through the corridors from the visitor center.

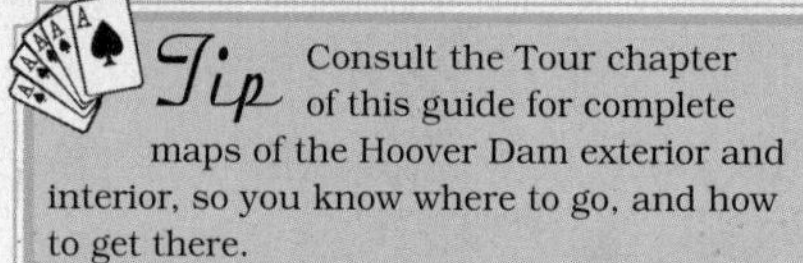

Tip: Consult the Tour chapter of this guide for complete maps of the Hoover Dam exterior and interior, so you know where to go, and how to get there.

Find the enemy commander, General Oliver.

Your forces should now be storming Hoover Dam Power Plant 01, and heading west. Each power plant consists of two tiered levels, with balcony routes along the east and west sides on two floors **(13)**, and a ground level with the massive power generators **(14)**. The upper level connecting doors are sealed, so you need to descend to the ground level.

During this time, expect heavy resistance from NCR forces. Your Legion brethren will absorb some of their attacks, but expect to cut a few foes down yourself. However, keep moving so you don't get bogged down (and sometimes overrun) in one particular area. Save your wrath for General Oliver, not every one of his minions!

SNEAK: If ever there was time for a Stealth Boy, it is now! You can leave the fighting to your Legion friends, and quickly maneuver down to the ground level. At this point, take the Secutus III option, which involves fewer run-ins with NCR soldiers.

Your goal is to reach General Oliver's compound at the very southern part of the Hoover Dam interior. You have some choices:

Secutus I: The Direct Way

The direct route involves wading through dozens of NCR Troopers attempting to waylay you, and methodically entering ground floor Power Plants 01, 02, 03, and finally 04 **(15)**. Cut through the troops as you go, until you reach the double blast doors leading to General Oliver's compound.

Secutus II: The Indirect Way

For slightly fewer combat opportunities, but less room to maneuver, you can locate the lower level of each power plant; it is a blast door on the ground floor of Power Plants 01, 02, 03, and 04. This allows you to frantically meander between the main power plant chambers, and their connecting turbine chambers below **(16)**. Ignore the machinery, and run as far along the lower level as you wish. You can rejoin Secutus I at any of the power plants although you must move back to the ground floor when you reach Power Plant 04 to reach the double blast doors leading to General Oliver's compound.

Secutus III: The Outside Shortcut

Another other option, which you can vary with the other paths, is to enter Power Plant 01, move into Power Plant 02 and ascend to the level above the ground floor, then locate the door to the exterior section of the dam. You appear at the base of the structure **(17)**, enabling you to push straight into Power Plant 04. Enter the only other door, and head back down to Power Plant 04 ground level to reach the double blast doors leading to General Oliver's compound.

Tip: During combat, you might find yourself thirsty, or close to death. Solve both problems, if you're not a stealthy sort, by sipping from the water valves on the floor of the power plants. These give you Health back, which is handy if you're saving your other survival aids.

Evinco Dux Ducis: Lee's Last Words

19

Push through into General Lee Oliver's Compound **(18)**, where the man himself **(19)** immediately stops you. He observes that you're the courier his reports mentioned, and that Hoover Dam will not fall while he draws breath. There are two ways to end this epic struggle. You can:

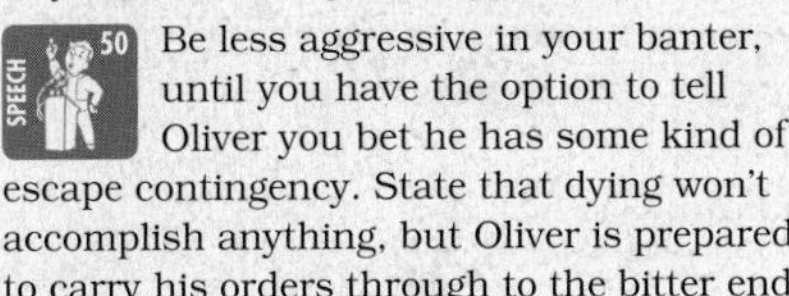

SPEECH 50 Be less aggressive in your banter, until you have the option to tell Oliver you bet he has some kind of escape contingency. State that dying won't accomplish anything, but Oliver is prepared to carry his orders through to the bitter end.

SPEECH 100 It takes all your powers of persuasion to convince Oliver that it is his responsibility to get his men out alive. Oliver agrees, flees, and you are immediately greeted by Legate Lanius, and the Quest concludes.

Return to the Legate and tell him that General Oliver has been driven off.

Any other conversational option leads to the inevitable; a final search and destroy mission with General Oliver as the prime target!

NCR Infamy Gained!

Kill General Oliver and the soldiers guarding him.

Evinco Dux Ducis: Lee's Last Stand

Oliver flees, putting up an energy wall designed to impede your progress. Aside from the man himself, you must also murder all of the soldiers guarding him. Begin by weaving through the office walls, dropping NCR Troopers **(20)**. Then head up the stairs to the balcony the general spoke to you from, killing as you go. Drop down when the balcony is blocked by the energy wall, and use a lower connecting corridor to reach the other side.

20

21

Use your Local Map to pinpoint the positions of Oliver and his remaining Ranger guards. Then roam the maze of office cubicles, taking care to avoid the Mines and Bear Traps while cutting down the well-armored NCR Rangers **(21)**. Clear the area methodically; Oliver has nowhere to run.

22

At the top of the next set of stairs, you run into Oliver's final defenses: around six NCR Heavy Troopers clad in Power Armor **(22)**. They take some beating. But they must be defeated, along with any stragglers and the general himself. All you have with you is your remaining ammunition, weapons, and any Companions you've brought along for the final push. Engage!

Return to the Legate and tell him that General Oliver has been killed.

Finis: Mortuus Ardeo

23

Return to the compound entrance where Oliver began his last stand, and speak with Legate Lanius, now resplendent in his full battle armor **(23)**. Your abilities and the spilling of NCR blood please him, and the rest of the dam is now fully under Legion control. With their commander dead, the NCR will pull out of this region, allowing unopposed conquest to the west! New Vegas will swell with slaves, and the tributes gathered will fund further campaigns. Perhaps in time, Legate Lanius may be granted the honor of conquering "California." But that is for later; now you are to witness the burning of the dead. The Main Quest concludes.

4,000 XP

Note "This is the end?" You cannot explore after the ending. When you watch the ending, it may gradually dawn on you that the multitude of actions you took during your adventure directly affected the ending. These decisions are broken down in the Appendices.

EUREKA!

ALLIED FACTION

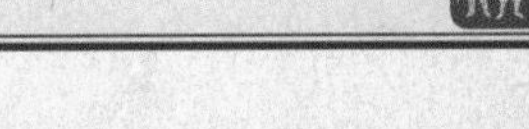

NEW CA. REPUBLIC

See flowchart on the following page

Preparation: Here's That Rainy Day

1

2

After Colonel Moore orders you to General Lee Oliver's Compound **(1)** inside the Hoover Dam [3.33], the final push for NCR victory in Nevada finally commences! Oliver **(2)** is convinced the NCR has the element of surprise, and he wants to bring the fight to the Legion's home turf. Oliver is in the beginning stages of planning an assault on The Fort [3.28]. Just then, an engineer interrupts you both. The general's plan has a shortfall: the Legion are attacking right now, streaming in from the Legate's Camp [3.34] to the east! Oliver thinks on his feet and orders you to take out the legate, and hamstring this attack.

NCR Emergency Radio

The Legion is attacking Hoover Dam, the Legate's camp must be destroyed to protect the dam.

Note Tune in to NCR Emergency Radio to listen to a variety of background information about the conflicts occurring elsewhere in the Wasteland, as well as the dam.

You can hear broadcasts from Camp Golf (which change depending on your actions during Side Quest: Flags of Our Foul-Ups).

There's chatter about Fiends near Camp McCarran (which is affected by the Fiend leaders you culled during Side Quest: Three-Card Bounty).

There are skirmishes over at Camp Forlorn Hope and Nelson (which are affected by decisions you made during Side Quests: Restoring Hope and We Are Legion respectively).

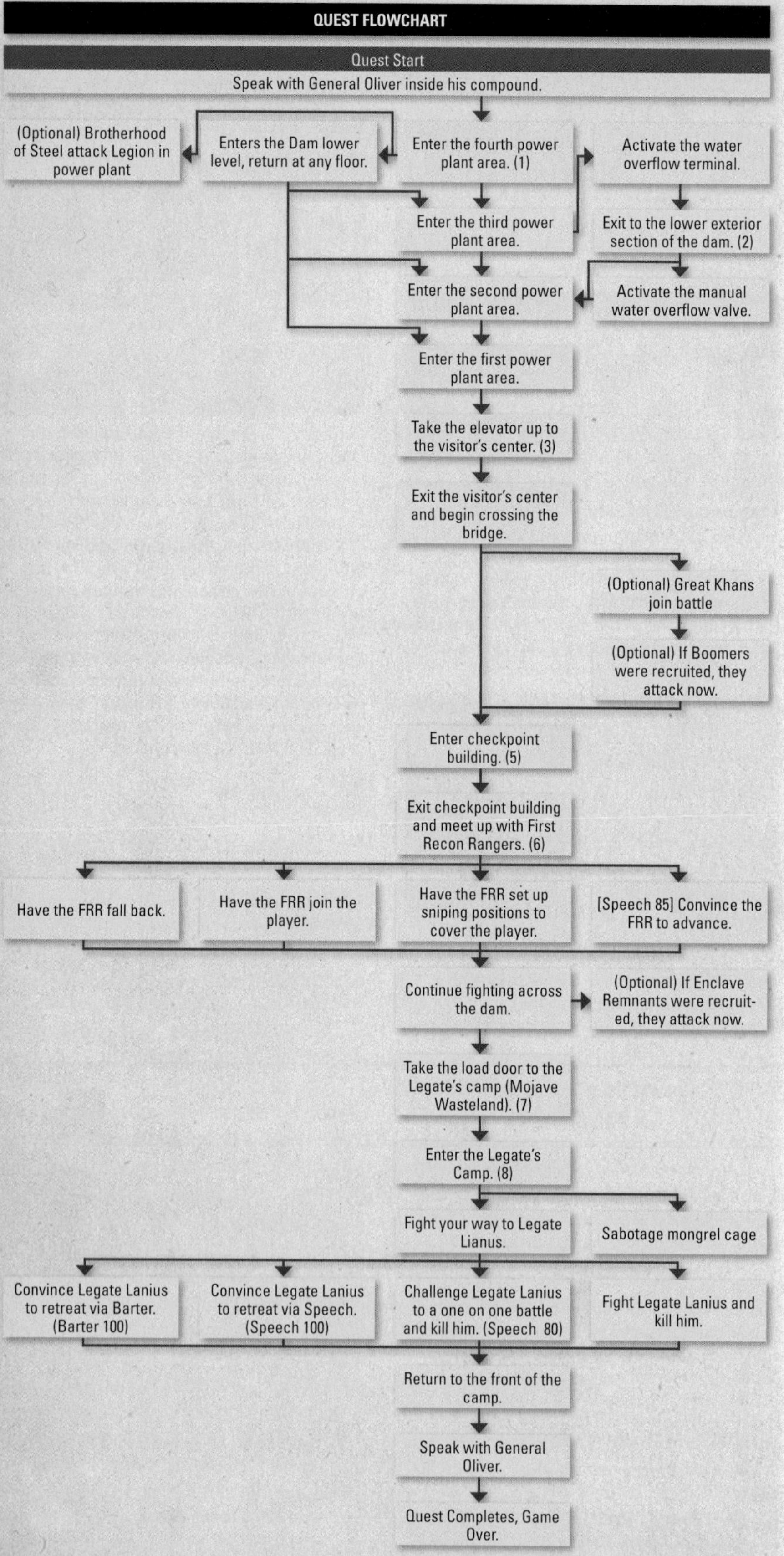

QUEST FLOWCHART

Quest Start

- Speak with General Oliver inside his compound.
- Enter the fourth power plant area. (1)
  - Enters the Dam lower level, return at any floor.
  - (Optional) Brotherhood of Steel attack Legion in power plant
  - Activate the water overflow terminal.
  - Exit to the lower exterior section of the dam. (2)
  - Activate the manual water overflow valve.
- Enter the third power plant area.
- Enter the second power plant area.
- Enter the first power plant area.
- Take the elevator up to the visitor's center. (3)
- Exit the visitor's center and begin crossing the bridge.
  - (Optional) Great Khans join battle
  - (Optional) If Boomers were recruited, they attack now.
- Enter checkpoint building. (5)
- Exit checkpoint building and meet up with First Recon Rangers. (6)
  - Have the FRR fall back.
  - Have the FRR join the player.
  - Have the FRR set up sniping positions to cover the player.
  - [Speech 85] Convince the FRR to advance.
- Continue fighting across the dam.
  - (Optional) If Enclave Remnants were recruited, they attack now.
- Take the load door to the Legate's camp (Mojave Wasteland). (7)
- Enter the Legate's Camp. (8)
  - Fight your way to Legate Lianus.
  - Sabotage mongrel cage
- Convince Legate Lanius to retreat via Barter. (Barter 100)
- Convince Legate Lanius to retreat via Speech. (Speech 100)
- Challenge Legate Lanius to a one on one battle and kill him. (Speech 80)
- Fight Legate Lanius and kill him.
- Return to the front of the camp.
- Speak with General Oliver.
- Quest Completes, Game Over.

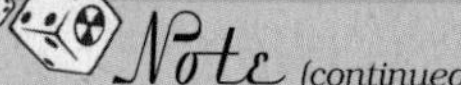

Note *(continued)*

There's also noise from The Strip, as the Omertas may make a move, depending on what you did during Side Quest: I Put a Spell on You.

It's hot as hell in here. But it's a dry heat. Listen for special chatter from the dam.

Caution Although you can complete this final battle without killing anyone, it requires considerable talents and skill. Therefore, if you haven't placed a fortuitous number of points into your Speech (and related) skills, "tool up" with all your finest hard-hitting projectiles and other favored weaponry before the Quest begins.

Oliver closes (and seals) the entrance to his compound, leaving you at the south end of Power Plant 04, deep inside the Hoover Dam. A frightened engineer named Mike Lawson **(3)** is also here, and he quickly lets you know that the Legion is using the dam's intake tunnels to storm into the structure. This needs to be stopped; preferably by diverting the flow of water into the generator turbines, grinding up the Legion like Brahminburger. Mike tells you the computer to activate the flow diversion is up ahead, but it's likely to need supplementing with a manual override from a water overflow valve outside.

[Optional] Mike Lawson suggested flushing the Legionaries through the turbines to stop their invasion of the station.

Tip Throughout the battle, sip from the water valves on the floor of the power plants. These restore you health, which is handy if you're saving your other means of food or Chem-induced survival.

Note For an overview map of Hoover Dam, consult the Tour chapter, which has complete maps of the Hoover Dam interior and exterior, so you know where to go, and how to get out.

Power Plant Pathways

Your overriding goal in this section is to make it topside and get out onto the top of the Hoover Dam. Your choices are:

Path 1: The Direct Way

4

The direct route involves wading through dozens of Legionaries attempting to waylay you, and methodically entering ground floor Power Plants 04, 03, 02, and finally 01 **(4)**. Cut through the troops as you go, until you reach the connecting corridors and elevator or double blast doors leading to the Visitor Center.

Path 2: The Indirect Way

5

For a battle close to where the Legion is emerging, and with less room to maneuver, locate the lower level of each power plant via blast doors on the ground floor of Power Plants 04, 03, 02, and 01. This allows you to frantically meander between the main power plant chambers, and their connecting turbine chambers below **(5)**. Ignore the machinery, and run as far along the lower level as you wish. You can rejoin Path 1 at any of the power plants, although you must move back to the ground floor when you reach Power Plant 01 to reach the elevator or double blast doors leading to the Visitor Center.

Path 3: The Outside Shortcut

6

The final path, which you can vary with the other paths (and which is essential for the optional objective), is to enter Power Plant 04 and then ascend to the floor above, and look for an exit door on the eastern wall, leading to the dam's exterior. You appear at the base of the structure **(6)**, enabling you to navigate through into Power Plant 02. Enter the only other door, and reach ground level, then continue into Power Plant 01 to reach either the elevators or the double blast doors leading to the Visitor Center.

Making Mincemeat of the Opposition

7

For a minimum number of additional Legion troops to battle through, heed Mike Lawson's advice. Crash through the door from General Oliver's Compound, and locate this terminal inside Power Plant 03 **(7)**; it's on the second floor, south side, above the door to Power Plant 04. When you access the terminal, you can:

Elect to turn on the overflow. This begins the process, but the final part of it must be finished manually.

[Optional] Activate the pressure release valve to flush the Legionaries through the turbines.

8

9

Step outside onto the walkway at the base of the dam **(8)**. Prepare for combat (or Sneaking) as you advance on a small squad of Legion troops; deal with them, and then locate this pressure release valve **(9)**, and hand-crank it to finish the flushing. Success! This doesn't hinder the progress of the Legion; it disperses them over a wide area. Of course, they're in tiny, turbine-chewed chunks, giving the NCR the advantage they need to finish the job! Now you face considerably fewer enemies as you cross the bridge.

The dam overflow has been diverted into the turbines, the Legion can no longer use them to access the power plant.

Dam Bridge Assault

Leave the relative safety of the Visitor Center exterior, and you realize the structure is under heavy Legion attack.

10

Ignore the guard and intake towers, and press on toward the middle of the bridge, and the Hoover Dam Checkpoint.

If you allied with the Boomers earlier in your Quest, Loyal lives up to his word (and name) and flies over the troops, dropping bombs and coating the Legion troops on the east side of the checkpoint building in fire **(10)**. Wait until the firestorm subsides, and continue to cross.

With no Boomer alliance, continue to battle across the heavily fortified sandbags, cutting down Legion troops with any NCR troopers left standing.

Caesar's Legion Infamy Gained!

11

If you brokered a Great Khan alliance, a team of warriors enters from the south, and provides some cannon fodder (and protection for you). They lob projectiles and attack the Legion on the curved dam bridge before succumbing to superior firepower and numbers. Battle along the dam bridge **(11)**.

Employ a Stealth Boy if you want to reach the checkpoint building unscathed and leave the fighting to the NCR and Legion.

12

Race to the checkpoint building **(12)**, and dive inside. There are some lockers to search, but the main area of interest is the desk to your right:

Hack a terminal here and you can read a Security Diagnostic stating that the generators may overload if the Generator Diagnostics program is run. Fortunately, the second menu allows you to Activate Generator Diagnostics!

With some tinkering, and a Remote Detonator (the kind used to detonate C-4), you plug into the terminal and set the primary trigger mechanism to begin the diagnostics. Activating the Detonator should cause the generators to explode.

No remote? Then no generator explosion!

Alpha Squad, Reporting In!

Exit through the eastern door, into the second part of the curved dam bridge, and you're immediately stopped by an NCR Ranger Veteran Commander of the First Recon Rangers **(13)**: Alpha Squad is reporting in! They thank you for your support, and have been assigned to ensure you reach the Legate's Camp. What assistance can they provide? You can:

Order them to push the advance on the enemy with their superior firepower. They take casualties, but this allows you to reach the Legate's Camp more or less unscathed.

You can request that snipers cover your advance, and they help take down some foes.

You can order First Recon Rangers to join you, tackling foes that are closer to attacking you.

Or you can shrug off this so-called "help"; you can take on the Legion without a chaperone!

When you've made your choice, set off to cover the rest of the bridge, letting the Rangers do their work **(14)**, or facing these ferocious foes, perhaps picking up and using their favored melee weapon **(15)**: the Power Fist!

If you recruited the Enclave Remnants, a Vertibird drops in near the fourth guard tower **(16)** and drops off Power-Armored veterans, who fight by your side as you push into Legate Lanius' territory.

Whether the Remnants (or Rangers) are with you or not, continue to push to the southeast, then east onto the remains of the overpass and road that winds through a small rocky enclave to a gate that leads into the Legate's Camp.

Commandeering Camp Carnage

Give the Praetorian Guard a taste of your vengeance **(17)** as you enter the inner gates, or Sneak by him using your impressively stealthy abilities. Enter the camp, and deal with any Legion soldiers that may be about, before checking the Mongrel Cage **(18)** to your right. The place is currently closed up, but to prevent the Legion from releasing these hounds, you can:

Remove the mechanism's springs to seal the gate shut.

Or, ignore them, and cut through these frothing canines during the last desperate times for the Legion.

Facing Down the Beast from the East

But now you face a more fearsome foe. Move to the steps cut into the earth, and follow them around and up toward the Legate's Tent. A mountain of a man approaches, wielding a blade just as tall and twice as sharp as a Deathclaw. Legate Lanius **(19)** has been waiting for you. You can:

Immediately engage him in combat. Large, chunky, highly explosive, and incredibly damaging weapons are obviously the key to whittling down his considerable constitution.

You can engage him in conversation too, although anything but the most deferential talk turns him violent. However, if you state "maybe you're willing to listen to reason," he notes that you fight with words, "like all beneath the flag of the bear." You can:

Tell him this battle is decided. He asks if you're here to surrender, and then goes on about killing people. Lots of people. You can try to Barter (see below), or tell him anything else so he turns violent, or:

Tell him this advancing he's so proud of took the Legion years. Lanius responds that the dam has never seen the massed strength of the East, only legates such as Graham, the Burned Man. You can tell him anything else to begin a fight, or:

Ask about what the East will become. Lanius says you're talking in circles, as HE is the personification of the might of the East! Respond with other words for a fight, or:

That if the Legion needs all the East to crush the West.... Lanius interrupts you, telling you victory here will be swift. The East will hold! Respond with fighting talk, or:

Say the weakness of the West will slow the Legion. Lanius is confused. Start verbal fisticuffs, or:

Note that the NCR's huge size means the Legion's whole army will be needed to hold the West. Lanius tells you that doesn't mean defeat. Once again, respond with fighting talk, or:

Tell him that moving the Legion's whole army West means losing the East. They can't hold both. Lanius verbally falters, blaming Caesar for drawing too much blood during the Eastern campaigns. But Lanius will not have Hoover Dam be the Legion's gravestone! He prepares to retreat!

Depending on how your conversation goes, you can:

Legate's Conclusion #1:

Tell him there is wisdom in victory, or that you don't believe you've seen the last of the Legion. When he responds, you can speak again with a final Speech check or other final utterances. And then he is gone.

Or you can ask if he's retreating. This infuriates Lanius; you know nothing of who he is! You can fight him and his troops (Legate's Conclusion #5), or:

Legate's Conclusion #2:

You can bluff him, and face him in combat one-on-one. He agrees to the duel **(20)**.

Tell him he could take the West, but not hold it. Lanius responds that anything the West sends against them will be broken. Respond with verbal threats, and combat begins. Or:

Tell him an army to fight them isn't necessary because the Legion's supply lines will kill them first. Lanius replies that they have The Fort and Hoover Dam, and that other communities will fall. Verbally attack, or:

Note that there are no communities to support them; the Legion has seen to that. He says there are many towns to harvest slaves from. Again, combat is but an offensive comment away, or:

Argue that the West settlements are not self-sufficient, they need the NCR and caravans. He tells you that you rely too much on the trappings of civilization. You can:

Ask him if he really believes that, or if he is taking a chance. This leads to Legate's Conclusion #3.

Tell him the taming of the West is defeating the Legion; the NCR's weakness is their defense, OR that the Legion can't supply all the West any better than the NCR. He tells you about Denver. This leads to Legate's Conclusion #3, #4, or #5 (below).

Or ask about Nipton, Searchlight, and Nelson. Lanius says Vulpes was responsible, and it was worth weakening the West. Ask if as a legate he really believes that, or if he's taking a chance. He tells you about Denver and a protracted battle. The West is a trap, and the bear is already caught in it. Respond with:

Legate's Conclusion #3:

Your faith; that trade has helped man survive the Great War, and will do so again. When he returns, he will put this to the test with his blades. Respond that you grant him that time, or await the day. Then he retreats!

Legate's Conclusion #4:

You seeing death as change and a strength. He talks about what war would have brought, the bullet scars you possess, and that you're more than a match for Vulpes. With that, he retreats!

Or, ask if he's retreating. This leads to Legate's Conclusion #2.

Legate's Conclusion #5:

Tell him anything else, and he turns violent, and attacks you with his men **(21)**. Pick the choicest blade and helmet from the appendages you've sliced!

Blade of the East

Legate's Helmet

Tip

Combat Legate Lanius one of three ways. Your alliance with the NCR allows you to talk him into retreating, preventing hostilities. Or fight at range, concentrating on his legs to cripple and slow him down so you can easily outrun him as you retreat and fire off powerful weaponry. Or use your very best armor-piercing weapons. Legate Lanius is a monster, so expect a tricky fight!

- If combat cannot be avoided, healing items are imperative, because Legate Lanius can inflict critical wounds in seconds, and he usually has Legion back-up.
- Armor-piercing (or similar) ammunition types are helpful if you're using Guns.
- If you're using Melee Weapons, remember to coat them with any of the Poisons you crafted at a campfire earlier. You did prepare for this fight, right?
- Crippling his legs or shooting his weapon are excellent ways to hold him back, as is scoring a knockdown or KO on him.
- Legate Lanius attacks with two bodyguards, who deliver massive damage with their Ballistic Fists, but aren't too hardy. Take them out first (especially if you specialized in Melee or Unarmed combat) so you're only attacked from one direction.

The battle has been won. Return to General Oliver.

Clean Up, Take Prisoners, and Watch the East

22

Either battle back to the Legate Camp's inner gate, using ranged weaponry to tag the Legion snipers from the upper rocky outcrops you can't reach, and then slaughter the remaining troops (and Mongrel Dogs if you didn't secure their pen); or walk there after successfully preventing bloodshed. As you approach the gate, an explosion rocks the entrance, and General Lee Oliver, flanked by NCR Rangers, strides into view **(22)**. He commends you on a fine piece of work, and is surprised you (and the dam) are still standing. You've secured the NCR's future, and the administration sends its thanks, for what that's worth. Answer the general in any way you like. He explains that the Legion is still running, but the NCR will always be watching the East. Choose your retirement plan from this adventure, and the general bids you farewell. The Main Quest concludes.

4,000 XP

Note

"Of everything that stands, the end?" You cannot explore after the ending. When you watch the ending, it may gradually dawn on you that the multitude of actions you took during your adventure directly affected the ending. These decisions are broken down in the Appendices.

Side Quests: Introduction

PREPARATION: MOJAVE MARAUDING

This chapter reveals the multitude of Side Quests that you can partake in throughout your adventure. Unlike Main Quests, Side Quests (AKA Miscellaneous Quests) can occur at any time, in any place, and can usually be completed whenever you wish. Here's how to use this chapter:

Caution Spoiler Alert! If you don't want to know what happens to Raul the Ghoul (or you're angered by the fact that "Raul the Ghoul" was even mentioned), then you now know the power of reading the following pages. Every major Quest that pops onto your Pip-Boy is solved optimally in this guide, so focus your gaze only on the Quests you want clues about.

What is a Side Quest?

A Side Quest is a series of Objectives that appear—along with your Main Quests—in the **Data > Quests** menu of your Pip-Boy. Conversations usually trigger Quests, but rummaging around on old terminals, shooting certain people, or stumbling across an item may affect Quests, too. The main reasons to complete Quests are for the thrilling adventure, cold hard Caps, and the Experience Points (XP).

Side Quest Guidance: An Explanation

The nearby table lists the Side Quests you can access. Note the following columns of information:

1. **Factions:** Each Quest involves different Factions. The table (and the start of each Quest) flags these Factions, so you know who you're dealing with, and more importantly, if you want to deal with them based on your current Reputation.

Note Some Quests pit one Faction against another. For example, Side Quest: Ghost Town Gunfight/Run Goodsprings Run forces you to choose sides; you can help the good folk of Goodsprings, or the bad men who've escaped the NCR Correctional Facility. As you progress, some Quests can't be attempted, simply because of who you're aligned with. Don't worry though; that's what multiple playthroughs are for!

2. **Follower:** Certain Quests involve a Follower, and these are flagged accordingly. To get a Follower to open up about their past—which is how you obtain their additional Perk, armor, or other item—you may need to bring them along on another Quest, so check their Quest introduction as soon as you can!

3. **Suggested Experience:** How do you know whether you'll breeze through a Quest, or be horribly out-classed and killed instantly? By checking this, of course! The length, difficulty, enemy types, and when the Quest becomes available are all taken into account, and a score of between 1 and 5 is given. These scores also appear at the beginning of each Quest. Here's what they mean:

●○○○○ **Simple:** Try this as soon as you stagger out into Goodsprings for the first time.

●●○○○ **Straightforward:** A relatively fraught-free series of Objectives allows you to ease you into adventuring.

●●●○○ **Cunning:** These tasks may test you, with one or two dangerous opponents to be wary of.

●●●●○ **Challenging:** Try this later in your Main Quest adventuring because it features tricky situations to overcome.

●●●●● **Hazardous:** This Quest is either horribly difficult, or requires you complete previous Quests or tricky situations first.

4. **Quest Number and Name:** The Side Quests are listed alphabetically in this guide because it's the easiest way to quickly find a Quest you want to read about. Don't read through the Quests though; check only the Quest you're interested in. t

5. **Integral to Main Quest:** Eight of the Side Quests (and these are usually the longest) are almost always accessed during your Main Quest, and involve interactions with a secondary faction such as the Boomers or Great Khans. You can complete the Quest without any associated Main Quest activities, so they are listed here. Check the Main Quest for more information, too.

Note Some Quests, such as "Don't Tread on the Bear," may occasionally appear on your Pip-Boy, as will notes you might collect that give hints at exploration. These are known as Free Quests (AKA Freeform Quests), and are covered in the Tour chapter, because they are usually short and related to a particular Primary Location.

Side Quests: Wasteland Wandering in 72 Parts

The following table shows information previously discussed, and should be checked every time you want an initial impression of a Side Quest.

FACTION 1	FACTION 2	FACTION 3	FACTION 4	FACTION 5	FOLLOWER	#	EXPERIENCE	QUEST NAME	ZONE	LOCATION
Great Khans	Crimson Caravan	Fiends				1	●●●○○	Aba Daba Honeymoon	[1.14]	Red Rock Drug Lab
Boomers						2	●●○○○	Ant Misbehavin'	[3.01]	Nellis Air Force Base
NCR	Caesar's Legion					3	●●○○○	Anywhere I Wander	[6.08]	Techatticup Mine
NCR	Caesar's Legion					4	●●○○○	Back in Your Own Backyard	[6.06]	Nelson
White Glove Society	The Strip					5	●●●○○	Beyond the Beef*	[2D.05]	Ultra-Luxe Casino
Van Graffs	Crimson Caravan	NCR	Caesar's Legion			6	●●●○○	Birds of a Feather	[2C.07]	Silver Rush
NCR	Crimson Caravan					7	●●○○○	Bitter Springs Infirmary Blues	[3.08]	Bitter Springs
NONE						8	●●●●○	Bleed Me Dry	[2.04]	The Thorn
Powder Gangers	Caesar's Legion					9	●●○○○	Booted	[4.30]	Nipton
NCR	Great Khans					10	●●○○○	Boulder City Showdown*	[3.32]	Boulder City
Omertas	Atomic Wrangler					11	●●●○○	Bye Bye Love	[2D.06] [2D.01]	Vault 21, or Gomorrah
NCR						12	●○○○○	Can You Find It in Your Heart?	[4.27]	Mojave Outpost
The Strip						13	●●●○○	Classic Inspiration	[2D.08]	Michael Angelo's Workshop
NCR	Great Khans					14	●●●○○	Climb Ev'ry Mountain	[3.08]	Bitter Springs
Caesar's Legion	NCR					15	●○○○○	Cold, Cold Heart	[4.30]	Nipton
Novac	Jason Bright	Super Mutant				16	●●●○○	Come Fly With Me	[5.18] [5.17]	Novac, REPCONN Test Site
Super Mutant					Raul	17	●●●●○	Crazy, Crazy, Crazy	[5.07]	Black Mountain
Great Khans	Followers OTA					18	●○○○○	Cry Me a River	[1.15]	Red Rock Canyon

FACTION 1	FACTION 2	FACTION 3	FACTION 4	FACTION 5	FOLLOWER	#	EXPERIENCE	QUEST NAME	ZONE	LOCATION
Atomic Wrangler						19	●●●○○	Debt Collector	[2C.06]	Atomic Wrangler
Great Khans	NCR					20	●●○○○	Don't Make a Beggar of Me	[4.03]	Great Khan Encampment
Primm	BoS	Followers OTA			ED-E	21	●○○○○	ED-E My Love	[4.17]	Primm
NCR	Caesar's Legion					22	●●○○○	Eye for an Eye	[6.16]	Camp Searchlight
BoS	Super Mutant					23	●●●●●	Eyesight to the Blind	[5.11]	Hidden Valley
NCR	Great Khans					24	●●●●○	Flags of Our Foul-Ups	[3.23]	Camp Golf
Followers OTA	Enclave				Arcade Gannon	25	●●●●●	For Auld Lang Syne	[2C.01]	Old Mormon Fort
The Kings	Followers OTA	NCR				26	●●○○○	G.I. Blues*	[2C.05]	King's School of Impersonation
Goodsprings	Powder Gangers					27	●○○○○	Ghost Town Gunfight/Run Goodsprings Run*	[4.05]	Goodsprings
Super Mutant					Lily	28	●●●●○	Guess Who I Saw Today	[1.10]	Jacobstown
NCR	Powder Gangers					29	●●●○○	Hard Luck Blues	[2.20]	NCR Sharecropper Farms
NCR	Crimson Caravan	Van Graffs			Cass	30	●●●●○	Heartache by the Number	[4.27]	Mojave Outpost
Followers OTA						31	●●○○○	High Times	[2C.01]	Old Mormon Fort
Omertas	The Strip	Fiends				32	●●●○○	How Little We Know*	[2D.01]	Gomorrah
BoS	NCR	Followers OTA			Veronica	33	●●●●○	I Could Make You Care	[5.02]	188 Trading Post
NCR						34	●○○○○	I Don't Hurt Anymore	[2.19]	Camp McCarran
NCR	Caesar's Legion				Boone	35	●●○○○	I Forgot to Remember to Forget	[5.18]	Novac
Powder Gangers	NCR	Primm				36	●●○○○	I Fought the Law	[5.15]	NCR Correctional Facility
Caesar's Legion	Boomers					37	●●○○○	I Hear You Knocking	[3.28]	The Fort
NCR	Caesar's Legion					38	●●●○○	I Put a Spell on You	[2.19]	Camp McCarran
NCR	Caesar's Legion					39	●○○○○	Keep Your Eyes on the Prize	[4.27]	Mojave Outpost
Caesar's Legion						40	●●○○○	Left My Heart	[2.22]	Aerotech Office Park
NCR						41	●○○○○	Medical Mystery	[6.02]	Camp Forlorn Hope
Primm	NCR	Powder Gangers				42	●○○○○	My Kind of Town	[4.17]	Primm
NCR	Great Khans	Caesar's Legion				43	●●○○○	No, Not Much	[3.08]	Bitter Springs
The Kings	Followers OTA	Fiends	Caesar's Legion	Super Mutant	Rex	44	●●●○○	Nothin' But a Hound Dog	[2C.05]	King's School of Impersonation
Great Khans	NCR	Caesar's Legion				45	●●●○○	Oh My Papa*	[1.15]	Red Rock Canyon
Novac					Boone	46	●○○○○	One for My Baby	[5.18]	Novac
White Glove Society	The Strip					47	●●○○○	Pheeble Will	[2D.05]	Ultra-Luxe Casino
Crimson Caravan						48	●●●○○	Pressing Matters	[2.09]	Crimson Caravan Company
NCR	Caesar's Legion					49	●●●○○	Restoring Hope	[6.02]	Camp Forlorn Hope
NCR						50	●●●●○	Return to Sender	[6.02]	Camp Forlorn Hope
NONE						51	●●○○○	Someone to Watch Over Me	[2.07]	North Vegas Square
BoS	Boomers	Super Mutant	Powder Gangers	NCR		52	●●●●○	Still in the Dark*	[5.11]	Hidden Valley
Boomers						53	●●○○○	Sunshine Boogie	[3.01]	Nellis Air Force Base
Chairmen	The Strip	Atomic Wrangler	Novac			54	●●○○○	Talent Pool	[2D.04]	The Tops Casino
BoS	Van Graffs					55	●●●●●	Tend to Your Business	[5.11]	Hidden Valley
NCR						56	●●○○○	That Lucky Old Sun	[5.13]	HELIOS One
NONE						57	●●●○○	The Legend of the Star/A Valuable Lesson	[2.17]	Sunset Sarsaparilla Headquarters
NCR						58	●●○○○	The Coyotes	[2.22]	Aerotech Office Park
Caesar's Legion	Omertas					59	●●○○○	The Finger of Suspicion	[3.28]	The Fort
Followers OTA	Mr. House (The Strip)					60	●●○○○	The Moon Comes Over the Tower	[2D.02]	Lucky 38 Casino
NCR	Omertas					61	●●○○○	The White Wash	[2.19]	Camp McCarran
NCR						62	●●●○○	There Stands the Grass	[2.19]	Camp McCarran
NCR	Fiends					63	●●●●○	Three-Card Bounty	[2.19]	Camp McCarran
Super Mutant	NCR					64	●●●○○	Unfriendly Persuasion	[1.10]	Jacobstown
Boomers	Crimson Caravan					65	●●○○○	Volare!*	[3.01]	Nellis Air Force Base
Atomic Wrangler	Followers OTA					66	●●●○○	Wang Dang Atomic Tango	[2C.06]	Atomic Wrangler
Caesar's Legion	NCR					67	●●●○○	We Are Legion	[6.06]	Nelson
NCR						68	●●●○○	We Will All Go Together	[6.16]	Camp Searchlight
Prospector	Powder Gangers					69	●●●●○	Wheel of Fortune	[6.16]	Camp Searchlight
Powder Gangers						70	●●●○○	Why Can't We Be Friends?	[1.21]	Vault 19
Crimson Caravan	NCR	Omertas	Gun Runners			71	●●●●○	You Can Depend on Me	[2.09]	Crimson Caravan Company
Boomers	Crimson Caravan					72	●●○○○	Young Hearts	[3.01]	Nellis Air Force Base

* INDICATES INTEGRAL TO MAIN QUEST

ABA DABA HONEYMOON

SUGGESTED EXPERIENCE

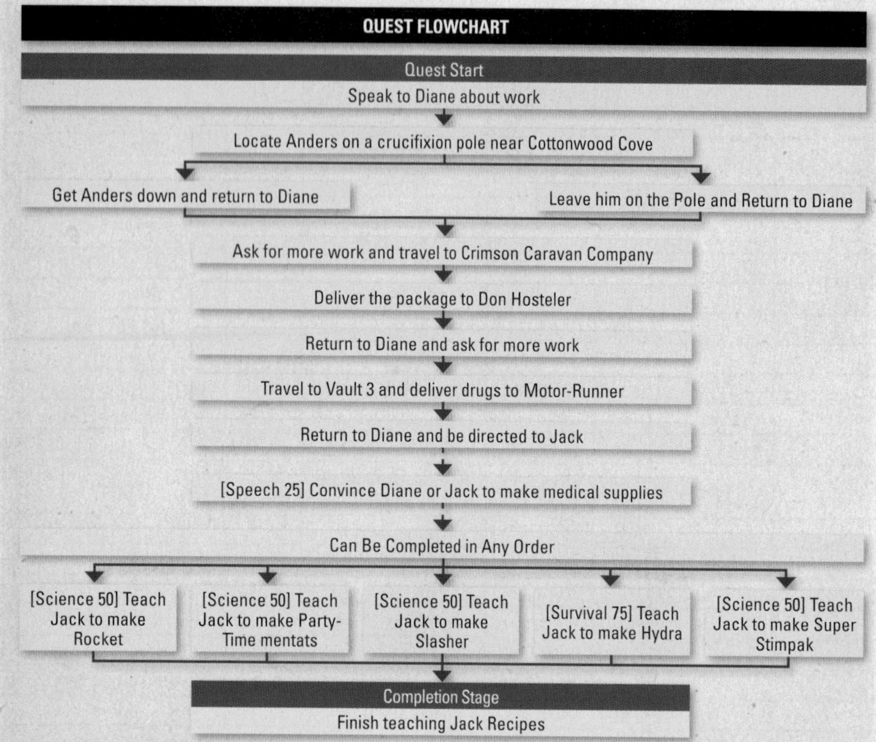

Main Factions

Two American Kids Doing the Best They Can

1

2

In the mountainous terrain known as Red Rock Canyon [1.15], the Great Khans' settlement dots the rugged landscape. But there's another location to find at the base of these mountains; the Red Rock Drug Lab **(1)** [1.14]. The rusting caravans are home to Jack, a stoic character who may be using his own Chems, and his partner Diane **(2)**. Talk to her about this line of work, and the Great Khans, before broaching the subject of making a few Caps. She tells you that Anders (one of her runners) hasn't reported back. Find him, and she'll have some real work for you. Agree to the work.

Find Jack and Diane's missing drug runner.

Job #1: Hung Up on Anders

3

Anders was last spotted in the area close to Cottonwood Cove [6.20], although you can also Fast Travel to the nearby Sniper's Nest [6.18] and scout the higher ground. The Legion seems to be teaching Anders a lesson; you'll find him crucified on a rocky outcrop just outside the settlement **(3)**. You can:

Talk to him to confirm that he's Anders before cutting him down. He (and the Great Khans) thank you. He heads back to camp.

Talk to him to confirm that he's Anders and then leave him on the crucifixion pole. The Legion don't go for drug-dealing, at least from outsiders.

Shooting him isn't nice, but it won't fail the Quest.

Return to Diane and tell her about Anders.

Whether you cut Anders down or not, return to Diane and explain his predicament. There's no love lost if Anders is still trussed up on the pole. But with him out of commission, Diane

Job #2: Don's Drug Mule

4

5

is shorthanded. She has an associate over at the Crimson Caravan Trading Company [2.09] who wants some merchandise. Agree to become a drug mule for the Quest to continue.

Mildly Suspicious Package

Deliver drugs to Don Hostetler at the Crimson Caravan.

Travel to the impressively fortified Crimson Caravan premises close to New Vegas itself, and enter the grounds. Inside the Crimson Caravan Main Office **(4)**, clad in a smart suit and natty hat, is the buyer, Don Hostetler **(5)**. Tell Don you have a package for him, and he quickly takes it off your hands and urges you to go. Comply if you want to continue, and return to Diane. She gives you a Cap payment for your troubles.

Caps 150

Great Khans Fame Gained!

Job #3: Get Your Motor-Runner Running

6

Diane's next task involves a shipment of Jet and Psycho that needs to be delivered to a man named Motor-Runner inside Vault 3 [2.24]. Agree to the job, but make sure you pay

attention to what Diane is telling you: the Fiends that Motor-Runner rules over are twitchy and the ones outside are outright hostile. However, those inside the vault don't bother a Khan. You're also given a Khan jacket so the Fiends inside the vault won't attack you on sight.

 **Highly Suspicious Package**

 **Great Khan Simple Armor**

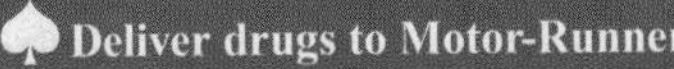

Deliver drugs to Motor-Runner.

If you think Jack and Diane seem like a couple of well-adjusted drug dealers, you can speak to Diane about making more helpful Chems, letting her know that medical supplies are always scarce and don't kill the buyer as often. Once the pair begin, trade with Jack for a variety of new health Chems. Teach him more at the end of this Quest.

The Fiends don't care for trespassers. Before you enter Vault 3 (and ideally as soon as the conversation with Diane concludes), put on the Khan jacket that she gave you (or any outfit you may already have that disguises you as a Great Khan). If you don't, expect Motor-Runner to attack you on sight!

Brandish your favored killing implement and journey eastward to Vault 3. The maze of ruined concrete and rusting shacks are "governed" by Fiends of a more primal nature; they attack you automatically.

 Fight them off with firepower, bludgeoning weapons, or your fists.

 Or silently skulk around to the vault entrance.

Back into the concrete building **(6)** leading to the giant Cog Door to Vault 3. Activate the Vault Door Control Pad to the right, and slip inside.

7

8

Once inside the vault perimeter, you're accosted by a Fiend **(7)**. Depending on your actions (and outfit), the following is possible:

 If you're dressed as a Great Khan, the Fiend is pleased to see you, and asks for some Psycho for herself.

Ask where the boss is, and that she's been hitting you up for freebies.

The Fiend backpedals quickly, and tells you where Motor-Runner is.

Even if you're dressed as a Khan, you can tell her you're not really one. The angry reply features a whole load of swearing.

 Quickly tell her what you're carrying, and that you don't deliver to the help. Attempt this with or without Khan armor.

- Or attack. Or leave.

Caution If you enter Vault 3 without a Great Khan get-up, you must succeed in the Speech check (above), or the Fiends inside turn hostile.

Follow the Fiend's directions, and you reach a server room, and finally a generator chamber where Motor-Runner **(8)** resides, flanked by his two mongrel hounds. Begin a conversation:

Tell Motor-Runner you have some Chems to sell. Mention Jack and Diane if you've already talked about the Fiends.

 You can also ask what happened to the residents of this vault. The answer isn't a surprise.

With the care package delivered, you can explore the vault if you wish, but returning to Diane continues this Quest. Diane is impressed that you're still alive.

 **Caps 300**

 **Great Khans Fame Gained!**

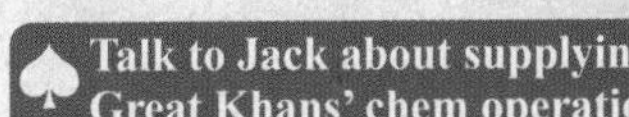

Talk to Jack about supplying the Great Khans' chem operation.

Job #4: Cooking Up a Batch (or Five)

9

Back at the drug lab, make sure you've convinced Diane or Jack to make Chems that are more medicinal in nature, and then speak to Jack **(9)** about earning an extra few Caps. He's always interested in new recipes.

You can:

- Trade or purchase Chems from him.
- Or teach him the following recipes, which can be attempted in any order:

 Teach Jack the recipe for Party-Time Mentats.

 Teach Jack the recipe for Rocket.

 Teach Jack the recipe for Slasher.

 Teach Jack the recipe for a Super Stimpak.

 Teach Jack the recipe for Hydra.

After you help Jack and Diane turn their two-Cap operation into a real Chem enterprise, the Quest concludes. Should you teach Jack all of the recipes, he has a special trick for you, the Khan Trick, which is an Unarmed Special Move.

 **Perk: Khan Trick**

 **300 XP (x5)**

ANT MISBEHAVIN'

SUGGESTED EXPERIENCE

See flowchart on the following page

Main Factions

BOOMERS

Exploding Antics

Begin by starting Side Quest: Volare! over at the Nellis Air Force Base [3.01] by dodging shells, reaching the gate, meeting Raquel, and then speaking with Mother Pearl. One of the tasks Pearl needs you to attend to is a Giant Ant problem. Locate Raquel, who may be in the

1

Barracks or patrolling outside **(1)**, and speak to her **(2)**. Ask about her "bug problem," and she tells you the power failed a few days ago due to Giant Ants tunneling into the base's Generator

2

room. Agree to help, and Raquel hands you a key to get in, and also mentions the ants must be eating gunpowder because they explode when struck by a flame-thrower or Laser Pistol. She warns you not to hit the artillery shells in the Generator building either. Explosive Giant Ants? Intriguing. Finally, she recommends that you visit Loyal, who has a weapon to use against the Ants.

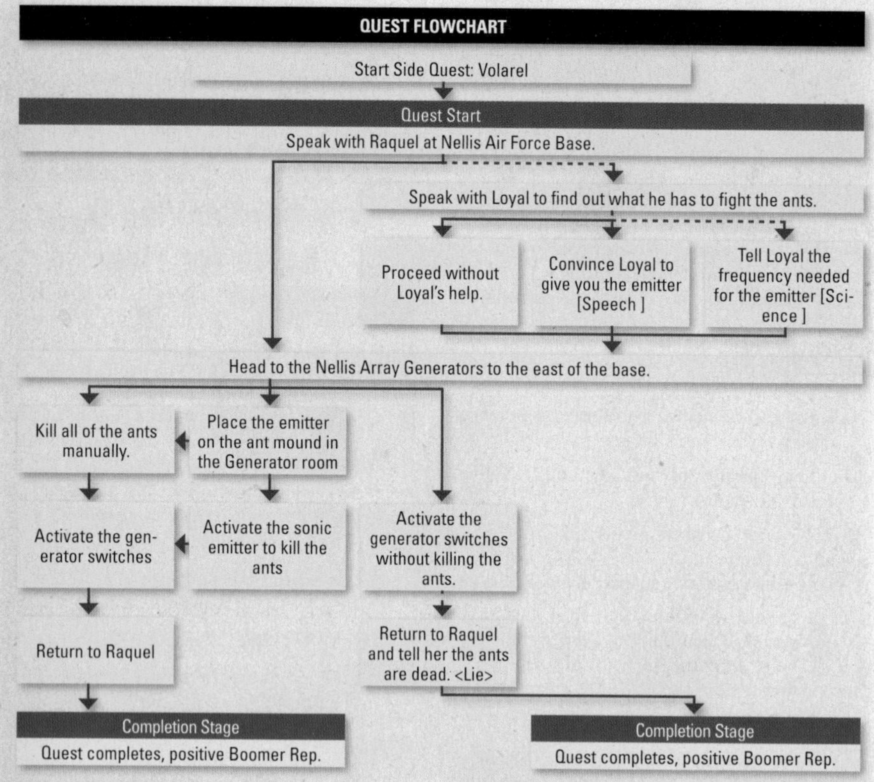

 **Nellis Generator Key**

Kill all ants in the generator room.

Restart the 2 array generators, then reset the main power breaker.

(Optional) Loyal may have something to help with the ants.

Note Some of the other Boomer quests are related to this one. First, speak with Mother Pearl to begin Side Quest: Volare! To complete the first part of this "overview" Side Quest, you must achieve the following:

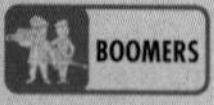 Become idolized with the Boomers. Achieve this by completing tasks within this Quest, as well as three additional linked Quests associated with this Faction (which are tagged throughout the guide).

- Complete Side Quest: Ant Misbehavin' (this Quest).
- Complete Side Quest: Sunshine Boogie.
- Complete Side Quest: Young Hearts.

These Quests (including this one) are all parts of Side Quest: Volare!

In addition, you can complete Free Quests connected to Nellis Air Force Base, which are detailed in the Tour Chapter.

Sounds Like a Good Idea

Journey around to the north side of the first Hangar **(3)** of the Nellis Hangars [3.02] and locate Loyal **(4)** who's usually inside, working with Jack. Loyal has his own tasks for you to complete, but for this Quest, tell him that Raquel mentioned the ant-culling weapon. He explains that he started to construct a Sonic Emitter, but he doesn't know the frequency to use. You can:

Ignore Loyal, and continue to the Generator building without his help.

 Tell him that any signal over 22,000 hertz at 150 decibels or more should do the trick.

 Or tell him you'll attempt a trial run. Either of the latter two options results in Loyal giving you the Emitter.

 **Sonic Emitter**

(Optional) Place Loyal's sonic generator on the ant mound.

An Anty Climax

Head east across the landing tarmac, toward the low-lying Nellis Array [3.03] with solar panels and a dish on the roof **(5)**. Locate the door to Nellis Array Generators, and open it using the key Raquel gave you. There are two entrances, but the optimal path is to take the one described:

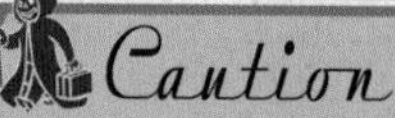

Caution Halt! Before you go any farther, be sure you understand the dangerous nature of the Generator station! More than a dozen Giant Ants roam this structure, ranging from small to Soldier-sized. The use of Incinerators and other weapons that shoot flame, or laser weapons, results in a mass Ant explosion, as will firing at the live artillery shells throughout the building. Only attempt this if you have enough armor and health to survive the blast!

Inside the Generator chambers **(6)**, Ants come scuttling toward you. You can:

 Shoot them with fire- or laser-based weapons, causing large-scale explosions. If you're tough, you can survive, and even use this tactic to dispatch all the Ants quickly.

 Shoot them with bullet-based weapons, melee weapons, or unarmed punching. All dispatch Ants without them exploding.

Or, you can avoid combat with Ants as you move deeper into the building.

(Optional) Activate the sonic emitter.

The Ant Mound itself **(7)** is on the lower ground, along the south wall. Expect a large swarm of Giant Ants to show up when you reach there. You can:

Ignore the mound completely, and manually kill the Giant Ants throughout the facility, until your Quest updates.

Or place the Sonic Emitter on the mound, and then activate it. This pops the Ants one by one, killing them all.

Or you can ignore the Giant Ants entirely.

Whether or not the Giant Ants are defeated, you haven't finished yet! Travel to the lower level, find the two Generators **(8)** along the western wall, and Activate the Electrical Switches attached to both of them. Then head west, to the gantry steps, and locate the Generator Main Power Switch halfway up on the metal landing before you reach the upper floor. Activate this, and the array powers back into life.

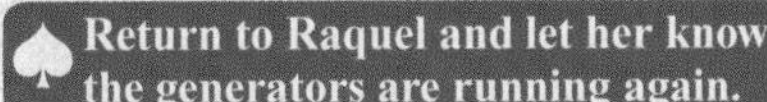

Return to Raquel and let her know the generators are running again.

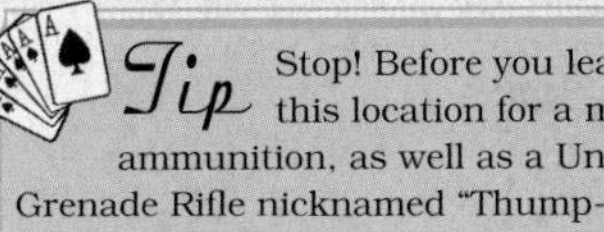

Tip Stop! Before you leave, check this location for a mass of ammunition, as well as a Unique Grenade Rifle nicknamed "Thump-Thump." The Tour Chapter has the exact location.

Raquel may be on patrol, in or near Pearl's Barracks, or waiting from her defenses **(9)** close to the main gate. Approach her, and let her know that the Ants have been exterminated, and the array is back online. Or, if you didn't kill all the Ants, lie and say you did to complete this Quest.

Boomer Fame Gained!

300 XP

ANYWHERE I WANDER

SUGGESTED EXPERIENCE

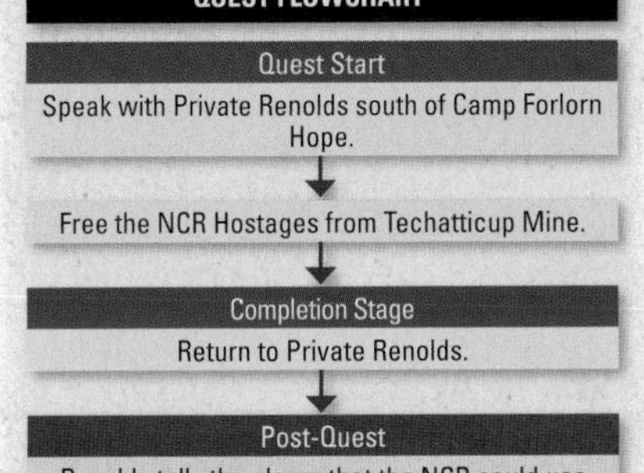

QUEST FLOWCHART

Quest Start
Speak with Private Renolds south of Camp Forlorn Hope.
↓
Free the NCR Hostages from Techatticup Mine.
↓
Completion Stage
Return to Private Renolds.
↓
Post-Quest
Renolds tells the player that the NCR could use them, and to report to Camp Forlorn Hope.

Main Factions

NEW CA. REPUBLIC, CAESAR'S LEGION

A Tempest in a Techatticup

While wandering the Mojave Wasteland, use the remains of the roads to guide you south of Nelson [6.06], toward the Techatticup Mine [6.08]. Mid-way between these points, along the blistered tarmac **(1)**, a wheezing Private Renolds **(2)** staggers up to you, and explains that his squad was ambushed by the Legion. "That bastard Alexus" was apparently the one responsible. Respond by:

- Letting him know you'll take a look.
- Better yet, answer, "You sure they're still alive?"

This allows you to Barter for a little "extra encouragement," in Cap form.

100 Caps

Rescue the NCR hostages from the Techatticup mine.

The Legion is holed up a few hundred yards farther along the road, in Techatticup Mine itself. Two Legion Recruits patrol the slightly elevated entrance in the rocky outcrop **(3)**. You may elect to step past, or fight them. Whatever your decision, look for and enter the scarred Door to Techatticup Mine.

Techatticup Mine (see the map in the Tour Chapter entry) consists of an entrance tunnel to an upper area filled with glowing fungus, radioactive barrels, Legion Recruits and their mongrel dogs, and two locked gates, each with an NCR prisoner behind it **(4)**. A lower chamber, linked by a long, winding tunnel, houses additional detritus, a few more Legion Recruits, and their leader Alexus **(5)**. The following options are available:

CAESAR'S LEGION: If you're Shunned or Vilified by the Legion, you're attacked on sight. Fight (using your favored weapons for tunnels) to the upper chamber, and optionally descend to the lower chamber for extra bloodshed.

CAESAR'S LEGION: If you're liked by the Legion, expect this to lessen if you want to free the prisoners. The Legion only attacks if you strike first, or open either of the gates with a prisoner behind.

You can try reasoning with Alexus, but to no avail. The prisoners will not be freed by sweet-talking or other verbal sparring. Choose to kill Alexus though, and you find a handy Techatticup Storage Key, which opens every gate in the mine.

SNEAK: You can try a more stealthy approach, moving past the troops (ideally with a Stealth Boy active). You can Pickpocket the Techatticup Storage Key from Alexus more easily, too. Alas, combat is inevitable once the gates to the prisoners are unlocked.

Techatticup Storage Key

Free both prisoners by opening each gate:

 You can employ Bobby Pins.

 **Or use the Techatticup Storage Key**

Once through the gate, untie the NCR squadmate and he flees the area, moving out of the mine quickly. You don't need to chaperone either of them, although it's usually better to kill off the Legion before freeing the prisoners. If both prisoners die, however, the Quest fails. So clear a path for them if you can!

Report back to Private Renolds.

Back on the road, Private Renolds is where you left him. Inform him of your triumph, and he lets you know the NCR could use someone like you. Camp Forlorn Hope is a good (and nearby) place to wander to next.

 **100 XP**

BACK IN YOUR OWN BACKYARD

SUGGESTED EXPERIENCE

QUEST FLOWCHART

Quest Start	
Speak with Ranger Milo west of Nelson.	
Completion Stage	Completion Stage
Kill the crucified NCR soldiers in Nelson.	Save crucified NCR soldiers by killing Caesar's Legion forces at Nelson

Main Factions

Note Depending on how violent you are toward the Legion, completing this Quest may jeopardise your Reputation with the Legion, making you unable to complete other Quests, such as Side Quest: We Are Legion. Pick a side!

Outmanned and Outgunned

West of Nelson [6.06], on the remains of the road that links this godforsaken settlement to Interstate 95 and the town of Novac [5.18] is a small NCR Ranger Checkpoint [6.S05] **(1)**, where a trio of soldiers stand guard. The head of the team here is Ranger Milo **(2)**. Approach, and he stops you; the entire area is locked down by the NCR until "some Legion snakes" are dislodged from Nelson. Speak with Milo:

Ask about the trouble with the Legion.

 Or, tell him your name (which doesn't ring any bells), and tell Milo you'll lend him a hand in ridding the area of the Legion.

Either way, his team is ill-equipped to deal with the Legion menace down in Nelson. So Milo wants you to take out the Legion's Trooper hostages. Milo is a Ranger, and the Troopers (both at the checkpoint, and imprisoned at Nelson) are different branches of the NCR. And the hostages are crucified down there **(3)**; a dirty trick designed to spread fear into the NCR. And it's working. Take out the hostages, and the Legion has "squat for leverage." Furthermore, Milo doesn't want more dead NCR Troopers; they're outnumbered ten-to-one as it is.

Kill the NCR Hostages.

Tip Before you leave the Ranger checkpoint, inspect the Footlocker under the shack guard post. Inside, you'll find two C-4 Explosives and a Detonator; perfect tools for your task to come. Grab them!

 **C-4 Explosive (2)**

 **Detonator**

A Quick Death, A Better Place

Milo runs off down the road, moving to some upper cliffs to provide covering fire while you do the dangerous dirty work. He's adamant that you kill the three NCR hostages with a single quick and deadly strike; not "plinked to death with some old Varmint Rifle." Oblige Milo by trying one of the following execution plans:

#1: Kill Everybody

   This first plan is unsubtle, dangerous, and only recommended for a combat maniac; just run down the rocky bluffs and drop anything wearing a red uniform. Continue this dance of red death until everything (including the Legion leader Dead Sea) is a bloodied corpse, or you are. The healing items you'll need can be offset by the scavenged items you'll find on the Legion. Dead Sea has a Unique Machete to covet, too.

 **Liberator**

#2: Kill the Hostages with a Modicum of Subtlety

 Crouch on the upper ridge and high ground on the southwest side of town **(4)**, and tag the three hostages with a high-powered Sniper Rifle. If you've crafted a high-power weapon with a silencer, then you won't have to deal with Legion Recruits storming your position, either.

#3: Silent Running

 Optionally use a Stealth Boy, and Sneak through the town's Legion guards to the central telephone pole crucifixion platform. You may be discovered by Dead Sea, but simply speak to him without attacking, and he leaves you alone. Drop both C-4 Explosives at the feet of two of the crucifixion poles, and retreat. Then press the Detonator **(5)**. The three hostages are blown sky-high, and the Quest updates, although the Legion are milling about, trying to find you; that's why you used the Stealth Boy and detonated from the cliffs near Milo's position.

- Drop Grenades at the crucifixion platform for a similar effect, but success is not guaranteed.
- Or, leave one C-4 Explosive on the platform, and the other on Dead Sea (by Pickpocketing then successfully placing a C-4 charge on him). That certainly demoralizes the Legion Recruits!

#4: Leave No Man Behind

Naturally, you can ignore Ranger Milo's orders, for the good of the crucified soldiers and your ongoing relationship with Boone, if he's with you as a Follower (especially as part of Side Quest: I Forgot to Remember to Forget). Despite what Milo requests, move to the NCR hostages and untie them, but don't kill them! Do this before or after combat, but beware: the Legion will attack you with all their forces in the area. Boone is actually annoyed at Ranger Milo's inaction at saving the hostages, so speak to Boone about this, as part of his Quest.

Return to Milo at the NCR Checkpoint.

Return to Milo to complete the Quest. He thanks you for your tactical prowess (or massacring abilities), and offers a small reward. Don't worry about the deaths of the hostages; nobody at the NCR of any worth will notice.

NCR Fame Gained!

150 XP

MAIN QUEST INTERSECTION

BEYOND THE BEEF

SUGGESTED EXPERIENCE

See flowchart on the following page

Main Factions

Before You Begin....

The Ultra-Luxe Hotel and Casino [2D.05] is the swankiest place on The Strip, and caters to a more...discerning customer with a taste for the finer things in life. This place is where one of The Strip's Families—the White Glove Society—has its base of operations. Depending on you and your Faction's ideals, the Society can become favored allies or freakish foes. Before you begin, it is worth knowing the numerous ways you can approach this Quest:

Note: To begin this Quest, you must have already accessed The Strip (check Main Quest: Ring-a-Ding Ding! for how to achieve this). In addition, to speak with Mortimer, you must have a "low" or "negative" Karma. Check your Karma "title" against the "Experience Points and Karma" section of this guide's Training Chapter and make sure it falls into the "evil" category. Finally, remember the Factions you may be working with during the Main Quest all want to ensure Society help (or destruction). To this end, you can:

Investigate before or at any time during the Main Quest.

MR. HOUSE Mr. House already has a professionally beneficial relationship with the Society. He doesn't need you to investigate them.

NEW CA. REPUBLIC Although they're neighbors, Ambassador Crocker (and Colonel Moore) don't want or need the Society investigating on their behalf.

CAESAR'S LEGION Caesar wants you to specifically ally with (and not defeat) the Society. Not for the forthcoming battle, but as supporters in the aftermath. Check Main Quest: Render Unto Caesar.

INDEPENDENT Yes Man gives you the names of the White Glove Society as part of Main Quest: Side Bets. All you need is to inquire about them. It is up to you to ally with or destroy them. You're the boss!

Stop! Beware of the Pheebles!

Note: It is incredibly important to realize that your actions during Side Quest: Pheeble Will directly affect the situation with Heck Gunderson, who is a major player in this Quest. Learn all the options of both Quests before committing any particularly spectacular (or violent) plans.

1

Move south through The Strip, past the Lucky 38 [2D.02] and The Tops [2D.04] to the imposing edifice known as the Ultra-Luxe Casino **(1)**. A White Glove Greeter (very politely) asks you to remove your weapons. You can:

Refuse, and be removed from the casino or begin to fight.

Or you can agree.

Or you can keep hold-out weapons.

There are two main ways this Quest can play out: either expose the Society for what they really are, or ally with them. The two different paths are set out below.

Exposure Path Part 1: One Heck of a Problem

2

3

Heck Gunderson is nursing a whiskey at the circular bar in the entrance foyer, with his armed guard **(2)**. Sidle up to Heck **(3)**, and he asks whether you've seen his boy. Lie or not; you can then speak to Heck about his ranching business, and most importantly, agree to find his lost son. Heck will pay a lot of Caps to get his son back, or to gain information on "the sons of bitches" responsible for taking him.

Ask around the Ultra-Luxe for information regarding Ted Gunderson's disappearance.

Get Ted back to his father if he is still alive.

Keeping Mum with Marjorie and Mortimer

4

5

Your next stop can be to speak with either Marjorie or Mortimer. Choose the former, and head to The Gourmand (restaurant) at the Ultra-Luxe **(4)**.

Marjorie **(5)**, standing near the curved desk, welcomes you politely. You can ask about Heck's Brahmin business with the Society, but you're really here to ask about Heck's missing son. She's a little agitated when you ask, and tells you she answered all her questions when an investigator came to see her. Ask her for more information on the investigator, and she points you in the direction of maitre d'; Mortimer. Before you go, you can also:

Ask if the White Glove Society used to feast on human flesh. Marjorie is furious and offended at such a baseless lie. Your Infamy with The Strip increases, but only if you ask this question.

The Strip Infamy Gained!

Inquire with Mortimer at the Ultra-Luxe about the investigator.

QUEST FLOWCHART

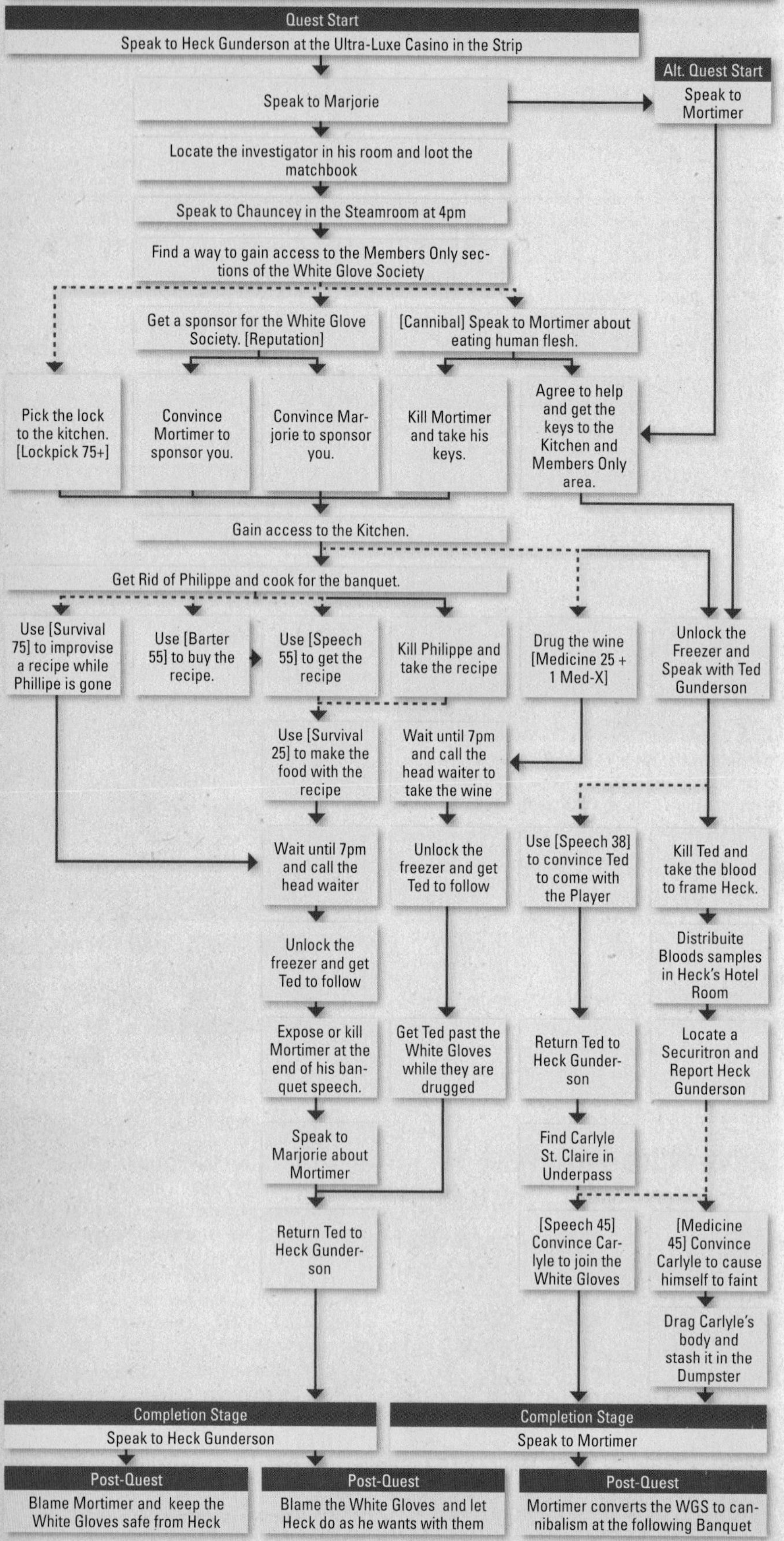

Quest Start

Speak to Heck Gunderson at the Ultra-Luxe Casino in the Strip

Alt. Quest Start

Speak to Mortimer

Speak to Marjorie

Locate the investigator in his room and loot the matchbook

Speak to Chauncey in the Steamroom at 4pm

Find a way to gain access to the Members Only sections of the White Glove Society

Get a sponsor for the White Glove Society. [Reputation]

[Cannibal] Speak to Mortimer about eating human flesh.

Pick the lock to the kitchen. [Lockpick 75+]

Convince Mortimer to sponsor you.

Convince Marjorie to sponsor you.

Kill Mortimer and take his keys.

Agree to help and get the keys to the Kitchen and Members Only area.

Gain access to the Kitchen.

Get Rid of Philippe and cook for the banquet.

Use [Survival 75] to improvise a recipe while Phillipe is gone

Use [Barter 55] to buy the recipe.

Use [Speech 55] to get the recipe

Kill Philippe and take the recipe

Drug the wine [Medicine 25 + 1 Med-X]

Unlock the Freezer and Speak with Ted Gunderson

Use [Survival 25] to make the food with the recipe

Wait until 7pm and call the head waiter to take the wine

Wait until 7pm and call the head waiter

Unlock the freezer and get Ted to follow

Use [Speech 38] to convince Ted to come with the Player

Kill Ted and take the blood to frame Heck.

Unlock the freezer and get Ted to follow

Distribuite Bloods samples in Heck's Hotel Room

Expose or kill Mortimer at the end of his banquet speech.

Get Ted past the White Gloves while they are drugged

Return Ted to Heck Gunderson

Locate a Securitron and Report Heck Gunderson

Speak to Marjorie about Mortimer

Find Carlyle St. Claire in Underpass

Return Ted to Heck Gunderson

[Speech 45] Convince Carlyle to join the White Gloves

[Medicine 45] Convince Carlyle to cause himself to faint

Drag Carlyle's body and stash it in the Dumpster

Completion Stage

Speak to Heck Gunderson

Completion Stage

Speak to Mortimer

Post-Quest

Blame Mortimer and keep the White Gloves safe from Heck

Post-Quest

Blame the White Gloves and let Heck do as he wants with them

Post-Quest

Mortimer converts the WGS to cannibalism at the following Banquet

6

7

Back in the Casino Floor area **(6)**, head to the elevated desk with the well-dressed gent scribbling away on his notepad. This is Mortimer **(7)**. Ask him about the Society, and other chit-chat if you wish. You may also begin the Alliance Path with him at this point (see below). But you're really here to ask about the private investigator. Tell him you wish to speak with the man, and Mortimer strangely agrees to give you his room key, "given the circumstances."

Investigator's Room Key

Get into the investigator's room at the Ultra-Luxe.

Chauncey's Last Chance

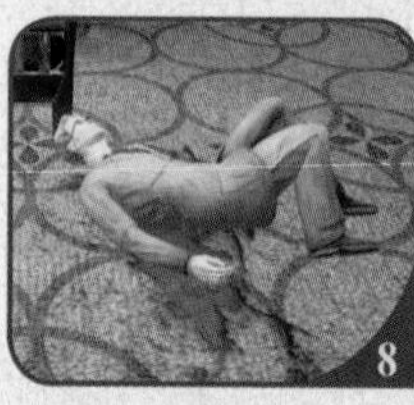
8

Enter the Ultra-Luxe Hotel Rooms area. Use the key Mortimer gave you to enter the only locked, unnamed suite. Inside, the body of the investigator is spread over the floor, blood slowly seeping into the expensive rug **(8)**. You barely have time to search the investigator

9

before you're set upon by two White Gloves **(9)**! Bring out your hold-out weapon, and beat them both down. Don't bring the fight out of the bedroom, or the ruckus causes the Society to get hostile. When you've taken down your attackers, secure a Matchbook from the investigator's corpse. Check your Pip-Boy's Data > Misc Menu for a note scrawled across the back of the Matchbook: "Steam Room. 4 PM."

Matchbook

Meet with the investigator's contact in the Ultra-Luxe steam room at 4 PM.

Head to the Ultra-Luxe Bathhouse **(10)** at around 16:00, or 4 PM, and wait for the only member of the White Glove Society not to wear a mask to show up. Chauncey **(11)** heads into the Steam Room. Follow him in

10

11

and speak with him. Explain who you are, and mention the dead investigator. Chauncey seems panicked: "they must know he was talking to someone on the inside." Press him, and Chauncey reveals that Mortimer is behind the disappearances—he's attempting to "regress" the Society into their old ways...of cannibalism! Ask about Ted, and Chauncey reckons he's still alive and being kept "fresh" for something special—a dining event at 7 PM! After you've exhausted Chauncey's knowledge, he crumples forward, shot by an assassin's bullet! Quickly attack the Mercenary **(12)** before you're killed, too!

12

Find a way to gain access to the Members Only section of The Gourmand.

(Optional) Find a sponsor to help you join the White Glove Society.

(Optional) Get rid of Philippe and cook for the banquet using his recipe for human flesh.

(Optional) Drug the wine at the White Glove Society banquet.

The game is afoot! You now have a choice of ways to enter the Ultra-Luxe Kitchen. You can:

- Ask Marjorie or Mortimer to sponsor you as a bona fide member of the White Glove Society. Their acceptance is based on your reputation around The Strip. Increase your Fame by completing Quests associated with the other Families, as listed in the nearby table.

THE STRIP If your Fame with The Strip is "Liked" or better, you are welcomed as a member and receive access to the kitchen.

THE STRIP If your Fame isn't to this level, you're not allowed to join. Raise your Fame, or try another option.

- Change to the "Alliance" path for this Quest, and speak to Mortimer about craving human flesh, and agree to help him.

If this is too tricky, you can always head over to the Door to Ultra-Luxe Kitchen, and pry it open with Bobby Pins.

SNEAK Or quietly sneak up to Mortimer and place a Grenade (or C-4) into his pocket, and then detonate it. Take the Kitchen Key from his corpse. If you're less subtle, you run the risk of turning all the Society against you.

Quests Related to The Strip

Location	Quest Name	Family
[2D.01] Gomorrah	How Little We Know	The Omertas
[2D.08] Michael Angelo's Workshop	Classic Inspiration	Michael Angelo
[2D.04] The Tops Casino	Talent Pool	The Chairmen

Alliance Path Part 1: The Craving

13

Heck Gunderson (who you can begin this Quest with) can be ignored, as you have a woman named Marjorie to meet with. Once on the Ultra-Luxe Casino Floor, head to the door marked "The Gourmand at the Ultra-Luxe," and enter **(4)**. Marjorie **(5)** welcomes you ever-so politely. Although you can ask her other questions (including that Caesar extends his offer of an alliance). Marjorie looks down her nose at you. You'll get no more from her.

14

Back in the Casino Floor area **(13)**, head to the elevated desk with the dandy man scribbling away on his notepad. This is Mortimer **(14)**. Ask him about the Society, Caesar's request (if you're allied with the Legion), and other chit-chat. Time to play the ace card; tell Mortimer you know his Society once dined on human flesh. You can:

Lie, and tell him you know what it is like to feel the Craving.

Or query whether it is true.

Return to Marjorie, and inquire about the White Glove Society's rumored penchant for human flesh. When she angrily replies, head to Mortimer, and ask about the Craving.

These options cause Mortimer to spill some beans; he's planning an exquisite Society dinner, but there's a problem with the main course. It has a powerful father named Heck Gunderson. Ted can be returned to his father, or his father can be framed for killing his son, and a replacement "meal"—a man named Carlyle St. Clair—needs to be "rounded up." To help you carry out his wishes, Mortimer hands you a Cattle Prod, and three keys. The Kitchen Key allows access to the general area where Ted is. The Penthouse Key is where Heck Gunderson is staying, and the Freezer Key leads to Ted's current whereabouts.

Cattle Prod

Ultra-Luxe Kitchen Key

Ultra-Luxe Penthouse Key

Ultra-Luxe Freezer Key

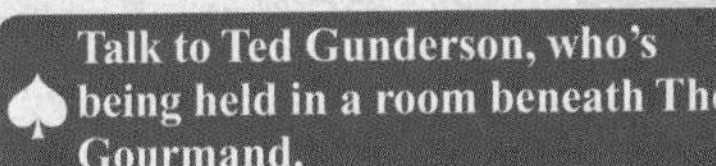
Talk to Ted Gunderson, who's being held in a room beneath The Gourmand.

Note Whether you used the Exposure or Alliance Path to get into the kitchens, you have one last opportunity to "switch paths." The two paths forming the second part of this Quest begin now!

Merged Path: Kitchen Nightmares

15

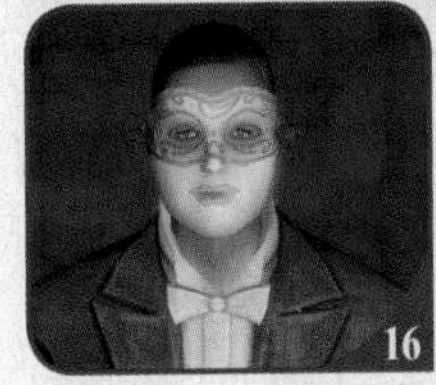
16

You're now in the kitchens. Pass the Brahmin roasting **(15)**, and head down the steps. You may be halted by a White Glove en route to the kitchen **(16)**. If so, keep your wits about you. You can:

Exposure: Tell him Mortimer has sent you to move the kid.

Alliance: Tell him Mortimer has sent you to move the kid (no Speech check is needed).

Lie about a burst water main.

Or tell him you're just passing through. The White Glove then follows you, barking warnings at you until he turns hostile, and the game is up. An unwise plan.

Once through, you have a variety of choices, depending on your chosen path:

With Exposure, you need to sabotage the banquet and sort out Ted Gunderson.
With Alliance, you only need to sort out the Ted Gunderson situation.

Exposure Path Part 2: Where's the Beef?

Try the Wine

17

To expose the Society, head to the wine cellar, adjacent to the main kitchen area. Head in here, and Examine the Banquet Wine Bottle **(17)** on the table. You can find the same wine in the kitchen, near Philippe. You can:

Do nothing, and try a different plan.

MEDICINE 25 You can spike the wine with a sedative. For this, you also need a Med-X. You should be carrying one in your inventory, but if you aren't, one place to purchase one is the New Vegas Medical Center [2.10], although this is a lengthy detour.

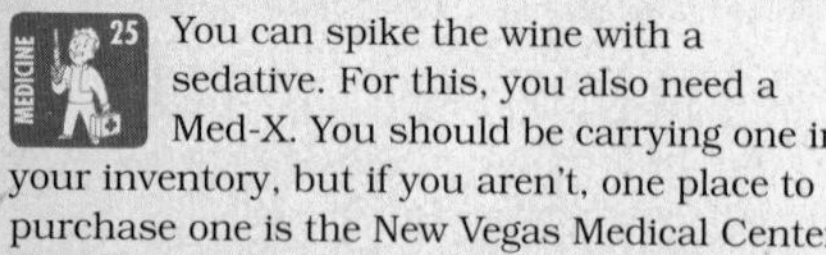
(Optional) Use the intercom to call in the head waiter.

Once you've spiked the wine, wait until the banquet starts, at 19:00 (7 PM), and then call for the waiter. At this point, you need to break Ted Gunderson out of the freezer. Once that occurs, you can hustle Ted out of the freezer and up through the casino, passing the snoozing banquet guests that you've drugged, and back to Heck Gunderson, where the Quest concludes.

Too Many Cooks

18

If you want to expose the White Glove Society, you need to incriminate Mortimer, and hope the more "evolved" members of the Society cast him out, and keep human meats off the menu. Mortimer mentioned that his chef was planning a superb meat course; this

19

needs to be changed to something more palatable. Enter the main kitchen area **(18)**, and confront Philippe **(19)**. He's high strung, and you may use this to your advantage after he mistakes you for the help. You can:

Lie, and tell him you're interested in putting out a cookbook.

Tell him his predisposition toward anger suggests unresolved issues.

Mention you saw a Radroach in the pantry, and that he should check it out.

Or kill him.

Or ignore him, wait for him to move away, and improvise the meal without a recipe.

Any of these options allows you to obtain the chef's recipes. Among them is one involving human flesh. This now needs to be mimicked.

Philippe's Recipes

20

There are various ovens in the kitchen, but this one **(20)** has all the ingredients necessary to cook a meal that Mortimer believes contains the meat he craves. You can:

Improvise the meal without a recipe.

Cook the meal using the recipe.

(Optional) Use the intercom to call in the head waiter.

(Optional) Bring Ted to the Members Only section to expose Mortimer at the end of his banquet speech.

Once the meal is cooked, wait until the banquet starts, at 19:00 (7 PM), and then call for the waiter. At this point, you need to break Ted Gunderson out of the freezer. Once that occurs, you can hustle Ted out of the freezer, optionally into the banquet to reveal Mortimer (after he has concluded his speech) as a crazed cannibal (and you as a reasonably adept chef), ready to send the Society tumbling back into its deviant past. Mortimer is caught, and Marjorie must be talked to. She thanks you for keeping this quiet. Well, that's for you and Heck Gunderson to decide! Bring Ted back to Heck Gunderson, where the Quest concludes.

Merged Paths: Son of a Gunderson

21

22

STEALTHBOY If you're not Allied with the White Glove Society, trying to obtain Ted before beginning this Quest, or without Mortimer's approval, causes you to be Shunned if you pick the lock to the kitchen. However, using the Stealth Boy negates this problem.

Whether or not you're Allying with the Society, you must head to the freezer **(21)**, and unlock it. You can:

Access the terminal, assuming you haven't had Mortimer's help, and unlock the door.

Unlock the door using skill and Bobby Pins.

Or using the key that Mortimer gave you.

Inside is Ted Gunderson **(22)**, and he's none-too-pleased being cooped up. In fact, he's threatening to tell Daddy. You can:

Calm Ted down, using any of the verbal options, but choosing "I could always leave you here if you aren't going to listen." Ted doesn't want that and agrees to follow you.

The revelations that his father is powerful and someone wishes to frame the White Glove Society also help to placate Ted and get him to trust you.

Or you can attack Ted, and quickly dispatch him in the freezer, or (with much more risk) at any time during your chaperoning.

FOLLOWER Or you can return to Mortimer and offer him one of your human companions as a replacement for Ted. He's certainly not going to be tasting the meat of Raul, Lily, or anything with robotic parts. Guide your unknowing Follower into the freezer, slowly shoving them in if they won't step inside, and then shut the door, using the terminal to engage the lock.

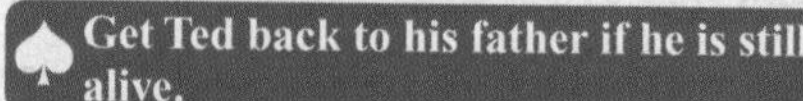
Get Ted back to his father if he is still alive.

Collect samples off of Ted's corpse for use in framing his father.

(Optional) Bring Ted to the Members Only section to expose Mortimer at the end of his banquet speech.

Herding the Ranch Hand

23

If Ted is alive, bring him with you through the casino all the way to the entrance foyer where Heck Gunderson and his bodyguard are

waiting **(23)**. Heck is overcome with joy. Talk to Heck Gunderson, who wants to skin the hides of those responsible. You can:

Lie and tell him you don't know who took him. This is the Society's preferred option, and allows you to continue your Quest with them (as well as receive Heck's Caps reward, and associated Fame gains). Now go and find a suitable "meat" for Mortimer. All the other options finish the Quest with Heck.

The Strip Infamy Gained!

White Glove Society Fame Gained!

You can blame Mortimer the cannibal, and leave Marjorie out of it.

Or you can blame the entire White Glove Society.

- Either option has Heck planning a blockade of The Strip. You can:

Tell him that's what they'd want, as they'd just start eating each other. You gain Fame.

Tell him not to be hasty. Heck rethinks his position. You gain Fame.

The Strip Fame Gained!

Or agree that it would be a fantastic idea. Heck goes off to begin the blockade, and you lose Fame.

- You can always start shooting the place up before (or after) Heck learns what the Society was going to do to his son. The battle is protracted.

If you side with Heck, you receive a Caps reward.

The Strip Infamy Gained!

White Glove Society Infamy Gained!

Caps (500)

Alliance Path Part 2: Fresh Meat

24

If you and Ted got violent in the freezer, quickly inspect the corpse. Gather Ted's blood samples so you can frame Heck Gunderson, and get this cattle ranching buffoon away from your lovely cannibal chums.

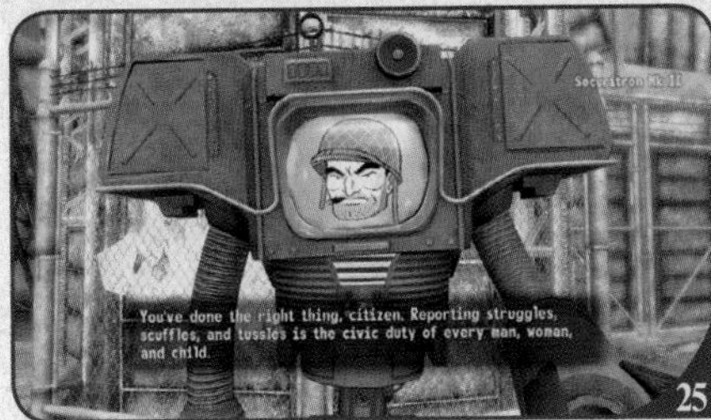

25

Ted's Blood Samples

Distribute your samples around Heck Gunderson's bed and sink in his Ultra-Luxe penthouse suite.

Now take the blood with you, and use the Penthouse Key that Mortimer gave you to enter Heck's penthouse suite, and liberally apply the blood to the room **(24)**.

Send a Securitron from The Strip to investigate Heck Gunderson's suite.

Now play the role of a good citizen, and leave the Ultra-Luxe, and locate a Securitron on the strip **(25)** and inform it of your "discovery." Heck is thus removed from the picture. But the meat isn't fresh, so find a suitable replacement for Mortimer.

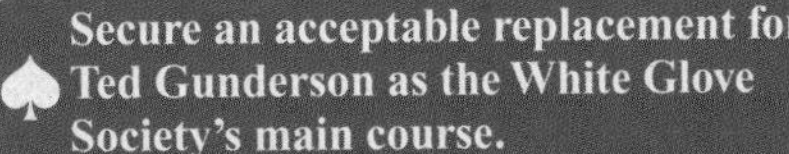
Secure an acceptable replacement for Ted Gunderson as the White Glove Society's main course.

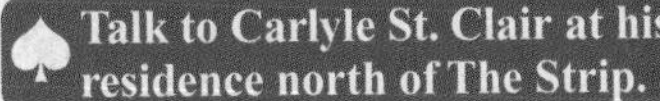
Talk to Carlyle St. Clair at his residence north of The Strip.

26

27

If you framed Heck, or delivered Ted to Heck but didn't reveal the Society's role in all of this, you can carry out Mortimer's final wishes by locating fresh meat. Close to the Freeside North Gate [2.08] or the Mole Rat Ranch [2.11] is the northern edge of the Mojave Wasteland. Journey past the perimeter road to a ramshackle shack **(26)** where Carlyle St. Clair III **(27)** is moping about. He asks what you want. You can:

Tell him to strip, and meet him in the dumpster for a good time.

- Tell him you're here to talk, and he moans on about his reputation, and that his family has blacklisted him. You can:

Go back to other responses.

Or recommend that he join the White Glove Society to clear his name. Tell him to speak to Mortimer. Carlyle agrees, and runs off to meet Mortimer. You don't need to follow him.

Pistol whip him into unconsciousness.

Or use the Cattle Prod until he falls over. Remember Carlyle needs to be incapacitated, and not killed!

- Ask if his neck is okay. He tells you he's been having problems sleeping. You can:

Apply a sleeper hold.

Get him to attempt some deep-breathing exercises until he passes out.

Apply a nerve strike to his neck.

If Carlyle is unconscious, the Objectives update:

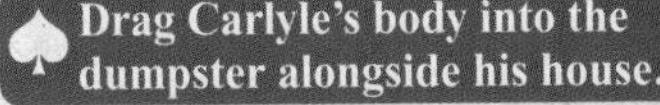
Drag Carlyle's body into the dumpster alongside his house.

Return to Mortimer in the Ultra-Luxe.

Back at Mortimer, inform him that Carlyle is either in the dumpster, or heading to the Casino. Mortimer is most grateful, and he's determined that dinner will be a success.

But he won't know until 19:00, or 7 PM tonight, when the banquet occurs. Wait or sleep until after that time, and return to Mortimer (it is unwise to enter The Gourmand, as the assembled guests don't want a nonmember seeing them tucking in to their Carlyle amuse bouche), and ask how the dinner is going. He's ecstatic, and the Quest concludes. The only other business is to persuade Marjorie to shift her stance and join Caesar, if you're allied with this Faction.

White Glove Society Fame Gained!

500 XP

You can persuade Marjorie to shift her stance and join with Caesar. Wait until the morning, when Marjorie returns to her desk at The Gourmand, and visit her then (and not at the banquet, unless you've already become a member during this Side Quest). Although she's unhappy with the hodgepodge of sporting equipment that passes for fashion with them, she agrees. You can return to Caesar with the result he ordered.

BIRDS OF A FEATHER

SUGGESTED EXPERIENCE

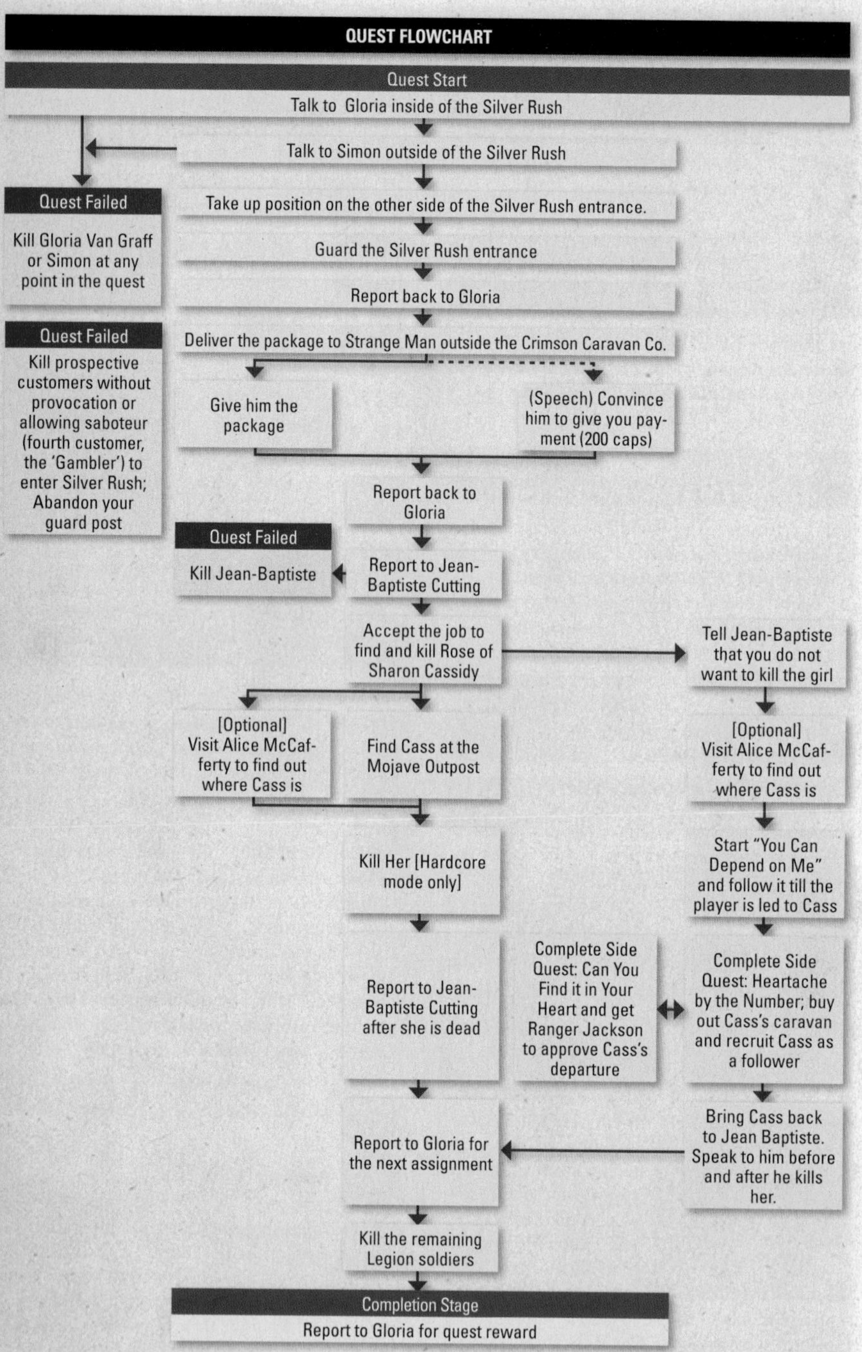

QUEST FLOWCHART

Quest Start

- Talk to Gloria inside of the Silver Rush
- Talk to Simon outside of the Silver Rush
- Take up position on the other side of the Silver Rush entrance.
- Guard the Silver Rush entrance
- Report back to Gloria
- Deliver the package to Strange Man outside the Crimson Caravan Co.
  - Give him the package
  - (Speech) Convince him to give you payment (200 caps)
- Report back to Gloria
- Report to Jean-Baptiste Cutting
  - Quest Failed: Kill Jean-Baptiste
- Accept the job to find and kill Rose of Sharon Cassidy
  - [Optional] Visit Alice McCafferty to find out where Cass is
  - Find Cass at the Mojave Outpost
  - Kill Her [Hardcore mode only]
  - Report to Jean-Baptiste Cutting after she is dead
- Tell Jean-Baptiste that you do not want to kill the girl
  - [Optional] Visit Alice McCafferty to find out where Cass is
  - Start "You Can Depend on Me" and follow it till the player is led to Cass
  - Complete Side Quest: Heartache by the Number; buy out Cass's caravan and recruit Cass as a follower ↔ Complete Side Quest: Can You Find it in Your Heart and get Ranger Jackson to approve Cass's departure
  - Bring Cass back to Jean Baptiste. Speak to him before and after he kills her.
- Report to Gloria for the next assignment
- Kill the remaining Legion soldiers

Completion Stage

Report to Gloria for quest reward

Quest Failed

Kill Gloria Van Graff or Simon at any point in the quest

Quest Failed

Kill prospective customers without provocation or allowing saboteur (fourth customer, the 'Gambler') to enter Silver Rush; Abandon your guard post

Full of Energy

The elderly Silver Rush Gambling Hall [2C.07] in Inner Freeside is now the exclusive domain

of the no-nonsense traders called the Van Graffs. Sidle up to the front door **(1)**, and you're greeted by Simon, and thugs with energy weapons once you enter the premises. You must:

Watch the conversation between the Van Graffs and a trading partner, which demonstrates just how ruthless and serious the Van Graffs are about their business.

Or you can try grabbing one of the dozens of highly prized energy weapon ammunition slugs, or shoot the place up, which fails the Quest automatically. Not good.

When the execution is over, you're allowed into the lower room where Gloria Van Graff **(2)** and her brother sell their top-of-the-line energy weapons. Her brother isn't the talkative type. You can:

Purchase a wide variety of energy weapons, parts to upgrade, ammunition, and projectiles from her.

Ask her about the business and neighborhood, and receive a wealth of background information.

Request some work. They need another body to guard the front entrance to the Silver Rush. Agree to this employment.

Go outside and talk to Simon.

Task #1: Client Supervisor

Return outside, speak to Simon **(3)** on the door, and follow his instructions. Accidental discharges of energy weapons ruin this Quest, so be civil, and change into the obligatory uniform: a Van Graff Combat Armor suit, and either a Laser or Plasma Rifle. (You can choose which, and learn the differences between them if you ask Simon. Lasers have a high rate of fire but not a lot of stopping power, while Plasmas are slow, but pack a kick). Now follow his instructions carefully; you're here to keep the riffraff away. "Drunks, punks, and Capless vermin" are to be turned away. Potential customers are permitted into the normal entrance, but only after a pat-down. And don't start fights!

 **Van Graff Combat Armor**

 **Laser Rifle**

 **Plasma Rifle**

Take up position on the other side of the Silver Rush entrance.

Guard the Silver Rush entrance.

Tip Although the Combat Armor is mandatory, you can swap your weapon to another Laser or Plasma Rifle, such as one you've already augmented with scopes or other accoutrements.

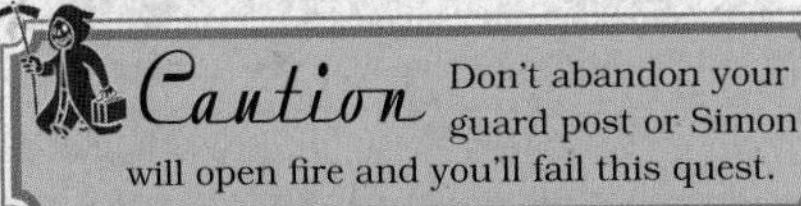

Caution Don't abandon your guard post or Simon will open fire and you'll fail this quest.

4

Begin your guard duties on the right side of the door, watching the Atomic Wrangler, as the flotsam and jetsam of Freeside pass you by **(4)**. Various people saunter over to try your patience. Expect the following:

5

A Drunk **(5)** wobbles over, asking about a laser gun. Simply refuse to let him in.

6

A Gambler **(6)** arrives, wanting to see some weapons. Tell him you have to search him first. No problems.

7

Another Gambler **(7)** with winnings at the Wrangler wants in. Refuse to let him in, or:

SPEECH 60 Convince him to be patted down first before letting him in.

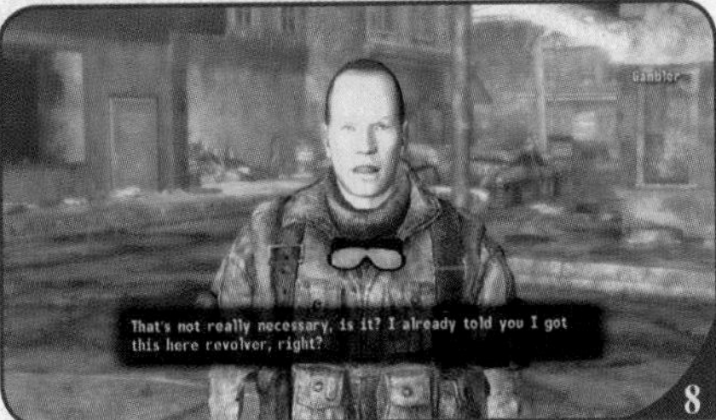

8

A "Gambler" **(8)** with a bulky, multi-pocket coat arrives, looking for something to replace his revolver. Stop him from entering the premises by insisting on a pat-down. He draws his weapon; quickly destroy him, because he's carrying a bomb! Allowing him in will result in a decimation of the Silver Rush denizens, and you will fail this Quest.

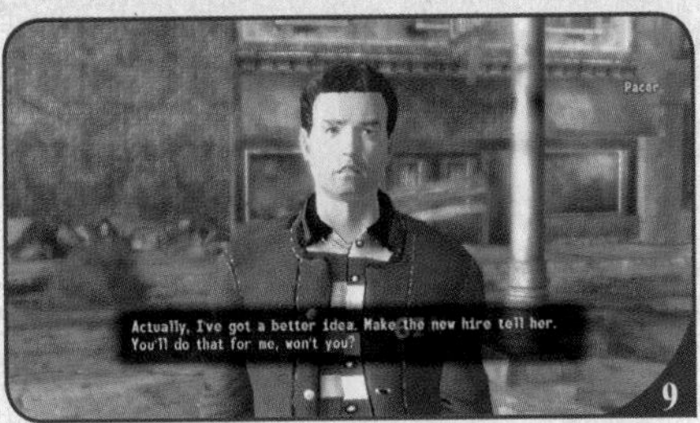

9

Once Simon clears the corpse off the sidewalk, wait for Pacer **(9)** from The Kings to arrive and speak with Simon. If Pacer has been killed in another quest, this won't occur. He wants you to give Gloria a message. Reply peacefully, and Pacer leaves. Answer aggressively, and you need to defeat Pacer (which causes problems with The Kings in other Quests, so be aware of this!). After this final visitor, your guarding duty is over.

Report back to Gloria.

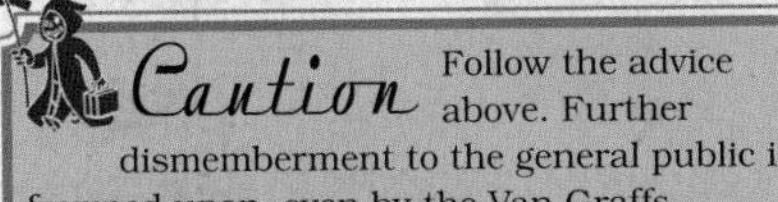

Caution Follow the advice above. Further dismemberment to the general public is frowned upon, even by the Van Graffs.

Task #2: Executive Liaison

Speak with Gloria, who critiques your guarding, and hands you your wages. She's found someone else to stand guard, freeing you for a different kind of task. You're to take a package of sample weapons to a client in a "discreet location." Gloria marks it on your World Map.

Caps (200)

Van Graff Package

Deliver the package to a man at the designated location.

10

The location in question is just east of Durable Dunn's Sacked Caravan [2.16] close to the Northeast Territories. You'll find your contact—a Strange Man—in the scrub **(10)**, waiting for the pick-up. He asks if you're the Van Graff's emissary. String him along or answer "yes," but don't kill him! Hand over the package, with the following options:

- Simply remove the package from your inventory.
- Or ask "where's the payment?" The man doesn't know what you're talking about:

SPEECH 75 Tell him your employer negotiated a small fee for this drop. The man reluctantly gives you 200 Caps.

Caps (200)

Any other verbal communication results in giving the package over without extra payment.

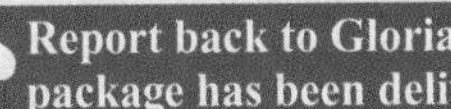

Report back to Gloria that the package has been delivered.

Task #3: Cass Wrangler

11

Tell Gloria how the drop went (and optionally get some information about the buyers). Gloria needs time to think, and points you to Jean-Baptiste Cutting **(11)** for another mission.

Talk to Jean-Baptiste to receive your next assignment.

Speak to him, and he tells you his sister is impressed with you. But he isn't, and doesn't think you have what it takes to work for this family. But he's willing to let you prove him wrong. Agree to tie up a "loose end" that might jeopardize a deal they've just inked. Jean-Baptiste needs you to find a girl named Rose of Sharon Cassidy. He wants you to bring her to him. Ask for more clues, and he tells you old Alice McLafferty over at the Crimson Caravans [2.09] might have more information on "Cass."

Find Rose of Sharon Cassidy and get her to follow you.

(Optional) Visit Alice McLafferty, who might know where Rose of Sharon Cassidy is currently located.

12

13

If you already know where Cass is, you can head straight there. But for a full set of choices, visit the large, enclosed Crimson Caravan compound **(12)**, and once inside, head toward the Main Office shed. Inside, ask Alice McLafferty **(13)** about Cass. Coincidentally, Alice is also looking for her; she's probably down at the Mojave Outpost [4.27]. You can:

- Agree to complete some work for Alice McLafferty, and begin Side Quest: You Can Depend on Me, complete the first task, and then head to Cass when this Quest opens up. Consult that Quest for detailed information.

Or you can leave, and head directly to the Mojave Outpost.

14

15

Trek to the southwestern edge of the Mojave Wasteland, into the Outpost under the two massive rusting statues, and locate the Barracks behind the mesh fence **(14)**. Inside, you'll find Cass **(15)** drinking with some NCR buddies. Engage her in conversation, and you can find out about her background. However, she isn't leaving this place until her caravan papers clear, or her title goes away. You can:

Plead, threaten, or verbally spar with her, but she's staying put.

Ask about buying out Cass' caravan, then recruit her as a Follower, but only as part of Side Quest: You Can Depend on Me, and you've received the request from Alice. Or, attempt this as part of Side Quest: Heartache By the Number, but with the knowledge that you'll double-cross Cass later.

 **Follower: Rose of Sharon Cassidy**

If you're playing in Hardcore Mode, you have the following two options:

You can kill Cass once she's your Follower, taking her somewhere nice and quiet, where the NCR won't see you.

Or you can kill Cass in cold blood. However, violence against patrons under NCR protection isn't particularly wise if you're allying with the NCR, and you need to fight your way out of the Outpost.

 **NCR Infamy Gain!**

Bring the Cassidy girl to Jean-Baptiste.

Back at the Silver Rush, head over to Jean-Baptiste, either with Cass in tow, or with the memory of her death. You can:

Present Cass to Jean-Baptiste, who then executes her.

Or tell Jean-Baptiste that Cass is dead (but only if you actually did the deed).

Or you can save Cass, and gain Infamy among the Van Graffs.

Once the deed is done, you receive your blood money, and report to Gloria for one last, and particularly violent job.

 **Caps (350)**

Report to Gloria Van Graff for your next assignment.

Task #4: One of the Team

16

Gloria tells you the client you delivered the sample to placed a massive order, and she wants to bring you in as an escort to ensure that the meeting goes smoothly. Agree to the task. You arrive clad in Van Graff gear, and Gloria looks worried. The clients, who appear to be a contingent of the Legion, are taking their sweet time inspecting the weapons. She has one last piece of business to attend to: when she gives you a signal, you're to follow her lead. It soon transpires the Van Graffs are as crazy as you'd previously thought; they double-cross and attack the Legion! You can:

Kill the remaining Legion troops.

Do nothing. The objective still completes if you stand by and let the Van Graffs do all the killing.

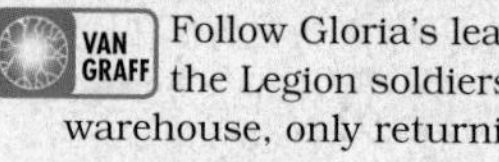 Follow Gloria's lead, and slaughter the Legion soldiers in the warehouse, only returning to her once anyone in a red uniform lies in a pile of goo or dust.

Or you can flip on Gloria, and attack your erstwhile comrades. The Quest fails, and the Legion still turn hostile toward you.

 **Caesar's Legion Infamy Gained!**

CAESAR'S LEGION To preserve your Reputation with the Legion, you must flee the warehouse without engaging any Legion in combat.

Tip Hacking the Legion allows you to loot some exceptionally potent weaponry. Don't leave without some choice armaments!

Report to Gloria Van Graff that all of the Legion troops are dead.

Assuming you kept it together and did as you were told, Gloria rewards you for your service with an impressive piece of armor, and the Quest concludes.

 **Van Graff Combat Armor**

 **Caps (1,000)**

 **NCR Reputation Gain!**

 **Freeside Reputation Gain!**

 **600 XP**

BITTER SPRINGS INFIRMARY BLUES

SUGGESTED EXPERIENCE

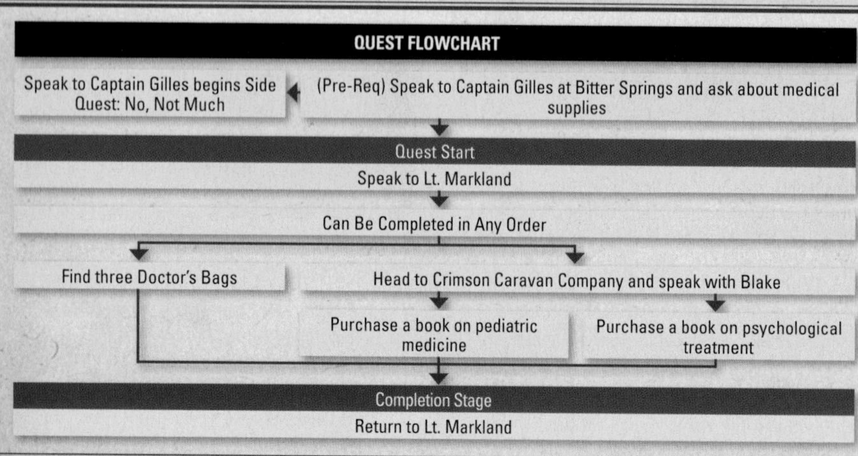

Supplies and Demands

1

Camp Bitter Springs **(1)** [3.08] is part military outpost, and part refugee camp. Captain Gilles **(2)** is overworked and overrun with those escaping the cold and bloody hand of the Legion. Meet her at the top of the camp, in her tent (or around the campfire), and ask what you can do to help. This begins the larger Side Quest: No, Not Much (see the nearby Note).

> **Note** The Bitter Springs Quests are interrelated. First, speak to Captain Gilles to begin Side Quest: No, Not Much. To complete the first part of that "overview" Side Quest, you must achieve the following:
>
> NEW CA. REPUBLIC Become Idolized with the NCR. Do this by completing Quests associated with this Faction (which are tagged throughout the guide).
>
> - Complete Side Quest: Bitter Springs Infirmary Blues (optional; this Quest).
> - Complete Side Quest: Flags of Our Foul-Ups.
> - Complete Side Quest: I Put a Spell on You.
> - Complete Side Quest: Restoring Hope.
> - Complete Side Quest: Climb Ev'ry Mountain (the part of the "overview" Quest).
>
> These five Quests are all parts of Side Quest: No, Not Much.

Talk to Lt. Markland about ways to help the medical situation at Bitter Springs.

Lieutenant Markland is treating the sick and infirm inside the doctor's tent **(3)** in the main cluster of tarp structures near the campfire. Head inside and meet him **(4)**. You can:

Ask for your wounds or radiation to be healed (for a price), and get some general background intel.

To begin this Quest, you need to tell Markland that Gilles has sent you to talk about getting medical aid for the camp. Markland is desperate for three Doctor's Bags, but what he really needs are two medical textbooks. He reckons Caravan Companies might be the best place to look for such tomes. The following tasks can be attempted in any order.

Find Lt. Markland a book on psychological treatment.

Find a book on pediatric medicine for Lt. Markland.

Bring Lt. Markland three Doctor's Bags.

Task #1: Excess Baggage

Assuming you aren't carrying three Doctor's Bags, Markland's information proves useful, and the New Vegas Medical Clinic [2.10] is the first stop to try to find Doctor's Bags. The building isn't particularly welcoming **(5)**, but pass the clinic guard, enter the structure, and locate Doctor Usanagi behind the counter **(6)**. You can:

Ignore the Quest and purchase Implants (nine, incredibly expensive Implant perks can be placed inside you, depending on your Endurance and funds), or receive healing.

Better yet, check her inventory: there's a Doctor's Bag (usually for around 60 Caps, so bring money or Trade with her).

Doctor's Bag

Task #1 (continued): Extra Baggage

Assuming you need another two Doctor's Bags, exit the clinic, and simply cross the street to the Crimson Caravan Company compound [2.09]. Once behind the walls, walk west along the road to a small shanty kiosk on your right **(7)**. Here you'll meet Blake **(8)**, one of the Crimson Caravan traders. You can:

Ask him about his life story, and about the Crimson Caravan Company itself.

Better yet, begin to Trade with Blake, and shuffle through his inventory. Bingo! There should be two Doctor's Bags for sale. Pay the man his 120 Caps!

Doctor's Bag (2)

Task #2: Blake's Books

Your interaction with Blake over at the Crimson Caravan Company kiosk doesn't end there, either: Also in his inventory are the two books Markland wants: "Stress and the Modern Refugee: A Primer," and "Tiny, Tiny Babies: All You Need to Know About Pediatric Medicine." Each costs 22 Caps. Pay Blake, say your farewells, and return to Camp Bitter Springs.

> **Note** You can't Pickpocket or kill Blake for these items.

Stress and the Modern Refugee: A Primer

Tiny, Tiny Babies: All You Need to Know About Pediatric Medicine

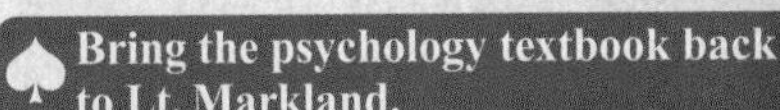

Bring the psychology textbook back to Lt. Markland.

Bring the pediatric medicine book back to Lt. Markland.

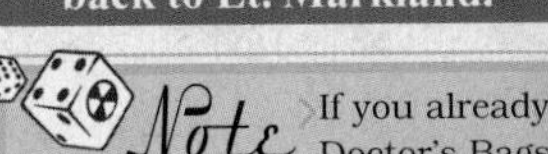

> **Note** If you already have Doctor's Bags in your inventory, you're in luck! It doesn't matter where you found them; just give them to Markland. The previous information simply provides an optimal path to quickly obtaining three bags.

> **Note** If Arcade is with you then the medical books are not needed. Arcade can help teach Lt. Markland more about medicine.

Special Delivery for Lt. Markland

Head back to the infirmary tent, and speak with Lieutenant Markland again. Hand over the three Doctor's Bags. Then hand over both books, and make the man's day.

NCR Fame Gained!

Markland is thrilled at the surplus of supplies he now has. Naturally, you can take advantage of this slip-up:

Ask for a little Medicine. You're given some Chems for your troubles.

Ask for a little Medicine, and your expenses to be covered. You're given Chems and Caps to cover your costs. Markland isn't quite as thrilled as he was to know you. But then, you're not quite as poor as you were, either.

Stimpaks, Rad-Xs, RadAways

Caps (100+40)

200 XP

BLEED ME DRY

SUGGESTED EXPERIENCE

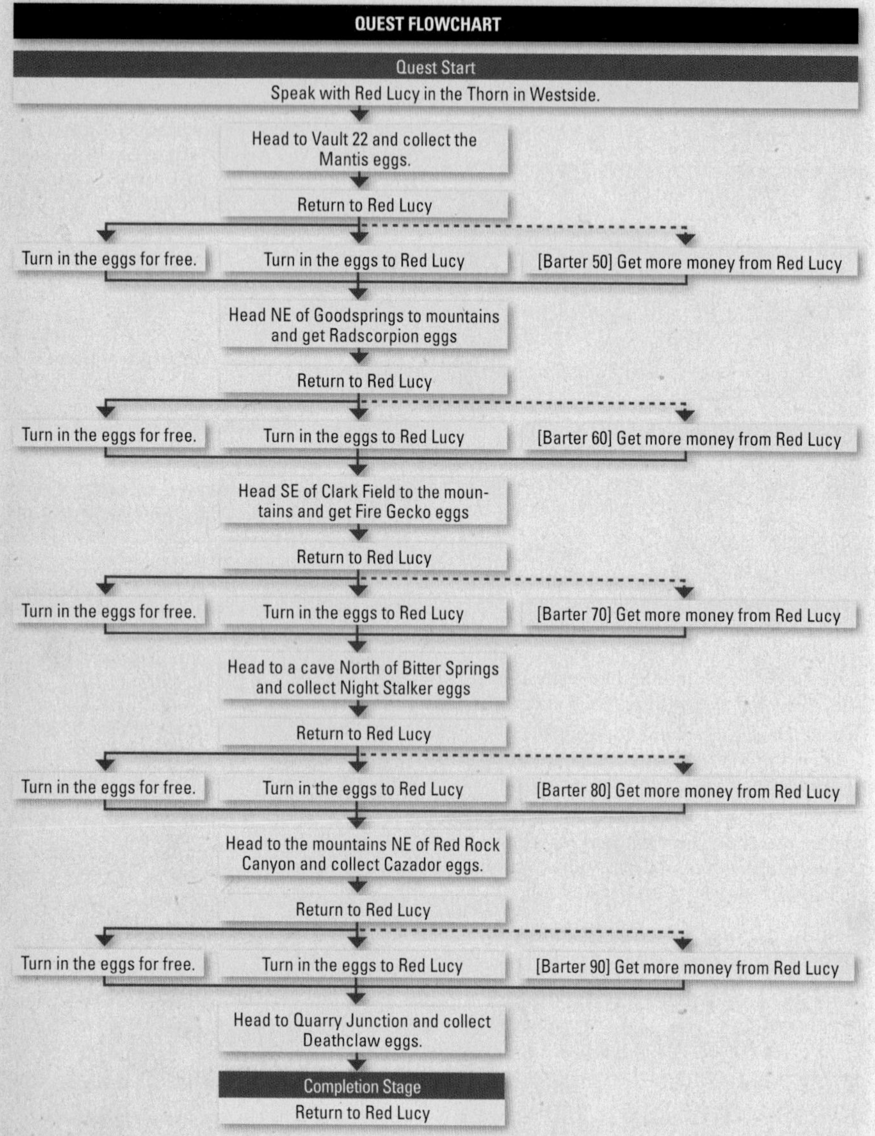

Seeing Red

1

2

The secret underground fighting arena known as Thorn [2.04] should be top of the list for places to visit on the Westside of New Vegas. Locate the sign **(1)**, and descend into the giant effluent chamber where citizens mill about, waiting for the next battle. Locate and speak to Red Lucy **(2)**, a comely sort who's usually waiting on one of the pit-side platforms. Speak to her about this operation, and be sure to place a bet on a forthcoming bout. Watch the bloodshed unfold (find more information about these fights in the Tour Chapter), and then return to speak to Red Lucy again, and ask how she trains the creatures.

She isn't telling, but does divulge how she finds the critters: she employs hunters. Ask if you can help The Thorn. Prove your worth, and Red Lucy shall reward your service! The Thorn needs newborn specimens; find the eggs, and expect greater tasks to come.

Red Lucy needs Giant Mantis' eggs. It's faster to gather them at a breeding ground, like Vault 22.

Hunt #1: A Dozen Giant Mantis' Eggs

3

4

Travel to the leafy entrance to Vault 22 [1.09]. To find the Mantis Eggs, you need to enter the Vault **(3)**. Beware of Spore Plants, Giant Mantises, and worse. Enter, open the door directly ahead of you, and run down the stairs. You can:

Repair the elevator in front of you (recommended).

Or leave the elevator, and descend through Oxygen Production, Food Production, and finally to the Common Areas. From there, take the elevator to the Fifth Level—Pest Control.

Once in Pest Control, step out of the elevator, and make a left at the four-way junction. Step over the plants and ascend the steps to a doorway on your right, which leads to a tree and vine-filled laboratory, and an easy-to-miss door on the left wall. Open the Door to Vault 22—Food Production. You appear in a rocky tunnel. At the first split in the tunnel, don't turn, but walk forward and pry open the eggs from the cluster **(4)**, and trek back out of the Vault.

Pile of Giant Mantis Eggs

While you're here, you might as well locate the HEPA Filters that the Brotherhood of Steel desperately needs during Side Quest: Still in the Dark.

I've got the Giant Mantis eggs that Red Lucy wants for The Thorn. I should return to her for my reward.

Back at The Thorn, tell Red Lucy you've found the eggs. She's impressed, and gives you some compensation. You can:

Tell her you deserve a bigger reward. She gives you extra Caps.

Agree that the Caps she's given you are sufficient.

Refuse to accept the Caps, and give her the eggs for free.

Caps (200 or 300)

100 XP

Whatever you choose, you can prepare for the next hunt.

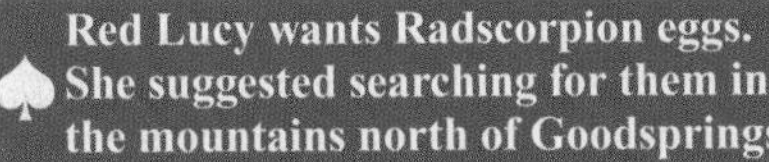

Red Lucy wants Radscorpion eggs. She suggested searching for them in the mountains north of Goodsprings.

Hunt #2: A Dozen Radscorpion Eggs

5

6

Head to the gulch just beyond the Goodsprings Cemetery [4.06] and prepare to repel the advancing Giant Radscorpions **(5)**. Prepare to attack at least six, before fleeing or resting. But don't leave the area until you've scooped the eggs from the nest near a small rocky outcrop **(6)**.

Pile of Radscorpion Eggs

I've got the Radscorpion eggs that Red Lucy wants for The Thorn. I should return to her for my reward.

Back at The Thorn, inform Red Lucy. She rewards you (the prizes include a Hunting Rifle and some .308 Ammo), and you have the same three choices:

Tell her you were planning to help snag deadlier creatures, but not without a raise. She gives you extra Caps.

Agree that the Caps she's given you are sufficient and ask about another hunt.

Refuse to accept the Caps, and give her the eggs for free. Ask for another hunt.

Caps (300 or 400)

Hunting Rifle and Ammo

150 XP

Red Lucy has asked me to find Fire Gecko eggs. She thinks I might find some near the Ireteba Peaks.

Hunt #3: A Dozen Fire Gecko Eggs

7

8

Travel to the Ireteba Peaks. In this remote and rugged wilderness, you're looking for the remote (and unmarked) Bootjack Cavern [6.S10], which is on the other side of the hill from Lucky Jim Mine [6.09]. Expect a small fracas before you enter, and additional combat as you head toward the northeastern dead-end passage **(7)**. Among the dead prospectors and bones is this egg cluster **(8)**. Claim your prize.

Pile of Fire Gecko Eggs

I've got the Fire Gecko eggs that Red Lucy wants for The Thorn. I should return to her for my reward.

Return to Red Lucy. She gives you some Caps, and you're permitted the following similar choices:

Tell her that her best hunter deserves the best rewards. She gives you extra Caps.

Agree that the Caps she's given you are sufficient and ask about another hunt.

Refuse to accept the Caps, and give her the eggs for free. Another hunt is available.

Caps (500 or 700)

200 XP

The elite hunters for The Thorn are looking for Nightstalker eggs. Red Lucy asked me to look at a cave near Bitter Springs.

Hunt #4: A Dozen Nightstalker Eggs

9

10

Bitter Springs [3.08] is the nearest habitable settlement to the Nightstalker cave (which was also used by the Great Khans as a Supply Cave), nestled in the red rocky terrain above the refugee camp. Locate the cave mouth and enter the gloom, attacking these hellish hounds as adeptly as you can **(9)**. Better yet, employ a Stealth Boy. Quickly pick the eggs along a far wall of the initial chamber **(10)**.

Pile of Nightstalker Eggs

I have bested the Nightstalkers at the Bitter Springs lair and acquired their eggs. Red Lucy needs to know about my feat.

Red Lucy is extremely impressed, and hands over a good number of Caps, as well as another gun and ammo. You can:

Tell her your reward should match your effort. She gives you extra Caps.

Agree that the Caps she's given you are sufficient and ask about another hunt.

Refuse to accept the Caps, and give her the eggs for free. Question her about another hunt.

Caps (700 or 1,000)

Hunting Revolver and Ammo

300 XP

The elite hunters of The Thorn are now in search of Cazador eggs. Red Lucy asked me to look for them near Red Rocks.

Hunt #5: A Dozen Cazador Eggs

11

12

Journey to Ranger Station Foxtrot [1.12] high in the northwest mountains, and venture farther up the gully to face down these deadly giant insects **(11)**. The egg cluster **(12)** is close to the ravine wall.

Pile of Cazador Eggs

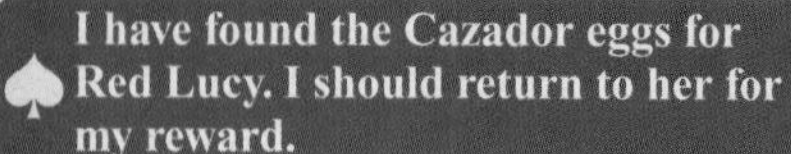

I have found the Cazador eggs for Red Lucy. I should return to her for my reward.

Red Lucy graciously takes the eggs from you, and hands over a good number of Caps. You can:

BARTER 90 Tell her there's nothing worse than Cazadores in the Wasteland. She gives you extra Caps.

Agree that the Caps she's given you are sufficient and ask about another hunt.

Refuse to accept the Caps, and give her the eggs for free. Question her about a final, fabled hunt.

Caps (1,000 or 1,500)

400 XP

Red Lucy has given me the most dangerous task a hunter could face. I'm to find Deathclaw eggs and bring them to her.

Hunt #6: A Dozen Deathclaw Eggs

13

Save your progress before you enter Quarry Junction [4.04], close to Sloan [4.08], and prepare for the most frightening hunt of all! You must cross the Deathclaw lair, ideally without summoning these clawing beasts to slaughter you **(13)**, and discover this rocky area. Study this picture carefully **(14)**; the eggs are in the dip to the right. Scrape away the bones, and bag yourself the ultimate incubated prize.

14

Tip Before entering Quarry Junction [4.04], you are wise to visit Sloan [4.08] and speak with Chomps Lewis to begin Free Quest: Claws Out; and Jas Wilkins to begin Free Quest: You Gotta Break Out a Few Eggs. You'll receive Stimpaks from Chomps, and should save a Deathclaw Egg for Jas, so she can give you the Recipe for the fabled Rose's Deathclaw Omelet. Consult the Tour section on Sloan for more information.

SNEAK By far the safest idea is to Sneak along the quarry, with a Stealth Boy activated (and more to use) unless you're extremely proficient in combat, have a Follower, can attack from long range and short, and have enough Stimpaks to heal an army!

Pile of Deathclaw Eggs

I've got the Deathclaw eggs for Red Lucy. I should return and let her know of my great deed.

Red Lucy hands over a spectacular Hunting Shotgun (with 12ga Ammo), and deems you the greatest hunter The Thorn has ever seen! You can:

Take the colossal haul of Caps she gives you. The Quest ends.

Caps (2,500)

Hunting Shotgun: Dinner Bell and Ammo

500 XP

I've become the greatest hunter that The Thorn has ever seen.

Hunt #	XP	Reward	Bartered Reward
1. Mantis Eggs	100	200	300
2. Radscorpion Eggs	150	300	400
3. Fire Gecko Eggs	200	500	700
4. Nightstalker Eggs	300	700	1,000
5. Cazador Eggs	400	1,000	1,500
6. Deathclaw Eggs	500	2,500	N/A
Totals	1,650	5,200	6,400

Hunt #7: Over Easy [Optional]

15

Red Lucy is impressed by your talents. And you've done enough for her to last many lifetimes. But she doesn't want you to leave and never return. Although you can say goodbye, you can also agree to head off somewhere a little more private. She agrees that she wants to know you deeper.... You'll find out exactly what that entails **(15)** when you accompany her to her room.

BOOTED

SUGGESTED EXPERIENCE

QUEST FLOWCHART

Quest Start

Speak with Boxcars in the Nipton General Store

↓

Travel to the Legion Raid camp

↓

Completion Stage

Save captured Powder Gangers

Main Factions

Putting Powder Gangers in Their Place

1

2

The Trading Post of Nipton [4.30] has recently succumbed to a Powder Ganger attack, and then the march of the Legion, whose savagery is visible from miles around. Enter the town, passing the numerous Gangers tied up to telephone poles, and move toward the general store near the Trading Post sign **(1)**. Inside is Boxcars **(2)**, the only Powder Ganger not baking on a cross or burning on a tire pile. Boxcars has a certain panache to his insults. Assuming you haven't shot him for his unpleasantness, you'll discover he's been crippled.

Give him a Med-X to continue the conversation. You won't get thanked.

Or save your Chems, and simply travel to the location without Boxcars' information.

Boxcars tells you about the town lottery; instigated after the Legion surrounded the settlement and gave the Powder Gangers a taste of brutality. Ask about some of the people being enslaved, and Boxcars mentions some Gangers were kidnapped and moved eastward. Agree to help them. Not that Boxcar cares.

Rescue the captives.

Caution Helping save a couple of criminal Powder Gangers is fine if you're feeling independent or want to help the NCR. However, if you plan to liaise with the Legion, rethink attacking their Raid Camp.

Caution Don't tread on the Bear! Beware the wrath of Caesar! If you've angered the NCR, or Caesar's Legion, you are likely to be attacked by assassination squads in the general vicinity of Nipton. And if you've annoyed both of these Factions (you have a low Reputation with them), expect attacks from both sides, and a large number of foes out for your blood!

3

4

The remaining survivors of the Nipton massacre are tied up and facing a grim future over at the Legion Raid Camp [5.29], which is more to the northeast than Boxcars described. When you reach the camp **(3)** consisting of a campfire, military tent, and some Legion camping structures, you can formulate a plan to rescue these captives:

You can speak to the Legion's leader in this small camp—the Legion Decanus—but he doesn't say much.

Sneak Attacks are a great way to begin the battle. Try crouching behind a tent and tagging Decanus with a Sniper Rifle, then dealing with the Recruits that charge in.

As freeing the hostages turns the Legion hostile, your only other course of action is to massacre the Recruits and Decanus with the same uncaring attitude they had for Nipton's population **(4)**. Grab any items from the Legion corpses if you wish (their outfits are helpful if you want to try disguising yourself as one of them).

Complete the Quest by untying the Powder Gangers around the campfire. Fortunately, you don't need to speak to Boxcars again.

Finally, you can wait for an NCR patrol to come across the camp and start a firefight. During the ruckus you can sneak in and untie the Powder Gangers with little risk.

Powder Ganger Fame Gained!

Take advantage of your surroundings; the camp's Footlockers can be ransacked for Legion weapons and other goods.

Caesar's Legion Infamy Gained!

100 XP

MAIN QUEST INTERSECTION

BOULDER CITY SHOWDOWN

SUGGESTED EXPERIENCE

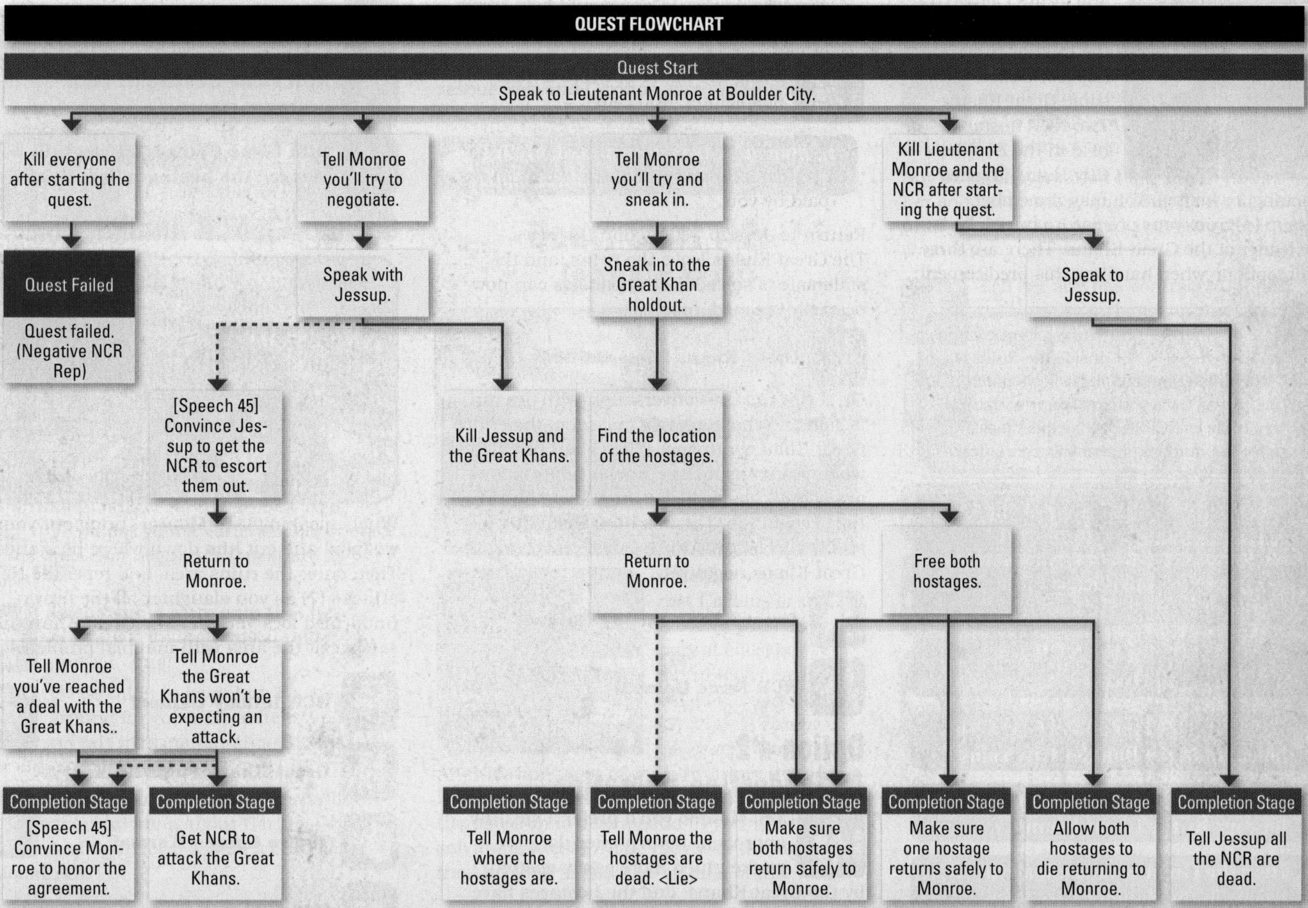

QUEST FLOWCHART

Quest Start
Speak to Lieutenant Monroe at Boulder City.

- Kill everyone after starting the quest.
  - **Quest Failed** — Quest failed. (Negative NCR Rep)
- Tell Monroe you'll try to negotiate.
  - Speak with Jessup.
    - (dashed) [Speech 45] Convince Jessup to get the NCR to escort them out.
      - Return to Monroe.
        - Tell Monroe you've reached a deal with the Great Khans..
          - **Completion Stage** — [Speech 45] Convince Monroe to honor the agreement.
        - Tell Monroe the Great Khans won't be expecting an attack.
          - **Completion Stage** — Get NCR to attack the Great Khans.
          - (dashed) **Completion Stage** — [Speech 45] Convince Monroe to honor the agreement.
    - Kill Jessup and the Great Khans.
- Tell Monroe you'll try and sneak in.
  - Sneak in to the Great Khan holdout.
    - Find the location of the hostages.
      - Return to Monroe.
        - (dashed) **Completion Stage** — Tell Monroe the hostages are dead. <Lie>
        - **Completion Stage** — Make sure both hostages return safely to Monroe.
      - Free both hostages.
        - **Completion Stage** — Make sure both hostages return safely to Monroe.
        - **Completion Stage** — Make sure one hostage returns safely to Monroe.
        - **Completion Stage** — Allow both hostages to die returning to Monroe.
- Kill Lieutenant Monroe and the NCR after starting the quest.
  - Speak to Jessup.
    - **Completion Stage** — Tell Jessup all the NCR are dead.

Completion Stage — Tell Monroe where the hostages are.

[2D.08]. Access the building **(1)**, which consists of an office, workshop, and large warehouse where Michael **(2)** crafts and repairs many of the signs you've seen on The Strip. You may also meet his assistant Kate. Clad in a Vault 21 Jumpsuit, Michael's startled and thinks you're here to request more billboards for Mr. House. You can:

Tell the truth, and begin this Quest.

Or lie, and Michael begins to sweat, apologizing for the late delivery of the billboards you know nothing about.

Retort that Mr. House doesn't appreciate failure, although you could be "persuaded" not to tell him. Michael asks what it would take.

Reply "300 Caps." You have one more chance to tell him you're kidding, or he hands the funds over, and is done dealing with you. Unfortunately, once you've shaken Michael down, he's unwilling to talk about his feelings, and the Quest cannot be started.

Caps (300)

Look at the spare parts and assembly tools and tell him Mr. House won't buy his excuses.

Or at any point, you can tell Michael to relax, you're a kidder.

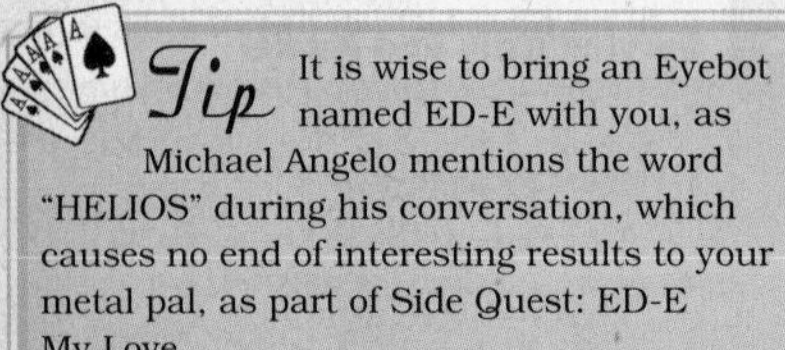
Tip It is wise to bring an Eyebot named ED-E with you, as Michael Angelo mentions the word "HELIOS" during his conversation, which causes no end of interesting results to your metal pal, as part of Side Quest: ED-E My Love.

Continue to steer the conversation toward Michael's background. He grew up in Vault 21, and he's increasingly frightened by the outside world, and longs for safe, warm corridors. This fear seems to be draining Michael of his creativity. But he needs you to keep quiet about it, as this information wouldn't be good for business. You can:

Diagnose him with clear symptoms of acute agoraphobia.

Ask about returning to Vault 21.

Or lie and laugh at his condition. Any of these three choices continues the conversation until Michael realizes he can bring the outside in. He produces a camera, and asks if you'd mind taking some photographs of inspiring landmarks. Agree to begin this Quest.

Codac R9000

Camera Film (24)

Michael Angelo wants pictures of famous signs around New Vegas.

Take a picture of the Bison Steve sign.

Take a picture of Novac's Dinosaur Thermometer.

Take a picture of the Sunset Sarsaparilla Headquarters Bottle sign.

Take a picture of the HELIOS One sign.

Take a picture of the McCarran Airfield sign.

Sights, Camera, Action!

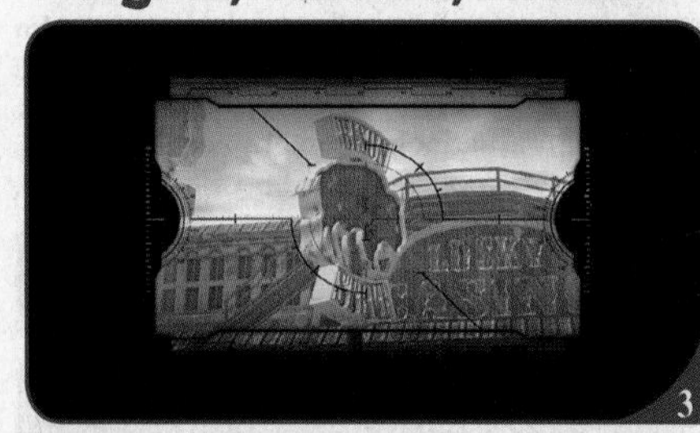
3

Take the camera, and remember you have 24 chances to take five good pictures, which should be more than sufficient. However, if you use up all 24 chances just ask Michael Angelo for more film. You can visit the following Mojave Wasteland landmarks in any order (they are presented alphabetically). On each occasion, stand so you have a good view of the sign. Optionally check for the sign in the camera's viewfinder **(3)**, and snap away (use "aim" as the viewfinder, and "shoot" to take the picture). Continue until the Quest Objective updates. The Cap value is the amount Michael awards you when you return (which you can do once all photos are done, or at any time during your photography trip).

The Bison Steve Sign

This is located in the town of Primm [4.17].

Dinky, the Dinosaur Thermometer

Find Dinky over at the town of Novac [5.18].

The HELIOS One Sign

As expected, this is at the front of the HELIOS One building [5.13].

The McCarran Airfield Sign

The sign is missing an "R," but it's still inspirational. Take at Camp McCarran [2.19].

The Sunset Sarsaparilla Headquarters Bottle

The big bottle of Sarsaparilla is the entrance to the company headquarters [2.17].

Picture #	Cap Payment
First	100
Second	125
Third	150
Fourth	175
Fifth	200
Completion	500

Return to Michael Angelo for your reward.

Back at his workshop, Michael is thrilled with your work, and awards you appropriately with some of the easiest Caps you've ever made!

500 XP

CLIMB EV'RY MOUNTAIN

SUGGESTED EXPERIENCE

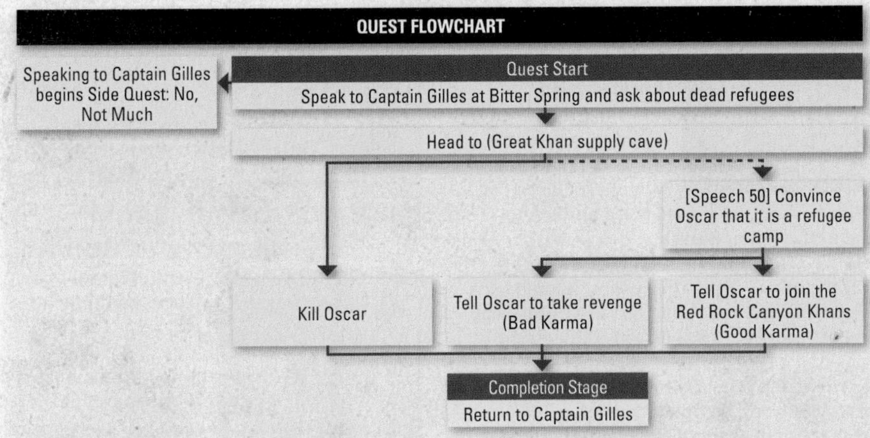

Beware the Moon

Camp Bitter Springs **(1)** [3.08] is in danger of being overrun by refugees trekking away from the Faction fighting across the Wasteland. Captain Gilles **(2)** is at her wit's end, and could do with some help from a Lone Wanderer. Greet her at the higher end of the camp, in her command tent area, and ask what you can do to help. This begins the larger Side Quest: No, Not Much (see the nearby Note). Continue the chat to begin an additional portion of the larger Quest (this one) by asking about the dead refugees. You're tasked with investigating nighttime raids on the camp.

The Bitter Springs Quests are interrelated. First, speak to Captain Gilles to begin Side Quest: No, Not Much. To complete the first part of that "overview" Side Quest, you must achieve the following:

Become Idolized with the NCR. Achieve this by completing Quests associated with this Faction (which are tagged throughout the guide).

Complete Side Quest: Bitter Springs Infirmary Blues (optional).

Complete Side Quest: Flags of Our Foul-Ups.

Complete Side Quest: I Put a Spell on You.

Complete Side Quest: Restoring Hope.

Complete Side Quest: Climb Ev'ry Mountain (this Quest; the second part of the "overview" Quest).

These five Quests are all parts of Side Quest: No, Not Much.

Find the source of the attacks on Bitter Springs.

Last of the Flails of God

After some difficult mountain-climbing, reach the farthest of the three caves in the sandstone mountains northwest of camp. The view from up here is spectacular **(3)**, but it's the cave in the rock wall behind you that needs investigating. Once inside the gloomy cavern, you're stopped only a few paces in by a gruff old coot clad in filthy Great Khan attire. This is Oscar Velasco **(4)**, and he's the nighttime raiding culprit. Speak to him next to his hanging meats, and confirm his guilt. You can:

- Ask him about the massacre. He counters with the fact that the camp was built on the blood of his people, an inconvenient fact forgotten by the NCR.
- Ask him about his people. He was part of a band of brothers known as the Flails of God. The NCR massacred everyone, including the women and children from his clan.

Tell him those in Camp Bitter Springs aren't responsible for the NCR atrocities. He agrees, but what else can he do?

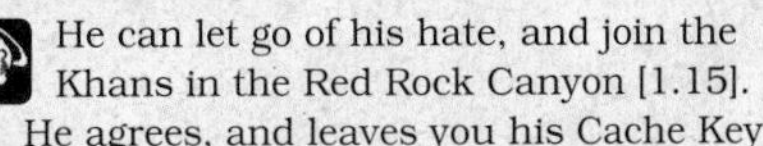

He can let go of his hate, and join the Khans in the Red Rock Canyon [1.15]. He agrees, and leaves you his Cache Key.

Great Khans Supply Cache Key

He can take revenge on those responsible and attack Camp McCarran [2.19]. He agrees, and sets off to an almost certain death. You're left without a key.

- Or you can finish the conversation quickly, and ignore him. This isn't wise, as he attacks if you try and open his Supply Cache gate.

The only other option is to kill Oscar Velasco, if your Speech skill is lacking.

> **Note** Assuming Oscar makes it back, you can run into him at Red Rock Canyon later in your adventure. Or, if you send him to Camp McCarran, the next time you're there, you'll witness his last (and pointless) stand.

Oscar's loot is behind a locked gate. You can:

Use the Great Khan's Supply Cache Key you were given, or looted from Oscar's corpse.

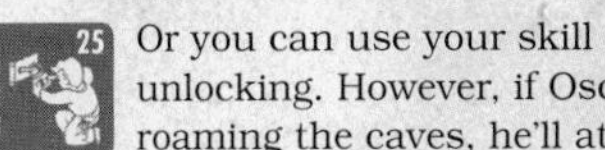

Or you can use your skill at unlocking. However, if Oscar is still roaming the caves, he'll attack you with Grenades and other deadly ordnance.

Behind the gate is a metal shelf **(5)** containing various items. Top of the list is the Great Khan Supply Cache. Grab it, and exit this gloomy place.

Great Khans Supply Cache

Tell Captain Gilles about Oscar Velasco.

Carefully retrace your steps, until you see Camp Bitter Springs below **(6)**. Return to Captain Gilles, and tell her that you've dealt with the attacks on the camp. They won't be a problem any more. Tell her there was a Great Khan raider up there. Quiz her further about the NCR massacre for her side of the story.

> **Note** Give Captain Gilles the Great Khan Supply Cache as part of the completion of Side Quest: No, Not Much. Refer to that Quest for further information.

NCR Fame Gained!

100 XP

COLD, COLD HEART

SUGGESTED EXPERIENCE

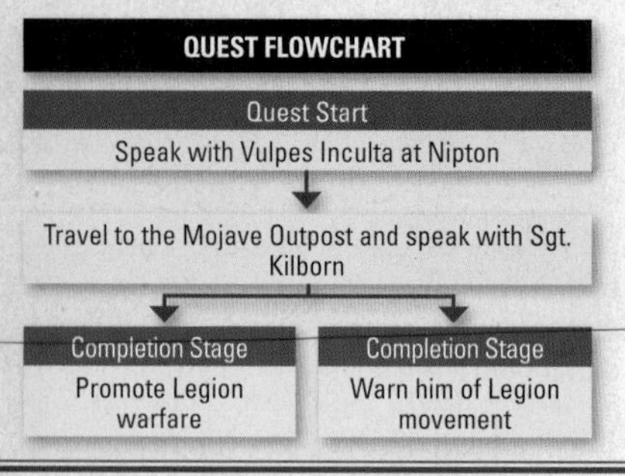

A Prelude to the Profligates

The town of Nipton, originally overrun by Powder Gangers, is now an example to the rest of the Mojave Wasteland of the

destructive power and horrific brutality of the Legion. Tire fires burn everywhere, and any remaining Powder Gangers have been tied to crucifixes fashioned from telephone poles and left to bake in the desert sun.

Move into Nipton and investigate the Town Hall **(1)**, toward the double doors. An imposing member of the Legion marches down the steps to meet you, clad in red armor and wearing some kind of dog-skinned helm. This is Vulpes Inculta **(2)**, and he tells you not to worry; you won't be nailed to a cross like the rest of these degenerates. If you admire his work in Nipton, you gain Legion fame.

Caesar's Legion Fame Gained!

Inculta wants you to memorize the fate of Nipton, then move west to the Mojave Outpost and let "the Profligates" know "the little sermon" he prepared here. You may already have come from here, investigating these occurrences for the NCR Ranger named Ghost (Side Quest: Keep Your Eyes on the Prize). You can continue the conversation at length, asking him about Caesar, before you're waved away to teach what you've learned here. "There will be more lessons in the days ahead," Inculta tells you, ominously.

Spread word of Legion atrocities.

Leave this unhappy place, and trek toward the NCR's Mojave Outpost [4.27] up the hill of rusting traffic, passing under the two massive metal statues **(3)**, and search out Sergeant Kilborn **(4)**. It is a simple matter to relay Inculta's warnings, although how you inform Kilborn can vary:

- You can warn him of the Legion's movement in and around Nipton.
- Or you can promote the Legion's aggressive tactics to the east. This option gains Legion fame but either option concludes this Quest.

Caesar's Legion Fame Gained!

You told the NCR about Vulpes attack at Nipton.

150 XP

COME FLY WITH ME

SUGGESTED EXPERIENCE

See flowchart on the following page

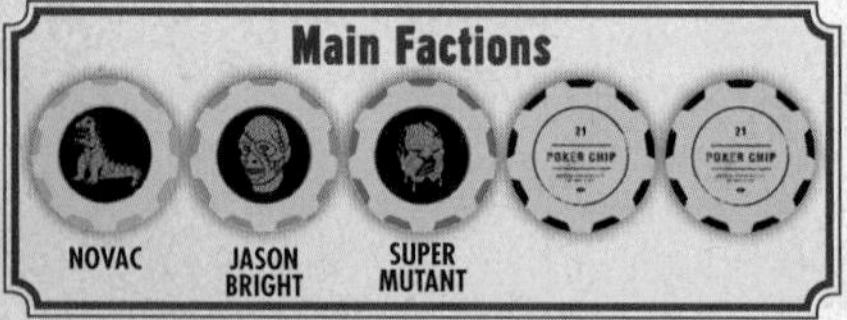

Novac's Ghoul Problem

The town of Novac [5.18] has been terrorized by Ghoul encroachments over the past few months, and the situation is now so bad that two snipers (Manny Vargas and Boone) take turns in the mouth of Dinky the Dinosaur **(1)** to guard the settlement from these Feral invaders. You can ask many of the townsfolk about this problem, but two of them give the most information. The first is Manny Vargas **(2)**.

During your search for the man with the checkered coat, in Main Quest: They Went That-A-Way, Manny requests your help regarding this issue. Indeed, if you don't have the necessary sweet-talking skills, you may have to finish this Quest before Manny reveals a clue to the man's whereabouts. It seems that Novac trades in junk, which is scavenged up the road at an old rocket test site. But a bunch of Ghouls showed up and took over. You need to remove the Ghouls, and Manny doesn't care how you do it.

Another Novac dweller who knows about the Ghouls lives in a tiny shack on the outskirts of town **(3)**. Enter the shack, negotiating the trinkets and *object d'art* strewn everywhere, and speak to No-bark Noonan **(4)**. You can threaten him, or listen to his particular brand of insane chatter, but to get some semblance of knowledge, ask if anything interesting is happening in the area. He mentions the Ghouls up by the old rocket factory, but tells you it's "sensationalist hooey." Ask who is actually at the factory, and No-bark replies that it's obviously commie ghosts "what don't know they're dead." At this point it might be wise to back slowly away, and begin this Quest.

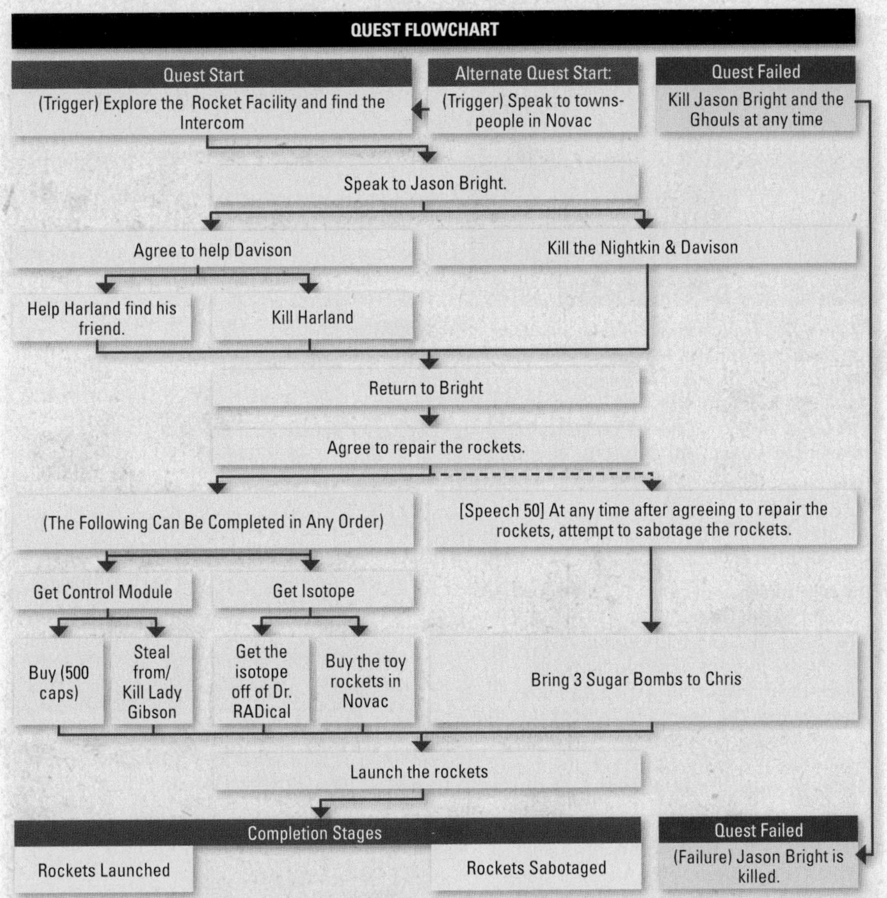

Head to the REPCONN facility west of Novac to investigate rumors of ghoul activity there.

Note: You don't need to speak to anyone in Novac to begin this quest. You can head to, or stumble upon the REPCONN Test Site without even heading into Novac. This Quest begins when you find the intercom inside the building, and speak with Jason Bright.

Some Bright Spark

5

The REPCONN Test Site [5.17] is almost due west of Novac, but the surrounding crags and mountains make a direct route almost impossible. Instead, find the remains of the road that begins close to the outskirts of Novac at a small electrical substation, and follow it through the rocky hillside. Ghoul bodies are strewn on the road, and live ones prowl and growl under a concrete bridge and security barrier. The road is littered with burned-out vehicles and partial defenses. Search these for items (especially the shelving and sandbags at the far end of the bridge area) before dropping down as the REPCONN facility looms into view ahead (and slightly right) of you **(5)**. Expect combat here with Ghouls in a variety of sickly hues.

Enter the facility and discover the source of the ghouls.

6

Climb either set of exterior steps up to a ruined concrete forecourt where more emaciated Ferals need executing (or Sneaking past). After dealing with them, move to the double doors and enter the facility. You're in the reception foyer **(6)** of the building, being verbally abused by a voice over a nearby intercom. You're instructed to get upstairs and speak with "Jason" before your unpleasant appearance causes vomiting. Agree to this, and step over the body of a dead Nightkin.

Launch Music signal found.

Head upstairs to meet with the owner of the voice from the intercom.

Speak with Jason Bright, the leader of the REPCONN ghouls.

7

8

The REPCONN Facility is a maze of rooms and corridors on two main levels. Wind through to a large warehouse area **(7)**, killing Feral Ghouls as you go. Climb the rusting catwalk steps in the warehouse that lead up and around to a covered walkway and a sealed door. Access the nearby intercom, where the same voice unlocks the door and says you he's watching you closely. Open the Door to REPCONN Research Labs.

The man on the intercom isn't actually a Ghoul; he's a scientist type called Chris Haversam. He's not as important as locating Jason Bright. Bright is checking the laboratory, so search the area until you find him **(8)**. He's certainly not Feral; in fact he's extremely civil, and tells you his true home awaits his people "in the Far Beyond." When he asks if you've come to help them "complete the Great Journey," you can:

- Attack any non-Feral Ghoul, Chris Haversam, or Jason Bright. If you do, this Quest automatically fails.
- Ask for copious information on the Great Journey, Far Beyond, and the human who let you in. You're given the Ghouls' cosmology, which makes interesting (if slightly deranged) listening.
- Tell Jason you're here because of the Feral Ghouls wandering into Novac. Jason hates to see "his flock" butchered, and had contained the Ghouls in the first floor of this facility. The demons must have let them out.

Naturally, ask for more information concerning these "demons." Jason seems to describe the method of attack by the Nightkin, whose incursions have apparently stopped "the Great Journey." Ask about the "raving" demon. This was a speech by their leader, warning the Ghouls to stay away. You're asked to help. To continue this Quest, agree to head underground and face these "demons." You're given a key to unlock the basement, which is otherwise inaccessible. Return to the large warehouse, drop down to the ground floor, and open the basement door.

REPCONN Basement Key

(Optional) Find the leader of the "demons" and speak with him.

Get rid of the Nightkin in the basement.

Battle in the Basement

Now you're in the REPCONN Basement, and you have a number of ways to help the Ghouls. Choose the plan you're most comfortable with:

Plan 1, Part 1: Antler Sings for Stealth Boys

9

Head south along the main corridor until you reach a right corridor junction, head down the few steps, and reach a door leading to a small storage room. This has been commandeered by a hulking Nightkin called Davison **(9)**. Taking orders, it appears, from a Brahmin skull called "Antler," Davison almost attacks, but (if you haven't killed any of his Nightkin, and optionally used a Stealth Boy to reach him) he instead asks what you're doing here. You can:

Find out more about Davison's particular type of psychosis.

Or tell him you're here on behalf of the Ghouls upstairs. He tells you that Antler has brought the Nightkin here to look for something. Tell him you can help.

Davison informs you that there's a shipping invoice for "hundreds" of Stealth Boys, apparently sent here. The Nightkin have searched everywhere for them—everywhere except one room. That room contains a "crack shot" Ghoul who sets traps and kills his kin. Agree to find the Stealth Boy stockpile as long as Davison and his Nightkin leave the place. "Antler" agrees, and Davison gives you a key.

 **Davison's Key**

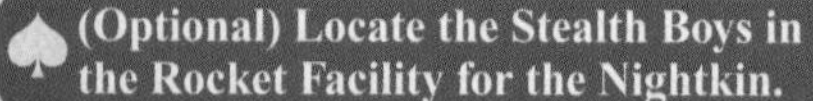
(Optional) Locate the Stealth Boys in the Rocket Facility for the Nightkin.

You can also choose to kill Davison (and all the Nightkin) at any point. Tips for dealing with Nightkin are listed under Plan 2.

Caution Watch out for Antler! It is an incredibly bad idea to touch the Brahmin skull Davison is taking orders from; picking up Antler or knocking it infuriates Davison, so prepare to fight him if this happens.

Plan 1, Part 2: Hardcore Harland

10

Davison's Key (which you'll find on his body if you decide to kill him instead) opens the door at the southern end of the first corridor, by the dead Nightkin and scattered barrels. It leads to a large, two-floor storage chamber with a Ghoul sniper, Harland **(10)**. He notices you're not 10-foot tall and blue, and holds his fire. You can:

Ask how he got trapped here, and about the Stealth Boys.

Tell him that he doesn't look like the other Ghouls from Bright's group. Then ask how you can help him get out of this room. He informs you that he had a friend who fled in the wrong direction; farther into the basement. She's probably dead, but Harland isn't leaving until he knows for sure. Agree to find this friend to begin Plan 1, Part 3.

Or, you can kill Harland, or advance into the room until Harland becomes hostile. This begins Plan 1, Part 4.

(Optional) Find Harland's friend, who has been imprisoned by the Nightkin.

Plan 1, Part 3: Missing That Crooked Yellow Smile

11

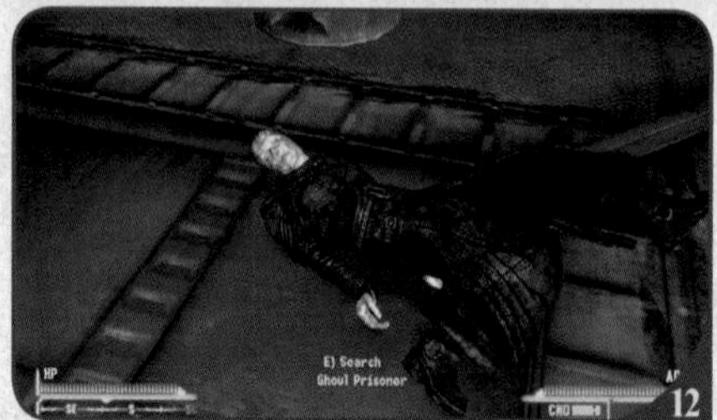

12

You must now (ideally using the map of the REPCONN Basement in the Tour Chapter) maneuver along the unsafe corridors to a two-floor control room with aggressive Nightkin, some armed with Grenade Launchers.

GUNS: You can attack normally, looking for the tell-tale signs of a shimmering Stealth Boy as Nightkin materialize in front of you. If you're swarmed, fire at their legs to slow down the charging Muties.

SNEAK: You can also try using the same Stealth technology as the Nightkin, and move about the basement without killing any, or as few Nightkin as possible.

Along the way, you'll encounter a Nightkin Jailer, and it's important to take the key from his corpse (or Pickpocket it) to allow access into the generator area **(11)**, which is accessed by a door. Once inside, turn left and open the door in the middle of the connecting wall. In both cases, you can:

LOCKPICK 25: Use Bobby Pins and a modicum of skill to open.

 **Use the Jail Key.**

 **Jail Key**

Once in the second generator room, the first barrel-storage room to your left (east) contains the remains of Harland's Ghoul-friend **(12)**.

(Optional) Return to Harland and let him know the bad news.

Inform Harland (back at his camping point) that his friend is dead. He'll miss her crooked, yellow smile. But with nothing left to worry about down here, he heads topside, allowing you to search this chamber thoroughly.

Plan 1, Part 4: Davison's Departure

13

Head up the stairs to the mezzanine level that Harland was viewing you from, and check the working terminal up here **(13)**. Read all three log entries: "Shipment Mistake?", "Workplace Misbehavior," and "Shipment Sent Back." The first and last missive provides all the evidence you need to let Davison know the Stealth Boys weren't even here to begin with.

 **Note: Stealth Boy Shipment Update**

Return to Antler and Davison, and tell him there are no stockpiles in this building. After some arguing with an inanimate skull, Davison agrees to take his remaining forces and locate the Stealth Boy shipment based on the updated information. The Nightkin threat in the basement has been removed!

Report to Jason Bright that the Nightkin are gone.

Tip Once Davison is hostile to your cause, every single Nightkin must be slain. There are around eight down here. Search the place thoroughly, until the Quest updates. Davison becomes violent if he hears you battling his brethren, so do your Nightkin killing away from his chamber, and close his door behind you.

Plan 2: Kill Everything That's Blue

14

For a more violent solution to the Nightkin menace, if don't care about a Ghoul's lost friend, enter the basement fully armed and ready to fight. When battling Nightkin **(14)**, remember these important points:

You can attack normally, looking for the tell-tale signs of a shimmering Stealth Boy as Nightkin materialize in front of you. If you're swarmed, fire at the legs to slow down the charging Muties.

You can also try using the same Stealth technology as the Nightkin, and move about the basement without killing any, or as few Nightkin as possible.

You don't even need to meet Harland using this plan, but if you do, his requests are irrelevant, as you aren't proving the location of Stealth Boys; you're eradicating the Nightkin menace.

Report to Jason Bright that the Nightkin are gone.

Preparation for the Great Journey

15

16

Ascend through the REPCONN building, all the way up to the Research Labs, and reconvene with Jason Bright. Inform him that the "demons" are gone. Bright is ecstatic and immediately makes plans to lead his flock through the basement to "the sacred site."

Head to the REPCONN basement and talk to Jason Bright about what comes next.

Backtrack down to the basement, and delve deeper into the twisting tunnels and connecting passageways, moving southward through the old sewer tunnels and radioactive storage rooms to an observation chamber overlooking a launch pad with a number of huge rockets sitting on it **(15)**. Speak with Jason once more. It seems the rockets that will carry Bright "to salvation" are missing vital components. You can speak to Jason one last time about Chris, or his Faction.

Speak to Chris Haversam about fixing the rockets.

Chris **(16)** doesn't like it, but he's been told to cooperate with you on the final tasks. Speak to him about this and you can:

- Ask how you can help. Haversam needs "shielded nuclear waste" for the fuel source, and thruster control systems for the missing computer parts. Set off to locate those at once, which can be done in any order.
- You can also ask what Haversam is doing here, and follow this line of questioning with dogged determination, asking why he isn't allowed on the launch pad, his humanity, past in Vault 34, lack of hair. And finally:

Reveal that Jason told you only Ghouls are making the trip. As expected with this kind of realization, Chris takes it badly. He instructs you to bring him three Sugar Bombs to sabotage the rockets, but only if you agree. You can change your mind at any time, too.

Find atomic fuel for the rockets.

Find parts to fix the rockets' thrust controllers.

(Optional) Bring 3 Sugar Bombs to Chris Haversam.

Rocket Part Reconnoiter

Reconnoiter #1: Control Modules

17

18

The first place to try looking for Thrust Control Modules is the Gibson Scrap Yard **(17)** [5.14]. Negotiate around the piles of junk to the garage itself, and find Old Lady Gibson **(18)**. You can ask her about other Quests and the HELIOS facility to the north. However:

You're mainly here for Thrust Control Modules. She has them, but they're 500 Caps.

You can figure out a trade with this attractive lady. She knows you don't mean it, but she gives you the modules for free, you flatterer!

Or Barter her down to 250 Caps.

Or use your charm to cut the price down to 250 Caps.

Or pay her the 500 Caps.

Or kill her and her dogs, and take the modules by force.

Or steal it when Gibson is away from the garage.

Thrust Control Modules

You can also ask whether they salvaged any containers of radioactive material from REPCONN. As it happens, they did, and it sat as a nightlight until it was recently purchased by a man in a radiation suit, who said he was heading over to Clark Field [6.07] to put the suit through its paces.

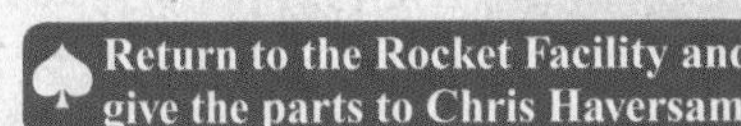
Return to the Rocket Facility and give the parts to Chris Haversam.

Reconnoiter #2A: Mr. RADical's Isotopes

19

20

If you spoke to Old Lady Gibson (or even if you didn't), you should follow up on her information regarding the man in the radiation suit. Head to Clark Field, and clamber through the ruins **(19)** until you spot a scavenger lying dead on the ground, clad in a radioactive suit **(20)**. Search the body (while watching your own RAD levels), and you find the Isotopes on his corpse, along with a Journal listing his (ultimately failed) suit tests.

Isotope-239 Igniting Agent

Mr. RADical's Journal

Reconnoiter #2B: Cliff Briscoe's Souvenirs

21

22

Another place to find the Isotopes you need is back in Novac. Visit the Dino Bite Gift Shop, and speak to Cliff Briscoe **(22)**. Ask what he sells, and deftly sidestep the issue of buying the T-rex figurines. Focus on asking him about the souvenir rockets; scale replicas of the ones in the REPCONN Facility. T hat makes them glow. Tell Briscoe you're here to purchase all his remaining rockets. He agrees, and offers to let you have the key to his storage room; take what you can carry for the cost of the key. You can:

Ask to see his inventory, and purchase the Storage Key for 75 Caps.

Tell him he has no other offers on the rockets. He offers you the key for 10 Caps.

Or pick the lock yourself, for free.

Or you can kill Briscoe and open the storage room, but that's a little excessive.

Inside the storage room **(21)**, there's a mass of rockets, as well as a huge stash in a crate. Simply grab the crate's worth; that's enough. Or take the individual ones, too.

Rocket Souvenir (49+)

Reconnoiter #2C: Schools of Learning

You don't need to hassle Cliff Briscoe for Rocket Souvenirs, because there are two other locations to scavenge them from. Visit the REPCONN Headquarters [2.35] and ransack the gift shop (and adjacent) area, gathering enough Rocket Souvenirs for your needs. There are also three Rocket Souvenirs inside the Elementary School inside Camp Searchlight [6.16]; but that isn't enough to complete this Objective.

Rocket Souvenir (15 + 3)

Return to the Rocket Facility and give the fuel to Chris Haversam.

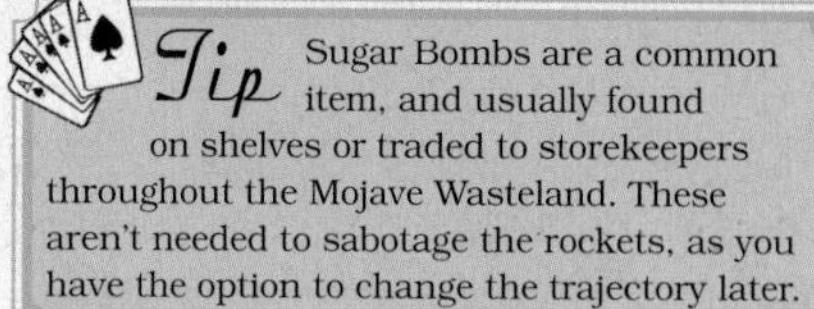

Tip Sugar Bombs are a common item, and usually found on shelves or traded to storekeepers throughout the Mojave Wasteland. These aren't needed to sabotage the rockets, as you have the option to change the trajectory later.

Bright Eyes, Burning Like Fire

Return to REPCONN, and return to the basement, and to the launch bay observation room. Speak with Haversam again. Hand him the Thrust Control Modules. Then hand him either the Rocket Souvenirs or the Isotope. Optionally hand over the Sugar Bombs if you definitely want to sabotage the rockets. With your part complete, head up to the viewing platform on the top floor of the facility, accessed via the Research Lab, where you first met Jason Bright.

Talk to Chris Haversam to begin preparations for the rocket launch.

Head up to the viewing platform and complete the launch sequence.

(Optional) Sabotage the rockets so that they crash on launch.

Once you have a commanding view of the launch pad dome, you have the sacred task of finishing the launch sequence. There are a variety of ways these rockets can launch.

The Rockets' Red Glare

23

Simply activate the launch button, ignoring the Navigation Console. The rockets launch successfully **(23)**.

Activate the Navigation Console, and examine the navigation data further, then alter the rockets' course so they arrive 12.5 percent closer to their destination. Now hit the Launch Button. The launch is a success **(25)**.

The Bombs Bursting in Air

24

Activate the Navigation Console, and set the rockets to crash into one another. Now hit the Launch Button. The launch is a failure **(24)**.

If Haversam found out he was human, and you convinced him that revenge was the only option (instead of telling him Jason Bright did it for Haversam's best interests), the launch is a failure no matter what you do **(24)**.

Novac Fame Gain!

XP 800 XP

XP 200 XP (for upgrading the trajectory)

Note Who's that wandering dejectedly around Novac? Why it's Haversam, who tells you what he's doing now that he has a new life, away from his old Ghoul-friends.

CRAZY, CRAZY, CRAZY

SUGGESTED EXPERIENCE

QUEST FLOWCHART

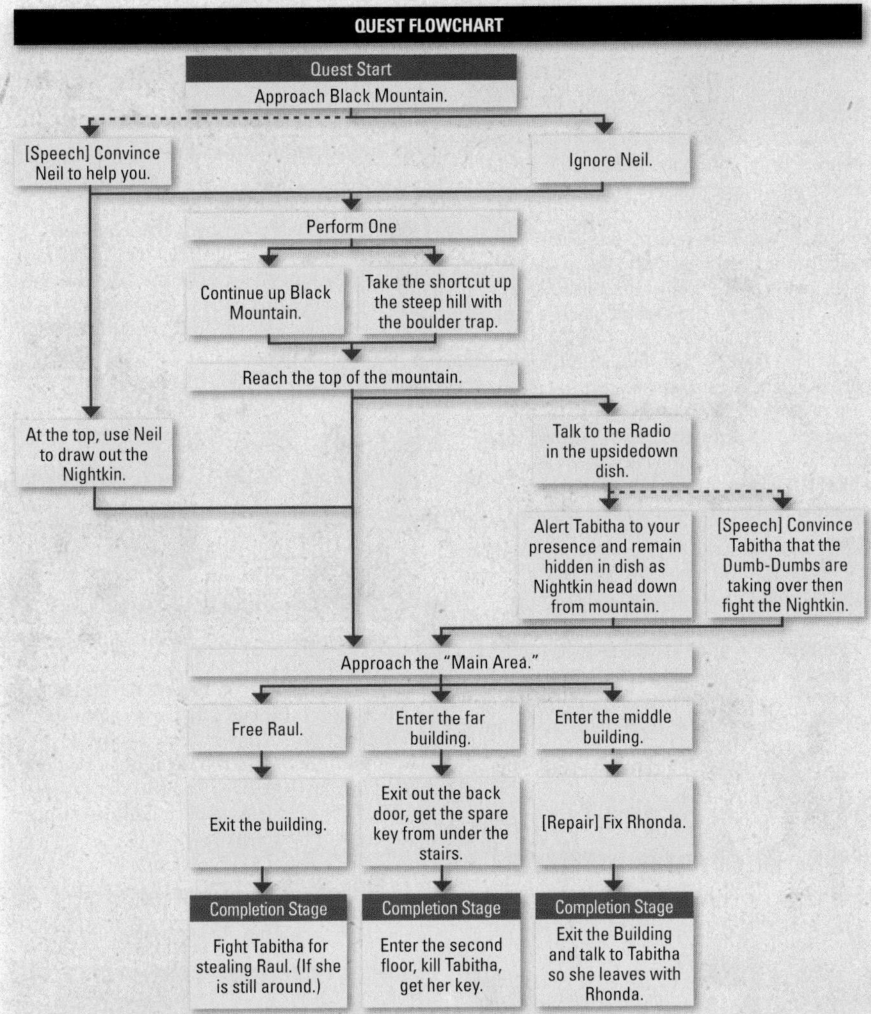

Entering the State of Utobitha

Black Mountain Radio

If, during your travels, you've tuned your Pip-Boy's Radio to Black Mountain Radio, you'll hear the dulcet tones of Tabitha, and her radio show of terror. If you've ever thought about scaling Black Mountain [5.07], prepare to pack more than a change of outfits; clusters of Deathclaws **(1)** roam the main road close to the Quarry Junction [4.04]. You can try clambering over the rocky ground to the east too, but you're likely to be ambushed by Nightkin: a particularly aggressive (and invisible) strain of Super Mutant. For the optimal path, keep to the right (east) side of the road as you head northeast up from Sloan [4.08], and take the remains of the road to the right when you see it. This leads to a winding series of switchbacks allowing access to Tabitha's mountaintop lair.

Although you can leave the road and scramble across the rocks, there are numerous Super Mutant shacks along the ascent. Instead, maneuver along the road as it winds right, to Neil's Shack [5.06]. At this point, you're waylaid by the shack's owner, a dark green Super Mutant named Neil **(2)**. You can:

Take out your weapon, ignoring what he has to say, and slaughter him.

Put away your weapon, and listen to him. This is the preferred plan, because you gain insight into this heavily fortified peak. Neil suggests you turn back, because that radio voice is Tabitha: the "supreme commander" of Black Mountain. Or as she calls it; "the State of Utobitha." She's ordered her troops—a mixture of crazed Nightkin and more reasonable "second-gen" Super Mutants—to shoot humans on sight. You can ask Neil for much more information, and the trouble to expect.

You can also ask Neil if he's had enough of Tabitha, and if he needs some help. Neil agrees, and tells you to meet him "in the village, up near the peak," where you can talk further. Without this Speech check, you're on your own.

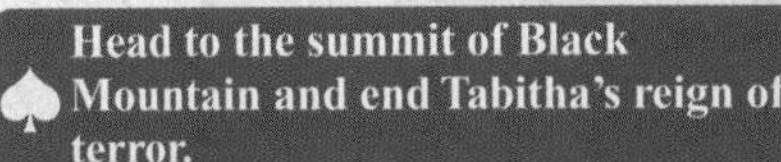
Head to the summit of Black Mountain and end Tabitha's reign of terror.

(Optional) Meet Neil in the village near the summit of Black Mountain.

There are two ways to scale Black Mountain. The first involves trekking up the switchbacks, while the second involves taking a shortcut.

Ascent: The Long, Horrifically Frightening Way

Choose to stay on the path, and you'll run into the following problems:

- There are three blockades **(3, 4, 5)**. Each contains two to four Super Mutants, and sometimes a disgusting Centaur. Attack from a distance, shooting the foes as they close in, and hobbling them with leg shots if they're too close.

You can also try sneaking close to each blockade, laying down mines or C-4, then backing up and revealing yourself, and hoping the Super Mutants charge into your trap.

- Expect periodic attacks from Nightkin **(6)**, which come out of thin air because these blue beasts use Stealth Boys to launch a surprise attack. Nightkin are mainly armed with melee weapons, so backing up and firing wildly is a plan.

7

- As you near the top, expect some toughened Super Mutants to take a swing at you **(7)**. Fortunately, you can see them coming. There are patrols of more than one Super Mutant to contend with, too. Now move into the shanty village.

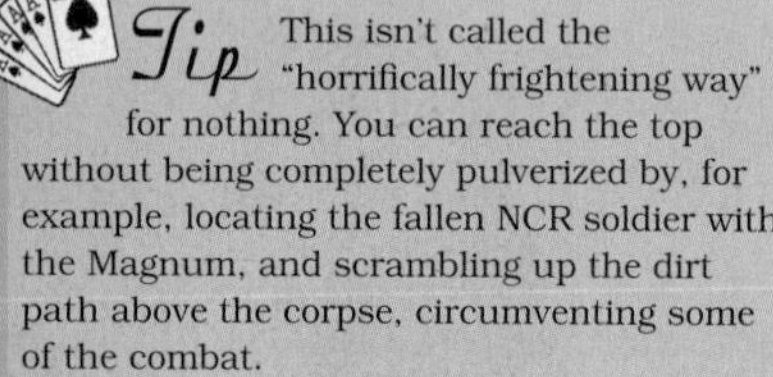

Tip This isn't called the "horrifically frightening way" for nothing. You can reach the top without being completely pulverized by, for example, locating the fallen NCR soldier with the Magnum, and scrambling up the dirt path above the corpse, circumventing some of the combat.

Ascent: The Short, Slightly Irradiated Way

8

9

10

The other, safer option involves a little stealth work. From the point where you spoke to Neil, follow the road around to the left until it straightens out, then peel off into the rocks on your right, locating a gravel path up the right (eastern) side of the mountain. Sneak and stay Hidden as you spot the second blockade **(8)** on your left. Quietly move across to a gate, and open it. This leads to a rocky mountainside where the path peters out. Expect to face a group of Evolved Centaurs **(9)** close to an impact crater. Turn north, and scramble up the rocks, heading for the cluster of radar dishes **(10)**, and climb all the way to the summit, and a second gate. You can:

Unlock the gate, and quietly sneak into any of the three summit buildings.

Or sidestep to the left, and take down Tabitha's Nightkin guard from behind the fence, before following it along until the fence ends, and entering the summit from the opposite end, close to the shanty town. This allows you to access any of the summit buildings.

Shanty Village and Summit: Not Receiving Visitors

11

Unless you took the shortcut, you'll arrive at the shanty village Neil described earlier **(11)**.

If Neil has made the ascent, speak to him, and use him to draw out the Nightkin from the cluster of three main buildings ahead (south) of you. These are Tabitha's personal guards, and having them de-cloak at a distance means taking them down is a lot easier. In fact, you're likely to be left with only a single Nightkin; the sniper guarding the radio mast on the summit.

An even better plan is to rendezvous with Neil, and then find a suitable hiding spot. Neil heads in, coaxes the Nightkin out, and they rush down the mountain after him, leaving you free to tackle just the sniper.

Whether Neil is with you or not, investigate the shanty town further, cutting down any green or blue adversaries as applicable. Then venture into the upturned radar dish.

This makeshift camp contains bedding and trunks you can scavenge (including two locked trunks with a mass of Caps and a Minigun inside).

Caps (around 400)

Minigun and ammo

Near one of the trunks is a transceiver. Talk into it, and you interrupt Tabitha's broadcast. She's furious. You can:

Alert her to your presence and she sends her Nightkin out to attack you. This is actually preferred because you're less prone to an ambush.

Infuriate her by convincing her that "dumb-dumbs" (her name for humans) are about to take over her radio station. This causes the Nightkin to come running into the area, making them easier to dispatch.

12

Press onward (south) along the path toward the summit buildings. Expect three or four Nightkin to attack you before, during, or after your arrival **(12)**, and pay particular attention to the Nightkin "sniper" armed with the Missile Launcher on the radio mast platform. You may have defeated Tabitha's forces, but she's still broadcasting her lunatic message. Choose from three plans here:

Plan #1: Rendezvous with Rhonda

13

14

15

Enter the middle of the three structures, marked "Storage Building." The place is a gigantic treasure trove of junk **(13)**, and three large trunks you can't unlock. Of more interest is a broken Mr. Handy (or in this case, a "Mrs. Handy") lying on a desk along one of the walls. The robot's nameplate says "Rhonda." You can:

Leave the robot alone, and try another plan.

Or check the robot's circuitry. You learn that the robot's AI is set to "hibernate" after being damaged. The robot was repaired, but not rebooted. Flipping the switch brings Rhonda back. Rhonda activates **(14)**, and immediately requests the location of her mistress. Tell her to head outside, and then follow her. As you emerge, Tabitha arrives, ready to crush you, until she spots Rhonda. Tabitha is overcome with joy that her friend is back **(15)**, and gives you a key. Perhaps losing Rhonda caused Tabitha's unpredictable behavior. They both leave together. Meanwhile, return to the storage room, and unlock the three trunks to find more ammunition and weapons than you can hope to carry. The Quest concludes.

Tabitha's Equipment Key

Plan #2: Shocked Jock

16

17

Enter the far structure, marked "Broadcast Building, 1st Floor" **(16)**. Inside, there's a terminal [EASY] with some old military logs, and a second [EASY] with Tabitha's diary, charting her interactions with a Super Mutant named Marcus, and her robot pal Rhonda, before her life took a turn for the strange. Exit this structure by the Door to Black Mountain, and you appear by a fence and some exterior metal steps. Check below the steps for a set of keys.

Tabitha's Room Key

Use the key at the top of the stairs to enter the second floor. Tabitha broadcasts from here, and she attempts to bludgeon you to death **(17)**. Search her corpse to find a second Room Key (that she used to lock herself in here), and an Equipment Key. This allows you to enter the storage room, and unlock three trunks. There's more ammunition and weapons in them than you can shake a Super Sledge at. The Quest concludes.

Plan #3: Libere al Espíritu Necrófago!

18

19

Enter the near structure, marked "Prison Building" **(18)**, and look around a small room with a Workbench and two terminals. One requires hacking [VERY HARD]. The other has six entries, written by what appears to be Tabitha's mechanic. Read all the entries, and you uncover a password.

Note: Black Mountain Password

The password allows you to activate the other terminal instead of hacking it, which in turn allows you to disengage the lock to the other door in this room. Open it, and meet Raul Alfonso Tejada **(19)**, the Ghoul from south of the border. You can ask about his life in Mexico City, and eventually learn that a mixture of fear and locked doors keeps Raul confined to the Black Mountain summit. To free Raul, you must exit the building, coming face-to-torso with Tabitha, and then defeating her. Raul is free to leave (although that Petro-Chico jacket might look good on you), while you can grab the Equipment Key from Tabitha's corpse, and enter the storage room, unlocking three trunks with more ammunition and weapons than the King has followers. The Quest concludes.

Tabitha's Room Key

Conclusion: Awesome Armaments and an Old-School Ghoul

Amid the masses of ammunition, be sure to inspect the trunks for a variety of (random) impressive armaments. When you're done ransacking, be sure you chat with Raul, whether you rescued him earlier, or you're unlocking his prison right now. He's happy to provide you with some exceptional Repair work, and you can bring him with you on a journey of past introspection: Free Quest: Old School Ghoul. This is well worth commencing.

Tabitha's Trunk Items (5 Trunks)

Follower: Raul

Perk!: Regular Maintenance

CRY ME A RIVER

SUGGESTED EXPERIENCE

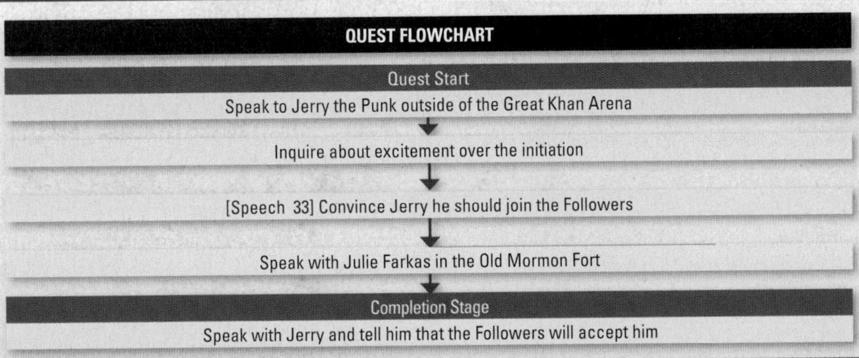

QUEST FLOWCHART

Quest Start

Speak to Jerry the Punk outside of the Great Khan Arena

↓

Inquire about excitement over the initiation

↓

[Speech 33] Convince Jerry he should join the Followers

↓

Speak with Julie Farkas in the Old Mormon Fort

↓

Completion Stage

Speak with Jerry and tell him that the Followers will accept him

Main Factions

Meeting the Punk Poet

Deep inside the Great Khan encampment in Red Rock Canyon [1.15] is a large circle of standing stones flanked by two standards **(1)**. This area, or the tent nearby, is where the snot-nosed (but sensitive) Jerry the Punk **(2)** is waiting around. Talking to Jerry takes some patience, as he's a petulant but frightened soul, attempting to psyche himself up for life with the Great Khans. You can listen to his poetry, which (like human flesh) is an acquired taste. His affection for poetry stemmed from interactions with the Followers of the Apocalypse during his youth. Jerry seems confused.

Suggest he's not happy being a Great Khan, and might be happier someplace else. Tell him you'll inquire at the Followers' base for him.

Talk to the Followers of the Apocalypse about letting Jerry the Punk join their order.

Note *The poetry stylings of Punk Poet Jerry:*

"There once was a fellow called Garret,
Whose sister she did love to bare it,
She flashed it around, all over town,
So if you would screw her, beware it."

Plan #1: Caring for a Sensitive Soul

To swell the ranks of the Followers, you must travel to the Old Mormon Fort **(3)** [2C.01] inside Freeside. Speak with Julie Farkas **(4)** once inside, and after a quick conversation about the Followers' lack of supplies and dire conditions, tell her you met a kid who's unsatisfied with his life, and ask if she can take him on. She agrees, even if he's doing inventory on the Pre-War Unexploded Munitions Collection back west.

Tell Jerry the Followers will accept him as a novice.

Back at the Great Khan Camp, Jerry is understandably elated when you tell him the news, and vows to flee "this crummy dump" forthwith.

350 XP

DEBT COLLECTOR

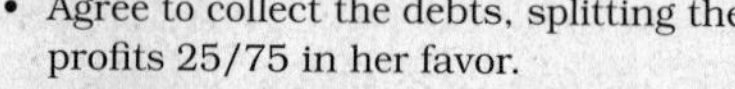

SUGGESTED EXPERIENCE

See flowchart on the following page

Halt. Tab. Delete.

Francine Garret, like her twin brother James, is the co-owner of the Atomic Wrangler Casino **(1)** [2C.06] in Inner Freeside [Zone 2C]. Pay her a visit, ideally after you've gained access to The Strip, or during your less-than-savory prostitute round-up, also known as Side Quest: Wang Dang Atomic Tango (check out Santiago's debt, below). Francine **(2)** is usually close to the lobby counter. Aside from asking about the area, a little "R&R," or for a room, request "work you need done around here." Francine says she needs an enforcer to gather some unpaid tabs. You can:

- Agree to collect the debts, splitting the profits 25/75 in her favor.
- Focus on asking her about the Caps you'll make. At this point, she offers a 25/75 split:

Inform her you're doing all the work around here. A 50/50 split is agreed upon.

Tell her a 50/50 split will cover your time and money. She agrees.

Or agree to her 25/75 terms, and wish you hadn't plowed all your points into Guns and Repair.

The "mixed bag of fruits" Francine needs tracking are Grecks, Santiago, and Lady Jane. You can elect to find them in any order, although there's a fourth option to consider, too.

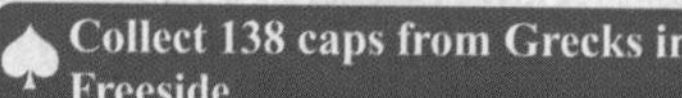

Collect 138 caps from Grecks in Freeside.

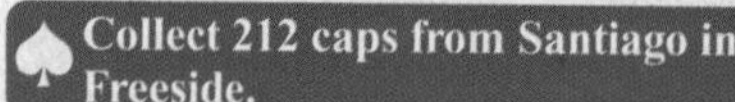

Collect 212 caps from Santiago in Freeside.

Find and collect 250 caps from Lady Jane.

Tip You can extract additional funds from each of the three debtors if you have the appropriate skills. Be careful with your fast-talking choices to ensure a maximum shakedown potential!

Note That shifty-looking fellow with the feather in his hat is Caleb McCaffery; the Atomic Wrangler's usual debt-collector. You can speak with him, but don't engage him in combat yet!

Debtor 1: Grecks the Ghoul

"Grecks is a bit cracked, but mostly harmless. Just don't mention anything about his lazy eye." Hanging out at the squatter camp in the northeast corner of Outer Freeside [Zone 2C] **(3)**, close to the Mormon Fort, is Grecks the Ghoul **(4)**. You can:

- Talk about the debt, which Grecks agrees to pay immediately.

You can conclude your conversation with 138 Caps.

Or you can press Grecks to cough up the rest, or he's "rat bait." He frantically hands over 179 Caps.

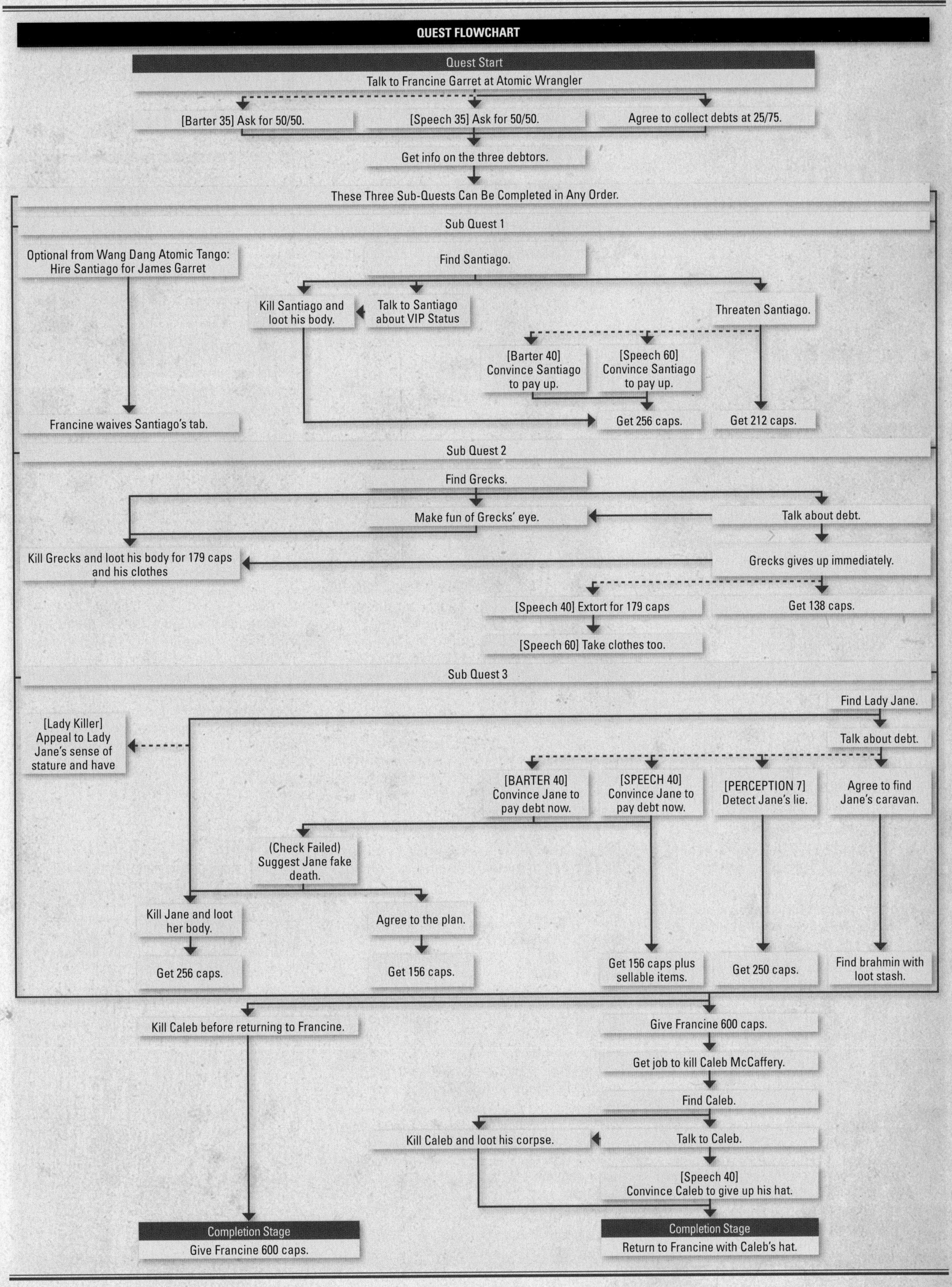
QUEST FLOWCHART
Quest Start
Talk to Francine Garret at Atomic Wrangler
[Barter 35] Ask for 50/50.
[Speech 35] Ask for 50/50.
Agree to collect debts at 25/75.
Get info on the three debtors.
These Three Sub-Quests Can Be Completed in Any Order.
Sub Quest 1
Optional from Wang Dang Atomic Tango: Hire Santiago for James Garret
Find Santiago.
Kill Santiago and loot his body.
Talk to Santiago about VIP Status
Threaten Santiago.
[Barter 40] Convince Santiago to pay up.
[Speech 60] Convince Santiago to pay up.
Francine waives Santiago's tab.
Get 256 caps.
Get 212 caps.
Sub Quest 2
Find Grecks.
Make fun of Grecks' eye.
Talk about debt.
Kill Grecks and loot his body for 179 caps and his clothes
Grecks gives up immediately.
[Speech 40] Extort for 179 caps
Get 138 caps.
[Speech 60] Take clothes too.
Sub Quest 3
Find Lady Jane.
[Lady Killer] Appeal to Lady Jane's sense of stature and have
Talk about debt.
[BARTER 40] Convince Jane to pay debt now.
[SPEECH 40] Convince Jane to pay debt now.
[PERCEPTION 7] Detect Jane's lie.
Agree to find Jane's caravan.
(Check Failed) Suggest Jane fake death.
Kill Jane and loot her body.
Agree to the plan.
Get 256 caps.
Get 156 caps.
Get 156 caps plus sellable items.
Get 250 caps.
Find brahmin with loot stash.
Kill Caleb before returning to Francine.
Give Francine 600 caps.
Get job to kill Caleb McCaffery.
Find Caleb.
Kill Caleb and loot his corpse.
Talk to Caleb.
[Speech 40] Convince Caleb to give up his hat.
Completion Stage
Give Francine 600 caps.
Completion Stage
Return to Francine with Caleb's hat.

 Making an example of Grecks, you can order him to strip, literally taking the clothes off his back. This is an unnecessary humiliation, unless you have a fetish for Dirty Pre-War Casualwear. But you aren't penalized.

 Or you can kill Grecks immediately, looting his corpse for 179 Caps.

  Or you can Pickpocket him.

Making fun of Grecks' weird eye at any point makes the Ghoul lose his cool. You'll need to kill him.

 **138 or 179 Caps**

Debtor 2: The Fabulous Santiago

"Santiago is a suave son of a bitch, but a total pansy when it comes to fisticuffs." By the blown-out building in the southeast corner of Freeside **(5)** is a squatter camp with a sharp-suited man standing nearby **(6)**. Ask Santiago about his debt, and he tells you he's a "Freeside VIP." It isn't wise to fall for Santiago's patter (which is also detailed in Free Quest: Smooth-Talking Criminal). Try one of the following:

- Immediately threaten Santiago:

Santiago hands over 212 Caps.

 Tell him Francine has put a bounty on his head. He hands over 256 Caps.

 Convince Santiago he must pay his debts. He agrees and forks over 256 Caps.

- Instead of threatening Santiago, you can take a softer approach. Ask about the "VIP status" and Santiago tells you for a mere 50 Caps, you can receive a "super secret code word" for a discount at Mick & Ralph's [2C.02]. You can:

Hand over the 50 Caps, and receive the word.

 Bargain Santiago down to 25 Caps for the word.

See through this ruse and threaten Santiago. See above.

 The third option is to simply kill Santiago, whether you've heard enough from him or not. Looting the corpse nets you 256 Caps.

  Or you can Pickpocket him.

If you're also looking for a male prostitute for James Garret during Side Quest: Wang Dang Atomic Tango quest, you can offer this line of work to Santiago, instead of collecting the Caps. Once Santiago agrees, his tab is waived when you speak with Francine.

 **212 or 256 Caps**

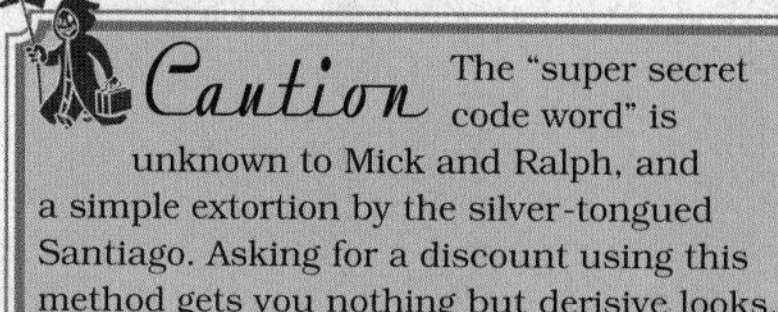

Caution The "super secret code word" is unknown to Mick and Ralph, and a simple extortion by the silver-tongued Santiago. Asking for a discount using this method gets you nothing but derisive looks.

Debtor 3: Lady Jane, the Impoverished Prospector

"Lady Jane fancies herself a high roller, but she's just another dirtbag NCR prospector." Usually in the vicinity of The Strip North Gate in Freeside [2.13] **(7)**, Lady Jane **(8)** presents herself as a highfalutin type, but there's more to her than well-coiffured hair. Speak to her about her debt, and she matter-of-factly tells you she hasn't the Caps to pay Francine. You can:

 Remark that you're sure a lady of her stature has sufficient honor to pay her debts. She agrees, handing over 250 Caps, and the location of her caravan, currently lost somewhere in the Mojave Wasteland.

 Tell her you're shocked she ran from the caravan without grabbing something.

 Or tell her there must be something of value she could put toward the debt.

A successful Barter or Speech check results in Lady Jane handing over some relatively innocuous salable items, as well as 156 Caps.

If you tried and failed the Barter or Speech checks, you can always suggest that she fake her own death. She tells you her plan, and you can agree to it (and receive 156 Caps), or just attack her (see below).

 You can tell Lady Jane is lying through her teeth about her lack of funds. She confesses, and you make off with 250 Caps.

  Or you can Pickpocket her.

 Or kill her and loot the Caps.

 **0, 156, or 250 Caps**

Find Lady Jane's caravan and collect caps from the remains.

Whether you received a Marker on your Pip-Boy or not, you can elect to search for Lady Jane's Caravan, savaged by Fire Geckos inside Bootjack Cavern **(9)** [6.S10], a Secondary Location not marked on your World Map, but one that's on the other side of the mountain from the Lucky Jim Mine [6.09]. There's usually a wandering prospector near the entrance to the cavern. Wind through the narrow tunnels to the dead-end, and search Jane's Brahmin **(10)** for a reasonable Bottle Cap haul.

 **276 Caps**

Cap-Collecting Conclusion

Return to Francine Garret with 388 caps.

Return to Francine Garret with 600 caps.

You can now return to Francine, back at the Atomic Wrangler. She doesn't care how you handled those "lumps of human refuse," as long the debts are paid. How you pay Francine is entirely up to you. The following table shows the Caps you could have accumulated, and your profit margins.

 In addition, at any time during this Quest, whether you've met any of the debtors or not, you can lie and give 600 Caps to Francine, telling her you've collected all the debts. She gives you your cut (150 or 300 Caps). This allows you to extort the debtors at your leisure.

The Bottle Cap Profit Share					
Debtor	Minimum Caps Needed (for Francine)	Maximum Caps Available (from debtor)	Your Cut (25/75)	Your Cut (50/50)	Your Maximum Profit Potential ([Max Caps - Min Caps] + 50% Cut)
Grecks	138	179	35	69	110
Santiago	212	256	52	106	150
Lady Jane	250	526	63	125	401
TOTALS:	600	961	150	300	661

Tip Maximize your profits by extorting the most out of Grecks (179); Santiago (256), don't agree to let him become a prostitute, or you don't receive a cut; and Lady Jane (250, plus the 276 from her dead Brahmin in the cave).

Hats Off to Caleb McCaffery

Once the first three debtors' payments have been received, a furious Francine tells you about a man named McCaffery, who's stolen a ton of Caps and run off to Vegas. McCaffery was the Atomic Wrangler's regular debt collector (in fact, he was in the hotel lobby at the start of this Quest). There's no love lost between the Garrets and McCaffery; she wants his hat as proof you've dealt with him.

Kill Caleb McCaffery

If you want access to The Strip, learn all the different methods listed in the Tour Chapter of this book, in the section on Freeside [Zone 2C]. Free Quest: The Strip Shakedown and Free Quest: Papers, Please have all the people to meet, and methods to try.

McCaffery is wandering close to The Strip **(11)** [Zone 2D], and is spoiling for a ruckus when you talk to him **(12)**. You can:

- Ask him to share the Caps he stole, and his hat; in return for his freedom. Caleb openly mocks you.

Tell him all you need is his hat, and you'll tell Francine he's dead. He's reluctant, but agrees.

57 Caps

- You can tell him no one crosses the Garret twins. All other options lead to combat. Put away Caleb and claim his Caps. The haul is improved once you loot his corpse:

165 Caps

Atomic Wrangler Room Key

Caleb McCaffery's Hat

Return to Francine with McCaffery's hat.

Upon your return to Francine, give her the hat, and she's as ecstatic as the Garret Twins get. She finds a place on her wall for the hat, and gives out 150 Caps (in addition to any you looted or were given by McCaffery). To further show her gratitude, she gives you an Atomic Wrangler Room Key to Caleb's old room (which you might already have looted from Caleb's corpse). The door is in the northeast corner, overlooking the entrance lobby.

150 Caps

Atomic Wrangler Room Key

500 XP

Post Quest Antics: Wham, Bam, Thanks Atomic Wrangler!

You're given your own room at the Atomic Wrangler, and it's up to you to use it! You can coax a variety of escorts (whether they be male, female, Ghoul, or Robot) into your room for a good time. Also take a moment to figure out the maximum Caps you could have gathered: 661 (three debtors) + 315 (Caleb and Francine's reward) = 976. Not a bad haul!

DON'T MAKE A BEGGAR OF ME

SUGGESTED EXPERIENCE

See flowchart on the following page

Main Factions

The Sloan Ranger

Begin at the Great Kahn Encampment [1.15], a couple of sleeping mats on a giant slab of partially quarried limestone **(1)** near a large red crane overlooking the quarry. A suspicious Melissa **(2)**, and her Great Kahn associates, greet you before you get too close for her comfort. Aside from a wealth of information about the Great Kahns (including initiation ceremonies), you can ask Melissa "what are you doing up here?" She replies she's waiting on a delivery, but it hasn't showed up. Pry further, and you learn it's supplies to make Chems. Tell her you'll help with her problem. She agrees to whatever reward you request, and tells you the suitcase with the shipment is likely to be in the nearby settlement of Sloan [4.08].

Search the suitcase at Sloan for the chemical supply shipment.

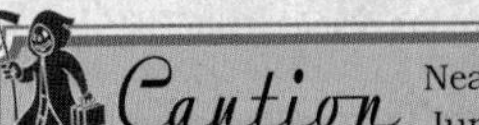

Caution Nearby Quarry Junction [4.04] is teeming with Deathclaws, and you must pass through Quarry Junction to reach the Great Khan Encampment. Prepare yourself with your best armor and weapons! If your level is too low, return to this Quest later.

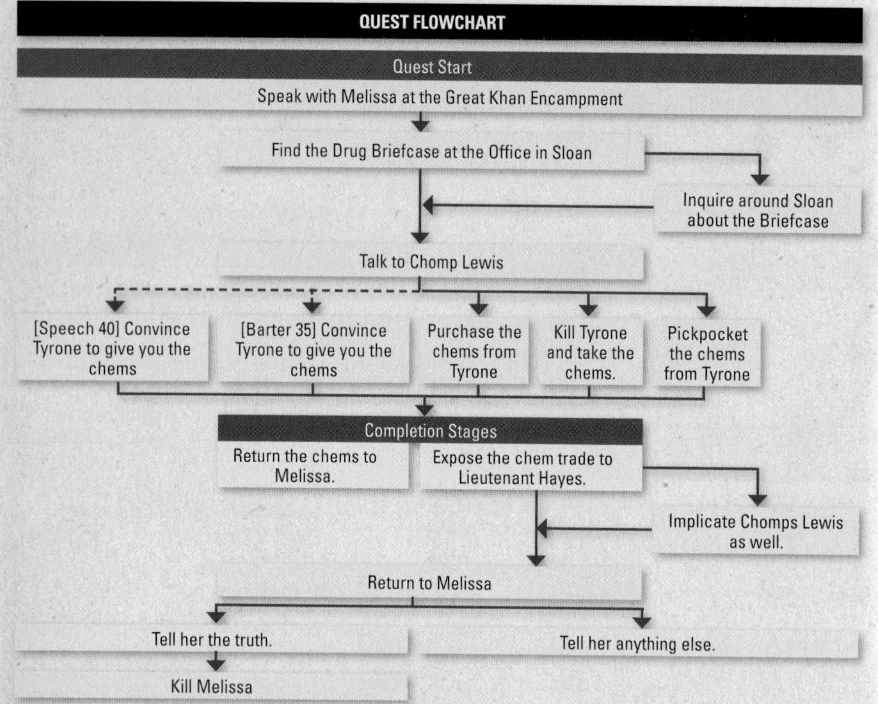

Keep to the quarry perimeter to avoid mass Deathclaw attacks, dealing with a few Radscorpions instead, en route to Sloan **(3)**. You're stopped on the highway close to the motley collection of rusting shacks by a man named Chomps Lewis **(4)**, telling you the road's unsafe due to Deathclaws. You can:

Tell Chomps that you'll take care of the Deathclaw problem. Whether you intend to or not is completely up to you; you're given five Stimpaks anyway!

Otherwise, Chomps doesn't reveal any evidence regarding the suitcase. Speak to him about Sloan, New Vegas, or the Powder Gangers if you want, before heading down into Sloan.

> *Tip* One of the inhabitants of Sloan is Snuffles the Mole Rat. Don't mistake him for a wild animal and shoot him, or you'll cause a ruckus with the quarry workers. Instead, check the animal's limp. There's a generator to fix, too. Both are detailed in the Tour Chapter of this guide.

Look for the Mining Office Shack, and head inside, and climb the stairs to the mezzanine office. The suitcase **(5)** is next to the desk with the Ham Radio on it. The suitcase may have a few common items, but not the supplies Melissa told you about. It's time to quiz old Chomps Lewis about this....

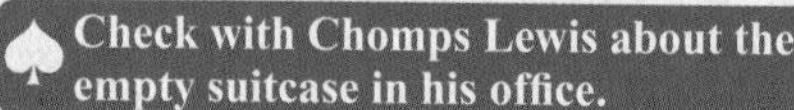

Check with Chomps Lewis about the empty suitcase in his office.

Trafficking with Tyrone

When you return to Chomps and ask where the delivery is, Chomps tells you Tyrone, the supplier in Primm, is a cheating son of a bitch and won't deliver the goods, even though he's been paid. You can further inquire about Chomps' loyalties to the NCR and Great Kahns before setting off to find Tyrone.

Acquire the chem shipment from Tyrone in Primm.

After a trek or Fast Travel south to the town of Primm [4.17], you should come across a small NCR camp **(6)** consisting of two tents and a small squad of soldiers. One of the tents leads to Lieutenant Hayes, so ignore that one. Inside the other tent is a soldier named Tyrone **(7)**, who's nervous about his clandestine operation, but still confident enough to refer to himself in the third person. Ask about the chemical supplies, and Tyrone tries to shake you down for an extra 300 Caps. You can:

Flex your muscles and ask Tyrone to repeat himself.

Threaten that someone else will start his deliveries.

Ask whether 300 Caps is worth being known as a deal-breaker.

Tell him he's already been paid in advance.

Shoot Tyrone. This is a terrible idea, because the NCR doesn't yet know that Tyrone's been selling their supplies, and will turn hostile, badly damaging your Reputation with the Faction.

The first three options cause Tyrone to hand over the chemicals. The fourth choice has no effect, although you can pay him if you have the necessary Caps. At this point, you have a couple of ways to complete this Quest:

Drug Chemicals

Return to Melissa with the chem shipment.

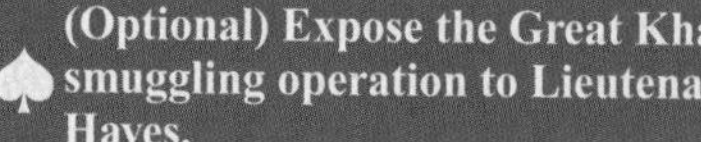

(Optional) Expose the Great Khan smuggling operation to Lieutenant Hayes.

Plan 1: Siding with the Great Kahns

You can actually return to Melissa without exposing this operation, and present the chems to her. She's surprised by your loyalty, takes the drugs, and pays you for your troubles. This plan is worthwhile because you receive a large number of Caps and finish the Quest.

150 Caps

Various chems

Great Kahns Fame Gained!

Plan 2: Siding with the NCR

While you're at the NCR camp in Primm, you can visit the other tent, and speak to Lieutenant Hayes **(8)**. He's an important man who can help you in a number of other Quests. Simply inform him that Tyrone has been selling chemical supplies to the Great Kahns and present the chemicals to Hayes. The Quest ends.

NCR Fame Gained!

Hayes takes the drugs, and asks if others were involved. You can:

Rat out Chomps Lewis over in Sloan.

Or lie, and tell him no one else was involved.

9

Neither option affects you or damages your Reputation.

Finally, if you've ruined this little smuggling operation, you can return to Melissa, and tell her that her supplier was exposed. When she asks what exactly happened, you can:

Tell her you turned him in. Melissa and crew immediately attack **(9)**. Flee or kill all three Great Kahns. Your Reputation doesn't suffer, and you can loot a reasonably large number of Caps from her corpse, as well as weapons and other helpful items.

85 Caps

Tell her Tyrone was sloppy and trusted the wrong person. Or lie, and tell her you don't know: She's annoyed, and heads off to Red Rock Canyon.

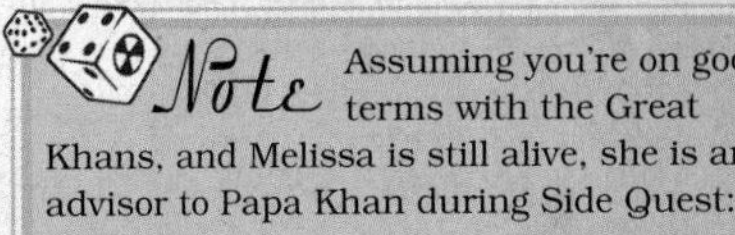
Note Assuming you're on good terms with the Great Khans, and Melissa is still alive, she is an advisor to Papa Khan during Side Quest: Oh My Papa.

100 XP

ED-E MY LOVE

SUGGESTED EXPERIENCE

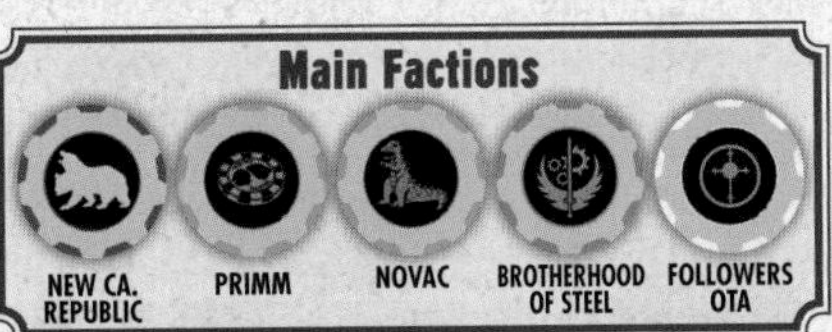

Companion Protocol: Begin!

1

2

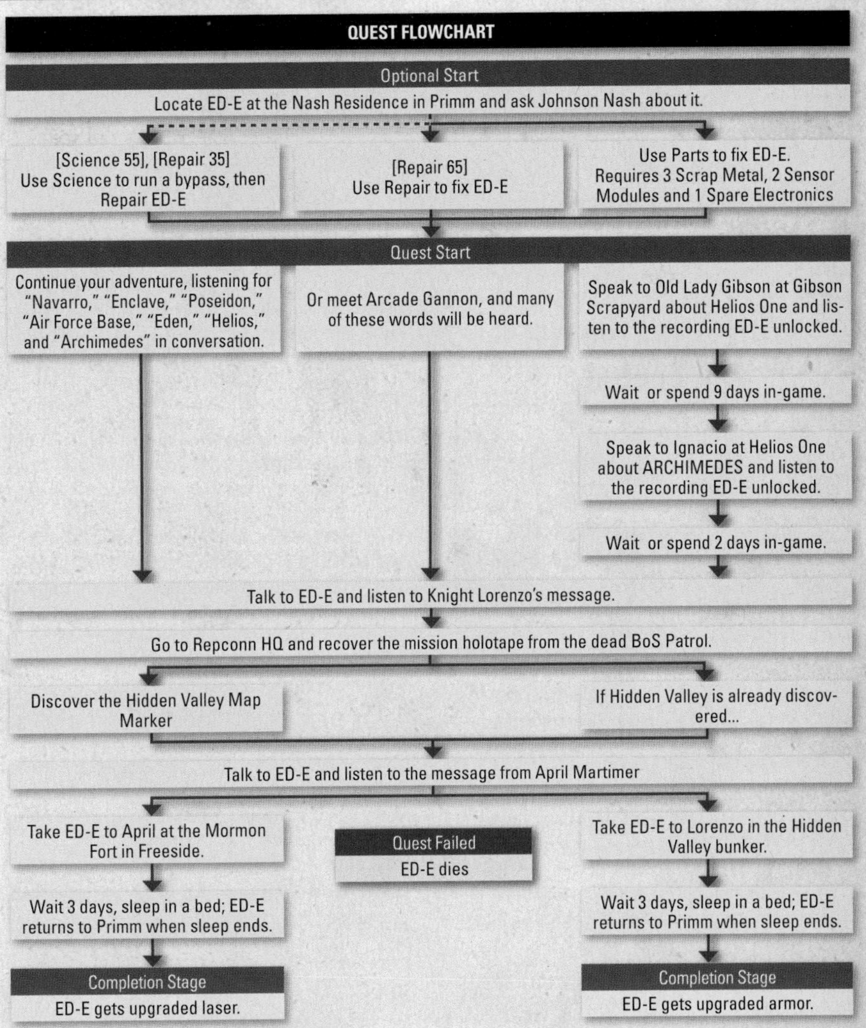

While you're in Primm [4.17], make sure you visit the Mojave Express Courier building **(1)**, the residence of Johnson and Ruby Nash, proprietors of the Vikki & Vance Casino. Focus your gaze on the Damaged Eyebot resting on the counter **(2)**. Examine it, and it appears to have suffered very little damage. Leave it alone, or head to the Vikki & Vance Casino and ask Johnson Nash about it. He's certainly fine with leaving it in your hands if you can fix it.

With enough skill, you can Repair it without any necessary parts.

Or examine the electronics and run a bypass.

Or, you can return with the following to Repair it: Scrap Metal (3), Sensor Module (2), and Scrap Electronics (1). Try rummaging in locations listed in the Tour section of this guide, particularly the gas station garage in Novac [5.18] that have "Scrap Metal" flagged as a pick-up item, for best (but not guaranteed) results. Or for more specific locations, try the following:

Scrap Metal (3): There are two pieces to steal on the same counter as ED-E. Or if Stealing isn't your thing, check Victor's Shack in Goodsprings [4.05] for two you can just take. Chet sometimes sells them at the Goodsprings General Store. Or check any Toolbox you see; there's a good chance you'll find one in there.

Sensor Module (2): There's one in the long trailer directly behind the saloon in Goodsprings, where you learned to shoot with Sunny. Chet sells one at the Goodsprings General Store.

Scrap Electronics (1): Steal one from one of the bungalows in Primm, just south of the Mojave Express. Or take one (without stealing) from Lone Wolf Radio [4.14] close by, to the north. Or take two from the Abandoned Shack just north of the Yangtze Memorial [4.07]. Or buy one from Chet at the Goodsprings General Store.

With all the necessary parts, the Repairs become a lot easier. Use the Magazines in the Mojave Express to increase your Repair and Science skills if they are too low.

Once ED-E has been activated, he becomes a Follower and grants you the Enhanced Sensors perk. Make sure you choose "<Companion Protocol::Begin>" so that ED-E actually becomes your Follower.

Follower: ED-E

Enhanced Sensors

Tip ED-E is an impressive combat Eyebot that acts as a faithful companion, and has the added benefit of not being dismissed if you locate and invite a "human" sized Follower (such as Arcade Gannon, Veronica, or even Lily). ED-E begins to reveal some of its secrets in unexpected ways:

More Than Meets the Eyebot

3

4

During your adventuring, visit to Old Lady Gibson at her Gibson Scrap Yard **(3)** [5.14], and start a friendly conversation **(4)**. During the course of the chit-chat, you both comment about the nearby solar array HELIOS One. As soon as the conversation is over, ED-E exhibits some strange behavior:

ED-E appears to have some Enclave log data stored that is triggered by some keywords.

ED-E launches a recording of a man named Whitley, a researcher at Adams Air Force base. Let the playback continue to its end, and you learn ED-E is a Duraframe Eyebot, and the last functional model of the test group. The recording mentions "significant improvements" and the name of Navarro before falling silent.

Note ED-E's recording is triggered by keywords uttered by entities you visit during the course of your adventure. If you don't feel like following the optimal (quest) path, expect recordings to start when the Eyebot hears the following words: "Navarro," "Enclave," "Poseidon," "Air Force Base," "Eden," "Helios," and "Archimedes." Simply look at the World Map, or meet Arcade Gannon, and many of these words will be heard.

5

6

Further recordings take time to be uncovered from ED-E's data banks. Wait or spend nine days continuing your adventure. Be sure you start to wait immediately, and then write down the day, date, and time that appears on-screen. Then figure out how much time is required to pass. For example, if it is "Tuesday, 10.31.81, 2:54 PM," you need to wait until the Wait menu is at: "Thursday, 11.09.81, 2:54 PM."

Now journey to HELIOS One **(5)** [5.13], optionally beginning Side Quest: That Lucky Old Sun, and proceed through the building until you meet Ignacio Rivas **(6)**, one of the scientists working there. Speak to him about ARCHIMEDES, and be sure to ask "You think ARCHIMEDES is a weapon they built here?" Note that if you have a spectacularly low (>3) Intelligence, this isn't an option thanks to your drooling, monosyllabic responses, and you must find others to utter trigger words. But assuming you can string sentences together, ED-E transmits another message.

This involves the results of the research on Duraframe Eyebots, and research into Poseidon Energy and projects in the Mojave area. Once you hear this recording, you must wait or spend an additional two days.

Technological Divergency

7

Once 48 hours have passed, ED-E should transmit with a new message, but this one is actually live. Knight Lorenzo of the Brotherhood of Steel is using ED-E as a relay to tell you he's extremely interested in examining

8

your tech. He gives you the coordinates of a Brotherhood patrol who can check it out. Your World Map updates.

Find the patrol Knight Lorenzo told you about to let the Brotherhood of Steel examine ED-E.

The patrol is in a static location inside the REPCONN Headquarters **(7)** [2.35]. Follow the infiltration advice detailed in this guide's Tour chapter for that particular location, or use fast talk or fast running to get around the Mobile Facial Recognition Scanners on each floor. When you reach the top floor, it appears the automated security got the better of the Brotherhood patrol, who are both dead **(8)**.

The patrol Lorenzo mentioned is dead, perhaps there is something on one of the corpses that may be useful.

Check the corpses of the fallen Paladins, and aside from Power Armor and Energy Weapons, there's a Holotape to take and listen to. There was a password on one of the corpses too, which seems to be an access code to the Brotherhood of Steel's main base, wherever that is hidden...your World Map updates with the location of Hidden Valley [5.11]. As the Quest updates, you may hear another voice emanating from ED-E. A woman named April Martimer has been monitoring your communications. She tells you she's with the Followers of the Apocalypse, who are much more liberal about sharing technology compared with the Brotherhood of Steel. She wants to mine ED-E for "the greater good."

Note April's greeting is contingent upon whether you've discovered Hidden Valley [5.11]. Is it on your World Map? Then this is the earliest time you hear this message. If you haven't, you won't hear the message until after you discover Hidden Valley.

Brotherhood of Steel Mission Holotape

Note: Mission Statement XV-56

There was a password on one of the Brotherhood corpses. Perhaps that could be used to bring ED-E to Lorenzo.

The Followers of the Apocalypse would like to see ED-E to get access to the logs he has stored.

At this point, you have two possible concluding paths:

Path A: A Taste of Cold Steel

Journey to Hidden Valley, and enter the western bunker **(9)**, and use the password "lives to fight another day" on the intercom, if you haven't already investigated this area. Or, bring Veronica with you because she can easily gain access. If this is your first time here, you must successfully complete the first part of Side Quest: Still in the Dark, and rid the area of an NCR Ranger. Once you're deemed trustworthy, and have the run of the bunker, visit Knight Lorenzo **(10)** down on bunker L2, and tell him about the Enclave-related recordings. He asks whether you can leave ED-E with him for a while. Agree to this, and then wait (or continue adventuring) for 72 hours. Then sleep for an hour, wake up so the Quest updates, and you are informed that ED-E has returned to Primm. Simply Fast Travel back to Primm and locate his marker on your World Map (or check back at the Mojave Express), and then greet him and ask him to rejoin you as a Follower. He's looking a little...different.

Path B: The Warmth of the Apocalypse

Journey to Freeside, and enter the Old Mormon Fort **(11)** [2C.01], and locate April Martimer **(12)**. Speak with her, and she tries to convince you to part with ED-E for a few days, to use the data for the good of humanity.

> **April Martimer with the Followers would like access to ED-E's data. She promises to upgrade its weapons while she works on it.**

Agree to this, and then wait (or continue adventuring) for 72 hours. Then sleep for an hour, wake up so the Quest updates, and you are informed that ED-E has returned to Primm. Simply Fast Travel back to Primm and locate his marker on your World Map (or check back at the Mojave Express), and ask him to rejoin you as a Follower. He's looking a little...happier to see you.

> **ED-E's upgrades are complete**

<Conclusion Protocol::Begin>

If you allowed ED-E to be tinkered with by the Brotherhood of Steel, he comes back with an upgraded suit of armor; it is no longer a patchwork of stickers and license plates **(13)**.

If you gave ED-E over to be manhandled by the Followers of the Apocalypse, he returns with an upgraded laser, and is generally cleaned up **(14)**. Either way, ED-E is now even more valuable!

EYE FOR AN EYE

SUGGESTED EXPERIENCE

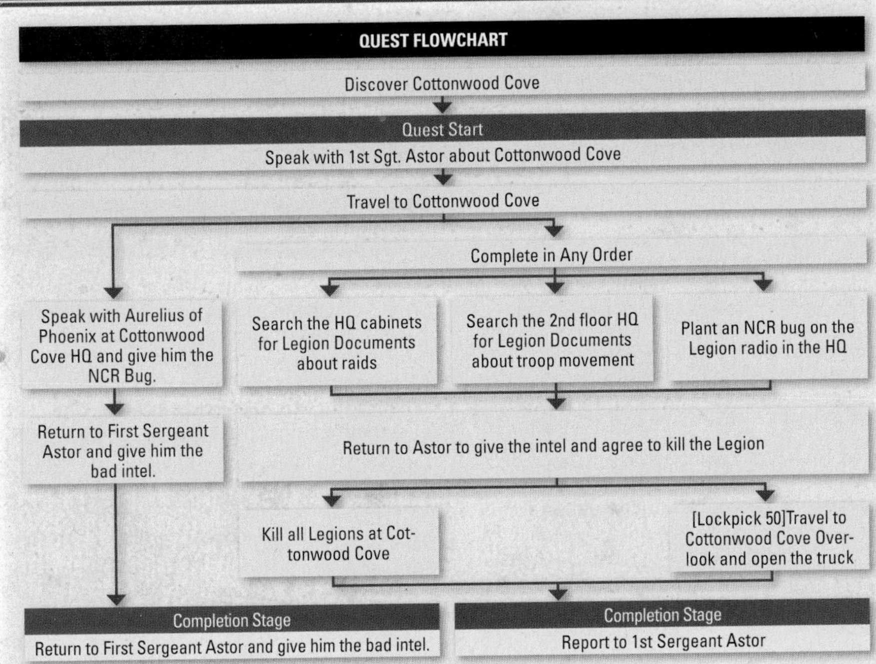

First Sergeant: Last Survivors

You cannot begin this Quest until you discover Cottonwood Cove [6.20] during the Main Quest (or by wandering). Check your Pip-Boy's World Map to see if it appears. The Quest begins due west of the cove on the remains of a road that bisects badly irradiated Camp Searchlight [6.16]. Just beyond the perimeter radiation signs, on the

west side of camp (1), is a small NCR outpost and a squad of NCR soldiers, led by First Sergeant Astor (2). He gladly tells you about "the incident" if you ask; legionaries snuck into the place and set off some kind of radiation bomb. Naturally, Astor wants revenge. Begin the Quest by mentioning Cottonwood Cove. Astor tells you the camp seems to be a primary crossing point for Legion raiding parties. Ask if he needs anything done, and he asks you to scout the camp, bringing back intel and planting a bug on their radio.

 **NCR Bug**

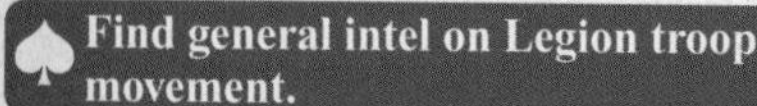

Find general intel on Legion troop movement.

(Optional) Tell Aurelius of Phoenix about NCR plans.

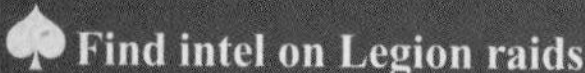

Find intel on Legion raids.

Plant the NCR bug.

Tip Although you may be siding with the NCR, the Legion, or hedging your bets, it is worth taking the Mark of Caesar from Vulpes Inculta at the tail end of Main Quest: Ring-a-Ding Ding! This provides evidence that you're here to help, even if you have ulterior motives.

Caution Watch out! If you are an enemy of the NCR, Astor will attack. Also, if you're an enemy of Caesar's Legion, the following Quest is much more difficult because the inhabitants of Cottonwood Cove will be hostile, and stealth becomes the preferred option.

Cove-rt Activities

Once you're hailed by a Legion Explorer at the entrance to Cottonwood Cove, you have the following verbal options:

 Inform him that you're a humble trader. He lets you through.

Tell him you're a friend of the Legion. If your Caesar's Legion reputation is high enough, he lets you through.

Tell him you'll go where you please, and run him through. This will make the Legion hostile and almost certainly prevent you from speaking with Aurelius of Phoenix. If you choose this option, flee and don't return until you've raised your Caesar's Legion reputation.

Once inside the camp, you're free to roam around, optionally collecting your own information from the likes of Decanus Severus. Your focus of this Quest is the main concrete building (3) housing the Office of Aurelius of Phoenix (top floor), and the Headquarters (ground floor). But where do your loyalties lie?

CAESAR'S LEGION Double-cross for the Legion!

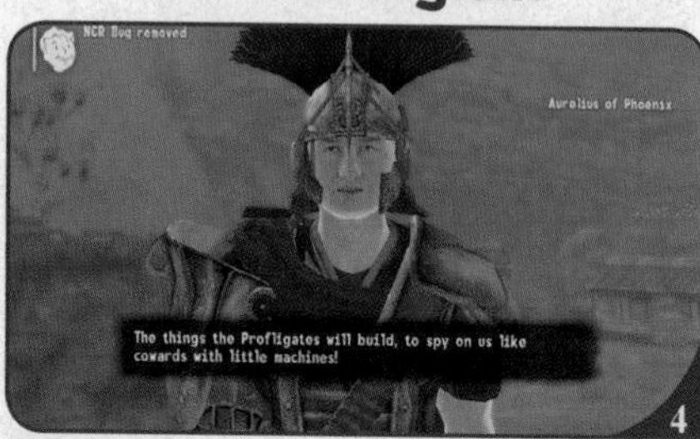

Enter the Headquarters, or the Office of Aurelius of Phoenix, and find the man himself (4). Wake him if applicable. Steer the conversation to informing Aurelius about the listening device, and give him the NCR bug. Aurelius spouts on about "the coward Profligates," and seizes the tactical opportunity to ambush the NCR squad responsible. He hands you an old patrol route map and other notes for you to fool Sergeant Astor with.

 **Old Legion Raid Plans, Notes, and Paperwork**

 **Caesar's Legion Fame Gained!**

(Optional) Give First Sergeant Astor the old intel.

Note Continue your crusade against the NCR by asking Aurelius if he pays for every NCR trooper you kill. This is Free Quest: Arizona Scavenger. Consult the Tour Chapter for more information.

Tip If you wish to return to Astor, it is wise to have previously located some adjacent Primary Locations so you can Fast Travel; although Camp Searchlight is nearby, it has dangerous radiation levels. Explore the Raided Farmstead [6.15] instead, then walk east, along the road.

Head back to Sergeant Astor, and hand over the notes that Aurelius of Phoenix gave you. Astor is amazed at the haul; it almost seems too good to be true! He hands you some Caps for your troubles, and the Quest concludes.

 **Caesar's Legion Fame Gained!**

 **You've lost Karma!**

 **Caps 150**

 **500 XP**

NEW CA. REPUBLIC Rooting for the Republic!

Enter the Headquarters (ground floor), and begin your clandestine operation. Inside the chamber (5), you'll find the following:

A Legion Radio. Activate it, and when prompted, plant the NCR Bug.

Farther along the same wall is a group of Filing Cabinets. Open them to discover the Legion Raid Plans.

 **Legion Raid Plans**

Head back outside, then climb the metal steps and enter the Office of Aurelius of Phoenix on the top floor of the same building. Open his rather grand desk, and take the Legion Patrol Notes (and anything else you want). Stealing is wrong, but it's a small Karmic price to pay to help the Republic!

 **Legion Patrol Notes**

Tip Don't attempt to grab the intel with the Legion around. You can sleep, or wait nearby and return at different points during the day when the rooms are empty. Or you can Sneak in, with an optional Stealth Boy. There's no excuse for being caught!

Return to First Sergeant Astor with the intel.

Head back to Sergeant Astor, and hand over the notes that you procured from the Headquarters and upper office. Astor is astounded at the intel; it almost seems too good to be true! He gives you some Caps for your troubles, and thanks you for your service. Ask him if he has anything else that needs taking care of.

 **NCR Fame Gained!**

 **Caps 150**

 **500 XP**

Kill all Legionaries in Cottonwood Cove.

That additional job entails wiping out the entire Legion presence back at Cottonwood Cove. Astor reckons killing the leadership would be a start, but permanently shutting down the dock would really help the cause. You have two options:

(Optional) Find a way to block off Cottonwood Cove.

Plan #1: Roll Out the Barrels

Perched precariously on the edge of the plateau above Cottonwood Cove's Legion camp are the rusting remains of a container truck **(6)**. The truck was carrying barrels of radioactive waste, which are leaking as you'll discover on your Rad Counter as you approach.

Scramble to the Trailer Door at the rear of the vehicle, and open it. Highly radioactive barrels cascade out, killing all of the troops below. Success!

Tip You may wish to bring Follower Boone with you to help with the massacre, as part of his Side Quest: I Forgot to Remember to Forget.

Caution If you want to loot the irradiated corpses below, it is wise to invest in Rad-X, RadAway, and/or a Radioactive Suit. If you haven't met Caesar at The Fort yet, and you don't want to cut off all contact with the Legion, check the Post Quest section, below..

Caution Killing enemies, whether leaders or legionaries, results in a Vilified Reputation with Caesar's Legion. If you wish to continue conversations with other Caesar's Legion adversaries, but still defeat them in the long run, an irradiated barrel-based death with no witnesses is the best way to keep your Reputation with them intact. If you were Idolized by the Legion, and then you massacre everyone in plain sight, your Reputation changes to "Wild Child."

Plan #2: Mad, Bad, and Dangerous to Know

Attacking Cottonwood Cove without irradiating the area requires a little cunning and the right weapons. The following plans are recommended for culling the Legion in this locale:

Kill Everybody

Simply race down the rocky bluffs carrying your favorite carnage-causing weapon, and slay anything wearing a red uniform. Continue until everybody is a twitching corpse, or you are. Although dangerous and lacking subtlety, this plan allows you to loot as many corpses as you can drop. Bring extra healing items! This obviously drops your Reputation with Caesar's Legion and very difficult to pull off.

Kill Everybody with a Modicum of Skill

The upper ridge and high ground on the southwest side of the camp is a perfect place to crouch and tag the initial Legion forces with a Sniper Rifle. Back up to the plateau and let the foes come to you instead of descending to them and being overwhelmed. Then you can move to the ground and finish the stragglers.

The Silent Assassin

Use a Stealth Boy or your Sneak skill to enter camp, then employ as many Sneak Attacks as you can on the Legion to buy some time before you're discovered. Remember you can retreat to the rocky ridge if you're in danger of being swarmed.

Waiting until many of the leaders are sleeping and then murdering them in their sleep thanks to the Mister Sandman perk is always a valid assassination tactic.

The Orbital Drop Shock

If you've found Euclid's C-Finder (as part of Side Quest: I Could Make You Care), you can launch orbital strikes from a distance, which is as entertaining as it sounds!

Cutting Off the Hydra Heads

Sometimes, checking your Pip-Boy's targets helps avoid unnecessary carnage. Astor doesn't need everyone gurgling up their blood and innards; he just wants a surgical strike, decapitating (literally, if you want) the two camp officers:

You can wade in, with all guns (or melee weapons) blazing.

Better yet, you can enter with two C-4 Explosives and a Detonator (Grenades or Mines work, too), and Pickpocket each officer, placing C-4 on their person without being seen, as long as you remain Hidden. Once both have explosives on them, press the Detonator and retreat, for a subtle but ruthless destruction of Legion morale!

Your primary targets are wandering around camp, inside the main concrete Headquarters building (try both floors), or sleeping inside or nearby this structure. Make sure that Decanus Severus **(7)** and the tough Aurelius of Phoenix **(8)** meet their maker. Don't forget to loot everybody; Aurelius has a particularly interesting Unarmed weapon created from the Dogtags of NCR troops.

Recompense of the Fallen

If combat is going badly, or you can't find one of your targets, flee to the container truck, and release the radioactive barrels. Do this even if you elect to slaughter everyone first, just to be doubly sure.

Return to First Sergeant Astor.

Astor LaVista, Caesar!

With the Legion reeling from your attack, return to First Sergeant Astor, and tell him of your triumph. He asks how you did it. You can reply in one of two ways (and you don't need to tell Astor exactly the way the fight played out). Naturally, Astor prefers it if you gave the Legion the same radioactive bath they did to his squad-mates. You're given a Caps reward, and the Quest concludes.

Caesar's Legion Infamy Gained!

NCR Fame Gained! (Large gain if you kill everyone in combat)

NCR Fame Gained! (Larger gain if you kill everyone with the radio-active barrels)

Caps 200 (250 if you kill everyone with the radioactive barrels)

1,000 XP

Post Quest Activities

If the NCR received incorrect information, this doesn't affect you personally.

If you released the radioactive barrels (and weren't spotted), you can still journey to The Fort [3.28] to meet Caesar. Lucullus has donned a Radiation Suit, and comments that he told the men of Cottonwood Cove to be wary of that truck.

If your Reputation with Caesar's Legion is Shunned, but the Legion doesn't attack you, you may take the barge to The Fort too, but you're likely to be attacked once on the peninsula. Bring Boone along for the massacre!

If you completed this Quest prior to beginning Main Quest: Render Unto Caesar, this past transgression is forgiven, and you can board the barge safely.

EYESIGHT TO THE BLIND

SUGGESTED EXPERIENCE

QUEST FLOWCHART

Complete Side Quest: Still in the Dark and have Elder McNamara stay in his position

Quest Start
Speak with Elder McNamara

Ask to become a Brotherhood of Steel

Bug the radio in Tabitha's room on Black Mountain

Completion Stage
Return to McNamara

Main Factions

SUPER MUTANT · BROTHERHOOD OF STEEL

Radio Wars

Note For this Quest to activate, you must side with Elder McNamara during Side Quest: Still in the Dark. Exit the Hidden Bunker area, and wait several days for the lockdown to be lifted. Then return and inquire about joining the Brotherhood of Steel. McNamara makes the following request:

Head to Black Mountain and install the remote signal transmitter in one of the consoles there.

1

This is a sister Quest to Side Quest: Tend to Your Business, and both are accessed depending on how you ended Side Quest: Still in the Dark. This Quest is only accessible once you side with Elder McNamara **(1).** Once he has given you your marching orders, leave the Hidden Bunker [5.11], and travel to Black Mountain [5.07], where the infamous Tabitha has been hosting her own brand of shock jockery. Carry a Remote Signal Transmitter, and consult (and complete) Side Quest: Crazy, Crazy, Crazy. This details all the pitfalls (and routes) up Black Mountain, and the specific ways you can deal with Tabitha.

Remote Signal Transmitter

2

3

Your trek takes you to the top of Black Mountain, past the numerous Super Mutant checkpoints **(2)**, or around and through a crater filled with lolloping Centaurs **(3)**. No matter which way you reach the summit, you usually have Nightkin to face en route to the Broadcasting Building. Enter the first floor, move to the exit, take Tabitha's Room Key from under the exterior metal steps, and scale them to the second floor, where Tabitha broadcasts from.

Tabitha's Room Key

4

5

Depending on how you finished Tabitha's Quest, she may be skipping away with her new pal Rhonda, or ready to crush you as an intruder with her Super Sledge **(4)**. Once she is out of the picture, move to the Radar Console **(5)**, and install the Remote Signal Transmitter as Elder McNamara instructed.

Report to McNamara that the device has been installed.

McNamara's Newest Paladin

6

Journey back to the Hidden Valley Bunker, and inform the Elder that the device has begun to transmit. McNamara thanks you for your help. In fact, you are given the title of Paladin of the Brotherhood, for meritorious service above and beyond the call of duty. There's no time for the usual ceremony, but McNamara gives you a suit of Power Armor **(6)** and trains you to use it, if you haven't learned that already. The Quest concludes with the elder informing you that you can trade or purchase the Brotherhood's full range of arms at the Armory inside the Bunker.

Power Armor Training

T-45d Power Armor

T-45d Power Helmet

Post Quest Activities

Now that you're a fully fledged member of the Brotherhood of Steel, and you have Elder McNamara's ear, you can use your influence to create a treaty with the NCR, and have the Brotherhood fight with them during the battle at Hoover Dam. In addition, Knight Torres sells some new (and powerful) items from the Bunker store: including the Laser RCW, Tri-beam Laser, Laser Rifles and Pistols, and even the infamous Gatling Laser. Consult the Tour Chapter for more information.

FLAGS OF OUR FOUL-UPS

SUGGESTED EXPERIENCE

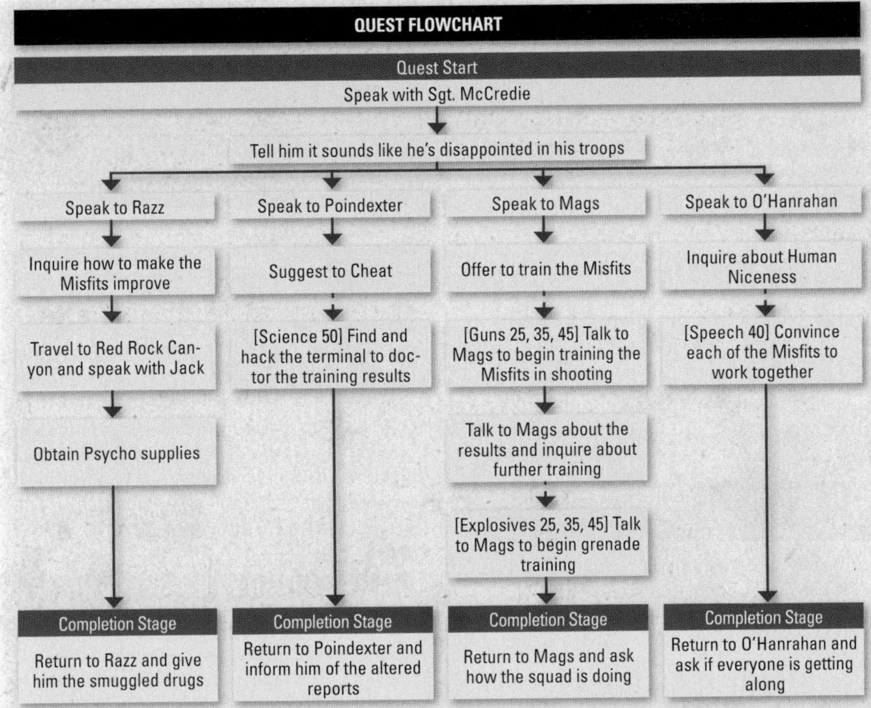

Main Factions

Once you're outside at the shooting range **(4)** with the team lined up, Mags asks for your words of wisdom:

Tell the squad to take positions where they can cover each other.

The squad needs to take their time and pick their shots while in communication with each other.

Exhaling before firing is the key. Squeeze, don't jerk!

Talk to Mags about further improvements.

Let the team shoot for a few moments before speaking to Mags again. The Misfits still have a grenade range inspection to pass. Agree to help.

Help the Misfits improve their grenade skills.

Speak with Mags once the team is in a line:

Tell the team to pull the pin, let it cook off for a count of three, and then throw.

The grenade shouldn't be pitched, but thrown with a good, solid arc.

Accuracy is less important; grenades are useful for breaking up clusters of foes.

Talk to Mags about the squad's readiness.

After the grenades have stopped flying, talk to Mags one more time. She tells you the team is progressing well, and the Quest concludes. Don't forget to tell McCredie!

An In-Tents Situation

1

2

Optionally begin by starting Side Quest: No, Not Much up at Camp Bitter Springs [3.08] by speaking with Captain Gilles. Or, simply travel here; the rows of tents and numerous troops makes Camp Golf [3.23] one of the largest NCR bases outside New Vegas. It is also where you find Sergeant McCredie, inside the larger tent **(1)** close to the House Resort. The sergeant **(2)** has little time for the likes of you, until you mention that Captain Gilles at Bitter Springs needs reinforcements. Keep the conversation going until you can mention that McCredie seems "a little disappointed" in his troops. He tells you he calls them "Misfits" for a reason; they're undisciplined, lazy, and lacking spirit. You're quite welcome to whip them into shape....

Leave the large tent, and find each of the recruits McCredie finds so objectionable (they're all in this camp). You need to turn one of the Misfits into a well-oiled fighting machine. Naturally, each takes a certain amount of skill on your part to complete successfully.

Note: Several Bitter Springs quests are interrelated. The following list shows any Quests you can undertake to improve your Reputation with the NCR. You don't have to complete any of them to begin this Quest, though.

- Complete Side Quest: Bitter Springs Infirmary Blues (optional).
- Complete Side Quest: Flags of Our Foul-Ups (this Quest).
- Complete Side Quest: I Put a Spell on You.
- Complete Side Quest: Restoring Hope.
- Complete Side Quest: Climb Ev'ry Mountain.

Note: These five Quests are all parts of Side Quest: No, Not Much.

Misfit #1: Gunplay and Grenades with Mags

3

Speak with Mags **(3)**, and ask her about squad unity. She'd have an easier time teaching Radroaches to march in formation. Mags needs the team to practice their marksmanship and explosives techniques, which are sorely lacking. Agree to take them out onto the range.

Help the Misfits improve their shooting skills.

Misfit #2: O'Hanrahan's Such a Nice Boy

5

Or, you can converse with Recruit O'Hanrahan **(5)**. He thinks the squad needs "a little more basic human niceness." You quiz his thinking, but he

wants the team to work more cohesively. But the idea shouldn't be his; it should be yours.

Convince the Misfits to work together.

Convince Mags to respect the squad and work with them.

Convince Razz to respect the squad and work with them.

Convince Poindexter to respect the squad and work with them.

Speak to each individual squad-mate, and ask about their backgrounds. Then mention their lack of fondness for each other.

Tell the squad-mates they should work together, and not against their common interest. Do this for each of the team members.

Return to O'Hanrahan.

Talk to O'Hanrahan again after the team agrees to put aside their differences. He tells you they're going to be "A-Okay!" The Quest concludes. Go speak to McCredie.

Misfit #3: Poindexter's Deception

Another option is the smart aleck Poindexter **(6)**, who has a theory and answer for everything, including the inadequacies in team dynamics. Poindexter thought a job in the NCR would mean coasting on an easy wave of mediocrity to a cushy government pension. Tell him to cheat in the forthcoming test. He's intrigued, but the company readiness reports are logged on the computer systems at the House Resort. Hack the system, and the records could be tweaked. Agree to this.

Fake the Misfits' readiness reports.

The House Resort **(7)** is the large stone edifice behind the tents. Head through the entrance double-doors to the grand foyer, and look for the Squad Readiness Reports Terminal **(8)** on the large curved desk below the main staircase.

Log on to the computer, which has four menu items. The first is for Squad CC554-2 ("Misfits") and the other shows troop movement for different Ranger detachments. The Misfits' rifle and grenade reports make depressing reading (unless you're aligned with the Legion). However, the third menu option—to "Alter Readiness Reports"—is worth checking. The team is now analyzed as "excellent."

NCR Infamy Gained!

Or, you can log into the Squad Readiness Reports Terminal (ideally when the Rangers aren't at their desks) in the offices behind the reception desk. This is easier to attempt without being spotted.

NCR Infamy Gained!

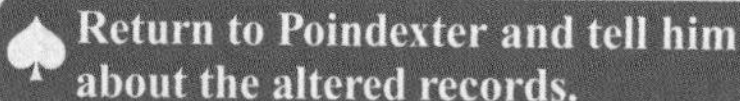

Return to Poindexter and tell him about the altered records.

Tell Poindexter the hack is complete, and he graciously calls himself a genius, with you running a close second. The Quest concludes. Go speak to McCredie.

Misfit #4: Juicing Up With Razz

The last of these miscreants is the partially hidden Razz **(9)**, who's adamant that the team needs "a healthy dose of angry juice." He means Psycho! He still has hookups; Jack at Red Rock Canyon [1.15] has the goods. Psycho is a bitch to quit though, so Razz reckons you might want to try another recruit.

Get drugs from Jack at Red Rock Canyon.

Head deep into Great Kahn territory, and visit the Red Rock Drug Lab **(10)** [1.14] connected to the main settlement. Here you'll find Jack and Diane. Tell Jack **(11)** that Razz wants "the usual," and you're handed a suspicious package. Speak to Jack if you want, then scarper.

Suspicious Package

Return the drugs to Razz.

Razz is jazzed at your return with the Psycho. It's going to be party time in the camp tonight! With the team feeling altogether more pumped for murdering the enemy, return to speak with McCredie.

Talk to Sgt. McCredie about the Misfits' improvement.

Although this Quest has concluded, remember that to finish Side Quest: No, Not Much, you need to return to Sergeant McCredie and request that reinforcements be sent to Captain Gilles at Bitter Springs. McCredie now agrees to this, and this specific Quest updates.

XP 200 XP

FOR AULD LANG SYNE

SUGGESTED EXPERIENCE

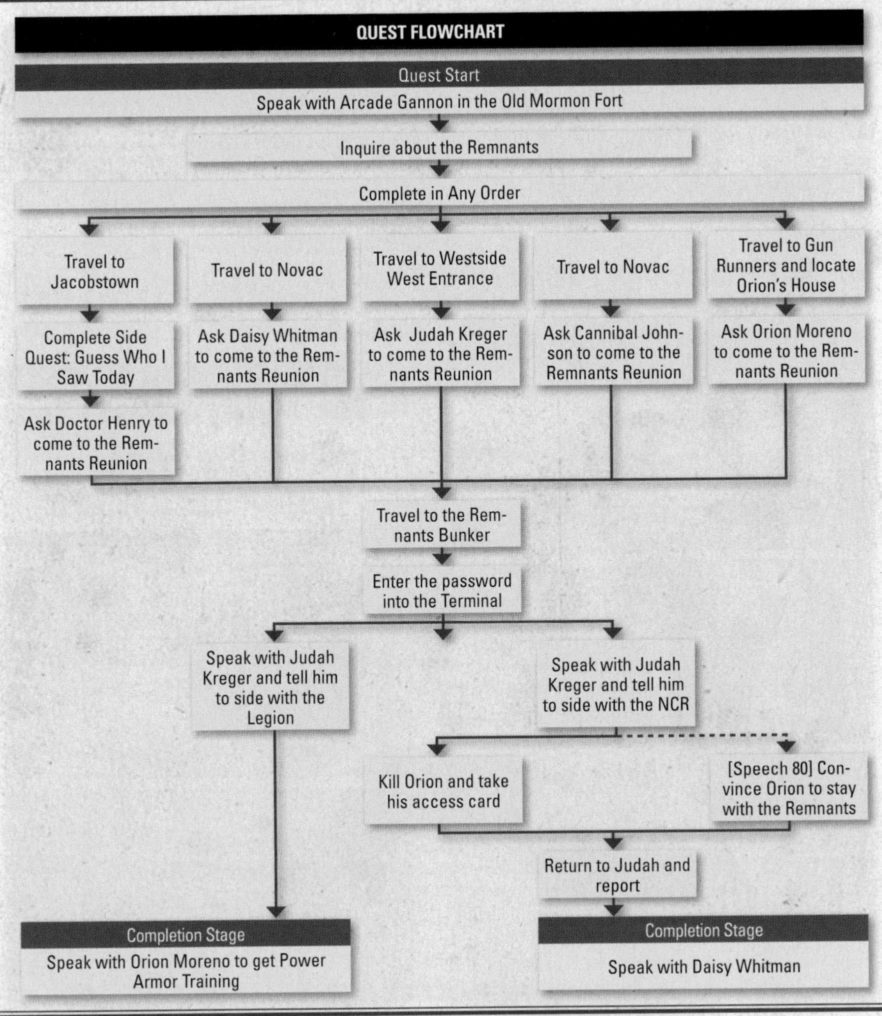

Main Factions

FOLLOWERS OTA | ENCLAVE

Pre-Quest: Gaining Ground with Gannon

This Quest has a few prerequisites, the first of which is to locate and have Arcade Gannon in your party. Do this by visiting the Followers Faction over at the Old Mormon Fort [2C.01] in Freeside **(1)**, and locating him **(2)**. Gannon is a friendly sort, and he's open to flattery. He also tells you about the research he's carrying out. In fact, this research, and Gannon's past, begins the conversation that eventually begins this Quest. But first, you need to gain Gannon's trust, which is scored in a "Points" system (see in the following table) based on actions that benefit the Followers. Once he likes you, you can inquire about Remnants; a hidden cabal of those who survived the extermination of the Enclave decades previously. The advancement in the Main Quest is vital, as (for example) the NCR begin to bring reinforcements, such as Power Armor Troops, into Camp Forlorn Hope, which triggers some of Arcade's dialogue. This conversation occurs when you've acquired two "Points," and the latter stages of your Main Quest are reached.

- Specifically, this means the following:

NEW CA. REPUBLIC / MR. HOUSE: You've completed most of Main Quest: For the Republic, Part 2, and you've dealt with the Brotherhood (either killed or scored a treaty with them).

CAESAR'S LEGION: You've successfully completed Main Quest: Render Unto Caesar.

INDEPENDENT: You've installed Yes Man, and completed Main Quest: Wild Card: Side Bets.

- **With Arcade, convince the Remnants to reunite for one last battle.**
- **Ask Doctor Henry to come to the Remnants reunion.**
- **Ask Daisy Whitman to come to the Remnants reunion.**
- **Ask Cannibal Johnson to come to the Remnants reunion.**
- **Ask Orion Moreno to come to the Remnants reunion.**
- **Ask Judah Kreger to come to the Remnants reunion.**

You must bring Arcade Gannon with you across the Mojave Wasteland to secure the support of five elderly survivors: the Remnants. You can find them in any order you wish. Already killed one or more of them? Bad news; the Quest is already over!

Only the Remnants Remain: Arcade Gannon's Progress

Location ID	Location Name	Associated Quest	Event	"Points"
[2.19]	Camp McCarran	Side Quest: The White Wash	Complete the Quest, arrest Anderson, but keep Westside supplied with water	+1
[2.19]	Camp McCarran	Side Quest: The White Wash	Complete the Quest, frame the Scorpion gang and kill them	+2
[2.19]	Camp McCarran	Side Quest: There Stands the Grass	After talking to Doctor Hildern about the OSI	+1
[3.28]	The Fort	Main Quest: Render Unto Caesar	Enter The Fort with Arcade, and tell him you only want to see what the Legion is up to; then quickly leave.	+3
[5.13]	HELIOS One	Side Quest: That Lucky Old Sun	Complete the Quest, and direct the power to Freeside	+1
[5.17]	REPCONN Test Site	None	Entering the vicinity, and sometimes the interior of the Test Site, triggers a reaction from Arcade	+1
[6.24]	Crashed Vertibird	None	Inspect the crash site, and Arcade remarks on the aircraft	+1

An Old Enclave: Cannibal Johnson

3

4

As you'd expect, Cannibal Johnson resides in the cave bearing his name [3.11], east of the main New Vegas conurbation. Locate the rocky outcrop **(3)**, enter the small cavern (watching for the Bear Traps underfoot), and speak to Johnson **(4)**. He's waiting for death, not a reunion. Ask him to join the reunion. He agrees, no matter what you say to him, and tells you of a five-word phrase needed to get into the Remnant Bunker. His word, appropriately enough, is "old." Although "deranged" would be closer to the mark. Afterward, speak with Arcade Gannon. Be sympathetic or sharp-tongued as you wish.

An Old Enclave: Daisy Whitman

5

6

The old pilot is currently residing at the Novac Motel **(5)**, in the town of the same name [5.18]. She's either on the balcony or in her room. Ask Daisy **(6)** to join, optionally inquiring about her past as a pilot, and she readily agrees to the reunion. Her word is "dear." You can ask how she enjoyed piloting Vertibirds for the Enclave before you leave. Gannon tells you more about his youth. Fake an interest.

An Old Enclave: Judah Kreger

7

The leader of the pack is on the streets of Westside, close to Miguel's Pawn Shop **(7)** [2.02]. Stop Judah **(8)** and ask him to join the crew. He asks why "a bunch of old warhorses" are needed. Respond as you desire, and he reluctantly agrees, telling you his word is "Navarro." You can then ask about the old squad, and Judah reveals there was a little tension among his team; Johnson and Moreno never got along. You can also inquire about the Enclave oil rig explosion and Navarro, familiar to scholars of recent history. Then speak and respond to Arcade once more.

8

An Old Enclave: Orion Moreno

9

10

Orion Moreno now lives in a small house on the other side of The Strip perimeter wall, just southeast of the Gun Runners establishment [2.14]. Locate the home **(9)**, and enter it. Moreno **(10)** has some choice words for the NCR. You can ask about his hatred of the NCR, and let him know that Arcade is gathering the Remnants. After he answers, butter him up or respond sarcastically if you wish; Moreno grudgingly agrees, but asks which Faction the team is planning to attack. Answer, and he makes sure you know he wants a piece of the NCR. His word is "Remember." Speak to Arcade once again.

An Old Enclave: Doctor Henry

11

12

The hardest of the Remnants to sway is Doctor Henry, who's currently experimenting with Stealth technology over in the remote north-western mountains. Trek to Jacobstown **(11)** [1.10], talk with Marcus the Super Mutant, and then enter the lodge. When you ask him to head to the reunion, Henry **(12)** says he's interested, but only after he completes his work here. At this point, you must successfully complete Side Quest: Guess Who I Saw Today. Refer to that Quest for detailed information, but briefly, you need to:

Agree to look for the source of the Nightstalker mutation.

Take Lily with you (if you wish) and explore the Charleston Cave [1.07] system to the north.

Battle Nightstalkers, and uncover the Chewed Stealth Boy from a slain Super Mutant.

Bring it back to Henry, coax Lily into being a test subject, then calm or deal with Keene.

Then keep the tests running, stop the tests, or solve the doctor's problem.

Henry is now amenable to the meet-up, and reveals his word to be "Friends." Now speak to Arcade Gannon.

♠ Gain access to the Remnants Bunker.

Dear Old Friends, Remember Navarro

13

14

Almost due east of Jacobstown in the north-western mountains is the Remnants Bunker [1.11], which is well hidden from view **(13)**. Locate the ground hatch in the rock alcove, and descend. Activate the door panel, and say the phrase "Dear old friends, remember Navarro." This only works if you've been told all five words! When the door unlocks, enter the bunker, and head into the Vertibird landing bay, complete with an astonishingly rare Enclave Vertibird **(14)**, as well as suits of Enclave Power Armor (which you can't take yet).

♠ Ask the Remnants to support the fight against the Legion or the NCR.

15

The whole team is here! Enter the command room **(15)**, and speak to the team. It soon becomes clear that old rivalries and loyalties are set in stone. Talk to Judah. You now have a choice, depending on whether you've allied with Caesar's Legion, or the NCR ("pro-NCR" plans include allying with Mr. House, or working independently).

Allied Faction	Remnants must fight against:
NCR	Caesar's Legion
Caesar's Legion	NCR
Mr. House	Caesar's Legion
Yes Man/Independent	Caesar's Legion

Siding with the NCR: Moreno is a No-Go

16

Choose "I want you to help the NCR hold onto the Dam," and Judah is okay with that, although Moreno won't be; he'll need talking to.

Try to convince Orion Moreno to stay.

Out in the hangar, Moreno has already tooled up in Remnant Power Armor for the battle ahead, although he isn't fighting for the NCR; he's ready to face you down! You can:

SPEECH 80 Tell him the team will show the NCR how its done. Amazingly, this works. Although Moreno won't be part of the battle, he does back off, allowing you to use his Power Armor and his keycard.

Any other choice results in a one-on-one battle between you and Orion Moreno **(16)**. Be sure to salvage his armor and keycard from the corpse.

 **Power Armor Training**

 **Remnants Power Armor**

 **Remnants Power Helmet**

 **Door Override Card**

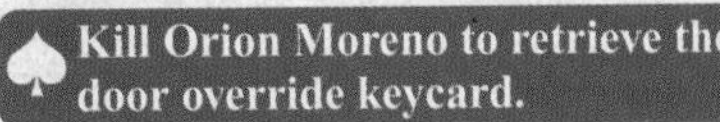

Kill Orion Moreno to retrieve the door override keycard.

Tell Judah Kreger what happened with Orion Moreno.

Back in the command room, Judah witnessed Orion's meltdown, and doesn't blame you. Speak to Daisy Whitman to be trained in Power Armor, if you haven't learned this Perk already (during Side Quests: Tend to Your Business or Eyesight to the Blind).

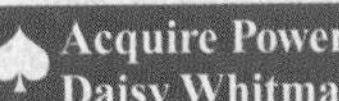

Acquire Power Armor training from Daisy Whitman.

Siding with Caesar: Johnson Isn't Eager

Choose "Help the Legion take over the Dam," and Judah agrees, although Johnson won't go along with it because he likes the NCR. He's a crack shot, and it's a shame not to take him along. He won't be convinced though. However, because Johnson isn't coming, there's an extra suit of Power Armor. Speak to Orion Moreno to be trained in it, if you haven't learned this Perk already.

 **Power Armor Training**

 **Remnants Power Armor**

 **Remnants Power Helmet**

Acquire Power Armor training from Orion Moreno.

Now leave the Remnants' command room so they can plan for the coming battle.

Post-Quest Activities: Reign of Death

You receive the Remnants Power Armor, and must leave the Remnants to plan for the attack on Hoover Dam [3.33]. Whenever you begin Act III of the Main Quest, the Remnants provide an extra line of fire and support on your behalf. During the battle, the Remnants swoop in, land, and kick a lot of ass. If you chose the path to convince Moreno and train with Daisy, you'll be wearing her Power Armor (because she's piloting the Vertibird).

 **500 XP**

G.I. BLUES

MAIN QUEST INTERSECTION

SUGGESTED EXPERIENCE

See flowchart on the following page

Before You Begin....

The King's School of Impersonation [2C.05] is a Freeside landmark, and the place where a Faction of likeminded and generally good-natured hoodlums attempt to keep order across town, and mimic the mannerisms of a long-dead and almost forgotten musician of ancient times. If you can earn The King's trust, this can be a powerful ally in the forthcoming battle for Mojave Wasteland supremacy. Before you begin, it is worth knowing the different ways you can approach this Quest:

There are no prerequisites to begin this Quest, so it can be started at any time. However, one of the Factions you may be working with during the Main Quest wants to ensure support (or annihilation) of the Kings for an incoming and ultimate battle. To this end, you can:

Investigate before you're allied to any one Faction in the Main Quest.

NEW CA. REPUBLIC Investigate on behalf of NCR Ambassador Crocker, to curb tension between the two Factions during Main Quest: King's Gambit. Check with this Quest for more specific, NCR-related information.

MR. HOUSE Mr. House is not interested in the services of the Kings.

CAESAR'S LEGION Caesar likes the altercation the Kings are having with the NCR, but doesn't consider them worthy enough to bother with.

INDEPENDENT If you're acting independently, Yes Man doesn't consider the Kings necessary to bring to your side, although it doesn't hurt to try.

Big Boss Man

1

2

Begin at the building with the giant neon guitar **(1)** promising open enrollments. Enter King's School of Impersonation, and head left to the locked door guarded by a slick-haired guy called Pacer **(2)** (or another one of King's henchmen if you've had an "altercation" with Pacer already). Pacer wants to know how much it's worth to get to meet the big man. You can:

QUEST FLOWCHART

Quest Start

Speak to The King at the King's School of Impersonation in Freeside

Speak to Orris near the northern gate of Freeside

Purchase Bodyguard services from Orris and follow him

Follow Orris until he says "I'll scout ahead" and turns the corner.

Observe Orris shoots his weapon outside of the player's view, then force greets the player

[Intelligence 6] Tell Orris that he fired three shots, but there are four bodies

[Medicine 30] Examine the bodies.

Fail all of the skill checks required to find out info on Orris

Return to the King. He will tell the player to hire Orris as many times as it takes to gain information.

Call Orris out on his scam, or Ignore

[Barter 51] Extort Orris

Kill Orris

Return to King and report what you've learned, then head to Old Mormon fort and find out who's been attacking locals

Speak to Wayne and then Roy at the Old Mormon Fort

Return to the King and inform him of the attacks

Head to the Old Mormon Fort and speak with Julie Farkas

Speak to the squatters, and inquire with The Missionary

Head to the train station at night and give the password "Hope"

Observe food distribution and return to the King

Return to the King and inform of the distribution

Follow Pacer and kill the NCR

Completion Stage

Speak to The King

Speak with Kieran and inquire about why the locals don't get food

Return to the King and inform him what happened

Head to the train station and tell Kieran of the misunderstanding

Completion Stage

Speak to the King

Shoot the place up, and fail the Quest impressively, which is also what happens if you try opening the door without Pacer's say-so.

60 You can tell him you want to pay your respects. Pacer likes that, and lets you in.

Or, you can offer five Caps (you're turned away in disgust), 50 Caps (Pacer lets you in), or 500 Caps (Pacer lets you in while you remember not to give away all your Caps).

The King himself, and his robot dog Rex **(3)** are both attempting to sit through an excruciating performance on the stage. He introduces himself (and his poorly hound dog) and you can ask him various questions. For Quest-related chatter, ask if he has any work for you. He wonders if you noticed the bodyguards for hire near the Freeside gates. One of them, called Orris, is making a little too much money, and he wants you to find out why. You're to hire him, and see what happens. The King gives you 200 Caps of hiring money.

Caps (200).

Hire a guard named Orris near the northern gate of Freeside.

Too Much Monkey Business

Head through the carriage doors, and up to the Freeside gate **(4)** where Orris and a few other folk are waiting. Orris **(5)** tells you that no one keeps you safer en route to the South Gate than him. Agree, and give him the 200 Caps the King just gave you. You didn't spend it, right?

Follow Orris to the south gate and watch for any suspicious behavior.

Orris sets off at an impressive pace, and it's sometimes tricky to keep up. Sheathe your weapon and you'll run faster. After a sprint to the southwest, accessing the carriage doors to Freeside, Orris jogs past the King's School of Impersonation, before making a left about a block before The Strip North Gate [2.13]. Shouting that he'll scout ahead, Orris turns the corner and sprints off. You hear gunfire, and by the time you arrive, he stops you and indicates four thugs lying on the road. Impressive, eh?

6 Not so fast; tell him he fired three shots and there are four guys here. He stammers that one of his bullets hit both men. Retort that he just faked this shooting to drum up repeat business. He thinks this is "an interesting theory." You can:

Extort all the money he has on him, or you'll head to the King and tell him. Orris grudgingly hands you all his Caps, and flees.

Caps (348)

Or you can keep Orris and continue, either if your Intelligence is too low, or instead of Bartering.

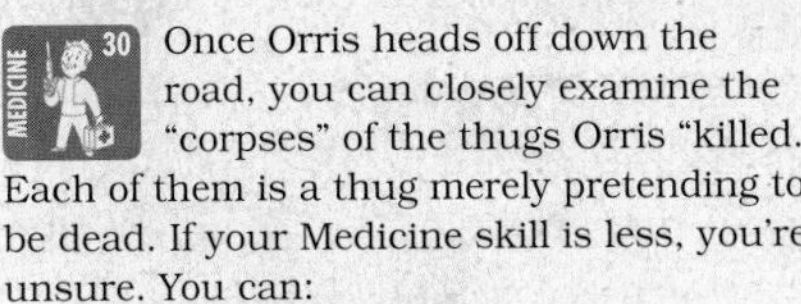

Once Orris heads off down the road, you can closely examine the "corpses" of the thugs Orris "killed." Each of them is a thug merely pretending to be dead. If your Medicine skill is less, you're unsure. You can:

Keep Orris, and continue.

Or plant a bullet or sharp object into the head of one of the dead thugs, or Orris **(6)**, and kill all five of these tricksters.

If you keep going, Orris eventually finishes his chaperoning. Return to the King.

Return to the King and report what you've learned about Orris.

Return to the King and report that Orris is dead.

A Big Hunk O' Love

7

Start a second talk with the King, who's usually right where you left him, but sometimes up in his apartment inside the same building **(7)**, and inform him what you learned about Orris:

If you didn't spot the scam, you must tell the King Orris seemed legit. He doesn't believe it, and tells you to hire Orris again. Repeat the chaperoning until you come back with the evidence the King needs! As Orris is now wise to your plan, he attacks you at the end of his chaperoning, so killing him is the only option.

If you spotted the scam (whether you killed Orris or let him live) the King thanks you for you help, and asks if you want to help with something more important.

It seems that many of the Freeside dwellers are resenting the influx of people who've swarmed the area recently. These newcomers, many of whom come from the NCR, aren't happy about being resented, and this sometimes leads to violence. This includes a few friends of the King's, and he wants you to find out who did it.

Go to the Old Mormon Fort and question some injured Locals about their assailants.

8

9

Head back out into Freeside, and locate the Old Mormon Fort [2C.01], and approach the large front entrance **(8)**. Check the first tent on the right as you enter, and you'll see three bruised and battered fellows named (from left to right): Wayne, Farris, and Roy **(9)**. Speak with Roy and then Wayne, telling them the King asked you to look into the attack. From your quizzing, you learn the attackers were big, young, and "better dressed than most Freesiders." And one of them was called "Lou." "Lou. Tenant." Make sure you're pleasant to these victims to increase your Fame.

Freeside Fame Gained!

Return to the King with your findings.

Back at the King's place, you surmise that the locals were attacked by NCR soldiers. The King doesn't like this, and hopes the NCR aren't about to take over Vegas. He'll ask around in case something big is going down. Part of this involves you heading back the way you came, to speak to folk at the squatter camps, or with Julie Farkas over at the Mormon Fort. She tends to know about these things.

Head to one of the Squatter camps in Freeside and learn why NCR soldiers have been entering the area.

(Optional) Talk to Julie Farkas and see if the Followers know anything about the situation.

In the Ghetto

10

Back at the Mormon Fort, locate Julie Farkas **(10)**, who is on the grounds, or inside one of the towers. Ask her about the NCR soldiers in Freeside, and she tells you her friend—Major Elizabeth Kieran—is handing out supplies to the poor in the western part of Freeside. Tell her the King thinks those troops have been attacking the locals, and Julie reckons you should speak to Kieran about it, and to mention her name so Kieran will open up.

(Optional) Talk to Major Elizabeth Kieran, and mention Julie Farkas if she's reluctant to help.

Ask around the Squatter camp to find a lead regarding why NCR soldiers are in Freeside.

Suspicious Minds

11

12

You can also find out more about these attacks at two squatter camps.

#1: The nearest is behind the Mormon Fort **(11)**, close to the Freeside perimeter wall. Grecks the ghoul is here, but the one doing the talking is a man named "the Missionary" **(12)**.

13

14

#2: The second is to the south of the Mormon Fort, one block southwest of Mick & Ralph's [2C.02] by Freeside's perimeter wall and a watchtower **(13)**. Santiago mooches around here, but the person to speak to is "the Missionary" **(14)**.

He asks if you're interested in free meals, but they're only for NCR citizens. Claim that you're a citizen, and "the Missionary"needs to verify your citizenship status with a few questions:

- "Who was the most popular president in NCR history: Peterson, Tibbett, Kimble, or Tandi?"

The answer is "Tandi."

- "What was the original name of the NCR capital: The Boneyard, Shady Sands, Aradesh, or Vault 13?"

The answer is "Shady Sands."

- "What animal is on the NCR's flag: A two-headed bear, an eagle, a two-headed snake, or a two-tailed lion?"

The answer is "A two-headed bear."

Answer all three questions correctly, and "the Missionary" tells you the meals are available up by the old train station in the northwest part of town. The password to tell the guards is "hope."

Answer any of the three questions incorrectly, or exhibit violence to the man, and you don't receive the password. You can retake the test as many times as you want.

Investigate rumors of free food and water being handed out nightly in the northwest part of Freeside.

Don't Be Cruel

15

16

Beneath the ruins of the partially collapsed freeway over on the western side of Freeside (get there by heading down the street, passing the Atomic Wrangler [2C.06], and then taking the door in the ruined house on your right), close to the boarded-up train station, is a Ruined Store [2C.03]. Approach the entrance **(15)**, and you're stopped by one of the two men guarding the place, who look like the guys that checked your citizenship. You can:

Leave, if you don't know the password.

 Tell them you're here to see Major Kieran on urgent business, and enter.

Or, if you learned the password via the citizenship test, tell them the password is "hope," and enter.

Squeeze past the hungry squatters and guards, and locate Elizabeth Kieran **(16)**. You can:

- Ask if she's with the military, and why locals aren't served. You can receive some food for you (and a nonexistent friend you're afraid wouldn't get served) if you want.
- Ask why locals aren't served. She isn't forthcoming, so:

Mention that Julie Farkas told you to ask her. Kieran explains that the NCR sent an envoy to the King, offering to coordinate the relief effort. He was brutally beaten, and the relief mission was scrapped. Kieran is currently functioning with greatly reduced NCR support.

Or witness the food operation without learning this rather pertinent fact.

Return to the King and inform him of the NCR supply drops.

(Optional) Inform the King that the NCR previously sent an envoy to discuss distributing supplies to Freeside.

Head back to see the King. Inside the School of Impersonation, after you've heard Kieran's story about the beaten NCR envoy, Pacer stops you and tells you the story is fake, and nothing to bother the King with. What's Pacer got to do to keep your mouth shut?

You can agree, or disagree, and make up your mind later.

Or you can extort some Caps, and make up your mind later.

 **Caps (200)**

 And then extort more Caps, and make your mind up later.

 **Caps (100)**

When you reach the King, inform him that you've seen the NCR distributing supplies near the old train station. At this point, you can:

Fail to mention anything about the NCR envoy, so that it appears the NCR is purposefully neglecting the majority of Freeside residents. This infuriates the King, and he orders you down there, to wipe out the NCR scum.

Or, you can choose to tell the King that "they said someone was sent to discuss the issue with you," and then explain that the man was beaten up. The King is shocked, and understands now why the NCR have been "all riled at us." Just then, the King is interrupted with news that Pacer is in a gunfight down by the train station. The King orders you to back him up.

Depending on your previous actions, and what you've told the King, you have two distinct conclusions to this Quest:

Head to the train station in northwest Freeside and try to negotiate with the NCR.

Kill all of the NCR troops holed up by the train station in northwest Freeside.

Head to the supply drop building and see if Pacer needs any help.

Conclusion #1: Fools Rush In (Where Angels Fear to Tread)

17

Head across Freeside to the train station, where the NCR citizens are milling about. Pacer may be cowering in a bus shelter, or not involved in this fight. Either way, you have a host of folk to mow down **(17)**. Tag them from afar, use the corners of the train station as cover, or Sneak in and lay Mines or pickpocket Grenades or C-4 into them; but don't leave until everyone (including Major Kieran) is dead.

 **NCR Infamy Gained!**

 **Freeside Fame Gained!**

 **1,200 XP**

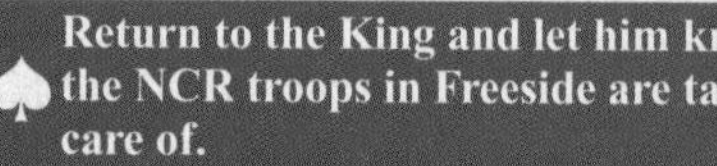
Return to the King and let him know the NCR troops in Freeside are taken care of.

Conclusion #2: Can't Help Falling in Love

18

Head across Freeside to the train station, where the NCR citizens are milling about nervously. Seek out Elizabeth Kieran **(18)**. You can tell her you're here to kill her (and start Conclusion #1), or state that the King wants to help with the relief effort. She warns you that the King might have a loose cannon among his men, and agrees to stand down.

 **Freeside Fame Gained!**

 **1,500 XP**

> *Note* If you've allied with the NCR, the best scenario for you is to keep the NCR Reputation up. Do this by:
>
> A. Convincing the King to curb the violence by talking to him before the Quest starts.
>
> B. Completing this Quest without killing the NCR citizens (Conclusion #2).
>
> C. Or eradicating every single member of the Kings.
>
> Check Main Quest: King's Gambit for more information.

Return to the King and let him know the situation with the NCR has been defused.

Post Quest Antics: A Little Less Conversation

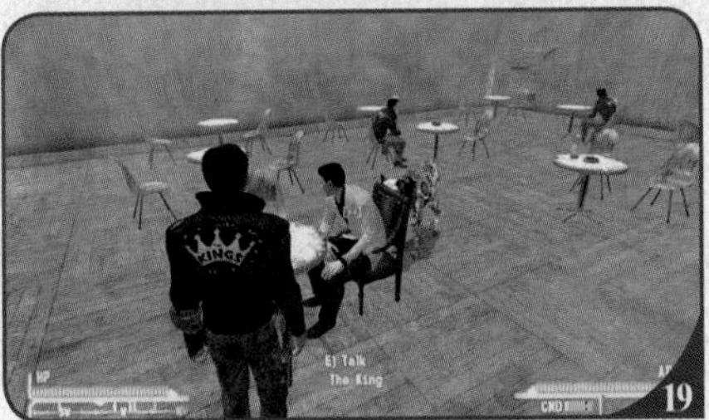

The King thinks either that "you helped us plenty," or that it's time for "a little more talkin' and a little less fightin'." He also offers you a reward: a single favor from the King. You can:

Join the Kings. The King doesn't usually do this, but he agrees to let you in. You can get your hair sculpted by Sergio (in the building), and wear the same type of amazingly stylish attire as the King himself **(19)**.

King's Outfit

Get access to The Strip. The King organizes a Passport, and tells you to pick it up from Mick & Ralph's.

You can receive a payment of Caps.

Caps (1,000)

Ask about Rex, the robot dog. Although his brain is slowly seeping out of its casing, he could be a faithful companion. See Side Quest: Nothin' But a Hound Dog for further details.

Finally, if you don't use the King's favor for any of the above listed options, you can approach the King during Main Quest: King's Gambit. Instead of killing Pacer for Ambassador Crocker, simply speak to the King and ask him to curb the violence as a favor to you. He agrees, allowing you to finish this Quest succinctly, and without doing any dirty work.

GHOST TOWN GUNFIGHT / RUN GOODSPRINGS RUN

SUGGESTED EXPERIENCE

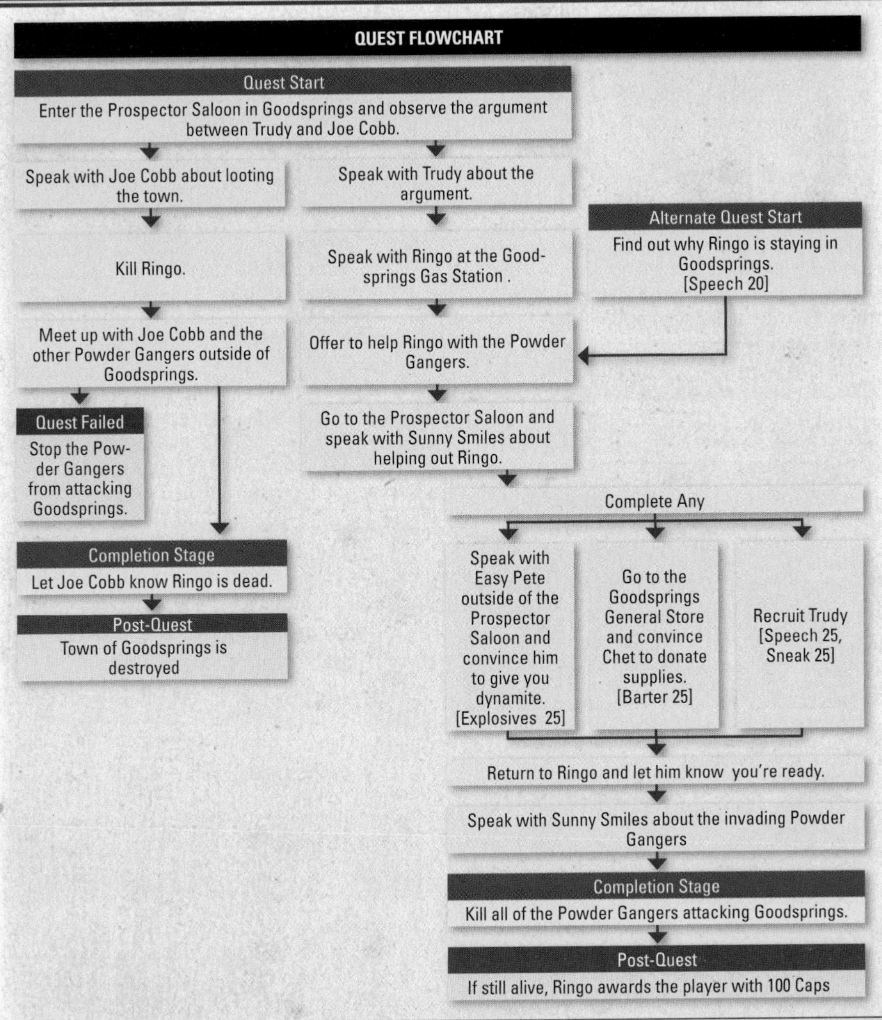

Ringo's Mistake Revealed

1

2

Although not mandatory, you might want to hone your talents with Sunny Smiles by completing Main Quests: Back in the Saddle and By a Campfire on the Trail, although you can start this Quest the moment you've shot the Sarsaparilla bottles with Sunny Smiles. Over at the Prospector Saloon **(1)** in the ghost town of Goodsprings [4.05], there's trouble brewing. Enter to watch a rather heated argument between a Powder Ganger named Joe Cobb, and the saloon proprietor Trudy **(2)**. After the verbal altercation, speak to both parties involved. Pick a side (ideally sticking to the Faction you've aligned yourself with), and the Quest splits into two main branches:

That guy in the gas station is Ringo; you can stumble across him without speaking to Trudy or Joe Cobb if you open the Goodsprings Gas Station, and find out why Ringo is in the area (with a successful Speech check).

Pick a Side #1: Goodsprings Townsfolk (Ghost Town Gunfight)

Talk with Trudy **(3)**. You can fix her radio, and talk at length about her knowledge of the Mojave Wasteland. But to continue, tell her you overheard the argument. She says a trader named Ringo came into town, with bad men after him. Goodsprings folk gave him a place to lie low, but the Powder Gangers have caught up with him. Murdering Joe Cobb isn't the towns-folk's way. Trudy hopes Ringo sneaks out. In fact, if you can help Ringo, you'd get a decent Reputation around here, even a discount at the saloon!

After some aimless wandering, you'll find Ringo inside the Goodsprings Gas Station **(4)**. Step inside, and you're met by a twitchy, but seemingly friendly Ringo **(5)**. You can:

Gun him down, switching sides to the Powder Gangers.

You can also play (and learn the rules of) Caravan. Ringo gives you your first deck.

Or speak to him about his predicament. He tells you that it would be wise to enlist the help of the Goodsprings population to help fight against the Powder Gangers. Agree to check out the following Objectives (you can complete any or none of the Optional ones).

Caravan Deck

Offer to help Ringo deal with the Powder Gangers.

Talk to Sunny Smiles about fighting the Powder Gangers.

(Optional) Enlist the help of Trudy.

(Optional) Convince Chet to open his store's stock to the town.

(Optional) Acquire Easy Pete's dynamite.

Task #1: All Smiles

Head back to the Prospector Saloon **(1)**, where Sunny Smiles **(6)** and her shaggy dog friend are waiting. Ask if she'll help, and she immediately agrees. Simple. You can now return to Ringo, or attempt to enlist more folk.

Return to Ringo and let him know that Sunny Smiles has agreed to help you fight the Powder Gangers.

Task #2: Trudy's True Calling

Back at the Prospector's Saloon **(1)**, Trudy **(7)** already knows your plans, and thinks it's a big risk. She needs convincing:

The battle will be full of bullets, explosions, and lots of fun.

The saloon and store are good ambush spots. If you had the help.

Either option works, although Trudy reckons everybody could be better-equipped if Chet could help out. You should also visit Doctor Mitchell for some medical supplies.

(Optional) Acquire additional medical supplies from Doc Mitchell.

Task #3: Stocking Up with Chet

Over at the General Store **(8)**, step up to the counter and speak with Chet **(9)**. Chet offers a wide variety of items for sale. Peruse his goods, then request some supplies to help fight off the Powder Gangers. Chet isn't about to invest 1,000 Caps-worth of equipment to this cause:

Tell Chet the Powder Gangers will take over, and finish your verbal flourish with some sarcasm. You're awarded some additional equipment (which you yourself should use).

Or you can give up sweet-talking Chet out of his goods.

Leather Armor

Tip

Chet is one of the first people you can meet who has specialized ammunition and weapon mod parts. It's a great idea to purchase some of his fine equipment. Consult the Guns and Gear Chapter of this guide for further information.

Task #4: For Pete's Sake

Sitting outside the Prospector Saloon **(1)** is an old timer called Easy Pete **(10)**. Ask about his dynamite, and he tells you the stuff is too dangerous. You can leave it at that, or:

Tell him you're familiar with the care and handling of Explosives. Pete agrees and tells you he'll have the stuff ready when the fight starts.

Task #5: Mitchell's Medical Prescription

Next to the Gas Station **(4)** is Doctor Mitchell's House **(11)**. Head inside and inform Doc Mitchell **(12)** of the current predicament. He has a bad leg, but lots of supplies. He'll give you what he can:

Ask about healing serious injuries, as you'll be using Explosives. This gives you an extra two Doctor's Bags.

Or thank him for his Stimpaks, ask him to heal you, speak about other matters, and then leave.

Stimpak (3)

Doctor's Bag (2)

Return to Ringo when you're ready for the gunfight with the Powder Gangers.

Now return to the Gas Station, and let Ringo know that Sunny's with you both, and it's time to face down the Powder Gangers (or you can wait until you're feeling more confident). The battle starts as soon as you agree to it!

Salvage what you can to add to your projectile threats in the combat to come.

Dynamite (3)

Defeat the Powder Gangers.

Join up with Sunny.

Last Hope at Prospector Saloon

13

Sunny joins you at the Gas Station and tells you the Gangers are here to play. She lets you know there's around six of them. Fortunately, Easy Pete came through for you, and she hands you some Dynamite.

 **Dynamite (5)**

Rush out of the Gas Station to the Prospector Saloon, and then look down the road to the south **(13)**. The Gangers are approaching from that direction. Sniping from higher ground is possible, or from behind the saloon or store buildings. But you'll save more lives if you soften up the foes by lobbing Dynamite at them before they split up. Most of the Gangers are armed with Melee Weapons, so you can back up and fire at them manually before they can reach you.

Assuming you defeat the Gangers, Ringo races up to you and hands over some Caps as thanks. Don't forget your Goodsprings discount at the saloon!

 **Caps (100)**

 **Goodsprings Fame Gained!**

 **Powder Gangers Infamy Gained!**

 **50 XP**

Tip Need to increase your Fame with Goodsprings still further? Then save the Goodsprings Settler from Geckos during Main Quest: Back in the Saddle, and fix Trudy's broken radio. Post-Quest, you also receive a discount on items from Chet's General Store. You are now Vilified with the Powder Gangers, and shot at on sight.

Pick a Side #2: Powder Gangers (Run Goodsprings Run)

14

Talk with Joe Cobb, and bring up the name he already mentioned; a man called Ringo. Joe tells you Ringo was some trader who decided to shoot instead of paying the Ganger toll. Ringo's hiding somewhere in Goodsprings. Cobb is almost at the point of shooting up the entire town for harboring the guy.

Ask if he's interested in taking over the town. Cobb quiets down and tells you to get out of town before you talk any more. If you want, follow him along the road heading southeast out of Goodsprings, to a building on the edge of town, where you and Cobb can hatch a plan **(14)**. Cobb wants to know why when there's nothing much worth stealing:

 Tell him the townsfolk will work for him, and pay him.

Or there's always the free food. Either response works, but first you'll need to settle matters with Ringo. He needs executing. Agree to this and Joe Cobb will return with his cohorts.

Kill Ringo.

Find Ringo inside the Goodsprings Gas Station **(4)**. Step inside, and you're met by a twitchy, but seemingly friendly Ringo **(5)**. You can:

Ask more about his problems; he has no chance against the gang on his own, although he saw you getting friendly with Cobb, and doesn't trust you. Convince him otherwise, and you can change your plans (Option #1).

Or, you can stop the conversation, and plant a bullet (or melee implement or fist) into Ringo. If you kill him, don't forget to loot the corpse for some Caps and a Caravan Deck.

 **Caravan Deck**

Tell Joe Cobb that Ringo is dead.

Back at your southeastern rendezvous point, check in with Joe Cobb, and let him know Ringo's dead. That's great and all, but Cobb needs to ensure his team isn't killed by a bunch of townies. You're tasked with the following objectives, which you can attempt, or ignore these requests, and tell Cobb to begin the battle.

 **Powder Gangers Fame Gained!**

(Optional) Shake down Chet for supplies.

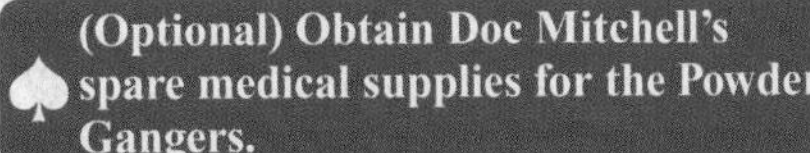

(Optional) Obtain Doc Mitchell's spare medical supplies for the Powder Gangers.

(Optional) Pick the lock on the Bighorner pen.

Let Joe Cobb know once you're ready to take over Goodsprings.

Task #1: General Store Shake Down

Move across the main drag to the General Store **(8)**, and walk up to Chet **(9)** who's manning the counter. Chet has a wide variety of items to purchase. Peruse his goods, but make sure you tell him the Powder Gangers need him to "donate" some supplies. Chet asks why.

 Let him know the supplies he gives up now mean his store won't be looted later.

 Tell him it's his chance to join the winning side. Either option works, and he hands over some leather armor and spare ammo.

Or rethink your ways, and talk about other matters.

 **9mm Rounds (30)**

 **Leather Armor**

 **Powder Gangers Fame Gained!**

Task #2: Bagging Mitchell's Medicine

Visit Dr. Mitchell's House **(11)** where you were treated for your wounds, and see the doctor again **(12)**. Lie, and tell him you need medical supplies for an injured man down the highway. When the doctor asks what the injuries are, you need to act quickly:

 Tell the doctor the man's breathing is uneven, and he's coughing up blood. The doctor quickly hands over what he can spare.

Or, you can stop the chat. You aren't fooling anyone.

 **Spare Medical Supplies**

Last Stand at Prospector Saloon

15

Return to Joe Cobb, and inform him of the tasks you've completed. Hand over the medical supplies. You keep the Leather Armor (wear it if you wish) and ammo. Cobb gives you back some of the medicine, in preparation for the battle. When you're ready to fight, tell him "let's take over Goodsprings!"

 **Powder Gangers Fame Gained!**

 **Stimpaks (5)**

 **Super Stimpak**

 **Buffout**

Let battle commence **(15)**! Head toward the Prospector Saloon, and engage Easy Pete, Trudy, Sunny Smiles, and the rest of those do-gooders, and cut them down where they stand. Naturally, you can snipe from a distance, run in and attack with guns, get even closer with melee or unarmed attacks, or stand back and let Joe Cobb and his crew feel the brunt of the attacks.

It's in your best interest to see the Powder Gangers win; there's no point in having a change of heart now! Also, with the Bighorners stampeding, the Goodsprings townsfolk become a little more distracted. Try keeping Joe Cobb safe too, as you'll speak to him after the battle, if he's still alive. You're now likely to be Vilified by the Goodsprings population and attacked on sight if you hang around here. However you're now Liked by the Powder Gangers.

Goodsprings Infamy Gained!

Powder Gangers Fame Gained!

Tip Now that you're allied with the Powder Gangers, you can visit the NCR Correctional Facility (where they broke out from) and speak to their leader, Eddie. This occurs as long as you didn't kill any Powder Gangers or side with the Goodsprings townsfolk.

Note The townsfolk have a few interesting items on their corpses. Trudy has a Prospector Saloon Expense List. The rest have guns and ammunition. Take what you want, and leave this place.

50 XP

GUESS WHO I SAW TODAY

SUGGESTED EXPERIENCE

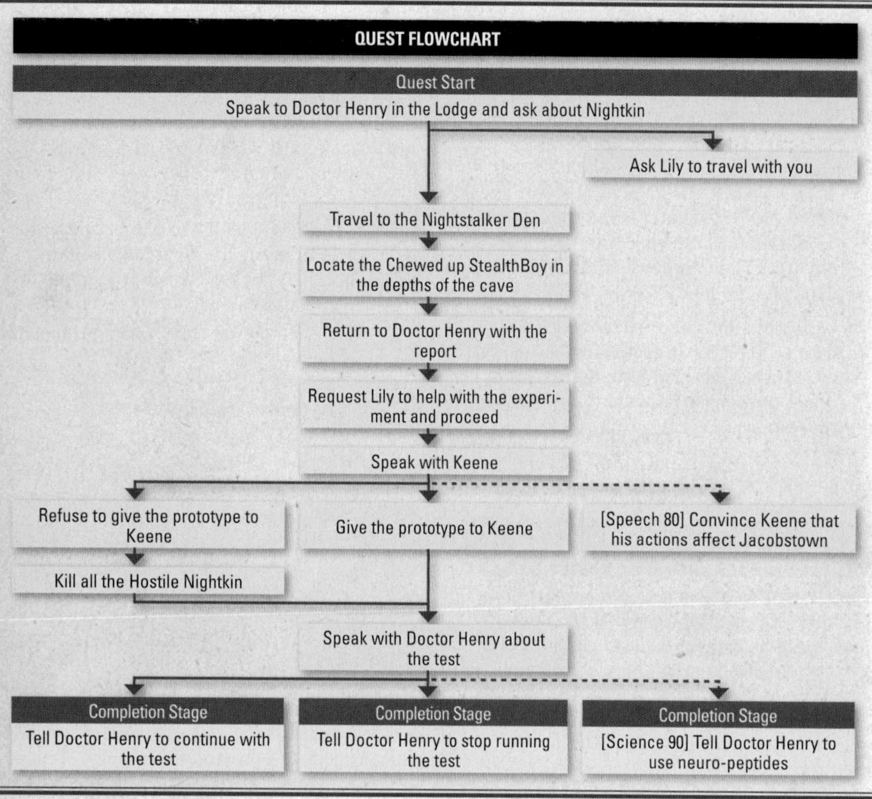

Main Factions

SUPER MUTANT

Here Be Monsters

1

2

The snow-capped northwestern mountains are a maze of warrens, trees, and the Super Mutant settlement of Jacobstown [1.10]. After meeting Marcus, and realizing that not all Super Mutants are half-deranged and addicted to Stealth Boys, readjust your viewpoint after entering the Jacobstown Lodge **(1)**. As you enter, you're harangued by the leader of the Nightkins in this area, a Mutant named Keene. Speak to Keene **(2)**, and he's very standoffish, but he's also having trouble with Marcus.

Ask why the Nightkin are here, and he tells you that Stealth Boys are having an adverse, cumulative effect on the minds of the Nightkin. This place is a sanctuary while the only other human here—Doctor Henry—works on a cure. But Keene's patience is wearing thin.

3

Turn right (north), staying on the ground floor, and enter Doctor Henry's large makeshift office. You can purchase and get repairs from his nurse assistant Calamity, but you're here to see Henry **(3)**. Speak with him, and although he's initially rude, he tells you he's been investigating the local Nightstalker population, because they've developed a natural stealth field. Henry also has a Stealth Boy Mark II prototype, but he needs to find the Nightstalker mutation first. This is where you come in, once you agree to help. Investigate the Nightstalker lair, and perhaps bring a Nightkin named Lily with you.

- **Talk to Lily about participating in Doctor Henry's experiment.**
- **(Optional) Ask Lily to help you investigate the Nightstalker mutations.**
- **Look for the source of the Nightstalker stealth mutation.**

Visiting Grandma Lily

4

5

Move outside to the Bighorner pens **(4)**, and speak to their keeper, a Super Mutant with a straw bonnet and farmer's ensemble. She mistakes you for "Little Jimmy," her grandson. It's best not to dwell too long on her exact mental condition, although it's well worth asking Lily **(5)** whether she wants to accompany you. She'd love to come, if only to seek revenge on the Nightstalkers who've been killing her Bighorners.

Tip Be sure no other Followers are with you, or Lily doesn't join in the expedition. Lily doesn't have to accompany you, but she's extremely handy in close-quarter fighting.

Tip Be sure no other Followers are with you, or Lily doesn't join in the expedition. Lily doesn't have to accompany you, but she's extremely handy in close-quarter fighting.

The Search for the Slobbered-On Stealth Boy

Head past Marcus (who's having trouble with some mercenaries—Side Quest: Unfriendly Persuasion), and exit the Jacobstown perimeter. Follow the large tree-trunk security wall heading roughly northwest, and go up into the tundra while the snow begins to coat the ground. Climb steadily until you reach a remote cave entrance, and bravely enter the Nightstalker Lair of Charleston Cave **(6)** [1.07].

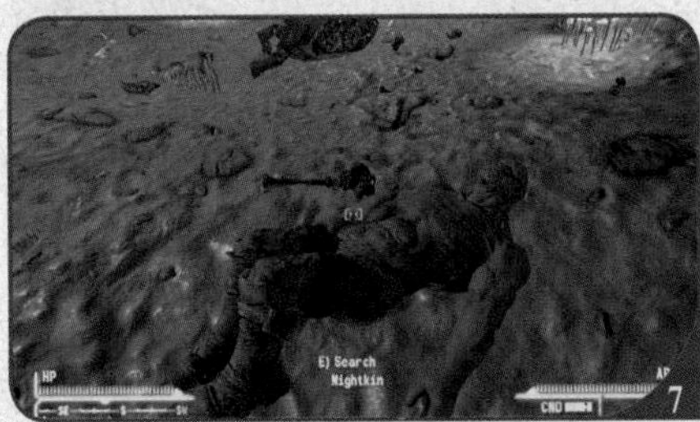

Once in the gloom of the cave, follow the tunnels and slowly descend, sweeping every opening, and watching out for strange, shimmering shapes. These are the Nightstalkers, and they're almost completely invisible. They turn violent when they spot you, so keep Lily calm or begin to cut them down, and advance farther into the cave system. Inside the main cavern **(7)** with the piles of animal bones and a recently killed Bighorner, you'll find the body of a Nightkin (near a Unique Weapon). Search the body for a Chewed Stealth Boy; you surmise this was slobbered on by the Nightstalkers, and created this odd mutation. Take the item, and return to the surface.

Unique Super Sledge: Oh, Baby!

Chewed Stealth Boy

Tell Doctor Henry you've discovered a potential cause for the Nightstalker mutations.

Now You See Her...

Descend the mountain, and bring Lily back to Doctor Henry's surgery. Tell him you found a Chewed Stealth Boy in the lair. After examining the unit, he concludes that he needs to run the Mark II Stealth Boy test on Lily.

If Lily isn't with you when you return to the doctor, speak to him first, and he recommends that she be used as a test subject. Exit and talk to her about the experiment. She gladly accompanies you back in.

Ask why Henry wants to experiment on Lily, and he answers that she's the least prone to bludgeoning you both to death, and has actually asked to help.

What are the risks? Well, there's a reason the Mark II Stealth Boys never got past the prototype stage. There's possibly immediate and permanent mental damage in Lily's future.

Talk to Lily about participating in Doctor Henry's experiment.

Tell Doctor Henry to proceed with the experiment once Lily is present.

Wait for Doctor Henry to complete the experiment.

The only way to conclude this Quest is for Lily to help with the experiment. Speak with her, and she'll tell you she knows the tests are dangerous, but it'll all turn out for the best in the end. Once you agree, she goes over to Doctor Henry, and the tests begin **(8)**. Lily vanishes into a shimmering cloak for a few moments, before returning to a visible state as the doctor concludes the experiment.

Keene on the Prototype

Speak with Keene and try to defuse the situation.

Kill the hostile Nightkin.

However, at this point Keene and his Nightkin brethren burst into the chamber and deliver a demand through clenched teeth **(9)**: give over the Stealth Boy prototype or the Nightkin will splatter the room with your insides. You can:

Tell Keene that his actions affect all the Mutants across the Wasteland. He replies sheepishly that he hadn't considered that, and the situation is defused peacefully.

You can ask what Keene plans to do with the prototype. Keene wants to locate all the other stashes of Stealth Boys and "improve" them, too. It is his decision, and he won't be swayed. You need to try a different tactic.

You can instruct Henry to give the Stealth Boy II prototype to Keene, who promptly leaves with his kin. The Quest concludes.

Or you can tell Keene he isn't getting the prototype. He flies into a rage, and must be defeated, along with his kin. Lily fights alongside you, bless her.

Speak with Doctor Henry.

Whether the prototype specs were given to Keene or not, the doctor correlated a lot of useful data from the experiment and is a lot closer to a cure. He suggests Lily wear the prototype for a longer period, so he can monitor the results. You can:

(Optional) Stabilize the Stealth Boy Mark II's stealth field.

Decide whether or not Lily should continue to wear the Mark II prototype and inform Doctor Henry.

Keep Lily alive.

Inform the doctor that neuro-peptide stimulators on a Nightstalker brain should be used. This kind of breakthrough is a brilliant and elegant solution!

You can stop the doctor from running the tests. Lily isn't harmed any more, and the prototype is dismantled.

You can instruct the doctor to fit the prototype onto Lily, despite her almost-certain death.

All three possibilities end the Quest. If Lily is with you, you can witness the effects that the prototype is having on her, and her (invisible) friend: Free Quest: Lily and Leo (consult the Tour Chapter for that information).

XP 500 XP

HARD LUCK BLUES

SUGGESTED EXPERIENCE

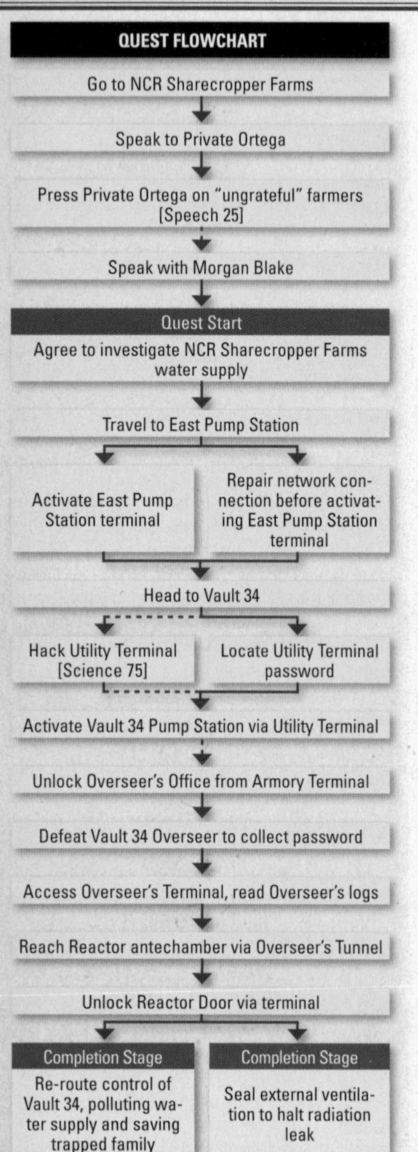

Coming a Cropper

1

2

The NCR have their tendrils in many facets of life in and around New Vegas, and growing crops is but one of their enterprises. The irrigation at the NCR Sharecropper Farms [2.20]—a vital resource to some, but an imposition on those outside of the NCR's rule—is an ongoing concern.

Main Factions

NEW CA. REPUBLIC
POWDER GANGERS

3

Visit the main gate **(1)**, and speak with Private Ortega **(2)**. She can tell you more about the Farms; they supply food to NCR outposts around the Mojave Wasteland, but some of the farmers are a little ungrateful. Ask who, and Ortega quiets down, unwilling to spread gossip.

Unless you press her on the subject, in which case she mentions Trent Bascom, who says the NCR isn't giving them the water they need. This is a reference to another irrigation-based Quest: Side Quest: The White Wash.

You can also ask about work (Major Dhatri is offering bounties on some Fiends), purchasing (the Crimson Caravan Company [2.09] is recommended), or a doctor (try the medic at Camp McCarran [2.19] or a civilian doctor to the northeast). When you're done chin-wagging, open the gates, and enter the Farm.

Here, you can speak with Morgan Blake **(3)**. Ask her what's going on, and she mentions that the East Pump Station [2.21] is a little run down. She asks if you can find anything strange going on. Agree to begin the Quest.

Investigate the East Pump Station.

4

Head east toward the Pump Station **(4)**, and locate the Door to the East Pump Station (not the Cistern). Access a Pump Station Terminal in the initial chamber, and you'll find some sort of data corruption has made the user interface illegible. You can:

Leave the terminal alone.

Repair the network connection and then activate the terminal.

Or simply activate the terminal.

If you can read the data, you uncover a radiation leak. This is unknown if you left the terminal alone, or tried to piece together the corrupted data. However, you can still complete the next Objective:

Find the source of the Radiation.

Pandemonium in Vault 34

5

The nearest area with a sizable radiation problem is Vault 34 [3.12]. Travel to either the Vault 34 entrance **(5)**, which is hidden in the wall of a rocky outcrop close to a parked military truck filled with radioactive barrels. Once inside the natural tunnels (Vault 34—1st Floor), explore the area, watching out for Golden Geckos, and keeping an eye on your radiation meter. When you reach the open Vault entrance door, prepare to face a troublesome Ghoul threat; it seems the Vault's inhabitants have gone Feral.

6

A complete reconnoiter of the Vault is now required. Dispatch the Ghouls, including technicians and those still wearing the remains of their uniforms **(6)**. Optionally access the terminals dotted throughout the place that warn about a reactor problem and flooding. You surmise that radiation is seeping into the ground water and causing the problems for the sharecroppers. Continue to descend into the Vault until you reach the level with the clinic and the locked Overseer's office door. Backtrack to a junction with a sign for both these locations, and take the side corridor to the water-filled steps. Water cascades down from the leaking pipe on your right.

7

Take a deep breath (and some radiation-abating Chems) and dive down the submerged steps. Follow the corridor west until it opens up into a debris-filled room, look immediately left, and search the already-dead Vault Technician **(7)** whose legs protrude from a desk. He carries the Vault 34 Utility Terminal Password. Grab this, and flee back to the dry corridor. Check the password.

 **Vault 34 Utility Terminal Password**

By now, you should have discovered that the Door to Vault 34—Reactor is closed and requires a key to open. The Password doesn't help directly, but if you progress farther into the Vault, culling more Feral Security Guards as you go, you'll reach another corridor with a small water cascade from a pipe, and the obligatory Ghoul inhabitant **(8)**. This is adjacent to an open doorway on your right (north) with some submerged steps. You can dive down into the steps, and secure a second Password from another submerged Vault Technician lying dead, under a desk. But a safer plan is to ignore that for the moment, and continue forward (west), until you reach the Utility Room on your left (south). This is close to the door to the Armory.

Note Vault 34 Armory is a great place to stock up. However, this is a purely optional plan, and not related to this Quest. Consult the Tour Chapter for details on what's inside the Armory, and how to unlock the necessary doors. The Overseer's Journal Fragments tell a terrible tale, also detailed in the Tour Chapter.

Enter the Utility Room and Activate the Terminal using the Password you found. The last menu option ("System") allows you to "Activate Pump Station." This pumps the water from the submerged steps in the doorway to the north. Head down these steps, and enter the dead-end room and secure a second Password from another submerged Vault Technician lying dead, under a desk. You now have the passwords to access the Vault areas necessary to this Quest.

 **Vault 34 Security Terminal Password.**

Now open the Door to Security Station A, and enter the Armory from this lower level; not the door adjacent to the Utility Room upstairs. Wind through the Ghoul-filled corridors to a larger office with barricaded desks and debris, and locate the terminal in the corner **(9)** near the Overseer's Journal Fragment.

 The hacking requires true mastery of your craft.

Or, if you have the Security Terminal Password, you can simply access the terminal without the need for impressive hacking.

This terminal allow you access to another "System" menu, where you can "Disengage the Lock to Overseer."

Note This chamber is also the place to scavenge parts from a Broken Mk III Auto-Doc, if you're working to heal Caesar during Main Quest: Et Tumor, Brute? You can only grab the parts if this Quest is active.

Someone's Gonna Suffer

With the Overseer's chamber open, move back to the 1st Floor and to the Reactor Room door, with "no access" written on it. This is now accessible, leading to more careful corridor navigating, along with some deft Ghoul removal. Locate the door with the barrel propping it open, which leads to the Overseer's Office **(10)**. The leader of Vault 34 is no longer of sound mind, so dispatch him and search his corpse. He is carrying the Password for his terminal, which is on the back (north) wall of the office. Activate the terminal, read the logs to update the Quest, and check the "System" menu to open the Armory door (which allows access to a large cache of weapons).

Shut down Vault 34's Reactor to help the Sharecropper Farms.

The computers to switch off the Vault's Reactors are easily accessed via the water-logged passageways you can reach from the Overseer's tunnel, under his desk. Open the heavy doors and drop glowing Ghouls until you reach this computer bank **(11)**, where you can Activate the Terminal and read the following messages:

SOS: This mentions a bomb planted in a pool that triggered an auto-lock on some of the Vault's doors, trapping a few survivors. Transferring control to a backup terminal could allow some non-Feral survivors to escape. The Quest updates.

You can also read a log, view two more commands, and open the Reactor Door (which is imperative). The Reactor Door opens, allowing you to access the master terminal.

In this chamber **(12)**, you must make a stark choice:

Seal external ventilation. This stops the radiation from seeping into the water table and outside air, solving the Sharecropper Farmers' problems. However, it also dooms a family of Vault Dwellers.

Or, you can reroute control of the Vault, which is what the SOS message requested. This allows the trapped Vault Dwellers to escape, but also releases a vast amount of radioactive matter, ruining the Sharecroppers' livelihood.

Either option concludes this Quest.

(Optional) Save Vault 34's trapped dwellers by leaving its Reactor intact, dooming the Sharecropper Farms.

 **NCR Fame Gained! (If you save Sharecropper Farms)**

 **100 XP (If you save Sharecropper Farms)**

 **150 XP (If you save the Vault Dwellers)**

HEARTACHE BY THE NUMBER

SUGGESTED EXPERIENCE

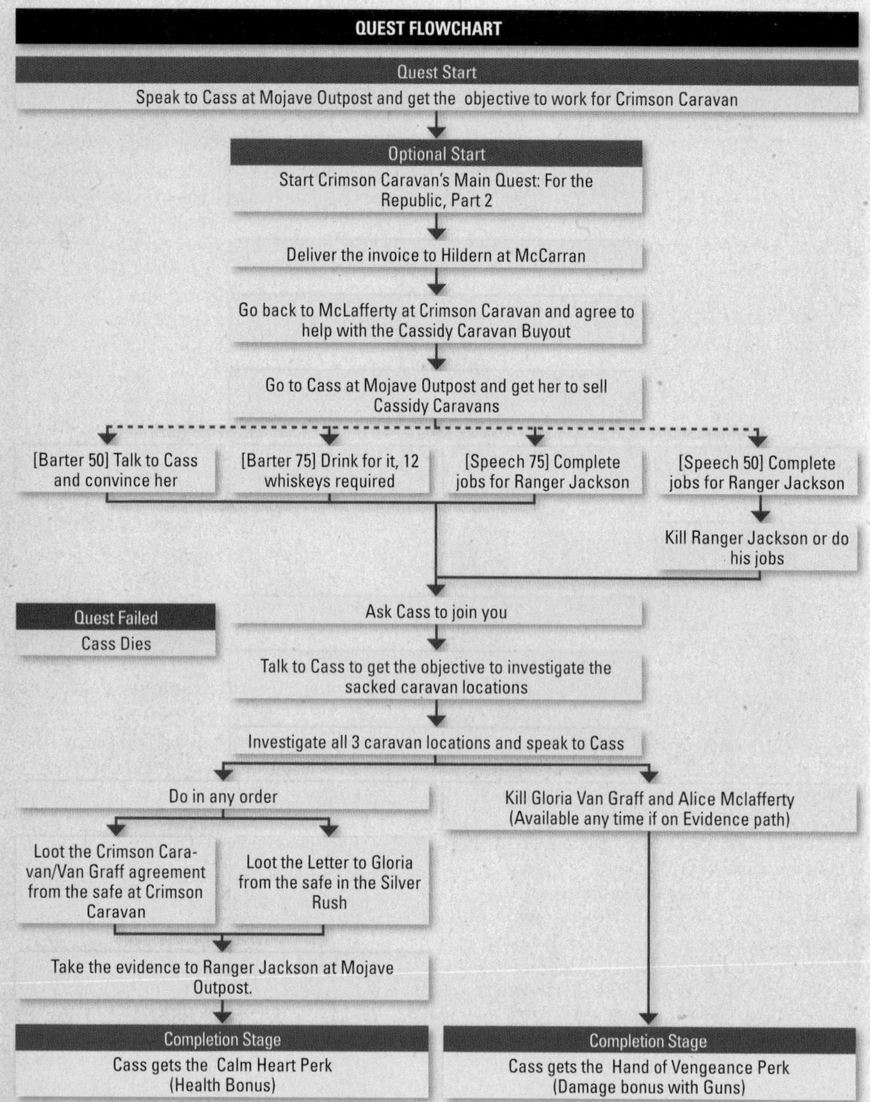

No Time for Gawkers

1

2

There are two ways to start this Quest. The first is to encounter Cass during Side Quest: You Can Depend on Me, while working for the Crimson Caravan Company. The second is to find Cass first. Achieve this by heading to the Mojave Outpost [4.27], and locating the barracks **(1)**, which has been partly transformed into a bar. Propped up against the counter is a young woman named Cass **(2)**. She seems standoffish when you speak to her, but continue the conversation (using any tact), and then ask Cass what she's trying to forget. She rants about losing her caravan, and the NCR's rather tepid response, that "roads aren't safe." She tells you she can't leave because she has caravan papers, and gives you a piece of advice:

Cass is drowning her sorrows at the Mojave Outpost. Her advice? Go work for the Crimson Caravan.

3

4

5

Follow this advice, and travel north into New Vegas, and locate the large walled Crimson Caravan Company compound [2.09]. Step inside, and find the main office **(3)**, where Alice McLafferty **(4)** has some work for you. Begin Side Quest: You Can Depend on Me (and refer to that Quest for more details), and take the invoice to Dr. Hildern **(5)** inside Camp McCarran [2.19], as Alice asked. You don't need to interrogate the doctor (unless other Side Quests are in your future); the Quest updates again, and you must return to Alice to let her know the first job has been done. She has additional jobs available, but the one that concerns this Quest is the "negotiation." Obtain further information on that before you leave.

Note: Crimson Caravan Invoice

Pitch in at the Crimson Caravan Company if you're looking for caravan work.

Deliver the Crimson Caravan invoice to Doctor Hildern at Camp McCarran.

Return to Alice McLafferty and let her know you've delivered the invoice.

Return to Cass and see if you can get her to part with the title for Cassidy Caravans.

Filling Out the Correct Paperwork

Return to the barracks bar at the Mojave Outpost, and inform Cass that you're here to buy out her caravan. This seems pointless to her, as it was recently ransacked by Raiders (or so she believes). Despite only having the clothes on her back, she still isn't selling the operation, simply on general principle. Present the offer and she declines it. At this point, you can:

Tell her you're not going to offer her money; you want to drink for it! She agrees to a competition, and it takes 12 Whiskeys (which will impair your other motor skills, and cost Caps to purchase) to drink her under the table.

If you're carrying a cache of Caps, you can buy her out with your considerable funds. She agrees, and you can begin the investigations.

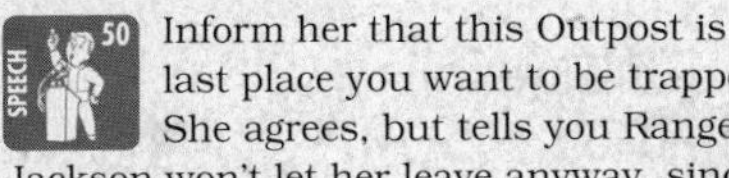

Inform her that this Outpost is the last place you want to be trapped. She agrees, but tells you Ranger Jackson won't let her leave anyway, since there's trouble on the Long 15 close by. If you could help Ranger Jackson with this job (or remove him as an obstacle), she'll sell the rights to her caravan. Plans #1A and 1B commence, and your Quest updates.

Or that if she made the caravan, she's responsible for killing it. This causes her hackles to rise, but as you explain, she realizes she's been thinking the same thing, but the whiskey had been killing those thoughts. She sells you the caravan and the Quest updates.

Clear the roads for Jackson in Mojave Outpost HQ to allow Cass freedom to leave.

(Optional) "Remove" Jackson as an obstacle without Cass or anyone the wiser.

Plan 1A: Visit the Mojave Outpost Headquarters **(6)**, and search the back (northeast) rooms for Ranger Jackson **(8)**. Ask about work, and he tells you he's having trouble with ants on the road to Ivanpah Lake. Simply complete Side Quest: Can You Find It in Your Heart, and kill all the Giant Ants at the intersection **(7)** close to the Nipton Road Pit Stop [4.29]. Return to Jackson for your reward, and then return to Cass, and let her know you cleared the road.

Plan 1B: Removing Jackson as a threat is only really an option if you're going to be working for allies other than the NCR. It's very difficult to pull off without anyone witnessing the murder.

One way is to Sneak around to the back of Ranger Jackson, Pickpocket him, and insert a Frag Grenade, and then retreat, with a Stealth Boy cloaking you to keep anyone from suspecting anything other than an accident. C-4 Explosives placed on Jackson also work.

Killing him in his sleep is also an excellent plan.

Then return to Cass, and tell her Ranger Jackson isn't going to keep her at the outpost any more.

Unfair Trading Practices

When speaking with Cass, convince her to join you, and she accepts. The Quest involving Alice McLafferty updates, but not this Quest until you speak to Cass in her new role as a Follower. She asks if you'd mind making a detour on your travels; she wants to check out the site where her caravan members died. Agree to this plan, and she tells you the location. Head to Cassidy Caravans Wreckage [2.31].

Pay your respects with Cass at her caravan's grave.

When you reach the wreckage **(9)**, Cass picks over the remains, and realizes there's nothing left. When she told you she'd heard the caravan had been burned, she was told of "ash" piles, but these were her men. She tells you anything you can scavenge is yours. Wait a minute or so, and she comes over and lets you know this wasn't the first caravan to be attacked in this manner. She wonders if the other caravan was hit by Energy Weapons too. Agree to check it out, even if it's a hell of a detour.

Investigate the wreckage of the Griffin Wares caravan with Cass.

As you arrive at Griffin Wares Sacked Caravan **(10)** [1.05], she tells you to poke around. Sure enough, there's another ash pile indicating the use of Energy Weapons. Not only that, but Cass finds a map showing caravan routes to the west, and another possible ambush spot! Time for another reconnoiter.

Track down Durable Dunn's missing caravan with Cass.

Trek all the way to Durable Dunn's Sacked Caravan **(11)** [2.16], and inspect the carnage. Somebody made camp here, and Cass didn't even know this had taken place. Something here stinks, and it's not just the corpse of the Van Graff thug Cass finds. She realizes the Crimson Caravan and the Van Graffs were behind the burnings. They must answer for these crimes! You have two ways to play this:

The Cass Way: Whiskey and Ammunition

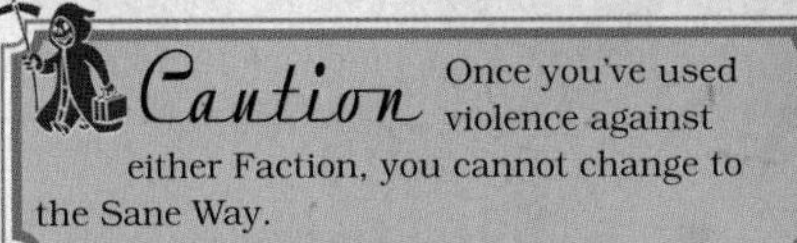

Caution Once you've used violence against either Faction, you cannot change to the Sane Way.

Find Alice McLafferty at the Crimson Caravan Camp and "settle accounts."

Find Gloria Van Graff at the Silver Rush in Freeside and make that bitch eat her hair.

Cass wasn't kidding about revenge being a dish best served with copious amounts of smoking bullet holes. If you agree to this bloodthirsty carnage, simply visit Alice McLafferty, and kill her **(12)**. Then locate the Silver Rush [2C.07] in Inner Freeside, cut down the guard, and lay waste to the (heavily armored) Van Graff thugs, plus Gloria Van Graff **(13)** and Jean-Baptiste Cutting. You might wish to bring a second Follower (such as ED-E), stock up on Grenades, or use the firepower inside the Silver Rush itself.

Of course, you could enter the premises calmly after surrendering your weapons, then wait for an opportunity to get close to Gloria, grab an Energy Weapon from the shop table (or better yet, buy one along with ammo), and gun her down with it before fleeing.

Once the combat is over, Cass gains the Hand of Vengeance perk, giving her a bonus to damage with Guns.

Hand of Vengeance

The Sane Way: Methodical Investigation

14

15

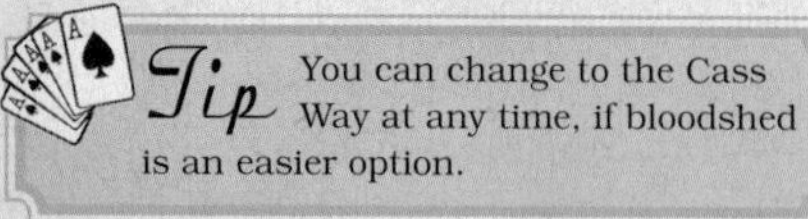

Tip: You can change to the Cass Way at any time, if bloodshed is an easier option.

Investigate the Crimson Caravan for reasons behind the attack.

Investigate the Silver Rush in Freeside for evidence on the Van Graffs' guilt.

Steady Cass' anger, and visit the Crimson Caravan Company. Once inside Alice's office, hide to the side of the desk, and open the safe [Average] **(14)**. Quickly take the Holotape inside, and close the safe before retreating outside, so no one spots you. Then inform Cass that this is part one of the evidence you can present to the NCR.

Note: Crimson Caravan–Van Graff Agreement

Locating evidence inside the Silver Rush is going to be much more difficult. As you approach the front door, you must surrender all your items. Oblige the guard, and tell Cass to wait outside for you; she isn't needed in here. Before you head to the Silver Rush, be sure you have a Stealth Boy and Bobby Pins. Then enter, watch Mr. Soren's "agreement," and then find a quiet spot and crouch so you're Hidden. Then activate the Stealth Boy.

Head to the locked door and pick it **(15)**, open the door, and head into the storage room beyond. There's a safe here; pick that, and obtain the Letter to Gloria from Alice, proving the two companies were in cahoots!

Before your Stealth Boy runs out, exit the building and rendezvous back with Cass.

Note: Letter to Gloria

Take the evidence of the Caravan attacks to Jackson at the Mojave Outpost.

Ask Cass who she knows in the NCR, and the answer is obvious. With the evidence in question, journey back to the Mojave Outpost, and present the information to Ranger Jackson. He'll see that the companies are punished using the rule of law, and he thanks you for not causing any unnecessary bloodshed.

Once the combat is over, Cass gains the Calm Heart perk, giving her a bonus to damage to Health.

Calm Heart

500 XP

HIGH TIMES

SUGGESTED EXPERIENCE

See flowchart on the following page

Main Factions

FOLLOWERS OTA

A Flickering Light in a Raging Storm

1

2

The Followers of the Apocalypse are fighting a battle for the hearts and minds of Freeside from their stronghold at the Old Mormon Fort [2C.01]. Enter the premises **(1)**, and search out a medic named Julie Farkas **(2)**. You can speak to her about her Faction's dire need of medical supplies (starting a couple of Free Quests in the process), and Freeside in general, as well as purchasing items and healing. To begin this Quest though, start by stating that "things are pretty rough here in Freeside."

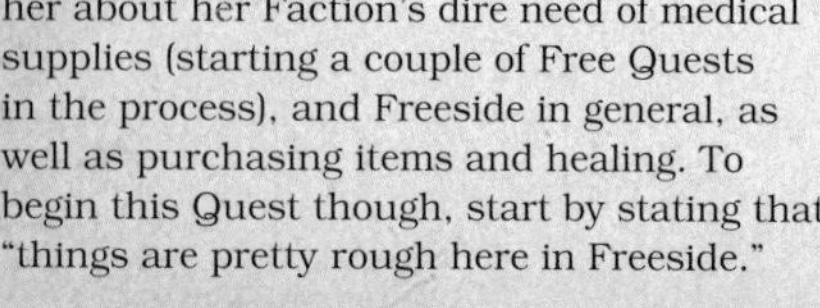

She agrees, but the Followers can only do so much. Ask if there's anything you can do to help. A couple of addicts could really help her cause, if only they'd sober up. Farkas also lists plans to trade with the Crimson Caravan Company, and mentions tensions in Freeside. Continue your questions by asking about helping addicts. She lists two folks; Old Bill Ronte and Jacob Hoff.

Ask about both men, and where you should start looking. Farkas suggests the Atomic Wrangler [2C.06], and the Quest begins.

Find Jacob Hoff.

Find Bill Ronte.

You can search for the two addicts in either order.

Low Life: Bill Ronte

3

Head through into the adjacent part of Freeside, past the Atomic Wrangler and the Silver Rush Gambling Hall [2C.07], to a ruined building on your right (west) side **(3)**.

4

Here you'll find Bill Ronte **(4)**, wheezing up against a wall with empty Whiskey bottles scattered at his feet. He immediately asks if you've seen Dixon.

You can inform Ronte that Farkas wants you to help him, and he understands, but remains in his stupor. It might be time to pay the facilitator a visit.

Help Bill Ronte with his alcoholism.

Low Life: Jacob Hoff

5

6

Journey south and southeast through Freeside, toward Mick & Ralph's [2C.02], and when you get there, turn right and look into the ruined building near the stumbling drunks **(5)**. Walk through the ruins and fallen masonry and you'll find

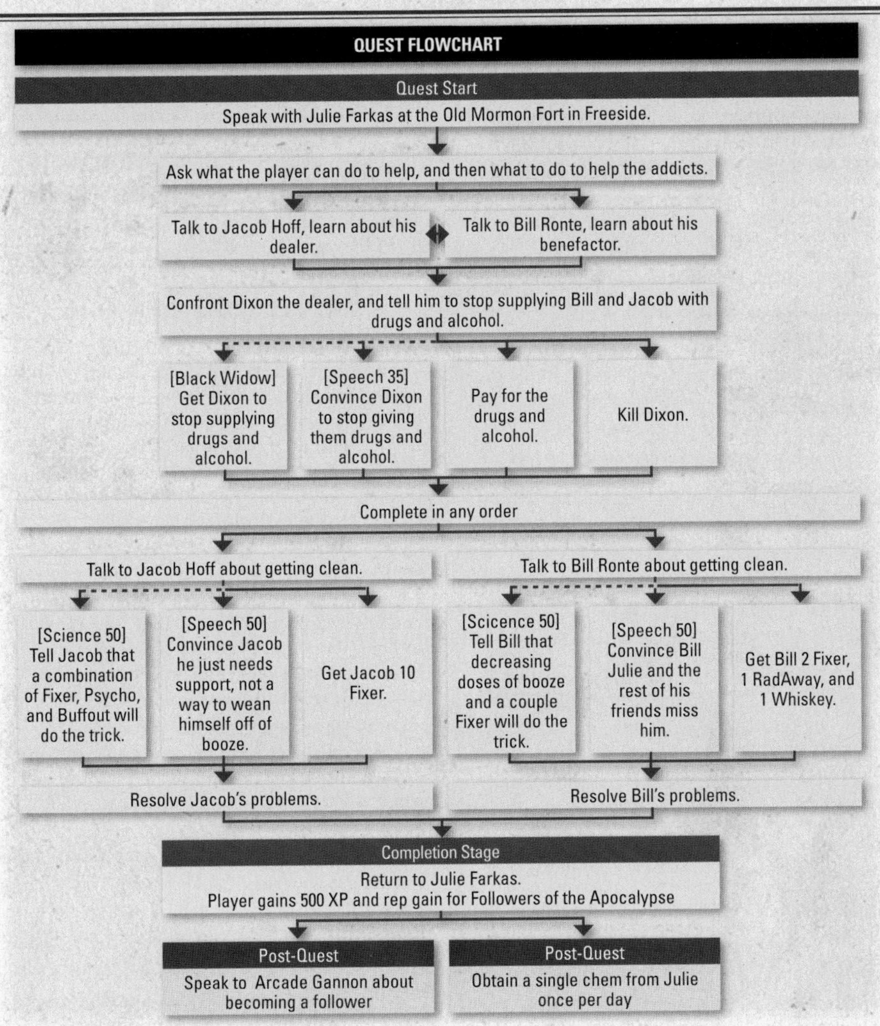

Jacob Hoff **(6)** slumped against a wall. He immediately asks you for Chems.

Help Jacob Hoff kick his addiction to Chems.

Whether you're being clever or genuinely concerned for his welfare, Jacob eventually tells you he'll feel better soon, once his guy arrives. Ask who the supplier is, and he mentions a man named Dixon. Jacob reckons something about him "seems sketchy."

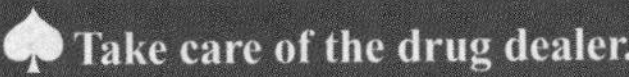

Take care of the drug dealer.

Dealing with Dixon

Dixon is usually very close to Jacob Hoff, among the same drunks populating the Freeside streets close to Mick & Ralph's. Holler at Dixon **(7)**, and he asks if you need a fix. You can:

Ask him about Bill and Jacob. He finds it hilarious that they're so "out of their domes."

Ask what he's selling, and buy or trade some of it.

Ask him why he wants to kill his customers. He replies that they're NCR; he loves seeing them in agony.

Tell Dixon to stop supplying them. Dixon considers this, and might be convinced if there was something in it for him.

Ask about a Cap payment. Dixon suggests Caps. Pay the man, and he walks away.

Shout about the NCR supplying him with cheap Chems to keep the population down.

Appeal to the man's more base nature, and stop him with your talents.

Or simply kill the man. No one else will mind in this squalor.

Fixing the Forlorn

Return to Jacob Hoff, and explain that you've taken care of his supplier. He's undestandably upset, and needs his fix, now! He wants Fixer—at least 10 shots—to calm his shakes and get him through the week. You can:

Agree to return with the 10 Fixers.

Use your powers of persuasion to tell Jacob to be strong; the support of friends and family will see him through this.

Or figure out that a combination of Fixer, Psycho, and Buffout would do it in a single shot. Jacob agrees.

Collect ten doses of Fixer for Jacob.

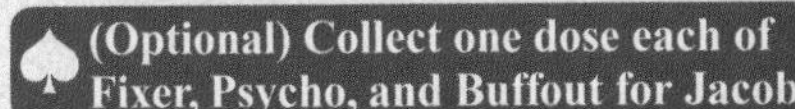

(Optional) Collect one dose each of Fixer, Psycho, and Buffout for Jacob.

All you have to do now is locate the nearest medical practitioner (Farkas back at the Old Mormon Fort, or Dixon before he scarpered are your best bets), and return to administer the Chems.

Return to Bill Ronte, and tell him that you've done away with his Whiskey specialist. Ronte isn't too pleased and wants his intoxicants immediately! He wants a concoction of booze and Chems. You can:

Agree to return with the necessary doses of Fixer, RadAway, and a bottle of Whiskey

Or tell him that Julie and the rest of his friends miss him, and they need his help. He feels guilty, and heads back to the Old Mormon Fort for some rest. You don't need to collect doses for him.

Or inform him that regulating decreasing doses of booze with some Fixer would be just as potent. Find these items, and administer them to him.

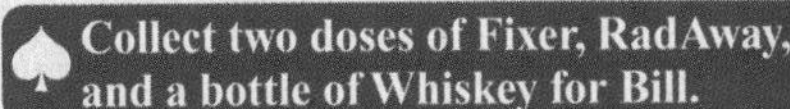

Collect two doses of Fixer, RadAway, and a bottle of Whiskey for Bill.

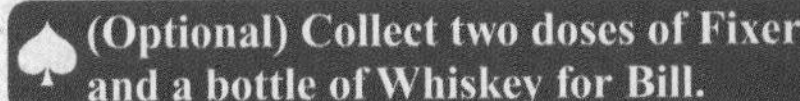

(Optional) Collect two doses of Fixer and a bottle of Whiskey for Bill.

Return to Julie Farkas.

Caution Both Bill Ronte and Jacob Hoff are skilled individuals. Don't execute them unless you want to decrease your Reputation with the Followers of the Apocalypse considerably.

Follower Favors

Back at the Old Mormon Fort, when you speak with Julie Farkas again, she's pleased at your compassion, and she's already helping her two fallen friends. She's happy to supply you with a single Chem of your choosing, once every hours.

Followers Fame Gained!

Freeside Fame Gained!

500 XP

MAIN QUEST INTERSECTION

HOW LITTLE WE KNOW

SUGGESTED EXPERIENCE

QUEST FLOWCHART

Quest Start

- Dealt with the Great Khans during Main Quest: For the Republic, Part 2
- Finish Side Quest: Bye Bye Love and speak to Joanna
- Player starts Main Quest: The House Always Wins, IV

- Ask around the Gamorrah about Cachino
- [Terrifying Presence] Ask around the Gamorrah about Cachino

- (Cachino will find the player and force greet) Ask about business on the side.

- [Lockpick] Pick lock into Cachino's room and loot his desk for Journal
- Pickpocket Cachino and take his Journal

- Confront Cachino about ledger. [Barter 60] +200 caps up front and +80xp

- Give Ledger back to Cachino for 100 caps
  - Can Be Completed in Any Order
    - Investigate Troike
      - Speak with Troike in the Zebra Club
        - Ask about killing the prostitute
          - [Medicine 30] Let Troike know something isn't right +30xp
          - Pickpocket Big Sal for the password, [Lockpick 75], or [Science 50] hack the terminal to unlock safe
          - Retrieve Blackmail Note from Sal's safe
        - Ask about guns, offer to help get Troike out of contract
          - Talk to Big Sal [Barter] or [Speech 53] to let Troike go
          - Return to Troike and let him know he is free
          - Use Troike's thermite to destroy the guns in the storage room
          - Have Troike destroy guns in the storage room
    - Investigate Clanden
      - Unlock the safe behind the dresser and steal the snuff tapes [Lockpick 75+]
      - Pickpocket Clanden and steal snuff tapes from the safe
      - Confront Clanden
        - Kill Clanden
        - [Speech 50] Convince Clanden to leave Vegas
  - Talk to Cachino about Troike and Clanden being handled. Player is instructed to kill Big Sal and Nero
    - **Completion Stage:** [Speech] Get Cachino to do it (Strip Rep Gain)
    - **Completion Stage:** Kill Big Sal and Nero (Strip Rep Gain)

- Tell Thug about ledger or [Speech 50] Convince Thug to let player tell Big Sal or Nero directly.
  - Talk to Big Sal (+1000 caps or [Barter 55] for +1200 caps and +55xp)
    - Attend Cachino's business meeting with Big Sal (wait for Big Sal to arrive, sit down in chair)
    - Offer to help Big Sal with Racket
  - Talk to Nero (+1000 caps)
    - Attend Cachino's business meeting with Nero (wait for Nero to arrive, sit down in chair)
    - Offer to help Nero with Racket
  - Can Be Completed in Any Order
    - Speak with Troike → Speak with Troike → Agree to disassembled weapons shipment near Sunset Sarsaparilla HQ → Retrieve disassembled weapons shipment from Fiends → Speak with Troike
    - Speak with Clanden → Speak with Clanden → Agree to help find Chlorine at the Ultra Luxe or Mick and Ralph's → Obtain Chlorine via sneak/lockpick at Ultra Luxe or purchase from Mick and Ralph's → Speak with Clanden
  - **Completion Stage:** Let Big Sal or Nero know that Troike and Clanden have been helped.

Main Factions

Before You Begin....

Gomorrah [2D.01] is one of the largest, seediest casinos on The Strip; it's the base of operations for the Omerta Family, a bunch of ruthless gangsters who run a number of rackets and are ready to launch some power-plays. They initially greet you with disdain, but depending on your actions, they can be neutralized, allied with, or even killed off. Before you begin, it is worth knowing the numerous ways you can approach this Quest.

You need to have access to The Strip (so you can enter Gomorrah). After that, you need to hear about the Omerta's plans to make a move on Mr. House so you can begin the Quest. To this end, you can:

Investigate after completing Side Quest: Bye Bye Love, and hearing rumors about Cachino from Joanna.

38 MR. HOUSE Investigate on behalf of Mr. House, during Main Quest: The House Always Wins, IV, with the intention of wiping the Omertas out.

NEW CA. REPUBLIC Investigate at the behest of NCR Ambassador Crocker, during Main Quest: For the Republic, Part 2.

INDEPENDENT Or investigate after commandeering Yes Man, during Main Quest: Wild Card: Side Bets.

CAESAR'S LEGION Although you may not be aware of this, the Omerta's plan to attack The Strip and usurp Mr. House has been instigated by Vulpes Inculta of the Legion. Meanwhile, Caesar is content to sit back and watch the plan unfold.

(Optional) Help Mick and Ralph get Omerta business again.

Let Mick and Ralph know the Omertas have room in their budget to buy guns from them again.

Loose Lips Sink Ships

1

2

Check yourself (and all except your hold-out weapons) in with the Omerta thug at the front desk of Gomorrah **(1)**. Your first task is to ask around for information. You can:

3

Ask the receptionist **(2)** for the "outstanding balance for some information. Tell me what the Omertas are up to." She mentions that Cachino, the lowest level lieutenant in the Omertas, is the man to speak to.

You can pry more information out of her by asking about the Family, then telling her you can keep secrets.

- Or, you can wander the casino floor, and bump into an Omerta thug **(3)**:

You can ask where Cachino is if you already know about him.

Or you can ask (rather unpleasantly) where Cachino is, and unnerve the thug.

> Talk to Cachino about suspicious Omerta activities; perhaps someone else in Gomorrah knows how to find him.

Cachino: Bad Lieutenant

4

5

You find out that Cachino is mooching around at Brimstone **(4)**, on the northeast side of the main level you're on. Head over there, and Cachino **(5)** stops you as you walk in, or around the bar. He asks—rather impolitely—why you've been asking questions. Tell him you've heard about his business on the side, and Cachino's bald head almost glows with fury. Then tell him he's been dealing with business off limits for the Family. He doesn't care what you think, and leaves you with a threat.

> Check Cachino's room or his person for some proof of his behavior. Perhaps someone has a key to his room.

6

7

You have three options to obtain proof that Cachino is engaged in some shady operations.

You can silently follow Cachino, and attempt to Pickpocket him **(6)**. Leave his Magnum, but be sure to take Cachino's Journal.

- Or, talk to the receptionist at the front desk. She reveals her disdain for Cachino. You can:

Convince her to give you the key to his room for free.

Use other means to convince her to hand over the key for free

Pay her 300 Caps for the key.

- You can also try to gain entry into Cachino's room, which is accessed via the bank of elevators. Choose "Suites Level," and step out into the long north-south corridor, where a thug guards Cachino's suite **(7)**. You can:

Employ a Stealth Boy, and move around the guard to the double doors behind him.

Or watch from the elevator banks as the guard walks away from the doors. Let him pass, and quickly scamper up to them.

Attacking the Omertas here is highly risky, but it's an option if no other Family members are stretching their legs.

The Door to Cachino's Suite is firmly locked. It requires some talent to jimmy open.

Once inside Cachino's suite, head up the stairs to the door leading to his expansive bedroom, and search the desk in the northeast corner. Inside, you'll find Cachino's Journal. Take it, and escape with as much subtlety as you displayed getting up here.

Cachino's Journal

Read the journal. The revelations inside mean you can keep Cachino on your side, or rat him out to the more important Family members.

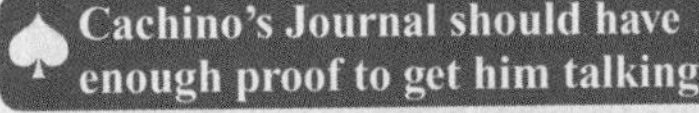

> Cachino's Journal should have enough proof to get him talking.

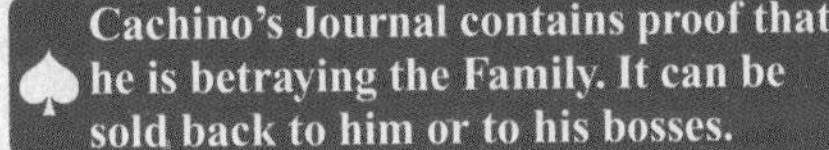

> Cachino's Journal contains proof that he is betraying the Family. It can be sold back to him or to his bosses.

Grabbing Cachino By the Short Hairs

8

Return to the main level, and confront Cachino with the ledger, proving his side businesses. Cachino's tone changes, as you both realize the information inside could get him killed. He asks what he can do for you. What you decide to do now affects the rest of this Quest, and sets you down one of two paths. You can:

Respond that you're going to keep this ledger for a little while. Cachino doesn't try to stop you. You can return and ask for Caps, or begin Path #2.

Tell him you'll consider giving him the ledger for some cash up front, and buy his friendship. He agrees, and hands you 200 Caps.

Caps (200)

Ask whether the journal is worth 100 Caps to him for your silence. It is; and he hands you 100 Caps. You can do this after the Barter check, pocketing a cool 300 Caps for your troubles!

Caps (100)

He then tells you he has some dirt on the Family that both the NCR and "Not-At-Home" (Mr. House) might find interesting. You can ally with Cachino at this point, and begin Path #1.

Or, you can execute Cachino **(8)**. You actually receive Karma for this action, but the Quest fails (this occurs if you shoot Cachino without explicit instructions from the Family).

Path #1: Siding with Cachino

Cachino tells you that the Family bosses—Big Sal and Nero—are arming themselves and using a guy named Troike to fulfill arms shipment orders. They've also brought in a specialist named Clanden. You can ask about both these men and what they're planning.

Troike is a Chem and hooker fiend who is usually down in the Zoara Club (Cachino hands you the key to get in). Clanden seems to have no vices at all, and keeps himself confined to his suite. Cachino lets you know you'll have a (mostly) free run of the place.

Zoara Club Key

> Talk to Troike about mysterious gun shipments.

> Find out what kind of work Clanden does for the Family.

At this point, you can investigate Troike or Clanden, in either order.

Troike: The Blackmailed Chem-Head

Head down to the lower lobby level (called "Brimstone"), and find the corridor leading to a door with an Omerta thug standing guard. This leads to the exclusive Zoara Club. Use the key Cachino gave you, pass a private elevator and a blast door, and enter the club **(9)**. Among the plush cushions and bouncers is a scruffy man named Troike **(10)**. He's already paranoid when you speak to him. You can ask what he does, but to really mine for information, try the following:

- Tell him Cachino sent you here to ask about some guns. Then tell him you're trying to help Cachino break up whatever the bosses are planning. Troike isn't particularly loyal, but the bosses have his number, and he won't help. You can:

Propose that you talk to the bosses about getting Troike out of his contract. He agrees, as long as he's kept out of the negotiations. Big Sal is the man to speak to. The Quest updates (See "Bargaining with Big Sal").

Or lie, and say you'll report him to the NCR. This works, and you can ask him about the guns the Omertas have (See "Cache Exchange").

Troike would like help talking Big Sal into letting him out of his contract.

- Ask him what happened with the prostitute, thanks to the tip Cachino gave you.

Troike spills the beans about spilling some hooker blood. When he woke up, she had stab wounds, and he was covered in her blood. Conveniently, he can't remember how that happened.

You can ask about the knife and inquire about the Chems he was taking. When he answers you can respond: "That seems like a lot of Chems," and end the conversation. But better yet:

Tell him that wasn't enough for him to lose the whole night. The story doesn't add up. The Quest updates. This is the only way to complete this line of questioning.

Ask him how the Family found out about it. Troike screamed, and a thug ran in and witnessed the aftermath. The thug offered to keep quiet if Troike agreed to help them obtain a massive cache of guns.

Something about Troike's story doesn't sit well. Talk to Big Sal, or look around for some evidence to exonerate him.

Big Sal is on the Gomorrah main level, so take the door from the Zoara Club, head up the stairs, and open the door to the balcony overlooking the main casino and entrance **(11)**. Big Sal **(12)** or Nero are up here, depending on the time of day. Don't head up to Big Sal's suite if he's sleeping; that causes the Omertas to turn hostile. Instead, wait or sleep until Big Sal is up and about, doing business on the comfy chairs of his mezzanine balcony. Speak with him.

Plan A: Bargaining with Big Sal

Tell Big Sal either that you want to get Troike out of his contract, or that there's something about Troike's story that doesn't sit right with you. When Big Sal responds, reply:

With a lie about Troike wanting to negotiate lower prices on weapons for the Omertas.

That Troike is pretty strung out, and more trouble than he's worth.

Or offer to purchase Troike's contract for 300 Caps.

Big Sal is amenable to any of these options, and you can return to ask Troike about the guns the Omertas have (See "Cache Exchange").

Big Sal agreed to let Troike out of his contract. Return to Troike and let him know the good news.

Plan B: Blackmail with Big Sal

If you don't want to speak to Big Sal, and want to find evidence to exonerate Troike instead, look for some juicy details inside Big Sal's office safe, which is up the stairs from the Brimstone bar. You can:

Follow Big Sal at a safe distance as he makes his rounds, or heads to or from his suite, then Pickpocket him **(13)**. Leave the ammo and concentrate on grabbing the key to his office, and his terminal password.

Big Sal's Password

Gomorrah Office Key

Whether you have Big Sal's Password or not, head up to the upstairs Zoara pool room, and approach the two doors on the east wall. The left one leads to Big Sal's office **(14)**. Enter, and sidle up to his desk area. You can:

Use the password and access Big Sal's terminal, disengaging the safe lock.

Or, you can apply some Science and hack into the terminal, then open the safe.

Or, you can move directly to the safe, and attempt to open it the old-fashioned way.

Inside the safe is a Holotape proving the bosses were blackmailing Troike.

Troike Blackmail Note

Show the blackmail proof from Big Sal to Troike.

Troike: Cache Exchange

Back at Troike, once you show him the blackmail evidence, or if his contractual disputes have been solved, ask him about the guns the Omertas have. He tells you the weapons cache is in a small utility section close by. You can ask how he smuggles in his weapons, and where they are from, but more importantly, ask how you both can take care of the weapons. He tells you he's been making some Thermite, which can melt almost anything. You can:

Order him to deploy the Thermite at the weapons cache, or you'll tell the bosses what he's been planning. After some swearing, he reluctantly agrees to sabotage his own stash, and tells you to head out of the casino; he'll take care of this while you're gone. The leads to Plan C.

Troike is going to destroy the guns for me. I should head out of the casino to give him time.

Or, ask for the Thermite and tell him you'll destroy the weapons yourself. He gladly obliges, and gives you a key to the cache room. The leads to Plan D.

Thermite

Gomorrah Utility Room Key

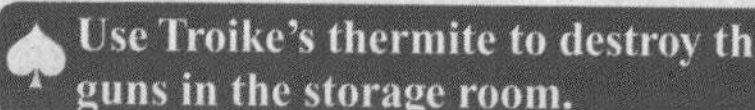

Use Troike's thermite to destroy the guns in the storage room.

Plan C: Troike's Sabotage

Is Troike blowing up the cache? Then stroll out of Gomorrah (optionally completing Clanden's side of the Quest if you wish), and head out onto The Strip. The Quest updates as Troike explodes the cache. This takes care of the Omertas' guns!

> **Troike should have had enough time to destroy the guns by now. Return to Cachino to let him know.**

Plan D: Caching Out

Blowing up the cache yourself? Then move to the blast door, and open it using the Gomorrah Utility Room Key Troike gave you. Head down the stairs, into the cache room, and Place Thermite on top of four large weapon crates **(15)**. Be sure you loot the Footlockers for free weapons and ammunition if you need them! When the Thermite is placed, step out of the room, and locate the Detonator: a light switch Troike rigged up. This takes care of the Omertas' guns!

> **Return to Cachino and let him know the guns have been destroyed.**

Clanden: Up to Snuff

The suspiciously squeaky-clean Clanden roams his expansive suite upstairs in Gomorrah **(16)**. Meet him in his room or the corridor **(17)** and begin to chat; he's noncommittal with his answers. You can even tell him Cachino sent you to talk to him, and you receive no evidence of any foul deeds. Another plan must be hatched. You can:

Follow him around and Pickpocket him, ideally without being spotted. Find his Room Key, along with a Key to the Zoara Club, if you don't have one. There's weaponry to grab, too.

Clanden's Room Key

Zoara Club Key

Or you can move to his suite doors at the south end of the corridor, and jimmy them open.

Inside Clanden's suite, there doesn't appear to be any incriminating evidence. That is, until you pay careful attention to the wall behind the two wardrobes, by Clanden's circular bed. Here you'll find a hidden safe **(18)**, which must be pried open using your Lockpick skill. Aside from a good many Caps, you also find a shocking surprise; some Snuff Tapes with Clanden engaged in all kinds of murderous debauchery!

Snuff Tapes

> **Show Cachino these tapes from Clanden's safe, or confront Clanden with them.**

Between the four suites, there are two storage rooms. One contains the usual array of cleaning products, but the other (complete with a very difficult lock) has the remains of a dead hooker. This is probably the prostitute Clanden murdered and set Troike up with.

You now have two main options: to confront Clanden himself, or take the tapes to Cachino.

If you meet Cachino, simply hand over the tapes, and Cachino is pleased with the evidence. He tells you to confront Clanden (see below).

If you meet Clanden, you can mention that the authorities would like to hear the tapes you found in his safe. Clanden calmly responds by telling you he should kill you before you get the chance. You can:

Return the tapes to Clanden, as long as he leaves Vegas, never comes back, and gives you 200 Caps.

Return the tapes to Clanden, as long as he leaves Vegas, and never comes back.

Tell him you can't give him the tapes. He draws his weapon; kill him.

Or just kill him where he stands.

> **Clanden has been taken care of, he won't be able to help the Omertas anymore. Cachino should be informed.**

Conclusion: Change in Management

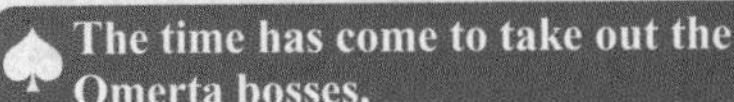

> **The time has come to take out the Omerta bosses.**

Now that both Troike and Clanden have been handled, return to Cachino in the bar area of Brimstone. He tells you the bosses (Big Sal and Nero) want to see you. Ask Cachino what the next step is. Cachino says it's to "cut off the head of the serpent." You can ask him why, or beat around the bush, but there's an inevitable conclusion here; Big Sal and Nero have to die. Cachino will slip you a gun during the meeting, and you both can take them out. You can:

Tell Cachino that's what the bosses will expect. But what they won't expect is if Cachino makes the hit. He agrees, and asks you to tell him when to start shooting.

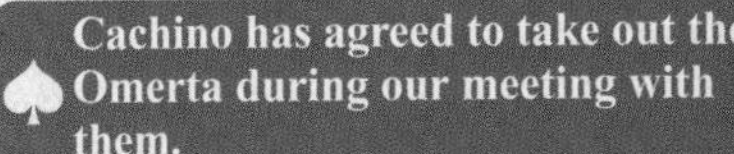

> **Cachino has agreed to take out the Omerta during our meeting with them.**

Or you can ask further questions, and finally agree to the boss takedowns.

When you agree, follow Cachino into the Zoara pool room, then into Nero's office **(19)**. Small talk soon turns into erupting gunfire, but not before Cachino quickly hands you some Stimpaks and a Sawed-Off Shotgun. Use this (or a concealed weapon), and start firing, killing both bosses. The Quest concludes, and you can optionally speak with Cachino, who promises to run a tighter ship. He comps you some chips if you ask him, too.

Gomorrah Chips (50)

The Strip Fame Gained!

300 XP

Tip Winning Troike his freedom pays dividends if you now go and speak to Mick and Ralph, and help them trade with the Omertas again. Consult "Post Quest Activities at the end of this Quest for the (completely awesome) reward!

Path #2: Siding with Big Sal and Nero

Cachino doesn't have the ledger, but the two bosses who run the Omerta operations—Big Sal and Nero—are likely to need this information. Head over to the Omerta thug guarding the entrance to the Zoara club stairs **(20)**. Tell this guy that you have business with his bosses. He's not letting you through, so:

You can tell him it involves Cachino, and him too if he doesn't let you through.

Or present the ledger to him as evidence.

Don't flee up the stairs or fight with the Omerta thug. If you do, the Omertas turn hostile, forcing you to flee for three days, or destroy every last one of them. The Quest usually fails at this point.

Either of the first two options gains you access up the stairs, and a Key to the Zoara Club downstairs.

Zoara Club Key

The door guard suggested I talk to Big Sal or Nero about Cachino's journal.

21

22

Up in the Zoara pool room, you can inspect the offices to the east (the left one is Big Sal's and the right is Nero's); but you're likely to find one of the bosses on the balcony overlooking the main casino floor. Depending on the time of day, you'll either meet Big Sal **(21)**, or Nero **(22)**. In either case, you can ask about their business. But more importantly, present proof that one of their lieutenants is dealing behind their backs. The boss asks to see it. You can:

Ask if it's worth 100 Caps to him. It is.

Caps (100)

Ask if it's worth 200 Caps to him. It is.

Caps (200)

Or ask other questions.

The boss isn't happy with this turn of events, and instructs you to meet him in his office.

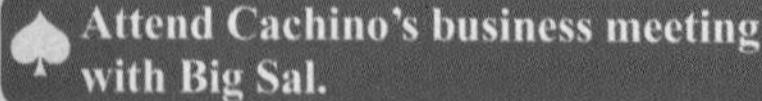

Attend Cachino's business meeting with Big Sal.

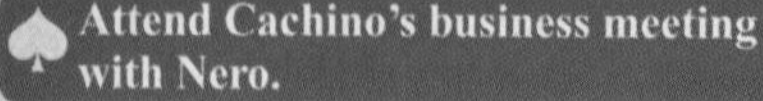

Attend Cachino's business meeting with Nero.

Sit-Down for You. Lie-Down for Cachino

23

Follow Big Sal or Nero to his office. You are soon joined by another associate (Button Man), and Cachino himself. The small-talk is soon interrupted by the associate's shotgun blowing large pieces of Cachino across the room. The sit-down concludes **(23)**. Speak to the boss, who's moderately upset about Cachino's death. Ask about their business, but also say that Cachino mentioned the bosses had something big planned. The boss says he was about to talk to you about that:

Two of the players in this racket—Troike and Clanden—have some problems that require solving. You're to help them out. This can be done in either order.

Talk to Troike to see what kind of help you can give him.

Check with Clanden to see what kind of help he needs.

Troike: Stolen Shipments

24

25

Head down to the lower lobby level (called "Brimstone"), and find the corridor leading to a door with an Omerta thug standing guard. This leads to the exclusive Zoara Club. Use the key the Omerta thug gave you to enter the place, pass a private elevator and a blast door, and enter the club **(24)**. Among the plush cushions and bouncers is a scruffy man named Troike **(25)**. He's a little paranoid when you speak to him. You can ask what he does, but to gain his trust, tell him the bosses sent you to see if he needed any help with his work.

Troike explains he obtains guns for the Omertas without the NCR finding out, and he needs "someone to cover my ass" with the last shipment. You can ask about his operations before quizzing him about the shipment. It seems a group of Chem-addled Fiends stole the weapons cache before he could get it into Vegas. You need to find it, and bring it back.

Recover a stolen shipment of weapon parts from the Fiends.

26

The shipment in question is sitting in hilly scrubland in the western foothills, close to the Sunset Sarsaparilla Headquarters [2.17] and a power transformer cluster. A small group of Fiends **(26)** shouldn't present too much of a problem for you. Destroy them, then look for the Disassembled Weapons Shipment **(27)** close to a burning barrel. Take the shipment, and return to Troike. He's impressed with your abilities.

27

Disassembled Weapons Shipment.

Clanden: Collecting Chlorine

28

29

The squeaky-clean Clanden roams his expansive suite upstairs in Gomorrah **(28)**. Meet him in his room or the corridor **(29)** and begin to chat; he's noncommittal with his answers. Say that the bosses sent you to offer assistance. He could use some help. In his role as an explosives expert, he sources demolition supplies, and has come up short. Ask what the bombs are for. Blowing stuff up, Clanden replies. Although there are other ways:

Such as a chlorine gas, perhaps? Clanden agrees.

Or ask what Clanden has in mind or needs.

The gas is what Clanden requires, and he knows that there's a swimming pool over at the Ultra-Luxe Casino [2D.05], although the White Glove Society wouldn't appreciate you "appropriating" it. Otherwise, you could try Freeside.

Bring chlorine to Clanden. Check near the pool at the Ultra-Luxe, or find out who supplies them.

Plan A: Pilfering Pool Supplies

30

31

Head out from Gomorrah, and across The Strip, moving southeast toward the Ultra-Luxe Casino **(30)**. Drop off your (non hold-out) weapons there, and enter the casino floor and continue toward a locked metal door **(31)** close to the elevator leading up to the penthouse.

The door opens only with skill and Bobby Pins. Do this when you aren't being watched (you might want to crouch so you know you're Hidden). Once inside the storage room, steal the Containers of Chlorine, then return to Clanden.

 **Container of Chlorine**

Plan B: Return to the Source

32

33

The other method of obtaining the Chlorine you need is to establish contact with the suppliers themselves. Visit Mick & Ralph's **(32)** [2C.02] in Outer Freeside, and speak to Ralph **(33)**. Ask him about the Chlorine, and he agrees to sell it to you once you begin to Trade with him.

Or you can convince him to give you the Chlorine for free.

 **Container of Chlorine**

♠ Let the bosses know that Clanden and Troike both have everything they need.

Conclusion: No Change in Management

Return to either Big Sal or Nero, and you're greeted as a good friend. Explain that your work commitments have been met, and the boss is pleased, awarding you with a sum of Caps for your troubles. Alas, the population of The Strip doesn't see it quite the same way.

 **Caps (400)**

 **The Strip Infamy Gained!**

 **300 XP**

Post-Quest Activities: Trading Up

For this to occur, you must have won Troike his freedom during this Quest. Once the Quest concludes, locate Troike again, and convince him to start Trading with Mick & Ralph, just as the Omertas used to do. Once he agrees, head to Mick & Ralph's, and tell them you bargained for them, and they can begin selling guns to this large supplier once more. You're duly rewarded for such a lucrative business deal with a token of their appreciation; the fanciest Pip-Boy around!

 **Pimp-Boy 3 Billion**

Post-Quest Activities: The Final Battle

- If you sided with Big Sal and Nero, the Omertas attack The Strip when the NCR is occupied at Hoover Dam. Clanden uses his Chlorine bomb to wipe out a huge part of The Strip's population almost immediately.
- If you attacked the Omertas, and failed this Quest, they still attack The Strip during the final battle, but Clanden doesn't have any Chlorine bombs.
- If you sided with Cachino, The Strip remains safe, and the Omertas do not attack.

I COULD MAKE YOU CARE

SUGGESTED EXPERIENCE

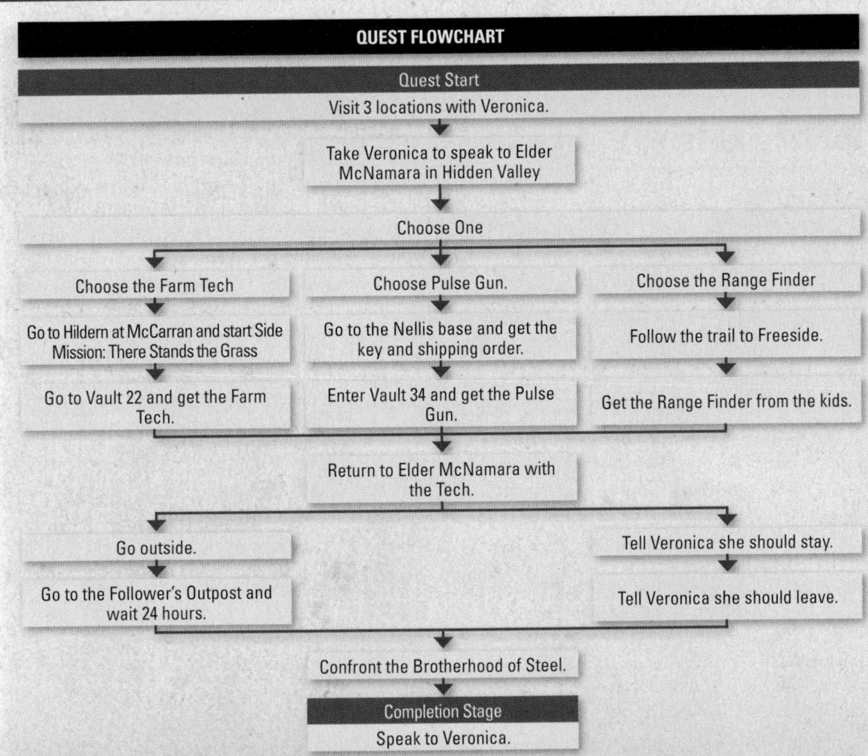

Pre-Quest: Out in the Big Wide World

1

This Quest requires a number of prerequisites, the first of which is to locate and agree to have Veronica in your party. Journey to the 188 Trading Post **(1)** [5.02], and search for Veronica **(2)**. You can speak to her at length regarding her relationship with the Brotherhood of Steel, other Factions, and life in the Mojave Wasteland in general.

To begin with, Veronica exhibits some consternation that the Brotherhood doesn't have much of a presence topside, because they are hidden away after defeats at the hands of the NCR. You can gradually coax more out of her when she witnesses and experiences more Wasteland occurrences. Take her on your travels, and perform any three of the following to get her to talk, and (after three) begin this Quest:

Go with Veronica to talk to the Brotherhood of Steel elder at Hidden Valley.

You'll know when the Quest starts, because Veronica approaches you and says the Brotherhood is failing. They need to change or die. And she needs to go home. You can agree or postpone this request. When you're ready to continue, depart to the inclement Hidden Valley [5.11], braving the strange storms as you reach one of the Hidden Valley Bunkers **(3)**; on the western side of the fenced-off zone. Descend the steps, and when you reach the locked door, Veronica steps forward and speaks some password phrases into the intercom. The bunker unseals.

> *Tip* To work with the Brotherhood of Steel yourself, begin Side Quest: Still in the Dark once Veronica opens the bunker. This is the easiest way into this tightly sealed stronghold. Consult the other Quest for more information on other choices and tasks when you meet Elder McNamara.

A Bunker Mentality

There's much to discover and many Brotherhood of Steel personnel to meet, but to focus on this Quest, head through the Bunker L1, then into the Bunker L2, and down to the main operations chamber **(4)**, where you both meet Elder McNamara **(5)**, leader of the remains of the Brotherhood of Steel in Nevada. Let Veronica speak with

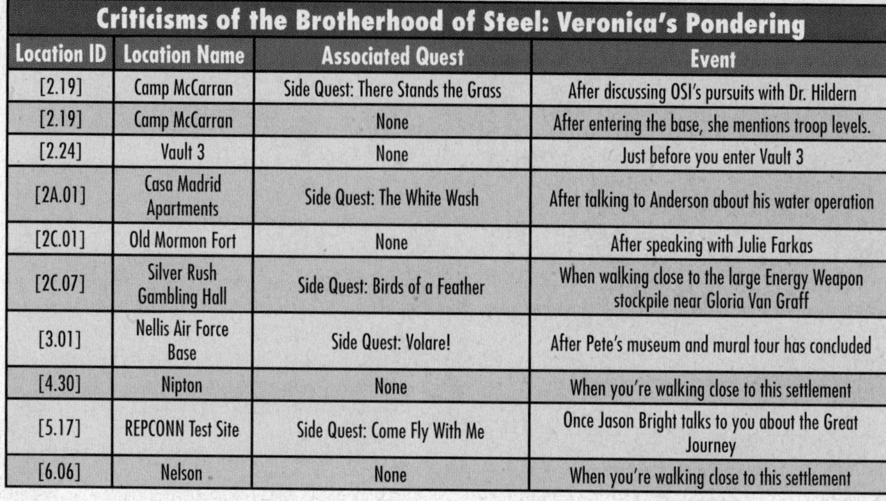

Criticisms of the Brotherhood of Steel: Veronica's Pondering			
Location ID	**Location Name**	**Associated Quest**	**Event**
[2.19]	Camp McCarran	Side Quest: There Stands the Grass	After discussing OSI's pursuits with Dr. Hildern
[2.19]	Camp McCarran	None	After entering the base, she mentions troop levels.
[2.24]	Vault 3	None	Just before you enter Vault 3
[2A.01]	Casa Madrid Apartments	Side Quest: The White Wash	After talking to Anderson about his water operation
[2C.01]	Old Mormon Fort	None	After speaking with Julie Farkas
[2C.07]	Silver Rush Gambling Hall	Side Quest: Birds of a Feather	When walking close to the large Energy Weapon stockpile near Gloria Van Graff
[3.01]	Nellis Air Force Base	Side Quest: Volare!	After Pete's museum and mural tour has concluded
[4.30]	Nipton	None	When you're walking close to this settlement
[5.17]	REPCONN Test Site	Side Quest: Come Fly With Me	Once Jason Bright talks to you about the Great Journey
[6.06]	Nelson	None	When you're walking close to this settlement

McNamara; she doesn't agree with his plan to "wait in a hole for everyone else to die." She isn't getting anywhere with the old man, and tells you to get out of here because she's just wasting her time.

Walk back out of the chamber until Veronica stops you and curbs her anger. She's fond of McNamara, despite his blinkered ways. She wants to change his mind, take a role in society, and attract new members—like the Followers of the Apocalypse, but with the technology to become powerful once again. She mentions Father Elijah, who had the right idea (to send Scribes out to look for beneficial technology) before his death. In fact, there's a comm terminal near here that might have his research on it.

 **Comm Station Password**

Access Father Elijah's notes at the comm terminal with Veronica.

Return with Veronica to the Brotherhood of Steel elder with evidence of the Brotherhood's misguided priorities.

In the Footsteps of Elijah

Exit the bunker to the outside, and find the comm terminal on your World Map; it is close to both HELIOS One [5.13] and the Gibson Scrap Yard [5.14]. At the base of a rocky outcrop, near some long-dead electrical power towers, is Gibson's Shack **(6)** [5.S10]. Head inside, and locate the Comm Station Terminal. Access and download the Research Notes. Veronica checks them out, and spots three separate pieces of technology that might be a good fit. Ask Veronica about each of them, and then choose one (and only one) to search for:

1. A Pulse Gun: a countermeasure to Power Armor.
2. A Rangefinder: a targeting device for some kind of doomsday weapon.
3. Farming technology: an NCR-related vegetation enhancer.

The Quest now splits into three paths. You can complete only one of them.

> *Tip* The "Pulse Gun" and "Rangefinder" options are available whether this Quest is active or not, so if you want to find them afterward, you can. You're sure to want to keep the Rangefinder, too!

Path #1: Pulse Gun

Look for information about the pulse gun at Nellis Air Force Base.

Father Elijah's notes indicate that evidence regarding the Pulse Gun lies at the Boomers' well-protected hidey-hole, the Nellis Air Force Base. Getting there is difficult and dangerous if you haven't already befriended (or beheaded) the Boomers. The optimal plan is to consult the start of Side Quest: Volare!, which takes you through the gauntlet run to get to the gate, and your talks with Raquel and Mother Pearl. Agree to help the Boomers, and then make a quick reconnoiter of Pearl's Barracks **(7)**, where you first speak to her. To avoid getting caught, wait until Raquel and Pearl have gone.

Check the filing cabinets near the corner desk. Steal two items of interest:

 **Colonel Blackwell's Key**

 **Inventory Transfer Order**

Caution Do not just take the Inventory Transfer Order. Take Colonel Blackwell's Key, or your trek is likely to take twice as long! You need the key to unlock the case that contains the weapon!

Recover the pulse gun from Vault 34 if it still exists.

Your Finger On the Pulse

The weapon was apparently transferred to Vault 34 [3.12] many moons ago. Head there (ideally with some radiation-abating Chems for yourself and Veronica), and locate the entrance in the side of the rocky outcrop **(8)**, cutting down Golden Geckos along the way. Consult the Tour Chapter for a comprehensive map of all the levels to this Vault, and Side Quest: Hard Luck Blues for more detail on the route through this maze of rusting walls and frothing Ghouls. To get to the Pulse Gun:

Tip Much of the vault is underwater, and to avoid a panicked drowning, you might wish to finish Side Quest: Volare! first, and obtain a Rebreather.

Head into the caves, and the first floor of the vault. Locate the locked Overseer's Office door. Backtrack to the junction with a sign for the Clinic and Overseer's Office. Take the side corridor with the leaky water pipe. Dive into the submerged steps. Swim along the corridor to the debris-filled room, look left, and search the Ghoulish Vault Technician **(9)**.

 **Vault 34 Utility Terminal Password**

Move to the corridor with a second leaky pipe, and open the door to the Utility Room. Access the terminal inside the Utility Room, click on "System," and pump the water from a nearby corridor.

 Or you can hack into the terminal.

Move to the door near the second leaky pipe. The stairs beyond are drained. Descend, and enter the dead-end room, and secure a second password from a dead (and Ghoulish) technician.

 **Vault 34 Security Terminal Password**

Open the Door to the Armory (not the Armory Door near the Utility Room). Activate the terminal in this area using the Security Password, click on "System," and disengage the Lock to the Overseer's Office.

 Or you can hack into the terminal.

Follow the signs back to the Overseer's Office, and open the Door to Reactor, near the green goo. Head into the Overseer's Office, and fight the remains of the Overseer **(10)**. Check his corpse.

 **Overseer's Password**

Activate the Overseer's terminal, click on "System," and open the Armory Door.

 Or you can hack into the terminal.

Return to the first floor, and locate the Armory Door near the Utility Room and second leaky pipe. Follow the signs for the Equipment Room, kill the remaining Ghouls, and uncover a massive weapons haul! However, the weapon you want is in the Gun Case **(11)**. Open it using Colonel Blackwell's Key. Take the Pulse Gun (which you can equip, but it has very little ammunition, and has no effect on enemies who aren't wearing Powered Armor)! Move to the end part of the Quest.

Bring the pulse gun back to the elder at Hidden Valley.

Path #2: Rangefinder

Visit the Pawn Shop in Freeside and the Vault 21 gift shop with Veronica.

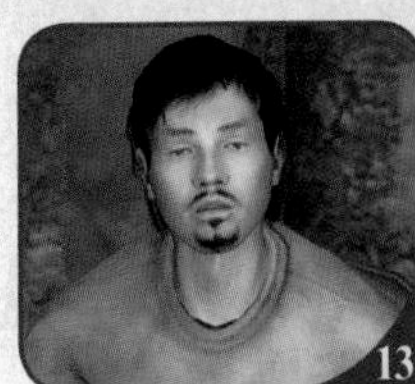

Veronica reckons the best bet is to locate a pawn shop in Outer Vegas, or a gift shop on The Strip that deals in pre-war antiques. Either of those would be a good place to start. The pawn shop in question is Miguel's Pawn Shop [2.02], accessed via the Westside West Entrance [2.01]. Optionally locate the shop itself **(12)**, and speak to the owner inside **(13)**. Tell Miguel you're looking for an antique rangefinder. Miguel is no help but you can restock or off-load some junk.

The other (and only) place where you'll find clues to this technology is the Vault 21 Gift Shop [2D.06] on The Strip. Enter the building **(14)** and speak to Sarah Weintraub the proprietor **(15)**. Ask her what kind of things she sells in her gift shop, and after she tells you, tell her you're looking for an antique rangefinder. She sold it to a "real twitchy, nervous sort of guy," with a "funny collar on." The man said he needed a concrete building, and Sarah instructed him to head for the ruins across from Mick & Ralph's [2C.02].

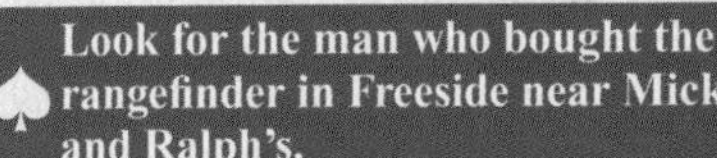
Look for the man who bought the rangefinder in Freeside near Mick and Ralph's.

Sifting Through Human Flotsam

The rag-tag drunks and thugs over on East Freeside congregate around Mick & Ralph's junk shop. Ignore most of the human detritus, and check the ruined building across the street. In the far right corner is a decapitated man **(16)**. This was the likely purchaser of the unit. But he doesn't have it any more.

Ask around to see what became of the rangefinder.

17

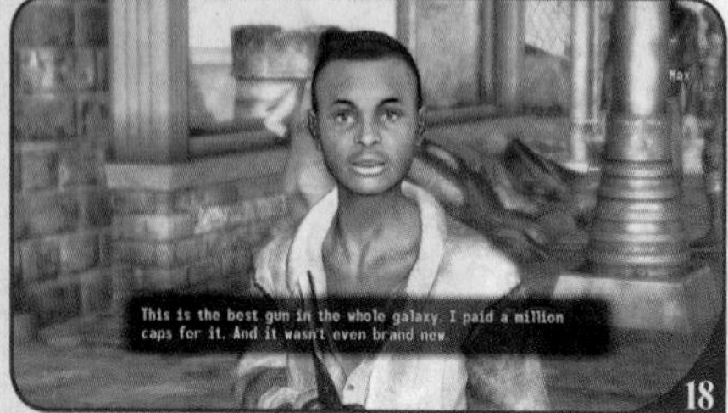

18

Sitting in the same shell of a building is Jacob Hoff (who you can attempt to save from a Chem-based malaise in Side Quest: High Times), but he isn't helpful. Try the vagrant on the street **(17)**. You can:

Tell him you're looking for someone carrying an antique gun. You get deranged cackling.

Ask if he'll accept a bribe of 100 Caps for the information.

Or threaten to "paint the curb with his brains" if he doesn't give you some information.

The latter two options elicit the response: "Kids." Be on the look-out for two of them. They might be roaming the streets, or playing inside Mick & Ralph's store.

Recover the rangefinder.

The little tykes in question are Max and Stacey (18) [2C.S12]. Stacey won't talk to you, but Max will if you catch up to him. You can:

- Ask to buy the "gun" from Max. He wants 1,000 Caps for it. You can:

Tell him the heavy use has depreciated the value, and give him 20 Caps.

Or give Max 1,000 Caps. Max is amazed, and you might want to rethink your conversation choices.

- Or you can wait until Max goes to bed (on top of the building adjacent to Mick & Ralph's), then Steal it from him.

Pickpocket it from him (whether this Quest is active or not).

Euclid's C-Finder

Find a way to enable the rangefinder at HELIOS One.

The ARCHIMEDES Principle

19

Travel to HELIOS One **(19)**, where Lieutenant Haggerty greets you at the door. This starts Side Quest: That Lucky Old Sun. Please refer to that Quest for specific speech conversations you can have with Haggerty, and any other named individual you may come into contact with. For the purposes of this Quest however, you simply need to enter the facility.

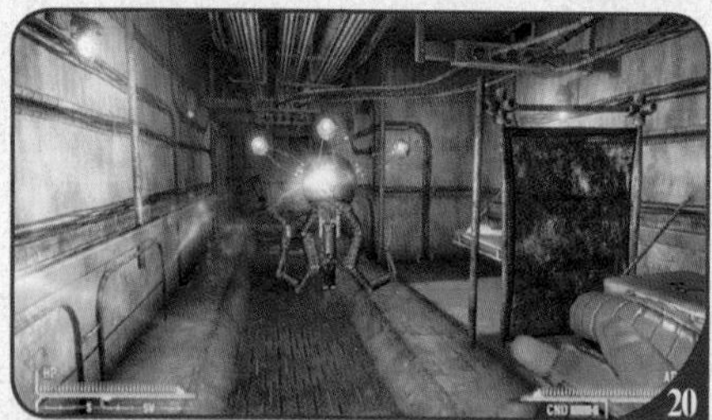
20

Enter the HELIOS One Power Plant Level, working your way through to the door with the amber light above it. Pass Fantastic, and exit to the array field. Move around the concrete foundations, and enter the Solar Collection Tower. Fight past the automated robot guards **(20)**, optionally pausing in the chamber with the Protectron Pods to secure a Poseidon Energy ID Card, and don't stop until you reach the Observation Level.

Poseidon Energy ID Card

21

Locate the Mainframe **(21)**, and power it up using the Auxiliary Generator.

Use your Repair skill and a piece of Scrap Metal.

Or activate PYTHON using your Poseidon Energy ID Card.

Or activate PYTHON using your Science skill.

Activate the HELIOS One Mainframe Terminal. Configure the Power Grid (to any location). Optionally, you can arm the ARCHIMEDES II Plant Defense System. The Quest objective updates. When the power is set to ARCHIMEDES II, you can move to the end part of the Quest.

Discuss your remaining options with Veronica.

Tip Remember! The power must be set to go to the ARCHIMEDES II, but the plant defenses don't have to be activated. If you have the rangefinder when the laser is powered up, it can be activated automatically. You can fire it once every 24 hours, and three targeting lasers descend from a sub-orbital laser cannon. Two seconds later, the ground around the target beams is fried in a massive surge of energy.

Bring the rangefinder to the elder at Hidden Valley.

Path #3: Vegetation Technology

Speak with the director of OSI about his research project.

22

23

Veronica thinks that the best place to start is the NCR OSI office itself, inside Camp McCarran [2.19]. Journey there, and enter the Terminal Building **(22)**, locating the offices behind the escalators on the far left (east) side of the interior building. Speak with Doctor Hildern **(23)**, the Director of Operations, OSI East. At this point, you should begin Side Quest: There Stands the Grass. Refer to that Quest for all the particular verbal details of this meeting, and agree to start the Quest.

Recover the experimental data from Vault 22.

24

25

Your next stop is the overgrown Vault 22 **(24)**. Your objectives are exactly the same as in the other Side Quest (although you don't need to find a Ghoul researcher named Keely). Enter the

Vault 22 Entrance Hall, and ideally mend the elevator. Battle the mutated plant life **(25)**. Head down to Fifth Level—Pest Control. Head through the level until you reach the door marked "No Access." Activate the terminal inside this room and download the experimental data.

At this point, you can also finish Side Quest: There Stands the Grass if you don't want to backtrack. Once you're outside the vault, head back to Hidden Valley. Move to the end part of the Quest.

Bring the data back to the elder at Hidden Valley.

Conclusion: Should I Stay or Should I Go?

26

Journey back to the Bunker L2 main operations chamber where the haughty McNamara and Veronica have a heated, and ultimately pointless discussion about the technology she has presented to him. He simply won't listen. After the impassioned speech, leave the chamber, waiting for Veronica to catch up and speak with you. Ask where that leaves her, and Veronica is unsure. You can:

Tell her this is her home and friends, and she should stay. She agrees.

Tell her leaving now is her only option. She agrees.

Tell her she's the only one who can make this decision, and she decides to stay.

You can leave her here, or continue to utilize her as a Follower. She needs some fresh air after this, and wants to head outside. Oblige her. It isn't until you're outside that the true extent of the elder's paranoia is revealed; a squad of heavily armed and armored Paladins stop you **(26)**. They won't stand for this! You can:

Placate them with statements. If Veronica has decided to stay, the Paladins don't listen, and combat begins.

Or attack them. Combat begins.

Or attack them after a particularly memorable description of their death throes. Combat begins.

In fact, the only way to avoid combat is if Veronica decided to leave. Tell the Paladin that, and he's happy she's headed into exile. Also be wary of attacking the Paladins before they shoot first, because Veronica frowns upon this, and the Quest fails.

This Is the End #1: I Should Stay

Did Veronica wish to stay with the Brotherhood? Then after the battle, she resigns herself to the fact that the first thing to go is trust. But she'll stay on regardless. Of course, she can still offer companionship, and has another perk (this one is for herself). The Quest concludes.

Bonds of Steel (Veronica)

1,000 XP

This Is the End #2: I Should Go

Did Veronica wish to leave the Brotherhood? Then the Paladins' actions outside only reinforce this notion. She tells you there's a Followers Outpost [3.21] near one of her old scavenging grounds. She wants to help out there.

Bring Veronica to check in with the Followers of the Apocalypse outpost.

27

28

When you reach the Outpost **(27)**, head up the steps and into the elevated signal operator's office, now appropriated by the Followers of the Apocalypse. Speak to Doctor Alvarez **(28)**. You can request medical attention, or tell her that Veronica (and/or yourself) is interested in joining the Followers. She tells you she's the wrong person to ask; Dr. Schiller makes these decisions, but he's out for the day on errands.

Return to the Followers of the Apocalypse outpost when Dr. Schiller is there.

29

30

You must wait 24 hours. Pass the time attempting other Quests, or simply wait away from the outpost. When you return, you're both shocked to discover that the place is the scene of a massacre. The Brotherhood of Steel squad followed you both here **(29)**, massacred the Followers, and is accusing you both of sharing knowledge with an outsider organization! They mean business, and Dr. Schiller is in no fit state to employ you **(30)**. The Paladins must be destroyed!

Talk to Veronica

In the aftermath of the carnage, Veronica blames herself. You can agree with her, or try to placate her; either way, she's not joining the Followers or returning home. She can stay as a Follower (Companion). The Quest concludes. You can still attempt Side Quest: Still in the Dark if you haven't done already, as long as you didn't attack the Brotherhood of Steel, or otherwise damage your Reputation with them. Veronica will wait outside Hidden Valley, though.

Causeless Rebel (Veronica)

1,000 XP

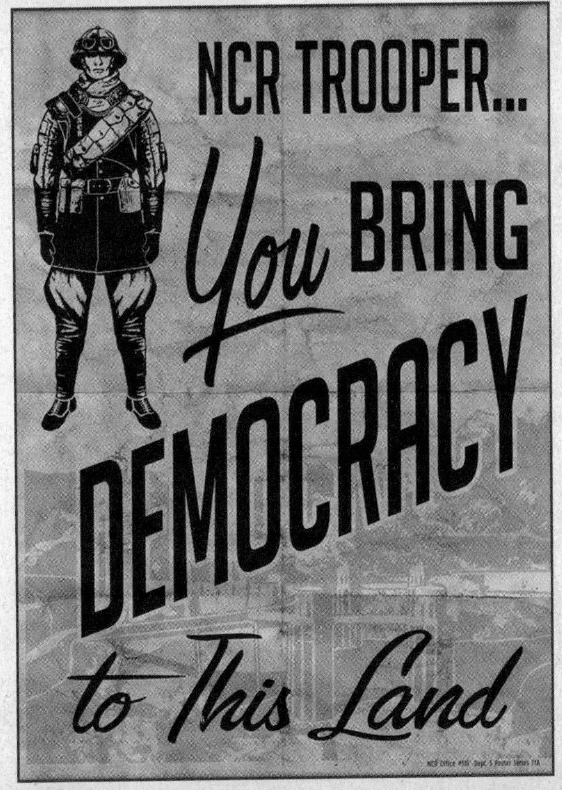

I DON'T HURT ANYMORE

SUGGESTED EXPERIENCE

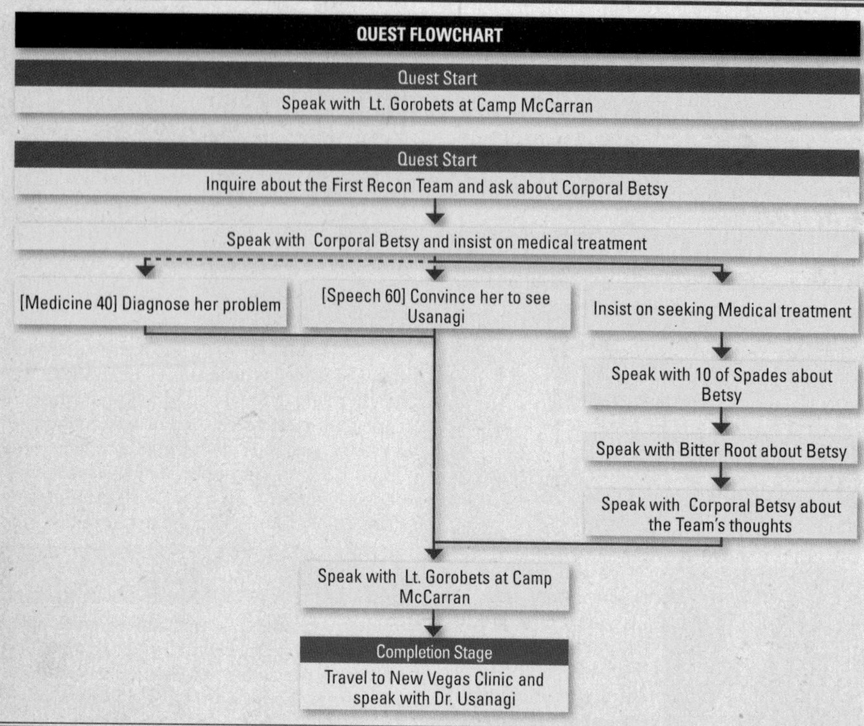

Rendezvous with First Recon

Camp McCarran [2.19] is home to many troops waiting for deployment, and most of them are situated in the expansive parking lot grounds, close to the Terminal Building. Locate the First Recon mess tents **(1)**, and speak with Lieutenant Gorobets **(2)** about his trained squad. He's suitably proud, but some of his team are scarred, like Betsy and Sterling.

Sterling was captured by the Legion, and they tortured him pretty badly. But his eyes still work, so he was transferred to Gorobets' sharpshooters.

Betsy was ambushed with 10 of Spades by a Fiend named Cook-Cook. They escaped, but only after Betsy was raped. She's shrugged the trauma off, but her behavior keeps getting worse. Agree to talk to Betsy for him.

Note Major Dhatri provides bounties for Cook-Cook and two other Fiends, as part of Side Quest: Three-Card Bounty.

Speak with Corporal Betsy about getting medical help for her trauma.

A Mental Reconnaissance

Locate Corporal Betsy **(3)**, and request that she get medical help. The Quest objectives update. With any other response than the two checks (below), you're tasked with speaking to her squadmates.

When Betsy doesn't comply with your request, you can:

Tell her mental trauma can slow her down or distract her, but it's treatable.

Tell her she's the weak link, and she needs to do something about it.

If either check is successful, Betsy agrees to receive help, and you can return to tell the lieutenant.

If you're male, you can ask for a date, but she isn't interested.

If you're female, she asks for more than a date, and you decline her advances.

Talk to the other members of First Recon about getting help for Betsy.

Speak with 10 of Spades.

Speak with Corporal Sterling.

You can approach the three members of First Recon in any order:

10 of Spades **(4)** was with her during the ordeal. You can:

Tell him you heard what happened, and ask him to describe the event. He tells you through stuttering lips that he was knocked unconscious.

Say he couldn't have done anything.

Ask why he thinks he let Betsy down.

Tell him you're trying to convince Betsy to see a doctor. He tells you that Sergeant Bitter-Root went to the clinic, too.

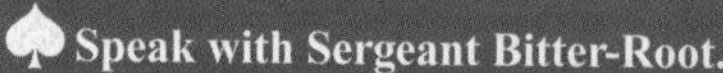

Corporal Sterling **(5)** is a man with a memory. You can:

Ask about his background.

Admire his Unique lever-action Weapon, which Sterling calls "La Longue Carabine."

Tell him you want Betsy to see a doctor. Sterling agrees, and says it's her pride that's keeping her from going.

Approach Sergeant Bitter-Root **(6)** only after you speak with 10 of Spades. You can:

- Ask about his unusual name. He asks if you're trying to start trouble.

Respond that you didn't mean to offend, and he replies that it's a Great Khan name. He proceeds (with some prompting) to tell you about his parents, and the NCR slaughter of Great Kahn at Bitter Springs [3.08]. Ask how he survived the massacre, and he gives you a long story, but not all of it:

Tell him he's not giving you the full story. This delves possibly too deep into his psyche.

Or tell him to forget you mentioned it.

- Tell him you're trying to get Corporal Betsy to see a doctor, and that he went to see Usanagi. He agrees that it helped.

Tell Corporal Betsy that the rest of First Recon agrees she needs help.

A Better Day for Betsy

When all three of First Recon's more "scarred" teammates have chimed in, return to Betsy, and tell her that the rest of First Recon all agree she should see Doctor Usanagi. She's indignant, telling you it's none of your business.

Tell her about 10 of Spades and his stuttering improvements.

Or Bitter-Root admitting that the doctor helped him.

Or Sterling saying that he wouldn't be in First Recon if he hadn't had to swallow his pride.

Any of these comments causes Betsy to rethink, and you can return to tell the Lieutenant.

Tell Lieutenant Gorobets that Corporal Betsy will start receiving treatment.

Return and tell Gorobets the news and he asks if you'd let Usanagi know that Corporal Betsy is coming, and make sure the clinic has time for her.

Deliver Gorobets' message to Doctor Usanagi at the New Vegas Medical Clinic.

7

8

The New Vegas Medical Clinic [2.10] is north of Camp McCarran. Trek there, and enter what looks like an old one-story store **(7)**. Doctor Usanagi **(8)** also sells the latest in Implant technology, but only if you have the Caps. You can buy, trade, and receive medical help, but you're here to tell her about the incoming corporal. She tells you she'll make time in her schedule.

NCR Fame Gained!

250 XP

I FORGOT TO REMEMBER TO FORGET

SUGGESTED EXPERIENCE

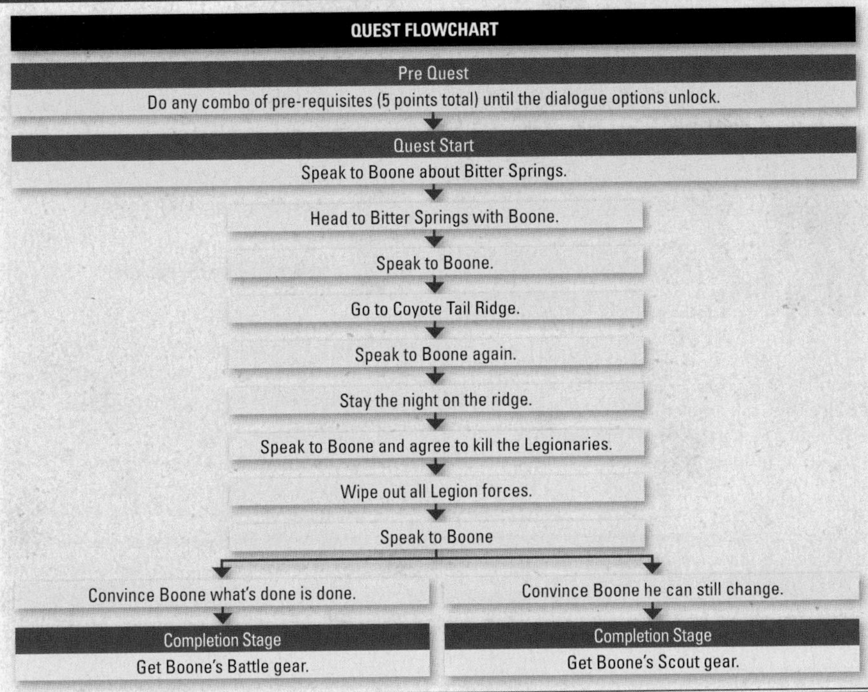

Main Factions

NEW CA. REPUBLIC · CAESAR'S LEGION

Pre-Quest: Out in the Big Wide World

1

This Quest has a number of prerequisites, the first of which is to locate and have Boone in your party. Do this by successfully completing Side Quest: One for My Baby, which takes place in and around Novac **(1)** [5.18]. Once you're buddies, you can speak to Boone **(2)**. You can speak to him at length about his past as an NCR sharpshooter and why he left them behind, and gain insight about other Factions and life in the Mojave Wasteland. Peel back Boone's past through a series of shared experienced across the Wasteland. Take him on your travels, and perform any of the following to get him to talk about his deceased wife, and the heavy burden he's been carrying. Each action is worth either one or two "points." When you reach five "points," Boone tells you enough to begin this Quest.

2

To get Boone to open up about Bitter Springs [3.08], you must speak with either Sergeant Bitter-Root, one of the First Recon in Camp McCarran [2.19], or Manny Vargas in Novac, and focus your conversation on Bitter Springs itself. This allows you to pry into Boone's past about what happened there.

Travel to Bitter Springs with Boone

The Canyons of His Mind

3

4

You'll know when this Quest starts, because Boone approaches you and mentions about a horrific ransacking of Bitter Springs that happened during his career with the NCR. He requests that you both head off to Bitter Springs. Choose either the entrance via the Great Khan graveyard **(3)**, or the main route up through the refugee caravans and shacks **(4)**. Once you near the middle of the camp,

Laying into the Legion: Boone's Progress				
Location ID	Location Name	Associated Quest	Event	"Points"
[2.19]	Camp McCarran	Free Quest: Silus Treatment	Kill Silus	+1
[2.19]	Camp McCarran	Side Quest: I Put a Spell on You	Kill Captain Curtis	+1
[3.28]	The Fort	Main Quest: Render Unto Caesar	Kill Caesar	+2
[4.30]	Nipton	Side Quest: Booted	Save and release the Powder Ganger hostages	+2
[4.30]	Nipton	None	Kill Vulpes Inculta	+1
[6.06]	Nelson	Side Quest: Back in Your Own Backyard	Save all the crucified NCR hostages	+2
[6.06]	Nelson	Side Quest: Back in Your Own Backyard	Kill all the crucified NCR hostages	+1
[6.20]	Camp Cottonwood	Side Quest: Eye for an Eye	Wipe out the Legion here completely	+2

Boone pipes up. This is where he was sent from Camp Golf to search for marauding Khans. He set up on a hump called Coyote Tail Ridge [3.15].

Go with Boone to Coyote Tail Ridge.

Talk to Boone about staying overnight at Coyote Tail Ridge.

5

Oblige Boone and head down the ravine to the red-rocked promontory **(5)** where Boone once committed a massacre. Once atop the ridge, Boone speaks again, indicating that the pass down there was known as Canyon 37. It was the Khan's only escape, and he guarded it while the main NCR force attacked. Remain interested in his stories, and he tells you the fleeing Khans were the sick, women, children, and the elderly. But Boone was forced to kill them all. Reply with varying degrees of sympathy, and agree to spend the night here.

Go to the Bitter Springs refugee camp and repel the Legion raid.

Unleash the Dogs of War

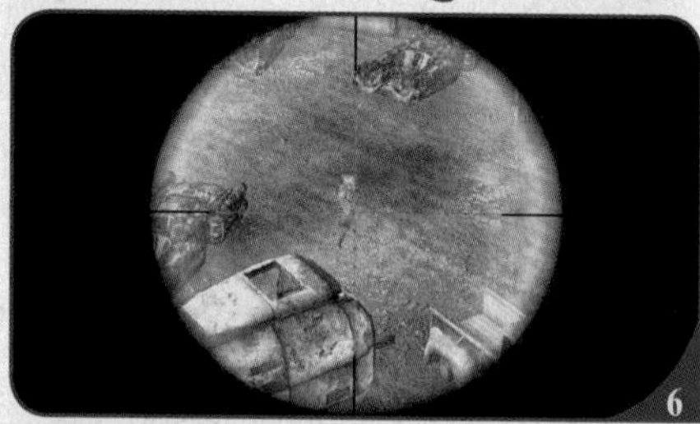
6

7

Time passes. Boone turns to you, and mentions that something is wrong. There's a Legion raiding party heading this way. You can flee, but to complete this Quest, agree to stay and face this horde. Immediately attack the troops you have visible contact with **(6)**, and then back up the canyon to Bitter Springs, as the Legion are not only after Boone for past transgressions, but they're out to murder the refugees, too. Locate the legionaries and cut them down. Pay special attention to the packs of Legion Mongrels because they can easily savage most of the refugees. Letting the enemy come to you is the best plan **(7)**.

You can also lay some Mines at the two entrances before heading to Coyote Tail to thwart the Legion's progress into the settlement.

Caesar's Legion Infamy Gained!

Talk to Boone.

After the fight, Boone beckons you over for a final philosophical discussion on life. His life, specifically, and why he didn't die in the preceding battle. You can:

- Tell Boone that he can't take back what he's done, but he can change and set himself on a better path.
- Or you can tell him to get over it. People die. It's war.

He agrees to either option, and puts on one of two pieces of armor. Choose the first option, and he receives 1st Recon Survival Armor. Have the second conversation, and he brings out 1st Recon Battle Armor. The Quest concludes.

1st Recon Survival Armor

1st Recon Battle Armor

Tip No, Boone didn't give the armor to *you*. But you can simply trade the item, swapping it (or taking it) by opening his Inventory. Boone doesn't mind. Remember you can have only one of the two types of armor, although they are statistically identical.

I FOUGHT THE LAW

SUGGESTED EXPERIENCE

See flowchart on the following page

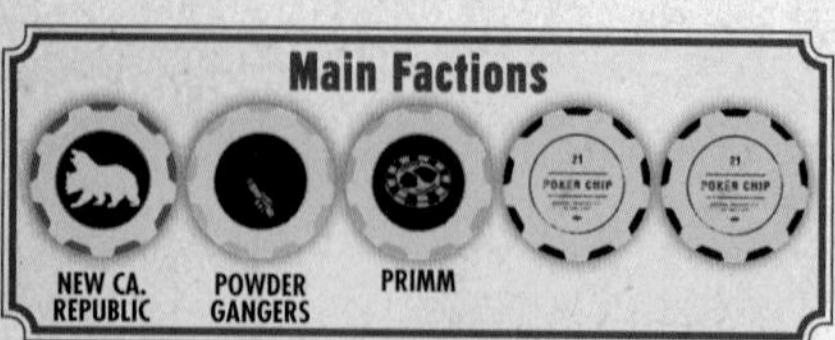

Dawes on the Door; Eddie Inside

1

2

What was once an important holding center for the NCR has now been overrun by Powder Gangers who escaped the very facility they now inhabit. The NCR Correctional Facility [5.15] is the base of power for the Gangers, and should be approached with caution (and while you're still on reasonably friendly terms with this Faction). Travel to the western gate **(1)**, open it, and move to where a man named Dawes **(2)** guards the entrance to the Visitor Center. Ask about the place, or what exactly a Powder Ganger is, and when you're ready, ask to go in. He asks for 100 Caps. You can:

Pay the man his 100 Cap entrance fee, and enter.

Or don't. But you can't access this Quest.

Violence isn't the answer, as it makes all the Powder Gangers hostile.

Of course, you could always try Pickpocketing the Caps from Dawes as you pass....

3

Inside the Visitor Center, pass the Gangers milling about (including Meyers, a possible

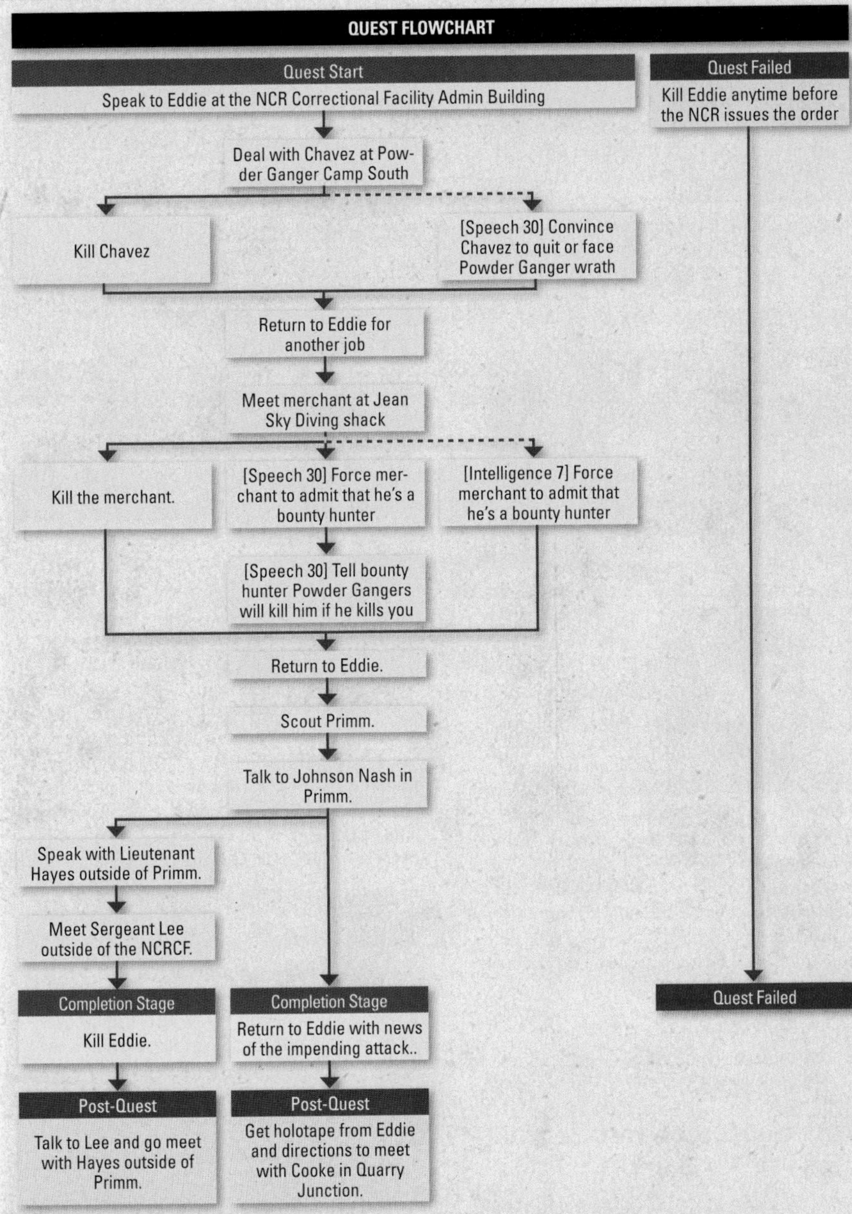

4

sheriff's candidate in Side Quest: My Kind of Town), and exit into the huge prison yard. Turn left, and look for the NCR CF Administration building between the two watchtowers **(3)**. Enter and climb the steps in the northwest corner, making a left at the top. Turn left again, into the operations room, where you'll find the leader of this band of miscreants: Eddie **(4)**. He asks for a reason not to kill you. Focus on requesting a job. Eddie tells you most folks know this is Powder Ganger territory, except a man named Chavez. He's been hitting traders with his own small crew. He wants you to bring Chavez down. Accept this offer of work. You can finish by talking about the prison, how the break-out occurred, and a man named Cooke.

Deal with Chavez.

Task #1: This Ganger Is a Goner

5

6

Chavez and his motley crew were last seen at the Powder Ganger Camp South [4.15]. Leave the facility and head there, looking for the half-tipped railroad carriage **(5)**. Chavez **(6)** and his crew are sitting around a campfire here. Speak to Chavez. He attempts to strong-arm you with some threats and a mugging.

Tell him that Eddie sent you. Chavez is less than impressed. You can:

Tell him that Eddie's determined, and Chavez should quit while he's still alive. Chavez agrees, and leaves peacefully.

Or attack him with words, then weapons.

Simply inform him that he's not going to live, and attack.

Or attack before you even engage these villains. They're easy pickings.

With Chavez dealt with using verbal or actual combat, return to Eddie to inform him of your success.

Powder Gangers Fame Gained!

Tell Eddie that you dealt with Chavez.

Task #2: Bounty Hunter

7

8

Inform Eddie that Chavez isn't a threat, and you're almost thanked. Eddie has another problem: Something feels "funny" about a merchant hanging around nearby. It's like he wants the Gangers to come and get him, rather than fleeing like most other traders. Agree to the job.

Track down the suspicious merchant and get rid of him.

The "merchant" in question is loitering on the corner of the Jean Sky Diving building **(7)** [4.12], northwest of the facility. Set out to find the man, simply known as the Traveling Merchant **(8)**. Choose from two primary options.

Option 1

He tells you to be careful of Powder Gangers roaming these parts.

You notice he's traveling light for a trader. He admits he's actually a bounty hunter.

You tell him a merchant would be much more worried about the Gangers. He admits he's actually a bounty hunter. You can:

Tell him to leave as the Gangers won't fall for this trick.

(A1) Tell him even if he kills you, the Gangers are already onto him. He backs off, and apologizes for trying to ambush you, and leaves.

Ask about the bounty, tell him about a toll, or about taking on the Gangers by himself. You're prompted to the Speech check (A1).

- Ask him to pay the Powder Ganger's toll. He tells you he's happy you showed up, as the NCR is likely to give him a bounty for your corpse. You're prompted to the Speech check (A1), or the following:

Ask about the bounty or about taking on the Gangers by himself. You're prompted back to the Speech check (A1).

Tell him he won't live to collect the bounty, and attack.

Or ask him what he's doing sticking around here.

Option 2

Shoot first and loot his corpse (there's a nice Stormchaser Hat).

When the "merchant" leaves the area, or this mortal coil, head back to the facility.

Powder Gangers Fame Gained!

Return to Eddie.

Task #3: Mojave Prison Blues

9

Eddie's happy (at least, his scowl has lessened slightly), but he wants you to haul ass to Primm, and see what the NCR is up to. You're to talk to the locals and find out if any of the troops stationed at Primm are heading his way. Agree to the task.

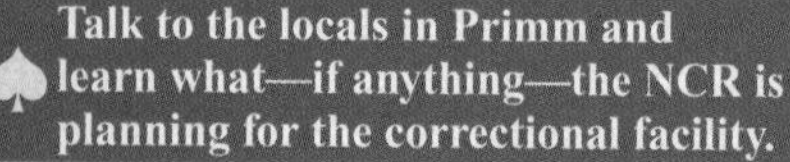

Talk to the locals in Primm and learn what—if anything—the NCR is planning for the correctional facility.

Trek southwest until you reach the outskirts of Primm **(9)** [4.17], or the adjacent California Sunset Drive-in [4.18]. Search out loose-lipped folk in two areas: the small NCR tent camp, and the Vikki & Vance Casino in Primm.

Area #1: Hayes' Tents

10

Approach the barrel fire and NCR troopers **(10)** and open the tent flap, leading to a conversation with Lieutenant Hayes **(11)**. You

11

can discuss other matters (or other Quests if active) with Hayes, but you're here to ask if the NCR has any plans to attack the prison. Naturally, the information is classified. Your conversation can linger at information on the Gangers, but you won't get any more intel from Hayes.

Area #2: Nash's Casino

12

13

Fight through the hostile Renegade Powder Gangers (no affiliation to Eddie, so kill without guilt, or Sneak around), and locate the main entrance to the Vikki & Vance Casino **(12)**. Watch for Layla the mercenary, if you didn't deal with her during the Main Quest: They Went That-A-Way. The co-owner of the place is Johnson Nash **(13)**. Ask him about the casino, talk about Primm (which is going to hell and needs a new sheriff), play Caravan, and more importantly, find out if the NCR plans to attack the prison. His memory needs jogging through currency, apparently:

Answer that you only ask politely the first time.

Or that you have 50 Caps you can give him.

Or hand him 100 Caps. If you have less, you need to return with the full 100. Attacking Nash isn't wise, as you can't mine information from a corpse.

Any of the three options gets Nash babbling about the NCR deciding that enough is enough, and sending a "mess of troops" to take the prison back any day now. Your options now fork:

Report back to Eddie with information on the NCR's planned attack.

(Optional) Betray Eddie by offering Lieutenant Hayes assistance in retaking the prison.

Plan A: Original Ganger

Back at the prison, traipse back to Eddie and inform him that the NCR is planning a raid. In fact, as you tell him, the sounds of gunfire erupt around you. They're already here! You're given your reward, and Eddie (along with his crew) take defensive positions. How you handle your weaponry on the way out determines whether you gain Fame or Infamy among either Faction.

Caps (100)

Chems

1,000 XP

Plan B: Proud Republican

14

15

Back at Hayes' tent, inform the lieutenant that you know of his plans to attack the prison. His annoyance soon turns to agreement if you tell him you want to help with the attack. Tell him the NCR will be wiped out if they attack. This comment falls on deaf ears, but you aren't attacked. If you want to help, Hayes agrees, and marks the staging area on your Pip-Boy's map. Sergeant Lee will be waiting there for you.

Rendezvous with Sergeant Lee.

The rendezvous point is the hilly area between the prison and the Powder Ganger Camp South. When you reach the hilltop **(14)**, speak with Sergeant Lee **(15)**. He's been given instructions to take down "some assbag" named Eddie, and the rest of the Gangers should surrender.

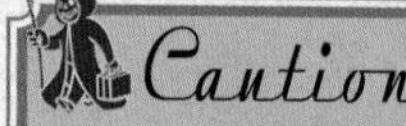

Caution Although your ultimate goal may be to kill Eddie, don't do it before Sergeant Lee tells you to, or you'll fail this Quest!

Note This Quest concludes before a huge battle between the NCR and the Powder Gangers, which you can fight in, alongside either Faction, kill everyone, or watch from a safe distance.

Kill Eddie.

16

The NCR troops then head down the hill and storm the facility. Follow them to the left, around the fencing to the entrance where

you met Dawes. You can hang back, or blast your way in. Sneaking is another option. But whatever your combat decision, you need to enter the Administration building, and slaughter Eddie in combat **(16)**. His henchmen make this difficult, so a try a slow, methodical series of executions and wall-hiding. Find a fair amount of quality weaponry and other goods on the bodies of Eddie's crew. For even more, loot the Administration Key from Eddie's corpse. It unlocks a door on the top floor leading to an item stash.

Administration Key

1,000 XP

I HEAR YOU KNOCKING

SUGGESTED EXPERIENCE

QUEST FLOWCHART

Quest Start

Speak with Lucius at The Fort

↓

Travel to Nellis Air Force Base and enter the Nellis Workshop

↓

Loot the Howitzer Firing Mechanism from the Gun Cabinet

↓

Return to The Fort

↓

[Repair 75] Repair the howitzer with the replacement firing mechanism

↓

Completion Stage

Return to Lucius

Note Gain access to The Fort by meeting and accepting Vulpes Inculta's invitation on The Strip [Zone 2D], at the end of Act I of the Main Quest: Ring-a-Ding Ding! Head to Cottonwood Cove [6.20] and take the boat to this island stronghold.

Negotium I: Apparatus Vacuus a Pectus Pectoris

1

2

During a stay at The Fort [3.28], and once you grace Caesar himself with your presence over at his tent **(1)**, speak to his subordinate, the mighty Lucius **(2)**. Verbally wrangle the conversation into a question about whether Lucius has any employment opportunities. He does: The Legion recently obtained an artillery weapon (which is currently aimed at Hoover Dam [3.33]), but they don't have the part or skill to fix it. Ask more questions, and he tells you a tribe called the Boomers is obsessed with such weapons. Perhaps the spare firing mechanism is there?

Get a replacement firing mechanism for the Legion's howitzer from the Boomers.

Note Accessing Nellis Air Force Base is tricky; The Boomers are dug in and use bombardment weaponry to deter visitors. However, it can be done using the techniques listed during Side Quest: Volare! You can attempt much of that Quest at the same time as this one.

Negotium II: Officina Praemium

3

4

Trek to the northeast corner of the Mojave Wasteland, and avoid the howitzer shells until you reach the front gates **(3)** of the Nellis Air Force Base [3.01]. You're stopped by a Boomer guard before a woman named Raquel takes over questioning. Maximize your life-expectancy by following her to a meeting with Mother Pearl **(4)**; the eldest of this tribe. Talk to her:

You can ask about obtaining a howitzer firing mechanism. But you certainly won't get one from her willingly.

You can also talk to her about helping out (for Side Quest: Volare).

This line of questioning appears to be going nowhere. But after your talk with Pearl, you're given free run of the base.

There is a way to get the firing mechanism without stealing it. Once you become Accepted with the Boomers, request it. Simply complete tasks within the base, and check your Pip-Boy until it informs you that your Fame has risen enough, then speak to Mother Pearl.

Retrieve the firing mechanism from the Boomers' workshop.

When you're free to wander without being shot at (assuming your Reputation is at "Hated" or better), head to the row of curved corrugated buildings **(5)** and enter the second from the end. Once inside the Nellis Workshop, move to the far end of the room, and begin ransacking the chamber.

5

6

Search the Gun Cabinet in the corner **(6)**. Among the items is a Howitzer Firing Mechanism. Grab it, and return to The Fort at your earliest convenience.

Howitzer Firing Mechanism

Install the replacement firing mechanism into the Legion's howitzer.

Negotium III: Telum Suscitatio

7

Back at The Fort, move west past Anthony and his canine, and search out the howitzer positioned on the cliff **(07)**. Examine the howitzer, and replace the firing mechanism. The NCR will be surprised once the Legion begins firing that immense cannon!

Inform Lucius that the howitzer has been repaired.

Move back into Caesar's tent and inform Lucius that the howitzer is now operational. Lucius is pleased because the device will prove useful against NCR snipers hidden in the hills near Hoover Dam.

Caesar's Legion Fame Gained!

100 XP

Should you complete this Quest and ally with Caesar's Legion during Act III of the Main Quest, the howitzer provides fire on the NCR snipers as you cross the dam and exit the checkpoint building.

I PUT A SPELL ON YOU

SUGGESTED EXPERIENCE

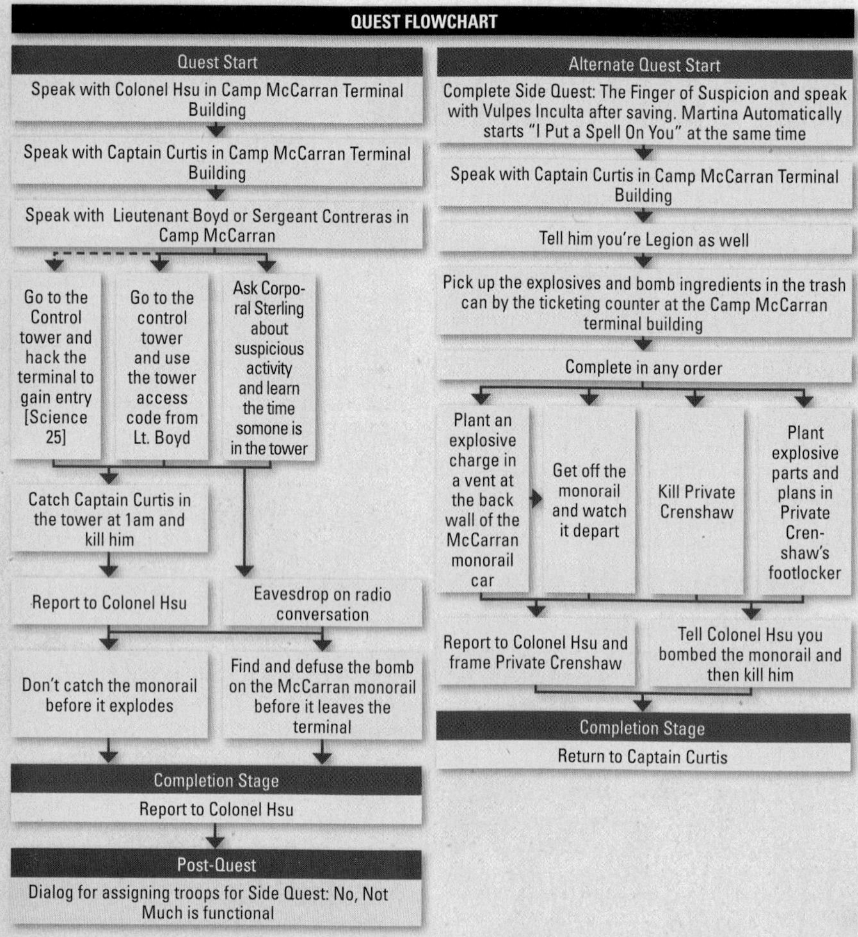

Path A: Terminal Problems

1

2

Enter Camp McCarran, and head for the Terminal Building **(1)**, and find Colonel James Hsu **(2)** in his northeast ground-floor office. Here, you can speak to him at length about various concerns. Ask what you can do to help, and he tells you the NCR is "fighting a lot of fires right now."

The Fiends keep pressing their position from Vault 3. Hsu sent an NCR Ranger called Bryce Anders after their leader, but he never came back. Now there's a bounty on Motor-Runner's head. You can agree to this job, and start Free Quest: Bounty Killer, I.

Note: Motor-Runner Bounty

The Legion captured an officer alive, but he isn't speaking. You can tell Hsu you bet you could make the Legion prisoner talk. He suggests talking to Lieutenant Boyd about it. You can agree to this job, and start Free Quest: Silus Treatment.

Hsu can't send a patrol on a bathroom break without them being ambushed; there's a leak at the base. Suggest that you help, and Hsu tells you that Captain Curtis is heading up the investigation right now.

Cracking Carrie's Code

3

Before You Begin (Satus Sententia)....

Camp McCarran [2.19] is a huge NCR stronghold on the outskirts of New Vegas, offering NCR soldiers and citizens a relatively safe monorail journey into The Strip. It's also the source of some Quests. Learn the numerous ways you can approach this Quest, which has two separate parallel paths depending on the Faction you're working with:

NEW CA. REPUBLIC With an Accepted NCR Reputation, you can start this Quest as a friend of the NCR's, seeking out Colonel James Hsu. This begins Path A.

CAESAR'S LEGION If you've decided to work with Caesar's Legion, you should have headed to the Fort [3.28], spoken to Vulpes Inculta, completed Side Quest: The Finger of Suspicion, and saved Martina. Speak to Vulpes Inculta once more. This begins Path B. However, you may have incurred NCR Infamy, and be susceptible to attack by the NCR (except for Captain Curtis, who you can speak with at any NCR Reputation level). The trick here is not to be caught by the NCR "sentries": Military Police (MPs), and Guard Dog patrols. These are the only troops aware of your Reputation; Sneak past them to gain access.

Note Several Bitter Springs quests are interrelated with this one. This is also a part of Side Quest: No, Not Much. However, it can be completed before or after. Here's how the Bitter Springs Quests break down: To complete the first part of Side Quest: No, Not Much, you must achieve the following:

NEW CA. REPUBLIC Become Idolized with the NCR by completing Quests associated with this Faction (which are tagged throughout the guide).

Complete Side Quest: Bitter Springs Infirmary Blues (optional).

Complete Side Quest: Flags of Our Foul-Ups.

Complete Side Quest: I Put a Spell on You (this Quest).

Complete Side Quest: Restoring Hope.

Complete Side Quest: Climb Ev'ry Mountain.

These five Quests are all parts of Side Quest: No, Not Much.

4

Captain Ronald Curtis' office is on the opposite side of the ground floor, behind the escalators **(3)**. Meet Curtis **(4)**, and extract some other information, then let him know Colonel Hsu wanted you to help him look into some recent intelligence leaks. Curtis says the mole is a slippery customer, and Curtis suggests speaking to Lieutenant Boyd or Sergeant Contreras (although Curtis is already suspicious of the latter). You can meet up with either soldier in any order.

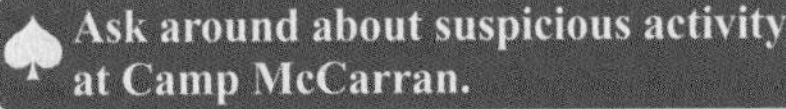
Ask around about suspicious activity at Camp McCarran.

5

6

Follow Curtis' advice, and seek out Lieutenant Carrie Boyd **(6)**, who is up the escalators near Curtis' office, and on the right side, in an interrogation office **(5)**. Ask if she's noticed anything suspicious.

Boyd's answers include soldiers going AWOL, break-ins, and thefts. These lead to four separate investigations:

The missing Ranger, which continues Free Quest: Bounty Killer, I.

A second missing soldier starts Side Quest: The White Wash.

The thefts, which starts Free Quest: Dealing with Contreras.

The break-ins. Strictly speaking, there was no sign of forced entry, just reports of someone sneaking into the camp's control tower at night. The odd part was that the criminal had an access code, which isn't widely distributed. When you ask for it, Lieutenant Boyd gives it over.

Control Tower Access Code

Investigate the late-night break-ins at the Camp McCarran control tower.

Note It isn't necessary to report back to Curtis at this point, but if you do, he continues to offer verbal support.

7

8

Head across to the upper floor Concourse area **(7)**, all the way to the boarded-up doors and entrance to the Camp McCarran Supply Shack. Inside, speak with Sergeant Daniel Contreras **(8)**. Ask him what he has for sale, inspect his wares, and then hint at some secret, under-the-table contraband. He's offended, so you can:

Stop this questioning.

Give him 50 Caps to open up his "extended" inventory.

Tell him you both could work out a deal.

Tell him you have connections, and work out an arrangement.

The latter three choices allow Contreras to tell you about his stash, but you need to complete a chore for him first, regarding Isaac at the Gun Runners [2.14]. This continues Free Quest: Dealing with Contreras. Note that meeting Contreras isn't necessary for this current Side Quest.

Note: McCarran Arms Request

Sabotage After Sundown

9

Back in the Terminal Building, head to the garage doors, and open them. This accesses the aircraft tarmac, and more temporary NCR military storage and structures. Across the yard is the Control Tower **(9)**. Approach the tower. You can:

Hack into the wall terminal, and discover the activity log entries. Look carefully at the "Enter" and "Exit" times, and you can see somebody was in the tower at around 01:00 on consecutive nights, and stayed there for about 15 minutes.

You can open the door to the tower by using the Key and Code Boyd gave you earlier. Inside, there's a Ham Radio on the desk, and a second receiver radio on the wall. Neither have any sounds coming from them.

With late-night break-ins reported, the logical step is to wait until late at night to continue your investigation. Using the activity log as a clue, crouch behind a corner wall or plane tail so you're Hidden, and wait until around 01:00. Somebody is walking across the yard! You can:

Stand up and greet him, which is an appalling idea. The man won't reveal his secrets without any incriminating evidence!

Instead, watch and wait for him to enter the Control Tower, and then (quietly) open the door and follow him.

You have two choices for the conclusion of this Quest: either silent listening and Sneaking away, or noisy confrontation and combat.

Eavesdrop on the radio transmission.

Plan #1: Quietly Does It

10

This option leads you to Conclusion #1. Inside the tower, the man is at the radio receiver **(10)**. Stay at the bottom of the steps and catch him in the act of verbally confirming the sabotage of the McCarran monorail system! The Quest updates.

Find and defuse the bomb on the McCarran monorail before it leaves the terminal.

Slip out of the tower, sprint across the yard to the garage doors, and enter the Terminal Building. Scale the escalators on your right, dash around the corner, and open the door to the outside.

Plan #2: Caught in the Act

11

This option leads you to Conclusion #2. Inside the tower, the man is at the radio receiver. Storm up the stairs (either before or after listening to the conversation) to confront this turncoat. It's Curtis! He's caught right in the middle of his conversation! Curtis tries to talk his way out, but there's only one solution. Curtis draws his weapon. Kill him **(11)**. There's no time to lose; report back to Hsu at once!

Report to Colonel Hsu.

Tell the colonel that you've plugged that intelligence leak. Tell him you caught Curtis radioing intel to Caesar's Legion and took him down. Hsu tells you Curtis assumed control of the monorail inspection crew today! Slightly panicked, Hsu orders you to get to the monorail; if it gets sabotaged, the NCR will be crippled here. Go! Scale the escalators above Hsu's office, dash around the corner, and open the door to the outside.

Find and defuse the bomb on the McCarran monorail before it leaves the terminal.

Conclusion #1: On the Right Track

12

Sprint onto the monorail platform, and quickly head into the open carriage door, turn left, and check the wall vent close to the adjoining carriage door for the Explosives **(12)**. Immediately defuse it, and breathe a sigh of relief.

Conclusion #2: Off the Rails

13

Wander onto the monorail platform, and nonchalantly wait around for the carriage doors to close. Then watch as the monorail begins its journey and promptly explodes on the line **(13)**. Either you were too slow, or you secretly wanted the NCR to suffer.

After either conclusion, return to Colonel Hsu. Explain what happened to the monorail, and he's either delighted or disappointed. Your reward is doled out, and this Quest concludes; and a portion of Side Quest: No, Not Much is completed, whether you started that "overview" Quest or not.

 **NCR Fame Gained!**

 **Caps (250) (If the bomb was defused)**

 **Caps (150) (If the bomb wasn't defused)**

 **500 XP (If the bomb was defused)**

 **350 XP (If the bomb wasn't defused)**

Bicallis B: Saluto Custodis

14

15

Ideally during Main Quest: Render Unto Caesar, and after you complete Side Quest: The Finger of Suspicion (Martina Groesbeck must be alive), return to The Fort [3.28], enter Caesar's Tent **(14)**, and conclude the Side Quest with Vulpes Inculta **(15)**. Inform him that "Martina said she sold her information to Captain Curtis in the NCR." He knows this captain well and suggests you go talk to him. You're responsible for keeping his identity (as a Legion spy) secret.

See if you can assist Captain Curtis in his operation at Camp McCarran.

16

Journey to Camp McCarran, and enter the Terminal Building and head for the office on the opposite side of the terminal ground floor, behind the escalators **(16)**. Tell Captain Ronald Curtis **(17)** you know who he is, and

17

that you're working for the Legion, too. He tells you to keep the noise down, but then sees an opportunity; Colonel Hsu knows about intelligence leaks, and Curtis has been put in charge of finding the culprit, the irony of which isn't lost on him. Keep asking, and he tells you about the plans to bomb the monorail. You're the bomber, and one of the NCR soldiers is the scapegoat. He explains the following objectives:

Pick up the explosives and bomb ingredients in the trash can by the ticketing counter at the Camp McCarran terminal building.

Plant a fission battery, conductor, Wonderglue, a box of Abraxo Cleaner, and the plans inside Private Crenshaw's footlocker.

Kill Private Crenshaw.

Plant an explosive charge in a vent at the back wall of the McCarran monorail car.

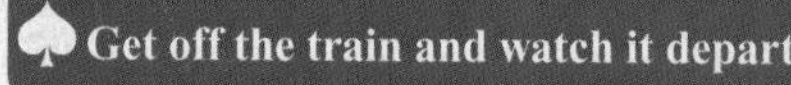

Get off the train and watch it depart.

You can ask Curtis to explain the plan again. After that, he urges you to speak with Hsu, and pretend you'll find the leak for him.

Offer to help Colonel Hsu find the spy.

18

19

In Colonel Hsu's northeast ground-floor office **(18)**, speak to him **(19)** at length about various concerns. Ask what you can do to help, and you're given the same information as if you were starting this Quest working with the NCR (Path A), not against them. Suggest that you help look into who's leaking NCR intelligence, and Hsu tells you he thinks you've done enough. He's one step away from shooting you. You can:

 Tell him you've been fighting for the wrong side, and you'll prove yourself to him. This is your last chance to switch sides, and follow Path A. You're told to speak with Curtis (which you've already done, so this is unnecessary).

Or carry on with the plan Curtis has hatched.

Recolligo Farrago

20

21

The first part of your terrorism involves taking the bomb ingredients. Move into the main terminal foyer, and head to the roped check-in area **(20)**, and search for the trash can **(21)** on the left side of the desks, close to the garage doors. Open the receptacle, and take every item inside; you need it all to frame Private Crenshaw.

 **Abraxo Cleaner**

 **Conductor**

 **Explosive Charge**

 **Fission Battery**

 **Monorail Sabotage Plans**

 **Wonderglue**

You can now enact the Curtis plan. Although it's easier to follow the order presented below, the following three tasks can be attempted in any order.

Dolosus Nex

22

23

Head upstairs to the concourse area **(22)**, and into the makeshift barracks of this large hexagonal structure. Find the footlocker at the foot of the bunkbed **(23)** and place the evidence inside Private Crenshaw's Footlocker. Place the Abraxo Cleaner, Conductor, Fission Battery, Monorail Sabotage Plans, and Wonderglue. Keep the Explosive Charge, or you'll find it very difficult to make the monorail go boom.

24

25

Fortunately, Curtis has Crenshaw patrolling a rarely trafficked area. Head down to the opposite end of the concourse, and open the Door to Camp McCarran Supply Shack. Trot past Sergeant Contreras and open the door near him, leading outside to the McCarran grounds. As Curtis described, Crenshaw is all on his own, patrolling the south wall **(24)**. You can attempt the following with Private Davey Crenshaw **(25)**:

Kill him at range.

Engage him in conversation. He talks about pranks being pulled. You can:

Tell him he'll be in trouble for blowing up the monorail, and slay him.

Add a touch of threatening whimsy to the last words the private ever hears. Then kill him.

Or try the old "here, hold this Grenade" trick. You'll need a Grenade, of course.

However you spill Crenshaw's blood, once it's done, you can pursue the final part of the sabotage.

Finis #III: Volatilis Plaustrum Cado

26

27

Back through the concourse to the mezzanine level of the Terminal Building, head right and around the corner to the door leading to the monorail platform **(26)**. Board the carriage, locate the small vent **(27)**, and place the Explosive Charge inside. Quickly vacate the monorail, step back onto the platform, and watch the doomed vehicle depart and explode.

Report to Colonel Hsu and frame Private Crenshaw.

Colonel Hsu needs to know what the hell happened, so tell him you've uncovered who blew up the monorail. You can:

- Tell him it was Private Crenshaw, who is dead now. Hsu finds it hard to believe.

Inform Hsu that he had explosives and plans. This succeeds in persuading him.

Tell Hsu Crenshaw confessed before he died, using the word "frumentarius" (the "secret service" of the ancient Roman Empire). This succeeds too.

Tell Hsu that Crenshaw confessed, but don't mention the Latin. You fail; Hsu doesn't believe you.

Or tell Hsu you'd be surprised what some people are capable of. This fails, too.

- Or attack the colonel, and kill him.

If you "succeeded," Hsu believes you. If you didn't, you're lucky to escape back to Curtis with your life, but Hsu doesn't attack.

Return to Captain Curtis.

Return to Curtis with Hsu still alive (whether you "succeeded" or not), and he is ecstatic, as the heat has shifted away from him. You're given a reward, and Caesar will hear of this triumph!

 **Caesar's Legion Fame Gained!**

 **Caps (250)**

 **500 XP**

Return to Curtis after killing Hsu, and when you mention this, Curtis is furious; he spent years earning that man's trust! The Quest ends, but not well.

KEEP YOUR EYES ON THE PRIZE

SUGGESTED EXPERIENCE

QUEST FLOWCHART

Quest Start
Go to the Mojave Outpost and talk with Ranger Ghost on top of one of the buildings
↓
Agree to investigate Nipton for Ranger Ghost
↓
Go to Nipton and speak with Vulpes Inculta about what happened there
↓
Completion Stage
Return to Ranger Ghost and tell her what happened

Main Factions

Ferocious Atrocities

Step past the giant rusting statues and snaking freeway jam to the NCR's Mojave Outpost **(1)** [4.27]. There are some oddballs in this settlement, and one of the most stoic is standing atop one of the buildings behind the wire fencing. Wind your way up to the roof via the sloping planks, and introduce yourself to Ranger Ghost **(2)**. She spots that you're a courier, and asks if you want a job. Reply in the affirmative, and Ghost tells you she thinks there's trouble in the town of Nipton [4.30]; there's no traffic and some billowing smoke. She tells you any survivors are likely to be inside the Town Hall. You're to report back any findings, but without endangering yourself unduly.

Recon the Nipton Town Hall for Ranger Ghost.

Follow the remains of the road across the desert, optionally passing the Morning Star Cavern [4.28] and Nipton Road Pit Stop [4.29] until you reach the settlement. Ghost was right to be worried; there are tire fires everywhere, and the Powder Gangers, who had previously run out the native population, are looking pretty tied up at the moment. Move toward the Town Hall **(3)** and approach the main double doors. A member of Caesar's Legion strides out, clad in some kind of red armor and dog skin. He introduces himself as Vulpes Inculta **(4)**, and tells you not to worry; you won't be nailed to a cross like the rest of these degenerates.

Inculta wants you to memorize the fate of Nipton, then move west to the Mojave Outpost and let "the Profligates" know "the little sermon" he prepared here. This begins Side Quest: Cold, Cold Heart. You can continue the conversation at length, asking him about Caesar, before you're waved away to teach what you've learned here. "There will be more lessons in the days ahead," Inculta warns.

Return to Ranger Ghost at Mojave Outpost.

Speak to Ghost again, and let her know the fate of Nipton. She's concerned—not by the atrocities, because the town was "a shithole asking to be burned"—but because Caesar's Legion is moving in, and war is inevitable.

 **100 XP**

 **NCR Fame Gained!**

LEFT MY HEART

SUGGESTED EXPERIENCE

See flowchart on the following page

Main Factions

A Frank Discussion

The old Aerotech Office Park **(1)** [2.22] on the east side of town is a refugee camp overflowing with human flotsam and jetsam. One of these sorrowful sorts is Frank Weathers **(2)**, a farmer who once owned 100 acres near Junktown. Ask him about the Legion if you wish, but definitely question him about his family; they were abducted by a band of Caesar's Legion slavers. You can:

Remark that you're sorry, or say that Frank wasn't a particularly good protector, and ask if he needs help.

Wonder aloud why Frank was spared. He admits he ran from his family.

When you're done admonishing or offering to help, Frank suggests beginning your search at Cottonwood Cove [6.20].

Cannibals, Slavers, and Worse!

Journey southward to Cottonwood Cove **(3)**, where the Legion's presence west of the Colorado River is strongest. You may be stopped by a Legion Explorer as you enter, but:

Showing the Mark of Caesar (given by Vulpes Inculta after you exit The Tops Casino)...

Telling him you're a passing trader...

Or calming him by explaining that you're a friend of the Legion all allow safe passage into camp.

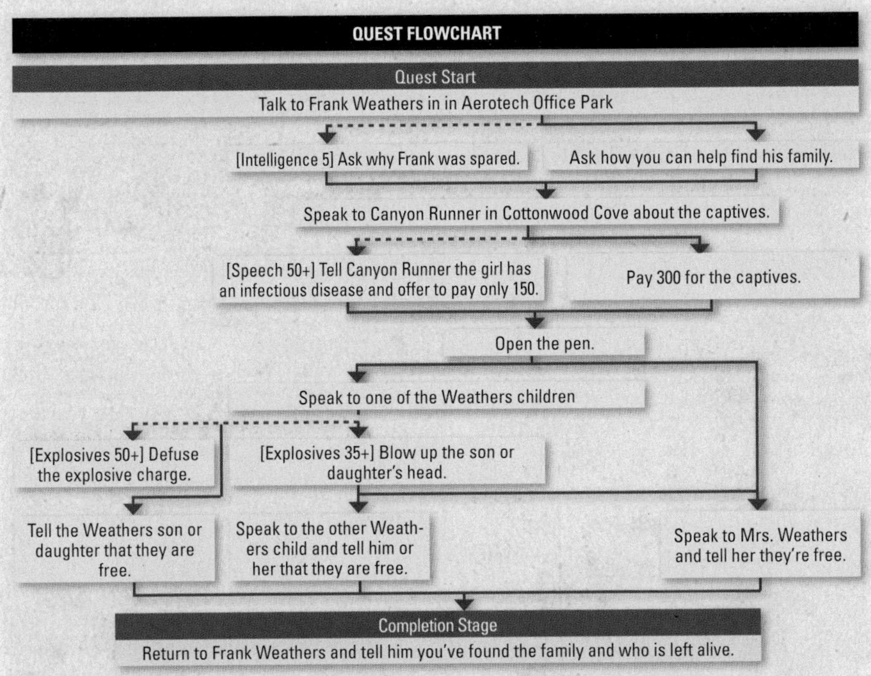

CAESAR'S LEGION Tell the explorer you're a friend, but if you have a poor Reputation ("Merciful Thug" or worse) you're recognized as an enemy and attacked.

Once inside, search for the Legion guard named Canyon Runner **(4)** standing near the mesh-fenced slave pens (attached to the main concrete building). Although you can talk about the Legion's movements and other matters, focus on the "slaves" he is in charge of.

5

6

7

The mother and two children inside the pen haven't earned the right to be called "slaves," and as a "Slavemaster," Canyon Runner professes to know his craft. Ask how much it would cost to purchase the three "captures." After reeling off an offensive list of problems with each of them, he asks for your offer:

Offer 300 Caps for the lot of them.

Lie, and point out that one of the children has all the symptoms of Pustular Hypomyalgia. Canyon Runner drops the offer to 150 Caps.

You can slay Canyon Runner, and everyone else in the camp, Vilifying your Reputation with the Legion. This is highly dangerous, and only for those with complete combat prowess.

With a mixture of Sneaky Lockpicking (or Canyon Runner's key, which you can Pickpocket from him), you can unlock the gate [Hard], and attempt to free the Weathers. This usually ends with them either headless or shot as they try to escape, so it's an initially cunning, but possibly sacrificial plan.

Once the transaction has taken place, open the gate using the Slave Key, and enter the pen. You're freeing Mrs. Weathers **(5)**, Sammy Weathers **(6)**, and Kenny Weathers **(7)**. There are two possible ways to free them.

Weathers Slave Key

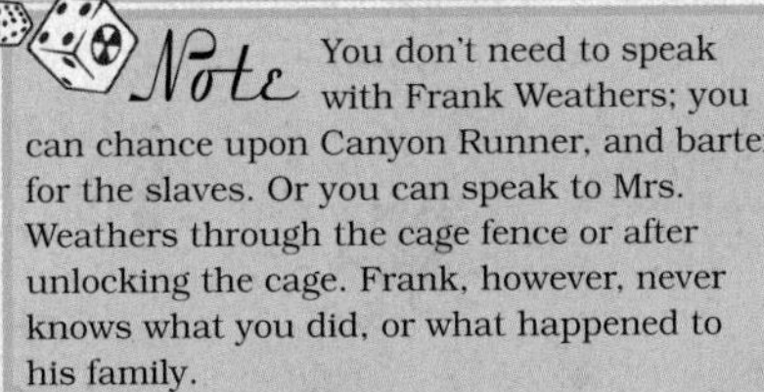
Note You don't need to speak with Frank Weathers; you can chance upon Canyon Runner, and barter for the slaves. Or you can speak to Mrs. Weathers through the cage fence or after unlocking the cage. Frank, however, never knows what you did, or what happened to his family.

Free the Weathers from slavery.

Weathers Forecast: Relief with a Chance of Freedom

After you speak to any of the three of them, and tell them that you've paid for them all and they are free to go, you automatically detach their explosive collars, and the Weathers leave their pens. They don't need chaperoning, but if you speak to them, they tell you they won't be reuniting with their father thanks to his abusive tendencies.

Weathers Forecast: Explosive with a Chance of Brains

This method is not recommended, but you can tell any Weathers family member that you're going to deactivate their collar. You can:

Tell them to hold still, and successfully deactivate the collar without it exploding.

Fail to stop the collar from exploding, decapitating the Weathers family member in question.

Or think about your Explosives skill, and rethink either plan.

Once done, any surviving members of the Weathers' family flee the area. They don't need chaperoning.

Caution If one of the Weathers family has an activating Slave Collar, the remaining family members will not agree to your threats or pleading. You must return with the Slave Key or purchase their freedom. Also be extremely aware that the family is likely to die during the escape if you haven't bargained for their freedom and a Legion patrol is close by!

Return to Frank Weathers.

Weathers Forecast: Alcoholic with a Chance of Redemption

Head back to the Aerotech Office Park and check in with Frank again, telling him you've saved his family. He immediately hands over some Caps, and asks where they are.

If you ask why you'd tell an abusive bastard like him, he asks what lies were spread by his wife:

Tell him his family doesn't want him around, but they would if he was sober. He agrees to get some help, which is a positive way to end his abusive relationship.

Or, that he's a yellow-bellied bastard. Pressing the subject causes Frank to blow his head off with a shotgun, which is one way of ending his abusive relationship.

You can extort Frank before you give him the information, and pocket some extra Caps for your troubles.

You can leave.

You can mention they were headed to the Old Mormon Fort [2C.01] in Freeside. As he's already been kicked out of there, he'll mooch around in case they leave, and doesn't attempt to get sober.

Caps 50 (unless all family members died)

35 (if Frank was extorted, agreed to sober up, or shot himself)

100 (if all family members died)

250 (if two family members died)

500 (if one family member died)

1,000 (if no family members died)

MEDICAL MYSTERY

SUGGESTED EXPERIENCE

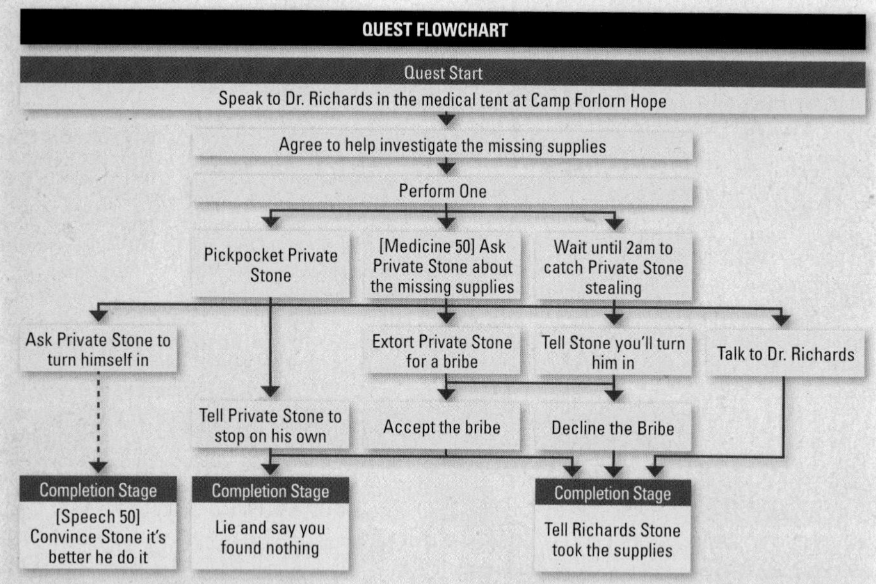

Bedside Manners

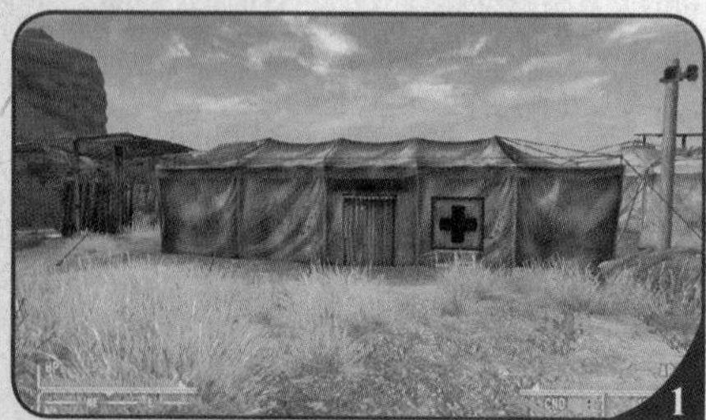

1

2

The grimly titled Camp Forlorn Hope [6.02] along the western cliffs is the hub for NCR communications and wounded soldiers. The staff are in desperate need of help (speak to Major Polatli to begin Side Quest: Restoring Hope, or Tech Sergeant Reyes to start Side Quest: Return to Sender). An overworked soul in the Medical Center **(1)** near the edge of town, Dr. Richards **(2)**, instantly takes a shine to you when you come in and speak to him. He's particularly chipper given the circumstances, but that doesn't mean he's fully stocked with medical supplies: Quite the opposite, in fact. Someone is stealing his supplies.

Ask more questions about this possible thievery, and he explains he's got less supply than he received, but not that he used. A simple deduction. The biggest problem is his supply of Hydra. You can:

Look into this for him, and begin the Quest.

Or ask what the symptoms of Hydra use are. This might help pinpoint a culprit.

Search Camp Forlorn Hope for clues about the missing medical supplies.

3

4

Smoking out the culprit takes some patience and perhaps a little luck, although knowing when to pounce on the thief is helpful too. Around the back of the camp **(3)**, between the ramshackle metal shack and the pond and rocky cliffs, stands a rather sad-looking soldier. You can try one of the following when you spot Private Stone **(4)**:

Gotcha! Plan #1

Immediately step up and ask him if he knows anything about Dr. Richards' missing supplies. Stone stammers a negative reply. You can:

Take this answer at face value, and leave him.

Confirm the dilated eyes and increased heart rate. Stone confesses, and asks to explain himself. See "Conclusion."

Gotcha! Plan #2

Skulk away, then keep a Hidden eye on Private Stone, moving slowly up behind to Pickpocket him. You'll find an Empty Hydra Syringe on him.

You can either confront Stone and ask him to explain himself, or return with the discovery to Doctor Richards. See "Conclusion."

Gotcha! Plan #3

Stake out the Camp Forlorn Hope Medical Center at night.

5

Or, you can wait around until 2 AM. Remain Hidden, with Private Stone in view, and follow him as he sneaks over to the Medical Tent to snag some more Chems. Follow him in, and catch him in the act **(5)**. Challenge Stone to explain himself. See "Conclusion."

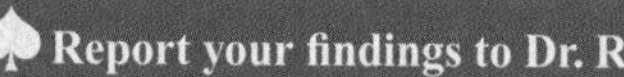

Report your findings to Dr. Richards.

Conclusion: Private Stoned

Once you've discovered that Private Stone is the thief, you can:

1. Head back to Dr. Richards, and tell him Stone is the culprit. Richards informs Major Polatli, and the Quest concludes.

2. Head back to Dr. Richards, and tell him you can't find the thief. Richards is disappointed, and the Quest concludes.

- Tell Private Stone you'll turn him in. He offers you a bribe. You can:

Accept the bribe, and choose Conclusion **1** or **2**.

Reject the bribe, and choose Conclusion **1** or **2**.

- Or you can ask for a bribe yourself. You're given some of what Stone stole. You can then choose **1** or **2**.

Jet (5)

- Ask Private Stone to turn himself in. He asks why. You can:

Tell him it's better than you doing it. Stone agrees. Return to Richards, and he thanks you for finding the criminal, and the Quest concludes.

Or you can change your mind, and tell him you'll turn him in, instead. See **1** or **2**.

NCR FameGained! (unless ending 2 is chosen)

300 XP

MY KIND OF TOWN

SUGGESTED EXPERIENCE

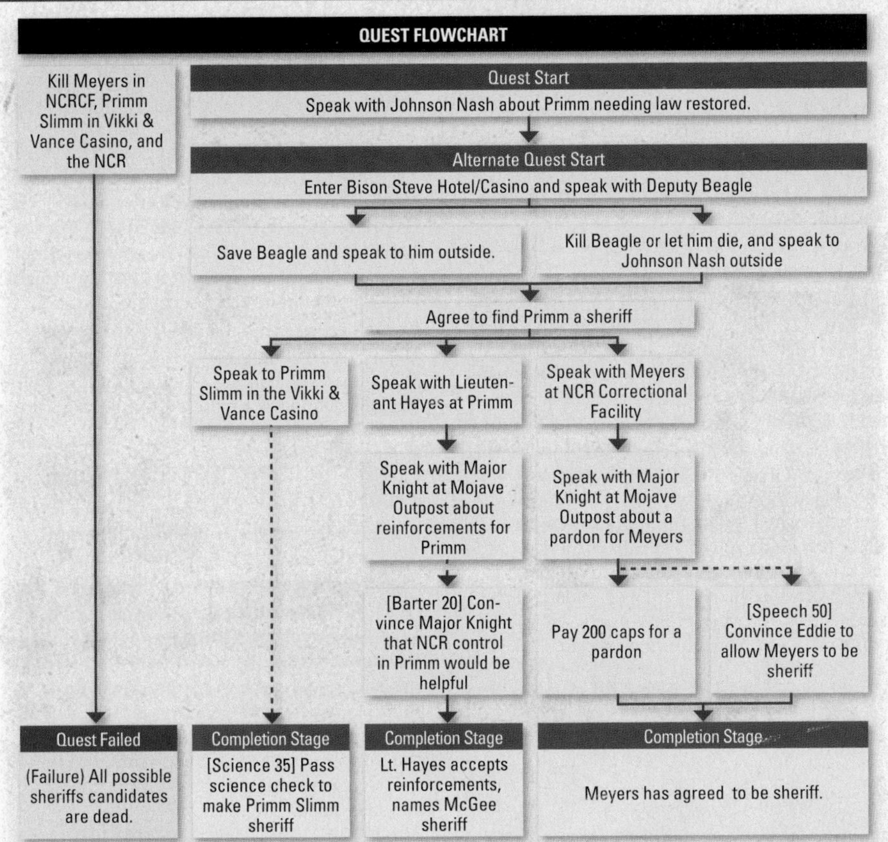

Main Factions

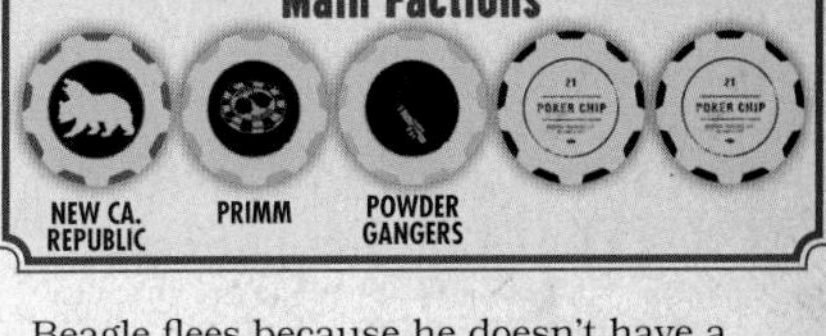

Primm and Proper

1

2

During a reconnoiter of Primm [4.17], after attacking or sneaking past the Renegade Powder Gang members (AKA convicts) loitering between the two casinos (and possibly during Main Quest: They Went That-A-Way), head directly into the Vikki & Vance Casino **(1)** to speak with the owner, Johnson Nash **(2)**. Everyone's a little uneasy because the whole town's gone to hell. Begin the Quest by asking Nash "what happened to Primm." It appears some reprobates broke out of the NCR Correctional Facility, and then got organized, and Primm's Deputy has been captured by them.

Primm's Deputy has been captured by Powder Gangers in Bison Steve and needs to be rescued.

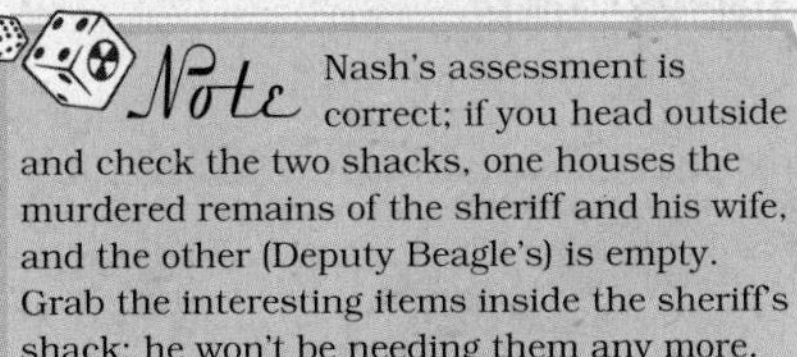

Note Nash's assessment is correct; if you head outside and check the two shacks, one houses the murdered remains of the sheriff and his wife, and the other (Deputy Beagle's) is empty. Grab the interesting items inside the sheriff's shack; he won't be needing them any more.

3

The other, dominating structure in Primm is the Bison Steve Hotel and Casino **(3)**, which comes with the remains of its own roller-coaster. Focus on the ground floor. Battle through to the kitchen area in the southeast corner, killing Renegade Powder Gangers as you go, and locate Deputy Beagle, kneeling and tied up. You can:

SPEECH 25

Free the deputy on the condition that he fight at your side. Beagle grudgingly accepts.

- You can free the deputy. He immediately scarpers back to the Vikki & Vance Casino, leaving you to fight any remaining enemies.

Beagle flees because he doesn't have a weapon for the job. If you speak to him, and hand over a spare weapon, he's more of an asset than a hindrance in the fracas to come.

Although, when you check his inventory, he's got a great suit of Leather Armor for you to "swap" (or take), which is well worth taking (without killing him) if you haven't found good armor yourself, yet.

- If Beagle dies (either during a firefight or by your hands), this Quest isn't over; go back and speak to Johnson Nash to continue.

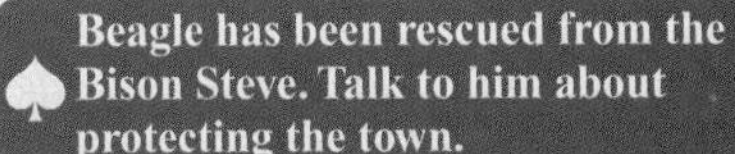

Beagle has been rescued from the Bison Steve. Talk to him about protecting the town.

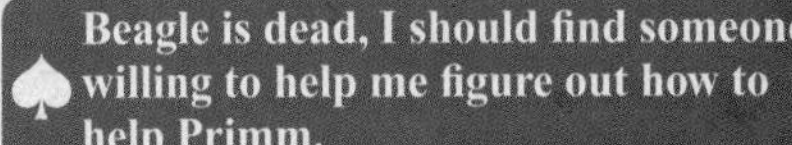

Beagle is dead, I should find someone willing to help me figure out how to help Primm.

Note A second way to begin this Quest is to ignore the Vikki & Vance Casino, and simply locate the trussed-up Deputy.

4

Assuming Beagle made it out of the Bison Steve Casino alive, speak to him back in his old stomping grounds, the Vikki & Vance Casino **(4)**. As well as delusions of grandeur, Beagle seems ill-equipped to handle another lawless attack. Beagle wants you to find Primm a sheriff, and he's suspiciously reticent to take over the role himself. Beagle offers up the name of Meyers, who's holed up in a nearby prison. Or, perhaps one of the NCR might help out. Select "I'll help bring law and order back to Primm."

If Beagle died during his escape, Johnson Nash fills you in on the town's desperate need for more law enforcement.

Note: They Didn't Shoot the Deputy

Beagle wants a new sheriff for Primm. He suggested an ex-sheriff at NCRCF and the NCR as potential candidates.

With Beagle dead, Johnson Nash requested help finding a new sheriff. He suggested the NCR or an ex-sheriff at NCRCF.

(Optional) Reprogram Primm Slimm to be sheriff of Primm.

Candidate #1: Primm Slimm

5

Ignore all this talk of out-of-towners taking over as sheriff, move farther into the Vikki & Vance Casino, and speak with the robotic tour guide: Primm Slimm **(5)**. He certainly has the cowboy hat for the promotion, but does he have the programming?

He does, but only if you reprogram him to serve as sheriff. Law Enforcement Protocols are reinstated. The Quest completes as soon as you've finished tinkering (there's no need to return to Nash or Beagle).

Candidate #2: Lieutenant Hayes

6

7

The next-nearest candidate to Primm is actually Lieutenant Hayes of the NCR. A small camp of troops is stationed on the west side of town, so visit the rubble-filled streets here, and locate the two tents **(6)**. Speak to Hayes **(7)** inside; aside from other Quest information he can impart, make sure you tell him that "Primm is in dire need of some real law." Hayes knows this, but doesn't have the guns or personnel to do anything but hold his current position. He needs more troops before he can even entertain your idea. A man named Knight at the Mojave Outpost [4.27] may be able to help.

Hayes and the NCR will protect Primm if they get some additional military personnel.

8

9

Trek south and a little west along the remains of the freeway to reach a massive, skeletal traffic jam, and two giant rusting statues that mark the entrance to the Mojave Outpost **(8)** [4.27]. Locate and enter the Mojave Outpost Headquarters building, past the mesh gate and sandbags. Major Knight **(9)** greets you as you enter. From flirting to details on this camp's own problems, you can converse with him at length. But to further this Quest, state "I'd like to talk to you about Primm." Knight says he'd like to help, but (as expected) can't spare the men. You can:

Reply that Primm's trade under NCR control would really help their main operations.

If you're successful, Knight radios for another unit to head to Primm.

Major Knight promised additional troops for Primm. Speak to Hayes about NCR protection for Primm.

Return to Lieutenant Hayes in his tent, and tell him "I got extra troop support for Primm." Hayes returns the favor, telling you that Sergeant McGee is to take over as sheriff, and the Rangers will be his deputies. But this comes at a price; the inhabitants must become registered NCR citizens and pay taxes for this protection. A shakedown or peace-of-mind? Choose the NCR to finish this Quest. Let Hayes know you'll think about the plan if you want to try a different candidate.

Candidate #3: Meyers

10

11

Your final choice is someone Beagle (or Nash) mentioned, named Meyers. He's locked away inside the NCR Correctional Facility **(10)** [5.15] to the northeast. Head here, with the appropriate methods of gaining entry to the west entrance, bypassing Dawes at the Door to the Visitor's Center. Meyers certainly has the cowboy hat for the promotion **(11)**, but does he have the mettle? Ask about him first, and then question his thoughts on being Primm's new sheriff. He's interested, but he needs a pardon and a guarantee he can run the place with a minimum of "due process." This sounds like more like a dictatorship than law enforcement.

Meyers, a former sheriff from NCRCF, is willing to be Sheriff of Primm if he gets a pardon from the NCR.

Caution The Gangers own the prison, and your Reputation with them is important. If you're Shunned or Vilified, expect to be shot at on sight, and you'll need to battle through to Meyers. Otherwise, expect little bloodshed, unless you start it first. The same caution must be applied if you're on the outs with the NCR, too.

The only NCR officer able to grant pardons is Major Knight at the Mojave Outpost. Visit the Headquarters, and talk to him about Primm. Tell him one of the NCRCF convicts is looking for a pardon so he can protect Primm. Knight is astonished; Meyers is a convict the NCR had been protecting Primm from! You can:

Tell Knight Meyers' sentence was almost up, and he isn't tied to the Gangers. Knight sees the trade route potential, and agrees.

Offer to "purchase" the pardon. Knight agrees.

Agree with Knight, and seek a different candidate.

Return to Meyers and let him know NCR has pardoned him and he can take over as sheriff.

Assuming you got him his pardon, return to Meyers (who may be in the prison, or in Primm depending on whether you're fighting the Powder Gangers at the prison) and tell him the news. He tells you he and his boys will take good care of Primm.

300 XP

Caution *This Quest fails* if Meyers, Primm Slimm, and the NCR around Primm are wiped out. Cool your jets!

Note You can return to Primm and speak to Deputy Beagle about the conditions the townsfolk are living under (tranquil peace under Primm Slimm, a military state under Sergeant McGee and the NCR, and a crazy backwater under Meyers). Good job!

Tip After the new sheriff has been appointed, wait three days before returning to the casino, and you'll find it's a hive of activity! Gambling is now available (you can complete Free Quest: Big Winner: Vikki & Vance), and there's trade available at this location (if you installed Primm Slim, you receive a discount).

NO, NOT MUCH

SUGGESTED EXPERIENCE

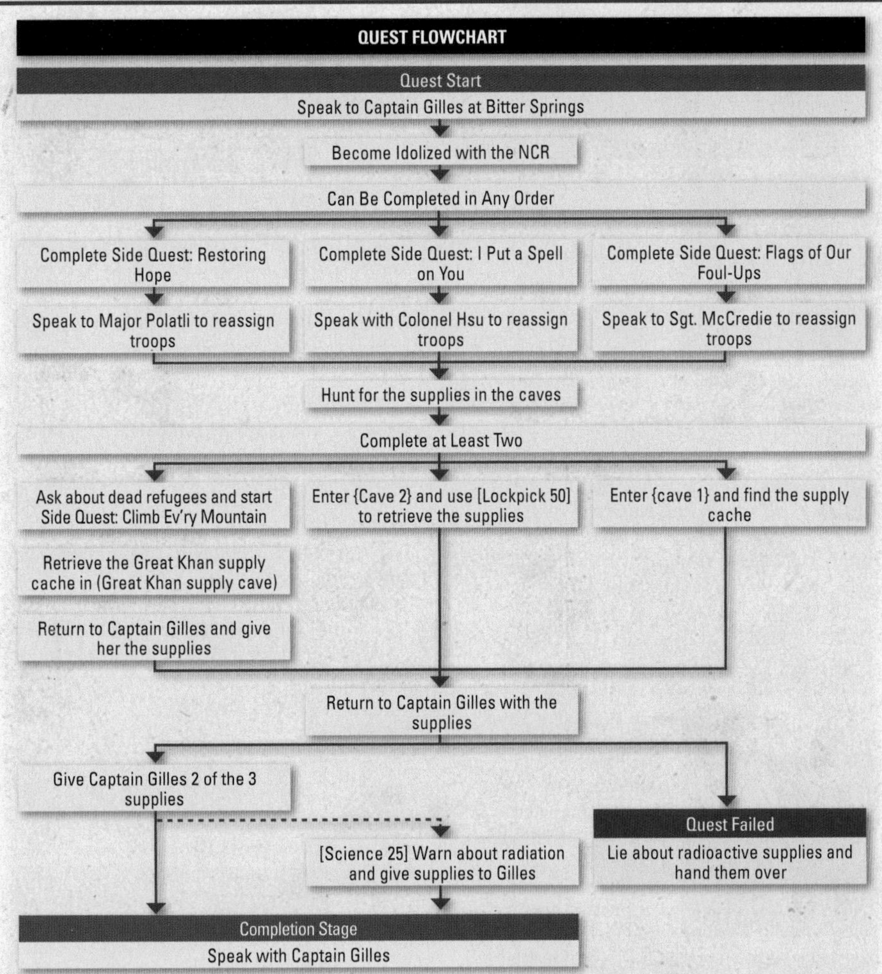

Complete Side Quest: Bitter Springs Infirmary Blues (optional).

Complete Side Quest: Flags of Our Foul-Ups.

Complete Side Quest: I Put a Spell on You.

Complete Side Quest: Restoring Hope.

Complete Side Quest: Climb Ev'ry Mountain.

These five Quests are all parts of Side Quest: No, Not Much.

This web of Quests now progresses. To complete this particular one, return to Captain Gilles once:

You're Idolized by the NCR.

- You've reassigned troops at Camp Golf [3.23], working with Sergeant McCredie (Flags of Our Foul-Ups).
- You've reassigned troops at Camp McCarran [2.19], working with Colonel Hsu (I Put a Spell on You).
- You've reassigned troops at Camp Forlorn Hope [6.02] working with Major Polatli (Restoring Hope).

The captain is worried about the camp's supplies, which are dangerously low. She swears someone is stealing them. You're tasked with finding where these supplies have ended up. She reckons they're in the caves in the mountains above camp.

Part 1: Actually, Quite a Lot

Camp Bitter Springs **(1)** [3.08] is only barely holding together due to the influx of refugees fleeing the Faction fighting across the Mojave Wasteland. Captain Gilles **(2)** is in charge of this mess. Locate her at the upper end of the camp, in one of her tents or around the campfire, and ask what you can do to help. This begins the "overview" Side Quest: No, Not Much. It also triggers access to four separate sub-Quests (see Note). She requests the following Objectives, which you can speak to her again about:

Find relief for Captain Gilles at Bitter Springs.

(This is the overall Objective of Side Quest: No, Not Much)

Talk to Camp Golf about reassigning soldiers to Bitter Springs.

(This is Side Quest: Flags of Our Foul-Ups)

Talk to Camp McCarran about reassigning soldiers to Bitter Springs.

(This is Side Quest: I Put a Spell on You)

Talk to Camp Forlorn Hope about reassigning soldiers to Bitter Springs.

(This is Side Quest: Restoring Hope)

Talk to Lt. Markland about finding medical supplies for the camp.

(This is Side Quest: Climb Ev'ry Mountain)

The Bitter Springs Quests are interrelated. First, speak to Captain Gilles to begin Side Quest: No, Not Much (this Quest). To complete the first part of that "overview" Side Quest, you must achieve the following:

NEW CA. REPUBLIC Become Idolized with the NCR. Achieve this by completing Quests associated with this Faction (which are tagged throughout the guide).

Find supplies for the camp.

Tip You decide how much to explore underground. Three caves lie northwest of Camp Bitter Springs: Great Khan Supply Cave 1 [3.S09]; Great Khan Supply Cave 2 [3.S10]; and Great Khan Supply Cave 3 [3.S11]. You only need to complete two of the following three parts (A, B, and C), although finishing all three gives you a greater reward.

Part 2A: Satisfactory Spelunking I

Begin your exploration by scaling the sandstone bluffs above the camp, and locating the lowest of the three cave entrances **(3)**. Enter the cave, and terminate the clusters of Giant Ants **(4)** scuttling about the dank natural tunnels. Follow the short (and slightly radioactive) tunnel to the northeast as it curves to the right, ending at a broken mesh fence and a dilapidated metal shelving unit, with a Radioactive Supply Cache resting on it **(5)**. You can bring the cache back to Gilles, or move farther up the bluffs to search the second cave.

Radioactive Supply Cache

Part 2B: Satisfactory Spelunking II

In the gravel dip between the sandstone mountains is a second, higher cave opening **(6)**. Head into the low-lit tunnels, and prepare to repel possible Nightstalker attacks **(7)**. Toward the northeast corner of the cave system is a locked gate.

Use your Bobby Pins and skill to unlock the gate, leading to a metal shelf containing some interesting items. Top of that list is the Great Khan Supply Cache **(8)**.

Great Khan Supply Cache

Part 2C: Climbing Ev'ry Mountain

The final cave, which holds a Great Khan named Oscar **(9)**, who's probably responsible for the lack of camp supplies, is its own Side Quest. Finish this successfully if you want to finish this Quest completely, and then return to Gilles.

Great Khan Supply Cache

Bring the supplies back to Captain Gilles.

Talk to Capt. Gilles for your reward.

Part 3: Almost Everything, In Fact

Back at Captain Gilles' command area, hand over the supply caches you've collected. You can:

Give Gilles the two non-irradiated supply caches. Gilles is understandably elated, and this convoluted Quest finishes with a flourish of good fortune.

Hand over the radioactive supplies, and tell her the supplies are irradiated, but with a Rad-X filter, they'll be safe. This counts as one of the two caches you must hand over. If Science isn't your strong skill, you must give her the other (non-irradiated) caches.

Give her the radioactive supplies, telling her they'll be helpful. This fails the Quest. Are you working for the Legion?!

NCR Fame Gained!

300 XP

You only need to provide two of the three sets of supplies to conclude this Quest. Take the irradiated supplies and use them to gain extra rewards by telling Gilles about the radioactivity. But if you give her the radioactive supplies without mentioning this, and return to Bitter Springs, the entire camp is sick....

NOTHIN' BUT A HOUND DOG

SUGGESTED EXPERIENCE

See flowchart on the following page

Nervous Rex

This Quest begins after you complete Side Quest: G.I. Blues. Once Orris has been dealt with, return to King's School of Impersonation **(1)** [2C.05] in Freeside, and speak with the King **(2)**, who you should be on

excellent terms with. Ask about King's robotic dog. Rex has been acting peculiar for some time now. Apparently, the Followers inspected him and said "his brain was bad." Say you'll help, and the King suggests you head over to Julie Farkas for some answers.

Move into the adjacent area of Freeside, and locate the Old Mormon Fort **(3)** [2C.01]; the hub of activity for the Followers Faction. Inside, speak to Julie Farkas **(4)** as recommended. It breaks her heart, but Rex's condition is beyond anything she can handle. Brain surgery and sophisticated cybernetics are required, and the only man capable of this lives up in the northwest mountains, in a place called Jacobstown [1.10]. Return to the King, and tell him the news. He's ecstatic, but too busy to make the trip. His idea is to "lend" Rex to you. Agree, and the Quest begins. Head almost due west, toward the hills.

Follower: Rex

Bring evidence of Karl's plan to Papa Khan.

Take it, and show it to Papa Khan, who takes great exception to the forthcoming butchery and slavery Karl was intending to attempt on the Great Khans. If Karl isn't already dead, he soon will be.

The Penny Drops for Papa

Papa Khan is now conflicted. Well, until he blew Karl's head off. But despite him coming around to his tribe's way of thinking, he wants to leave a legacy of greatness when he dies. He doesn't want them cowering in a canyon and living off scraps, and joining Caesar was an attempt to find lost glory. You can:

Tell him his tribe is already proud and strong; he must claim his own glory!

Ask what legacy his tribe has? It is nothing but ghosts and martyrs.

Or ask where you can find past inspiration for him. He thinks the Followers of the Apocalypse might have some data.

In either Speech check, Papa agrees, and your Quest moves to the discussion under "A Khan Do Attitude" (below).

Talk to the Followers of the Apocalypse about the Great Khans.

The Path of the Righteous Man

15

16

Journey to the Old Mormon Fort [2C.01] in Freeside, open the front gate **(15)**, and speak to Julie Farkas **(16)**. Tell her things seem pretty rough, then ask what you can do to help. These pleasantries allow you to then ask whether she knows of something that could inspire the Great Khans. She tells you they were taught reading, writing, and basic science to make medicine. But they made Chems. Ezekiel would know more. He's a Follower with particular knowledge of tribal cultures. He's currently wandering the eastern Mojave wastes.

Talk to Ezekiel about the history of the Great Khans.

Just down the hill from the 188 Trading Post **(17)** is a wandering man called Ezekiel **(18)**. Tell him Julie Farkas told you to ask about the Great Khans. He gives you a potted

17

18

history. Ask for a smaller pot, and he gives you a book from ancient times, about a tribe he thinks the Khans built their culture on.

Pretty Pretty Horses: A History of the Mongol Empire

Bring the history book back to Papa Khan.

A Khan Do Attitude

Back in Red Rock Canyon, seek out Papa Khan one more time, and show him the book.

Tell him to read about the mighty Mongol Empire if he wants inspiration. This is the exact symbol his tribe can unite behind! Or, tell him to read this if his thugs want to ape the glories of the past. The results are the same, although Papa is slightly more insulted.

Wish him the best, and the Quest concludes (unless you need to report back to Moore).

Tell him as long as he isn't fighting with Caesar, you don't care what he does. The Quest concludes (unless you need to report back to Moore).

Or, ask if he'd consider joining the NCR instead of Caesar. You may wince at his response, which is a resounding "no." Perhaps Regis might be more amenable? The Objective updates.

Great Khans Fame Gained!

Talk to Regis about the NCR.

Your final conversation is with Regis. Ask him about the NCR, and he seems more amenable to working with them, but Papa Khan would never agree to this. And as long as Papa Khan is alive, he won't be swayed. Which should get you thinking:

Moore's Law: Useful Machete Fodder

Return to Colonel Moore as soon as you find out that Regis is amenable to allying with the NCR. She doesn't dismiss it out of hand, until you request a diplomatic solution. There's no time for that, although she could still work with the Khans if Papa Khan was executed. Using stealth, of course. You're given a Locksmith's Reader to help with your Lockpicking, and told to wait until night, or to surprise him when he's alone.

Locksmith's Reader

Bobby Pins (5)

Assassinate Papa Khan without being detected.

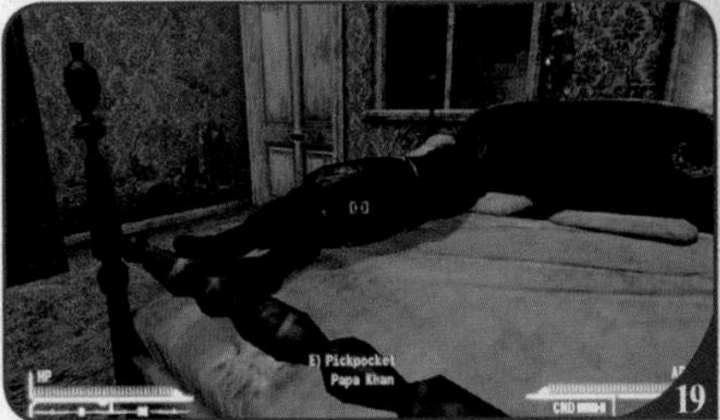

19

Return to the longhouse during the night (when Papa Khan is sleeping in the rear bedroom), and creep around the back.

Bring out your Bobby Pins (and read the magazine if you need to) and pick the lock. Once you're inside the bedroom, check the bed. Papa Khan should be sleeping here. If he isn't, either wait or return later.

Sneak around behind him **(19)**, and attempt a Pickpocket. You can then choose to murder him.

Talk to Regis about the Khans' allegiance.

Now head out and find Regis, and ask him to lead the Khans against Caesar and fight for the NCR. Without Papa's guidance, he has little choice. He agrees, and the Khans appear during the final battle.

Great Khans Fame Gained!

Wipe out the Great Khans at Red Rock Canyon.

Return to Red Rock Canyon and speak to Papa Khan.

Moore's Law: No Khan Do

20

There is one additional interaction you can attempt after receiving your marching orders from Colonel Moore during Main Quest: For the Republic, Part 2: Enter Red Rock Canyon and murder anyone wearing a black Brahmin-skin jacket and handlebar moustaches **(20)**. Kill every single Khan in a ballet of blood, and return to Moore. This will fail this Side Quest, and is ill-advised for completionists, but it does quickly progress the Main Quest.

500 XP

ONE FOR MY BABY

SUGGESTED EXPERIENCE

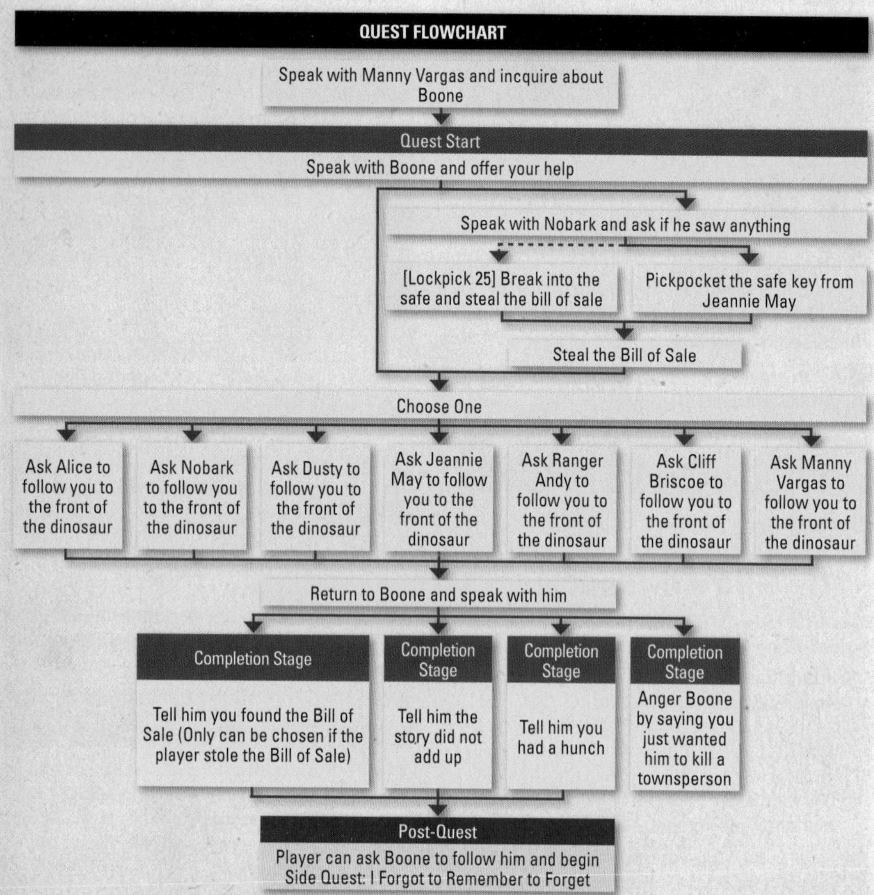

Into the Mouth of Sadness

1

2

Novac [5.18] is a town on edge, not least because of the advancements the Legion is making to the east. To this end, Novac has snipers posted in the mouth of its greatest tourist attraction: Dinky the Dinosaur **(1)**. There are two snipers: Manny Vargas takes the day watch (from 9 AM to 9 PM) while Boone has the nighttime operations.

Begin this Quest by visiting either of the snipers in the mouth of Dinky, using the door in the beast's sides. Pass the gift shop, and step out from the belly of the beast.

Manny Vargas provides information on your attackers, and requests your help to take out the roving Ghouls in the area (Side Quest: Come Fly With Me). He'll also provide background on Boone if you ask.

Boone is a sniper, and they used to spot for each other when they were enlisted with the NCR. They settled in Novac, but Manny and Boone aren't on the best of terms right now. Boone's wife didn't see eye-to-eye with Manny on some things. She's now missing, and Boone isn't speaking to Manny.

Press Manny on these matters, and he tells you about his gang past, and how this "bitch" wanted to take Boone away from a soldier's life.

Note: Nighttime Sniper

Return after 9 PM and speak with Boone **(2)** inside Dinky's mouth. Boone isn't in the best mood, and asks why you're here:

Steer the chatter to Boone looking for someone in particular. He answers that he's looking for Legion.

Conversation is stilted, but politely persevere and Boone eventually tells you "I need someone I can trust." Boone wants you to find something out for him. Somebody took "Carla," and he wants to know who set it up. She's dead now, but Boone wants the son of a bitch who sold her. Find who's responsible, and bring them in front of the dinosaur while Boone is on duty. Wear Boone's Beret to signal that you're with the person Boone needs to enact revenge on.

Boone's Beret

(Optional) Ask around Novac for information about who kidnapped Boone's wife.

Send someone in front of Dinky the Dinosaur. Put on the beret to signal to Boone that this is the culprit.

Part 1: Hearsay and Gossip

Bring up the Local Map on your Pip-Boy, and you'll see various possible townsfolk to speak with about Boone's wife. Although it isn't necessary to go to all (or any) of them, it's a good idea to learn everybody's possible motives.

Suspect #1: Cliff Briscoe

3

4

The first suspect is the one who has the most opportunity to eavesdrop: Cliff Briscoe, who works inside Dinky in the Dino Bite Gift Shop **(3)**. Speak with Cliff **(4)** about Boone and his betrothed. Cliff didn't speak to them much, especially the wife because Boone did most of the purchases. She was in the store once, but didn't stay long.

Coax Cliff Briscoe out for a nighttime constitutional around to the front of Dinky, if you feel the need.

Suspect #2: Manny Vargas

5

6

The most obvious suspect is Manny Vargas. You can find him in his room at the motel **(5)** during the night, or on watch inside Dinky during the day.

Speak to him **(6)** about Boone's wife. Carla didn't have a friend in town, and didn't want any. She sat in her room. She was rude. You wouldn't have liked her. Manny's first thought (when he heard she'd been kidnapped) was relief. But he thought Boone would come after him, and their friendship wouldn't be the same. Which it hasn't been.

You can ask him to join you in front of the dinosaur, if you want.

Suspect #3: Jeannie May Crawford

7

8

The Dino Dee-lite Hotel's **(7)** proprietor may know something. Enter the door to the front desk, and speak with Jeannie May Crawford **(8)**. She seems friendly, and you can ask all about her, and the town. Ask about Boone's wife, and she's sympathetic, but reckons she might have run away on her own. Carla liked the lights of New Vegas. Perhaps she got tired of waiting, and went back there?

You can ask her to walk with you to the front of the dinosaur, if you wish.

Suspects #4 and #5: Dusty and Alice McBride

9

10

11

The modest McBride house toward the town's southwestern edge **(9)** is home to Dusty McBride **(10)** and his wife Alice **(11)**. Dusty says he doesn't really know about Boone and Carla. But Carla seemed to have an edge about her, that she'd rather be someplace else. Meanwhile Alice only just remembers Boone, "that sniper fella." She only met them once or twice. They seemed like nice folk. Alice may not even know Carla is dead.

You can request that Dusty or Alice accompany you on a stroll toward Dinky, if you're that way inclined.

Suspect #6: No-Bark

12

13

Behind the motel, on Novac's northwest perimeter, is a shoddy shack **(12)** belonging to No-Bark **(13)**. Enter the shack, and navigate his "decorations," before speaking to the old coot about Carla:

You can intimidate No-Bark with your sheer physicality.

Or weave through a few more questions.

No-Bark says he saw the abduction take place. Some "shadowy folk" came and went to the motel, and possibly the lobby, too. He thought they were cannibals, so he kept away. But the culprits were actually "Molerat men," coming up from "the Underneath" to steal women with the promises of "fancy mud mansions." Although this is obviously the drooling warbling of an addled lunatic, the lobby might be worth checking out.

But No-Bark is obviously deranged. Perhaps he'd like to come with you and see the big dinosaur?

(Optional) Look for evidence of the guilty party inside the Dino Dee-lite lobby.

Acting on No-Bark's Bite

14

[Optional] Return to the motel lobby, where you spoke with Jeannie May Crawford, and look for evidence. The only area of interest is the floor safe **(14)**. You can:

Pickpocket the Safe Key from Jeannie May. You may need to wait until daylight for her to appear, if there's nobody in the lobby.

Safe Key

Or pry open the Safe with your Bobby Pins and a modicum of skill. To avoid hostilities, make sure Jeannie isn't in the vicinity, or use a Stealth Boy.

The safe holds a Bill of Sale. Take it, and read it in the Misc Menu of your Pip-Boy's Data.

Bill of Sale

Part 2: A Shot in the Dark

With the Bill of Sale, you have all the evidence you need: one of the townsfolk sold Carla, and Boone's unborn child, to the Consul Officiorum (The Legion)!

Head back to the suspect mentioned in the Bill of Sale, and request that they accompany you to the front of the dinosaur. Remember to wear Boone's Beret before you get there.

Or, head back to any of the people you've previously spoken with (or those listed above), and get them to follow you instead. Wear Boone's Beret if you want to end their life.

> **Caution** SPOILER ALERT
>
> Having trouble figuring out who the guilty party is? Can't locate the Bill of Sale? The person responsible for Carla's abduction runs the motel (but not the gift shop). It's always the quiet ones....

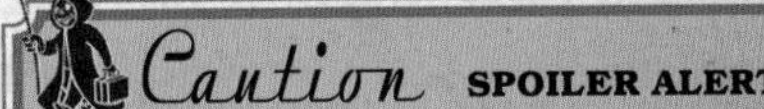

Return to Boone.

Part 3: Mopping Up

Back in the mouth of Dinky, reconvene with Boone, who's very keen to learn how you knew who was guilty. You can:

- Show Boone the Bill of Sale, which proves who the guilty party was. This brings closure to Boone's nightmare. That is, of course, if you stole the bill from the safe, and Boone executed the correct person!
- You can tell Boone that the person's story didn't add up, or that you had a hunch. Boone is livid that you didn't get any proof:

You can alleviate his fears by telling him you deduced the guilty party through a process of elimination.

Or you can provide less-than-adequate replies about the executed party being the closest to proof there was, or that you needed someone to blame and it didn't matter who. Boone refuses to speak with you and may turn violent.

You can tell Boone you just wanted him to kill the helpless lamb you led to the slaughter. Boone goes crazy, and you'll need to kill him.

Assuming you didn't anger Boone to the point of battle, you get some Caps and another special Beret, and the Quest ends. But your conversation shouldn't. Now that his wife's killer is dealt with (at least, in Boone's mind), he won't be staying at Novac.

- Offer to partner up, with both of you going after the Legion. Boone is hesitant.

Tell him you'll kill more of them if you team up.

Or tell him you thought snipers worked in teams.

Either option leads Boone to leave Novac and become your Follower. This is the only way to begin Side Quest: I Forgot to Remember to Forget.

Caps (100)

1st Recon Beret

150 XP

> *Tip* Executing townsfolk isn't wise, even in these lawless parts. Boone will turn hostile if you kill the victim that he wanted to execute. Furthermore, if you bring an innocent to Dinky for a brain evacuation, you'll need some clever wit not to get a sniper bullet to the face when you return to speak with Boone (although you can still complete the Quest).

PHEEBLE WILL

SUGGESTED EXPERIENCE

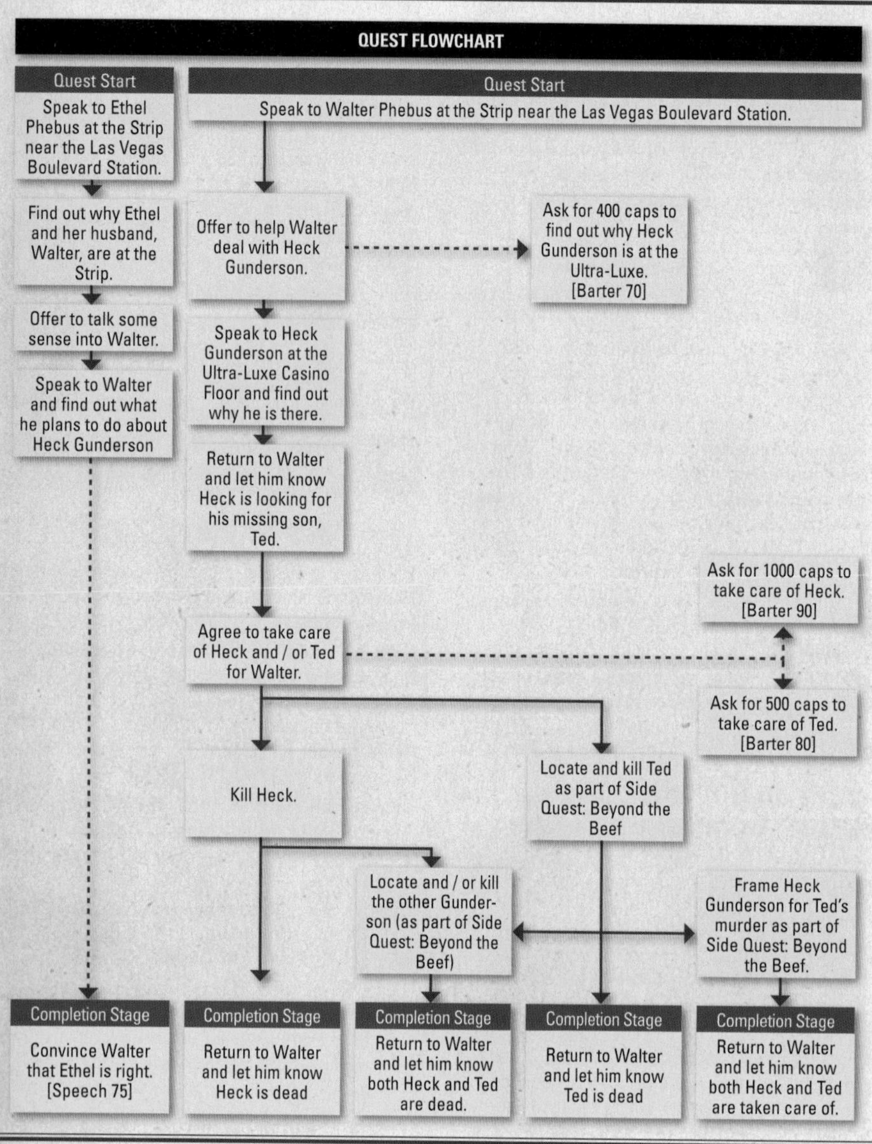

Meet the Pheebles

Close to the New Vegas Boulevard Station **(1)** [2D.03], between the Ultra-Luxe [2D.05] and Lucky 38 casinos [2D.02] is a spot for sightseers on The Strip. Among them are Ethel and Walter Phebus, and something is bothering each of them. Speak to either of them to see what the problem is and begin the Quest.

Part #1: Clear-Headed Ethel

Ethel **(2)** seems preoccupied with her husband. She's from a small ranch west of here, called "Phebus Ranch," where they recently lost some land to Heck Gunderson. You can ask what it's like being a rancher, and what they're up to on The Strip. She tells you to speak to Walter if you want more information on Heck (which starts Walter's story). Now ask if you can help her. She says she can't leave until her husband finishes his feud with Gunderson.

> **(Optional) Ethel Phebus wants her husband, Walter, to forget about Heck Gunderson and return to their ranch.**

Part #2: Walter's Red Mist

Talk to Ethel's husband Walter **(3)**, either before or after speaking to her. You can steer the conversation to what Ethel was telling you. But to get to the bottom of this, you need to:

Tell Walter he looks more than just hot and bothered.

He tells you he's got a score to settle. He has a lot of grievances that Heck Gunderson must answer for; out west, you have to "sell" your ranch to Gunderson, or you die. Walter isn't the kind of man who gets trampled over. At this point, you can:

- Tell him you could help. This leads to Part #3.

Tell him the best doesn't come cheap, and you'll fight on his behalf for a 400 Cap fee. This leads to Part #3.

> **Find out the purpose behind Heck Gunderson's visit to the Ultra-Luxe.**

- Conclusion #1. Or tell him that Ethel is right, and vengeance only leads to more death. He's not buying it. You can:

Tell him he's giving Heck just the excuse he needs. Walter agrees, and decides to leave the city and head back home to a better life. The Quest concludes.

Walter has let go of his will for revenge, and can now return with Ethel to their ranch.

Part #3: Gunning After Gunderson

Walter wants you to find out what Heck Gunderson's story is. The chiseler is blowing hot air over at the Ultra-Luxe **(4)**. Head inside, give your weapons (minus hold-outs) to the White Glove Greeter, and speak with Heck Gunderson **(5)**. The man is preoccupied with the disappearance of his son, Ted. Continue that line of questioning, and you begin Side Quest: Beyond the Beef. You don't have to decide to help Heck, but you can go tell Walter what Heck is doing.

Heck Gunderson is looking for his disappeared son. Talk to Walter Pheebus about this.

Walter wants to get even, and now that Gunderson has been spotted, inform Walter that Gunderson's barely protected, and his son is missing. You can suggest separate courses of action, assuming you don't want the Phebuses to leave Gunderson and New Vegas (Conclusion #1). You can:

- Suggest that Heck might listen to your pleas if his son's life was at stake. Walter isn't interested.
- Use your Barter skill to talk prices:

Agree to deal with Heck for 1,000 Caps.

Agree to sort out Heck's son, Ted, for 500 Caps.

- Talk prices without using Barter.

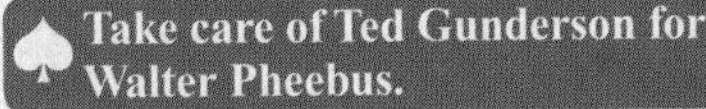

Take care of Ted Gunderson for Walter Pheebus.

Take care of Heck Gunderson for Walter Pheebus.

At this point, Side Quest: Beyond the Beef begins in earnest. Consult that Quest for all the details of dealing with the White Glove Society. What follows are brief highlights on the different ways to sort out either Ted or Heck.

Better off Dead, Ted

Ted is locked up inside the Ultra-Luxe's kitchen freezer: Follow the Beyond the Beef Quest until you gain access to the kitchen door, then head down to the freezer, open it, and shoot Ted **(6)** before he starts moaning. Then you can:

- Conclusion #2: Return to Walter, and claim your prize without finishing Beyond the Beef.

Ted's a goner. Talk to Walter about this.

- Conclusion #3: Or take Ted's blood, smear it all over Heck's penthouse suite, locate a Securitron, frame Heck for murder, and return to Walter. This deals with both Ted and Heck.

Heck, and Ted, Gunderson are taken care of. Talk to Walter about this.

Heck Gets it in the Neck

- Conclusion #4: Or, once you've met Heck (and/or killed Ted), you can shoot him and his bodyguard **(7)**, which fails Side Quest: Beyond the Beef, drops your Fame with the White Gloves and The Strip considerably, but it does help out Walter's cause immeasurably. Flee the Ultra-Luxe, and tell Walter the good news. He leaves New Vegas ecstatic.

White Glove Society Infamy Gained!

The Strip Infamy Gained!

Heck Gunderson's dead. Talk to Walter about this.

Now you can inform Walter Phebus that the plan you hatched is complete. Walter gives you the reward you decided on (or you can claim you don't want it, if you're crazy), and Walter departs with his wife, sickened by the violence. The Quest concludes.

Walter was happy to hear of Heck Gunderson's demise. He decided to take Ethel back to their home.

The following Caps and XP rewards are available depending on your actions and general competence:

Barter Checks Passed?	Who Did You Sort Out?	Caps Reward	XP Reward
None	Heck	700	100
None	Heck and Ted	950	200
None	Ted	450	100
Just the first one	Heck	900	100
Just the first one	Heck and Ted	1,150	200
Just the first one	Ted	650	100
All of them	Heck	1,400	100
All of them	Heck and Ted	1,900	200
All of them	Ted	900	100
None	No one; sided with Ethel	200	300
First one	No one; sided with Ethel	400	300

PRESSING MATTERS

SUGGESTED EXPERIENCE

QUEST FLOWCHART

Complete Side Quest: You Can Depend On Me

Quest Start
Speak with Alice McLafferty

Travel to Sunset Sarsaparilla Headquarters

Disable the bottle cap press

Completion Stage
Speak with Alice

Main Factions

Note This Quest only becomes active after you've completed Side Quest: You Can Depend on Me.

Meeting Alice the Overseer (Again)

1

2

Now that you're well established with the Crimson Caravan Company [2.09], enter the office **(1)** and ask Alice McLafferty **(2)** if she has any tasks. She certainly does; it appears prospectors have been trading with new Bottle Caps they've been pressing themselves, over at the old Sunset Sarsaparilla Headquarters [2.17]. You must find the press and disable it. You can also ask Alice about Caps, and receive an expert opinion on the state of Bottle Cap trading along the west coast. Head to the plant at your leisure.

Disable the bottle cap press.

Cap a Load of This

3

4

5

Journey to the Sunset Sarsaparilla Headquarters **(3)**, and enter the premises via the doors behind the giant bottle. Expect Protectron Security and shipping robots to impede your progress through the corridors before reaching the shipping warehouse **(4)**. The bottle cap press **(5)** is roughly in the center of the room. Activate it and you can see that the press has been used recently, backing up Alice's claim. Strip all the important-looking bits out of the machine.

Return to Alice McLafferty and let her know the bottle cap press is out of action.

Back at the Crimson Caravan, Alice rewards you with a load of (legitimate) Caps. The only other thing you need to talk to Alice about is to release Janet from her contract as part of Side Quest: Young Hearts.

100 XP

500 Caps

RESTORING HOPE

SUGGESTED EXPERIENCE

See flowchart on the following page

Main Factions

A Major Undertaking

1

2

Close to the mighty Colorado River is a communications center and triage hub for wounded NCR soldiers: the unapologetically titled Camp Forlorn Hope [6.02]. The personnel are in desperate need of assistance (speak to Dr. Richards to begin Side Quest: Medical Mystery, or Tech Sergeant Reyes to start Side Quest: Return to Sender). In the Command Center **(1)**, the camp leader, Major Polatli **(2)**, needs your adventuring prowess, although he's initially dismissive of you. You can question him about the NCR, but asking what he needs help with begins this Quest. What he really needs is to get his camp back in order, so he can win back Nelson [6.06] from the Legion. Your first task is to find Quartermaster Mayes and see what he needs.

Talk to Quartermaster Mayes.

Task #1: Supplies and Demands

3

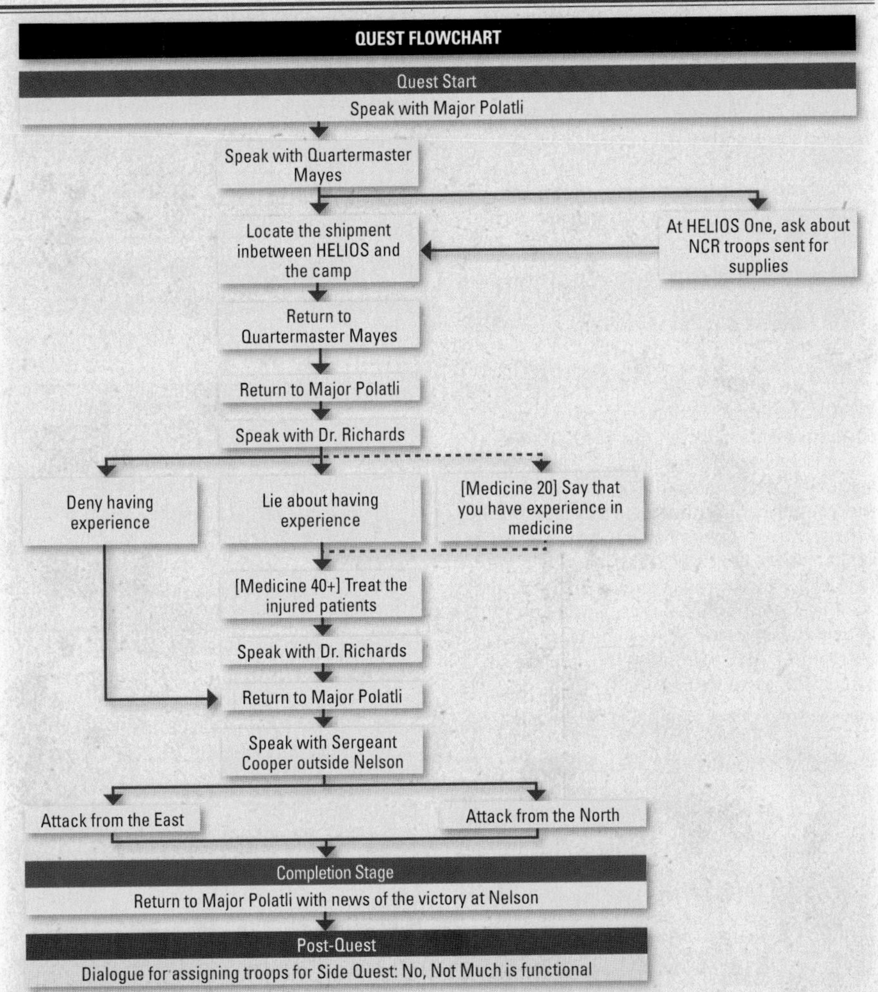

4

Near or inside one of the storage tents **(3)** just south of the Command Center is Quartermaster Mayes **(4)**. You can ask him how the camp is doing, but inform him Major Polatli has sent you to help. The camp is short of both personnel and supplies. Ask how you can help with the supplies, and he tells you NCR soldiers were supposed to return with some, but they were likely victims of a Legion raiding party. The supplies are likely to be stuck somewhere between the camp and HELIOS One [5.13] where the supplies were picked up. That's your next stop.

Go to HELIOS One to ask about Forlorn Hope supplies.

5

6

Although you can chance upon the supplies as you wander over to HELIOS One **(5)**, you receive pinpoint information once you're challenged at the entrance by Lieutenant Haggerty **(6)**. You can challenge her and begin another Quest at this point (Side Quest: That Lucky Old Sun), but your first choice is to ask about the troopers sent from Camp Forlorn Hope. She says your Pip-Boy should be able to pick up the GPS marker on the supply crate they attached, and sure enough, the Camp Forlorn Hope Supply Shipment [6.S01] pops up just northeast of the Southern Nevada Wind Farm [6.03], west of Camp Forlorn Hope.

Follow the GPS marker to the Forlorn Hope supplies.

7

8

Trek there with your weapon drawn and ready for combat. The suspiciously quiet rocky ground of baked rubble and tufts of grass **(7)** hides three dead NCR troopers. Their limb loss suggests a Legion attack. Search the corpses for their Dogtags (Free Quest: Tags of Our Fallen). Two of the troopers have a Forlorn Hope Letter. But the main prize is the Camp Forlorn Hope Supply Crate. Open it and remove the shipment. This prompts an ambush by Legion Recruits **(8)**. You can:

Flee the combat zone, with the foes chasing you until you reach Camp Forlorn Hope.

Attack the three foes, tagging the enemy with the long-range rifle first, then backing up from the machete-wielding enemies if you're having problems dropping these Legion punks.

Or, coax the nearby Fire Geckos into combat with the Legion, watch the ensuing massacre, and mop up the survivors as you wish (or quietly leave).

 **NCR Dogtag (3)**

 **Forlorn Hope Letter 1**

 **Forlorn Hope Letter 8**

 **Camp Forlorn Hope Supply Shipment**

Return the supplies to Quartermaster Mayes.

Back at the camp, return to Quartermaster Mayes, and tell him you've found the supplies he was looking for. You can also trade, or play Caravan with Mayes. He suggests you check in with the major.

Speak to Major Polatli.

Task #2: Triage Time

Back in the Command Center (or a nearby tent with a mattress the major is sleeping on, after you've woken him up), tell Polatli you've found some supplies. That solves one short-term problem, but the lack of troops is a real issue. You're to liaise with Dr. Richards to see if he needs any help getting the wounded troops back on the front line.

Meet with Dr. Richards.

Inside the Camp Forlorn Hope Medical Center **(9)**, just north of the Command Center (or sleeping in a tent close by) is Dr. Richards **(10)**, who takes more than a shine to you. You can ask how things are around camp, for medical treatment, and most importantly, what help he needs. He asks if you have some medical experience:

You can answer that you do.

You can lie about having experience.

Or, you can tell him you don't, in which case you should report back to the major.

Help Dr. Richards with his patients.

Inside the Medical Tent are three patients with horrific injuries that need your attention **(11)**. In each case, improper treatment will kill them (although you aren't allowed to just delve in with a machete unless you want to sever your ties with the NCR as well as a patient's appendage). Treat them accordingly:

Patient #1 has multiple machete wounds. You can:

Leave him alone.

Treat him using your Medicine skill.

Or use medical equipment to treat: Return with Med-X, Whiskey, and Surgical Tubing.

Patient #2 has a serious leg injury. You can:

Leave him alone.

Treat him using your Medicine skill.

Or use medical equipment to treat: Return with a Medical Brace, Med-X, and a Bonesaw.

Patient #3 has close range blast trauma. You can:

Leave him alone.

Treat him using your Medicine skill.

Or use medical equipment to treat: Return with Tweezers, Med-X, and a Super Stimpak.

You should be able to collect all medical equipment during your travels, or from the Medical Center itself. If you successfully operate on the three patients (using your skill or equipment), or simply leave them alone, speak with Dr. Richards again for his sincere thanks.

Return to Major Polatli.

Task #3: Assault on Nelson

Tell the major you've finished helping Dr. Richards, and Polatli is impressed, but there are still the Legion forces in Nelson to deal with. If the NCR retake the town, it will help in the looming confrontation at Hoover Dam. You can ask about the troops, and any intel on the Legion forces, after which the major tells you that killing the Legion commanders in Nelson would severely cripple them, allowing the NCR to hold the location. You're to meet up with Sergeant Cooper just outside Nelson. His small squad is there to assist you.

Meet with Sergeant Cooper.

Between the rocky bluffs behind the town of Nelson **(12)**, find Sergeant Cooper **(13)** and his squad. Speak to the sergeant, and he asks you which direction they should focus their attack; from the north, or the ridge on the east. You can choose either, or (prior to speaking with Cooper) check out the topography of the area. Choose an option, and launch the attack!

The Morale Imperative

The number of troopers available with Sergeant Cooper for this assault varies depending on the NCR Morale, which is detailed in the following tables:

Morale Bonuses: How to Obtain

Side or Free Quest Name	Action	Morale Bonus
Restoring Hope	Helping Mayes	+1
Restoring Hope	Helping Richards	+1
Medical Mystery	Completed	+1
An Ear to the Ground	Every 10 Legion Ears collected	+1 (to a maximum of +3)
Tags of Our Fallen	Every 5 NCR Dogtags collected	+1 (to a maximum of +3)
Return to Sender	Completed	+3

Morale Bonuses: Forces with Sergeant Cooper

Morale Bonus	Forces Available
0–3	Troopers (2)
4–6	Troopers (4)
7–9	Patrol Rangers (4)
10+	Combat Rangers (4)

Defeat the Legion at Nelson.

There are benefits of choosing either direction to attack from:

The north **(14)** allows you to swarm the enemy, which is useful if you're using close combat weapons, such as shotguns, melee, or unarmed weapons, and your armor is strong.

The east **(15)** allows you to "cover" your team and take up a sniping position, tagging troops from a commanding position using larger and more powerful ranged weaponry.

While it's helpful if Sergeant Cooper and his forces survive the assault, it's not too problematic if they don't. Unless you're feeling a real affinity to the NCR or the troopers serving in its army, you can be the only survivor.

You don't actually need to rendezvous with Sergeant Cooper at all. You can completely circumvent him and launch an attack on Nelson all by yourself!

Caution Before the attack, consider how it will affect your standing in these two other Quests: Side Quest: Back in Your Own Backyard and Side Quest: We Are Legion. The former involves executing NCR captives for Ranger Milo (so visit him first before you launch the attack, although you can save the captives, too). The latter involves killing all of Camp Forlorn Hope for Dead Sea, the Nelson commander. That won't be happening unless you switch allegiances right now!

Expect to take down 8–10 Legion Explorers and Recruits as you proceed through Nelson. Pay special attention to those in the wooden guard towers, perhaps tagging them and then taking a commanding position from there yourself. As with other assaults on settlements, you can:

Kill everybody using your most ferocious-looking weapon.

Modicum of Skill: Kill everybody using the height (and cover) of the high ground to your benefit and tagging more foes before dropping to the ground and finishing the stragglers.

The Silent Assassin: Sneak into camp, then use as many Sneak Attacks as you can before you're discovered. Remember that you can retreat behind or into buildings.

Death of Dead Sea: Focus on the black-feathered foe. Dead Sea **(16)** is in charge here, and his death demoralizes the Legion. Watch where he goes because he can hide in the buildings close to the hanging NCR captives. Don't forget to grab his Unique Weapon afterward.

Liberator

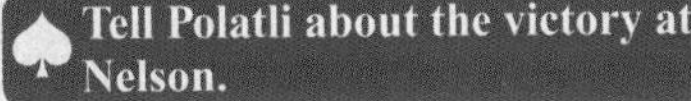

Tell Polatli about the victory at Nelson.

Return to Camp Forlorn Hope, and speak with the major one last time. He's happy about the outcome, and once you start the Quests relating to Bitter Springs [3.08]—Side Quest: No, Not Much—you can request troops on behalf of Captain Gilles. Refer to that Quest for more information.

NCR Fame Gained!

Caesar's Legion Infamy Gained!

300 XP

Note The Bitter Springs quests are interrelated with this one. First, speak to Captain Gilles during this Quest to begin Side Quest: No, Not Much. To complete the first part of that "overview" Side Quest, you must achieve the following:

- Become Idolized with the NCR. This is achieved by completing Quests associated with this Faction (which are tagged throughout the guide).
- Complete Side Quest: Bitter Springs Infirmary Blues (optional).
- Complete Side Quest: Flags of Our Foul-Ups.
- Complete Side Quest: I Put a Spell on You.
- Complete Side Quest: Restoring Hope (this Quest).
- Complete Side Quest: Climb Ev'ry Mountain.

These five Quests are all parts of Side Quest: No, Not Much.

RETURN TO SENDER

SUGGESTED EXPERIENCE

See flowchart on the following page

Just Another Charlie-Foxtrot Assignment

The communications hub for the NCR along the western side of the Mojave Wasteland is the demoralized Camp Forlorn Hope [6.02]. You can speak to Major Polatli (Side Quest: Restoring Hope), but for this Quest head inside the Camp Forlorn Hope Command Center **(1)** to meet Reyes **(2)**. If she's not on duty, she's sleeping in a tent nearby.

She needs somebody to figure out some inconsistencies in her reports, especially regarding the interception of hostiles. She reckons the radio security codes have been compromised, and hands you code upgrades to take to all six Ranger stations. You're to take a Holotape with the code on it to the Comm Officer at each station, and these are scattered throughout the entire Mojave Wasteland!

Deliver the radio security upgrade codes to each of the Ranger Stations.

Upgrade Ranger Station Alpha.

Upgrade Ranger Station Bravo.

Upgrade Ranger Station Charlie.

Upgrade Ranger Station Delta.

Upgrade Ranger Station Echo.

Upgrade Ranger Station Foxtrot.

Note You can visit them in any order, but they're listed here alphabetically.

Job 1A: Ranger Station Alpha

On the rocky shores of Lake Mead is Ranger Station Alpha **(3)** [3.30]. Track down Comm Officer Castillo **(4)**. Castillo heard from Reyes that new codes were coming, but finds it odd she sent a civilian. After the codes are given over, Castillo tells you area is reasonably secure, thanks to the detachment of Ranger snipers on the job.

Job 1B: Ranger Station Bravo

QUEST FLOWCHART

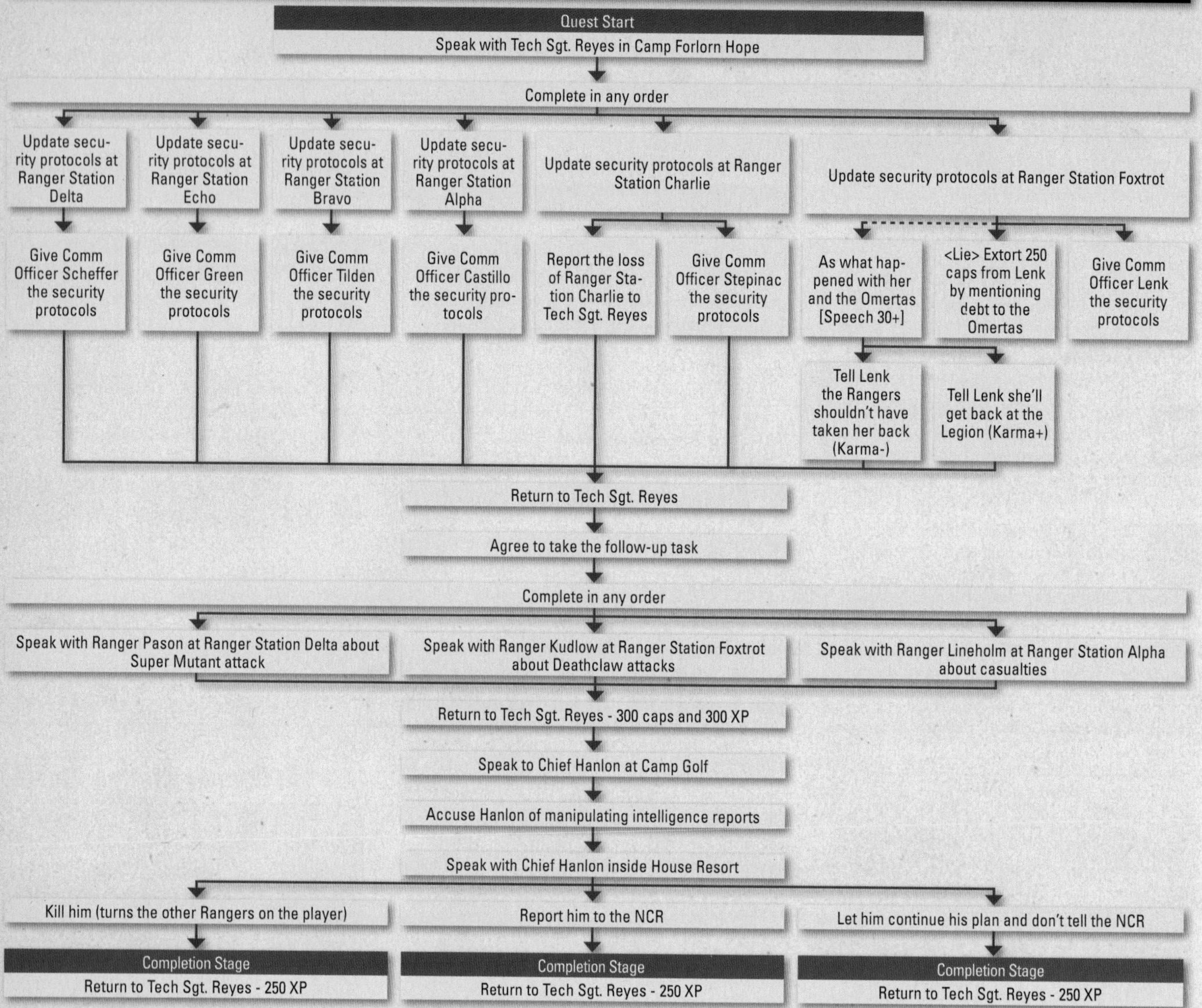

Quest Start

Speak with Tech Sgt. Reyes in Camp Forlorn Hope

Complete in any order

- Update security protocols at Ranger Station Delta
  - Give Comm Officer Scheffer the security protocols
- Update security protocols at Ranger Station Echo
  - Give Comm Officer Green the security protocols
- Update security protocols at Ranger Station Bravo
  - Give Comm Officer Tilden the security protocols
- Update security protocols at Ranger Station Alpha
  - Give Comm Officer Castillo the security protocols
- Update security protocols at Ranger Station Charlie
  - Report the loss of Ranger Station Charlie to Tech Sgt. Reyes
  - Give Comm Officer Stepinac the security protocols
- Update security protocols at Ranger Station Foxtrot
  - As what happened with her and the Omertas [Speech 30+]
  - <Lie> Extort 250 caps from Lenk by mentioning debt to the Omertas
    - Tell Lenk the Rangers shouldn't have taken her back (Karma-)
    - Tell Lenk she'll get back at the Legion (Karma+)
  - Give Comm Officer Lenk the security protocols

Return to Tech Sgt. Reyes

Agree to take the follow-up task

Complete in any order

- Speak with Ranger Pason at Ranger Station Delta about Super Mutant attack
- Speak with Ranger Kudlow at Ranger Station Foxtrot about Deathclaw attacks
- Speak with Ranger Lineholm at Ranger Station Alpha about casualties

Return to Tech Sgt. Reyes - 300 caps and 300 XP

Speak to Chief Hanlon at Camp Golf

Accuse Hanlon of manipulating intelligence reports

Speak with Chief Hanlon inside House Resort

- Kill him (turns the other Rangers on the player)
  - **Completion Stage**: Return to Tech Sgt. Reyes - 250 XP
- Report him to the NCR
  - **Completion Stage**: Return to Tech Sgt. Reyes - 250 XP
- Let him continue his plan and don't tell the NCR
  - **Completion Stage**: Return to Tech Sgt. Reyes - 250 XP

Over in the rocky northeast is the desolate Ranger Station Bravo **(5)** [3.09]. Open the Junk Door and speak with Comm Officer Tilden **(6)**. He doesn't want anything you're selling. Give him the update, and he tells you to let Reyes know they don't need any more ammunition, just water. He tries the radio, but all he gets is Camp Golf [3.23].

Job 1C: Ranger Station Charlie

Tucked away in the mountains southwest of Camp Forlorn Hope is a walled yard with

numerous junked trailers and electrical towers. Ranger Station Charlie **(7)** [5.23] has a concrete-walled office. Enter and speak to Comm Officer Stepinac **(8)**. He takes the codes, although he doesn't reckon the Legion is sophisticated enough to be listening in.

Job 1D: Ranger Station Delta

On the cliffs close to the Colorado River, Ranger Station Delta **(9)** [3.36] is a small outpost based around a ruined house. Talk

to Comm Officer Scheffer **(10)**. She's direct, and tells you to let Reyes know the station is secure. You can also speak (but not at great length) to her about the NCR Rangers and the service they provide to the Republic.

Job 1E: Ranger Station Echo

Almost directly south of Camp Forlorn Hope, Ranger Station Echo **(11)** [6.10] is surrounded on two sides by junk walls.

12

Comm Officer Green **(12)** takes the codes, although he's annoyed because he just changed them. Green keeps an eye on the Legion at Cottonwood Cove [6.20], but there's little going on at the moment.

Job 1F: Ranger Station Foxtrot

13

14

Hidden in the northwest mountains is the small and understaffed Ranger Station Foxtrot **(13)** [1.12]. Rendezvous with Comm Officer Lenk **(14)** who immediately thinks you're from the Omertas, attempting a shakedown! Give her the codes and you can:

Convince her to tell the story of how she lost her nerve after a Legion attack, and has been racking up gambling debts.

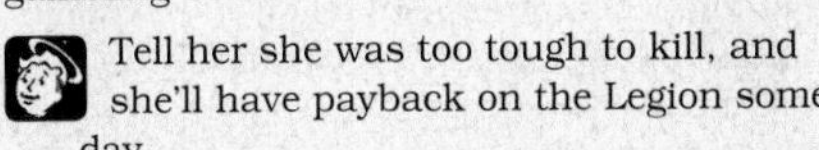
Tell her she was too tough to kill, and she'll have payback on the Legion some day.

Or lie, and tell her you are with the Omertas, and she needs to pay up what she has.

Caps (250)

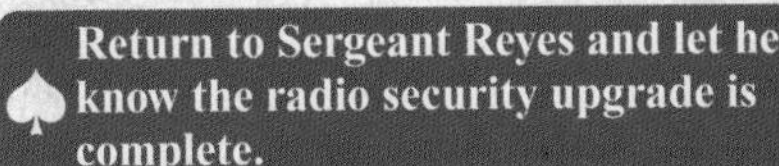
Return to Sergeant Reyes and let her know the radio security upgrade is complete.

I Call Bravo-Sierra on These Transmissions

Return to Tech Sergeant Reyes, and inform her that all six of the Ranger Stations have received their updated codes. She has another job, although she's almost apologetic for offering it to you. It entails returning to three of the previous Ranger Stations. Reyes is getting disturbing reports of casualties, and she doesn't think these are accurate. Are trained Deathclaws really attacking Foxtrot? The oddities she's heard about are listed in the following updated Objectives (you're to investigate only the three most alarming or suspicious reports):

Ask Ranger Lineholm about the battle losses at Ranger Station Alpha.

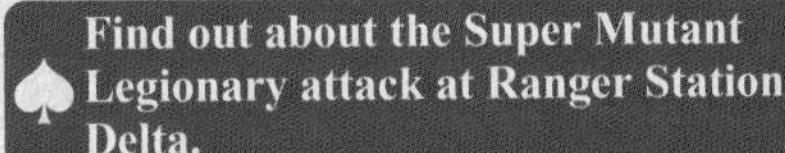
Find out about the Super Mutant Legionary attack at Ranger Station Delta.

Investigate the Deathclaw attacks on Ranger Station Foxtrot.

Job 2A: High Mortality at Alpha?

15

Head back to Ranger Station Alpha, and speak to Ranger Lineholm **(15)** at the camp, asking her to explain the high casualties at the station. She's surprised at this; there's a report of a broken ankle, but nothing more. But any injury, illness, or death gets radioed to Ranger HQ at Camp Golf. Chief Hanlon compiles the reports and sends out reinforcements. Perhaps some wires are crossed?

Job 2B: Super Mutants at Delta?

16

Return to Ranger Station Delta, and move along the rough terrain heading for a Hoover Dam [3.33] vista point where Ranger Pason **(16)** is on the lookout with his Robobrain. After initial alarm, Pason calms down when you ask about the report he filed about the Super Mutants wiping out an NCR patrol. The patrol was wiped out, but by incompetent use of a grenade.

Job 2C: Trained Deathclaws at Foxtrot?

17

Head back to the remote Ranger Station Foxtrot, and speak with Ranger Kudlow **(17)**. She would remember any report she'd sent that featured trained Deathclaws rampaging the premises, and she certainly hasn't filed any such report. With this evidence collected, you can return to Tech Sergeant Reyes with the evidence (or lack thereof) that she needs.

Tell Sergeant Reyes that her suspicions about misinformation being fed to the NCR was correct.

Float-Testing Hanlon's Answers

Back at Camp Forlorn Hope, inform Reyes that the Rangers' versions of the reports they sent to Camp Golf don't match what she received. She thought as much, rewards you for your efforts, and requests that you take this evidence to Chief Hanlon and confront him with it.

Caps (300)

NCR Fame Gained!

Inform Chief Hanlon what you and Sergeant Reyes discovered.

18

19

Journey to the operations base at Camp Golf [3.23], and navigate the tents, heading for the large Resort House **(18)** where Chief Hanlon resides. Enter the house, and exit onto the large balcony immediately above the front doors, where Hanlon **(19)** is relaxing, looking out at the view of Lake Las Vegas [3.22] and a giant water pipe. As you approach, Hanlon nods toward the water, and tells you how mankind neglected the lakes and dams in the past.

Chief Hanlon likes to talk. When you're ready, steer the conversation to the intel problems. Hanlon then gives you a complex explanation of how data is organized and evaluated. Keep the questions civil, asking why intel isn't sent directly to the troopers. A better conversation starter is to accuse Hanlon of manipulating intelligence data. He ushers you back into the Resort House, to somewhere more quiet.

Speak to Chief Hanlon in his office.

Once in his office, you can tell Hanlon he's been inventing his own intelligence reports. Hanlon responds by telling you it's misdirection (which, ironically, he seems to be attempting on you). Hanlon goes on about his life, the wretched nature of man, and the constant threats from the Legion. Ask him what he thinks you should do about this, and eventually (after Hanlon talks about tactical shortcomings on Hoover Dam), it dawns on you that you have three different possibilities to end this:

You can let Hanlon continue his plan, without informing the NCR.

You can report him to the NCR (in this case, a Ranger down in Camp Golf), even if you tell him otherwise. Once you leave the office, however, Hanlon's door shuts, and he begins a broadcast that ends (sadly) with him taking his own life. The confession is made, and the Quest ends. You need not return to Reyes. Afterward, you may hear the NCR talking about Hanlon's suicide.

Chief Hanlon's Confession

Or you can attack him, which turns all the Rangers around Camp Golf hostile.

NCR Infamy Gained!

500 XP

SOMEONE TO WATCH OVER ME

SUGGESTED EXPERIENCE

QUEST FLOWCHART

Quest Start

Speak with Crandon near H&H Tools Factory

- [Barter 35] Convince him to pay you for help
- [Speech 45] Offer to help

Talk to Bill at the playground

- Attack him
- Pay him 50 caps to leave
- [Speech 45] Ask him nicely to leave

Return to Crandon

Agree to deal with the troublemakers in the sewers

Take the entrance to the North sewers and speak to Greasy Johnny

- Attack him
- Pay him 100 caps to leave
- [Barter 50+] Pay him 50 caps to leave
- [Speech 65+] Tell him the locals are getting edgy

Return to Crandon

Speak with Mrs. Hostetler and agree to find info on her daughter's new friends

Look for Alice Hostetler and her friend, Andy, in the building named The Gray.

Talk to the thug outside Andy's room.

- Attack him and grab the key to Andy's room from his corpse
- [Speech 70+] Lie and tell him Mrs. Hotetler's outside, break into Andy's room

Grab henchman note on TV stand

Andy forcegreets you outside his room.

- Kill Andy.
- Talk to Andy and learn Alice wants to leave New Vegas
- [Speech 65+] Lie and tell him you were just passing through

Return to the Hostetler house. Alice forcegreets you.

- Let them sort it out → Completion Stage: Alice kills her mother and runs out
- Tell her Andy sent you.
  - Show Alice the note.
  - Tell Alice to go ahead and attack her mother if she wants.
  - Tell her you knew she couldn't do it → Completion Stage: Alice kills her mother and runs out

Tell her to give you her gun.

- Tell her to leave New Vegas. → Alice leaves New Vegas unhappily
- Tell her to stay with her parents. → Alice stays in New Vegas.
- [Speech 75+ or Intelligence 7+] Ask Alice why she's doing this → Alice leaves New Vegas to find her own path

Talk to Mrs. Hostetler.

Completion Stage	Completion Stage	Completion Stage	Completion Stage	Completion Stage
Alice kills her mother and runs out	<Attack> her, take 1000 caps from her corpse	Accept 200 caps.	Don't accept a reward	[Barter 65+] Ask for more caps, get 500 caps

Main Factions

Crandon's North New Vegas Crawl

Near the H&H Tools Factory [2.06], in the enclosed portion of the Mojave Wasteland [Zone 2B] close to North Vegas Square is a particularly desolate stretch of road **(1)**, with but a few settlers. The self-appointed leader of this area wants to keep it that way, too: Locate Crandon **(2)** and ask him about North Vegas. Aside from warning you against looting the Tools Factory, Crandon (when prompted) tells you his name, and his role: to keep an eye out for trouble. Ask if he needs a helping hand, and Crandon isn't convinced. You can:

Respect his independence, but tell him you're good at eliminating trouble.

Explain your skills and the reward you expect for your work. You're awarded 50 Caps as down-payment.

Crandon accepts either of these bluffs, and otherwise the Quest cannot begin.

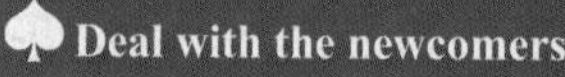

Task #1: Dealing With the Detritus

Your first task involves some squatters who've taken up residence where they don't belong, over by the playground **(3)**. Near this playground, you might spot a man named Jules (who has his own Free Quest: Meeting an Equal). The ne'er-do-wells are huddling around a flaming barrel by the swings. Squatter Bill **(4)** is their spokesman. Tell Bill to move on, and he reacts negatively. You can:

Pay Bill and his brethren to vacate the playground.

Ask nicely. You only do this one time.

Or attack, and wipe out Bill and his two companions.

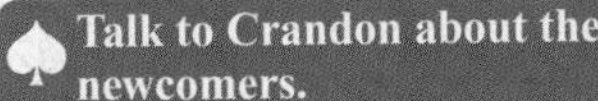

Talk to Crandon about the newcomers.

When you've spoken to Bill, or shed squatter blood, report back to Crandon who's still wandering the area. Crandon sees that you handled yourself well, and now has a more difficult task: a handful of greasers down in the sewers are causing trouble.

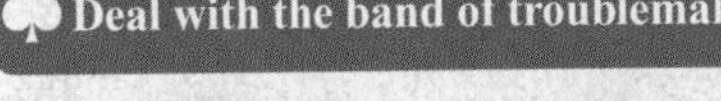

Deal with the band of troublemakers.

Task #2: Flushing Out the Effluent

5

6

7

The sewers under North New Vegas are a complex series of interconnected tubes and walkways, but the nearest entrance is easy to find; head back through the junk door, and descend through the Manhole to North Sewers **(5)** [U2.N]. Then follow the tunnels methodically through to the junction chamber **(6)** where the greasers are hanging around. The head of this ragtag bunch of vermin is Greaser Johnny **(7)**.

Attack the quintet of greasers using your preferred weaponry, until they're all dead.

Talk to Crandon about the greasers in the sewers.

When the greasers are no longer stinking up the place, scramble back to the surface, and return to Crandon. He's pacing around in the usual place, but he's most happy when you mention you've skimmed the scum off the lower tunnels. He has one additional job for you, and it involves brain power:

Task #3: The Hostile Hostetlers

Talk to Mrs. Hostetler.

8

9

Crandon informs you that a Mrs. Hostetler, who lives near the Crimson Caravan Company [2.09], thinks her daughter is making bad "friends." Your first task is to talk to the mother. She lives in a reasonably pleasant section of what passes for suburbia, south of the New Vegas Medical Clinic [2.10]. Look for the Hostetler Home **(8)** [2.S05] on your Pip-Boy's Local Map. Enter the premises, and calm Mrs. Hostetler down **(9)**. Ask her for work, and she wants you to snoop on her daughter. Agree to this.

Find information about Alice Hostetler's new friends.

Look for Alice Hostetler and her friend, Andy, in the building named The Gray.

10

11

Travel back to North New Vegas where Crandon is located, and head to the far western end of the street, looking for a seedy apartment building called The Gray **(10)** [2B.01]. Its front fascia lives up to the name; open the doors, and proceed left (west) to a Thug standing guard outside Andy's Room **(11)**. It seems Alice and her sweetheart aren't at home.

No sign of either Alice or Andy. Inspect The Gray for clues to their whereabouts.

The Thug greets you with monosyllabic cursing. You can:

- Explain you're looking for Alice Hostetler and Andy. Keep the line of questioning civil (even as the Thug continues his threats). When prompted, you can then:

Lie to the Thug that Mrs. Hostetler is outside, brandishing a shotgun. The Thug races off to quell the nonexistent confrontation, allowing you to access Andy's Room.

- React aggressively to this fool, and waste him. Andy's Room Key is on his corpse.

Andy's Room Key

Beware of a second Thug attacking; you may wish to execute a Sneak Attack and take him down first.

Try Pickpocketing the Thug. Even if this works, as soon as you try to unlock the door (assuming you're using a Stealth Boy), the Thug spots you and attacks.

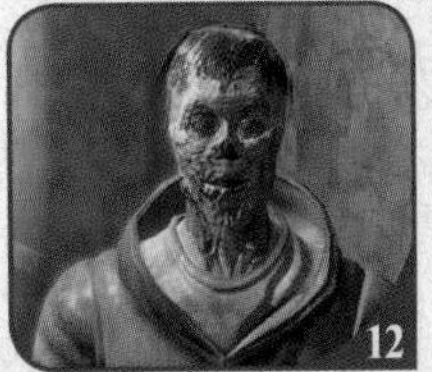

12

Whether you attack the Thug or not, getting into Andy's Room requires unlocking the door:

Using Bobby Pins, or

Using Andy's Room Key.

Once inside the room, inspect the shelf underneath the television for a Note explaining a proposed Crimson Caravan heist. Take this, and leave the room as the Quest updates.

Henchman Message to Andy Scabb

On the way out of the building, you run into Andy Scabb himself **(12)**. You can:

Tell him to relax, and leave without speaking to him.

Let him know you've found out about his plans for Alice (Andy is manipulating her into betraying her family, and Alice has little else to hang her hope onto). Agree to take a cut from the Hostetler's money that Alice and Andy intend to steal.

Or you can slay this lumpy-skinned freak where he stands.

Tell Mrs. Hostetler about Andy's plan to steal the Crimson Caravan money.

(Optional) Help Andy with his plan to steal the Crimson Caravan money from the Hostetlers.

13

Whatever your decision, return to the Hostetler Home. Alice Hostetler accosts you as you enter the premises **(13)**, and after a marathon argument session with her mother, she's in no mood for pleasantries. Specific actions become very important from this point on. Listen to her vent, then respond:

- A1. Tell her you're not here to hurt her. She asks what the hell you want.

 A2. Say you just want to talk. Then tell her Andy is just using her to get at the Hostetler money.

- A3. She doesn't believe you. Show her the note you found. She's understandably (and violently) upset.
- A4. At this point, you can ask "what do you really want, Alice?" Alice tearfully tells you about her parents, and the grim life they have together. You can:

Tell her they care.

 Then tell her only she can answer her dreams (Completion Consequence #1).

Tell her to leave and never return, or follow her own path (Completion Consequence #2 or #5).

- B1. At any point during the previous conversation, or after her first blurted utterances, you can tell her that Andy sent you to help her (assuming you didn't kill the Ghoul). After that, you can:

Show her the note (continue at A3).

Tell her to attack her mother (continue at C1).

Ask for her gun (continue at A4).

Or coax her into massacring her mother (also continue at C1).

- C1. At any point during the initial stages of the conversation, you can state "Actually, just sort this out on your own," or tell her to attack her mother if she wants. This prompts Alice into finding and gunning down her mother (Completion Consequence: #3 or #4).
- D1. During the conversation at certain points, you can ask where the money is. Alice tells you her mother has it, and she'll kill her for it. You can:

 Ask if she really wants to do this (continue at A4).

Or you can show her the note you found in Andy's room (continue at A3).

Completion Consequences

The Quest continues (and sometimes ends) with one of the following:

#1. Alice attacked her house. She decided to let go and stay with her parents.

#2. Alice attacked her house. She decided to run away from New Vegas.

#3. Alice attacked her house. She died after attacking her mother.

#4. Alice attacked her house. After attacking her mother, both of them died.

#5. Alice attacked her house. She left New Vegas to find her own path.

Completion Consequences: Crimson Caravan Caps

The Crimson Caravan haul should be foremost in your mind as the Quest concludes. Depending on whether Mrs. Hostetler is dead or alive, the following options are available:

If Mrs. Hostetler is alive, you can speak with her, and refuse any of the family's reserve.

Or you can accept a partial amount of the reserve (200 Caps).

Or you can Barter Mrs. Hostetler up to giving you half of the reserve (500 Caps).

Or, if Mrs. Hostetler is dead (either by your hands or Alice's), loot the corpse for the full amount (1,000 Caps).

 **150 XP**

 **0, 200, 500, or 1,000 Caps**

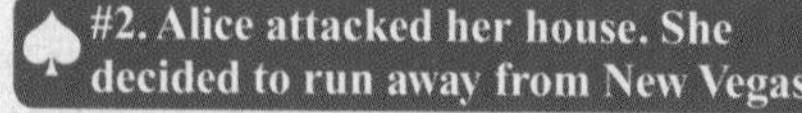

STILL IN THE DARK

MAIN QUEST INTERSECTION — SUGGESTED EXPERIENCE

See flowchart on the following page

Main Factions

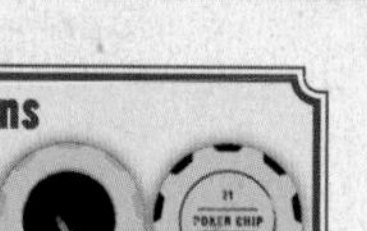

Before You Begin....

The Hidden Valley [5.11] is a ghostly place, covered in a mysterious storm of sand and dirt, and seemingly home to nothing except Radscorpions and Bark Scorpions. It is home to the remains of the Brotherhood of Steel's West Coast chapter, who have been driven underground, literally, after battles against the NCR. Depending on your Main Quest overlords, the Brotherhood can become staunch allies, or they can be wiped out. Before you begin, it is worth knowing the numerous ways you can approach this Quest:

Note There are no prerequisites to begin this Quest; it can be started at any time. However, the Factions you may be working with during the Main Quest all want to ensure Brotherhood support (or annihilation) for an incoming and ultimate battle. To this end, you can:

Investigate before you're embroiled in any Main Quest politicking, either with Veronica, or on your own. You will need to "Prove Yourself" before the Quest starts if you're alone.

MR. HOUSE: Investigate at the insistence of Mr. House, during Main Quest: The House Always Wins, V.

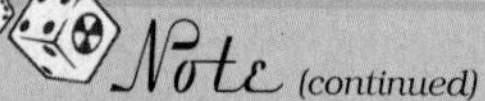

Note *(continued)*

 Investigate on behalf of NCR Colonel Moore, during Main Quest: For the Republic, Part 2.

 Investigate as a centurion of Caesar's, during Main Quest: Render Unto Caesar.

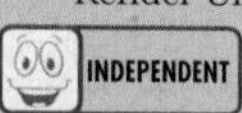 Or investigate after speaking with Yes Man, during Main Quest: Wild Card: Side Bets.

Check these Quests first, because some Faction commanders have specific plans in mind for the Brotherhood of Steel; all want Brotherhood of Steel annihilation, but only the NCR (and you, working independently) will accept a treaty.

I Hear You Knocking...

Enter the Hidden Valley, and inspect the area behind the perimeter fence to see four sealed bunkers, each daubed with graffiti from long ago **(1)**. Two of the bunkers are empty, another shows recent signs of an NCR Ranger sleeping there, but the one you should enter is on the valley's western side. Head down the steps, past the cargo containers, and inspect the blast door, where there's an intercom. You can:

Speak into the intercom. You hear nothing. Continue to speak into the intercom, and you continue to hear nothing.

 You can use your not-inconsiderable talents and pry the blast door open, and begin the Quest as an intruder, rather than a friend. See "Detour: Prove Yourself Worthy."

HOLOTAPE: Or, you can read the information listed under "The Doomed Patrols." The three dead Brotherhood of Steel patrols each yield a Holotape with a password to enter this base. Find any (they can be obtained whether this Quest is active or not), bring it to this door, and you reveal the password and begin "Detour: Prove Yourself Worthy."

 Or, you can bring Veronica with you **(2)** from the 188 Trading Post. This place is her home. She runs up to the intercom, and begins a password-infused conversation. The door swings open.

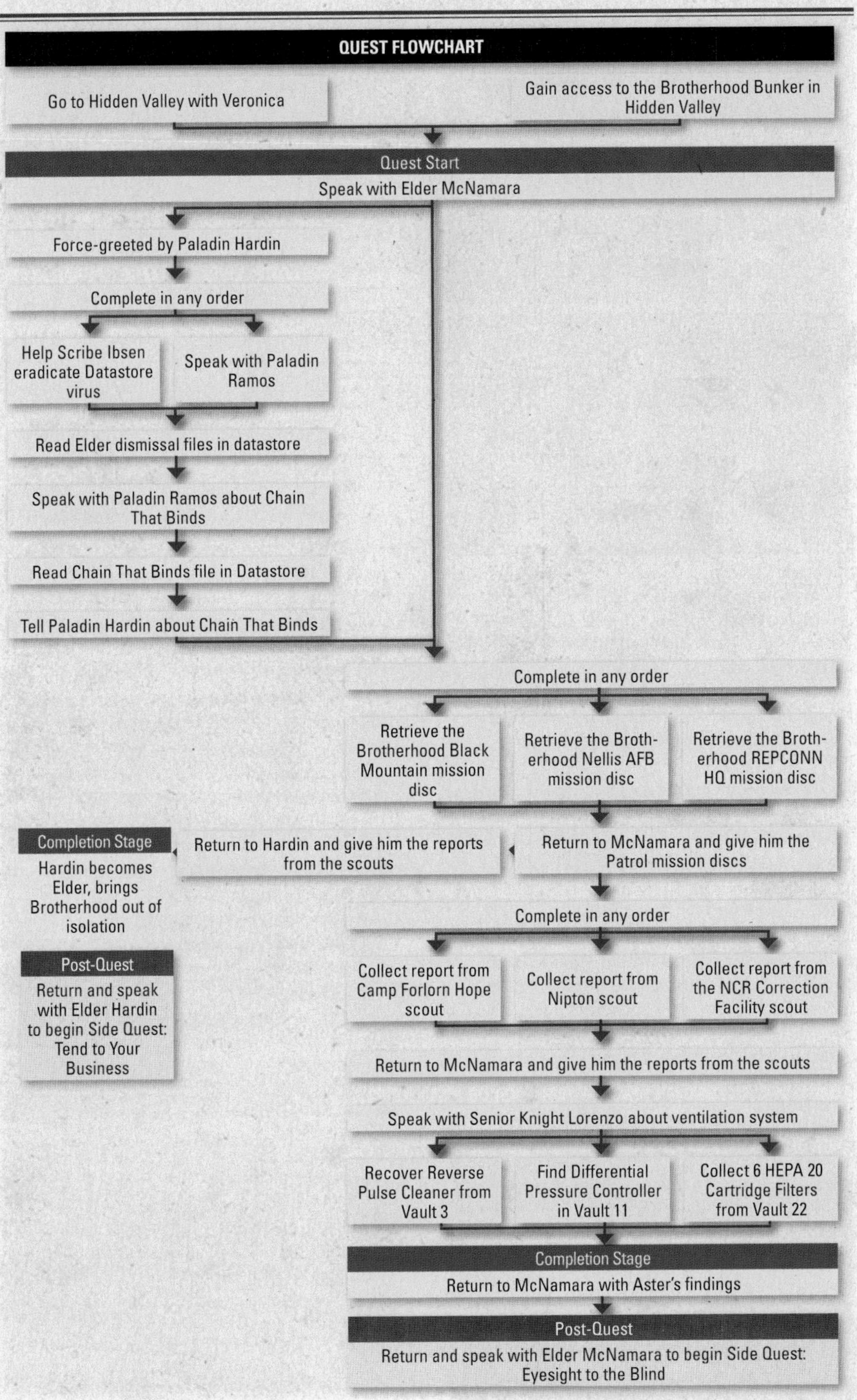

QUEST FLOWCHART

- Go to Hidden Valley with Veronica
- Gain access to the Brotherhood Bunker in Hidden Valley

Quest Start
Speak with Elder McNamara

- Force-greeted by Paladin Hardin
- Complete in any order
  - Help Scribe Ibsen eradicate Datastore virus
  - Speak with Paladin Ramos
- Read Elder dismissal files in datastore
- Speak with Paladin Ramos about Chain That Binds
- Read Chain That Binds file in Datastore
- Tell Paladin Hardin about Chain That Binds

Complete in any order
- Retrieve the Brotherhood Black Mountain mission disc
- Retrieve the Brotherhood Nellis AFB mission disc
- Retrieve the Brotherhood REPCONN HQ mission disc

Return to McNamara and give him the Patrol mission discs

Return to Hardin and give him the reports from the scouts

Completion Stage
Hardin becomes Elder, brings Brotherhood out of isolation

Post-Quest
Return and speak with Elder Hardin to begin Side Quest: Tend to Your Business

Complete in any order
- Collect report from Camp Forlorn Hope scout
- Collect report from Nipton scout
- Collect report from the NCR Correction Facility scout

Return to McNamara and give him the reports from the scouts

Speak with Senior Knight Lorenzo about ventilation system
- Recover Reverse Pulse Cleaner from Vault 3
- Find Differential Pressure Controller in Vault 11
- Collect 6 HEPA 20 Cartridge Filters from Vault 22

Completion Stage
Return to McNamara with Aster's findings

Post-Quest
Return and speak with Elder McNamara to begin Side Quest: Eyesight to the Blind

Detour: Prove Yourself Worthy

At the bottom of the first set of stairs, Paladin Ramos **(3)** stops you with a gruff rebuke. Normally he would have shot you, but the elder wishes to speak with you. You can agree (and begin the Quest), leave, or refuse (in which case the entire base turns hostile).

Down in the command room **(4)**, approach the large circular desk, and engage Elder McNamara **(5)** in conversation. He asks how you got here, and explains he takes pains to minimize exposure topside, but needs

an "outsider" to accomplish certain tasks. He has a test for you; an NCR Ranger has set up post in one of the bunkers up top. McNamara wants him driven off. Agree to take care of the Ranger. The elder makes sure you know it isn't necessary to kill him. You're then fitted with an explosive collar, which will detonate if you wander away from Hidden Valley.

Explosive Collar

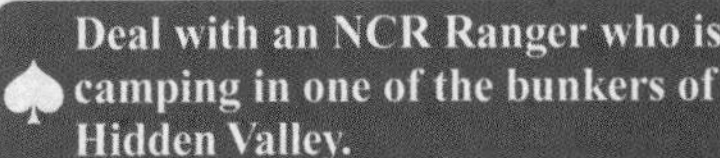

Dobson's Choice

You're unceremoniously dumped outside the bunker door with a bomb around your neck. Don't forget that your equipment will be in the chest to your right. To begin this task, head outside and consult your map. Depending on the time of day, Ranger Dobson may be on patrol or in the bunker. During daylight hours, he watches the NCR Correctional Facility in the distance **(6)**; your collar allows just enough distance to reach it. Otherwise, wait for him (or sleep) in "his" bunker, with the campfire, radio, and journal. At night, he stops you as you enter the bunker. Speak to Dobson **(7)** and he draws his weapon, thinking you're a Powder Ganger. You can:

Retort with verbal boisterousness. Dobson laughs off his joke.

Explain that you're not a Powder Ganger, or leave.

You can now ask Ranger Dobson some questions. One of them is "you have to get out of here." He asks why.

Tell him the Brotherhood of Steel has a base inside one of the bunkers. He can't believe it. Show him your explosive collar, and he takes it off, and tells you to come back to his bunker to go over what you saw. Should you try this, the Brotherhood of Steel will not let you back into the bunker, and they track you down and attempt to assassinate you from time to time. The Quest fails.

Lie and tell him the Powder Gangers use the bunkers as hideouts. He's worried, and thanks you for the tip. He then leaves, completing this Objective.

Or talk about something else.

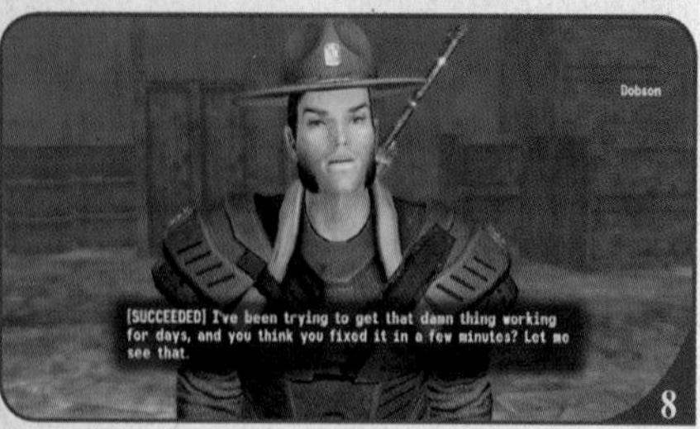

8

Back in "his" bunker **(8)**, you can speak to Ranger Dobson again, or check out his journal and his radio. The journal shows that he hasn't found out about the Brotherhood of Steel yet. With the radio, you can:

- Leave it alone. If Dobson sees you, he asks what you've been doing to it. You tell him nothing.

Touch the radio again, and Dobson attacks.

- Rig the radio to explode when used. If Dobson sees you, he asks what you've been doing to it. You can:

Lie and tell him you fixed it. He goes over to inspect it, and is blown into smaller pieces.

You can tell him you rigged it to explode. He goes do-lally, and must be killed.

Or tell him nothing. Touch the radio again, and Dobson attacks.

- Or smash the radio. Do this when Dobson can see you, and he's understandably violent. Kill him.

So, Dobson can be removed as a threat to the Brotherhood by:

1. Killing him by rigging his radio up as a bomb.
2. Touching his radio too many times.
3. Shooting him.
4. Telling him that the area is a Powder Ganger hideout.
5. Or destroying the radio when Dobson is away from the bunker. When he returns, he feels unsafe about his hidey-hole, and leaves.

All of these are acceptable. What isn't acceptable is mentioning the Brotherhood of Steel at any time during the conversation with Dobson. Do this, and once Dobson has been dealt with, the Paladins storm your location and attack.

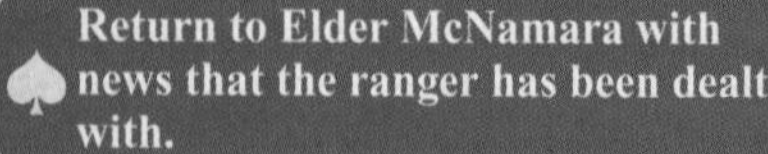
Return to Elder McNamara with news that the ranger has been dealt with.

Return to the bunker and head down the steps until you reach Elder McNamara. You have a conversation about how you handled the Ranger, and then he requests your presence in the command room.

If you killed Dobson, McNamara isn't pleased and you need to explain yourself. Complete the Speech check, or you're attacked by the Brotherhood of Steel!

Subterranean Shut-Ins

9

10

Once you've completed the "detour" and you're trusted by the Brotherhood, or if Veronica is with you, head past Paladin Ramos' office **(9)** toward the head of security, who directs you to Elder McNamara's main command operations chamber **(10)**. Head down the stairs, across Hidden Valley Bunker L1, to the L2 door, and into the chamber itself.

Speak to Elder McNamara in the command room.

The chamber is circular, with a couple of guards stationed at the entrance. Elder McNamara is willing to trust you if you're willing to help. He informs you that his soldiers rarely venture outside (aside from Veronica), but when they do, it is to retrieve materials deemed too important to ignore. However, some of them haven't returned, and you're to look for them, bringing the brothers (or their Holotapes) back to the bunker. Agree to do this.

Find the missing Brotherhood patrol at REPCONN HQ and retrieve their mission holotape.

Find the missing Brotherhood patrol at Nellis AFB and retrieve their mission holotape.

Find the missing Brotherhood patrol at Black Mountain and retrieve their mission holotape.

Building an Insurrection

11

Leave the command room, and as you're about to leave Bunker L2, you're stopped by Head Paladin Hardin **(11)**, who seems annoyed about McNamara's "desperate measures": that is, you. But he has a veneer of friendliness as he tells you the chapter is in trouble and the elder is in the center of it all. You can:

Listen to what he has to say, or ask why he should be trusted, and then listen.

Or tell him you won't listen to him.

Assuming you listen, Hardin tells you morale has plummeted as the chapter continues to live in this underground hermitage. This will only change if a new elder is installed. You can see where this is going. He wants McNamara out. He's combed the Brotherhood records for a dismissal precedent, but not found any. Those likely to help him are all allied with McNamara. He asks for your help. You can:

Agree to see what you can do. This allows you to ignore Hardin later, without cutting off your options. This also sets up the Brotherhood to be an ally, which is vital if you want them on your side for a forthcoming battle! You're told to speak with Ramos and rummage in the Brotherhood's datastore. Finally, if McNamara gives you tasks, Hardin wants to know about it.

Or refuse, and take your cues only from McNamara.

Speak to Hardin again as soon as you're given your first task by McNamara. Tell him the elder has you looking for the lost patrols and retrieving their mission info. He asks you to let him know if you find anything.

[Optional] Help Head Paladin Hardin find a way to oust Elder McNamara from his position.

[Optional] Talk to Senior Paladin Ramos on Hardin's behalf.

[Optional] Look at Brotherhood's history files related to elders being dismissed from their positions.

[Optional] Talk to Senior Scribe Ibsen about accessing the Brotherhood's datastore.

[Optional] Return to Hardin with the lost patrols' mission discs.

> *Note* Icon Definitions:
>
> From this point, whenever there are actions that are only necessary if you're helping Head Paladin Hardin, they are flagged with this icon.
>
> Tasks ordered by Elder McNamara comprise the majority of this Quest. These are flagged with this icon (do these whether you're helping Hardin or not).

Partition Party

12

Before you leave, you can begin Hardin's two immediate tasks. Farther into Bunker L2 is the datastore **(12)**. Manning it is the slightly frazzled Scribe Ibsen **(13)**, who's having a bad day. Ask what the problem is, and Ibsen tells

13

you an exploratory patrol brought back a data disc with a virus on it that shut them out of their own cataloging program. You can ask about the patrols, but focus on the virus. He asks if you have any ideas:

Suggest the virus be partitioned so read-access is only provided by the kernel administrator. Ibsen agrees this would work; it just needs someone to seal a portion of the virus to a particular terminal. Agree to attempt this.

To continue this, you must know your Science; there's no other way to begin.

The virus is a nasty little blighter, but here's the plan. Wait until Scribe Ibsen tells you that "the virus has jumped," and immediately access a terminal.

14

If you see this appearing on the terminal screen **(14)**, ignore the terminal and move onto the next.

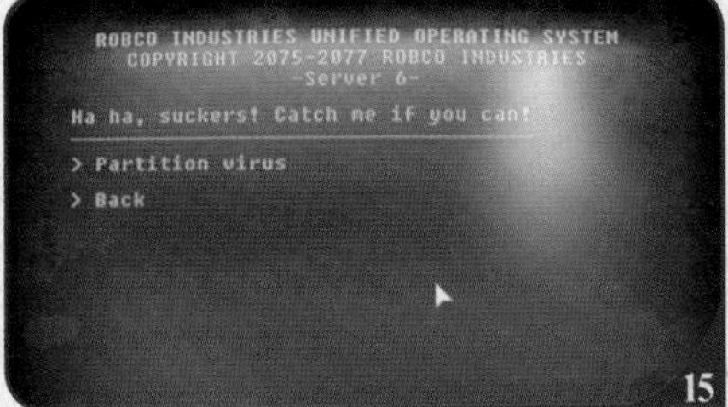

15

If you see this **(15)**, or some other mildly offensive message from the hacker, partition the virus immediately!

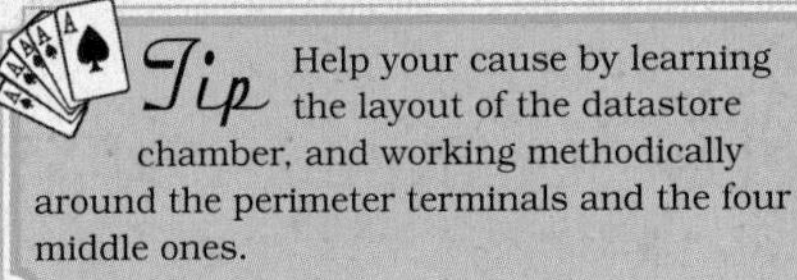

Tip Help your cause by learning the layout of the datastore chamber, and working methodically around the perimeter terminals and the four middle ones.

Continue this until your time runs out (and you have to begin again), or until you've successfully partitioned the virus three times. The affected terminals are completely random each time you attempt this puzzle.

Ibson congratulates you on your partitioning prowess, and says you can now access the nonclassified topics:

Bunker Information

Project Goals: Hidden Valley

System Overview

To obtain more topics (and complete this optional Objective), you need to get a senior-level member of the chapter to unlock a topic for you. Paladin Ramos is the one to ask about this.

Chains That Bind

16

17

Venture up to the security office on Bunker L1 to speak with Ramos. He explains that there are "only a few cases of elders being dismissed" and encourages you to read through the reports **(16)**. Now that Ramos has unlocked the entry in the datastore, you can head back downstairs to access the files **(17)**. There are three reports, although only the second is of interest. Apparently, one elder was deposed for breaking a rule called the "Chain That Binds."

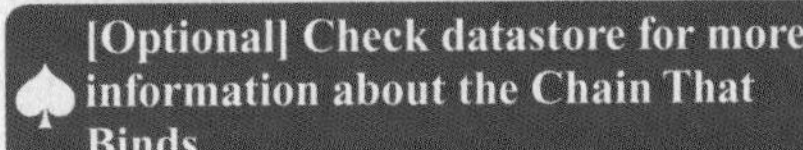

[Optional] Ask Paladin Ramos about the Chain That Binds.

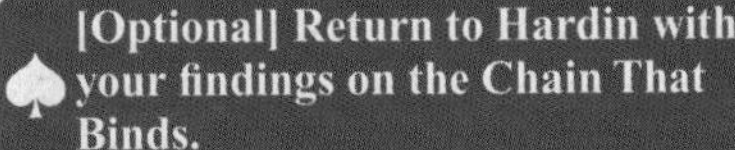

[Optional] Check datastore for more information about the Chain That Binds.

[Optional] Return to Hardin with your findings on the Chain That Binds.

18

19

Return to Ramos armed with questions about the Chain That Binds. He unlocks an entry in the datastore regarding the rule, noting that you're probably the first person to read the file in years **(18)**. Go back to Bunker L2 and access the datastore file. Once you've read up on the Chain That Binds, you can pass the information to Paladin Hardin, who may leverage it in his plot to oust Elder McNamara.

Hardin is dismissive of your research until you highlight an obscure part of the rule that dictates any superior who breaks the chain of command and issues orders to his subordinate's squad members shall be punished. Finding evidence of McNamara's wrongdoing is now top priority, Hardin insists **(19)**. It's time to search for the missing patrols as requested by Elder McNamara with an eye for such evidence.

Task #1: The Doomed Patrols

Now leave the bunker and search for the three missing patrols. These can be found in any order.

A Black Day at Black Mountain

20

21

Equidistant between Scorpion Gulch [5.12], Black Mountain [5.07], and Hidden Valley is a large crater **(20)**. You can easily trek there on-foot from the bunker. As you near the crater, with the Black Mountain radar dishes visible nearby, begin to cull the Centaur population from the surrounding rocks. Then descend into the steep crater, locating the bodies of two Paladins **(21)** and obtain the first Holotape. Grab the Power Armor and Laser Rifle weaponry and ammunition, too.

Brotherhood of Steel Mission Holotape

Power Armor

Laser Rifle and Ammunition

Tip You are trained to wear Power Armor during Side Quest: For Auld Lang Syne, or (if you play your cards right) at the end of the Quests that proceed from this one: Side Quest: Eyesight for the Blind or Side Quest: Tend to Your Business. So take the Power Armor if you want to wear it in the near future!

Terminated on the Top Floor

22

Travel to the REPCONN Headquarters [2.35], and approach the double doors **(22)**, and enter the main floor. If you want to thoroughly inspect this building, placating

the security robots in the process (Free Quest: Access Powers), consult the Tour Chapter. For a quicker infiltration, head upstairs. Here's the route to take:

Either watch the Mister Handy robots give you a tour of the facility.

Or, pry (or hack) the door open to your right (north), near the dead bodies in the foyer.

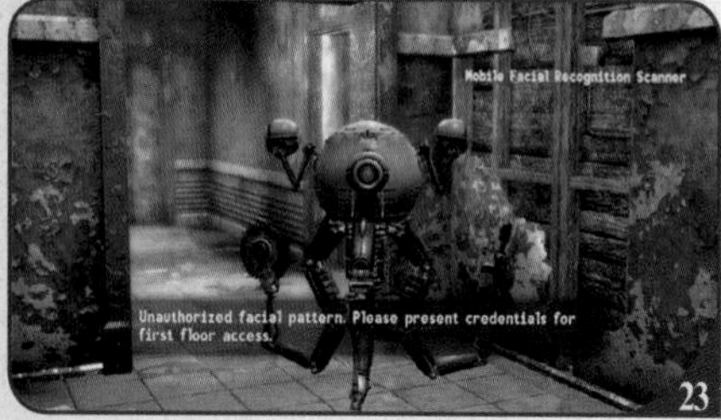

23

Head out of the Pod room, and open the door on your right (north), and head up the stairs. You may be stopped by Mobile Facial Recognition Scanners **(23)** along the way. You can:

- Answer them without appropriate attribute, skill, or perk prowess. They give you 30 seconds to leave before summoning security robots.
- Attack them immediately.
- Or answer depending on the question:

Confuse the one on the stairs.

Confuse the one on the second floor corridor.

Correctly say the executive password.

Tip Free Quest: Access Powers enables you to launch the Rocketeer Tour. Obtain an employee keycard at the end of the tour and use it to access the first computer on the left of the locked door from the Reception room. You can now head up to the next floor, find another computer (to the left as you enter), which allows for further access. Consult the Tour Chapter entry for REPCONN Headquarters for the entire route.

24

Open the Door to REPCONN Office 2nd Floor, turn left, and head south along the long corridor, turn right, head up the stairs, and enter the top floor.

Just inside the door to your right (northeast) is a section of collapsed concrete, and a Paladin slumped against a wall **(24)**. Take his Holotape. Then retrace your steps out of here.

Brotherhood of Steel Mission Holotape

Bombing Run

25

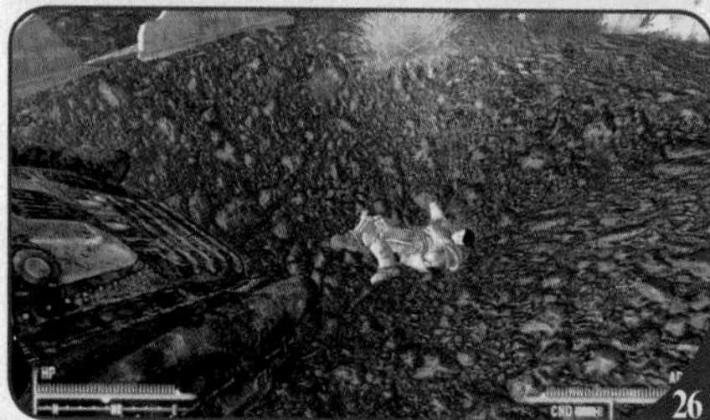
26

The third patrol caught fire investigating the Boomers up near the Nellis Air Force Base [3.01]. The nearest safe areas to move to are Raul's Shack [3.05] or the Fields' Shack [3.04]. Head up the road, and you'll run into George, who asks if you want to pay for information on how to approach the Boomers' stronghold safely. The recommended steps are as follows:

Read the start of Side Quest: Volare!, which has all the necessary steps for safely reaching the Nellis Air Force Base.

It is far safer, although slightly longer, to contact the Boomers and begin that Quest, after which their bombardment abates.

Or, you can run the gauntlet and scramble up the road, and search for this section **(25)** of ruins; note the concrete wall and burned-out vehicle.

Step into the small crater near the vehicle, salvage the last Holotape from the corpse **(26)**, and retreat.

Brotherhood of Steel Mission Holotape

Return to Elder McNamara with the three patrol mission holotapes.

Task #2: Scouting Reports

Return to the Hidden Valley, enter the correct bunker, and proceed to Bunker L2. Approach the junction to the command room, where Head Paladin Hardin is waiting. You can:

Ignore him, and enter the command room.

Or update him about the patrols, and show him the mission discs. Hardin is furious that McNamara gave his men orders without telling him. This builds up Hardin's evidence for ousting McNamara.

Back in the command room, give the Holotapes over to Elder McNamara (or find out more about the bunker lockdown and the crazy surface sandstorm), and he isn't surprised that they all died. The Brotherhood, it seems, has many enemies. He tells you about some scouts already in the field, who were told to hold position and maintain radio silence. You are to contact those scouts and gather their reports.

Leave the command room, and exit to the surface.

Leave the command room, and tell Hardin that you're contacting scouts. He thinks it's a good idea, and one he's wanted to implement for years. Exit to the surface.

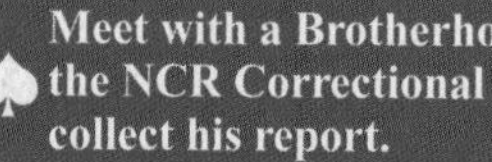
Meet with a Brotherhood scout near the NCR Correctional Facility and collect his report.

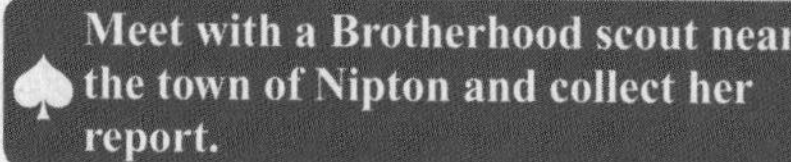
Meet with a Brotherhood scout near the town of Nipton and collect her report.

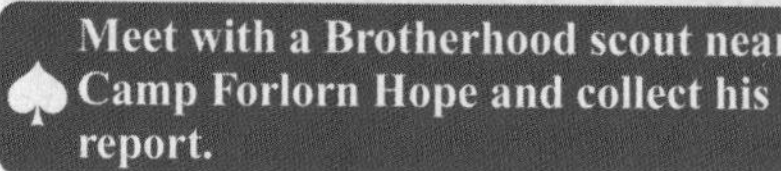
Meet with a Brotherhood scout near Camp Forlorn Hope and collect his report.

Are the Bears Still Hunting?

The three scouts maintaining radio silence can be found in any order:

27

This Brotherhood scout **(27)** is crouched on a large pile of stones just outside the perimeter fence overlooking the NCR Correctional Facility. You can:

Attack the Brotherhood scout and kill him without the Brotherhood knowing.

Or speak to the scout using the passphrase. The scout tells you about the Powder Gangers' takeover of the facility. What's puzzling is why the NCR hasn't taken it back. The report is handed over.

Brotherhood Scout Report #1

28

Move to either the Hidden Supply Cave [5.27] or the Coyote Den [5.26] along the railroad tracks, and take to the rocky bluffs above. The Brotherhood scout **(28)** is perched on a rocky promontory offering distant views of Nipton [4.30]. You can:

Blast the Brotherhood scout, and defeat her without any payback from the Brotherhood.

Or use the pass-phrase. This scout was watching as the small town to the south was attacked and most inhabitants were slain. She hands you the report.

 **Brotherhood Scout Report #2**

29

The last scout is standing on a clifftop between Camp Forlorn Hope [6.02] to the north, and Nelson [6.06] to the south. You can head there from any direction, but beware if you're approaching via the Southern Nevada Wind Farm [6.03] because there are some vicious Cazadors to fight. If they follow you, they can target and kill the scout. When you reach the scout **(29)** on a rocky buttress, you can:

Defeat him, or let the Cazadors finish him off without any problems from the Brotherhood.

Or recite the pass-phrase. This scout has been watching the altercations between Nelson and the NCR Camp. He hands you his report.

 **Brotherhood Scout Report #3**

Return to Elder McNamara with the three scouts' reports.

Task #3: In the Air Tonight

30

31

Move back to the Hidden Valley bunker, and head toward the command room where Head Paladin Hardin is still waiting.

Back with McNamara, hand over the scout reports, and the elder thanks you. You're a trusted outsider, and McNamara can now confide in you. He needs you to find some components to fix the bunker's air filtration system. Senior Knight Lorenzo has the details; he brought the matter to McNamara's attention and is the only other person aware of it.

Speak to Senior Knight Lorenzo regarding the failing air filtration system.

Pass by Hardin, and head through Scribe Ibsen's datastore chamber before following the corridor ahead around. Turn left (east), and enter the bunker workshop and server room **(30)**. Locate Senior Knight Lorenzo here **(31)**. Tell him you're here to help retrieve air filtration components. Lorenzo mumbles something about having your death on his conscience; the task ahead is fraught with danger! He gives you a list of components, which are likely to be somewhere inside the vaults dotted about the Mojave Wasteland.

Search the vaults in the region for a differential pressure controller.

Search the vaults in the region for a reverse pulse cleaner.

Search the vaults in the region for several HEPA cartridge filters.

Approach the junction to the command room and Bunker L1, where Head Paladin Hardin is waiting. You can:

 Ignore him, and exit the bunker to the surface.

 Or inform Hardin what you're up to. He's shocked and surmises (correctly) that the system's in real trouble. Hardin can't believe there aren't more Paladins working on this. Leave him, and move up to Paladin Ramos' office. Speak to Ramos, and tell him you've discovered proof that the chapter is in danger, and that McNamara covered it up. He says he'll investigate this on his own, and if it corroborates your story, he'll consider switching his vote from McNamara to Hardin.

The three separate components can be found in any order. For a full list of what each vault contains, check the Tour Chapter.

Vault 3: Fiendish Behavior

32

Head to Vault 3 [2.24], battling (or Sneaking past) Fiends until you reach the sloping entrance **(32)**. Activate the Vault Door Control Pad to the right, and step into this Fiend-filled location, which is Motor-Runner's domain. Here's the route to take to reach the component:

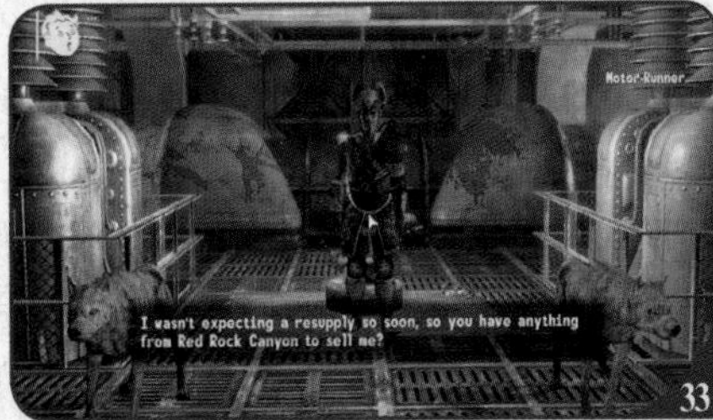

33

Step into the entrance area, where you're harangued by a Fiend.

You can kill her, which turns all the Fiends inside the vault hostile.

 Or you can tell her you're carrying Chems. She lets you through and nobody gets hurt.

Head through the doorway, and make a right and an immediate left. Move past the two closed doors to the corridor junction, and turn right, down the steps. A quick left, then right down another set of steps leads to the Door to Vault 3—Maintenance Wing. Open it, and step through into a connecting room, and open the door opposite.

Step into a large metal tunnel and make a left, then a right, and open the door into the server room. Open the door on the right wall, and approach Motor-Runner and his two hounds **(33)**. You can:

 Ask what happened to the vault residents.

Deliver some Chems, if you're here as part of Side Quest: Aba Daba Honeymoon.

Or kill Motor-Runner. Or stop talking and leave him be.

34

Look to the left, and locate the two lockers **(34)**. The left one has the component you need.

 **Reverse Pulse Cleaner**

Vault 11: Rodent Rampage

35

Journey to Vault 11 [5.05], entering from the rocky exterior cave entrance **(35)** and through the Giant Mantis and Rat-filled corridors. Here's how to reach the component you need:

36

Open the steel door in the entrance chamber, and turn right. Head through the doorway, turn right into the corridor, and left, down the steps. Follow the corridor along and descend another set of steps. Turn right and follow the corridor to another set of steps down, and open the Door to Vault 11 Living Quarters.

Conclusion: All Aces

When you've found all the performers, or after each has been given a business card (it doesn't matter when), return to the Aces Theater, and speak to Tommy Torini once again, inquiring about each act:

- Billy Knight was "one hell of a haggler" (if you Bartered with Billy and coached him to negotiate).

 **90 (3%) or 150 (5%) Caps**

If you didn't tell Billy to haggle, Torini tells you Knight "practically begged" him to hire the guy, and your cut is substantially lower. You can:

Take the cut

 **45 (3%) or 75 (5%) Caps**

 Tell Torini that Billy is worth three times that much, and he doubles up your fee.

 **90 (3%) or 150 (5%) Caps**

 **The Strip Fame Gained!**

- The cowboy has "chops, baby, real chops, and I ain't just talking about that mustache."

 **100 (3%) or 166 (5%) Caps**

 **The Strip Fame Gained!**

- Mr. Isaac? "That cat's gonna bring me money like you wouldn't believe!"

 **100 (3%) or 166 (5%) Caps**

 **The Strip Fame Gained!**

- The ugly mug with the razor tongue? "One hell of a novelty act!"

 **150 (3%) or 250 (5%) Caps**

 **The Strip Fame Gained!**

 **500 XP**

 Note: You receive a Fame Gain with The Strip for each performer you wrangle, and an additional boost when the Quest is over. Come back between 4 PM and 1 AM any day to watch these new acts!

TEND TO YOUR BUSINESS

SUGGESTED EXPERIENCE

QUEST FLOWCHART

Complete Side Quest: Still in the Dark making Hardin the Elder
↓
Quest Start
Speak with Hardin
↓
Ask to become a Brotherhood
↓
Travel to Freeside and enter the Silver Rush
↓
Eliminate the Van Graffs
↓
Completion Stage
Return to Hardin

Main Factions

And Now We're Full of Energy

Note: For this Quest to activate, you must side with Head Paladin Hardin during Side Quest: Still in the Dark. Exit the Hidden Bunker area, and wait several days for the lockdown to be lifted. Then return, and inquire about joining the Brotherhood of Steel. Hardin has the following request:

Kill the Van Graffs and their men.

This is a sister Quest to Side Quest: Eyesight to the Blind, and both are accessed depending on how you ended Side Quest: Still in the Dark. This Quest is only accessible

once you side with Head Paladin Hardin **(1).** Once newly appointed Elder Hardin has given you instructions, ascend the steps and depart from the Hidden Bunker [5.11]. Head for Freeside, moving through to the Silver Rush Gambling Hall [2C.07], where the ruthless Van Graffs have been selling their own highly impressive energy weapons that Hardin has his eye on. Check out (and optionally complete parts of) Side Quest: Birds of a Feather. This details the plans that the Van Graffs have for you, and it might be wise to finish them (and claim your rewards) before the killing starts.

Don't burst in with all guns blazing **(2)**, because Gloria Van Graff **(3)** and Jean-Baptiste Cutting **(4)** are crack shots, and their thugs (around six in the store, and Simon outside) wear armor and carry the latest in energy weapon technology. Begin by making sure you're carrying a sizable number of Caps or tradable items, and buy as much as you want from Gloria's shop. Once she's dead, the store dies with her. Then try any of the following options:

 Gather as much C-4 as you can, along with a Detonator, before you arrive. Pickpocket Gloria and Jean-Baptiste and place C-4 into their inventory, then do the same for as many thugs as you have C-4 for. Then trigger an extremely explosive mass murder.

 If you must stand and fight, choose highly damaging weapons (such as Plasma), and if the situation becomes a little too taxing, back into the residence, dropping Mines or Grenades along your route to soften up the pursuers.

Or, you could complete the vast majority of Side Quest: Birds of a Feather, and simply let them face the Legion during the final part of that Quest. Then kill any survivors.

An even easier plan is to simply begin Side Quest: Birds of a Feather, and when you're standing on the door with Simon, patting everyone down who enters, wait for the fourth potential "customer." He's actually a suicide bomber, but instead of discovering this, allow him to enter the premises. The explosion kills the Van Graffs, and you can congratulate yourself for not getting your hands dirty, or your Reputation soiled.

 Tip: Don't forget to destroy Simon (the Van Graff thug on the front door, outside).

Return to Elder Hardin with the news that the Van Graffs have been eliminated.

Hardin's Newest Paladin

5

Journey back to the Hidden Valley Bunker, and inform Hardin that the Van Graffs have been defeated. Hardin considers this a small step in the right direction. In fact, he bestows on you the title of Paladin of the Brotherhood, for your meritorious service in its name. Normally, this would come with a ceremony, but there's no time. Hardin gives you a suit of Power Armor, and trains you to use it, if you haven't learned that already. The Quest concludes with the elder telling you that you can trade or purchase the Brotherhood's full range of arms at the Bunker Armory **(5)**.

Power Armor Training

T-45d Power Armor

T-45d Power Helmet

Post Quest Activities

Now that you're a fully fledged member of the Brotherhood of Steel and have Head Paladin Hardin's ear, you can use your influence to create a treaty with the NCR, and have the Brotherhood fight with them during the battle at Hoover Dam. In addition, Knight Torres sells some new (and powerful) items from the Bunker store: including the Laser RCW, Tri-beam Laser, Laser Rifles and Pistols, and even the infamous Gatling Laser. Consult the Tour Chapter for more information.

THAT LUCKY OLD SUN

SUGGESTED EXPERIENCE

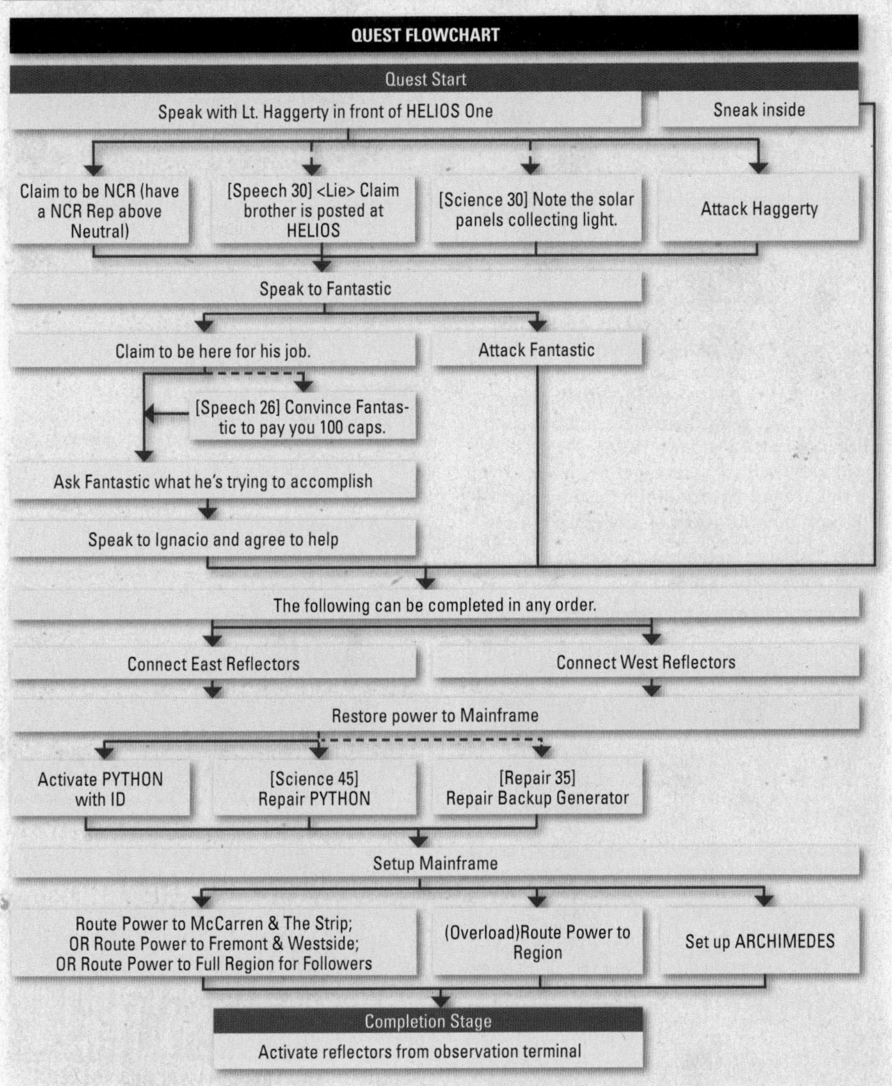

An Ancient Monument to the Sun

1

2

The giant solar array and power plant known as HELIOS One [5.13] is currently under the jurisdiction of the NCR. Journey to the front gates **(1)**, where you're stopped short by Lieutenant Haggerty **(2)**, who instructs you to state your business. You can:

Have snuck in around Haggerty without her even seeing and challenging you.

Claim to be with the NCR (if your Reputation is Neutral or above), and ask if they require help. You're told to speak to Fantastic, and the Quest begins.

Inform her you're pale death and come to bear her to perdition. You must then attack the NCR, which causes severe Reputation problems.

Or you can just attack, which has the same effect, but without any fancy threats.

Otherwise, you need to tell Haggerty you'd like to enter the power plant. She asks why she'd consider doing that. You can:

Tell her the solar tower isn't collecting much sunlight, and you can help.

Lie and tell her your brother works here.

Any other verbal choice results in her politely but firmly denying you entry. Assuming you've been allowed in, Haggerty suggests you speak with the power plant's expert, although he's actually an idiot. Even a saboteur couldn't do a worse job than him.

Talk to the idiot wearing sunglasses in the back of the HELIOS One plant building.

Fantastic and the Follower

3

4

Open the doors behind Haggerty, and meander through the power plant's connecting chambers to the northeast living quarters **(3)**, where the idiot in question resides. Fantastic **(4)** (the name isn't winning him any additional fans) is wearing a scientist's coat, but otherwise seems to be a complete sham. He thinks you're here to replace him. He may be right. Speak to him, and it doesn't take long to realize he's a grifter.

- Tell him you're not here to replace him, and ask him what he's trying to accomplish.

He's getting power, but the outside mirrors aren't aiming correctly, so the array is running at one-percent efficiency. Which apparently isn't good enough for "some assholes." The problem is that the controls for the plant are in the tower area complete with a pre-war security system that the NCR set off. He isn't going anywhere near it. But you can.

Ask about the mirrors, and he tells you about two outside terminals that control the mirrors. And if you're ever at the mainframe, the power needs to be sent to the correct location: "The Strip and McCarran." Before your conversation finishes, you're given a password to one of the outside terminals.

Western Reflector Control Terminal Password

- Or, you can confirm that you're here for his job. Fantastic freaks out. You can then:

Tell him to pay you a stack of Caps and you'll forget about ousting him. He obliges.

Caps (100)

Or recant your previous information, and ask what he's trying to accomplish. See above.

At any time you can attack and kill Fantastic without any repercussions from the NCR.

Connect to the HELIOS One mainframe from the western reflector control terminal.

Connect to the HELIOS One mainframe from the eastern reflector control terminal.

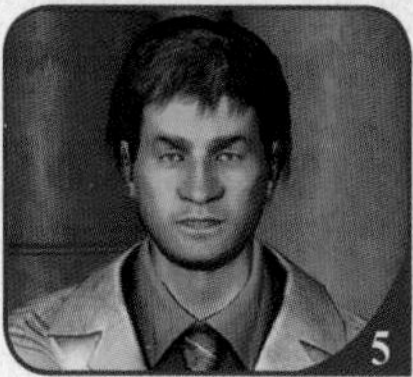
5

After the idiot talk is over, you can optionally speak with Ignacio Rivas **(5)** in an adjacent chamber. He starts asking if you're a soldier or a scientist. Your answer isn't important. Rivas then asks if you're with a particular group. You can answer:

That it's more fun to keep it a mystery.

That this is his territory, and you want to know who he is with. He tells you his identity.

Or another choice, an allegiance to others, or to yourself.

Rivas explains he's a Follower of the Apocalypse, and although he isn't against the NCR using this technology, he believes the base has "things best left buried with the old world." But he does give you some helpful information that once the mainframe is restored, you can route power wherever you choose, without the NCR even knowing. He offers you a password to the other outside terminal. He then tells you about equipment marked with pre-war symbols used by the military. All had a codeword: "ARCHIMEDES." No wonder the Brotherhood of Steel wouldn't give this place up without a fight. And the NCR have no knowledge of this weapon...yet.

Eastern Reflector Control Terminal Password

6

7

Take the door out to the Mojave Wasteland, and enter the fenced-off area where the vast solar mirror arrays are standing, pointed in the incorrect direction around the tower structure. Run to either the eastern **(6)** or the western **(7)** reflector control terminal. Beware of some minor traps (such as a Frag Mine or Rigged Shotgun) as you approach.

Using the passwords given, log on, and "Reset Mainframe Connection." You can optionally read more about the ARCHIMEDES testing, and a military visit from long ago. Then move to the Door to the Solar Collection Tower, and enter it. This is *not* the door you exited from!

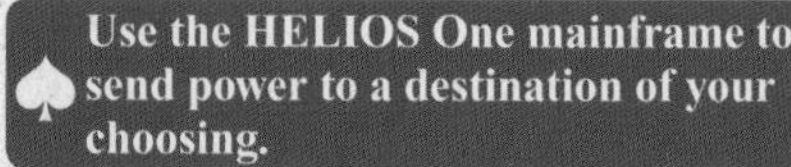
Use the HELIOS One mainframe to send power to a destination of your choosing.

[Optional] Arm ARCHIMEDES security system to wipe out all nearby NCR soldiers.

Gaining Power for a Solar Shower

8

Proceed through the pre-war robot guardians of the Solar Collection Tower, heading toward the HELIOS One observation level.

Along the way, you can optionally deactivate turrets.

And neutralize a variety of robots, too **(8)**.

Wind down sewer tunnels, up and down gantry stairs, past Protectrons in stasis, pausing in an adjacent chamber to optionally grab an Employee ID Card (there are two), and locating an elevator.

Poseidon Energy Employee ID Card (2)

9

10

Now in the observation level, which is one large chamber with a huge mainframe in the middle of it **(9)**, your next task is to restore power to the mainframe, which lacks enough power to operate.

Restore power to the HELIOS One mainframe via an auxiliary generator.

Close to the mainframe is an auxiliary generator. Inspect it, and you'll see that it's in reasonable shape, but requires the following to activate:

A piece of scrap metal (which you may be carrying, or can easily find rummaging back in the previous part of the power plant, or in a toolbox on the metal shelving in this chamber).

- Climb up the gantry stairs to a command control room, where the shell of a worker robot named PYTHON lies dormant. It has specialized tools for maintenance. You can:

Use the Poseidon Energy ID Card you took from the lower research room, and slot it into the robot's head.

Or hard-wire the robot to run on autopilot in repair mode.

With either option, PYTHON moves down to the generator, and fixes the wiring **(10)**.

Activate the HELIOS One Mainframe Terminal **(11)**, and read about the initial trials and ARCHIMEDES testing. But the reason you're here is to "Configure the Power Grid." Once you make this choice, you can choose again, but only up until you activate the reflectors from the observation terminal. Where do you want the power to go?

1. McCarran and Las Vegas Strip. This is the NCR's favored result, and you're rewarded with Fame accordingly.

NCR Fame Gained!

2. Fremont and Westside. This is the Followers' favored result, and you're rewarded with Fame too.

Followers Fame Gained!

3. Full Region. This provides just enough power for everyone, making the Followers very happy.

Followers Fame Gained!

4. ARCHIMEDES II. This will destroy the NCR, and is the favored result if you aren't aligned with them.
5. Full Region (Emergency Output Level): Aside from an ending change, this works the same as choice 3.

Followers Fame Gained!

Initiate reflector retargeting from the console on the tower observation deck.

Tip The Follower (and also Companion Follower) called Arcade Gannon has his own Quest (Side Quest: For Auld Lang Syne), and bringing him along to this Quest is both helpful and advisable for gaining his trust.

Tip Arming the ARCHIMEDES II is an excellent idea if you wish to obtain the full power of the sun, and have a weapon called Euclid's C-Finder. Although finding this device is optional (and a possible part of Veronica's Side Quest: I Could Make You Care), if HELIOS One is functional, you can order an ARCHIMEDES blast down on a set of opponents once per day.

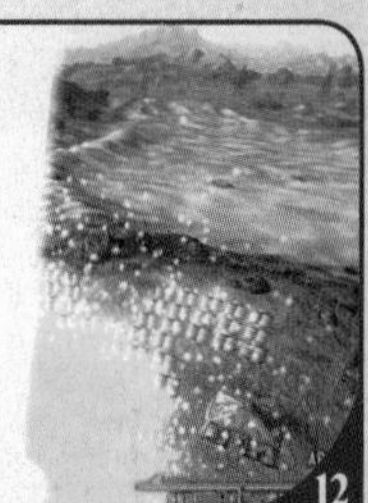

The final step is to activate the reflector retargeting. Head up the gantry stairs to the command control room where PYTHON was found, and exit into the Mojave Wasteland. You should appear high above the reflector array, with a commanding view of the desert. Descend and locate the Reflector Control Panel, and activate it between the hours of 09:00 and 15:00, during peak sunlight hours. The result is a spectacular light show of ancient technology **(12)**!

Talk to Ignacio. Talk to Fantastic.

Finish this Quest by speaking to Ignacio again, informing him that the energy-collecting nature of the HELIOS One has been restored. He thanks you, and awards you with a couple of Stimpaks for your troubles. The Quest concludes, but there are wide-reaching implications depending on where the power is routed to!

Stimpak (2)

800 XP

THE LEGEND OF THE STAR AND A VALUABLE LESSON

SUGGESTED EXPERIENCE

See flowchart on the following page

Main Factions

Your Plastic Pal Who's Fun to Be With!

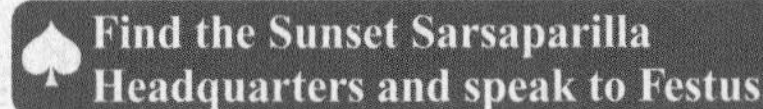

Find the Sunset Sarsaparilla Headquarters and speak to Festus.

The Sunset Sarsaparilla Headquarters [2.17] on the west side of town was once home to a corporation that would challenge the Nuka-Cola Corporation in terms of beverages sold and harmful ingredients ingested by its customers. The building itself **(1)** has a main entrance once you step into the giant Sarsaparilla bottle, and open the Door to the Factory Floor. You can search the premises and bump into the (hostile) robot guardians if you wish. Or look for the Sunset Saloon machine in the foyer, and say hello to Festus **(2)**!

This cowboy pal introduces himself, and gives instructions on how to "talk" with him. Say you're "pleased to meetcha," and he asks whether you're here to redeem your Sunset Sarsaparilla Stars. At this point:

It's wise to say "Star Info."

You can also play a game of Lucky Horseshoes by saying "I feel lucky." If you beat Festus, you're likely to win a few Caps, and never get those last couple of minutes of your life back.

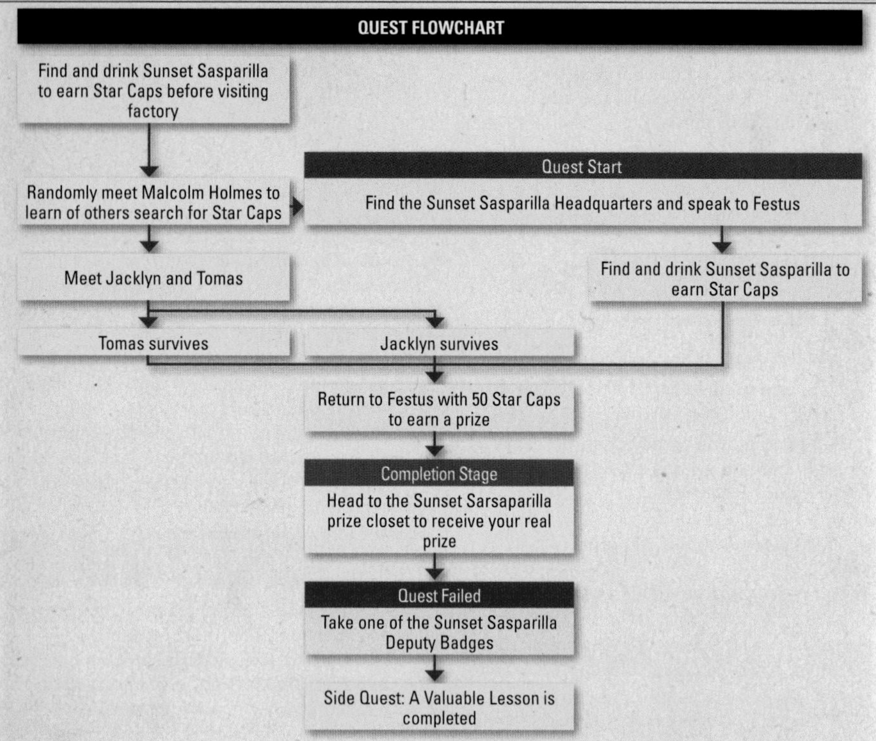

 **Caps (a few)**

And you can inquire about the health advisory by stating "Silly Ol' Advisory." You may need to say this multiple times; perhaps your accent is difficult for Festus to pick up?

Tip Here's how you play Lucky Horseshoes: Cards are numbered two through ten, along with aces, which count as one. You and Festus take turns drawing cards (the blue button). Each card is added to your totals. The totals need to add up as close to 21 without going over. You should "hold" (the red button) once you get up close to 21. If either of you draws a card that brings both totals to the same number, the other player's total goes up by one. The winner is the player who is closer to 21, after they hold at 21 or below, or if the other player's total is 22 or higher, and they "bust." Remember you can still lose, even if you're on 21! Or to put it another way, this is Blackjack without being able to know your cards. Naturally, it is geared toward a Festus victory.

Festus explains that select Sunset Sarsaparilla bottles have a special cap with blue stars printed on them. These Star Caps (which are not legal tender) are known as Sunset Sarsaparilla Stars. Find enough of them, and you win a prize!

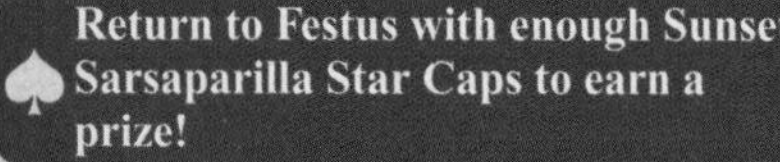
Return to Festus with enough Sunset Sarsaparilla Star Caps to earn a prize!

The Great Sunset Sarsaparilla Star Cap Hunt

3

4

The Mojave Wasteland is littered with 100 of these Star Caps, and the colossal scavenger hunt begins now! For example, you can journey to the Smith Mesa Prospector Camp **(3)** [6.29] and rummage around under the rocky outcrop for Sunset Sarsaparilla Star Cap on top of a concrete block **(4)**. When you have a bunch of caps, return one, some, or all of them to Festus, and place them in his "slot." He keeps a running total, and when you've collected 50 of them, you get a fabulous reward!

Elementary Advice, My Dear Holmes

5

If you pick up a Star Cap without visiting Festus, and don't know what it is, you may receive a visit (randomly) from an old prospector named Malcolm Holmes **(5)**. He tries to bluff you with some trading talk, but he's really been following you "for a good bit now," Assuming you let him continue talking, he offers an explanation of exactly why those shiny blue caps are so prized, and then leaves with a warning. Beware of a man called Allen Marks; some Star Cap hunters have been known to kill for their collection! You can:

Let Malcolm leave, and start your hunt now that you have a rather fanciful account of Festus.

 Crouch and Pickpocket Malcolm, or kill him, to check whether he was telling the truth about not being interested in Star Bottle Caps. He's holding some, so he won't mind if you take them, will he?

 **Sunset Sarsaparilla Star Bottle Cap (6)**

Tackling Tomas or Jostling with Jacklyn

6

Malcolm Holmes was right; other adventurers are prepared to kill for the chance of Star Cap prizes. Randomly occurring in the Mojave Wasteland **(6)** during your search, you may run across a woman named Jacklyn, who hollers at you to help her kill a young man named Tomas, who has "gone crazy!" You can:

 Side with Jacklyn, and take out Tomas.

Side with Tomas, and bring down Jacklyn.

Watch the combat, which usually (but not always) results in a victory for Tomas.

Now speak to the survivor.

7

If Tomas **(7)** survived, he immediately explains that the woman just attacked him without provocation. You can ask why, or if he knew her, or leave. If you're talking to him, he explains they were traveling (and flirting) together before her psychotic episode. He reckons it might have something to do with his lucky charm necklace made from blue caps. You can:

 Tell him that all sorts of nasty folk are looking for those Caps, and he'd be safer without it. He believes you, and asks how to get rid of them. You can:

Tell him you'll hold onto them, and he hands them over.

Tell him to discard them anywhere, and he leaves, still carrying the necklace.

He's to hand over the necklace or you gut him like a fish. He obliges, and flees.

Or tell him to be on his way, and he leaves.

If Tomas leaves, simply follow him and Pickpocket or murder him. He's carrying a small Journal backing up his story, plus seven Star Caps if he has the necklace.

Sunset Sarsaparilla Star Bottle Cap (7)

Note: Tomas' Journal

If Jacklyn **(8)** survived, she quickly goes over to Tomas' corpse, and retrieves something. Then she explains that Tomas was out to kill her. You can ask if she's okay, or what he wanted, but you should take interest in what she extracted from Tomas' corpse. So she doesn't just leave, ask her what she took. She blusters something about a necklace being made from special blue caps, and asks if you have any. You can:

Say you have nothing like the Star Caps she already has. She agrees, after which you can inform her that the necklace isn't really hers, because it's made from Star Caps! She turns violent and must be defeated.

Or answer that you don't, and she leaves.

If Jacklyn leaves, simply tail her and Pickpocket or kill her. She's carrying two Star Caps, plus another seven if she has the necklace.

Sunset Sarsaparilla Star Bottle Cap (2 or 9)

Tip

Sunset Sarsaparilla Star Caps are flagged in the Tour Chapter of this guide at each location where one can be found. Find all 100 at a glance in the chart in the Appendices Chapter. Set off into the sunset, happy hunting, and remember; you only need 50 to finish this Quest!

There's a 10 percent chance of obtaining a Star Cap when you open a Sarsaparilla Bottle (not an empty one!). Find Bottles in the following places:

- In situ, scattered in locations across the Mojave Wasteland.
- In some crates with the Sunset Sarsaparilla logo stamped on them.
- Or from some Sunset Sarsaparilla Vending Machines.

A Valuable Lesson

Now comes the real story behind Sunset Sarsaparilla: The Legend of the Star! Festus goes on (and on) with this story until you reach the conclusion and the Quest fails. You didn't do anything wrong. There just wasn't a fabulous treasure, just a drawn-out sales patter from a half-broken robot. Voice your protest, and Festus agrees to give you a real prize. Side Quest: A Valuable Lesson now automatically begins.

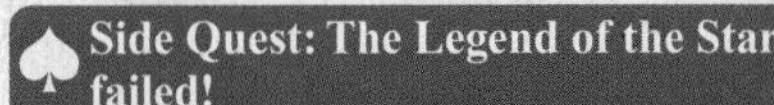

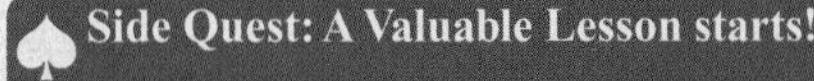

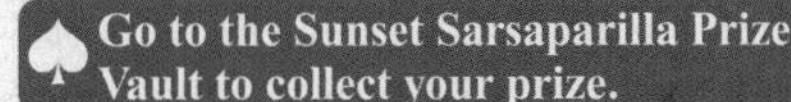

The prize closet is, unfortunately, on the other side of a corridor that is blocked with fallen masonry, so employ the following route through the Sunset Sarsaparilla Headquarters: Open the door to the right (north), head across the corridor to another door and open it, heading into an open-plan cubicle office with a fallen ceiling. Climb up the ceiling section (or ascend to the upper floor from the bottling area to the north), and then dash through the corridors, passing the stairs down, to an office with a wall safe above a hole in the floor **(9)**. Naturally, the wall safe [Average] has a Star Cap to take! Drop down the hole, and open the double doors to a Prize Vault that has been sealed up until this point. Check the area for dozens of Sunset Sarsaparilla Deputy Badges. Congratulations! Wait, there's a much better, non-sanctioned prize in the corner, by the corpse of the man Malcolm Holmes warned you about: Allen Marks **(10)**. A Holotape details the real story of the Star Caps and Marks' final moments. Take his Unique Laser Pistol, too. The Quest concludes.

Sunset Sarsaparilla Crate Items (10)

Sunset Sarsaparilla Deputy Badge (319)

"Pew-Pew" Laser Pistol

1,500 XP

THE COYOTES

SUGGESTED EXPERIENCE

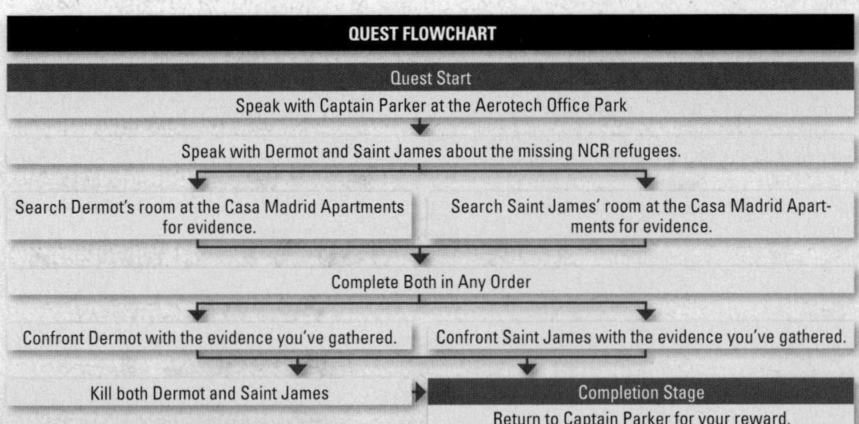

Getting the Dirt on Dermot and Saint James

1

2

The Aerotech Office Park **(1)** [2.22] on the east side of the New Vegas suburbs is a temporary refugee camp, under the jurisdiction of NCR Captain Parker **(2)**, who is seriously overworked and understaffed. This is where drifters from the Republic, locals who can't turn a dime, or drunken reprobates end up. Recognize the chaotic nature of this place, and offer to help. He's happy to task you to investigate the disappearance of some of the camp's refugees. They don't seem to follow a pattern (young, old, male, female...) although a family with a little blond girl carrying a Teddy Bear is etched into his memory. Keith could provide the clues needed; he's a two-bit hustler running a gambling den out of his shack, and he wins far too often. He might be dealing Chems too. Ultimately, Keith provides little information; check him out to complete Free Quest: Keith's Caravan Charade. Some of the missing folks did business with Dermot and Saint James; some Westside [Zone 2A] scavengers.

Note: Investigate Keith's gambling and drug operations

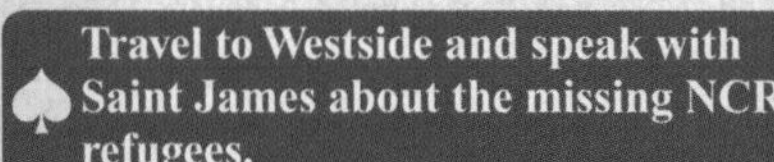
Travel to Westside and speak with Saint James about the missing NCR refugees.

Scavengers...or Slavers?

3

4

Head across town to the Westside West Entrance [2.01] or Miguel's Pawn Shop [2.02], and situate yourself in this rough-and-tumble part of town. Focus your search on the Casa Madrid Apartments [2A.01]. Pass Marco at the front entrance **(3)** and enter the premises. Around the corner to your left, you should spot Dermot **(4)** and Saint James **(5)** heading out of their apartment rooms. Dermot is the silent type, so waylay Saint James with some patter:

5

- Tell him that some missing people were last seen with him. Saint James tells you he doesn't know anything about the Aerotech camp disappearances.

  Verbally pounce on this slip-up. Saint James can't explain his gaff, and masks it with blue language and a swift exit.

- You can also attack these thugs in scavenger clothing. But you lose later interrogation choices.

Search Dermot's room at the Casa Madrid Apartments for evidence.

Search Saint James' room at the Casa Madrid Apartments for evidence.

6

7

The Scavengers have locked their apartment doors firmly. You can:

Unlock the doors to both apartments (with two Lockpick attempts).

Optionally kill both Saint James and Dermot in cold blood. That's one (overly violent) way to conclude the Quest.

Mosey on into Dermot's place first **(6)**, and search around. Of particular interest is Dermot's Ledger. Pick it up and read the notes on your Pip-Boy; it's pretty damning evidence. Over in Saint James' apartment, the place is empty, except for a Teddy Bear near the bed **(7)**. The little blond girl's favorite toy?

Dermot's Ledger

Teddy Bear

(Optional) Confront Dermot or Saint James with the evidence you've gathered.

(Optional) Kill Saint James and Dermot.

Tell Captain Parker what happened to the missing refugees.

8

Dermot and Saint James are still within chasing distance, so get after them! Confront them on the streets of Westside, and begin an altogether more aggressive line of questioning.

Stop Dermot and let him know that you've figured out what they've been doing based on the ledger evidence. A fight immediately erupts.

Stop Saint James and show him the Teddy Bear. He blusters, but tells you he found it salvaging.

Try telling him you found the ledger in Dermot's room. Saint James' Power Fist twitches into life. Fight!

Or realize that reasoning is impossible and just kill these two sickos **(8)**.

Or leave the two to walk free, and return to Captain Parker.

Tell Parker the truth about Saint James and Dermot, whether they're dead or not. Parker thanks you for clearing up this matter, takes away your Teddy Bear, and hands out a small reward.

Caps (150)

250 XP

THE FINGER OF SUSPICION

SUGGESTED EXPERIENCE

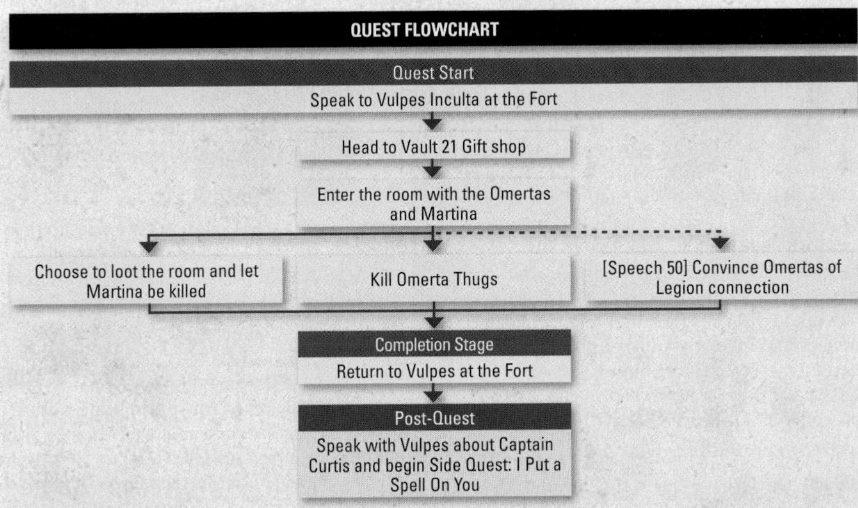

Note Access The Fort by meeting and accepting Vulpes Inculta's invitation on The Strip [Zone 2D], at the end of Act I of Main Quest: Ring-a-Ding Ding! Head to Cottonwood Cove [6.20] and take the boat to this island stronghold.

Negotium I: Servo Custodis

1

2

During your visit to The Fort [3.28], after exchanging pleasantries with Caesar in his tent (**1**), speak to Vulpes Inculta, a man with many disguises. But this is the uniform he wears most proudly **2**). Steer the conversation toward whether he has a task for you. A gambler, Martina Groesbeck (who has a knack for learning other people's secrets and passing that along to the Legion) is under the watch of the Omertas (who run the iniquitous Gomorrah [2D.01] on The Strip). You're to intercede and keep her safe. She's likely to be at the Vault 21 Gift Shop [2D.06].

Find Martina Groesbeck.

Eliminate the Omerta thugs sent to kill Martina.

Negotium II: Insolitus Famulatus

3

4

5

Complete your obligations to Caesar (or Mr. House, or Yes Man) in the Securitron Vault (AKA Weather Station) before you can leave The Fort. Then travel to The Strip North Gate, and enter The Strip, moving past the large clubs toward Vault 21. Enter the premises (**3**), gazing in wonder at the pristine Vault walls and memorabilia of the Gift Shop, and then descend into the cool underground labyrinth of connecting corridors. Search for the Diner toward the middle of the Vault; Martina is likely to be in a chamber to the west.

You're greeted by an Omerta Thug, who tells you to leave while you still have legs to carry you. You can:

SPEECH 50 Inform these cretins that Martina is under the Legion's protection. The thug backs off immediately, and the goon squad leaves to talk over this interaction with their boss. Speak to Martina.

XP **50 XP**

Or, you can attack the Omerta thugs (**4**). Be very careful that your attacks don't strike Martina! Loot the corpses, then speak to Martina.

Or, you can attack everyone, and bring down Martina too, locating her Room Passcard in the process.

Or, you can tell the Omerta thugs to do whatever they want; you're here to loot the room. They make short and bloody work of Martina. You're left with little but Martina's Room Passcard to scavenge from her body.

Martina's Room Passcard

Return to Vulpes and let him know Martina's safe.

Return to Vulpes and let him that Martina is dead.

Speaking to Martina (**5**) uncovers some interesting facts. She's been feeding the NCR some information, but nothing clandestine; Martina just eavesdrops on the activities of the New Vegas families. You're left wondering why the Legion are so keen on protecting her, especially as she hates slavers.

This question is answered when you return to Caesar's tent and speak with Vulpes Inculta again:

Tell him that Martina's safe, and the Omerta thugs have left, or are dead. This buys her some time. The Quest concludes.

You can optionally tell Vulpes Inculta that Martina sold her information to Captain Curtis in the NCR (if Martina is dead, you can read about Curtis on her terminal inside Vault 21). Vulpes isn't the least bit surprised; he knows the captain well! Of course, you're now responsible for keeping this NCR infiltrator's true allegiances to yourself. This line of questioning is one way to start Side Quest: I Put a Spell on You.

Caesar's Legion Fame Gained!

XP **100 XP**

THE MOON COMES OVER THE TOWER

SUGGESTED EXPERIENCE

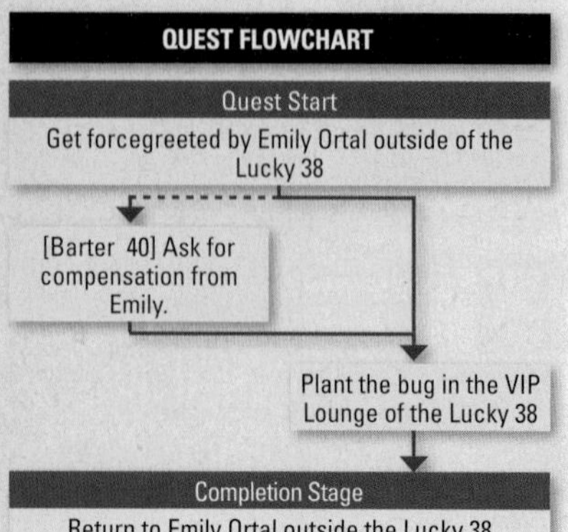

Learning About Longevity

Once you've made a name for yourself with the residents of The Strip (the easiest way to do this is by completing Main Quest: Ring-a-Ding Ding!, then speaking to Mr. House), locate the massive Lucky 38 sign [2D.02], and the nearby steps **(1)** and then the lady in the corner, who introduces herself as Emily Ortal **(2)**. She asks about your antics, then tells you that some of the Followers of the Apocalypse have been interested in Mr. House's technology; specifically how he stays alive. This is where you come in. You can:

Agree to begin the Quest.

Or agree to begin the Quest after a little compensation. She agrees to give you some medical supplies after a successful operation.

After either verbal confirmation, enter the Lucky 38.

Bug an access point to the Lucky 38's data network for the Followers of the Apocalypse.

Return to Victor, and enter the Casino level **(3)**. Case the joint, moving up the steps to the VIP lounge on the western side of the two-level Casino chamber. Close to a refrigerator, by the counter, is a terminal; it's the only one on the Casino level you can bug **(4)**. Access it and bug the network, and leave.

Return to Emily Ortal on the New Vegas strip with news that the tower has been bugged.

Back at Emily, confirm you've bugged the tower, and Emily responds that the bug was deactivated a few minutes after it went online. There are some countermeasures in place to prevent eavesdropping, but the Followers will get through eventually. Not today, however. If you Bartered for them, you receive some medical supplies, and the Quest concludes.

 **Stimpak (5)**

 **Doctor's Bag (2)**

 **Super Stimpak (2) Med-X (2)**

 **Today's Physician (2)**

 **Followers of the Apocalypse Fame Gained!**

 **500 XP**

THE WHITE WASH

SUGGESTED EXPERIENCE

See flowchart on the following page

The White Stuff

Camp McCarran [2.19] is the largest NCR stronghold in the Mojave Wasteland, and the source of a number of Quests. This one is activated a little differently. First, enter the Terminal Building **(1)** and locate

Colonel James Hsu **(2)** in his northeast ground-floor office, and speak to him at length about various matters, including the start of Side Quest: I Put a Spell on You. He mentions a lost Ranger, and that Captain Curtis has further details for this, so head across the concourse to his ground floor office to speak to him **(3)**, asking about the intelligence leaks. Curtis suggests speaking with Lieutenant Boyd or Sergeant Contreras. This is all well and good, but it doesn't start this Quest!

But Curtis did mention Lieutenant Carrie Boyd, who is interviewing a Legion prisoner in the holding cell above Curtis' office. Speak to her **(4)**, and ask if she's noticed anything suspicious. Her answers include

soldiers going AWOL, break-ins, and thefts. These lead to four separate investigations to ask about:

A missing soldier starts Free Quest: Bounty Killers, I.

A second missing soldier starts this Quest.

The break-ins start Side Quest: I Put a Spell On You.

The thefts start Free Quest: Dealing with Contreras.

Ask who is missing, and she lists Anders, a Ranger. Colonel Hsu sent him on a dangerous assignment. Ask for more information on Anders. She suggests returning to Colonel Hsu for further information. But there's a second man, Corporal White. Ask "anyone else missing?" for her to talk about White. Be sure to tell Boyd "I'll see what I can find out about Cpl. White for you," to begin this Quest. Boyd lets you know White had been in regular "contact" with a hooker named Dazzle

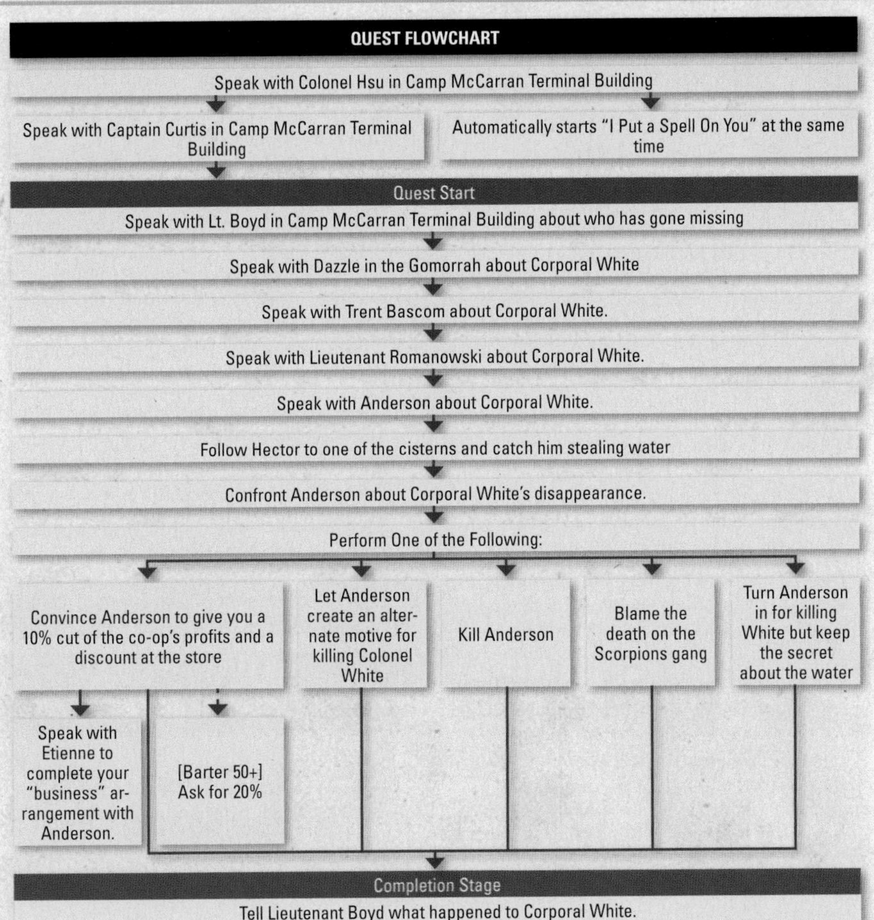

at Gomorrah Casino [2D.01]. His belongings are up in the barracks in the concourse building. That's a good place to start.

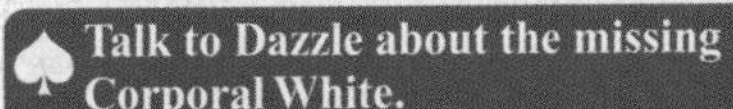

Talk to Dazzle about the missing Corporal White.

Leave Boyd and head south on the upper mezzanine floor, toward the Camp McCarran Concourse **(5)**. Step inside, and turn left as the place opens up into a wide chamber. On your left is a makeshift barracks. Inspect the first bunkbed area you see **(6)**; open Cpl. White's Locker and secure his Journal. White was investigating some odd computer read-outs from a water pump station. The evidence doesn't currently add up, so head over to find Dazzle.

Corporal White's Journal

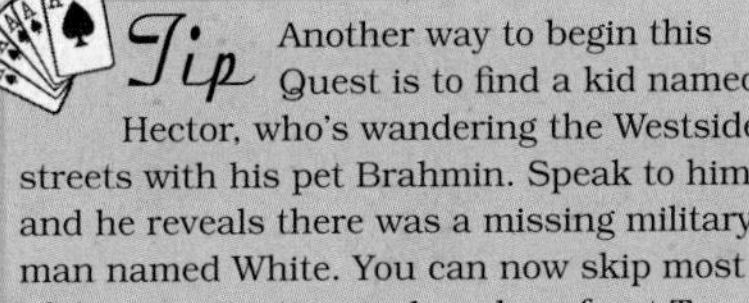

Tip Another way to begin this Quest is to find a kid named Hector, who's wandering the Westside streets with his pet Brahmin. Speak to him, and he reveals there was a missing military man named White. You can now skip most of the investigative work and confront Tom Anderson (see below).

Dazzling Conversation

Journey up through Freeside, and negotiate your entrance into The Strip [Zone 2D]. Once inside, head directly to Gomorrah **(7)**, a monument to adult pleasures. Check your weapons (all but your hold-out ones) at the door with the Omerta Thug, and head across the lobby, around the side of the elevator bank to the left, through the bar and dancing stage, to the Door to Courtyard. This leads to an open pool area, complete with palm trees, and "relaxation" tents **(8)**. Find Dazzle **(9)** along the left side of these tents. Her speech tells you she's ready for a good time, but her lifeless eyes tell a different story. You can "party" with her if you wish, but you must ask her if she spent time with a trooper named White. She says yes, but asks why. You can be pleasant or mean in your response; Dazzle tells you White used to talk about the farms east of The Strip, and a farmer named Bascom, who was having problems with the NCR.

Find out what Trent Bascom knows about Corporal White.

Crop a Load of This

Depart The Strip, and head out to the eastern Sharecropper Farms [2.20], fields of irrigated dirt **(10)**. Head over to Trent Bascom **(11)**, who is likely to be tending to his crop of maize. You can ask about his background, but speak to him about Corporal White. Apparently White was looking into a water shortage plaguing this farm, and Bascom hasn't heard back from him. The last person Bascom saw talking to White was Lieutenant Romanowski **(12)**.

Speak with Lieutenant Romanowski about Corporal White.

This NCR soldier is standing guard close to one of the Sharecropper structures. Speak with him, and you can ask a host of questions, ranging from why the NCR are guarding these fields, to the lack of water. Romanowski tells you White was "solving the mystery of the Great Water Shortage," and you can tell he wasn't buying White's conclusions. White went over to Westside [Zone 2A] to talk to a Follower of the Apocalypse called Tom Anderson.

This water shortage can't be a coincidence then, you can inform Romanowski, who's uninterested in your hypotheses.

You can also ask about the Followers, whether he's heard from White, or if he had anything against White. Romanowski thinks White is a "glory hound."

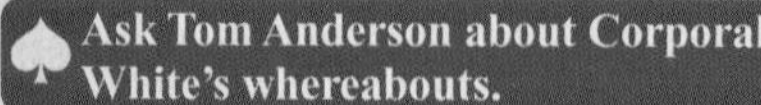

Confessions in Casa Madrid

13

14

Travel to either the Westside West Entrance [2.01] or Miguel's Pawn Shop [2.02], and search the rubble-strewn block for the entrance to the seedy Casa Madrid Apartments **(13)** [2A.01]. Pass Marco on the door, and step inside, heading around the ground floor hallway until you bump into Anderson standing near one of the rooms **(14)**. You can ask Anderson what he does, and importantly, about Corporal White. Strangely, he tells you no one by that name came around here. He seems forthcoming and pleasant. You can:

Point your finger at Anderson as the culprit to the water shortage. This immediately leads you to the "Conclusion" part of this Quest (below).

Or you can Pickpocket Anderson, and take his Confession, and confront him with it (see "Conclusion," below).

Anderson's Confession

Otherwise, you need to find somebody else in the area who was involved in White's disappearance.

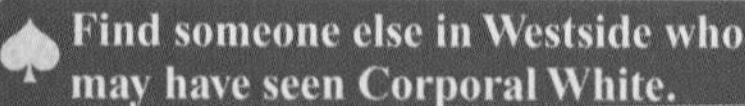

Kidding Around

15

If you didn't get the full story from Anderson, you need to find more proof. Head outside into Westside, and head east, passing Mean Sonofabitch en route to the area close to

16

Klamath Bob's Liquor Store **(15)** [2A.03] or the nearby allotments, where a little boy named Hector **(16)** is hanging around with his Brahmin pal. You can ask what he does here, as well as:

- Ask him if he knows anything about Corporal White. He stammers a response, sheepishly.

You can tell him he won't get into trouble.

You can tell him it's the right thing to do.

Or ask if he's sure he doesn't know anything. He doesn't give out any solid information, meaning you need to plan a small surveillance operation to catch the kid in the act of stealing water.

- Or, you can watch from a safe distance, and patiently follow Hector, until he eventually steals some water at the cisterns.

Follow Hector during the day and find out where he's getting his water.

In any of these cases, the evidence that Hector provides points to Anderson as the person responsible for White's disappearance. Return to the Casa Madrid Apartments and confront Anderson with this new information.

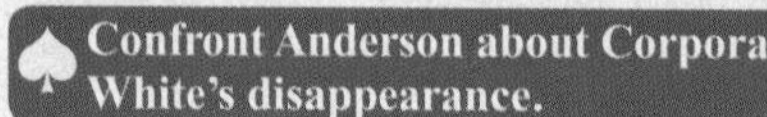

Conclusion: Westside's Water Problem

Back in the Casa Madrid Apartments, you can:

Point your finger at Anderson as the culprit to the water shortage, just as before.

Or tell him Hector revealed everything.

Anderson freely admits that he removed White to protect Westside's self-reliance. It was a rash decision that he now regrets. But what to do now? There are a few choices:

The first choice is to say you'd rather not turn him in, but someone else might come looking for him. Anderson gives you an alternate story: blame White's death on the Scorpions Gang. You can:

(A1) Agree to this, and Westside keeps getting water. And you can report back to Lieutenant Boyd.

(A2) Agree to this for a price.

If you choose the latter option, Anderson is agreeable to this and suggests a co-op with you receiving 10 percent of the profits.

Tell Anderson he can keep his profits, and you'll go with the Scorpions Gang story (A1).

Coax him into giving up 20 percent of the profits. Locate Etienne, then return to Boyd with the Scorpions Gang story (A1).

Or agree that 10 percent is fair. Check in with Etienne, then return to Boyd with the Scorpions Gang story (A1).

Or tell him it's less hassle just to murder him. Kill Anderson (A3).

Another option is to tell Anderson that he needs to answer for his crimes. He says he'll surrender as long as the water keeps flowing to Westside, and the NCR doesn't know about it. The excuse Anderson will use is that he and White fought over a woman. You can:

(A4) Agree to the deal. Anderson surrenders and you can report back to Lieutenant Boyd.

Ask what's in it for you. You can sort out a cut of profits (A2).

Tell Anderson you won't lie for him. This drives him to combat. Kill Anderson (A3).

Tell Anderson you're taking him out. This drives him to combat. Kill Anderson (A3).

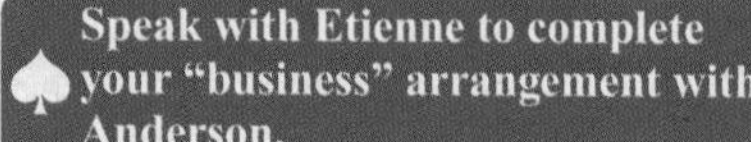

[Optional] Cooperation from the Cooperative

17

18

If you've agreed to keep quiet for a cut of the profits, you need to locate the Westside Co-op **(17)** [2A.02] and sidle up to Clayton Etienne at the counter **(18)**. Inform him of your new arrangement, and then request your "special" order from him. This is 10 percent (or 20 percent) of the profits, and you can return every two days to claim a similar amount.

Cap (~170 every 48 hours)

Tell Lieutenant Boyd what happened to Corporal White.

19

Back at Camp McCarran, return to Lieutenant Carrie Boyd, and tell her you have an update on White. Her guess (that he married a hooker) is wrong. Tell her the story you and Anderson concocted, or that he's guilty, or that you killed him (Conclusions A1, A2, A3, or A4). She's happy the case is over, and because you saved her a whole lot of extra work, you're welcome to the contents of a confiscated goods trunk **(19)** over by the prison cells across the hall. Open this now for handy items:

NCR MP Confiscated Goods Trunk Key

Boxing Times

Locksmith's Reader

Patriot's Cookbook

¡La Fantoma!

500 XP

THERE STANDS THE GRASS

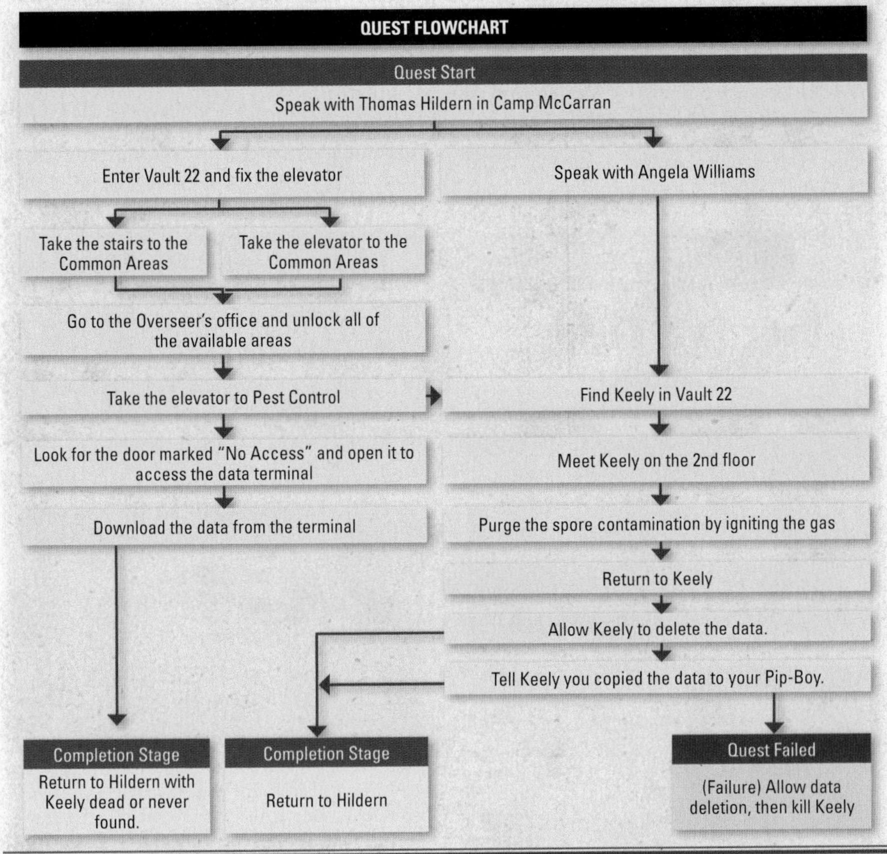

Organically Grown

Although Camp McCarran [2.19] is the NCR's largest tactical presence in the urban sprawl of New Vegas, some noncombatants work within the high walls of the sprawling compound. Head into the Terminal Building **(1)**, and reach the chamber behind the escalators in the southeast corner of the ground floor. This is where Doctor Thomas Hildern **(2)** and his assistant Angela Williams **(3)** both work for the NCR OSI. Speak to Hildern, and ask about the Office of Science and Industry; and receive a wealth of information from the director. Steer the conversation to a job offer, and Hildern mentions some research data that the doctor requires downloading from Vault 22 [1.09]. Agree to this employment opportunity.

Enter Vault 22 and download the research data found there.

Also speak to Angela Williams **(3)**. Confirm the Quest you're embarking on, and Williams tells you you're not the first person sent to the vault. There were a lot of mercs too. And none of them came back. Then there's Keely, an unusual scientist.... Williams asks if Hildern mentioned this. He didn't. Before you finish chatting, Williams says she's prepared to pay you to make sure Keely is safe. You can agree or decide not to help, and then ask Williams a lot more questions.

(Optional) Find Keely, a researcher who has gone missing at Vault 22.

Before you go, challenge Hildern for his lack of information. He doesn't think it makes any difference and lets you cancel or confirm that you're ready for the Quest. However, you can:

Demand double the Caps, or you'll spout off about him. He reluctantly agrees.

In the Weeds

Vault 22 is northwest of your current position, in the mountain foothills. As you arrive **(4)**, the place is covered in thick, lush grass, and home to a group of Giant Mantis insects. Avoid or slay them, and open the Vault Door to Vault 22. Enter the Entrance Hall and descend the steps to the junction with the elevator in front (east) of you. You can:

Inspect the elevator, which isn't working until you tinker with a nearby panel. At this point, all the vault levels are accessible. Quest-related actions are performed down on the Fourth level—Common Area. Descend there.

Or leave the elevator, and descend through Oxygen Production, Food Production, and finally to the Common Areas.

Along the way, you can optionally inspect nearby chambers, accessing terminals to discover just what bizarre experiments were being performed here. Soon enough, you encounter them yourself, such as Giant Mantises, Spore Plants, and Spore Carrier Savages **(5)**.

6

7

Once in the Common Areas level, make sure you visit the Overseer's Office **(6)**, and Activate the Terminal on the desk. You need to:

Unlock Crew Quarters.

Unlock Data Backup.

Unlock Cavern Access.

This opens the rest of the vault so you can cover all areas. Now take the elevator to the Pest Control (fifth level). Carefully work through the overgrown flora and fauna, cutting down (or Sneaking past) the carnivorous foliage **(7)**. At this point, your paths split, as you have a second, and optional way to complete this Quest and to locate Keely. Or you can continue with Hildern's original plan without searching for her.

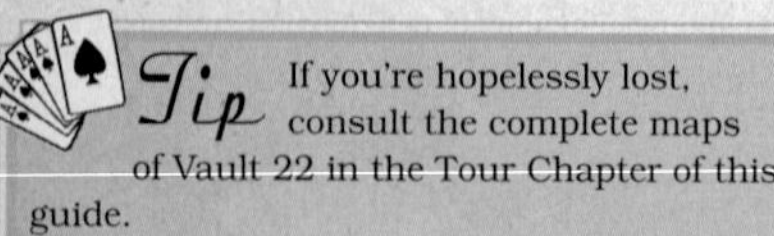

If you're hopelessly lost, consult the complete maps of Vault 22 in the Tour Chapter of this guide.

Option #1: Data Dash

8

9

Who needs Keely anyway? First, locate the door by a small corridor plant blockade with "No Access" written on it **(8)**. This leads to the data you need. Access the Terminal **(9)**, and Download Research Data. You can now leave Vault 22 and head back to Hildern; see the "Conclusion" portion of this Quest. Or, you can search for Keely, with or without this data.

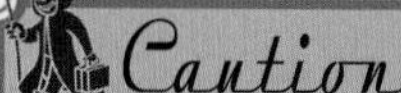

Stop! If you plan to take Veronica down here as part of Side Quest: I Could Make You Care, you need to reach this point in the Quest with her, as she needs the data as well (although you can choose another option with Veronica and visit a different location, if you wish).

Return to Dr. Hildern at Camp McCarran with the research data.

Option #2: Keely's Revenge

10

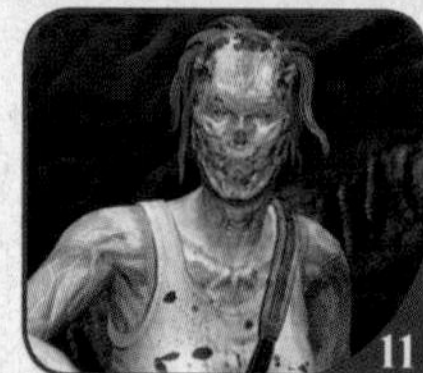

11

First, locate the door by a small corridor plant blockade with "No Access" written on it—this leads to the data Hildern needs. Then look west along the adjacent corridor for a locked door you just passed.

Pry open the door, and enter a cultivating chamber with a large hole in the northern wall. Shoot anything green and mean, and enter the rocky tunnel leading to a sprawling cave system with a giant cavern in the middle, filled with carnivorous plant life **(10)**. After some judicious pruning, sprint to the northwest edge of this huge cavern, to a small dead-end tunnel, where Keely **(11)** is waiting to be rescued.

Speak with her, and she tells you the plants in the vault have gotten completely out of control, but she's got a plan to deal with them. You can accept, refuse, or ask for payment. Keely tells you to meet her back on the second level (Oxygen Production).

Meet Keely at her base of operations on the second level.

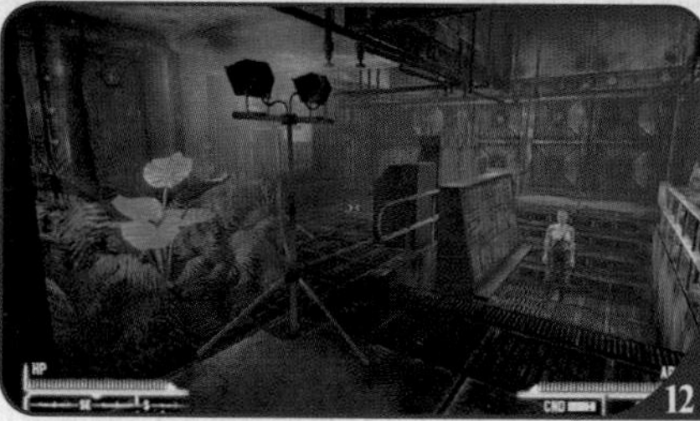

12

Follow Keely, and take the elevator (which she fixes if you haven't yet), and look for her marker on your Local Map; she heads into a lab area with UV lighting **(12)**. Speak to Keely and she asks if you're ready to begin. You can refuse, agree, or remind her of the payment. The last two options get Keely talking: She explains that the vault is filled with toxic spores, and you need to get rid of them. Keely has pumped the place full of flammable gas to counteract the spores. The only problem is that the gas must be ignited close to the leak. This sounds dangerous.

Find the vents Keely is pumping gas through and somehow ignite the gas.

Keely seems to be a firm friend, but she's very focused in her task. She locks the vault, which means you cannot leave until you've either helped ignite the gas or you kill her.

13

Battle back down to Pest Control on the fifth floor, and search out the escaping gas **(13)**, coming from a vent close to the "No Access" door, at the end of the long corridor near the cultivation room and cavern tunnel entrance. To ignite the gas without suffering horrific damage, lob Dynamite or a Grenade and step into the cultivation room so you're not struck by the rolling blast. Or you can lay down C-4 Explosives, step to a safe distance, and detonate. Or lob in a Grenade through the door then close the door so the explosion is contained.

Return to Keely and let her know the spores have been purged.

Back at the lab, inform Keely of your spore-searing success, and she's pleased, as well as being ready to complete the final part of her mission, which you should have already figured out is diametrically opposed to Doctor Hildern's. She wants the "research that led to these abominations" erased. You can:

- Allow her to delete the files.
- Yell at her to stop and not delete the files. She's startled, and asks you why. You can:

Tell her Dr. Hidern specifically sent you to find them.

Change your mind, and let her delete the files.

Or tell her that in the right hands, the files could do a lot of good. At this point, you can leave with, or without the data.

- If you already downloaded the data from the terminal, you can inform Keely that the data is copied onto your Pip-Boy. Keely isn't happy, but she can't do anything about it, unless you wipe it yourself.

Return to Camp McCarran and tell Dr. Williams that Keely is safe.

Return to Dr. Hildern at Camp McCarran with the research data.

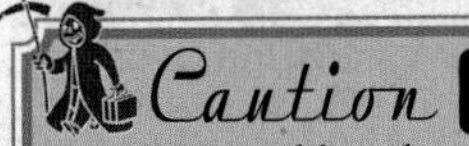

Killing Keely is just bad Karma, although you do pick up a few Frag Grenades and Keely's Password to her terminal. Finish the Quest by taking the data to Doctor Hildern. If Keely deleted the data and you kill her, the Quest fails.

Conclusions: Cap-itulation

Back at Dr. Hildern's office in Camp McCarran, you have a variety of ways to end this Quest. You can:

- Speak to the doctor, and hand him the data you brought back from Vault 22. He decodes it, and is thrilled with the result. You receive payment accordingly (regardless of your Bartering at the beginning of this Quest).

Caps (1,200)

You can shake Hildern down for more Caps, too.

And even more Caps if you succeed in a Barter or Speech check, and tell him he cut an under-the-table deal with you, and without the knowledge of the NCR.

Caps (600)

- You can tell the doctor the data isn't available. He may go all red-faced and twitchy, but there's little he can do about it. But you'll get no reward from him.
- Speak to Angela Williams about saving Keely, who awards you for keeping her friend safe.

Caps (800)

XP **1,000 XP (Hildern receives data, Keely isn't found)**

XP **1,200 XP (Keely is found, data is deleted)**

XP **1,500 XP (Keely is found, Hildern receives data)**

XP **400 XP (Keely is killed, data is deleted)**

THREE-CARD BOUNTY

SUGGESTED EXPERIENCE

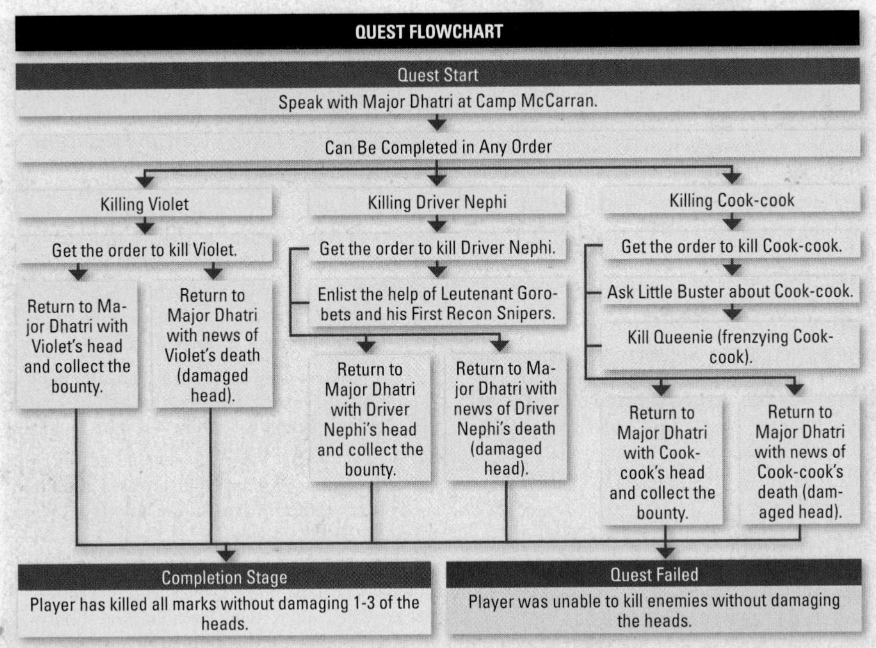

The NCR pays good Caps to Wanderers with the necessary combat skills to remove certain troublesome foes. Check in at Camp McCarran **(1)** [2.19], and visit Major Dhatri **(2)**, who's usually somewhere in the parking lot camp, or outside the doors to the Terminal Building. He's been having real problems with three Fiends nearby. He wants them dead, and he doesn't care how it's done. But he warns you: you're in for one hell of a fight. Also, no headshots. The head needs to be recognizable to Dhatri's superiors. You're taking the head back to him, by the way. Don't get careless!

Kill Violet and acquire her head—preferably intact.

Kill Driver Nephi and acquire his head—preferably intact.

Kill Cook-Cook and acquire his head— preferably intact.

Major Dhatri has bounties available. Speak to him about receiving a mission or turning in a bounty.

Just a Head's Up

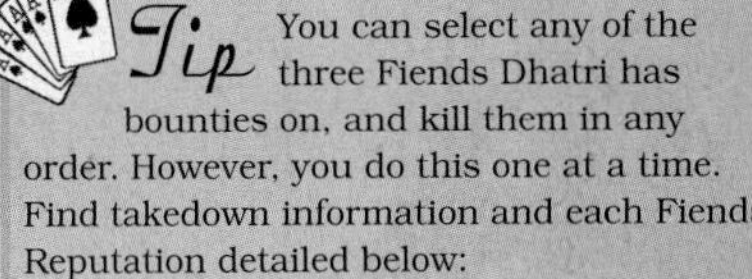

You can select any of the three Fiends Dhatri has bounties on, and kill them in any order. However, you do this one at a time. Find takedown information and each Fiends' Reputation detailed below:

Fiendish Takedown Tactics

3

4

Fiends are less than cunning but unflinchingly aggressive. You'll need to prepare for the battles ahead. Be mindful of the following before attacking the concentrations of Fiends southwest of New Vegas:

Long-range sniping is an excellent way to whittle down the ranks of the Fiends.

V.A.T.S. is particularly useful in these type of battles **(3)**, as you can ensure that no stray shots hit the bounty target's head. Fire from cover, ideally at the legs of incoming enemies to cripple them, slowing them down considerably.

Fighting at closer quarters presents more of a challenge because you're out in the open. Dart around corners and use the numerous ruined buildings as cover. You might wish to draw the enemy into a trap you've created, such as a cluster of primed Mines.

Bring along a Follower who can draw the enemy's fire, either by sniping, watching your back, or charging in while you provide the cover. But be wary of Followers (especially Boone) aiming at the heads of the Fiends you wish to defeat, which quickly ruins the greater rewards. Leave these sharpshooters behind if they become too adept!

You can't aim at the head of the specific Fiend you're tracking, but you can decapitate the others **(4)**! Just check the name before you fire.

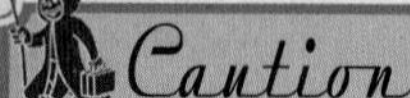
Caution: Beware! Violet, Driver Nephi, and Cook-Cook are extremely competent at spotting intruders, and will detect anyone Sneaking up to them, even with 100 Sneak skill, and with a Stealth Boy active.

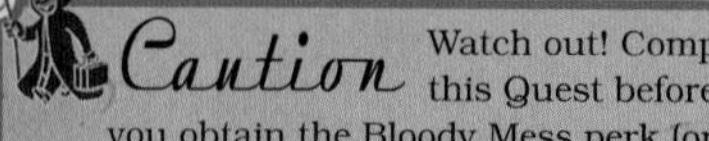
Caution: Watch out! Complete this Quest before you obtain the Bloody Mess perk (or save your game before each fight); if the shot that takes the Fiend down explodes them, the heads become damaged even if you aimed elsewhere.

WANTED: Violet

5

6

"We know less about her than the other two. Just watch out for the dogs. She raises them herself. Might as well be their mother—they never leave her side." Travel to Poseidon Gas Station [1.17], just north of the Violet and Violetta Trailer Compound **(5)** [1.S22] where Violet **(6)** makes her home. Mooch around behind the trailers, using them as cover, and destroy all the Dogs. One of these Fiend Guard Dogs is called Violetta, and she has a very special brain. Consult Side Quest: Nothin' But a Hound Dog before killing her.

This is a valuable perk during the assault on Violet's Trailer Compound; her Guard Dogs won't attack you, allowing you to defeat her much more easily and directly.

Take down Violet with any violent action except for a headshot. Don't forget to collect the head!

Violet's Head

Return to Major Dhatri with Violet's head and collect the bounty.

Speak to Major Dhatri, and hand over the head. He's pleased with the results of your hunt. Take your reward, and choose any remaining bounties.

Caps (50) (damaged head)

Caps (250) (intact head)

NCR Fame Gained!

WANTED: Driver Nephi

(Optional) Enlist the help of Lieutenant Gorobets and his First Recon snipers to take down Driver Nephi.

7

8

The optional plan has you staying in the NCR Camp that's sprung up around the terminal building **(7)** and locating Lieutenant Gorobets **(8)** sitting with Sergeant Bitter-Root in the nearby mess tent. Tell Gorobets you require his help, and he instantly agrees; they've been after Nephi for a while and there's a debt to settle.

9

10

With the First Recon Unit of snipers with you (or not; it's an optional but recommended plan), you can investigate the ruins **(9)** close to Vault 3 [2.24] where Driver Nephi and his cohorts hang out. Move there with the snipers, rather than Fast Traveling, so you all arrive together, and attempt one of the following plans:

- Run into the mass of Fiends and begin to slaughter them without a care.
- Use the cover and the various buildings, railroad tracks, burned-out vehicles, and other scenery as cover, and plug away at the foes, letting them come to you.
- Or coax the Fiends back to where the First Recon snipers are, and let them help you in the takedowns.

You must dispatch at least a dozen Fiends before you face down Driver Nephi **(10)**. Make sure you're back-pedaling (or shooting the weapon out of his hands) or you'll face a devastating attack from his Unique Melee Weapon. Once he's defeated, remove the head and the driver.

Driver Nephi's Head

Nephi's Golf Driver

Return to Major Dhatri with Driver Nephi's head and collect the bounty.

Speak to Major Dhatri, and hand over the head. He's satisfied with the evidence presented and can order the snipers down to Camp Forlorn Hope [6.02] now. Take your reward, and choose any remaining bounties.

 **Caps (50) (damaged head)**

 **Caps (250) (intact head)**

 **NCR Fame Gained!**

WANTED: Cook-Cook

(Optional) Speak with Little Buster about Cook-Cook.

11

12

This gem of a human being was almost killed by an NCR recruit named Buster (at least, according to Buster). Buster is close to one of the shacks near some parked trucks **(11)** taking his frustrations out on a Super Mutant dummy. Speak with Buster **(12)**, and you'll find out that Cook-Cook keeps a herd of Brahmin to roast whenever he's peckish, but he's grown attached to one of them. Put a bullet into that hide, and Cook-Cook might get careless with rage.

(Optional) Kill Cook-Cook's favorite Brahmin, Queenie, to cause him to go berserk and attack friends and foes alike.

13

14

Cook-Cook holds the ground close to the South Vegas Ruins West Entrance [2.23], although the Poseidon Gas Station is nearby, too. When you reach Cook-Cook's camp, try one of the following:

Your usual takedown tactics, against a half-dozen or more tough, well-armed Fiends and their leader. Distant takedowns diminish the threat of being cook-cooked alive.

 Or, you can Sneak (or dash) into camp, or snipe from a distance, and aim at the Brahmin named Queenie **(13)**. Once she's been turned to mince, Cook-Cook becomes inconsolable, stooping to look at the remains of his beloved animal. After which, you can finish the freak off **(14)**.

 **Cook-Cook's Head**

 **Incinerator**

Return to Major Dhatri with Cook-Cook's head and collect the bounty.

Back with Major Dhatri, return the head for a sizable reward (assuming it's recognizable). Then select the remaining bounties, if this isn't your last.

 **Caps (50) (damaged head)**

 **Caps (250) (intact head)**

 **NCR Fame Gained!**

Once you've turned in all three heads, Major Dhatri rewards you with additional Caps and a verbal pat on the back.

 **Caps (500)**

 **500 XP**

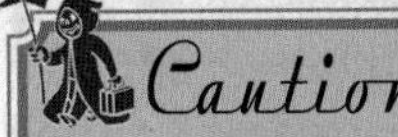

If you manage to mangle every single head, then precision warfare may not be your strongest suit. As long as one of the heads is returned, the Quest completes. If all three look like mushed offal, there's less of an XP reward, but the Quest can still be completed. Once this Quest concludes, the First Recon snipers eventually move to Camp Forlorn Hope if they survive the attack on Driver Nephi.

UNFRIENDLY PERSUASION

SUGGESTED EXPERIENCE

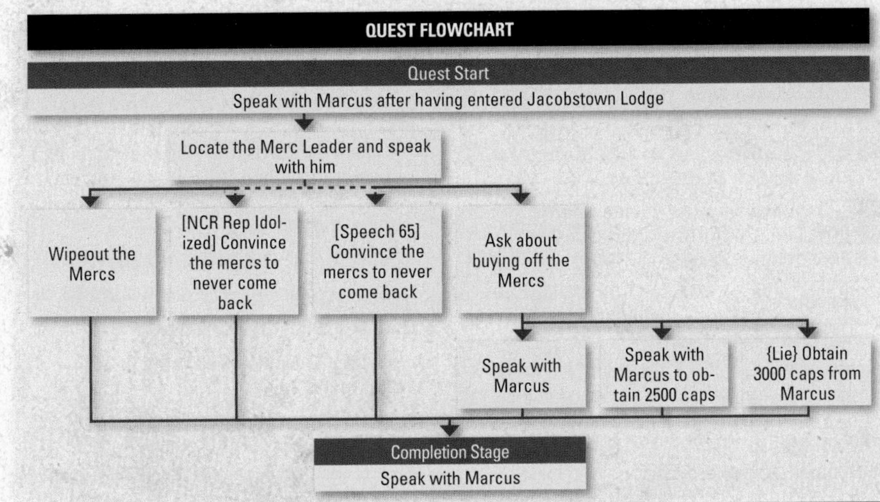

Stopping the Mutie-baiting Mercenaries

1

2

The snowy north-western mountains are home to the Super Mutant settlement of Jacobstown **(1)** [1.10], where Nightkin, friendly first-generation Super Mutants, and a strange Super Mutant named Lily live in a strange, otherworldly alliance. Head there without any murderous thoughts on your mind.

and locate one of the Super Mutants named Marcus **(2)**. He welcomes you to town, but the next time you meet, he presents you with a problem. It seems NCR mercs are harassing the town, and have shown up again, just past the perimeter. Marcus isn't sure who these intruders are aligned with, and violence will just cause the NCR to roll over their settlement. Marcus wants you to talk to them and get them to leave through persuasion or payment, with killing only as a very last resort. Agree to the task.

Speak with the leader of the mercenaries harassing Jacobstown.

Come to a peaceful arrangement with the mercenaries.

(Optional) Wipe the mercenaries out.

3

4

Travel east a few hundred feet out of Jacobstown on the remains of the road **(3)**, and you'll spot a group of well-armed humans (two on the rocks to the left, two on the right, and the leader on the road). Speak to their leader, a man named Norton **(4)**. His business is with the "muties," not you. You can:

Ask him some general questions, including finding out who's paying him.

 NEW CA. REPUBLIC Let Norton know just who he's speaking to, and your association with the NCR. Norton agrees to leave.

SPEECH 65 Threaten to deal with them, as well as the Mutants. Norton agrees to leave.

Figure that since they're mercenaries, Caps should make them go away. Norton replies that the group who hired his squad still owes him half the payment: the princely sum of 2,500 Caps. Pay up, and they'll leave. The Quest updates. You can:

Return to Marcus.

(Optional) Ask Marcus for money to pay off the mercenaries.

- Pay Norton his piffling 2,500 from your own coffers, and let him be on his way.
- Or return to Marcus, and when he asks what's on your mind, tell him:

You need 2,500 Caps to pay the mercenaries. He grudgingly hands over the funds.

Take a little off the top, and request 3,000 Caps. This will wipe out the town's treasury. But Marcus gives you the funds.

Any of these options allows a peaceful arrangement with the mercenaries to be reached.

5

NEW CA. REPUBLIC Matters can take a turn for the violent **(5)**, but only if you're particularly careless with your verbiage, or discharge a weapon in one of the mercenary's extremities. If a fight breaks out, Marcus and a Super Mutant compadre help bludgeon the humans. Judging by the Reputation you're losing, you're pretty sure you know who sent Norton and his gang now.... Loot Norton's corpse for the following two rare items:

 **NCR Infamy Gained!**

 **Mercenary Note**

 **Sunset Sarsaparilla Star Bottle Cap**

Now return to Marcus to complete the Quest. The NCR, or anybody else looking for an excuse to attack Jacobstown, won't get it from these reasonable Super Mutants.

This isn't the case if you massacred Norton and his team. Marcus is philosophical about the outcome though; at least the town coffers are full (unless you asked for the funds, and then executed Norton's team), and Marcus has time to build up the town defenses.

 **250 XP**

VOLARE!

MAIN QUEST INTERSECTION

SUGGESTED EXPERIENCE

See flowchart on the following page

Before You Begin...

Nellis Air Force Base [3.01] is an abandoned and sprawling compound now home to a Faction called the Boomers. Known for their extremely potent howitzer defenses, they are initially extremely aggressive to visitors, but they calm down and can become staunch allies once you prove your worth. Before you begin, learn the numerous ways you can approach this Quest:

There are no prerequisites to begin this Quest; it can be started at any time. However, the Factions you may be working with during the Main Quest all want to ensure Boomer support (or annihilation) for an incoming and ultimate battle. To this end, you can:

Investigate before you're embroiled in any Main Quest politicking.

 MR. HOUSE Investigate at the behest of Mr. House, during Main Quest: The House Always Wins, II.

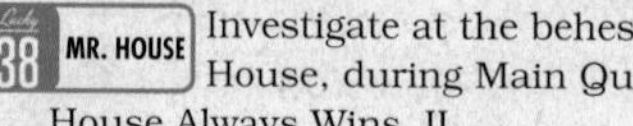 Investigate on behalf of NCR Ambassador Crocker, during Main Quest: Things That Go Boom.

 Investigate as an emissary of Caesar, during Main Quest: Render Unto Caesar.

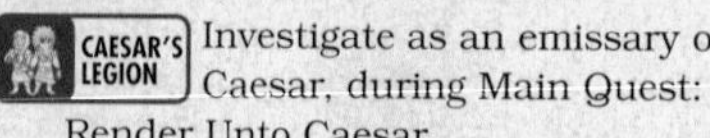 Or investigate after allying with Yes Man, during Main Quest: Wild Card: Side Bets.

It would be wise to check these Quests first, because some Faction commanders don't mind if you ally with, destroy, or ignore the Boomers.

The Boomer Quests are interrelated. First, speak with Mother Pearl to begin Side Quest: Volare! (this Quest). To complete the first part of this "overview" Side Quest, you must achieve the following:

BOOMERS Become Idolized with the Boomers. This is achieved quickly by completing tasks within this Quest, as well as three additional linked Quests associated with this Faction (which are tagged throughout the guide). You can gain reputation with Free Quests but it takes longer.

Complete Side Quest: Ant Misbehavin'.

Complete Side Quest: Sunshine Boogie.

Complete Side Quest: Young Hearts.

These three Quests are all parts of Side Quest: Volare!

You can also complete the following Free Quests for more Reputation:

Free Quest: Malleable Mini Boomer Minds and Bear Necessities

Free Quest: Iron and Stealing

Free Quest: Missing a Few Missiles

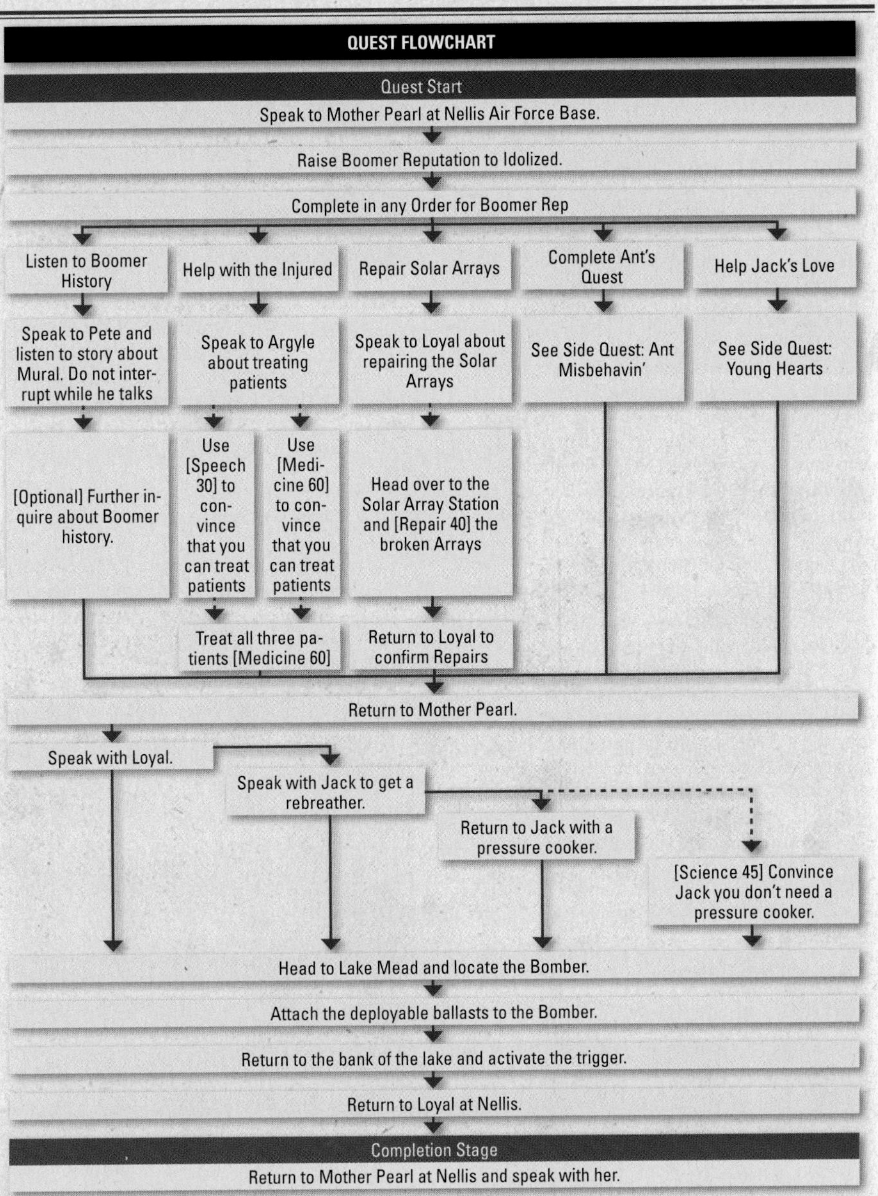

QUEST FLOWCHART

Quest Start

Speak to Mother Pearl at Nellis Air Force Base.

↓

Raise Boomer Reputation to Idolized.

↓

Complete in any Order for Boomer Rep

Listen to Boomer History	Help with the Injured		Repair Solar Arrays	Complete Ant's Quest	Help Jack's Love
Speak to Pete and listen to story about Mural. Do not interrupt while he talks	Speak to Argyle about treating patients		Speak to Loyal about repairing the Solar Arrays	See Side Quest: Ant Misbehavin'	See Side Quest: Young Hearts
[Optional] Further inquire about Boomer history.	Use [Speech 30] to convince that you can treat patients	Use [Medicine 60] to convince that you can treat patients	Head over to the Solar Array Station and [Repair 40] the broken Arrays		
	Treat all three patients [Medicine 60]		Return to Loyal to confirm Repairs		

↓

Return to Mother Pearl.

↓

Speak with Loyal. → Head to Lake Mead and locate the Bomber.

Or: Speak with Jack to get a rebreather. → Head to Lake Mead and locate the Bomber.

Or: Speak with Jack to get a rebreather. → Return to Jack with a pressure cooker. → Head to Lake Mead and locate the Bomber.

Or: Speak with Jack to get a rebreather. → [Science 45] Convince Jack you don't need a pressure cooker. → Head to Lake Mead and locate the Bomber.

↓

Head to Lake Mead and locate the Bomber.

↓

Attach the deployable ballasts to the Bomber.

↓

Return to the bank of the lake and activate the trigger.

↓

Return to Loyal at Nellis.

↓

Completion Stage

Return to Mother Pearl at Nellis and speak with her.

Highway to the Danger Zone

To reach the Boomers, trudge northeast toward the Fields' Shack [3.04]. Up ahead is a road over a rise **(1)**, and a man named George **(2)** who forces you to stop. He warns you to slow down, or you'll get blown up like the rest of the scavenging idiots heading into Boomer territory. George offers information, for a price. You can:

Threaten a kicking. George talks you out of it, but doesn't give up his instructions.

- Or, keep talking until he offers a wager: pay him 300 Caps, and he'll give you instructions on how to safely reach the Boomer base. And if you make it back, he'll pay you double! You can:

Convince him to make the wager 200 Caps.

Pay George 300 Caps.

- Or ignore George entirely, and head into the danger zone.

If you shook George down or made the bet, he hands you a note, but tells you it's all in the timing as you move from building to building.

Nellis Artillery Timing Details

Tip This note gives you all the necessary knowledge to minimize damage you'll take as the Boomers bombard you up ahead. This guide reveals all, so obviously you don't need to pay George (but he does stick around, giving you the full 600 Caps if that was the wager). Here are the highlights:

Move from building to building up the northwest side of town toward the front gate.

Stick to the high cover in the northeast corner of the two buildings.

Then make a bee-line for the gate.

The Boomers won't shoot their own people, so stick to the fence until you reach the gate.

An old tunnel enters the area from the south, but no one has returned to say it's safe.

Pearl of Wisdom

The optimal path to the Boomer's perimeter gate **(3)** is to follow the first part of the instructions to the letter; run (without your weapon drawn so you move faster) up the road, and keep left as the path widens to reveal a number of ruined houses. Head for the end of the home that's most intact, between the rocky outcrop shield to your left, and the ruins on your right. Dive into the house, and then sprint down to the fence, where the Boomers stop firing. Then edge along the fence to the front gate, where you're greeted by a guard **(4)**. After a tense talk, he tells you Raquel will arrive to deal with you.

Tip Or, you can simply run along the rock wall to the left when you reach the top of the road; you might be struck by the outer splash damage once or twice, but you won't take a direct hit.

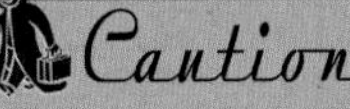

Caution Leave any Companions at George's location. If you don't, they suffer horrible damage from the howitzers (and usually die in Hardcore mode). Return for them once you have free access to Nellis.

Note At the Fields' Shack, you can head to the right, ignoring the road, and locate a railroad track. Follow that as the track sweeps around, and ends in an open area (where you must run to avoid howitzer bombardment), and a train tunnel. The entrance door is firmly locked [VERY HARD]. If you somehow manage to open this door, the tunnel is filled with Ghouls, and the opposite exit [VERY HARD] leads away from the Boomers' base. If you're approaching from the south, you can head through the tunnel, and spend some tense moments running along the remains of the track to a secondary base gate, which is unmanned and sealed tight. Edge along the fence to the gate from this point.

Raquel **(5)**, the master-at-arms for the Nellis homeland, appears and informs you that Mother Pearl wishes to speak with you. You can ask who she or Mother Pearl is before being escorted into the base. You appear inside the Nellis Air Force Base barracks where Mother Pearl **(6)** greets you with a friendly smile. You can speak with her at length about the Boomers, the area, history, and other Factions. But you should ask whether you might assist her. Mother Pearl answers vaguely. You can:

Ask how you both can trust each other if they keep secrets. Pearl answers it's because they haven't let an outsider into their homeland for decades.

Or you can get on with contacting the other members of her tribe that require assistance. You have free rein of the base, but any hostilities will be met with lethal force. Side Quest: Volare! begins. Complete the following tasks (some of which are their own Quests) in any order to become Idolized with the Boomers.

You can also begin a terrifying bloodbath, killing all the Boomers if it's in your interest, or that of your Faction patron. Expect a hard-fought and difficult battle.

Boomers Infamy Gained!

Help the Boomers around Nellis.

Note Tasks are available from Raquel, Doc Argyll, Loyal, Jack, and Pete. Find them at any time, and in any order. You can start multiple Quests at once. Also note you don't have to complete all the tasks to become Idolized.

A. and B. Raquel's Task: Missing a Few Missiles and Ant Misbehavin'.

Speak to Raquel, who is either in the barracks, patrolling the outside of the large hangars **(7)**, or standing on her reinforced spotter platform across from the main gate. Tell her Mother Pearl mentioned she had a "bug problem." She explains that the base's generator room is overrun with Giant Ants. This begins Side Quest: Ant Misbehavin'. Consult that Quest in this guide for further information.

Free Quest: Missing a Few Missiles: Ask her for other work once this Quest is over, and she tells you she'll dispense Caps if you return with quantities of Missiles for her. Naturally, these should be gathered off-base! You receive Boomer Fame for any you bring back, as well as 10 Caps per Missile.

Note: Nellis Missile Metal

Boomers Fame Gained!

C. Loyal's Task: Sunshine Boogie

Both Loyal and Jack are usually inside the first giant hangar (part of the Nellis Hangars [3.02]) northeast of Pearl's barracks. Head inside **(8)**, and speak to Loyal **(9)**. You can:

Ask him about some kind of weapon to fight Giant Ants, if Side Quest: Ant Misbehavin' is under way.

Or tell him you're here to make yourself useful. He replies that the generator building has a number of solar arrays on the roof, and they need repairing. This begins Side Quest: Sunshine Boogie. Consult that Quest in this guide for further information.

D. and E. Jack's Tasks: Iron and Stealing, and Young Hearts

Free Quest: Iron and Stealing: Both Loyal and Jack are usually inside the first giant hangar northeast of Pearl's barracks. Head inside and ask Jack **(10)** he has any work, and he tells you he'll pay you Caps if you bring him with quantities of Scrap Metal. Naturally, these should be gathered off-base! You receive Boomer Fame for any you bring back, as well as 10 Caps per Scrap Metal.

Note: Nellis Scrap Metal

Boomers Fame Gained!

Jack also has a rather personal matter, but he's reluctant to share it with you. Press him on this subject, and Side Quest: Young Hearts begins. Consult that Quest in this guide for further information.

F. Pete's Task: For Pete's Sake

To learn the (unabridged) history of the Boomers, head over to the trio of curved corrugated sheds to the northwest, and enter the Nellis Boomer Museum **(11)**. Inside, standing proudly near a large mural, is Pete **(13)**, who knows you'll be eager to hear the story of the Boomers. He's recently taken over from Don, who's dead. Say that you'd "like to know all about your people," and tell him you can spare the time. Pete gets up, and proceeds to regale you with a thrilling history of the tribe. Gaze at the mural **(12)**, and don't interrupt Pete at any time or skip anything he's saying! Otherwise, you'll have to hear it all again! Keep listening until you gain some Fame.

Boomers Fame Gained!

If you're a history buff (or glutton for punishment), you can ask Pete some additional questions afterward.

- Ask why his ancestors left the safety of the vault. Any other response is fine, but a reasoned utterance (granting you further Fame) is called for.

 Mention that any detonation with a yield of less than half a ton is boring.

 **Boomers Fame Gained!**

- Tell Pete you were surprised Nellis was empty when the Boomers found it. Then go for the following, Fame-related check:

 Surmise that the Boomers brought Geiger counters to ensure the base was safe.

 **Boomers Fame Gained!**

- Ask how the Boomers survive, if they are cut off from the world. Then mention the following Fame-related comment:

 Hypothesize that they must cultivate soy or legumes and grains too.

 **Boomers Fame Gained!**

 Hypothesizing that they must feast on human flesh results in a failed response, and no Fame reward.

- Ask what the howitzers are doing at an Air Force base. Pete replies they were dragged here. You should respond with:

 Awe; the howitzer battery is a monument to the grit and resolve of the Boomers.

 **Boomers Fame Gained!**

- Ask how Nellis has taught the Boomers to fly. Pete replies that after restoring power, they learned that some elaborate chairs they'd been sleeping in were actually VR machines. But Pete can't allow you to use them. Reply:

 "Oh, to slip the surly bonds of Earth and dance amid the soaring birds!"

 **Boomers Fame Gained!**

- Finally, ask how Pete learned where to find an old bomber. Apparently Loyal found a magazine with the information in it; the bomber crashed into Lake Mead on July 21, 1948; more than 300 years ago! Reply:

 That attaching ballasts to the plane would allow it to be hauled here for repairs.

 **Boomers Fame Gained!**

The history lesson is over. You can now continue the tasks. There's also a Snow Globe in here, so make sure you snap it up.

 **Snow Globe Nellis AFB**

Note A cabinet in the adjacent workshop contains a howitzer firing mechanism. This is critical to Lucius of the Legion. Consult Side Quest: I Hear You Knocking for more information.

G. Argyll's Task: Medical Antics

14

15

In the southwest corner are two curved corrugated sheds **(14)**, one of which is the medical station, housing Argyll and his patients. You can ask for medical treatment or supplies yourself, but you're really here to make yourself useful. Argyll **(15)** has three gravely injured patients. He asks if you have medical training:

 Reply that you do.

 Reply that you do, whether you do or not.

Now look at each Injured Boomer:

 Patient #1 has a serious infection. You can:

Leave him alone.

Treat him using your Medicine skill.

 **Boomers Fame Gained!**

 Patient #2 has a very bad leg injury. You can:

Leave him alone.

Treat him using your Medicine skill.

 **Boomers Fame Gained!**

 Patient #3 has swelling around his face and neck, and difficulty breathing. You can:

Leave him alone.

Treat him using your Medicine skill.

 **Boomers Fame Gained!**

Return to Pearl.

Arise, Oh Lady of the Lake

16

When you've done enough to earn the Boomers' trust, return to Mother Pearl, who is pleased with your progress. Although she won't commit troops to a forthcoming battle, she does believe the time has come for you to show your value in full. You're to find Loyal.

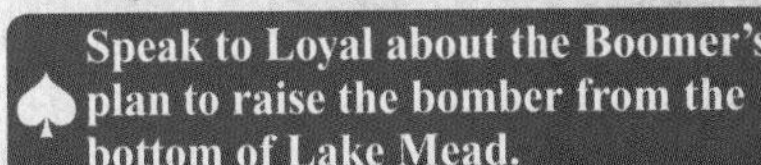
Speak to Loyal about the Boomer's plan to raise the bomber from the bottom of Lake Mead.

Find Loyal in his usual haunt: the hangar interior **(16)**. He says it's time to tell you about the Lady in the Water, a Crashed B-29 Bomber [3.26] that lies at the bottom of Lake Mead. The plan is to attach ballast to the plane, lifting it up to the surface using a Detonator (which you're handed). If you ask about getting to the bottom of Lake Mead without drowning, he suggests you speak with Jack (who's likely to also be in the hangar).

 **Deployable Ballast (2)**

 **Detonator**

Attach the ballast from Loyal to the B-29 at the bottom of Lake Mead.

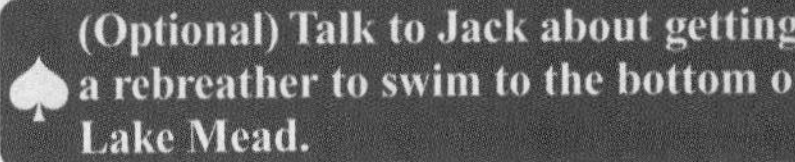
(Optional) Talk to Jack about getting a rebreather to swim to the bottom of Lake Mead.

Speak with Jack, and say Loyal mentioned he could help you breathe under water. Jack agrees, but says he needs some parts from a pressure cooker to create a hermetic seal for the rebreather.

(Optional) Jack needs some parts from a pressure cooker to finish his rebreather.

You can:

Leave the base, and return with a pressure cooker salvaged on your travels.

 Note that corn silk, a rubber hose, and removable adhesive would work, too. He agrees, and completes the rebreather using your idea, and hands it over.

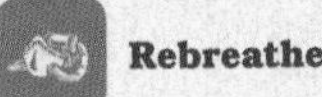 **Rebreather**

Or you can ignore this, and hold your breath when you begin to dive.

The Plane Truth: Boomers Allied

Leave the Boomers' base, and travel to Lake Mead. Callville Bay [3.18] is the closest shoreline to the B-29 bomber, so head there, watching for Cazadors to kill. Leap from the jetty into the water, and from Callville Bay harbor **(17)**, swim south on the surface of Lake Mead, peering down until you spot the wreckage of the plane **(18)**. Dive down, and attach both the ballasts, one under each wing. If you aren't wearing the rebreather, surface as soon as you run out of oxygen to minimize health loss.

♠ Return to the shore near the tow winch and use Loyal's detonator to float the B-29 to the surface.

Swim back to the concrete pier **(19)** on the Callville Bay shoreline, and listen for Loyal's Detonator to begin to beep as you near a large harpoon winch. When you hear the beeping, produce the Detonator (it is in your Weapons inventory) and activate it. The B-29 rises to the surface, amazingly intact!

♠ The B-29 is up from the bottom of the lake, return to Loyal to let him know.

Head back to the hangar at Nellis Air Force Base, and tell Loyal that the operation was a success. He's thrilled and tells you to meet up with Mother Pearl again. You can optionally ask how he's going to get the plane back here, and he tells you that his robots are going to handle it. You can bid him farewell, or:

Mention that others will be looking for this plane, and that diversionary tactics are likely to be used to draw enemy attention away from this find. Loyal concurs.

♠ Loyal is going to start recovering the B-29, let Pearl know your job is done.

Pearl is in her barracks, or wandering the base. Let her know the B-29 is on the way, and she's thrilled, calling this news "a miracle." You're now considered a trusted friend. At this point, you can ask if they'll assist in the upcoming battle at Hoover Dam. Mother Pearl agrees that she'd be happy to lend her support to you, and whatever benefactor you're currently scheming with. The Quest ends with you receiving some Unique gifts as an honorary Boomer. Consult Act III of the Main Quest for the other, more bombardment-based gifts they bring.

 **Boomers Fame Gained!**

 **Boomers Flightsuit**

 **Boomers Helmet**

400 XP

WANG DANG ATOMIC TANGO

SUGGESTED EXPERIENCE

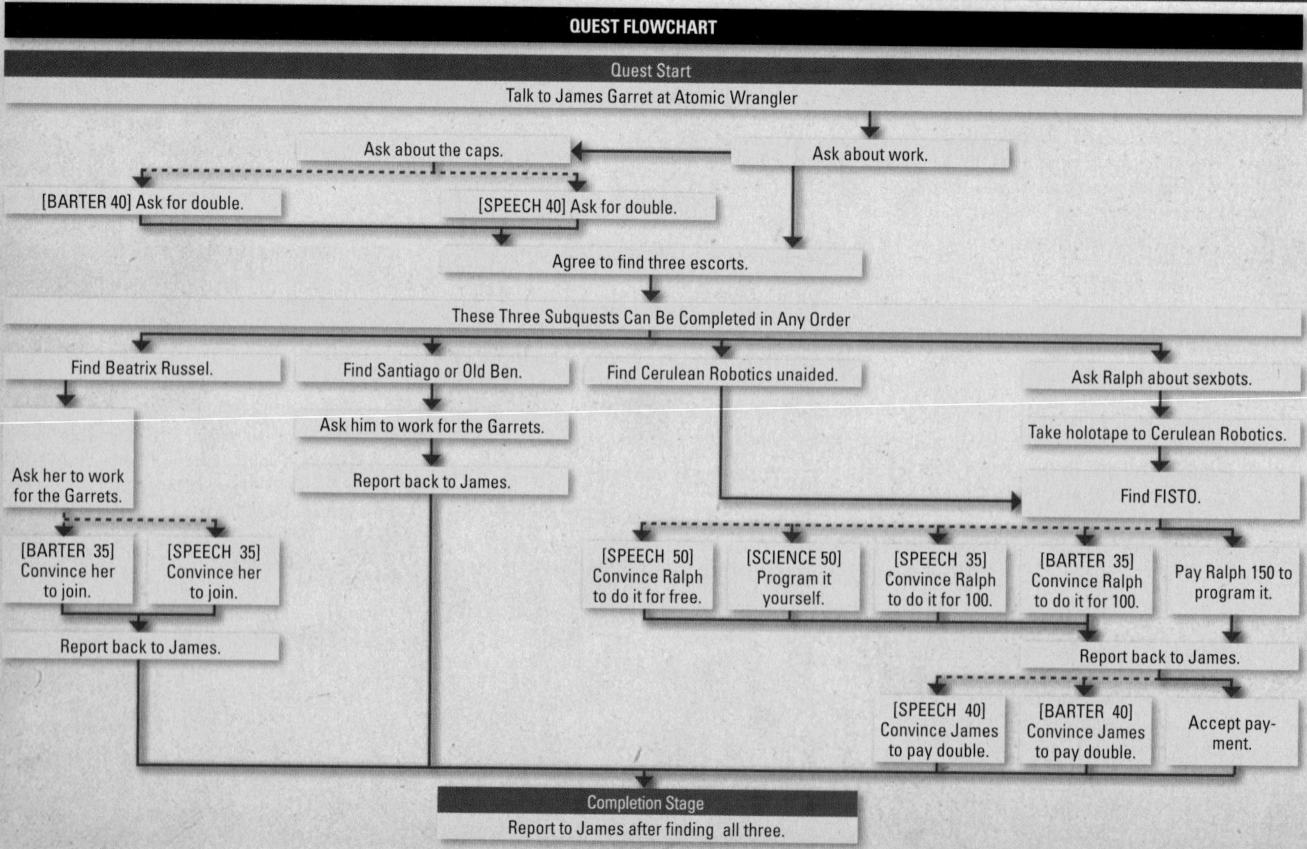

QUEST FLOWCHART

Quest Start

Talk to James Garret at Atomic Wrangler

- Ask about work.
  - Ask about the caps.
    - [BARTER 40] Ask for double.
    - [SPEECH 40] Ask for double.
- Agree to find three escorts.

These Three Subquests Can Be Completed in Any Order

- Find Beatrix Russel.
  - Ask her to work for the Garrets.
    - [BARTER 35] Convince her to join.
    - [SPEECH 35] Convince her to join.
  - Report back to James.
- Find Santiago or Old Ben.
  - Ask him to work for the Garrets.
  - Report back to James.
- Find Cerulean Robotics unaided.
  - Find FISTO.
- Ask Ralph about sexbots.
  - Take holotape to Cerulean Robotics.
  - Find FISTO.
    - [SPEECH 50] Convince Ralph to do it for free.
    - [SCIENCE 50] Program it yourself.
    - [SPEECH 35] Convince Ralph to do it for 100.
    - [BARTER 35] Convince Ralph to do it for 100.
    - Pay Ralph 150 to program it.
  - Report back to James.
    - [SPEECH 40] Convince James to pay double.
    - [BARTER 40] Convince James to pay double.
    - Accept payment.

Completion Stage

Report to James after finding all three.

Escort-Recruiting Ain't Effortless

1

2

James Garret, along with his twin sister Francine, is the co-owner of the Atomic Wrangler Casino **(1)** [2C.06]. Visit this den of iniquity in Inner Freeside [Zone 2C] and speak with Francine, beginning Side Quest: Debt Collector (check out Santiago's recruitment, below). James **(2)** is stationed behind or around the lobby bar counter. As well as asking about the other "services" the hotel provides, quiz him on whether he has any work that needs doing. He mentions some "unusual requests" from some of his wealthier customers. You're tasked with recruiting escorts to match these "proclivities," without roughing up any of them. You can:

- Agree to the work.
- Tell James you'll expect 100 Caps minimum for each candidate you bring in. James agrees. You can:

Agree to the work.

Inform him that these escorts are critical to his business, and you want double. James agrees.

Tell him your travel and other costs mean you need double. James agrees.

If you ask James where the hell a "sexbot" is likely to be found, he directs you to Ralph, over at the store he shares with his associate, Mick.

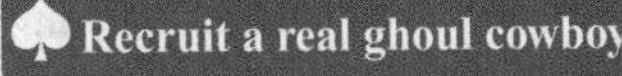

Recruit a real ghoul cowboy.

Recruit a suave talker.

Recruit a sexbot.

Note Side Quest: Talent Pool also involves James Garret, who owns the contract to the Ghoul comedian Hadrian, also on the premises. Ask James about Hadrian if this Quest is active.

Escort 1 (Option A): The Suave-Talking Old Ben

3

4

Your nearest recruit is standing close to the Securitrons at the entrance to The Strip, in Freeside **(3)**. Locate Old Ben **(4)**, who provides information to you prior to you interacting with the robots guarding The Strip entrance. During your talks, Old Ben lets slip that he's had a variety of jobs, from gun-for-hire to butcher. One of them was an escort. Ask Old Ben if he'd like to work for the Garrets. The job is a "real boyfriend experience" for more discerning patrons. Ben asks why you think he'd go back to that kind of degradation:

Reply that he's a work of art, shining a beacon of light into the depressing existence of others. He buys your line.

Reply that he gives clients a precious respite from the ills of the world. He buys your sweet-talking.

Reply that the pay's good and he can make his own hours. This fails to entice Old Ben.

Or you can ignore Old Ben and try talking to Santiago.

Tell James Garret Old Ben will be joining the Wrangler.

Escort 1 (Option B): The Sultry Santiago

5

6

Around the blown-out building in the southeast corner of Outer Freeside **(5)** [Zone 2C] is a squatter camp with a rather well-put-together gent standing close by **(6)**. Assuming you have started both this and Side Quest: Debt Collector, you can ask Santiago whether he'd be interested in becoming an escort. Negotiations become extremely fluid soon afterward, as Santiago agrees immediately, and races off to see James; Francine's debts are forgiven. This is an easier option than Old Ben, but means you can't shake Santiago down for his debt, because he'll now be using other methods.

Tell James Garret Santiago will be joining the Wrangler.

Tip You can choose either Santiago or Old Ben, but not both.

Escort 2: A Real Ghoulfriend Experience

7

8

James Garret requested a male Ghoul cowboy willing to submit to degrading pleasures, but finding one is impossible. In fact, the only Ghoul sporting an old western get-up is Beatrix Russell **(8)**, inside the Mormon Fort [2C.01] **(7)**. Locate and speak to her, and after the pleasantries, ask if she's "interested in working for the Garrets." She replies "that pig" McCaffery is working as a guard there already. Continue to press upon her that her role would be less "guard," and more "prostitute" until she understands "weirdos into bullwhips and necrosis" is a fetish Garret can get behind. But Beatrix "ain't no whore," and needs convincing:

Rattle off some guff about her being independent, and having a deep discount on the hotel booze. She agrees.

Tell her she'd have a discount on room rates, booze, and other alcohol. She agrees.

Any other verbal recourse results in Beatrix being interested, but not enough to pursue this option.

Tell James Garret Beatrix will be joining the Wrangler.

Escort 3, Part 1: Finding FISTO: The Tradesman's Entrance [Optional]

9

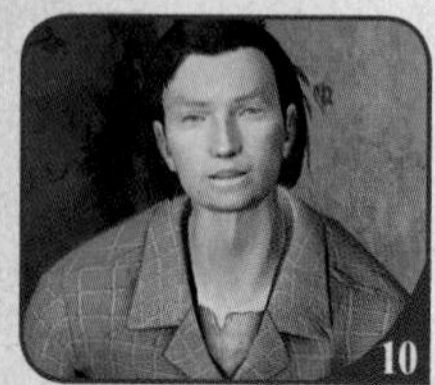

The "sexbot" may be the trickiest of all to source. There are two methods (Part 1 or 2); you'll find your next clue if you visit Mick & Ralph's **(9)** [2C.02] in Freeside, and speak to Ralph **(10)**. He responds to your request with a smile, replying that Cerulean Robotics is the only place he knows about, but it's been overrun with vermin for years. He tells you where the place is (see Part 2). You can:

- Thank him, and try to find the place (see Part 2).
- Or, you can ask him if there's "a Holotape or anything" you need to reprogram the sexbot. Ralph replies he could manufacture one, but it would take "a few days and some Caps." You can:

Tell him data modules are useless, and drive down the price of his work to 100 Caps.

Inform him that you've been a loyal customer (even if this is your first time here). He agrees to 100 Caps.

Let Ralph know you've been steering business his way (even if you haven't). He agrees to program it for free, as a favor to you.

- Or you can pay the man his asking price.

Whatever monies you part with, the Holotape won't be ready for two entire days. Return (or wait) until you can ask about the Holotape again, and procure it from Ralph. A terminal is required to upload the data into a robot.

Ralph's Sexbot Holodisk

Escort 3, Part 2: Finding FISTO: Backdoor Antics

Cerulean Robotics, one of the many abandoned buildings in the Freeside area, is in the rarely tracked western side, and the entrance is, as Ralph puts it; "on the back side of the building" **(11)**. You can find this location, and enter with or without Ralph's help. Inside the structure, tag any aggressive Rats, then move to the northeast corner, where two Protectron robots are standing, motionless. One of them—marked "FISTO"—needs to be reprogrammed, and woken up.

This is achieved via the Protectron Programming Interface, on the wall to the left. This also allows you to ignore Ralph's Holotape plan if you have a competent-enough Science skill.

Or you can use the Holotape Ralph provided for you, which has a bypass for this terminal.

Escort 3, Part 3: Fiddling with FISTO

There are two way to power up FISTO **(12)**:

You can program the Sexbot Routine yourself, from the Programming Interface next to the robot.

Or, you can upload Ralph's Sexbot Routine once you've spoken to Ralph, waited for the routine to be made, and taken it from Ralph.

The Fully Integrated Security Technetronic Officer creaks into life. After shortening that name to "FISTO," the robot orders you to "assume the position." You can:

Immediately halt the robot's advances.

Or, you can take one for the team, and test out the robot's "enhancements" before handing it over to the Garrets.

Whether engagement was cancelled or encouraged, inform the robot that James Garret is its new owner. Then walk (or hobble) back to see James at the Atomic Wrangler.

Tell James Garret FISTO will be joining the Wrangler.

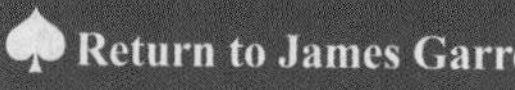

Return to James Garret.

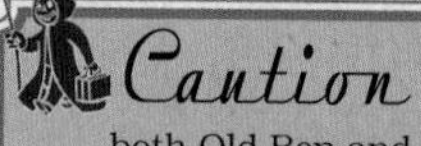

Caution: If you have an itchy trigger-finger and both Old Ben and Santiago die, the Quest fails. You can still complete the Quest if either one of them survives, since you're only required to recruit one of them.

Sleazy Money: Finishing Off with James

Garret can be approached after each escort is hired, or once all of the necessary escorts are found:

Whether you've found Santiago or Old Ben, James is happy and rewards you with 50 (or double) Caps.

When you inform James you've found a Ghoul cowboy, you tell him Beatrix is female. James doesn't mind (and the customer might not even notice the difference). You're rewarded with 50 (or double) Caps.

Reporting that you've procured a sexbot sends James into a beaming tizzy. Play on this enthusiasm:

Make sure he knows FISTO is heavy-duty, and built to last.

Tell James this wasn't a cakewalk. With either successful check, you're paid double, on top of your original finder's fee (50 + 50 Caps, or 100 + 100 if you doubled the finder's fee).

Or you can simply tell Garret the robot is already programmed to respond to commands. After more than a little giddiness, Garret settles with you (for the original, agreed amount of 50 or double).

150–400 Caps

450 XP

WE ARE LEGION

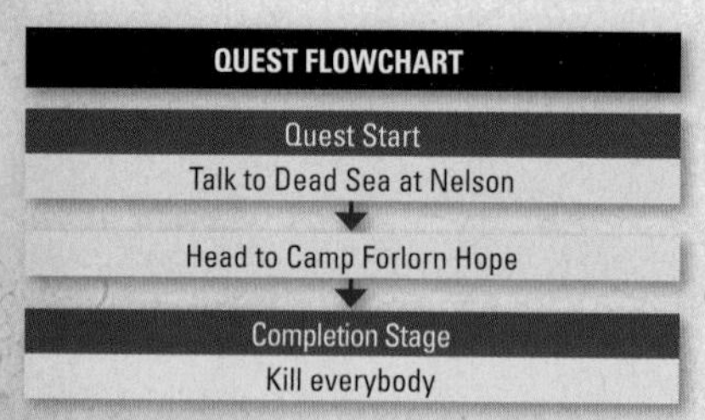

Dead Sea Scolds

The *Evocati* (veteran soldier) in charge of tying NCR soldiers to crucifixes in the overrun town of Nelson **(1)** [6.06] is a feather-helmed man named Dead Sea **(2)**. As long as you're not Shunned or Vilified by the Legion, you can venture into Nelson without being attacked. Speak to a guard to receive an escort to Dead Sea's location, or hang around at the crucifixes long enough, and Dead Sea shows up. Converse with this psychotic to learn that his battle tactics include a whole lot of melee hacking. When you've heard enough (or before you piss him off), ask Dead Sea if you can help "the stalemate," and Dead Sea tells you to attack Camp Forlorn Hope all by yourself. Well?

Kill all NCR Officers at Camp Forlorn Hope

Caution You'd better be *extremely* sure of which side you're on if you want to complete this Quest! Attacking Camp Forlorn Hope Vilifies you in the eyes of the NCR, and you're shot at on sight by their troops!

Camp No Hope

Attacking Camp Forlorn Hope **(3)** [6.02] requires some degree of forethought, planning, and weaponry. The following possibilities are mainly beneficial to your survival and standing within the Legion:

Kill Everybody

Charge in, carrying your most ferocious-looking weapon, and butcher anything wearing a brown uniform. Don't stop until they're all dead, or you are. This plan is unsubtle and highly dangerous, but the items you can loot from corpses almost outweighs the healing items you'll use up.

Kill Everybody With a Modicum of Skill

The high ground on the west side of the camp is a perfect place to crouch and tag the perimeter guards with a Sniper Rifle. Then you can descend to the rooftops, using the height (and cover) to your benefit, tagging more foes, before dropping to the ground and finishing the stragglers.

The Silent Assassin

Use a Stealth Boy or your Sneak skill to enter the camp, then employ as many Sneak Attacks as you can on the troops to buy some time before you're discovered. Remember you can retreat to the rocky ridge if you're in danger of being swarmed.

Waiting until many of the officers are sleeping and then murdering them in their sleep thanks to the Mister Sandman perk is always a valid assassination tactic.

Vilified Stealth

You can still enter the camp, even if your Reputation with the NCR is Vilified due to past atrocities. However, you must avoid the MPs, and any Dogs that detect you. Should this occur, your only options are to attack or flee.

The Orbital Drop Shock

If you've found Euclid's C-Finder (as part of Side Quest: I Could Make You Care), you can launch orbital strikes from a distance, which is as entertaining as it sounds!

Cutting Off the Hydra Heads

Sometimes, reading your Pip-Boy Objective pays dividends. Dead Sea doesn't mind if you slaughter everybody, but your actual task is a surgical strike, decapitating (literally, if you want) the four camp officers.

You can wade in, with all guns (or golf clubs) blazing.

Better yet, you can enter with four C-4 Explosives and a Detonator (Grenades or Mines work, too), and Pickpocket each officer, placing C-4 on their person without being seen. Once all four have Explosives on them, press the Detonator and retreat. Minimal bloodshed, and maximum NCR demoralization!

Your primary targets are Dr. Richards **(4)**, usually found in the Medical Center; Quartermaster Carl Mayes **(5)**, located in his own tent; Tech Sergeant Reyes **(6)**, and Major Polatli **(7)**, both found in the Command Center. If they're not in these locations, find them sleeping in a nearby tent (making an execution by explosives an even-easier option.

Tip Don't forget to loot the camp afterward!

Caution Completing these killing Objectives always results in you being Vilified in the eyes of the NCR, unless your attack is completed without detection; then no one knows who mysteriously killed the officers of Camp Forlorn Hope, and your Reputation remains unchanged! If you were Idolized by the NCR, and then massacre everyone in plain sight, your Reputation changes to "Wild Child."

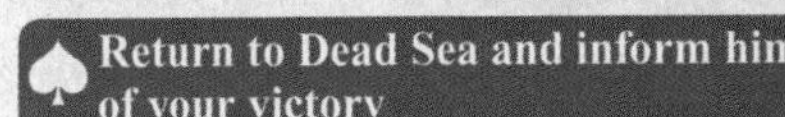

Return to Dead Sea and inform him of your victory

Liberator of the Legion!

When the four intended victims (or everyone in the camp) have succumbed to your bloodlust, return to Nelson and confront Dead Sea, boasting of your successful slaughter. He doesn't quite have the bark he once had, and he tells you he'll send word of your achievement. He then gives you his Machete, his own blade. He must now perform a similar deed to earn such a weapon. Take the Liberator or leave it, with or without a cutting remark to finish.

 **NCR Infamy Gained! (No change if undetected)**

 **Caesar's Legion Fame Gained!**

 **Liberator**

 **300 XP**

WE WILL ALL GO TOGETHER

SUGGESTED EXPERIENCE

QUEST FLOWCHART

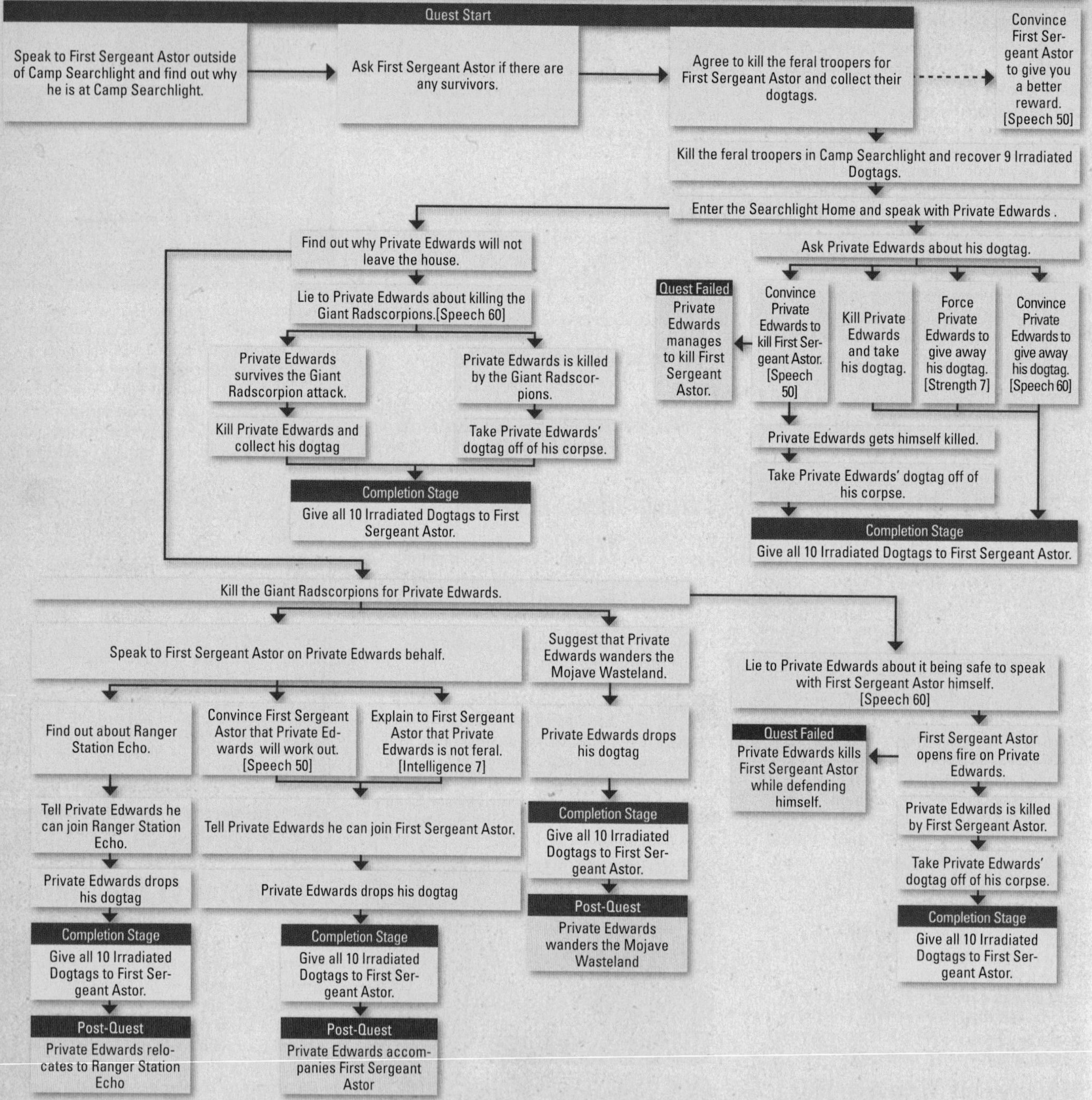

Quest Start

Speak to First Sergeant Astor outside of Camp Searchlight and find out why he is at Camp Searchlight.

Ask First Sergeant Astor if there are any survivors.

Agree to kill the feral troopers for First Sergeant Astor and collect their dogtags.

Convince First Sergeant Astor to give you a better reward. [Speech 50]

Kill the feral troopers in Camp Searchlight and recover 9 Irradiated Dogtags.

Enter the Searchlight Home and speak with Private Edwards .

Ask Private Edwards about his dogtag.

- Convince Private Edwards to kill First Sergeant Astor. [Speech 50]
  - **Quest Failed**: Private Edwards manages to kill First Sergeant Astor.
  - Private Edwards gets himself killed.
  - Take Private Edwards' dogtag off of his corpse.
- Kill Private Edwards and take his dogtag.
- Force Private Edwards to give away his dogtag. [Strength 7]
- Convince Private Edwards to give away his dogtag. [Speech 60]

Completion Stage: Give all 10 Irradiated Dogtags to First Sergeant Astor.

Find out why Private Edwards will not leave the house.

Lie to Private Edwards about killing the Giant Radscorpions.[Speech 60]

- Private Edwards survives the Giant Radscorpion attack.
  - Kill Private Edwards and collect his dogtag
- Private Edwards is killed by the Giant Radscorpions.
  - Take Private Edwards' dogtag off of his corpse.

Completion Stage: Give all 10 Irradiated Dogtags to First Sergeant Astor.

Kill the Giant Radscorpions for Private Edwards.

Speak to First Sergeant Astor on Private Edwards behalf.

- Find out about Ranger Station Echo.
  - Tell Private Edwards he can join Ranger Station Echo.
  - Private Edwards drops his dogtag
  - **Completion Stage**: Give all 10 Irradiated Dogtags to First Sergeant Astor.
  - **Post-Quest**: Private Edwards relocates to Ranger Station Echo
- Convince First Sergeant Astor that Private Edwards will work out. [Speech 50]
- Explain to First Sergeant Astor that Private Edwards is not feral. [Intelligence 7]
  - Tell Private Edwards he can join First Sergeant Astor.
  - Private Edwards drops his dogtag
  - **Completion Stage**: Give all 10 Irradiated Dogtags to First Sergeant Astor.
  - **Post-Quest**: Private Edwards accompanies First Sergeant Astor

Suggest that Private Edwards wanders the Mojave Wasteland.

- Private Edwards drops his dogtag
- **Completion Stage**: Give all 10 Irradiated Dogtags to First Sergeant Astor.
- **Post-Quest**: Private Edwards wanders the Mojave Wasteland

Lie to Private Edwards about it being safe to speak with First Sergeant Astor himself. [Speech 60]

- First Sergeant Astor opens fire on Private Edwards.
  - **Quest Failed**: Private Edwards kills First Sergeant Astor while defending himself.
  - Private Edwards is killed by First Sergeant Astor.
  - Take Private Edwards' dogtag off of his corpse.
  - **Completion Stage**: Give all 10 Irradiated Dogtags to First Sergeant Astor.

First Sergeant: Last Men Standing

1

2

The irradiated town and NCR base known as Camp Searchlight [6.16] is now a horrific shell, with roaming Feral Ghouls, still clad in their NCR uniforms. A small camp just beyond the western perimeter of the town's radiation signs **(1)** contains a squad of soldiers led by First Sergeant Astor **(2)**. Ask him about the incident, and begin Side Quest: An Eye for an Eye. Not only does Astor want revenge,

but he tells you he was stationed at Camp Searchlight before the incident. Ask him if there were any other survivors, and he mentions his ex-teammates, now slobbering Feral Ghouls. He hasn't the heart to execute him, but wonders if you could do the humane thing, and put them down. They deserve a clean death. You need to return with their Dogtags to show you've done the deed. Astor offers some Caps for each Dogtag, and "an old rifle" if you bring in at least 10. You're given something to offset the radiation in the area, too.

Bargain with Astor to increase your reward.

Rad-X (2)

RadAway (2)

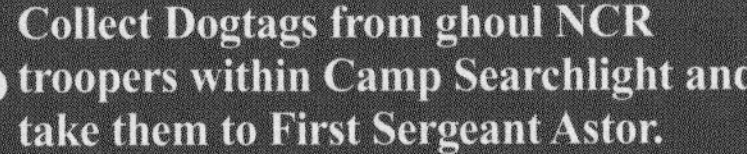
Collect Dogtags from ghoul NCR troopers within Camp Searchlight and take them to First Sergeant Astor.

Although Astor mentions "at least" 10 Dogtags to find, there are only 10 in the Camp Searchlight area, and they're different from regular NCR Dogtags because they're "irradiated." You can't simply go off, cull some NCR soldiers, and return with their identification! Instead, move forward into the township, and spend the next few minutes thoroughly searching the streets for Ghouls. Cull them all, but pay special attention to those wearing NCR uniforms. Search every one, and although you don't find Irradiated Dogtags on every corpse, you should find nine. Having trouble finding them all? Here's where to look:

Cross the bridge, and tackle a group of Ghouls close to the Police Station **(3)**.

Some usually lurk on or near the main crossroads by the Fire Station **(4)**.

Don't forget the Ghouls close to the chapel and NCR storage area on the west side of town **(5)**.

Don't overlook a couple of foes near the turrets on the far east side of town **(6)**.

Other Dogtags: Although these are the usual locations, you may not find all nine Dogtags from these Ghouls due to them (for example) begin slain and looted before you arrive here. If you're short on Dogtags, search the dwellings in and around town, and locate any additional bodies in there, to bring your total up to a minimum of nine (or 10 if you don't want to deal with Private Edwards).

Irradiated NCR Dogtag (9)

Saving (or Slaying) Private Edwards

Another elusive Dogtag is around the neck of an NCR soldier sitting in despair, inside a Searchlight Home **(7)** close to the west-side chapel. Enter the house and confront the final irradiated soldier: Private Edwards **(8)**. You can:

Fire on, or otherwise kill Private Edwards, and obtain his Dogtags.

Or you can try Pickpocketing the private, and grab the Dogtags.

Or begin a conversation (which you can end by killing him at any point). He introduces himself as Private Kyle Edwards. He's still a competent soldier, but after the irradiation, he'll be shot at by his former colleagues before he can explain he's not a threat. You can have a long conversation about him, but to aid him and progress this Quest, tell him you've noticed he's wearing an NCR Dogtag. At this point, you can:

- Ask for the Dogtag, which he won't give up:

Tell him his humanity is a part of him, and not the Dogtag. He gives it up.

Order him to give you the Dogtag. He gives it up.

Or tell him there's an NCR soldier outside who wants you to kill him for it. Tell him it's because he thinks Edwards is suffering. After that you can the change conversation, or:

Coax him into killing Astor. He agrees and leaves the home. At this point, he may be savaged by Radscorpions, shot by you, or (eventually) shot by Astor or his team. If Astor dies, the Quest fails; so prevent this!

You can also ask "there must be someplace you can go." Edwards says he's afraid of the radiation. Ask if that's "the only thing you're afraid of," and Edwards admits he's scared of Radscorpions, too. At this point, you can:

- Lie to Edwards about having killed all the Radscorpions. Thinking it is now safe to leave, Edwards departs, and is set upon by these monsters.

  He can die, and you can loot the Dogtag.

  He can survive, and you must kill him, and loot the Dogtag.

- Head outside, kill every last Radscorpion, and return to Edwards, and explain the eradication.

Edwards still won't leave the house. Return to First Sergeant Astor, and explain Edwards' predicament. Although Astor would shoot him on sight, he tells you there's a Ranger Station north of here that might be interested in taking him in; they have Ghouls there too. Tell Edwards this, and he hands you his Dogtag, and sets off for Ranger Station Echo.

Irradiated NCR Dogtag

All ghoul Dogtags found, return to First Sergeant Astor.

When the Private Edwards situation has been resolved, return to First Sergeant Astor, and cash in your Dogtags. You can do this at any time. You're given Caps per Dogtag, and a larger reward when Astor has all 10.

Caps (25) (per Dogtag)

Caps (250) (for 10th Dogtag)

Service Rifle and Ammo (for 10th Dogtag)

25 XP (per Dogtag)

100 XP (for 10th Dogtag)

WHEEL OF FORTUNE

SUGGESTED EXPERIENCE

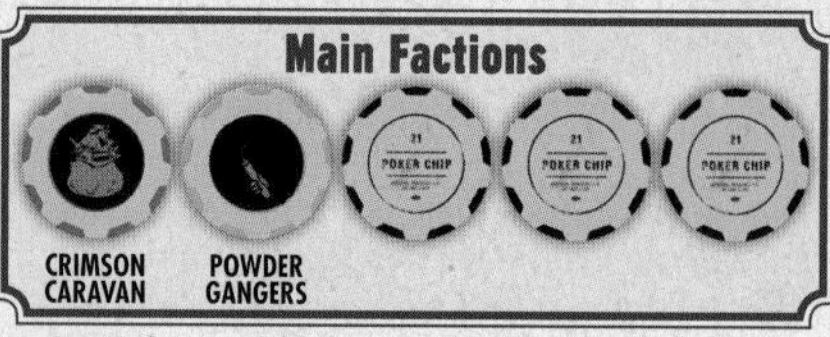

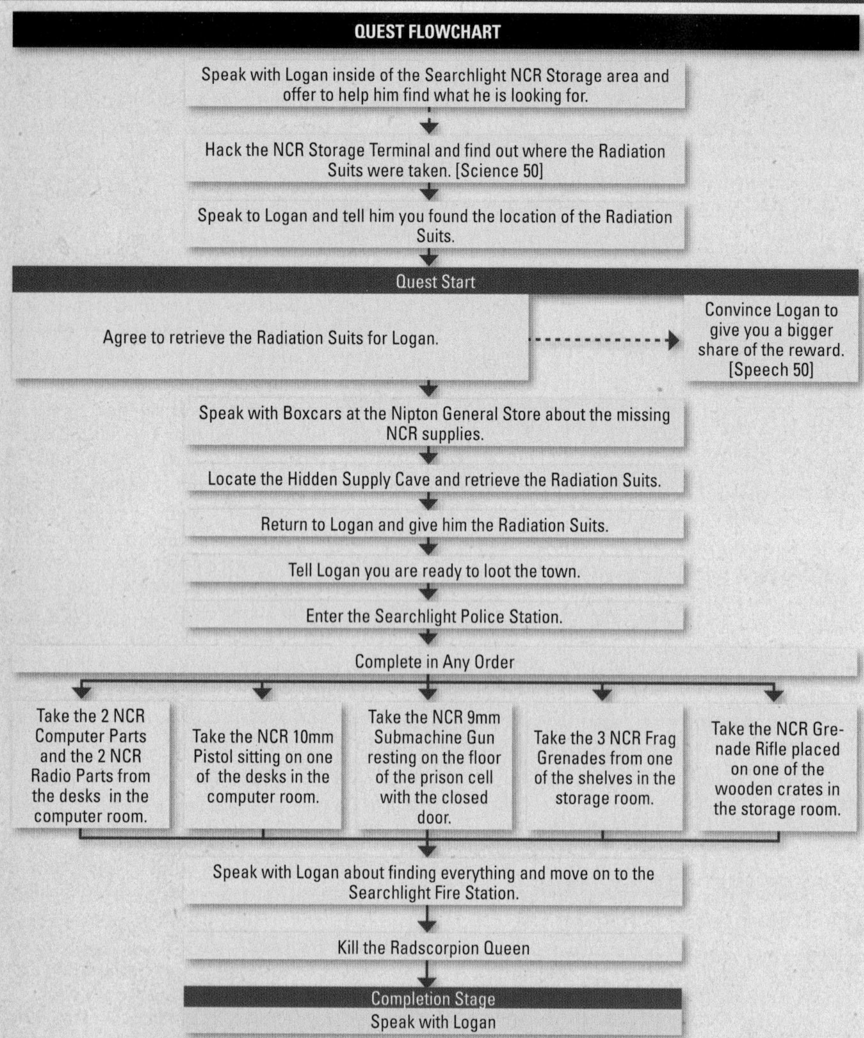

Dirty Old Town

1

2

Camp Searchlight [6.16], a town once commandeered into an NCR base before a Legion radiation bomb wreaked untold havoc, is a nightmare of Ghoulish soldiers and irradiated death. But there are still prospectors in the area. One of them is usually searching in the small cellar under the west-side remains of a chapel **(1)**. Open the Cellar Door to Searchlight NCR Storage and you'll find Logan **(2)** rummaging through NCR supplies.

Pleasantries don't work on this unpleasant scavenger (although you can find out he's working with the Crimson Caravan Company [2.09]), so ask him if he's looking for something. Then ask if you can help. He tells you to "hack that damn computer over there," because it has the location of some Radiation Suits.

Head on over and hack the NCR Storage Database, and read the Log Entries. There's no other way to begin this Quest. Unlock the floor safe for some minor items if you wish.

There's always the option to attack Logan and loot two keys from his corpse. These open the Police and Fire Stations, but fail this Quest.

Return to Logan and tell him you've found the location of the suits. Logan tells you to bring them back, and you'll loot the town together, and receive a share of the spoils.

Agree, and the Quest begins.

Or demand a bigger share of the reward. Which Logan agrees to.

Speak with someone in Nipton about the missing Radiation Suits.

A Suit for Any Occasion

3

4

The database referenced Nipton [4.30], so head there next, and search for the Trading Post **(3)**. Inside, mine the equally odious Boxcars **(4)** for information. Ask about the recent Legion razing of the place, or more importantly, if he knows "anything about some NCR supplies." He informs you that he saw some "Legion assholes" carrying crates to a cave north of here.

Find suits in a nearby cave.

5

6

The aptly titled Hidden Supply Cave [5.27] northeast of Nipton is the likely spot.

When you've found the entrance between the rock fissures **(5)**, use Bobby Pins and talent to open the door.

The single cavern is strewn with various boxes and metal crates. Stoop to take a Radiation Suit (which you should wear while scavenging Camp Searchlight), and open the adjacent Footlocker **(6)** to discover the Radiation Suit Package referenced in the database.

Radiation Suit

Radiation Suit Package

Return with the suits to Logan.

7

8

Logan and his two silent friends are still milling about in the NCR storage cellar. Tell him you found the suits **(7)** and his teammates don the outfits **(8)**. You can also ask where you're all going, and what they hope to find. When you're ready to scavenge, agree to move out.

Go with Logan to search the Police Station.

Scavenger Hunt #1: Police Station

9

Head up to the surface streets, and begin to clear a route across the main town's cross-street to the far side and around to the left. Minimize the chances of Logan dying under an assault of Feral Ghoul claws by trying the following safety techniques:

Take the turrets offline at the nearby terminals.

Battle the Ghouls prior to returning to Logan, removing most of the threats between the chapel and the Police Station.

When you're on the streets with Logan's team, be sure you're focusing on Logan himself. His teammates are Ghoul fodder as far as you're concerned, but for the Quest to continue, Logan must survive. If he's being savaged, help kill his attackers. Your destination is the Police Station **(9)** where you can use the key Logan gave you to open the front door.

Is Logan dead? Then search his corpse for two keys, and scavenge the NCR items on your own.

Searchlight Police Station Key

Searchlight Fire Station Key

10

The interior of the Police Station **(10)** consists of an entrance room, a row of cells, bathrooms, a storage room, and a central communications room. Remove any Ghoul threats, and check the following table to learn where to search for the following NCR supplies:

Room Description	NCR Equipment	Location
Southeast Storage Room	NCR Grenade Rifle	On the wooden crates
Southeast Storage Room	NCR Frag Grenade (3)	On the metal shelf
Communications Room	NCR 10mm Pistol	On a desk
Communications Room	NCR Computer Parts	Inside two separate desks
Communications Room	NCR Radio Parts	Inside two separate desks
Cell Row	NCR 9mm Submachine Gun	Inside right-side cell, below mattress

Once all the NCR-related equipment has been found, return to Logan, and tell him the scavenge is complete in this location. He gives you the Fire Station Key, and orders you to head over there next.

Searchlight Fire Station Key

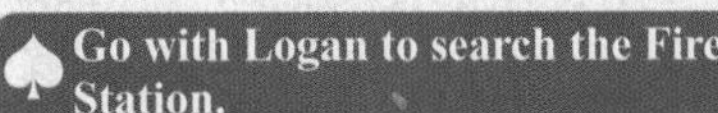

Go with Logan to search the Fire Station.

Scavenger Hunt #2: Fire Station

11

Move across town to the central thoroughfare, and destroy any adversaries close to Logan's team before moving into the Fire Station **(11)**. Prepare to take the lead, because the Fire Station is home to the largest Radscorpion

12

you've ever seen **(12)**! Battle this Radscorpion Queen, and any nearby minions, until she bursts apart. The pressurized canisters near the wall can help damage her. If Logan dies in this battle, the Quest ends. When you've scavenged your fill of Radscorpion Glands, search the floor. Here you'll find a dead legionary with some orders to optionally read. But the NCR equipment is upstairs.

13

At the top of the stairs is a long corridor with a red carpet. Find the following equipment:

Room Description	NCR Equipment	Location
Fire Officer's Southwest room	NCR 9mm Submachine Gun	On a wooden bookcase
Fire Officer's Southwest room	NCR Frag Grenade (2)	On a wooden bookcase
Eastern Barracks/ Mess Room	NCR Radio Parts (2)	On a small table
Eastern Barracks/ Mess Room	NCR Computer Parts (2)	Inside a duffle bag
Eastern Barracks/ Mess Room	NCR Computer Parts (2)	Inside a duffle bag

Once you've acquired all the NCR equipment (plus a magazine and other helpful items, which are listed in the Tour Chapter), return to Logan. Hand over the haul, and you're half-surprised when Logan turns his gun on you. Return the favor, and murder the bum, along with his prospector friends **(13)**. The Quest then concludes. Afterward, check the bathroom stalls to find a Unique Fire Axe.

Unique Weapon: Knock-Knock

100 XP

WHY CAN'T WE BE FRIENDS?

SUGGESTED EXPERIENCE

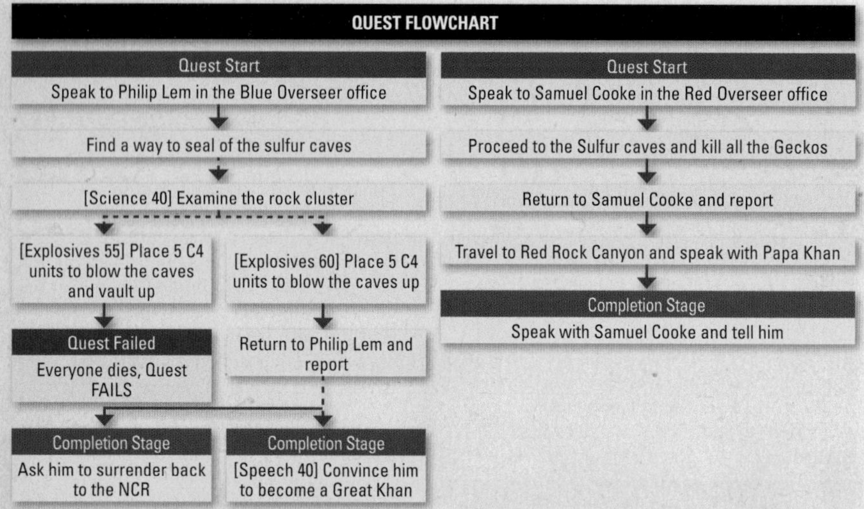

Too Many Cookes

A man named Samuel Cooke, whispered about by Powder Gangers, and already on the NCR's radar, is holed up in the confines of Vault 19 [1.21]. Approach the vault's unassuming entrance in an abandoned parking lot **(1)**, and descend through the manhole cover. Activate the Vault Door Control Pod to open the giant cog door, and enter the vault, stopping as you reach the corridor with the signs pointing left and right. This vault had two separate Overseer's Offices **(2)**. The reasons for this become clear if you read the information on the various terminals dotted throughout. But now these offices each contain a Powder Ganger leader, each vying for power.

Tip You choose which Powder Ganger to work for. You can talk to both Philip Lem and Samuel Cooke, claim both Red and Blue Sector Keycards (essentially giving you full access to the vault), and complete some of the parallel paths to this Quest. But at some point, you need to pick a side. The following information shows both parallel paths in their entirety.

Samuel Cooke's Path: The Great Gecko Hunt

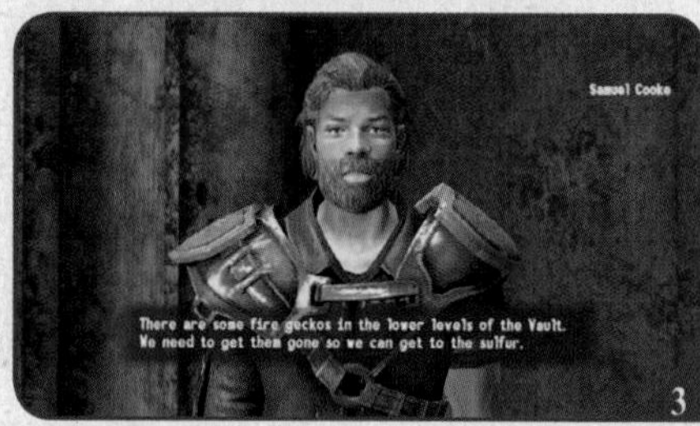

To the right, the office contains Samuel Cooke **(3)**, who's a little on edge. He tells you that the "coward Lem" is thinking of surrendering to the NCR, and his men are confused over just who is leading this Powder Ganger splinter group. You can ask him about the prison break from the NCR Correctional Facility [5.15]. He also explains the various groups, both human and animal, that live nearby. Before you go, be sure to ask Cooke if he's got any work. He needs you to eliminate the Fire Geckos in the vault's lower levels so they can reach some sulfur deposits. Agree to the task while Cooke keeps an uneasy eye on Lem. He gives you a keycard that opens only Red Sector doors.

 **Red Sector Keycard**

Eliminate the fire geckos in the caves under the vault.

Fire Gecko Cooking

Head around to the door marked "Quarters," and open it using your keycard. Proceed through the first floor. (Avoid combat with the Powder Gangers wandering the area or the Quest fails). Locate the Elevator to the Vault 19 Living Quarters, and descend. Down in this lower level, the Gangers have failed to push the Fire Geckos back, so expect combat with them as you access the main mezzanine area. Locate the giant hole in the ground **(4)** near the pool tables, and drop into the Sulfur Cave.

The Sulfur Cave consists of portions of the reactor level of the vault, and a labyrinth of natural cave tunnels, dotted with Fire Geckos **(5)**. Expect to kill at least eight, and usually around 12 of these fire-breathing beasts as you methodically search every nook and cranny. Beware of Nightstalkers farther in the caves, which aren't necessary to cull. Continue the Gecko cull until your Objective updates.

Report back to Samuel Cooke.

Traipse back up to the first floor and to Cooke's office, and inform him that the deed is done. He asks if you're interested in another job. Reply in the affirmative, and Cooke tells you to head to Red Rock Canyon [1.15] northwest of here. You're to find Papa Khan and ask him if he'd allow Cooke's Gangers to join up with them.

Speak with Papa Khan in Red Rock Canyon.

After some additional Mojave Wasteland trekking, you should arrive at the impressive canyon and locate the leader of the Great Khan, who is inside his longhouse, wandering the cluster of buildings nearby **(6)**, or in his

outhouse. You may have other Quests related to Papa Khan, but the verbal choice you're interested in is the offer of alliance from the Powder Gangers at Vault 19. Mention bombs, and the Great Khan **(7)** is keen, and agrees—as long as they pass the Khan initiation test.

Report back to Samuel Cooke.

Trudge back to Vault 19, let Samuel Cooke know, and he sets about telling his brethren, and the Quest concludes.

300 XP

Philip Lem's Path: Subterranean Explosions

8

To the left, the office contains Philip Lem **(8)**, who's a little annoyed. Especially at that "overambitious prick" Cooke, who's going to get them all killed. You can ask him about the prison break from the NCR Correctional Facility. Be sure to ask Lem if he's got any work. He tells you that he has some Caps if you can cut off access to the sulfur in the caves below the vault. If the sulfur can't be mined, then explosives can't be primed, and Cooke will lose his influence. Agree to the task while Lem keeps a suspicious eye on Cooke. You're given a keycard that opens only Blue Sector doors.

Blue Sector Keycard

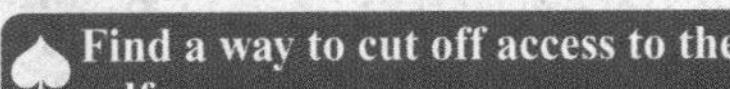

Find a way to cut off access to the sulfur.

Note Blowing up sulfur deposits is dangerous, but to complete this Quest path, you must bring at least three units of C-4 Explosives. If you don't have them, go off and find or purchase some, and then return.

Tip You can find two lots of C-4 already in this vault. Consult the Tour chapter for more information.

Tip You can obtain C-4 for free in the footlocker at Ranger Milo's Checkpoint, east of Novac [5.18].

Tip If you speak to Mick, over at Mick & Ralph's [2C.02], and ask to see his "special" cache of weapons, you can buy C-4.

Tip If you're Idolized by the Boomers, visit the Nellis Hangars [3.02] and trade with the munitions manager inside the northeast hangar; he occasionally sells C-4.

Having a Blast

9

Head around to the door marked "Quarters," and open it using your keycard. Proceed through the first floor. (Avoid combat with the Powder Gangers wandering the area or the Quest fails). Locate the Elevator to the Vault 19 Living Quarters, and descend. Down in this lower level, the Gangers have failed to push the Fire Geckos back, so expect combat with them as you access the main mezzanine area. Locate the giant hole in the ground **(9)** near the pool tables, and drop into the Sulfur Cave.

10

The Sulfur Cave consists of portions of the reactor level of the vault, and a labyrinth of natural cave tunnels, dotted with Fire Geckos. You can optionally kill as many as threaten you, or that you wish to dispatch. Beware of Nightstalkers farther into the caves, which aren't necessary to cull. Continue until you reach the large grotto area to the southwest **(10)**. Deal with any threats, and then investigate the large crystal deposits in the Microcline Rock. The crystals seem to indicate a pocket of potassium nearby. Strategically placed C-4 could be enough to destroy both the cave and the vault. You can:

Leave this alone. This is also the choice if you have no C-4.

Plant enough C-4 to destroy the caves (three units).

Or plant enough C-4 to destroy the caves and the vault (five units). Although spectacular, this option is the very definition of "overkill" because it blows the entire vault, and the Powder Gangers, to smithereens. The Quest fails.

Report back to Philip Lem.

With the C-4 primed, return back to Philip Lem, and tell him the sulfur deposits have been sealed off. Cooke's plans have been foiled, and the Gangers can now turn themselves in to the NCR.

Or, you can convince Philip Lem that the Great Khans would be happy to take them in. Refer to the final part of Cooke's Quest and visit Papa Khan to seal the deal.

Or agree with Lem, and let them surrender.

300 XP (If you convince Lem or Cooke to join the Khans)

YOU CAN DEPEND ON ME

SUGGESTED EXPERIENCE

See flowchart on the following page

Meeting Alice the Overseer

1

The Crimson Caravan Company [2.09] owns a fortified plot of land in northeast urban New Vegas. Travel to either of the two entrances **(1)**, and enter the premises. Inside, you can speak

2

to the Caravaneers, inspect the Brahmin grazing land, and even speak to Blake. But when you're ready, enter the Crimson Caravan Main Office in the southeast corner, and mosey on over to the main desk, where Alice McLafferty resides **(2)** during daylight hours. She can tell you all about the history of the company; in fact she's come up from California to help this branch out. Ask for work to discover she need a runner. You're to deliver an invoice to a Dr. Hildern somewhere inside Camp McCarran [2.19].

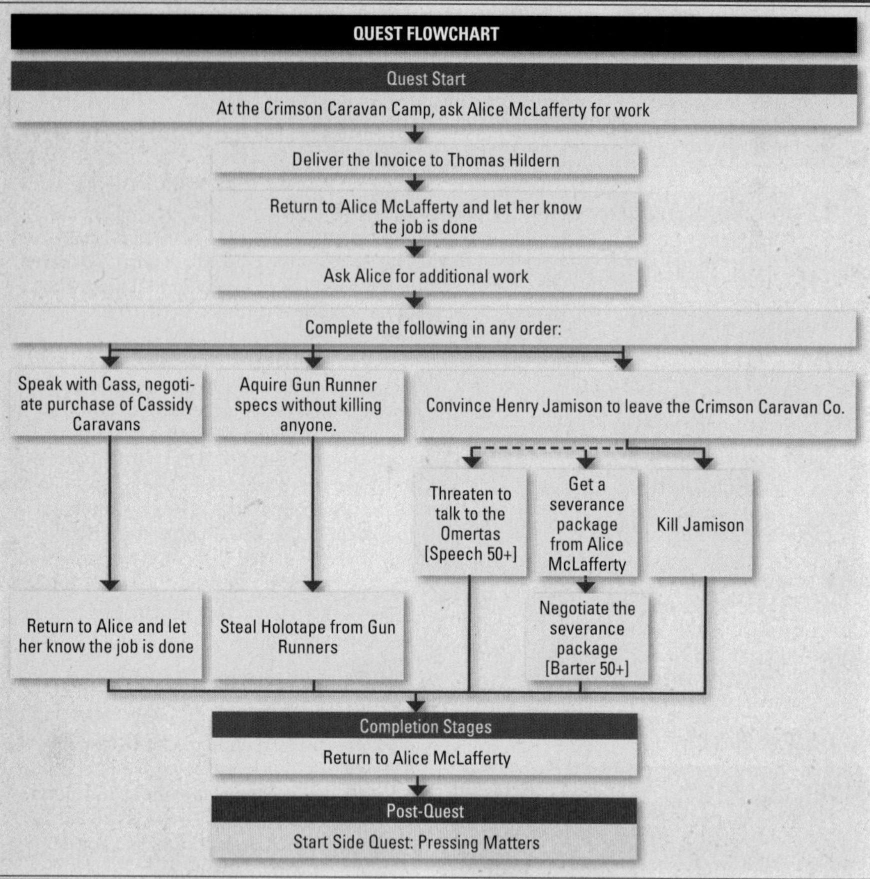

Note: Crimson Caravan Invoice

♠ **Deliver the Crimson Caravan invoice to Doctor Hildern at Camp McCarran.**

Note Read the note via the Misc menu on your Pip-Boy. The invoice is for various bits of scientific equipment shipped from Shady Sands, California. For those with long memories, this is interesting....

Tip If you've met Cass over at the Mojave Outpost [4.27], this Quest intersects, and it is worth weighing your options by reading Side Quest: Heartache by the Number before continuing.

Job #1: Direct to the Director of Operations, OSI East

3

4

Travel to the NCR stronghold of Camp McCarran, and enter the massive walled enclosure **(3)**. Run southward, across the large forecourt (now appropriated into training areas and barracks) and enter any of the Doors to Camp McCarran Terminal Building. Hildern is in his office, on the ground floor in the southeast corner. Pass by his assistant Angela, and introduce yourself to the doctor **(4)**. Speak to him about Vault 22 (Side Quest: There Stands the Grass), then hand him the invoice.

♠ **Return to Alice McLafferty and let her know you've delivered the invoice.**

Back at McLafferty's office, she pays you a modest sum, and asks if you're interested in more important jobs. Agree, and she lets you know of the following:

She wants a negotiation with a smaller trading outfit resolved as soon as possible.

Henry Jamison is an unwanted employee with tricky family connections. He needs to go.

Finally, the Gun Runners manufacturing specifications need to be "acquired," but without incident.

Accept all of these jobs now to minimize returning to Alice. Choose the one you want to attempt first (they can be tried in any order).

Caps 50

Crimson Caravan Fame Gained!

♠ **Alice McLafferty, owner of the Crimson Caravan Company, has additional jobs available.**

♠ **Negotiate with Cass to buy out Cassidy Caravans for the Crimson Caravan Company.**

♠ **Convince Henry Jamison to quit his position at the Crimson Caravan Company.**

♠ **(Optional) Acquire the Gun Runners' secret manufacturing specifications from their factory.**

Job #2: Picking the Whiskey Rose

5

6

Cass had a small caravan operation that Alice wants in on, but finding the proprietor isn't easy. She's usually in the southwestern desert, at the NCR's Mojave Outpost [4.27]. Open the gate on the left behind the sandbags, and locate the Mojave Outpost Barracks **(5)** where Cass **(6)** is drowning her sorrows. She's initially aggressive, but once you explain that the Crimson Caravan wants to buy her out, she calms down. However, her stock and animals have burned to ash. Even though Cassidy Caravans is simply the woman and the items she's carrying, she still won't sell. Press her, and she doesn't budge. When she says "Just doesn't feel right, trading history for a slip of paper," you can respond:

That you'll drink for it. Match Cass' drinking until one of you passes out. You may have underestimated this lady.

That she made the caravan and now is responsible for killing it. This angers but eventually persuades her.

That this is the last place she wants to be trapped in. You're right, of course.

Or you can kill her at any time, although the NCR aren't too happy about that. This is also a prerequisite of Side Quest: Birds of a Feather, involving the Van Graffs over at the Silver Rush [2C.07].

Any of the first three responses, along with logical additional conversation, results in Cass joining you as a Follower, if you wish. During this time, she provides you with the Whiskey Rose perk.

 **Follower: Cass**

 **Whiskey Rose**

Note: The Whiskey Rose perk grants you Damage Resistance when drinking Whiskey, and no Intelligence loss from consuming alcohol, and ignores the negative effects of alcohol addiction. Here's to your very good health!

Tell Alice McLafferty that the Crimson Caravan Company now owns Cassidy Caravans.

Tell Alice McLafferty that Cass is dead.

Back at Alice's desk, your payment depends on the outcome of your altercation with Cass:

 **0 Caps if she died.**

 **250 Caps if she lived and you bought her out.**

 **Crimson Caravan Fame Gained! If she lived and you bought her out.**

Job #3: Targeted for Termination

7

8

A Crimson Caravan employee not living up to his true potential is Henry Jamison. You'll find him, usually slumped against a slot machine, inside the Atomic Wrangler Casino **(7)** [2C.06] inside Freeside. Tell him you're here to talk about ending his employment. Jamison **(8)** refuses; his daddy told him he'd be in charge of the branch. And he's in trouble with the Omertas. How can he gamble without his Crimson Caravan cash?

 Let him know you'll tell the Omertas he doesn't have their money.

- Ask him what he wants in exchange for quitting. His answer is a vast severance package.

 Considerably lessen the severance package by telling him you'll walk away, and leave the Omertas to get him.

Or tell him you'll inform Alice there's a deal to be made.

- Or you can kill the workshy freeloader. Follow him to his room so the place doesn't erupt into a firefight.

 The easiest way to accomplish this without being attacked is to utilize a Stealth Boy, make sure your Sneak is high, and use a live Explosive (C-4 or a Grenade) and Pickpocket him. Just don't return any time soon once you hightail it out of here!

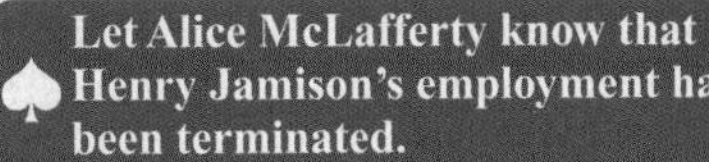

Let Alice McLafferty know that Henry Jamison's employment has been terminated.

Back at Alice's desk, your reward depends on the outcome of Henry Jamison's conversation.

 **150 Caps if you kill Henry**

 **300 Caps if you pay off his debt and give him a severance package**

 **500 Caps if you "convince" him to quit**

 **400 Caps if you only have to pay off his gambling debt**

 **Crimson Caravan Fame Gained!**

Job #4: Running, No Gunning

9

10

The trickiest of the remaining jobs takes place inside the well-guarded Gun Runners facility [2.14]. Move to the Vendortron manning the store kiosk **(9)** and inquire about weaponry (purchasing any you wish). However, the Gun Runners have their establishment sealed up tighter than Raven Rock. You can speak to Isaac **(10)** who's usually near the Reloading Bench, but it won't do any good. No amount of sweet-talking gets into the facility. Try another way:

 The only way is to pick the lock of the gate to the left of the kiosk. If you do this when Isaac or any other Gun Runner is around, you'll be attacked.

 Therefore, it is wise to be Sneaking while you're wrestling with Bobby Pins. Using a Stealth Boy is extremely important, too. And time your unlocking so that no one else is around; check your Pip-Boy's radar so you know where everyone is.

 Using less subtle methods to obtain the information usually fails the Quest.

11

Once through the gate, step quickly forward and open the Door to Gun Runner Headquarters, and head south down the long corridor to a Smithy filled with Workbenches and other machinery **(11)**. Locate the Gun Runner Terminal in the northwest corner. Of the four menu items, you only need to click the first ("Download manufacturing specifications"). Do this without being spotted by any of the Gunsmiths.

 Or try out your own ordnance on the Gunsmiths if you wish, now you're inside the premises. This isn't advisable though, as it may fail the Quest.

Hand the Gun Runners' manufacturing specifications over to Alice McLafferty.

Back at Alice's desk, your payment depends on the outcome of your actions at the Gun Runners.

 **300 Caps if anybody attacked you, or was attacked by you. Don't you listen to instructions?**

 **500 Caps if you infiltrate the gun runners with no alarms or casualties**

 **Crimson Caravan Fame Gained!**

Conclusion: Pressing Matters

When any or all of the three jobs are complete, return to collect your payment. After all jobs are done, speak to Alice once again, and ask if there's anything else she needs you to do. As it happens, there is. Side Quest: Pressing Matters now begins....

 **500 XP**

YOUNG HEARTS

SUGGESTED EXPERIENCE

QUEST FLOWCHART

Quest Start
Go to Nellis Air Force Base and begin Side Quest: Volare!

Quest Start
Speak to Jack at the Hangar about helping out.

Quest Start
Find out about Jack's "personal matter". [Speech 35]

Quest Start
Agree to find Jack's love interest.

Go to the Crimson Caravan Company and locate Janet.

Speak with Janet and ask if she ever watches the Boomers.

Tell Janet about Jack.

- Explain that Jack is not worth dying for.
- Explain that Jack is a catch. [Black Widow]
- Explain that Jack is special. [Lady Killer]
- Explain that Jack is naive.

Look into obtaining permission for Janet to enter Nellis.

Quest Failed
Lie to Janet about having permission to enter Nellis. [Speech 55]

Post-Quest
Janet is killed by the Boomers' artillery fire.

Return to Nellis and speak with Pearl about Janet.

- Appeal to Pearl's romantic side to allow Janet into Nellis [Lady Killer]
- Reassure Pearl that Janet will not be a threat. [Idolized by Boomers]
- Convince Pearl to allow Janet into Nellis. [Speech 35]

Speak with Jack and tell him that Janet feels the same way.

Tell Jack that Janet needs a way of getting past the Boomers' artillery.

Return to Janet and tell her she can enter Nellis.

Enter the Crimson Caravan Main Office and speak to Alice McLafferty about Janet.

- Kill Alice.
- Agree with Alice that Janet should not be paid her lost wages.
- Negotiate with Alice to pay Janet her lost wages. [Barter 65]
- Convince Alice to pay Janet her lost wages. [Speech 75]

Return to Janet and inform her of Alice's decision / fate.

Escort Janet to Nellis.

Quest Failed
Janet dies while travelling to Nellis.

Completion Stage
Speak with Jack after he speaks with Janet.

Never Be Hung Up

1

Begin by starting Side Quest: Volare! over at the Nellis Air Force Base [3.01] by dodging

2

shells, reaching the gate, meeting Raquel, and then speaking with Mother Pearl. One of Pearl's tasks involves Jack. Locate him inside the Nellis Hangars **(1)** [3.02] and ask about the Scrap Metal he needs collecting. But to begin this Quest, continue to listen, and Jack **(2)** reveals a second, rather personal matter. You can:

Main Factions

Tell him where you come from, personal matters are discussed all the time.

For a handsome guy like Jack, you bet there's a girl involved.

Either option causes Jack to spill the beans; there's Crimson Caravan Outpost [2.09] near here. and once in a while, Jack watches through spotter binoculars at a "special girl." And sometimes she watches him back!

Tell Jack that you could talk to her for him. He eagerly explains that she has short red hair. Then he has a light panic and a queasy stomach. Tell him you'll look into it.

Note: Jack's Love Story

Find Jack's love interest.

Note The Boomer Quests are all related. First, speak with Mother Pearl to begin Side Quest: Volare! To complete the first part of this "overview" Quest, you must achieve the following:

BOOMERS Become Idolized with the Boomers. Do this by completing tasks within this Quest, as well as three additional linked Quests associated with this Faction (which are tagged throughout the guide).

- Complete Side Quest: Ant Misbehavin'.
- Complete Side Quest: Sunshine Boogie.
- Complete Side Quest: Young Hearts (this Quest).

These three Quests (including this one) are all parts of Side Quest: Volare!

I Just Can't Break Away

3

4

Journey west to the Crimson Caravan Company Headquarters **(3)**, and open the main gates. Once inside (and during daylight hours), locate the Brahmin paddock, and find the short, red-haired girl in there. Ask whether she watches the Boomers over in Nellis, and Janet **(4)** stops sweeping, and asks who wants to know. Explain that there's a young man who has a crush on her, and she responds positively, asking what he's like. You can:

Tell her that he's nice, and a little naive, and convinced she's the love of his life.

Tell her he's a special guy for a special gal.

Explain that Jack is a real catch.

Tell her he's okay, but not worth dying for.

Any of the responses elects a positive outcome from Janet, and she wonders if there's a way for the Boomers to let her visit Nellis. You can:

Tell her that you'll ask Mother Pearl to make an exception for you.

Or lie, and tell her permission has been granted, and that they know she's coming.

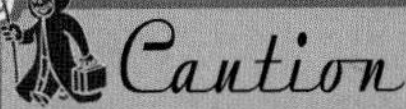
Ask Pearl for permission for Janet to enter Nellis.

Caution You just lied, and Janet ran off to the Boomer's Base, but everything is pretty far from okay. If you choose this option, Janet races toward the Nellis AFB, and is blown into tiny, tiny pieces by their howitzers. The Quest fails.

Assuming you didn't lead Janet to the slaughter, head back to the Nellis AFB, and look for Mother Pearl in her barracks or strolling the compound. Tell her that Jack is interested in a girl, and that she works for the Crimson Caravan (or she's some "kooky dame"). This is a problem, because Jack isn't allowed to leave, and Janet wouldn't make it through the artillery barrages. Suggest the following:

Tell her it would mean a lot to Jack if Janet could come to Nellis.

Reassure Pearl that Janet is no threat to the Boomers.

Or appeal to Pearl's romantic side.

She agrees on the condition that Jack take responsibility for her.

Tell Jack Janet is interested in him.

Run Free

5

6

Back in the hangar, Jack is getting a little antsy. He asks if you've seen the redhead of his dreams. Explain that you've spoken to Pearl, and Janet needs a way past the artillery. Jack has a plan; he hands you a Boomer outfit, and says he'll let the gunners know she's coming, and not to fire on her.

Boomer Outfit for Janet

Take the Boomer Outfit to Janet.

Return to the Crimson Caravan Headquarters, and speak with Janet **(5)** again. You can:

Tell her you have a Boomer uniform for her to wear while she crosses to Nellis. Hand it over, and she puts it on **(6)**.

Or lie, and tell her permission has been granted, and that they know you're coming. Watch out! This gets her killed, too!

Of course, there's "one more thing." Apparently Janet has a work contract with the Crimson Caravan, and if she leaves, she loses her wages. Janet asks if you'd speak to Alice McLafferty about the matter.

Speak to Alice McLafferty on behalf of Janet.

7

8

Search out the Crimson Caravan Main Office shack **(7)**, and locate Alice **(8)** sitting behind her desk. Tell her that Janet has asked you to talk about releasing her from her contract. Alice already knows about this puppy love and informs you that Janet is free to leave, but she'll forfeit her wages. You can:

Ask if she's really going to ruin a time of happiness for Janet.

Wonder whether opening a trade route to the Boomers wouldn't be a bad thing.

Or make the deal.

Or kill Alice, lowering your standing considerably among the Crimson Caravan Faction, and flee, ideally with Janet. This isn't a wise move.

The first two options give Janet the monies she's owed. The latter two don't.

Let Janet know McLafferty agreed to pay her.

Let Janet know McLafferty won't be paying her.

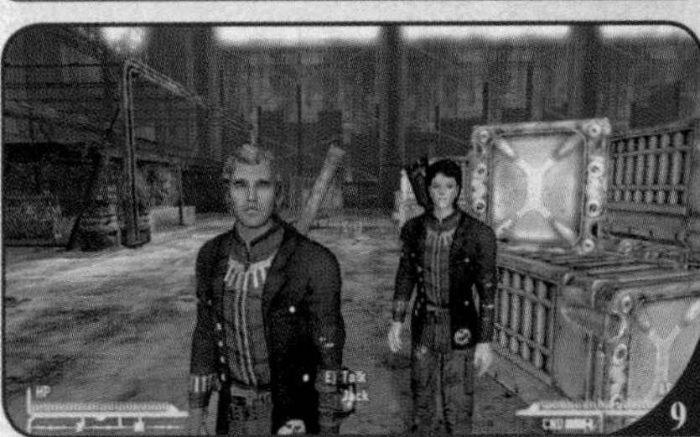
9

Return to Janet, letting her know the decision you reached with Alice. She's either ecstatic (and you receive a Boomer Fame Gain), or she's less than ecstatic, but still willing to make the trip. She hurries off to pack. You can escort her back to Nellis, or let her go on her own, although she might be killed by a wandering or rogue enemy between the two settlements. Now return to see Jack at your earliest convenience (but give Janet a couple of hours to reach the base, if you're not chaperoning her).

Boomer Fame Gained!

Meet Janet back at Nellis

Return to Jack.

When you finally meet the lovebirds **(9)**, Jack explains that he's never been happier. The Quest concludes, and your heart melts, just a little bit.

Boomer Fame Gained!

300 XP

Tour of the Mojave Wasteland

WELCOME TO THE MOJAVE WASTELAND

For an overall perspective on the Mojave Wasteland, refer to the poster map included in this guide. The poster map shows the entire wasteland divided into six zones; each zone is usually bounded by roads so you can easily locate yourself on the map using your Pip-Boy. The poster map reveals information like locations to explore, underground links, and areas where your Reputation has effects. When you want to know more about each zone and the locations it contains, this Tour of the Mojave Wasteland covers it all. Here's how to use this chapter:

Map Overview and Legend

Interior maps will help you explore major locations and locate any important or valuable items within. Interior maps are labeled with:

- ● **Reputation Marker:** These locations show up with a Reputation reference on your Pip-Boy's World Map.
- ① **Map Marker:** This shows the general area to search for one or more important items, or a major junction or route, in an interior map.
- Ⓐ **Threshold Marker:** This signifies a door (with a corresponding letter to the text description), a locked door (a blank marker), or a blockade in a corridor (also a blank marker). If this is linked via a red line, it shows the threshold between two levels or floors of a structure.

Measuring Your V.I.T.A.L. Statistics

Every location in this chapter is detailed with a "V.I.T.A.L." or Vault-Tec Informational Topographical Asset List. Every location features its name, zone number, a fly-by photograph of its exterior, and notes. Additional information lets you quickly ascertain what the location has to offer. Here's what all the V.I.T.A.L. statistics mean:

STATISTIC	DESCRIPTION
RELATED QUESTS: REFERENCES TO THE THREE TYPES OF QUEST TO UNDERTAKE.	
Main	Visited during a Main Quest.
Side	Visited during a Side Quest.
Free	A Free Quest, usually at this location.
THREAT LEVEL: PLAYER EXPERIENCE NEEDED AND OVERALL DANGER.	
●○○○○	Extremely light: An easy-to-dispatch foe or animal.
●●○○○	Light: A couple of Fiends or a few small creatures.
●●●○○	Moderate: A small Super Mutant camp or single large creature.
●●●●○	Problematic: Expect heavy resistance and multiple entities.
●●●●●	Extreme: Exceptionally strong or legendary foes.
FACTIONS: THE TYPE OF FRIENDS OR FOES THAT INHABIT EACH LOCATION.	
Name	The Faction type, as detailed in the Factions and Bestiary chapter.
Entities	The specific individuals, or monster types that inhabit this locale.
SERVICES: INDIVIDUALS OR VENUES THAT OFFER A PARTICULAR TYPE OF ASSISTANCE.	
Caravan Player	An entity is willing to play a few games of Caravan if you ask.
Gambling	Blackjack, Roulette, or Slots may be available at this venue.
Healer/Dealer	You can be healed, or purchase ingestible goods here.
Repairer	You can get your weapons and equipment repaired here.
Trader	You can trade for new or improved items at this location.
CRAFTING: DEVICES THAT HELP YOU CREATE HELPFUL ITEMS FROM ASSORTED INGREDIENTS.	
Campfire	A place to cook up Recipes, based on ingredients you've collected.
Reloading Bench	A bench to break down and create new ammunition types.
Workbench	A bench to create new and helpful items and weapons.
Upgrade	A Trader with modifications you can easily install onto a weapon.
DANGERS: HAZARDS THAT YOU MUST BE EXTREMELY WARY OF, OR RISK HEALTH LOSS.	
Traps	Beware of a Bear Trap, Chain Trap, Grenade Bouquet, Shotgun, or other trap here.
Radiation	Exposure to (usually) low radiation at this location.
Mines	Beware of Frag or Pulse Mines. Deactivate them to use yourself.

STATISTIC	DESCRIPTION
COLLECTIBLES: PARTICULARLY HELPFUL ITEMS TO FIND, GATHER AND THEN USE, OR SELL.	
Caravan Cards	Won or stolen from a player, or found on a corpse. Cards are random.
Hollowed-Out Rock	A "false" (graffiti-daubed) rock with random items hidden inside.
Skill Book	A book that permanently increases a particular skill.
Skill Magazine	A magazine that temporarily increases a particular skill.
Snow Globes	A fancy trinket of a particularly large location. Mr. House collects them.
Sunset Sarsaparilla Star Cap	A blue star cap; collect them for Festus.
Unique Item	An item of clothing or inventory equipment that is very rare, or one-of-a-kind.
Unique Weapon	A unique and usually powerful weapon.
MISCELLANEOUS: OTHER STATISTICS THAT PROVIDE A FINAL LAYER OF INFORMATION AND HELP.	
Area Is Locked	Part of this location requires a special key or high Lockpick/Science to enter.
Follower	One of eight Companion Followers can be found here.
Guns and Ammo	Weaponry (whether Guns, Energy Weapons, Melee Weapons, or Unarmed) is here.
Health, Chems, or Water	Find Health, Chems, or clean drinking Water here.
Highly Visible	Tall or imposing structure; used to get your bearings.
Home Sweet Home	You are rewarded with a safe residence here.
Interior Exploration	There is more to this location than just the surface.
Lots O' Caps	Expect to find a large windfall of Caps at this location.
Perk!	You are awarded a perk at this location, which could be for you or a Companion.
Quest Item	An item integral to a Quest is found here; some only if the Quest is active.
Radio Signal	Your Pip-Boy picks up a narrow-band radio signal.
Sleeping Quarters	You can sleep here.
Underground Connection	This links to an underground area, which connects to other locations.
Wasteland Vegetation	Naturally growing plant life is abundant here.
Weapons, Please!	You are ordered to disarm when entering this location.
Wild Wasteland	A strange oddity based on this trait is seen here.

Caution Take care when using explosives, heavy weapons, or ordnance! Many of the Collectible items are small and light, and may move if hit by such weaponry. Be sure to search around if an item isn't where it should be.

A Few Words About Free Quests

This Tour section also lists (and solves) more than 90 "Free Quests." These are tasks that never appear in your Pip-Boy's Quest menu. Clues to some appear in your Notes menu, and you'll simply stumble across others. These are usually short, offer a small XP (Experience Point) bonus, and are yet another entertaining diversion from your Main Questing. The following table lists all available Free Quests. To read more, turn to the location listed under "Location Start."

MAIN FACTION / FOLLOWER	#	QUEST NAME	LOCATION START
Super Mutant	1	Wind-Brahmin Wrangler	[1.01] Brooks Tumbleweed Ranch
Super Mutant/Lily	2	Lily and Leo	[1.10] Jacobstown
NCR	3	Lenk's Bad Debts	[1.12] Ranger Station Foxtrot ●
NONE	4	Strategic Nuclear Moose	[1.13] Brewer's Beer Bootlegging
Primm	5	A Pair of Dead Desperados, II	[1.S05] Wins Hideout

MAIN FACTION / FOLLOWER	#	QUEST NAME	LOCATION START
The Thorn	6	Fight Night	[2.04] The Thorn
Followers OTA	7	Harder, Better, Faster, Stronger	[2.10] New Vegas Medical Clinic
Mr. House (The Strip)	8	Strip Search	[2.13] The Strip North Gate
NCR	9	A Final Plan for Esteban	[2.19] Camp McCarran
NCR	10	Bounty Killer, I	[2.19] Camp McCarran
NCR	11	Dealing with Contreras	[2.19] Camp McCarran
NCR	12	Don't Poke at the Bear	[2.19] Camp McCarran : Mojave Wasteland (Random)
NCR	13	Don't Tread on the Bear	[2.19] Camp McCarran : Mojave Wasteland (Random)
NCR	14	Emergency Radio Waves	[2.19] Camp McCarran : Mojave Wasteland (Random)
NCR	15	Not Worth a Hill of Corn and Beans	[2.19] Camp McCarran
NCR	16	Rest and Resupply	[2.19] Camp McCarran
NCR	17	Silus Treatment	[2.19] Camp McCarran
NCR	18	Keith's Caravan Charade	[2.22] Aerotech Office Park
NCR	19	Bounty Killer, II	[2.24] Vault 3
NONE	20	I Love Bananas	[2.24] Vault 3
NONE	21	Access Powers	[2.35] REPCONN Headquarters
NONE	22	Honorary Rocketeer	[2.35] REPCONN Headquarters
Westside	23	A Bit of Slap and Tickle	[2A.01] Casa Madrid Apartments
North Vegas	24	Meeting an Equal	[2B.S04] Jules
Followers OTA	25	Short-Term Treatment	[2C.01] Old Mormon Fort
Followers OTA	26	Long-Term Care	[2C.01] Old Mormon Fort
Followers OTA	27	Friend of the Followers	[2C.01] Old Mormon Fort
The Kings	28	Papers, Please	[2C.02] Mick & Ralph's
Atomic Wrangler	29	Big Winner, Atomic Wrangler	[2C.06] Atomic Wrangler
Atomic Wrangler	30	Hat's Entertainment	[2C.06] Atomic Wrangler
NONE	31	Maud's Muggers	[2C.S11] The Granny Gang
Freeside	32	Reach for the Sky, Mister!	[2C.S12] Max and Stacey
Freeside	33	Rotface's Loose Lips	[2C.S15] Rotface
Freeside	34	Flogging a Dead Corpse	[2C.S19] An Unsubtle Mugging
Freeside	35	Smooth-Talking Criminal	[2C.S20] Squatter Camp #2
The Strip	36	Big Winner, The Gomorrah	[2D.01] Gomorrah
The Strip	37	Playing on the Old Joana	[2D.01] Gomorrah
The Strip	38	Razzle Dazzle!	[2D.01] Gomorrah
Mr. House (The Strip)	39	The House Has Gone Bust!	[2D.02] Lucky 38 Casino
Mr. House (The Strip)	40	Useless Baubles or Fancy Trinkets?	[2D.02] Lucky 38 Casino
The Strip	41	Big Winner, The Tops	[2D.04] The Tops Casino
The Strip	42	Big Winner, Ultra-Luxe	[2D.05] Ultra-Luxe Casino
Brotherhood of Steel/ Veronica	43	You Make Me Feel Like a Woman	[2D.05] Ultra-Luxe Casino
The Strip	44	Suits You, Sarah	[2D.06] Vault 21
The Strip	45	Tourist Traipse	[2D.06] Vault 21
Mr. House (The Strip)	46	We Must Stop Meeting Like This, IV	[2D.S02] Victor at the Lucky 38
NONE	47	Cajoling a Cudgel	[U2.EC] East Central Sewers
Boomers	48	Malleable Mini Boomer Minds	[3.01] Nellis Air Force Base
Boomers	49	Bear Necessities	[3.01] Nellis Air Force Base
Boomers	50	Missing a Few Missiles	[3.01] Nellis Air Force Base
Boomers	51	Iron and Stealing	[3.02] Nellis Hangars
NONE	52	All Fired Up!	[3.12] Vault 34
NCR	53	Help for Halford	[3.19] Camp Guardian
Caesar's Legion	54	A Trusted Aide	[3.28] The Fort
Caesar's Legion	55	Beware the Wrath of Caesar!	[3.28] The Fort : Mojave Wasteland (Random)
Caesar's Legion	56	Caesar's Favor	[3.28] The Fort : Mojave Wasteland (Random)
Caesar's Legion	57	Laurifer Gladiator	[3.28] The Fort
Caesar's Legion	58	Powder to the People	[3.28] The Fort
Caesar's Legion	59	Saving (or Savaging) Sergeant Teddy	[3.28] The Fort
NCR	60	Defacing the Humble Stone	[3.32] Boulder City
Mr. House (The Strip)	61	We Must Stop Meeting Like This, III	[3.32] Boulder City
Boomers	62	Highway to the Danger Zone, I	[3.S03] Boomer Territory Road
Boomers	63	Highway to the Danger Zone, II	[3.S04] Bombarded Houses
Goodsprings	64	Ringo's Caravan Rules	[4.05] Goodsprings
Goodsprings	65	We Must Stop Meeting Like This, I	[4.05] Goodsprings
Goodsprings	66	We Must Stop Beating Like This	[4.05] Goodsprings
Goodsprings	67	Trudy's Radio Repair	[4.05] Goodsprings
Goodsprings	68	Exhumin' Nature	[4.06] Goodsprings Cemetery
NONE	69	Claws Out	[4.08] Sloan
NONE	70	You Gotta Break Out a Few Eggs	[4.08] Sloan
NONE	71	Power to the People	[4.08] Sloan
NONE	72	Claws Mended	[4.08] Sloan
Goodsprings	73	Barton the Fink	[4.11] Goodsprings Source
Primm	74	A Pair of Dead Desperados, I	[4.17] Primm
Primm	75	A Team of Moronic Mercenaries	[4.17] Primm
Primm	76	Big Winner, Vikki & Vance	[4.17] Primm
Primm	77	Gland for Some Home Cooking	[4.17] Primm
NONE	78	Thought for the Day	[5.02] 188 Trading Post
NONE	79	Democracy Inaction	[5.05] Vault 11
Super Mutant/ Raul	80	Old School Ghoul	[5.07] Black Mountain
Brotherhood of Steel	81	Pistol Packing	[5.11] Hidden Valley
Brotherhood of Steel	82	Brotherhood Bond, I	[5.11] Hidden Valley
Brotherhood of Steel	83	Brotherhood Bond, II	[5.11] Hidden Valley
Powder Gangers	84	Eddie's Emissary	[5.15] NCR Correctional Facility
Novac	85	Andy and Charlie	[5.18] Novac
Novac	86	Getting a Leg Up from Andy	[5.18] Novac
Novac	87	Straus Calls	[5.18] Novac
Novac	88	The Screams of Brahmin	[5.18] Novac
Novac	89	We Must Stop Meeting Like This, II	[5.18] Novac
NCR	90	An Ear to the Ground	[6.02] Camp Forlorn Hope
NCR	91	Tags of Our Fallen	[6.02] Camp Forlorn Hope
Caesar's Legion	92	Arizona Scavenger	[6.20] Cottonwood Cove
Caesar's Legion	93	Caching in at the Cove	[6.20] Cottonwood Cove

ZONE 1: NORTHWEST MOUNTAINS

Topographical Overview

The terrain is steep and wild for much of this region, which is dominated by a huge sandstone formation known as Red Rock Canyon, the base of a tribe with a violently nomadic past. Areas of parkland and small villages are now home to mutated animals and Chem-addled raiders. Fiends have encroached from the east and are threatening Trail 160. Hidden vaults await an inquisitive traveler (one is already home to escaped Powder Gangers while the other holds more shocking secrets), and while there are a scattering of drifters and grifters in the old farmsteads north of New Vegas, the other dominant force is the settlement of Jacobstown, named for an old friend of a Super Mutant named Marcus. Visit him in the snowy peaks to the west, and he may yet achieve his dream of peace.

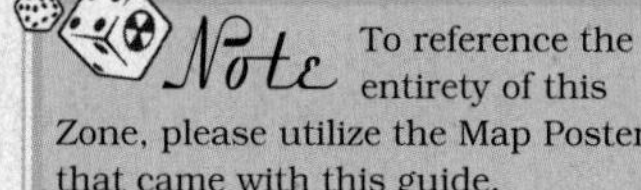

To reference the entirety of this Zone, please utilize the Map Poster that came with this guide.

Highways and Byways

The northwestern end of Highway 95 cuts through the tip of this zone, and there's a rough road along the northern edge where farmers long abandoned their livelihoods to Raiders or worse. Generally, the main roads are now nothing more than trails: 157 winds into the Pine Ravines and mountainous region leading to Jacobstown. Unmarked pathways allow easy access around Red Rock Canyon, and a second trail—the 160—takes you around the foothills to the boundary at the edge of the New Vegas Conurbation.

Available Services, Crafting and Collectibles

- Services: Caravan Players: [0/15]
- Services: Gambling: [0/15]
- Services: Healers/Dealers: [2/31]
- Services: Repairers: [1/9]
- Services: Traders: [2/33]
- Crafting: Campfires: [15/109]
- Crafting: Reloading Benches: [4/36]
- Crafting: Workbenches: [3/41]
- Crafting: Weapon Upgrades: [1/10]
- Collectibles: Snow Globes: [1/7]
- Collectibles: Caravan Cards: [0/30]
- Collectibles: Hollowed-Out Rocks: [8/42]
- Collectibles: Skill Books: [6/51]
- Collectibles: Skill Magazines: [21/213]
- Collectibles: Star Bottle Caps: [8/100]
- Collectibles: Unique Items: [9/95]
- Collectibles: Unique Weapons: [7/42]

Primary Locations

[1.01] Brooks Tumbleweed Ranch
[1.02] Northern Passage
[1.03] Ruby Hill Mine
[1.04] Followers Safehouse
[1.05] Griffin Wares Sacked Caravan
[1.06] Horowitz Farmstead
[1.07] Charleston Cave
[1.08] Silver Peak Mine
[1.09] Vault 22
[1.10] Jacobstown
[1.11] Remnants Bunker
[1.12] Ranger Station Foxtrot
[1.13] Brewer's Beer Bootlegging
[1.14] Red Rock Drug Lab
[1.15] Red Rock Canyon
[1.16] Chance's Map
[1.17] Poseidon Gas Station
[1.18] Spring Mt. Ranch State Park
[1.19] Nopah Cave
[1.20] Bonnie Springs
[1.21] Vault 19
[1.22] Whittaker Farmstead

Secondary Locations

[1.S01] Radioactive Road Block
[1.S02] Hovering Anomaly/Mercenary Camp
[1.S03] Electrical Transformer Station
[1.S04] Sharecroppers' Lament
[1.S05] Wins Hideout
[1.S06] Abandoned Farmstead
[1.S07] Jackal Shack
[1.S08] New Vegas Home
[1.S09] Rusting Pickup Truck
[1.S10] Carlyle St. Clair's House
[1.S11] Mojave House
[1.S12] Brahmin Paddock and Farmstead
[1.S13] Trail 157 Junction
[1.S14] Ruby Hill Grave
[1.S15] Mountain Vista
[1.S16] Pine Ravines Pathway
[1.S17] Red Rock Pathway
[1.S18] Westside Turnaround and Playground
[1.S19] Abandoned Home
[1.S20] Cazadors' Duffle Bag
[1.S21] Disassembled Weapons Shipment
[1.S22] Violet and Violetta Trailer Compound
[1.S23] Radioactive Pools
[1.S24] Red Rock Canyon Commemorative Stone
[1.S25] Spring Mountain Pathway
[1.S26] Hovering Anomaly
[1.S27] Sulfur Cave

PRIMARY LOCATIONS

[1.01] Brooks Tumbleweed Ranch

- Free Quest: Wind-Brahmin Wrangler
- Threat Level: ●●●●●
- Faction: Super Mutant
  - Entity: Nightkin
  - Entity: Wind-Brahmin
- Collectibles:
  - Skill Book: [Speech] [1/4] [1/6]
  - Sunset Sarsaparilla Star Cap [1/100]
- Health, Chems or Water
- Interior Exploration
- Sleeping Quarters
- Wasteland Vegetation

North of the remains of Highway 95, this ranch consists of a derelict shack, a fallen feed silo, and a house. The ranch house has a Wind-Brahmin you can "pet," and various junk on the ground floor along with some First Aid Boxes; check the pantry for a Sunset Sarsaparilla Star Bottle Cap on the floor near the empty bottles. Find another Wind-Brahmin and some mattresses upstairs, along with a Skill Book on the locker shelf.

- First Aid Box (2)
- Sunset Sarsaparilla Star Cap [1/100]
- Skill Book: Lying, Congressional Style [Speech] [1/4] [1/6]
- Cattle Prod

Free Quest: Wind-Brahmin Wrangler

Outside, step into the paddock where the Wind-Brahmins are gamboling about, and you're surprised by a Nightkin. He asks if you want to buy the Wind-Brahmin. All of them. For all of your Caps. You can:

Kill this crazy Super Mutant, and optionally any "Wind-Brahmin" you don't see eye to eye with.

Or part with all your Caps, and "own" a piece of the tumbleweed action. Naturally, bring a low number of Caps if you want a "bargain."

[1.02] Northern Passage

- Threat Level: ●●●●●
- Faction: None
- Collectibles: Hollowed-Out Rock [1/42]
- Wasteland Vegetation

Beyond the dying sharecropper farms and the decaying power line is a ramshackle hut and a small, steep hill path to a large cavern filled with rocks you can cannot shift. The Northern

Passage is currently blocked, and cannot be accessed. Check the grave (use a Shovel), and be sure to look for the Hollowed-Out Rock across from the Banana Yuccas.

- Hollowed-Out Rock [1/42]
- Grave Items

[1.03] Ruby Hill Mine

- Threat Level:
- Faction: Abomination
  - Entity: Lakelurk
- Collectibles:
  - Hollowed-Out Rock [2/42]
- Unique Weapon [1/42]
- Wasteland Vegetation
- Interior Exploration

Nestled in a rock face west of the winding Trail 157 and grazing Bighorners is a rickety door leading to an abandoned mine. Note the Hollowed-Out Rock next to the entrance. The water-logged mine, now filled with Lakelurks, is the final resting place of a Jackal Gang explorer.

- Hollowed-Out Rock [2/42]

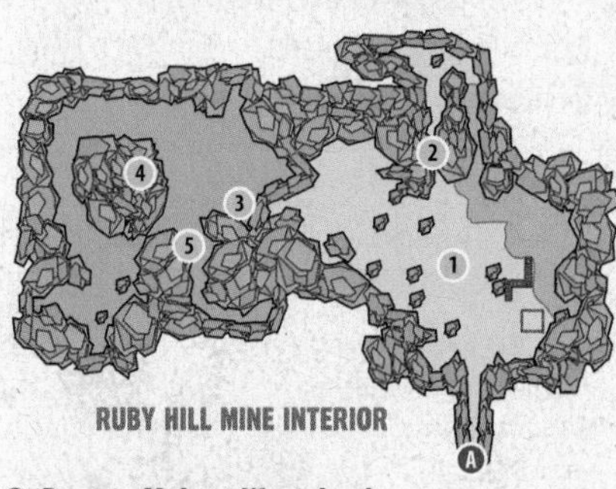

A Door to Mojave Wasteland

1 Initial Chamber

To the right (east) of the entrance, rickety stairs lead to an empty platform and a rocky ledge. The chamber itself is strewn with rocks, rusting mine carts, and wandering Lakelurks.

2 Connecting Passage (Under and Above)

Accessible from the western grotto or the upper rocky ledge in the initial chamber, this passage connects these areas, and features an alcove with Explosives. The lower (western) exit is underwater.

- Explosives Crate Items (2)

3 Connecting Passage (Ground Level)

Most the Lakelurks reside here.

4 Grotto

This offers little to scavenge, aside from a Super Mutant corpse floating over a strange, skeletal underwater card game. Check the natural pillar for more Explosive Crates.

- Explosives Crate Items (3: 1 = Average, 1 = Hard)

5 Jackal Gang Member (Deceased)

Uncover her small haul (the Worn Key unlocks the Hard Crate at Location #4), including a Unique Weapon.

- Knife
- Unique Weapon: Pushy [1/42]
- Worn Key

[1.04] Followers Safehouse

- Free Quest: Friend of the Followers
- Threat Level:
- Faction: Followers of the Apocalypse
  - Entity: Doctor Luria
- Services:
  - Healer [1/31]
- Crafting: Workbench [1/41]
- Collectibles: Skill Book: [Medicine] [1/4] [2/6]
- Area Is Locked
- Health, Chems, or Water
- Home Sweet Home
- Interior Exploration
- Sleeping Quarters

On a rocky bluff overlooking the ruined farmsteads and North New Vegas is a concrete bunker bearing the insignia of the Followers of the Apocalypse. The door can only be opened with the Followers Safehouse Key, accessed after Julie Farkas and the others at the Old Mormon Fort [2C.01] grow to like you (Free Quest: Friend of the Followers). Once inside, locate the following:

- Workbench [1/41]
- Skill Book: D.C. Journal of Internal Medicine [Medicine] [1/4] [2/6]

Much like other Safehouses across the Mojave, this offers a place of rest and healthy solace. The following benefits occur:

1. Any bed you sleep in at this location gives you a "Well Rested" bonus.
2. A water fountain here allows you to sip purified water without radiation.
3. If the location has a fridge, it is restocked with items once per day.
4. Aside from the fridge, you can store items int containers without them disappearing. Choose a metal box, footlocker, or other chest type, place a low value item inside, then return after a day to ensure your items haven't been taken.
5. This location has a medical practitioner (Doctor Luria), who visits every Monday and Thursday. You can check the day of the week when you attempt to Wait or Sleep. Doctor Luria hands over one set of the following, each time she visits (so you can choose items twice a week, assuming you're there when the doctor is).

- Healer: Doctor Luria [1/31]
  - Super Stimpak
  - Stimpak (3)
  - RadAway (2) and Rad-X

[1.05] Griffin Wares Sacked Caravan

- Side Quest: Heartache By the Number
- Threat Level:
- Faction: Prospector

Griffin is nowhere to be seen, but his Pack Brahmin and Guards are slowly rotting in the sun. Bring Cass here during Side Quest: Heartache By the Number for further revelations.

- Sunset Sarsaparilla Crate
- Plasma Rifle and Ammo

[1.06] Horowitz Farmstead

- Threat Level:
- Faction: Viper Gang
- Crafting:
  - Campfire [1/109]
  - Reloading Bench [1/36]
- Dangers: Mines
- Collectibles: Sunset Sarsaparilla Star Cap [2/100]
- Guns and Ammo
- Health, Chems, or Water
- Sleeping Quarters

The western cluster is empty, save for a possible wandering Cazador and a Reloading Bench. The southern and eastern buildings are sealed up. The northern building (watch for Frag Mines!) is home to a small Viper Gang camp. Once you've killed them, check the back of the rusting pickup for a Hunting Shotgun and ammo.

- Reloading Bench [1/36]
- Campfire [1/109]
- Frag Mine
- Ammo Box Ammunition (3) [1 = Average]
- Hunting Shotgun and Briefcase
- First Aid Box and Healing Powder (2)
- Produce Sack
- Sunset Sarsaparilla Crate (3) and Bottles
- Sunset Sarsaparilla Star Cap [2/100]
- Sleeping Quarters

[1.07] Charleston Cave

- Side Quest: Guess Who I Saw Today
- Threat Level:
- Faction: Mutated Animal
  - Entity: Nightstalker (Stealth strain)
- Crafting: Campfire [2/109]
- Dangers: Radiation
- Collectibles:
  - Hollowed-Out Rock [3/42]
  - Magazine: [Medicine] [1/19] [1-3/21]
  - Magazine: [Repair] [1/27] [1-3/21]
  - Magazine: [Survival] [1/30] [1-3/21]
  - Unique Weapon [2/42]
- Guns and Ammo
- Health, Chems, or Water
- Interior Exploration
- Quest Item
- Sleeping Quarters

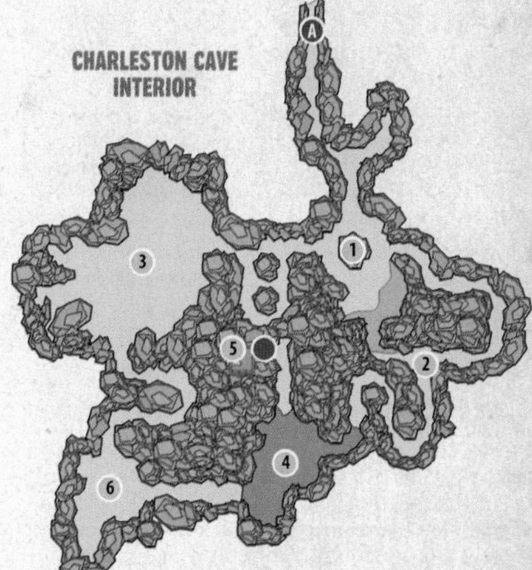

Full of stunning stalactites and other ancient rock formations, Charleston Cave has remained closed for hundreds of years since its discovery in the early 1960s, and subsequent geological instability. Once the home to a hold-out during the Great War, strange mutant critters known as Nightstalkers roam these empty chambers. A new and even more terrifying strain can shroud themselves in Stealth Boy–like invisibility. Don't forget to inspect the nearby rock!

- Hollowed-Out Rock [3/42]

A Door to Mojave Wasteland

1 Entrance Camp

Among the mattresses is a Campfire, and a half-buried Ammo Box [Locked: Easy].

- Campfire [2/109]
- Ammo Box [Locked: Easy]
- Sleeping Quarters

2 Eastern Bone Zone

Access this via the eastern passage that winds down, past a connecting corridor, to a small cavern filled with long-dead Nightstalker snacks.

3 Big Cavern (West)

Nightstalkers prowl this large natural chamber.

4 Water-Logged Cavern Junction

Offering three routes out, and filled with ankle-deep and lightly irradiated ground water, this is the cavern's lowest point.

5 Blast Door to One-Man Vault

Chiseled out of the cavern is a long-abandoned storage room. Pick the lock [HARD] and ransack the shelves for the following items.

- Assorted Tools
- Ammo Box Ammunition (3)
- Hunting Shotgun
- Grenade Box Ammunition
- Stimpaks, RadAway, and Rad-X
- Holotape: Post-War Audio Log
- Magazine: Today's Physician [Medicine] [1/19] [1/21]
- Magazine: Fixin' Things [Repair] [1/27] [2/21]
- Magazine: Lad's Life [Survival] [1/30] [3/21]
- Purified Water (10)
- Sleeping Quarters

6 Nightstalker Larder

This medium-sized cave holds a variety of half-eaten Bighorner parts, and scattered human skeletal remains, and a Unique Weapon. Enter this chamber, and search the dead Nightkin in here, to uncover a Quest-critical item: the Chewed Stealth Boy. The Nightkin isn't here unless this Quest is active.

- Quest Item: Chewed Stealth Boy
- Unique Weapon: Oh, Baby! [2/42]

[1.08] Silver Peak Mine

- Threat Level: ●●●●●
- Faction: Mutated Insect
  - Entity: Cazador
- Crafting: Workbench [2/41]
- Collectibles:
  - Hollowed-Out Rock [4/42]
  - Sunset Sarsaparilla Star Cap [3/100]
  - Skill Book: [Lockpick [1/4] [3/6]
  - Unique Item [1/95]
- Guns and Ammo
- Interior Exploration
- Sleeping Quarters

Up the rocky embankment to the west of Trail 157 is a small opening cut into the rock face, and a mine shack entrance. Inspect the Hollowed-Out Rock at the entrance, before heading inside.

- Hollowed-Out Rock [4/42]

A Door to Mojave Wasteland

1 Mine Shack Interior

The two-room shack has scattered tools and scrap metal, and the following, including a Shovel (useful for grave-robbing). Check the floor by the ransacked lockers for a Skill Book.

- Shovel
- Scrap Metal (3)
- Ammo Box Ammunition (3)
- Skill Book: Tumblers Today [Lockpick] [1/4] [3/6]
- Sunset Sarsaparilla Star Cap [3/100]
- Varmint Rifle
- Teddy Bear and Toy Box
- Sleeping Quarters
- Workbench [2/41]

B Door to Silver Peak Mine

C Door to Silver Peak Mine Shack

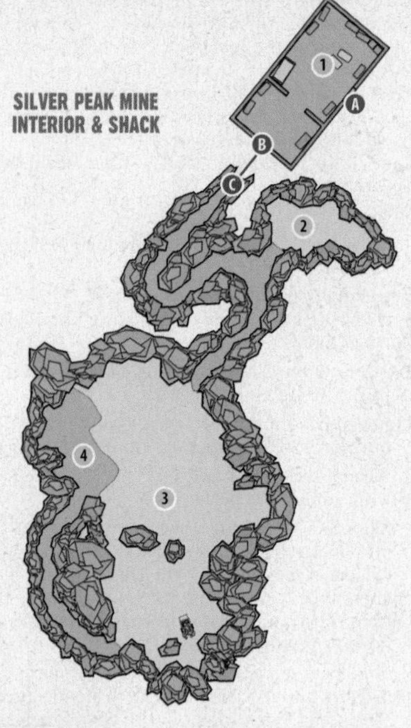

2 Storage Cavern

Halfway down the snaking and descending passage, an opening on your left leads to a small mine cavern with cluttered boxes and mine carts, and little else.

3 Cazador Cavern

This cavern houses a small (but ferocious) population of Cazadors. Ignore the high ledge. There is an exit tunnel near some Explosive Crates in the southwest wall.

- Explosives Crate Items (2)

4 Passage and Upper Ledge

Use this passage to reach the ledge above. This leads to a gate; open it and procure the following from the skeletal remains of an Enclave hold-out:

- Explosives Crate Items (2)
- Chems (Hydra)
- Unique Item: Remnants Power Helmet [1/95]

[1.09] Vault 22

See maps on the following page

- Side Quest: Bleed Me Dry
- Side Quest: I Could Make You Care
- Side Quest: Still in the Dark
- Side Quest: There Stands the Grass
- Free Quest: Suits You, Sarah
- Threat Level: ●●●●●
- Faction: Abomination
  - Entity: Keely
  - Entity: Giant Mantis
  - Entity: Spore Carrier
  - Entity: Spore Plant
- Collectibles:
  - Hollowed-Out Rock [5/42]
  - Skill Book [Barter] [1/4] [4/6]
  - Magazine [Science] [1/23] [4/21]
  - Unique Weapon [3/42]
- Area Is Locked
- Guns and Ammo
- Health, Chems, or Water
- Interior Exploration
- Sleeping Quarters
- Wasteland Vegetation
- Quest Item

Vault 22 was a "green" vault, filled with scientists dedicated to their experiment: keeping the entire population of the vault alive with plants grown with its confines. The experiment could be said to have exceeded all expectations, but with horrific side-effects. Many have attempted to locate the data the scientists left behind, but so far nobody has returned alive. The vault is open, but warning signs surround it from people lucky enough to survive their initial encounter with the vault's inhabitants. Don't forget to check the Hollowed-Out Rock on the right side of the gulley, across from the "Keep Out!" sign.

- Hollowed-Out Rock [5/42]

First Level: Vault 22—Entrance Hall

A Exit to Mojave Wasteland

1 Restored Terminal and Bedding

Find an explorer's bedding, a Magazine sandwiched between two Pre-War Books, and a rusting (but workable) Restored Terminal on the raised floor adjacent to the Vault Door. The terminal has two menu entries from a Vault 22 Expedition.

> Vault 22 Expedition, entry 1
> Vault 22 Expedition, entry 2

- Magazine: Programmer's Digest [Science] [1/23] [4/21]
- Duffle Bag Items
- Sleeping Quarters

2 Broken Elevator

This crossroads has a Vending Machine to bang on, as well as the door to an elevator [B]. You can:

Repair the elevator, which allows access to all five floors of this vault.

Or leave it alone. Your other option is to head left (south), down the stairs to the unlocked door [C].

B Broken Elevator

C Door to Vault 22—Oxygen Recycling

Second Level: Vault 22—Oxygen Recycling

B Broken Elevator

C Door to Vault 22—Entrance Hall

3 Stairwell Junction

This area allows quick access up or down to the Entrance Hall or Food Production, allowing you to avoid all chambers in this level.

D Door to Vault 22—Food Production

4 Laboratory Entrance

Thick vines snake up through the central ventilation area. This place is in ruins.

5 U-Shaped Corridor

This is the main conduit on this level. Note Keely's Laboratory to the south.

6 Small Incubation Room

Plants have thrust through the vents in this tiny chamber.

7 East Laboratory

Flora is running rampant. There's a very faint chittering noise. Another Restored Terminal contains an entry complaining about a "noise" in the duct work. It isn't written by Keely.

8 Keely's Laboratory

Check Keely's terminal for three more entries. You can also step into a viewing chamber to the east; this area (Location #32) is currently blocked and you can't access it.

> Vault 22 Expedition, entry 3
> Vault 22 Expedition, entry 4
> Vault 22 Expedition, entry 5

- Duffle Bag Items

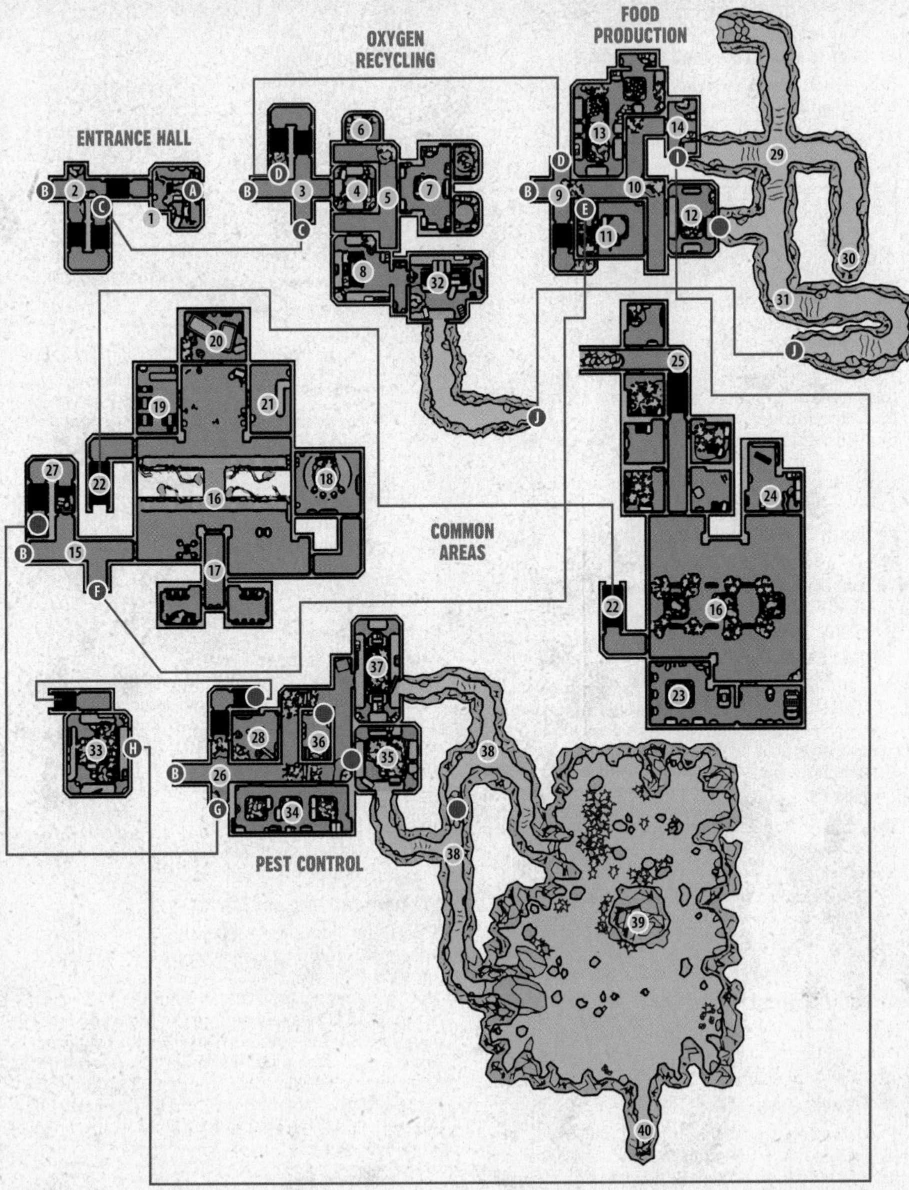

OXYGEN RECYCLING

FOOD PRODUCTION

ENTRANCE HALL

COMMON AREAS

PEST CONTROL

Ⓚ Door to Vault 22—Food Production

This leads back to a cave tunnel system that is first accessed down at the fifth level.

32 Viewing Laboratory

This is the laboratory you could see through the windows from Keely's Laboratory (#8). There's a vital (and unique) Quest Item inside the northeast locker, which is accessible whether you have Side Quest: Still in the Dark active or not. Grab this so you don't have to return. You must now traipse all the way back to Pest Control.

- Quest Item: HEPA 20 Cartridge Filer (6)

Third Level: Vault 22—Food Production

Ⓑ Broken Elevator

Ⓓ Door to Vault 22—Oxygen Recycling

9 Spore Carrier's Staircase

Brace for an attack from a horrific plant/humanoid hybrid called a Spore Carrier. It usually leaps from the clusters of plants growing on the ground. Expect more attacks throughout the rest of the vault. These stairs lead down to the Common Areas, or up to Oxygen Recycling, allowing you to avoid all chambers in this level.

Ⓔ Door to Vault 22—Common Areas

10 Spore Carrier's Corridor

Expect camouflaged Spore Carriers to leap from the foliage as you progress.

11 Water Purification

Strange ultraviolet lamps shine in one corner, and Keely's continuing (and startling) expedition Journal entries can be read on the terminal here.

> Vault 22 Expedition, entry 6

> Vault 22 Expedition, entry 7

12 Crop Laboratory and Cave Door Access

This small laboratory has the remains of crop plants, and a reinforced blast door in the eastern wall. The door requires a key, and the wall terminal doesn't give you permission to open it. Locate the Vault 22 Cave Door Keycard in Location #25, then swipe the wall terminal to release the lock, and access the cave system. The desk terminal has some alarming (but ancient) missives:

> Security Request

> Medical Emergency

> Help!

13 Food Production

More powerful Spore Carrier Brutes lurk in this L-shaped chamber. The northern raised computer room contains a monitor with some grim yield reports from the time the vault was active.

> Status Report 9228

> Status Report 9253

> Status Report 9312

- Food Additive

14 Observation Chamber

Open the door to a room providing a look out at a (currently inaccessible) part of the cavern system. Giant Mantises may be seen here.

Ⓘ Door to Vault 22—Pest Control

This is underneath, and leads to the winding cavern chambers to the east of here.

29 Cave Tunnel Junction

This area is accessed from Location #28; the Upper Laboratory on Fifth Level—Pest Control. Defeat the Giant Mantises here (there are at least six in the caves) before picking a path. The tunnel to the north is inaccessible.

30 Dead-End Tunnel

Face the largest Giant Mantis, a female guarding her ootheca, and then open it from the end of the tunnel. Inside is a Mantis Egg. This is handy if you're collecting these for Red Lucy, as part of Side Quest: Bleed Me Dry.

- Quest Item: Mantis Egg

31 Winding Tunnel

Head right (south), and pass the (still sealed) door to Location #12, and follow the tunnel all the way to the end to a door.

Ⓙ Door to Vault 22—Oxygen Recycling

You can now access the chamber on the other side of the glass wall from Keely's Laboratory (Location #8). Refer back for that information.

Fourth Level: Vault 22—Common Areas

Ⓑ Broken Elevator

Ⓕ Door to Vault 22—Food Production

15 Entrance Corridor

The stairs that continue down to Pest Control are blocked, and can never been accessed from this point, forcing you east to the mezzanine door.

16 (Upper and Lower) Mezzanine

This large, two-story location has been choked with vines. This hub area has multiple doors and doorways. Expect Spore Carrier attacks, mainly occurring downstairs.

17 (Upper) Restrooms

Beware of Spore Carriers in the ladies' stalls! The water is slightly irradiated, and unnecessary to drink unless you're parched.

18 (Upper) Overseer's Office

The terminal here is of specific interest. There are three menus, and you should unlock all locations:

> Unlock Crew Quarters. This locks the door to Location #25.

> Unlock Data Backup. This locks the door to Location #36.

> Unlock Cavern Access. This isn't possible due to the override.

19 (Upper) Cafeteria

The western cafeteria has some Fresh Fruit, and more Food in the fridge.

- Food

20 (Upper) Break Room

There are signs of a disturbance in this room, and odd UV lamps are active. Check the wall terminal, which has two additional entries (and progress) that Keely has made.

> Vault 22 Expedition, entry 8

> Vault 22 Expedition, entry 9

- Pool Cue (2)

21 (Upper) Bar

One corner contains some items, including some valuable Cave Fungus you could use in a Recipe.

- Cave Fungus
- Beer, Wine, Scotch and Vodka
- First Aid Box

22 (Upper and Lower) Stairs

If you don't want to jump from the mezzanine, this is the longer, slightly safer way to descend.

23 (Lower) Utility Rooms

Locate the doorway with the "Utility" sign in the south wall. The first room is a small generator area with a terminal and tool cabinet. The terminal has a couple of worrying emails. The adjoining chamber to the west has a sparking transformer and some weapons.

> Ticket 1—Strange noises

> Ticket 2—Gas leak?

- Tool Cabinet Items (4)
- Laser Pistol and Ammo
- Flamer and Ammo

24 (Lower) Clinic

There's a terminal to check, which has a number of cases of vault dwellers with unusual viral infections.

> Case 162 (and three updates)

> Case 164 (group)

> Case 173 (group)

- Tool Cabinet Items (3)
- First Aid Box

25 (Lower and Upper) Crew Quarters [Average]

This area is locked, unless you unlocked it in the Overseer's office. A corridor leads to some stairs, with two doors on either side. Three of the doors lead to a small room and bed to sleep on. Check the first door on the left (west) for an ambush from three Spore Carriers and overwhelming fernery! Don't forget your Vault 22 Jumpsuit souvenir from any of the dressers (especially if you're collecting them for Sarah at Vault 21), and the Vault 22 Cave Door Keycard, allowing access at Location #12). At the top of the steps is a vicious Spore Plant and two more rooms contain Spore Carriers. The fallen rocks ahead stop further progress.

- Scrap Metal
- Teddy Bear (2) Quest Item: Vault 22 Cave Door Keycard
- Sleeping Quarters
- Vault 22 Jumpsuit

27 Common Areas Blocked Staircase

Head down to the fifth level, enter the Entrance Corridor [26], and then look for the Door to Vault 22—Common Areas [Very Easy], which is locked. Head back up the stairs to the blockage, fighting a couple of Giant Mantises on the stairwell. The detour is worth it; a skeleton lies next to an AER14 Prototype Laser Rifle and some scattered ammo.

- Unique Weapon: AER14 Prototype Laser Rifle [3/42]

Fifth Level: Vault 22—Pest Control

B Broken Elevator

G Door to Vault 22—Common Areas [Very Easy]

Unlock this door to return to the previous floor's stairwell to secure a Unique Item.

26 Entrance Corridor

The long, branching (no pun intended) corridor stretches off to the east.

28 (Upper) Laboratory Classroom

Take the stairs to the north and enter this laboratory classroom, fighting off Spore Carriers as you go. There's a Skill Book on the side table, and the teacher's terminal is still active. This provides evidence of the "non-walking" plants that the vault dwellers had spliced together. A reinforced blast door allows access back into the cave system of the Food Production level.

> Species 1

> Species 2

> Species 3

- Skill Book: Tales of a Junktown Jerky Vendor [Barter] [1/4] [4/6]

H Door to Vault 22—Food Production

Note which previous locations you should visit before continuing.

33 (Lower) Office

Head east down the Entrance Corridor (#26), and ignore the first door on the right. Kill any Spore Carriers, and make a left, because the way ahead is blocked. This leads to an L-shaped corridor with another blockade and enemies. Check the door on the left (west) wall. It leads to a small office with UV lamps keeping a Spore Plant at bay.

34 Cultivation Chamber

The only way to reach farther into this level is to access the first door on your right (south) from the Entrance Corridor (#26), which leads into this Cultivation Chamber. Nullify the Spore Plants before exiting the door farther along the room, circumventing the plant blockade back in the corridor.

35 South Cultivation Chamber [Hard]

The door to this location is locked. Usually, you'd access this on your return from the Giant Cavern (#39), unlocking the door via the wall terminal on the inside of the room.

36 Data Room

This chamber with the "No Access" door has all of the data that the vault dwellers collected before their unfortunate demise. This information is critical two Side Quests. There is a single menu that you should access:

> Download research data

This data is important to three interested parties, and it is recommended that you have these Quests active:

Doctor Thomas Hildern, as part of Side Quest: There Stands the Grass.

Keely, as part of Side Quest: There Stands the Grass.

Veronica, as part of Side Quest: I Could Make You Care.

37 North Cultivation Chamber

Note that this set of tunnels is completely separate from the ones on the higher floors. Watch out for Spore Plants.

38 Tunnels (Two Sections)

Check both paths at the junction. One is blocked, so take the other into the Giant Cavern (no matter which section of tunnel you're in).

39 Giant Cavern

This huge, subterranean cavern is brimming with snapping plants, Giant Mantises, and scattered oothecae you can grab Mantis Eggs from. Head south to locate a small alcove tunnel. Note that the exit to the other section of tunnel is via ascending a large, curved rock.

- Mantis Egg

40 Keely's Antechamber

The scientist who survived longer than the Mercenaries Doctor Hildern sent down here is in this antechamber, waiting for rescue, as part of Side Quest: There Stands the Grass.

[1.10] Jacobstown

See maps on the following page

- Side Quest: For Auld Lang Syne
- Side Quest: Guess Who I Saw Today
- Side Quest: Nothin' But a Hound Dog
- Side Quest: Unfriendly Persuasion
- Free Quest: Lily and Leo
- Threat Level: ●●●●●
- Faction: Super Mutant
  - Entity: Marcus
  - Entity: Lily
  - Entity: Keene
  - Entity: Doctor Henry
  - Entity: Calamity
  - Entity: Super Mutant
  - Entity: Nightkin
  - Entity: Bighorner
- Services:
  - Repairer [1/9]
  - Trader [1/33]
- Crafting: Reloading Bench [2/36]
- Dangers: Radiation
- Collectibles:
  - Hollowed-Out Rock [6/42]
  - Skill Book [Melee Weapons] [1/4] [5/6]
  - Magazine [Repair] [2/27] [5-8/21]
  - Magazine [Science] [2/23] [5-8/21]
  - Magazine [Survival] [2/30] [5-8/21]
  - Magazine [Unarmed] [1/11] [5-8/21]
  - Snow Globe [1/7]
  - Sunset Sarsaparilla Star Cap [4/100]
  - Unique Item [2/95]
- Follower
- Guns and Ammo
- Health, Chems or Water
- Interior Exploration
- Perk!
- Sleeping Quarters
- Wasteland Vegetation
- Quest Item

Marcus, a mild-mannered Super Mutant sheriff of Broken Hills took it upon himself to find a refuge for the "broken-minded" of his kind: low-intelligence Super Mutants and schizophrenic Nightkin. It proved to be more difficult than holding on to Broken Hills, but he eventually decided Jacobstown was a good spot to set up a community. Despite splinter groups (Davison and Tabitha), Marcus does his best to take care of Lily and the other Super Mutants and Nightkin at Jacobstown.

1 Town Entrance and Marcus

Check the clump of rocks to the right (north) of the guards to find a Hollowed-Out Rock. Step forward to receive welcome from Marcus. He tells you to keep any alliance with the NCR to yourself, and to avoid baiting the Nightkins. You can ask him more about the place, and what he thinks about the major Factions. The second time you enter this place (after visiting the lodge), Marcus informs you he's being hassled by Mercenaries. This starts Side Quest: Unfriendly Persuasion.

- Hollowed-Out Rock [6/42]

2 Town Sign and Lodge Exterior

The small pond is slightly irradiated. You can explore the perimeter and behind the lodge, but there's nothing to find but melting snow.

3 Jacobstown Bungalow #1 (South)

Only three of the seven bungalows are accessible. One has the following:

- Skill Book: Grognak the Barbarian [Melee Weapons] [1/4] [5/6]
- Unique Item: Nuka-Cola Victory [2/95]
- Carton of Cigarettes
- Sleeping Quarters

4 Jacobstown Bungalow #2 (North)

A card game ended in one player (now skeletal) losing everything.

- Sunset Sarsaparilla Star Cap [4/100]
- Footlocker Items (2)
- Food and Drink
- Sleeping Quarters

5 Jacobstown Bungalow #3 (West) [Average]

Pick the lock to enter another wrecked chalet.

- Service Rifle and Ammo
- Dino Toy
- Sleeping Quarters

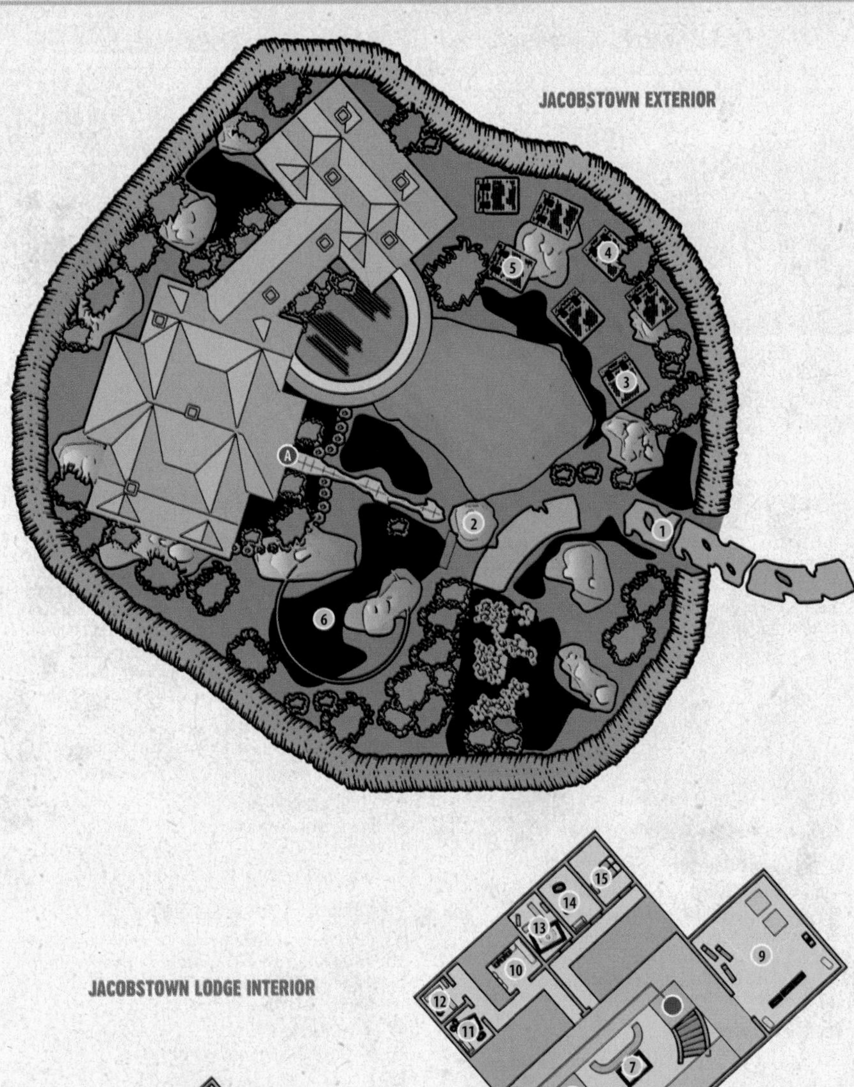

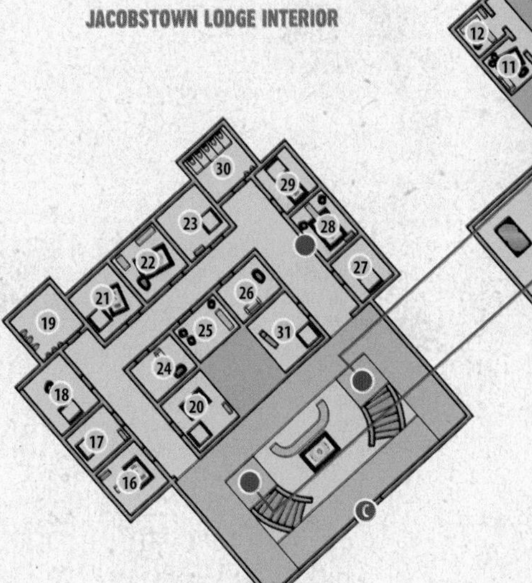

6 Lily's Bighorner Pen

Speak to a Nightkin named Lily, who's mistaken you for her grandson Jimmy. She's obviously delusional, but very sweet and seemingly loyal. Ask her to join you as part of, and also optionally at the end of Side Quest: Guess Who I Saw Today. She's also featured in Free Quest: Lily and Leo. She also has a fascinating history, including information on The Master.

- Follower: Lily
- Perk!: Stealthgirl

A Door to Jacobstown Lodge

Jacobstown Lodge

B Door to Jacobstown Exterior (Ground)

7 (Ground and Upper Floor) Entrance Hall and Keene

Nightkin wander the lodge interior, and Keene slightly berates you at the entrance. This uneasy peace between the Nightkin and Doctor Henry is extremely delicately balanced. Between the curved staircases is the front desk with a Snow Globe.

- Snow Globe—Mt. Charleston [1/7]

Note You found a Limited Edition Mojave Landmark Snowglobe! These rare, Pre-War artifacts are widely considered to be useless baubles, but rumor has it some collectors will pay dearly for them.

C Door to Jacobstown Balcony (Upper)

The outside balcony has a couple of Super Mutants enjoying the view.

8 (Ground Floor) Pool Room

While the Nightkins stomp about complaining about their pain, you can glance at this large room with pool tables.

- Pool Cue (5)

9 (Ground Floor) Doctor Henry's Clinic

Doctor Henry and his Ghoul assistant Calamity run a clinic for Super Mutants, but Henry's main research is into Stealth technology and curing the Nightkin's craziness.

- Repairer: Calamity [SKILL 60] [1/9]
- Trader: Calamity: [1/33] Possibility of items such as:
  - Doctor's Bag
  - Skill Magazines (not counted toward Collectibles total)
  - Stimpaks and Super Stimpaks

He's initially annoyed at your presence, but once you're pleasant, Doctor Henry asks you to help him with his research. So begins Side Quest: Guess Who I Saw Today. This is also how to get Lily as a Follower, and is necessary when completing elements of the other listed Side Quests: when requesting that he reunite with his old Enclave buddies as part of Side Quest: For Auld Lang Syne; or whether he can help save the brain of Rex, as part of Side Quest: Nothin' But a Hound Dog. You can also read the notes on Doctor Henry's terminal:

> Nightkin Test Data

> Mark II Prototype

> Keene

- Quest Item: Stealth Boy Mark II Prototype
- Sleeping Quarters

10 (Ground) Lodge Kitchens

Expect a bit of a mess, and some Food.

11 (Ground) Small Lounge #1

- Carton of Cigarettes

12 (Ground) Small Lounge #2

- Sleeping Quarters

13 (Ground) Small Lounge #3

- Sleeping Quarters

14 (Ground) Small Lounge #4

This is the middle room in the right-side corridor behind the front desk.

- Sensor Module (2)

15 (Ground) Staff Bedroom

- Footlocker Items
- Ammo Box Ammunition (2)
- Sleeping Quarters

16 (Upper) Left Corridor Bedroom #1

- Sleeping Quarters

17 (Upper) Left Corridor Bedroom #2

- Sleeping Quarters

18 (Upper) Left Corridor Bedroom #3

This has a small science experiment in one corner.

- Teddy Bear
- Sleeping Quarters

19 (Upper) Left Corridor Restrooms (Gentlemen)

You can sip radiation-free water from the sinks here.

20 (Upper) Left Corridor Bedroom #4

- Footlocker Items
- Ammo Box Ammunition
- Floor Safe Items [Average]
- Sleeping Quarters

21 (Upper) Connecting Corridor Bedroom #1

This is a junkie's room, with scattered syringes and Chems.

- Chems (Buffout, Fixer, Rebound)
- Sleeping Quarters

22 (Upper) Connecting Corridor Bedroom #2

This contains the remains of a pinball machine, imported all the way from Point Lookout!

- Sleeping Quarters

23 (Upper) Connecting Corridor Bedroom #3

- Magazine: Boxing Times [Unarmed] [1/11] [5/21]
- Chems and Bobby Pins
- Sleeping Quarters

24 (Upper) Connecting Corridor Lounge #1

- Sensor Module (2)

25 (Upper) Connecting Corridor Lounge #2

- Sleeping Quarters

26 (Upper) Connecting Corridor Lounge #3

- Magazine: Fixin' Things [Repair] [2/27] [6/21]
- Magazine: Programmer's Digest [Science] [2/23] [7/21]
- Sleeping Quarters

27 (Upper) Right Corridor Bedroom #1

- Ammo Box Ammunition (2)
- Footlocker Items (2)
- Sleeping Quarters

28 (Upper) Marcus' Room [Hard]

Pry the lock open to enter this chamber, which is mostly empty.

- Carton of Cigarettes
- Sleeping Quarters

29 (Upper) Right Corridor Bedroom #3

Sleep on the bed if you can avoid the radio equipment.

- Weapon Repair Kit
- Sleeping Quarters

30 (Upper) Right Corridor Restrooms (Ladies)

Sip radiation-free water from the sinks here.

31 (Upper) Right Corridor Bedroom #4

This looks to be a dump for tinkering and medical equipment.

- Reloading Bench [2/36]
- Doctor's Bag
- Magazine: Lad's Life [Survival] [2/30] [8/21]
- Carton of Cigarettes (2)
- Ammo Box Ammunition (2)
- Sleeping Quarters

Free Quest: Lily and Leo

After Side Quest: Guess Who I Saw Today is over, you can speak to Lily once again, and ask her to accompany you as a Follower. You immediately receive the Stealthgirl perk, and an impressive combat machine. However, once you've left Jacobstown and entered combat, Lily sometimes falls early, or rampages without regard for her safety, which is troubling. After the fight, ask her what happened. She tells you she listens to Leo, but sometimes she forgets to take medicine. These psychotic episodes are due to this "Leo" character; an aspect of Lily's personality just as real to her as you are.

Ask about her tactics, and you can tweak her combat effectiveness, but to significantly change Lily's mental state, you can choose how much medicine she takes:

1. Tell her to take her medicine every time she is supposed to. She no longer suffers from psychotic breaks, but her combat effectiveness is greatly reduced.
2. Tell her to take her medicine half as often as she is supposed to. She will still suffer psychotic breaks if her health reaches one quarter, but she will break off combat if you begin Sneaking.
3. Tell her to stop taking her medicine: She will suffer psychotic breaks if her health reaches one-half, but her combat abilities are significantly improved.

- Follower: Lily
- Perk!: Stealthgirl

[1.11] Remnants Bunker

See map below

- Side Quest: For Auld Lang Syne
- Threat Level: ●●●●●
- Faction: Enclave
- Collectibles:
  - Hollowed-Out Rock [7/42]
  - Unique Item [3/95]
  - Unique Item [4/95]
- Area Is Locked
- Guns and Ammo
- Interior Exploration
- Perk!
- Quest Item

Off the beaten track in the rocky and wooded wilderness is a rocky outcrop with an overhang and a small hatch at its base. Right of this easy-to-miss opening is a Hollowed-Out Rock. The hatch is unlocked.

- Hollowed-Out Rock [7/42]

Note: Aside from the entrance corridor, the following interior locations can only be accessed during Side Quest: For Auld Lang Syne.

A Ladder to Mojave Wasteland

1 Bunker Door Control

The panel responds to a passphrase; "Dear old friends, remember Navarro." This is only accessible once you've met and agreed to facilitate a reunion with Doctor Henry, Daisy Whitman, Cannibal Johnson, Orion Moreno, and Judah Kregar.

2 Vertibird Hangar

The hangar holds a pristine Enclave Vertibird (which only Daisy Whitman can fly). Against the south wall are six suits of Remnants Power Armor that must be earned during the Quest, along with the necessary perk to control them properly.

- Ammo Box Ammunition (2)
- Perk! Power Armor Training
- Remnants Power Armor
- Remnants Power Helmet
- Unique Item: Gannon Family Tesla Armor [3/95]
- Unique Item: Gannon Family Tesla Helmet [4/95]
- Quest Item: Door Override Card

3 Command Room

The Remnants meet up in this small, circular chamber after you reunite them.

[1.12] Ranger Station Foxtrot ●

- Side Quest: Return to Sender
- Free Quest: Lenk's Bad Debts
- Threat Level: ●●●●●
- Faction: NCR
  - Entity: Ranger Kudlow
  - Entity: Comm Officer Lenk
- Fame/Infamy
- Crafting:
  - Campfire [3/109]
  - Reloading Bench [3/36]
- Guns and Ammo
- Health, Chems, or Water
- Interior Exploration
- Lots O' Caps
- Sleeping Quarters
- Wasteland Vegetation

Nestled at the foot of a radio mast in a dead-end mountainous gulch is the small ranger station with four solders, run by Comm Officer Lenk. Aside from the Scotch scattered around camp, this looks to be a reasonably well-run outpost, which keeps a look-out for the nearby Great Khans.

- Campfire [3/109]
- Reloading Bench [3/36]
- Produce Sack Items
- Sunset Sarsaparilla Crate Items
- Purified Water (3)
- First Aid Box [Very Easy]
- Ammo Box Ammunition
- Mine Box Ammunition [Very Easy]
- Sleeping Quarters

Free Quest: Lenk's Bad Debts

As soon as you speak with Comm Officer Lenk, she blurts out that you must tell your Omerta masters that she needs more time. She's mistaken you for a collector. You can:

A1. Lie, and tell her that's why you're here, and to pay what she owes. She obliges.

NCR Infamy Gained!

Caps (250)

- A2. You can ask what happened, and she tells you about money the Omertas lent to her. Now they want it back. You can lie (A1), ask again (A2), or tell her your opinion of the Rangers (A3).
- A3. You can tell her you thought the NCR were brave. Lenk doesn't want to talk. You can:

Ask to hear her version, not someone else's. She tells you that her patrol was ambushed by the Legion, all were killed except her, and the remorse she felt lead to gambling, and the aforementioned debts. You can:

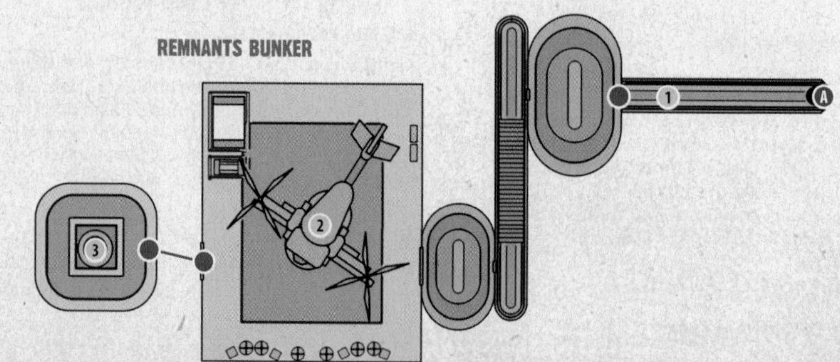

 Tell her she was tough to kill, and she'll get payback.

Talk about something else.

 Or tell her she's pathetic, then try another option.

Or talk about something else (A4).

- A4. You can also talk about what she's doing here (checking on the movements of the Great Khans).

[1.13] Brewer's Beer Bootlegging

- Free Quest: Strategic Nuclear Moose
- Threat Level: ●●●●●
- Faction: Mutated Insect
  - Entity: Cazador
  - Entity: Gourd (Deceased)
- Crafting: Campfire [4/109]
- Collectibles:
  - Skill Book: [Science] [1/4] [6/6]
  - Sunset Sarsaparilla Star Cap [5/100]
- Guns and Ammo
- Health, Chems, or Water
- Interior Exploration
- Sleeping Quarters

In the hills to the west of New Vegas, after a short ascent along a rocky pathway is a small shack. Among the prowling Nightstalkers is the body of a man named Gourd.

- Sunset Sarsaparilla Crate Items

Shack Entrance Room

The place is a mess, and includes a Campfire inside the structure (hardly safe!). Check the top of the low shelf nearest the cellar door for a Star Cap and the key that opens the cellar door.

- Campfire [4/109]
- Chems and Alcohol
- Sunset Sarsaparilla Star Cap [5/100]
- Key
- Sleeping Quarters

Bootlegger's Storage

Open the Cellar Door [Average] and descend into a two-room cellar.

- Explosives Crate Items (2) [1 = Average]
- BB Gun and Ammo (20)
- First Aid Box
- Gun Cabinet Items [Hard]
- Ammo Box Ammunition (2)
- Crate Items (3)
- Sleeping Quarters

Free Quest: Strategic Nuclear Moose

The back of the two-room chamber sports a small distillery, with the phrase "Strategic Nuclear Moose: And God said, let them have beer" advertising Gourd's concoction. The dozens of Beer Bottles here can get you alarmingly drunk. Don't forget the Skill Book on the table!

- Beer (51)
- Skill Book: Big Book of Science [Science] [1/4] [6/6]

[1.14] Red Rock Drug Lab

- Side Quest: Aba Daba Honeymoon
- Side Quest: Oh, My Papa
- Threat Level: ●●●●●
- Faction: Great Khan
  - Entity: Jack
  - Entity: Diane
- Services: Healer/Dealer [2/31]
- Crafting: Campfire [5/109]
- Collectibles:
  - Magazine: [Medicine] [2/19] [9-10/21]
  - Magazine: [Science] [3/23] [9-10/21]
- Health, Chems, or Water
- Lots O' Caps
- Perk!
- Sleeping Quarters

In the northern end of the Red Rock Canyon, where the Great Khans have their encampment, are two Chem dealers named Jack and Diane. They sell to folks looking

for a fix from across the Mojave. Their base of operations is a cluster of rusting trailers. The two longer ones have their "cooking" implements and their bedding. Jack and Diane are part of Papa Khan's more influential brethren, consulted during Side Quest: Oh, My Papa. They have their own Quest, where you can do odd jobs for Diane, leading to some sizable Caps rewards, and teach Jack how to make new Chems (he rewards you with an Unarmed Move called the Khan Trick). Otherwise, Jack sells you Chems.

- Campfire [5/109]
- Healer/Dealer: (Jack) [2/31]
- Footlocker Items (2)
- Cave Fungus (3)
- Magazine: Today's Physician [Medicine] [2/19] [9/21]
- Magazine: Programmer's Digest [Science] [3/23] [10/21]
- Perk! Khan Trick
- Sleeping Quarters

[1.15] Red Rock Canyon ●

- Main Quest: For the Republic, Part 2
- Main Quest: Wild Card: Side Bets
- Side Quest: Aba Daba Honeymoon
- Side Quest: Cry Me a River
- Side Quest: Oh My Papa
- Threat Level: ●●●●●
- Faction: Great Khan
  - Entity: Papa Khan
  - Entity: Regis
  - Entity: Karl
  - Entity: Jerry the Punk
  - Entity: Great Khan
- Fame/Infamy
- Trader [2/33]
- Crafting:
  - Campfire [6/109]
  - Campfire [7/109]
  - Campfire [8/109]
  - Campfire [9/109]
  - Reloading Bench [4/36]
  - Workbench [3/41]
  - Weapon Upgrade [1/10]
- Collectibles:
  - Magazine: [Guns] [1/11] [11-13/21]
  - Magazine: [Science] [4/23] [11-13/21]
  - Magazine: [Survival] [3/30] [11-13/21]
  - Unique Item [5/95]

RED ROCK CANYON EXTERIOR

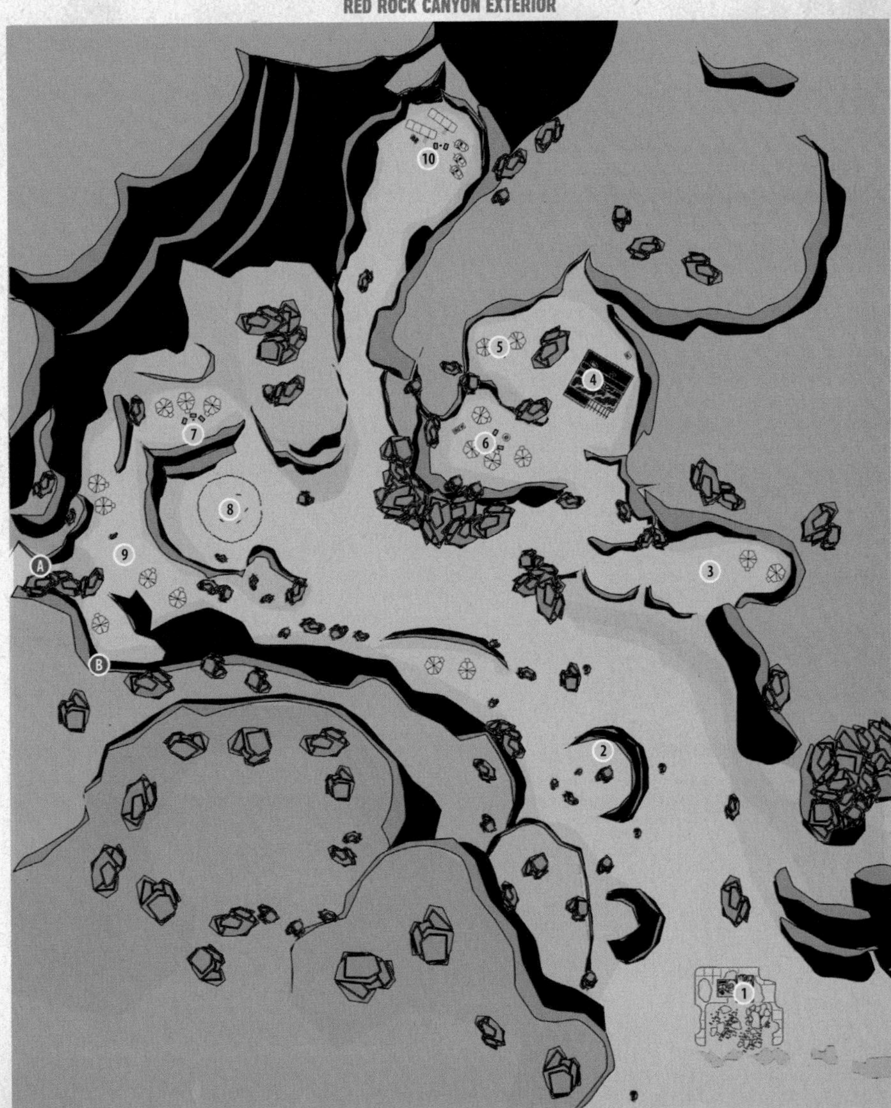

- Guns and Ammo
- Health, Chems or Water
- Highly Visible
- Interior Exploration
- Sleeping Quarters
- Wasteland Vegetation
- Quest Item

Pre-War, Red Rock Canyon was a popular tourist attraction. Remnants of Pre-War campsites and ancient petroglyphs still dot the area even though it has been completely dominated by the Great Khans. The Great Khans have their camps and outposts spread throughout the area, though most of them are concentrated in one area near the red rocks themselves. The Great Khans relocated here after the Bitter Springs Massacre, where NCR accidentally killed a large number of noncombatants during an otherwise normal skirmish between the two groups. Today, the Great Khans while away their time, dreaming of past glories while resorting to petty drug-dealing and battles by proxy (the Fiends) with the NCR.

1 Great Khan Armory

Hidden in the basement of the burned-out dwelling are the Great Khan Armorer and her bodyguard. They aren't so talkative until your Reputation with the Great Khans is "Liked" or better. Then you can Trade with the Armorer.

- Reloading Bench [4/36]
- Workbench [3/41]
- Trader: Great Khan Armorer [2/33]
- Trader [Great Khan Armorer]: Weapon Upgrades [Guns] [1/10]

Otherwise, the following items are behind the cell doors [Hard].

- Ammo Box Ammuntion (4)
- Dynamite
- Gun Cabinet Items (2)
- Scrap Metal and Hydra

2 Rocky Promontory

This offers some of the best views of the settlement.

3 Petroglyph Tents

4 Great Khan Longhouse

This is the main dwelling, and home to Papa Khan himself. You can speak to him about his past, the tribe, and a number of other matters related to Side Quest: Oh My Papa. Regis usually joins in for a feast, and Karl is an emissary from Caesar's Legion. Consult the Side Quest for the conversation options with him.

Across from the feasting tables (there's plenty of Food and Fruit both there and in the kitchen, but you'll need to steal it) is a fireplace with a Campfire. Opposite the kitchen is Karl's bedroom, containing a footlocker with some interesting Journal entries. The other bedroom [Hard] can be pried open from inside or outside, and is where Papa Khan rests.

- Campfire [6/109] (When lit, this cannot be used for Crafting)
- Fruit, Wine, and Food
- Quest Item: Karl's Journal
- Gun Cabinet Items
- Unique Item: Papa Khan's Helmet [5/95]

5 Upper Tents

6 Regis' Campfire and Tents

A Brahmin roasts on a Campfire. Grab the following from the two tents you can enter:

- Campfire [7/109]
- Campfire [8/109]
- Magazine: Milsurp Review [Guns] [1/11] [11/21]
- Magazine: Programmer's Digest [Science] [4/23] [12/21]
- Magazine: Lad's Life [Survival] [3/30] [13/21]
- Duffle Bag Items
- Footlocker Items
- Sleeping Quarters

7 Upper Tents

- Campfire [9/109]
- Footlocker Items (2)
- Duffle Bag Items

8 Training Circle

Great Khans are adept in unarmed combat, and all are practicing in this arena except Jerry the Punk, who's more inclined to write poetry: Side Quest: Cry Me a River.

9 Western Tents

The south mountain paths leads up and around to Spring Mt. Ranch State Park's pond [1.18]. The one to the west cuts up through the northwest mountains, bringing you out toward Jacobstown [1.10].

- Footlocker Items
- Duffle Bag Items
- Sleeping Quarters

A Entrance to Red Rock Pathway [1.S17]

B Entrance to Pine Ravines Pathway [1.S16]

10 Red Rock Drug Lab [1.14]

[1.16] Chance's Map

- Threat Level: ●●●●●
- Faction: Prospector
  Entity: None
- Collectibles: Hollowed-Out Rock [8/42]
- Wasteland Vegetation

By a couple of route markers for Trail 160, and close to a Hollowed-Out Rock, is a patch of ground with a variety of junk items strewn through it. This is Chance's Map. You can find out where Chance is now [4.S01]!

- Hollowed-Out Rock [8/42]

[1.17] Poseidon Gas Station

- Threat Level: ●●●●●
- Faction: Fiend
- Dangers: Radiation
- Collectibles: Magazine: [Crit. Chance] [1/11] [14/21]

North of the Violet and Violetta Trailer Compound [1.S22] at the head of trail 160, is a dumping ground of half-buried radioactive barrels. Beware of Fiends operating in this area, and check the police car for duct tape, and the following:

- Magazine: True Police Stories [Crit. Chance] [1/11] [14/21]
- Weapon Repair Kit

[1.18] Spring Mt. Ranch State Park

- Threat Level: ●●●●●
- Faction: Mutated Animal
  Entity: Giant Mantis
- Dangers: Radiation
- Wasteland Vegetation

A section of rough gravel road leads to a couple of fenced areas of scrubland, a parking area, and two ruined buildings containing nothing but rubble. Farther west still are two picnic areas and a small, slightly irradiated lake, now overrun by Giant Mantises. Across the lake is a foot trail allowing you access into the mountains, ending up at the far end of the Great Khan encampment.

[1.19] Nopah Cave

- Threat Level: ●●●●●
- Faction: Mutated Animal
  Entity: Fire Gecko
- Collectibles: Unique Item [6/95]
- Interior Exploration

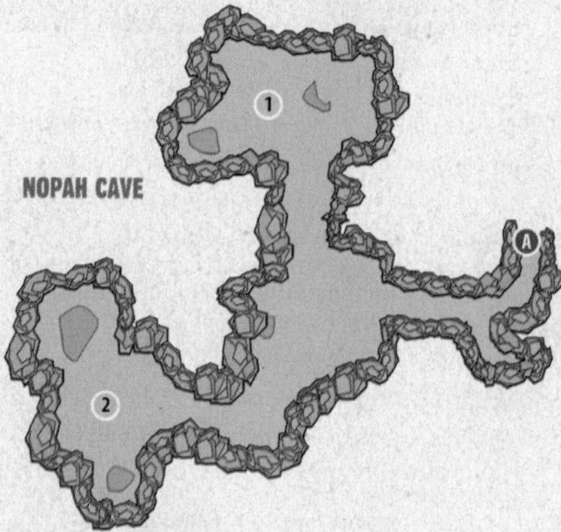

These ancient caverns were once famed for trilobite fossils, but Fire Geckos roam here now.

A Exit to Mojave Wasteland

1 North Cavern

Expect a half-dozen Fire Geckos of various sizes.

2 Southwest Cavern

This is a second breeding ground for Fire Geckos. Also search the dead Super Mutant, and locate the skeleton next to a well-stocked pack.

- Gecko Meat and Hide
- Unique Item: Adventurer's Pack [6/95]

[1.20] Bonnie Springs

- Threat Level: ●●●●●
- Faction: Viper Gang
  Entity: Viper Gang Leader
  Entity: Viper Gang Member
- Crafting: Campfire [10/109]
- Collectibles:
  Sunset Sarsaparilla Star Cap [6/100]
  Sunset Sarsaparilla Star Cap [7/100]
  Unique Weapon [4/42]
- Highly Visible
- Wasteland Vegetation

Slowly fading from memory and crumbling into the dirt is the old mining ghost town of Bonnie Springs. Use this location as a landmark. The ghost town itself is being ransacked by around six Viper Gang members with two Leaders. Be sure to loot a Unique set of Spiked Knuckles from the one who tries hand-to-hand combat with you. Then check the second building porch for a couple of Star Caps.

- Campfire [10/109]
- Sunset Sarsaparilla Star Cap [6/100]
- Sunset Sarsaparilla Star Cap [7/100]
- Unique Weapon: Love and Hate [4/42]

[1.21] Vault 19

- Side Quest: Why Can't We Be Friends?
- Free Quest: Suits You, Sarah
- Threat Level: ●●●●●
- Faction: Powder Ganger (Escaped Convict)
  - Entity: Samuel Cooke
  - Entity: Philip Lem
  - Entity: Escaped Convict
  - Entity: Fire Gecko
  - Entity: Nightstalker
- Dangers: Mines
- Collectibles:
  - Sunset Sarsaparilla Star Cap [8/100]
  - Magazine [Medicine] [3/19] [15-16/21]
  - Magazine [Science] [5/23] [15-16/21]
- Guns and Ammo
- Health, Chems, or Water
- Interior Exploration
- Sleeping Quarters
- Underground Connection
- Quest Item

Vault 19's "social experiment" involved the segregation of the dwellers into two different colored sections, with minimal contact. After the sulfur from the cave system beneath the vault unexpectedly began to leak through the ventilation system, a sense of paranoia grew, and the place became abandoned, although records are pretty sketchy. The vault has two entrances: via a parking lot, or the caves themselves [1.S27]. The Great Khans avoided the place (as historically, they haven't had the best of times squatting in vaults) as they moved north. No other group has been aggressive enough to attempt to displace the Fire Geckos from the vault. Powder Gangers, searching for a place to turn into a base, explored the upper floor of Vault 19 and found that it was "mostly clear." Now they wait, with a fragmented leadership.

Vault 19—First Floor

Ⓐ Ladder to Mojave Wasteland

1 Vault Door and Entrance Room

This involves descending from a Manhole cover on the surface.

2 Overseer's Office #1: Samuel Cooke

Enter the Overseer's office, where you meet an agitated Samuel Cooke. You can ask him about work, and what's got him worked up. He requests you clear the Sulfur Caves of marauding Geckos. This begins Side Quest: Why Can't We Be Friends? You receive a Red Keycard, allowing you to enter any of the locked doors marked red on the guide map.

- Quest Item: Red Sector Keycard

3 Overseer's Office #2: Philip Lem

Head through the open doorway, and enter the Overseer's office, where you meet a laid-back, but rather annoyed Lem. He needs you to cut off access to the Sulfur Caves, to prevent Cooke from mining them. This also begins Side Quest: Why Can't We Be Friends? You receive a Blue Keycard, allowing you to enter any of the locked doors marked blue on the guide map. There is also a working terminal here, and the following menus:

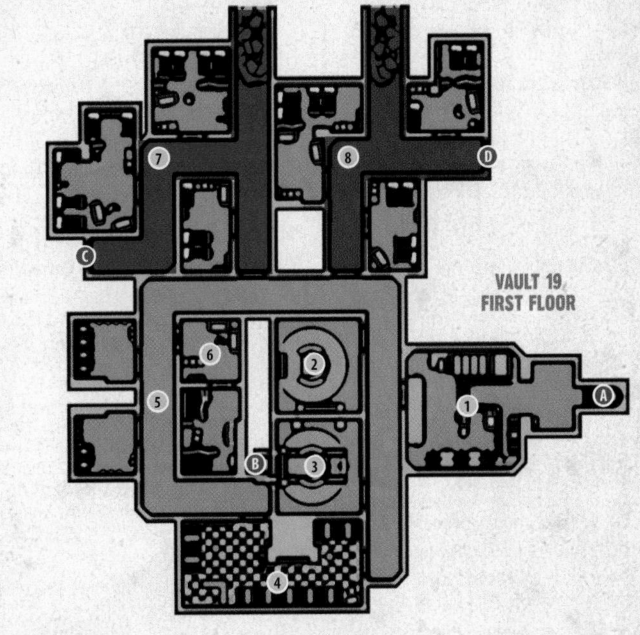

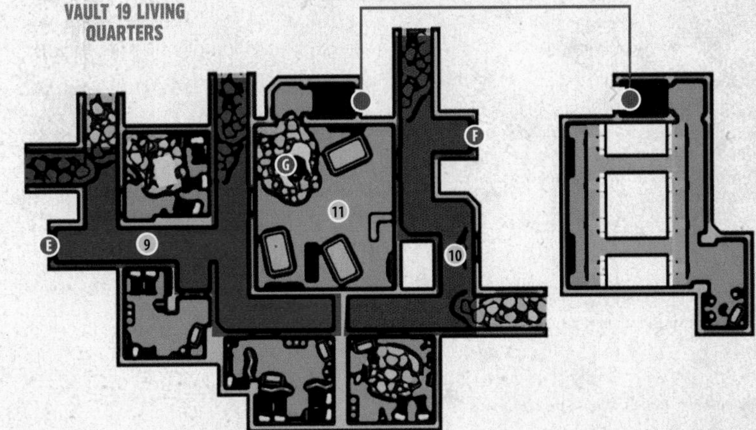

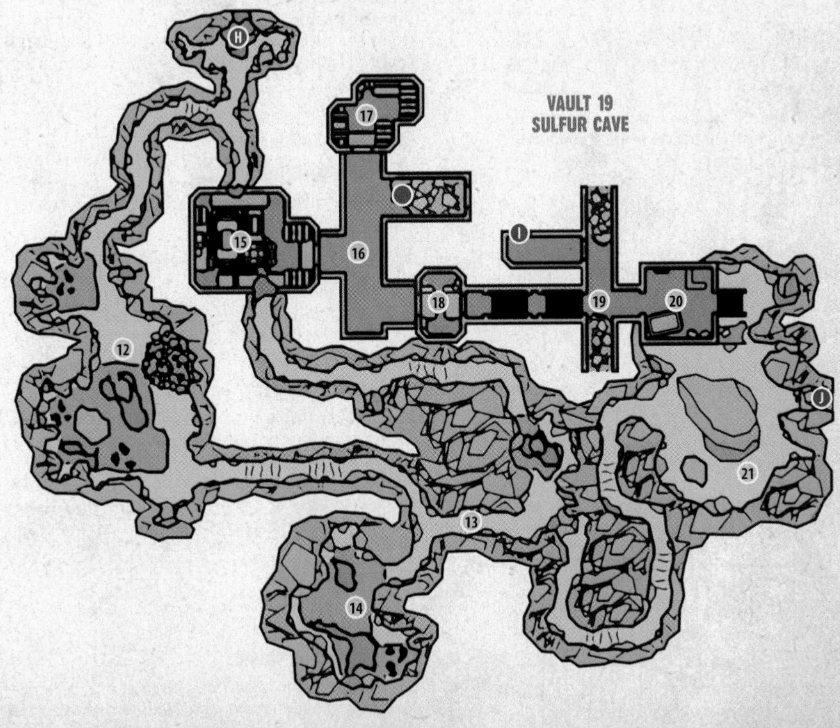

> Recover Data

> -data corrupted-: Read this to uncover a password to reach back here from the Reactor area.

- Quest Item: Blue Sector Keycard

B Elevator—To Sulfur Caves (inaccessible, and under Overseer desk)

This is inaccessible from here, but you can return from the Sulfur Caves, opening the floor of the Overseer's office via a wall terminal [Average].

4 Diner

A few Escaped Convicts mooch about. Check the Vending Machines in the southeast corner for some hidden C-4.

- Quest Item: C-4 Plastic Explosive
- First Aid Box

5 Restrooms and Connecting Corridor

- First Aid Box (2)

6 Clinic

The doctor's desk, aside from the Skill Magazine, has a number of scattered Holotapes detailing deranged mental states of patients brought here.

- Doctor's Bag (2) and Stimpaks
- First Aid Box (3) and Teddy Bear
- Magazine: Today's Physician [Medicine] [3/19] [15/21]
- Holotape: Patient 1648654
- Holotape: Patient 1687865
- Holotape: Patient 3905698
- Holotape: Patient 5498465
- Holotape: Patient 6525645
- Sleeping Quarters

7 Blue Sector: Dormitories

Access the door in the connecting corridor using the key Lem gives you. Escaped Convicts roam the three dormitory rooms here, and most carry keycards. Don't forget to collect your Vault 19 Jumpsuit from any dresser or locker!

- Vault 19 Jumpsuit
- Sleeping Quarters

The first dormitory has a terminal with the following messages:

> A Message from the Overseer: Telling the dwellers there's trouble with the water purification system.

> Journal #138

> Journal #139

- Magazine: Programmer's Digest [Science] [5/23] [16/21]

The second dormitory has a terminal with more psychotic logs, and a Blue Sector Keycard.

> Log #479

> Log #480

> Log #481

> Log #482

> Log #483

> Log #484

- Quest Item: Blue Sector Keycard
- Footlocker Items

The third dormitory also has an active terminal, with Journal entries about being poisoned.

> A Message from the Overseer

> Journal #209

> Journal #210

- Quest Item: Blue Sector Keycard

C Blue Sector Elevator to Vault 19—Living Quarters

8 Red Sector: Dormitories

Access the door in the connecting corridor using the key Cooke gives you. There are three dormitory rooms here, and an elevator exit to Vault 19—Living Quarters.

- Vault 19 Jumpsuit
- Sleeping Quarters

The first dormitory has a terminal with the following messages:

> A Message from the Overseer: Telling the dwellers there's trouble with the water purification system.

> My Journal: Entry 74

- Carton of Cigarettes and Teddy Bear
- Quest Item: Red Sector Keycard

The second dormitory has two terminals with more frightened Journal entries.

> A Message from the Overseer

> My Journal: Entry 65

> My Journal: Entry 98

- Carton of Cigarettes (2)
- Footlocker Items
- Quest Item: Red Sector Keycard

The third dormitory also has an active terminal, with two Log entries about being poisoned.

> Log #45

> Log #46

D Red Sector Elevator to Vault 19—Living Quarters

Vault 19—Living Quarters

E Blue Sector Elevator to Vault 19—1st Floor

9 Blue Sector: Fire Gecko Corridors

There are Mines down this corridor, so watch your step. Continue east down the corridor, to a door on your right (south) leading to a second dorm. Check the desk for a Star Cap, search the dressers and lockers, and unlock a Floor Safe before checking the terminal with Bobby Pins on top of it. There are two more entries from fearful members of this odd, separated, and sickly vault. This includes paranoia regarding the Star Cap itself! The southern part of the corridor has another chamber with one more terminal and two Log entries.

> A Message from the Overseer

> Journal Entry 194

> Journal Entry 206

> Log Entry 56

> Log Entry 74

- Frag Mine (2)
- Sunset Sarsaparilla Star Cap [8/100]
- Floor Safe Items
- Vault 19 Jumpsuit
- Sleeping Quarters

F Blue Sector Elevator to Vault 19—1st Floor

10 Red Sector: Fire Gecko Corridors

Watch for Mines! Right in front of you is a Red Sector Door leading to the Break Room (Location #11). The map shows two dormitories off this corridor, but the eastern one is inaccessible.

- Frag Mine (3)

The southern dorm features a place to sleep, a dresser with items in it, and a terminal, which you can access for more information on this bizarre, segmented, and sickened vault.

> A Message from the Overseer

> Journal Entry #86

- Sleeping Quarters

11 Break Room

A rather large (and steaming) hole leads down into the Sulfur Caves. Also be aware of stairs up to the mezzanine level, but there's nothing up here (except a place to rain fire down on the Geckos).

- First Aid Box

G Hole to Sulfur Caves

Vault 19—Sulfur Caves

This entire area has an influx of Fire Geckos. Expect to face at least eight.

H Hole to Vault 19—Living Quarters

12 Microcline Rock

Here you can lay C-4 Explosives and bring the entire cave system down, helping Philip Lem as part of the Side Quest.

13 Sulfur Passages

Clear all of the Fire Geckos out, only if you wish to ally with Samuel Cooke as part of the Side Quest. At this point, there's a rock pile to the southeast that you can climb up, which is easily missed. This is one way to reach the Nightstalker Cavern. The other way is through the vault chambers.

14 Dead-End Cave

Don't head down here if you're being chased by Fire Geckos!

15 Transformer Room

Sparking transformers and large server pods are in this damaged chamber, which is used to head deeper into the vault or cave structure.

16 Connecting Corridor

The corridor to the reactor is impassable.

17 Systems Room

There's nothing but a Fire Gecko and banks of dormant servers.

18 Utility Room

Check the terminal for a single Diary entry. More weird noises!

> Diary Entry #86

19 Overseer's Passage

To the left is another corridor. It leads to a secret elevator.

- Footlocker Items

I Elevator to Vault 19—Overseer's Office [Hard]

Note the C-4 Plastic Explosive here. Pick the lock to return to the first floor, and then open the floor of the Overseer's office via a wall terminal [Average].

- Quest Item: C-4 Plastic Explosive

20 Bar Room

This offers access into the Nightstalker Cavern.

21 Nightstalker Cavern

J Ladder to Mojave Wasteland

You can climb this ladder to escape, or descend down it from the hole in the hillside just northwest of the Whittaker Farmstead [1.22].

[1.22] Whittaker Farmstead

- Threat Level: ●●●●●
- Faction: Powder Gangers
- Crafting: Campfire [11/109]
- Collectibles: Magazine: [Energy Weapons] [1/10] [17/21]
- Guns and Ammo
- Health, Chems, or Water
- Interior Exploration
- Sleeping Quarters

On the northern side of Trail 159 is a small farmstead, recently taken over by a splinter group of Cooke's Powder Gangers. Attack, or Sneak around to the east side of the house and pick the lock [Easy] (and check the table outside for some ammo). On the hall table is more ammo, Buffout, and the last message from Ranger Teresa Lutz. Check the rocks nearby for two graves; rob them with a Shovel.

- Campfire [11/109]
- Steak and Ammo
- Sunset Sarsaparilla Crate
- Machete
- Magazine: Future Weapons Today [Energy Weapons] [1/10] [17/21]
- Buffout
- Note: Ranger Holodisk Message
- Grave Items (2)
- Sleeping Quarters

ZONE 1: SECONDARY LOCATIONS

[1.S01] Radioactive Road Block

- Threat Level: ●●●●●
- Crafting: Campfire [12/109]
- Dangers: Radiation
- Wasteland Vegetation

This is the end of the road for Highway 95. Note the Campfire to the southeast. The crater with the rusting cars is radioactive.

- Campfire [12/109]

[1.S02] Hovering Anomaly/ Mercenary Camp

- Threat Level: ●●●●●
- Faction: Alien/Mercenary
  - Entity: Alien Captain
  - Entity: Alien
  - Entity: Mercenary
- Crafting: Campfire [13/109]
- Collectibles:
  - Unique Weapon [5/42]
  - Unique Weapon [6/42]
- Guns and Ammo
- Wasteland Vegetation
- Wild Wasteland!

Something odd is glinting off the rocks forming the northern boundary of the Mojave Wasteland. On closer inspection (assuming you have the Wild Wasteland trait), you see a strange, circular craft and three spindly forms. These are hostile and must be defeated! Be sure you take the Unique Weapon (and all ammunition) from the captain.

- Unique Weapon (Wild Wasteland Only): Alien Blaster [5/42]

Without the Wild Wasteland trait, you spot movement among the rocks forming the northern boundary of the Mojave Wasteland. On closer inspection, you stumble across a Mercenary Camp. Be sure you pry the Unique Weapon (and all ammunition) from the leader.

- Campfire [13/109]
- Unique Weapon (Unavailable with Wild Wasteland): Gauss Rifle: YCS/186 [6/42]

[1.S03] Electrical Transformer Station

- Threat Level: ●●●●●
- Main Trading Route

Providing some of the power for The Strip, this deserted location is actually in working order!

[1.S04] Sharecroppers' Lament

- Threat Level: ●●●●●
- Faction: Fiend
  - Entity: Fiend
- Collectibles: Magazine [Explosives] [1/12] [18/21]
- Sleeping Quarters
- Wasteland Vegetation

Abandoned and now home to Fiends, this dwelling is almost a ruin. Abandoned buildings stand near the line of power towers stretching west to east.

- Chems and Dirty Water
- Scrap Electronics
- Magazine: Patriot's Cookbook [Explosives] [1/12] [18/21]
- Sleeping Quarters

[1.S05] Wins Hideout

- Free Quest: A Pair of Dead Desperados, II
- Threat Level: ●●●●●
- Faction: Idiot
  - Entity: Pauline Wins
  - Entity: Sammy Wins
- Collectibles:
  - Unique Item [7/95]
  - Unique Item [8/95]
  - Unique Weapon [7/42]
- Guns and Ammo
- Health, Chems, or Water
- Interior Exploration
- Sleeping Quarters
- Wasteland Vegetation

Head inside the shack to meet Sammy and Pauline Wins; a couple of smartly dressed folk with big ideas. If you want to hear them, start the Free Quest. Otherwise, search the room for free Food (in the fridge), and an amazingly difficult Safe [Very Hard]. There's an easier way to open it....

- Ammo Box Ammunition (2)
- Sleeping Quarters

Free Quest: A Pair of Dead Desperados, II

This Quest makes more sense if you head to Primm [4.17] and visit the Vikki & Vance Casino first. Sammy and Pauline Win look familiar, and they have an extremely ambitious plan for holding up all the Vegas casinos. Pauline tells you the plan in detail. You can:

Tell them that plan is going to get them both killed.

SPEECH 55 — Lie that the plan is the greatest plan you've ever heard.

Gun them both down.

Assuming you used Speech, Pauline realizes what a crazy plan that really was, and tells you to talk to Sammy about giving you Vance's Gun, the same gun stolen from the Vikki & Vance Casino! Then tell the brawn of this two-bit operation to give you the gun, and he obliges. It's in the safe, and he tells you the combination.

Kill the incompetent pair for two more Unique Items.

- Unique Item: Vance's Lucky Hat [7/95]
- Unique Item: Vikki's Bonnet [8/95]
- Unique Weapon: Vance's 9mm Submachine Gun [7/42]

[1.S06] Abandoned Farmstead

- Threat Level: ●●●●●
- Wasteland Vegetation

This is boarded up and inaccessible, but there may randomly be a Magazine in the mailbox.

[1.S07] Jackal Shack

- Threat Level: ●●●●●
- Faction: Jackal Gang
  - Entity: Jackal Gang Member
  - Entity: Coyote
- Crafting: Campfire [14/109]
- Health, Chems, or Water
- Wasteland Vegetation

Two ill-equipped Jackal Gang members eke out an existence here.

- Campfire [14/109]
- Brahmin Steak and First Aid Box [Average]
- Sleeping Quarters

[1.S08] New Vegas Home

- Threat Level: ●●●●●
- Interior Exploration
- Sleeping Quarters
- Wasteland Vegetation

Scavenge items from the fridge of this otherwise-empty dwelling.

- Sleeping Quarters

[1.S09] Rusting Pickup Truck

- Threat Level: ●●●●●
- Wasteland Vegetation

Check the flatbed for some ammo.

- Ammo Box Ammunition [Easy]

[1.S10] Carlyle St. Clair's House

- Side Quest: Beyond the Beef
- Threat Level: ●●●●●
- Faction: Wastelander
  - Entity: Carlyle St. Clair III
- Interior Exploration
- Wasteland Vegetation
- Quest Item

This one-room shack has no owner until Side Quest: Beyond the Beef is active. Then you can ask Carlyle St. Clair III about his relationship with the White Glove Society. Find ingestibles in the fridge, and note the handy dumpster.

- Sleeping Quarters

[1.S11] Mojave House

- Threat Level: ●●●●●
- Faction: Wastelander
- Area Is Locked
- Guns and Ammo
- Health, Chems, or Water

- Interior Exploration
- Sleeping Quarters
- Wasteland Vegetation

On the porch is a fridge with Beer, and a mailbox to check before you pry open either door [Average] and search inside, where you'll find a hidden maize-growing operation complete with hydroponic lighting. There's drink in the interior fridge, too.

- Maize (a whole load)
- First Aid Box
- Ammo Box Ammunition (2)
- Wall Safe Items
- Moonshine
- Sleeping Quarters

[1.S12] Brahmin Paddock and Farmstead

- Threat Level: ●●●●●
- Faction: Wastelander
  - Entity: Brahmin
- Sleeping Quarters
- Wasteland Vegetation

The farmstead is sealed up, and so is the shack, but the windmill has a place to sleep. Brahmin roam the area.

- Sleeping Quarters

[1.S13] Trail 157 Junction

- Threat Level: ●●●●●
- Faction: Mutated Animal
  - Entity: Bighorner
  - Entity: Giant Mantis
- Wasteland Vegetation

Locate this road and you can follow it all the way to Jacobstown [1.10], or head into the wild mountain ravines, to a pathway that leads into Red Rock Canyon. This is the northeast end of the road; the other end is in Jacobstown.

[1.S14] Ruby Hill Grave

- Threat Level: ●●●●●
- Faction: Mutated Animal
  - Entity: Bighorner
- Wasteland Vegetation

Near the grazing Bighorners, against the rocky walls is a grave. Unearth some random items using a Shovel.

- Grave Items

[1.S15] Mountain Vista

- Threat Level: ●●●●●
- Faction: Mutated Animal
  - Entity: Bighorner
  - Entity: Giant Mantis
- Highly Visible
- Wasteland Vegetation

Stand atop the mountain and survey the path to Ranger Station Foxtrot [1.12], and view The Strip (Zone 2) in the distance. This is an excellent vista spot.

[1.S16] Pine Ravines Pathway

- Threat Level: ●●●●●
- Faction: Mutated Animal
  - Entity: Bighorner
  - Entity: Cazador
- Wasteland Vegetation

A Bighorner pathway through the pine ravines in this area ends at Ranger Station Foxtrot. This helps you find your way in this wilderness.

[1.S17] Red Rock Pathway

- Threat Level: ●●●●●
- Faction: Mutated Animal
  - Entity: Cazador
- Wasteland Vegetation

This ravine pathway allows access between the Pine Ravines and Red Rock Canyon [1.15] to the southeast. Beware of multiple Cazador nests.

[1.S18] Westside Turnaround and Playground

- Threat Level: ●●●●●
- Crafting: Campfire [15/109]
- Wasteland Vegetation

Outside the protective Westside West Entrance [2.01] perimeter is a road turnaround, with a rusting playground and picnic tables. Notice the remains of the Campfire.

- Campfire [15/109]

[1.S19] Abandoned Home

- Threat Level: ●●●●●
- Faction: Fiend
  - Entity: Fiend
- Dangers: Traps
- Interior Exploration
- Sleeping Quarters
- Wasteland Vegetation

This concrete home is the only accessible one in the area. It's empty aside from some grub in the fridge. Tamper with the Explosive in this mailbox, and rig it to explode in 10 seconds or when someone walks nearby, because you're likely to face a Fiend ambush as you exit (around three of the punks).

- Sleeping Quarters

[1.S20] Cazadors' Duffle Bag

- Threat Level: ●●●●●
- Faction: Mutated Animal
  - Entity: Cazador
- Guns and Ammo
- Health, Chems or Water

To the west of Brewer's Bootlegging Shack [1.13] are some rocky foothills filled with Cazadors, and among these is a collection of bones by a small clump of rocks. Check the area closely for a Duffle Bag with tons of useful items.

- Duffle Bag Items

[1.S21] Disassembled Weapons Shipment

- Side Quest: How Little We Know
- Threat Level: ●●●●●
- Faction: Fiend
  - Entity: Fiend
- Lots O' Caps
- Wasteland Vegetation
- Quest Item

Three Fiends guard this footlocker, whether Side Quest: How Little We Know is active or not. The footlocker is handy for this Quest.

- Quest Item: Disassembled Weapons Shipment

[1.S22] Violet and Violetta Trailer Compound

- Side Quest: Nothin' But a Hound Dog
- Side Quest: Three-Card Bounty
- Threat Level: ●●●●●
- Faction: Fiend
  - Entity: Violet
  - Entity: Violetta
  - Entity: Fiend Guard Dog
- Collectibles:
  - Magazine: [Energy Weapons] [2/10] [19-21/21]
  - Magazine: [Science] [6/23] [19-21/21]
  - Magazine: [Sneak] [1/10] [19-21/21]
  - Unique Item [9/95]
- Guns and Ammo
- Health, Chems, or Water
- Sleeping Quarters
- Wasteland Vegetation
- Quest Item

Just south of the Poseidon Gas Station [1.17] is a large collection of massed trailers. This is the home of a hated Fiend leader named Violet and her vicious dogs, the most ferocious of which is called Violetta. Check Side Quests: Three-Card Bounty and Nothin' But a Hound Dog first, and keep Violet's head intact!

- Ammo Box Ammunition (4)
- Doctor's Bag and Super Stimpak (2)
- Purified Water (2)
- Human Flesh (30)
- Chems and Beer
- First Aid Box
- Footlocker Items
- Magazine: Future Weapons Today [Energy Weapons] [2/10] [19/21]
- Magazine: Programmer's Digest [Science] [6/23] [20/21]
- Magazine: ¡La Fantoma! [Sneak] [1/10] [21/21]
- Unique Item: Nuka-Cola Quartz [9/95]
- Quest Item: Violet's Head
- Quest Item: Violetta's Brain
- Sleeping Quarters

[1.S23] Radioactive Pools

- Threat Level: ●●●●●
- Faction: Fiend
- Dangers: Radiation

Avoid the three shallow, polluted pools of effluent and ground water.

[1.S24] Red Rock Canyon Commemorative Stone

- Threat Level:
- Faction: Mutated Animal
  - Entity: Big Horner
- Wasteland Vegetation

A large hewn rock welcomes you to the area.

[1.S25] Spring Mountain Pathway

- Threat Level:
- Faction: Mutated Animal
  - Entity: Cazador
  - Entity: Giant Mantis

This allows an alternate route into the back of the Great Khan's camp in Red Rock Canyon [1.15], and is accessed via the ravine on the far side of the pond at Spring Mt. Ranch State Park [1.18].

[1.S26] Ravine Path

- Threat Level:
- Faction: Mutated Animal
  - Entity: Cazador

This allows quick access between Sprint Mt. Ranch State Park [1.18] and the ransacked Tribal Village [4.01]; a handy shortcut.

[1.S27] Sulfur Cave

- Threat Level:
  - Entity: Fire Gecko
  - Entity: Nightstalker

This cave is an alternate entrance and exit to and from Vault 19 [1.21], if you don't want to use the parking lot.

ZONE 2: NEW VEGAS CONURBATION [EXTERIOR ZONES]

Topographical Overview

The magic of New Vegas and the glittering towers of The Strip are out of reach for most folks eking out an existence in this mainly "exterior" zone. Aside from the five interior districts detailed in Part 2, the western side of town consists of a tight-knit Westside cooperative, with society gradually breaking down the farther south you go, where city blocks are violently run by Chem-addicted raiders known as Fiends. They have quite a territory to the southwest, but don't dare risk heading toward the NCR's main base at Camp McCarran, with its adjacent locations devoted to irrigated farming and refugees. To the east and north, independent businesses such as the Gun Runners and Crimson Caravan Company flourish, although they are mainly concerned with the weapons trade. Finally, take a trip to Freeside; it's the only way to enter fabulous New Vegas itself!

> **Note** This section details all the Primary Locations you can see with your Pip-Boy's World Map function, their associated Secondary Locations, and Manhole Covers accessing the New Vegas Sewers. Five additional zones detail interior "districts" of New Vegas, which are contained in the second part of the Zone 2 Tour.

> **Note** To reference the entirety of these Zones, please utilize the Map Poster that came with this guide.

Highways and Byways

The Conurbation is dominated by a grid of streets too numerous to mention, but keep a lookout for a few roads, including the Long 15 which runs to the west (and outside) of The Strip until it becomes elevated (and inaccessible). Similarly, Highway 95 on the eastern side winds north and northwest; follow it to the eastern entrance to Freeside. Also elevated is a monorail linking Camp McCarran to The Strip, although you need to be inside either location to access (and ride) it. Don't forget to use the roads on the edge of this zone to find your way about.

Available Services, Crafting, and Collectibles

Services: Caravan Players: [3/15]
Services: Gambling: [1/15]
Services: Healers/Dealers: [4/31]
Services: Repairers: [0/9]
Services: Traders: [6/33]
Crafting: Campfires: [4/109]
Crafting: Reloading Benches: [7/36]
Crafting: Workbenches: [7/41]
Crafting: Weapon Upgrades: [2/10]
Collectibles: Snow Globes: [0/7]
Collectibles: Caravan Cards: [4/30]
Collectibles: Hollowed-Out Rocks: [0/42]
Collectibles: Skill Books: [6/51]
Collectibles: Skill Magazines: [56/213]
Collectibles: Star Bottle Caps: [19/100]
Collectibles: Unique Items: [10/95]
Collectibles: Unique Weapons: [6/42]

Primary Locations

[2.01] Westside West Entrance
[2.02] Miguel's Pawn Shop
[2.03] Westside South Entrance
[2.04] The Thorn
[2.05] South Cistern
[2.06] H&H Tools Factory
[2.07] North Vegas Square
[2.08] Freeside's North Gate
[2.09] Crimson Caravan Company
[2.10] New Vegas Medical Clinic
[2.11] Mole Rat Ranch
[2.12] Monte Carlo Suites
[2.13] The Strip North Gate
[2.14] Gun Runners
[2.15] Freeside's East Gate
[2.16] Durable Dunn's Sacked Caravan
[2.17] Sunset Sarsaparilla Headquarters
[2.18] El Rey Motel
[2.19] Camp McCarran
[2.20] NCR Sharecropper Farms
[2.21] East Pump Station
[2.22] Aerotech Office Park
[2.23] South Vegas Ruins West Entrance
[2.24] Vault 3
[2.25] South Vegas Ruins East Entrance
[2.26] New Vegas Steel
[2.27] West Pump Station
[2.28] Samson Rock Crushing Plant
[2.29] The Basincreek Building
[2.30] Allied Technologies Offices
[2.31] Reed Imports Sacked Caravan
[2.32] Grub n' Gulp Rest Stop
[2.33] Ant Mound
[2.34] Hunter's Farm
[2.35] REPCONN Headquarters

Secondary Locations

[2.S01] Ruined Buildings
[2.S02] Ruined Store
[2.S03] Ruined Store
[2.S04] Ruined Building with Locked Cache
[2.S05] Hostetler and Isaac Homes
[2.S06] Orion Moreno's House
[2.S07] Destroyed Freeway Bridge
[2.S08] NCR Patrol
[2.S09] Elevated Freeway and Billboards
[2.S10] Apartment Allotment
[2.S11] Westside Playground
[2.S12] Summer Springs Boarding House
[2.S13] Tiki Tonga Burned-Out Ranch Homes
[2.S14] Sarsaparilla Burned-Out Ranch Homes
[2.S15] Elevated Long 15
[2.S16] Long 15 Mines
[2.S17] New Vegas Sign
[2.S18] Cook-Cook's Territory
[2.S19] NCR Sandbag Defenses
[2.S20] Long 15 Pedestrian Steps
[2.S21] Long 15 Overturned Train Carriage
[2.S22] Driver Nephi's Territory
[2.S23] Long 15 Mines 2
[2.S24] Abandoned Warehouse
[2.S25] NCR Checkpoint and Burned Buildings
[2.S26] Abandoned Buildings and Ranger Morales' Corpse

Zone 2: Underground Access Entrances/Exits

[2.SU01] Manhole to North Sewers
[2.SU02] Manhole to North Sewers
[2.SU03] Manhole to North Sewers
[2.SU04] Manhole to East Central Sewers
[2.SU05] Manhole to East Central Sewers
[2.SU06] Manhole to East Central Sewers
[2.SU07] Manhole to East Central Sewers
[2.SU08] Manhole to Central Sewers

PRIMARY LOCATIONS

[2.01] Westside West Entrance

- Threat Level: ●●●●●
- Faction: Westside Militia
  - Entity: Westside Militia
- Highly Visible
- Interior Exploration
- Wasteland Vegetation

This conduit location is accessed numerous times during Quests.

With Fiends a constant problem, the Westside Militia has created an impressive, two-tier approach to defending the gate that leads to Westside [Zone 2A]. The Militia are suspicious, but not violent if you haven't interacted with them before. Note the small garden (with plants ripe for picking) and a second, southern entrance [2.03].

[2.02] Miguel's Pawn Shop

- Side Quest: I Could Make You Care
- Free Quest: Dealing with Contreras
- Threat Level: ●●●●●
- Faction: Westside Militia
  - Entity: Miguel
- Services: Trader [3/33]
- Crafting: Reloading Bench [5/36]
- Interior Exploration

Inside the store, you can sift through the junk (or steal it), or locate Miguel, who Trades with you. You can buy stuff, or ask him about Westside (he took over from his grandfather, who founded the shop, after he was killed). There's not much more than junk on offer here.

- Trader: Miguel [3/33]
- Reloading Bench [5/36]

[2.03] Westside South Entrance

- Threat Level: ●●●●●
- Faction: Westside Militia
  - Entity: Westside Militia
- Highly Visible
- Interior Exploration
- Wasteland Vegetation

This less-trafficked area is close to the underground fighting establishment known as The Thorn [2.04].

[2.04] The Thorn

- Side Quest: Bleed Me Dry
- Free Quest: Fight Night
- Threat Level: ●●●●●
- Faction: Red Lucy
  - Entity: Red Lucy
  - Entity: Guard
  - Entity: New Vegas Citizen
  - Entity: Various Caged Entities
- Collectibles: Unique Item [10/95]
- Area Is Locked
- Interior Exploration
- Lots O' Caps
- Sleeping Quarters
- Underground Connection

Close to the Westside South Entrance [2.03] is a large scrawled sign for this den of iniquity, which is closed during nighttime hours. Descend into the Manhole to access a large fighting arena.

Ⓐ Ladder to Westside

① Upper Corridors

Almost completely surrounding the main arena is a perimeter corridor that allows access into the arena, as well as The Thorn's Cages below (through any of five blast doors). The sealed door to the north cannot be accessed until you offer yourself in the arena.

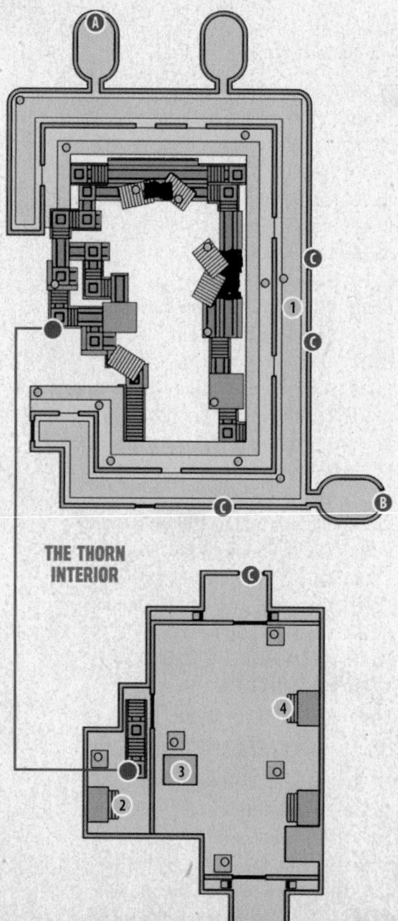

Ⓑ Exit to Sewer System

This allows access to the New Vegas North Sewers [U2,N] and is the only Primary Location with a direct link to and from this area. All other surface access points are from Manhole Covers.

② To Red Lucy's Chamber

This is where Red Lucy takes those who prove brave enough, and they help her test her bed's mattress springs. Check her terminal [Very Easy] to find three menus. In The Thorn's Mainframe Control, you can shut down the power to free all the beasts from their pens (creating havoc and causing a problem completing the Side Quest).

③ Arena and Red Lucy

You can talk about her, Westside, or the fighting arena she's set up, and begin Free Quest: Fight Night. She's wearing a very rare outfit.

- Unique Item: Bounty Hunter Duster [10/95]

④ To Creature Pens

The Thorn's cages are separated into two areas. The eastern section has Cazadors, Giant Mantises, and Fire Geckos. The southern (separate) section has Deathclaws, Nightstalkers, Radscorpions, and a tunnel to a Manhole Cover and the creature gate (inaccessible).

Ⓒ Entrances to The Thorn's Cages

The northern entrance is accessible only if you put yourself into a bout.

Free Quest: Fight Night

Speak to Red Lucy about the types of fights she offers. They come in three varieties:

1. You can bet on a fight between two creatures, or creature(s) and Fiend(s). This is a low-risk, low-reward strategy. Witness the battle, and receive a modest profit if your creature wins. For a 50 Cap bet, for example, expect to make 15–20 Caps profit if your critters are the winners.
2. You can fight the creature (of your choosing) yourself. This is higher risk. Prepare for the fight accordingly (tooling up with weapons you wish to use, bringing Health items with you). The rewards are higher; typically 150–200 Caps. If you don't die.
3. Or, you can spend some Caps and create your own match-ups! Ever wanted to see a Fiend take on a Deathstalker? Then choose that fight. This is for entertainment purposes more than anything, and you don't receive a reward.

> **Tip** Option #2 is an exceptionally good way to level your character up! You get to choose creatures you want to fight, you receive XP and Caps upon victory, and the arena is relatively "safe"; you're never ambushed by more than the allotted Deathclaw when you choose to fight one, for example.

[2.05] South Cistern

- Threat Level: ●●●●●
- Faction: NCR
  - Entity: NCR Military Police
  - Entity: NCR Trooper
- Health, Chems, or Water
- Interior Exploration

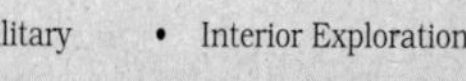

A small concrete block building, the Cistern is part of the vast treatment works spread across New Vegas. Two NCR soldiers guard this location. Drink from the valve for radiation-free water (not the trough below!).

[2.06] H&H Tools Factory

- Threat Level:
- Faction: Robot
  - Entity: Crazed Mister Handy
  - Entity: Robobrain
  - Entity: Mark II Turret
- Dangers:
  - Traps
  - Radiation
  - Mines
- Collectibles:
  - Magazine [Sneak] [2/10] [1-2/56]
  - Magazine [Unarmed] [2/11] [1-2/56]
- Guns and Ammo
- Interior Exploration

Long before the war, H&H Tools Company provided Nevada and California with high-quality robotics equipment. Owned by the half-brother of Robert Edwin House (the founder of RobCo, and—were it not for the 200 year gap—the same man who lives in the Lucky 38 Casino). When their father was killed in an accident, the elder brother swindled Robert out of the family fortune, and assumed control of the company.

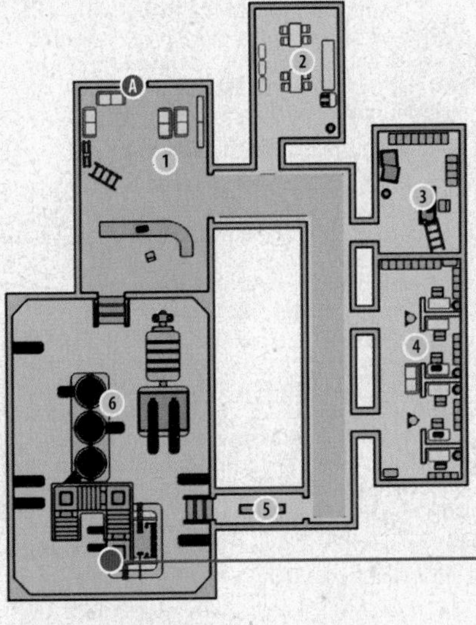

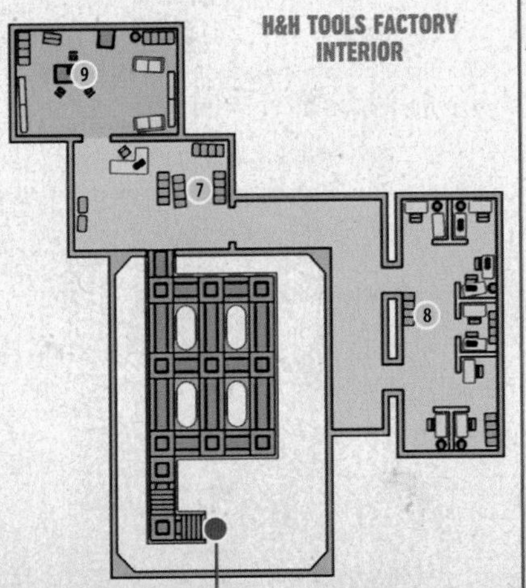

Robert went on, through his dealings with RobCo and their lucrative contracts, to become one of the wealthiest men on earth. His half-brother meanwhile, became increasingly paranoid, seeking to guard himself against a vengeance that never came, and inflicting all manner of strange HR rules on his workforce. The remains of this factory still stand, surrounded by husk-like remains of North Vegas' industrial area.

A Door to the Mojave Wasteland

1 Tool Company Foyer

This large entrance area is a mess of ruined books. In the warehouse beyond, robots are milling about in water, and elsewhere, other robots are hitting the odd Frag Mine. The bookcase on the left (east) wall holds a Magazine and another lies on the main desk. Check the desk for a terminal, which reveals some interesting (and ancient) emails, detailing some increasingly draconian HR measures thanks to the company's head, a "Mr. H."

- > HR e-mail 05/14/2020
- > HR e-mail 07/25/2022
- > HR e-mail 11/08/2023
- > Access Hidden Network Drive: This accesses another Journal entry.
- > Journal Entry 07/12/2062: No one crosses the House!
- Frag Mines
- Magazine: iLa Fantoma! [Sneak] [2/10] [1/56]
- Magazine: Boxing Times [Unarmed] [2/11] [2/56]

2 Break Room and Kitchen

Strewn Food lies everywhere.

3 Executive Office

Beware the quintet of Frag Mines and Tripwire at the entrance. Check the interior for Med-X, and a terminal with the same revelatory emails, as well as a message from a worried man named Dobson.

- > HR e-mail 05/14/2020
- > E-mail from Dobson O'Gill
- > HR e-mail 07/25/2022
- > HR e-mail 11/08/2023
- Frag Mine (5)

4 Office Cubicles

Without the proper ID, the Mark II Turrets shoot you on sight. One of the terminals has a missive from Alan Dalton, a RobCo representative. Another terminal has emails from a worried Jack Maynard, and seedy conversations between Jenny DeSoto and Alan Dalton.

- > HR e-mail 05/14/2020
- > E-mail from Jack Maynard
- > E-mail from Jenny DeSoto
- > E-mail from Alan Dalton (2)
- > HR e-mail 07/25/2022
- > HR e-mail 11/08/2023

5 Steel Bar Trap Corridor

Watch out for the pressure plate, or feel an steel bar in your face.

6 Waterlogged Warehouse

Robobrains move through the water here, shooting at you. Escape to the gantry steps, but watch for the Frag Mines on the way up.

- Frag Mine (4)

7 (Upper) Receptionist Office and Filing

Receptionist Cindy-Lou used to work in this office, which now has a couple of Mines at the entrance. Check the terminal for the usual HR emails, and the following:

- > Access Hidden Network Drive: This accesses another Journal entry.
- > Journal Entry 04/15/2077: Cindy-Lou can no longer save him.
- Frag Mine (2)

8 (Upper) Office Cubicles

Down the corridor is another set of cubicles. The four terminals have the HR emails, and the following hidden messages:

> E-mail from Jenny DeSoto: Regarding the hiring of a private investigator.

> Journal Entry 04/06/2068: Thought energy can be stolen via haircuts. It's not crazy; it's a FACT.

> Journal Entry 12/27/2074: Oh boy, somebody is a dull boy.

9 (Upper) Anthony House's Office

Beware the Rigged Shotgun trap; duck and disarm the Tripwire. The highlight of your search is a Lucky 38 VIP Keycard. There's also Anthony House's terminal to hack [Average].

- > Journal Entry 05/14/2061: About missing his father, and his family's history.
- > Journal Entry 01/19/2062: A half-brother might be taking over the company. Not for long!
- > Journal Entry 06/19/2077: The Reds have attacked? Or just the employees that must pay?
- > Lucky 38 Executive Override: You can start this from here.
- Quest Item: Lucky 38 VIP Keycard

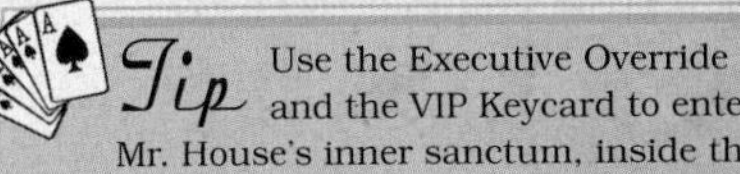

Use the Executive Override and the VIP Keycard to enter Mr. House's inner sanctum, inside the Lucky 38 Casino, if you haven't met him yet and lack the necessary Science skill to hack his security terminals.

[2.07] North Vegas Square

- Threat Level:
- Faction: North Vegas Resident
- Entity: None
- Interior Exploration

The fragmented citizens of New Vegas have sealed themselves into different defensible quadrants, and this tactic is just as apparent at the Junk Doors leading into North Vegas Square. Enter North Vegas Square [2B] to meet its citizens, including their self-imposed leader Crandon, and the only other Primary Location, The Gray [2B.01].

[2.08] Freeside's North Gate

- Threat Level:
- Faction: The Kings
- Entity: The Kings Gang Member
- Interior Exploration

The main fortified portions of New Vegas, Freeside [Zone 2C], and The Strip [Zone 2D] are accessed through one of two Freeside gates. This is the northern one. This gate can be seen from miles around due to the huge "Freeside" sign riveted above the inaccessible freeway overpass.

[2.09] Crimson Caravan Company

- Side Quest: Aba Daba Honeymoon
- Side Quest: Birds of a Feather
- Side Quest: Bitter Springs Infirmary Blues
- Side Quest: Heartache by the Number
- Side Quest: Pressing Matters
- Side Quest: Volare!
- Side Quest: You Can Depend on Me
- Side Quest: Young Hearts
- Threat Level: ●●●●●
- Faction: Crimson Caravan Company/NCR
  - Entity: Caravaneer
  - Entity: Caravan Guard
  - Entity: Blake
  - Entity: Janet
  - Entity: Alice McLafferty
  - Entity: Don Hostetler
- Fame/Infamy
- Services: Trader [4/33]
- Crafting:
  - Campfire [16/109]
  - Workbench [4/41]
  - Weapon Upgrade [2/10]
- Collectibles:
  - Caravan Cards [1/30]
  - Magazine [Crit. Chance] [3-4/56]
  - Magazine [Sneak] [3/10] [3-4/56]
  - Sunset Sarsaparilla Star Cap [9/100]
- Guns and Ammo
- Health, Chems, or Water
- Highly Visible
- Interior Exploration Lots O' Caps
- Main Trading Route
- Sleeping Quarters
- Wasteland Vegetation
- Quest Item

The Crimson Caravan Company is the largest supplier to the NCR of military-grade weaponry, and an assortment of provisions and other equipment types. Their base of operations is a highly fortified walled base just east of the main Freeside and Strip area, alarmingly close to their rivals; the Gun Runners. There are two entrances to this location (east and west).

A B Doors to Mojave Wasteland

1 Caravaneer Barracks

The Caravaneers like to sweep, even inside their barracks, which is spotless. Check the restroom for clean drinking water.

- Footlocker Items (8) [1 = Very Easy, 1 = Easy, and 1 = Average]
- First Aid Box
- Magazine: ¡La Fantoma! [Sneak] [3/10] [3/56]
- Sleeping Quarters

2 Guard Barracks

Against an exterior wall, there's a Workbench. Inside, there's little except sleeping Guards. The restroom has clean drinking water.

- First Aid Box (2)
- Footlocker Items (3)
- Ammo Box Ammunition [Easy]
- Sleeping Quarters
- Workbench [4/41]

3 Water Tower

Don't forget to pick some plants under the tower and around camp.

4 Campfire and Caravans

- Campfire [16/109]

5 Brahmin Paddock

The Caravaneers are here, sweeping up the Brahmins' waste, and tending to them. Among them is a young lady named Janet. She has a secret admirer over at the Boomer's Nellis Air Force Base [3.01]; Side Quest: Young Hearts.

6 Blake's Wares

Blake is an honest, if a little cocksure Trader who offers some fine items for sale. You can ask more questions about Caravaneering, before buying something. Note the two non-skill books are bought for Lieutenant Markland.

- Trader: Blake [4/33]
  - Random Magazines
  - Doctor's Bags
- Trader (Blake): Weapon Upgrades [Energy Weapons, Guns] [2/10]
- Trader (Blake): Caravan Cards [1/30]
- Goods to Steal:
  - First Aid Box (3) [Very Easy, Easy, Average]
  - A couple of hats
  - Ammo Box Ammunition (2) [Very Easy, Average]
  - Carton of Cigarettes (3)
  - Purified Water (7)

7 Crimson Caravan Main Office

Alice McLafferty runs the New Vegas operations from here with a stern countenance. She can be hit up for work, or more information about the history of this company. Also in the office is Don Hostetler, but he doesn't have much to say (unless you have a Chem delivery from Jack and Diane). You can take your life in your hands (and your Infamy levels to new heights) by killing Alice for some Caps (around 100), or accessing the following:

Caps (100+)

Alice's terminal has information on a New Canaan branch, notes on Henry Jamison, a failed Gun Runner tariff, and problems with the War Effort.

Alice's safe [Average] contains her agreement with the Van Graffs. It can be opened with the key you'll find on her. The agreement is shocking news to independent Caravaneers, such as Cassidy's Caravans (find Cass at the Mojave Outpost [4.27], as part of Side Quest: Heartache by the Number.

- Holotape: Crimson Caravan–Van Graff Agreement

Desk [Very Easy] contains nothing of interest.

Don's terminal [Average] contains some memorandums from a lady Don is more than befriending.

- First Aid Box
- Sunset Sarsaparilla Star Cap [9/100]
- Magazine: True Police Stories [Crit. Chance] [2/11] [4/56]

CRIMSON CARAVAN EXTERIOR

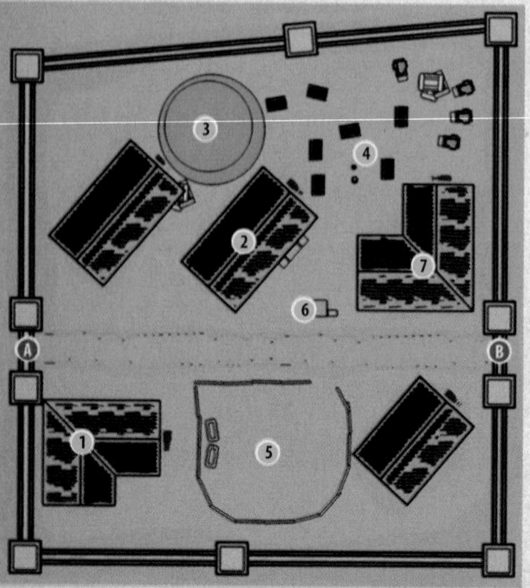

[2.10] New Vegas Medical Clinic

- Main Quest: Et Tumor, Brute?
- Side Quest: Bitter Springs Infirmary Blues
- Side Quest: I Don't Hurt Anymore
- Free Quest: Harder, Better, Faster, Stronger
- Threat Level: ●●●●●
- Faction: Followers of the Apocalypse
  - Entity: Doctor Usanagi
- Fame/Infamy
- Healer/Dealer [3/31]
- Collectibles:
  - Magazine [Medicine] [4/19] [5-7/56]
  - Magazine [Repair] [3/27] [5-7/56]
  - Magazine [Speech] [1/12] [5-7/56]
- Health, Chems, or Water
- Interior Exploration
- Perk! Hypertrophy Accelerator [1/9]
- Perk! Optics Enhancer [2/9]
- Perk! Nociception Regulator [3/9]
- Perk! Empathy Synthesizer [4/9]
- Perk! Logic Co-Processor [5/9]
- Perk! Reflex Booster [6/9]
- Perk! Probability Calculator [7/9]
- Perk! NEMEAN Sub-Dermal Armor [8/9]
- Perk! PHOENIX Monocyte Breeder [9/9]
- Sleeping Quarters
- Quest Item

Across the road from the eastern entrance to the Crimson Caravan Company [2.09], and just above a Manhole Cover to the North Sewers [U2,N] is an unassuming storefront. However, this has a Follower of the Apocalypse emblem above the door. A small sign also indicates the medicinal nature of this establishment.

1 Doctor Usanagi's Waiting Room

Run by the selfless Doctor Usanagi, the clinic offers a reasonable array of medical supplies and an unmatched array of Implants. Pass the bodyguards to speak to Doctor Usanagi herself. You can speak about her role or (if you're engaged in a Quest) another matter, but you can make a 500 Cap donation to the Followers (for a Fame gain), and also purchase medical supplies and the Skill Magazines on the tables around the waiting room. You can also steal these, which causes Follower Infamy and everyone becomes hostile. Also, if you're ready for computerized enhancements of a more robotic kind, why not begin Free Quest: Harder, Better, Faster, Stronger?

Followers of the Apocalypse Fame Gained!

- Healer: Usanagi [3/31]
- Healer Highlight (Usanagi): Doctor's Bag (3), Skill Magazines (3), Stimpak (22)
- Skill Magazine: Today's Physician [Medicine] [4/19] [5/56]
- Skill Magazine: Fixin' Things [Repair] [3/27] [6/56]
- Skill Magazine: Meeting People [Speech] [1/12] [7/56]

NEW VEGAS MEDICAL CLINIC

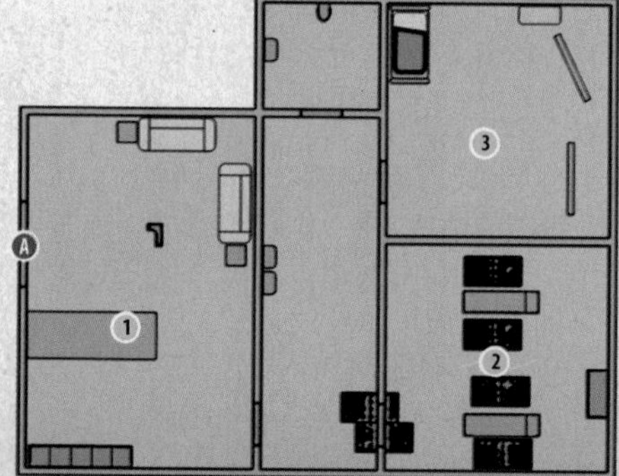

2 Surgery

This is where the Implant operations are performed (although you don't remember them). There's a Mk I Auto-Doc here, but its parts are useless.

3 Recovery and Class Room

A Followers Medical Student is usually in this place of learning (and sleeping).

- Sleeping Quarters

Free Quest: Harder, Better, Faster, Stronger

Collect a sizable number of Caps or bring trading items, and consult with Doctor Usanagi about Implants. She informs you that they are safe, durable, and costly. Usanagi is also prepared to cut you a deal, offering a 1,000 Cap discount for statistics she deems in critical need of improvement (attributes that are low). The number of Implants you can take is equal to your Endurance, up to nine (and available Caps).

Request	Implant Name	Ability	Cost (Caps)
"I want more Muscles."	Hypertrophy Accelerator [1/9]	STR +1	3,000–4,000
"Make me see better."	Optics Enhancer [2/9]	PER +1	3,000–4,000
"Make me tougher."	Nociception Regulator [3/9]	END +1	3,000–4,000
"Make people like me better."	Empathy Synthesizer [4/9]	CHR +1	3,000–4,000
"I want to be smarter."	Logic Co-Processor [5/9]	INT +1	3,000–4,000
"To make me quicker."	Reflex Booster [6/9]	AGL +1	3,000–4,000
"Make me luckier."	Probability Calculator [7/9]	LCK +1	3,000–4,000
"Sub-what?"	NEMEAN Sub-Dermal Armor [8/9]	Armor	8,000
"I'd like regenerating ability."	PHOENIX Monocyte Breeder [9/9]	Regen.	12,000

[2.11] Mole Rat Ranch

- Threat Level: ●●●●●
- Faction: Mutated Animal
  - Entity: Mole Rat

Aside from a few dead Mole Rats, this locale appears to have been abandoned.

[2.12] Monte Carlo Suites

- Threat Level: ●●●●●
- Faction: Scorpion Gang
  - Entity: Scorpion Gang Member
  - Entity: Roller
  - Entity: Yvette
- Crafting:
  - Reloading Bench [6/36]
  - Reloading Bench [7/36]
  - Workbench [5/41]
- Area Is Locked
- Guns and Ammo
- Health, Chems, or Water
- Interior Exploration
- Sleeping Quarters

On the western edge of the New Vegas Conurbation and north of the Sunset Sarsaparilla Headquarters [2.17] is a run-down hotel littered with burned-out vehicles, mostly used for cover and not barricades. This is the lair of the Scorpion Gang, a scrappy and overconfident bunch of mercenaries. They don't listen to reason, so Sneak or attack the first gang member at the entrance.

A Doors to Mojave Wasteland: 12 O'Clock: Entrance

Unlock the Entrance Doors [Easy] and prepare for a fight with Scorpion Gang members, including the leaders Roller and Yvette. All must die (or be avoided). Conduct a clockwise sweep around the hotel. If a room has a fridge in it, expect Food inside.

1 1 O'Clock: Room

2 2 O'Clock: Room

- Sleeping Quarters

3 4 O'Clock: Room

Find Jet and a small amount of ammo here.

4 5 O'Clock: Room

- Sleeping Quarters

5 7 O'Clock: Room [Easy]

This is locked. Inside, there are mattresses and a locked footlocker [Average], which usually contains Chems.

- Sleeping Quarters

6 8 O'Clock: Room

Roller's room includes ammo, Food in a fridge, two Reloading Benches and Workbench.

- Scrap Metal (4)
- Crate Items
- Ammo Box Ammunition [Average]
- Reloading Bench [6/36]
- Reloading Bench [7/36]
- Workbench [5/41]

7 10 O'Clock: Room

- Teddy Bear (2)

8 11 O'Clock: Room

Check the ovens in these rooms for the odd snack, too.

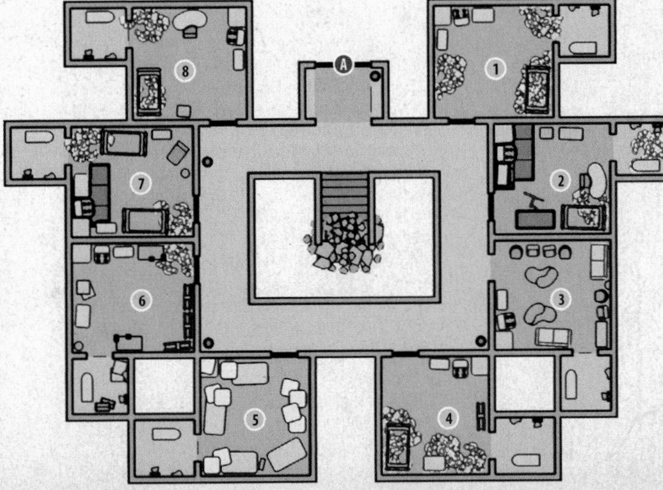

[2.13] The Strip North Gate

- Side Quest: Wang Dang Atomic Tango
- Side Quest: Debt Collector
- Free Quest: Strip Search
- Free Quest: Papers, Please
- Threat Level: ●●●●●
- Faction: Mr. House/The Strip
  - Entity: Old Ben
  - Entity: Securitron Gatekeeper
  - Entity: Securitron Mk I
- Area Is Locked
- Highly Visible
- Interior Exploration
- Radio Signal [Black Mountain]
- Quest Item

At the southwestern end of Freeside is a huge barricade, with a neon welcoming sign, the excitement of which is tempered somewhat by the Securitron presence. These are robots in the service of Mr. House over at the Lucky 38 Casino. Before you enter, Old Ben greets you, and tells you to watch your step. You can ask him about The Strip, and his own checkered past. Then you can inspect the Campfires to the side of this gate (there are three) where a Squatter named Lady Jane (Side Quest: Debt Collector) is known to hang out. These are locations Squatter Camp #3 and Old Ben [2C.S27], and Squatter Camp #4 [2C.S28].

Finally, attempt to access The Strip if you wish:

Free Quest: Strip Search

The Securitron Guards at The Strip North Gate [2.13] require proof of your high-rolling status. You can:

Hand over 2,000 Caps; the "credit check" to prove you're not a "less-reputable person." The bad news? You'll need to scrounge together the necessary Caps. The good news? The check is just to see that you're good for the money, and you get to keep the Caps!

Answer "1C 3C R34 M," verbally hacking and confusing the Gatekeeper into letting you in.

Or you can attack the toughened Gatekeepers. Prepare for a protracted battle.

Or, you can complete Side Quest: G.I. Blues, and request a passport from the King, as a reward.

Or, you can visit Mick & Ralph's [2C.02], speak to Ralph, and have him craft a Passport for you.

NEW CA. REPUBLIC Finally, if you're wearing NCR armor (Faction Clothing), you can journey to Camp McCarran [2.19] instead of The Strip, enter the Terminal Building, and wait (without being seen) until 6 PM, when the guards change shift. Then board the monorail, and ride it to the Vegas Boulevard Station [2D.03]. Exit, and you're greeted by Victor. This method is dangerous and can severely impede your standing with the NCR.

[2.14] Gun Runners

- Side Quest: You Can Depend on Me
- Threat Level: ●●●●●
- Faction: Gun Runners
  - Entity: Isaac
  - Entity: Vendortron
  - Entity: Gun Runner Guard
  - Entity: Gun Runner Gunsmith
- Services:
  - Caravan Player [1/15]
  - Trader [5/33]
- Crafting:
  - Reloading Bench [8/36]
  - Reloading Bench [9/36]
  - Reloading Bench [10/36]
  - Workbench [6/41]
  - Workbench [7/41]
  - Workbench [8/41]
  - Workbench [9/41]
  - Weapon Upgrade [3/10]
- Collectibles:
  - Caravan Cards [2/30]
  - Sunset Sarsaparilla Star Cap [10/100]
  - Magazine: [Energy Weapons] [3/10] [8-10/56]
  - Magazine: [Explosives] [2/12] [8-10/56]
  - Magazine: [Medicine] [5/19] [8-10/56]
- Area Is Locked
- Guns and Ammo
- Health, Chems, or Water
- Interior Exploration
- Lots O' Caps
- Sleeping Quarters
- Quest Item

Exterior: Gun Runner Kiosk

This heavily fortified armory is a small but extremely impressive operation. The Gun Runners supply only the finest hardware to the most discerning of customers, including the NCR. Approach the kiosk outside the gates of the building, and speak with either the Vendortron, or Isaac, near the Reloading Bench. You can ask about the Gun Runners, inquire about touring the factory (you can't), and play a game of Caravan.

- Reloading Bench [8/36]
- Caravan Player [Isaac] [1/15]
- Caravan Cards [Isaac] [2/30]

The Vendortron can't allow you into the factory but can sell you a wealth of weaponry, including upgrades for existing ordnance. Check the Vendortron's in-game store menu for enhanced ammunition. Note that all weapons are in perfect condition.

- Trader: Vendortron [5/33]
- Trader (Vendortron): Weapon Upgrades [Energy Weapons, Explosives, Guns] [3/10]

Breaking into the Gun Runners factory alerts the three patrolling guards, and nullifies the Vendortron's sales routine, stopping you from purchasing these rare items. Unlock the gate [Average], and head to the Gun Runner Headquarters front doors just beyond.

Ⓐ Doors to Gun Runner Headquarters

① Entrance Foyer

Find Fresh Apples, as well as a Star Cap in the small crate of empty Sarsaparilla Bottles.

- Carton of Cigarettes
- Sunset Sarsaparilla Star Cap [10/100]

② Kitchen

As you'd expect, there's scattered Food to claim, usually under heavy fire from the Gun Runners you've angered.

③ ④ Restroom and Dormitory

There are usually some goodies inside the Duffle Bag near the bathtub, and three Magazines to grab on or near the stalls.

- Magazine: Future Weapons Today [Energy Weapons] [3/10] [8/56]
- Magazine: Patriot's Cookbook [Explosives] [2/12] [9/56]
- Magazine: Today's Physician [Medicine] [5/19] [10/56]

⑤ Gun Smithy

The care and attention the Gun Runners give their weaponry is unsurpassed, and their Smithy is where this fine work takes place. Unlock a Locker [Average] for a nice item. The middle of the room has four Workbenches and two Reloading Benches, one of which has an Assault Carbine on it, and another holds a Laser Rifle. Finally, you can access the Gun Runner Terminal, where there's information on naming the Vendortron (not "Bob"), an order for Camp McCarran, and "Persona Non Grata." A final option appears during the Side Quest: You Can Depend on Me (and only then), allowing you to download some Manufacturing Specifications onto a Holotape.

> Vendortron Naming
> Camp McCarran Order #172
> Persona Non Grata

- Reloading Bench [9/36]
- Reloading Bench [10/36]
- Workbench [6/41]
- Workbench [7/41]
- Workbench [8/41]
- Workbench [9/41]
- Scrap Metal (2)
- Assault Carbine
- Laser Rifle
- Weapon Repair Kit

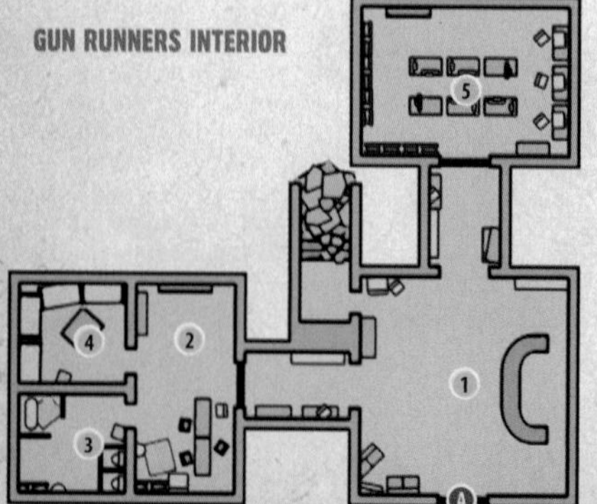

[2.15] Freeside's East Gate ●

- Threat Level: ●●●●●
- Faction: None
- Interior Exploration

This is the eastern Freeside gate, allowing access to the main fortified portions of New Vegas: Freeside [Zone 2C] and The Strip [Zone 2D]. Visible from Sharecropper Farms [2.20], and next door to the Gun Runners [2.14], this gate is usually the quickest way to reach Freeside and The Strip the first time you wander toward the New Vegas fortification. It also offers impressive views of The Strip's main casinos. There usually isn't a guard at these gates.

[2.16] Durable Dunn's Sacked Caravan

- Side Quest: Heartache by the Number
- Threat Level: ●●●●●
- Faction: Crimson Caravan / Van Graff
  - Entity: Caravan Guard (Deceased)
  - Entity: Van Graff Thug (Deceased)
  - Entity: Pack Brahmin (Deceased)
- Crafting: Campfire [17/109]
- Guns and Ammo

Dunn's Caravans may be durable, but they're certainly not bullet-proof; as indicated by the dead Brahmin and guards on the rickety bridge close to the East Pump Station [2.21]. The "island" between the two bridges has a Campfire, and the bodies of Van Graff Thugs to check. Bring Cass here during Side Quest: Heartache by the Number for further revelations.

- Campfire [17/109]
- Laser Rifle and Ammo

[2.17] Sunset Sarsaparilla Headquarters

See map on the following page

- Side Quest: The Legend of the Star/A Valuable Lesson
- Side Quest: Pressing Matters
- Threat Level: ●●●●●
- Faction: Robot
  - Entity: Bottling Robot
  - Entity: Shipping Worker
  - Entity: Sunset Sarsaparilla Security
  - Entity: Mr. Janitor
- Services: Gambling [Lucky Horseshoes] [1/15]
- Collectibles:
  - Magazine [Science] [7/23] [11-12/56]
  - Magazine [Speech] [2/12] [11-12/56]
  - Unique Weapon [8/42]
- Area Is Locked
- Guns and Ammo
- Health, Chems, or Water
- Interior Exploration
- Lots O' Caps
- Quest Item

The old headquarters of the well-known and loved "Beverage of the West Coast," this structure features a many-faceted glass bottle of the company's signature drink, Sunset Sarsaparilla. Before the war, an urban legend circulated that if you collected bottle caps marked with a star, you could send them in to the Sunset Sarsaparilla Headquarters and receive a prize. Now, this legend has taken on a life of its own; crazed individuals stalk the Wasteland searching for "SSSs" (Sunset Sarsaparilla Stars), a fact exacerbated by an automated robotic attendant, Festus, who prompts people with an option to present their Sunset Sarsaparilla Stars. Dare you find out the truth?

Sunset Sarsaparilla Factory Floor

Ⓐ Door to Mojave Wasteland

① Sunset Sarsaparilla Foyer

The ruined foyer still has a semblance of thrill and razzle-dazzle.

- Caps (a few)
- Magazine: Programmer's Digest [Science] [7/23] [11/56]

② Festus

Sitting in his rundown saloon, Festus is the mascot of the old Sunset Sarsaparilla Company, and here to bring you great news of a competition, and the official word on that health advisory (keep asking!). Requesting information on Star Bottle Caps begins Side Quest: The Legend of the Star. Returning with 50 or more

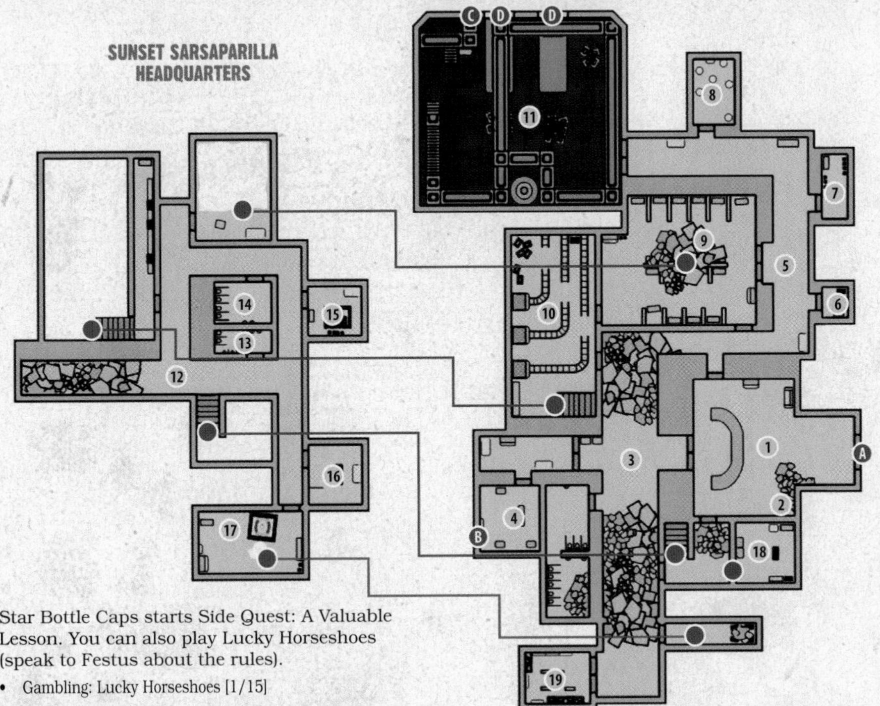

Star Bottle Caps starts Side Quest: A Valuable Lesson. You can also play Lucky Horseshoes (speak to Festus about the rules).

- Gambling: Lucky Horseshoes [1/15]

3 Main Corridor (Blocked) and Restrooms

One of the rubble piles has the remains of a Broken Shipping Worker you can salvage. Check both the restrooms here. There's Jet in one of the stalls.

- First Aid Box and Jet

4 Break Room to Outside Patio

Find some Food in the fridge, and an exit leads toward the Northwest Mountains [Zone 1]. Check one of the picnic tables for a Magazine.

- Magazine: Meeting People [Speech] [2/12] [12/56]

B Door to Mojave Wasteland (Outside Patio)

5 Northeast U Corridor

This U-shaped corridor is the central conduit to most of the locations. Check the Broken Shipping Workers for Energy Cells or Fission Batteries.

6 Storage Closet

- Scrap Metal (2)

7 Mr. Janitor's Closet

Mr. Janitor is currently offline. Access the nearby terminal [Average], and bring up the following menu options:

> Check mail
> Water Leak: Apparently there was a water leak in the upstairs meeting room. Was there possible long-term damage? See location #9 for more information!
> Great Job: The automated Janitor system is a great success!
> Check maintenance system
> Activate Work MHDY135: This causes Mr. Janitor to make a sweep of the main rooms, looking for trash, before returning here to deactivate.

8 Break Room

This small room has cluttered tables and bits of Food.

9 Upstairs Meeting Room (now Downstairs)

The upper floor has fallen in on a cubicle office below. Note the exits; out to the warehouse, and up the rubble to the upper floor.

10 Bottling Room (Ground and Upper)

Don't confuse this with the larger shipping warehouse. Expect attacks from the Bottling and Security Robots. There's a possibility of a Star Bottle Cap in an unopened bottle, so check them all! Beware of more robots on the upstairs balcony.

- Sunset Sarsaparilla Crate Items (36)

11 Shipping Warehouse

Beware the hostile Robot Shipping Workers, and if you thought the Bottling Room had a huge number of crates, check this place out! Hack the terminal [Average]. There are two entries as the march of time brought robots into the workplace, forcing out humans. There is also a pressing plate for the bottle caps in here. It must be destroyed, but only if Side Quest: Pressing Matters is active.

> Check message
> Check draft

- Sunset Sarsaparilla Crate Items (203)

C D Doors to Mojave Wasteland (Loading Alley)

12 (Upper) Corridor

Find a Broken Custodial Robot to scavenge for parts, and stairs to the south.

13 (Upper) Restrooms (Gentlemen)

- First Aid Box

14 (Upper) Restrooms (Ladies)

- First Aid Box

15 (Upper) Foreman's Office

A Broken Custodial Robot lies in this blood-specked room.

- Sunset Sarsaparilla Crate Items (2)

16 (Upper) Sales Office

- Sunset Sarsaparilla Crate Items (2)

17 (Upper) Executive Office

A Broken Personal Assistant lies in this room with a hole in the floor, leading to the sealed storage, and four tool cabinets. Check the desk, Vending Machine, and wall safe [Average] for the usual items; except the safe, which may have a Star Cap (which isn't counted toward the 100 you can find lying about, visible to you). Check the terminal [Very Easy] for the following missives:

> Check saved inbox messages
> What contest?
> How's your new toy?
> Check saved sent messages
> RE: What contest?
> While the iron is hot
> RE: How do you like your new toy?

- Tool Cabinet Items

18 (Lower) Mr. Brody's Office [Very Hard]

Check the terminal for these messages:

> Check automated messages
> Go to page 1, 2, 3: Charting the security breaches in the building.

- Scrap Metal
- Tool Cabinet Items

19 Sealed Storage

Accessed only after Side Quest: A Valuable Lesson begins. Drop down the hole from Location #16, and open the door, which is otherwise sealed. The following is in this chamber, including a hapless adventurer called Allen Marks, his last words recorded on Holotape, and his Unique Weapon.

- Holotape: Allen Marks
- Sunset Sarsaparilla Crate Items (10)
- Sunset Sarsaparilla Deputy Badge (319)
- Unique Weapon: Pew Pew [8/42]

[2.18] El Rey Motel

- Threat Level:
- Faction: Wastelander / Mutated Animal
  - Entity: Bark Scorpion
  - Entity: Chem Addict
- Collectibles:
  - Sunset Sarsaparilla Star Cap [11/100]
- Unique Item [11/95]
- Area Is Locked
- Guns and Ammo
- Health, Chems, or Water
- Interior Exploration
- Sleeping Quarters

Chem addicts hang out here, mainly because they aren't usually hassled by Fiends due to the motel's proximity to Camp McCarran [2.19]. This is also between two access points to the Central Sewers [U2.C].

A Doors to Camp McCarran [2.19]

B Manhole to Central Sewers [U2.C]

1 New Vegas Sign [2.S17]

2 Ground Floor Room

There scattered Beer, Chems, and a few Bark Scorpions to quickly get rid of before you turn woozy. Read the Threatening Note on the table. It's suitably intimidating.

- Eyeglasses and Beer
- Note: Threatening Note

EL REY MOTEL EXTERIOR

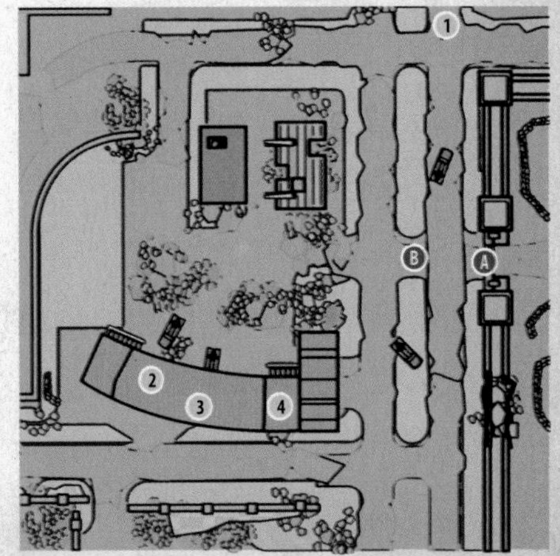

3 Upper Floor Room #1 [Very Easy]

Unlock or force the lock and check out this dead guy, sprawled with a Med-X in his hand and close to a Nuka-Cola Victory!

- Teddy Bear (2) and Scrap Metal
- Unique Item: Nuka-Cola Victory [11/95]

4 Upper Floor Room #2 [Very Easy]

Force or unlock the door and enter this rather festive chamber, which takes a turn for the bloody as a Crazed Chem Addict launches at you!

- Knife (2)
- Sunset Sarsaparilla Star Cap [11/100]

[2.19] Camp McCarran

- Main Quest: King's Gambit
- Side Quest: No, Not Much
- Side Quest: I Don't Hurt Anymore
- Side Quest: There Stands the Grass
- Side Quest: The White Wash
- Side Quest: I Put a Spell on You
- Free Quest: A Final Plan for Esteban
- Free Quest: Bounty Killer, I
- Free Quest: Dealing with Contreras
- Free Quest: Don't Poke at the Bear
- Free Quest: Don't Tread on the Bear
- Free Quest: Emergency Radio Waves
- Free Quest: Not Worth a Hill of Corn and Beans
- Free Quest: Old School Ghoul
- Free Quest: Rest and Resupply
- Free Quest: Silus Treatment
- Threat Level: ●●●●●
- Faction: NCR
  - Entity: Colonel James Hsu
  - Entity: Major Dhatri
  - Entity: Captain Ronald Curtis
  - Entity: Lieutenant Carrie Boyd
  - Entity: Lieutenant Gorobets
  - Entity: Sergeant Bitter-Root
  - Entity: Sergeant Daniel Contreras
  - Entity: Corporal Walter Hornsby
  - Entity: Corporal Betsy
  - Entity: Corporal William Farber
  - Entity: Corporal Sterling
  - Entity: 10 of Spades
  - Entity: Private Christina Morales
  - Entity: Private Davey Crenshaw
  - Entity: Doctor Kemp
  - Entity: Doctor Thomas Hildern
  - Entity: Angela Williams
  - Entity: NCR Trooper
  - Entity: NCR Ranger
  - Entity: NCR Guard Dog
  - Entity: Silus
- Fame/Infamy
- Services:
  - Caravan Player [2/15]
  - Healer/Dealer [4/31]
  - Healer/Dealer [5/31]
  - Trader [6/33]
  - Caravan Cards [3/30]
- Crafting:
  - Reloading Bench [11/36]
  - Workbench [10/41]
- Collectibles:
  - Magazine [Barter] [1/16] [13-29/56]
  - Magazine [Guns] [2/11] [13-29/56]
  - Magazine [Guns] [3/11] [13-29/56]
  - Magazine [Guns] [4/11] [13-29/56]
  - Magazine [Lockpick] [1/12] [13-29/56]
  - Magazine [Medicine] [6/19] [13-29/56]
  - Magazine [Medicine] [7/19] [13-29/56]
  - Magazine [Energy Weapons] [4/10] [13-29/56]
  - Magazine [Repair] [4/27] [13-29/56]
  - Magazine [Repair] [5/27] [13-29/56]
  - Magazine [Sneak] [4/10] [13-29/56]
  - Magazine [Speech] [3/12] [13-29/56]
  - Magazine [Survival] [4/30] [13-29/56]
  - Magazine [Survival] [5/30] [13-29/56]
  - Magazine [Survival] [6/30] [13-29/56]
  - Magazine [Survival] [7/30] [13-29/56]
  - Magazine [Survival] [8/30] [13-29/56]
  - Sunset Sarsaparilla Star Cap [12/100]
  - Unique Item [12/95]
  - Unique Weapon [9/42]
  - Unique Weapon [10/42]
  - Unique Weapon [11/42]
- Area Is Locked
- Follower
- Guns and Ammo
- Health, Chems, or Water
- Highly Visible
- Interior Exploration
- Lots O' Caps
- Main Trading Route
- Sleeping Quarters
- Underground Connection
- Quest Item

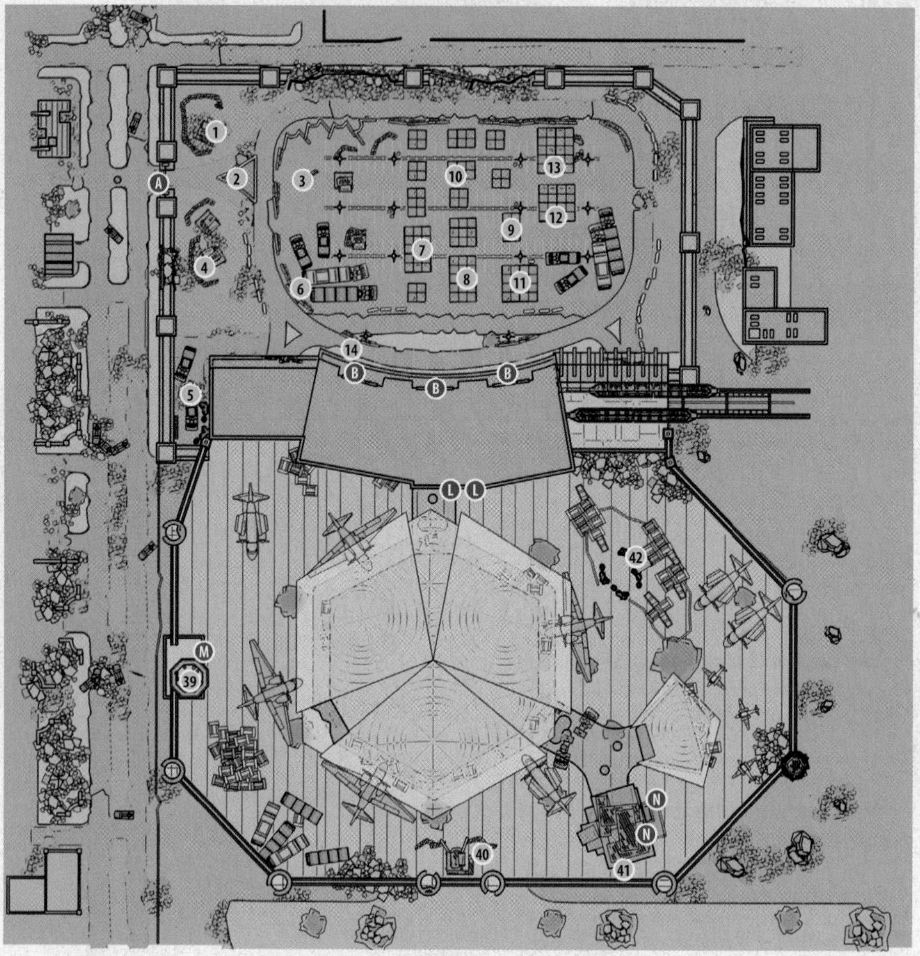

Camp McCarran is the main base for NCR military operations in southern Nevada. Formerly McCarran International Airport, the structure now houses and trains NCR's sizable battalions. Camp McCarran is the hub of activity in the area, and constantly has soldiers moving into and out of it. Despite this, security is tight and there are only a few ways in. A monorail connects Camp McCarran and The Strip, but it's heavily guarded.

CAMP MCCARRAN EXTERIOR

Camp McCarran Parking Lot

A Gate to Mojave Wasteland (near The Las Vegas Sign)

1 Northwest Sentry Post

Some of this ammunition must be stolen if you wish to obtain it.

CAMP MCCARRAN SUPPLY SHACK

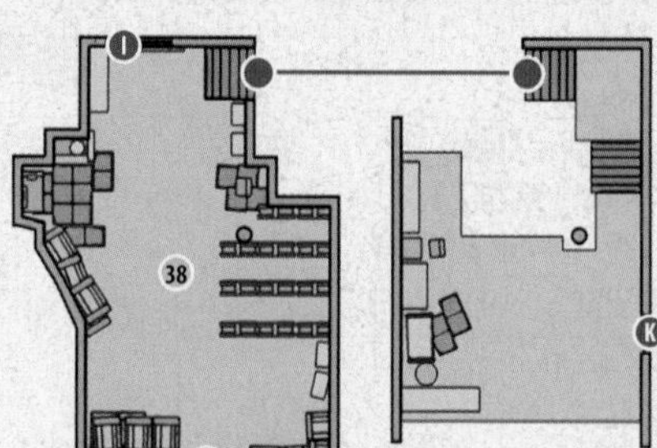

- Ammo Box Ammunition (2)
- Grenade Box Ammunition

2 Sandbag Road Defenses

- Grenade Box Ammunition

3 Firing Range and Sentry Post

Close to the tent city is a firing range. Major Dhatri is sometimes at this location, when he isn't wandering the area, or standing in front of the Terminal Building. Consult him to begin Side Quest: Three-Card Bounty.

- Ammo Box Ammunition (3)
- First Aid Box (2)
- Gun Cabinet Items (2)

4 Western Sentry Posts

There are two here.

- Ammo Box Ammunition (4)
- First Aid Box

5 Truck Mechanic Area

- Scrap Metal (10)

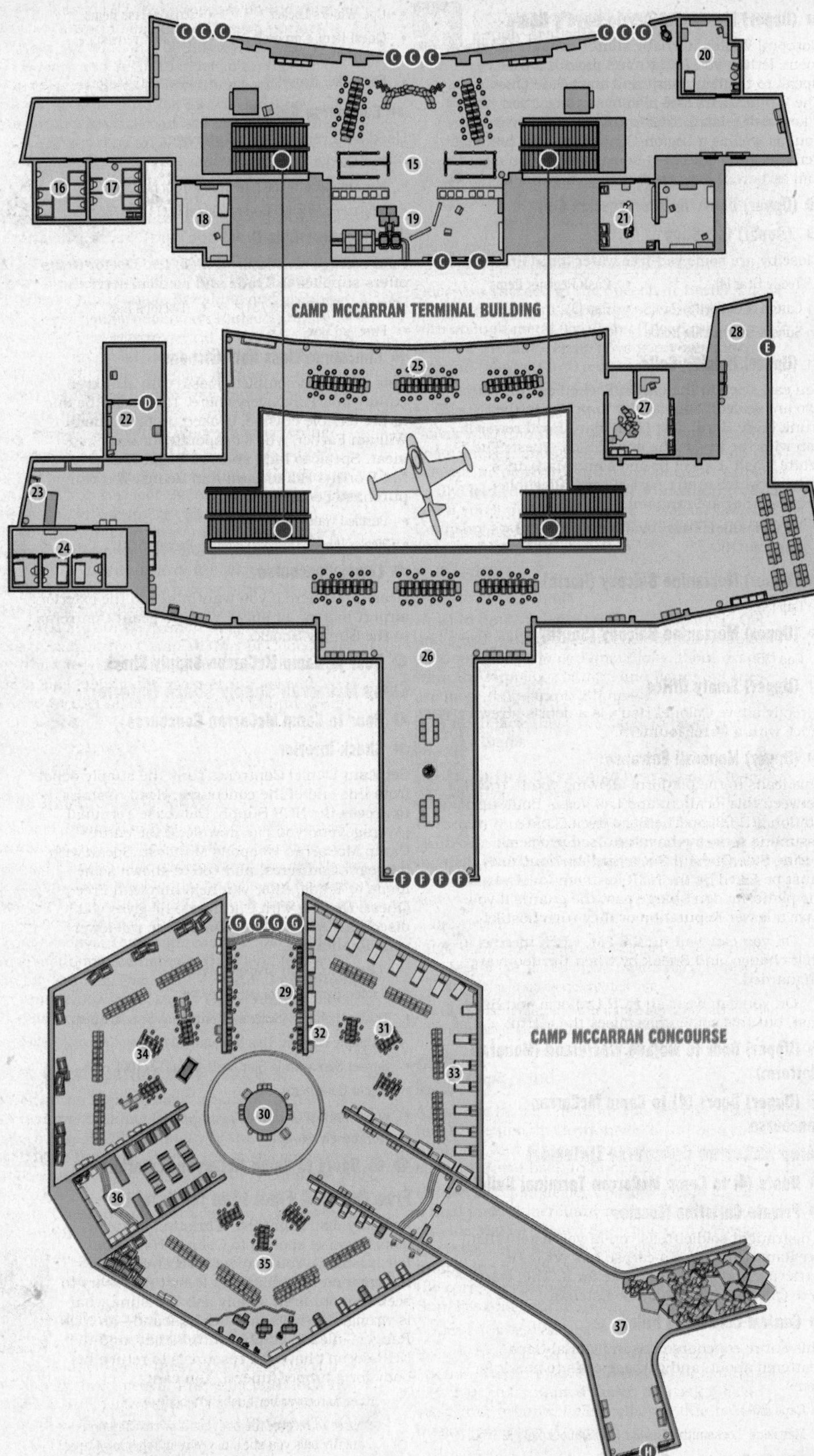

6 Little Buster's Punching Bag

There's a Sentry Post here, and a diminutive soldier with a big ego taking it to the Super Mutant dummy. You can speak to him about his plans (being a Bounty Hunter) and the Fiends he's taken down. He hints about the jobs Major Dhatri can offer you, and more importantly, he plays a mean hand of Caravan. He also has a mean hand claw: a Unique Bladed Gauntlet you can Pickpocket or kill him for.

- Caravan Player: Little Buster [2/15]
- Caravan Cards: Little Buster [3/30]
- Unique Weapon: Cram Opener [9/42]
- Scrap Metal

7 First Recon's Tents

The NCR's best sniper company resides in this area, led by Lieutenant Gorobets. Ask him about his team, and he tells you he's worried about two of his squad: Betsy and Sterling. Ask for more information to begin Side Quest: I Don't Hurt Anymore. Other members include 10 of Spades (with a stammer), Corporal Betsy, (who is sarcastic and rude to males and overly flirtatious to females,) Corporal Sterling (who survived Malpais, covets his Unique Weapon, and is part of Raul's Free Quest), and Sergeant Bitter-Root (a tough man with a troubled past).

- Unique Weapon: La Longue Carabine [10/42]
- Ammo Box Ammunition (2)
- Footlocker Items (3)
- Sleeping Quarters
- Magazine: ¡La Fantoma! [Sneak] [4/10] [13/56]
- Magazine: Milsurp Review [Guns] [2/11] [14/56]

8 Communications and Weapons Tent

Hack a terminal [Very Easy] for the following messages, which don't seem to be official NCR business-related:

- > Redhead
- > **Reminder ***
- > Hi there!
- Ammo Box Ammunition (2)
- Grenade Box Ammunition [Average]
- Gun Cabinet Items (3)

9 Officer's Tent

- Footlocker Items

10 Tent City

This group of eight tents is north of First Recon's tents, where more of the NCR Troopers reside.

- Footlocker Items (8)
- Magazine: Salesman Weekly [Barter] [1/16] [15/56]
- Magazine: Fixin' Things [Repair] [4/27] [16/56]
- Magazine: Fixin' Things [Repair] [5/27] [17/56]
- Magazine: Meeting People [Speech] [3/12] [18/56]
- Magazine: Lad's Life [Survival] [4/30] [19/56]
- Duffle Bag Items (3)
- Carton of Cigarettes
- Sleeping Quarters
- Cap (18)
- Silenced .22 Pistol
- Bobby Pin
- Teddy Bear
- Ammo Box Ammunition (2)

11 Storage Tent

- Chems and Stimpaks
- Purified Water (3)
- Doctor's Bag (3)
- Magazine: Future Weapons Today [Energy Weapons] [4/10] [20/56]
- Magazine: Milsurp Review [Guns] [3/11] [21/56]
- Magazine: Today's Physician [Medicine] [6/19] [22/56]
- Food
- Carton of Cigarettes (3)
- Footlocker Items
- Ammo Box Ammunition (2)
- First Aid Box (2)

12 Medical Tent

- Magazine: Lad's Life [Survival] [5/30] [23/56]
- Magazine: Today's Physician [Medicine] [7/19] [24/56]
- First Aid Box (3)
- Purified Water (2)
- Chems and Blood Pack
- Doctor's Bag

13 Mess Hall Tent

Expect a small variety of Food on one of the tables, and more in a box by the cooking pans on the barrels outside.

- Magazine: Lad's Life [Survival] [6/30] [25/56]
- Magazine: Lad's Life [Survival] [7/30] [26/56]

14 McCarran Airport Frontage

Major Dhatri may be here once you've investigated the Terminal Building, ready to give out Side Quest-related bounties.

B Doors (3 sets) to Camp McCarran Terminal Building

L Garage Doors (2) to Camp McCarran Terminal Building

and figure that a good (but not completely accurate) rule of thumb is to request help when you're within Zone 2. You can call the following:

- NCR Supply Support: A Supply Cache is dropped close to your location, and if you make "Emergency Radio" your active Quest, you can see the location. Run and scavenge the items inside.

NCR Supply Cache Items

- NCR Trooper Support: An NCR Trooper is sent to your location, and acts as a Follower (although in less-difficult modes, he or she dies instead of falling unconscious).

Follower: NCR Trooper

- NCR Ranger Support: An NCR Ranger is sent to provide longer-range support, and acts as a Follower (although he or she dies if taking enough enemy damage, too).

Follower: NCR Ranger

The Trooper and Ranger don't take orders, and won't be dismissed; they are simply here as fire support. To use the radio again (only after a Trooper or Ranger dies, or you pick up supplies), wait 24 hours.

> **Note** Despite being a Free Quest, this appears on your Pip-Boy's Quest Log if you choose "NCR Supply Support."

Free Quest: Not Worth a Hill of Corn and Beans

Over in the Camp McCarran Concourse Kitchens (Location #36), Corporal William Farber is furious over a crooked health inspector, and the quality of food he's forced to serve the Troopers. With only corn and beans on the menu, the men are getting restless (and flatulent). Ask if there's something you can do to improve the supplies. Three problems need solving:

Farber requires a continuous supply of fresh meat. Fitz, Nash, and Crimson Caravan all might have the meat he needs.

His food processor has broken down and requires a wealth of parts to fix. He provides a list if you ask. Try the various Traders in the desert, or over at Westside. He also recommends a place called "House Tools."

He also needs some spices to give his meals a kick. The Crimson Caravan Company might have some.

- Note: Meat Vendor List
- Note: Food Processor Parts List

Farber mentioned an NCR department that works on spices. This is the OSI, although they've much more important research to undertake. Visit the office inside the terminal. Once you've spoken with both Doctor Hildern and Angela Williams over at the OSI office, you can mention to Williams that you hear the food around here is pretty bad. Williams recommends that you speak with Contreras about finding some supplies, although it's going to cost some Caps. This doesn't help with your current Free Quest; but it hints at another (Dealing with Contreras).

Tasks #1 (and #3): Putting Meat (and Spices) on the Menu

Fitz: At his Grub n' Gulp Rest Stop [2.32], peruse his selection of meats to discover he's purely small-time and can't supply enough for Farber.

Ruby Nash: Travel to the town of Primm [4.17], and meet Ruby Nash over at the Vikki & Vance Casino. Ask her what she cooks, and she mentions a delicious Radscorpion Venom Casserole. Ask for some, and she's happy to cook some up, as long as you provide the Radscorpion Glands. Check the Tour of Primm for this Free Quest. Return with Glands, and you're given Ruby's Casseroles in increments of five (based on the Glands you recover). Unfortunately, Farber isn't interested in such small quantities.

- Quest Item: Ruby's Casserole (5)

Blake: Visit the Crimson Caravan Company [2.09] and speak with Blake, letting him know McCarran needs a regular shipment of Brahmin meat and spices. The only problem is the payment. You can:

Tell Blake that if he gives the NCR a deal on the price, he'll have the upper hand in future negotiations.

Say he could arrange a trade as McCarran has plenty of vegetables.

Or let McCarran worry about the costs.

Task #2: Putting the Processor Back to Work

The contraption is the kitchen's food processor, and it's completely busted. Check your Note to find out what parts are needed:

Equipment Part	# Required
Pilot Lights	2
Pressure Cookers	2
Conductors	2
Firehose Nozzles	2
Fission Batteries	4
Steam Gauge Assemblies	2
Sensor Modules	2
Scrap Metal	5
Pot	1

You can find them (as Farber recommended) over at the H&H Tools Factory [2.06], but a Gas Station in Novac [5.18] also has some of these parts. Anywhere you find Scrap Metal may have the parts. You can:

Collect the parts, and then return and fix the machine.

Or jury-rig the machine without the parts, using your exceptional Repair talents.

Now speak with Farber, and he gives you a discount when you Trade with him from now on.

Free Quest: Rest and Resupply

When you've done a few tasks and Quests for the NCR, visit Colonel James Hsu, who is pleased with your progress. Once you're Liked by the NCR, Hsu tells you about an out-of-the-way Safehouse [5.03] where you can rest and resupply your inventory. You're given a key and can now access this location.

- NCR Safehouse Key

Free Quest: Silus Treatment

Speak with Colonel James Hsu, and he mentions that Lieutenant Boyd is having a difficult time with a captured Legion Centurion who's not talking. Perhaps you could provide a different approach to obtaining the information? You're given a Note with this information on it.

- Note: Silus Treatment

Speak to Boyd at length about the prisoner in her custody. Ask about beating the man senseless. Boyd is happy with that plan, but restrictions from President Tandy's administration prevent her from using violence. But that doesn't prevent you! Whether you have moral objections about this or not, agree to the plan and watch Boyd verbally spar with Silus about slave collars, until you're beckoned in.

You have to surrender your weapons when you head into the cell, so gun combat isn't an option. Talk to Silus and he immediately rants at you. You can:

Verbally spar continuously with Silus. This gets him gradually more furious.

Or you can attack him with your fists.

No other action gets the job done. After some verbal (or real) attacks, Silus stops, and you must speak with Boyd again. She heads in to talk to Silus, who still refuses to talk. Head back in to inflict more punishment courtesy of your forked tongue or meaty hands.

After a final bout of sparring (don't kill Silus!), the Centurion wilts, and gives you some extremely helpful information: Caesar is ill, and there's a Legion infiltrator somewhere in the camp! Report back to Boyd, who rewards you.

Caps (175)

NCR Fame Gained!

[2.20] NCR Sharecropper Farms

See map on the following page

- Side Quest: Hard Luck Blues
- Side Quest: The White Wash
- Threat Level: ●●●●●
- Faction: NCR
  - Entity: Private Ortega
  - Entity: Morgan Blake
  - Entity: Lieutenant Romanowski
  - Entity: Trent Bascom
- Collectibles:
  - Sunset Sarsaparilla Star Cap [13/100]
  - Skill Book [Sneak] [1/4] [1/6]
- Health, Chems, or Water
- Interior Exploration
- Lots O' Caps
- Sleeping Quarters
- Wasteland Vegetation
- Quest Item

The NCR provides protection (and water thanks to a pipe up from Lake Las Vegas [3.22]) to New Vegas Sharecroppers to tend a large allotment southeast of Freeside's East Gate [2.15]. You can speak to Private Ortega at the gate, who tells you that some of the workers aren't particularly grateful for this arrangement.

Press her for information, and she mentions Trent Bascom, who reckons the NCR isn't providing enough water for them to meet harvest quotas.

You can also ask about her posts, and information about various places around town.

Once inside the camp, speak with Morgan Blake; she provides you with some information and indicates a Pump Station in need of your investigating, beginning Side Quest: Hard Luck Blues.

Lieutenant Romanowski provides information from an NCR perspective. He's more helpful after Side Quest: The White Wash is active, aiding you in your investigations.

Trent Bascom is usually working the fields. You can ask him about the Thaler Act, the NCR, and his "bum deal." But he doesn't reveal more information unless Side Quest: The White Wash is active. You can also Pickpocket Bascom to discover a Note from Corporal White, which helps in this Quest. Both Bascom and Morgan Blake also have a few NCR Dollars.

- Quest Item: Note to Corporal White
- NCR $$$

You can now check out the plants growing in each greenhouse, and perhaps pick one or two (if you aren't spotted).

A Orion Moreno's House [2.S06]

B Manhole to East Central Sewers [U2.EC]

1 Greenhouse #1

- Fresh Water (from a valve)
- Pinto Beans
- Maize

2 Greenhouse #2

- Fresh Water (from a valve)
- Pinto Beans

NCR SHARECROPPER FARMS EXTERIOR

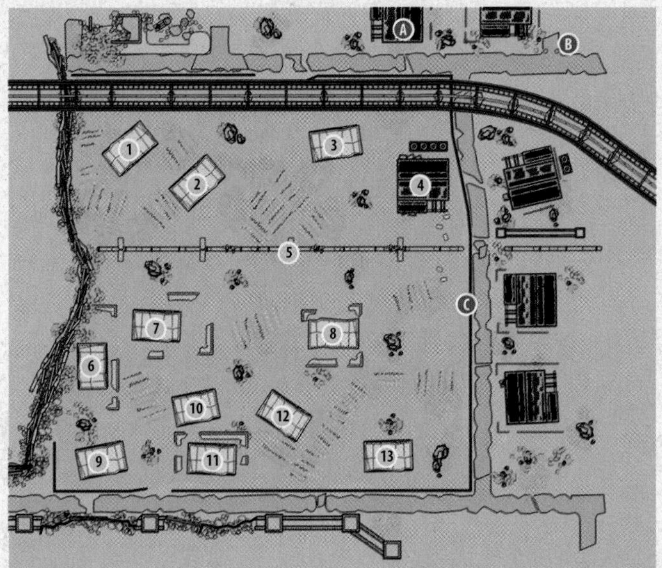

3 Greenhouse #3 [Easy]

- Fresh Water (from a valve)
- Honey Mesquite
- Maize

4 Sharecropper Barracks

You'll find Trent Bascom sleeping here when he isn't working. It's easy to Pickpocket everyone if you wait until they're sleeping.

- Sunset Sarsaparilla Star Cap [13/100]
- Skill Book: Chinese Army: Spec Ops. Training Manual [Sneak] [1/4] [1/6]
- Footlocker Items (2)
- First Aid Box

5 Irrigation Pipe

Sip from the valves here for a little rad-free sustenance.

C Entrance Gate

There is an NCR flagpole here (and Private Ortega). To the east are three ranch homes, all boarded up. Check the mailboxes to occasionally find a Magazine.

6 Greenhouse #4

- Fresh Water (from a valve)
- Pinto Beans
- Maize

7 Greenhouse #5

- Fresh Water (from a valve)
- Maize

8 Greenhouse #6

- Fresh Water (from a valve)
- Honey Mesquite

9 Greenhouse #7

This is an incubation house.

- Fresh Water (from a valve)
- Maize

10 Greenhouse #8

- Fresh Water (from a valve)
- Maize

11 Greenhouse #9

- Fresh Water (from a valve)
- Maize

12 Greenhouse #10

This is abandoned, and partly used for storage.

13 Greenhouse #11

This is abandoned, and partly used for storage.

- Fresh Water (from a valve)

[2.21] East Pump Station

- Side Quest: Hard Luck Blues
- Threat Level: ●●●●●
- Faction: NCR
  - Entity: None
- Fame/Infamy
- Collectibles: Magazine [Repair] [6/27] [30/56]
- Health, Chems, or Water
- Interior Exploration

This location is of paramount importance to the NCR, because it is responsible for filtering the water being pumped along the giant water pipe from Lake Las Vegas [3.22], and then into the Sharecropper Farms [2.20]. There are actually two buildings: the East Cistern, and the facility itself, plus two nearby Manhole Covers allowing access into the sewers [U2]. Inside the cistern is a Water Tower Valve (allowing you to sip clean water), and a blown-out terminal with a Magazine next to it.

- Skill Magazine: Fixin' Things [Repair] [6/27] [30/56]

A matching Pump Station lies to the west [2.27], but this one is on the outskirts of the Sharecropper Farm area. Enter and inspect the interior.

A Door to Mojave Wasteland

EAST PUMP STATION

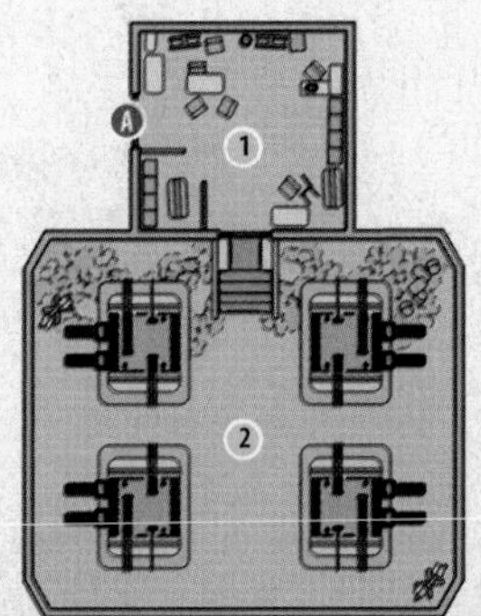

1 Office

Activate the Pump Station Terminal, and you can:

Leave it alone.

Repair the network connection. This nets you some XP, but isn't necessary to read the warning.

Activate the terminal to read the warning about radiation being detected in the filtration system, but not in this facility (it is actually in Vault 34 [3.12]). This begins Side Quest: Hard Luck Blues.

2 Pump Room

This is operational, but empty.

[2.22] Aerotech Office Park

See map on the following page

- Side Quest: Left My Heart
- Side Quest: The Coyotes
- Free Quest: Keith's Caravan Charade
- Threat Level: ●●●●●
- Faction: NCR
  - Entity: Captain Parker
  - Entity: Bert Gunnarsson
  - Entity: Frank Weathers
  - Entity: Keith
  - Entity: Refugee
  - Entity: Junky
- Fame/Infamy
- Services:
  - Caravan Player [3/15]
  - Healer/Dealer [6/31]
- Collectibles:
  - Caravan Cards [4/30]
  - Magazine: [Barter] [2/16] [31-32/56]
  - Magazine: [Medicine] [8/19] [31-32/56]
  - Sunset Sarsaparilla Star Cap [14/100]
- Guns and Ammo
- Health, Chems, or Water
- Interior Exploration
- Sleeping Quarters
- Quest Item

Close to a Manhole to the East Central Sewers [U2.EC], and adjacent to the Sharecropper Farms [2.20] and Camp McCarran [2.19] is a fortified refugee camp re-purposed from an old office park. The elevated monorail track surrounds this location. Open the Junk Door, and you can speak to Captain Parker about ongoing humanitarian problems. Occasionally present is a Ghoul named Bert Gunnarsson (a member of the Followers of the Apocalypse), who can heal you. Ask him about the refugees.

- Healer: Bert Gunnarsson [6/31]

1 Courtyard

The downtrodden roam this rubble-filled area.

2 Aerotech Tent

It is better (for your Karmic soul) to receive medical attention from Bert than steal the items in this room. Frank Weathers is also here. Ask him about his family, and you can begin the hunt for them: Side Quest: Left My Heart.

- Quest Item: Note on Frank Weathers' Family
- First Aid Box (4)
- Chems
- Sleeping Quarters

3 Aerotech Suite 200

Search through the strewn mess of hobos and debris. The entrance foyer has some Chems, ammo, and a Caravan Shotgun. Find Keith in here to begin the Free Quest.

- Chems
- Caravan Shotgun and Ammo
- Sleeping Quarters

AEROTECH OFFICE PARK EXTERIOR

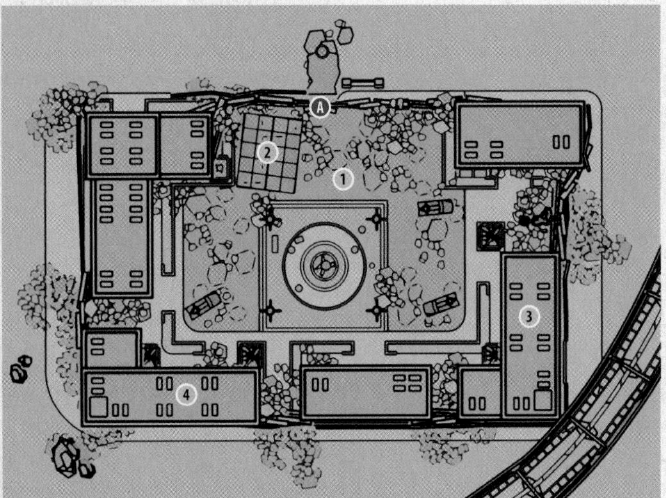

4 Aerotech Suite 300

The other Aerotech suite is in a little better condition, and houses the more stable long-term patients. One of the restrooms is locked [Easy] with ammo (and a skeleton) inside.

- Magazine: Salesman Weekly [Barter] [2/16] [31/56]
- Magazine: Today's Physician [Medicine] [8/19] [32/56]
- Food and Chems
- Sunset Sarsaparilla Star Cap [14/100]

Free Quest: Keith's Caravan Charade

Keith, wearing a red jumpsuit, offers to play Caravan with you. You can:

Ask what he wants, and he invites you to play some games. You can also play Caravan with him. If you do, don't expect to win.

Tell him gambling isn't your scene, but that you want something "medical." He offers Jet for 35 Caps. Take it and continue, or leave it and the conversation.

- Jet

Ask him what his con trick is. You realize he's using marked cards, making victory at Caravan pretty much an impossibility. You can take this information to Parker.

- Caravan Player: Keith [3/15]
- Caravan Cards: Keith [4/30]

[2.23] South Vegas Ruins West Entrance

- Threat Level: ●●●●●
- Faction: Fiend
  - Entity: Cook-Cook
  - Entity: Fiend
- Interior Exploration
- Radio Signal [Black Mountain: Zone 2E only]

Three entrances/exits allow access into this Fiend stronghold, ruled over by the iron fist and crazy brain of Motor-Runner in Vault 3 [2.24]. Of the three entrances (including the one not shown as a Primary Location on your Pip-Boy's World Map), this is by far the most dangerous, because you must deal with the lunatics and deviant Cook-Cook, in his ruins hideout just north of here [2.S18], if you aren't Sneaking.

[2.24] Vault 3

See maps on the following page

- Side Quest: Aba Daba Honeymoon
- Side Quest: Still in the Dark
- Free Quest: Bounty Killer, II
- Free Quest: I Love Bananas
- Free Quest: Suits You, Sarah
- Threat Level: ●●●●●
- Faction: Fiend
  - Entity: Motor-Runner
  - Entity: Fiend
  - Entity: Daniel
  - Entity: BoneGnash
  - Entity: GnashBone
  - Entity: Bryce Anders
  - Entity: Rick Lancer
  - Entity: Dennis
  - Entity: Rachel
  - Entity: Carter (Deceased)
- Dangers:
  - Traps
  - Mines
- Collectibles:
  - Skill Book [Sneak] [2/4] [2/6]
  - Magazine [Guns] [5/11] [33-44/56]
  - Magazine [Lockpick] [2/12] [33-44/56]
  - Magazine [Lockpick] [3/12] [33-44/56]
  - Magazine [Lockpick] [4/12] [33-44/56]
  - Magazine [Lockpick] [5/12] [33-44/56]
  - Magazine [Lockpick] [6/12] [33-44/56]
  - Magazine [Medicine] [9/19] [33-44/56]
  - Magazine [Medicine] [10/19] [33-44/56]
  - Magazine [Repair] [7/27] [33-44/56]
  - Magazine [Repair] [8/27] [33-44/56]
  - Magazine [Repair] [9/27] [33-44/56]
  - Magazine [Speech] [4/12] [33-44/56]
  - Sunset Sarsaparilla Star Cap [15/100]
  - Unique Item [13/95]
- Area Is Locked
- Guns and Ammo
- Health, Chems, or Water
- Interior Exploration
- Sleeping Quarters
- Quest Item

Vault 3, which is now completely within South Vegas Ruins (AKA "Fiend Territory") was once an ordinary, happy vault. It wasn't built above a sulfur cave, or to feature Vault-Tec "experiments" that could drive dwellers mad. In fact, the place was functioning normally until a slight water leak turned the lower chambers soggy and forced the inhabitants out to the surface, in search of humanity on the topside. Instead, they met the Fiends.

Vault 3—Recreation Area

A Door to South Vegas Ruins

1 (Upper) Entrance Door

You're greeted by a rather unpleasant Fiend, and assuming you aren't already engaged in combat, you can:

Tell her you're carrying Chems, and you don't deliver to the help. This is available whether or not Side Quest: Aba Daba Honeymoon is active.

GREAT KHANS If you're dressed as a Great Khan as part of the Side Quest, the Fiend is pleased to see you, and asks for some Psycho for herself.

- Ask where the boss is, and that she's been hitting you up for freebies.

The Fiend backpedals quickly, and tells you where Motor-Runner is.

Even if you're dressed as a Khan, you can tell her you're not really one. The angry reply features a whole load of swearing.

Any other option results in you leaving, or the entire vault of Fiends turning hostile.

2 (Upper) Storage [Easy]

Unlock via the "No Access" blast door.

- First Aid Box
- Tool Cabinet Items (2)
- Teddy Bear (4)
- Scrap Metal

3 (Upper) Diner

If you're not slaughtering them, Fiends complain about Motor-Runner's Chem distribution in this central chamber.

- Scrap Metal (3)
- Chems and Stimpaks
- Bobby Pins

4 (Upper) Kitchen [Easy] and Pantry

The door in the eastern wall allows access to the pantry.

- First Aid Box and Food
- Purified Water

5 (Lower) Thoroughfare and Restrooms

A few Fiends hang around here like a bad smell, which also seems to be coming from the restrooms.

- Bobby Pins and Scrap Metal
- First Aid Box [Very Easy]

6 (Lower) Doctor's Office [Hard]

- RadAway (3)
- Fixer (2)
- Doctor's Bag
- First Aid Box
- Magazine: Today's Physician [Medicine] [9/19] [33/56]

7 (Lower) Filing Room [Easy]

Find Bobby Pins by the door, near the gurney.

- Bobby Pins
- First Aid Box
- Magazine: Fixin' Things [Repair] [7/27] [34/56]

B Door to Vault 3—Living Quarters

8 (Upper and Lower) Mezzanine and Fiend Sleeping Area

Spanning two levels, this unkempt mezzanine is now strewn with mattresses and pool tables. Doors lead to and from the upper balcony. Check the Vending Machines.

- Chems and Stimpaks
- Scrap Metal
- Pool Cue (6)
- Sleeping Quarters
- Ammo Box Ammunition

9 (Lower) Projector Room

- Doctor's Bag
- Chems and Stimpaks
- Ammo Box Ammunition (2)
- 10mm Pistol
- Teddy Bear

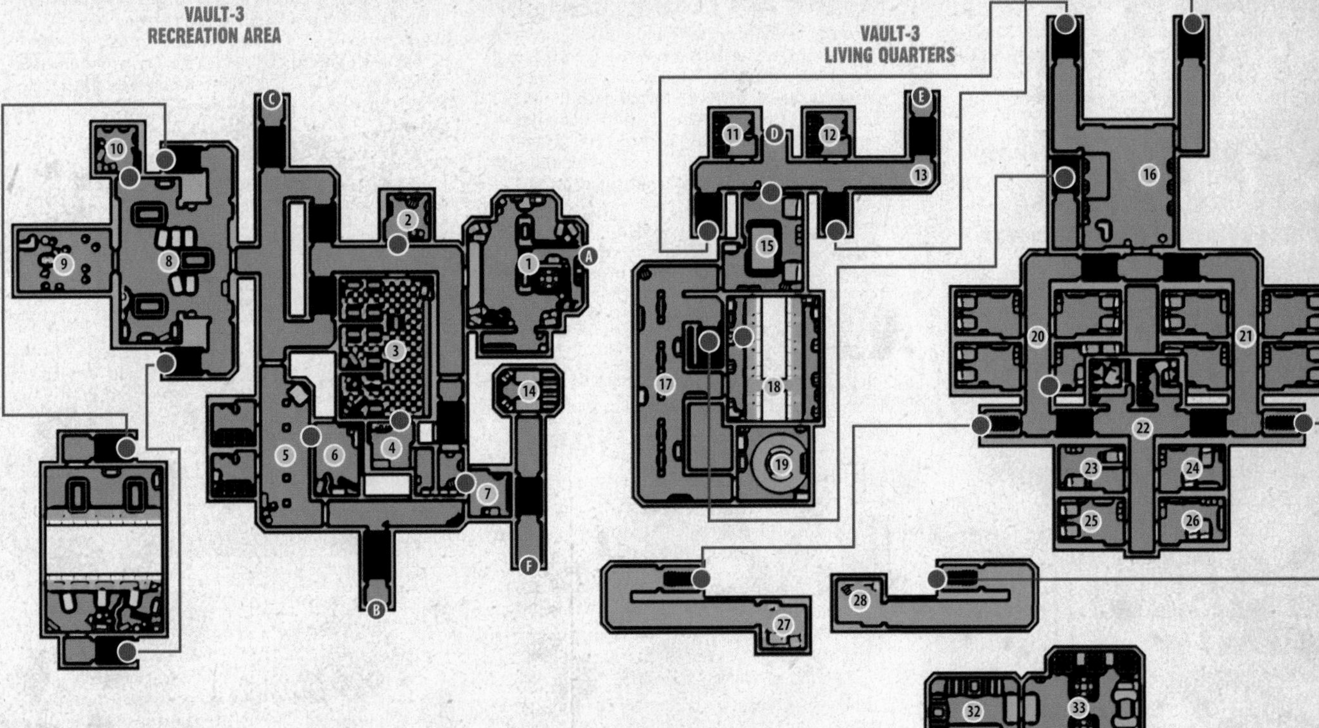

10 Storage [Very Easy]

- Tool Cabinet Items
- Pool Cue (23)
- Unique Items: Nuka-Cola Victory [13/95]

C Door to Vault 3—Maintenance Wing

F Door to Vault 3—Maintenance Wing

14 Server Room

This is only accessible from the booby-trapped staircase (Location #13) in the Living Quarters. A wounded NCR Ranger named Bryce Anders is holed up in this room. Speak to him for Free Quest: Bounty Killer, II (which "officially" begins in Camp McCarran). Anders also carries a key that he can give you during conversation, or you can Pickpocket or kill him. Hack a terminal [Very Easy] to open the access panel in the north wall, allowing a quick exit.

- Mine Box Ammunition
- Ammo
- Quest Item: Vault 3 Maintenance Key

Vault 3—Living Quarters

D Door to Vault 3—Recreation Area

11 12 (Upper) Restrooms

13 (Upper) Booby-Trapped Staircase

Step over the dead Fiend and watch for Frag Mines at the foot and top of the steps, along with a Tripwire and Grenade Bouquet.

- Frag Mine (2)
- Frag Grenades (3)

E Door to Vault 3—Recreation Area

15 (Upper) Executive Dorm [Average]

This chamber is accessed from the north corridor via a wall terminal [Average] or door [Average], and is the only way to reach the mezzanine area and Overseer's office. The door to the southwest leads to Location #17.

- Teddy Bear and Dino Toy (2)
- Skill Book: Chinese Army: Spec. Ops. Training Manual [Sneak] [2/4] [2/6]
- Magazine: Locksmith's Reader [Lockpick] [2/12] [35/56]
- Magazine: Today's Physician [Medicine] [10/19] [36/56]
- Magazine: Meeting People [Speech] [4/12] [37/56]

16 (Lower) Holding Cells Mezzanine

Fiends hold three prisoners here: a Ghoul named Dennis, a woman called Rachel, and the talkative leader Rick Lancer. Speak to Rick to begin Free Quest: I Love Bananas. Should you complete this task, you receive the Password to the Overseer's Office Terminal.

- Quest Item: Vault 3 Overseer Password

17 (Upper) Concourse

Access this area above the steps leading down to the Holding Cells Mezzanine through either the Executive Dorm [Average] or lower Holding Cells Door [Average] or wall terminal (which isn't locked once you have the Overseer Password, but is otherwise [Average]). Check the door to the east halfway along the concourse to reach the Upper Mezzanine. The door around the corner to the south accesses the Overseer's Office (Location #19).

- Carton of Cigarettes
- Binoculars
- Scrap Metal

18 (Upper) Holding Cells Mezzanine

Unless you access the locked door below [Average], the Holding Cells and this area can't be accessed unless you drop from this spot.

19 (Upper) Overseer's Office

There's a small amount of Food here, and a large Overseer's Terminal. Hack it [Hard] or use the Overseer Password for the following menu options:

> Happy Birthday!: Uncle George wishing young Janet a happy sweet 16th.

> Upcoming Election: A friend of George's hopes his candidacy for Overseer won't spoil a friendship.

> Thank You!: George Stault continues to be the Overseer.

> Weapon Lockers: Michelle thinks Michael may be planning a coup, and to keep the weapons in storage.

> Unlock Storage Room Doors: This unlocks the submerged storerooms (Locations #27 and #28).

- Hunting Rifle and Ammo
- Binoculars

20 (Lower) Western Dorms

These four rooms contain a few sleeping Fiends and beds, as well as Vault 3 Jumpsuits to grab from most dressers.

- Vault 3 Jumpsuit
- Sleeping Quarters

21 (Lower) Eastern Dorms

These four rooms, accessed via the same stairs or connecting corridor from the Western Dorms, have comatose Fiends and scattered Chems. A working terminal in the southeast dorm offers little help.

- Sleeping Quarters

22 (Upper and Lower) Connecting Restroom Corridor

23 (Upper) South Dorm #1

- Magazine: Locksmith's Reader [Lockpick] [3/12] [38/56]
- Ammo Box Ammunition
- Sleeping Quarters

24 (Upper) South Dorm #2

- Sunset Sarsaparilla Star Cap [15/100]
- Sleeping Quarters

25 (Upper) South Dorm #3

The terminal here offers the following messages:

> The Water Situation: Rationing occurs due to leaks, and a committee is formed to create ties to the outside.

> External Relations: Thanks from Lincoln (whose terminal this is likely to have been) to Michelle.

> Your Endorsement: Thanks from Lincoln to George Stault.

- Teddy Bear
- Sleeping Quarters

26 (Upper) Daniel's Dorm

A Fiend called Daniel resides here, near his terminal. The other working terminal gives little information. Pickpocket or kill Daniel for two important keys (to help with a Free Quest).

- Scrap Metal and Dino Toy
- Sleeping Quarters
- Quest Item: Fiend Prisoner Key
- Quest Item: Vault 3 Maintenance Key

27 28 (Underwater) Submerged Storeroom A [Hard] and B [Hard]

These are unlocked if you access the Overseer's Terminal. They are at the end of two separate corridors, and are not connected to each other. Be quick and don't run out of air, and watch for constant (but low-level) radiation poisoning from the water. Magazines are in the east storeroom (#27).

- Magazine: Milsurp Review [Guns] [5/11] [39/56]
- Magazine: Locksmith's Reader [Lockpick] [4/12] [40/56]
- Magazine: Locksmith's Reader [Lockpick] [5/12] [41/56]
- Magazine: Fixin' Things [Repair] [8/27] [42/56]
- Teddy Bear
- Gun Cabinet Items (2)

Vault 3—Maintenance Wing

G Door to Vault 3—Recreation Area

This area cannot be accessed from the Living Quarters.

29 Server Room

This provides access to the main corridor to the north. Vincent's terminal near a couple of server boxes displays the following messages:

> Water Leak: A water leak has proved more serious than first thought.

> Dinner?: An invite from "Vin" to "Jenny" for another dinner date.

> Re: Dinner?: Jenny agrees, and perhaps breakfast is in the cards, too!

> Thank You!: Salutations to William Mayson for his date help.

30 Locked Storage [Average]

Access this area via a wall terminal or door. Check the lockers for possible Utility Jumpsuits, which have some helpful benefits.

- Carton of Cigarettes
- Magazine: Locksmith's Reader [Lockpick] [6/12] [43/56]
- Vault 3 Utility Jumpsuit

31 Locked Storage [Average]

Access this area via a wall terminal or door, at the eastern end of the main corridor.

- Beer
- Magazine: Fixin' Things [Repair] [9/27] [44/56]

32 Server Room

33 Reactor: Motor-Runner's Sanctuary

Assuming you're not fighting, you can speak to the Fiends' leader: Motor-Runner. But first, check the two lockers to the left of the entrance. One of them holds a Reverse Pulse Cleaner, which is vital to salvage for Side Quest: Still in the Dark. Flanked by his two Guard Dogs, Motor-Runner stands to greet you, if you're not at war with the Fiends. You can:

Conclude any Chem business you have with him, as part of Side Quest: Aba Daba Honeymoon.

Sell him Chems independent of that Quest.

Ask what happened to the residents of the Vault. You can guess the answer.

Dispatch Motor-Runner to conclude Free Quest: Bounty Killer, II.

Or leave.

He carries a Chainsaw, which is a particularly gruesome Melee Weapon to steal.

- Quest Item: Reverse Pulse Cleaner
- Chainsaw

Free Quest: Bounty Killer, II

Up in the locked Server Room of the Recreation Area (Location #14) sits a wounded NCR Ranger named Bryce Anders. You may have heard the name before if you've talked with Colonel Hsu over at Camp McCarran, and (optionally) completed Bounty Killer, I. You can (optionally) ask Bryce about the vault and the Fiends. But to get the real information, ask what an NCR Ranger is doing here.

Lie and tell him you're an independent contractor, and he tells you he's here from Colonel Hsu over at Camp McCarran [2.19] to exterminate Motor-Runner.

Lie and tell him Hsu sent you to find him.

Or, if you completed Bounty Killer, I; you don't have to lie.

After this, two possible conversation options are helpful.

- Tell Anders that the colonel was concerned he missed a check-in. Ask what the hold-up is, and he points to his leg. You can:

Tell him it is infected. Anders asks if you can fix him up. You can:

Tell him he should leave for McCarran, and he opens the access panel and sprints for it. You can tackle Motor-Runner yourself.

Return with a Doctor's Bag (the nearest one is in Location #6 of this structure), and heal him.

Or leave him here.

Or, tell him you'll have to work together to defeat Motor-Runner.

- Tell Anders that Hsu thinks he needs additional support. Anders indignantly asks what kind of support. You can:

Tell him you want to rescue hostages. You're on your own for this one.

Or that you'll have to work together to defeat Motor-Runner.

Or that you can take care of Motor-Runner. Anders thinks it's a bad idea. You can:

State that you found Anders just fine. He agrees and gives you the key.

Or leave him to his wounds and head on alone.

- Quest Item: Vault 3 Maintenance Key

There are four conclusions after the conversation with Bryce Anders, as you progress with murderous intentions toward Motor-Runner:

- You and Bryce can battle through the Fiends to reach and defeat Motor-Runner.
- You can use the Maintenance Key to reach and defeat Motor-Runner.
- You can take the Maintenance Key from Anders by Pickpocket or murder, or from a Fiend named Daniel, as part of Free Quest: I Love Bananas.
- You can ignore Bryce, Hsu, and everyone, kill Motor-Runner, and then return to Hsu to tell him. Your Fame increases.

NCR Fame Gained!

Free Quest: I Love Bananas

Down in the Holding Cells part of Vault 3's Living Quarters, a group of kidnapped Caravaneers await torture or worse. Rick Lancer speaks for the trio, once a quartet before Carter died in the cell. Rick pleads for his freedom. You can:

Unlock the Cell Door [Hard] without speaking to any of them, and watch as they attempt an escape.

- Speak with Rick, getting more information on the vault and the Fiends, and Rick also mentions he's found a password for the Overseer's Office Terminal (Location #19). You can:

Agree to help him escape, in return for the password.

Intimidate Rick into giving you the password without a necessary rescue.

Assuming you wish to release the prisoners, Rick tells you a Fiend named Daniel has the necessary key. He's in his dorm room (Location #26). Pickpocket or kill Daniel for two important keys (the other is a Maintenance Key useful during Free Quest: Bounty Killer, II). Return and unlock the cage, freeing the prisoners.

- Quest Item: Fiend Prisoner Key
- Quest Item: Vault 3 Maintenance Key
- Quest Item: Vault 3 Overseer Password

[2.25] South Vegas Ruins East Entrance

- Threat Level: ●●●●●
- Faction: Fiend
  - Entity: Fiend
- Interior Exploration
- Radio Signal [Black Mountain: Zone 2E only]

Three entrances/exits provide access into this Fiend stronghold, ruled over by the steely gaze and Chem-addled attitude of Motor-Runner in Vault 3 [2.24]. Of the three entrances (including the one not shown as a Primary Location on your Pip-Boy's World Map), this is farthest into Fiend Territory, and adjacent to New Vegas Steel [2.26].

[2.26] New Vegas Steel

- Threat Level: ●●●●●
- Faction: Fiend/Robot
  - Entity: Crazed Mister Handy
  - Entity: Mr. Steel
- Dangers: Traps
- Collectibles:
  - Magazine [Explosives] [3/12] [45-48/56]
  - Magazine [Melee Weapons] [1/9] [45-48/56]
  - Magazine [Repair] [10/27] [45-48/56]
  - Magazine [Science] [8/23] [45-48/56]
  - Sunset Sarsaparilla Star Cap [16/100]
  - Guns and Ammo
- Interior Exploration

NEW VEGAS STEEL

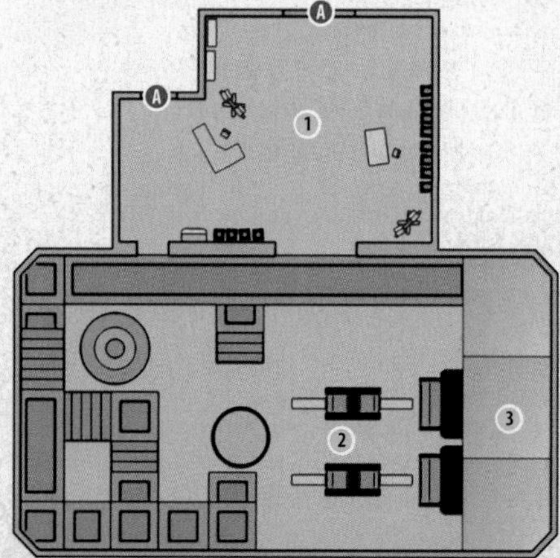

Caution Watch out! The molten steel is dangerous to touch, and you can fall into the vat bucket if you're particularly hapless!

Deep in Fiend Territory along the southwestern side of New Vegas, this steel plant still operates with its robot staff. Note the nearby access to South Vegas Ruins [Zone 2E].

Ⓐ Doors (2) to Mojave Wasteland (Fiend Territory)

1 Foreman's Office

Access the terminal and hit the "Lucky 38 Executive Override," which allows access into Mr. House's control chamber. Check the plastic bins next to the desk for magazines.

- Magazine [Patriot's Cookbook] [Explosives] [3/12] [45/56]
- Magazine [Tæles of Chivalrie] [Melee Weapons] [1/9] [46/56]
- Magazine [Fixin' Things] [Repair] [10/27] [47/56]
- Magazine [Programmer's Digest] [Science] [8/23] [48/56]
- Sunset Sarsaparilla Star Cap [16/100]

2 Smelting Chamber

This is full of hostile robots, and a gantry leads to a booth.

- Ammo Box Ammunition (2)

3 Smelting Booth

[2.27] West Pump Station

- Side Quest: Hard Luck Blues
- Threat Level: ●●●●●
- Faction: Fiend
  - Entity: None
- Interior Exploration

A matching pump station is to the east [2.21], but this one is on the outskirts of Fiend territory.

Ⓐ Door to Mojave Wasteland (Fiend Territory)

1 Office

There's a radio and various junk plus a little Food and other comestibles. Activate the Pump Station Terminal, and you can:

Leave it alone.

Repair the network connection. This nets you some XP, but isn't necessary to read the warning.

Activate the terminal to read the warning about radiation being detected in the filtration system, but not in this facility (it is actually in Vault 34 [3.12]). This begins Side Quest: Hard Luck Blues.

WEST PUMP STATION

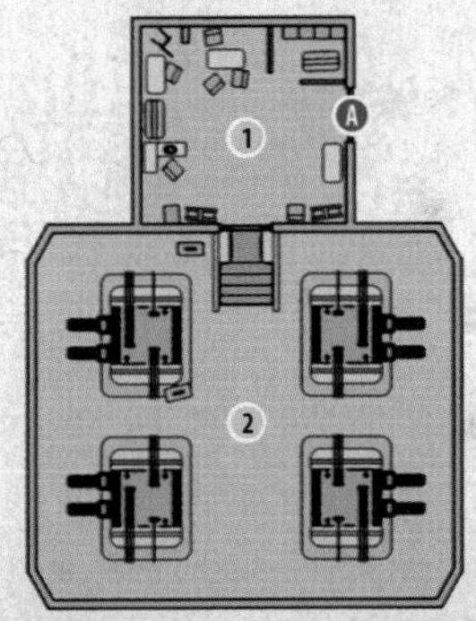

2 Pump Room

This is operational, but empty.

[2.28] Samson Rock Crushing Plant

- Threat Level: ●●●●●
- Faction: None
  - Entity: None
- Highly Visible
- Wasteland Vegetation

Composed of four sealed concrete buildings to the north and the main workings to the south, surrounded by the remains of a fence, this Quarry has been disintegrating for decades. Abandoned by prospectors due to the influx of Fiends, the area offers nothing but a few wild plants. Use the buildings as cover after retreating from Fiends, or the structure as a marker for the southwest corner of the New Vegas Conurbation.

[2.29] The Basincreek Building

- Threat Level: ●●●●●
- Faction: Mutated Animal
  - Entity: Giant Soldier Ant
  - Entity: Radroach
- Collectibles:
  - Magazine [Crit. Chance] [3/11] [49-50/56]
  - Magazine [Melee Weapons] [2/9] [49-50/56]
- Interior Exploration

One of the many office structures close to Camp McCarran [2.19], this one is just east of the Long 95, as it dips into its sunken section. There is only one entrance, by a burned-out car and garbage can. It borders Fiend territory, so be aware of these lunatics when exploring.

Ⓐ Door to Mojave Wasteland

1 Foyer

The ceiling has collapsed, exposing an upper (and inaccessible) office. There are drink machines to bang on, and a small corner table holds a well-hidden Magazine.

- Magazine: True Police Stories [Crit. Chance] [3/11] [49/56]

2 Main Corridor

Face the Giant Soldier Ant and two smaller foes, then inspect this corridor.

- Note: Help Me!

3 Locked Office

Someone locked himself in his office and couldn't find the key. His skeletal remains lie on the other side of the door.

- Magazine: Tæles of Chivalrie [Melee Weapons] [2/9] [50/56]

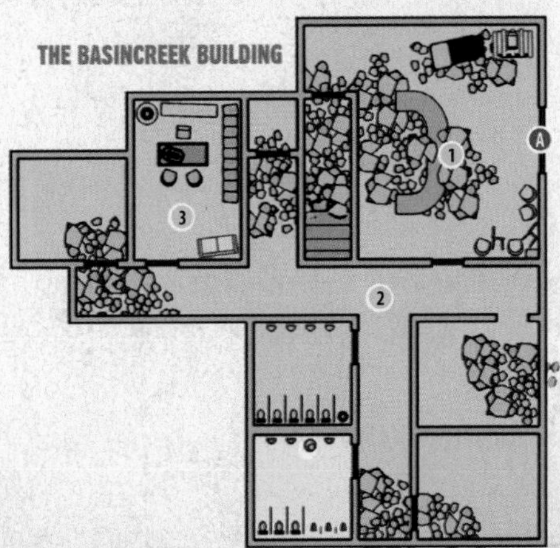

[2.30] Allied Technologies Offices

- Threat Level: ●●●●●
- Faction: Mutated Insect
  - Entity: Giant Ant
- Collectibles:
  - Skill Book [Barter] [2/4] [3/6]
  - Magazine [Crit. Chance] [4/11] [51-52/56]
  - Magazine [Melee Weapons] [3/9] [51-52/56]
  - Sunset Sarsaparilla Star Cap [17/100]
  - Sunset Sarsaparilla Star Cap [18/100]
- Health, Chems, or Water
- Interior Exploration

Ⓐ Door to Mojave Wasteland

1 Entrance Foyer

Face down the Giant Soldier Ant before inspecting the two doors you can open.

- Magazine: True Police Stories [Crit. Chance] [4/11] [51/56]

2 Offices

The door to the right (east) accesses a small office of cubicles, and a Giant Ant. Find Fixer and two Star Caps on the desks.

- Sunset Sarsaparilla Star Cap [17/100]
- Sunset Sarsaparilla Star Cap [18/100]

3 Office and Break Room

Open the broken door to an L-shaped corridor and another room with a couple of Giant Ants and broken terminals.

- Skill Book: Tales of a Junktown Vendor [Barter] [2/4] [3/6]
- Magazine: Tæles of Chivalrie [Melee Weapons] [3/9] [52/56]

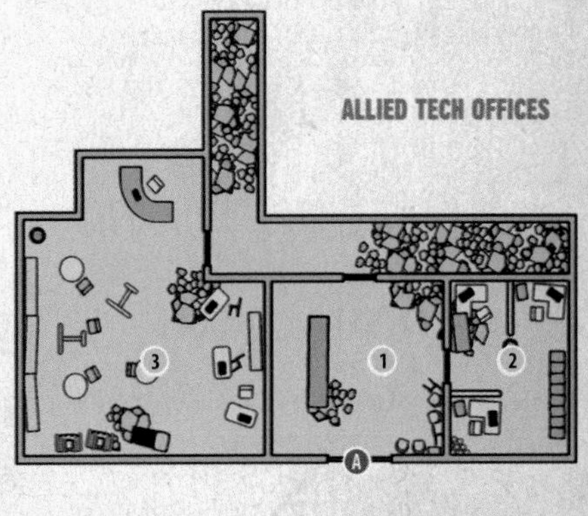

[2.31] Cassidy Caravans Wreckage

- Side Quest: Heartache by the Number
- Side Quest: You Can Depend on Me
- Threat Level:
- Faction: Crimson Caravan Company
  - Entity: None

This caravan, which belongs to Cassidy, a contractor with the Crimson Caravan Company [2.09], has been ransacked, and all its (useful) items stolen. There's slim pickings here besides the information you can provide to the Crimson Caravan's boss, Alice McCaffery, or Cass herself, who is down south at the Mojave Outpost [4.27].

[2.32] Grub n' Gulp Rest Stop

- Threat Level:
- Faction: Prospector
  - Entity: Fitz
  - Entity: Lupe
  - Entity: Brahmin
- Services:
  - Trader [7/33]
  - Trader [8/33]
- Crafting: Campfire [18/109]
- Collectibles:
  - Magazine [Barter] [3/16] [53/56]
  - Sunset Sarsaparilla Star Cap [19/100]
- Health, Chems, or Water
- Sleeping Quarters

This shanty rest stop lies at the end of the east-west road from here to the Samson Rock Crushing Plant [2.28], and Highway 95, which soon becomes elevated, inaccessible, and flanked with billboards for The Strip's many hotels and casinos. You can't enter the hut; all your trading must be done with Fitz and his partner Lupe.

- Campfire [18/109]
- Magazine: Salesman Weekly [Barter] [3/16] [53/56]
- Sunset Sarsaparilla Star Cap [19/100]
- Sleeping Quarters

You can ask Fitz about a place to buy weapons and armor (he recommends the Gun Runners [2.14] over by the Freeside gate), the location of a doctor (Doctor Usanagi is his choice, over at New Vegas Medical Clinic [2.10]). You can also Trade with him. Also speak to Lupe about the water she sells (it's taken via the NCR pipeline), and about the Fiends, New Vegas, and a number of other subjects. Then you can buy water from her (irradiated, or pure).

- Trader: Fitz [7/33]
- Trader: Lupe [8/33]

[2.33] Ant Mound

- Threat Level:
- Faction: Mutated Animal
  - Entity: Fire Ant Soldier
  - Entity: Giant Worker Ant
  - Entity: Giant Ant Queen
- Guns and Ammo
- Interior Exploration
- Radio Signal [Black Mountain]
- Wasteland Vegetation

A once-fertile plain between the outskirts of New Vegas and the rugged desert terrain is now devoid of crops. Beware of Fiends heading down from the McCarran airstrip to the north, close to the Allied Technologies Officers [2.30], but a bigger concern are the Giant Fire Ants scuttling out of their mound, inside an old barn.

- Ammo Box Ammunition
- Grenade Box Ammunition

A Ant Tunnel to Mojave Wasteland

1 Ant Mound Passage

Head left at this location, because the other corridors are dead-ends.

2 First Cavern

3 Queen's Chamber

A gigantic Queen Ant lurks at the bottom of the passage (if you're high enough level), in her chamber. Harvest the Queen Ant Pheromones from her body, then sort out the remaining Soldiers. Check a couple of Wastelander corpses here, too.

- Giant Ant Pheromones

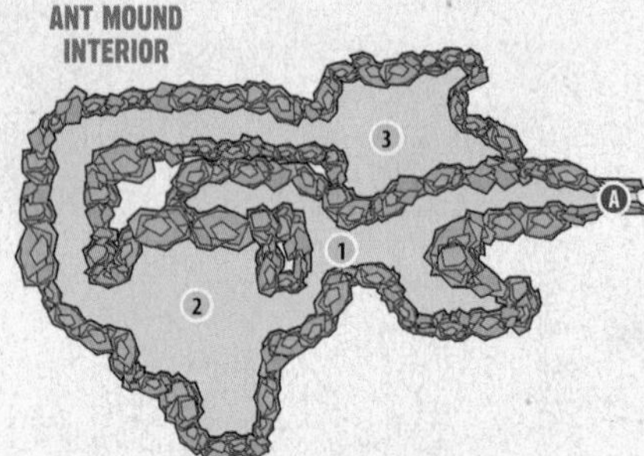

[2.34] Hunter's Farm

- Threat Level:
- Faction: Powder Ganger
  - Entity: Powder Ganger
  - Entity: Fire Gecko
- Collectibles:
  - Sunset Sarsaparilla Star Cap [20/100]
  - Sunset Sarsaparilla Star Cap [21/100]
- Interior Exploration
- Radio Signal [Black Mountain]
- Sleeping Quarters
- Wasteland Vegetation

Due to increased Fiend activity, Powder Ganger escapees, and a lack of irrigation, the old farmsteads are in a depressed state. The farmland behind hasn't mustered any crops, but you can harvest wild plants.

- Sunset Sarsaparilla Star Cap [20/100]
- Sunset Sarsaparilla Star Cap [21/100]
- Sleeping Quarters

[2.35] REPCONN Headquarters

See maps on the following page

- Side Quest: Come Fly With Me
- Side Quest: ED-E My Love
- Side Quest: Still in the Dark
- Free Quest: Access Powers
- Free Quest: Honorary Rocketeer
- Threat Level:
- Faction: Robot
  - Entity: Maintenance Robot
  - Entity: Tour Guide
  - Entity: Mobile Facial Recognition Scanner
  - Entity: Sentry Bot
- Collectibles:
  - Skill Book [Energy Weapons] [1/4] [4-6/6]
  - Skill Book [Energy Weapons] [2/4] [4-6/6]
  - Skill Book [Science] [2/4] [4-6/6]
  - Sunset Sarsaparilla Star Cap [22/100]
  - Sunset Sarsaparilla Star Cap [23/100]
  - Sunset Sarsaparilla Star Cap [24/100]
  - Sunset Sarsaparilla Star Cap [25/100]
  - Sunset Sarsaparilla Star Cap [26/100]
  - Unique Item [14/95]
  - Unique Item [15/95]
  - Unique Item [16/95]
  - Unique Item [17/95]
  - Unique Weapon [12/42]
- Area Is Locked
- Guns and Ammo
- Health, Chems, or Water
- Highly Visible
- Interior Exploration
- Radio Signal [Black Mountain]
- Quest Item

REPCONN Corporation was an up-and-coming regional aerospace firm, and keen contributor to Las Vegas political campaigns. They operated a test facility in the Black Mountains to the south (much to the chagrin of the local populations, who long complained of the "REPCONN bombs" landing in their fields and destroying property). The company was purchased by the giant RobCo Company just before the Great War, in a hostile takeover. New security countermeasures were installed, and more militaristic plans were undertaken, especially after the discovery of a special radioactive igniting agent that interested certain senior RobCo members. These counter-measures are still in effect, so investigate this building with caution.

Exterior: REPCONN Train Station

Close to the deserted playground is the railway station serving the REPCONN Headquarters. It is eerily quiet. Check the interior for the following items:

- Carton of Cigarettes (2) Doctor's Bag

Exterior: REPCONN Headquarters

The immediate perimeter is patrolled by a few mostly harmless Maintenance Robots. There is only one entrance.

Interior: REPCONN Office Main Floor

A Door to the Mojave Wasteland

1 Entrance Foyer

A trio of (dead) Fiends attempted to access the locked door to the north of this dirty, but intact foyer. They were stopped by REPCONN Maintenance Robots, and a larger (and more ferocious) Tour Guide. Speak to the Tour Guide (about the history of the company), to begin a room-to-room information trek, and Free Quest: Honorary Rocketeer. You can ignore the tour if you don't want to learn about the history of REPCONN, although the Tour Guide helps unlock the door to the Solar System Exhibit (Location #8). Begin your tour HERE, Rocketeer!

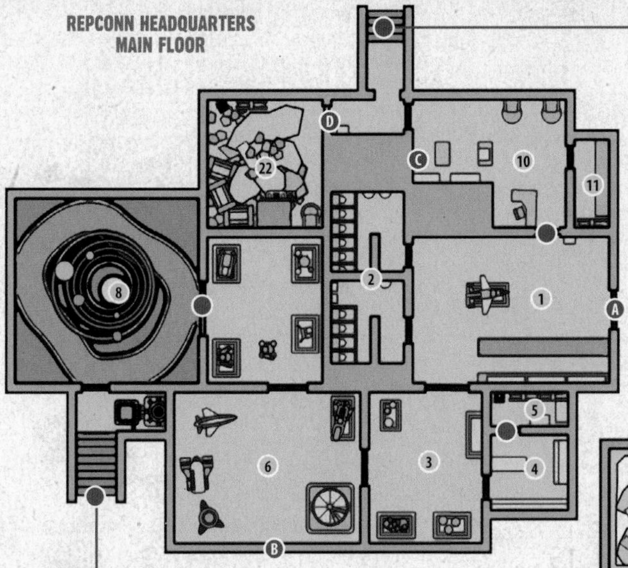

REPCONN HEADQUARTERS MAIN FLOOR

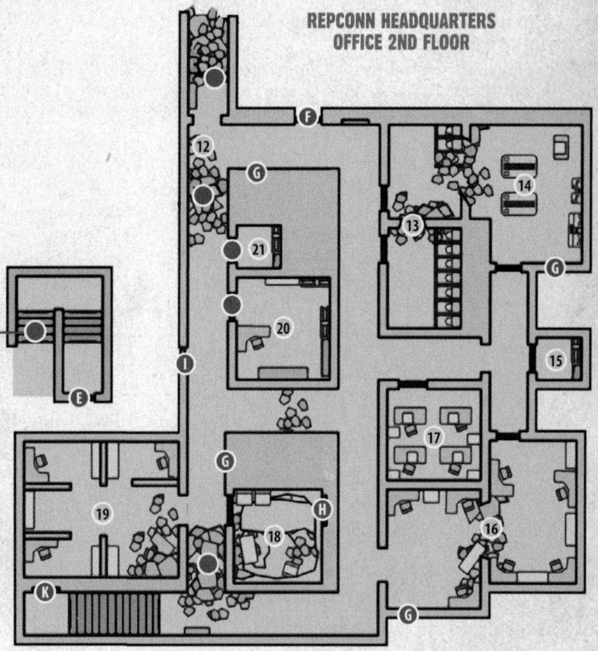

REPCONN HEADQUARTERS OFFICE 2ND FLOOR

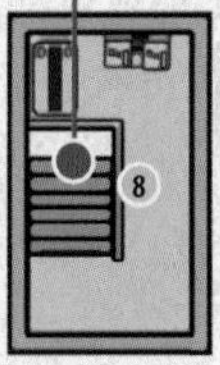

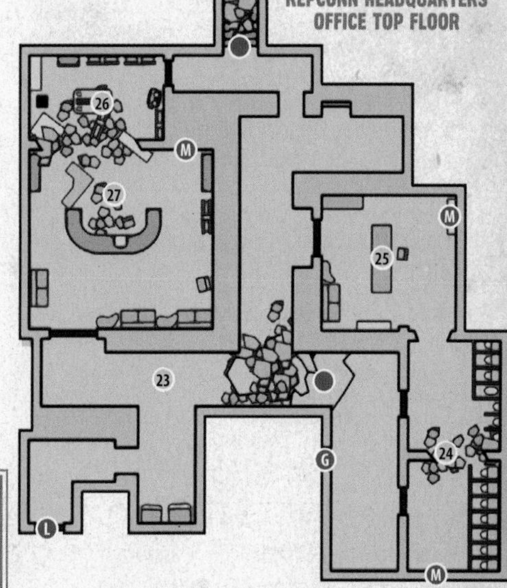

2 Restrooms

Aside from the irradiated water, these are empty.

3 Tour Chamber #1: Radiation—Myths and REPCONN's Reality

Inspect the plaque at each exhibit for further information. Optionally listen as the Tour Guide gives more asides.

> Exhibit A: "Boring Old Rod? Or...": A fuel rod that once powered REPCONN rockets was here, but it has disappeared.

> Exhibit B: "Radioactive Waste?": A group of barrels and a discussion about the "fiction" of radiation.

> Exhibit C: "Nuclear Family!" A representation of safety barrels, all nestled together!

> Exhibit D: "Plas-Ma What?": This is a new way to power rockets, without the worrying health risks!

4 Gift Shop

A Rocket Souvenir is worth scavenging; it is a possibly useful item during Side Quest: Come Fly With Me. Otherwise, check the counter for a Star Cap.

- Rocket Souvenir
- Sunset Sarsaparilla Star Cap [22/100]

5 Gift Shop Store Room [Hard]

Pry open the lock to access a tiny storage room with some big-ticket items:

- Rocket Souvenir (14)
- Sunset Sarsaparilla (2)
- Floor Safe Items [Average]
- Skill Book: Big Book of Science [Science] [2/4] [4/6]
- Unique Item: Nuka-Cola Quartz [14/95]
- Unique Item: Nuka-Cola Quartz [15/95]
- Unique Item: Nuka-Cola Victory [16/95]
- Unique Item: Nuka-Cola Victory [17/95]

6 Tour Chamber #2: Rockets—Prototype Success Stories

Pause to inspect the plaque at each exhibit for additional information. Before you leave, inspect the wall to the south.

> Exhibit E: "Rockets Away!": A prototype radiation-propulsion rocket, made in partnership with RobCo.

> Exhibit F: "Ready, Set, Launch!": A scale model of the Test Site Dome, where rockets shot up... and came down on nearby settlements.

> Exhibit G: "Green Bean": It got the name thanks to where it exploded; in the backyard of some friendly local.

> Exhibit H: "Big Fat Fiery Fred": Aside from the re-entry mishap, this rotund rocket's orbital flights were a success!

> Exhibit I: "Needlenose": This used fossil fuels and plasma to launch into space.

B Hidden Wall (Location #6)

This portion of wall is actually an automated door. You can:

Leave it alone, or

REPAIR 65 Jam the opening mechanism, so it can't open.

Caution Jamming hidden walls throughout this facility prevents activation of REPCONN robot reinforcements, should you stumble into an area deemed "restricted" without proper authorization. It's all part of Free Quest: Access Powers.

7 (Lower) Tour Chamber #3: RobCo—And Now a Word from Our Sponsor

REPCONN was "pleased" to have a chamber sponsored by the robotics corporation RobCo. Check out some of their lesser-known robots:

> Exhibit J: "Watch Your Step!" This Sentry Bot variant takes no prisoners. Beware because they're hidden in the walls of this building!

> Exhibit K: "The 'I' in 'Eyebot'": All the sights and sounds of your TV, blasted at you on the street!

> Exhibit L: "The 'Hand' in 'Handy'": The first of the friendly Mr. Handy models is shown.

> Exhibit M: "It's Got Wheels!": The Protect-O-Bot may have failed safety standards, but it's still one mean machine!

8 Tour Chamber #4: Riches Beyond the Stars [Average]

If the Tour Guide doesn't open the door for you, pry it open, and watch the tiny model rockets race about this still-functioning solar system model.

> Exhibit N: "Our Rich, Rich Solar System": (Not actual size) There's always more places to mine!

9 Exhibit Server Room

South of the solar system chamber are steps up to a control panel, upon which rests Jenny Millet's Security Keycard. This opens the locked door (with the wall terminal) in the foyer.

- Quest Item: Jenny Millet's Security Keycard

10 Robot Recharge and Security Office [Average]

Access this area using Bobby Pins and talent, or Jenny Millet's Security Keycard, and enter an L-shaped security room. Access the only working terminal [Average], and immediately choose the first menu option. With your face scanned, you can visit this part of the building without any problems from robot busy-bodies. Then check the desk behind for a Star Cap.

> Add user Facial Data to Database

> Inter-office Correspondence #345759: About the new security measures.

> Inter-office Correspondence #345776: From the new VP, Carl Rook.

- Sunset Sarsaparilla Star Cap [23/100]

Between this chamber at the next floor, you bump into the first Mobile Facial Recognition Scanner, who asks for identification. Depending upon your exploration (and wit), there are a variety of options. You can:

Confuse the robot with your double-talk, and it lets you past. This only occurs if you haven't secured Jenny Millet's Security Keycard or submitted your facial data.

If you have the keycard, but didn't submit your facial data, the scanner asks you to check in with security before continuing.

If you've already checked in with security (with or without the keycard), you're let through without any problems.

Or you can apologize and tell the scanner you're leaving. The scanner recognizes this as an "invalid response," and gives you 30 seconds to flee before "security" is summoned.

Or you can begin to destroy all the robots in the building in a gigantic firefight.

Caution: If the scanner summons security, the entire building goes into a panicked lockdown, and REPCONN Sentry Bots are summoned. Fight, or flee. Naturally, there's a more sedate way to explore this facility.

11 Security Office Storage [Average]

Well worth picking, the locked door opens into a narrow storage room with the following:

- Ammo Box Ammunition (2)
- Microfusion Cell (20 x 15)
- Plasma Pistol
- First Aid Box and Med-X
- Plasma Rifle

C Hidden Wall (Location #10)

This portion of wall is actually an automated door. You can:

Leave it alone, or

Jam the opening mechanism, so it can't open.

D Door to Shipping Room (Location #22) [Very Hard]

An incredibly difficult door and wall terminal prevent all but the most adept thief from entering the chamber beyond. You can access from here, or from an upper floor. You can also open this door if you have the Third Floor Security Card, found in Location #17.

E Door to REPCONN Office 2nd Floor

J (Upper) Door to REPCONN Office 2nd Floor

This is an alternate method of accessing the Shipping Room.

22 (Upper and Lower) Ruined Office and Shipping Room

The ceiling has fallen in on this shipping area, which can be accessed via the locked door or wall terminal in Location #10 or the second floor. The trek here is well worth it, once you grab the following:

- Scrap Metal (3)
- First Aid Box
- Microfusion Cell (20 x 11)
- Skill Book: Nikola Tesla and You [Energy Weapons [1/4] [5/6]
- Floor Safe Items
- Unique Weapon: Q-35 Matter Modulator [12/42]

REPCONN Office 2nd Floor

F Door to REPCONN Office Main Floor

12 Corridor

Rubble blocks the corridor and stairs to the west. Hide here until the scanner passes, so you can infiltrate this floor without raising the alarm (if your Intelligence is less than 7).

Between this chamber at the next floor, another Mobile Facial Recognition Scanner requests identification. Depending upon your exploration (and wit), there are a variety of options. You can:

Rapidly bark out a series of numbers that the scanner thinks is the correct ID. This only occurs if you haven't submitted your facial data on this floor yet.

If you've already submitted your facial data (in Location #14), you're let through as "Ms. Wang" without any problems.

Or you can apologize and get 30 seconds to flee before "security" is summoned.

Or you can test out your new plasma weapons on these bags of bolts. Engage!

G Hidden Wall (Locations #12, 14, 16, Corridor near 18)

This portion of wall is actually an automated door. You can:

Leave it alone, or

Jam the opening mechanism, so it can't open.

13 Restroom (Open Plan)

Walls have fallen, leaving massive gaps between the two restrooms and the Northeast Server Control. Cut through there to quickly attempt your second facial data submission in Location #14.

- First Aid Box

14 Northeast Server Control

The quickest way to enter this room is via the holes in the walls from the restrooms (#13). Quickly locate the terminal [Very Easy], and access the following, which prevents the alarm from being raised if you haven't met a scanner yet. Check the Skill Book next to the terminal.

> Add user Facial Data to Database

> Inter-office Correspondence #3457785: Someone is sending confidential data; possibly to the Poseidon Corp.!

> Inter-office Correspondence #3458631: Sara Wang reckons this could be insider information!

> Inter-office Correspondence #3458642: Carl Rook thanks her for her diligence, and company privacy.

> Inter-office Correspondence #3458648: The old VP data needs clearing off this terminal.

- Skill Book: Nikola Tesla and You [2/4] [6/6]

15 Storage Room

16 Southeast Offices

The dividing wall between these offices has fallen.

17 East Office

Hack the terminal [Hard] in the far corner to obtain an Executive Security Badge, allowing access to any door leading to the top floor, or back to the main floor! This means you can enter the Door to REPCONN Office Main Floor (#H; which accesses the Shipping Room). There's also a Star Cap by the bottle on the desk.

> Print Executive Security Badge

> Inter-office Correspondence #3262725: Leonard Steeple has resigned. Julia Hasters is overseeing his departments.

- Quest Item: REPCONN Second Floor Security Card
- Quest Item: REPCONN Third Floor Security Card
- Sunset Sarsaparilla Star Cap [24/100]

18 (Lower and Upper) South Kitchen

The ceiling has collapsed, but you can clamber up the rubble to the third floor kitchen, and a door [Easy] to the top floor.

H Door to REPCONN Office Top Floor [Easy]

Unlock with Bobby Pins or the Third Floor Security Card.

19 Southwest Offices

20 Hacker's Office [Average]

This can only be unlocked using Bobby Pins and talent. Inside is a terminal [Easy] with some rather interesting messages:

> Encrypted Message: About intercepting the "Q-35."

> Q-35 Release Notes: Information on the Quantum Plasma Modulation Matter Injection Rifle.

> Inter-office Correspondence #3262173: Regarding a hostile takeover of REPCONN by RobCo.

> Inter-office Correspondence #3262178: A reply from Julia Masters (CFO) about halting the takeover.

> Inter-office Correspondence #3262719: A no-confidence measure on Leo.

21 Ammo and Medical Storage [Average]

This can only be unlocked using Bobby Pins and talent. Grab the following from inside:

- Tool Cabinet Items
- First Aid Box and Stimpak
- Doctor's Bag
- Ammo Box Ammunition (2)

I Door to REPCONN Office Main Floor [Hard]

Unlock this with sheer talent or the Third Floor Security Card. It leads back to the main floor, Location #22.

K Door to REPCONN Office Top Floor

REPCONN Office Top Floor

L Door to REPCONN Office 2nd Floor

23 Executive Level Corridor

Head out of the L-shaped smaller corridor into a larger one, with two Vending Machines to check, and a scanner waiting in front of the doors to the CEO's office to the left. Greet the scanner, or Sneak past the two dead Brotherhood of Steel Paladins, and into the next corridor (Location #24).

On this floor, two Mobile Facial Recognition Scanners may stop to tell you that this area is for Executives only. You can:

Answer with a password that happens to be correct. You're free to wander about the floor.

Or you can blurt out "ice cream," which shockingly, happens to be correct!

Or you can apologize and get 30 seconds to flee before "security" is summoned.

Or you can test out your new plasma weapons on these bags of bolts. Engage!

Tip: A better way would be to enter via the other entrance (Location #N) from the kitchens, and sneak up through the restrooms to the two Executive Offices.

Two Brotherhood of Steel Paladins lie on the ground, one partially covered in fallen masonry. Searching them allows you to grab their armor, items, and a Holotape that's vital for Side Quest: Still in the Dark and ED-E My Love. Take this whether these Quests are active or not.

- Brotherhood T-51b Power Armor (2)
- Laser Rifle and Ammo (2)
- Quest Item: Brotherhood of Steel Mission Holotape

M Hidden Wall (Locations #24, 25, 27)

This portion of wall is actually an automated door. You can:

Leave it alone, or

Jam the opening mechanism, so it can't open.

N Door to REPCONN Office 2nd Floor

24 Restrooms

These are more-easily accessible via the second entrance to this floor. The interior walls are destroyed, providing access into Executive Office #1.

25 Executive Office #1: Leonard Steeple's Office

Be warned; a scanner is likely to enter soon after you! Check the desk for a Star Cap, and a terminal [Very Hard] for the following menu options:

> Inter-office Correspondence #3262091: From Piers, regarding a possible RobCo buy-out.

> Inter-office Correspondence #3262099: An irate Steeple wishing to send back "the package."

> Inter-office Correspondence #3262105: This is a sweet deal, about to turn very sour for REPCONN.

> Inter-office Correspondence #3458503: From Carl Rook to Xuan Duang about completing the Q-35.

> Disable Robots: This shuts down all the robots in the entire facility, enabling you to come and go as you please.

- Sunset Sarsaparilla Star Cap [25/100]

26 Executive Level: Server Room

Open a floor safe [Easy].

- Floor Safe Items

27 Executive Office #2: Piers Isley's Office

Check the bottles on the ground by the bookcases for a Star Cap. Hack the terminal [Easy] for the following menu options:

> Unlock Safe: Unlocks the Server Room Safe

> RE: RobCo: Carl sends Piers a message about dramatically increasing security in the building.

> Inter-office Correspondence #3457477: To the launch facility Project Manager about the increase in security.

- Sunset Sarsaparilla Star Cap [26/100]

Free Quest: Access Powers

If you've managed to infiltrate this building, find all three keycards, take the Q-35, read all the terminal entries, and deactivate the robots without firing a shot or being challenged without the correct security clearance, then consider yourself an impressive adventurer. And one with an impressively massive Plasma Rifle.

Free Quest: Honorary Rocketeer

Take the full tour, from the foyer to the solar system, with the Tour Guide at your side, and read every plaque. Then grab all 15 Souvenir Rockets in the gift shop and storeroom, and you can consider yourself an official Rocketeer! Well done!

ZONE 2: SECONDARY LOCATIONS

[2.S01] Ruined Buildings

- Threat Level: ●●●●●
- Health, Chems, or Water

The half-block of buildings to the west of the H&H Tools Factory [2.06] has taken damage in recent years, and most of the structures are nothing but rubble.

- First Aid Box

[2.S02] Ruined Store

- Threat Level: ●●●●●

In this devastated city block are the remains of a shop without a roof (making it a good place to retreat to if you're attacked).

- Cash Register Items

[2.S03] Ruined Store

- Threat Level: ●●●●●

Close to one of the Manhole Covers and Sewer Entrances (to U2.N: North Sewers) are the remains of a store, with good sniping opportunities from the upper floor.

[2.S04] Ruined Building with Locked Cache

- Threat Level: ●●●●●
- Dangers:
  - Traps
  - Mines
- Collectibles:
  - Magazine [Crit. Chance] [5/11] [54-56/56]
  - Magazine [Explosives] [4/12] [54-56/56]
  - Magazine [Lockpick] [7/12] [54-56/56]
- Area Is Locked
- Guns and Ammo
- Health, Chems, or Water
- Interior Exploration

A block to the east of the Mole Rat murders [2.11] are a group of crumbling brick structures. Check the northeast corner store, watching for Frag Mines (and a Magazine inside the front door). Or, you can use the back door (watch for the Tripwire and Grenade Bouquet); either allows access to a locked Metal Door [Hard]. Pry that open to reach a hidden cache of items including more Magazines.

- Frag Mine (2)
- Frag Grenade (3)
- 9 Iron
- Magazine: [True Police Stories] [Crit. Chance] [5/11] [54/56]
- Magazine: [Patriot's Cookbook] [Explosives] [4/12] [55/56]
- Magazine: [Locksmith's Reader] [Lockpick] [7/12] [56/56]
- Scrap Metal
- Sniper Rifle and Ammo
- First Aid Box
- Doctor's Bag
- RadAway and Purified Water (2)

[2.S05] Hostetler and Isaac Homes

- Side Quest: Someone to Watch Over Me
- Threat Level: ●●●●●
- Faction: Wastelander
  - Entity: Mrs. Hostetler
  - Entity: Alice Hostetler
- Collectibles: Sunset Sarsaparilla Star Cap [27/100]
- Guns and Ammo
- Health, Chems, or Water
- Interior Exploration
- Main Trading Route
- Sleeping Quarters
- Quest Item

Check the three mailboxes for a random Magazine. Inside the Hostetler house, you'll find Mrs. Hostetler, who asks you (in no uncertain terms) to vacate the premises. She has additional opinions if Side Quest: Someone to Watch Over Me is active, and her daughter Alice may also be here. Check her abode for items to steal including Food in the fridge and on the dining room table. Don't forget the Star Cap between the sofas on the small table! Isaac is almost always at the Gun Runners, so his house is pretty bare; find scraps of Food in the fridge and a bed, but little else.

- Carton of Cigarettes
- Sunset Sarsaparilla Star Cap [27/100]
- Knife
- Sleeping Quarters

[2.S06] Orion Moreno's House

- Side Quest: For Auld Lang Syne
- Threat Level: ●●●●●
- Faction: Enclave
  - Entity: Orion Moreno
- Collectibles: Unique Item [18/95]
- Interior Exploration

- Sleeping Quarters

An old man named Orion Moreno lives in a ranch house here. This and an adjacent house may have Magazines in their mailboxes. Except for a fully stocked fridge, Moreno's house lacks items. Speak to him though, and you can learn about his deep-seated hatred of the NCR. He is a key player in Side Quest: For Auld Lang Syne, so don't kill him unless you're aware of the consequences!

- Unique Item: Explorer's Gear [18/95]

[2.S07] Destroyed Freeway Bridge

- Threat Level: ●●●●●
- Wasteland Vegetation

Across from the entrance to the East Central Sewers are the remains of a freeway bridge, now fallen into the dry riverbed below. This is the extreme eastern border of Zone 2.

[2.S08] NCR Patrol

- Threat Level: ●●●●●
- Faction: NCR
  - Entity: NCR Trooper

Two NCR Troopers are here, and a trio patrols the area around the Aerotech Office Park [2.22]. Ask them about how their tours are going.

[2.S09] Elevated Freeway and Billboards

- Threat Level: ●●●●●

Just north of the Grub n' Gulp Rest Stop [2.32] are a number of casino billboards, and the raised freeway section of Highway 95. This elevated platform, which you cannot stand on, stretches up and around to Freeside's East Gate [2.15].

[2.S10] Apartment Allotment

- Threat Level: ●●●●●
- Faction: Westside/Fiend
    - Entity: Westside Resident
    - Entity: Fiend
- Wasteland Vegetation

Just south of The Thorn [2.04] is a blue apartment with a large garden allotment of unripe plants. Expect Fiend encroachment from the south.

[2.S11] Westside Playground

- Threat Level: ●●●●●

This urban area can be confusing, so look for this flat ground with a rusting play area near The Thorn [2.04] to help situate yourself.

[2.S12] Summer Springs Boarding House

- Threat Level: ●●●●●

This apartment building is sealed up tight but has its name emblazoned on the side. It's close to the Monte Carlo Suites [2.12] and also to Scorpions Gang Territory.

[2.S13] Tiki Tonga Burned-Out Ranch Homes

- Threat Level: ●●●●●
- Faction: Fiend

An area of decimation at the northern edge of Fiend Territory, this location takes its name from the apartments just north. One of the mailboxes may contain a Magazine.

[2.S14] Sarsaparilla Burned-Out Ranch Homes

- Threat Level: ●●●●●
- Faction: Fiend

Just one block north of Sunset Sarsaparilla Headquarters [2.17] is a block of burned-out homes and a play area. Check the mailboxes for Magazines.

[2.S15] Elevated Long 15

- Threat Level: ●●●●●

This is where the Long 15, which you can follow all the way from the Mojave Outpost [4.27], becomes elevated and inaccessible. Use it as a landmark from this point; it cuts through Zone 2C (Freeside) and across toward Boomer Territory.

[2.S16] Long 15 Mines

- Threat Level: ●●●●●
- Dangers: Mines
- Guns and Ammo

The NCR have placed Frag Mines across this section of road to prevent Fiend access from the west.

- Frag Mine (5)

[2.S17] New Vegas Sign

- Threat Level: ●●●●●
- Highly Visible

This has been a Vegas landmark since before anyone can remember. It is occasionally used by NCR Rangers to snipe at Fiends to the south, but you can't climb on it. Use it as a landmark when you're nearing Camp McCarran [2.19]

[2.S18] Cook-Cook's Territory

- Side Quest: Three-Card Bounty
- Threat Level: ●●●●●
- Faction: Fiend
    - Entity: Cook-Cook
    - Entity: Fiend
    - Entity: Queenie
    - Entity: Fiend Brahmin
- Crafting: Campfire [19/109]
- Dangers: Mines
- Collectibles: Unique Item [19/95]
- Guns and Ammo
- Health, Chems, or Water
- Quest Item

A terrible Fiend named Cook-Cook, who rapes those NCR soldiers that he captures, is holed up in these ruins to the north of South Vegas Ruins West Gate [2.23]. He's surrounded by sycophants and his pet Brahmin Queenie (which you can hurt to drive him into a rage). Keep Cook-Cook's head intact if you're doing Side Quest: Three-Card Bounty. Beware of a concealed Mine, and don't leave without stealing a Recipe from the steel shelves.

- Campfire [19/109]
- Unique Item [Recipe]: Cook-Cook's Fiend Stew [19/95]
- Food
- Frag Mine
- Quest Item: Cook-Cook's Head

[2.S19] NCR Sandbag Defenses

- Threat Level: ●●●●●
- Faction: Fiend
- Guns and Ammo

The NCR face periodic entanglements with the Fiends in this area, and have recently pulled back from these defenses.

- Mine Box Ammunition [Easy]

[2.S20] Long 15 Pedestrian Steps

- Threat Level: ●●●●●
- Dangers: Mines
- Guns and Ammo

This allows access to the Fiend Territory east and west if you find yourself wandering down the Long 15. Watch for the Frag Mine and extinguisher trap on the western steps adjacent to New Vegas Steel [2.26].

- Frag Mine (2)

[2.S21] Long 15 Overturned Train Carriage

- Threat Level: ●●●●●
- Faction: Fiend

Require a quick escape up into Fiend Territory from the sunken section of the Long 15? Then climb up the dangling train carriage here, and sit on the roofs to snipe.

[2.S22] Driver Nephi's Territory

- Side Quest: Three-Card Bounty
- Threat Level: ●●●●●
- Faction: Fiend
    - Entity: Driver Nephi
    - Entity: Fiend
- Collectibles: Unique Weapon [13/42]
- Guns and Ammo
- Health, Chems, or Water
- Sleeping Quarters
- Quest Item

Famous for his vicious golf club swing, Driver Nephi rules the Fiend Territory to the south of Zone 2E, and has a base within a ruined building close to the Samson Rock Crushing Plant [2.28]. This is quite open, so use the building rubble as cover, prepare for combat with close to a dozen Fiends, and take care not to mangle Driver Nephi's head if you're engaged in Side Quest:

Three-Card Bounty. Nephi's base is a weird collection of Vegas signs and platforms.

- Unique Weapon: Nephi's Golf Driver [13/42]
- Quest Item: Driver Nephi's Head
- Super Stimpak and Ammo
- Grenade Box Ammunition [Average]
- Sleeping Quarters

[2.S23] Long 15 Mines 2

- Threat Level: ●●●●●
- Dangers: Mines
- Guns and Ammo

The NCR have placed Frag Mines across this section of road to prevent Fiend access from the Driver Nephi's Territory.

- Frag Mine (8)

[2.S24] Abandoned Warehouse

- Side Quest: Birds of a Feather
- Threat Level: ●●●●●
- Faction: Fiend
- Interior Exploration
- Main Trading Route

Just east of the Allied Technologies Offices [2.30] is a large Abandoned Warehouse teeming with Fiends. Inside is an expansive, single-chamber warehouse with Garage Doors and a Metal Door to enter and exit. Take your time rummaging to find the following:

- Sunset Sarsaparilla Crate (27)
- Fridge Food and Wine (11)
- Scrap Metal (2)

[2.S25] NCR Checkpoint and Burned Buildings

- Free Quest: A Final Plan for Esteban
- Threat Level: ●●●●●
- Faction: NCR
  - Entity: NCR Trooper

On the ring road north of REPCONN Headquarters [2.35] is an NCR Checkpoint, but this is only visible during Free Quest: A Final Plan for Esteban, one of the Camp McCarran [2.19] Free Quests. This is where Ranger Morales' body must be taken. Otherwise, there are four ruined buildings to the north here, with scattered minor items to salvage.

[2.S26] Abandoned Buildings and Ranger Morales' Corpse

- Free Quest: A Final Plan for Esteban
- Threat Level: ●●●●●
- Faction: Fiend
  - Entity: Fiend
  - Entity: Ranger Jackson (Deceased)
  - Entity: Ranger Morales (Deceased)
- Dangers:
  - Traps
  - Mines

This becomes a new Primary Location on your Pip-Boy during Free Quest: A Final Plan for Esteban. Otherwise deserted, this place has four Fiends patrolling the roofs and forecourt of this place, which is also booby-trapped with Mines and a Rigged Shotgun. The bodies of Ranger Jackson and Morales lie here, but only if the Free Quest is active.

ZONE 2: UNDERGROUND ACCESS ENTRANCES/EXITS

The following Manhole Covers offer access into the New Vegas Underground Sewer System; Zone U2. Consult that part of the Tour for interior information.

[2.SU01] Manhole to North Sewers

- Threat Level: ●●●●●
- Interior Exploration
- Underground Connection

On the Zone 2 perimeter road, close to the entrance to Zone 2B: North Vegas Square [2.07].

[2.SU02] Manhole to North Sewers

- Threat Level: ●●●●●
- Interior Exploration
- Underground Connection

Just northeast of the entrance to Freeside's North Gate, on the road.

[2.SU03] Manhole to North Sewers

- Threat Level: ●●●●●
- Interior Exploration
- Underground Connection

On the north-south road by the east entrance to Crimson Caravan Company [2.09], close to New Vegas Medical Clinic [2.10].

[2.SU04] Manhole to East Central Sewers

- Threat Level: ●●●●●
- Interior Exploration
- Underground Connection

On the east-west road east of Freeside's East Gate [2.15], near the ruined building and parking lot.

[2.SU05] Manhole to East Central Sewers

- Threat Level: ●●●●●
- Interior Exploration
- Underground Connection

At the junction with the flaming barrels and Mesquite Honey tree, just east of Orion Moreno's House [2.S06].

[2.SU06] Manhole to East Central Sewers

- Threat Level: ●●●●●
- Interior Exploration
- Underground Connection

On a sewer pipe near the lower, dry bed just east of East Pump Station [2.21], adjacent to a blocked pipe.

[2.SU07] Manhole to East Central Sewers

- Threat Level: ●●●●●
- Interior Exploration
- Underground Connection

On the road just in front of the Aerotech Office Park [2.22].

[2.SU08] Manhole to Central Sewers

- Threat Level: ●●●●●
- Interior Exploration
- Underground Connection

Right in front of the entrance to Camp McCarran [2.19].

ZONE 2: NEW VEGAS CONURBATION [INTERIOR ZONES]

Topographical Overview

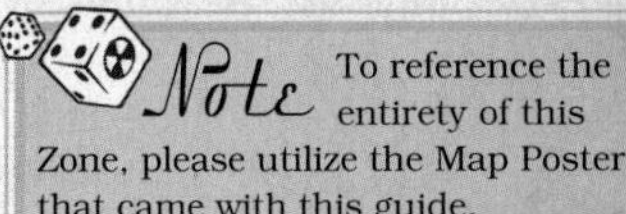

Note: To reference the entirety of this Zone, please utilize the Map Poster that came with this guide.

The Great New Vegas skyline is dominated by the Lucky 38 Tower, and other monuments to excess, but visiting such ostentatious structures requires more than just knocking on a door. There are five "Interior zones" within the New Vegas Conurbation, and all offer a glimpse into the way of life for the inhabitants. Zone 2A (Westside) consists of a cooperative of crop-growers and militia, all vying for water from the NCR. Zone 2B (North New Vegas) is a squatter camp with few amenities. Zone 2C (Outer and Inner Freeside) is a sprawling series of large roads, structures, and casinos that don't quite have the razzmatazz of those on The Strip. The Kings, Followers of the Apocalypse, Garrets, and Van Graffs, along with Mick & Ralph inhabit Freeside. The Strip itself is a neon-clad architectural triumph, but heavily fortified and guarded by Securitrons in the service of Mr. House, who rules the three Families (the Omertas at the Gomorrah, the Chairmen at The Tops, and the White Glove Society at the Ultra-Luxe) with an iron fist. The NCR also has an embassy here, and a brother and sister live and work for Mr. House, building more neon signs and showing rich folk around Vault 21. Finally, Zone 2E is Fiend Territory, and the only part of New Vegas where you're actively hunted by hostile forces.

Highways and Byways

Access to the interior zones is almost exclusively via gates, which are guarded by gang members or militia of the Faction you're about to meet inside. Inside each zone, there are main streets and alleys; especially in Freeside you should learn the layout so you can gauge (for example) which gate is nearest your destination. For example, always take the Freeside North Gate if you're heading to the Old Mormon Fort, and the Freeside East Gate if you want to visit Mick & Ralph's. There are Sewer entrances to Zones 2A and 2B (not the others). To reach Zone 2D (The Strip), you must enter Zone 2C (Freeside) first.

Available Services, Crafting and Collectibles

Services: Caravan Players: [4/15]
Services: Gambling: [11/15]
Services: Healers/Dealers: [12/31]
Services: Repairers: [1/9]
Services: Traders: [7/33]
Crafting: Campfires: [8/109]
Crafting: Reloading Benches: [2/36]
Crafting: Workbenches: [11/41]
Crafting: Weapon Upgrades: [1/10]
Collectibles: Snow Globes: [3/7]
Collectibles: Caravan Cards: [5/30]
Collectibles: Hollowed-Out Rocks: [0/42]
Collectibles: Skill Books: [4/51]
Collectibles: Skill Magazines: [37/213]
Collectibles: Star Bottle Caps: [2/100]
Collectibles: Unique Items: [22/95]
Collectibles: Unique Weapons: [5/42]

Primary and Secondary Locations

Zone 2A: Westside

[2.01] Westside West Entrance
[2.02] Miguel's Pawn Shop
[2.03] Westside South Entrance
[2A.01] Casa Madrid Apartments
[2A.02] Westside Co-op
[2A.03] Klamath Bob's Liquor Store
[2A.04] North Cistern
[2A.S01] The Chessboard
[2A.S02] Manhole to North Sewers
[2A.S03] Marco
[2A.S04] Mean Sonofabitch
[2A.S05] Building Alcove
[2A.S06] Westside Allotment (West)
[2A.S07] Makeshift Bedding
[2A.S08] Makeshift Bedding
[2A.S09] Westside Allotment (East)
[2A.S10] Hector and the Water Brahmin

Zone 2B: North Vegas Square

[2.07] North Vegas Square
[2B.01] The Gray
[2B.S01] Cranden
[2B.S02] Manhole to North Sewers
[2B.S03] Owned Bedding
[2B.S04] Jules
[2B.S05] Squatter Bill
[2B.S06] Playground

Zone 2C: Freeside

[2.08] Freeside's North Gate
[2.13] The Strip North Gate
[2.15] Freeside's East Gate
[2C.01] Old Mormon Fort
[2C.02] Mick & Ralph's
[2C.03] Ruined Store
[2C.04] Cerulean Robotics
[2C.05] King's School of Impersonation
[2C.06] Atomic Wrangler
[2C.07] Silver Rush
[2C.S01] Bodyguards-For-Hire
[2C.S02] Genaro's Fodder
[2C.S03] Dead Man's Dumpster
[2C.S04] Genaro's Little Helpers
[2C.S05] Squatter Camp #1
[2C.S06] Mick and Ralph's Crier
[2C.S08] Tapper and the Water Supply
[2C.S09] Train Station
[2C.S10] Signal Box Tower
[2C.S11] The Granny Gang
[2C.S12] Max and Stacey
[2C.S13] Vagrants and Thugs
[2C.S14] Dixon the Dealer
[2C.S15] Rotface
[2C.S16] Bodyguards-For-Hire
[2C.S17] Jacob Hoff
[2C.S18] Dead Man
[2C.S19] An Unsubtle Mugging
[2C.S20] Squatter Camp #2
[2C.S22] Atomic Wrangler Crier
[2C.S23] Silver Rush Crier
[2C.S24] Bill Ronte
[2C.S25] Ruined Building
[2C.S26] Dead Thugs
[2C.S27] Squatter Camp #3 and Old Ben
[2C.S28] Squatter Camp #4

Zone 2D: New Vegas Strip

[2.13] The Strip North Gate
[2D.01] Gomorrah
[2D.02] Lucky 38 Casino
[2D.03] Vegas Boulevard Station
[2D.04] The Tops Casino
[2D.05] Ultra-Luxe Casino
[2D.06] Vault 21
[2D.07] NCR Embassy
[2D.08] Michael Angelo's Workshop
[2D.S01] Mister Holdout
[2D.S02] Victor at the Lucky 38
[2D.S03] Emily Ortal
[2D.S04] Billy Knight
[2D.S05] Street Vendor
[2D.S06] Vulpes Inculta or Alerio
[2D.S07] Walter and Ethel Phebus
[2D.S08] The Tops Promoter
[2D.S09] NCR Embassy Gates

Zone 2E: South Vegas Ruins

[2.23] South Vegas Ruins West Entrance
[2.24] Vault 3
[2.25] South Vegas Ruins East Entrance
[2E.01] Zapp's Neon Signs
[2E.S01] Sentry Post Mattress
[2E.S02] Neon Sign Graveyard
[2E.S03] Lean-To Shack
[2E.S04] Ruined Concrete Outbuilding
[2E.S05] Southwest Exit to and from Fiend Territory

Zone U2: New Vegas Sewers

[U2.N] North Sewers
[U2.EC] East Central Sewers
[U2.C] Central Sewers
[U2.?] Sealed Sewers

ZONE 2A: WESTSIDE

[2A.01] Casa Madrid Apartments

- Side Quest: The Coyotes
- Side Quest: The White Wash
- Free Quest: A Bit of Slap and Tickle
- Threat Level: ●●●●●
- Faction: Westside Militia/Followers of the Apocalypse
  - Entity: Pretty Sarah
  - Entity: Dermot
  - Entity: Saint James
  - Entity: Tom Anderson
  - Entity: Maude
  - Entity: Jimmy
  - Entity: Sweetie
- Collectibles:
  - Magazine [Barter] [4/16] [1-3/37]
  - Magazine [Lockpick] [8/12] [1-3/37]
  - Magazine [Speech] [1-3/37]
- Area Is Locked
- Guns and Ammo
- Health, Chems, or Water
- Interior Exploration
- Sleeping Quarters
- Quest Item

The sounds of ecstasy (or more likely, agony) emanate through the walls of this low-rent knocking shop. Step through the dilapidated front doors, and prepare for some offers you can definitely refuse.

Ground Floor

A Doors to Westside

1 Pretty Sarah's Lobby

The table just inside the door has a couple of Magazines, but these belong to the scarred woman by the stairwell, who turns hostile if you snag them and she's watching. Pretty Sarah is a pimp; you can speak to her about her "merchandise."

- Magazine: Salesman Weekly [Barter] [4/16] [1/37]
- Magazine: Locksmith Reader [Lockpick] [8/12] [2/37]

2 Marco's Apartment [Average]

Marco may be sleeping, or out on his rounds. Speak with Marco and you can ask more each inhabitant here, once you've met them, including the horrific battering Pretty Sarah took from a Fiend named Cook-Cook.

- Ammo Box Ammunition

3 Dermot's Apartment

When he's not mooching around the streets near Westside Co-op [2A.02], Dermot works as a salvager. The Ledger is only available during the Quest.

- Quest Item: Dermot's Ledger

CASA MADRID APARTMENTS

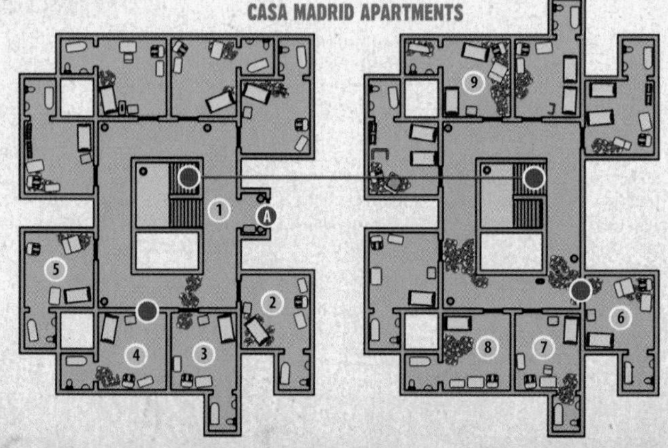

4 **Saint James' Apartment [Average]**

Saint James is just as helpful as his less-intelligent friend when it comes to your prying questions, unless Side Quest: The Coyotes is active. The Teddy Bear is only available during the Quest.

- Quest Item: Teddy Bear

5 **Anderson's Apartment**

Tom Anderson is a member of the Followers of the Apocalypse, and he's working hard to make sure the Co-op flourishes. Although he doesn't come out and say it, he's having a bit of trouble with the NCR; for the full details, consult Side Quest: The White Wash.

Upper Floor

6 **Pretty Sarah's Apartment**

- Chems

7 **Maude's Apartment**

If you're looking for a woman with "experience," you can't do much better than Maude. You can talk to her about Sweeties and Jimmy too. 75 Caps gets you full sex, as long as you don't go putting anything "someplace it was never intended."

- Sexy Time!

8 **Jimmy's Apartment**

Aside from the usual Food, Jimmy has a Magazine on the table; not that he needs help with his confidence. Speak to him and you can:

Tell him back rubs are a specialty of yours.

Ask about Maude, Sweetie, and Pretty Sarah.

Get down to business. 200 Caps gets you an evening that'll leave you "without a care in the world."

- Magazine: Meeting People [Speech] [5/12] [3/37]
- Sexy Time!

9 **Sweetie's Apartment**

Sweetie is young, free, and single-minded; leaving the Gomorrah to ply her own trade, where she earns less, but isn't addicted to Chems. You can ask about the others, herself, or for a good time. She'll "do things you didn't think were possible" for 300 Caps. You can also ask about Saint James' "proclivities," for 200 Caps.

Or 100 Caps. She then tells you about his creepy time with a Teddy Bear. You can return to ask Saint James about this, but his responses aren't revealing, and do involve swearing.

- Sexy time!

Other Apartments

The other rooms on the ground and upper floors (including the two locked ones [Very Easy, Average] have a place to sleep, and some fridge Food (and occasionally Drink) to rummage through.

- Sleeping Quarters

Free Quest: A Bit of Slap and Tickle

Whether your preference is male, female, or elderly, there's something for any lost and lonely soul here in Casa Madrid! Simply speak to any of the "good time guys and gals" in Pretty Sarah's care. How fast can you waste those Caps with a spot of "sexy time"?

- Sexy time!

[2A.02] Westside Co-op

- Threat Level: ●●●●●
- Faction: Westside Militia
  - Entity: Clayton Etienne
- Services: Trader [9/33]
- Collectibles:
  - Magazine [Barter] [5/16] [4-5/37]
  - Magazine [Survival] [9/30] [4-5/37]
- Health, Chems, or Water
- Interior Exploration
- Lots O' Caps
- Radio Signal [Black Mountain; Westside streets only]
- Wasteland Vegetation

A reasonably intact old Uptown Drugs Store is now the base of operations of a fledgling business known as the Westside Co-op, and guarded by a tongue-tied Super Mutant called Mean Sonofabitch (who's actually quite pleasant).

Clayton Etienne runs the Co-op. If you've finished Side Quest: The White Wash with an "understanding," Etienne is the guy to come back to for your Caps. If you're not shaking him down, you can ask about his story (he tells you about the crime families of New Reno), the co-op (he talks about help they got from Tom Anderson and the Followers), and what he has for sale. You can then purchase, or steal from him. There's a wealth of Caps if you want to turn Westside hostile, and more in the floor safe [Average].

- Trader: Clayton Etienne [9/33]
- Magazine: Salesman Weekly [Barter] [5/16] [4/37]
- Magazine: Lad's Life [Survival] [9/30] [5/37]
- Caps (600+)

[2A.03] Klamath Bob's Liquor Store

- Threat Level: ●●●●●
- Faction: Westside Militia
  - Entity: Klamath Bob
- Services:
  - Trader [10/33]
  - Caravan Player [4/15]
- Collectibles: Caravan Cards [5/30]
- Guns and Ammo
- Health, Chems, or Water
- Interior Exploration
- Radio Signal [Black Mountain; Westside streets only]

You can elect to steal or purchase some fine libations from Klamath Bob himself. You can ask him if he's from Klamath (he mentions some history regarding "a tribal from Arroyo"), the various small Factions in the area (mainly the Scorpions at the Monte Carlo Suites [2.12] and the Fiends), as well as the more colorful characters in Westside. You can also play a hand of Caravan with him, or take the Magnum under his cash register. He has few Caps if you're thinking about a hold-up.

- Caravan Player [Klamath Bob] [4/15]
- Caravan Cards [Klamath Bob] [5/30]
- Trader: Klamath Bob [10/33]
- .357 Magnum Revolver and Ammo

[2A.04] North Cistern

- Threat Level: ●●●●●
- Faction: Westside Militia
  - Entity: None
- Health, Chems, or Water
- Interior Exploration

This offers a Water Tower Valve (allowing you to sup from clean water), and (unless you like collecting Sporks) little else of value.

ZONE 2A: SECONDARY LOCATIONS

[2A.S01] The Chessboard

- Side Quest: For Auld Lang Syne
- Threat Level: ●●●●●
- Faction: Westside
  - Entity: Judah Kregar
  - Entity: Westside Citizen

Judah Kregar is usually near or standing around this location, although he walks the streets of Westside, too. Mean Sonofabitch also loiters here, close to the Pawn Shop.

[2A.S02] Manhole to North Sewers

- Threat Level: ●●●●●
- Underground Connection

This allows easy access to and from the North Sewers [U2.N].

[2A.S03] Marco

- Threat Level: ●●●●●
- Faction: Westside Militia
  - Entity: Marco

Marco is likely to be found sitting outside the building he manages.

[2A.S04] Mean Sonofabitch

- Threat Level: ●●●●●
- Faction: Westside Militia
  - Entity: Mean Sonofabitch

The inaccurately named Mean Sonofabitch is a pleasant, almost humorous First Generation Super

Mutant, who lumbers around town. Ask around, and you learn his speech impediment was caused by his tongue being cut out of his mouth.

[2A.S05] Building Alcove

- Side Quest: The Coyotes
- Threat Level: ●●●●●
- Faction: Westside Militia
  - Entity: Saint John
  - Entity: Dermot

If they aren't inside the Casa Madrid Apartments, two unpleasant Scavengers are hanging around here like a bad smell.

[2A.S06] Westside Allotment (West)

- Threat Level: ●●●●●
- Faction: Westside Cooperative
  - Entity: Westside Citizen

- Sleeping Quarters
- Wasteland Vegetation

One of two allotments the Westside Citizens are attempting to cultivate.

- Sleeping Quarters

[2A.S07] Makeshift Bedding

- Threat Level: ●●●●●
- Sleeping Quarters

This is one of a number of locations across Westside where you'll find Makeshift Bedding.

- Sleeping Quarters

[2A.S08] Makeshift Bedding

- Threat Level: ●●●●●
- Sleeping Quarters
- Sleeping Quarters

[2A.S09] Westside Allotment (East)

- Threat Level: ●●●●●
- Faction: Westside Cooperative
  - Entity: Westside Citizen
- Sleeping Quarters
- Wasteland Vegetation

The second of two allotments where the Westside Citizens are attempting to grow vegetation.

- Sleeping Quarters

[2A.S10] Hector and the Water Brahmin

- Side Quest: The White Wash
- Threat Level: ●●●●●
- Faction: Westside Cooperative
  - Entity: Hector
  - Entity: Water Brahmin

A small child walks with his pet Brahmin and siphons water from the barrels the NCR delivers from their Sharecropper Farms.

ZONE 2B: NORTH VEGAS SQUARE

[2B.01] The Gray

- Side Quest: Someone to Watch Over Me
- Threat Level: ●●●●●
- Faction: North Vegas Resident, Thug
  - Entity: Alice Hostetler
  - Entity: Andy Scabb
  - Entity: Thug
  - Entity: North Vegas Resident
- Crafting: Reloading Bench [12/36]
- Collectibles: Sunset Sarsaparilla Star Cap [28/100]
- Guns and Ammo
- Interior Exploration
- Radio Signal [Black Mountain, in North Vegas Square only]
- Sleeping Quarters
- Quest Item

The small fortified camp of North New Vegas, run by Crandon and the stoic Jules has but one large location, close to the manhole cover leading to the North Sewers [U2.N]; the Gray Hotel. Once you enter, prepare for a quick-thinking, or fast-drawing altercation with the chem-addled thugs here. One is guarding a runaway girl's room, who has shacked up here with her boyfriend; a Ghoul named Andy. They only appear if the Side Quest involving them is active.

Ⓐ Door to North Vegas Square

① Ground Floor

Conduct a clockwise search through the rooms. While some have a bounty of useless items (such as a collection of Tin Cans or Empty Syringes and a Toaster in the bath), the following items are of interest:

- Quest Item: Henchman Message to Andy Scabb (only if Quest is active)
- Strange Meat
- Dino Toy
- Sleeping Quarters

② Upper Floor

Now do the same upstairs, with similar results.

- Sleeping Quarters

③ 9 O'Clock Room (Upper)

- Sunset Sarsaparilla Star Cap [28/100]
- Sleeping Quarters

④ 1 O'Clock Room

This chamber has a Reloading Bench. Note the Teddy verses Dino Toy confrontation!

- Reloading Bench [12/36]
- Strange Meat
- Teddy Bear and Dino Toy
- Combat Knife
- Knife
- Sleeping Quarters

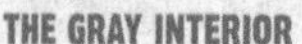
THE GRAY INTERIOR

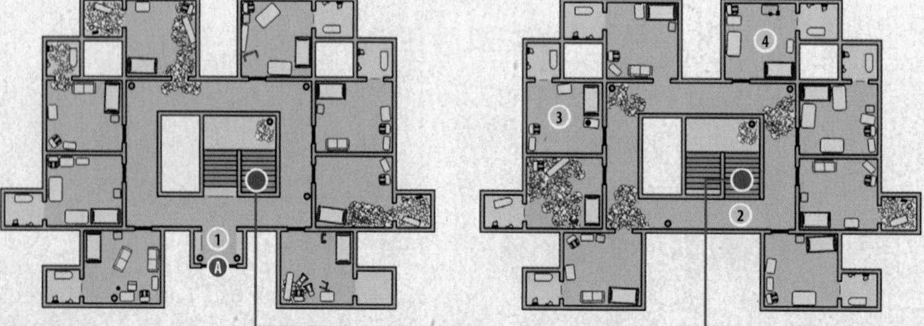

ZONE 2B: SECONDARY LOCATIONS

[2B.S01] Cranden

- Side Quest: Someone to Watch Over Me
- Threat Level:
- Faction: North Vegas
  - Entity: Cranden

You'll find Cranden wandering these streets, muttering about the influx of squatters.

[2B.S02] Manhole to North Sewers

- Threat Level:
- Underground Connection

This allows easy access to and from the North Sewers [U2.N].

[2B.S03] Owned Bedding

- Threat Level:

This Makeshift Bedding belongs to Crandon and Jules, and can't be slept on.

[2B.S04] Jules

- Free Quest: Meeting an Equal
- Threat Level:
- Faction: North Vegas
  - Entity: Jules
- Services: Caravan Player [5/15]
- Collectibles:
  - Caravan Cards [6/30]
  - Unique Item [20/95]

If you can match him (verbally) in Guns and Survival skills, he greets you as an equal. He also plays a mean hand of Caravan, and can give you information on the area, the NCR, and the Fiends to the southwest.

- Caravan Player: Jules [5/15]
- Caravan Cards [6/30]

Free Quest: Meeting an Equal

Strike up a conversation with Jules the old gunslinger, and ask why he's suspicious, and he tells you he's seen a lot. You can:

Indicate that Jules can take care of himself, and point to his revolver. He asks if you can handle "more than just a weapon." He asks if you know yourself.

Tell him you're one with the land. He thought himself too old to find an equal! He then tells you how to make a special form of .44 ammunition.

- Unique Item: Schematics—.44 Magnum, Hand Load [20/95]

[2B.S05] Squatter Bill

- Side Quest: Someone to Watch Over Me
- Threat Level:
- Faction: Squatter
  - Entity: Squatter Bill

A rather grumpy man, Squatter Bill has taken over North Vegas with a bunch of companions, much to Crandon's chagrin.

[2B.S06] Playground

- Side Quest: Someone to Watch Over Me
- Threat Level:
- Faction: Squatter
  - Entity: Squatter

A couple of rather rude Squatters don't take kindly to being disturbed.

ZONE 2C: FREESIDE

[2C.01] Old Mormon Fort

- Main Quest: Kings Gambit
- Side Quest: Cry Me a River
- Side Quest: For Auld Lang Syne
- Side Quest: G.I. Blues
- Side Quest: High Times
- Side Quest: Nothin' But a Hound Dog
- Side Quest: Oh My Papa
- Side Quest: Wang Dang Atomic Tango
- Side Quest: ED-E My Love
- Free Quest: Short-Term Treatment
- Free Quest: Long-Term Care
- Free Quest: Friend of the Followers
- Threat Level:
- Faction: Followers of the Apocalypse / Freeside
  - Entity: Julie Farkas
  - Entity: Arcade Gannon
  - Entity: April Martimer
  - Entity: Beatrix Russel
  - Entity: Followers Doctor
  - Entity: Followers Guard
  - Entity: Gambler
  - Entity: Roy, Farris, and Wayne
  - Entity: Child
  - Entity: Giant Rat
- Fame/Infamy
- Services: Healer/Dealer [7/31]
- Collectibles:
  - Magazine [Medicine] [11/19] [6/37]
  - Snow Globe [2/7]
  - Unique Item [21/95]
  - Unique Item [22/95]
- Follower
- Health, Chems, or Water
- Interior Exploration
- Main Trading Route
- Perk!
- Sleeping Quarters

At the north end of Freeside, an Old Mormon Fort has been converted into the base of operations for the Followers of the Apocalypse, a quasi-religious organization hellbent on helping humanity, while ensuring nothing like the Great War ever occurs again. The courtyard of the fort is used for general triage and care, with the old (heavily damaged) adobe fort buildings themselves being for Followers' storage and residences. Despite the historic name of the place, there are no serious fortifications—just fences and gates with a few armed Followers inside.

Ⓐ Door to Freeside; Fort Courtyard Entrance

① Sandbag Defenses

You'll meet a guard or two, and Beatrix Russel, in this location. She's a cowgirl Ghoul with a heart of gold, and a rare coat. You can ask her (at length) about her past, Freeside, and all the Factions therein.

- Unique Item: Bounty Hunter Duster [21/95]

② Roy, Farris, and Wayne's Tent

Although this place mainly caters to those down on their luck, these three Freeside residents look like they've been beaten up. They aren't speaking about it, and won't until you quiz them as part of Side Quest: G.I. Blues.

- Sleeping Quarters

OLD MORMON FORT EXTERIOR

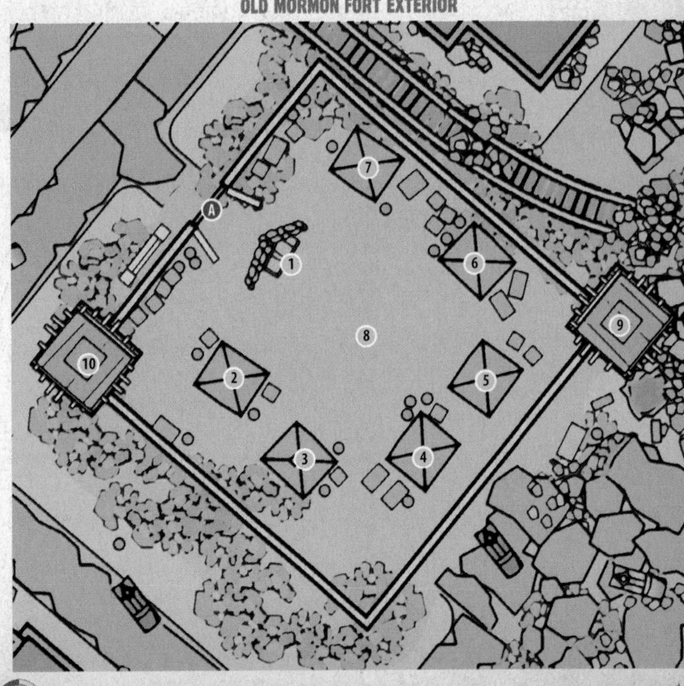

3 Arcade Gannon's Tent

One of the Followers Doctors—a man named Arcade Gannon—sits or stands around here, although he puts himself down as a researcher, and not a particularly good one. He's better at Latin though. He seems interested if you ask him to help your cause, but he points you in the direction of Julie Farkas if you want to really help the Followers. Persist, and he asks why he should go with you. You can:

Tell him things are bad here, and you'd I'd to make a difference with him at your side.

That he's really smart, and you're really dumb. He can help you do...things.

That you need a good-looking doctor in this big, bad wasteland.

Or move on to other matters. Any of the three previous options allows Arcade to come with you. This also begins his Side Quest: For Auld Lang Syne.

- Follower
- Perk! Better Healing
- Sleeping Quarters

4 5 Storage and Rest Tents

There's usually a couple of gamblers in the Rest Tent, sleeping off a heavy night.

- Sleeping Quarters

6 7 Guard Tent and Doctor's Tent

April Martimer is either here, or around camp, but only if Side Quest: ED-E My Love is active.

8 Julie Farkas

The leader of the Followers of the Apocalypse is Julie Farkas, a soft-spoken woman with a heart as big as a Bloatfly. You can speak to Julie about her problems with a lack of medical supplies. You can also speak to her about two chem addicts who need saving (High Times), The King in Freeside, and specifically his relationship with the NCR (G.I. Blues and King's Gambit), The King's dog Rex (Nothin' But a Hound Dog), and about a sensitive Great Khan who wishes to hang up his biker jacket for a doctor's coat (Cry Me a River). Farkas really is a lynch-pin of Freeside.

Farkas also is proficient at fixing you up, but at a cost. Finally, you can speak to her about returning with medical supplies for her (Free Quest: Short-Term Treatment), or setting up some kind of discount with local vendors (Free Quest: Long-Term Care).

- Healer: Julie Farkas [7/31]
- Unique Item: Follower's Lab Coat [22/95]

9 Eastern Tower

This storage area has rotting crates and rusting Tin Cans everywhere.

10 Western Tower

This accesses a small surgery room with poor lighting. There's a Filing Cabinet here to check: If Side Quest: High Times is active, you can pull the records of one of the affected Freeside dwellers. If Main Quest: King's Gambit, or Side Quest: G.I. Blues is active, you can read the medical records of Pacer, one of The King's Gang members.

- Quest Item: Pacer's Patient Record
- Quest Item: Jacob Hoff's Patient Record

Upstairs is Julie's office, complete with a magazine on her desk (which must be stolen), and a Snow Globe on the book shelf (which can be snagged without any Karmic worries).

- Magazine: Today's Physician [Medicine] [11/19] [6/37]
- Snow Globe—Mormon Fort [2/7]

> **Note** You found a Limited Edition Mojave Landmark Snow Globe! These rare, Pre-War artifacts are widely considered to be useless baubles, but rumor has it some collectors will pay dearly for them.

Free Quest: Short-Term Treatment

Julie Farkas is in desperate need of Med-X, RadAway, and Fixer. Simply find any or all three of these Chems during your travels, and then hand them back in to her. After a few kind gestures, Julie offers to sell you a box of Magazines she received. Trade with her for them if you want them. The Magazines don't count toward the total Collectibles, as they are random.

- Followers of the Apocalypse Fame Gained!
- Skill Magazines (18)

Free Quest: Long-Term Care

Julie Farkas isn't just looking for a few spare Chems; she's hoping you might be able to broker a permanent trade deal with one of the three local merchants; and suggests you speak to Mick & Ralph [2C.02], The Garrets over at the Atomic Wrangler [2C.06], and the Crimson Caravan Company [2.09].

Mick & Ralph don't have the technology or wherewithal all to supply Chems to anyone, but they recommend speaking to the Garrets.

The Crimson Caravan isn't interested in working with the Followers; this is a dead-end.

James Garret is taken with the idea; in return for the Followers using their technology to mend the Atomic Wrangler's alcohol-producing stills, they can provide as much Med-X as they need. Farkas isn't too happy about this, but agrees, and after you reconfirm with James, then Farkas once more, the trading begins.

Broker a successful deal for a Reputation gain, and a discount on your medicine.

- Followers of the Apocalypse Fame Gained!
- Freeside Fame Gained!

Free Quest: Friend of the Followers

Should you become increasingly helpful to the Followers' plight, it begins to pay dividends. Continue to earn Followers of the Apocalypse Fame, and during one conversation with Julie Farkas, she presents you with a special key. This opens the door to the Followers Safehouse [1.04], where you can rest, and relax. Consult that location for more information.

- Followers Safehouse Key

[2C.02] Mick & Ralph's

- Side Quest: How Little We Know
- Free Quest: Papers, Please
- Threat Level: ●●●●●
- Faction: Freeside
  - Entity: Mick
  - Entity: Ralph
- Services:
  - Repairer [2/9]
  - Trader [11/33]
  - Trader [12/33]
- Crafting: Workbench [11/41]
- Collectibles:
  - Magazine [Medicine] [12/19] [7-9/37]
  - Magazine [Melee Weapons] [4/9] [7-9/37]
  - Magazine [Science] [9/23] [7-9/37]
  - Unique Item [23/95]
  - Unique Weapon [14/42]
- Area Is Locked
- Guns and Ammo
- Health, Chems, or Water
- Interior Exploration
- Lots O' Caps
- Wasteland Vegetation
- Quest Item

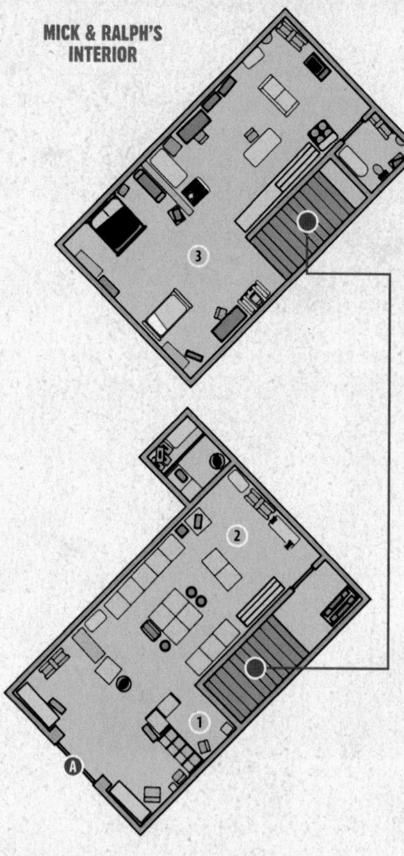

Providing some of the finest quality trinkets to discerning customers, while serving the riff-raff the usual low-grade armaments, Mick and his colleague Ralph run a thriving business from the seedier side of Freeside. Their store is a treasure-trove of objets d'art, mass-produced crap, and almost everything you've found on your Wasteland journeys; even those weird little dolls people say are from a place back East called Point Lookout. Sometimes, Max and Stacey run around in here. Max has an interesting toy gun for you to check:

- Unique Weapon: Euclid's C-Finder [14/42]

1 Ralph's General Supplies

Ralph runs the front of the store, and he sells general supplies. You can ask him what he has in stock, and Trade with him. If you're after some Chlorine during Side Quest: How Little We Know, this is the place to obtain it.

- Trader: Ralph [11/33]
- Trader Highlight (Ralph): Container of Chlorine

You can also request a bounty of information on the various Factions inside Freeside. You can also ask if he offers "any other services." This begins Free Quest: Papers, Please.

2 Mick's Weapons

Mick is at the back of the store, near his Workbench, and sells guns. You can ask to see the guns that he has for sale, and Trade with him.

- Trader: Mick [12/33]
- Trader Highlight (Mick): Hidden Cache of Weapons

You can also ask how business is. He tells you it has slowed down since The Omertas stopped buying, and asks if you could find out the reason. You'll know why if you commence Side Quest: How Little We Know, and you can return to Mick and tell him.

- Note: Omertas Stopped Buying From Mick

You can also ask Mick to Repair any of your equipment. He's extremely proficient.

- Repairer [Mick]: Repair Skill 75 [2/9]

You can also ask if he's got any special items for sale. He's suspicious, and asks if you work for any of the casinos.

Reply "Yes," and he tells you there are no Vegas-banned items here.

Reply no. He opens up a hidden wall, into a storage room brimming with only the most impressive, eye-popping (literally and figuratively) hardware.

- Unique Item: Naughty Nightwear [23/95]

3 Upper Apartment

You can also ransack the store, which isn't recommended as you don't get to steal everything Mick and Ralph sell, although there's a Caps haul. Go upstairs, and there's water to drink in the bathroom.

- Workbench [11/41]
- Caps
- Carton of Cigarettes (5)
- Food (including a delicious Potato!)
- Dino Toy (2) and Teddy Bear
- Magazine: Today's Physician [Medicine] [12/19] [7/37]
- Magazine: Tæles of Chivalrie [Melee Weapons] [4/9] [8/37]
- Magazine: Programmer's Digest [Science] [9/23] [9/37]

Free Quest: Papers, Please

If you ask Ralph about his special services, he tells you he can offer you something, but only after you've impressed the King. You can:

- Inquire about the King, and then complete Side Quest: G.I. Blues, and then return here with the King's blessing.

Or, you can ask Ralph if he has something on the side. He agrees to tell you that he's perfected a craft of Passport counterfeiting. Obviously, he wants to keep this low-key. The Passport is going to cost you 500 Caps. You game?

Without enough Caps, you can agree to come back later.

With 2,000 Caps to burn, you can tell him you've got enough to pass the credit check at The Strip North Gate [2.13].

You can agree, and purchase the passport for 500 Caps.

Or you can bargain Ralph down to 375 Caps.

- Quest Item: Counterfeit Passport

[2C.03] Ruined Store

- Side Quest: G.I. Blues
- Threat Level: ●●●●●
- Faction: NCR
  - Entity: Elizabeth Kieran
- Area Is Locked
- Health, Chems, or Water
- Interior Exploration
- Radio Signal [Black Mountain]

In an oft-overlooking part of Freeside, two "Men" guarding this location are actually NCR soldiers attempting to win hearts and minds (and to some, usurp the power of The Kings Gang) by feeding the Squatters of Freeside. Approach, and the Men ask for a Password. You can:

Tell them the password, as part of Side Quest: G.I. Blues.

Tell him you were already let in. They step aside.

Or say you don't know, barring you from entering until you return with a password.

Once inside, you see a soup kitchen run with almost military precision. Speak to Elizabeth Kieran, and you soon discover it *is* a military operation.

- Doctor's Bag
- Food (a huge supply)
- Purified Water (enough to drown you)

[2C.04] Cerulean Robotics

- Side Quest: Wang Dang Atomic Tango
- Free Quest: Maud's Muggers
- Threat Level: ●●●●●
- Faction: Mutated Animal, Robot
  - Entity: Giant Rat
  - Entity: Protectron
  - Entity: FISTO!
- Crafting:
  - Reloading Bench [13/36]
  - Workbench [12/41]
- Collectibles:
  - Sunset Sarsaparilla Star Cap [29/100]
  - Skill Book [Speech] [2/4] [1/4]
- Area Is Locked
- Interior Exploration
- Radio Signal [Black Mountain]
- Quest Item

In a lonely and occasionally traversed section of Freeside is a monolithic office building, which was home to Cerulean Robotics. You can freely enter the facility. On your way out, don't be surprised if you're accosted by Malefic Maud and her ruthless band of octogenarian muggers (Free Quest: Maud's Muggers; related to Freeside itself)!

A Door to Freeside

1 Entrance Foyer

Beware the odd Giant Rat intrusion.

2 Break Room

Over in the corners appears to be the remains of an ancient Protectron fight with a now-deceased worker.

- Sunset Sarsaparilla Star Cap [29/100]

3 Open-Plan Office and Workshop

This section of the large room houses a few desks and a conveyor belt where components once sped along.

- Skill Book: Lying, Congressional Style [Speech] [2/4] [2/4]
- Scrap Metal

4 Protectron Pods

Aside from the junk, and another disused Protectron, there's another, blue Protectron still encased in his pod. Close by is a wall terminal with a Protectron Programming Interface [Average]. You can:

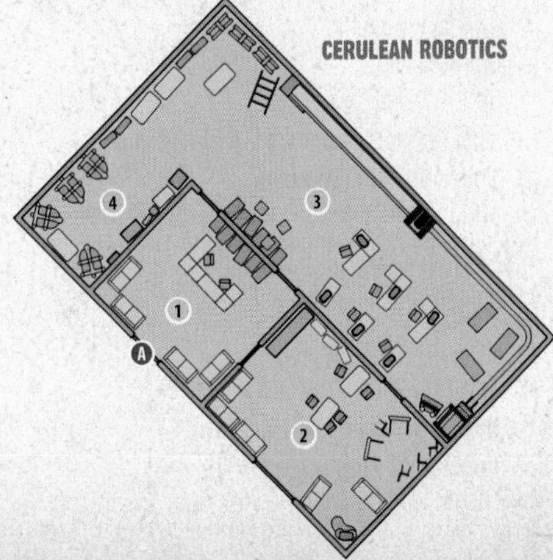

Hack into the terminal, and then Run a Diagnostic Routine, and Upload a Programming Routine. You don't have the Programming Routine unless you acquired it during the Side Quest. Only then, can FISTO! activate!

- Workbench [12/41]
- Reloading Bench [13/36]
- FISTO!

[2C.05] King's School of Impersonation

See map on the following page

- Main Quest: King's Gambit
- Side Quest: G.I. Blues
- Side Quest: Nothin' But a Hound Dog
- Free Quest: Papers, Please
- Threat Level: ●●●●●
- Faction: Kings Gang / Freeside
  - Entity: The King
  - Entity: Rex
  - Entity: Pacer
  - Entity: Sergio
  - Entity: Kings Gang Member
  - Entity: Groupie
- Fame/Infamy
- Collectibles:
  - Magazine [Unarmed] [3/11] [10/37]
  - Unique Item [24/95]
  - Unique Weapon [15/42]
- Area Is Locked
- Follower: Rex
- Perk!
- Guns and Ammo
- Health, Chems, or Water
- Interior Exploration
- Lots O' Caps
- Sleeping Quarters
- Quest Item

The most powerful individual in Freeside, the King is the leader and undisputed ruler of The Kings Gang, a group of tough guys that dominate the center of the community. The King models himself on a singer from ancient times, after discovering some old recordings, and is charming, rebellious, and well-dressed. He sits and vets newcomers to the gang, and those that wish to impersonate the King himself, who in turn, is an impersonation. He's accompanied by his dog Rex, a cybernetic hound around since Pre-War times, who's a little worse for wear.

Floor 1: Bar, Stage, Bedrooms and Recreation

A Door to Freeside

1 The King's Bar

Inside the King's School of Impersonation is a bar, where you can steal a Beer or Sunset Sarsaparilla. Pacer is also here, guarding the entrance to the Stage Room. To get into see the King, you can:

Tell Pacer you're here to pay your respects. Pacer likes that, and lets you in.

Or, you can offer five Caps (you're turned away in disgust), 50 Caps (Pacer lets you in), or 500 Caps (Pacer lets you in while you remember not to give away all your Caps).

Pickpocketing Pacer allows you to take his key, which opens up Location #2.

- Pacer's Key

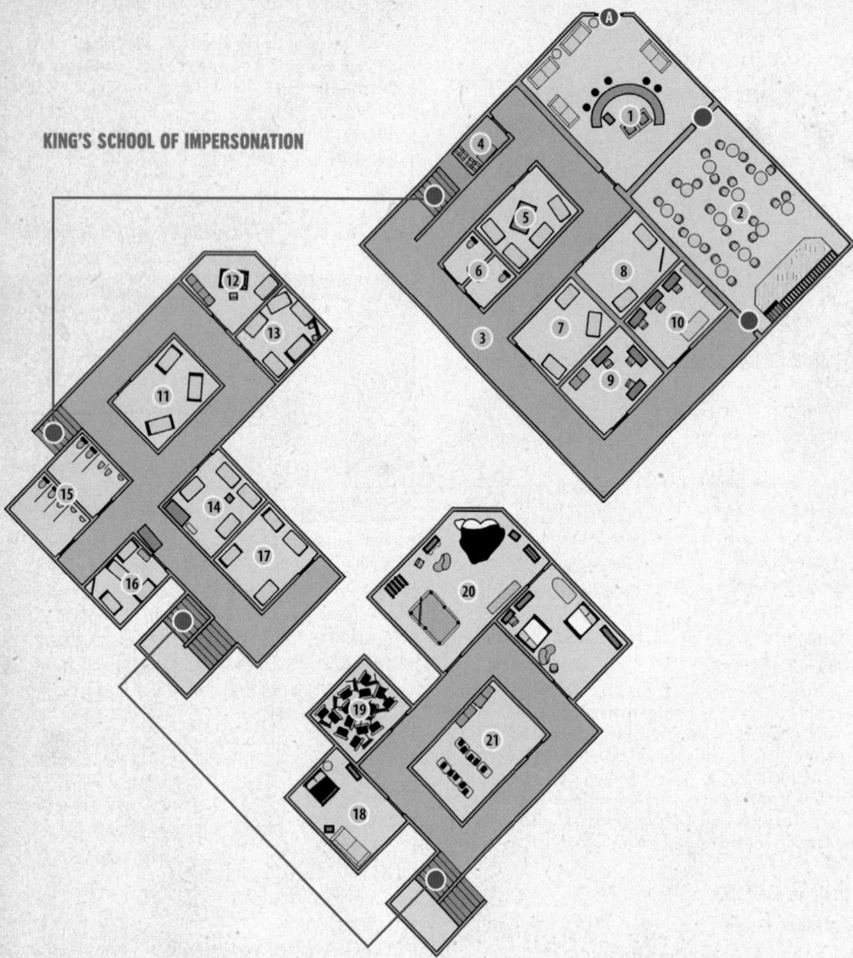

2 Stage Room

Once inside the Stage Room, meet the King and Rex. You can converse with him to begin Side Quest: G.I. Blues, and also inquire about him ceasing violence against the NCR as part of Main Quest: King's Gambit. The King also has a key (which opens the other door in this room), and a unique outfit, but you'll need to pry them off his corpse.

- The King's Key
- Unique Item: Viva Las Vegas [24/95]
- Follower: Rex
- Perk! Search and Mark

3 (Ground) Corridor

As long as you don't try anything too brazen, the Kings Gang lets you wander.

4 (Ground) Storage Room

5 (Ground) Beer-Pong Room

- Sleeping Quarters.

6 (Ground) Restrooms

There's radiation-free water to drink in either of these rooms.

7 (Ground) Spin-the-Bottle Bedroom

- Sleeping Quarters.

8 (Ground) Chalkboard Bedroom

- Sleeping Quarters.

9 (Ground) Make-up Room

10 (Ground) Sergio's Stylings

Sergio works his greased-back magic here, but can't offer you a styling yet. Complete Side Quest: G.I. Blues, and the King allows it, enabling you to complete your look. Sergio carries a Unique Straight Razor, too.

- Unique Weapon: Figaro [15/42]

Floor 2: Bedrooms and Recreation

11 Pitch-and-Putt Bedroom

- 9 Iron
- Sleeping Quarters

12 Groupie's Bedroom

- Sleeping Quarters

13 Windowed Bedroom

- Sleeping Quarters

14 Chess Bedroom

- Footlocker Items
- Sleeping Quarters

15 Restrooms

There's radiation-free water to drink in either of these rooms.

- Straight Razor
- First Aid Box (2)

16 Bedroom by the Stairs

- Carton of Cigarettes
- Sleeping Quarters

17 Back Bedroom

- Scrap Metal
- Sleeping Quarters
- Switchblade (2)

Floor 3: Master Bedrooms and Storage

18 (Upper) Pacer's Bedroom

The King's right-hand man is a guy called Pacer, who isn't quite as easy-going as the big man. Find his secret stash under the bed; important for the associated Quests.

- Switchblade
- Quest Item: Pacer's Jet Stash
- Sleeping Quarters

19 (Upper) School Desk Graveyard

20 (Upper) The King's Boudoir

This huge, high-ceiling chamber is where the King sleeps; on his ostentatious bed (which you can try out, too). In the en-suite chamber are additional beds for his Groupies.

- Magazine: Boxing Times [Unarmed] [3/11] [10/37]
- Pool Cue
- Carton of Cigarettes
- Jailhouse Rocker (2)
- King's Outfit (3)
- Sleeping Quarters

21 (Upper) Outfit Storage

The Kings Gang has a throwback style, and its important to maintain a uniform appearance.

- King's Outfit (30)

[2C.06] Atomic Wrangler

See maps on the following page

- Side Quest: Bye Bye Love
- Side Quest: Debt Collector
- Side Quest: Talent Pool
- Side Quest: Wang Dang Atomic Tango
- Free Quest: Big Winner, Atomic Wrangler
- Free Quest: Hat's Entertainment
- Threat Level: ●●●●●
- Faction: Freeside
  - Entity: James Garret
  - Entity: Francine Garret
  - Entity: Caleb McCaffery
  - Entity: Hadrian
  - Entity: Escort
  - Entity: Atomic Wrangler Guard
  - Entity: Cashier
  - Entity: Gambler
- Fame/Infamy
- Services;
  - Gambling: Blackjack [2/15]
  - Gambling: Roulette [3/15]
  - Gambling: Slots [4/15]
- Collectibles:
  - Unique Item [25/95]
  - Unique Item [26/95]
  - Unique Item [27/95]
- Area Is Locked
- Guns and Ammo
- Health, Chems, or Water
- Home Sweet Home
- Interior Exploration
- Lots O' Caps
- Sleeping Quarters
- Wasteland Vegetation
- Quest Item

The Atomic Wrangler, the only active casino in Freeside (featuring a neon sign of a futuristic cowboy riding a stylized atom), is also a flophouse, brothel, and source of chems, located just down the main drag. It is run by the Garret Twins, protected by their thugs, and is a common hangout for the Van Graffs and Kings. Many caravaneers and poor (but not impoverished) NCR folks can also be found here.

Atomic Wrangler—First and Second Floor

A Door to Freeside

1 Entrance Lounge

If you're really into your scavenging, there's a scattering of around eight Caps on the floor. There a few jokers in this pack that you can speak to, including:

- Gambling: Slots [4/15]

Caleb McCaffery, who thinks you're a kid, and isn't very pleasant, or helpful. There's a reason for this, as you'll discover during the associated Side Quests. He's wearing some Unique items, though.

Hadrian the Ghoul insult comic. You're encouraged to play along and insult the fella back. Then he tells you he's famous, but isn't pulling in the Caps in this dump. You're encouraged to find a new gig for him, as part of Side Quest: Talent Pool. See that hip cat Tommy Torini for all the details, man!

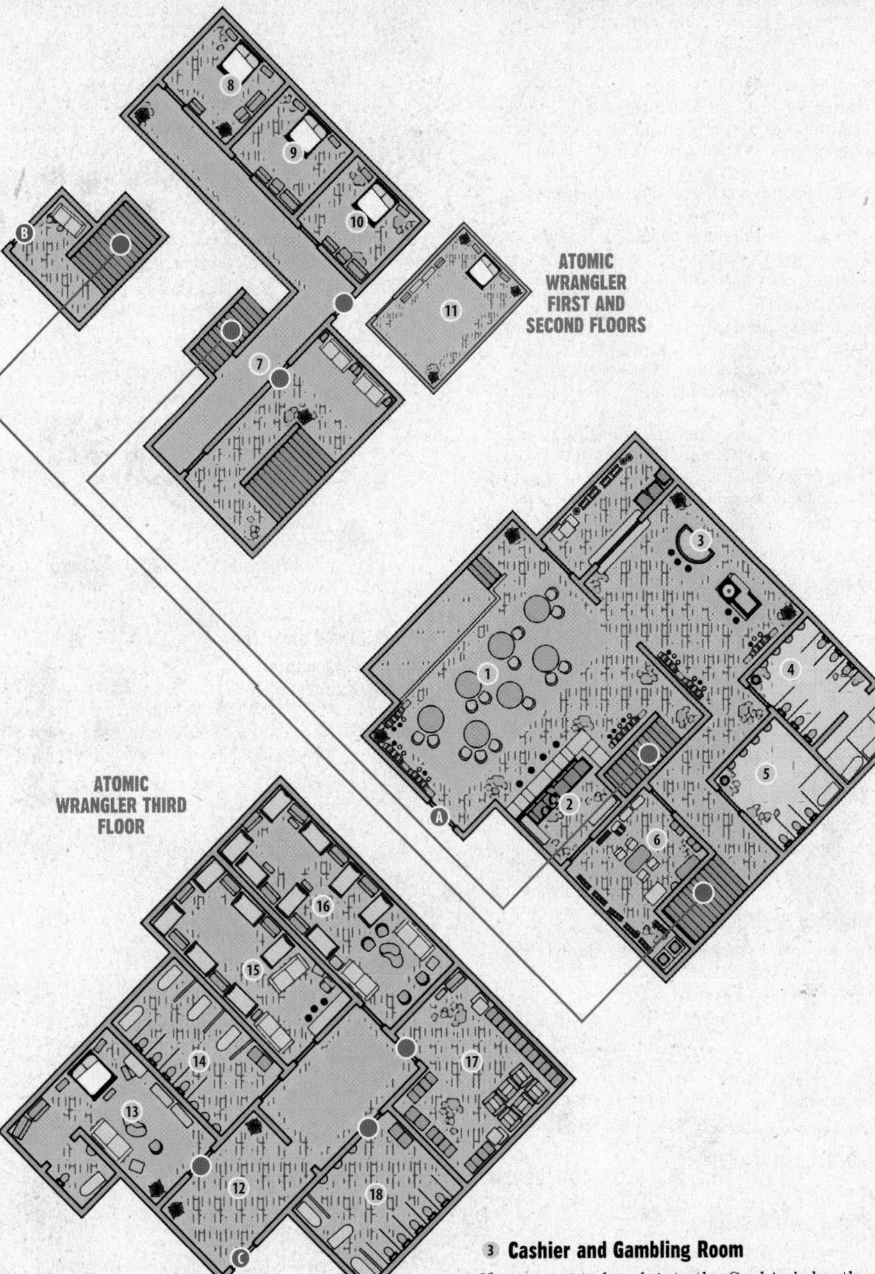

The Atomic Wrangler Guards are hired to blend into the background, then blend your head into a shade of crimson if you start any trouble. They can be over-powered, but only if you're a psychotic who needs a low Rep in Freeside.

- Unique Item: Caleb McCaffery's Hat [25/95]
- Unique Item: Bounty Hunter Duster [26/95]

2 Entrance Check-in and Bar

Francine and James Garret work behind the bar of the joint they own. Speak to them to begin a conversation about the neighborhood, and each has their own Side Quest. Should you Pickpocket or kill them, they each have a couple of keys; a Bank Key (that opens the cashier's booth and the wall safes) and the Upstairs Key (opening Francine's bedroom).

- Atomic Wrangler Bank Key (2)
- Atomic Wrangler Upstairs Key (2)
- Carton of Cigarettes (4)
- Drink
- Cash Register Items
- Lever-Action Shotgun

3 Cashier and Gambling Room

If you want to break into the Cashier's booth from the lounge via the guarded door [Very Hard], there's a ton of useless Pre-War Money, and seven safes. Four are on the wall [Hard] and none have anything like the haul you're expecting; just some random items and a few Caps.

- Gambling: Cashier
- Floor Safe Items (3)
- Floor Safe Items (4) [Hard]
- Gambling: Blackjack (Dealer must draw to 16, and stand on all 17s) [2/15]
- Gambling: Roulette [3/15]

4 Restroom (Ladies)

If you're after a drink of rad-free water, this is the place.

5 Restroom (Gentlemen)

And this is the other place.

6 Kitchens

There's a huge variety of items to steal from this preparation and eating area for the Garrets. The door from the back corridor to here is locked [Very Hard].

- Medical Cabinet Items
- Gun Cabinet Items
- Knife
- Food (including Plants and Fruit)
- Drink (including Beer and Spirits)

7 Upper Balcony

Escorts (both male and female) prowl this area, looking to service the clientèle. This includes you, but only after you're comped a suite.

8 North Bedroom

9 Northeast Bedroom [Average]

10 East Bedroom [Average]

11 Comped Suite [Requires Key]

At the end of their Side Quests, the Garrets give you this room to use as you see fit. You can now bring Escorts back here.

B Door to Atomic Wrangler—Third Floor

Atomic Wrangler—Third Floor

C Door to Atomic Wrangler—Second Floor

12 Hallway

This allows access to all the rooms on this floor.

13 Francine's Bedroom [Very Hard]

Hidden under the bed is a floor safe [Very Hard] There's rad-free water in the bathroom.

- Unique Item: Nuka-Cola Victory [27/95]
- Floor Safe Items [Very Hard]

14 Restroom (Ladies)

This has individual bathtubs for "discerning" clients, and the following:

- First Aid Box
- Medical Cabinet Items

15 Party Room

There's a number of mattresses in here, some cabinets to look through, and personal footlockers to rummage in. Oh, and three Caps on a silver Briefcase.

- Personal Footlocker Items (2)
- Briefcase Items (2)
- Sleeping Quarters

16 Guard Room

Some slumbering guards are usually found here.

- Teddy Bear
- Personal Footlocker Items (4)
- Sleeping Quarters

17 Dusty Storage Room [Hard]

- Footlocker Items
- Gun Cabinet Items

18 Restroom (Gentlemen) [Hard]

This has a group of bathtubs for "discerning" clients, and the following:

- First Aid Box
- Medical Cabinet Items

Free Quest: Big Winner, Atomic Wrangler

Need a little gambling with your good times? Then learn when to take the Atomic Wrangler for as much as you can, without being banned from the facility. Locate a Blackjack or Roulette table, or try the Slots, and the Floor Manager comes around to sweet-talk you when your Luck starts to hold:

At 1,250 Chips won, you're congratulated.

At 2,500 Chips won, you're congratulated again.

At 3,750 Chips won, you're the talk of the venue.

But once you hit 5,000 Chips won, the Garrets cut you off to stop you from fleecing them. However, your Reputation doesn't suffer. What, no comped suite?!

Free Quest: Hat's Entertainment

Obtaining your own Comped Suite at the Atomic Wrangler is the ultimate goal at the end of Side Quest: Debt Collector. It also involves murdering McCaffery, which isn't really a problem, as he's an unconscionable annoyance. Take the room key from his corpse, when you fight him in Freeside. Take his hat as proof to Francine, and you receive an identical key from her. Only one is needed to enter your suite (Location #12). You have the run of the Atomic Wrangler, coaxing a variety of escorts (whether male, female, Ghoul, or robot) into your room.

- Atomic Wrangler Room Key

[2C.07] Silver Rush

- Main Quest: King's Gambit
- Side Quest: Birds of a Feather
- Side Quest: Heartache by the Number
- Side Quest: Tend to Your Business
- Threat Level: ●●●●●
- Faction: Van Graff/ Freeside
  - Entity: Gloria Van Graff
  - Entity: Jean-Baptiste Cutting
  - Entity: Simon
  - Entity: Van Graff Thug
  - Entity: Mr. Soren
- Fame/Infamy
- Services: Trader [13/33]
- Crafting: Weapon Upgrade [4/10]
- Collectibles: Unique Item [28/95]
- Area Is Locked
- Guns and Ammo
- Health, Chems, or Water
- Interior Exploration
- Lots O' Caps
- Quest Item
- Weapons, Please!

"Vegas' best source of laser and plasma weapons." So says the thug guarding the door to the Silver Rush, an old casino transformed into a heavily guarded Energy Weapons trader's paradise. It's run by Gloria Van Graff, the younger of the two siblings, and her brother Jean-Baptiste Cutting. She is the person responsible for the New Vegas van Graffs' general strategy, including striking up a deal with Alice McLafferty of the Crimson Caravan Company to wipe out the competition in New Vegas (the Gun Runners and Cassidy Caravans). Jean-Baptiste Cutting is the muscle of the Van Graff operation, and handles all of Gloria's dirty work. Jean-Baptiste is a nasty, mean-spirited son-of-a-bitch. Despite the family's tendency to deal in energy weapons, Jean-Baptiste is a connoisseur of big guns and explosives. He threatens people for looking at him the wrong way and is far from all talk; he will go from zero-to-murder in two seconds.

The Van Graff Thug at the front door is actually Simon, and you get introduced once you speak to Gloria Van Graff, and begin the Side Quest. If you want to annoy him, open his crate of ammunition (or crouch behind a barrel so he doesn't see you). Before you enter, you're searched for any weapons and those that aren't Energy Weapons or likely to cause a problem are temporarily confiscated. If you're out to shoot the place up, do so after befriending Gloria.

- Dark Metal Crate [Very Easy]

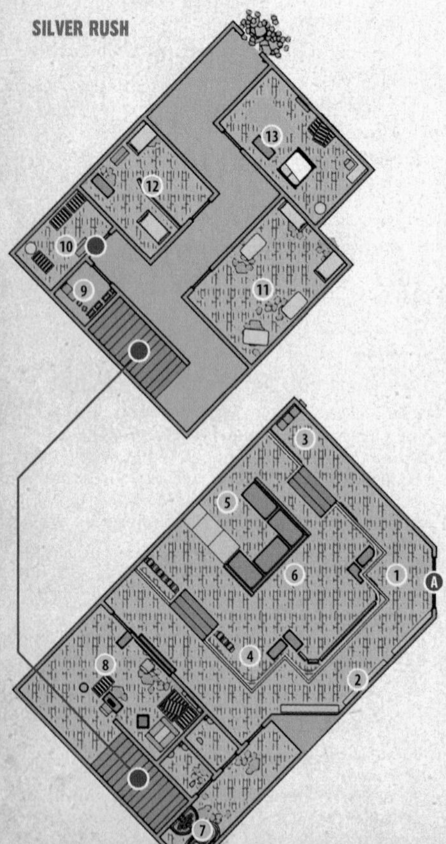

A Door to Freeside

1 Entrance Holding Area

Four heavily armed thugs stop you from progressing any further until Gloria Van Graff and Jean-Baptiste Cutting demonstrate what happens to those who make a late payment, to a business man named Mr. Soren. He quickly leaves.

Caution Mr. Soren was complaining about the poor quality of the merchandise. This may be the case when you purchase too; so be ready to Repair anything you buy.

2 Weapons Shelf

A huge amount of ammunition, Grenades, and Mines are showcased on this shelf. All must be stolen (or bought).

- Recharger Rifle
- Laser Rifle
- Plasma Grenade
- Laser Pistol (3)
- Microfusion Cell (20 x 5)
- Energy Cell (20 x 15)
- Electron Charge Pack (20 x 6)
- Flamer Fuel (12 x 2)
- Plasma Mine (4)

3 Gun Cabinet (Open)

- Laser Rifle (4)

4 Jean-Baptiste Cutting

An unpleasant man with an apt surname doesn't speak to you until you become a hire, and begin Side Quest: Birds of a Feather. Kill him, and you'll find a number of impressive Energy Weapons.

5 Gloria Van Graff

The slightly less intimidating matriarch of this operation is Gloria, at her table of Energy Weapons. You can ask her a number of questions about her business, the area, and what she thinks of the major Factions. But the real reason you're here is for the Trading. Note that some (but not all) of the weapons listed are neatly spread out on the tables. Also note that she provides you with items throughout Side Quest: Birds of a Feather, including Unique combat armor.

- Quest Item: Van Graff Package
- Unique Item: Van Graff Combat Armor [28/95]
- Trader: Gloria Van Graff [13/33]
- Trader: Gloria Van Graff Upgrades [Energy Weapons] [4/10]

Caution If you are thinking of holding up the joint, be warned that killing Gloria means her Upgrades die with her. Resist this temptation, or attack only after securing the Upgrades you want.

6 Van Graff's Table

The table from where Gloria sells her quality merchandise has the following weapons to steal:

- Laser Pistol
- Laser Rifle
- Tri-beam Laser Rifle
- Plasma Caster
- Pulse Mine (2)
- Pulse Grenade (2)
- Laser RCW
- Energy Cell (20 x15)
- Flamer
- Flamer Fuel (12 x 2)
- Plasma Rifle
- Plasma Mine (2)
- Recharger Pistol
- Plasma Pistol
- Multiplas Rifle
- Plasma Grenade (8)
- Plasma Defender

7 Restrooms

This corridor, with removed gambling tables at one end, allows access to clean water you can sip.

8 Reinforced Kiosk [Hard]

This locked location isn't for outsiders to enter, so you may have to fight the Van Graffs before entering here. Behind the counter is a storeroom and a floor safe. Find a Note here with shocking revelations during Side Quest: Heartache By the Number.

- Laser Pistol
- Floor Safe Items [Hard]
- Quest Item: Note: Letter to Gloria

9 (Upper) Tool Closet [Hard]

- Microfusion Cell (20 x 5)
- Energy Cell (20 x 3)
- Plasma Rifle
- Tool Cabinet Items

10 (Upper) Weapons Storage [Hard]

- Grenade Box Ammo (2)
- Gun Case Items
- Ammo Box Ammunition

11 Bedroom

12 Jean-Baptiste's Bedroom

- Scrap Metal (2)

13 Gloria Van Graff's Bedroom

A more lavish affair, with empty storage cases and some Vodka.

- Plasma Pistol

ZONE 2C: SECONDARY LOCATIONS

Note As previously noted, there are 28 separate Secondary locations within Outer (1-20) and Inner (21-28) Freeside. Expect to be attacked by thugs at any time!

[2C.S01] Bodyguards-For-Hire

- Side Quest: G.I. Blues
- Threat Level: ●●●●●
- Faction: Freeside
    - Entity: Bodyguard for Hire
    - Entity: Kings Gang Member
    - Entity: Orris
    - Entity: Gambler
- Follower

Just inside this gate are three rough-and-tumble individuals, ready for you to hire them during your stay in Freeside. For the sum of 100 Caps, you get their protective services; they act as a Follower, but work on their own, and protect you from thug attackers and pickpockets. One of the men is called Orris, and he charges double. He's also a person of interest during the Side Quest.

- Follower: Bodyguard for Hire
- Follower: Kings Gang Member
- Follower: Orris

[2C.S02] Genaro's Fodder

- Threat Level: ●●●●●
- Faction: Freeside
    - Entity: Genaro
- Services: Healer [8/31]
- Health, Chems, or Water

If you enjoy a more down-to-earth cuisine, speak with Genaro, who sells you Food that some Scavengers wouldn't touch.

- Healer (food): Genaro [8/31]

[2C.S03] Dead Man's Dumpster

- Threat Level: ●●●●●
- Faction: Freeside
    - Entity: Freeside Thug

Check the dumpsters and bodies for loot.

[2C.S04] Genaro's Little Helpers

- Threat Level: ●●●●●
- Faction: Followers of the Apocalypse
    - Entity: Child
    - Entity: Giant Rat

Dashing along the streets of Outer Freeside are three children chasing a Giant Rat. You surmise this is one way Genaro is kept in raw food for his cuisine. Sometimes, the children disappear into the Old Mormon Fort. Kill the rodent, and the children can feast.

[2C.S05] Squatter Camp #1

- Side Quest: G.I. Blues
- Side Quest: Debt Collector
- Threat Level: ●●●●●
- Faction: Freeside
    - Entity: Squatter
    - Entity: Grecks
    - Entity: The Man
- Sleeping Quarters

Visit this location during Side Quest G.I. Blues and speak to Grecks the Ghoul (as part of Side Quest: Debt Collector), as well as an NCR "Man."

- Sleeping Quarters

[2C.S06] Mick and Ralph's Crier

- Threat Level: ●●●●●
- Faction: Freeside
    - Entity: Mick and Ralph's Crier

This child bellows advertising for Mick & Ralph's store, informing you where the place is ([2C.02]).

[2C.S07] Freeside Entrance (Outer)

- Threat Level: ●●●●●
- Faction: Freeside

Learn the location of this bank of mangled vehicles and metal; it is the thoroughfare between Outer and Inner Freeside, and the quickest route to and from The Strip.

[2C.S08] Tapper and the Water Supply

- Threat Level: ●●●●●
- Faction: Freeside/The Kings
    - Entity: Tapper
- Health, Chems, or Water
- Services: Healer [9/31]
- Sleeping Quarters

A Kings Gang Member appropriately called Tapper mans a large water valve in this area, and is happy to quench your thirst; for a price.

- Healer (Water): Tapper [9/31]
- Purified Water

[2C.S09] Train Station

- Side Quest: G.I. Blues
- Threat Level: ●●●●●
- Faction: Freeside / NCR

This location is sealed up tight, but major conflict erupts in this location during a major Side Quest.

[2C.S10] Signal Box Tower

- Side Quest: G.I. Blues
- Threat Level: ●●●●●
- Faction: Freeside/ NCR
- Services:
    - Campfire [20/109]

If you choose a more violent end to the Side Quest, expect combat in this location; a rotting signal box close to the Train Station.

- Campfire [20/109]

[2C.S11] The Granny Gang

- Threat Level: ●●●●●
- Free Quest: Maud's Muggers
- Faction: Freeside
    - Entity: Malefic Maud
    - Entity: Irate Ida
    - Entity: Rancorous Ruth
- Wild Wasteland!

Maud's Muggers

This is a frightened city. Over these houses, over these streets hangs a pall of fear. Fear of a new kind of violence which is terrorizing the city. Yes, gangs of old ladies attacking defenseless fit young couriers. This occurs randomly, but there's a high chance if it happening when you exit Cerulean Robotics.

[2C.S12] Max and Stacey

- Side Quest: I Could Make You Care
- Free Quest: Reach for the Sky, Mister!
- Threat Level: ●●●●●
- Faction: Freeside
    - Entity: Max
    - Entity: Stacey
- Collectibles:
    - Unique Weapon [14/42]
- Guns and Ammo

Two troublesome tykes are racing around this otherwise-unpleasant part of town; Max is chasing Stacey with a "toy gun," which is actually something far more impressive. Talk to Max as part of the Side Quest, and if you want to start the Free Quest.

- Unique Weapon: Euclid's C-Finder [14/42]

[2C.S13] Vagrants and Thugs

- Threat Level: ●●●●●
- Faction: Freeside
    - Entity: Freeside Thug
    - Entity: Vagrant

You may be attacked near to this street junction, or watch the wretched drunks and vagrants slump on the sidewalks.

[2C.S14] Dixon the Dealer

- Side Quest: High Times
- Threat Level: ●●●●●
- Faction: Freeside
  - Entity: Dixon
- Services: Healer/Dealer [10/31]
- Health, Chems, or Water

Dixon has a few items designed to pick you up and keep you coming back for more.

- Healer/Dealer: Dixon [10/31]
- Dixon's Jet
- Dixon's Whiskey

[2C.S15] Rotface

- Side Quest: G.I. Blues
- Free Quest: Rotface's Loose Lips
- Threat Level: ●●●●●
- Faction: Freeside/Ghoul
  - Entity: Rotface

Slumped against a wall near Mick & Ralph's is a Ghoul who looks like just another vagrant. But speak to him, and he's a fountain of knowledge; beginning the Free Quest.

[2C.S16] Bodyguards-For-Hire

- Threat Level: ●●●●●
- Faction: Freeside
  - Entity: Bodyguard for Hire
  - Entity: Kings Gang Member
- Follower
- Sleeping Quarters

Just inside this gate are three rough-and-tumble individuals, ready for you to hire them during your stay in Freeside. For the sum of 100 Caps, you get their protective services; they act as a Follower, but work on their own, and protect you from thug attackers and pickpockets. Also check the ruined building behind them; there's a place to sleep here.

- Follower: Bodyguard for Hire
- Follower: Kings Gang Member
- Sleeping Quarters

[2C.S17] Jacob Hoff

- Side Quest: High Times
- Threat Level: ●●●●●
- Faction: Followers of the Apocalypse
  - Entity: Jacob Hoff
- Health, Chems, or Water

Surrounded by empty Jet inhalers, Jacob Hoff is a wretched sight, and only here if the Side Quest is active.

[2C.S18] Dead Man

- Side Quest: I Could Make You Care
- Threat Level: ●●●●●
- Collectibles: Unique Item [29/95]

Slumped corpses aren't that rare in Freeside, but this one is sporting an interesting piece of neck attire; useful during the Side Quest.

- Unique Item: Destroyed Collar [29/95]

[2C.S19] An Unsubtle Mugging

- Free Quest: Flogging a Dead Corpse
- Threat Level: ●●●●●
- Faction: Freeside
  - Entity: Freeside Thug

Investigate here, and you may fear for your life; check the Free Quest for more information.

[2C.S20] Squatter Camp #2

- Side Quest: Debt Collector
- Side Quest: G.I. Blues
- Side Quest: Wang Dang Atomic Tango
- Free Quest: Smooth-Talking Criminal
- Threat Level: ●●●●●
- Faction: Freeside
  - Entity: Squatter
  - Entity: Santiago
  - Entity: The Man
- Services:
  - Campfire [21/109]
  - Campfire [22/109]
- Sleeping Quarters

Visit this location during Side Quest G.I. Blues and speak to Santiago the fancy man, as well as an NCR "Man." Santiago is quick to offer you a deal (Smooth Talking Criminal) and you have a proposition for him too; if Side Quest: Wang Dang Atomic Tango or Debt Collector are active.

- Campfire [21/109]
- Campfire [22/109]
- Sleeping Quarters

Note: The following Secondary Locations are in Inner Freeside, through either set of doors.

[2C.S21] Freeside Entrance (Inner)

- Threat Level: ●●●●●
- Faction: Freeside

This is the main thoroughfare between Outer and Inner Freeside, and the quickest route to and from The Strip. The second entrance near the Silver Rush is rarely used.

[2C.S22] Atomic Wrangler Crier

- Threat Level: ●●●●●
- Faction: Freeside / Atomic Wrangler
  - Entity: Atomic Wrangler Crier

Hungry, thirsty, or horny? Then the Atomic Wrangler Crier tells you all about the services this nearby casino offers.

[2C.S23] Silver Rush Crier

- Threat Level: ●●●●●
- Faction: Freeside / Van Graff
  - Entity: Silver Rush Crier

If you're looking for a bit more energy—weapons, that is—check out what this man is yelling.

[2C.S24] Bill Ronte

- Side Quest: High Times
- Threat Level: ●●●●●
- Faction: Followers of the Apocalypse
  - Entity: Bill Ronte
- Health, Chems, or Water

Sitting in his own filth next to scattered and empty Whiskey bottles, Bill Ronte is a pathetic sight, and only here if the Side Quest is active.

[2C.S25] Ruined Building

- Threat Level: ●●●●●
- Sleeping Quarters

Adjacent to the Silver Rush is a ruined two-story town-home with mattresses aplenty.

- Sleeping Mattress

[2C.S26] Dead Thugs

- Side Quest: G.I. Blues
- Threat Level: ●●●●●
- Faction: Freeside
  - Entity: Orris
  - Entity: Freeside Thug

If Orris is showing you around Freeside as part of the Side Quest, he reveals his amazing gun-toting prowess and stands proudly over the bodies of four dead thugs. But only three shots were fired.... This is also where you must lead Joana during Side Quest: Bye Bye Love.

[2C.S27] Squatter Camp #3 and Old Ben

- Side Quest: Debt Collector
- Side Quest: Wang Dang Atomic Tango
- Threat Level: ●●●●●
- Faction: Freeside
  - Entity: Old Ben
  - Entity: Lady Jane

- Crafting:
  - Campfire [23/109]
  - Campfire [24/109]

Old Ben usually stands in front of the Securitrons at The Strip gate, and warns you that you require a passport to enter. You can also speak to him at length about his checkered past, and possible future job if a Side Quest is active. Lady Jane usually sits on a bench, refusing to give you any Caps during Side Quest: Debt Collector.

- Campfire [23/109]
- Campfire [24/109]

[2C.S28] Squatter Camp #4

- Threat Level: ●●●●●
- Crafting: Campfire [25/109]

A rarely used Campfire glows close to the glitz of The Strip North Gate.

- Campfire [25/109]

Free Quest: Reach for the Sky, Mister!

Whether you're engaged in Side Quest: I Could Make You Care or not, flag Max down [2C.S12] (Stacey is fleeing so she won't talk to you). You can:

Order Max to give you the gun. He's reluctant to. Try another option.

Tell Max you're a space soldier, and that you need the gun to stop an alien invasion. He gladly gives you the gun, but wants it back.

Or ask to buy the "gun" from Max. He wants 1,000 Caps for it. You can:

Tell him the heavy use has depreciated the value, and give him 20 Caps.

Or give Max 1,000 Caps. Max is amazed, and you might want to rethink your conversation choices.

This weapon looks to be useless, but it certainly isn't, if you conclude the Side Quest with Veronica.

- Unique Weapon: Euclid's C-Finder [14/42]

Free Quest: Rotface's Loose Lips

Local Ghoul gossip Rotface [2C.S15] has a wealth of random information for you, if you pay him a Cap each time. Below are all 30 of his revelations, and what they actually mean:

Rotface revelation	What it means
FREESIDE GOSSIP	
Think twice before hiring a body guard at the gates; they aren't all saints.	He's speaking of Orris, and events at the start of Side Quest: G.I. Blues.
Freeside is run by "a pack of yahoos" called the Kings. Their leader—the King—is trying to prevent an all-out riot in Freeside.	The events set to transpire in Side Quest: G.I. Blues
He saw the King take his robo-dog over to the Old Mormon Fort [2C.01]. The dog was "flipping out."	This refers to Side Quest: Nothin' But a Hound Dog.
Pacer pissed off the Van Graffs big time, and now they want him dead.	A handy fact to know if you're attempting Main Quest: King's Gambit.
The Followers run a place in the Old Mormon Fort, and they're great for healing.	This is the truth.
Mick & Ralph run a store just down the street and sell some unexpected wares.	The store is at Location 2C.02, and speak to Mick about a hidden cache of weapons he sells.
Ralph is no slouch at the keyboard, and has competently reprogrammed in his time.	This is great news if you're wanting a passport.
Apparently, some of the clientele over at the Atomic Wrangler [2C.06] are making strange "escort" requests, including the services of Ghouls.	The events set to transpire in Side Quest: Wang Dang Atomic Tango.
Apparently the Garrets over at the Atomic Wrangler are having a hard time collecting monies owed to them.	This refers to Side Quest: Debt Collector.
At the northwest end of Fremont Street is a place run by the scary Van Graffs, but if lasers are your thing, it's the place to go.	Rotface is referring to the Silver Rush [2C.07].
Mention the NCR in Freeside, and people get on edge. There's talk that they are going to roll over New Vegas.	A possible plan if you ally with the NCR during the Main Quest.
There are two types of folk inside Freeside; those that have lived here all their lives (Locals), and those who came in with the NCR (Squatters). Each blame the other for problems.	Another truism.
There's no life for Squatters in Freeside; those arriving for a better life just got stuck.	True recent history.
Life has been bad for the Squatters, but lately they are a bit more optimistic.	The optimism is due to events in Side Quest: G.I. Blues.

Rotface revelation	What it means
Drugs are everywhere in Freeside, and then affect the lives of those you wouldn't normally expect: Jacob Hoff was a brilliant chemist before he turned to Chems. A King called Pacer is also a fan of a Jet, but it is dangerous for his heart.	These facts are correct, and help slightly during Side Quest: High times and Main Quest: King's Gambit respectively.
THE STRIP GOSSIP	
No one knows the first thing about Mr. House. He just showed up a few years ago. Who the hell is he?	True ancient history.
The Strip is run by three families who owe their allegiance to Mr. House, who told them to ally with him, or leave.	True history.
Those "big metal murder machines" stop anyone from entering The Strip. But if you know the right people, you can get through without being rich.	The Securitrons at the Strip's North Gate [2.13]. The "right people" is the King.
The Chairmen run The Tops Casino [2D.04]. But security is tight, and you can't bring weapons in there.	As described.
The Omertas are one of Mr. House's Three Families, and they run a casino called Gomorrah [2D.01] on the Strip. It lives up to its name and reputation.	As described.
Rumor has it that the White Glove Society was an all-Ghoul gang, which is why they wear those masks.	This is a false myth.
There's a guy on the main drag who sells second-hand adventuring gear. But where does it come from?	Rotface is referring to Mr. Holdout and his inventory of stealth weapons.
MOJAVE WASTELAND GOSSIP	
A passing traveler told everyone there's a "plant paradise" to the west where food is abundant. Some people listened to him, left to find it, and never came back.	Rotface is talking about Vault 22 [1.09].
There's some kind of underground fights going on, pitting beasts against each other. By "underground", he literally means "under the ground."	He's talking about The Thorn [2.04].
The Gun Runners [2.14] sell just about every kind of firearm you could imagine, and some you probably couldn't.	As described.
East of Freeside is a air force base, but no one knows what's inside, as anyone who approaches has been violently blown up.	He's talking about the Boomer territory and Nellis Air Force Base [3.01].
Rotface reckons there's a huge army camped to the east, massing to attack the NCR.	He's talking about The Fort [3.28] and Legate's Camp [3.34]
Traders are griping that the old Interstate 15 is too dangerous. Steer clear of it unless you're armed to the teeth.	He's talking about the area near Sloan [4.08]; Quarry Junction [4.04] where Deathclaws roam.
A town to the south was attacked, and the lack of refugees means the attack was either not so bad, or very, very bad.	Although Nelson was razed, Rotface is likely talking about Nipton [4.30].
The NCR used to run a prison to the southwest, but they don't talk about it any more.	He's referring to the NCR Correctional Facility [5.15].

Free Quest: Flogging a Dead Corpse

A Freeside Thug waves to you from the alleyway [2C.S19], across from Squatter Camp #2. Investigate, and you're shown a corpse between two dumpsters. Speak to the thug, and he makes it clear you're about to join the previous victim. Simply cut these punks down, flee the scene, or let your bodyguard take care of the situation.

Free Quest: Smooth-Talking Criminal

Approach Santiago at Squatter Camp #2 [2C.S20] during Side Quest: Debt Collector, and he insists he's actually a VIP at the Atomic Wrangler. He also tells you he has a super-secret password for Mick & Ralph's to give you discounts. You can:

Ignore this bluster, and obtain the monies owed to Francine Garret.

Pay him 50 Caps for the password.

Or knock him down to 25 Caps.

The code word is "extravaganza." You can visit Mick himself and tell him. He tells you that you're not the first to be ripped off by Santiago. Return to Santiago, and he tells you he's nothing left to give you. You can:

Believe this sob-story, and walk away 50 (or 25) Caps poorer.

Or Pickpocket (or kill and loot) Santiago for the Caps he's still kept.

ZONE 2D: NEW VEGAS STRIP

[2D.01] Gomorrah

- Side Quest: How Little We Know
- Side Quest: Bye Bye Love
- Side Quest: The White Wash
- Free Quest: Big Winner, The Gomorrah
- Free Quest: Razzle Dazzle!
- Free Quest: Playing on the Old Joana
- Threat Level: ●●●●●
- Faction: The Strip / Omertas
  - Entity: Big Sal
  - Entity: Nero
  - Entity: Cachino
  - Entity: Dazzle
  - Entity: Joana
  - Entity: Troike
  - Entity: Clanden
  - Entity: Receptionist
  - Entity: Omerta Thug
  - Entity: Omerta Floor Manager
  - Entity: Gambler
  - Entity: Dancer
- Fame/Infamy
- Services:
  - Gambling: Blackjack [5/15]
  - Gambling: Roulette [6/15]
  - Gambling: Slots [7/15]
  - Healer [11/31]
  - Healer [12/31]
  - Healer [13/31]
- Collectibles:
  - Skill Book [Guns] [1/4] [3/4]
  - Magazine [Barter] [6/16] [11-16/37]
  - Magazine [Crit. Chance] [6/11] [11-16/37]
  - Magazine [Explosives] [5/12] [11-16/37]
  - Magazine [Guns] [6/11] [11-16/37]
  - Magazine [Lockpick] [9/12] [11-16/37]
  - Magazine [Speech] [6/12] [11-16/37]
- Area Is Locked
- Guns and Ammo
- Health, Chems, or Water
- Highly Visible
- Interior Exploration
- Lots O' Caps
- Sleeping Quarters
- Quest Item
- Weapons, Please!

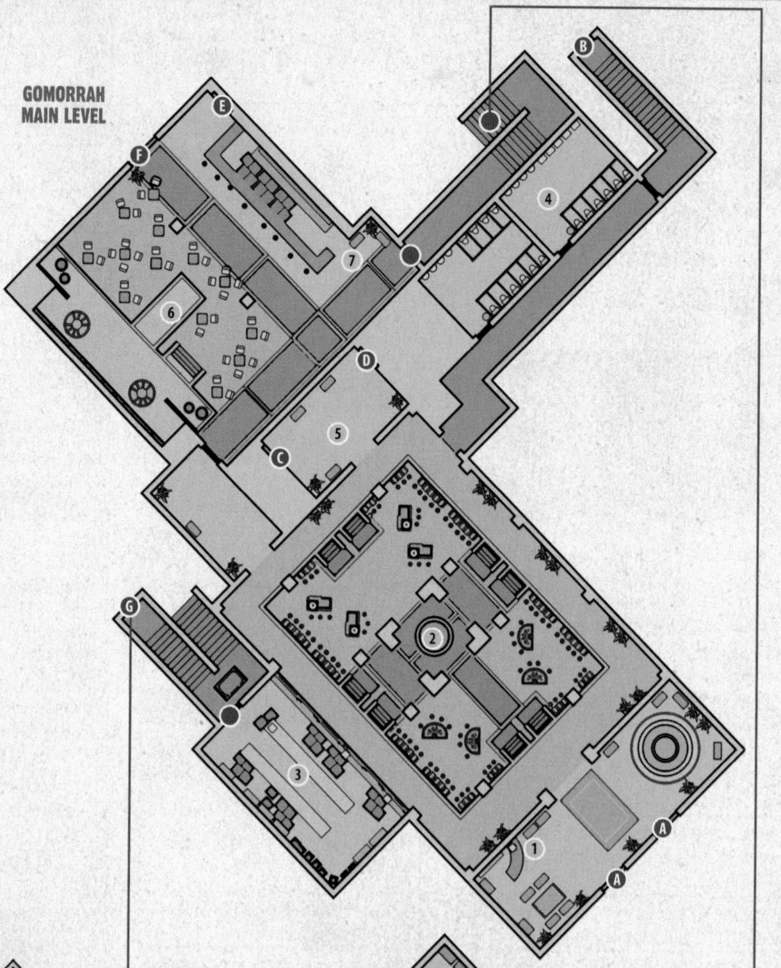

GOMORRAH MAIN LEVEL

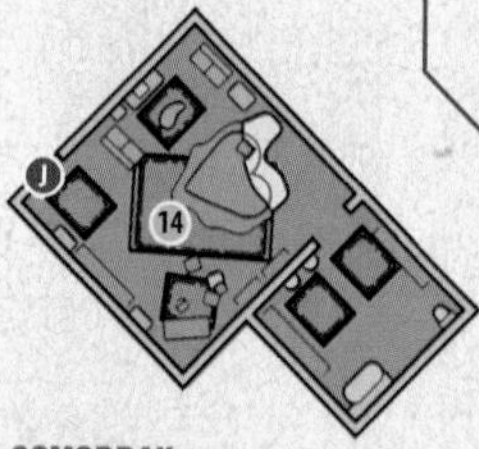

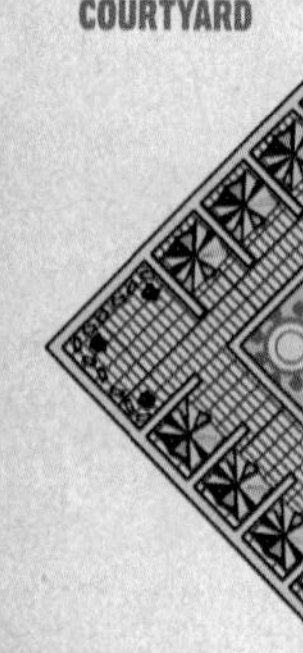

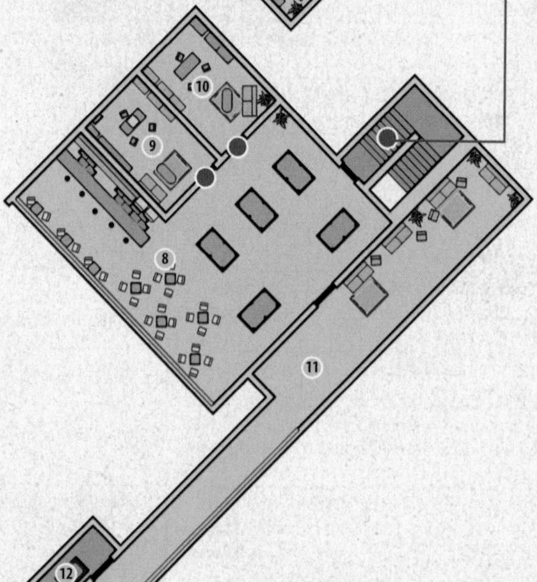

GOMORRAH JOANNA'S ROOM

GOMORRAH LOWER LOBBY

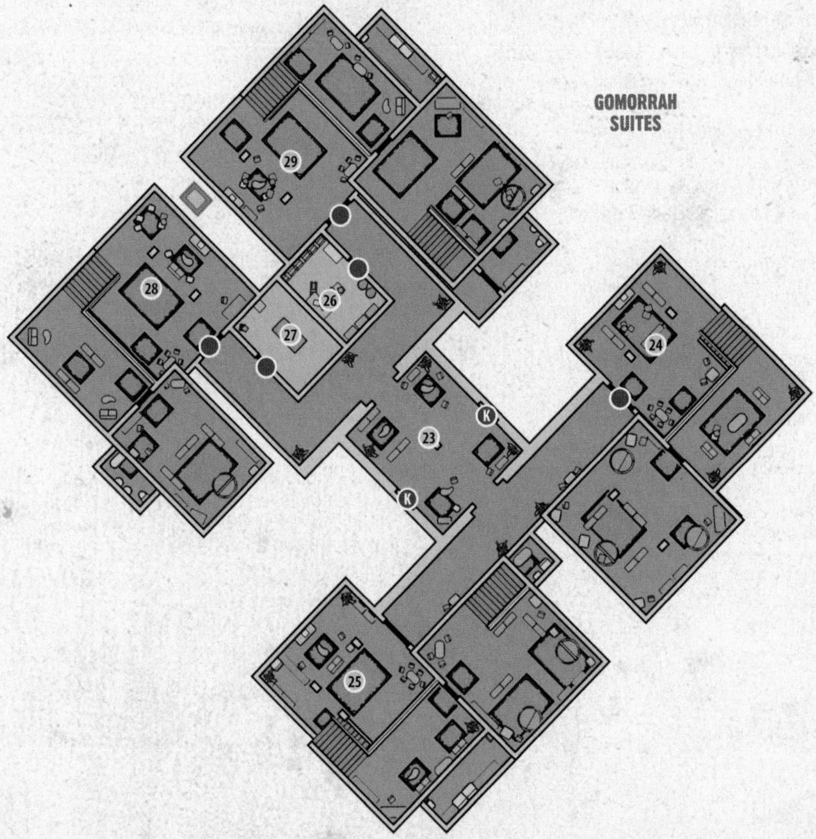

GOMORRAH SUITES

Where The Strip's other casinos are refined, the Gomorrah is rough around the edges, and coarse, as it offers sleazy sex for sale. Top of the attractions list is the sex (any type you want with anyone you want); then the booze and drugs, and finally the Food and Gambling. The casino's entire theme is excessive debauchery. While casino games are available, they are the Omertas' secondary interest. Unlike the Chairmen, the Omertas think little of their clientele and will beat the crap out of them as soon as look at them. Unknown to everyone else on the strip (although Mr. House has some idea), the head of the Gomorrah, Nero, may be orchestrating a racket with unknown parties.

Gomorrah Main Level (Interior)

A Doors (2) to The Strip

1 (Ground) Reception Front Desk

Once inside, an Omerta Greeter immediately asks for your weapons. You can:

Oblige, and hand them over. They are returned once you leave.

Oblige, but keep your holdout weapons.

Refuse twice, and start combat, or leave the hotel.

Afterward, you can ask where your weapons are (in the bank), and what there is to do in the place. A nearby Receptionist is also behind a large curved desk. Ask her about the dirt on the place and she stops herself from telling you. You can:

Tell her you'd love to loosen those lips.

Tell her you can keep secrets.

Or ask about something else. To get her to talk about the Omertas, you must have Side Quest: How Little We Know active.

2 (Ground) Gambling Hall

Surrounding a mystical woman's silhouette are the gambling tables and slot machines where you can pay to play, and try to become a (Free Quest) Big Winner, Gomorrah.

- Gambling: Blackjack (Dealer must hit soft 17s) [5/15]
- Gambling: Roulette [6/15]
- Gambling: Slots [7/15]

3 (Ground) Bank and Cash Room

Talk to the Gomorrah Cashier about exchanging Caps, NCR, or Legion money for increments of up to 1,000 Tops Casino Chips, before you go gambling. If you want an extreme bloodbath and The Strip Reputation ruination, try attacking the cashier and unlocking the Cash Room [Very Hard] from the stairs accessible from the Lower Lobby. Open three safes for some quick cash.

- Gambling: Cashier

4 (Ground) Restrooms (Male and Female)

Pure water can be consumed from the faucets or toilets.

B (Ground) Door to Gomorrah Lower Lobby

5 (Ground) Elevator Bank

There are two elevators, and you can remain where you are, or travel down to the Lower Brimstone (Lower Lobby) level, or up to the Suites.

C D (Ground) Elevator to Lower Brimstone and Suites Levels

6 (Ground) Brimstone

Exotic dancers take the stage in this upscale, yet seedy strip show. Cachino roams this area looking for you, but only during Side Quest: How Little We Know. Ask the bartender for a drink (or information), and there's more alcohol to steal on the back shelves.

- Gambling: Slots [7/15]
- Healer (Drinks and Chems): Bartender [11/31]

7 (Ground and Upper) Zoara Club Entrance

An Omerta Thug stands by this locked door [Average] and won't let you up onto the Pool Room. You can:

Convince him, when the Side Quest is active.

Kick off a fight with him.

Or Pickpocket the key to open the door from him.

- Quest Item: Zoara Club Key

E (Ground) Elevator to Gomorrah Lower Lobby

F (Ground) Doors to Courtyard

8 (Upper) Zoara Club Pool Room

Once you reach this exclusive pool club you can inspect the balcony, sit and watch the stage dancers, and order more drinks (or Chems) from the bar. Steal items from the fridge if you dare.

- Healer (Drinks and Chems): Bartender [12/31]

9 (Upper) Big Sal's Office [Very Hard]

One of the Omerta bosses conducts "interviews" and business from this location, as part of the Side Quest. Big Sal's Terminal [Average] contains the lock disengage for the wall safe [Hard], which has some interesting Holotape information regarding Troike; part of the Side Quest: How Little We Know.

- Skill Book: Guns and Bullets [Guns] [1/4] [3/4]
- Quest Item: Troike Blackmail Note

10 (Upper) Nero's Office [Very Hard]

The other Omerta boss conducts business from here.

11 (Upper) Balcony

You'll find the Omerta Bosses use this to hang out; expect to find either Big Sal or Nero, depending on the time of day. Pickpocket or kill the boss to find the following items, which unlock the terminal and safe in his office:

- Big Sal's Password
- Quest Item: Gomorrah Office Key

12 (Upper and Lower) Stairs to Cash Room

You shouldn't come down here except to face a hostile guard. The stairs end in a door leading to the Lower Lobby.

G (Ground) Door to Gomorrah Lower Lobby

Courtyard

H Door to Gomorrah Main Level

13 (Ground and Upper) Courtyard Grounds

A special area for clients to come and be entertained in the most adult ways possible. The shallow pool has rad-free water to wade through or drink. There are prostitutes you can talk and bargain with. Among the throng of gyrating dancers is a woman named Dazzle. She proves helpful during Side Quest: The White Wash. There's a second dancer, called Joana, who's thrusting in one corner. She has a sad and seedy side of the Omertas' operations, and helps with Side Quest: Bye Bye Love, once she's spilled the beans inside her room.

I (Upper) Door to Joana's Room

Joana's Room

J Door to Courtyard

14 Joana's Room

One of the Omerta's best girls is Joana, and you can visit her boudoir (and attempt to woo her during the Free Quest, or start the Side Quest in here). The place itself has rad-free water, but nothing worth stealing.

- Sleeping Quarters

Gomorrah Lower Lobby

K L Elevators to other floors

15 Lower Brimstone Lobby

This allows access to the main Lower Brimstone, offering more of the same debauchery, as well as access to the exclusive Zoara Club.

16 Lower Brimstone Party Room

M Door to Gomorrah Main Level

17 Lower Brimstone Stage and Bar

Whether you're in the mood for a woman, man, or Ghoul, there's something for everyone. In the middle is a bar with scattered bottles of Beer and spirits to steal.

- Healer (Drinks and Chems): Bartender [13/31]

N Elevator to Gomorrah Main Level

18 19 Zoara Club Entrances

An Omerta Thug stands by either of these locked doors [Average] and won't let you up onto the Zoara. You can:

Convince him, when the Side Quest is active.

Kick off a fight with him.

Or Pickpocket the key to open the door from him.

- Quest Item: Zoara Club Key

O Express Elevator to Suites [Very Hard]

This offers quick access between the Lower Lobby and Suites. Use the Zoara Key to access it.

20 Weapon Storage [Very Hard]

A cache of weapons is hidden in a chamber beyond this blast door, which is easily accessible with a key from Troike. The final plan for the weapons is dependent on your completion of Side Quest: How Little We Know.

- Weapon Footlocker Items (2)

20 21 Zoara Club Upper and Lower Party Rooms

This exclusive club features plush pillows and reclining couches, and a man named Troike, who's integral to Side Quest: How Little We Know. Make sure you come here with an invitation from Cachino or one of the bosses, or the Omerta Thugs turn hostile.

P Door to Gomorrah Main Level

Gomorrah Suites

Q Elevator to other floors

RE Express Elevator to Lower Lobby [Very Hard]

This offers quick access between the Lower Lobby and Suites. Use the Zoara Key to access it.

23 Elevator Lobby

Omerta Thugs patrol this floor, and the elevators, so keep your wits about you if you're Sneaking.

24 (Upper and Lower) Cachino's Suite

Restroom rad-free water is available. Check the desk for a Journal that makes interesting reading as part of Side Quest: How Little We Know.

- Carton of Cigarettes
- Magazine: Milsurp Review [Guns] [6/11] [11/37]
- Sleeping Quarters

25 (Upper and Lower) Clanden's Suite

Restroom rad-free water is available. Clanden himself is usually somewhere in this apartment suite, and you can ask him a number of questions, especially once SIde Quest: How Little We Know is active. There's a hidden wall safe to find behind the cabinets, too, implicating Clanden in the most horrific of crimes.

- Carton of Cigarettes
- Teddy Bear
- Magazine: True Police Stories [Crit. Chance] [6/11] [12/37]
- Sleeping Quarters
- Wall Safe items [Hard]
- Caps (100+)
- Quest Item: Snuff Tapes

26 Storage [Easy]

- Scrap Metal (2)
- Intact Garden Gnome

27 Gomorrah's Secret [Very Hard]

Misadventures in film-making are hard to miss in this tiny room.

- Combat Knife
- Doctor's Bag
- Sexy Sleepwear

28 (Upper and Lower) Big Sal's Suite [Hard]

Restroom rad-free water is available. Big Sal won't take kindly to your snooping, so be careful who sees you enter this place. The boss has a key.

- Magazine: Patriot's Cookbook [Explosives] [5/12] [13/37]
- Quest Item: Gomorrah Office Key
- Sleeping Quarters

29 (Upper and Lower) Nero's Suite [Hard]

Restroom rad-free water is available. Nero will be here if Big Sal is running the casino, and he'll be extremely angry if awakened, so be careful how you move around this place. The boss has a key.

- Magazine: Salesman Weekly [Barter] [6/16] [14/37]
- Magazine: Locksmith's Reader [Lockpick] [9/12] [15/37]
- Magazine: Meeting People [Speech] [6/12] [16/37]
- Carton of Cigarettes (2)
- Footlocker Items
- Bottle Cap (10)
- Quest Item: Gomorrah Office Key
- Sleeping Quarters

Free Quest: Big Winner, The Gomorrah

Need a little gambling with your strip shows? Then learn when to take the Gomorrah for all you can, without being banned from the facility. Locate a Blackjack or Roulette table, or try the Slots, and the Floor Manager comes around to sweet-talk you when your Luck starts to hold:

At 2,250 Chips won, you're awarded a couple of Brahmin Steaks to enjoy now or later.

At 4,500 Chips won, you're given some delicious Mentats.

At 6,750 Chips won, there's an impressive piece of Combat Armor to take.

But once you hit 9,000 Chips won, the Omertas become a little agitated and stop you from fleecing them. However, your Reputation doesn't suffer. What, no comped suite?!

Free Quest: Playing on the Old Joana

Visit the Courtyard, and locate Joana, who is dancing with some patrons. Sidle over to her, and begin some sexy chit-chat.

Tell her you always have what it takes. She likes your witty comebacks.

Reply using double-entendres. She's enthralled, and agrees to "party" with you free of charge. Any other conversation options end with a fee. Once inside her boudoir, you can get it on, or talk to her to begin Side Quest: Bye Bye Love. Conclude this Free Quest with a Well Rested bonus after bedtime frolics!

Free Quest: Razzle Dazzle!

One of the Gomorrah ladies wants to know if you want to party with her by her tent in the Courtyard. All she wants is 100 Caps. You can:

Tell her you girls must stick together and ask for a better deal.

Tell her she's the one getting the deal.

Or party with her and hand over the 100 Caps. Either of the first two options halve the price of admission, so to speak. The Free Quest concludes once the screen fades to black.

[2D.02] Lucky 38 Casino

- Main Quest: For the Republic: Part 2
- Main Quest: Wild Card: A Change in Management
- Main Quest: Wild Card: Finishing Touches
- Main Quest: The House Always Wins, I
- Main Quest: The House Always Wins, II
- Main Quest: The House Always Wins, III
- Main Quest: The House Always Wins, IV
- Main Quest: The House Always Wins, V
- Main Quest: The House Always Wins, VI
- Main Quest: The House Always Wins, VII
- Main Quest: Render Unto Caesar
- Side Quest: The Moon Comes Over the Tower
- Free Quest: The House Has Gone Bust!
- Free Quest: Useless Baubles or Fancy Trinkets?
- Threat Level: ●●●●●
- Faction: The Strip / Mr. House
    - Entity: Mr. House
    - Entity: Victor
    - Entity: Jane
    - Entity: Securitron
- Fame/Infamy
- Crafting: Workbench [13/41]
- Collectibles:
    - Magazine [Critical Chance] [7/11] [17-23/37]
    - Magazine [Energy Weapons] [5/10] [17-23/37]
    - Magazine [Energy Weapons] [6/10] [17-23/37]
    - Magazine [Medicine] [13/19] [17-23/37]
    - Magazine [Medicine] [14/19] [17-23/37]
    - Magazine [Unarmed] [4/11] [17-23/37]
    - Magazine [Unarmed] [5/11] [17-23/37]
    - Snow Globe [3/7]
    - Unique Weapon [16/42]
- Area Is Locked
- Guns and Ammo
- Health, Chems, or Water
- Highly Visible
- Home Sweet Home
- Interior Exploration
- Lots O' Caps
- Sleeping Quarters
- Quest Item

LUCKY 38 BASEMENT

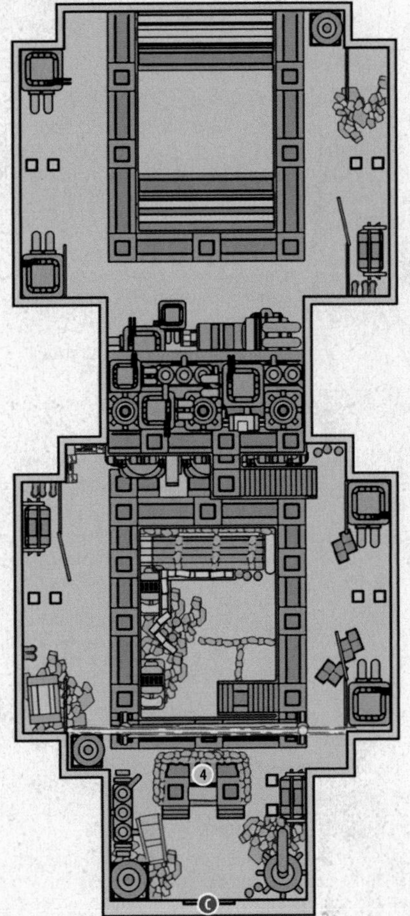

The towering superstructure of the Lucky 38, which has been the base of operations for Mr. House for as long as anyone can remember (even the non-feral Ghouls), the giant monolith seems more like a well-maintained mausoleum of Pre-War Vegas glory once you enter. Though it is not an active casino, it is an enduring monument to Mr. House's vision of Las Vegas: luxury without decadence, refinement without elitism, class without snobbery. This is still the ultimate lure of Vegas: the one that tells anyone that they too could be a winner, just like Mr. House. Even with multiple wings and floors shut off, the rare visitors that enter the premises soon understand that the Lucky 38 is enormous.

This is the most prominent location in the Mojave Wasteland skyline, and should be used to situate yourself when wandering. Waiting outside the foot of the giant tower is Victor, who cheerfully beckons you in the first (and subsequent) times you visit.

Lucky 38 Casino Floor (Interior)

A Doors to New Vegas Strip

1 Casino Floor

This place has been put into a lockdown, and is guarded by Securitrons, by the order of the increasingly reclusive Mr. House. Although there are tables and slots, none are active.

- Rawhide Cowboy Hat
- Carton of Cigarettes (5)
- Sunset Sarsaparilla Bottle (5)

LUCKY 38 PRESIDENTIAL SUITE

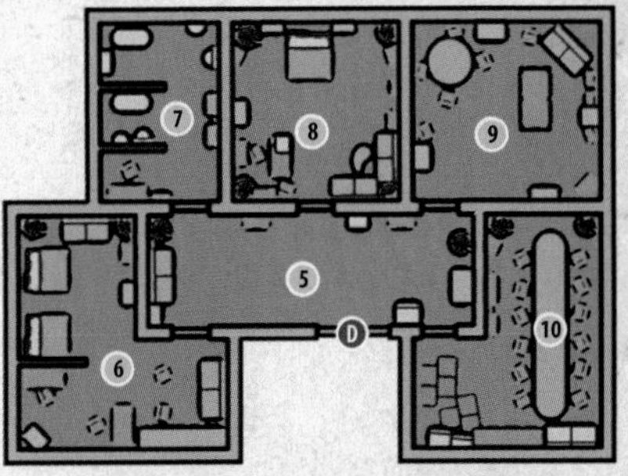

LUCKY 38 CASINO FLOOR

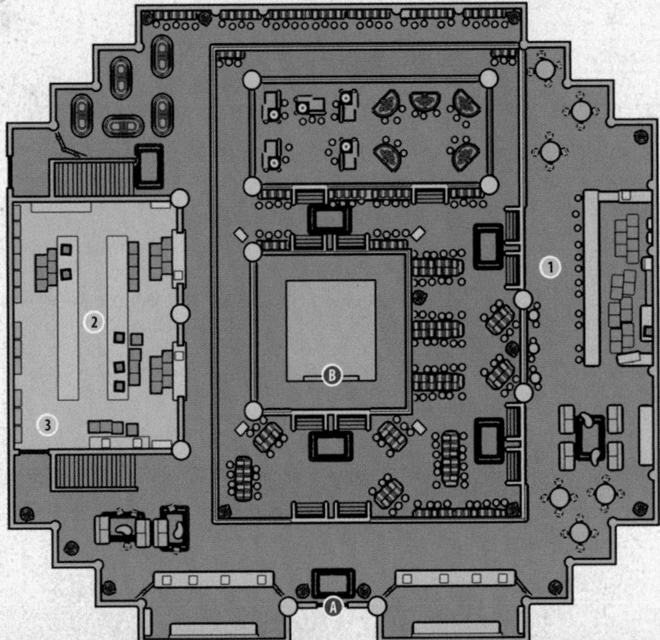

LUCKY 38 COCKTAIL ROOM

LUCKY 38 PENTHOUSE

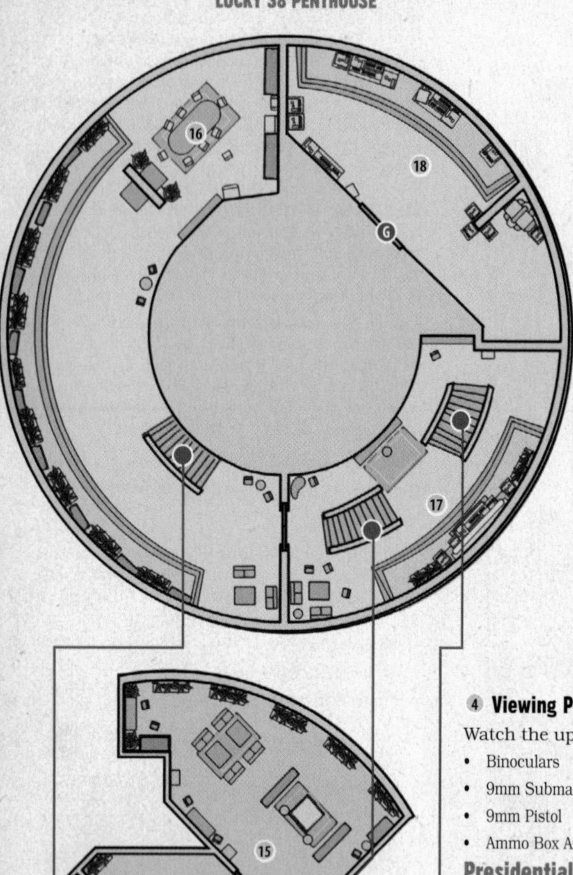

LUCKY 38 CONTROL ROOM

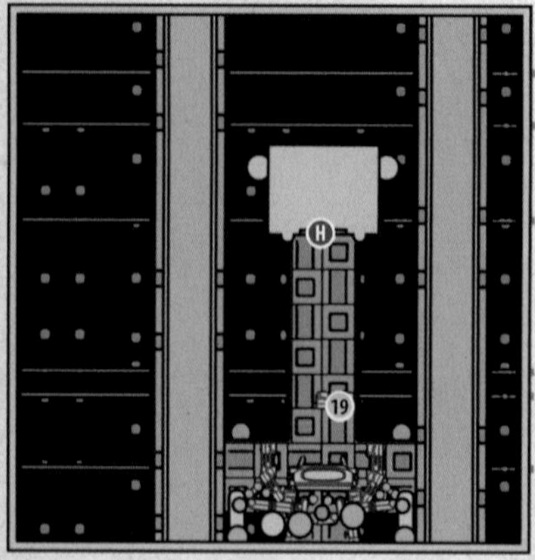

B Lucky 38 Elevator Bank

Victor waits here to chaperone you to the floor of your choice; dependent on your standing with Mr. House, and the progression of Main Quests.

2 Lucky 38 Cashier

- Carton of Cigarettes (6)
- Safe Items (4)

3 Mezzanine Bar

The Access Point Terminal is hacked as part of Side Quest: The Moon Comes Over the Tower. Don't leave without a pair of Golden Gloves, with a commemorative Skill Magazine to grab, too!

- Sunset Sarsaparilla Bottle (8)
- Magazine: Boxing Times [Unarmed] [4/11] [17/37]
- Unique Weapon: Golden Gloves [16/42]

Basement

C Lucky 38 Elevator Bank

This Securitron area and Lucky 38's reactor can be visited only once during the Main Quest, when either Mr. House or Yes Man commands it.

4 Viewing Platform

Watch the upgrade of the Securitrons here.

- Binoculars
- 9mm Submachine Gun
- 9mm Pistol
- Ammo Box Ammunition

Presidential Suite

D Lucky 38 Elevator Bank

This swanky home becomes accessible only after Mr. House grants you access to it during the Main Quest, usually after the end of Main Quest: You'll Know it When it Happens.

5 Suite Lobby

Victor stands by the elevators to ensure you visit the correct floors. Check the wall terminal, and you can thoroughly upgrade this pad, assuming you have the funds. Here's what's on offer (all of it usually comes to around 1210 Caps):

Furniture or Item	Effect
Crafting Locker 1	Store crafted items inside this.
Crafting Locker 2	Store crafted items inside this.
Fridge	Store Food, Drink, and Chems inside this.
Guest Wardrobe 1	Store outfits inside this.
Guest Wardrobe 2	Store outfits inside this.
Master Wardrobe 1	Store outfits inside this.
Master Wardrobe 2	Store outfits inside this.
SS Vending Machine	Obtain Sunset Sarsaparilla Bottles (and a chance of a Star Cap).
Weapon Trunk 1	Store Weapons inside this.
Weapon Trunk 2	Store Weapons inside this.
Workbench [13/41]	Use as directed.

The rest of the Tour of this floor presupposes you've purchased these items.

6 Office and Guest Bedroom

- Guest Wardrobe Items (2)
- Sleeping Quarters
- Basketball

7 Bathroom

If you require Rad-free water, sip from the sinks in here.

- Bobby Pins
- Magazine: Today's Physician [Medicine] [13/19] [18/37]

8 Master Bedroom

Sleep on your own personal, and rather lavish bed.

- Master Wardrobe Items (2)
- Weapons Truck 1 Items
- Magazine: Today's Physician [Medicine] [14/19] [19/37]
- Your Sleeping Quarters

9 Games Room

Take from the Vending Machine, and also place all the Snow Globes you've collected, and not sold, on this plinth (as shown).

- Pool Cue (6)
- Teddy Bear
- Magazine: Future Weapons Today [Energy Weapons] [5/10] [20/37]
- Snow Globe Plinth
- Vending Machine Items

10 Dining Room

There's a small amount of Food here, and items inside the fridges. In one corner is a Workbench you purchased.

- Carton of Cigarettes (4)
- Crafting Locker Items (2)
- Workbench [13/41]

Lucky 38 Cocktail Lounge

E Lucky 38 Elevator Bank

This floor, which is directly under Mr. House's Penthouse, becomes accessible once Mr. House grants you access to it during the Main Quest, usually after the end of Main Quest: You'll Know it When it Happens.

11 12 13 14 Lounge Floor

Mr. House has sealed off this area. There's a floor safe to open [11], which usually has an impressive weapon inside. Check a couple of the tables [12, 13] for Magazines, and a locked Briefcase [Hard] with random items (one of which could be another Magazine). Finally, be sure to find the Snow Globe [14]!

- Cash Register Items
- Floor Safe Items [Average]
- Suitcase Items [Hard]
- Magazine: True Police Stories [Crit. Chance] [7/11] [21/37]
- Magazine: Future Weapons Today [Energy Weapons] [6/10] [22/37]
- Magazine: Boxing Times [Unarmed] [5/11] [23/37]
- Snow Globe—"Test Site" [3/7]

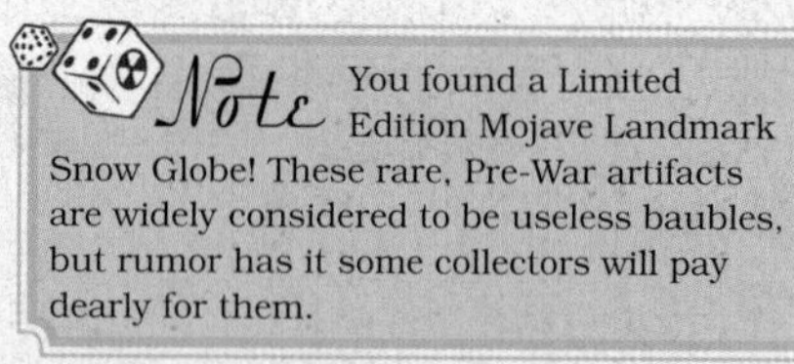

Note: You found a Limited Edition Mojave Landmark Snow Globe! These rare, Pre-War artifacts are widely considered to be useless baubles, but rumor has it some collectors will pay dearly for them.

Lucky 38: Mr. House's Penthouse

F Lucky 38 Elevator Bank

You're on top of the world, and at the top of the Lucky 38 tower.

15 (Upper) Mr. House's Bedroom and Living Room

Mr. House doesn't seem to be about, and the Protectrons aren't active, so you can sleep here, and take what you need. You also may find a Vault 3 Jumpsuit in one of the dressers.

- Carton of Cigarettes (3)
- Sleeping Quarters

16 (Lower) Mr. House's Dining Room and Kitchen

17 (Upper and Lower) Mr. House's Command and Control

Aside from the huge collection of Pre-War Books, Mr. House has a number of Securitrons acting as guards and companions. Meet and speak with Jane; she keeps Mr. House "entertained." You can ask her about New Vegas, and her master. Don't forget to compliment her on their new looks once you upgrade the Securitrons over at The Fort [3.28] as part of Main Quest: The House Always Wins, II. You can also bring her Snow Globes, as part of Free Quest: Useless Baubles or Fancy Trinkets.

The gigantic screen and computers are where Mr. House speaks with you during multiple Main Quests (The House Always Wins Quests). It is also the location where you can speak with Yes Man if you decide to ally with him (Wild Card Quests). Under the stairs to the left of the computer bank is a wall terminal [Hard]. Access this, and you can open a hidden door.

18 (Lower) Mr. House's Control Room Security Override

Dash into this room if you're being attacked; a Security Terminal shuts down the offensive posture of the Securitrons.

G (Lower) Elevator to Lucky 38 Control Room [Hard]

Access the wall terminal, and you can unlock the elevator doors, and ride the elevator down.

Lucky 38 Control Room

H Lucky 38 Elevator to Penthouse

19 Gantryway and LS Chamber

This chilling chamber has a large stasis device at one end, and an "LS chamber." You might want to investigate further. The klaxons that are sounding suggest you might be in trouble if you do; see Free Quest: The House Has Gone Bust!.

Free Quest: The House Has Gone Bust!

Technically a Side Quest message in your Pip-Boy, this Free Quest occurs if you decide to shut down Mr. House once and for all; and achieve this epoch-making event! This occurs during the Main Quest if you seek an Independent Vegas, or at the whim of the Faction you're allied with. Naturally, this never occurs if you're Mr. House's right-hand man or woman.

Free Quest: Useless Baubles or Fancy Trinkets?

Collecting Snow Globes, of which there are seven scattered throughout the Mojave Wasteland, is not only fun, but can win you copious Caps from Mr. House if you sell them to his "friend" Jane. Simply locate a Snow Globe (the Appendices chapter of this guide lists all seven), and exchange them for 2,000 Caps per globe.

[2D.03] Vegas Boulevard Station

- Threat Level: ●●●●○
- Faction: NCR
  - Entity: NCR Trooper
  - Entity: Securitron Mk I
- Fame/Infamy
- Area Is Locked
- Health, Chems, or Water
- Interior Exploration
- Underground Connection

The LVB, or Las Vegas Boulevard Station offers a monorail service between here and Camp McCarran [2.19]. This is mainly for the benefit of NCR citizens and military.

A Doors to The Strip

1 Processing Office

A Securitron Mk I is here to make sure you don't loiter (and to maintain a tense, but professional relationship with the NCR). Head further in and an NCR Trooper warns you that most weapons are banned by Mr. House when entering casinos.

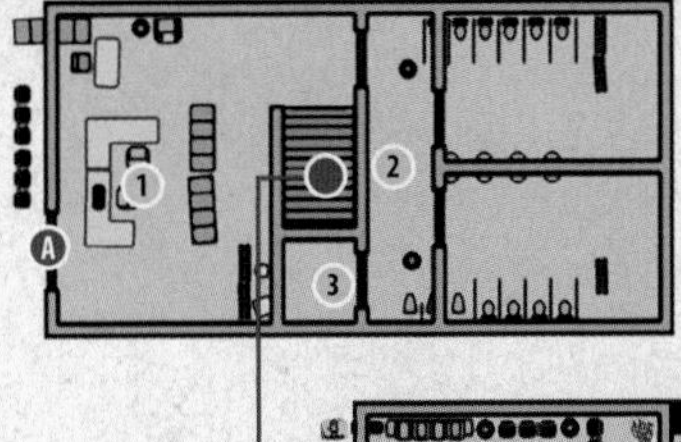

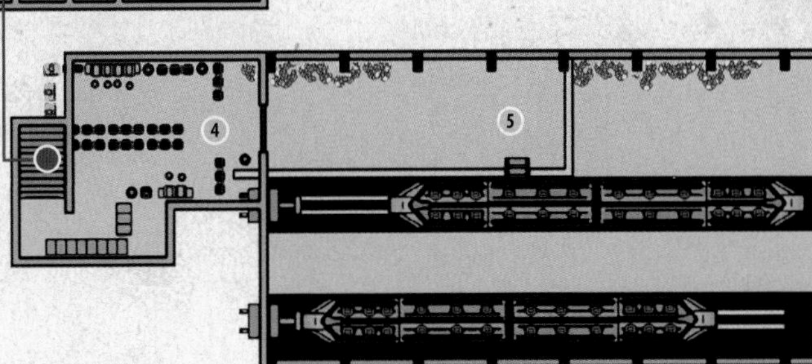

You can also speak to the Trooper about the Casinos, and other fun times to be had on The Strip, if it's your first time here.

2 Restrooms

Both these rooms have water you can drink, from sinks (or toilets or urinals) without radiation.

3 Storage

Unless you're collecting Plungers, there's no items of worth in here.

4 Departure Lounge

You must have a Reputation that is "Liked" or higher for the Troopers to let you through. Otherwise, prepare for a fight!

Tip Or, you can wait until the shift change at 6 PM, and Sneak through to board the monorail. Or, dress as an NCR Trooper, and hope you're not spotted. Either can get you to and from The Strip (without being stopped by Securitrons at The Strip North Gate [2.13], at the risk of being discovered.

5 Monorail Station

Board the monorail, and ride it south to the Camp McCarran Terminal Building. If you're being shot at by NCR Troopers, expect the alarm to be raised when you reach McCarran, too!

[2D.04] The Tops Casino

See maps on the following page

- Main Quest: They Went That-A-Way
- Main Quest: Wild Card: A Change in Management
- Main Quest: Wild Card: You and What Army?
- Main Quest: Wild Card: Side Bets
- Side Quest: Talent Pool
- Free Quest: Big Winner, The Tops
- Threat Level: ●●●●○
- Faction: The Strip / Chairmen
  - Entity: Benny
  - Entity: Yes Man
  - Entity: Swank
  - Entity: Tommy Torini
  - Entity: Chairman Greeter
  - Entity: Chairman
  - Entity: Chairman Bodyguard
  - Entity: Chairman Floor Manager
  - Entity: The Tops Cashier
  - Entity: Gambler
  - Entity: Rad Pack Dancer
- Fame/Infamy
- Services:
  - Gambling: Blackjack [8/15]
  - Gambling: Roulette [9/15]
  - Gambling: Slots [10/15]
  - Healer [14/31]
  - Healer [15/31]
- Collectibles:
  - Skill Book [Unarmed] [1/4] [4/4]
  - Magazine [Barter] [7/16] [24-33/37]
  - Magazine [Barter] [8/16] [24-33/37]
  - Magazine [Critical Chance] [8/11] [24-33/37]
  - Magazine [Lockpick] [10/12] [24-33/37]
  - Magazine [Melee Weapon] [5/9] [24-33/37]
  - Magazine [Melee Weapon] [6/9] [24-33/37]
  - Magazine [Science] [10/23] [24-33/37]
  - Magazine [Speech] [7/12] [24-33/37]
  - Magazine [Survival] [10/30] [24-33/37]
  - Magazine [Survival] [11/30] [24-33/37]
  - Unique Item [30/95]
  - Unique Item [31/95]
  - Unique Item [32/95]
  - Unique Item [33/95]
  - Unique Item [34/95]
  - Unique Item [35/95]
  - Unique Weapon: [17/42]
- Area Is Locked
- Health, Chems, or Water
- Highly Visible
- Home Sweet Home
- Interior Exploration
- Lots O' Caps
- Sleeping Quarters
- Quest Item
- No Weapons, Please!

The Tops offers a classic Vegas experience, with cool, hip, fun, and macho posturing to entice those with a sense of style. This is a place for manly men with a dame on each arm; here to see the Rad Pack as they perform their routine "The Four Taps" over at the Ace Theater. Choose a fine wine, order the Brahmin steak rare, and have a good time, baby! The place is run by The Chairmen, who talk tough, but most of them don't take things too seriously; they're just too cool and laid back to let anything get to them. Well, all but one of them....

The Tops Casino Main Floor (Interior)

A Doors (8) to The Strip

1 (Ground) Reception Front Desk

Once inside, a Chairman Greeter immediately asks for your weapons. You can:

Oblige, and hand them over. They are returned once you leave.

Oblige, but keep your holdout weapons.

Refuse twice, and start combat, or leave the hotel.

Afterward, you can ask where your weapons are (in the bank), and what there is to do in the place.

Swank is also behind the large curved reception desk. You can tell him some shocking stories about Benny (and obtain a Key), as part of Main Quest: Ring-a-Ding Ding!, or ask about Vegas, every major Faction, the Strip, or the Tops itself.

- Quest Item: Benny's Suite Key

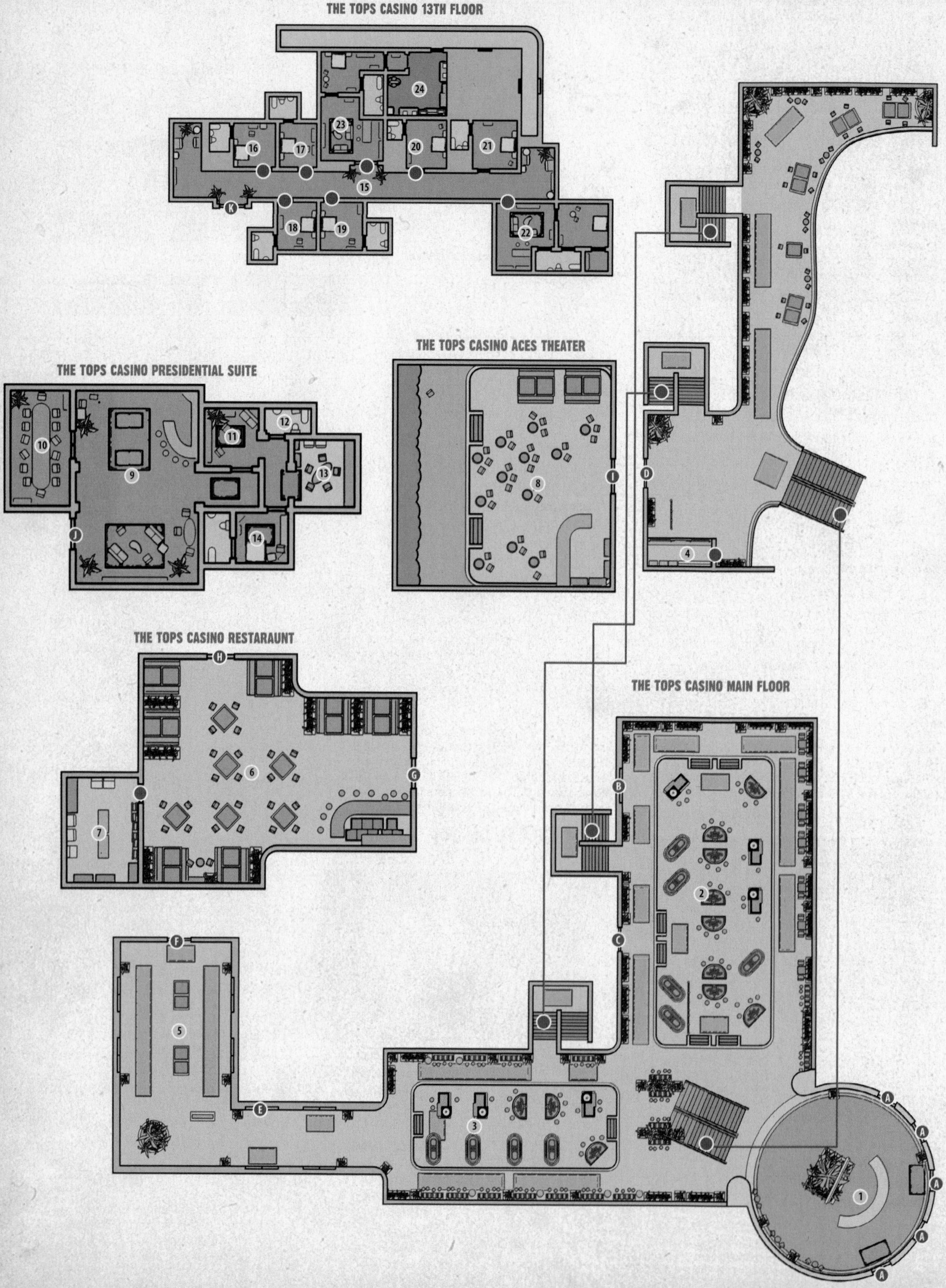
THE TOPS CASINO 13TH FLOOR
24
23
16
17
20
21
15
K
18
19
22
THE TOPS CASINO ACES THEATER
8
I
D
4
THE TOPS CASINO PRESIDENTIAL SUITE
10
9
11
12
13
14
J
THE TOPS CASINO RESTARAUNT
H
6
G
7
THE TOPS CASINO MAIN FLOOR
B
2
C
F
5
E
3
1
A
A
A
A
A
A

2 (Ground and Upper) Gambling Hall (North) and Mezzanine Balcony

The giant northern wing of the casino has a multitude of gambling tables and slot machines to play on. Once you've visited the cashier, you can begin gambling, and possibly begin Free Quest: Big Winner, The Tops. Benny is also usually found in this area. There's also a Floor Manager, Chairmen, and a Bodyguard keeping a look-out for sharks.

- Gambling: Blackjack (Dealer must draw to 16, and stand on all 17s) [8/15]
- Gambling: Roulette [9/15]
- Gambling: Slots [10/15]
- Magazine: Tæles of Chivalrie [Melee Weapons] [5/9] [24/37]

B Elevator to The Tops Presidential Suite

C Door to The Tops Restaurant

3 (Ground) Gambling Hall (West)

A slightly more intimate setting, without the roulette.

- Gambling: Blackjack (Dealer must draw to 16, and stand on all 17s) [8/15]
- Gambling: Slots [10/15]

4 (Upper) Bank [Very Hard]

Speak to The Tops Cashier about exchanging Caps, NCR, or Legion money for increments of up to 1,000 Tops Casino Chips, before you go gambling. If you want an extreme bloodbath and The Strip Reputation ruination, try attacking the cashier and unlocking the metal door [Very Hard], and opening three lockers [Hard], for some quick cash.

- Gambling: Cashier

D (Upper) Door to The Aces Theater

E (Ground) Elevator to 13th Floor

You can access this (and only this) elevator as part of Main Quest: Ring-a-Ding Ding! You need a key (from Swank, for example).

5 Elevator Bank [Out of Order]

This offers access to the exterior courtyard.

F Door to Courtyard

[Not on Map] Courtyard

This closed-in exterior location offers views of the Lucky 38 Tower, a swimming pool of rad-free water, and access between The Tops Restaurant and the Casino Main Floor.

The Tops Restaurant

G Door to The Tops Casino Main Floor

6 (Ground) Restaurant and Bar

This place is spotless, and has a few slot machines around the bar, where you can purchase a beverage or two.

- Healer (Drinks): Bartender [14/31]
- Gambling: Slots [10/15]

7 (Ground) Kitchen [Average]

Pick the lock (this won't cause problems unless you're blatant), and inspect the kitchen for Food in the fridge, and well-stocked shelves:

- Alcohol and Food
- Purified Water (15)
- Unique Item: Nuka-Cola Quartz [30/95]
- Unique Item: Nuka-Cola Quartz [31/95]
- Unique Item: Nuka-Cola Quartz [32/95]
- Unique Item: Nuka-Cola Quartz [33/95]
- Unique Item: Nuka-Cola Quartz [34/95]

H Door to Courtyard

The Aces Theater

I Door to The Tops Casino Main Floor

8 Theater Hall

Head in here at around 6:00 PM for a Rad Pack performance on stage, and then speak to Tommy Torini about the theater, and perhaps finding some acts for it; which begins Side Quest: Talent Pool. You can also order a cocktail or Vodka over at the Theater bar, too.

- Healer (Drinks): Bartender [15/31]
- Quest Item: Tommy Torini's Business Card (4)

The Tops Presidential Suite

J Door to The Tops Casino Main Floor

This elevator is only accessible with the Presidential Suite Key, which is given out during Main Quest: Ring-a-Ding Ding by Benny under certain circumstances.

9 Foyer

Sometimes, Benny is here (or you can talk to him over the Intercom) as part of the Main Quest.

- Wine, Alcohol, and Fruit
- Carton of Cigarettes
- Skill Book: Pugilism Illustrated [Unarmed] [1/4] [4/4]
- Magazine: Meeting People [Speech] [7/12] [25/37]
- Pool Cue (2)
- Wall Safe Items [Average]

10 Conference Room

- Food

11 Lounge

- Alcohol

12 Bathroom

Rad-free water is available to drink here.

13 Kitchen

There's Food in the fridge, and water to drink from a wall sink.

- Carton of Cigarettes
- Magazine: Tæles of Chivalrie [Melee Weapons] [6/9] [26/37]
- Cap (10)

14 Bedroom and Ensuite

A comfy bed and an ensuite bathroom with all the non-irradiated toilet water you can drink. Ain't life grand?

- Magazine: True Police Stories [Crit. Chance] [8/11] [27/37]
- Sleeping Quarters

The Tops 13th Floor

K Door to The Tops Casino Main Floor

This elevator is only accessible with Benny's Room Key, given during Main Quest: Ring-a-Ding Ding.

15 Main Corridor

Steal from the Vending Machines at the far east and west ends, along with water fountains with pure water to sip.

16 Room #1301 [Average]

Break and enter this room for some rad-free bathroom water, dressers and wardrobes to search, and a Strip Letter.

- Note: Strip Letter 6: Mark tells Tracy he's on to a winner at roulette.
- Magazine: Salesman Weekly [Barter] [7/16] [28/37]
- Sleeping Quarters

17 18 19 20 21 Rooms #1302, #1304, #1305, #1306, #1307 [Average]

Jimmy the lock to an almost identical room, but without a Strip Letter. Room #1307 is used by the Chairmen, who don't mind you checking the place out, if your Reputation is okay. Room #1305 has a Magazine.

- Magazine: Programmer's Digest [Science] [10/23] [29/37]
- Sleeping Quarters

22 High Roller's Suite

This is only opened using the key you're awarded as part of Free Quest: Big Winner, The Tops. Check the fireplace mantle for some goods.

- Carton of Cigarettes
- Magazine: Lad's Life [Survival] [10/30] [30/37]
- Home Sweet Home
- Sleeping Quarters

23 Benny's Suite

You may access this using a key that's available during various Main Quests. If you've invited Benny to bed, you can kill him or let him live here (or grab his Unique suit).

- Carton of Cigarettes
- Magazine: Salesman Weekly [Barter] [8/16] [31/37]
- Locksmith's Reader [Lockpick] [10/12] [32/37]
- Magazine: Lad's Life [Survival] [11/30] [33/37]
- Unique Item: Benny's Suit [35/95]
- Unique Weapon: Maria [17/42]
- Sleeping Quarters

24 Yes Man's Chamber

Through the door at the back of the bedroom is a chamber with a strange Securitron called Yes Man. This friendly face is programmed to follow orders without question, and you can become firm allies, and begin the Wild Card Alliance route and associated Main Quests.

Free Quest: Big Winner, The Tops

Like to gamble? Then learn the difference between becoming a firm friend of the Chairmen, and outstaying your welcome. Sidle up to a blackjack table, spin a little roulette, or sit down for some slots, and the floor manager comes around to congratulate you as soon as your winnings start to pile up.

At 2,000 Chips won, you're given a free Vodka (which you can keep for later).

At 5,000 Chips won, you're handed a nice Brahmin Steak (which can be pocketed for afterward).

At 7,500 Chips won, you're comped the High Roller's Suite Key, which opens Location #22. You can stay there as long as you wish, but the place is closed once you leave The Strip.

At 10,000 Chips won, the Chairmen change their tone, and ban you from gambling (although your Reputation doesn't suffer). They just can't take these losses!

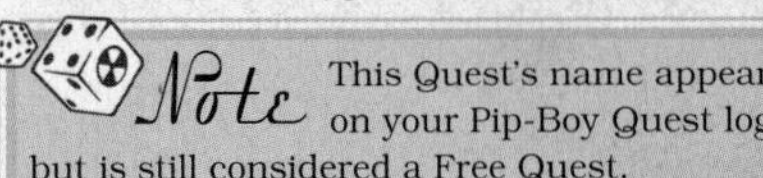

This Quest's name appears on your Pip-Boy Quest log, but is still considered a Free Quest.

[2D.05] Ultra-Luxe Casino

See maps on the following page

- Main Quest: Render Unto Caesar
- Side Quest: Beyond the Beef
- Side Quest: How Little We Know
- Side Quest: Pheeble Will
- Free Quest: Big Winner, Ultra-Luxe
- Threat Level:
- Faction: The Strip / White Glove Society
  - Entity: Mortimer
  - Entity: Marjorie
  - Entity: Philippe
  - Entity: Chauncey
  - Entity: Heck Gunderson
  - Entity: Ted Gunderson
  - Entity: White Glove Greeter
  - Entity: White Glove
  - Entity: White Glove Bodyguard
  - Entity: White Glove Floor Manager
  - Entity: Ultra-Luxe Cashier
  - Entity: Gambler

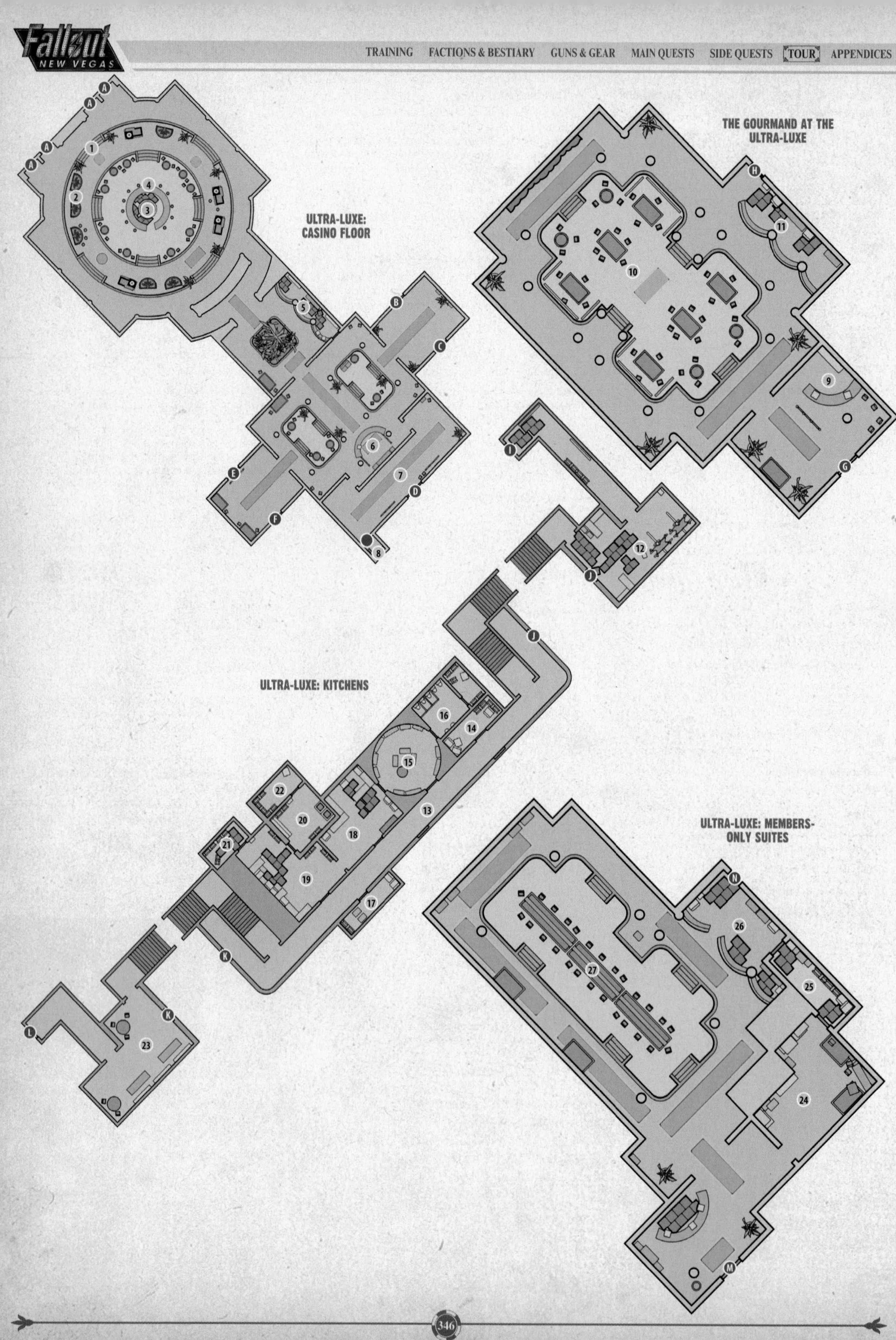
ULTRA-LUXE: CASINO FLOOR
THE GOURMAND AT THE ULTRA-LUXE
ULTRA-LUXE: KITCHENS
ULTRA-LUXE: MEMBERS-ONLY SUITES

ULTRA-LUXE: BATHHOUSE

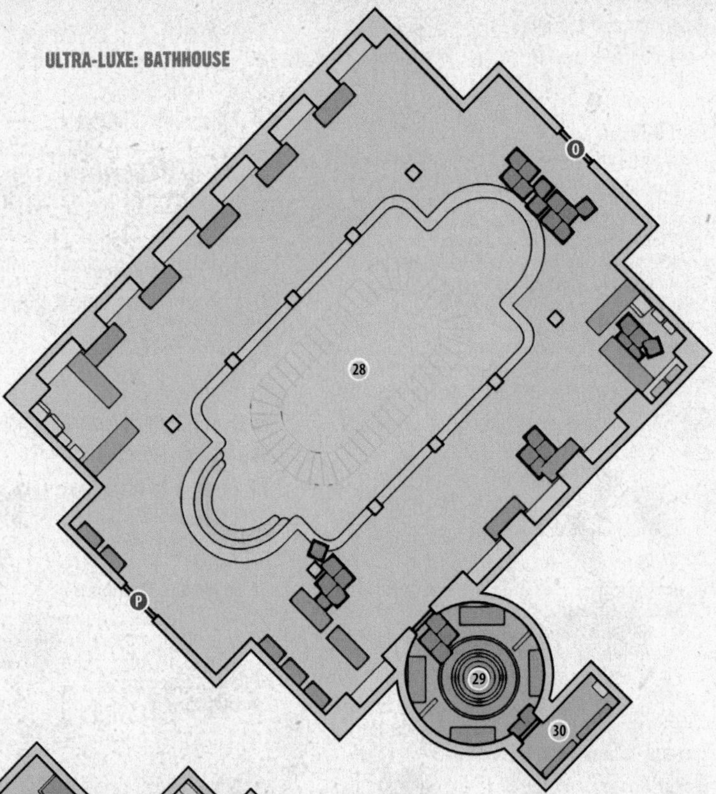

ULTRA-LUXE: HOTEL ROOMS

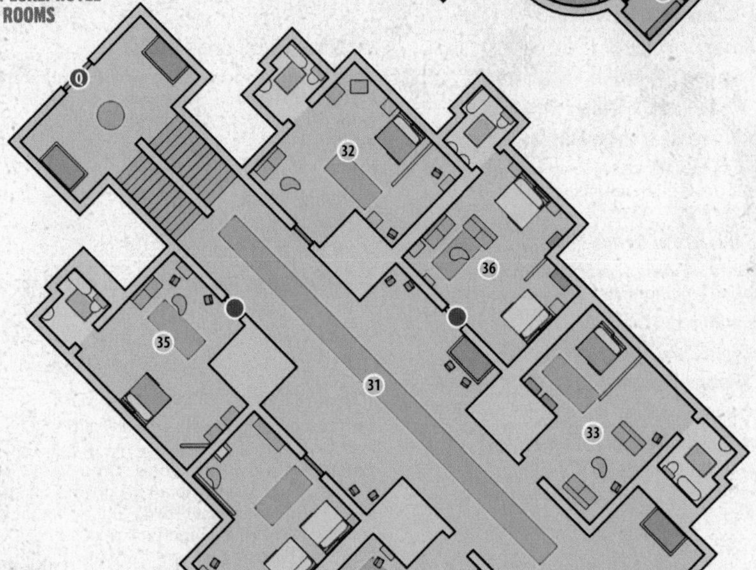

ULTRA-LUXE: PENTHOUSE SUITE

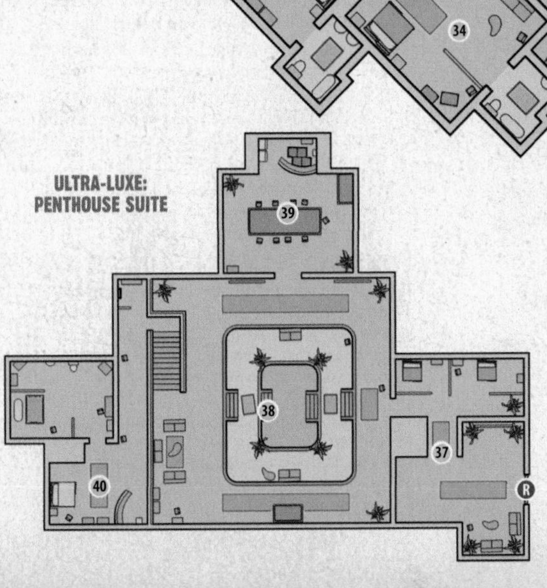

- Fame/Infamy
- Services:
  - Gambling: BlackJack [11/15]
  - Gambling: Roulette [12/15]
  - Healer [16/31]
  - Healer [17/31]
- Collectibles:
  - Unique Item [36/95]
- Area Is Locked
- Guns and Ammo
- Health, Chems, or Water
- Highly Visible
- Home Sweet Home
- Interior Exploration
- Lots O' Caps
- Perk!
- Radio Signal [Ultra-Luxe]
- Sleeping Quarters
- Quest Item
- Weapons, Please!

The Ultra-Luxe is an establishment of incredible refinement that delicately conceals its operators' more questionable tendencies. Run by the Sawneys, the Ultra-Luxe pampers its clients and provides The Strip's most elite casino experience. A dress code is strictly enforced. All of the staff and family members are well-dressed, well-spoken, and well-behaved. The casino's prime attractions are its meat-oriented restaurant, The Gourmand, its cocktail lounge, Top Shelf, and its art gallery. Roulette and blackjack are the only games offered.

Ultra-Luxe Casino Floor (Interior)

A Doors (4) to The Strip

1 Ultra-Luxe Grand Entrance

Once inside this pristine, circular lobby, a White Glove Greeter politely requests that you remove all weaponry before entering. You can:

Agree, or ask why he needs your guns. They are kept in the Bank until you leave.

Keep your holdout weapons, and agree.

Or face him down and start a war with the White Glove Society, which isn't helpful for your good Reputation.

2 Gambling Steps

Once inside, the stepped surrounding has roulette and blackjack tables to play on, and start Free Quest: Big Winner, Ultra-Luxe. What are you, a Philistine? There are no slots in here!

- Gambling: Blackjack (Dealer must draw to 16, and stand on all 17s) [11/15]
- Gambling: Roulette [12/15]

3 The Top Shelf

The circular bar with the leaf motif is called the Top Shelf. Speak to the bartender; this is a good spot for (an overpriced) drink. You can also buy a fancy (and Melee Weapon friendly) Dress Cane here, too. Otherwise, there's only a couple of Sarasaparilla Bottles to steal.

- Healer (Drinks): Bartender [16/31]

4 Heck Gunderson and Company

Propping up the bar with his shotgun-toting hired hand is a rancher named Heck Gunderson. Speak to him at length about his troubles.

5 Bank [Very Hard]

Speak to The Ultra-Luxe Cashier about exchanging Caps, NCR, or Legion money for increments of up to 1,000 Tops Casino Chips, before you go gambling. If you want to ruin your standing with the White Gloves and risk The Strip Reputation, try attacking the cashier and unlocking the metal door [Very Hard], and opening safe and floor safe [Average], for some quick cash.

- Gambling: Cashier

6 Concierge and Guest Services

Mortimer waits here in his finery, and is happy to extol the virtues of this establishment, and its delicious meats. He has a number of (mainly Quest-related) keys you can steal:

- Quest Item: Ultra-Luxe Freezer Key
- Quest Item: Ultra-Luxe Kitchen Key
- Quest Item: Ultra-Luxe Penthouse Key

7 Rear Hallway

This allows access to the Penthouse, and Chauncey is here. He's not like the other White Gloves; he's forgotten his mask, and doesn't have the same, eerie way about him.

8 Rear Storage [Easy]

Among this detritus is a Container of Chlorine; a vital ingredient if you're helping the Omertas during Side Quest: How Little We Know.

- Quest Item: Container of Chlorine

B Door to The Gourmand at the Ultra-Luxe

C Door to Ultra-Luxe Bathhouse

D Elevator to Ultra-Luxe Penthouse [Hard]

You must have an appropriate key (as part of Side Quest: Beyond the Beef), or unlock the elevator manually.

E Door to White Glove Members Only Section

You must become sponsored by the White Gloves as part of Side Quest: Beyond the Beef to access this area, use Marjorie's key, or Sneak in via the Kitchen.

F Door to Ultra-Luxe Hotel Rooms

The Gourmand at the Ultra-Luxe

G Doors to Ultra-Luxe Casino Floor

9 Gourmand Entrance

Marjorie works here at the front desk, but she's much more than a slightly snooty greeter; speak to her when Side Quest: Beyond the Beef is active for much more conversation topics. She also has a Key on her (which you can Pickpocket); useful for getting into the Members-Only area of this place (Door #E).

- Quest Item: White Glove Society Members Key

10 Gourmand Floor

The patrons are enthusing about Chef Philippe's cooking. This location plays an important role during Side Quest: Beyond the Beef.

11 Gourmand Refreshment Dispensary

The bar is well-stocked, and the Gourmand Food Supplier is happy to provide you with a meal (once you pay him!).

- Healer (Food): Gourmand Food Supplier [17/31]

H Door to Ultra-Luxe Kitchen [Easy]

Unless you've made plans with Mortimer, you must pick this lock to reach the kitchens. Stay Hidden, or lose Reputation.

Ultra-Luxe Kitchen

I Doors to The Gourmand at the Ultra-Luxe

12 Brahmin Flambéing Room

The Brahmin meat gets a good roasting here, and infected portions are cut out. There's pure water to drink from the sinks here.

- Infected Brahmin Meat (6)
- Sunset Sarsaparilla Crate (3)
- Knife

J Elevator to and from Ultra-Luxe Kitchen

13 Kitchen Corridor

This lengthy and narrow corridor stretches past all the major rooms, and a White Glove usually stops you here to ask what you're doing. You can:

Lie and tell him the water main has burst and you're here to check for damage.

Tell him you're passing through, and he forces you out with his cane drawn. Attack or leave.

Attack him to suffer a Reputation hit.

14 Storage

- Sunset Sarsaparilla Bottle

15 Wine Cellar

There's a bottle on the small table, but only if Side Quest: Beyond the Beef is active. Use the intercom on the wall for this Quest, too.

- Wine (25)

16 Restroom and Storage

This place is spotless. Drink rad-free water here without worry.

- First Aid Box

17 Staff Storage

- Sunset Sarsaparilla Bottle
- Sunset Sarsaparilla Crate

18 19 Kitchens

These are two connected rooms (also connected to the Wine Cellar), where Philippe creates his amazing cuisine. Unless Side Quest: Beyond the Beef is active, Philippe isn't usually here. Sip water from the sink, and check both chambers for a variety of Food on the counters and in fridges. In the second kitchen, there's an intercom to call the Head Waiter (during the Side Quest), and a Recipe you'll want to keep!

You can also drug the Banquet Wine on the shelf with Med-X.

- First Aid Box (2)
- Knife (4)
- Unique Item [Recipe]: Brahmin Wellington [36/95]

20 21 22 Pantries and Freezer

These have a variety of items to steal. Activate the Freezer Access Terminal [Very Easy] to check out a few slabs of meat. During the Side Quest, you may find another meat here. Also on the shelves are two human skulls; strange mementos to keep near Food.

- Purified Water (8)

K Elevator to and from Ultra-Luxe Kitchen

23 Locker Room

- Carton of Cigarettes

L Door to White Glove Members Only Section

White Glove Members Only Section

Access by unlocking Door #M from the other side using Marjorie's Key, or sneak in via the Kitchens (Door #N).

M Doors to Ultra-Luxe Casino Floor

Enter here without being sponsored, and expect your Reputation to plummet when you're spotted.

24 Office and Storage

- Sunset Sarsaparilla Crate (3)

25 Narrow Storage Passage

- Sunset Sarsaparilla Crate (3)

26 Members-Only Refreshment Dispensary

There's water to sip from a sink, food in the fridge, and a load of Alcohol and Sarsaparilla Bottles to steal.

- Sunset Sarsaparilla Bottle (9)

27 Members-Only Banquet Hall

This is where the real delicacies are tasted, and a possible place where Side Quest: Beyond the Beef culminates.

N Door to Ultra-Luxe Kitchen

Ultra-Luxe Bathhouse

O Doors to Ultra-Luxe Casino Floor

28 Swimming Pool

Hotel guests are in their skivvies, and the water both in the pool and in the bar sinks are safe to drink. Check the fridges for Food.

- Sunset Sarsaparilla Crate (2)

29 30 Sauna Steam Room

Check the sauna for some Alcohol, and the steam room for some conversation, if you know the time to chat; as part of the Side Quest.

- Cattleman Cowboy Hat
- Beer and Wine

P Doors to Ultra-Luxe Hotel Rooms

Ultra-Luxe Hotel Rooms

Q Doors to Ultra-Luxe Casino Floor

31 Main Hall

32 33 34 Rooms #A, B, and C

- First Aid Box

35 Private Investigator's Room

There was a P.I. staying here, and you'll uncover the key if you speak with Mortimer as part of Side Quest: Beyond the Beef. The evidence is as shocking as it is bloody.

- Quest Item: Matchbook

36 Bon Vivant Room

This is only opened using the Bon Vivant Room Key you're awarded as part of Free Quest: Big Winner, Ultra-Luxe.

- Wine
- Sleeping Quarters
- Home Sweet Home

R Doors to Ultra-Luxe Bathhouse

Ultra-Luxe Penthouse

S Elevator to Ultra-Luxe Casino Floor

This is locked from the other side [Hard]. Unlock using a key from Mortimer, or your own ingenuity.

37 Foyer and Bedrooms

Expect a Gunderson Hired Hand to thwart your progress if you aren't Sneaking. Unless you're wishing to attempt a spot of redecorating as part of Side Quest: Beyond the Beef, it isn't necessary to enter this locale.

- Teddy Bear
- Sleeping Quarters
- Food

38 Grand Withdrawing Room

The reflecting pool in this spectacular chamber has water to drink. Beware of another Hired Hand; this is Heck Gunderson's suite you're infiltrating!

- Wine (2)

39 Dining Room

- Brahmin Steak (2)
- Sunset Sarsaparilla Bottle (2)
- Wine (4)

40 Balcony Bar, Master Bedroom and Bathroom

- Wall Safe Items
- Sleeping Quarters
- Sunset Sarsaparilla Bottle (2)
- Carton of Cigarettes
- First Aid Box

Free Quest: Big Winner, Ultra-Luxe

Do you have a preference for a wager? Then understand the difference between becoming a firm friend of the White Glove Society, or a slight outcast. Step on over to a blackjack table, or place your roulette bets, and a floor manager comes around to commend you as soon as your winnings start to pile up.

At 3,750 Chips won, you're given a complementary Atomic Cocktail (which you can keep for later).

At 7,500 Chips won, you're handed a delicious Brahmin Wellington (which can be pocketed for afterward).

At 11,250 Chips won, you're comped the Bon Vivant Suite Key, which opens Location #36. You can stay there as long as you wish, but the place is closed once you leave The Strip.

At 15,000 Chips won, you're cut off, and banned from gambling (although your Reputation doesn't suffer). They simply need to remain solvent!

Free Quest: You Make Me Feel Like a Woman

If you quiz Veronica (who is located at 188 Trading Post) thoroughly, all she really wants is a dress. A nice dress. They make her feel like a woman. The fancier the better; in fact, if you return with a White Glove Society Attire Dress (which you'll need to kill a member inside the Ultra-Luxe for), then trade items with her, Veronica puts it on, and enthusiastically teaches you the Scribe Counter (an Unarmed Special Move).

- Perk! Scribe Counter

[2D.06] Vault 21

- Side Quest Bye Bye Love
- Side Quest The Finger of Suspicion
- Free Quest: Suits You, Sarah
- Free Quest: Tourist Traipse
- Threat Level: ●●●●●
- Faction: The Strip / Mr. House
    - Entity: Sarah Weintraub
    - Entity: Gambler
    - Entity: Traveler
    - Entity: Carlitos
    - Entity: Omerta Thug
    - Entity: Martina Groesbeck
- Fame/Infamy
    - Services: Trader [14/33]
- Collectibles: Snow Globe [4/7]
- Area Is Locked
- Health, Chems, or Water
- Highly Visible
- Home Sweet Home
- Interior Exploration
- Lots O' Caps
- Radio Signal
- Sleeping Quarters

A vault where its dwellers used to settle their differences via games of chance, is now a hotel and gift shop. The top floor is just the gift shop and front desk for the hotel. Visitors can buy Vault 21 jumpsuits, toasters, and other souvenir items, and view displays and read authentic details about the history of Vault 21. The vault itself is kept in pristine condition, aside from the subterranean eastern section, which was sealed by Mr. House; much to the annoyance of the last remaining residents Sarah (and her brother Michael) Weintraub. Aside from the ostentatious signage, the initial kiosk welcoming visitors to the vault lacks the spectacular nature of The Strip's other venues. But step inside, and you're transported back in time.

Vault 21 Gift Shop

Ⓐ Door to New Vegas Strip

① Entrance and Shop

Prepare to visit an almost-pristine vault, courtesy of Mr. House! Sarah is happy to speak with you, although you have a feeling she has some pent-up some frustration. You can ask about the history of the vault, get her ranting about Mr. House, She also sells vault gear in her shop. This begins Free Quest: Suits You, Sarah. Ask again, and you can view her (frankly pitiful) selection of trinkets.

- Trader: Sarah Weintraub [14/33]

You can also ask Sarah for a room, which she cheerfully rents out for one night, for 20 Caps. You can:

Take the room.

SPEECH 55 Or negotiate a special price for a permanent rental agreement. She reduces the rate to 10 Caps per night. Then she quickly tells you that the room is near the game room; make a left, and it's on the left-hand side. This is actually Location #8 (see below), and it's easy to miss her instructions. Especially as she doesn't repeat them!

Keep asking (nicely) about the vault, and she soon tells you that she's happy to give you a personal tour. This begins Free Quest: Tourist Traipse.

Pickpocket or murder her to severely damage your Strip Reputation, but obtain Caps, and a couple of keys (to Locations #8 and #9).

- Cap (300)
- Sarah's Dresser Key
- Sarah's Room Passcard

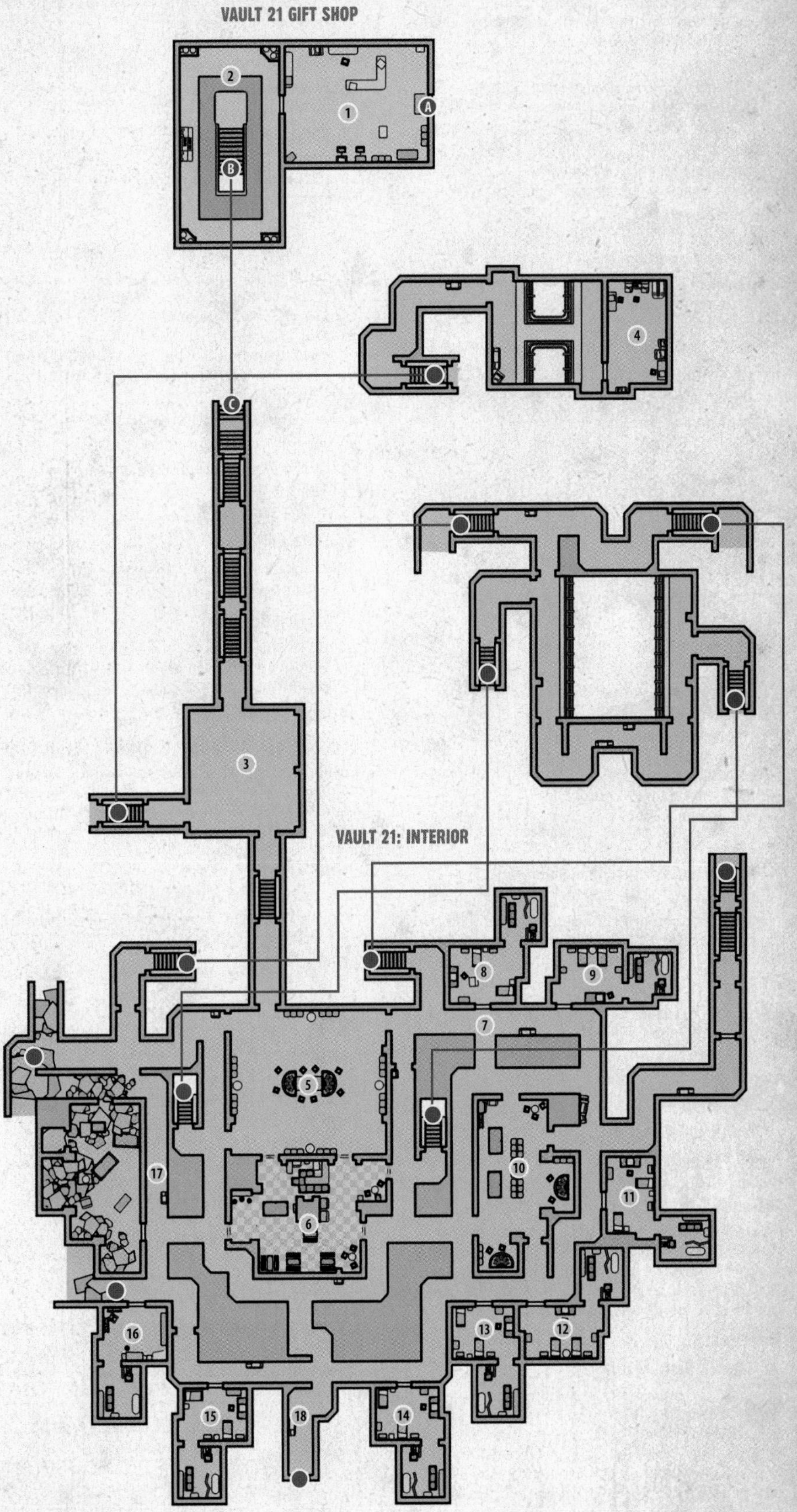

VAULT 21: INTERIOR

The Vault 21 Reception Terminal [Very Hard] is difficult to hack, and you risk severe Infamy attempting this in front of Sarah (so make her start the tour first). On the terminal are the following Sarah Weintraub's Mail:

> Messages

> New Message from Sheldon Weintraub: Sarah's big brother is lamenting his time stuck in a cold warehouse, thanks to Mr. House dumping concrete inside their Vault.

> Our Influential Friends: Complements from Charlene Tann about this chic "cramped underground hole."

> Sent Messages

> Hey, you!: A message back to Sheldon: Sarah remains chirpy, despite being cheated.

Also in the room is a tiny Vault 21 Terminal, which you can activate to obtain the following messages:

> Services

> Diner Menu

> Gift Catalogue

> Convenience

> History of Vault 21

> Vault 21—A Paradise of Equality

> Opening to a New World

> A Tribute to Mr. House

> Mail Messaging

2 Bunker

B Door to Vault 21

Vault 21

C Door to Vault 21 Gift Shop

3 (Lower and Upper) Entrance Mezzanine

This offers a thoroughfare into the rest of the vault. Take the stairs up and around to the Mezzanine, and you can access the Control Room.

4 (Upper) Control Room

There are two Vault 21 Control Terminals in here, and either accesses the following menus (all of which cannot be hacked into, due to Mr. House's mainframe dominance):

> Vault Security

> Vault Access Control

> Vault Life Support

5 (Lower and Upper) Main Game Hall

Highfalutin travelers and grumbling gamblers speak in hushed tones in here, but gambling isn't available; just access to the snaking corridors to all areas of the vault.

6 Diner

Carlitos, a dejected man with a lost love, can be spoken to, which begins Side Quest: Bye Bye Love.

- Purified Water (6)
- Pool Cue (2)
- First Aid Box and Food

7 Guest Room Corridor

Sarah concludes her Free Quest: Tourist Traipse here.

8 Guest Suite

Assuming you've paid for the room (otherwise the beds can't be slept in), this is a home away from home. Sip water from the sink, and check out the Vault 21 Guest Terminal, offering the same information as the one in the Gift Shop.

- Home Sweet Home
- Sleeping Quarters

9 Sarah's Suite [Average]

This can be unlocked using cunning skill, or by Pickpocketing the keys from Sarah herself (or searching her corpse). Take (without penalty) the Snow Globe from the bedside table. There's also Sarah's Dresser [Hard]. She also has her own terminal [Easy] with some interesting messages; the same ones that appear on her Gift Shop Terminal.

- Dresser Items [Hard]
- Snow Globe—The Strip [4/7]

Note You found a Limited Edition Mojave Landmark Snow Globe! These rare, Pre-War artifacts are widely considered to be useless baubles, but rumor has it some collectors will pay dearly for them.

10 Game Room (East)

Originally, the vault had two of these, but Mr. House blocked off the western one. Check the Vending Machines.

- Pool Cue (3)

11 12 13 14 15 Suites #1, 2, 3, 4, and 5

These offer the same amenities as your room. The doors are open or unlocked. On the computer table in Rooms #1 #3, and #5 is a Note to steal. If Side Quest: The Finger of Suspicion is active, Suite #4 is where you'll usually find a bunch of Omerta Thugs roughing up Martina Groesbeck.

- Note: Strip Letter 1: Lenny lost all his money.
- Note: Strip Letter 2: Sue lost all her Caps.
- Note: Strip Letter 3: Dennis lost all his money to a real classy lady.
- Sleeping Quarters

16 Suite #6

This has a less pristine atmosphere.

- First Aid Box
- Tool Cabinet Items

17 Eastern Corridor

All of the chambers east of here are blocked, although you can view the rubble through some of the windows.

18 Dead-end Corridor

Free Quest: Suits You, Sarah

While talking with Sarah, and as long as you keep your more smart-ass comments to yourself, you can stop Sarah after she fails to impress you with her vault goodies. She's really looking for more Vault Jumpsuits, and she's hoping you can help. You can:

Tell her you'll help her out.

Mention you might be persuaded. You can then Barter (see below), or agree to help.

A bit of sweet-talking convinces her to work together with you.

But tell her not to say "here, now!"

Mention Boomer Suits, and she says she'll definitely pay a good number of Caps for them, too!

At this point, you can begin to explore the Mojave Wasteland, and obviously the vaults, before bringing back anything you can scavenge. Vault Jumpsuits are almost always found in dressers, some lockers, and occasionally folded up on shelves. Here's what Sarah takes. Expect to receive 30 Caps per Vault Suit, and 15 per Boomer Suit (which she only accepts after the Barter check).

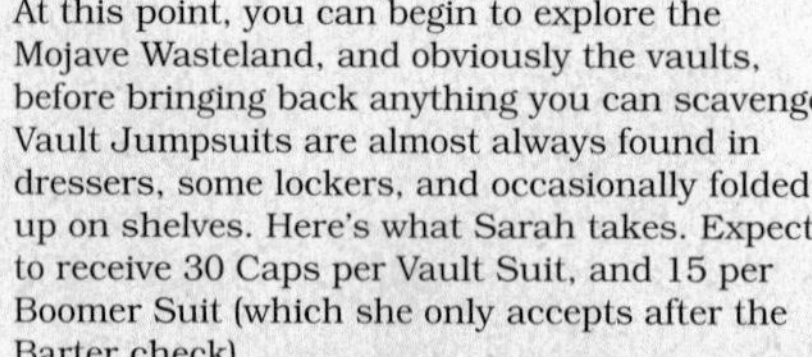

Location Number	Location Name	Item Description	Price Paid (Caps)
[1.09]	Vault 22	Vault 22 Jumpsuit	30
[1.21]	Vault 19	Vault 19 Jumpsuit	30
[2.24]	Vault 3	Vault 3 Jumpsuit	30
[3.01]	Nellis Air Force Base	Boomer Suit	15
[3.01]	Nellis Hangars	Boomer Suit	15
[3.12]	Vault 34	Vault 34 Jumpsuit	30
[5.05]	Vault 11	Vault 11 Jumpsuit	30

Free Quest: Tourist Traipse

If you're adept at polite conversation, steer it toward Sarah's knowledge of the vault, and you soon receive the option to take a personal tour. Agree to it to begin this Quest. The following route (and information snippets) are revealed:

Location # and Name	Information
Location #2: Bunker	Thick steel and stone to protect the vault interior.
Location #3: Entrance Mezzanine	Above are the life-support controls. The vault is no longer symmetrical, thanks to Mr. House.
Location #5: Main Game Hall	Disputes were gambled upon, and the winner made the decisions.
Location #6: Diner	Huge, and difficult-to-clean parties were held here.
Location #7: Guest Room Corridor	Your room is to the left. No snooping next door in Sarah's room!
Location #7: Guest Room Corridor	Close by is a game room that each side of the Vault had, before Mr. House filled one with cement.

[2D.07] NCR Embassy

See maps on the following page

- Main Quest: Things That Go Boom
- Main Quest: King's Gambit
- Side Quest: How Little We Know
- Threat Level: ●●●●●
- Faction: NCR
  - Entity: Liza O'Malley
  - Entity: Ambassador Dennis Crocker
  - Entity: Private Jake Erwin
  - Entity: Captain Marie Pappas
- Services:
  - Caravan Player [6/15]
  - Caravan Player [7/15]
- Collectibles:
  - Caravan Cards [7/30]
  - Caravan Cards [8/30]
  - Unique Item [37/95]
- Guns and Ammo
- Health, Chems, or Water
- Interior Exploration
- Radio Signal [Black Mountain]
- Sleeping Quarters

The NCR has a sizable presence on The Strip, commanding the Las Vegas Boulevard Station [2D.03] to Camp McCarran [2.19], and they have an Embassy on this part of The Strip, which is separated into two buildings. There's the NCR Military Police HQ to the right (south), and the Embassy itself on the left (north) after you walk through the gate. Troopers (who are on duty throughout the Mojave Wasteland) and Military Police (responsible for The Strip) mill about here.

NCR Military Police Headquarters

A Doors to The Strip

1 NCR Military Police HQ Office

The locked desk [Average] holds the keys to the cells. The terminal on top of the desk [Easy] can be hacked, and you can read a Strip Security Notice, MP Shift Reports, and a Trooper Behavior Report.

- NCR Embassy Cell Key

2 Cells

The restrooms and corridor have access to pure water. The cells require a key to open. Check the table for another Strip Letter.

- Note: Strip Letter 10
- Sleeping Quarters

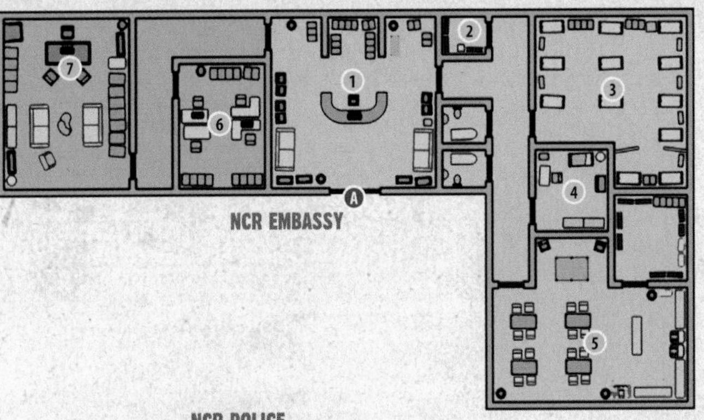

NCR EMBASSY

NCR POLICE HEADQUARTERS

3 Equipment Storage

The door to this is locked [Hard], and the reasons become clear; there's a number of items here to steal:

- Combat Knife (and other Melee Weapons)
- 10mm Pistol and Ammo
- Ammo Box Ammunition (2)
- First Aid Box
- Cattle Prod (3)
- NCR Trooper Armor

NCR Embassy

A Doors to The Strip

1 Reception

LIza O'Malley is the receptionist, and you can request a meeting with Ambassador Crocker with her (only if the Main Quest is active). She also has some gossip (when the Main Quest calls for it) regarding the Omertas over at the Gomorrah [2D.01]. Hack into her terminal (if you want your Infamy to increase), and read the Embassy Report, Captain Pappas' Report (checkpoints lack security), and Liza's Personal Notes (she's super-busy!).

2 Storage

3 Barracks

The barracks is across from the two restrooms (where you can drink water), and you can sleep here if you wish. One of the tables has a Strip Letter to grab too; from Lt. Ashville admonishing Private Erwin for his pranks. Private Jake Erwin's bunk is next to this table. Liza O'Malley and He sleeps here at night.

Private Jake Erwin can be talked to about The Strip, NCR members, and challenged to a game of Caravan.

Captain Marie Pappas is either in a bunk, or walking the Embassy. She gives you a dressing down when she sees you. You can ask about Erwin, the Strip, herself, or the Ambassador. The responses are curt.

- Note: Strip Letter
- Caravan Player [Private Jake Erwin] [6/15]
- Caravan Cards [Private Jake Erwin] [7/30]
- Sleeping Quarters

4 Ambassador Crocker's Bedroom

Crocker sleeps here (and can be woken without penalty) during the night. He can be murdered if you want that suit of his, and need to be shunned by the NCR.

5 Recreation Room and Larder

A food hall and pool room usually has a resting Military Policeman or two.

- Pool Cue (2)
- Note: Strip Letter 9

6 Filing Room

A couple of MPs are usually in here, working on paperwork. The Holotape gives some information on the Strip's three Families (The Omertas, Chairmen, and White Glove Society).

- Holotape: Ambassador Phillip Granger's Final Report

7 Ambassador Dennis Crocker's Office

This large chamber with comfy sofas and a large desk is where Crocker works (and where you report to him) during the day-time. There's nothing of value to steal, except a Holotape on the bookshelf, detailing the frustrations the NCR have had dealing with Mr. House. Speak to Ambassador Crocker and ask him about the NCR, Strip, play Caravan, and begin the Main Quests if you want to ally yourself with the NCR. You can also hack into Ambassador Crocker's Terminal [Average] (if you want your Infamy with the NCR to increase), and read an Informant Report (the Omertas are unhappy with Mr. House), Freeside Report (a rise in violence of NCR citizens, and Pacer may be involved), Farm Report (east side farms are producing a good amount of crops), and Fiend Report (they are more active outside New Vegas).

- Holotape: Ambassador Susanna Edith's Final Report
- Caravan Player: Ambassador Dennis Crocker [7/15]
- Caravan Cards: Ambassador Dennis Crocker [8/30]
- Unique Item: Ambassador Crocker's Suit [37/95]

[2D.08] Michael Angelo's Workshop

- Side Quest: Classic Inspiration
  Threat Level: ●●●●●
- Faction: The Strip
  - Entity: Kate
  - Entity: Michael Angelo
- Crafting
  - Workbench [14/41]
  - Workbench [15/41]
  - Workbench [16/41]
  - Workbench [17/41]
  - Workbench [18/41]
- Collectibles:
  - Unique Item [38/95]
  - Unique Item [39/95]
- Health, Chems, or Water
- Interior Exploration
- Lots O' Caps
- Radio Signal [Black Mountain]
- Quest Item

At the far end of The Strip, past the big casinos and Vault 21 [2D.06], is a workshop of the talented (and ex-Vault 21 resident) Michael Angelo, who is responsible for most of the working neon across The Strip, especially have Zapp's Neon Signs closed a couple of hundred years ago.

A Door to The Strip

1 Entrance and Reception

You can meet Kate here, and ask her about her boss, or herself. There's some radiation-free water to sip from the fountain, too.

2 Workshop Gantry Chamber

The main part of this building is taken up by a large open warehouse with gantry walkways to roam around, and a small enclosed foreman's area.

- Workbench [14/41]
- Workbench [15/41]

MICHAEL ANGELO'S WORKSHOP

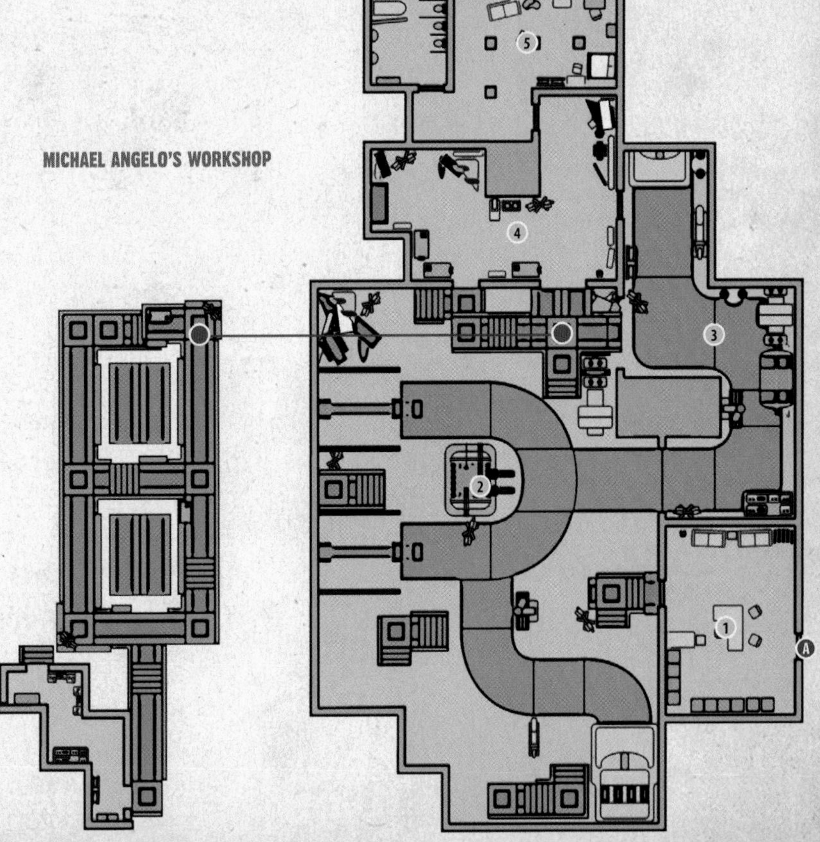

3 Northeast Generators and Workshop

4 North Workshop

This is where Michael Angelo spends some of his time forging new signs. There's (yet) more Workbenches here, another water fountain, and Schematics for a Billboard (which is just for show). Speak to Michael Angelo to start Side Quest: Classic Inspiration, and you're given a camera too.

- Workbench [16/41]
- Workbench [17/41]
- Workbench [18/41]
- Unique Item [Schematics]: Billboard [38/95]
- Unique Item: Codac R9000 [39/95]

5 Living Quarters

Michael lives modestly, and his living room is accessed via a door in the North Workshop. There's a bathroom off this area, allowing more water drinking from the sinks (and the toilets). Of more interest is Michael Angelo's Terminal, which has a message from a man named Sheldon Weintraub (Michael's actual name).

ZONE 2D: SECONDARY LOCATIONS

[2D.S01] Mister Holdout

- Threat Level: ●●●●●
- Faction: The Strip
  Entity: Mister Holdout
- Services: Trader [15/33]
- Guns and Ammo

If you're worried about defending yourself inside the casinos with a "gun-free" policy, step over to this shady-looking gentlemen close to the Gomorrah Hookers, who's happy to sell you some weapons you can conceal on your person. You can refuse, purchase, or:

Or you can inform him that you're already skilled in the art of hiding weapons from casino guards. You can still trade with him afterward.

- Trader: Mister Holdout [15/33]

[2D.S02] Victor at the Lucky 38

- Main Quest: Things That Go Boom
- Main Quest: The House Always Wins, I
- Side Quest: The Moon Comes Over the Tower
- Free Quest: We Must Stop Meeting Like This, IV
- Threat Level: ●●●●●
- Faction: The Strip/Mr. House
  Entity: Victor
  Entity: NCR MP Officer
  Entity: Emily Ortal
- Quest Item

The first time you enter The Strip, VIctor appears (yet again), and the Free Quest begins. From this point onward, he remains close to the Lucky 38. This is also the location where you're stopped by an NCR MP Officer and given a Note regarding Ambassador Crocker; beginning Main Quest: Things That Go Boom. And once you've befriended Mr. House, you're stopped by a woman named Emily Ortal, to begin Side Quest: The Moon Comes Over the Tower.

Free Quest: We Must Stop Meeting Like This, IV

The very first time you successfully navigate past the Securitrons at The Strip North Gate [2.13] and enter The Strip itself, Victor trundles out to greet you once again. You can ask what he's doing here, and Victor insists you visit The Lucky 38 Casino and meet Mr. House, who's bound to be a firm friend and is itching to make your acquaintance. Whether you agree to visit Mr. House or not, Main Quest: The House Always Wins, I begins.

[2D.S03] Emily Ortal

- Side Quest: The Moon Comes Over the Tower
- Threat Level: ●●●●●
- Faction: The Strip
  Entity: Emily Ortal
- Services: Healer [18/31]
- Health, Chems, or Water
- Wasteland Vegetation

This is where you're approached by Emily Ortal, at the start of her Side Quest.

[2D.S04] Billy Knight

- Side Quest: Talent Pool
- Threat Level: ●●●●●
- Faction: The Strip
  Entity: Billy Knight
- Lots O' Caps

A street comedian works his patter here. Listen to the zingers, and then speak to him; you get much more out of him if the Side Quest is active, and you can make his dreams come true.

[2D.S05] Street Vendor

- Threat Level: ●●●●●
- Faction: The Strip
  Entity: Street Vendor
- Services: Healer [18/31]
- Health, Chems, or Water
- Wasteland Vegetation

Standing in front of the Las Vegas Boulevard Station is a Street Vendor, who's happy to provide some items to purchase or trade. The selection can best be described as "limited."

- Healer: Street Vendor [18/31]

[2D.S06] Vulpes Inculta or Alerio

- Main Quest: Render Unto Caesar
- Threat Level: ●●●●●
- Faction: Caesar's Legion
  Entity: Vulpes Inculta
  Entity: Alerio
- Quest Item

When you exit, you're likely to be stopped early in your adventuring by Vulpes Inculta (or Alerio if Vulpes is dead), to begin a new Main Quest path, and receive the Mark of Caesar.

- Quest Item: Mark of Caesar

[2D.S07] Walter and Ethel Phebus

- Side Quest: Pheeble Will
- Threat Level: ●●●●●
- Faction: None
  Entity: Walter Phebus
  Entity: Ethel Phebus

Fresh off the monorail and looking for Heck Gunderson, Walter and Ethel are a pair of country folk looking to settle a score. Speak to either of them to begin the Side Quest.

[2D.S08] The Tops Promoter

- Threat Level: ●●●●●
- Faction: The Strip / Chairmen
  Entity: Tops Promoter

This is the general location of a promoter whose job it is to get you into the casino.

[2D.S09] NCR Embassy Gates

- Main Quest: Things That Go Boom
- Main Quest: For the Republic, Part 2
- Threat Level: ●●●●●
- Faction: NCR
  Entity: NCR Military Police

A plaque commemorating the opening of this Embassy at the behest of President Aaron Kimball is adjacent to the perimeter gate, which is also guarded by an NCR MP. Speak to him about general happenings on The Strip.

ZONE 2E: SOUTH VEGAS RUINS

[2E.01] Zapp's Neon Signs

- Threat Level: ●●●●●
- Faction: Fiend
  - Entity: Fiend
- Crafting:
  - Workbench [19/41]
  - Workbench [20/41]
  - Workbench [21/41]
- Dangers:
  - Traps
  - Mines
- Collectibles:
  - Magazine [Repair] [11/27] [34-37/37]
  - Magazine [Sneak] [5/10] [34-37/37]
  - Magazine [Survival] [12/30] [34-37/37]
  - Magazine [Unarmed] [6/11] [34-37/37]
  - Unique Item [40/95]
  - Unique Item [41/95]
- Guns and Ammo
- Health, Chems, or Water
- Interior Exploration
- Radio Signal [Black Mountain: Zone 2E only]
- Sleeping Quarters

You should be instantly familiar with Zapp's actual neon signs, as the Fiends have welded many of them together to form impassable perimeter walls. The actual building is a graveyard of ancient signs, including the feet of a Tall Boy statue. Inside, expect more Fiends, and additional traps.

Ⓐ Door to South Vegas Ruins (Fiend Territory)

① Entrance Office

Be extremely careful in this area, as there's a Tripwire and a Grenade Bouquet at the top of the stairs, and a patrolling Fiend on the stairs below. Deactivate the Tripwire, and gather the Grenades directly above. Watch for the terminal too; it is rigged to explode. Descend the stairs carefully; stoop and deactivate (or shoot from range) three Frag Mines.

- Frag Grenade (3)
- First Aid Box
- Magazine: Fixin' Things [Repair] [11/27] [34/37]
- Magazine: ¡La Fantoma! [Sneak] [5/10] [35/37]
- Frag Mine(3)

② Workshop

Clear the Fiends from this area before you inspect it. Adjacent, up a small ramp, is a storage garage.

- Workbench [19/42]
- Workbench [20/42]
- Workbench [21/42]
- Ammo Box Ammunition
- Sleeping Quarters

③ Upstairs Foreman's Office

Ascend the steps, disarming three sets of two Frag Mines, or face lacerations as they detonate along with a fire extinguisher. Inside the office itself, conduct a search of the shelving and desk for the following items, and hack the terminal [Easy] to read about two Shipping Invoices and an accident report.

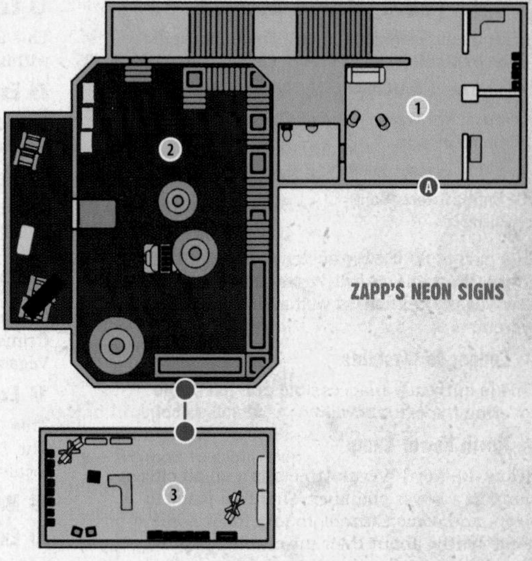

- First Aid Box
- Carton of Cigarettes
- Nuka-Cola Quartz [40/95]
- Nuka-Cola Quartz [41/95]
- Magazine: Lad's Life [Survival] [12/30] [36/37]
- Magazine: Boxing Times [Unarmed] [6/11] [37/37]
- Ammo Box Ammunition
- Grenade Box Ammunition
- 9mm Submachine Gun and Ammo

ZONE 2E: SECONDARY LOCATIONS

[2E.S01] Sentry Post Mattress

- Threat Level: ●●●●●
- Faction: Fiend
  - Entity: Fiend
- Crafting: Campfire [26/109]
- Health, Chems, or Water

A Fiend on a mattress near a Campfire guards the western entrance to this zone. Remember to check the nearby dumpsters.

- Campfire [26/109]
- First Aid Box
- Sleeping Quarters

[2E.S02] Neon Sign Graveyard

- Threat Level: ●●●●●
- Faction: Fiend
  - Entity: Fiend
- Health, Chems, or Water

Among the rusting and faded signs of yesteryear are some shelves with the following:

- First Aid Box

[2E.S03] Lean-To Shack

- Threat Level: ●●●●●
- Faction: Fiend
  - Entity: Fiend
- Crafting: Campfire [27/109]
- Guns and Ammo
- Health, Chems, or Water

Scavenge these items when the coast is clear. The Produce Sack has a number of items you can use in Recipes.

- Campfire [27/109]
- Grenade Box Ammunition [Easy]
- Produce Sack Items
- Sleeping Quarters

[2E.S04] Ruined Concrete Outbuilding

- Threat Level: ●●●●●
- Faction: Fiend
  - Entity: Fiend
- Guns and Ammo
- Health, Chems, or Water

Adjacent to the Lean-To Shack are the remains of a concrete outbuilding, with a large haul of items you must grab!

- Scrap Metal
- Mine Box Ammunition
- Doctor's Bag
- Service Rifle
- Sledgehammer

[2E.S05] Southwest Exit to and from Fiend Territory

- Threat Level: ●●●●●
- Faction: Fiend
  - Entity: Fiend
- Interior Exploration

This is unmarked on your Pip-Boy's World Map, but is another entrance and exit into Zone 2E; handy if you wish to flee to the south.

[3.21] Follower's Outpost
[3.22] Lake Las Vegas
[3.23] Camp Golf
[3.24] Mountain Shadows Campground
[3.25] Scavenger Platform
[3.26] Crashed B-29
[3.27] Lake Mead Cave
[3.28] The Fort
[3.29] Deserted Shack
[3.30] Ranger Station Alpha
[3.31] Boulder Beach Compound
[3.32] Boulder City
[3.33] Hoover Dam
[3.34] Legate's Camp
[3.35] Cazador Nest
[3.36] Ranger Station Delta
[U3.A] Train Tunnel

Secondary Locations

[3.S01] Power Transformer
[3.S02] Chem Addicts' Camp
[3.S03] Boomer Territory Road
[3.S04] Bombarded Houses
[3.S05] Vault 34 Alternative Entrance
[3.S06] NCR Truck and Dead Trooper
[3.S07] Mole Rat Hole
[3.S08] Cazador Nests
[3.S09] Great Khan Supply Cave 1
[3.S10] Great Khan Supply Cave 2
[3.S11] Great Khan Supply Cave 3
[3.S12] The One (and Super Mutant Camp)
[3.S13] Road Turnabout
[3.S14] Camp Guardian Cave
[3.S15] NCR Water Pipeline
[3.S16] NCR Sentry Nest
[3.S17] Lake Mead Scenic Overlook
[3.S18] Sunken Sarsaparilla Supplies
[3.S19] Sunken Boat
[3.S20] Boulder City Billboard Sign
[3.S21] Sunset Sarsaparilla Billboard (Lonesome Drifter)
[3.S22] Ranger Pason's Patrol Overlook

PRIMARY LOCATIONS

[3.01] Nellis Air Force Base

- Main Quest: Things That Go Boom
- Main Quest: Render Unto Caesar
- Main Quest: The House Always Wins, III
- Main Quest: Wild Card: Side Bets
- Side Quest: Ant Misbehavin'
- Side Quest: Sunshine Boogie
- Side Quest: Young Hearts
- Side Quest: Volare!
- Side Quest: I Hear You Knocking
- Free Quest: Malleable Mini Boomer Minds
- Free Quest: Bear Necessities
- Free Quest: Missing a Few Missiles
- Free Quest: Iron and Stealing
- Free Quest: Old School Ghoul
- Threat Level: ●●●●●
- Faction: Boomers
  - Entity: Mother Pearl
  - Entity: Raquel
  - Entity: Loyal
  - Entity: Jack
  - Entity: Pete
  - Entity: Argyll
  - Entity: Lindsay
  - Entity: Boomer
  - Entity: Mini Boomer
  - Entity: Boomer Chef
  - Entity: Boomer Munitions Manager
- Fame/Infamy
- Services: Healer/Dealer [19/31]
- Crafting:
  - Campfire [28/109]
  - Reloading Bench [14/36]
  - Workbench [22/41]
- Collectibles:
  - Skill Book [Explosives] [1/3] [1/9]
  - Skill Book: [Repair] [1/4] [2/9]
  - Magazine [Explosives] [6/12] [1-9/52]
  - Magazine [Explosives] [7/12] [1-9/52]
  - Magazine [Medicine] [15/19] [1-9/52]
  - Magazine [Melee Weapons] [7/9] [1-9/52]
  - Magazine [Repair] [12/27] [1-9/52]
  - Magazine [Repair] [13/27] [1-9/52]
  - Magazine [Science] [11/23] [1-9/52]
  - Magazine [Sneak] [6/10] [1-9/52]
  - Magazine [Unarmed] [7/11] [1-9/52]
  - Snow Globe [5/7]
- Area Is Locked
- Guns and Ammo
- Health, Chems, or Water
- Highly Visible
- Interior Exploration
- Lots O' Caps
- Sleeping Quarters
- Wasteland Vegetation
- Quest Item

NELLIS AIR FORCE BASE EXTERIOR

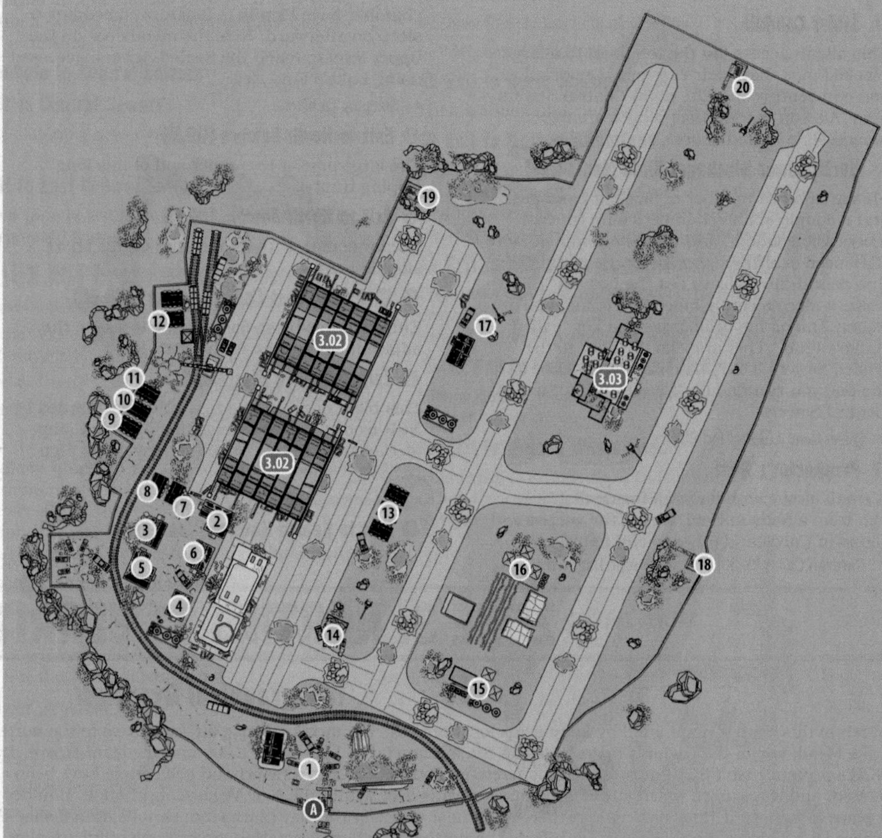

Nellis Air Force Base: Exterior

Ⓐ Gates to Mojave Wasteland

1 Boomer Gate

This is the main entrance to the base, and two Boomers are patrolling, each armed with Missile Launchers. You're stopped here, and brought to Pearl's Barracks at the start of Side Quest: Volare! Aside from the guard tower and gate hut, there's no items to find here (unless you're attacking the Boomers to collect their weapons).

2 Pearl's Barracks

Mother Pearl is usually here, or on her rounds circling the Hangars. The restroom has pure water to sip. The copy of Duck and Cover! is between the other books on the shelf above the Grenade Rifle.

- First Aid Box
- Grenade Rifle and Ammo
- Skill Book: Duck and Cover! [Explosives] [1/3] [1/9]

3 4 Nellis Women's Barracks #1 and #2

The restrooms have pure water to sip.

- First Aid Box (2)
- Sleeping Quarters

5 Nellis Men's Barracks

The larger male barracks (adjacent to a tent where there's more mattresses to sleep on) has a few snoozing Boomers, and some stuff to steal. The restroom has pure water to sip.

- First Aid Box
- Gun Cabinet Items (3)
- Footlocker Items (2)
- Magazine: Patriot's Cookbook [Explosives] [7/12] [1/52]
- Scrap Metal
- Sleeping Quarters

6 Nellis Children's Barracks

The kids who wander the base, and attempt to play with you (Free Quest: Malleable Mini Boomer Minds) slumber here. The restroom has pure water to sip.

- First Aid Box
- Toy Box Items (7)
- BB Gun and Ammo
- Baseball Bat
- Magazine: Today's Physician [Medicine] [15/19] [2/52]
- Sleeping Quarters

7 Nellis Schoolhouse

The Boomer Teacher is usually in here. Inside her desk [Very Easy], there are more items.

- Magazine: Fixin' Things [Repair] [12/27] [3/52]
- Magazine: Programmer's Digest [Science] [11/23] [4/52]
- Magazine: Boxing Times [Unarmed] [7/11] [5/52]

8 Nellis Medical Station

Doctor Argyll runs this small hut, and currently has three injured Boomers thanks to the Ant infestation in the Array. Consult Side Quest: Volare! for your options on healing them. You can be healed by the doctor if you're well-liked.

- Healer: Argyll [19/31]
- First Aid Box
- Food and Purified Water

9 Loyal's House

One of three corrugated sheds to the west of the hangars. When he's not in the hangar, Loyal sleeps here.

- Skill Book: Dean's Electronics [Repair] [1/4] [2/9]
- Sleeping Quarters

10 Nellis Workshop

This one is usually empty, meaning you can scavenge and steal. The Gun Cabinet to the right is especially important as it contains a Howitzer Firing Mechanism you can take to help Caesar's Legion in Side Quest: I Hear You Knocking, and this can be done at any time.

- Reloading Bench [14/36]
- Workbench [22/41]
- Magazine: Fixin' Things [Repair] [13/27] [6/52]
- Quest Item: Howitzer Firing Mechanism
- Sleeping Quarters

11 Nellis Boomer Museum

Pete runs this museum, which consists of a large mural painted to show the history of this clan of vault dwellers, and their fascination with the skies. Listening to Pete's story is part of Side Quest: Volare!; so be sure to ask additional questions afterward for a large Fame and Reputation boost! There's a Snow Globe you can take here without penalty, too.

- Snow Globe—Nellis AFB [5/7]
- Magazine: Patriot's Cookbook [Explosives] [6/12] [7/52]
- Magazine: Tæles of Chivalrie [Melee Weapons] [7/9] [8/52]
- Magazine: ¡La Fantoma! [Sneak] [6/10] [9/52]
- BB Ammo
- Boomer Fame Gained!

Note

You found a Limited Edition Mojave Landmark Snow Globe! These rare, Pre-War artifacts are widely considered to be useless baubles, but rumor has it some collectors will pay dearly for them.

12 Biodiesel Refinery

An old curve-roofed storage hangar now used by the Boomers to make Biodiesel fuel from Maize. Caution! Any sparks (such as a fired weapon) causes the place to go up, and you with it!

- Maize (really quite a lot of it)

13 Disused Corrugated Sheds

There's a military truck, and Raquels' Southern Howitzer Defenses nearby.

14 Raquels' Southern Howitzer Defenses

Raquel guards from this point when she isn't running other errands.

15 Water Filtration System

These two tents hold water purification equipment inside (which can't be taken). There's a howitzer close by, and an abandoned (and sealed) concrete air base building no longer in use. Expect a couple of Boomer Robot patrols around here, too.

16 Boomer Greenhouses

The greenhouses and cultivated Maize can't be accessed.

- Campfire [28/109]
- Sleeping Quarters

17 Northern Howitzer Defenses

18 19 20 North, Northeast, and Eastern Guard Towers

These ramped towers offer sniping potential, and an early warning for the Boomers.

Free Quest: Malleable Mini Boomer Minds

Mini Boomers are playing around the Air Force Base, close to Raquel's Defenses. Speak to any of them.

One of them is a little girl. She's excited to see a stranger. You can:

Tell her you battled mutated animals, and braved other dangers. Apparently, you're awesome.

- Boomer Fame Gained!

Or tell her you're passing through.

A second Mini-Boomer asks you to pay a toll to pass. You can:

State that a fair traveller may pass through the gate. You're let through the invisible gate.

- Boomer Fame Gained!

Or tell the scamp you're passing through.

A cheeky little Mini Boomer thinks she's La Fantoma. You can:

Tell her that you hope to fight for the forces of good by her side. She agrees that a sidekick would be cool.

- Boomer Fame Gained!

Or tell her you're passing through.

Put up your dukes, stranger! The Red-Brick Kid (a ginger-haired little tyke) approaches. You can:

Mock surrender, fleeing as you're no match for his fighting style. You'd better run!

- Boomer Fame Gained!

Or tell him you're passing through.

A Mini Boomer with a penchant for aircraft controlling wants to know if you're ready for take-off. You can:

Slightly patronize her, letting her know she'll fly a plane when she's bigger. She agrees. It'll be awesome!

- Boomer Fame Gained!

Or tell her you're passing through.

Roar! This Mini Boomer is actually a dinosaur! You can:

Roar back, because you're a vicious velociraptor. ROAR! Ooo; you know a lot about dinosaurs!

- Boomer Fame Gained!

Or tell him you're passing through.

A Mini Boomer is missing his toys, and he wants something fun to play with. You can:

Tell him he doesn't need toys; he should try a game of "boomers and targets." That's a sweet idea!

- Boomer Fame Gained!

Or tell him you're passing through.

Free Quest: Bear Necessities

Another Mini Boomer you can speak with is Lindsay, who's missing Mister Cuddles. You can:

Ask who Mister Cuddles is. It's her Teddy, and she lost him. She can't remember where. You can:

Ask her to think really hard about what she was doing the last time she saw him.

- Quest Item: Note: Mr. Cuddles

Agree to look for the Teddy. Or ignore her.

Ignore her.

Look for Mister Cuddles. He's inside the Nellis Hangar [3.02] that Loyal and Jack work in, among a stack of large containers (see [3.02], Location #5 for more information). When you return to her, she asks if he's been spotted. You can:

Tell her he's dead. She runs off, crying. This heartless act can be attempted with or without the Teddy Bear.

- Boomer Infamy Gained!

Give her Mister Cuddles if he's been found. She's very happy!

- Boomer Fame Gained!

Free Quest: Missing a Few Missiles

Once you've proved your Ant-killing skills and completed Side Quest: Ant Misbehavin', return to Raquel and ask if she's got any further work for you. She tells you the Boomers are low on missiles, and she'll take any that you have. Return with quantities of Missiles for her. Naturally, these should be gathered off-base, although you can make sure you're Hidden, and grab a few from the gun cabinet in the hangar kitchens, and give them back to her as if they were yours! Your Fame with the Boomers increases for Missiles you give.

- Quest Item: Note: Nellis Missile Metal
- Boomer Fame Gained!

[3.02] Nellis Hangars

See maps on the following page

- Free Quest: Iron and Stealing
- Free Quest: Old School Ghoul
- Threat Level: ●●●●●
- Faction: Boomer
  - Entity: Loyal
  - Entity: Jack
  - Entity: Boomer
  - Entity: Boomer Chef
  - Entity: Munitions Manager
- Fame/Infamy
- Services:
  - Healer/Dealer [20/31]
  - Trader [16/33]
- Crafting:
  - Reloading Bench [15/36]
  - Reloading Bench [16/36]
  - Workbench [23/41]
- Collectibles:
  - Sunset Sarsaparilla Star Cap [30/100]
  - Sunset Sarsaparilla Star Cap [31/100]
  - Unique Item [42/95]
  - Unique Item [43/95]
  - Unique Item [44/95]
- Guns and Ammo
- Health, Chems, or Water
- Highly Visible
- Interior Exploration
- Lots O' Caps
- Sleeping Quarters
- Wasteland Vegetation
- Quest Item

Dominating the otherwise flat landscape of the Air Force Base are two massive hangar buildings. The southwest hangar is still a place where Loyal (a venerable Boomer) dreams of dredging a B-29 Bomber from Lake Mead and repairing it. The northeast building is now a Mess Hall and Munitions Storage. You'll usually find Loyal and Jack inside the hangar.

Southwest Hangar

A Doors to Nellis Air Force Base

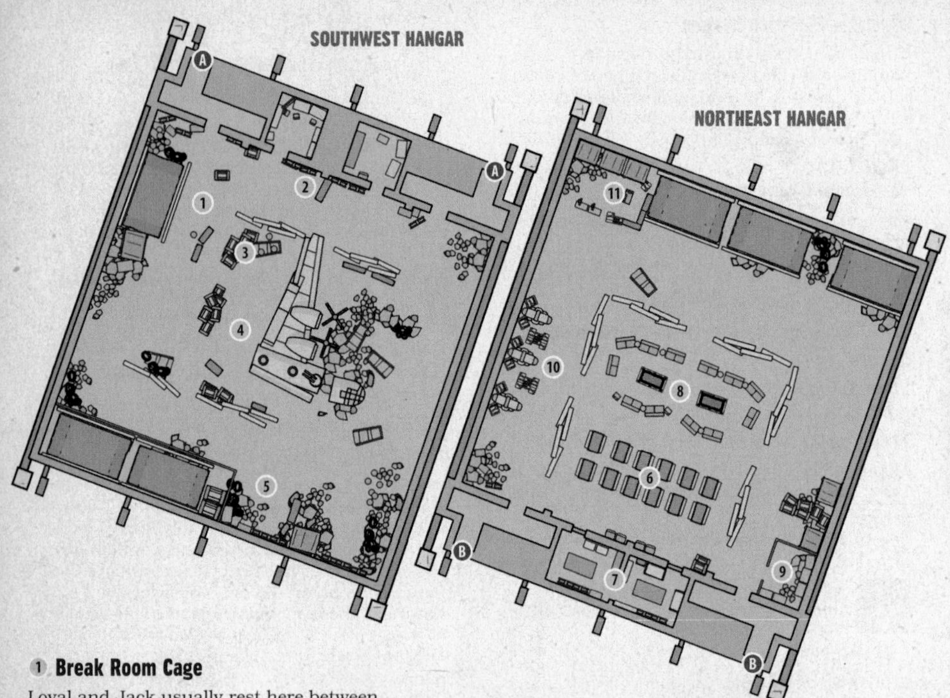

1 Break Room Cage

Loyal and Jack usually rest here between tinkering.

- Ammo Box Ammunition (2)
- Armor Case Items (8)
- Grenade Box Ammunition

2 Storage and Offices

- First Aid Box (2)
- Scrap Metal
- Carton of Cigarettes

3 Mr. Cuddles

Lindsay, a Mini Boomer, lost her Teddy Bear, and wants you to find it (Free Quest: Bear Necessities). He's lying around in the pile of large container crates.

- Quest Item: Mr. Cuddles

4 B-29 Bomber Sections

The remains of a giant fuselage section, wing, and nose of an ancient aircraft lie in the middle of this hangar.

5 Storage Shelves

Don't forget to check the metal shelving on the wall for a unique Schematic.

- First Aid Box (2)
- Carton of Cigarettes
- Scrap Metal
- Unique Item: [Schematic] Rock-It Launcher [43/95]

Loyal and Jack

Speak to Loyal and you can ask him about some kind of weapon to fight Giant Ants, if Side Quest: Ant Misbehavin' is under way. Or tell him you're here to make yourself useful. He replies that the generator building has a number of solar arrays on the roof, and they need repairing. This begins Side Quest: Sunshine Boogie. Consult that Quest in this guide for further information. Further into Side Quest: Volare!, Loyal gives you a Detonator and Ballasts that should help you rise a plane from Lake Mead. Talk to Jack for a Rebreather to help you conserve oxygen underwater at this point. You should also bring Raul with you when you speak to Loyal, as part of Free Quest: Old School Ghoul.

Talk to Jack, and you can ask him about the Boomers, and if there's any help that he needs. This begins Free Quest: Iron and Stealing. Jack also has a rather personal matter, but he's reluctant to share it with you. Press him on this subject, and Side Quest: Young Hearts begins.

- Quest Item: Sonic Emitter
- Quest Item: Deployable Ballast (2)
- Quest Item: Detonator
- Unique Item: Rebreather [42/95]

Free Quest: Iron and Stealing

Jack tells you he's looking for some Scrap Metal, if you can spare any. Return with quantities of Scrap Metal for him. Naturally, these should be gathered off-base, although you can make sure you're Hidden, and grab a couple of pieces from the hangar and give them back to Jack as if they were yours! Your Fame with the Boomers increases for Scrap Metal you give. Scrap Metal is scattered throughout the Wasteland; usually in industrial locations such as factories.

- Quest Item: Note: Nellis Scrap Metal
- Boomer Fame Gained!

Northeast Hangar

B Doors to Nellis Air Force Base

6 Mess Hall Tables

The Mess Hall tables have some scattered Caps (to steal).

- Sunset Sarsaparilla Star Cap [30/100]
- Sunset Sarsaparilla Star Cap [31/100]

7 Kitchens

"Hungry for grub?" The Boomer Chefs allows you to purchase Food, but only if you're "Liked."

- Healer (Food): Boomer Chef [20/31]
- Healer Highlight (Boomer Chef): Sunset Sarsaparilla (30)

There's also a footlocker and gun cabinet to check; the cabinet usually has a large quantity of Missiles; useful for cunningly bringing to Raquel during her Free Quest: Missing a Few Missiles.

- Gun Cabinet Items
- Sleeping Quarters

8 Pool Room

- Pool Cue (4)

9 Munitions Store

The shelving is brimming with ordnance; speak to a Munitions Manager to purchase items. This occurs only when you're "Liked" by the Boomers. Below are the munitions stored here if you want to grab them without payment.

- Trader: Boomer Munitions Manager [16/33]
- Ammo Box Ammunition (17)
- Gun Box Items (2)
- Grenade Rifle (4)
- Missile (3)
- Missile Launcher (3)
- Plasma Grenade (6)
- Pulse Grenade (7)
- Frag Grenade (7)
- Unique Item: Mini-Nuke [44/95]

10 Nellis Flight Simulators

They can't be accessed.

11 Workshop

This is a godsend to the tinkerer.

- Reloading Bench [15/36]
- Reloading Bench [16/36]
- Workbench [23/41]
- First Aid Box (2)
- Weapon Repair Kit
- Broken Missile Launcher

[3.03] Nellis Array ●

- Main Quest: See Location [3.01]
- Side Quest: Ant Misbehavin'
- Side Quest: Sunshine Boogie
- Threat Level: ●●●●●
- Faction: Boomer / Mutated Insect
  - Entity: Giant Worker Ant
  - Entity: Giant Soldier Ant
- Fame/Infamy
- Collectibles:
  - Unique Item [45/95]
  - Unique Item [46/95]
  - Unique Weapon [19/42]
- Area Is Locked
- Guns and Ammo
- Interior Exploration
- Quest Item

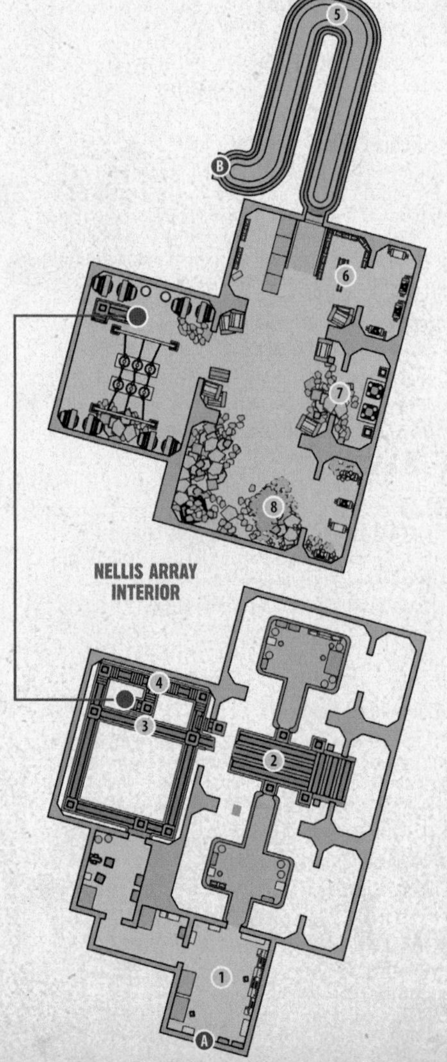

The Nellis array is the second-most impressive piece of solar-power engineering in the Mojave Wasteland, after HELIOS One [5.13]. The place's exterior is peppered with solar reflectors, five of which are broken. Fixing them is part of the Side Quest. There is an Array Control Interface too; which is currently offline, but can be checked during the Quest.

Array Interior

Ⓐ Door to Nellis Air Force Base (Exterior)

1 Entrance Control Rooms

This is one of two ways to enter the building, using the key given to you by Raquel. Search the Dead Boomer by the doorway; he's usually carrying some quality items (such as a Grenade Launcher, Grenade Rifle, and ammo). There's a second Dead Boomer in the adjacent room, near an Assault Carbine. The four linked rooms bring you out on one of two gantries, with a gap to jump between them.

- Grenade Launcher and/or Rifle and Ammo
- Assault Carbine

2 Central Gantry

Directly below is the generator floor, and a number of Giant Ants. Jump the gap to get to and from the northwest gantry, and beware; you can fall from up here!

3 Northwest Gantry

Some Ants have infiltrated the northwest gantry, too. Leap and land on one of the container boxes, and launch Grenades down onto the Ants from safety.

4 Gantry Steps

Halfway down the stairs is the Generator Main Power Switch, which is only active once you've powered the generators.

5 Access Tunnel

If you want to enter this area from the outside, and wish to emerge on the generator floor immediately, use this access point.

6 Lower floor Munitions Storage

There's a mass of bullets and other ammunition in this corner, which is well worth grabbing after the Side Quest is over, and you're safe.

- Ammo Box Ammunition (21)
- .308 Round (24 x 12)
- .500 Round (100 x 11)
- 40mm Grenade (12 x 2)
- Unique Item: Mini-Nuke [45/95]
- Unique Item: Mini-Nuke [46/95]

7 Generators

The two generators are in good working order, but can only be switched on (via the lever panels on them) after ridding the place of the Giant Ant problem.

8 Ant Mound

This disgusting mound of sinew is where the Giant Ants attack from. Place a Sonic Emitter here, or simply destroy all the insects. Be sure you check the destroyed mini-generators to the east, as there's a skeleton lying next to a prized Grenade Rifle.

- Unique Weapon: Thump-Thump [19/42]
- 40mm Grenade (12)

Ⓑ Door to Nellis Air Force Base (Exterior)

[3.04] Fields' Shack

- Threat Level: ●●●●●
- Faction: None
- Collectibles:
  Sunset Sarsaparilla Star Cap [32/100]
- Unique Weapon [20/42]
- Guns and Ammo
- Interior Exploration
- Sleeping Quarters

The old caretaker shack near the power transformer [3.S01] is now a place where George (on the road to the Boomers) occasionally likes to lay his head.

- Ammo Box Ammunition (4)
- Sunset Sarsaparilla Star Cap [32/100]
- Sleeping Quarters
- Unique Weapon: Abilene Kid LE BB Gun [20/42]

[3.05] Raul's Shack

- Free Quest: Old School Ghoul
- Threat Level: ●●●●●
- Faction: Ghoul
  Entity: Nightstalker
  Entity: Brahmin
- Crafting: Workbench [24/41]
- Collectibles: Skill Book: [Guns] [2/4] [3/9]
- Follower
- Guns and Ammo
- Health, Chems, or Water
- Interior Exploration
- Sleeping Quarters
- Wasteland Vegetation

Raul is a Ghoul, currently away from his shack; otherwise engaged up in Black Mountain [5.07]. You interact with him during Side Quest: Crazy, Crazy, Crazy, but should only return here if he becomes a Companion.

- Skill Book: Guns and Bullets [Guns] [2/4] [3/9]
- Doctor's Bag and Stimpak
- Ammo Box Ammunition (2)
- Frag Grenade (3)
- Workbench [24/41]

[3.06] Brotherhood of Steel Safehouse

- Side Quest: Still in the Dark
- Free Quest: Brotherhood Bond, II
- Threat Level: ●●●●●
- Faction: Brotherhood of Steel
  Entity: Paladin Sato
- Services: Repairer [3/9]
- Crafting:
  Reloading Bench [17/36]
  Workbench [25/41]
- Area Is Locked
- Health, Chems, or Water
- Home Sweet Home
- Interior Exploration
- Sleeping Quarters

This shack can only be opened if you have the Brotherhood of Steel Safehouse Key, awarded by the leader of the Brotherhood at the conclusion of Side Quest: Still in the Dark. In the rocky terrain near a small band of marauding Fire Geckos is an unassuming shack, shrouded in a rock alcove.

Safehouse Bunker [Interior]

This one-room bunker allows you to rest on any of the cots, sip from the radiation-free water fountain, and tinker on both a Work and Reloading Bench.

- Reloading Bench [17/36]
- Workbench [25/41]
- Weapon Repair Kit

Much like other Safehouses across the Mojave, this offers a place of rest and healthy solace. The following benefits occur:

1. Any bed you sleep in at this location gives you a "Well Rested" bonus.
2. There is a water fountain here allowing you to sip purified water without Radiation.
3. If the location has a fridge, it is restocked with items once per day.
4. Aside from the fridge, there are containers you can store items without them disappearing. Choose a metal Box, footlocker, or other chest type, place a low value item inside, then return after a day to ensure your items haven't been taken.
5. This location is visited by Paladin Sato, who is here every Sunday and Wednesday. You can check the day of the week when you attempt to Wait or Sleep. Paladin Sato is an extremely proficient Repairer, and can tinker on any item you want for as long as he's at the Safehouse.

- Repairer: Paladin Sato [Skill 100] [3/9]

[3.07] Bloodborne Cave

- Threat Level: ●●●●●
- Faction: Abomination
  Entity: Nightstalker
- Crafting: Campfire [29/109]
- Dangers: Traps
- Collectibles:
  Hollowed-Out Rock [9/42]
- Guns and Ammo
- Health, Chems, or Water
- Interior Exploration
- Lots o' Caps

Known for the red-hued sandstone rocks flanking it, Bloodborne is off the beaten track, near a cluster of Fire Geckos, and three unmarked Great Khan Supply Caves to the east [3.S09, 10, 11]. Locate the cave mouth in the perimeter rock wall, and the nearby Hollowed-Out Rock.

- Hollowed-Out Rock [9/42]

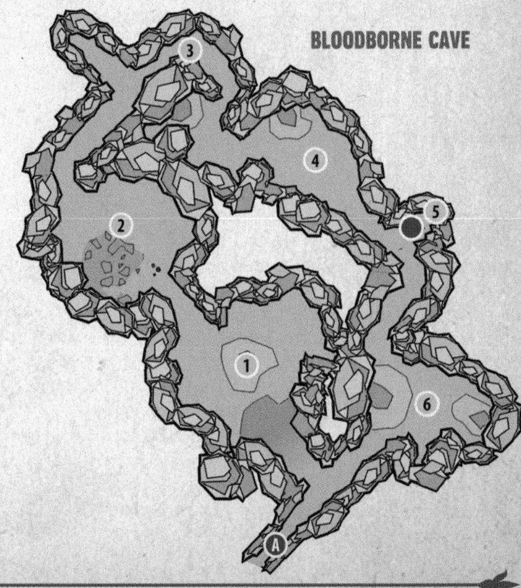

Ⓐ Exit to Mojave Wasteland

1 Ledge Cavern

Drop down from the ledge above, accessed via the initial corridor. Search two corpse (one fresh, the other skeletal) for the following:

- Service Rifle
- Frag Grenade
- 12.7mm Pistol and Ammo

2 Sulfur Cavern

Check the ancient Campfire for the skeletal remains of a family of hunters.

- Campfire [29/109]
- Hunting Revolver and Ammo
- Hunting Shotgun and Ammo
- Dino Toy
- Key

3 Dead Legionary

4 Bone Cavern

More ancient remains lie here.

- Knife

5 Locked Gate [Very Hard]

This difficult lock is easier if you use the key sitting on the Campfire from Location #2. Watch for the Tripwire when you open the gate, or face a Frag Grenade attack.

- Frag Grenade Bouquet (3)
- 12.7mm Submachine Gun and Ammo
- First Aid Box and Purified Water
- Trunk Items [Average]
- Caps (a huge amount!)

6 Empty Cavern

[3.08] Bitter Springs ●

- Side Quest: No, Not Much
- Side Quest: Climb Ev'ry Mountain
- Side Quest: Bitter Springs Infirmary Blues
- Side Quest: I Forgot to Remember to Forget
- Threat Level: ●●●●●
- Faction: NCR
  - Entity: Captain Gilles
  - Entity: Lieutenant Markland
  - Entity: NCR Trooper
  - Entity: Refugee
- Fame/Infamy
- Services: Healer/Dealer [21/31]
- Crafting:
  - Campfire [30/109]
  - Campfire [31/109]
  - Campfire [32/109]
  - Campfire [33/109]
- Collectibles:
  - Magazine [Barter] [9/16] [10-12/52]
  - Magazine [Barter] [10/16] [10-12/52]
  - Magazine [Repair] [14/27] [10-12/52]
- Guns and Ammo
- Health, Chems, or Water
- Sleeping Quarters
- Wasteland Vegetation
- Quest Item

In the past century, Bitter Springs was used by the Great Khans as a semi-permanent community. Due to prolonged conflict with NCR, the Great Khans were eventually tracked back to Bitter Springs by NCR forces. The assault that rapidly followed was known as the "Bitter Springs Massacre" due to the NCR's First Recon mistakenly shooting down dozens of young, old, and wounded Khans who attempted to escape through a southern slot canyon from a location called Coyote Tail Ridge [3.15]. Today, Bitter Springs hosts refugees from settlements Caesar's Legion are razing; a situation that is becoming increasingly untenable. Currently, there are rumors of an NCR-hating ghost that comes down from the mountains to frighten refugees and Troopers alike. The actual settlement itself is almost completely surrounded by rocks, and is in a gully. It can be accessed via the southern slot canyon refugee camp, the western Great Khan graveyard, or the northern bluffs.

1 Southern Slot Canyon Entrance

Pass the sign of the NCR Bear, and weave through the mangled array of twisted metal trailers and carriages fashioned as rudimentary shelters.

- Sleeping Quarters

2 Great Khan Graveyard

Twelve graves from the site of the Great Khan massacre lie in situ. Find a Shovel and dig up items from each grave, and steal the helmets adorning the gravestones. This offers another route into and out of the settlement.

- Grave items

3 Tent City

A mixture of Great Khan tents, scrap-metal lean-tos, and other detritus masquerading as protection from the sun, are gathered in a jumble of flat land between the canyon walls. One of the refugees—a little girl—offers you a Barnabas Bear, then tells you she's sleepy.

- Campfire [30/109]
- Campfire [31/109]
- Campfire [32/109]
- Magazine: Salesman Weekly [Barter] [9/16] [10/52]
- Sleeping Quarters

4 Lieutenant Markland's Infirmary

Unwell refugees lie in beds here, as the overworked Lieutenant Markland does the best he can. The doctor offers to heal you, but the prices are high. He can't sell you medical supplies, as there aren't any. Speak to Captain Gilles, then back to Markland to uncover the exact items he requires, and start Side Quest: Bitter Springs Infirmary Blues.

- Doctor's Bag
- Healer: Lieutenant Markland [21/31]

5 Captain Gilles' Camp

The top of Bitter Springs is a Campfire surrounded by tents. Speak to Gilles, and ask what you can do to help, and you begin the colossal Side Quest: No, Not Much. Within that Quest, you can investigate the strange goings-on up the in the mountains (Great Khan Supply Caves 1, 2, 3 [3.S09, 10, 11]), as part of Side Quest: Climb Ev'ry Mountain.

- Campfire [33/109]
- Footlocker Items (3)
- Ammo Box Ammunition
- Magazine: Salesman Weekly [Barter] [10/16] [11/52]
- Magazine: Fixin' Things [Repair] [14/27] [12/52]
- Sleeping Quarters

BITTER SPRINGS EXTERIOR

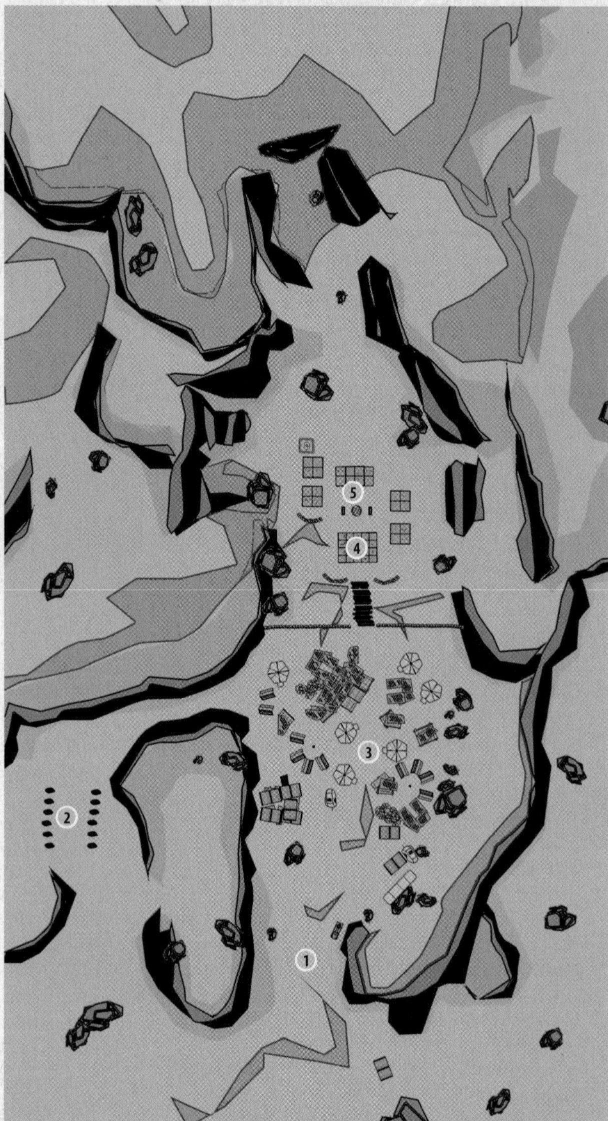

[3.09] Ranger Station Bravo ●

- Side Quest: Return to Sender
- Threat Level: ●●●●●
- Faction: NCR
  - Entity: Ranger Ericsen
  - Entity: Comm Officer Tilden
- Fame/Infamy
- Collectibles: Magazine [Repair] [15/27] [13/52]
- Guns and Ammo
- Health, Chems, or Water
- Highly Visible

In the highlands northeast of Bitter Springs [3.08] is a collection of reinforced metal and wood walls, truck containers, and cargo pods arranged in a defensive pattern, designed to keep the nearby Ghouls out. Run by Ranger Ericsen and Comm Officer Tilden, the NCR are watching Legion activity on the strip of the Colorado River known as "The Narrows." You can take Purified Water here, but the Ammunition won't be hauled away without a fight!

- Purified Water (5)
- Ammo Box Ammunition (10) [5: Average]
- Magazine: Fixin' Things [Repair] [15/27] [13/52]

[3.10] The Devil's Throat

- Threat Level: ●●●●●
- Faction: Abomination
  - Entity: Centaur
  - Entity: Evolved Centaur
- Dangers: Radiation
- Collectibles: Unique Weapon [21/42]
- Guns and Ammo

A dangerous and radioactive maw inhabited by Centaurs and their ironically monikered "Evolved" cousins. It is better to drop them from a distance before inspecting a container truck and its dumped contents; barrels that offer nothing but sickness. However, inside the truck is a Prospector (who looks to have overdosed with Jet) and a considerable array of loot, including Reinforced Combat Armor, and a Party Hat! But the big prize is his weapon.

- 5mm Round (333)
- Combat Armor, Reinforced
- Switchblade
- Party Hat
- Unique Weapon: CZ57 Avenger [21/42]

[3.11] Cannibal Johnson's Cave

- Side Quest: For Auld Lang Syne
- Threat Level: ●●●●●
- Faction: Enclave
  - Entity: Cannibal Johnson
- Crafting:Campfire [34/109]
- Dangers: Traps
- Collectibles:
  - Skill Book [Melee Weapons] [2/4] [4/9]
  - Hollowed-Out Rock [10/42]
  - Magazine [Survival] [13/30] [14/52]
- Guns and Ammo
- Health, Chems, or Water
- Interior Exploration
- Sleeping Quarters

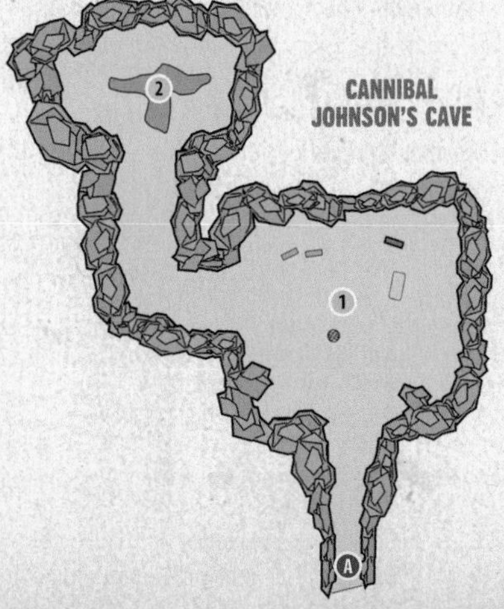

On the bluffs northwest of Camp Golf [3.23], close to Vault 34 [3.12], is a slit in the rocks above a steep gully, which sports a battered old door. Check the Hollowed-Out Rock at the entrance. Enter, and watch your step!

- Hollowed-Out Rock [10/42]

A Exit to Mojave Wasteland

1 Cannibal's Chamber

Deactivate the Bear Trap on the floor. Speak with Cannibal Johnson, and he greets you as an old friend. It's only when you talk more that you realize he was hoping it was death. At this point, you can speak to him about "mean old" drill Sergeant Dornan, his time in the military, and whether he's a Cannibal. He isn't saying.

But recalls a story where he bit the heart out of a Raider when he was surrounded.

He also mentions his tribal wife, with pretty eyes. She's dead a long time, now.

Kill Johnson, and you only gain a Hunting Rifle and .357 Magnum.

- Campfire [34/109]
- Enclave Footlocker Ammo [Average]
- Skill Book: Grognak the Barbarian [Melee Weapons] [2/4] [4/9]
- Magazine: Lad's Life [Survival] [13/30] [14/52]
- .357 Magnum Revolver and Ammo
- Hunting Rifle
- Knife
- Sleeping Quarters

2 Johnson's Coolhouse

Cannibal Johnson looks like an accomplished hunter. There's also ground-water to drink, which is cleaner than it appears.

[3.12] Vault 34

See maps on the following page

- Main Quest: Et Tumor, Brute?
- Side Quest: I Could Make You Care
- Side Quest: Hard Luck Blues
- Free Quest: All Fired Up!
- Free Quest: Suits You, Sarah
- Threat Level: ●●●●●
- Faction: Ghoul
  - Entity: Golden Gecko
  - Entity: Vault Overseer
  - Entity: Vault Security Officer
  - Entity: Vault Security Guard
  - Entity: Vault Technician
  - Entity: Vault Dweller
- Crafting: Reloading Bench [18/36]
- Dangers: Radiation
- Collectibles:
  - Skill Book: [Guns] [3/4] [5/9]
  - Magazine: [Crit. Chance] [9/11] [15-20/52]
  - Magazine: [Explosives] [8/12] [15-20/52]
  - Magazine: [Explosives] [9/12] [15-20/52]
  - Magazine: [Guns] [7/11] [15-20/52]
  - Magazine: [Guns] [8/11] [15-20/52]
  - Magazine: [Repair] [16/27] [15-20/52]
  - Magazine: [Repair] [17/27] [15-20/52]
  - Magazine: [Repair] [18/27] [15-20/52]
  - Unique Weapon: [22/42]
  - Unique Weapon: [23/42]
- Area Is Locked
- Guns and Ammo
- Health, Chems, or Water
- Interior Exploration
- Quest Item

Vault 34's social experiment was a fully armed society. The residents had an enormous armory and everyone had free access to it. For the first hundred years or so, things went well enough. When population problems became problematic, violence broke out. Large factions within the vault suggested limited reproductive rights. This caused more violence, leading to the Overseer stating that all weapons would be confiscated. Rather than accept this, a large faction of the vault dwellers left the vault, eventually settling at Nellis Air Force Base as the Boomers. The remaining vault dwellers chafed under increasingly restrictive overseer rule until a group of rebels staged an attack on the armory. In the weeks of fighting that ensued, the vault's reactor was damaged, leaking radiation throughout the area, and dooming most of the survivors into a long-suffering and feral existence.

Climb the hills to the east of the East Pump Station [2.21] for a commanding view of New Vegas, and a drop-in entrance on the vault itself. The exterior of the vault is a large hill with roving Golden Geckos, and a couple of parked military trucks with radioactive barrels on them close to the other entrance. To the northeast of the vault entrances is a dead NCR Trooper with a Radiation Suit you can don for the interior investigation. Otherwise, be sure to bring Rad-X, RadAway, or obtain the Lead Belly Perk to prevent Radiation sickness.

Vault 34—1st Floor (Interior)

A Door to Mojave Wasteland

1 2 Gecko Caverns

Toxic waste barrels illuminate the east and west alcoves. Beware of Golden Geckos.

B Opening from Mojave Wasteland

You can drop in from the top of the hill the vault is under, but not return in this direction.

3 Vault Entrance Tunnel

Check the bend in the tunnel for a skeleton.

- 10mm Pistol and Ammo

4 (Floor 2) Vault Entrance

Your first Ghoul attack occurs here. Check the control booth to the north for a Journal Fragment; the first of many in this vault. This details overcrowding in the vault that lead to violence, and guards at the Vault Armory.

- Note: Overseer's Journal Fragment (p64)
- Lead Pipe

5 (Floor 2, Floor 1, Floor B1) Mezzanine, Hall, and Systems Room

Although initially a balcony overlooking a hall, the hole in the ground allows you to drop into the Server Room below. Cross the Mezzanine bridge to a couple of barricades and a skeleton with a Magazine near his stash of Pork N' Beans. Don't forget to check the dressers for Vault 34 Jumpsuits. The main floor has barricades by each of the exit doors. The Systems Room has ammo and First Aid.

- Magazine: Fixin' Things [Repair] [16/27] [15/52]
- Lead Pipe
- Police Baton
- 10mm Submachine Gun and Ammo
- First Aid Box
- Vault 34 Jumpsuit

6 (Floor 2) Barricaded Map Room

Check the dressers for Vault 34 Jumpsuits, and the table for a gun and a terminal with the following messages:

> Welcome: A partially scrambled welcome message.

> Warning: Flooding: All doors to the third floor have been sealed.

> Warning: Reactor: Moderate damage and high radiation levels on the fourth floor.

> Log: A jumbled missive about riots.

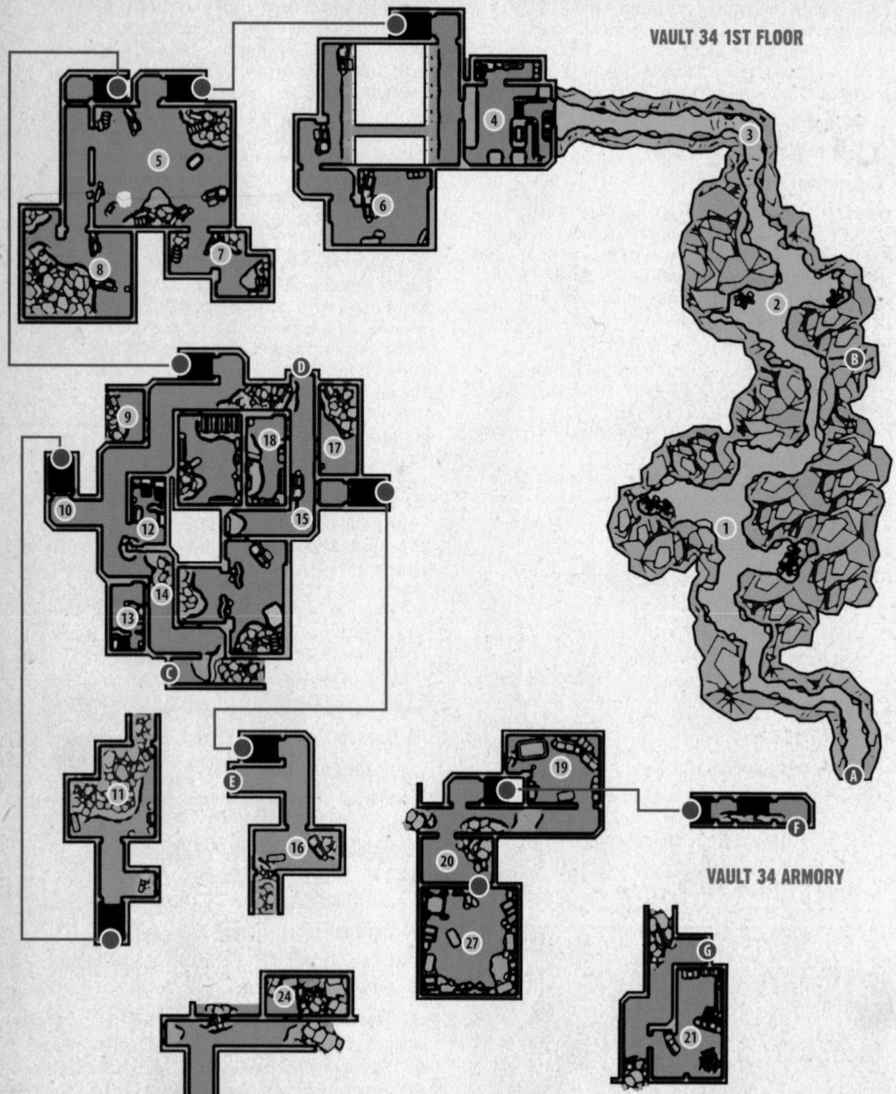

VAULT 34 1ST FLOOR

VAULT 34 ARMORY

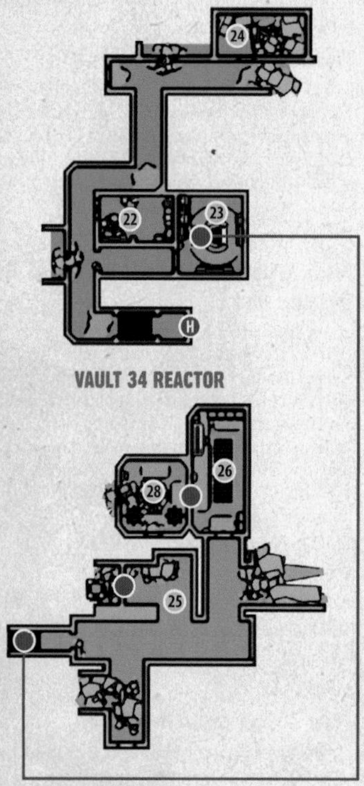

VAULT 34 REACTOR

- 10mm Submachine Gun
- Vault 34 Jumpsuit

7 (Floor 1) Barricaded Room

8 (Floor 1) Barricaded Diner

- Lead Pipe (2)
- Magazine: Patriot's Cookbook [Explosives] [8/12] [16/52]
- 10mm Submachine Gun
- Doctor's Bag
- First Aid Box

9 (Floor B1) Operations Room

Ghouls are stuck in here until you return from the waterlogged area (Location #11).

- Magazine: Fixin' Things [Repair] [17/27] [17/52]
- First Aid Box
- Vault 34 Jumpsuit

10 (Floor B1) Burst Pipe Corridor

Look for the burst pipe as this can be used as a marker to ensure you're diving into the correct irradiation location.

- Lead Pipe

11 (Floor B1 Underwater) Technician's Room

Swim down here to secure the only necessary item, on the Ghoulish and irradiated remains under the desk. This unlocks the terminal in Location #18.

- Holotape: Vault 34 Utility Terminal Password

12 (Floor B1) Dorm Room #1

- Magazine: Patriot's Cookbook [Explosives] [9/12] [18/52]
- Vault 34 Jumpsuit
- Sleeping Quarters

13 (Floor B1) Dorm Room #2

- Magazine: Milsurp Review [Guns] [7/11] [19/52]
- 10mm Submachine Gun
- Vault 34 Jumpsuit

14 (Floor B1) Clinic

Don't miss the exit door in the north wall.

- First Aid Box
- Wall Safe Items [Average]
- 10mm Pistol
- Vault 34 Jumpsuit

C Door to Vault 34 Reactor (Overseer's Quarters)

This is sealed, and opens only after you unlock it in Location #21.

15 (Floor B1) Burst Pipe Corridor #2

Look for the burst pipe above the barricade as this can be used as a marker to ensure you're diving into the correct irradiation location.

16 (Floor B1 Underwater) Technician's Room

Swim down here to secure the only necessary item, on the Ghoulish and irradiated remains under the desk. This area is drained once you access the Utility Station Room Terminal (Location #18). The password accesses the terminal in the Security Station A (Location #21).

- Holotape: Vault 34 Security Terminal Password

17 (Floor B1) Storage

Warning! Escaping Gas! Don't fire a weapon, or you'll detonate the gas. There are three Ghouls in here, and another Overseer Fragment. With the population getting out of control, the Overseer rerouted the Armory locks to his own terminal.

- Note: Overseer's Journal Fragment

D (Floor B1) Door to The Armory

This gets you into the Armory, but not to the cache of weapons.

18 (Floor B1) Utility Room

Use the Utility Terminal Password, or unlock the terminal [Very Hard] in here. Check the following:

> Warning: Flooding: All doors to the third floor have been sealed.

> Warning: Reactor: Moderate damage and high radiation levels on the fourth floor.

> Log: A jumbled missive about riots.

> System: Activate Pump Station to drain the water and allow progress to Security Station A.

- 10mm Pistol and Ammo
- Vault 34 Security Armor
- Vault 34 Security Helmet

E (Floor B1) Door to Security Station A

This is accessible only after the water is drained from the area.

Vault 34 Armory

F Door to Vault 34 1st Floor

19 Recreation Room

Check the area at the end of the corridor dotted with green radioactive acid for the following:

- Reloading Bench [18/36]
- Pool Cue
- First Aid Box
- Skill Book: Guns and Bullets [Guns] [3/4] [5/9]
- 10mm Pistol (2)

20 Equipment Room Entrance

The door in this room is locked, and cannot be opened until you access the Overseer's Terminal.

G Door to Vault 34 1st Floor

21 Security Station

Inspect the Mk III Auto-Doc for a piece of machinery to help during Main Quest: Et Tumor, Brute (which is only accessible if the Quest is active). Use the Security Terminal Password, or unlock the terminal [Very Hard] in here, which is near another Overseer's Journal Fragment. The Journal charts the doomed battles across the vault. Now check the terminal:

> Warning: Flooding: All doors to the Third Floor have been sealed.

> Warning: Reactor: Moderate damage and high radiation levels on the fourth floor.

> Log: A jumbled missive about riots.

> System: Disengage the Lock to the Overseer's Office (Location #C). Now return there.

- Note: Overseer's Journal Fragment (p66)
- Vault 34 Security Armor
- Vault 34 Security Helmet (2)
- Quest Item: Diagnostic Scanning Unit

27 Armory and Equipment Room Cache

Locked up by the Overseer, the door can only be unlocked from his terminal. Inside the room, gather armaments from the following, and ensure Veronica is here as part of Side Quest: I Could Make You Care, for a particular use regarding the Pulse Gun locked in the Gun Case [Very Hard]. There's a second Unique Weapon on the floor (an upturned table) here, too.

- Crate Items (2)
- 40mm Grenade (12 x 2)
- Ammo Box Ammunition (16)
- Grenade Launcher (2)
- Minigun
- Assault Carbine (2)
- Marksman Carbine
- Riot Shotgun
- 10mm Submachine Gun (5)
- Sniper Rifle (2)
- 10mm Pistol (9)
- Vault 34 Security Armor (4)
- Vault 34 Security Helmet (3)
- Police Baton
- Detonator
- Missile Launcher
- Combat Armor
- Combat Helmet
- C-4 Plastic Explosive (2)
- Unique Weapon: All-American [22/42]
- Gun Case [Very Hard]
- Unique Weapon: Pulse Gun [23/42]

Vault 34 Reactor

H Door to Vault 34 1st Floor

22 Security Room

There's a terminal here on the table with the Magazine, but the messages are the same.

- Lead Pipe
- Vault 34 Security Armor
- Vault 34 Security Helmet
- Magazine: Milsurp Review [Guns] [8/11] [20/52]

23 Overseer's Room

Fight off the Feral Overseer, and search his corpse for a password. Or you can hack [Very Hard] the Overseer's Terminal. Select the System Menu. There's also another Journal Fragment on the computer bank. It details the end of the vault in harrowing detail.

> System: Open the Armory Door. This allows access to the door at Location #20.

- Quest Item: Overseer's Password
- Note: Overseer's Journal Fragment (p67)
- First Aid Box

24 Security Room

Danger! Escaping Gas! Don't fire a weapon, or you'll cause an explosion.

- Doctor's Bag
- Magazine: True Police Stories [Crit. Chance] [9/11] [21/52]

25 Waterlogged Overseer Passage

Danger! Radiation! The door here leads to a reactor room completely blocked with debris.

26 Waterlogged Computer Bank

Danger! Radiation! Access this Mainframe to complete Side Quest: Hard Luck Blues, and save either some remaining vault dwellers, or help the Sharecropper Farms. Consult the Quest for details. The following messages are available:

> SOS: From the vault dwellers still alive in this hellhole.
> Log: A manual override has been attempted.
> Open Reactor Door
> Close exterior vents
> Reroute vault control

- Magazine: Fixin' Things [Repair] [18/27] [22/52]
- First Aid Box

28 Reactor Room

Danger! Radiation! This room can only be unlocked from the Computer Bank in the adjacent room. The terminal in here allows you to make a final choice during the Side Quest. Beware of Glowing Ones as you return!

> Seal external ventilation
> Reroute control of the vault

Free Quest: All Fired Up!

It is important that you don't overlook what is the Mojave Wasteland's most abundant collection of firepower. Locating both passwords from the underwater sections of the vault, or hacking the terminals, and then unlocking the Armory Equipment room from the Overseer's Terminal, is a Free Quest worth taking. Additional kudos if you read all of the Overseer's Journal entries.

[3.13] Gypsum Train Yard

- Threat Level: ●●●●●
- Faction: Abomination
  - Entity: Deathclaw
  - Entity: Giant Ant
- Dangers: Radiation
- Collectibles: Sunset Sarsaparilla Star Cap [33/100]
- Health, Chems, or Water
- Interior Exploration
- Wasteland Vegetation

This old Gypsum quarry is now home to a half-dozen Deathclaws, prowling the slightly irradiated water at the base of the quarry face, and conveyor belt. There's little but death outside in the quarry or around the rusting carriages (including Cazadors to the southeast). Check the office shack for the following:

- Sunset Sarsaparilla Star Cap [33/100]
- First Aid Box
- Ant Egg Clutches

[3.14] Cap Counterfeiting Shack

- Threat Level: ●●●●●
- Faction: Mutated Animal
  - Entity: Cazador
- Collectibles:
  - Skill Book [Barter] [3/4] [6/9]
  - Sunset Sarsaparilla Star Cap [34/100]
  - Sunset Sarsaparilla Star Cap [35/100]
  - Sunset Sarsaparilla Star Cap [36/100]
- Guns and Ammo
- Health, Chems, or Water
- Interior Exploration
- Sleeping Quarters

Inside, the shack offers spartan comforts, and a few Ammo Boxes (one empty) and a bunk bed.

- Varmint Rifle
- Teddy Bear and Beer
- Ammo Box Ammunition (2)
- Sleeping Quarters

If you've a hankering for Sunset Sarsaparilla, there's some in the crates down in the cellar. Then check the tables with the bottles on them; there are worthless Counterfeit Caps, Bottle Caps, and three Star Caps to grab. Lastly, check the back room for a rare Skill Book, and the following:

- Sunset Sarsaparilla Crate Items (3)
- Caps
- Sunset Sarsaparilla Star Cap [34/100]
- Sunset Sarsaparilla Star Cap [35/100]
- Sunset Sarsaparilla Star Cap [36/100]
- Ammo Box Ammunition (2)
- Gun Cabinet
- First Aid Box
- Skill Book: Tales of a Junktown Jerky Vendor [3/4] [6/9]

[3.15] Coyote Tail Ridge

- Side Quest: I Forgot to Remember to Forget
- Threat Level: ●●●●●
- Faction: None
- Highly Visible
- Wasteland Vegetation

These foothills were a good, defendable position for the First Recon Snipers during their massacre of the Great Khans. Boone tells you more about this past atrocity during his Side Quest. Other than a few scattered plants, this is simply a thoroughfare to Bitter Springs.

[3.16] Bitter Springs Recreation Area

- Threat Level: ●●●●●
- Faction: Mutated Animal
  - Entity: Giant Rat
- Collectibles:
  - Skill Book [Lockpick] [2/4] [7/9]
  - Magazine [Sneak] [7/10] [23/52]
  - Sunset Sarsaparilla Star Cap [37/100]
  - Sunset Sarsaparilla Star Cap [38/100]
- Health, Chems, or Water
- Interior Exploration
- Wasteland Vegetation

Now little more than a collection of doomed vehicular hulks rusting in the sun, this once-bustling vista spot now sports a single, large shack within the concrete barricade perimeter. Inside the shop, there's the following:

- Sunset Sarsaparilla Star Cap [37/100]
- Sunset Sarsaparilla Star Cap [38/100]
- Skill Book: Tumblers Today [Lockpick] [2/4] [7/9]
- Magazine: ¡La Fantoma! [Sneak] [7/10] [23/52]
- Safe Items [Average]

[3.17] Fisherman's Pride Shack

- Threat Level: ●●●○○
- Faction: Abomination
  - Entity: Lakelurk
- Crafting: Campfire [35/109]
- Collectibles:
  - Skill Book [Unarmed] [2/4] [8/9]
  - Hollowed-Out Rock [11/42]
  - Sunset Sarsaparilla Star Cap [39/100]
- Guns and Ammo
- Health, Chems, or Water
- Interior Exploration
- Sleeping Quarters
- Wasteland Vegetation

This shack offers great views of Lake Las Vegas (and an abundance of water to drink). Beware of nearby Lakelurks, and check the Hollowed-Out Rock and Campfire close to the shack itself before entering. Inside is a tiny, dim room with the following items:

- Hollowed-Out Rock [11/42]
- Campfire [35/109]
- Sunset Sarsaparilla Star Cap [39/100]
- Skill Book: Pugilism Illustrated [2/4] [8/9]
- BB Gun and Ammo
- Sleeping Quarters

[3.18] Callville Bay

- Side Quest: Volare!
- Threat Level: ●●●●○
- Faction: Mutated Animal
  - Entity: Cazador
  - Entity: Giant Rat
- Collectibles:
  - Sunset Sarsaparilla Star Cap [40/100]
  - Sunset Sarsaparilla Star Cap [41/100]
  - Magazine: [Survival] [14/30] [24/52]
- Health, Chems, or Water
- Interior Exploration
- Wasteland Vegetation

Once a small port and boat launch, Callville Bay is a derelict no-man's land overrun by Cazadors from their nest inside the corrugated warehouse that has fallen in on itself. There's a (currently inactive) harpoon winch on the launch itself. Lake Mead is a great source of drinking water, so sip yourself healthy, and don't forget to visit Captain Dean's Boat Rentals. Deal with the rodent infestation, before rummaging through the store shelves for the following:

- Bobby Pin (2)
- Knife (3)
- First Aid Box
- Sunset Sarsaparilla Star Cap [40/100]
- Sunset Sarsaparilla Star Cap [41/100]
- Magazine: Lad's Life [Survival] [14/30] [24/52]
- Carton of Cigarettes (2)
- Floor Safe Items [Average]

[3.19] Camp Guardian

- Free Quest: Help for Halford
- Threat Level: ●●●○○
- Faction: Mutated Animal
  - Entity: Coyote
  - Entity: Radscorpion
  - Entity: Bark Scorpion
  - Entity: Giant Rat

CAMP GUARDIAN EXTERIOR

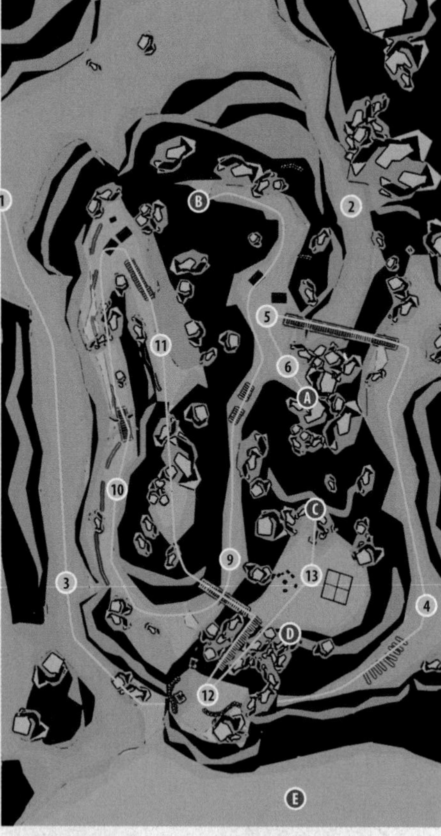

- Collectibles: Hollowed-Out Rock [12/42]
- Guns and Ammo
- Interior Exploration
- Radio Signal [Camp Guardian]
- Wasteland Vegetation

> **Note** Camp Guardian is the scrawled name of the ancient looping pathways up these rocky crags. However, the NCR camp at the summit is known as Guardian Peak [3.20] on your Pip-Boy. You must first scale this location to reach the peak.

When the main road from Callville Bay [3.18] ends at a Road Turnabout [3.S13] and an old scenic overlook. Explore the pathways in this maze of craggy rock formations, small tunnel systems, and finally a (now abandoned) NCR post high atop Guardian Peak. You can also approach the area from Lake Mead to the south, and Ranger Station Bravo [3.09] to the north. As you approach, you can hear an SOS if you tune your Pip-Boy to Camp Guardian Radio!

- Radio: Camp Guardian Radio

1 To Overlook Turnabout

From the road turnaround with the two burned-out cars and Scenic Overlook sign, move into the gully. Note the remains of a picket fence along the cliff above. You can follow the gully to the right (south) to Location #3 and the climb up to Guardian Peak, or explore to the left (northeast) toward Location #2.

2 Radscorpion Gully

The road to the northeast splits to the right (east) and winds around to the south, under a rickety bridge to a dead-end.

3 Guardian Peak Sign

Close to the shore of Lake Mead is a sign and the beginning of the Guardian Peak trail, near a graffiti-daubed sign, and Hollowed-Out Rock. Coyotes roam this area. A few steps fsrther up the picket-fenced path is a garbage can, and two notes (one among some loose rocks, and the other two on bushes) about rock-clearing by NCR soldiers to reach the Peak.

- Hollowed-Out Rock [12/42]
- Note: Camp Guardian Log Page 7
- Note: Camp Guardian Log Page 3
- Note: Camp Guardian Log Page 18

4 Sleeper Steps and Crevasse Pass

Expect more pages as you progress along the path; look down to find them on the steps and bushes. As you reach the steps, look up at the cliff face to your left, and bring out your Local Map. There's an entrance to the interior of the Guardian Peak Caves [3.20], which (with careful jumping) you can actually reach, circumventing the rest of this climb!

- Note: Camp Guardian Log Page 12
- Note: Camp Guardian Log Page 20

5 Gully Bridge and Picnic Area

There are Giant Rats near an outhouse, and plants to pick along this route, which takes you to the bridge you couldn't reach from Location #2. At the picnic area, check the sandbags to the right (north) for some Grenade crates. The path splits to the left (Location #9), doubles back to the southwest (Location #6) and right (Location #8) at this point.

- Frag Grenade (7)

6 Sloping Path to Camp Guardian Cave

Climb to the cave mouth that overlooks the Gully Bridge you just used. Enter the cave.

A Entrance to/from Camp Guardian Cave

7 Main Cavern (interior)

Inside the Cave, there's a short passage to a large open chamber with Giant Rats to contend with. Drop down, and you can't get back up.

8 Camp Guardian Cave Passage Loop (interior)

This leads along a winding, natural cave tunnel, with Giant Rats to deal with, and exits back out to a the lower sandbags with a Super Mutant dummy, Radscorpions, and the path back up to the Picnic Area.

B Entrance to/from Camp Guardian Cave

9 Narrow Bridge Gully

The only way onward is to continue up the sets of steps dug into the gully earth, and through the next gully area to a cliff edge.

10 Cliff Ledge Picket Path to Picnic Area #2

Turn right (northwest) at the Broc Flower and grab two more Notes as you carefully traverse the ground over a small bridge, to a second picnic area and more steps leading still farther upward.

- Note: Camp Guardian Log Page 13
- Note: Camp Guardian Log Page 5

11 Peak Ascent

Follow the trail up more steps, and finally into Guardian Peak Camp [3.20], crossing the narrow bridge above Location #9. The search of the camp, and discovery of a large cave structure not properly surveyed by the NCR, is discussed at the next location:

[3.20] Guardian Peak

- Free Quest: Help for Halford
- Free Quest: Tags of Our Fallen
- Threat Level: ●●●●●
- Faction: Abomination
  - Entity: Private Halford
  - Entity: Lakelurk

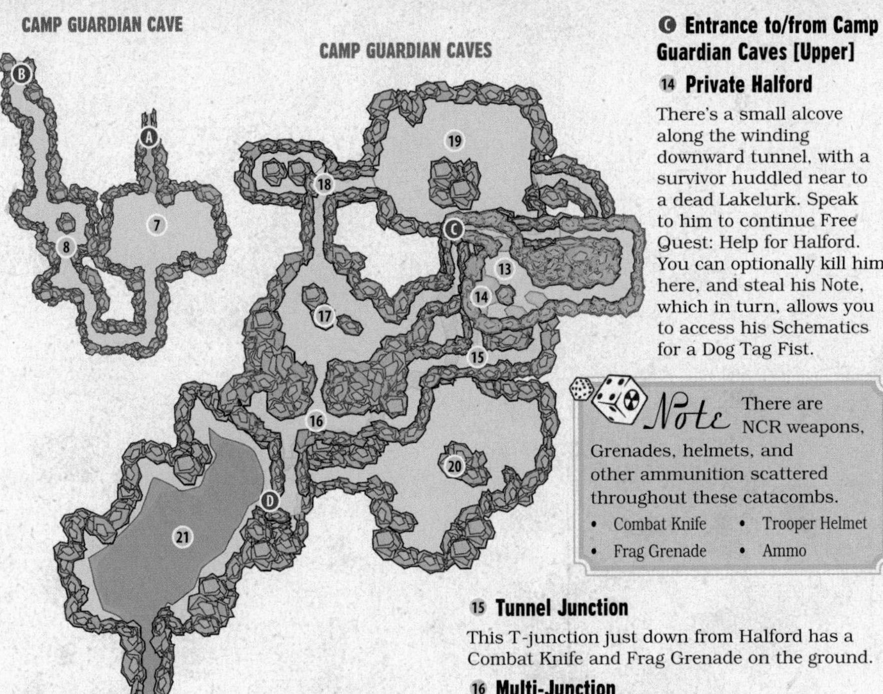

- Entity: Lakelurk King
- Crafting: Campfire [36/109]
- Collectibles:
  - Sunset Sarsaparilla Star Cap [42/100]
  - Unique Item [47/95]
- Guns and Ammo
- Health, Chems, or Water
- Interior Exploration
- Radio Signal [Camp Guardian]
- Sleeping Quarters

The only remaining survivor of a Lakelurk attack is hiding inside these caverns, and starts Free Quest: Help for Halford.

This is the camp that the NCR finally cleared to. Consult the previous location (Camp Guardian [3.19]) for the route to get here. Grab the Note at the entrance, just after the bridge. Then check the Campfire for some Water and Food, as well as a Star Cap. There's signs of scavenging inside the tent, but there's more Food, bedding to sleep on, and footlockers to scavenge from.

- Campfire [36/109]
- Sunset Sarsaparilla Star Cap [42/100]
- Note: Camp Guardian Log Page 8
- Sleeping Quarters

12 Radio and Vista

Check the steps for another two Notes, and a Ham Radio, along with an amazing view of Lake Mead and the mountains. There's more food, some ammo, another Note by an armchair with Binoculars to take. By now, you should have read most of the available Notes (some are lost to the wind forever). Apparently, the NCR might have been sitting on some kind of nest they didn't know about before it was too late....

- Note: Camp Guardian Log Page 15
- Note: Camp Guardian Log Page 19
- Note: Camp Guardian Log Page 14
- Ammo Box Ammunition (2)
- Binoculars

13 Camp Guardian Caves Entrance [Exterior and Interior]

North of the tent is a hole in the rocks; the last, and possibly most frightening, part of this excursion. In the initial chamber, there's a crate with the following on or near it. The cave tunnel continues downward.

- 9mm Pistol
- C-4 Plastic Explosive (2)
- Combat Knife

C Entrance to/from Camp Guardian Caves [Upper]

14 Private Halford

There's a small alcove along the winding downward tunnel, with a survivor huddled near to a dead Lakelurk. Speak to him to continue Free Quest: Help for Halford. You can optionally kill him here, and steal his Note, which in turn, allows you to access his Schematics for a Dog Tag Fist.

Note There are NCR weapons, Grenades, helmets, and other ammunition scattered throughout these catacombs.

- Combat Knife
- Frag Grenade
- Trooper Helmet
- Ammo

15 Tunnel Junction

This T-junction just down from Halford has a Combat Knife and Frag Grenade on the ground.

16 Multi-Junction

There are two tunnels in the north wall; the latter leads to a dead-end, so take the other one, into the Small Central Cavern.

17 Small Central Cavern

This has a few Lakelurks to worry about.

18 Long Spiral, or Short Drop

The north of the Small Central Cavern leads to a winding passage into the North Cavern, or a ledge allowing you to drop down.

19 Northern Cavern

A huge cavern with multiple Lakelurks, centered around a massive natural column dotted with unnatural glowing fungi. The only exit is deeper and down; a tunnel in the south wall with NCR Trooper corpses. Grab the Dogtags if you're collecting them for Camp Forlorn Hope's Quartermaster Mayes [6.02] as part of his Free Quest. There are eleven corpses, leading you into the next chamber.

- NCR Dogtag (11)

20 Lair of the Lakelurk King

The NCR squad made their last stand here, in another massive cavern with five Lakelurks and their dreaded King. Fight them off if you're trying to save Private Halford, and then search for Clutches of Lakelurk Eggs if you wish. There's an NCR Pack Brahmin carrying a number of items.

- Pack Brahmin Items
- Lakelurk Eggs

21 Lake Mead Exit Cavern

There are another six Lakelurks in here, so prepare to fight them in the culmination of the battle with the King.

D Exit to Cliff Ledge

This allows access to a short cliff ledge, and back down to the path with the picket fence.

E Exit to Lake Mead

This brings you bobbing up here a rusting underwater boat wreck, close to the cliffside path of Camp Guardian. You can enter from this location, too.

Free Quest: Help for Halford

At location #14, inside the Guardian Peak caves, you'll find a frightened NCR soldier called Private Halford. You can read about his squad's exploits in the Notes scattered throughout these adjacent areas, and hear his alarm signals if you tuned your Pip-Boy to Camp Guardian Radio. You can ask what happened, and what's wrong with him:

MEDICINE 50 Which you can postulate is a dislocated joint and laceration.

At this point, you can:

Leave Halford and clear the caves on your own, then return to him. He gives you a Note as a reward.

Have Halford accompany you until he either dies or survives (it is likely to be the former). Take the Note from his corpse, or as a reward if he survives.

Tell Halford to leave, and he heads off back to California, but leaves you a Note.

The Note itself is actually a Schematic for making a Dog Tag Fist weapon.

- Halford's Note
- Unique Item: [Schematics] Dog Tag Fist [47/95]

[3.21] Follower's Outpost

- Side Quest: I Could Make You Care
- Threat Level: ●●●●●
- Faction: Followers of the Apocalypse
  - Entity: Doctor Alvarez
  - Entity: Doctor Schiller
- Services: Healer/Dealer [22/31]
- Collectibles: Hollowed-Out Rock [13/42]
- Health, Chems, or Water
- Interior Exploration
- Sleeping Quarters
- Wasteland Vegetation

An old train junction and signal box is the location for the Followers' outpost, where Prospectors can come and get treated for their ailments. Note the Hollowed-Out Rock at the base of the signal box. Climb up to the balcony above, and enter the wooden tower. Sitting behind her desk is Doctor Alvarez, who runs the place Doctor Schiller (who is out making the rounds) as well as her fellow practitioners and guards.

- Hollowed-Out Rock [13/42]
- Healer: Doctor Alvarez [22/31]

[3.22] Lake Las Vegas

- Threat Level: ●●●●●
- Faction: NCR
- Health, Chems, or Water
- Wasteland Vegetation

Dammed at its northeastern end by the NCR, who have a sizable presence at the adjacent Camp Golf [3.23], this provides a good source of water for the Sharecropper Farms to the northwest, thanks to the snaking pipeline. The lake itself holds nothing but a few submerged golf carts, and other minor detritus, although there's a Campfire to the east, at the Scenic Overlook [3.S17].

[3.23] Camp Golf ●

- Side Quest: No, Not Much
- Side Quest: Flags of Our Foul-Ups
- Side Quest: Return to Sender
- Threat Level: ●●●●●
- Faction: NCR
  - Entity: Chief Hanlon
  - Entity: NCR Ranger
  - Entity: Sergeant McCredie
  - Entity: Doc Sawbones
  - Entity: O'Hanrahan
  - Entity: Razz
  - Entity: Poindexter
  - Entity: Mags
- Fame/Infamy
  - Services: Healer/Dealer [23/31]
- Crafting:
  - Campfire [37/109]
  - Campfire [38/109]
- Collectibles:
  - Caravan Cards [10/30]
  - Magazine: [Energy Weapons] [7/10] [25-37/52]
  - Magazine: [Energy Weapons] [8/10] [25-37/52]
  - Magazine: [Explosives] [10/12] [25-37/52]
  - Magazine: [Lockpick] [11/12] [25-37/52]
  - Magazine: [Melee Weapons] [8/9] [25-37/52]
  - Magazine: [Repair] [19/27] [25-37/52]
  - Magazine: [Repair] [20/27] [25-37/52]
  - Magazine: [Science] [12/23] [25-37/52]
  - Magazine: [Science] [13/23] [25-37/52]
  - Magazine: [Speech] [8/12] [25-37/52]
  - Magazine: [Survival] [15/30] [25-37/52]
  - Magazine: [Survival] [16/30] [25-37/52]
  - Magazine: [Unarmed] [8/11] [25-37/52]
  - Sunset Sarsaparilla Star Cap [43/100]
  - Sunset Sarsaparilla Star Cap [44/100]
  - Sunset Sarsaparilla Star Cap [45/100]
  - Unique Item [48/95]
  - Unique Item [49/95]
  - Unique Item [50/95]
  - Unique Item [51/95]
  - Unique Item [52/95]
- Guns and Ammo
- Health, Chems, or Water
- Highly Visible
- Interior Exploration
- Sleeping Quarters
- Wasteland Vegetation
- Quest Item

Adjacent to Lake Las Vegas [3.22] are the remains of a golf course, now overgrown grass and scrub with a large NCR camp in the middle of the course. The NCR have a heavy presence here as they are guarding a giant water pipe that stretches off to the north, to water the Sharecropper Farms [2.20] plants and keep the NCR's belly full.

1 Southwest Guard Tower

The perimeter of this location follows the road around from this tower overlooking the lake.

2 West Guard Tower

3 Target Range

The tee-off for the fourth hole is now a concrete-block construction of targets for the NCR raw recruits being trained here to hone their talents. This is where you bring the Misfits.

4 Camp Golf Mess Tent

There are two entrances, and the one out back leads to some cooking pots and a couple of Knives. There's Food here, but you must steal it.

- Knife (2)

The Misfits

As you'd expect, if you can't find O'Hanrahan, Poindexter, Mags, or Razz sitting around or wandering the camp or in their tent, they're likely to be over-filling their bellies here. Speaking with any of them allows you to find out more about them, but you won't begin the Quest until you speak to Sergeant McCredie first. Note that Poindexter has some Caravan Cards on his person.

- Caravan Cards [10/30]

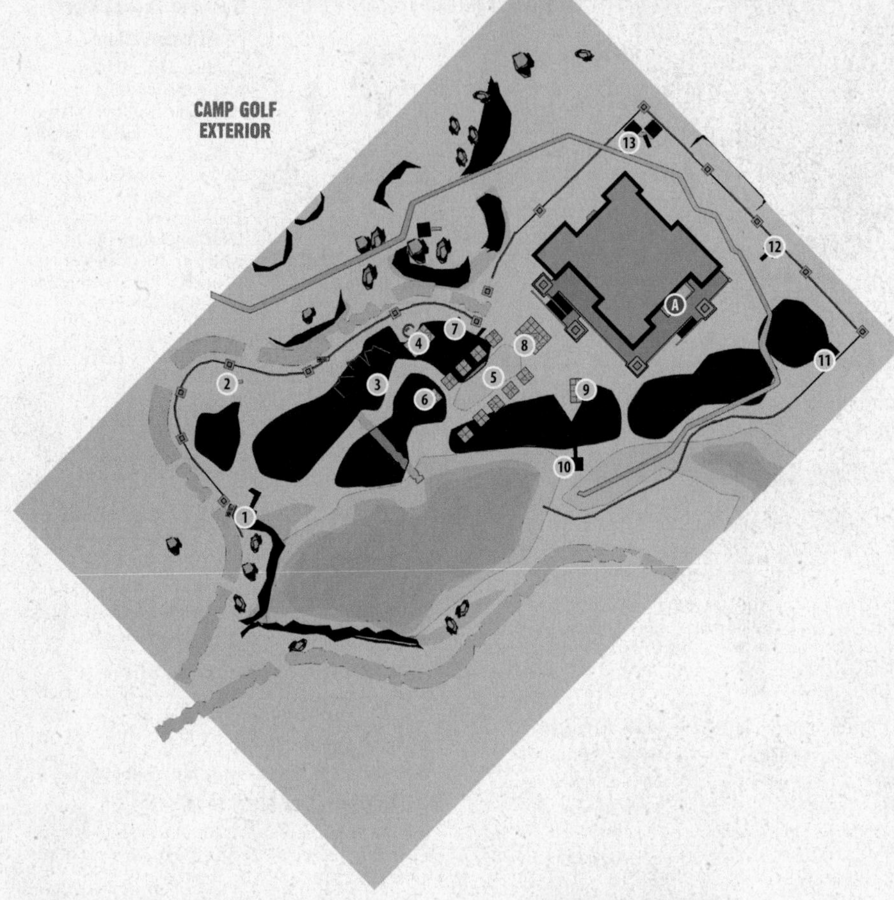

5 Camp Golf Trooper Tents

There are 10 tents and a Campfire here. The first nine all have the following possible items inside:

- Campfire [37/109]
- Carton of Cigarettes
- Footlocker Items
- Sleeping Quarters

6 Misfits' Tent

This is where you should return to during the Side Quest, if the Misfits aren't about. Check the Duffle Bags and grab a couple of Magazines if your Karma can take it.

- Magazine: [Future Weapons Today] [Energy Weapons] [7/10] [25/52]
- Magazine: [Patriot's Cookbook] [Explosives] [10/12] [26/52]

7 Northwest Guard Tower

8 McCredie's Communications Tent

Sergeant McCredie is a gruff and no-nonsense soldier who signed up at 16, and is attempting to whip the new recruits into shape while dealing with constant Legion incursions. Offer to help out to begin Side Quest: Flags of Our Foul Ups. The communications room itself has a couple of staff, and the following items to steal.

- Ammo Box Ammunition
- Scrap Metal
- Magazine: [Lad's Life] [Survival] [15/30] [27/52]
- Magazine: [Programmer's Digest] [Science] [12/23] [28/52]

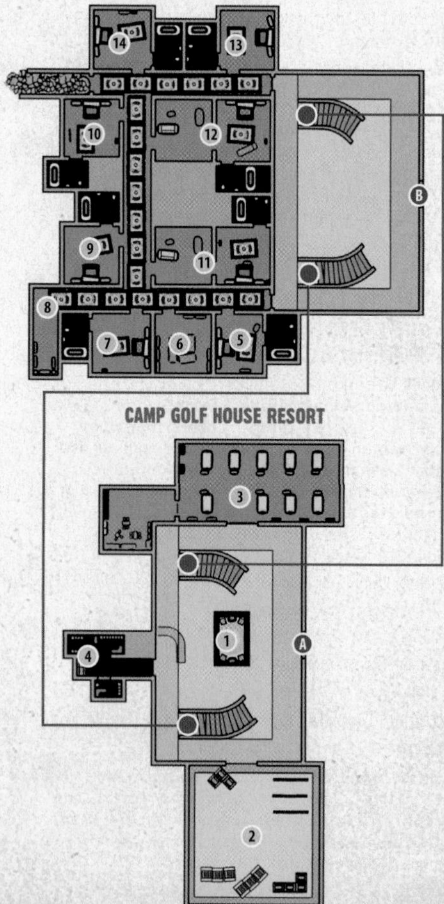

9 Infirmary Tent

Doc Sawbones runs this place, which is currently empty of the injured. He's able to fix you up for a price, and that price is 100 Caps. But he has little else to say.

- Healer: Doc Sawbones [23/31]
- Blood Pack (2)
- Health and Chems
- Doctor's Bag

10 South Guard Tower

11 Northeast Guard Tower

12 North Guard Tower

13 North Double Guard Tower

House Resort

This lodge-style building named after the benefactor and ex-owner of the place, is now the base for the NCR Rangers in the region. It is also the location of Chief Hanlon; an important cog in the machinery of Side Quest: Return to Sender.

A Entrance to/from House Resort

1 (Ground and Upper) Grand Foyer

A suitably grand entrance. At the curved reception desk is a Squad Readiness Reports Terminal with the following data (most of which is redacted, but the Misfits report is necessary for Side Quest: Flags of our Foul-Ups):

> Squad CG554-2 "Misfits"
  > Rifle Range Report
  > Grenade Range Report
> Ranger Detachment Alpha
> Ranger Detachment Bravo
> Ranger Detachment Charlie

B (Ground and Upper) Door to Camp Golf and Upper Balcony

There are two pairs of double-doors; the first you used to enter, and the second out to an exterior balcony directly above. Chief Hanlon is out here, staring wistfully at Lake Mead, and starts rambling on about the water problems of other states. Afterward, you can quiz him at length about Caesar's Legion, and the Rangers. He's also part of the culmination of Side Quest: Return to Sender; but only if this Quest is active. He carries a rare, but not unique gun, too.

- Ranger Sequoia

2 (Ground) Storage Hall

A once-grand dining room, which still sports a painting of (what is surely an ancestor of) Mr. House standing by one of his robotic creations, has been cleared and is now an almost-empty storage chamber.

- Campfire [38/109]
- First Aid Box
- Ammo

3 (Ground) Barracks and Mess Hall

Rangers occasionally sleep, and when they do, it's usually in here. There's an adjoining Mess Hall.

- Combat Knife
- Combat Armor and Helmet
- Footlocker (9) and Duffle Bag (4) Items
- Scrap Metal
- Carton of Cigarettes
- Purified Water (17)
- Food, Drink, and Alcohol
- Unique Item: Nuka-Cola Quartz [48/95]
- Unique Item: Nuka-Cola Quartz [49/95]
- Unique Item: Nuka-Cola Quartz [50/95]
- Unique Item: Nuka-Cola Quartz [51/95]
- Unique Item: Nuka-Cola Quartz [52/95]

4 (Ground) Offices

Behind the reception desk are two offices. The one to the left has a special keycard, obviously left by a previous owner, that allows access to the inner sanctum of the Lucky 38 Casino. The other, Squad Readiness Reports Terminal [Hard], is more difficult to access, as the NCR isn't happy if you attempt a hacking. Not to worry; it simply has the same information as the reception terminal.

> Activate Luck 38 executive override
> Squad CG554-2 "Misfits"
  > Rifle Range Report
  > Grenade Range Report
> Ranger Detachment Alpha
> Ranger Detachment Bravo
> Ranger Detachment Charlie

- Lucky 38 VIP Keycard

5 (Upper) Left Corridor Bedroom #1

The door to this room is open. Inside, someone has been tinkering with an engine.

- Carton of Cigarettes
- Magazine: Fixin' Things [Repair] [19/27] [29/52]
- Scrap Metal
- Sleeping Quarters

6 (Upper) Left Corridor Bedroom #2

- Purified Water (4)

7 (Upper) Left Corridor Bedroom #3

- Teddy Bear
- Magazine: Meeting People [Speech] [8/12] [30/52]
- Sleeping Quarters

8 (Upper) Hall Office

There's a broken terminal here.

- Magazine: Future Weapons Today [Energy Weapons] [8/10] [31/52]

9 (Upper) Connecting Corridor Bedroom #1

This is a junkie's room, with scattered syringes, and Chems.

- Chems (Jet, Buffout, Fixer, Rebound)
- Sleeping Quarters

10 (Upper) Connecting Corridor Bedroom #2

- Magazine: Boxing Times [Unarmed] [8/11] [32/52]
- Bobby Pins
- Sleeping Quarters

11 (Upper) Connecting Corridor Lounge #1

- First Aid Box
- Footlocker Items
- Floor Safe Items
- Ammo Box Ammunition

12 (Upper) Connecting Corridor Lounge #2

- Magazine: Fixin' Things [Repair] [20/27] [33/52]
- Magazine: Programmer's Digest [Science] [13/23] [34/52]
- Doctor's Bag
- First Aid Box
- Sleeping Quarters

13 (Upper) Right Corridor Bedroom #1

- Magazine: Locksmith's Reader [Lockpick] [11/12] [35/52]
- Magazine: Tæles of Chivalrie [Melee Weapons] [8/9] [36/52]
- Magazine: Lad's Life [Survival] [16/30] [37/52]
- Sunset Sarsaparilla Star Cap [43/100]
- Sunset Sarsaparilla Star Cap [44/100]
- Sunset Sarsaparilla Star Cap [45/100]
- Sleeping Quarters

14 (Upper) Right Corridor Bedroom #2

- Frag Grenade (3)
- Sleeping Quarters

[3.24] Mountain Shadows Campground

- Threat Level: ●●●●●
- Faction: None
- Crafting: Campfire [39/109]
- Collectibles:
  - Magazine [Medicine] [16/19] [38-39/52]
  - Magazine [Survival] [17/30] [38-39/52]
  - Sunset Sarsaparilla Star Cap [46/100]
- Sleeping Quarters

Mountain Shadows is actually three separate picnicking spots separated by faint rocky paths. Traverse these rocky warrens carefully to avoid a broken limb, or use the remains of the road leading across the railroad and back to the 188 Trading Post [5.02] to find your way to the main camp. The western picnic area below offers little but rusty kitchen wares and some food. The two picnic tables to the east, near the two burned-out cars, offer some scraps of food, and a Lad's Life.

- Campfire [39/109]
- Magazine: Today's Physician [Medicine] [16/19] [38/52]
- Magazine: Lad's Life [Survival] [17/30] [39/52]
- Sunset Sarsaparilla Star Cap [46/100]
- Sleeping Quarters

[3.25] Scavenger Platform

- Threat Level: ●●●●●
- Faction: Abomination
  - Entity: Lakelurk
- Crafting: Campfire [40/109]
- Collectibles:
  - Skill Book [Survival] [1/4] [9/9]
  - Sunset Sarsaparilla Star Cap [47/100]
- Guns and Ammo
- Health, Chems, or Water
- Highly Visible
- Lots O' Caps
- Sleeping Quarters

Useful to scramble back to during underwater investigations of Lake Mead, this quartet of linked, floating shacks on the lake is now home to around half a dozen Lakelurks.

- Campfire [40/109]
- Caps
- Skill Book: Wasteland Survival Guide [Survival] [1/4] [9/9]
- Sunset Sarsaparilla Star Cap [47/100]
- Ammo Box Ammunition (2)

[3.26] Crashed B-29

- Side Quest: Volare!
- Threat Level: ●●●●●
- Faction: Boomer
- Area Is Locked
- Health, Chems, or Water

In surprisingly good condition considering the years spent lying at the bottom of Lake Mead, this ancient Bombing aircraft is the ultimate salvage project of a Boomer named Loyal, over at Nellis Air Force Base [3.01]. However, it can't be raised to the surface without proper ballasts; acquired during the Side Quest. Otherwise, this is a large marker you should use when locating Lake Mead Cave [3.27].

[3.27] Lake Mead Cave

- Threat Level: ●●●●●
- Faction: None
- Collectibles: Magazine: [Survival] [18/30] [40/52]
- Guns and Ammo
- Health, Chems, or Water
- Interior Exploration

Caution You are wise to consider a Rebreather to avoid running out of air; or simply surface in the initial cave chamber, as there are air pockets here. Beware entering the Main Chamber; there's no air at all in here!

A Exit to Lake Mead

1 Initial Cave Chamber

This sunken trove is illuminated by strange pink fungi.

- Sunset Sarsaparilla Crates
- First Aid Box (2)
- Ammo Box Ammunition

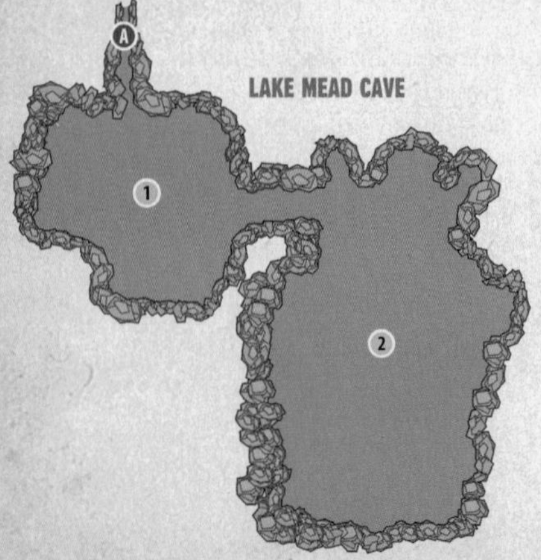

2 Main Chamber

Accessed via an opening in the eastern wall, this is a terrifying chamber if you don't have breathing apparatus. Keep to the ground, and search the southwest area for a group of suitcases, between which is a Lad's Life. The pink fungi reveals where to look. Remember: the exit passage is to the northwest!

- Magazine: Lad's Life [Survival] [18/30] [40/52]
- Ammo Box Ammunition

[3.28] The Fort ●

See maps on the following page

- Main Quest: Ring-a-Ding Ding!
- Main Quest: Render Unto Caesar
- Main Quest: The House Always Wins, I
- Main Quest: The House Always Wins, II
- Main Quest: Wild Card: You and What Army?
- Side Quest: I Forgot to Remember to Forget
- Side Quest: I Hear You Knocking
- Side Quest: Nothin' But a Hound Dog
- Side Quest: Oh My Papa
- Side Quest: The Finger of Suspicion
- Free Quest: A Trusted Aide
- Free Quest: Beware the Wrath of Caesar!
- Free Quest: Caesar's Favor
- Free Quest: Laurifer Gladiator
- Free Quest: Powder to the People
- Free Quest: Saving (or Savaging) Sergeant Teddy
- Threat Level: ●●●●●
- Faction: Caesar's Legion
  - Entity: Caesar
  - Entity: Lucius
  - Entity: Vulpes Inculta
  - Entity: Anthony
  - Entity: Otho
  - Entity: Siri
  - Entity: Dale Barton
  - Entity: Melody
  - Entity: Legionary
  - Entity: Legionary Instructor
  - Entity: Legionary Blacksmith
  - Entity: Legionary Decanus
  - Entity: Legionary Vexillarius
  - Entity: Other Legionary Forces
- Fame/Infamy
- Services:
  - Caravan Player [8/15]
  - Healer/Dealer [24/31]
  - Repairer [4/9]
  - Trader [17/33]
- Crafting:
  - Campfire [41/109]
  - Campfire [42/109]
  - Weapon Upgrade [5/10]
- Collectibles:
  - Caravan Cards [11/30]
  - Unique Item [53/95]
- Area Is Locked
- Guns and Ammo
- Health, Chems, or Water
- Highly Visible
- Interior Exploration
- Lots O' Caps
- Sleeping Quarters
- Underground Connection
- Wasteland Vegetation
- Quest Item
- No Weapons, Please!

Also known as Fortification Hill, this is on the Arizona side of the Colorado River. After the first Battle of Hoover Dam, the NCR secured and held this section of river against Caesar's subsequent strikes. Caesar's remaining troops regrouped at Fortification Hill, overlooking Lake Mead and the dam. When Caesar himself arrived, he dealt with his failed commander, Joshua Graham, by having him set on fire and hurled down the cliff face into the lake. Although beaten, the Legion were not defeated. And now, smoke continuously rises from Caesar's camp and the sounds of activity can be heard from the dam. It is an ominous and looming threat to the security of Hoover Dam and New Vegas itself.

Outer Gate and Fortification Hill

A Gate to Cottonwood Cove

1 Gate Entrance

This is where you are deposited from your journey up the Colorado River from Cottonwood Cove. A Legionary Main Gate Guard greets you and orders you to disarm. You can:

- Keep your holdout weapons and disarm.
- Disarm.
- Refuse (and return to Cottonwood Cove).
- Refuse (and attack; if this is a plan, be sure to bring Boone along as part of Side Quest: I Forgot to Remember to Forget).

Ask what is considered a banned item, and then tell the guard you have a medical condition. You get to keep your Chems and healing items.

Or you can give up your weapons, Pickpocket the Weapons Footlocker Key from the guard, but your Reputation plummets when you try and open the footlockers by the gate.

2 Crucifixion Posts

Mainly corpses, and a near-dead Legionary who committed theft against Caesar.

3 Legate's Gate

The area behind the gate is inaccessible, but a wandering Caravaneer called Dale Barton is here, and he's happy to Trade with you. You can also find out more about Caesar and Dale from speaking with him. He isn't the greatest Repairer, but he can fix your stuff, too. Finally, he can play a hand or two of Caravan with you.

- Caravan Player: Dale Barton [8/15]
- Repairer: Dale Barton [Skill 30] [4/9]
- Trader: Dale Barton [17/33]
- Trader (Dale Barton) Weapon Upgrades [5/10]
- Trader (Dale Barton) Caravan Cards [11/30]

4 Northeast Trench

Between the inner gate drawbridge is a long trench winding around the perimeter of the camp. Head around to the northeast, and you can spot dozens of red tents on the inaccessible side of Lake Mead. To the north, you can just make out Guardian Peak [3.20].

- Ammo Box Ammunition (2)

5 Drawbridge

6 Perimeter Wall (South)

This affords good views of Hoover Dam [3.33] to the southwest, and you can climb the rocks to inspect more crucifixes.

7 Perimeter Wall (North)

- First Aid Box

8 Steps to Inner Fort

This is the main thoroughfare to the top of Fortification Hill. Along the way, you can watch a Legionary Instructor and his child soldiers learn the ways of violence.

- Sleeping Quarters

Caesar's Fort

9 Fort Entrance

There are tents either side and bedrolls to sleep on, as well as footlockers to steal from. Blacksmiths are sharpening Machetes here. You may also run into various troop types.

- Footlocker Items (10)
- Sleeping Quarters

10 Arena

Speak with Otho by the Arena entrance if you wish to prove your worth, and begin Free Quest: Laurifer Gladiator.

11 Victus Aula (Food Hall)

Speak to Siri to begin Free Quest: Powder to the People. Otherwise, this place has a scattering of Brahmin Steaks it probably isn't worth getting killed over.

- Healer: Siri [24/31]

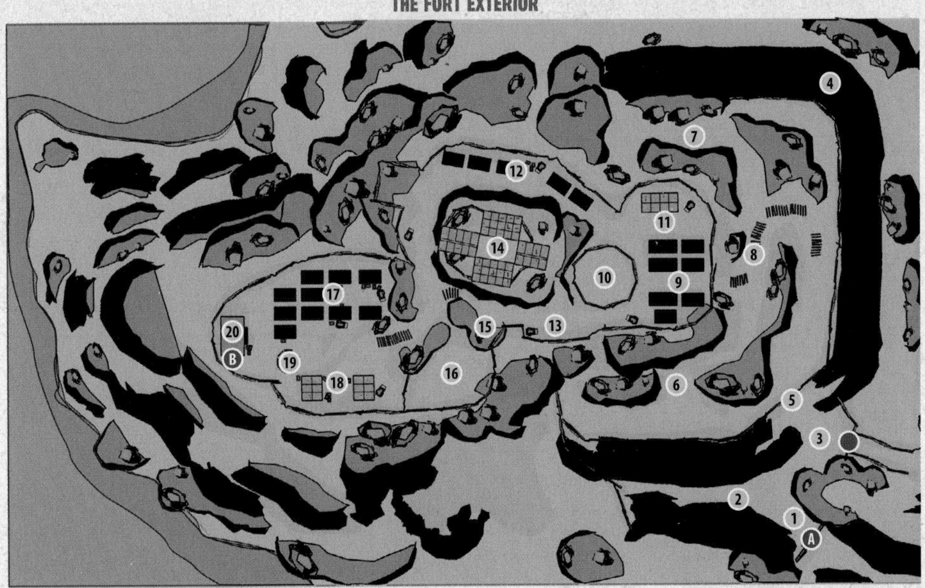

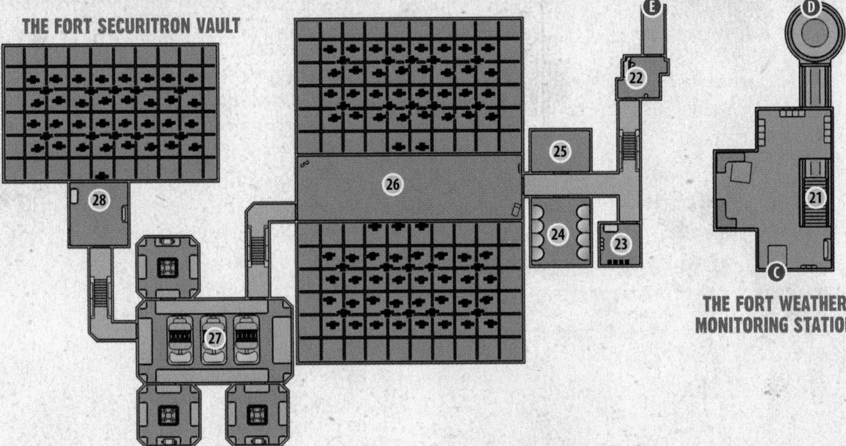

12 Northern Tents

- Footlocker Items (9)
- Sleeping Quarters

13 Anthony and Lupa

Waiting on the south side of Caesar's Tent is Anthony and the Legion's most ferocious hound, Lupa. You can ask Anthony about the Legion, Burned Man, Sergeant Teddy (if Free Quest: Saving (or Savaging) Sergeant Teddy is active) and how they breed their dogs. You can also figure out a mutually beneficial way to utilize Lupa during Side Quest: Nothin' But a Hound Dog, but only if the Side Quest is active.

14 Caesar's Tent (Exterior and Interior)

Guarded by the most senior guard, this is where the leader of the Legion resides. Inside is one large chamber with Caesar's resting area behind his throne. Search the tables on the side tents for the Legion Slave Ledger; which is essential for Side Quest: Oh My Papa, and worth taking as early as possible. If Benny escaped during Main Quest: Ring-a-Ding Ding!, he's tied up here. Over in Caesar's bedroom is a broken Mk III Auto-Doc, and a footlocker [Very Hard] with a large number of Caps inside to steal.

Caesar himself is flanked by the indomitable Vulpes Inculta and Lucius, who takes Caesar's place should the "emperor" die. The first time you meet Caesar, you can begin to work for him, and start Main Quest: Render Unto Caesar. Other quests, such as Main Quest: Et Tumor, Brute? and Side Quests: The Finger of Suspicion, and I Hear You Knocking, begin from this location. Speak with these three individuals for a wealth of information on The Legion.

- Quest Item: Legion Slave Ledger.
- Footlocker Items [Very Hard]
- Caps (2,000)
- Unique Item: Caesar's Armor [53/95]

15 Broken Howitzer

Inspect this howitzer, and you'll discover it is missing a firing mechanism. Help with that, as part of Side Quest: I Hear You Knocking.

16 Brahmin Pen

A rather gruesome-looking puddle, a small child named Melody, and a Brahmin await you here. Speak with Melody to begin Free Quest: Saving (or Savaging) Sergeant Teddy.

- Sleeping Quarters

17 Western Tents

- Footlocker Items (4)
- Sleeping Quarters

18 Blacksmith's Forge

- Campfire [41/109]
- Footlocker Items (8)
- Machete (3)
- Scrap Metal
- Sleeping Quarters

19 Training Area

- Campfire [42/109]

20 Weather Monitoring Station

The entrance is firmly sealed until you've spoken to Caesar, and agreed to enter the area, as part of Main Quest: Render Unto Caesar. This location is actually a Securitron Vault, and is also known as a "bunker," too.

B Door to Weather Monitoring Station

Weather Monitoring Station (Interior): Entrance

C Door to The Fort

21 Upper Monitoring Room

Weather Station Guards give your possessions back (and take them away when you head back into The Fort). Slot the Platinum Chip into the Console to open the floor doors.

D Elevator Door to Securitron Vault

Weather Monitoring Station (Interior): Securitron Vault

E Elevator Door to Weather Monitoring Station

22 Mr. House Remote Relay

Mr. House's (or Yes Man's) face beams in from the Lucky 38. Speak to him before you can open the door to the Securitron Vault. On the wall is a Vault Status Terminal unrelated to the door with the following information:

> Status Log: Untoward happenings in the vault since the security system was armed.

> Turret Status: Active

> Protectron Status: Active

> Sentry Bot Status: Standby

23 Security Room

Aside from the helpful items to grab, there are three wall terminals here; the Protectron Operations Terminal [Hard], Turret Operations Terminal [Average], and Sentry Bot Operations Terminal (not locked). The latter is a dummy terminal, but the first two can be hacked, and all the Protectrons and Turrets in the vault powered down, helping you immensely.

- Plasma Rifle
- Ammo Box Ammunition
- Grenade Box Ammunition (2)

24 Protectron Pod Chamber

This was activated when you first entered the vault, and the Protectrons in this vault came from this room, which is mostly empty.

- Scrap Metal

25 Sentry Bot Chamber and Junction Box

Six Sentry Bots wait until an alarm is triggered; usually once you conclude the Main Quest path you've decided upon. The room is small and empty, so there's no need to fight the Sentry Bots into it. On the outside of the door is a junction box. You can:

Leave it alone.

Override the door controls and disconnect the door from the automated security system.

Once inside the chamber, you can Pickpocket each Sentry Bot, and deactivate it, nullifying these possible enemies completely.

26 Securitron Viewing Chamber

Protectrons and Turrets are encountered here, along with a bank of windows showing an (inaccessible) hall on each side where Mr. House's dormant Securitron army wakes to be awakened.

- Scrap Metal

27 Generator Room

Large generators rumble in this area which has four Protectrons, and three secondary rooms. Each of these has a Power Regulator. Examine one and you'll learn that the reactor core of this vault will overload if all three are destroyed. Choose whether to destroy them (attack with any weapon you want) depending on your Main Quest alliances.

28 Computer Room

Watch for turrets on the stairs and in the corners of this room. The only active machinery is the Securitron Operations Console. Insert the Platinum Chip into here to install the Mk. II upgrade software for the Securitrons.

Free Quest: A Trusted Aide

Should you become increasingly subservient to Caesar's will, it begins to pay dividends. Continue to earn Fame with the Legion, and during one conversation with Lucius, he steps forward to present you with a special key. This opens the door to the Caesar's Legion Safehouse [6.22], where you can rest, and relax. Consult that location for more information.

- Caesar's Legion Safehouse Key

Free Quest: Beware the Wrath of Caesar!

Caution The Legion has spies everywhere. If you continue to work against its interest, you will be marked an enemy.

This Objective appears as you progress along the Main Quest path, but choose not to align with Caesar's Legion. Appearing as a Quest in your Pip-Boy, this is deemed "Free" because Caesar's wrath is random. However, during your treks across the Mojave Wasteland, you are first warned, and after a day or so, randomly attacked by Legion Assassins, charging at you with their toughened armor and vicious weapons. These skirmishes are part of your alliance decision, and cannot be predicted or avoided.

Free Quest: Caesar's Favor

This is a similar Free Quest to Caching in at the Cove, but under slightly different circumstances. When you're Liked by Caesar's Legion, an "agent" in disguise approaches you, and tells you about Legion drop-boxes, along with instructions on a Note. A Quest Marker appears on your Pip-Boy showing you a (randomly) placed drop-box, which usually contains Legion Coins and confiscated items from those the Legion has enslaved. Your continued support to the Legion is encouraged!

- Quest Item: Note on Drop-Boxes

Free Quest: Laurifer Gladiator

Otho runs the arena, and he's always looking for challengers to his stable of indentured gladiators. This is a purely small-time operation, but you can ask to compete in the arena, as well as learning the rules (only a Machete, Melee Weapon combat, and light armor). To the death! You can also ask him about how the arena fights work, the Legate, and the Burned Man. For every battle you win, you receive Fame, and the chance to fight a more seasoned opponent.

Battle #	Opponent
Arena Battle #1	Slave (2)
Arena Battle #2	NCR Sergeant Andrews
Arena Battle #3	NCR Ranger Stella

- Caesar's Legion Fame Gained!

Free Quest: Powder to the People

Siri is a slave, gathered up and forced into servitude as Caesar's army swept up through New Mexico. She can tell you about her life, how women are treated, and her Healing Powder, which see gladly gives those that have an Accepted or better Reputation with the Legion.

You can inform her that she should use one Broc Flower per Xander Root. She realizes her mistake, and you receive some Fame.

Whether or not you solve her problem, you can return, once per day, to ask and receive Healing Powder from Siri, which is obviously more potent if you've refined the recipe for her.

- Healing Powder (6)

Free Quest: Saving (or Savaging) Sergeant Teddy

Melody helps out at the Brahmin Pen. Drop in on her, and she tells you she can't talk to you. You can:

Tell her you won't tell if she won't.

Say you're a friend and it's okay to talk to friends.

Tell her that Brahmin say "Moo!"

These break the ice, allowing her to tell you that the nasty man Anthony has taken Sergeant Teddy from her, and she wants it back.

- Quest Item: Note: Sergeant Teddy

Anthony stands with his dog Lupa. Tell him you're here for Melody's bear, and he makes you a deal; fight four of his best mongrels, and the bear is yours. You can:

Tell him the mongrels won't touch you, as you're their friend. Anthony thought his hounds were being too affectionate toward you. He gives up Sergeant Teddy without a fight (or a Fame gain).

Reduce the number of dogs from four to two.

Or agree to the fight.

After a moderately, or very difficult fight with the mongrels, return to Anthony, who grudgingly gives you the bear, and you receive a Fame gain.

- Caesar's Legion Fame Gained!
- Sergeant Teddy

Return to Melody, and show her that you have Sergeant Teddy, You can:

- Ask what she has to trade. She has nothing, leaving you either of the following choices:

Give her the Teddy.

Rip the Teddy in half in front of her. She yells that she hates you. But you gain Fame!

- Caesar's Legion Fame Gained!

[3.29] Deserted Shack

- Threat Level: ●●●●●
- Wasteland Vegetation
- Faction: None

In the scrubland by the railroad track where the dust devils like to roam is a tumbledown shack with an antenna sticking out the rock bluff it is attached to. There's little here but a lack of hope.

[3.30] Ranger Station Alpha ●

- Side Quest: Return to Sender
- Threat Level: ●●●●●
- Faction: NCR
  - Entity: Ranger Lineholm
  - Entity: Comm Officer Castillo
- Fame/Infamy
- Crafting: Campfire [43/109]
- Collectibles: Magazine [Survival] [19/30] [41/52]
- Guns and Ammo
- Health, Chems, or Water
- Highly Visible
- Sleeping Quarters

Another NCR Ranger Station with commanding views of The Fort [3.28] and Lake Mead, these troops keep their eyes open for movement along "The Narrows." Ranger Lineholm (who tells you the story of the bomber that crashed into the lake, how great Rangers are, and the role the station plays) commands this place, and Comm Officer Castillo (who you can ask similar questions to) are stationed here.

- Campfire [43/109]
- Mine Box Ammunition [Easy]
- Ammo Box Ammunition (2) [1 = Easy, 1 = Average]
- Magazine: Lad's Life [Survival] [19/30] [41/52]
- Sleeping Quarters

[3.31] Boulder Beach Campground

- Threat Level: ●●●●●
- Faction: Abomination
  - Entity: Lakelurk
- Crafting: Campfire [44/109]
- Collectibles: Hollowed-Out Rock [14/42]
- Health, Chems, or Water

The wharf is populated with Lakelurks. Beware, but also make sure you find the Hollowed-out Rock on the roadside. The actual campground has numerous picnic tables and wrecked cars, but offers no handy items. There is a Campfire to the south, surrounded by tires.

- Hollowed-Out Rock [14/42]
- Campfire [44/109]

[3.32] Boulder City ●

See map on the following page

- Main Quest: They Went That-A-Way
- Main Quest: Ring-a-Ding Ding!
- Side Quest: Boulder City Showdown
- Free Quest: Defacing the Humble Stone
- Free Quest: We Must Stop Meeting Like This, III
- Threat Level: ●●●●●
- Faction: NCR/Great Khan
  - Entity: Ike
  - Entity: Private Kowalski
  - Entity: Lieutenant Monroe
  - Entity: NCR Trooper
  - Entity: Private Ackermann
  - Entity: Private Gilbert
  - Entity: Great Khan
  - Entity: Jessup
- Fame/Infamy
- Services: Healer [25/31]
- Collectibles:
  - Sunset Sarsaparilla Star Cap [48/100]
  - Magazine: [Crit/Chance] [10/11] [42-45/52]
  - Magazine: [Sneak] [8/10] [42-45/52]
  - Magazine: [Sneak] [9/10] [42-45/52]
  - Magazine: [Unarmed] [9/11] [42-45/52]
  - Unique Item [54/95]
  - Unique Item [55/95]
  - Unique Item [56/95]
  - Unique Item [57/95]
- Area Is Locked
- Guns and Ammo
- Health, Chems, or Water
- Interior Exploration
- Main Trading Route
- Radio Signal [Black Mountain]
- Sleeping Quarters
- Wasteland Vegetation
- Quest Item

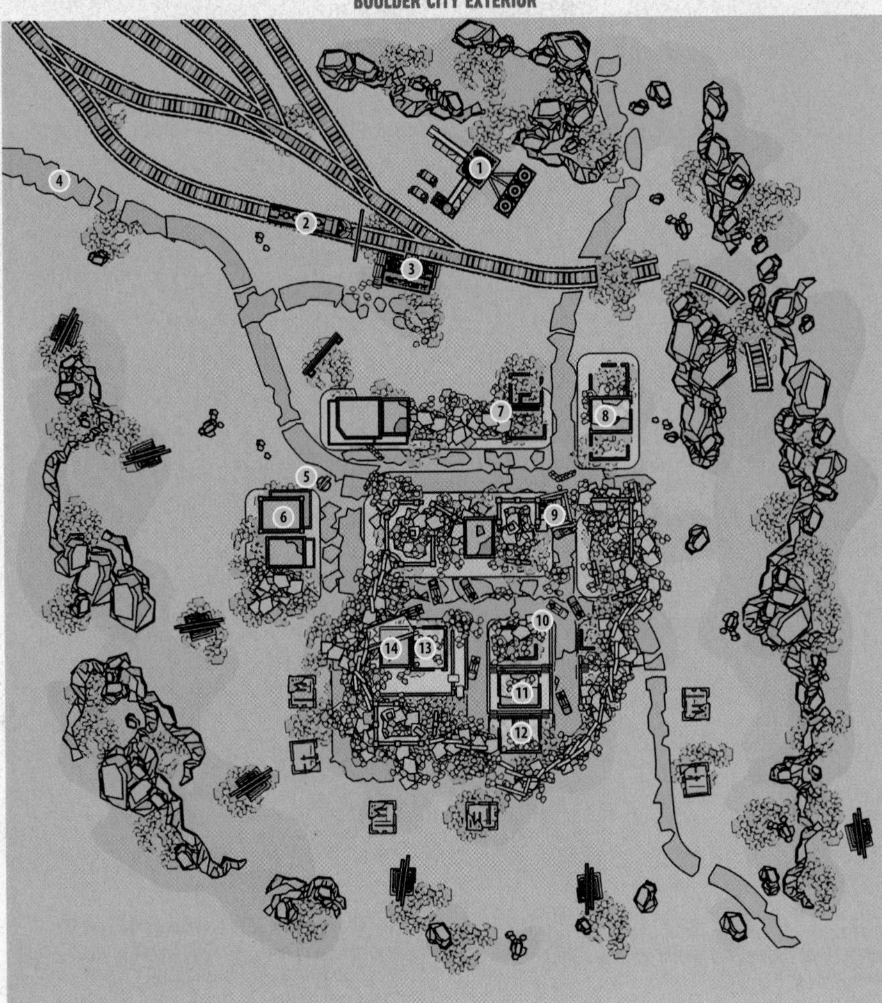

Boulder City, sprawling though its ruins are, has never been a sizable settlement post-war. It is a minor location, mostly notable for its proximity to Hoover Dam [3.33] and the 188 Trading Post [5.02]. It's a common resting spot for people on their way to New Vegas and for troops moving to and from the dam. There are not many intact buildings, as it was the site of intense fighting between NCR and Caesar's Legion during the first Battle of Hoover Dam. The Rangers lured some of the toughest veteran Legionaries into the town and blew it to pieces with explosives that had been strategically placed ahead of time.

Boulder City Train Yard

1 The Old Cement Works

A small quarry where freight trains were loaded is just north of town.

- Magazine: Boxing Times [Unarmed] [9/11] [42/52]
- Magazine: ¡La Fantoma! [Sneak] [8/10] [43/52]

2 The Barstow Express

A rusting green locomotive with a skeleton close by.

- Hunting Rifle and Ammo

3 Train Station

Beware the Bark Scorpion in here. Check both Vending Machines, and behind the counter for a terminal [Average], which you can use to unlock the floor safe [Hard].

- Floor Safe Items [Hard]

Boulder City Exterior

4 Northwest Entrance

This is the main thoroughfare into town, past the large billboard for the nearby Hoover Dam [3.33].

5 War Memorial

A slab of limestone carved with the names of those who gave their lives during the first Battle of Hoover Dam. Private Kowalski is paying his respects here. Carve additional indents into the War Memorial to begin Free Quest: Defacing the Humble Stone.

6 Big Horn Saloon

Ike is the owner of this watering hole; speak with him about the history (and recent destruction) of Boulder City. You can purchase (or steal) a few drinks from him, too. Check the back room for more Drink, Food, and a Shotgun.

- Sunset Sarsaparilla Star Cap [48/100]
- Healer: Ike [25/31]
- Unique Item: Nuka-Cola Quartz [54/95]
- Unique Item: Nuka-Cola Quartz [55/95]
- Unique Item: Nuka-Cola Quartz [56/95]
- Crate Items (6)
- Lever-Action Shotgun and Ammo

7 Northeast Rubble

- Machete

8 Ranger Lutz's Last Stand

On the upper floor is a Holodisk with Ranger Teresa Lutz's last message.

- Machete
- Ranger Hat
- Holotape: Ranger Holodisk Message
- Service Rifle

Boulder City Ruins

9 Ruins Entrance

As you approach the ruins entrance, Lieutenant Monroe warns you that the place is locked down; the NCR are attempting to bargain with some Great Khans who have taken some of their forces hostage. This begins Side Quest: Boulder City Showdown. Your actions also influence Main Quest: They Went That-A-Way and Main Quest: Ring-a-Ding Ding!. You can only enter the ruins when you agree to help Monroe.

10 NCR Troopers Location

11 Half-Demolished Store #1

- Jet
- Magazine: True Police Stories [Crit/ Chance] [10/11] [44/52]
- Magazine: ¡La Fantoma! [Sneak] [9/10] [45/52]
- Sleeping Quarters

12 Half-Demolished Store #2

- 10mm Submachine Gun and Ammo
- Buffout
- Grenade Box Ammunition [Average]
- Sleeping Quarters

13 Great Khan Demolished Store

A Great Khan is holding two NCR Privates—Ackerman and Gilbert—in the back room. You can access them via the back door [Easy] if you're sneaky. There's likely to be a Great Khan or two on the roof.

- Sleeping Quarters

14 Great Khan Hideout

You can creep around the entire building in a clockwise route without being spotted, if you're sneaky. Inside the store hideout you'll find some Food and Sarsaparilla bottles, but the person you're really here to see helped shoot you in the head: Jessup. You have a variety of verbal and combat options with this lowlife, as part of the Side Quest. Behind him is a Great Khan named McMurphy who's recently taken terminal wounds. There are Quest Items on Jessup's corpse (some of which he gives you), and a good set of armor.

- Ammo and Ammo Box Ammunition (2)
- Quest Item: Chairman Job Offer
- Quest Item: Engraved Cigarette Lighter
- Great Khan Suit Armor
- Unique Item: Jessup's Bandana [57/95]
- Sleeping Quarters

Free Quest: Defacing the Humble Stone

At the War Memorial (Location #5), Private Kowalski is paying his respects to his brother, who died during the Battle of Hoover Dam. You can ask about Kowalski, the memorial, Point your weapon at the memorial, and Kowalski warns you to be careful. Shoot a small chunk (or strike it with a Melee or Unarmed attack), and Kowalski is furious, pointing his Service Rifle at you. You can:

Apologize for your rude and disrespectful behavior.

Call him a little bitch. This doesn't end well; usually for Kowalski. Your Reputation with the NCR sinks.

Reply with a "whatever," which results in Kowalski keeping his cool: Just.

Shoot the memorial again, and Kowalski gets violent.

- NCR Infamy Gained!

Free Quest: We Must Stop Meeting Like This, III

As you meander around the settlement, and you haven't yet met Mr. House at the Lucky 38 Casino, you may spot a Securitron zipping around on its single tire. Why, it's Victor, the good-time cowpoke Securitron! If you spot him in Boulder City, you can thank him for rescuing you from a shallow grave, ask what he's doing, ask about the men who jumped you, or to stay out of your way. Although he might be tailing you, he's not prepared to become a Follower. You can shoot at him too, but he has no items to loot.

[3.33] Hoover Dam

- Main Quest: For the Republic, Part 2
- Main Quest: You'll Know It When It Happens
- Main Quest: Arizona Killer
- Main Quest: No Gods, No Masters
- Main Quest: All or Nothing
- Main Quest: Veni, Vidi, Vici
- Main Quest: Eureka!
- Threat Level: ●●●●●
- Faction: NCR
  - Entity: President Aaron Kimball
  - Entity: General Lee Oliver
  - Entity: Colonel Cassandra Moore
  - Entity: Ranger Grant
  - Entity: Ranger Stevens
  - Entity: Private Watson
  - Entity: Cato Hostilius
  - Entity: NCR Ranger
  - Entity: NCR Trooper
  - Entity: NCR Heavy Trooper
  - Entity: Engineer
  - Entity: Quartermaster Bardon
  - Entity: Mike Watson
- Fame/Infamy
- Services: Trader [18/33]
- Dangers:
  - Traps
  - Radiation
  - Mines
- Collectibles:
  - Snow Globe [6/7]
  - Magazine [Lockpick] [12/12] [46-49/52]
  - Magazine [Repair] [21/27] [46-49/52]
  - Magazine [Science] [14/23] [46-49/52]
  - Magazine [Science] [15/23] [46-49/52]
  - Unique Item [58/95]
  - Unique Item [59/95]
  - Unique Item [60/95]
  - Unique Item [61/95]
- Area Is Locked
- Guns and Ammo
- Health, Chems, or Water
- Highly Visible
- Interior Exploration
- Lots O' Caps
- Sleeping Quarters

All of the Main Quest in Act III centers around this location, as do the Main Quests involving the visit of President Aaron Kimball. A stronghold of extreme strategic importance for centuries, this location has seen recent turmoil between major Faction too. A few years before current events, Caesar's Legion rolled in, led by ex-Mormon missionary Joshua Graham, Caesar's legate. Not considering NCR's army to be a serious threat, Graham exercised somewhat lax control over the Legion. During the Battle of Hoover Dam, NCR Rangers and Sharpshooters from First Recon employed risky tactics against the Legion with the help of the enlisted Troopers, and despite horrific loss of life, Caesar's forces were pushed back, but not routed.

The NCR has been holding the dam continuously since, and have fortified positions along the dam and up and down the west side of the Colorado River. Recently, the Legion pushed the NCR off of the east side of the river at the Battle of Willow Beach (which destroyed an NCR military camp) and the Battle of Arizona Spillway. Day to day military operations at the dam are under the command of Colonel Moore. While troopers are active here, there are also a large number of civilian contractors who are trying to keep the dam running. They are of a secondary concern to Moore, who is preparing from for an impending attack by Caesar and a visit by President Kimball.

Hoover Dam (Exterior)

HOOVER DAM EXTERIOR

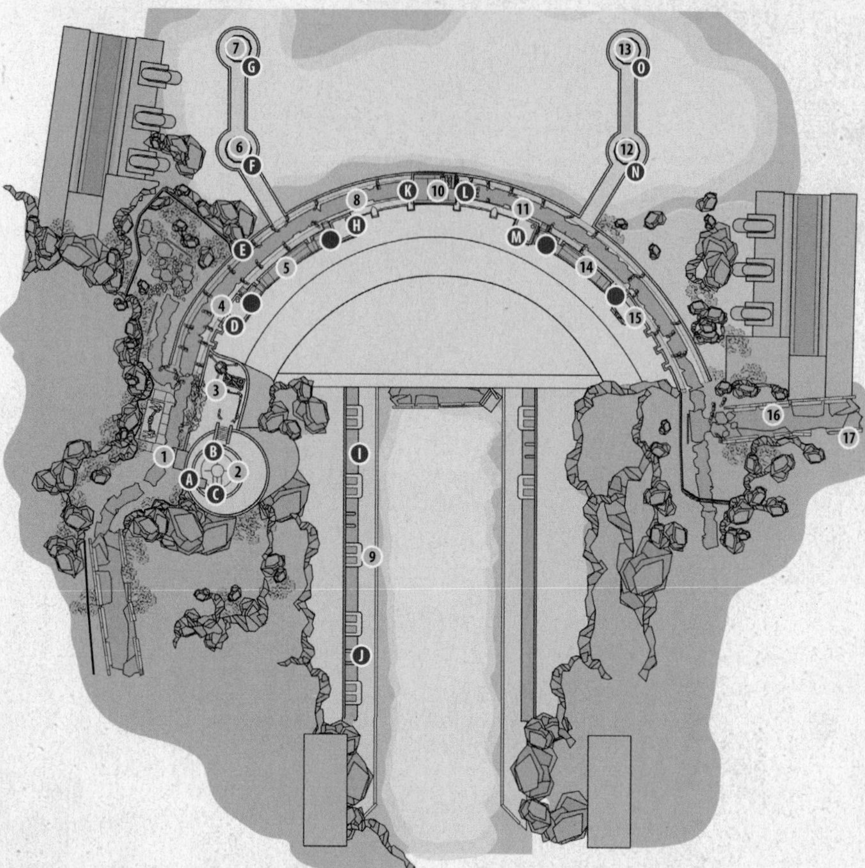

1 Entrance Road

This is the usual method of entering this location, via the remains of a bridge and a winding road from Boulder City [3.32]. Rangers patrol this area, and you'll meet specific ones (Ranger Stevens and Ranger Grant) if President Kimball is visiting the troops during Main Quest: You'll Know It When It Happens and: Arizona Killer. Note the remains of a memorial on the west side of the road.

2 Visitor Center

This is a tactically beneficial location with views of the entire facility, and four entrances inside, including the one from the roof which also acts as a Vertibird landing pad. There's a Ham Radio and Gun Control Console, which are useful during the president's visit. Note the ladder to reach the roof.

- Unique Item: President Kimball's Suit [58/95]

A B C Doors to/from Visitor Center Interior

3 Presidential Stage

President Aaron Kimball speaks with the troops, and offers a commendation to one of them (Private Watson), assuming an assassination attempt doesn't occur, as part of the two previously mentioned Main Quests. If you're working with the Legion, Cato Hostilius will be waiting here for your signal.

4 Dam Bridge and Guard Tower #1

Unless you're involved in a final attack, this location is populated by patrolling Troopers and Engineers. You can enter the guard tower, or climb the ladder, and reach the roof, which is the perfect location for an assassination attempt! This guard tower isn't connected to the Hoover Dam Interior.

D Doors and Hatches to/from Guard Tower #1

5 Dam Tower Access Defenses [Hard]

If you want to move between Guard Towers #1 and #2, unlock either of the rickety doors and move along the underside of the defenses, which are a little safer.

E Hatch from Water

If you fall off the north side of the dam bridge, there's a ladder leading up to this point. You can't open this hatch the other way.

6 7 Hoover Dam Intake Towers 01 and 02

Check the locker inside Tower 02 for some items. These locations are utilized during Act III of the Main Quest.

F G Doors to Hoover Dam Intake Towers 01 and 02

8 Dam Bridge and Guard Tower #2

This is another excellent sniping spot. The elevator inside allows access to the Hoover Dam Offices (Interior) and is the only other way (aside from the Visitor Center) to enter the dam interior. Check Guard Tower #2's bathroom stalls for a Magazine. During Act III, you can access Guard Tower #3, too.

- First Aid Box
- Ammo
- Magazine: Programmer's Digest [14/23] [46/52]

H Doors and Hatches to/from Guard Tower #2, and Hoover Dam Offices

I Door to Hoover Dam Power Plant 02

9 Lower Exterior Walkway

Only accessible if you're heading from the interior of the dam outside, and then back again, this provides a short-cut during Act III. There is a valve here, and Legion attackers during the final battle.

J Door to Hoover Dam Power Plant 04

> **Note** Any exterior location from this point onward is Inaccessible until Act III of the Main Quest.

10 Hoover Dam Checkpoint Building

Halfway along the Dam Bridge is a ramshackle hut blocking your path. The door is Inaccessible, and remains so until Act III of the Main Quest. Inside, there are lockers to search, and a ladder up to a sniper's nest outside.

(K) (L) Doors to Hoover Dam Checkpoint Building

11 Dam Bridge and Guard Tower #3

This is another excellent sniping spot. The elevator inside allows access to the Hoover Dam Offices (Interior), but only after certain Quest-related Objectives have occurred during Act III.

- First Aid Box

(M) Doors and Hatches to/from Guard Tower #3, and Hoover Dam Offices

12 13 Hoover Dam Intake Towers 03 and 04

These locations are utilized during Act III of the Main Quest.

(N) (O) Doors to Hoover Dam Intake Towers 03 and 04

14 Dam Tower Access Defenses [Hard]

If you want to move between Guard Towers #3 and #4, unlock either of the rickety doors and move along the underside of the defenses, which are a little safer.

15 Dam Bridge and Guard Tower #4

This tower has taken heavy damage and cannot be accessed.

16 Arizona Spillway

This giant overflow slide is dangerous; Beware of taking damage if you drop down (which is a pointless exercise).

17 Road to Legate's Camp

Expect heavily armed Legion troops along this road, streaming out of Legate's Camp [3.34], which is behind the large gate.

Hoover Dam Visitor Center (Interior)

> *Note* The interior locations have a numbering and lettering structure unrelated to the exterior of the Hoover Dam.

(A) (Lower) Door to Hoover Dam (Exterior)

(B) (Lower) Door to Hoover Dam Power Plant 01

(C) (Lower) Door to Hoover Dam Power Plant 01 (Stairs)

1 (Lower and Upper) Visitor Center

This circular entrance area is a staging post during the final battle for NCR Rangers. Before that, NCR troops are milling about. Be sure to check the central reception desks for a Snow Globe. Upstairs, there's roof access

- Snow Globe—Hoover Dam [6/7]

> *Note* You found a Limited Edition Mojave Landmark Snow Globe! These rare, Pre-War artifacts are widely considered to be useless baubles, but rumor has it some collectors will pay dearly for them.

(D) (Lower) Door to Supply Closet

Inside the closet are a couple of lockers, one of which has an Engineer's Jumpsuit

- Engineer's Jumpsuit

(E) (Upper) Door to Hoover Dam (Exterior)

(F) (Upper) Door to Offce [Very Hard]

The office behind these doors has a few items in a desk, but nothing unique.

(G) (Upper) Stairs to Hoover Dam (Exterior)

Hoover Dam Power Plant 01

> *Note* The Power Plant locations have four levels: Upper, Middle, Ground, and Lower.

(H) (Upper) Door to Hoover Dam Visitor Center

(I) (Upper) Elevator to Hoover Dam Visitor Center

2 (Upper and Middle) Stairwell and Connecting Chamber

You can reach the two northern balconies from here, or after descending the steps and opening the Blast Door to the east. Or, you can reach the western balconies (Upper and Middle).

3 (Upper and Middle) Northern Balconies

These are two separate locations. From here, you can access either floor of the Dam Offices, and look over the massive Power Plant 01. Check the Upper Balcony desk for a Magazine.

- Magazine: Locksmith's Reader [Lockpick [12/12] [47/52]

(J) (Upper and Middle) Doors to Hoover Dam Offices

These are two separate locations. The Upper Door allows quick access to meet Colonel Moore.

4 (Upper and Middle) Western Balconies

The door in the western wall allows access between floors. There's a gantry bridge to the Eastern Balcony (Upper). The Middle Western Balcony has access across to the northern and eastern balconies (Middle), and a Blast Door to Power Plant 02 at its south end, which is locked from the other side. It also has access down to the Ground level, and across to the Eastern Balcony (Middle).

5 (Upper and Middle) Eastern Balconies

The door in the eastern wall allows access between floors. There's a gantry bridge to the Western Balcony (Upper). The Middle Eastern Balcony has access across to the northern and western balconies (Middle), and a Blast Door to Power Plant 02 at its south end, which is unlocked. It also has access down to the ground level, and across to the Western Balcony (Middle). You can wander around the giant turbine balconies here, too.

- Scrap Metal

6 (Ground) Power Plant Floor

This is a giant, noisy expanse of gigantic turbines and generators. Turn large valves to sip pure water. A door in the western wall leads down to connect to the Dam Lower Level. A door in the south wall allows access to an almost identical Power Plant 02.

- Scrap Metal (2)
- Sunset Sarsaparilla Bottle

(K) (Middle) Doors to Hoover Dam Power Plant 02

The western one is sealed, and can only be opened from Hoover Dam Power Plant 02. The eastern one is open.

(L) (Ground) Door to Hoover Dam Power Plant 02

(M) (Ground and Lower) Door to Hoover Dam Lower Level

Hoover Dam Offices

See map on the following page

(N) (Upper and Middle) Doors to Hoover Dam Power Plant 01

These are two separate doors leading to two separate corridors eventually connecting via the stairs to the west.

- Footlocker and Locker Items (Middle only)

7 (Upper) Restroom

You can drink rad-free water from here.

8 (Middle) Quartermaster's Store

Quartermaster Bardon works at this location. If your Reputation isn't high enough, he won't be willing to speak or sell you anything. Return when you're Liked, and you can obtain information about the NCR and the Dam, but Bardon is still unsure about selling you anything.

Tell him you completely understand, but you are working for the good of the NCR. He makes an exception; just for you.

- Trader: Quartermaster Bardon [18/33]

Or, you can ransack his chamber for the following:

- Footlocker Items (4)
- Weapon Repair Kit
- First Aid Box and Cateye
- Scrap Metal (2)
- Doctor's Bag
- Carton of Cigarettes (2)

9 (Middle) Northwest Dorms

- Teddy Bear
- Duffle Bag Items
- Footlocker Items (4)

10 (Middle) North Dorms

- Teddy Bear
- Duffle Bag Items
- Footlocker Items (3)
- Carton of Cigarettes

11 (Upper) Colonel Cassandra Moore's Office

You receive your marching orders during Main Quest: For the Republic, Part 2, from this location, or nearby. Moore is a no-nonsense soldier, and has knowledge of the NCR and the surrounding area. She has little time for sightseers. In the corner of the corridor outside, between Moore's two offices is a lantern with a Magazine.

- Magazine: Fixin' Things [Repair] [21/27] [48/52]

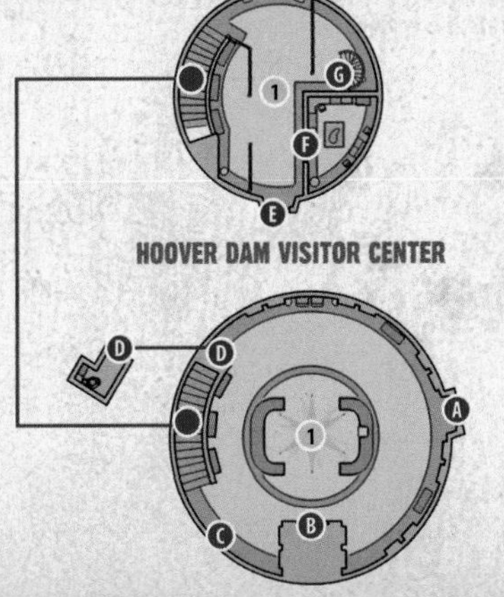

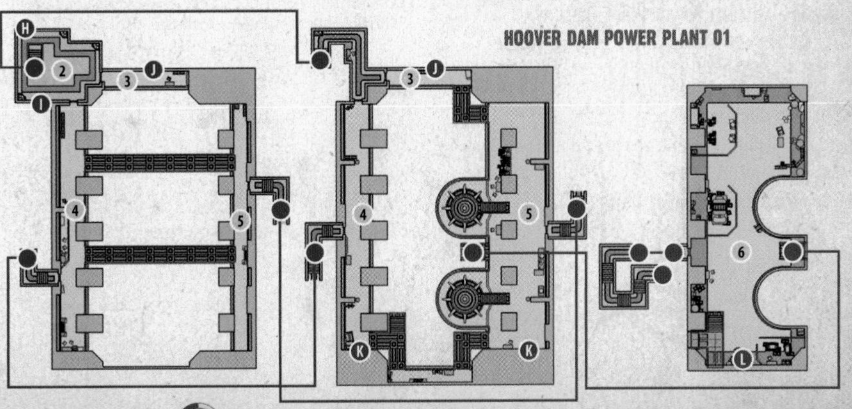

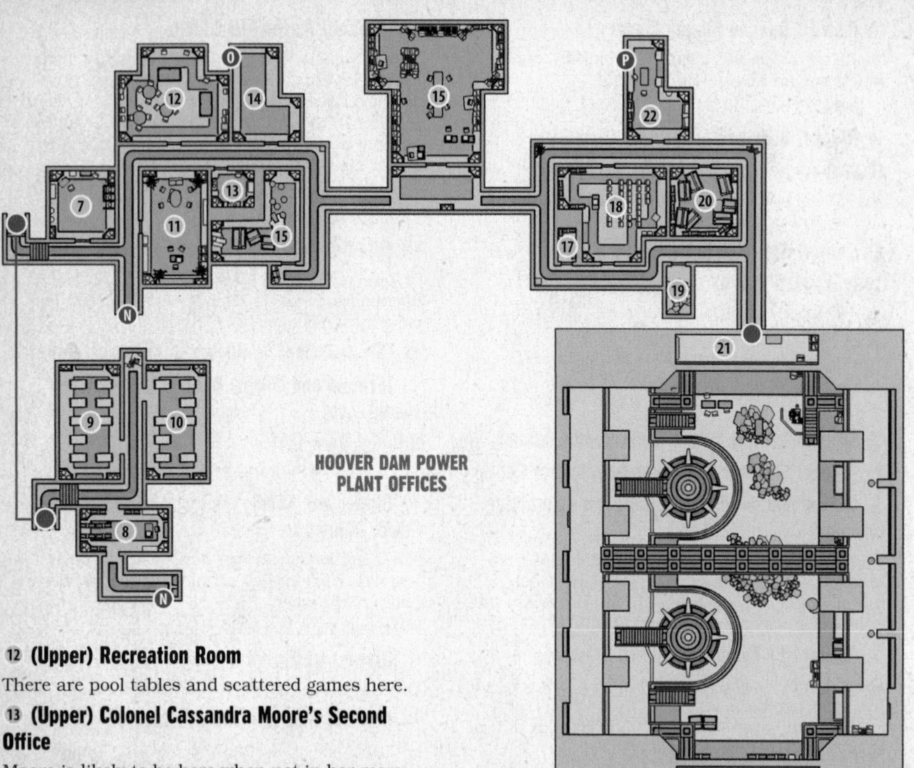

12 (Upper) Recreation Room

There are pool tables and scattered games here.

13 (Upper) Colonel Cassandra Moore's Second Office

Moore is likely to be here when not in her more expansive chamber. The terminal in has some interesting missives to read, including information on some odd suits that turned up, and were promptly stolen.

> Initial Inventory Report

> No Clue What These Are

> Great. Just Great.

- Magazine: Programmer's Digest [15/23] [49/52]

14 (Upper) Connecting Chamber

O (Upper) Door to Hoover Dam Tower

This leads to the second guard tower on the Exterior Dam Bridge.

15 (Upper) Radioactive Barrel Storage

Check the middle stack of crates for an amazing piece of foreign stealth technology!

- Unique Item: Chinese Stealth Armor [59/95]

16 (Upper) Central Control and Relay Room

This has no function until Act III, when it becomes an integral part of the action if you're with Mr. House or Yes Man.

17 (Upper) Storage

- Scrap Metal
- Carton of Cigarettes

18 (Upper) Briefing Room (with Projector)

- Scrap Metal

19 (Upper) Debris Room

20 (Upper) Crate Storage Room

21 (Upper) Eastern Power Plant Balcony

This location can't be entered; only the upper balcony is accessible, and only once certain obligations to Mr. House and Yes Man are made.

22 (Upper) Kitchenette

Check the fridge and shelves for Food and items.

- Sunset Sarsaparilla Bottle

P (Upper) Door to Hoover Dam Tower

This leads to the second guard tower on the Exterior Dam Bridge. This is inaccessible until Act III.

Hoover Dam Power Plant 02

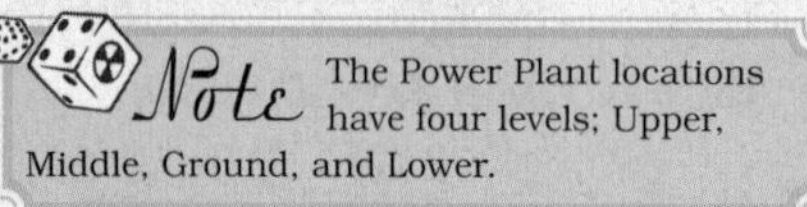

Note: The Power Plant locations have four levels; Upper, Middle, Ground, and Lower.

Q (Middle) Doors to Hoover Dam Power Plant 01

The western one has a wall terminal [Hard] to open the door. The eastern one is open.

R (Ground) Door to Hoover Dam Power Plant 01

23 (Middle) Northern Balcony

From here, you can look over the massive Power Plant 02. It is accessed via the West or East Middle Balconies. There is an identical balcony to the south.

24 (Upper and Middle) Western Balconies

The door in the western wall allows access between floors. There's a gantry bridge to the Eastern Balcony (Upper). The Middle Western Balcony has access across to the northern and eastern balconies (Middle), and a Blast Door to Power Plant 03 at its south end. It also has access down to the Ground level, and across to the Eastern Balcony (Middle).

25 (Upper and Middle) Eastern Balconies

The southern door in the eastern wall allows access between floors, while the northern one (Middle) allows access outside, for a quick detour to Power Plant 04. There's a gantry bridge to the Western Balcony (Upper). The Middle Eastern Balcony has access across to the northern and western balconies (Middle), and a Blast Door to Power Plant 03 at its south end, which is unlocked. It also has access down to the Ground level, and across to the Western Balcony (Middle). You can also wander around the giant turbine balconies here, too.

- Scrap Metal

S (Middle) Door to Hoover Dam (Exterior)

This allows exterior access to and from Power Plants 02 and 04.

26 (Ground) Power Plant Floor

This is a giant, noisy expanse of gigantic turbines and generators. There is a large valve you can turn to sip pure water. There is a door in the western wall leading down to connect to the Dam Lower Level. There's a door in the south wall allowing access to an almost identical Power Plant 03.

- Scrap Metal (2)
- Sunset Sarsaparilla Bottle

T (Ground and Lower) Door to Hoover Dam Lower Level

U (Middle) Doors to Hoover Dam Power Plant 03

V (Ground) Door to Hoover Dam Power Plant 03

Hoover Dam Power Plant 03

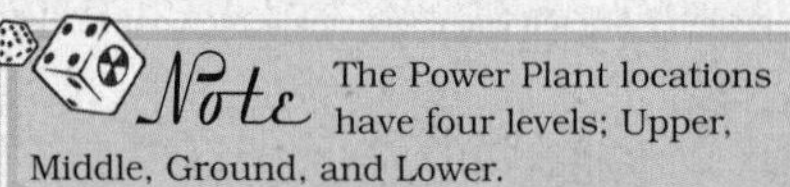

Note: The Power Plant locations have four levels; Upper, Middle, Ground, and Lower.

W (Middle) Doors to Hoover Dam Power Plant 02

Both are accessible.

X (Ground) Door to Hoover Dam Power Plant 02

27 (Middle) Northern Balcony

From here, you can look over the massive Power Plant 03. It is accessed via the West or East Middle Balconies. There is an identical balcony to the south.

28 (Upper and Middle) Western Balconies

The door in the western wall allows access between floors. There's a gantry bridge to the Eastern Balcony (Upper). The Middle Western Balcony has access across to the northern and eastern balconies (Middle), and a Blast Door to Power Plant 04 at its south end. It also has access down to the Ground level, and across to the Eastern Balcony (Middle).

29 (Upper and Middle) Eastern Balconies

The door in the eastern wall allows access between floors. There's a gantry bridge to the Western Balcony (Upper). The Middle Eastern Balcony has access across to the northern and western balconies (Middle), and a Blast Door to Power Plant 04 at its south end, which is unlocked. It also has access down to the Ground level, and across to the Western Balcony (Middle). You can wander around the giant turbine balconies here, too.

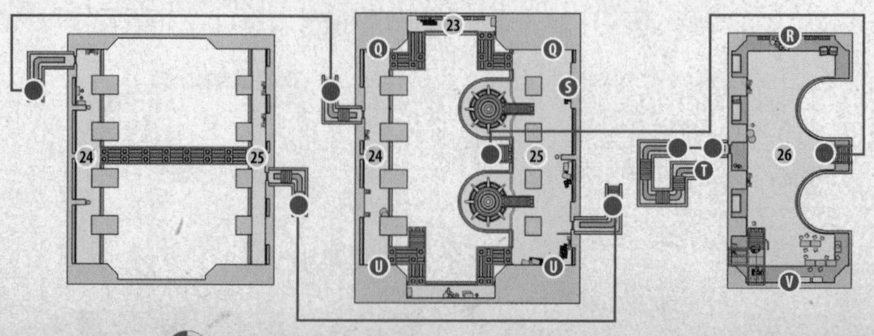

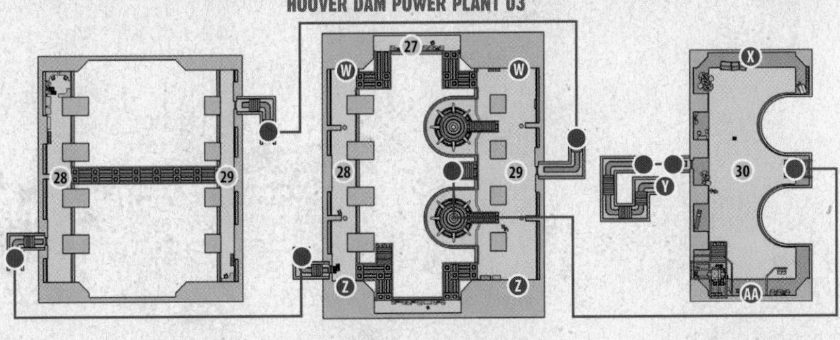

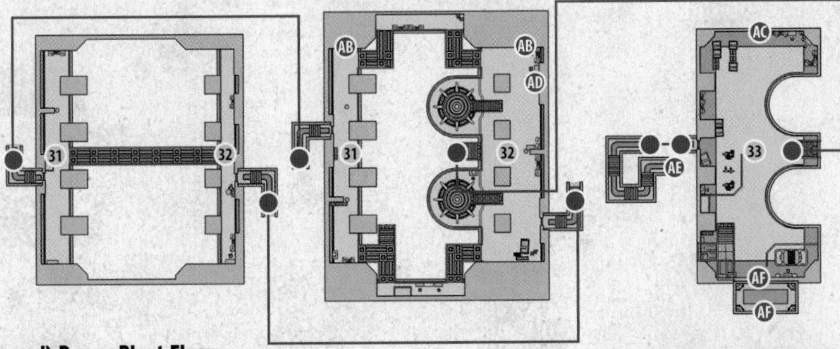

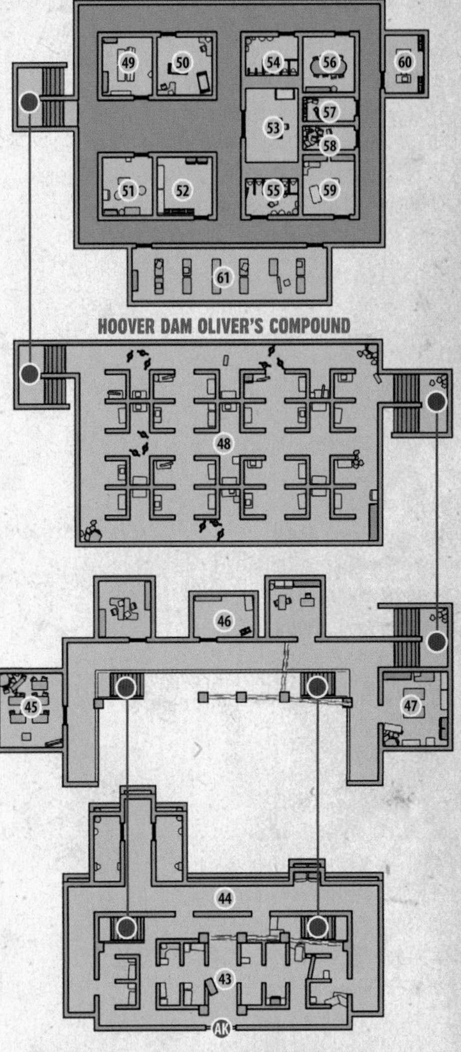

30 **(Ground) Power Plant Floor**

This is a giant, noisy expanse of gigantic turbines and generators. A door in the western wall leads down to connect to the Dam Lower Level. There's a door in the south wall allowing access to an almost identical Power Plant 04.

- Footlocker Items
- Ammo Box Ammunition (6)

(Y) (Ground and Lower) Door to Hoover Dam Lower Level

(Z) (Middle) Doors to Hoover Dam Power Plant 04

(AA) (Ground) Door to Hoover Dam Power Plant 04

Hoover Dam Power Plant 04

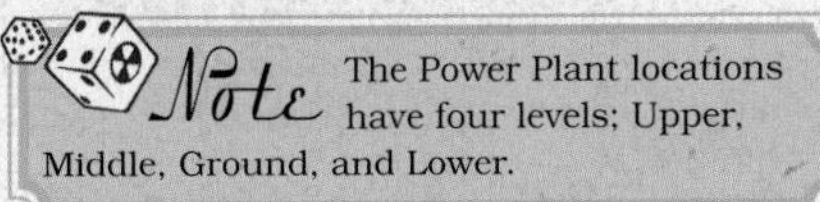
Note: The Power Plant locations have four levels: Upper, Middle, Ground, and Lower.

(AB) (Middle) Doors to Hoover Dam Power Plant 03

Both are accessible.

(AC) (Ground) Door to Hoover Dam Power Plant 03

31 **(Upper and Middle) Western Balconies**

The door in the western wall allows access between floors. There's a gantry bridge to the Eastern Balcony (Upper). The Middle Western Balcony has access across to the northern and eastern balconies (Middle). There are no doors to the south end (except the one on the Ground Floor). It also has access down to the Ground level, and across to the Eastern Balcony (Middle).

- Scrap Metal

32 **(Upper and Middle) Eastern Balconies**

The southern door in the eastern wall allows access between floors, while the northern one (Middle) allows access outside, for a quick detour to Power Plant 02. There's a gantry bridge to the Western Balcony (Upper). The Middle Eastern Balcony has access across to the northern and western balconies (Middle). There are no doors to the south. It also has access down to the Ground level, and across to the Western Balcony (Middle). You can also wander around the giant turbine balconies here.

- Teddy Bear

(AD) (Middle) Door to Hoover Dam (Exterior)

This allows exterior access to and from Power Plants 02 and 04.

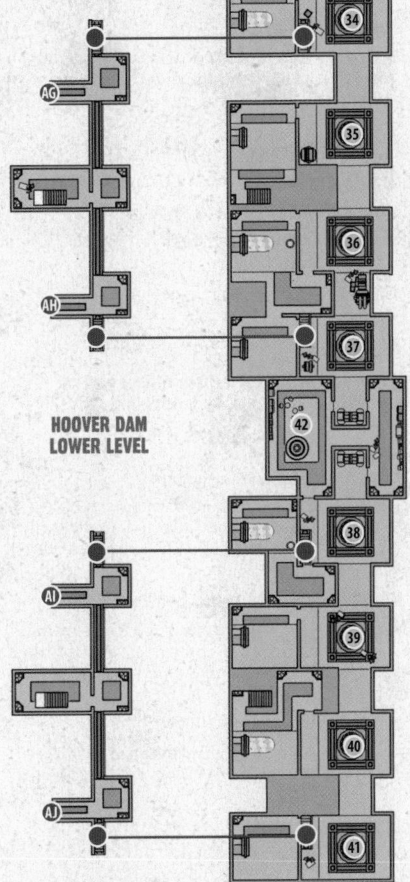

33 **(Ground) Power Plant Floor**

This is a giant, noisy expanse of gigantic turbines and generators. There are valves you can sip water from, and a door in the western wall leading down to connect to the Dam Lower Level. There's a door in the south wall allowing access to an almost identical Power Plant 04.

- Footlocker Items
- Ammo Box Ammunition (6)

(AE) (Ground and Lower) Door to Hoover Dam Lower Level

(AF) (Ground) Outer and Inner Doors to General Oliver's Compound

This remains sealed until Act III. If you're allied with the NCR, you may speak to an Engineer named Mike Lawson about important matters before the doors are breached, as part of Main Quest: Eureka!.

Hoover Dam Lower Level

34 35 36 37 38 39 40 41 **Turbines N1-8**

Some are functioning, and some are not. To the west are giant water pipes, where the Legion appears during Act III.

- Scrap Metal (2)

42 **Break Room**

- Beer

(AG) Door to Hoover Dam Power Plant 01

(AH) Door to Hoover Dam Power Plant 02

(AI) Door to Hoover Dam Power Plant 03

(AJ) Door to Hoover Dam Power Plant 04

General Lee Oliver's Compound

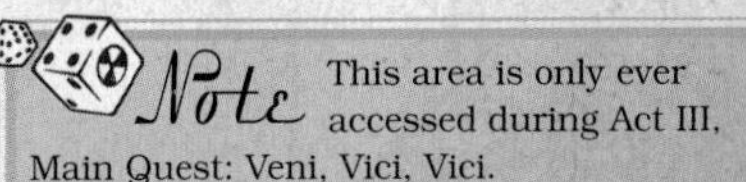
Note: This area is only ever accessed during Act III, Main Quest: Veni, Vici, Vici.

(AK) Door to Hoover Dam Power Plant 04

43 **(Lower) Offices**

You confront General Oliver here.

44 (Lower) Lower Passage

There are Vending Machines to raid, and a way around the energy wall.

45 (Ground) West Briefing Room

46 (Ground) Concrete Rooms

All are empty except one with fridge items.

47 (Ground) East Office

48 (Upper) Open-Plan Office

Take your shots here, using the cubicle walls as cover. Beware of Rigged Shotgun and Bear Traps throughout this area.

- Danger! Bear Trap
- Danger! Rigged Shotgun Trap
- Danger! C-4 MIne
- First Aid Box
- Ammo

49 (Top) Storage

- Footlocker Items (2)

50 (Top) Office

51 (Top) Break Room

There's a Water Fountain in here.

52 (Top) Filing Room

53 (Top) Large Office

You are attacked by Heavy NCR Troopers here. General Lee Oliver is in this general vicinity; be sure you loot his corpse to obtain some Unique Items.

- Sleeping Quarters
- Unique Item: General Oliver's Cap [60/95]
- Unique Item: General Oliver's Uniform [61/95]

54 55 (Top) Restrooms

Rad-free water is available.

56 (Top) Conference Room

57 (Top) Storage Closet

58 (Top) Chair Closet

59 (Top) Sleeping Area

- Sleeping Quarters

60 (Top) Northeast Office

61 (Top) Mail Room

[3.34] Legate's Camp

- Main Quest: No Gods, No Masters
- Main Quest: All or Nothing
- Main Quest: Veni, Vidi, Vici
- Main Quest: Eureka!
- Threat Level: ●●●●●
- Faction: Caesar's Legion
  - Entity: Legate Lanius
  - Entity: Praetorian Guard
  - Entity: Prime Legionary
- Crafting:
  - Campfire [45/109]
  - Campfire [46/109]
- Dangers:
  - Radiation
- Collectibles:
  - Unique Item [62/95]
  - Unique Weapon [24/42]
- Area Is Locked
- Guns and Ammo
- Health, Chems, or Water
- Interior Exploration
- Sleeping Quarters

Caesar's Legate, a man-mountain named Lanius, is camped in this location, which is inaccessible until you're forced to assault it (or from it) during the last Act of the Main Quest. The following exploration can occur only after this time.

LEGATE'S CAMP EXTERIOR

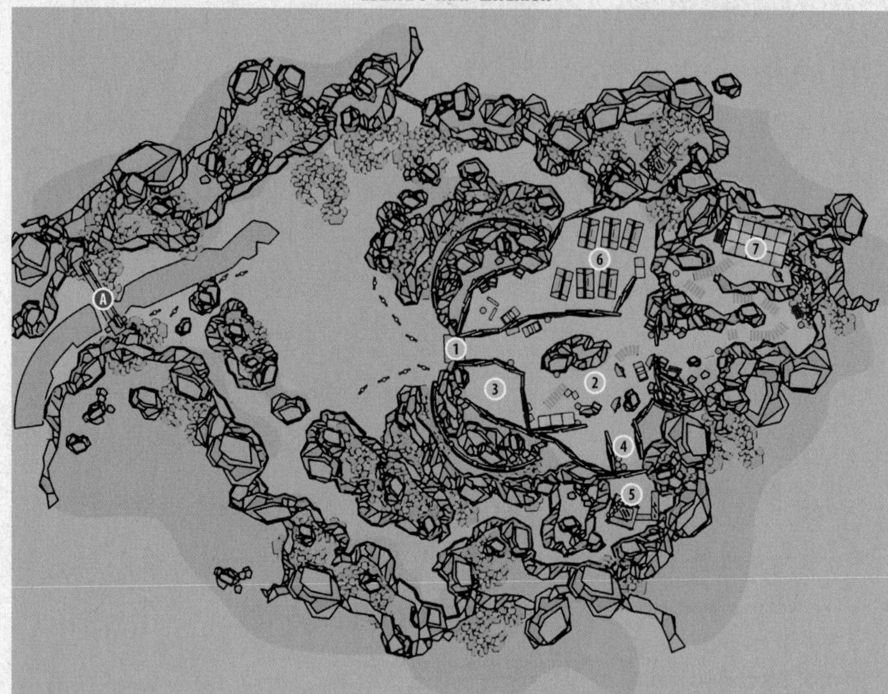

A Perimeter Gates

These lead to and from Hoover Dam [3.33], and the road continues to an impenetrable barricade, which is in the general direction of The Fort [3.28].

1 Interior Drawbridge

Meet Caesar's elite Praetorian Guard here.

2 Training Arena

Expect over a dozen Prime Legionaries here.

- Campfire [45/109]
- Machete (5)
- Footlocker Items (2)

3 Mongrel's Cage

This has a gate with a tampered locking mechanism designed to keep the gate shut. You can:

Leave it alone.

Remove the springs and seal the cage.

Preventing the dogs from attacking frees up the forces against Caesar (you included) to deal with only human foes. Naturally, if you're allied with Caesar, leave this well alone.

4 Brahmin Pens and South Entrance

This is where you can enter if you're infiltrating the camp using Sneak. Simply head around the outside perimeter edge, and open the gate at this point, to slip in quietly.

5 Guard Tower

You can optionally head up here, deal with the single guard, and set up sniping volleys and cut down countless Legion foes, if you're so inclined.

6 Legionaries Camp

- Campfire [46/109]
- Footlocker Items (10)

7 Legate's Tent

Pass the mildly irradiated pond, and scale the steps to the Legate's Tent, where you battle, or speak with Legate Lanius, a giant of a man skilled in the arts of battle and conversation.

- Unique Item: Legate's Helmet [62/95]
- Unique Weapon: Blade of the East [24/42]

[3.35] Cazador Nest

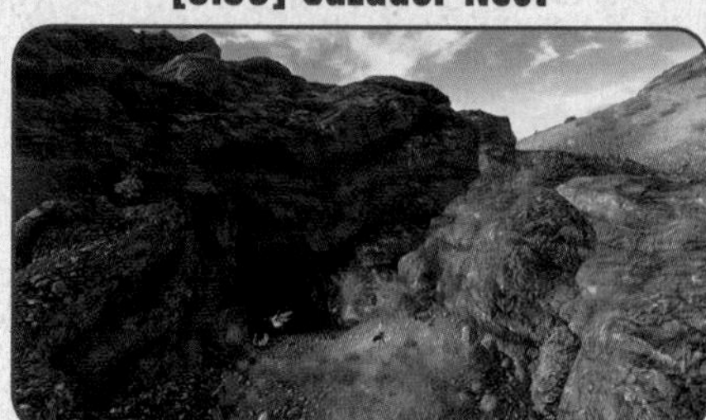

- Threat Level: ●●●●○
- Faction: Mutated Animal
  - Entity: Cazador
- Crafting:
  - Campfire [47/109]
  - Campfire [48/109]
- Collectibles: Hollowed-Out Rock [15/42]

There is a nest (and a Hollowed-Out Rock) in the alcove where the Cazadors are congregating. Check the rocky terrain nearby; there's a Campfire on the rounded summit of the hill northwest of the nest, overlooking Boulder City; and a second one due west of the nest, on the rocky terrain southwest of the road to Boulder City.

- Campfire [47/109]
- Campfire [48/109]
- Hollowed-Out Rock [15/42]

[3.36] Ranger Station Delta ●

- Side Quest: Return to Sender
- Threat Level: ●●●○○
- Faction: NCR
  - Entity: Ranger Pason
  - Entity: Comm Officer Scheffer
- Fame/Infamy
- Crafting:
  - Campfire [49/109]
  - Reloading Bench [19/36]
- Collectibles:
  - Magazine [Guns] [9/11] [50-51/52]

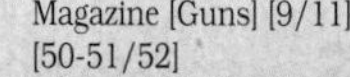

- Magazine [Survival] [20/30] [50-51/52]
- Guns and Ammo
- Health, Chems, or Water
- Highly Visible
- Interior Exploration
- Sleeping Quarters

This Ranger Station was erected on the remains of a ruined farmstead, which is still visible. Ranger Pason is looking for Legion crossing the river. You can ask him, or Scheffer what they're doing, and what the Rangers do. Outside is a Campfire, and a rather grim outhouse, but the real reason for visiting is the cellar under the house ruins. Pick open the lock [Average], and search the pool-table room for a well-hidden Magazine!

- Campfire [49/109]
- Ammo Box Ammunition (3) [2 = Easy]
- Magazine: Milsurp Review [Guns] [9/11] [50/52]
- Magazine: Lad's Life [Survival] [20/30] [51/52]
- Gun Case
- Reloading Bench [19/36]
- First Aid Box
- Gun Cabinet [Average]
- Pool Cue
- Sleeping Quarters

[U3.A] Train Tunnel (Underground)

View from the south, looking north.

- Threat Level: ●●●●●
- Faction: Ghoul
  - Entity: Feral Ghoul
- Dangers:
  - Traps
  - Mines
- Collectibles: Magazines
- Area Is Locked
- Guns and Ammo
- Interior Exploration
- Underground Connection

You can enter this location from the north [Very Hard] or south [Very Hard]. Inside, expect heavy resistance from Ghouls. Be sure to check the desiccated corpse of a Wastelander; he may be carrying a couple of random Magazines. There are Frag Mines dotted throughout this hellish passage, and Bear Traps at the north end. Why come down here? As an alternate way to get to and from Boomer territory.

- Frag Mine (9)
- Danger! Bear Trap!
- Fire Helmet
- Magazines (Random)

ZONE 3: SECONDARY LOCATIONS

[3.S01] Power Transformer

- Threat Level: ●●●●●
- Crafting: Campfire [50/109]
- Wasteland Vegetation

This is a junction for power towers you can follow to the south and west.

- Campfire [50/109]

[3.S02] Chem Addicts' Camp

- Threat Level: ●●●●●
- Faction: None
  - Entity: Chem Addict
- Crafting: Campfire [51/109]
- Sleeping Quarters
- Wasteland Vegetation

A couple of wretched specimens huddle on mattresses by a Campfire.

- Campfire [51/109]
- Sleeping Quarters

[3.S03] Boomer Territory Road

- Side Quest: Volare!
- Free Quest: Highway to the Danger Zone, I
- Threat Level: ●●●●●
- Faction: None
  - Entity: George
- Wasteland Vegetation
- Quest Item

Free Quest: Highway to the Danger Zone, I

When starting Side Quest: Volare!, meet a man named George here who forces you to stop. He warns you to slow down, or you'll get blown up like the rest of the scavenging idiots heading into Boomer territory. Now you're listening George says he has a little information for you. At a price. You can:

Threaten a kicking. George talks you out of it, but doesn't give up his instructions.

Keep talking, until he offers a "wager"; pay him 300 Caps, and he'll give you instructions on how to safely reach the Boomer base. And if you make it back, he'll pay you double! You can:

Convince him to make the wager 200 Caps.

Pay George 300 Caps.

Or ignore George entirely, and head into the danger zone.

If you shook George down or made the bet, he hands you a note; but tells you it's all in the timing as you move from building to building. Consult the next Secondary Location for details on maneuvering.

- Quest Item: Nellis Artillery Timing Details

[3.S04] Bombarded Houses

- Side Quest: Still in the Dark
- Side Quest: Volare!
- Free Quest: Highway to the Danger Zone, II
- Threat Level: ●●●●●
- Faction: Boomer
- Guns and Ammo
- Wasteland Vegetation
- Quest Item

Free Quest: Highway to the Danger Zone, II

George's Note gives you all the necessary knowledge to minimize damage you'll take as the Boomers bombard you up ahead. Which obviously means you don't need to pay George (who naturally, isn't there to hand a rube like you 600 Caps when you return). Here are the highlights:

Move from building-to-building up the northwest side of town toward the front gate.

Stick to the high cover in the northeast corner of the two buildings.

Then make a bee-line for the gate.

The Boomers won't shoot their own people, so stick to the fence until you reach the gate.

There's an old tunnel which enters the area from the south [U3.A], but no one has returned to say it's safe.

Spend time in this location, and you may stumble across the remains of two Brotherhood of Steel Paladins. Strip them of useful items, including a Holotape useful during Side Quest: Still in the Dark.

- Quest Item: Brotherhood of Steel Mission Holotape

[3.S05] Vault 34 Alternative Entrance

- Main Quest: Et Tumor, Brute?
- Side Quest: I Could Make You Care
- Side Quest: Hard Luck Blues
- Free Quest: All Fired Up!
- Threat Level: ●●●●●
- Faction: Mutated Animal
  - Entity: Golden Gecko
- Dangers: Radiation
- Interior Exploration

Climb to the top of this hill that Vault 34 [3.12] was hewn into; not only for the spectacular Vegas view, but for the mine shaft entrance.

[3.S06] NCR Truck and Dead Trooper

- Main Quest: Et Tumor, Brute?
- Side Quest: I Could Make You Care
- Side Quest: Hard Luck Blues
- Free Quest: All Fired Up!
- Threat Level: ●●●●●
- Faction: Mutated Animal
  - Entity: Golden Gecko
- Dangers: Radiation

Search the Trooper for a helpful items before you explore Vault 34 [3.12].

- Radiation Suit and RadAway

[3.S07] Mole Rat Hole

- Threat Level: ●●●●●
- Faction: Mutated Animal
  - Entity: Mole Rat
- Wasteland Vegetation

Roaming the rocky gulches are a group of Mole Rats to kill and skin.

[3.S08] Cazador Nests

- Threat Level: ●●●●●
- Faction: Mutated Animal
  - Entity: Cazador
- Wasteland Vegetation

If you're picking the copious wild vegetation in this zone, beware of the area north of the road; there are a number of Cazador Nests and around a dozen of these vicious insects.

[3.S09] Great Khan Supply Cave 1

- Side Quest: Climb Ev'ry Mountain
- Side Quest: No, Not Much
- Threat Level: ●●●●●
- Faction: Great Khan
  Entity: Oscar Velasco
- Dangers:
  Traps
  Mines
- Area Is Locked
- Guns and Ammo
- Health, Chems, or Water
- Interior Exploration
- Sleeping Quarters
- Quest Item

A Exit to Mojave Wasteland

1 Locked Gate and Supply Cache

Beware of the Frag Mines below the gate; deactivate them before opening the gate itself [Easy]. Enter the gate to pilfer from the supply cache. Oscar has the key that opens all the caches in this, and the two adjacent caves.

- Frag Mine (2)
- Quest Item: Great Khan Supply Cache
- Combat Knife
- Scrap Metal
- Hunting Rifle and Ammo
- Ammo Box Ammunition
- Footlocker Items
- Quest Item: Great Khans Supply Cache Key

2 Connecting Passage

Watch out for a Bear Trap at one end, and Frag Mines at the other.

- Frag Mine (3)

3 Oscar's Hideout

The Great Khan responsible for Bitter Springs tormenting keeps a few items near his cooking Brahmin.

- Ammo Box Ammunition (2)
- Sleeping Quarters

[3.S10] Great Khan Supply Cave 2

- Side Quest: Climb Ev'ry Mountain
- Side Quest: No, Not Much
- Threat Level: ●●●●●
- Faction: Great Khan/Mutated Animal
  Entity: Nightstalker
- Area Is Locked
- Guns and Ammo
- Health, Chems, or Water
- Interior Exploration
- Quest Item

1 Large Cavern

Search this cave as part of two Side Quests. This has a few scattered flesh bits, and some Nightstalkers chewing on them.

2 Supply Cache [Easy]

Open the gate using the key found in Location [3.S10], or pry the gates open [Easy]. Note the Great Khan petroglyphs on the walls.

- Quest Item: Great Khan Supply Cache
- Footlocker Items
- Frag Grenade (3)
- Machete
- Carton of Cigarettes
- Ammo Box Ammunition (2) [1 = Average]
- Produce Sack Items
- Explosives Crate Items

[3.S11] Great Khan Supply Cave 3

- Side Quest: Climb Ev'ry Mountain
- Side Quest: No, Not Much
- Threat Level: ●●●●●
- Faction: Great Khan / Giant Ant
  Entity: Giant Ant Soldier
  Entity: Giant Ant Worker
- Dangers: Radiation
- Interior Exploration
- Quest Item

1 Radioactive Dump

Search this cave as part of two Side Quests. The main chamber has been used to dump radioactive barrels, and this has had a mutative effect on the local Ant population.

- Ant Nectar
- Ant Egg Clutch Items

2 Radioactive Cache

The gate is off its hinges, allowing easy access to the following items:

- Quest Item: Radioactive Supply Cache
- Chems and Dirty Water

[3.S12] Super Mutant Camp

[3.S12] The One (and Super Mutant Camp)

- Threat Level: ●●●●●
- Faction: Super Mutant
  Entity: Super Mutant
  Entity: Glowing One
- Crafting: Campfire [52/109]
- Dangers: Radiation
- Guns and Ammo
- Sleeping Quarters
- Wasteland Vegetation
- Wild Wasteland!

In the irradiated northeast is an old nuclear bomb that appears to be a dud, but also explains the large numbers of Glowing Ones in the area. Check it out:

It appears the core components can be salvaged for some choice Energy Weapon ammo!

- Energy Cell (150)
- Microfusion Cell (50)
- Sensor Module (2)

Close by (also if you have Wild Wasteland perk) are some unfriendly Super Mutants bathing in the radiation. Cull them to take some of the biggest weapons you can carry!

- Campfire [52/109]
- Sleeping Quarters

[3.S13] Road Turnabout

- Threat Level: ●●●●●
- Free Quest: Help for Halford
- Radio Signal [Camp Guardian]

This is the end of the road that takes you through the northeast part of the Wasteland; ending at a scenic overlook of Camp Guardian [3.19].

[3.S14] Camp Guardian Cave

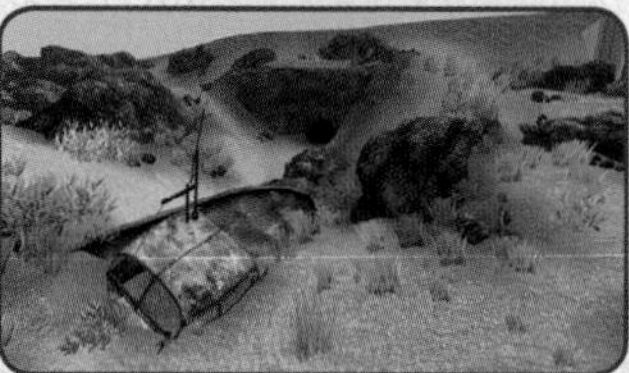

- Free Quest: Help for Halford
- Threat Level: ●●●●●
- Interior Exploration
- Radio Signal [Camp Guardian]
- Underground Connection

Underwater, in Lake Mead is a cave entrance close to the remains of a gambling boat. This is an alternate entrance to reach the interior of Camp Guardian Caves, usually accessed via Guardian Peak [3.20].

[3.S15] NCR Water Pipeline

- Threat Level: ●●●●●
- Faction: Mutated Animal
  Entity: Bloatfly
  Entity: Bighorner
- Highly Visible
- Main Trading Route
- Wasteland Vegetation

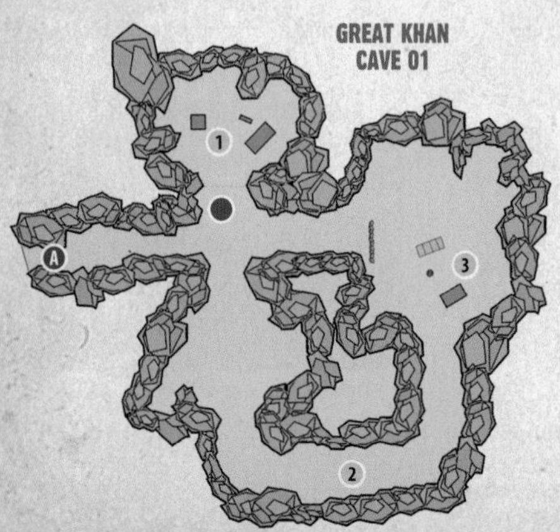

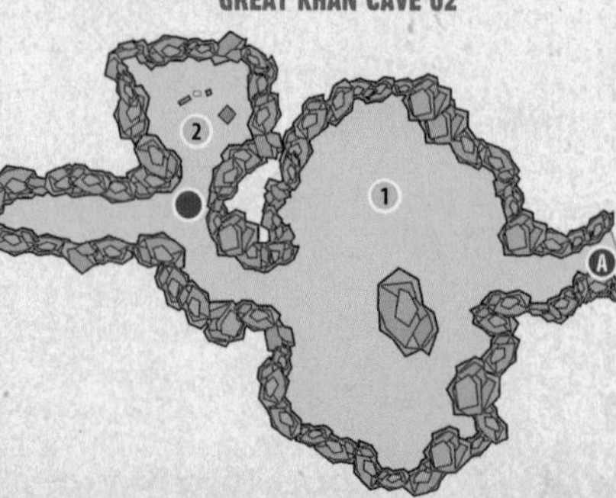

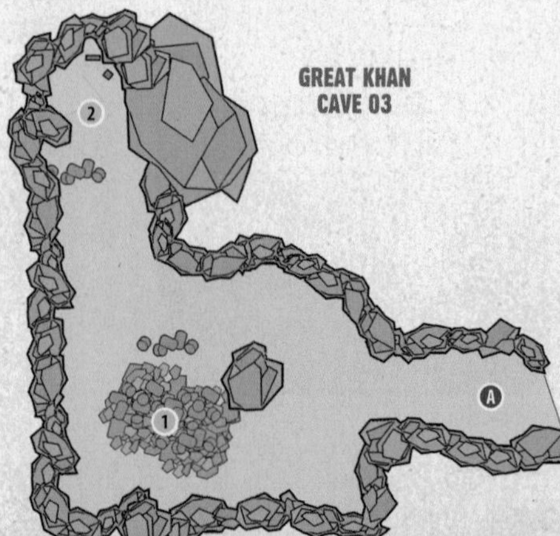

The giant, rusting pipe running around Camp Golf [3.23] and then northward toward the NCR Sharecropper Farms [2.20] is easy and useful to follow when situating yourself.

[3.S16] NCR Sentry Nest

- Threat Level: ●●●●●
- Faction: NCR
    Entity: NCR Trooper
- Wasteland Vegetation

This is on a hill outside the perimeter boundary of the base, and is therefore a great place to use as a sniping position, raining long-range death down on the NCR below.

[3.S17] Lake Mead Scenic Overlook

- Threat Level: ●●●●●
- Crafting: Campfire [53/109]
- Collectibles: Magazine [Survival] [21/30] [52/52]
- Sleeping Quarters

Close to Lake Las Vegas [3.22] and the massive Lake Mead itself, this has a small trailer with the following:

- Campfire [53/109]
- Carton of Cigarettes
- Magazine: Lad's Life [Survival] [21/30] [52/52]
- Sleeping Quarters

[3.S18] Sunken Sarsaparilla Supplies

- Threat Level: ●●●●●
- Collectibles:
    Sunset Sarsaparilla Star Cap [49/100]
    Sunset Sarsaparilla Star Cap [50/100]
    Sunset Sarsaparilla Star Cap [51/100]

A jackknifed container truck rests at the bottom of Lake Mead, with its spilled contents of (mostly empty) Sunset Sarsaparilla Bottles strewn out from the open container. There is actually a Star Cap among the debris; don't move any crates and be very gentle when looking, or the Cap may shift under a crate!

- Sunset Sarsaparilla Star Cap [49/100]
- Sunset Sarsaparilla Star Cap [50/100]
- Sunset Sarsaparilla Star Cap [51/100]
- Cap (a few scattered)
- Sunset Sarsaparilla Crate (18)

[3.S19] Sunken Boat

- Threat Level: ●●●●●
- Faction: Abomination
    Entity: Lakelurk
- Health, Chems, or Water

One of Lake Mead's secrets is a rusting boat with a single Hydra to pick up as you swim around the skeletal, and half-imbedded vessel.

[3.S20] Boulder City Billboard Sign

- Threat Level: ●●●●●
- Highly Visible

One of two either side of the 95 Highway, use this to situate yourself with the nearby roads and Primary Locations.

[3.S21] Sunset Sarsaparilla Billboard (Lonesome Drifter)

- Side Quest: Talent Pool
- Threat Level: ●●●●●
- Faction: Wastelander
    Entity: Lonesome Drifter
- Crafting: Campfire [54/109]
- Collectibles:
    Unique Item [63/95]
    Unique Item [64/95]
    Unique Weapon [25/42]
- Guns and Ammo
- Highly Visible
- Main Trading Route
- Sleeping Quarters
- Wasteland Vegetation

Note this sign for Sunset Sarsaparilla east of the El Dorado Dry Lake [5.09], as this is where the Lonesome Drifter resides. Speak to him when Side Quest: Talent Pool is active, to help him find his way. You may even win him over, and accept a Unique Weapon as a gift. That Acoustic Guitar, however, is only going to be pried out of his cold, dead hands.

- Campfire [54/109]
- Unique Item: Acoustic Guitar [63/95]
- Unique Item: Regulator's Duster [64/95]
- Unique Weapon: Mysterious Magnum [25/42]
- Sleeping Quarters

[3.S22] Ranger Pason's Patrol Overlook

- Side Quest: Return to Sender
- Threat Level: ●●●●●
- Faction: NCR
    Entity: Ranger Pason
    Entity: Robobrain
- Guns and Ammo
- Quest Item

At the end of the gully pathway from Ranger Station Delta [3.36] is a Robobrain belonging to Ranger Pason, who is looking out over the Hoover Dam [3.33] to the north for signs of The Legion. Speak to him as part of Side Quest: Return to Sender. He is also carrying an "unremarkable" Report.

- Binoculars
- Quest Item: Ranger Pason Report

ZONE 4: SOUTHWEST DESERT

Topographical Overview

The Southwest Desert is something of a paradox; offering your first tentative steps into the world in and around the settlement of Goodsprings; but with arguably the most dangerous area in the Wasteland just to the northeast; inside the Deathclaw-filled Quarry Junction [4.04], and the hapless workers in need of your help in the adjacent settlement of Sloan [4.08]. It is worth spending some time in Goodsprings to start, learning how to Craft and purchasing upgrades, before romping south. The seedy town of Primm [4.17] is farther south on the arterial Long 15 road, flanked on either side by radioactive rural locales; the Mesquite Mountain Crater [4.19] and Jack Rabbit Springs [4.26]. Dominating the southern desert is the Ivanpah Dry Lake [4.24], stretching across a road and all the way to a giant scar in the earth. Two more major settlements on the California border are the NCR stronghold of the Mojave Outpost [4.27], and the recently razed town of Nipton [4.30], where the ruthless atrocities of Caesar's Legion are witnessed first-hand.

> **Note** To reference the entirety of this Zone, please utilize the Map Poster that came with this guide.

Highways and Byways

The north-south road of choice used to be the Long 15, which bisects this zone all the way from the northeast corner, and meanders southward, past Goodsprings, through Primm, and ends at the Mojave Outpost. A smaller, desert road winds through Goodsprings from the remote northwest area and joins the Long 15, and along the northern zone border, Trail 160 links the two roads. Keep in mind that the entire eastern edge of this location is the railroad track, and you can become spatially competent when exploring. To the south, Trail 164 breaks off from the Long 15 near the Mojave Outpost, and continues east through the Ivanpah Dry Lake and into Nipton; winding all the way to Camp Searchlight [6.16] in Zone 6.

Available Services, Crafting and Collectibles

Services: Caravan Players: [4/15]
Services: Gambling: [3/15]
Services: Healers/Dealers: [3/31]
Services: Repairers: [1/9]
Services: Traders: [3/33]
Crafting: Campfires: [18/109]
Crafting: Reloading Benches: [6/36]
Crafting: Workbenches: [3/41]
Crafting: Weapon Upgrades: [1/10]
Collectibles: Snow Globes: [1/7]
Collectibles: Caravan Cards: [12/30]
Collectibles: Hollowed-Out Rocks: [9/42]
Collectibles: Skill Books: [12/51]
Collectibles: Skill Magazines: [32/213]
Collectibles: Star Bottle Caps: [18/100]
Collectibles: Unique Items: [7/95]
Collectibles: Unique Weapons: [3/42]

Primary Locations

[4.01] Tribal Village
[4.02] Makeshift Great Khan Camp
[4.03] Great Khan Encampment
[4.04] Quarry Junction
[4.05] Goodsprings
[4.06] Goodsprings Cemetery
[4.07] Yangtze Memorial
[4.08] Sloan
[4.09] Goodsprings Cave
[4.10] The Devil's Gullet
[4.11] Goodsprings Source
[4.12] Jean Sky Diving
[4.13] Powder Ganger Camp West
[4.14] Lone Wolf Radio
[4.15] Powder Ganger Camp South
[4.16] Canyon Wreckage
[4.17] Primm
[4.18] California Sunset Drive-in
[4.19] Mesquite Mountains Crater
[4.20] The Prospector's Den
[4.21] Mesquite Mountains Camp Site
[4.22] Nipton Road Reststop
[4.23] Nevada Highway Patrol Station
[4.24] Ivanpah Dry Lake
[4.25] Ivanpah Race Track
[4.26] Jack Rabbit Springs
[4.27] Mojave Outpost
[4.28] Morning Star Cavern
[4.29] Nipton Road Pit Stop
[4.30] Nipton
[4.31] Mojave Drive-in
[4.32] Crescent Canyon West
[4.33] Crescent Canyon East

Secondary Locations

[4.S01] Chance's Grave
[4.S02] Warning Signs on Goodsprings Road
[4.S03] Scorpion Valley
[4.S04] The Dead Survivalist
[4.S05] Abandoned Shack
[4.S06] 6A, 6B, 6C Goodsprings Water Wells (3)
[4.S07] Broken Radio Tower and Dead Body Overhang
[4.S08] Archeologist's Fridge
[4.S09] Deathclaw Trailer
[4.S10] Corvega Atomic Billboard
[4.S11] Railroad Bridge
[4.S12] Ammo Stash
[4.S13] Jackknifed Truck
[4.S14] The Desiccated Adventurer
[4.S15] Powder Ganger Junction
[4.S16] Bloatfly Flats
[4.S17] The Devil's Carbunkle
[4.S18] Trash Ditch
[4.S19] Prospector's Lean-To
[4.S20] Bright's Darkness
[4.S21] Mesquite Mountains Lean-To
[4.S22] Super Mutant Camp
[4.S23] Nipton Junction
[4.S24] Californian Exodus
[4.S25] Crashed Cargo Plane
[4.S26] Radscorpion Burrow
[4.S27] Mole Rat Burrows
[4.S28] Sealed Train Tunnel

PRIMARY LOCATIONS

[4.01] Tribal Village

- Threat Level: ●●●●●
- Faction: Mutated Animal
  Entity: Cazador
- Crafting: Campfire [55/109]
- Collectibles: Hollowed-Out Rock [16/42]
- Health, Chems, or Water
- Sleeping Quarters
- Wasteland Vegetation

This is close to the mountainous stretch of Trail 160. Keep your wits about you as you spot a series of burned bodies dotted along side path that leads to a massacre at an old Tribal Village. Deal with the airborne threats.

- Hollowed-Out Rock [16/42]
- Campfire [55/109]
- First Aid Box, Chems and Stimpaks
- Armor Case Items
- Sleeping Quarters

[4.02] Makeshift Great Khan Camp

- Threat Level: ●●●●●
- Faction: Great Khan
  Entity: None
- Crafting: Campfire [56/109]
- Collectibles: Hollowed-Out Rock [17/42]

This recently abandoned camp has a few empty Whiskey bottles and a Campfire, but little else. It is on the edge of the 160 trail.

- Campfire [56/109]
- Hollowed-Out Rock [17/42]

[4.03] Great Khan Encampment

- Side Quest: Don't Make a Beggar of Me
- Side Quest: Oh My Papa
- Threat Level: ●●●●●
- Faction: Great Khan
  Entity: Melissa
  Entity: Great Khan
- Services: Caravan Player [9/15]
- Crafting: Campfire [57/109]
- Collectibles: Caravan Cards [12/30]
- Sleeping Quarters

This sounds more impressive than what is essentially three Great Khans and some light bedding on the rocky perimeter of Quarry Junction [4.04]. Melissa, the leader of this motley crew, stops and asks suspiciously about your intentions. You can:

Ask about the Great Khans that took your Platinum Chip when you sustained your head injuries. She doesn't know, or isn't telling.

Ask what she's doing here. Pursue this line of questioning for an alternate start to Side Quest: Don't Make a Beggar of Me.

Speak to her about switching allegiances, but only if Side Quest: Oh My Papa is active.

Or ask about the history of the Great Khans, and play Caravan with her.

- Caravan Player: Melissa [9/15]
- Caravan Cards: [12/30]
- Campfire [57/109]
- Chems and Beer

[4.04] Quarry Junction

See map on the following page

- Side Quest: Bleed Me Dry
- Free Quest: Claws Out
- Free Quest: You Gotta Break Out a Few Eggs
- Threat Level: ●●●●●
- Faction: Abomination
  Entity: Deathclaw
  Entity: Deathclaw Mother
  Entity: Alpha Male Deathclaw
- Dangers: Radiation
- Collectibles:
  Unique Items [65/95]
  Unique Items [66/95]
  Unique Weapon [26/42]
- Guns and Ammo
- Health, Chems, or Water
- Highly Visible
- Lots O' Caps
- Radio Signal [Black Mountain]
- Quest Item

Arguably the most dangerous area of the Mojave Wasteland, and the reason the Long 95 is currently closed to all but the bravest (or most inept) wanderers, Quarry Junction is a massive, sprawling rock quarry with numerous tiers to it, and over a dozen ferocious Deathclaws, including larger entities that require all your stamina (and firepower) to defeat! The workers at Sloan [4.08] live a fearful (and unprofitable) existence with this menace still prevalent. There's a reason warning signs have been constructed as far away as the Yangtze Memorial [4.07]....

1 Quarry Entrance

A dead Powder Ganger and warning daubed on a crane are too late; unless you're Sneaking, you're already being set upon by Deathclaws! Try entering the Quarry via the upper ridges, close to the Great Khan Encampment [4.03].

2 Northern Tiered Plateau

There is, at least, a chance of survival up here, as the Deathclaws in the main area don't climb up as quickly as they descend. Try leaping on the large crushing conveyor belts or digging cranes so you're less exposed to attacks.

QUARRY JUNCTION EXTERIOR

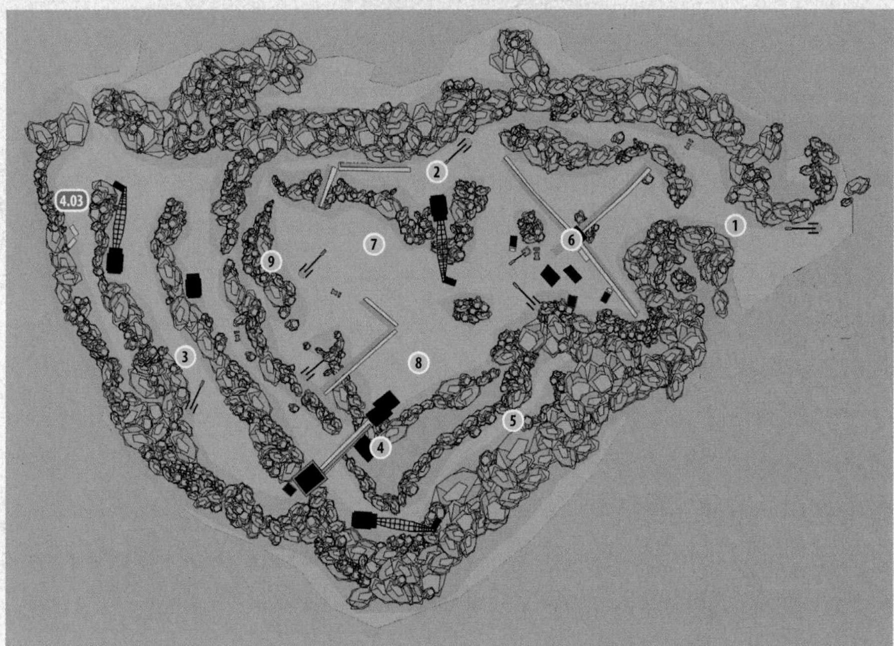

3 Southwest Rock Tiers

This allows ascension to the Great Khan Encampment, and to a number of rocky tiers, although there's no escape if you're being pursued by Deathclaws.

4 Southern Conveyor Machines

Sniping from the top of this structure (or the roof of the hut near the conveyor belt itself) affords you to some time. The lower conveyor belt allows you to escape from the Silt Pools.

5 Southeastern Rocky Ridge

You can't scramble up here from the Quarry floor, so this isn't an escape route; it's a place to survey the beasts below, and optionally snipe them.

6 Quarry Floor and Main Conveyor Crusher

Expect constant, overwhelming Deathclaw attacks if you're fool-hardy enough to venture into this area. The giant triple-conveyor belt crusher should be used to jump on and race up, so you can fight without being surrounded.

7 8 Silt Pools

Two shallow ponds of irradiated water are farther into the quarry. This is where the Deathclaw Mother and Alpha Male are prowling: Vicious, terrifying giant abominations! Don't forget to scavenge the Fat Man by the south pool (this is the only one lying around, but there are more on corpses to scavenge).

- Unique Weapon: Fat Man [26/42]
- Unique Item: Mini Nuke [65/66]

9 Deathclaw Nest

The Mother is guarding a small alcove nest, with three Deathclaw Eggs still intact. Gather them all; for the Quests that need them, and the value if you're planning to sell them (200 Caps each). There's more to grab around the skeletons in the nest, too:

- Quest Item: Deathclaw Egg (3)
- Light Machine Gun and Ammo
- Super Stimpak
- Unique Item: Mini-Nuke [66/95]

[4.05] Goodsprings ●

See map on the following page

- Main Quest: Ain't That a Kick in the Head
- Main Quest: They Went That-A-Way
- Main Quest: Back in the Saddle
- Main Quest: By a Campfire on The Trail
- Side Quest: Ghost Town Gunfight
- Side Quest: Run Goodsprings Run
- Free Quest: Ringo's Caravan Rules
- Free Quest: Trudy's Radio Repair
- Free Quest: We Must Stop Meeting Like This, I
- Free Quest: We Must Stop Beating Like This
- Threat Level: ●●●●●
- Faction: Goodsprings
  - Entity: Trudy
  - Entity: Doc Mitchell
  - Entity: Sunny Smiles
  - Entity: Cheyenne
  - Entity: Victor
  - Entity: Easy Pete
  - Entity: Ringo
  - Entity: Joe Cobb
  - Entity: Settler
- Fame/Infamy
- Services:
  - Caravan Player [10/15]
  - Healer/Dealer [26/31]
  - Healer/Dealer [27/31]
  - Trader [19/31]
- Crafting:
  - Reloading Bench [20/36]
  - Workbench [26/41]
  - Weapon Upgrade [Guns] [6/10]
- Collectibles:
  - Caravan Cards: [13/30]
  - Caravan Cards: [14/30]
  - Caravan Cards: [15/30]
  - Skill Book: [Sneak] [3/4] [1/12]
  - Magazine: [Barter] [11/16] [1-14/32]
  - Magazine: [Barter] [12/16] [1-14/32]
  - Magazine: [Barter] [13/16] [1-14/32]
  - Magazine: [Lockpick] [Given by Sunny]
  - Magazine: [Medicine] [17/19] [1-14/32]
  - Magazine: [Repair] [22/27] [1-14/32]
  - Magazine: [Repair] [23/27] [1-14/32]
  - Magazine: [Science] [16/23] [1-14/32]
  - Magazine: [Science] [17/23] [1-14/32]
  - Magazine: [Speech] [9/12] [1-14/32]
  - Magazine: [Speech] [10/12] [1-14/32]
  - Magazine: [Speech] [11/12] [1-14/32]
  - Magazine: [Survival] [22/30] [1-14/32]
  - Magazine: [Survival] [23/30] [1-14/32]
  - Magazine: [Unarmed] [10/11] [1-14/32]
  - Sunset Sarsaparilla Star Cap [52/100]
  - Sunset Sarsaparilla Star Cap [53/100]
- Guns and Ammo
- Health, Chems, or Water
- Interior Exploration
- Lots O' Caps
- Main Trading Route
- Sleeping Quarters
- Wasteland Vegetation
- Quest Item

Goodsprings is a small, barely active town that had been a mining community since the early days of Nevada. Most recently, it was settled under a grant from NCR to develop a low-risk mining environment near a reliable source of potable water. Even so, there are only a dozen or so people in the town due to trade along I-15 drying up. Signs along I-15 direct people to Goodsprings for water, but they do the town no good if no one is on the highway to read them.

> **Tip** There are a number of mailboxes in this settlement. Check each one for the possibility of a random item, or Magazine.

1 2 3 4 Abandoned Homesteads (North)

There are four home sites, and a rusting trailer here.

- BB Gun
- Sensor Module
- Magazine: Meeting People [Speech] [9/12] [1/32]
- Sleeping Quarters

5 Goodsprings Gas Station

There's no gas, but the station still has an inhabitant inside. Before you enter, check the Vending Machine, and the back of the pickup truck (as there's sometimes Dynamite in a crate there). To actually enter the premises, you must have the key, having talked with Sunny Smiles and began Main Quest: Ghost Town Gunfight. Inside, a jittery Ringo almost fills you full of lead. You can ask him about the area, what he's doing and his run-ins with the Powder Gangers, and he's extra-helpful in explaining the rules of a new card game: Free Quest: Ringo's Caravan Rules. Ringo has some Caps on him too, although you'll have to kill him for them.

Inside the Gas Station there's a variety of items to sift through.

- Caravan Player: Ringo [10/15]
- Caravan Cards: [13/30]
- Caravan Cards: [14/30]
- Crate (3) and Sack Items
- Cash Register Items
- Floor Safe Items [Easy]
- Carton of Cigarettes
- Doctor's Bag
- Magazine: Boxing Times [Unarmed] [10/11] [2/32]
- Caps (150+)
- Sleeping Quarters

6 Goodsprings Home

A settler is usually outside, tending to crops. Check inside for the following:

- Ammo Box Ammunition
- Knife
- Magazine: Lad's Life [Survival] [22/30] [3/32]
- Sunset Sarsaparilla Star Cap [52/100]

7 Goodsprings Main Drag

8 Goodsprings General Store

Chet runs the General Store, which has a few scattered supplies outside the small worn storefront. Of particular use are a Reloading Bench and Workbench between the store and the saloon.

- Crate Items (7)
- Sack Items (2)
- Reloading Bench [20/36]
- Workbench [26/41]

GOODSPRINGS EXTERIOR

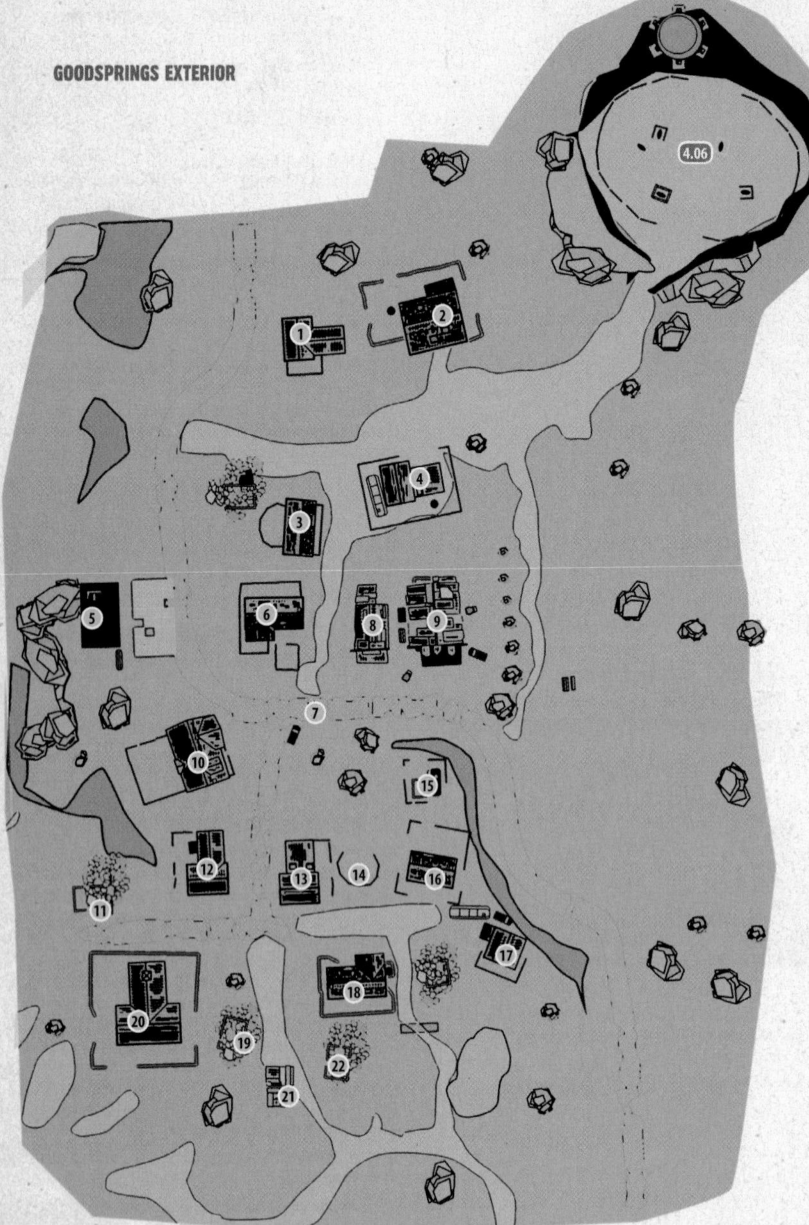

Inside the store, there's a variety of items to steal, if you don't feel like purchasing:

- Magazine: Salesman Weekly [Barter] [11/16] [4/32]
- Silenced .22 Pistol
- Scrap Metal
- Cash Register Items (2)
- Armor Case Items
- Food

Meet Chet himself, and he patiently explains the differences between the ammunition types and weapon modifications (Upgrades) that he sells, and the reasons "surplus" ammo isn't that good. You can also ask about your attackers, but the real reason you're here is to upgrade your guns!

- Trader: Chet [19/33]
- Trader (Highlight): Caravan Cards [15/30]
- Trader (Highlight): Weapon Upgrades [Guns] [6/10]

Caution It's never a good idea to kill those who can help you, and Chet is among these folk. Offing him results in his copious collection of Weapon Upgrades disappearing with him; so let him live if you're going down the path of a murderer.

9 Prospector Saloon

The hub of Goodsprings is this ramshackle tavern. Easy Pete may be sitting in his rocking chair on the porch, and he's excellent for getting some information (and Dynamite) out of. There are four exterior doors; two at the front (one is locked [Very Easy]), one at the back, and one that leads to a secret moonshine shed [Very Easy] attached to the building, close to the fence where Sunny Smiles has you shoot off bottles during Main Quest: Back in the Saddle. Inside the shed, you find the following:

- Scrap Metal
- Moonshine (5)

Inside the saloon, you can meet Sunny Smiles and her dog Cheyenne, and begin Main Quest: Back in the Saddle. Make sure you ask her about employments, so she tells you about the locked safe inside the Schoolhouse, and gives you a Magazine (which isn't counted toward the total you can find lying around) and Bobby Pins. She also has a wealth of knowledge about the surrounding area and Factions. Check the sideboard in this area for another Magazine.

- Magazine: Locksmith's Reader [Lockpick]
- Magazine: Fixin' Things [Repair] [22/27] [5/32]
- Bobby Pins

At the back is a bathroom you can sip rad-free water from. There are some items you can steal (although you're better off buying them from Trudy if you care about your Reputation). Trudy's office has a couple more magazines, and a Terminal [Easy] you can hack to disengage a floor safe [Hard].

- Magazine: Salesman Weekly [Barter] [12/16] [6/32]
- Magazine: Meeting People [Speech] [10/12] [7/32]
- Pool Cue
- Sunset Sarsaparilla Crate Items
- Floor Safe Items [Hard]
- .357 Magnum Revolver

Once you've spoken with Sunny and aimed at her bottles, you can meet Trudy the "den mother" of Goodsprings. She's having some problems with a Powder Ganger called Joe Cobb (Side Quest: Ghost Town Gunfight). You can speak to her about it, the lay of the land, the men who shot you, Victor, and Goodsprings itself. Keep talking to her to begin Free Quest: Trudy's Radio Repair. She also sells wares, and offers a discount once you finish the Quest in Goodsprings' favor.

- Healer: Trudy [26/31]
- Healer Highlight (Trudy): Magazines and Moonshine (that you didn't steal)

10 Doc Mitchell's House

This was the place where you recuperated after your dirt nap. Return to Doc Mitchell again and obtain more medical supplies. Doc Mitchell was a resident of Vault 21 (hence the Jumpsuit he gave you), and offers more information on the area, Victor, the men who tried to kill you, and other matters. He can also heal you (usually for 50 Caps), and sell you medical supplies.

- Healer: Doc Mitchell [27/31]

You can also make a thorough sweep of the doctor's home:

You can repair the Submachine Gun and add it to your inventory.

You can create Stimpaks, or Chems (Psycho, Buffout, Mentats, Steady, or Rebound) at the Chemistry Experiment.

- Cap (9)
- Gun Case Items
- Stimpaks and Chems
- Magazine: Today's Physician [Medicine] [17/19] [8/32]
- Magazine: Fixin' Things [Repair] [23/27] [9/32]
- Broken 9mm Submachine Gun
- Sunset Sarsaparilla Crate Items
- Blood Pack
- Ammo Box Ammunition
- First Aid Box (2)
- Carton of Cigarettes

11 12 Ruined House and Abandoned Home

13 Goodsprings Home

Check inside to steal the following:

- Teddy Bear
- Purified Water and Food
- Ammo
- First Aid Box
- Briefcase Items
- Safe Items

14 Bighorner Pen

You can startle the Bighorners in this unkept during Side Quest: Ghost Town Gunfight.

15 Ruined Home and Water Tank

- Ammo

16 Goodsprings Home

- Sleeping Quarters

17 Trailer, Boarded-up, and Destroyed Home

Check the mailbox by the boarded-up home for a possible Magazine.

18 Goodsprings Home

A small crop of plants and a Bighorner are behind the house to the south.

- Skill Book: Chinese Army: Spec. Ops. Training Manual [Sneak] [3/4] [1/12]
- Sunset Sarsaparilla Bottle
- Sunset Sarsaparilla Star Cap [53/100]
- First Aid Box
- Single Shotgun and Ammo

19 Ruined House

20 Goodsprings Schoolhouse

Sunny recommends you scavenge in here, and she's correct. Inside, deal with the Giant Mantis Nymphs, optionally hack into the terminal [Easy] to open the safe (or unlock it using Bobby Pins). The safe usually has a large number of Caps and a Doctor's Bag. Check the room for multiple Magazines.

- Magazine: Salesman Weekly [Barter] [13/16] [10/32]
- Magazine: Programmer's Digest [Science] [16/23] [11/32]
- Magazine: Programmer's Digest [Science] [17/23] [12/32]
- Magazine: Meeting People [Speech] [11/12] [13/32]
- Magazine: Lad's Life [Survival] [23/30] [14/32]
- Mantis Egg
- Footlocker Items
- Bobby Pins
- Safe Items [Easy]

21 Victor's Shack

When he's not trundling down from the cemetery, you may find Victor sitting outside his shack. You can speak to him (Free Quest), or head inside for a snoop and a sleep. The sink water is a little too irradiated, though.

- Ammo Box Ammunition (2)
- Weapon Repair Kit
- Scrap Metal
- Sleeping Quarters

22 Ruined House

Free Quest: Ringo's Caravan Rules

Don't shoot Ringo in the gas station, and instead speak with him, and you can receive a patient tutelage regarding the rules of Caravan. He also provides you a starter deck, which is extremely kind of him, along with Holotape rules to refer to any time you like. Now go out and build up your deck, and find other players across the Mojave!

- Note: How to Play Caravan
- Caravan Deck

Free Quest: We Must Stop Meeting Like This, I

As you meander around the settlement, and you haven't yet met Mr. House at the Lucky 38 Casino, you may spot a Securitron zipping around on its single tire. Why, it's Victor, the good-time cowpoke Securitron! If you spot him in Goodsprings, you can thank him for rescuing you from a shallow grave, ask what he's doing, ask about the men who jumped you, or to stay out of your way. Although he might be tailing you, he's not prepared to become a Follower. You can shoot at him too, but he has no items to loot.

Free Quest: We Must Stop Beating Like This

As you get your bearings in and around the settlement of Goodsprings, you may inadvertently get into combat scrapes; usually with Geckos or Powder Gangers during Side Quest: Ghost Town Gunfight. Should this occur, and Victor is close by, he evens the score and demolishes anyone foolish enough to challenge you. He's looking out for you. But why?

Free Quest: Trudy's Radio Repair

Keep the chatter up with Trudy at the Prospector's Saloon, and she tells you she's having real problems with her Radio. Agree to fix it for 25 Caps, or Barter her up to 50 Caps. You're offered a slight discount when the tunes come back on.

Goodsprings Fame Gained!

[4.06] Goodsprings Cemetery

- Main Quest: Ain't That a Kick in the Head
- Main Quest: By a Campfire on the Trail
- Free Quest: Exhumin' Nature
- Threat Level: ●●●●●
- Faction: Goodsprings
  - Entity: None
- Collectibles: Snowglobe—Goodsprings [7/7]
- Guns and Ammo
- Lots O' Caps (depending on Luck)
- Wasteland Vegetation
- Quest Item

Although you may have started your days thinking you were ending them right here, in the courier's shallow grave dug by Benny and his cohorts, Victor's rescue from this location allowed you to explore, and this should be one of your first perusals after checking out Goodsprings. There are graves to dig up, and more importantly, a Snow Globe resting against one headstone. Use this elevated position to check the horizon; you can see The Strip and Camp McCarran [2.19] to the northeast, and Bonnie Springs [1.20] to the north. Use the Water Tower as a landmark on your travels.

- Snowglobe: Goodsprings [7/7]

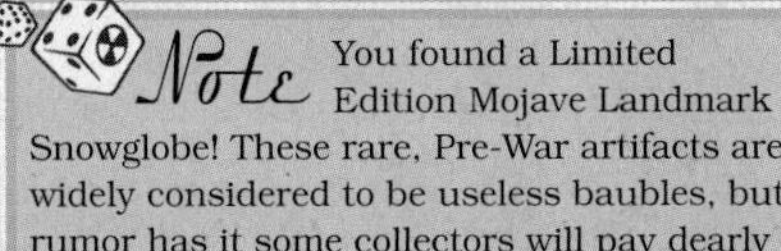

Note You found a Limited Edition Mojave Landmark Snowglobe! These rare, Pre-War artifacts are widely considered to be useless baubles, but rumor has it some collectors will pay dearly for them.

Free Quest: Exhumin' Nature

There are a number of grave sites on this promontory plot, including your own. However, excavating them is impossible without a Shovel. Purchase one from Chet at the Goodsprings General Store (15 Caps), and return to start your ghoulish digging.

- Grave items
- Ammo (bits and bobs)
- Caps (a few)

[4.07] Yangtze Memorial

- Threat Level: ●●●●●
- Faction: None
- Collectibles: Hollowed-Out Rock [18/42]
- Highly Visible

Most locals can't rightly remember the exact reason for the large cross on the hill northeast of Goodsprings [4.05], but it honors the fallen of the Yangtze Campaign after the Chinese invaded Alaska in 2066, and the United States fought back, deploying to the Chinese mainland in a long and bloody war that ended with the 2077 holocaust. There's a Hollowed-Out Rock here, and a warning of Deathclaws in the Quarry Junction [4.04] to the northeast. Northwest is an Abandoned Shack [4.S05] that's well worth checking out. Use the memorial as a landmark.

- Hollowed-Out Rock [18/42]

[4.08] Sloan ●

- Side Quest: Don't Make a Beggar of Me
- Free Quest: Claws Out
- Free Quest: You Gotta Break Out a Few Eggs
- Free Quest: Power to the People
- Free Quest: Claws Mended
- Threat Level: ●●●●●
- Faction: Quarry Workers / NCR
  - Entity: Chomps Lewis
  - Entity: Jas Wilkins
  - Entity: Quarry Worker
  - Entity: Snuffles
- Fame/Infamy
- Services: Healer/Dealer [28/31]
- Crafting: Workbench [27/41]
- Collectibles:
  - Sunset Sarsaparilla Star Cap [54/100]
  - Skill Book [Explosives] [3/4] [2/12]
  - Skill Book [Repair] [2/4] [3/12]
  - Unique Item [67/95]
- Health, Chems, or Water
- Interior Exploration
- Lots O' Caps
- Radio Signal [Black Mountain]
- Sleeping Quarters
- Quest Item

A camp of mining shacks off the Long 19 was once a place where workers earned a good living. That was until the Deathclaws moved in. You're likely to enter the place traveling along this freeway, and you'll be stopped by Chomps Lewis; who's still the foreman of this small settlement. He tells you to loop around via Primm [4.17] if you want to avoid a mauling. You can ask him about New Vegas, and the operation: They make cement for the NCR using the limestone quarry. Ask him for a more detailed explanation. You can then begin Free Quest: Claws Out. Chomps also has a Letter to Tyrone, which is useful during the Side Quest.

- Quest Item: Letter to Tyrone

1 Sandbag Defenses

Sloan itself is comprised of a couple of sandbag walls on the Long 95, and fenced-off rocky depression with four shanty huts. Check the sandbag table for Binoculars.

2 Worker Barracks

To the right of the entrance is a high shelf with a radio, Dino Toy, and Skill Book. On the cabinet at the far end is a second Skill Book, and a couple of Lockers [1 = Easy]. Check out the following items, and take any bunk bed for some rest.

SLOAN EXTERIOR

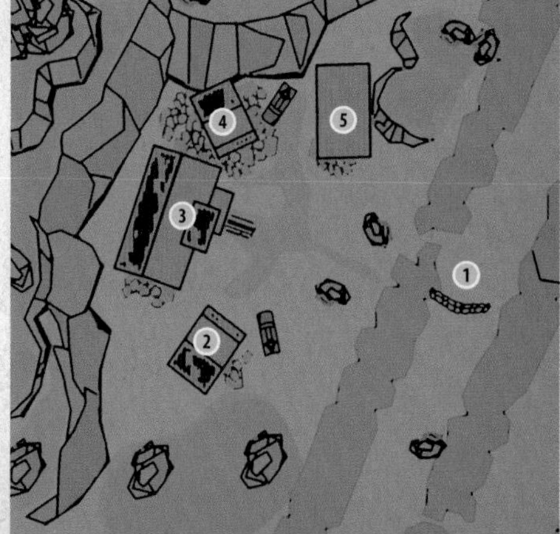

- Skill Book: Duck and Cover! [Explosives] [3/4] [2/12]
- Skill Book: Dean's Electronics [Repair] [2/4] [3/12]
- First Aid Box
- Carton of Cigarettes (2)

3 Mining Office

Upstairs is where there's a haul to Sneak out with; two trunks behind the picnic table are likely to be filled with Caps, and there's more inside the safe [Average]. There's also a suitcase by the side of the desk upstairs too. It has nothing of worth unless Side Quest: Don't Make a Beggar Out of Me is active. Then the lack of drugs allows you to quiz Chomps about it.

- Pool Cue (2)
- Caps a-plenty

4 Machine Shop

- Workbench [27/41]
- Scrap Metal (3)

5 Mess Hall

Jas Wilkins is the jovial cook inside this rudimentary restaurant, and aside from asking about her family omelet recipe (Free Quest: You Gotta Break Out a Few Eggs), she sells you any of the Food she has. Check the round table nearby for a Star Cap. There's also a large amount of food in the pantry behind her, but that has to be stolen.

- Healer: Jas Wilkins (Food) [28/31]
- Sunset Sarsaparilla Star Cap [54/100]

Free Quest: Claws Out

Chomps Lewis, at his sandbag post on the Long 95, is having a heck of a time with the Deathclaws that have moved into his quarry. After a talk, tell him you could take care of his Deathclaw problem. Chomps hands over some medical supplies to help you get the job done. He also gives you some advice; to take down the Deathclaw Mother and Alpha Male.

- Stimpak (5) and Super Stimpak (5)

Attacking these Deathclaws is pretty much suicidal. Remember you only have to shoot the Mother and Alpha Male, and it's recommended you bring all the ammo you can carry, perhaps using a Sniper Rifle from afar, with a Mini-gun or Light Machine Gun as back-up, and Sneak to the top of a crane so you aren't savaged. Return to Chomps to tell him the deed is done, and you're rewarded with some NCR funds, and fame.

- NCR $100 (5)
- NCR Fame Gained!

Tip It is worth asking about the Deathclaws and agreeing to kill them just for the free Stimpaks!

Free Quest: You Gotta Break Out a Few Eggs

What's the tastiest thing you've ever eaten? That's what Jas Wilkins wants to know in the Sloan Mess Hall. Respond with:

People.

Ghouls and Super Mutants.

Anything that wasn't made 200 years ago.

Or ask why. She has an Aunt Rose from Modoc, California, who swears that a Deathclaw Omelet is the best. She tells you her back-story. She wants you to snag one, and she can't pay with money, but will share the recipe. You can guess where the eggs are, can't you?

You can visit Quarry Junction [4.04], and use the map and information in the Tour to locate and take the three Deathclaw Eggs. Sneaking, and coming down from the Great Khan Encampment [4.03] is the easiest plan. Return to Jas, and she's ecstatic, cooking up the Omelet just for you, and giving you the Recipe.

- Deathclaw Egg (3)
- Wasteland Omelet
- Unique Item [Recipe]: Rose's Wasteland Omelet [67/95]

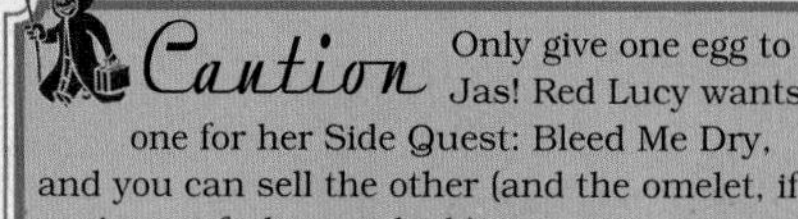
Caution Only give one egg to Jas! Red Lucy wants one for her Side Quest: Bleed Me Dry, and you can sell the other (and the omelet, if you're not feeling peckish).

Free Quest: Power to the People

Somebody with a distinct lack of competence assembled Sloan's generator, which is found next to the Mining Office. Inspect it, and you can:

Leave it alone.

Properly assemble the generator. Then return to Chomps Lewis to tell him, and he's grateful. Although he's paying you in NCR Dollars.

- NCR $100 (2)
- NCR Fame Gained!

Or permanently disable it. You get some Scrap Metal, a Conductor, and Sensor Module.

- Scrap Metal (5)

Free Quest: Claws Mended

The camp's pet Mole Rat, Snuffles is feeling under the weather. But it's an injured leg that's the problem. You can:

Attempt to speak to Snuffles, with little interest.

Or clean the wound with antibiotics and expertly bind the leg. You get an excited snuffle! Return to Chomps Lewis to tell him, for a Fame reward.

- NCR Fame Gained!

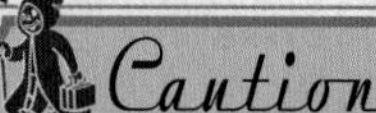
Caution Don't mistake Snuffles for vermin, as peppering the camp mascot with gunfire results is a massive Infamy gain!

[4.09] Goodsprings Cave

- Threat Level: ●●●●●
- Faction: Mutated Animal
  - Entity: Coyote
- Collectibles: Hollowed-Out Rock [19/42]
- Health, Chems, or Water
- Interior Exploration
- Wasteland Vegetation

Southeast of Goodsprings [4.05] is a small cave system perfect for amateur spelunkers to explore. It is guarded by a few Coyotes, and features a Hollowed-Out Rock; open it for some random items.

- Hollowed-Out Rock [19/42]

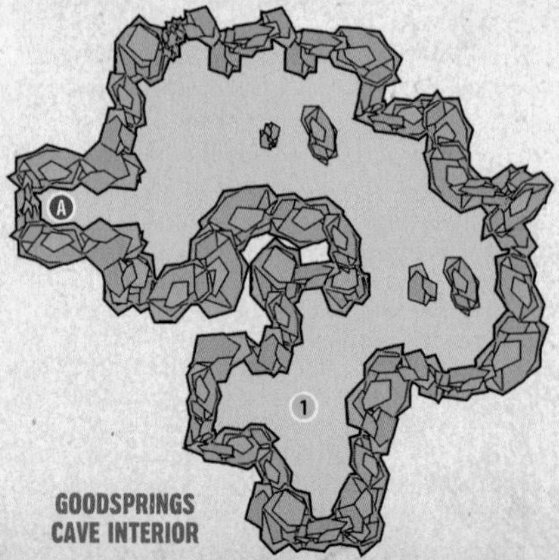

A Exit to Mojave Wasteland

1 Coyote Bone Bath

The cave is a single winding passage leading to a collection of bloody bones still being gnawed on by Coyotes. The water is bloody, but drinkable. Further back are more skeletal remains and the bodies of two Prospectors. Both are carrying weapons and items. Check the Duffle Bag too.

- Duffle Bag Items

[4.10] The Devil's Gullet

- Threat Level: ●●●●●
- Faction: Mutated Animal
  - Entity: Coyote
- Collectibles: Sunset Sarsaparilla Star Cap [55/100]
- Health, Chems, or Water

A smaller maw than the Devil's Throat [3.10], this hole in the ground (found if you search for the broken perimeter fence) offers a steep descent from the Coyote hills above, and scattered debris at the bottom.

- Sunset Sarsaparilla Star Cap [55/100]

[4.11] Goodsprings Source

- Main Quest: Back in the Saddle
- Main Quest: By a Campfire, on the Trail
- Free Quest: Barton the Fink
- Threat Level: ●●●●●
- Faction: Goodsprings/ Mutated Animal
  - Entity: Gecko
- Crafting:
  - Campfire [58/109]
  - Campfire [59/109]
  - Campfire [60/109]
- Health, Chems, or Water
- Wasteland Vegetation

The "source" in question refers to clean, drinkable water that follows from a small, windmill-powered pump in the ground, among the low rocks. Sunny Smiles heads down this way to teach you elementary Campfire-making techniques, and there's no shortage of Campfires to try out Recipes here. There are three separate water sources as you make your way southward from Goodsprings [4.05]. During this time, you may have to save a Goodspring resident from Geckos, who are lurking in this area. At the lowest point of Goodsprings Source are the three Campfires, and nearby is a Prospector's Trailer, where Barton Thorn and his Free Quest lurk.

- Fresh Water
- Campfire [58/109]
- Campfire [59/109]
- Campfire [60/109]
- Sleeping Quarters

Free Quest: Barton the Fink

Wandering dejectedly outside his small trailer is a man named Barton Thorn. He's in a bit of a pickle; his girl is trapped by Geckos on a nearby ridge, and she's going to die without your help! He tells you to head up past the broken radio tower to the top of the trail. You can agree (and look for the radio tower) or refuse (and end this Quest).

Locate the Broken Radio Tower [4S.07A], then head southwest and then northwest, moving up the ridge path, taking care of any Geckos you wish. At the top, you're greeted with Bear Traps, not a girlfriend in peril. Gunshots back down the trail announce the arrival of Barton, who's happy you helped clear a path to the treasure up here, and then attacks you! Swiftly end his life, before claiming the items up at the Dead Body Overhang [4S.07B] yourself!

- Danger! Bear Trap! (3)
- Fridge Items
- Footlocker Items (Caps)
- Ammo Box Ammunition

[4.12] Jean Sky Diving

- Side Quest: I Fought the Law
- Threat Level: ●●●●●
- Faction: Powder Gangers
  - Entity: Powder Gangers
  - Entity: Bloatflies
- Collectibles: Sunset Sarsaparilla Star Cap [56/100]
- Interior Exploration

At the junction of the Long 15 and the road that winds into Goodsprings [4.05] are the remains of an old sky-diving school, now overrun by a few Powder Gangers. The small plane still sits, slowly rusting into the ground. The nearest you can get to the skies is up on the roof, allowing views of the scrubland, and Bloatflies you can shoot. Inside the shack are the following items:

- Weapon Repair Kit
- Sunset Sarsaparilla Star Cap [56/100]

[4.13] Powder Ganger Camp West ●

- Threat Level: ●●●●●
- Faction: Powder Ganger
  - Entity: Powder Ganger
- Fame/Infamy
- Crafting: Campfire [61/109]
- Dangers: Radiation
- Guns and Ammo
- Sleeping Quarters

On the Long 15, past the ruined buildings and the rusting vehicles, is a trailer and a jackknifed container truck on the east side of the road, opposite the sign for the Vikki & Vance Casino in Primm [4.17]. The truck backs onto a lower effluent pool where the truck's contents spilled out. On the earthen mound above are a couple of Gangers guarding a Campfire.

- Campfire [61/109]
- Note: Powder Ganger Note
- Ammo Box Ammunition (2)
- Dynamite (3)

[4.14] Lone Wolf Radio

- Threat Level: ●●●●●
- Faction: Mutated Animal
  - Entity: Gecko
- Collectibles:
  - Sunset Sarsaparilla Star Cap [57/100]
  - Skill Book [Survival] [2/4] [4/12]
- Sleeping Quarters
- Wasteland Vegetation

On the rocky terrain northwest of Primm [4.17], and west of the Long 15, is a wide trailer with numerous antennae. It is quite empty of life.

- Sunset Sarsaparilla Star Cap [57/100]
- Skill Book: Wasteland Survival Guide [Survival] [2/4] [4/12]

[4.15] Powder Ganger Camp South ●

- Side Quest: I Fought the Law
- Threat Level: ●●●●●
- Faction: Powder Ganger
  - Entity: Chavez, Powder Ganger
- Fame/Infamy
- Crafting: Campfire [62/109]
- Collectibles: Magazine [Survival] [24/30] [15/32]
- Guns and Ammo
- Sleeping Quarters

Chavez and his tiny gang of Powder Gangers that have split with Eddie and the main Ganger outfit over at the NCR Correctional Facility [5.15] hang out at this poor excuse for a hideout. Chavez is only here if this Quest is active. The Note relates to Samuel Cooke's Ganger offshoot, currently exploring Vault 19 [1.21].

- Campfire [62/109]
- Dynamite (2)
- Note: Powder Ganger Note
- Magazine: Lad's Life [Survival] [24/30] [15/32]
- Sleeping Quarters

[4.16] Canyon Wreckage

- Threat Level: ●●●●●
- Faction: Mutated Animal
  - Entity: Coyotes

The remains of a jackknifed truck and a mass of twisted metal jammed into a canyon, preventing progress westward. Odd messages are daubed on the wreckage, which is impassable. Close by are two graves you can rob for some random items. Check the truck's trailer for some tiny skeletons, and smuggled grenades in the "XXX" crates.

- Frag Grenades
- Crate Items (3)
- Grave Items (2)

[4.17] Primm

See map on the following page

- Main Quest: They Went That-A-Way
- Side Quest: I Fought the Law
- Side Quest: My Kind of Town
- Side Quest: Don't Make a Beggar Out of Me
- Side Quest: ED-E My Love
- Free Quest: A Pair of Dead Desperados, I
- Free Quest: A Team of Moronic Mercenaries
- Free Quest: Big Winner: Vikki & Vance
- Free Quest: Gland for Some Home Cooking
- Threat Level: ●●●●●
- Faction: Primm / Powder Gangers / NCR
  - Entity: Lieutenant Hayes
  - Entity: Sergeant McGee
  - Entity: Sheriff McBain (Deceased)
  - Entity: Mrs. McBain (Deceased)
  - Entity: Deputy Beagle
  - Entity: Johnson Nash
  - Entity: Ruby Nash
  - Entity: Primm Slim
  - Entity: Layla
  - Entity: Tyrone
  - Entity: Escaped Convict
  - Entity: Convict Leader
- Fame/Infamy
- Services:
  - Caravan Player [11/15]
  - Gambling: Blackjack [13/15]
  - Gambling: Roulette [14/15]
  - Gambling: Slots [15/15]
  - Trader [20/33]
- Crafting:
  - Campfire [63/109]
  - Campfire [64/109]
  - Campfire [65/109]
  - Reloading Bench [21/36]
- Dangers: Radiation
- Collectibles:
  - Caravan Cards: [16/30]
  - Hollowed-Out Rock [20/42]
  - Skill Book: [Barter] [4/4] [5/12]
  - Magazine: [Barter] [14/16] [16-20/32]
  - Magazine: [Guns] [10/11] [16-20/32]
  - Magazine: [Repair] [24/27] [16-20/32]
  - Magazine: [Repair] [25/27] [16-20/32]
  - Magazine: [Science] [18/23] [16-20/32]
  - Sunset Sarsaparilla Star Cap [58/100]
  - Sunset Sarsaparilla Star Cap [59/100]
  - Unique Weapon: [27/42]
- Follower
- Guns and Ammo
- Health, Chems, or Water
- Highly Visible
- Interior Exploration
- Lots O' Caps
- Perk!
- Sleeping Quarters
- Wasteland Vegetation
- Quest Item

Pre-War, Primm was "budget Vegas," a tiny town where Californians could go to gamble, the shortest distance between their wallets and a hole in the ground. Now it's not much of a settlement at all, poorly populated to begin with and more treacherous since the Powder Gangs broke out of prison. Wastelanders have scouted out Primm for settlement in recent years, but even at its "prime," it was unlikely to have had a large population. To attempt to woo potential travelers along the then-freeway, two "themed" casinos where built around the exploits of two desperadoes from ancient history, and an archaic (and now highly dangerous) rollercoaster.

1 Long 95 and NCR Flag

This stretch of freeway bisects Primm to the west, and you can head into the sunken underpass, or climb on the walls to reach the level ground of the casino forecourts and gas station. The flag of the NCR is tied to a nearby lamppost. Check the rocks to the west; there's a flat area with a Campfire to use above you.

- Campfire [63/109]

PRIMM EXTERIOR

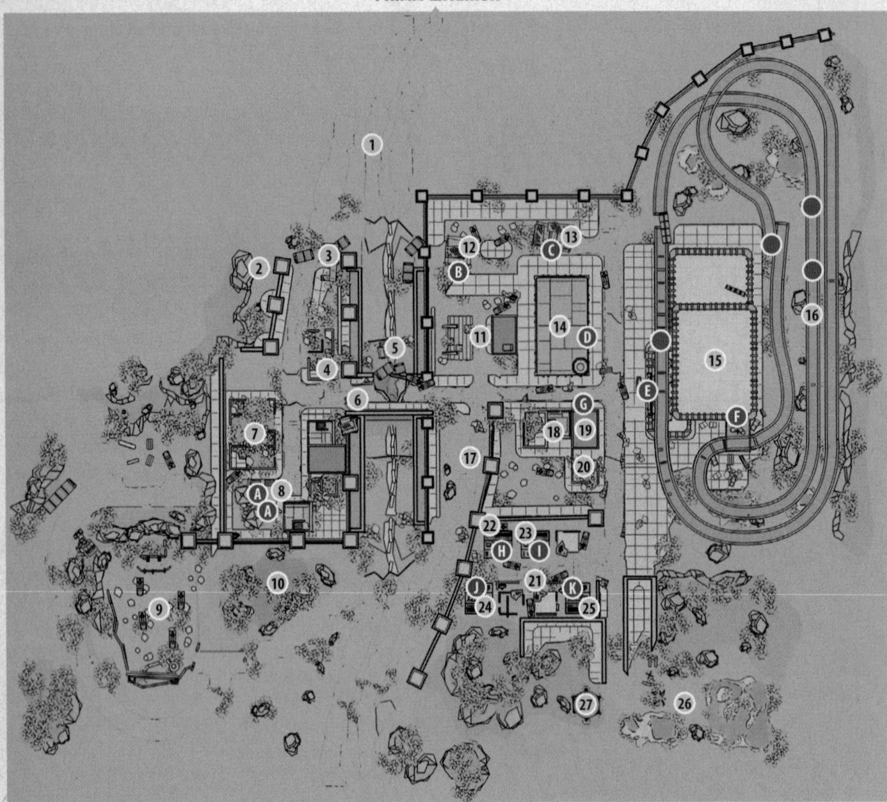

2 Hollowed-Out Rock

Just above the perimeter wall is an already-ransacked fake rock, with scattered Chems below. These are all over the Mojave Wasteland!

- Hollowed-Out Rock [20/42]
- Chems

3 NCR Sentry Shack

You're usually stopped by an NCR Trooper telling you that Primm is off-limits. You can ask what's going on, and he tells you the town is overrun by Escaped Convicts, and two Raider gangs are active in the area. He mentions Lieutenant Hayes if you want to speak to someone about helping the townsfolk. Any ammo in this location must be stolen. You can climb on the tin roof and use it as a defendable sniping area, too.

- Ammo Box Ammunition (4)
- Sleeping Mattress

4 Ruined Building (Sniper Nest)

The rubble and remaining wall of a building can be climbed to a bedroll, and a small platform offering excellent views across to the Casinos.

- Ammo Box Ammunition
- Sleeping Quarters

5 (Lower) Long 95 Blockade

Down on the underpass of the Long 95, there's a sentry shack and a burned Coach Liner designed to impede attacks from the road. To get back to the walled Primm perimeter, you need to head back up the sloping road.

- Ammo Box Ammunition (3)

6 Bridge Defenses

A beaten shack with equally weathered NCR Trooper holds the bridge from the lawless east side of town.

- Ammo Box Ammunition (4)

7 Ruined Building

- First Aid Box

A Tent Flaps (2) to NCR Tent Interior

8 NCR Camp and Tents

A small band of NCR Troopers, along with Sergeant McGee who originally from the Hub, are stationed in a walled-off corner southwest of town. You can ask McGee about his life, and then visit Lieutenant Hayes inside his tent, or the adjacent supply tent. Should you kill or Pickpocket Hayes, you can check his Military Orders (which are to hold Primm when not preparing for an attack on the Powder Gangers over at the NCR Correctional Facility [5.15]). During Side Quest: Don't Make a Beggar of Me, there's a military "supplier" stationed inside the second tent called Tyrone. You can speak to Hayes about him, too (when the Quest is active), as well as telling him news of any impending Powder Ganger attack during Side Quest: I Fought the Law. Finally, you can agree with Hayes that Sergeant McGee would make a fine sheriff during Side Quest: My Kind of Town.

- Note: Military Orders
- Armor Case Items
- Ammo Box Ammunition (2)
- Sleeping Quarters
- Scrap Metal (2)

9 California Sunset Drive-in [Primary Location 4.18]

10 Irradiated Pond Danger! Radiation!

11 Poseidon Gas Station

The beginning of the battle with the Escaped Convicts begins here. Use the open garage, dumpsters, and walls of the Vikki & Vance Casino for cover opportunities.

B Door to Deputy Beagle's Residence

12 Deputy Beagle's Residence

Beagle is currently being held against his will inside the Bison Steve Casino, but you can enter his shack and have a look around at the posters on his walls, and Gun Case [Very Easy] by his bed.

- Gun Case Items

C Door to Primm Sheriff's Office

13 Primm Sheriff's Office

Sheriff McBain is no longer the law in these parts, as you'll discover when you find his body on the bed of his shack, along with his dead wife. Grotesquely, you can sleep on the bed, and conduct a search of handy items.

- Reloading Bench [21/36]
- Brahmin-Skin Outfit
- Sheriff's Duster
- Ammo Box Ammunition
- Sheriff's Hat
- .308 Round (24 x2)

D Door to The Vikki & Vance Casino

14 The Vikki & Vance Casino

Head here to meet the hold-outs from the Escaped Convict town infiltration. Consult the Interior Map information below.

E F Doors (Lower and Upper) to The Bison Steve Hotel

15 The Bison Steve Hotel

Enter these premises if you want to rescue Deputy Beagle, and take down some Escaped Convicts. Conduct a quick sweep of the exterior walls to delve into some dumpsters. Consult the Interior Map information to come.

16 El Diablo Rollercoaster

The red marks on the guide map indicate sections of track that can't be accessed, usually from one direction. This is a favored sniping spot for two to three Escaped Convicts, so beware of being shot when you investigate the coaster tracks. You can also move up onto the lower of the two roof sections, and the awning above the ground entrance (where there's the following items). Use the coaster to reach the upper entrance into the Bison Steve Hotel (Location F) if you want to Sneak down and tackle the foes. Otherwise, this offers excellent views, or sniping attack points down to the Convicts milling about the street between the Casinos.

- Chems and Binoculars

17 Slip Road

This offers an escape route back onto the Long 95 (or an entrance right into town).

18 Ruined Building

Sneak up here to the roofless upper floor for some prime sniping views across to the Casinos, and the following items by a bed frame:

- Ammo Box Ammunition (2)
- Magazine: Milsurp Review [Guns] [10/11] [16/32]

19 Mojave Express Couriers (Nash Residence)

Are you starting to remember? Do you recognize Daniel Wyand? Perhaps in time; he's a courier just like you, but didn't survive a bullet to the brain, and is slumped outside the Mojave Express. Search his corpse for a Note. Compare it to the one you started with, and you'll see they're written by the same hand. This one mentions a different delivery package.

- Note: Mojave Express Delivery Order (4 of 6)

G Door to Nash Residence

Inside the Mojave Express, which is the home of Johnson and Ruby Nash who run the Vikki & Vance Casino, there are two of Ruby's Casseroles on the table. They look delicious and pack quite a punch. Check the fridge for items to steal, and the bedside table for some Magazines to pilfer. Of more importance is a Damaged Eyebot sitting on the counter. Consult Side Quest: ED-E My Love for information on activating it.

- Ruby's Casserole (2)
- Magazine: Fixin' Things [Repair] [24/27] [17/32]
- Magazine: Programmer's Digest [Science] [18/23] [18/32]
- Scrap Metal (2)
- Follower: ED-E
- Perk! Enhanced Sensors

Once ED-E has been activated, he becomes a Follower and grants you the Enhanced Sensors Perk. His Side Quest: ED-E My Love now begins!

20 Rubble

- Safe Items

H I J K Doors to Primm Houses

21 Primm Residential Street

Remember to check the mailboxes for possible items to scavenge.

- Campfire [64/109]

22 Primm House #1

This house has been cleaned out, aside from the skeleton with a Switchblade in his head, and a wall safe cunningly hidden behind a bookcase.

- Lead Pipe
- Wall Safe Items [Average]

23 Primm House #2

There's some scattered Food (and Baseballs) in here, along with Scrap Electronics.

- Baseball Bat
- Sleeping Quarters
- Teddy Bear

24 Primm House #3

This has a stocked fridge and a place to sleep.

- Ruby's Casserole and Beer
- Sleeping Quarters

25 Primm House #4

Don't forget the Star Cap on the bookcase, fridge, and kitchen cabinet.

- Sunset Sarsaparilla Star Cap [58/100]
- First Aid Box
- Sleeping Quarters

26 Playground and Bloatfly Swamp

27 Water Tower

You can sip from the valve here, but the water is slightly radioactive.

The Vikki and Vance Casino

A Door to Mojave Wasteland (Primm)

1 Entrance and Johnson Nash

The proprietor of this establishment greets you when you first enter the premises, telling you the town's gone to hell. You can ask who he is, and the history of Primm, as well as information on the men who shot you (Main Quest: They Went That-A-Way, as well as the six couriers who were sent). You can also find out more information about ED-E, and even play a hand of Caravan. He's also a good sounding board when you're trying to sort out a new sheriff for the settlement (Side Quest: My Kind of Town). You should also see what Nash is selling (these include Magazines); you receive a discount if you complete the Side Quest!

- Caravan Player: Johnson Nash [11/15]
- Trader: Johnson Nash [20/33]
- Caravan Cards: Johnson Nash [16/30]

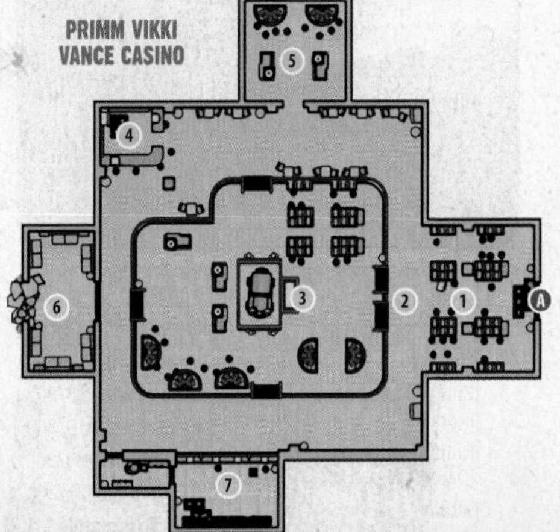

2 Gambling Floor

Due to the Convict problem, gambling has been temporarily suspended; complete Side Quest: My Kind of Town and wait three days, and the Gambling is back on! You can check the Vending Machines for bottles, but you'll lose Fame in doing so. You can also meet Johnson's wife Ruby Nash, and speak to her. You might as well begin Free Quest: Gland for Some Home Cooking while you're at it.

- Gambling: Blackjack (Dealer must hit soft 17) [13/15]
- Gambling: Roulette [14/15]
- Gambling: Slots [15/15]

3 The Authentic Vikki & Vance Museum Experience

Speak to Primm Slim, the cowpoke Protectron for a potted history of this place, and the exhibit. Although the items have long since been stolen (aside from the vehicle), you can inspect the mannequins and cases that once held clothes and weapons Vikki and Vance once used (Free Quest: A Pair of Dead Desperados). And if you're thinking that Primm might need a new sheriff as part of a Side Quest; well Primm Slim might be the robot you're looking for.

4 Bar

There's a Cash Register to turn over, but the hassle isn't really worth it unless you're sneaky.

5 High Rollers Room

- Combat Knife
- Silenced .22 Pistol and Ammo

6 Lounge

There are two Magazines to steal, and a safe to pick in front of the fallen rubble.

- Magazine: Salesman Weekly [Barter] [14/16] [19/32]
- Magazine: Fixin' Things [Repair] [25/27] [20/32]

7 Bank

The wall of safes has three that are still locked [Easy, Easy, and Hard], and another one with contents not yet stolen. There's extra ammo on the floor.

- Cash Register Items (3)
- 9mm Submachine Gun and Ammo
- Chems
- Safe Items (3) [Easy, Easy, Hard]

The Bison Steve Hotel Ground Floor (Interior)

A Door to Mojave Wasteland (Primm)

1 (Ground) Reception

Expect Convict battles as you progress eastward into the building. Check behind the reception desk for a terminal [Easy] that allows access to an otherwise locked door [Hard].

2 (Ground) Manager's Quarters

Open the locked door to enter this small room with a small amount of Food and the following items, which includes a key to open the maintenance door in the lobby area.

- Cap (4)
- Blood Pack
- Rad-X and Med-X (3)
- Bison Steve Maintenance Key
- 9mm Pistol
- First Aid Box and Mentats

3 (Ground) Gift Shop

Be sure you salvage the Skill Book by the floor safe behind the counter. Be sure to open the safe; the Unique .357 Magnum is well worth the Bobby Pin loss!

- Teddy Bear (6)
- Cap (9)
- Floor Safe Items [Hard]
- Skill Book: Tales of a Junktown Jerky Vendor [Barter] [4/4] [5/12]
- Unique Weapon : Lucky [27/42]

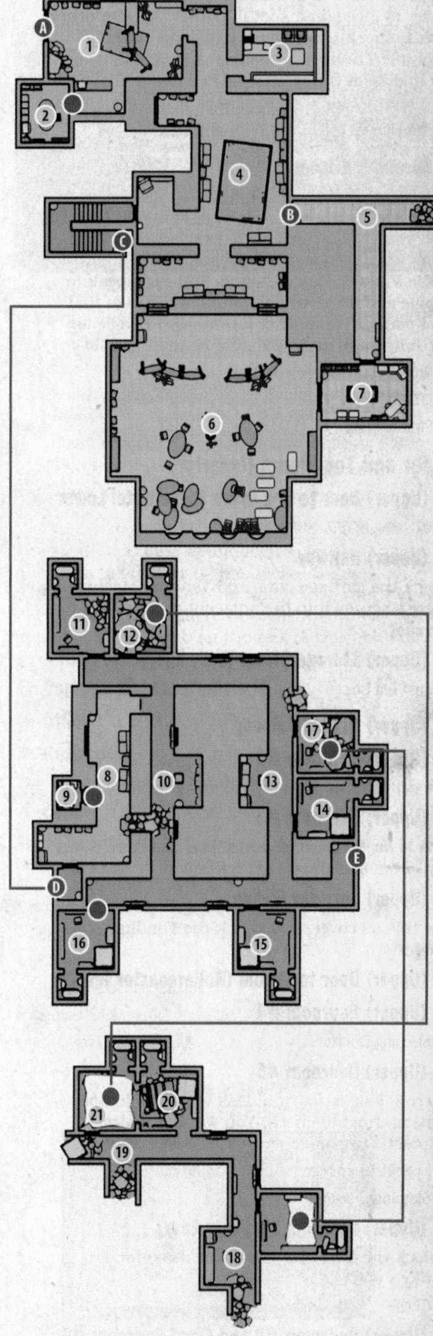

4 (Ground) Lobby

Expect combat to occur here; use the walls and alcoves to hide behind. Check the Vending Machine, and the side table on the east side for a Star Cap. Check the Maintenance Door [Easy] for a Sneak-based way into the kitchen where Deputy Beagle is

- Sunset Sarsaparilla Star Cap [59/100]

B (Ground) Maintenance Door [Easy]

This can be opened using the Maintenance Key.

C (Upper) Door to the Bison Steve Hotel Upper Floor

5 (Ground) Maintenance Corridor

Useful for a quick approach in and out of the building.

[4.24] Ivanpah Dry Lake

- Threat Level:
- Faction: Mutated Animal
  - Entity: Bark Scorpion
  - Entity: Radscorpion
- Entity: Giant Ant
- Highly Visible
- Wasteland Vegetation

A massive flat expanse of sand and fetid air, this dry lake stretches (trail 167 bisecting it to the south) all the way to Crescent Canyon [4.32/33] to the south. At its northern-most edge, expect Escaped Convicts and the odd Ghoul to wander these parts, as well as the Jackal Gang holed up inside the Nevada Highway Patrol Station. To the northeast edge, expect a few Bark Scorpions. The perimeter of the Dry Lake follows the Long 15 southward to the west, and past Jack Rabbit Springs and Nipton to the east. Periodically, there are low piles of rocks, and the odd plant to harvest. In the middle of the north section, is the Race Track [4.25], where Giant Ants roam. The Dry Lake is bisected by the remains of the 164, and Nipton Road Pit Stop. The southern part of the Lake features a Radscorpion Burrow [4.S26].

[4.25] Ivanpah Race Track

- Threat Level:
- Faction: Mutated Animal
  - Entity: Giant Ant
- Wasteland Vegetation

The large oval indent in the middle of Ivanpah Dry Lake isn't a crater, but the remains of a racetrack; now home to an extended family of Giant Ants. Beware the Soldier Ants particularly. They pour out of an inaccessible tunnel toward the middle of the track.

[4.26] Jack Rabbit Springs

- Threat Level:
- Faction: Abomination
  - Entity: Centaur
  - Entity: Evolved Centaur
  - Entity: Super Mutant
- Fame/Infamy
- Services: Repairer
- Crafting: Campfire [68/109]
- Collectibles: Hollowed-Out Rock [21/42]
- Dangers: Radiation
- Guns and Ammo

One of the most spoiled areas of this zone, the jackrabbits have long gone, but their warrens are still there, now inhabited by deviant abominations known as Centaurs, and their even more grotesque Evolved cousins. Be wary not only of their spittle, and the pools of radioactive water, but also the small Super Mutant Campfire to the east, at the top of the warrens. When you're done larking, inspect the hump with the protruding rods; a marker for a skeleton, and the following goods, then check for the Hollowed-Out Rock south of the radiation pools, on the edge of the Dry Lake.

- Campfire [68/109]
- Hollowed-Out Rock [21/42]
- Ammo Box Ammunition (2)
- Weapon Repair Kit
- Hydra and Stealth Boy

[4.27] Mojave Outpost

- Side Quest: Birds of a Feather
- Side Quest: Can You Find It in Your Heart
- Side Quest: Cold, Cold Heart
- Side Quest: Heartache by the Number
- Side Quest: Keep Your Eyes on the Prize
- Side Quest: My Kind of Town
- Side Quest: You Can Depend on Me
- Threat Level:
- Faction: NCR
  - Entity: Ranger Jackson
  - Entity: Ranger Ghost
  - Entity: Cass
  - Entity: Major Knight
  - Entity: Lacey
  - Entity: Caravaneer
  - Entity: NCR Trooper
  - Entity: Mercenary
  - Entity: Traveling Merchant
  - Entity: Brahmin
- Fame/Infamy
- Services:
  - Caravan Player [12/15]
  - Repairer [5/9]
  - Trader [21/31]
- Collectibles:
  - Caravan Cards [23/30]
  - Skill Book [Explosives] [3/3] [11/12]
  - Sunset Sarsaparilla Star Cap [67/100]
  - Unique Item [68/95]
  - Unique Item [69/95]
  - Unique Item [70/95]
- Follower
- Guns and Ammo
- Health, Chems, or Water
- Highly Visible
- Interior Exploration
- Lots O' Caps
- Main Trading Route
- Perk!
- Sleeping Quarters
- Wasteland Vegetation
- Quest Item

The place where Mojave Outpost now stands was originally a checkpoint between California and Nevada. After the war, it stood empty and vacant for well over a century. Ten years ago, the NCR Rangers and the Desert Rangers of Nevada (who had been dwindling in numbers) met at what had become known as the I-15 Mojave Outpost, to establish terms of the Ranger Unification Treaty. In its current form, Mojave Outpost serves as the link between NCR and the Mojave Wasteland.

1 Unification Monument

At the peak of the traffic graveyard are the gigantic statues of scrap metal, commemorating the Ranger Unification Treaty. Check the plaque between the two massive figures for a historical footnote. This is the ceremonial and actual entrance.

2 Sergeant Kilborn

A gruff, bearded, but friendly sort, Kilborn can help you find work, and provide a little history. He's also the person to tell about the atrocities performed in Nipton, as part of Side Quest: Cold, Cold Heart.

3 Brahmin Pens

Mercenaries and Traders place their Brahmin in gated pens here.

- Sleeping Quarters

4 Checkpoint

Now sealed off from travelers, this area has a couple of booths, and a small armed guard.

- Binoculars

5 Ranger Ghost's Post

The particularly pallid Ranger usually watches the horizon from here, and she's ready to answer questions about this place, any news from the west, and she wants some help; Side Quest: Keep Your Eyes on the Prize.

- Binoculars

A Mojave Outpost Headquarters

Major Knight runs the front desk of this office, but Ranger Jackson is in charge of this Outpost. Knight needs to note down your details.

You can flirt with him, too.

Knight is an incredible tinkerer, and offers up his unsurpassed Repair skill for the right price. Nearby is a Vending Machine, offices empty of items you need, and a corridor leading to Ranger Jackson. He's also able to speak to you about NCR Troop levels, as part of Side Quest: My Kind of Town.

- Repairer: Major Knight [SKILL 100] [5/9]

The rear of the building has a number of rooms with the usual fridge Food and scraps to optionally check. But you're here to see Ranger Jackson, who you can quiz about the state of the Outpost, and who offers you a job of clearing Ants; Side Quest: Can You Find It in Your Heart. You're given some Caps and a weapon, plus Food, depending on your demeanor. Jackson also plays a secondary role in Side Quest: Heartache By the Number.

- Caps

MOJAVE OUTPOST EXTERIOR

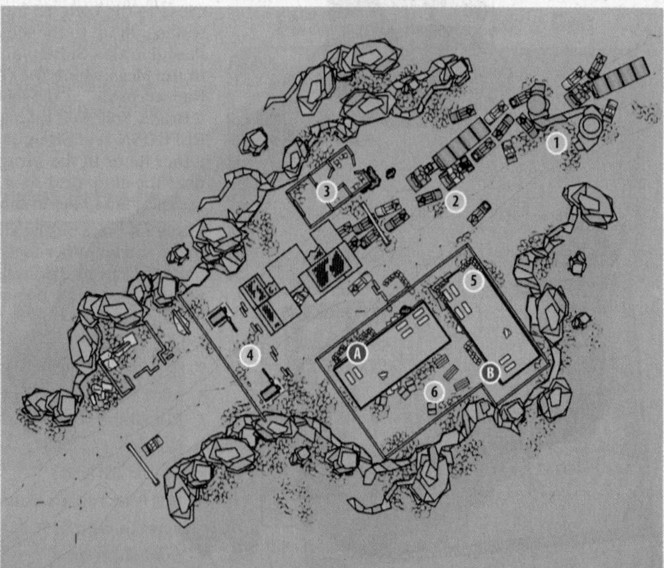

6 Picnic Area

Outside of the bar are a couple of splintered picnic tables, near the creeping Buffalo Gourd growing everywhere in this location. Check the immediate area for Sunset Sarsaparilla Crates, and Sacks of Food.

B Outpost Barracks

NCR Troopers, Caravaneers, and a young lady named Cass all use this watering hole, sometimes crashing on a mattress in the adjacent room. You can sleep there, too. Lacey is the barkeep (there's a Star Cap on her bar), and she has some information on the Outpost. She plays a keen hand of Caravan too, as well as having a copious amount of goods to Trade with you. Cass is initially aggressive, but (depending on the Side Quests), she may require some coaxing to become a Follower. Consult those Quests for the answers, and Cass can join you, along with her associated Perk.

- Caravan Player: Lacey [12/15]
- Trader: Lacey [21/33]
- Trader Highlight (Lacey): Upgrades [Guns]
- Caravan Cards [23/30]
  Sunset Sarsaparilla Star Cap [67/100]
- Follower: Cass
- Perk! Whiskey Rose

Lacey keeps a well-stocked bar, which requires you to steal items to keep them. There's a Skill Book below the counter, too.

- Skill Book: Duck and Cover! [Explosives] [3/3] [11/12]
- Sunset Sarsaparilla (19)
- Carton of Cigarettes (7)
- Unique Item: Nuka-Cola Quartz [68/95]
- Unique Item: Nuka-Cola Quartz [69/95]
- Unique Item: Nuka-Cola Quartz [70/95]
- Tool Cabinet Items
- Food, Beer, Wine, Whiskey, Nuka-Cola, Purified Water, and Spirits
- Sleeping Quarters

[4.28] Morning Star Cavern

- Threat Level: ●●●●●
- Faction: Abomination
  Entity: Nightstalker
- Collectibles: Hollowed-Out Rock [22/42]
- Interior Exploration
- Wasteland Vegetation

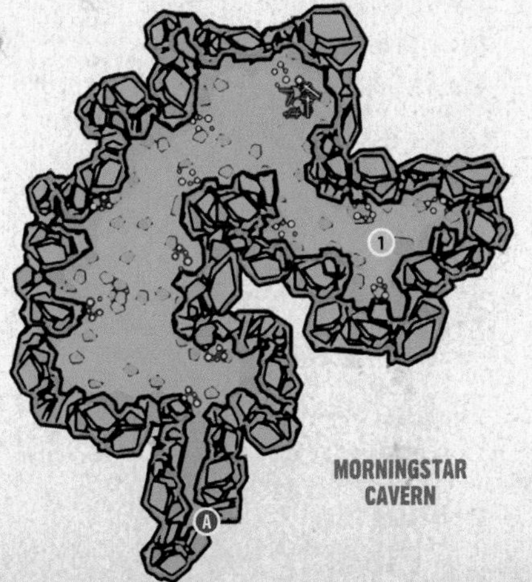

In the southwestern corner of the Ivanpah Dry Lake are a series of flat, tiered rocks leading up to a Nightstalker pack and an opening in the rock wall. Check the Hollowed-Out Rock before entering this dark cavern.

- Hollowed-Out Rock [22/42]

A Exit to Mojave Wasteland

1 Cavern Interior

This winding cavern curves around past a couple of corpse and bone piles, to a large rear alcove where more Nightstalkers are ready to pounce, near a Mercenary corpse.

- Duffle Bag Items

[4.29] Nipton Road Pit Stop

- Threat Level: ●●●●●
- Faction: Jackal Gang
  Entity: Jackal Gang
- Crafting
  Campfire [69/109]
- Guns and Ammo
- Health, Chems, or Water
- Sleeping Quarters

As the crows scatter and the Radscorpions and Giant Ants fight over supremacy of Ivanpah Dry Lake, head cautiously into the pit stop; now three razed buildings. The Jackal Gang are active here; deal with them, then check the Campfire for the following:

- Campfire [69/109]
- Mine Box Ammunition
- Grenade Box Ammunition [Easy]
- Healing Powder (2)
- Sleeping Quarters

[4.30] Nipton

See map on the following page

- Main Quest: They Went That-A-Way
- Side Quest: Booted
- Side Quest: Cold, Cold Heart
- Side Quest: I Forgot to Remember to Forget
- Side Quest: Keep Your Eyes on the Prize
- Threat Level: ●●●●●
- Faction: Caesar's Legion
  Entity: Vulpes Inculta
  Entity: Legionary
  Entity: Legion Mongrel
  Entity: Oliver Swanick
  Entity: Boxcars
  Entity: Mister Gutsy
  Entity: Radroach
  Entity: Giant Mantis Nymph
- Crafting:
  Campfire [70/109]
  Reloading Bench [24/36]
  Workbench [28/41]
- Dangers:
  Traps
  Mines
- Collectibles:
  Skill Book: [Science] [3/4] [12/12]
  Magazine: [Barter] [15/16] [21-24/32]
  Magazine: [Energy Weapons] [9/10] [21-24/32]
  Magazine: [Guns] [11/11] [21-24/32]
  Magazine: [Science] [19/23] [21-24/32]
  Sunset Sarsaparilla Star Cap [68/100]
  Unique Item [71/95]
- Area Is Locked
- Guns and Ammo
- Health, Chems, or Water
- Highly Visible
- Interior Exploration
- Lots O' Caps
- Sleeping Quarters
- Wasteland Vegetation
- Quest Item

Forces of Caesar's Legion, under the command of Vulpes Inculta, have swept around the poorly defended Camp Searchlight [6.16] to sack Nipton and kill every living creature within. Ironically, this camp had previously been terrorized by Powder Gangers, who were routing the regular population before they fell to the Machetes and bloodlust. The signs of devastation are obvious from outside this settlement; black smoke rises from the town, corpses are strewn on pyres, and victims crucified to telephone poles.

1 Oliver Swanick

Enter the settlement traveling east along Trail 164 from the Mojave Outpost, and you run into the luckiest Powder Ganger of all. Oliver doesn't make much sense, but it appears the Legion drew Lottery Tickets to see who would be crucified, and who would live to retell their witnessing of these atrocities. Oliver flees after speaking to you.

- Lottery Ticket

2 Good Luck Trailer Park

The last hold-outs from the Legion raid fought in this scrubland trailer park; and the evidence of the fight is still visible. Search the trailers for (bloody) sleeping mattresses, and scavenge the area within the remains of the mesh fence for the following:

- Caravaneer
- Lottery Ticket (4)
- Campfire [70/109]
- Carton of Cigarettes
- Purified Water (3)
- Laser Rifle
- Scrap Metal
- Sleeping Quarters

3 Nipton House (Southwest)

The bedroom of this ransacked building has a Star Cap on the broken bookshelf. There's Food in the fridge.

- Sunset Sarsaparilla Star Cap [68/100]
- Purified Water
- Sleeping Quarters

4 Nipton House (Southeast)

This is adjacent to the pyre burning on the main road. There's Food in the fridge.

- Carton of Cigarettes
- Sleeping Quarters

5 Nipton House (West)

This lies north of the road, by the tire pyre and roasted crucified Powder Ganger skeleton. It has been ransacked, although there's Beer, and more (plus Food) in the fridge.

- Sleeping Quarters

6 Nipton Trading Post: General Store

The Legion have left their mark on this store, and the Powder Ganger who had taken it over. Scattered Food is everywhere, and the Ganger named Boxcars is so unpleasant, you're shocked the Legion didn't string him up too. You can ask him about the Lottery (he came second, so he lived, but at a cost). The mayor (who's been writing Journal entries found in the locations nearby) didn't get off so lightly. You can start Side Quest: Booted by agreeing to help the Powder Ganger hostages who weren't crucified.

You can give him a Med-X to Boxcars if you have one. He's as thankful as you'd expect.

Check the counter for a Magazine. The upstairs of the store, accessed via the door behind the counter [Easy], leads to a wrecked apartment room, and another Magazine, as well as a floor safe to check.

- Magazine: Salesman Weekly [Barter] [15/16] [21/32]
- Magazine: Milsurp Review [Guns] [11/11] [22/32]
- Floor Safe Items
- Sleeping Quarters

NIPTON EXTERIOR

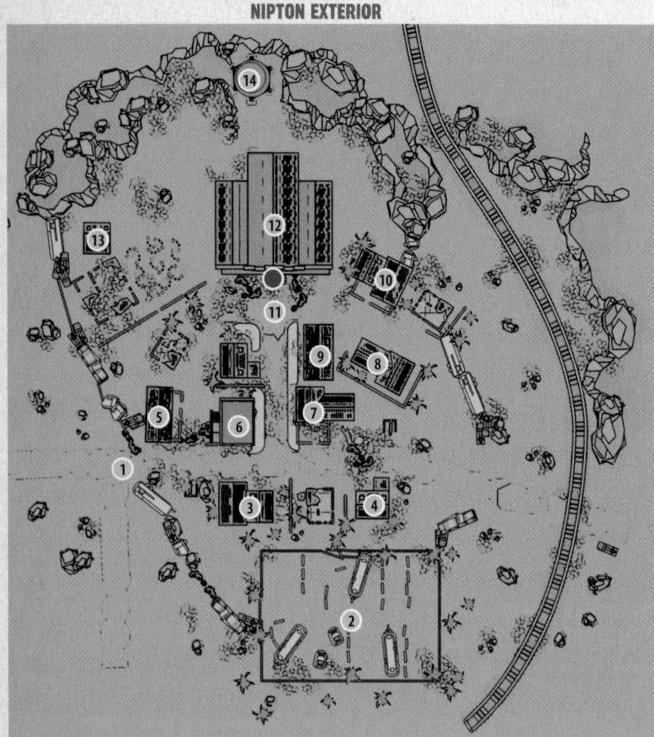

NIPTON TOWN HALL ASSEMBLY

NIPTON TOWN HALL MAYOR STEYN'S OFFICE

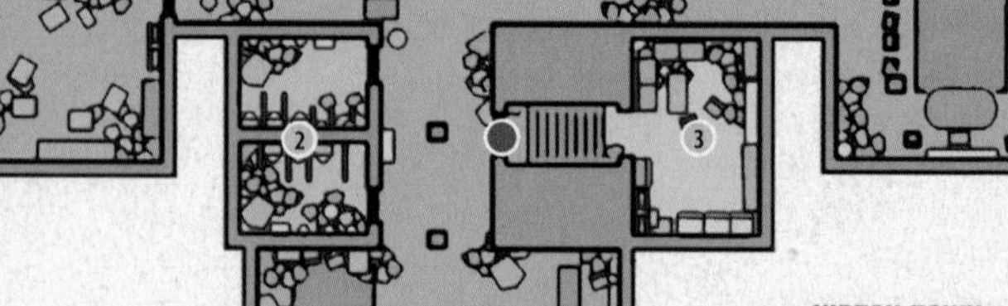

NIPTON TOWN HALL FIRST FLOOR

7 Bark Scorpion Nipton House

The Legion have captured some poisonous Bark Scorpions, which are inside a cage [Average], which you can open if you want to fight them at close quarters. There are also Frag Mines here, making this a death-trap. Disarm the ones you don't step on (there's one in every room). The kitchen has a Shotgun Trap across the door, so stop and disarm the Tripwire first. Food in the fridge [Easy] and a Legionary to search, and a cabinet to open [Average]. Check the Tool Cabinet for a Note written by a hold-out from the previous mayor.

There's a Rigged Shotgun Trap in the bedroom doorway as well, and a cabinet [Easy] and desk [Very Easy] to open. Finally, check the bed for a footlocker, and the bathroom for a safe with some decent firepower, and a random Magazine.

- Note: Declaration of Vital Essence
- Frag Mine (4)
- Magazine

8 Gutsy Nipton House

East of the central crucified road is a house with a floating Mister Gutsy that attacks you on sight. When you've defeated it, check the room it was guarding; a workshop with scattered junk and a Workbench, as well as a terminal with two menu options; the latter of which reveals the story behind this place. The kitchen has a load of Food. The bedroom has a Single Shotgun, a 9 Iron in the bathroom, and a Laser Rifle in the bath. Open the floor safe and search the dead Legionary before you leave.

> Reset Mainframe Connection (which does nothing)

> Specifications (which reveals a slightly creepy Journal Entry)

- Tool Cabinet Items (2)
- Workbench [28/41]
- Single Shotgun
- 9 Iron
- Laser Rifle
- Knife
- Floor Safe Items [Average]
- Sleeping Quarters

9 Nipton Corner House

This is the closest to the Town Hall, where the Legion are currently camped. Inside there's some BB ammo, Food, and a place to sleep.

- Sleeping Quarters

10 Northeast Nipton House

This has a Reloading Bench, and some freshly prepared Food in the kitchen.

- Reloading Bench [24/36]
- Sleeping Quarters

11 Crucified Powder Gangers

A few Legionaries with the mark of the wolf are waiting in front of Nipton Town Hall. Their leader is Vulpes Inculta, and he's not incognito (like he dresses when he accosts you on The Strip). He was responsible for this. He wants you to teach everyone the lesson the Powder Gangers learned from this ransacking.

You can insult his headgear, and attack.

You can do as he asks.

Or you can ask more questions.

Anything other than attacking allows you to agree to tell the tale of Nipton, which begins Side Quest: Cold, Cold Heart. The crucified Powder Gangers themselves are too close to death to help.

12 Nipton Town Hall

This structure is where Vulpes Inculta and his Legionaries are camped, although they're about to move back to The Fort. Search this location using the information below.

13 Nipton Hotel

Close to the razed remains of the hotel rooms is the office itself. Inside are the corpses for four NCR Troopers. Pick at them, check the Cash Register [Easy], then leave.

- Caps
- NCR Dogtags (4)

14 Water Tower

There's a valve to sip from behind the Town Hall, but the water is slightly irradiated.

Nipton Town Hall—First Floor

A Double Doors to Nipton

1 Reception Area

Check behind the reception desk where the dead Wastelander is, but watch for a Frag Mine. Legion Mongrels walk these corridors. The Worn Key opens the cellar.

- Frag Mine
- Worn Key
- Lottery Ticket (6)

2 Restrooms

There's nothing but slightly irradiated water and corpses with common clothing in both rooms, and in the corridor.

- Lottery Ticket (2)

3 Cellar [Hard]

There's a large amount of scattered Food here, and some Turbo.

- Explosives Crate Items
- First Aid Box, and Turbo (2)
- Gun Cabinet Items
- Lottery Ticket (5)

4 Classrooms

There's nothing but decaying bodies and Radroaches. Some can be searched.

5 Ransacked Office

Check the Filing Cabinets for items. The double doors here are inaccessible.

6 Conference Room

7 **Meeting Room**

Giant Mantis Nymphs can be crushed underfoot. Don't waste ammo on them. There are more bodies to search, scattered about.

B **Stairs to Town Hall Assembly Floor**

The eastern steps have the remains of a fight between dog and man. Neither won.

Nipton Town Hall—Assembly Floor

C **Door to First Floor**

8 **Landing Corridor**

9 **Offices**

Beware the booby-trapped body in here.

- Frag Mine

10 **Assembly Room**

- Lottery Ticket (6)

D **Stairs to Mayor Steyn's Office**

Nipton Town Hall—Mayor Steyn's Office

E **Door to Assembly Floor**

11 **Hallway**

There's Food and Drink in the fridge and Vending Machines.

12 **Restroom**

- First Aid Box

13 **Executive Office #1**

14 **Executive Office #2 [Very Easy]**

15 **Mayor's Office**

Check the Mayor's fancy desk and cabinet for a Skill Book, two Magazines, Mentats, and his personal terminal, which has the following entries:

> Reset Mainframe Connection

> Prison Break: Notes from a trickster-turned-mayor. Unpleasant notes.

> High Roller: An attempt to make money from the recent break-out from the NCR Correctional Facility.

> Testing...: A man with the Legion offers a deal Steyn passes up. It will be his undoing.

- Skill Book: Big Book of Science [Science] [3/4] [12/12]
- Magazine: Programmer's Digest [19/23] [23/32]
- Magazine: Future Weapons Today [Energy Weapons] [9/10] [24/32]
- Bobby Pins
- Laser Pistol and Ammo
- Lottery Ticket (7)

16 **Mayor's Storage Room [Average]**

Pry the lock open for the following items:

- Footlocker Items
- Chems and Food
- Carton of Cigarettes
- 10mm Pistol and Ammo
- Unique Item: Nuka-Cola Victory [71/95]
- Gun Cabinet Items

[4.31] Mojave Drive-in

- Threat Level: ●●●●●
- Faction: None
- Entity: None

Located at the tail-end of Nipton near the Trailer Park, and the only area not filled with piles of Powder Gangers on a pyre, the Mojave Drive-in is in arguably worse condition than its Primm counterpart.

[4.32] Crescent Canyon West
[4.33] Crescent Canyon East

- Threat Level: ●●●●●
- Faction: Mutated Animal
  - Entity: Golden Gecko
  - Entity: Protectron
- Dangers: Radiation
- Collectibles:
  - Hollowed-Out Rock [23/42]
  - Hollowed-Out Rock [24/42]

The giant crescent canyon is a wonder of nature, and now a breeding ground for Golden Geckos. At the very southern edge of the Ivanpah Dry Lake [4.24], the western edge is close to an unmarked Radscorpion Burrow [4.S26]. Descend heading south, moving from west to east, and after the initial Gecko encounter, check the fallen vehicle for a Hollowed-Out Rock and Lottery Ticket. Progress further into the canyon, and the floor becomes wet with oozing radiation, and masses of strewn barrels. Even the tumbleweed is radioactive.

Pass the container truck with the barrels, and look east to see the remains of a bridge above. Continue to the remains of the fallen bridge and railroad carriages, along with an irradiated (and tough) Protectron guard. The canyon base of the eastern entrance also yields a Hollowed-Out Rock. Up on the railroad line, there's nothing at the collapsed bridge except a red carriage, and a spectacular view northward.

- Lottery Ticket
- Hollowed-Out Rock [23/42]
- Hollowed-Out Rock [24/42]

ZONE 4: SECONDARY LOCATIONS

[4.S01] Chance's Grave

- Threat Level: ●●●●●
- Collectibles: Unique Weapon [28/42]

The final resting place of Chance is here, at the top of a hill, close to the Tribal Village [4.01]. Bring a Shovel and unearth the following items:

- Unique Weapon: Chance's Knife [28/42]
- Great Khan Simple Armor

[4.S02] Warning Signs on Goodsprings Road

- Threat Level: ●●●●●

The road north of Goodsprings [4.05] warns of danger to come; this refers to the Cazadors in the Tribal Village, but otherwise this is a great thoroughfare to reach Zone 1.

[4.S03] Scorpion Valley

- Threat Level: ●●●●●
- Faction: Mutated Animal
  - Entity: Radscorpion
- Wasteland Vegetation

A small gulch where Radscorpions roam. Cull them for Glands you can give to Ruby Nash in Primm [4.17], or avoid the area.

[4.S04] The Dead Survivalist

- Threat Level: ●●●●●
- Faction: Mutated Animal
  - Entity: Radscorpion
- Collectibles: Magazine [Survival] [25/30] [25/32]
- Guns and Ammo

The skeleton of a long-dead adventurer lies near the copy of Lad's Life he didn't read. There may be a dead Mercenary to search, too.

- Magazine: Lad's Life [Survival] [25/30] [25/32]
- Switchblade

[4.S05] Abandoned Shack

- Threat Level: ●●●●●
- Crafting: Reloading Bench [25/36]
- Collectibles: Magazine [Survival] [26/30] [26/32]
- Guns and Ammo
- Health, Chems, or Water
- Interior Exploration
- Sleeping Quarters
- Wasteland Vegetation

North of the Yangtze Memorial [4.07] is a shack at the south end of Scorpion Gulch. Enter and locate the following:

- Reloading Bench [25/36]
- Ammo Box Ammunition
- Scrap Electronics (2)
- Machete
- 9 Iron

- First Aid Box, Chems and Doggie Treat
- Magazine: Lad's Life Survival [26/30] [26/32]
- Sleeping Quarters

[4.S06] 6A, 6B, 6C Goodsprings Water Wells (3)

- Main Quest: Back in the Saddle
- Threat Level: ●●●●●
- Faction: Mutated Animal
  - Entity: Gecko
  - Entity: Goodspring Settler
- Guns and Ammo

Location S6A is a water well. Location S6B is a small caravan trailer. Location S6C are two water wells; one is destroyed, while the other works. You can sip pure water from the working wells, or the troughs. Note there is another working well at Goodsprings Source [4.11] itself.

- Shovel

[4.S07] 7A: Broken Radio Tower [4.S07] 7B: Dead Body Overhang

- Free Quest: Barton the Fink
- Threat Level: ●●●●●
- Faction: Mutated Animal
  - Entity: Barton Thorn
  - Entity: Gecko
- Dangers: Traps
- Guns and Ammo
- Lots O' Caps
- Sleeping Quarters
- Wasteland Vegetation
- Wild Wasteland!

These are the two locations to trek to during Free Quest: Barton the Fink, which begins in Goodsprings Source [4.11]. Pay special attention to the traps up at the top of the ridge path connecting the two locations.

At the top is a dead Prospector, with some items to loot.

At the top is the corpse of the bespectacled Johnny Five-Aces, with a glass pitcher and five scattered aces around him. On the cliff are four balls in a line. You wonder how time works....

- Danger! Bear Trap! (3)
- Fridge Items
- Footlocker Items (Caps)
- Ammo Box Ammunition
- Sleeping Quarters

[4.S08] Archaeologist's Fridge

- Threat Level: ●●●●●
- Wild Wasteland!

Over by the side of the road is a discarded fridge with the door wrenched off.

Inside are the skeletal remains of an archaeologist. Only his hat is salvageable.

- Suave Gambler Hat

[4.S09] Deathclaw Trailer

- Threat Level: ●●●●●
- Faction: Abomination
  - Entity: Deathclaw
- Crafting: Campfire [71/109]
- Sleeping Quarters

South of the Whittaker Farmstead [1.22] is a caravan trailer and deserted fields at the foothills of Quarry Junction [4.04]. The lack of humans is due to the prowling Deathclaws.

- Campfire [71/109]
- Sleeping Quarters

[4.S10] Corvega Atomic Billboard

- Threat Level: ●●●●●
- Faction: Abomination
  - Entity: Deathclaw
- Highly Visible

Billboards are dotted about the landscape, and serve as simple landmarks, but this one is very useful as it marks the northern perimeter of the Deathclaws' territory outside Quarry Junction [4.04]. If you see this billboard, beware!

[4.S11] Railroad Bridge

- Threat Level: ●●●●●
- Highly Visible

The railroad runs parallel along the Long 15, and is the easiest way to judge which zone you're in. This bridge has a dead Ghoul under it; this Bright Brotherhood follower has traveled far from their REPCONN Test Site [5.17] base.

- Bright Brotherhood Robe

[4.S12] Ammo Stash

- Threat Level: ●●●●●
- Guns and Ammo

By a small bush and low rock just off Long 15, there's some forgotten ammunition.

- Ammo Box Ammunition (2)

[4.S13] Jackknifed Truck

- Threat Level: ●●●●●
- Faction: Mutated Animal
  - Entity: Coyote
- Health, Chems, or Water

This rusting container has a number of items to scavenge.

- Sunset Sarsaparilla Crate Items (2)
- Doctor's Bag

[4.S14] The Desiccated Adventurer

- Threat Level: ●●●●●
- Guns and Ammo
- Health, Chems, or Water

On the flat rocks overlooking Long 15, an adventurer has shuffled off this mortal coil.

- First Aid Box
- Ammo
- Knife

[4.S15] Powder Ganger Junction

- Threat Level: ●●●●●
- Faction: Powder Ganger
  - Entity: Powder Ganger
- Collectibles: Magazine [Medicine] [18/19] [27/32]
- Guns and Ammo
- Highly Visible

At the junction on the Long 15 that allows access to the NCR Correctional Facility [5.15], there's a wrecked trailer, and two dead Caravan Guards. Beware of Powder Gangers (and their lobbed explosives) in this vicinity. Use the trailer as a route marker afterward.

- Ammo Box Ammunition
- Magazine: Today's Physician [Medicine] [18/19] [27/32]

[4.S16] Bloatfly Flats

- Threat Level: ●●●●●
- Faction: Mutated Animal
  - Entity: Bloatfly

If you're using Bloatflies for a Recipe, or simply need target practice, check the fetid pools between the Long 15 and railroad track, just southeast of Jean Sky Diving [4.12]

[4.S17] The Devil's Carbunkle

- Threat Level: ●●●●●
- Faction: Mutated Animal
  - Entity: Bloatfly
  - Entity: Radroach
- Dangers: Radiation
- Collectibles: Magazine [Sneak] [10/10] [28/32]
- Health, Chems, or Water

The trash ditch, once an old stream bed that runs from the Long 15, ends up in this irradiated mess. Check the garbage can, and find the following under a rusting car.

- Magazine: ¡La Fantoma! [Sneak] [10/10] [28/32]
- Chems and Doctor's Bag

[4.S18] Trash Ditch

- Threat Level: ●●●●●
- Faction: Mutated Animal
  Entity: Gecko

Run-off from the hills collects in a (now irradiated) pond to the east, and the old stream is now a ditch for refuse, and a path to follow to the Devil's Carbunkle.

[4.S19] Prospector's Lean-To

- Threat Level: ●●●●●
- Crafting: Campfire [72/109]
- Collectibles:
  Magazine [Critical Chance] [11/11] [29-30/32]
  Magazine [Survival] [27/30] [29-30/32]

North of California Sunset Drive-in is a rusting playground and Prospector's Lean-to. Find two Magazines in these parts. Try hitting Tin Cans as target practice, too.

- Campfire [72/109]
- Teddy Bear
- Magazine: True Police Stories [Crit. Chance] [11/11] [29/32]
- Magazine: Lad's Life [Survival] [27/30] [30/32]

[4.S20] Bright's Darkness

- Threat Level: ●●●●●

At the foot of the electrical power tower that you can use as a landmark are the remains of a dead Ghoul in a cowl. Expect an Energy Weapon on the corpse too.

- Bright Brotherhood Robe

[4.S21] Mesquite Mountains Lean-To

- Threat Level: ●●●●●
- Faction: Ghoul
  Entity: Feral Ghoul
- Dangers: Radiation
- Collectibles:
  Magazine [Repair] [26/27] [31-32/32]
  Magazine [Science] [20/23] [31-32/32]
  Sunset Sarsaparilla Star Cap [69/100]
- Sleeping Quarters

Close to the bubbling radiation of the Mesquite Mountains Crater is a lean-to affixed to the rock, affording shelter from the perpetual Ghoul problem. Watch out; that road cone has a mine under it!

- Frag Mine
- Tire Iron and Vodka
- Sunset Sarsaparilla Bottle
- Hockey Mask
- First Aid Box
- Magazine: Fixin' Things [Repair] [26/27] [31/32]
- Magazine: Programmer's Digest [Science] [20/23] [32/32]
- Sunset Sarsaparilla Star Cap [69/100]
- Sleeping Quarters

[4.S22] Super Mutant Camp

- Threat Level: ●●●●●
- Faction: Super Mutant
  Entity: Super Mutant
  Entity: Evolved Centaur
  Entity: Centaur
- Crafting: Campfire [68/109]
- Dangers: Radiation
- Guns and Ammo

Soaking in the radiation of Jack Rabbit Springs [4.26] are a small band of Super Mutants and their disgusting Centaur pets. The Campfire was flagged at Jack Rabbit Springs (#68).

- Rebound
- Sleeping Quarters

[4.S23] Nipton Junction

- Side Quest: Can You Find it in Your Heart
- Threat Level: ●●●●●
- Faction: Mutated Animal
  Entity: Giant Ant Soldier
  Entity: Giant Ant Worker
- Main Trading Route

This is the Long 15 junction with Trail 164 that takes you east to Nipton and Camp Searchlight [6.16]. The place is deserted, until you rid the area of Giant Ants during a Side Quest.

[4.S24] Californian Exodus

- Threat Level: ●●●●●
- Faction: NCR
- Highly Visible
- Main Trading Route

The remains of an ancient traffic jam lead up to the Mojave Outpost [4.27]. There's little but Food and a couple of Tool Boxes to check out in the back of the containers. However, the chained explosions the vehicles make (especially if you "daisy-chain" them with Frag Mines or C-4) is pointlessly impressive!

[4.S25] Crashed Cargo Plane

- Threat Level: ●●●●●
- Faction: Mutated Animal
  Entity: Radscorpion
- Guns and Ammo
- Wasteland Vegetation

The remains of a rusting plane in the sands of the south Ivanpah Dry Lake [4.24] hold a small find in the sand.

- Ammo Box Ammunition

[4.S26] Radscorpion Burrow

- Free Quest: Gland for Some Home Cooking
- Threat Level: ●●●●●
- Faction: Radscorpion1
  Entity: Radscorpion Queen
  Entity: Radscorpion
- Interior Exploration
- Wasteland Vegetation
- Quest Item

A clump of rocks with a swarm of Radscorpions reveals itself to be a burrow. Once inside, the burrow opens up into a large cave with a ferocious Radscorpion Queen to contend with, and well as a number of smaller beasts. Assuming you survive, you can collect copious items from the bodies of four Prospectors and a Jackal Gang Member, and gather Radscorpion Glands if you're wanting some of Ruby Nash's infamous Casseroles (Free Quest: Gland for Some Home Cooking).

- Radscorpion Gland

[4.S27A and 4.S27B] Mole Rat Burrows

- Threat Level: ●●●●●
- Faction: Mutated Animal
  Entity: Mole Rat
- Wasteland Vegetation

Some Mole Rats are living dangerously close to the Radscorpions. Although visible, their burrows are too small to fit through.

[4.S28] Sealed Train Tunnel

- Threat Level: ●●●●●
- Wasteland Vegetation

This is the end of the line of the railroad that borders this zone, which you can follow north all the way to New Vegas.

ZONE 5: CENTRAL MOUNTAINS

Topographical Overview

This undulating zone features a host of large locales, but is dominated to the north by Black Mountain, and the remains of a radar station now overrun by a Super Mutant named Tabitha. Those that seek solace in the mountains don't want to be found, as the denizens of Hidden Valley would certainly concur. Beware of Bark Scorpions in the maze-like gulch, and concentrate on investigating the larger structures south of the El Dorado Dry Lake; HELIOS One with its incredible solar panel array; the REPCONN Test Site where Ghouls and Super Mutants are waging war against one another, and there's always time to take in Dinky the Dinosaur over at Novac, where the settlers are always friendly, if a little on edge. South of Novac are less populated mountains, and a number of caves to explore; be sure you know which ones contain Geckos, and which have Deathclaws! Don't forget Primm Pass either; a great direct path to and from Zone 4. The western area has its own problems as you'll discover if you set foot inside the perimeter of the NCR Correctional Facility, where the inmates are quite literally running the asylum.

> *Note* To reference the entirety of this Zone, please utilize the Map Poster that came with this guide.

Highways and Byways

The border of this zone is perhaps the easiest to pinpoint, as it takes in the major roads and railroad in the region. To the west, the perimeter follows the route of the railroad tracks all the way from Junction 15 Railway Station to the north, down to Nipton in Zone 4. To the north is the continuation west to east of Trail 160, which meets up at the 188 Trading Post, and then continues southward down Highway 95, taking in the major sights along the way. The southern perimeter is the continuation of Trail 164 which began at the Mojave Outpost in Zone 4, and the road continues all the way to the northern edge of Camp Searchlight in Zone 6. As for the middle of this map? Aside from a second north-south road to Novac, the mountains mainly have pathways to lose yourself in, and a winding road to the top of Black Mountain itself.

Available Services, Crafting and Collectibles

Services: Caravan Players: [2/15]
Services: Gambling: [0/15]
Services: Healers/Dealers: [2/31]
Services: Repairers: [4/9]
Services: Traders: [9/33]
Crafting: Campfires: [22/109]
Crafting: Reloading Benches: [7/36]
Crafting: Workbenches: [11/41]
Crafting: Weapon Upgrades: [4/10]
Collectibles: Snow Globes: [0/7]
Collectibles: Caravan Cards: [5/30]
Collectibles: Hollowed-Out Rocks: [10/42]
Collectibles: Skill Books: [6/51]
Collectibles: Skill Magazines: [10/213]
Collectibles: Star Bottle Caps: [15/100]
Collectibles: Unique Items: [20/95]
Collectibles: Unique Weapons: [6/42]

Primary Locations

[5.01] Junction 15 Railway Station
[5.02] 188 Trading Post ●
[5.03] NCR Ranger Safehouse
[5.04] El Dorado Substation
[5.05] Vault 11
[5.06] Neil's Shack
[5.07] Black Mountain
[5.08] Black Rock Cave
[5.09] El Dorado Dry Lake
[5.10] Powder Ganger Camp North ●
[5.11] Hidden Valley
[5.12] Scorpion Gulch
[5.13] HELIOS One ●
[5.14] Gibson Scrap Yard
[5.15] NCR Correctional Facility ●
[5.16] Powder Ganger Camp East ●
[5.17] REPCONN Test Site
[5.18] Novac ●
[5.19] Emergency Service Railyard
[5.20] Primm Pass
[5.21] Harper's Shack
[5.22] Dead Wind Cavern
[5.23] Ranger Station Charlie ●
[5.24] Highway 95 Viper's Encampment
[5.25] Wrecked Highwayman
[5.26] Coyote Den
[5.27] Hidden Supply Cave
[5.28] Walking Box Cavern
[5.29] Legion Raid Camp
[5.30] Broc Flower Cave
[5.31] Snyder Prospector Camp

Secondary Locations

[5.S01] Fetid Pond
[5.S02] Boulder City Billboard Sign
[5.S03] Savaged Brahmin
[5.S04] Gore Bag
[5.S05] Quarry Junction Cargo Platform
[5.S06] Pack of Wild Dogs
[5.S07] Correctional Parking Lot
[5.S08] Powder Ganger Alcove
[5.S09] Tower Relay Alcove
[5.S10] Gibson's Shack
[5.S11] End of the Road
[5.S12] REPCONN Test Site Checkpoint
[5.S13] Sealed Train Tunnel
[5.S14] Radioactive Barrels
[5.S15] Wrecked Biker
[5.S16] Bright's Darkness
[5.S17] Legion Camp
[5.S18] Mole Rat Burrow
[5.S19] Viper Gang Ambush
[5.S20] Viper Gang Alcove
[5.S21] Signpost 164
[5.S22] Fancy Lads Billboard
[5.S23] Astor's Recon Camp
[5.S24] Highway 95: All Signs Point To Novac

PRIMARY LOCATIONS

[5.01] Junction 15 Railway Station

- Threat Level: ●●●●●
- Faction: Abomination
  - Entity: Deathclaw
- Collectibles: Sunset Sarsaparilla Star Cap [70/100]

This marks the unofficial spot where the rugged terrain of the Mojave desert flattens out into the New Vegas plains, and is also a good place to situate yourself to if you're following the roads and rail tracks; Long 15 winds up past the farmland to the northwest, while the REPCONN Headquarters is visible to the northeast. You're usually in mortal danger of Deathclaws advancing down the tracks from Quarry Junction though, so be ready to flee if you aren't able to deal with three or four attacking at once. The platform building is sealed up tight.

- Sunset Sarsaparilla Star Cap [70/100]

[5.02] 188 Trading Post ●

- Side Quest: I Could Make You Care; Oh My Papa
- Free Quest: Thought for the Day
- Threat Level: ●●●●●
  Faction: NCR, Brotherhood of Steel, Gun Runner, FOTA
- Entity: Michelle Kerr
- Entity: Samuel Kerr
- Entity: Veronica
- Entity: Arms Merchant
- Entity: Alexander
- Entity: The Forecaster
- Entity: Ezekiel
- Fame/Infamy
- Services:
  - Repairer [6/9]
  - Trader [22/33]
  - Trader [23/33]
  - Trader [24/33]
  - Trader [25/33]
- Crafting: Upgrades [7/10]
- Crafting: Reloading Bench [26/36]
- Collectibles: Sunset Sarsaparilla Star Cap [71/100]
- Follower
- Guns and Ammo
- Health, Chems, or Water
- Main Trading Route
- Perk!
- Sleeping Quarters
- Quest Item

Formed after the Powder Ganger break-out down at Primm [4.17] forced traders northward, the intersection of the 95 and 93 (hence "188") is now a bustling Trading spot, catering to the NCR from Boulder City [3.32] and Hoover Dam [3.33] as well as offering good connections down the 95. Start on the eastern side of the intersection.

188 Slop & Shop: "It's Better Than Nothing."

Michelle (daytime) and Samuel Kerr (nighttime) run this store, and you can ask either of them for a little local flavor, as well as the Legion raids. They have a variety of items to trade, including a few weapons, and Doctor Bags. Remember the selection changes depending on who is on duty; you can wake the other Kerr from the mattress under their blue metal shack. Don't forget to check out their shack; there's a small bar with a Star Cap on it, and a Reloading Bench around the back.

- Repairer: Samuel Kerr [Skill 40] [6/9]
- Trader: Michelle Kerr [22/33]
- Trader: Michelle: Upgrades [Guns] [7/10]
- Trader: Samuel [23/33]
- Reloading Bench [26/36]
- Sunset Sarsaparilla Star Cap [71/100]
- Reloading Bench [26/36]

Veronica, Who Lives in a Hole in the Ground

The hooded figure standing close to the Slop & Shop is Veronica, who you can engage in conversation. She lives in a bunker, and is here picking up supplies for her "family." If you want her to join you, answer her question about the Brotherhood of Steel:

Tell her that they shoot lasers from their eyes. This impresses her, but not in a good way.

Answer with a polite reply that doesn't involve killing them, and Veronica asks to join you. Veronica has received training in Power Armor, and primarily focuses on Melee Weapons.

Tell her that you kill Brotherhood of Steel on sight, and she ignores you.

- Follower: Veronica
- Perk: Scribe Assistant

Arms Merchant: Bravo Company's Finest?

Cross the bridge (there's a long trailer with mattresses to sleep in) to the western side of the overpass, and check the tent for more mattresses. Close by is a parked military truck, with an Arms Merchant. She's been discharged from the NCR for three years, since an "incident" during the first Legion attack on the dam. Ask her about that, as well as seeing what she has for sale (it's usually cheaper than Michelle):

- Trader: Arms Merchant [24/33]
- Sleeping Quarters

Gun Runners: For the Discerning Customer

Speak to Alexander under the bridge, who runs a satellite operation for the Gun Runners [2.14] and isn't about to sell his wares to the likes of you. You can ask about the Gun Runners, or his attitude, but he won't sell you anything.

You can ask him about his wares being a fan of guns yourself. Only then will he open his inventory.

- Trader: Alexander [25/33]

Ezekiel the Explorer

A member of the Followers of the Apocalypse is hanging around outside the northern edge of this Post. He doesn't say much, unless you're inquiring about Great Khan history, as part of Side Quest: Oh My Papa.

- Quest Item: Pretty Pretty Horses: A History of the Mongol Empire

Free Quest: Thought for the Day

Sitting on the concrete below the overpass is a child known as The Forecaster. He's wearing some kind of head brace (which he believes is his "medicine"), and isn't selling anything; not even the bric-a-brac surrounding him. He's selling thoughts, at 100 Caps a pop. You can ignore him, or pay up. There are three "thoughts" to buy:

"Me": Rapidly changing conditions (vague premonitions about your Main Quest).

"Everywhere:" Rain of blood will flood the desert and not purify it (more about the decisions you must make).

"Here:" Cloudy with a chance of friendship (about Veronica, and her "key").

[5.03] NCR Ranger Safehouse

- Free Quest: Rest and Resupply
  Threat Level:
- Faction: NCR
  - Entity: Ranger Gomez
  - Trader [26/33]
- Crafting: Reloading Bench [27/36]
- Area Is Locked
- Guns and Ammo
- Health, Chems, or Water
- Home Sweet Home
- Interior Exploration
- Sleeping Quarters

A well-hidden door along a gully leads into a Safehouse only accessible with the appropriate key, obtained once you complete the Free Quest with Colonel Hsu.

A Exit to Mojave Wasteland

1 Canteen

Inside the Safehouse is a structure built into the natural cavern. The canteen has a Reloading Bench and Water Fountain.

- Reloading Bench [27/36]

2 Barracks

Much like other Safehouses across the Mojave, this offers a place of rest and healthy solace. The following benefits occur:

1. Any bed you sleep in at this location gives you a "Well Rested" bonus.
2. There is a water fountain here allowing you to sip purified water without Radiation.
3. If the location has a fridge, it is restocked with items once per day.
4. Aside from the fridge, there are containers you can store items without them disappearing. Choose a metal box, footlocker, or other chest type, place a low value item inside, then return after a day to ensure your items haven't been taken.
5. This location is visited periodically by Ranger Gomez, who is usually here every Wednesday and Saturday. You can check the day of the week when you attempt to Wait or Sleep. Gomez hands over (for free) one set of the following, each time the Ranger visits (so you can choose items twice a week, assuming you're there when the Ranger is).

- Trader: Ranger Gomez [26/33]
- Regular Gun Ammo
- Energy Weapon Ammo
- Explosives

NCR RANGER SAFEHOUSE

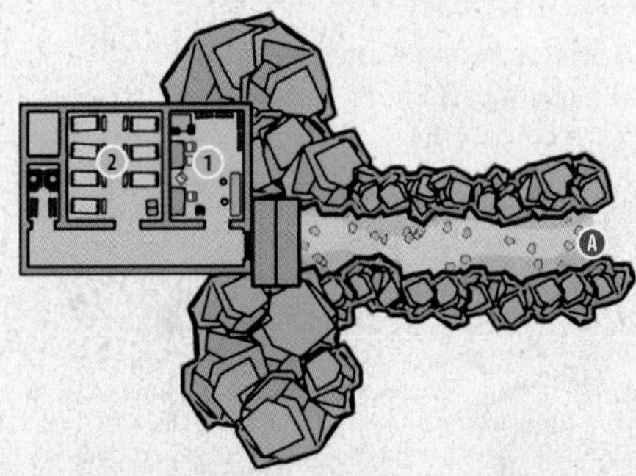

[5.04] El Dorado Substation

- Main Quest: Wild Card: Finishing Touches
- Main Quest: The House Always Wins, VII
- Threat Level:
- Faction: NCR
  - Entity: NCR Trooper
- Collectibles: Sunset Sarsaparilla Star Cap [72/100]
- Guns and Ammo
- Interior Exploration
- Radio Signal [Black Mountain]
- Sleeping Quarters

Taking the incredible energy from HELIOS One [5.13] and converting it into usable electricity occurs here, at the substation and adjacent transformer yard, both of which are guarded by NCR Troops that give you strict instructions not to trespass on the property. Open the Garage Door to the Substation. A terminal allows access to power areas of the Mojave Wasteland based on your alliance needs, and at the expense of NCR friendliness.

- Ammo Box Ammunition
  Sunset Sarsaparilla Star Cap [72/100]
- Sleeping Quarters

[5.05] Vault 11

See maps on the following page

- Side Quest: Still in the Dark
- Free Quest: Democracy Inaction
- Free Quest: Suits You, Sarah
- Threat Level:
- Faction: Mutated Animal
  - Entity: Giant Mantis
  - Entity: Giant Rat
  - Entity: Robot
- Dangers:
  - Traps
  - Radiation
  - Mines
- Collectibles:
  - Skill Book [Unarmed] [4/4] [1/6]
  - Hollowed-Out Rock [25/42]
  - Unique Item [72/95]
- Area Is Locked
- Guns and Ammo
- Health, Chems, or Water
- Interior Exploration
- Radio Signal [Black Mountain]
- Sleeping Quarters
- Quest Item

Vault 11 was a social experiment vault to see if the residents would periodically select and kill a fellow vault dweller to avoid the threat of total vault extermination. Each year, the vault computer informed the residents that one currently living member of the vault had to be placed in a special chamber, where they would be "terminated" for the good of the vault. Failure to comply, the computer said, would result in a total and irrevocable shutdown of the vault's life support. The vault dwellers followed the instructions for decades, picking victims through numerous methods. But eventually, something changed...

An old wooden door, in close proximity to a Hollowed-Out Rock, greets those who dare enter this rocky tomb.

- Hollowed-Out Rock [25/42]

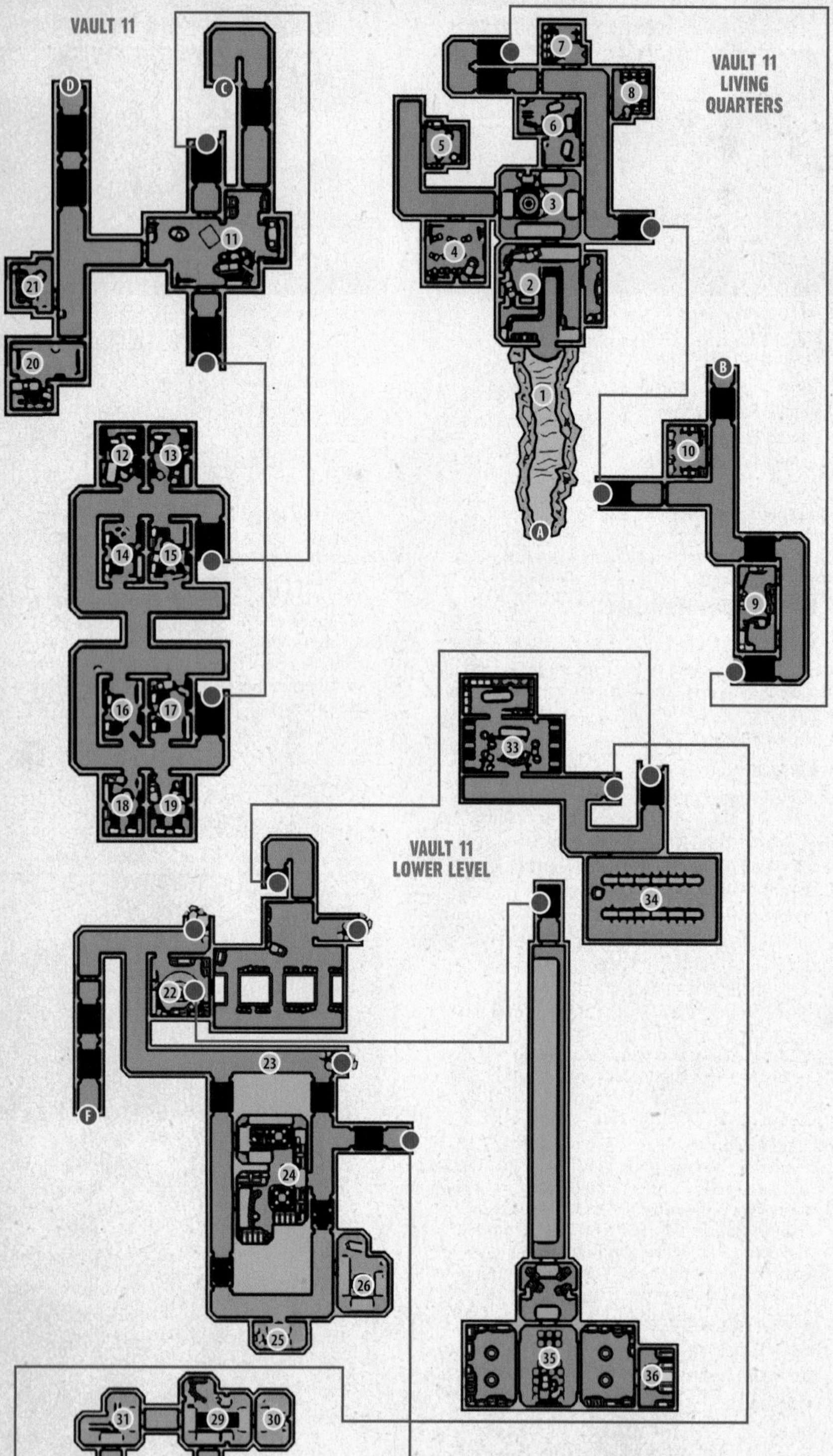

VAULT 11

VAULT 11 LIVING QUARTERS

VAULT 11 LOWER LEVEL

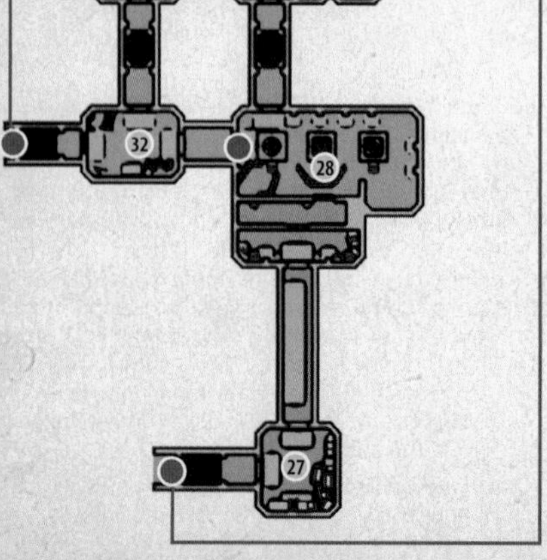

Vault 11 Entrance Level

Ⓐ Door to Mojave Wasteland

1 Rocky Tunnel

There are two Bark Scorpions to avoid as you reach the massive vault door, which is currently open. The Vault Door Control Pod (on either side) closes and opens it again.

2 Entrance Chamber

Stamp out the Giant Mantises, then peer around the room, which has some odd posters lampooning a couple of unknown persons in what appears to be a vault election. Check the terminal above the box of ammo to download a security recording: The four corpses at the front entrance of Vault 11 (in the Clinic) and a strange recording point to sinister events. This is Free Quest: Democracy Inaction.

> Security Recording: Vault Entrance

- Note: System Recording: Vault 11 Front Entrance
- Note: Vault 11

3 Filtration Room

A round filtration device dominates this room, with four exits, and the first of many Giant Rats to deal with. Study the graffiti on the posters closely. The sign above the door to the north reads "Clinic."

4 Classroom

Giant Mantises are in this small classroom, which has a public terminal to access. This gives lists of the candidates: Henry Glover (a family man with six children, who oddly ends his election spiel with a request to vote for "Nate Stone"). Donna Haley (who is aware of the rumors circulating, but then finishes with a self-harming flourish, telling the reader "my administration would be a disaster"). Then there's Nate Stone (who complains about dirty backroom politics).

> Vault 11 Election Guide: See above.

> Notice of Postponement (regarding "murders" that forced the election to be stalled).

> Overseer Order 745: Katherine Stone (the Overseer) opts for random election proceedings.

5 Cigar Lounge

Pass the NCR Trooper corpse, and into this Giant Mantis-filled room. Check the fridge for Food before you leave.

- Carton of Cigarettes (2)

6 Clinic

The place is crawling with Giant Mantises, and there are four skeletons on the gurneys, and a fifth on the ground.

- First Aid Box (2)

7 8 Restrooms

The gentlemen's restroom has a shelf of cleaning products.

9 (Mid-Level) Laboratory

Between the ground and lower floors of this level is a long laboratory room. The public terminal contains the same information as the one in the classroom (Location #4).

> Vault 11 Election Guide > Overseer Order 745

> Notice of Postponement

10 (Lower) Computer Room

Both stairs and corridors lead here. There are two terminals; one is a trap and the other has the Public information on it.

> Vault 11 Election Guide > Overseer Order 745

> Notice of Postponement

Ⓑ Door to Vault 11 Living Quarters

Vault 11 Living Quarters

Ⓒ Door to Vault 11 Entrance Level

11 Recreation Room and Bar

Giant Mantises and Rats co-exist with animosity here. The place is a bit of a mess, and there's nothing but junk (and a few Fission Batteries. Note the three exits (Male and Female Dorms, and Admin).

12 13 14 15 (Lower) Male Dorm Rooms #1, #2, #3, #4

Don't forget to check the dressers for a Vault 11 Jumpsuit! Dorm Room #3 has a personal terminal [Very Easy] to hack, which downloads a Security Recording to your Pip-Boy. Roy Gottlieb from the Justice Bloc wants to usurp the Overseer, and is ready to arm up, take to the lower floors to hold out until he gets what he wants.

> Security Recording

- Note: Justice Bloc HQ Security Tapes
- Vault 11 Jumpsuit
- Footlocker Items (2)
- Sleeping Quarters

16 17 18 19 (Lower) Female Dorm Rooms #1, #2, #3, #4

Doom Room #1 has a Skill Book by an overturned dresser.

- Skill Book: Pugilism Illustrated [Unarmed] [4/4] [1/6]
- Footlocker Items (2)
- Sleeping Quarters

20 Security

Accessed on the upper corridor from Location #11, this has some ammo to gather, as well as a security terminal with the usual messages, and one additional one: A Deposition, in which Overseer Katherine Stone reveals shocking (and sexual) problems between her and (alledgedly) all of the Justice Bloc.

> Deposition

- 25mm Grenade (20)
- Ammo Box Ammunition (4)

21 Locked Storage [Hard]

Accessed via a wall terminal [Hard] or Door [Hard], to secure the contents of this room:

- Ammo Box Ammunition (3)
- Mine Box Ammunition
- Unique Item: Mini-Nuke [72/95]
- Flamer Fuel (12)
- 25mm Grenade (20 x 2)
- Energy Cell (20 x 4)
- Microfusion Cell (20 x 5)

E Door to Vault 11 Lower Level

Vault 11 Lower Level

F Door to Vault 11 Living Quarters

22 Overseer's Office

Beware of a Rigged Shotgun trap at the door; disarm the Tripwire and deactivate it. As well as a load of Scrap Metal, the room contains the Overseer's Terminal, which requires a password to access it, found in the Atrium. Return here and you can open the Sacrificial Chamber.

> Open Sacrificial Chamber

23 Utility and Atrium Corridor

The corridor section to the east is blocked, which makes it impossible to reach the Atrium from this direction. Head south, down either staircase.

24 Utility Room: Roy Gottlieb's Last Stand

There are three entrances to choose from depending on which corridor you've accessed. The northeast entrance has a Tripwire and Grenade Bouquet; watch out! The eastern entrance (facing west) has a steel beam that swings down to hit you; stoop and untie the Tripwire to deactivate that. Judging by the skeletons, it seems Roy's plan was put into practice, but they died down here.

- Frag Grenade (3)
- First Aid Box
- Ammo Box Ammunition (2)

25 (Underwater) Pump Control Room

The underwater chambers are slightly irradiated, so be quick, but don't worry about running out of air; there's some in the cavity above the water, as these passages aren't completely submerged. Be doubly sure you open the Locker inside this chamber, as it has a Differential Pressure Controller in it; a vital piece of equipment needed during Side Quest: Still in the Dark. Take this right now (the Quest does not have to be active), and don't sell it!

- First Aid Box
- Quest Item: Differential Pressure Controller

26 (Underwater) Auxiliary Pump

There's little in here except a slight case of radiation poisoning.

- Ammo Box Ammunition

27 Reactor Area: Storage #1

28 (Waterlogged) Sub-Reactor Room

Enter through the control room with the Ammo Boxes to the right (east). There's a loudspeaker to activate, but nothing happens. The reactors themselves are flooded, and there are skeletons from the past vault fracas. The door to the left (west) is locked [Average].

- Ammo Box Ammunition (5) [1 = Average]

29 30 (Completely Underwater) Main Reactor and Storage

Exit via the door to the north and take a deep breath; enter the reactor room and don't drown! There are more skeletal defenders, and a storage room to the east with the following:

- First Aid Box
- Ammo Box Ammunition (2)

31 (Completely Underwater) Connecting Chamber

Access Location #32 if you can't unlock the door in the Sub-Reactor Room.

32 (Waterlogged) Reactor Area: Storage #2

The door to the west leads to steps up to the Atrium area.

33 Cafeteria

Another place where democracy ended in bloodshed. Watch the Frag Mine as you walk in, and the Grenade Bouquet as you reach the back room (a Giant Mantis may already have triggered it).

- Frag Mine
- Purified Water (4)
- Ammo Box Ammunition
- First Aid Box
- Footlocker Items
- Cabinet Trunk Items

34 (Lower and Upper) Atrium

The corridor branches south. Follow it to a door, and upstairs to a second door; both lead to the Atrium. On the upper mezzanine is an Atrium Terminal, with the Prepared Speech of Gus Olson, Ombudsman. There is a Holodisc offering the same, shocking revelations about the vault's mainframe, and the yearly Overseer activities that could chill you to the core! Gus knows how to tear at the heartstrings! Now you know the password for the Overseer's Terminal.

- Holodisc: Prepared Speech of Gus Olson, Ombudsman, for the Annual Overseer Election

35 Overseer's Walk

After a long walk and a bright light from the risen Overseer's desk, you reach a small movie projector. Close the door, and sit down for a relaxing viewing of a picture show entitled "Happy Trails." It doesn't stay happy for long!

36 Vault 11 Mainframe

If you're determined to complete the Free Quest, it might be wise to head here, and access the mainframe. The following menus are present; and the second option reveals the real truth!

> Override Lockdown.

> Automated Solution Response

> System Recording: Vault 11 Solution

Free Quest: Democracy Inaction

Figuring out exactly what happened to the residents of Vault 11, and understanding the Overseer's long walk, as well as accessing the Mainframe, gives you a whole new perspective on the Vault-Tec Corporation, and completes this Quest.

[5.06] Neil's Shack

- Side Quest: Crazy, Crazy, Crazy
- Threat Level: ●●●●●
- Faction: Super Mutant
  - Entity: Neil
  - Entity: Nightkin
  - Entity: Super Mutant
  - Entity: Deathclaw
- Guns and Ammo
- Radio Signal [Black Mountain]
- Sleeping Quarters

At the foot of the Black Mountain switchbacks is a dilapidated shack. Neil, a friendly first-gen Super Mutant, is close by, and speaking to him allows you to find out more about the area, and the Nightkin that guard Tabitha at the top of the Mountain.

- Frag Grenade (2)
- Sleeping Quarters

[5.07] Black Mountain

See map on the following page

- Side Quest: Crazy, Crazy, Crazy
- Free Quest: Old School Ghoul
- Threat Level: ●●●●●
- Faction: Super Mutant
  - Entity: Neil
  - Entity: Nightkin
  - Entity: Super Mutant
  - Entity: Raul
  - Entity: Rhonda
  - Entity: Tabitha
- Services: Repairer [7/9]
- Crafting:
  - Campfire [73/109]
  - Campfire [74/109]
  - Campfire [75/109]
  - Reloading Bench [28/36]
  - Workbench [29/41]
  - Workbench [30/41]
- Dangers:
  - Traps
  - Radiation
- Collectibles:
  - Sunset Sarsaparilla Star Cap [73/100]
  - Unique Item [73/95]
  - Unique Weapon [29/42]
- Area Is Locked
- Follower
- Guns and Ammo
- Health, Chems, or Water
- Highly Visible
- Interior Exploration
- Lots O' Caps
- Perk!
- Perk!
- Perk!
- Radio Signal [Black Mountain]
- Sleeping Quarters
- Quest Item

A slightly unhinged Super Mutant named Tabitha (and also Rhonda) has installed herself (with the indentured help of a Ghoul named Raul) in this mountain-top radar installation, and is broadcasting her particular brand of insanity throughout much of the Wasteland. There are two ways to reach her lair; both of which are covered in the Side Quest.

1 Road Entrance

Take this exit off the Long 95 just after the Quarry Junction [4.4]. You're likely to be attacked by multiple Deathclaws unless you're keeping to the eastern side and moving through the rocks carefully.

2 Neil's Shack [5.06]

This is where you meet Super Mutant Neil, who's ready to help in the assault on Black Mountain, as part of the Side Quest. Consult his Primary Location for further details.

3 Danger! Falling Rocks!

This section of road allows you to view the first Super Mutant blockade [4], and the traps the Muties have readied for intruders. However, there's a path off to the right (south) that skirts around and bypasses the road, ending up at a gate (Location [7]).

BLACK MOUNTAIN EXTERIOR

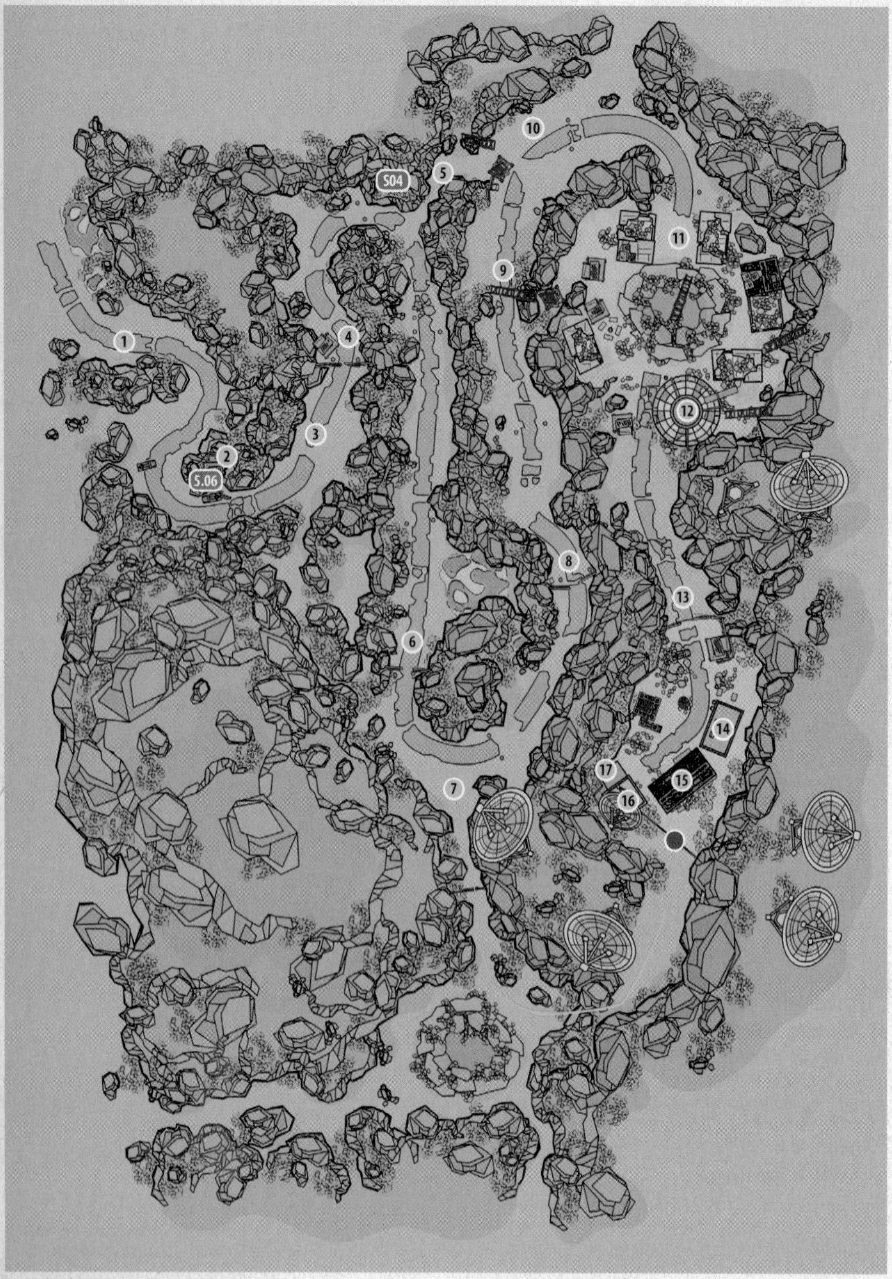

4 Super Mutant Blockade #1

Expect at least three Super Mutants, and a couple of Nightkin to attack near here. The blockade hut itself has a footlocker to scavenge, and some ammo.

- Ammo Box Ammunition

5 Bear-Trap Gully

Expect more attacks from Super Mutants and Nightkin as you progress around the bend, passing two flaming barrels. You may have had to dodge a pushed boulder at this point, too. The road continues up (south), but there's a small gully here, with a dead NCR Trooper and a Magnum. This gully leads to a boulder trap, and the Scenic Overlook (Location [10]).

- .357 Magnum Revolver
- Bear Trap! (6)

6 Super Mutant Blockade #2

Expect at least two or three more attacks before you reach this metal wall and barrels, and a few more Muties to tackle. You can peel off to the east, into a small patch of radioactive ground water, and up a tiny gully if you want a dangerous shortcut.

7 Danger! Falling Rocks Again!

As the road curves around to the left (northeast) again, there's another warning sign, and a gate off to your right (southeast). This is the shortcut to take to reach Tabitha's broadcasting building (Location [#16]) as you advance into the northern edge of Scorpion Gulch [5.12]. Head up the mountain, around the giant radar dishes to reach a second gate [Locked: Hard].

8 Super Mutant Blockade #3

This has a few hefty fellows and insane Nightkin to worry about, and a couple of items to scavenge between battles.

- Frag Grenade (3)
- Ammo Box Ammunition

9 Ruined Radio Mast

Further along the road is a fallen radio mast, and more Mutie mayhem. There's a steep path to the right, allowing a shortcut into the shanty village. Otherwise, cut down Super Mutants and Centaurs and continue onward and upward.

10 Scenic Overlook

This is the top of Bear Trap Gully, where the boulder was launched from. Trek the winding bend up to the village.

11 Shanty Village

This was once a collection of radio masts and monitoring stations. Now it is dominated by a giant crater, and badly erected shanty huts, which are empty. Keep a look-out for more Muties (expect at least three). There's a Campfire and bedding to use once the coast is clear.

- Campfire [73/109]
- Sleeping Quarters

12 Dome Home

Tabitha and her brethren have turned a fallen radar dish into a moderately successful storage area. There a Campfire inside, and there are trunks to open [1 = Average], and each contains a haul of Caps. Around the back is a third trunk (with a Minigun inside) and a Transceiver. Speak to Tabitha (as part of the Side Quest) here.

- Campfire [74/109]
- Minigun and Ammo
- Caps (900+)

13 Summit

Take the (southern) road from the Dome Home, and expect a final wave of Nightkin attacks (especially if you spoke to Tabitha about a "dumb-dumb revolt"). Once at the Summit itself, beware of the Mutie with the Unique Missile Launcher on the radio mast. Check the small satellite dish on the ground for a Campfire. There's a particularly disgusting dumpster here, too.

- Campfire [75/109]
- Unique Weapon: Annabelle [29/42]

14 Prison Building

This two-room chamber is where Raul is being locked up. The first room has a locked door, Workbench, and two terminals. Check the accessible one for six entries that Raul has written about the madness he's suffered. Or just read Entry #6 for the Password to the second terminal, which is otherwise difficult to hack [Very Hard]. The second terminal unlocks the door. Raul is inside, and you can speak to him at length about his history, horrendous working conditions under Tabitha, and ask him to join you as a Follower if you wish.

- Note: Black Mountain Prison Password
- Workbench [29/41]
- Workbench [30/41]
- Follower: Raul
- Perk!: Regular Maintenance

15 Storage Building

In addition to being a radio personality, Tabitha is a hoarder, and this chamber is proof of it. Although the main prizes are what's contained within the two trunks (that can only be unlocked with Tabitha's Key), there's other items to scavenge beforehand, including a Star Cap on the bottom shelf with the bottles. On a table, there's Rhonda, a deactivated Mister Handy that you can reactivate [Science] for Tabitha, for a happier Quest ending.

- Reloading Bench [28/36]
- Missile Launcher
- Sunset Sarsaparilla Star Cap [73/100]
- Super Stimpak
- Ammo
- Frag Grenade (2)
- Quest Item: Rhonda

When you've successfully open the trunks using Tabitha's Key, the following mass of weaponry can be hauled out of here (use Raul to help if you're unable to carry it all):

- Tabitha's Trunk #1, #2, and 3 Items (Guns and Ammo)

16 Broadcast Building (First Floor)

Inside is a terminal [Easy] charting an astonishing series of logs from ancient times, when this installation took a direct hit. The final entry is from Marcus, when he first arrived at this place to set up camp. The second terminal [Easy] charts Marcus' removal from Black Mountain, and Tabitha's descent into madness.

17 Broadcast Building (Second Floor)

This is the broadcasting booth where Tabitha speaks from, and is accessed using Tabitha's Room Key, found under the metal stairs you just climbed up. Inside are two more trunks you can scavenge from (with her Equipment Key), a Note ordering Raul to fix something, and a Sheet Music Book that's worth 100 Caps. If you killed Tabitha, there's a Super Sledge on her corpse.

- Super Sledge
- Note: Repair Note #3
- Unique Item: Sheet Music Book [73/95]
- Tabitha's Trunk #4 and 5 Items (Guns and Ammo)

Free Quest: Old School Ghoul

Once you rescue Raul, you can opt to have him as a Follower, where he brings an impressive Repair Skill (and visit Raul's Shack [3.05] to help him utilize his tinkering equipment). But if you speak to Raul at length, and listen to his thoughts on various factions as well as his life in Mexico City before the bombs dropped, there's a tinge of sadness to his voice. Raul is getting old—even for a Ghoul—and needs to figure out his lot in life. And for that, he needs your help, and the wisdom of those more elderly Mojave residents (who can be visited in any order).

- Follower: Raul
- Perk!: Regular Maintenance

Wise Old Soul #1: Ranger Andy

Visit Novac [5.18], and speak with Ranger Andy, making sure you ask him about his leg wound. When you exit the building, Raul comes up to you, and asks what you thought of Ranger Andy. You can:

Answer positively, about this hero of the NCR.

Or negatively, about this waste of space.

You're affecting Raul's introspection with your answers, but whatever your opinions, Raul begins to share his past with you. You can stop him at any time, but to continue this Quest, listen to Raul's entire story about growing up at the Hidalgo Ranch, and the fire. It seems Raul is feeling a little nostalgic for the past. You can continue on with other Quests.

Wise Old Soul #2: Loyal

Head into Boomer Territory, and seek out Loyal in the Nellis Air Force Base [3.01], in the Hangars area [3.02]. Speak to him about the Solar Array, and begin Side Quest: Sunshine Boogie. After the conversation, Raul tells you it's good to see that Loyal guy making himself useful to his people, especially as he's getting up there in years. You can answer with varying degrees of positivity.

The conversation brought up old memories about the time after the Ranch fire, journeying to Mexico City, and living like a scavenger, and finding something to cover his horrific burns. He once spotted a vaquero outfit hanging in a shop. His sister laughed, and he started to build up a legend. Then he left for the Gulf Coast and the old Petro-Chico refinery. He stops the story for now.

Wise Old Soul #3: Corporal Sterling

Inside Camp McCarran where First Recon are polishing their sniper rifles, the old guard (literally) has joined their ranks. Speak with Corporal Sterling about his past, his gun, and even his wounds as part of Side Quest: I Don't Hurt Anymore. After the conversation is over, Raul stops you and says he admires Sterling; retiring from the service and coming back to do more. Answer with varying degrees of positivity.

Raul reveals that he headed north to Tuscon, found a little shack, and started to fix stuff. He stayed for another 75 years until Claudia showed up, until Dirty Dave showed up, and caused pain that Raul relives to this day. After a story of vengeance and almost impossible survival, Raul left and ended up at Black Mountain, and in Tabitha's grasp.

Gunslinger or Gun Repair?

After all three Wise Old Souls have been visited, Raul tells you that although he's been having doubts about becoming the gunslinger he once was, he's decided to leave the fighting to you. You can:

Agree that if he thinks that's best, you won't stop him.
Raul agrees, and Regular Maintenance Perk is replaced by an enhanced version. And a slightly snazzier outfit.

- Repairer: Raul Tejada [Skill 100] [7/9]
- Perk! Full Maintenance

SPEECH 66 Or that you think Raul is great with a pistol. Raul agrees, and puts on his gunslinging outfit, giving himself an additional perk, which increases his rate of fire with revolvers and lever-action firearms by 33 percent.

- Perk! Old Vaquero

[5.08] Black Rock Cave

- Threat Level: ●●●●●
- Faction: Super Mutant
  Entity: Nightkin
- Collectibles:
  Hollowed-Out Rock [26/42]
- Unique Weapon [30/42]
- Guns and Ammo
- Interior Exploration
- Radio Signal

An opening in the rock face, below the giant radar dishes. Beware of Radscorpions, and check the rocks for the hollow one on the way in.

- Hollowed-Out Rock [26/42]

A Exit to Mojave Wasteland

1 Danger! Nightkin!

Be very mindful of the deranged trio of heavily armed Nightkin. Fighting them is worth it though:

2 Prospector's Loot

Inspect the Prospector corpse in the northeast end of the cavern to uncover a Unique Zap Glove: the Paladin Toaster!

- Unique Weapon: Paladin Toaster [30/42]

BLACK ROCK CAVE

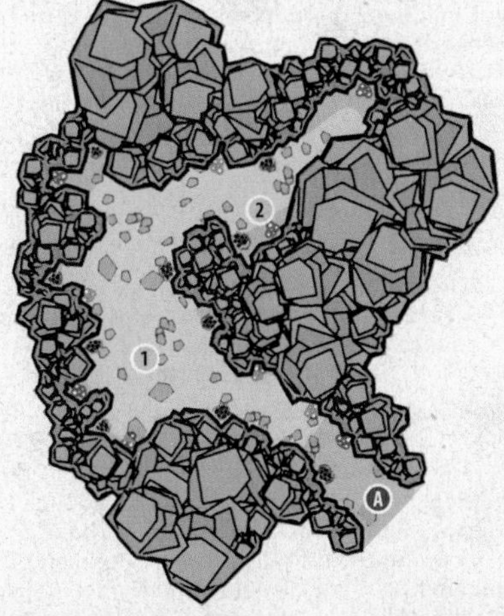

[5.09] El Dorado Dry Lake

- Threat Level: ●●●●●
- Faction: Mutated Animal
  Entity: Giant Ant
- Collectibles: Hollowed-Out Rock [27/42]
- Highly Visible
- Radio Signal
- Wasteland Vegetation

Although the wind whipping the sand up can be mesmerizing, this Dry Lake is just as dangerous as its larger cousin to the southwest (Ivanpah Dry Lake [4.24]), due to the large number of Giant Ants inhabiting the flat earth. Be sure to check the Hollowed-Out Rock in the central-east area near a Jalapeno plant. Otherwise, the half-covered picnic area to the north, and the military truck barricade stuck in the middle of the sand are devoid of major scavenged items.

- Hollowed-Out Rock [27/42]

[5.10] Powder Ganger Camp North ●

- Threat Level: ●●●●●
- Faction: Powder Ganger
  Entity: Powder Ganger
- Crafting
  Campfire [76/109]
- Fame/Infamy
- Radio Signal
- Sleeping Quarters
- Wasteland Vegetation

This small shack within spitting distance of the NCR Correctional Facility [5.15] is a northern guard post for the Powder Gangers. There are modest defenses, only three Gangers to deal with. Check the footlocker for a Note, telling others of the Faction to congregate to the north, perhaps to join Samuel Cooke's Ganger offshoot, currently exploring Vault 19 [1.21].

- Campfire [76/109]
- Note: Powder Ganger Note
- Sleeping Quarters

[5.11] Hidden Valley

See map on the following page

- Main Quest: Wild Card: Side Bets
- Main Quest: The House Always Wins, V
- Main Quest: Render Unto Caesar
- Main Quest: For the Republic, Part 2
- Side Quest: Eyesight for the Blind
- Side Quest: ED-E My Love
- Side Quest: I Could Make You Care
- Side Quest: Still in the Dark

HIDDEN VALLEY EXTERIOR

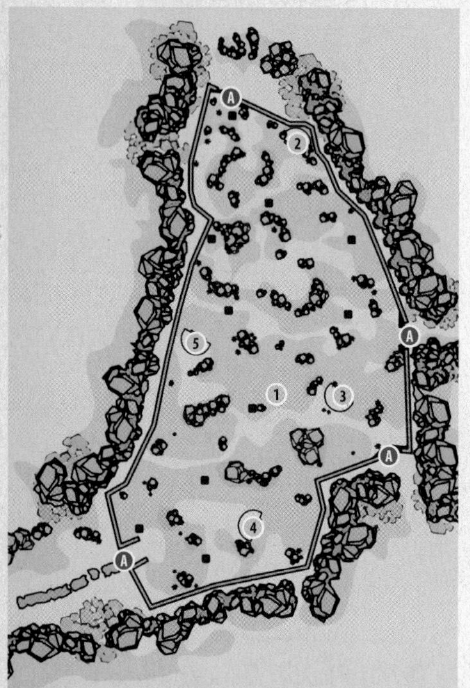

- Side Quest: Tend to Your Business
- Free Quest: Pistol Packing
- Free Quest: Brotherhood Bond, I
- Free Quest: Brotherhood Bond, II
- Threat Level: ●●●●●
- Faction: Brotherhood of Steel
  - Entity: Elder McNamara
  - Entity: Head Paladin Hardin
  - Entity: Head Scribe Taggart
  - Entity: Paladin Ramos
  - Entity: Senior Scribe Schuler
  - Entity: Scribe Isben
  - Entity: Senior Knight Lorenzo
  - Entity: Knight Torres
  - Entity: Brotherhood Paladin
  - Entity: Apprentice Watkins
  - Entity: Initiate Stanton
  - Entity: Brotherhood Initiate
- Fame/Infamy
- Services:
  - Healer/Dealer [29/31]
  - Repairer [8/9]
  - Trader [27/33]
- Crafting:
  - Campfire [77/109]
  - Campfire [78/109]
  - Reloading Bench [29/36]
  - Workbench [31/41]
  - Upgrades [8/10]
- Collectibles:
  - Skill Book [Energy Weapons] [3/4] [2/6]
  - Hollowed-Out Rock [28/42]
  - Unique Item [74/95]
  - Unique Item [75/95]
  - Unique Item [76/95]
  - Unique Item [77/95]
- Area Is Locked
- Guns and Ammo
- Health, Chems, or Water
- Interior Exploration
- Sleeping Quarters
- Quest Item
- Weapons, Please!

Hidden Valley is housed in the remnants of a USAF bunker near the heart of the valley. Abandoned even before the war, the area around the bunker is littered with junk. Signs on the roads and peaks leading into the valley warn that it is a USAF testing range and stretches of drooping wire fences form a pathetic barrier in post-apocalyptic times. Upon entering the outer region of the actual bunkers, surviving Prospectors have reported an eerie feeling, and four bunkers, each with an intercom and complete, almost deafening silence on the other side. Others tell of seeing armored figures exiting the Valley from within a raging sandstorm that seems to arrive every evening and stay for the night. The main entrance is from the south gates, at the end of the side road from Long 95 that passes north of the NCR Correctional Facility [5.15]. There are periodic breaks in the perimeter fence, including a large breach to the north.

Ⓐ Entrances (or Breaks in the Fence)

① Hollowed-Out Rock

Once inside the perimeter, you may experience severe and localized inclement weather. This may not be naturally occurring. Beware of Bark Scorpions as you scout the undulating terrain. Inside the valley you'll find a Hollowed-Out Rock, and four bunkers to investigate.

- Hollowed-Out Rock [28/42]

② Hidden Valley Bunker (North)

Enter and descend the steps. This chamber is partially collapsed, with large containers. The intercom yields nothing. Open the interior Blast Door [Average] and the way ahead is completely blocked, although the following items are among the fallen masonry:

- Ammo
- Unique Item: Mini-Nuke [74/95]
- Unique Item: Mini-Nuke [75/95]

③ Hidden Valley Bunker (East)

Enter and head down the steps. This room has a Campfire, and a devastated ceiling, crushing some long-dead bunker dwellers on a makeshift bed. The intercom has you repeating yourself, so unlock the Blast Door [Easy]; this confirms the area is sealed and cannot be entered.

- Campfire [77/109]
- Sleeping Quarters
- Wine

④ Hidden Valley Bunker (South)

Enter and descend the steps. Depending on the time of day, and whether Side Quest: Still in the Dark is active, you may run into an NCR Ranger named Dobson here; he's using this bunker as a base of operations while he checks on the Powder Gangers nearby. Read his Journal if you wish. Unlock the Blast Door [Hard], and you can tell there's no further progress to be made, although clambering over the fallen masonry yields the following items among the concrete:

- Campfire [78/109]
- Ammo Box Ammunition (3)
- Sack Items
- Scrap Metal (2)
- Quest Item: Dobson's Journal
- Unique Item: Mini-Nuke [76/95]
- Frag Grenade
- Sleeping Quarters

⑤ Hidden Valley Bunker (West)

Enter and head down the stairs and open the Blast Doors. This lower chamber is filled with scattered (and giant) immovable containers. At the far end is a Blast Door, and an intercom. Speaking into it has you talking to yourself again. You can:

Unlock the Blast Door [Very Hard], and enter the chamber beyond.

Recite the password, which you may have found on the corpses of three sets of Paladins across the Wasteland. Consult Side Quest: Still in the Dark for more details.

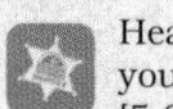

Head down here with Veronica (who joins you if you visit her at the 188 Trading Post [5.02]).

Either option allows you to progress two Side Quests: Still in the Dark, and I Could Make You Care. Beyond the first Blast Door is a second, unfamiliar door type, leading into Hidden Valley Bunker L1.

HIDDEN VALLEY BUNKER L1

Hidden Valley Bunker L1

Ⓐ Door to Hidden Valley Bunker

① Entrance Chamber

You are stopped here by Paladin Ramos, and report to Elder McNamara here, as part of Side Quest: Still in the Dark. If Free Quest: Brotherhood Bond is active, there's ammunition inside an Ammo Box here, restocked as part of Free Quest: Brotherhood Bond, I.

- Ammo Box Ammunition

② Security Chamber

Paladin Ramos, the head of security for the Brotherhood of Steel, resides here. You can ask a variety of questions, but check his terminal [Very Easy] if you want to incur his wrath. The following messages (recent thoughts from Ramos) are available. You can also Hack into the wall terminal [Hard] and disengage the turrets on this floor, or change their targeting parameters (even better!) so they attack the Brotherhood! Kill Ramos, and he has a key on him, as well as some excellent equipment.

- > Read Journal 651
- > Read Journal 652
- > Read Journal 653
- Quest Item: Hidden Valley Bunker Key

③ (Upper and Lower) Dormitory

Note the grating underneath, which leads to a lower sub-floor where Brotherhood of Steel personnel also access. Stealing isn't tolerated

- Brotherhood Footlocker Items (16)
- Sleeping Quarters

Ⓑ Ⓒ Ⓓ Stairs Between Grating

④ (Upper and Lower) Senior Scribe Schuler's Office

Schuler is usually in her office or sleeping nearby, and you can ask her about the goings on in the Bunker as part of Side Quest: Still in the Dark, getting information on dissent for Head Paladin Hardin. Schuler is also an accomplished doctor. Check her plastic waste bin for a Skill Book. Access her terminal to read Journal Entries, and sever your Reputation if you're seen.

> Journal Entry 01
> Journal Entry 260
> Journal Entry 261

- Healer: Senior Scribe Schuler [29/31]
- Skill Book: Nikola Tesla and You [Energy Weapons] [3/4] [2/6]

5 (Upper and Lower) Shooting Range

You can aim at the Super Mutant dummies at the far end, as long as you're using your own weapons and ammunition.

6 (Upper and Lower) Equipment Depot

Knight Torres guards this location, and you can't purchase any of the impressive array of technology without first raising your Reputation with the Brotherhood of Steel to "Liked" or better, and you've agreed to help the elder find his lost patrols as part of Side Quest: Still in the Dark. You can then access "lesser wares." For access to purchasing all of the Brotherhood's items, complete the Side Quest: Still in the Dark, and then become a member of the Brotherhood of Steel after completing Side Quests: Eyesight to the Blind, or Tend to Your Business. Torres is also missing a Laser Pistol; consult the Free Quest for more information. Return it, and she repairs some items for free!

- Trader: Knight Torres [27/33]
- Trader: Knight Torres Upgrades [Explosives and Guns] [8/10]
- Repairer: Knight Torres [Skill 100] [8/9]

The door under the grating requires the Depot Key, which is only available if you Pickpocket Knight Torres; no mean feat, but possible! This allows you to steal the following items:

- T-45d Power Armor
- T-45d Power Helmet
- Laser Rifle
- Plasma Rifle
- Ammo Box Ammunition (7)

7 (Upper) Dining Room

There's items in the two fridges, and rad-free water in the fountain.

8 9 (Lower) Under Dorms

Looking for a particular Brotherhood of Steel member? They may be sleeping here.

- Sleeping Quarters

10 (Lower) Eastern Dorms

You may find initiates and others sleeping here. One of them may be Apprentice Watkins, who you can quiz at length about the Brotherhood of Steel, and even the battle at HELIOS One [5.13].

11 (Lower) Lorenzo's Under Dorm

This place is spartan except for a terminal [Average], which has some of Senior Knight Lorenzo's Journal Entries. These may help if you're siding with Head Paladin Hardin.

> Journal Entry 745
> Journal Entry 746
> Journal Entry 747

- Sleeping Quarters

12 13 14 15 (Lower) Under Dorms

Looking for a particular Brotherhood of Steel member? They may be sleeping here.

- Sleeping Quarters

16 (Upper) School

Where Initiates are taught the primary elements of gun metals and other useful knowledge.

17 18 (Upper) Restrooms

Rad-free water can be drunk here.

E Door to Hidden Valley Bunker L2

Hidden Valley Bunker L2

F Door to Hidden Valley Bunker L1

19 Connecting Chamber

This is a thoroughfare during the Side Quests; you may be stopped by Head Paladin Hardin here. Pickpocket or kill him, and he has a keycard you can utilize.

- Quest Item: Head Paladin's Keycard

20 Command Center

Elder McNamara surveys the Mojave Wasteland from this circular epicenter of the bunker structure. He is the most important and senior member of the Brotherhood of Steel, and has a wealth of knowledge you can talk to him about. He's also a major player in all four related Side Quests. Pickpocket or kill him, and he has a keycard you can utilize.

- Quest Item: Elder's Keycard
- Unique Item: Brotherhood Elder's Robe [77/95]

21 Elder McNamara's Bedroom

Power Armor is placed on a table along with weaponry here.

- Super Sledge
- T-45d Power Armor
- T-45d Power Helmet
- Plasma Pistol
- Plasma Rifle
- Sleeping Quarters

22 Head Paladin Hardin's Bedroom

A sparse affair; Hardin sometimes sits and contemplates the future of the Brotherhood from the desk here.

- Sleeping Quarters

23 Scribe Ibsen's Bedroom

- Sleeping Quarters

24 Data System Chamber

Scribe Ibsen is having a devil of a time with a hacker's program infecting the numerous wall terminals in this lattice-shaped chamber. Speak with him as part of Side Quest: Still in the Dark, and fix these error messages.

25 VR Chamber

The VR pods are currently (and permanently) offline, but Head Scribe Taggart is here, and can speak to you during Side Quest: Still in the Dark. Pickpocket or kill him, and he has a keycard you can utilize. Apprentice Watkins is sometimes here, too. She has a lot to say. Mainly about herself. On the perimeter wall of this location is a Self-destruct Authorization Terminal, and a Self-destruct Terminal [Very Hard]. Should the Faction you're working with want complete annihilation of the Brotherhood, and you're okay with the plan, this is where you can make a clandestine attempt at destroying the entire Bunker.

- Quest Item: Head Scribe's Keycard

26 Head Scribe Taggart's Bedroom

- Sleeping Quarters

27 Forge and Operations Chamber

The delicate study of technology, the running of the Bunker's life-support systems, and tinkering with weapons still malfunctioning are all taken care of here under the competent gaze of Senior Knight Lorenzo. He's in desperate need of some items too, as part of Side Quest: Still in the Dark, and is also very interested in the technology of ED-E, if you brought him as part of Side Quest: ED-E My Love. Feel free to use the benches in this chamber, and speak to Lorenzo about his thoughts and feelings. Steal stuff only if you want to harm your Reputation (or if you want to Pickpocket Lorenzo's Zap Glove).

- Workbench [31/41]
- Reloading Bench [29/36]
- Scrap Metal (9)
- Jammed Minigun
- Malfunctioning Super Sledge
- Broken Laser Rifle
- Broken Recon Armor (2)
- Broken Power Armor (2)
- Broken Power Helmet (2)
- Zap Glove

Free Quest: Pistol Packing

Speak with Knight Torres at the Equipment Depot, and she's one Laser Pistol short. This won't sit well with Head Paladin Hardin, so she asks you to help, and hands over a Note. Step into the range next door, and ask the Paladin there if he knows about the missing weapon. He tells you Initiate Stanton checked the gun out, but checked it in again a day later.

- Note: Missing Laser Pistol

Locate Initiate Stanton, who may be wandering Bunker L1, or sleeping in one of the dorms. Speak to him, and he tells you that him and Apprentice Watkins snuck outside into Scorpion Gulch [5.12] to shoot Bark Scorpions, and lost the weapon. To continue the Quest, ask Stanton to be specific about where he dropped it. He tells you it was near a "big rock" with a "corpse near it." You can also talk to Watkins too, but she's not concerned with the situation.

Head out and brave the Bark Scorpions of the Gulch [5.12], and search for this mound of rocks with the Wastelander corpse. The Laser Pistol is atop the rocks. Grab it! Return to Torres, and present her with the Pistol. She's duly thankful, and in return gives you a Tri-Beam Laser Rifle. Torres is also happy to mend any of the weapons you own to get more practice, too.

- Quest Item: Missing Laser Pistol
- Tri-Beam Laser Rifle
- Brotherhood of Steel Fame Gained!
- Repairer: Knight Torres

Free Quest: Brotherhood Bond, I

Become Idolized with the Brotherhood, and a member of the this subterranean family, an initiate will greet you upon your return, and let you know there's a collection of recycled Energy Weapon ammunition, which is restocked every 24 hours. Grab what you need, and come back for more when you need to.

- Energy Ammo

Free Quest: Brotherhood Bond, II

Should you become increasingly helpful to the Brotherhoods' plight, it begins to pay dividends. Continue to earn Followers of the Apocalypse Fame, and once you complete Side Quest: Still in the Dark, you're presented with a special key. This opens the door to the Brotherhood of Steel Safehouse [3.06], where you can rest, and relax. Consult that location for more information.

- Brotherhood of Steel Safehouse Key

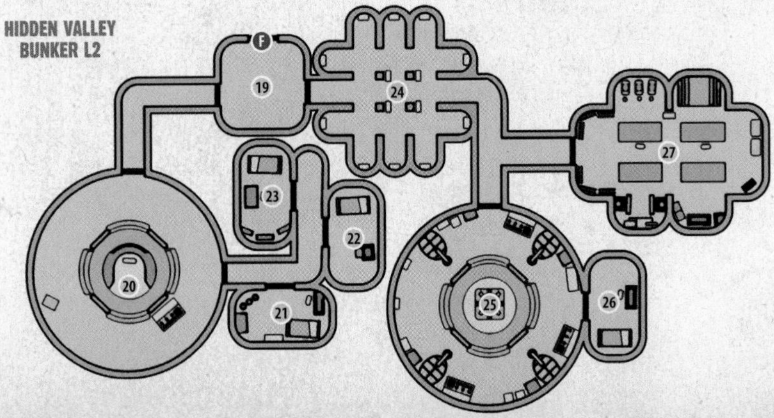

HIDDEN VALLEY BUNKER L2

F 19 24 27 23 22 20 21 25 26

[5.12] Scorpion Gulch

- Side Quest: Still in the Dark
- Free Quest: Pistol Packing
- Threat Level: ●●●●●
- Faction: Mutated Animal, Abomination
  - Entity: Radscorpion
  - Entity: Bark Scorpion
- Dangers: Radiation
- Collectibles: Caravan Cards [24/30]
- Guns and Ammo
- Radio Signal [Black Mountain]
- Quest Item

Although this maze-like warren appears incredibly complicated to traverse, the rock passages lead to one of three different locations; Hidden Valley to the west, Black Mountain to the north, and HELIOS One to the east. The rocks are too steep to climb to the REPCONN Test Site [5.17]. The entire area has Radscorpions, and the smaller, hallucinatory Bark Scorpions to contend with.

1 HELIOS One Access Point

This rocky ravine has a metal ramp up to a Grave you and rob, and a dead Prospector to search. Among the usual weapons and items, you'll find cards on his corpse.

- Caravan Cards [24/30]

2 South Junction

Check a dead Wastelander in the middle of the junction for some common items. If Free Quest: Pistol Packing is active, the missing Laser Pistol is on the rock here, too.

- Quest Item: Missing Laser Pistol

3 Hidden Valley Access Point #1

4 Winding Gully Junction

Along the east path, which winds around to the north, you can scramble up gravel and stand on the mesa in the middle of both paths.

5 Hidden Valley Access Point #2

From Location #4, there's a couple of parallel paths, all leading to another opening in the eastern perimeter mesh fence to Hidden Valley.

6 Abominable Crater

Leading to Black Mountain's switchbacks or a cunning path right up to Tabitha's Broadcast Building, this area is dominated by a large crater, and a host of disgusting Centaurs. The bottom of the crater (which is irradiated!) contains the corpses of two Brotherhood Paladins.

- Note: Mission Statement CB-03
- T-45d Power Armor and Helmet (2)
- Laser Rifle and Ammo (2)

SCORPION GULTCH EXTERIOR

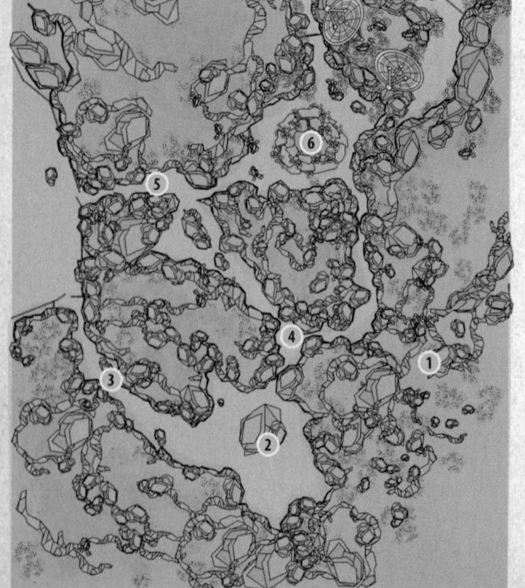

[5.13] HELIOS One ●

- Side Quest: ED-E My Love
- Side Quest: I Could Make You Care
- Side Quest: Sunshine Boogie
- Side Quest: That Lucky Old Sun
- Threat Level: ●●●●●
- Faction: NCR
  - Entity: Lieutenant Haggerty
  - Entity: NCR Trooper
  - Entity: NCR Guard Dog
  - Entity: Sentry Bot
  - Entity: Mister Gutsy
  - Entity: Turret
  - Entity: PYTHON
  - Entity: Fantastic
  - Entity: Ignacio Rivas
- Fame/Infamy
- Dangers:
  - Traps
  - Mines
- Collectibles:
  - Skill Book [Medicine] [3/4] [3/6]
  - Magazine [Repair] [27/27] [1-2/10]
  - Magazine [Science] [21/23] [1-2/10]
- Guns and Ammo
- Health, Chems, or Water
- Highly Visible
- Interior Exploration
- Radio Signal [Black Mountain]
- Sleeping Quarters
- Quest Item

Constructed Pre-War by Poseidon Energy, HELIOS One is a concentrated solar energy plant consisting of an enormous array of reflectors and the power plant itself (housing steam turbines and all of the machines required to transform the energy into usable electricity). The plant has been damaged extensively since the war (including recent incursions between the NCR and the remaining Brotherhood of Steel forces in the Mojave). Now, only a third of its reflectors still fully intact and able to fully rotate. To make matters worse, various issues in the plant itself make the energy transfer inefficient, meaning the plant is operating far under potential. NCR doesn't possess the scientific knowledge to get the plant in ideal shape and both the Followers of the Apocalypse and Brotherhood of Steel are reticent to help for political reasons. Due to its fragility, Caesar has no serious interest in HELIOS One, but his troops perform occasional raids on it to keep NCR's forces spread out.

HELIOS One Exterior

A Door to HELIOS One Power Plant

This is the main entrance to the plant. It is usually wise to speak with Lt. Haggerty first.

1 Main Entrance

The main entrance to the building is guarded by a small NCR force under the command of Lieutenant Haggerty. She stops you, and asks your business. You can:

Lie and tell her you're with the NCR and ask if she needs help. This begins Side Quest: That Lucky Old Sun.

Tell her you want to investigate the place.

Ask for Food.

Attack, either after a fear-inducing utterance, or after you start hacking or shooting.

B Door to HELIOS One Power Plant [Very Easy]

Although you can Sneak in via a side Blast Door, you risk annoying the NCR.

F Door to HELIOS One Power Plant (Interior)

You emerge from this door on the other side of the perimeter fence, allowing access to the following locations:

HELIOS ONE EXTERIOR

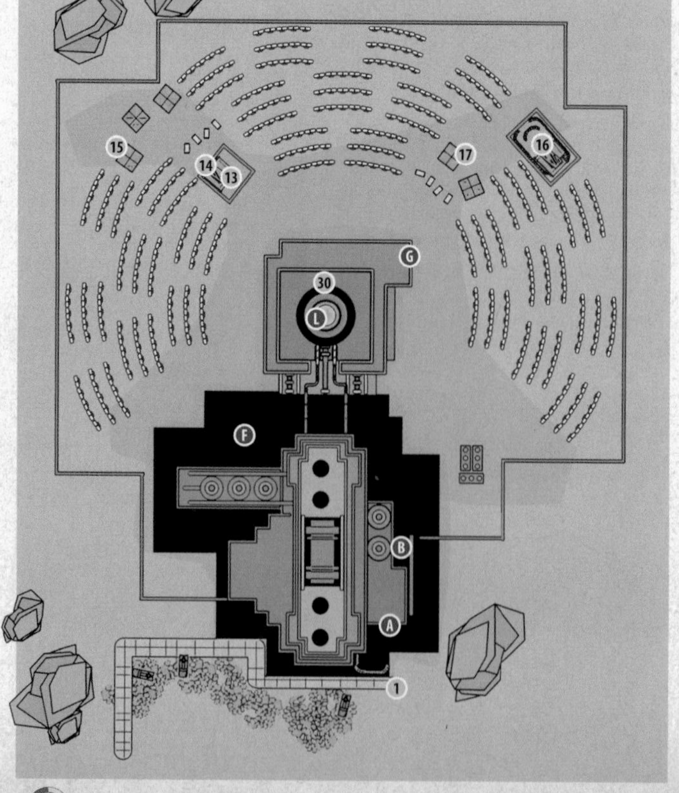

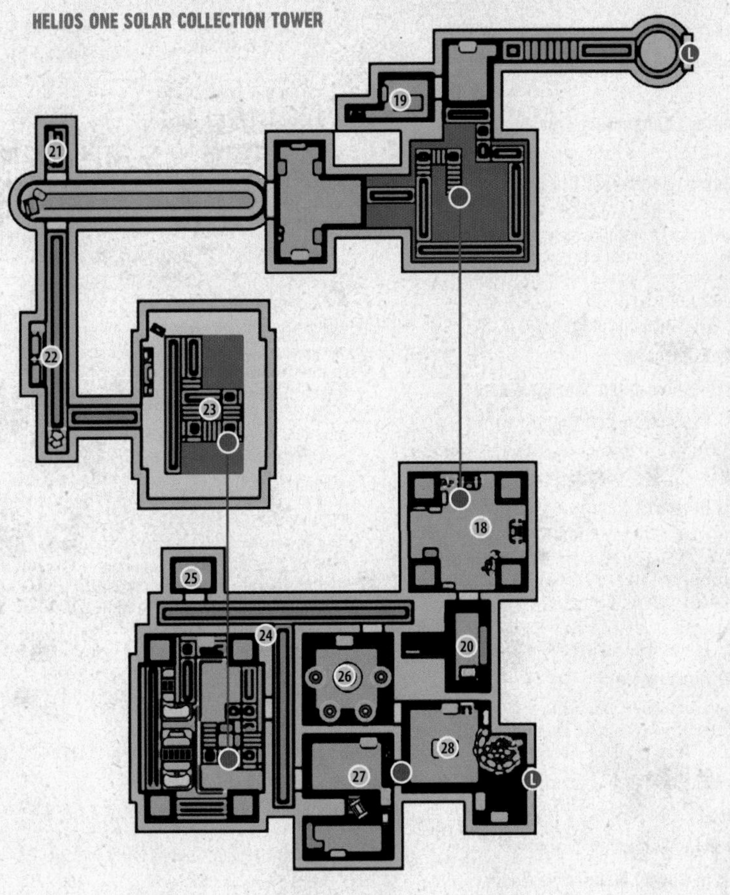

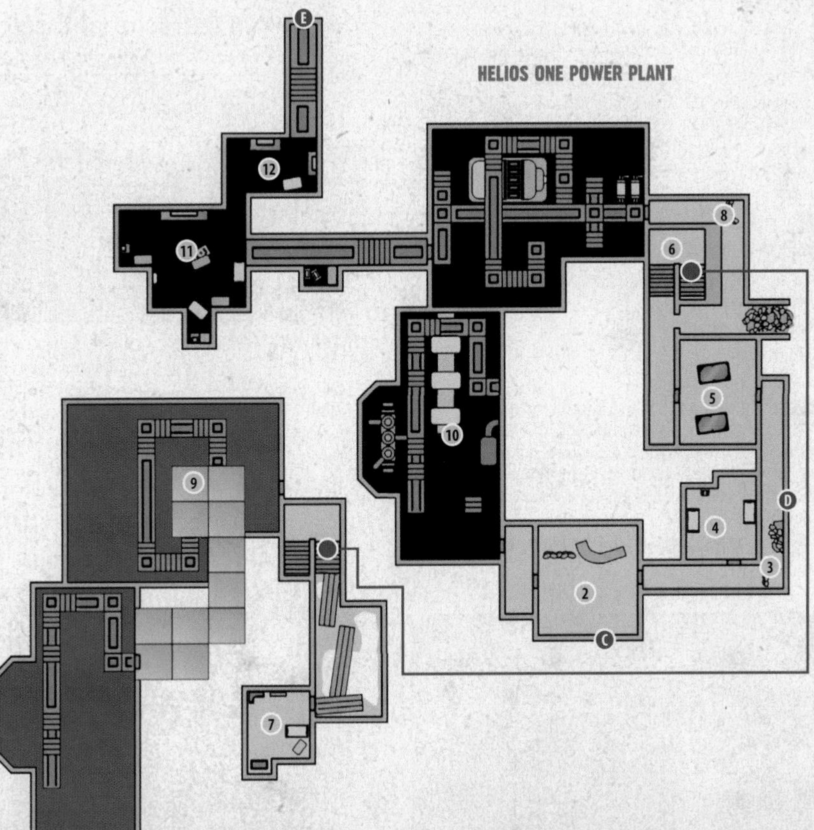

13 Western Reflector Control [Hard]

The solar panel array is an impressive feat of engineering, but is devoid of items except at this location; beware of extensive traps! Disarm Frag Mines, Bear Traps, and a Tripwire rigged to a Shotgun. Then access the Control Terminal [Hard]. If you have the password, this terminal does not need to be hacked. In addition, behind the shack the Control Terminal is under are some tents with the following:

> Reset Mainframe Connection: Accessed as part of Side Quest: That Lucky Old Sun.

> ARCHIMEDES Testing: Previously available to read.

> Upcoming Visit: Previously available to read.

- Frag Mines (3)
- Sleeping Quarters
- Ammo Box Ammunition (2)

14 Broken Solar Reflector #1

At this, and any other Broken Solar Reflector in this area, you can activate it to salvage some of the array's parts. This is useful to do as part of Side Quest: Sunshine Boogie, or whenever you wish.

- Quest Item: Solar Array Parts

15 Broken Solar Reflector #2

- Quest Item: Solar Array Parts

16 Eastern Reflector Control [Hard]

In front of the shack the Control Terminal is under are a couple of tents with mattresses and ammo. Then access the Control Terminal [Hard] inside the gated and sandbagged area. If you have the password, this terminal does not need to be hacked.

> Reset Mainframe Connection: Accessed as part of Side Quest: That Lucky Old Sun.

> ARCHIMEDES Testing: Previously available to read.

> Upcoming Visit: Previously available to read.

- Ammo Box Ammunition [Easy]

17 Broken Solar Reflector #3

- Quest Item: Solar Array Parts

G Door to Solar Collection Tower

L Door to HELIOS One Observation Level

30 (Upper) Reflector Control Panel

Located at the top of the accessible part of the tower, use this to focus the reflector array and attempt a massive impulse of power, during either related Side Quest.

HELIOS One Power Plant (Interior)

C Door to Mojave Wasteland

2 Reception

A small defensive position and two NCR Troopers guard this location. There's also a desk terminal; log onto PoseidoNet for the following messages:

> ARCHIMEDES Testing: Regarding a past test of this epic laser system.

> Results: Aside from collateral damage, the test is deemed successful.

> Upcoming Visit: From Brig. Gen. Scott Lowe of the U.S. Army to an indefinite stay.

> "Can I Tell Him?": An excerpt from a Poseidon Energy Publication. Short answer; "no, you can't."

- Sack (3) and Cabinet Items
- Ammo

3 Connecting Corridor

Debris-filled from past battles with the Brotherhood of Steel, this allows access from the exterior.

- Carton of Cigarettes (2)
- Basketball
- Ammo

D Door to Mojave Wasteland

4 Small Dorm

Expect a couple of NCR Troopers in here. There's rad-free water from a fountain in this room.

- Sack Items (2)
- Sleeping Quarters

5 (Lower) Pool Room and (Upper) Hallway

You can drop down here from above.

6 (Upper and Lower) Stairs

Take these to reach the Upper Hallway.

7 (Upper) Office

This upper office is worth visiting during your Side Questing, as a Holotape provides a password for an otherwise-difficult Eastern Reflector Control Terminal (Location #16). Check the terminal for the same messages as the reception terminal, and don't forget the Skill Book on the bed.

- Skill Book: D.C. Journal of Internal Medicine [Medicine] [3/4] [3/6]
- Footlocker and Sack Items
- Quest Item: Eastern Reflector Control Terminal Password
- Sleeping Quarters

8 (Lower) Connecting Corridor

- Ammo

9 (Lower and Upper) Generator Chamber #1

Head up into the enclosed control room for a bunk bed area, and a second blast door; this leading to Location #10.

- Footlocker Items

10 (Lower and Upper) Generator Chamber #2

Access this area from the Reception (Location #2), or the previous Generator Chamber. A Trooper and Dog usually patrol here.

- Teddy Bear
- Scrap Metal
- Ammo

11 Fantastic's Laboratory

Run by part-time scientist and full-time grifter, speaking to Fantastic at this location is a major part of the start of Side Quest: That Lucly Old Sun. Through a competent and lengthy conversation (or Pickpocketing), you can obtain something of worth from him:

- Quest Item: Western Reflector Control Terminal Password
- Sleeping Quarters

12 Ignacio Rivas' Laboratory

Ignacio is a lot more competent, but a lot less confident than Fantastic, and he hopes you can divert the power of this Facility to the Followers of the Apocalypse's structures, as part of the Side Quest. Additional chats or Pickpocketing allows another Password to be uncovered. Also speak to him about ARCHIMEDES to uncover more of ED-E's recordings, during Side Quest: ED-E My Love.

- Quest Item: Eastern Reflector Control Terminal Password

E Door to Mojave Wasteland (HELIOS One Exterior)

HELIOS One Power Plant (Interior)

H Door to Mojave Wasteland (HELIOS One Exterior)

18 (Upper and Lower) North Stairwell

Enter the Turret Control Room first. Then, from the entrance (with the water fountain you can drink rad-free from), you can battle past the Sentry Bots and down to debris-strewn lower level, and storage room (Location #20).

- Magazine: Programmer's Digest [Science] [21/23] [1/10]

19 (Upper) Turret Control Room

Beware four Frag Mines (on the floor and on the shelving), then access the Turret Control System Terminal [Easy]. Hack it to turn off the turrets in this structure.

> Re-configure Targeting Parameters: Which causes the turrets to attack you, or the Sentry Bots.
> Deactivate Turret System
> System Information

20 (Lower) Storage Room

- Sack Items
- Wall Safe Items [Average]
- Pulse Grenade (2)

21 (Descending) Tunnel Storage Room

- First Aid Box
- Scrap Metal

22 (Descending) Connecting Corridor

- Sleeping Quarters

23 (Descending) Southwest Stairwell

Descend down while staying on the gantries, pausing at the perimeter walkway halfway down to grab a Magazine from a table. There are robots to face, and rad-free water to drink from a sink at the bottom floor.

- Magazine: Fixin' Things [Repair] [27/27] [2/10]

24 (Lowest) T-Passage

25 (Lowest) Rubble-filled Storage Room

26 (Lowest) Protectron Pod Room

Four Protectrons are in this chamber.

- First Aid Box

27 (Lowest) Research Room

There's a modicum of junk strewn about, but there are two ID Cards that make controlling a robot in a future chamber (Location #29) much easier. The door to the kitchenette is locked [Average].

- Quest Item: Poseidon Energy Employee ID Card (2)

28 (Lowest) Kitchenette

Parts of this room have been filled with rubble. Check the elevator up to the Observation Level, and a door back to the Research Room [Average].

I Door to HELIOS One Observation Level

HELIOS One Observation Level (Interior)

J Door to Solar Collection Tower

29 (Lower and Upper) Mainframe Room

This has a large mainframe computer, which is currently lacking power. Close by is an auxiliary generator. You can:

Use a piece of Scrap Metal and your know-how, and connect the generator, improving the output bandwidth.

- Head upstairs, and inspect PYTHON; a maintenance robot with a keycard slot. You can:

Hardwire the robot to run on autopilot.

Fit the Poseidon Energy ID Card into the slot. In either case, PYTHON fixes the generator for you.

With the mainframe computer online, you can view the following:

> Configure Power Grid: See below.
> Initial Trials
> ARCHIMEDES Testing

Consult Side Quest: That Lucky Old Sun, as well as Side Quest: I Could Make You Care, for all pertinent plans relating to powering this massive solar array up. Then exit to complete the tour, back into the Mojave Wasteland (but atop the solar tower).

K Door to Mojave Wasteland (HELIOS One Exterior)

[5.14] Gibson Scrap Yard

- Side Quest: Come Fly With Me
- Side Quest: ED-E My Love
- Side Quest: Nothin' But a Hound Dog
- Threat Level: ●●●●●
- Faction: Prospector/Novac
  - Entity: Old Lady Gibson
  - Entity: Audaz, Basura, Colmillo, Fiel, Reina, and Rey
- Services:
  - Repairer [9/9]
  - Trader [28/33]
- Crafting:
  - Workbench [32/41]
  - Upgrade [9/10]
- Collectibles:
  - Caravan Cards [25/30]
  - Sunset Sarsaparilla Star Cap [74/100]
  - Unique Weapon [31/42]
- Guns and Ammo
- Interior Exploration
- Radio Signal [Black Mountain]
- Quest Item

Old Lady Gibson has been running this modest scrapyard for the last few years since the passing of her husband. All she has now are memories, and a collection of hounds that she dotes on. Inside the garage is where Reina and Rey stay, and Old Lady Gibson rests. There's a metal box [Average] to open, either via Bobby Pins and talent, or by acquiring Gibson's through Pickpocketing or killing her. The box contains the Thrust Control Modules; vital for a Side Quest if it is active. Unless you're heartless, there's no reason to get on the bad side of Gibson. Speak to her, and she can tell you about HELIOS One, as well as Repairing your items or Trading with you; she's one of the best in the Mojave! Finally, kill Gibson to take her Unique Sawed-Off Shotgun; Big Boomer.

- Workbench [32/41]
- Old Lady Gibson's Key
- Repairer: Old Lady Gibson [Skill 65] [9/9]
- Trader: Old Lady Gibson [28/33]
- Trader: Old Lady Gibson Upgrades [Energy Weapons] [9/10]
- Trader (Old Lady Gibson): Caravan Cards [25/30]
- Sunset Sarsaparilla Star Cap [74/100]
- Quest Item: Thrust Control Modules
- Unique Weapon: Big Boomer [31/42]

[5.15] NCR Correctional Facility ●

See map on the following page

- Side Quest: I Fought the Law
- Side Quest: My Kind of Town
- Side Quest: Still in the Dark
- Free Quest: Eddie's Emissary
- Threat Level: ●●●●●
- Faction: Powder Ganger
  - Entity: Dawes
  - Entity: Powder Ganger
  - Entity: Carter
  - Entity: Hannigan
  - Entity: Scrambler
  - Entity: Eddie
- Fame/Infamy
- Services: Trader [29/33]
- Crafting:
  - Campfire [79/109]
  - Workbench [33/41]
- Collectibles:
  - Caravan Cards [26/30]
  - Sunset Sarsaparilla Star Cap [75/100]
  - Skill Book [Speech] [3/4] [4/6]
  - Magazine [Explosives] [11/12] [3-4/10]
  - Magazine [Melee Weapons] [9/9] [3-4/10]
  - Unique Item [78/95]
- Area Is Locked
- Guns and Ammo
- Health, Chems, or Water
- Highly Visible
- Interior Exploration
- Lots O' Caps
- Radio Signal [Black Mountain]
- Sleeping Quarters
- Quest Item

Slightly ironically, after

NCR CORRECTIONAL FACILITY

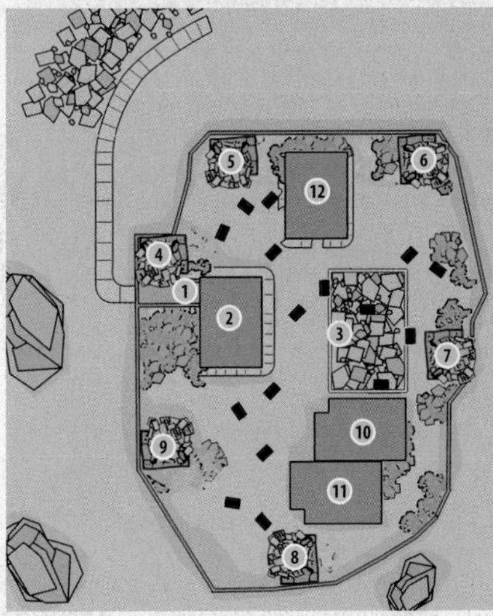

breaking out of this very facility, which used to be operated by the NCR, the dregs of humanity known as the Powder Gangers decided to form a Faction and stay in this heavily fortified place, with plans of expansion. They already established camps outside the prison (North [5.10], South [4.15], East [5.16], and West [4.13]), but infighting between the violent and possibly Chem-addled leadership has caused splinter groups to form. The NCR is still too widely stretched by the Legion to form a force that can take back the place.

1 Dawes on the Doors

A man named Dawes mans the doors to the Visitor Center. You can ask about him, the break-out, and how to get in; it's either pay up (100 Caps) or shoot everyone in blue (plummeting your reputation with the Gangers).

2 Visitor Center

The Ganger in here are threatening, but not violent unless you stay around in here; in which case your Fame plummets and they become hostile. You can speak to Meyers about his possible role as Primm's new Sheriff.

- Sunset Sarsaparilla Star Cap [75/100]
- Magazine: Tæles of Chivalrie [Melee Weapons] [9/9] [3/10]

3 Prison Yard

The following guard towers surround the premises, too (some of the items in the tower may need to be stolen, and some have a Powder Ganger guard):

- Campfire [79/109]
- Workbench [33/41]
- Explosives Box Ammunition
- Machete

4 Guard Tower #1

- Ammo
- Sleeping Quarters

5 Guard Tower #2

- Varmint Rifle and Ammo

6 Guard Tower #3

- Super Stimpak
- Stimpak (2)

7 Guard Tower #4

- Ammo
- Food and Dirty Water

8 Guard Tower #6

- Caps (5)
- First Aid Box

9 Guard Tower #7

- Ammo Box Ammunition [Very Easy]
- Chem and Food

10 Cell Block A

This place has been wrecked during the riot. There's a few wandering and slumbering Gangers to Pickpocket and/or Murder. Check the explosives crate in one cell. The southeast cell (with the door still on its hinges) has a better haul:

- Explosives Box Ammo
- Grenade Box Ammo
- Mine Box Ammo [Easy]
- Armor Case (2) [1 = Average]
- Magazine: Patriot's Cookbook [Explosives] [11/12] [4/10]

11 Cell Block B and Carter the Trader

This is where Carter, one of the Powder Gangers with an enterprising streak, runs a small Trader's business. Before you meet him, check the cells for a few Chems and a Footlocker [Very Easy]. The only locked cell door [Easy] contains a stack of Caps inside an Ammo Box, and Schematics for Powder Charge, so expect Carter to go ballistic if you try unlocking it. You can ask Carter about himself and the prison, before Trading.

- Unique Item [Schematic] Powder Charge [78/95]
- Caps (150+)
- Trader: Carter [29/33]
- Trader: Carter: Caravan Cards [26/30]

12 NCR CF Administration Building

Eddie and his cohorts run the place from here. Check the metal shelves in the entrance room for a gun case, and speak with Hannigan who's in the "surgery" across from the entrance. You can ask him about himself and the current situation, but he isn't prepared to heal you. Check out his room for some key items (which you can only steal). The rest of the downstairs rooms have little to salvage (except some Sarsaparilla bottles from a Vending Machine).

- Gun Case Items
- Doctor's Bag (2)
- First Aid Box [Easy]

Upstairs in the hall is a Gun Cabinet [Average], and a ruined office to the northeast with a Skill Book you must snag.

- Skill Book: Lying, Congressional Style [Speech] [3/4] [4/6]

Inside the Warden's Room is Eddie, who you can talk at length to about the breakout and Cooke, and begin Side Quest: I Fought the Law. Next to him is Scrambler, who's a nasty piece of work. Behind him is a wall safe [Average] with a large number of Caps (which you can't get without the Gangers going hostile). Eddie has a key and Plasma Pistol on him:

- Wall Safe Items
- Administration Key
- Caps (200+)
- Plasma Pistol

The Administration Key opens the locked office room to the southeast [Average] containing Ammo and Caps. Check one of the metal boxes for a random Magazine.

- Explosives Crate Ammo
- Magazine
- Ammo and Caps (20+)

Free Quest: Eddie's Emissary

If you complete Side Quest: I Fought the Law, and side with the Powder Gangers, winning over Eddie's suspicious mind (and increasing your Fame among them); the Powder Gangers are no longer hostile to you; as they usually are when encountered away from the NCR Correctional Facility.

[5.16] Powder Ganger Camp East

- Threat Level:
- Faction: Powder Ganger
  - Entity: Powder Ganger
- Fame/Infamy
- Crafting: Campfire [80/109]
- Collectibles: Hollowed-Out Rock [29/42]
- Guns and Ammo
- Health, Chems, or Water
- Radio Signal [Black Mountain]
- Sleeping Quarters
- Wasteland Vegetation

Approach it from the southwest to locate a Hollowed-Out Rock near a Honey Mesquite tree. Lightly fortified, and with only a trio of Gangers to worry about, these are easy pickings.

- Hollowed-Out Rock [29/42]
- Campfire [80/109]
- Purified Water and Chems
- Healing Powder
- Ammo Box Ammunition (2)
- Sleeping Quarters

[5.17] REPCONN Test Site

See maps on the following page

- Side Quest: Come Fly With Me
- Threat Level:
- Faction: Ghoul / Nightkin
  - Entity: Jason Bright
  - Entity: Chris Haversam
  - Entity: Davison
  - Entity: Antler
  - Entity: Harland
  - Entity: Ghoul
  - Entity: Nightkin
- Crafting:
  - Reloading Bench [30/36]
  - Workbench [34/41]
  - Workbench [35/41]
  - Workbench [36/41]
- Dangers:
  - Traps
  - Radiation
  - Mines
- Collectibles:
  - Unique Item [79/95]
  - Unique Item [80/95]
  - Unique Item [81/95]
  - Unique Item [82/95]
  - Unique Item [83/95]
  - Unique Item [84/95]
  - Unique Item [85/95]
  - Unique Item [86/95]
  - Unique Item [87/95]
  - Unique Item [88/95]
  - Unique Item [89/95]
  - Unique Item [90/95]
- Area Is Locked
- Guns and Ammo
- Health, Chems, or Water
- Highly Visible
- Interior Exploration
- Lots O' Caps
- Radio Signal [Black Mountain]
- Sleeping Quarters
- Quest Item

The remains of the old REPCONN (Rocket Engineering Production Company of Nevada) test plant, along with its landmark rocket launch dome, have sat idle over the years, and are now home to Feral Ghouls who come to terrorize the inhabitants of nearby Novac [5.18]. However, within the facility, there's a prolonged stalemate going on between a band of Nightkin, devolved from Marcus' forces up at Jacobstown [1.10] and lead by a deranged man-mountain named Davison. They are attempting to locate shipments of Stealth Boys. The (marginally) sane ghouls are led by an intelligent, messianic glowing ghoul who dreams of escaping with his followers in the plant's remaining rockets.

Test Site Exterior Entrance

The site itself is completely surrounded on three sides by rugged and inaccessible mountains; you reach it via the road from Novac, passing through the REPCONN Test Site Checkpoint [5.S12]. The rocket dome and radar dishes to the south are unable to be reached. There is a hatch in the ground to the basement, but this is only accessible from the ground to the surface. The still-impressive site building is teeming with Ghouls, and has a life-size rocket sculpture in front of the main steps. A scattered corpse of a Ghoul with Bright Brotherhood Robes lies in the ground.

- Bright Brotherhood Robe

To the right (eastern) side of the building is a gated area, allowing you to creep up through the fallen sections of wall and enter without engaging the Ghouls. Or, you can scale the rocky bluffs east of the base to snipe the Ghouls. To the southwest is an irradiated sunken dry pond with a skeleton near some Chems. To the west is a collapsed tunnel and access around the rear perimeter, to a corner of broken fencing, and the northwest entrance to the interior.

- Bright Brotherhood Robe (2)
- Ammo Box Ammunition (4)
- Machete

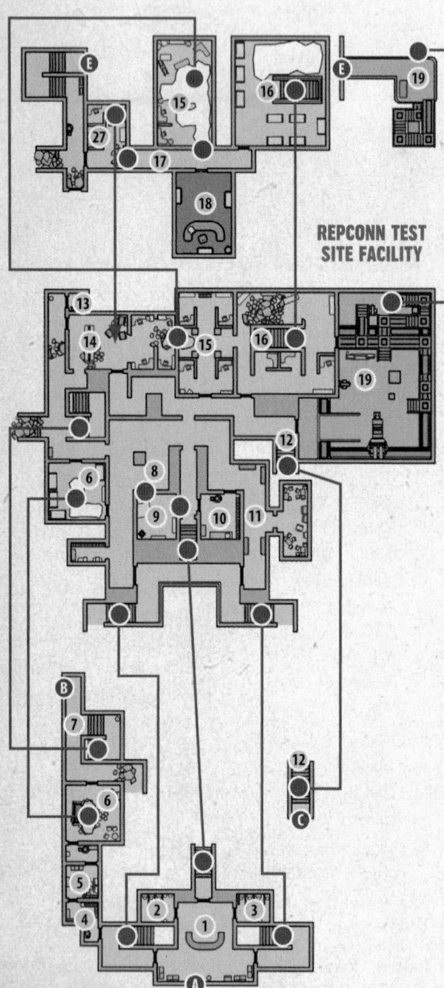

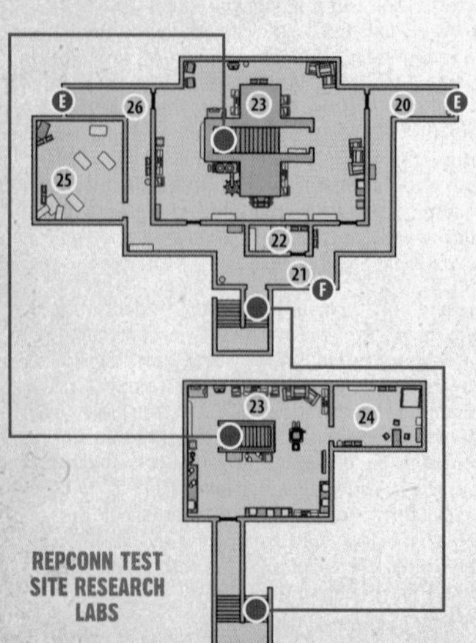

REPCONN Facility (Interior)

A Door to REPCONN Test Site (Exterior)

1 (Lower and Upper) Reception

Consult Side Quest: Come Fly With Me for more information. There are multiple exits from this chamber, and a balcony (with two dead robed Ghouls) to drop down from (which cannot be accessed from the ground). Check the Vending Machine, and check the dead Nightkin and Ghoul here. There's a locked Door [Easy] in the north wall behind the desk allowing access to stairs to the upper floor. Finally, you can utilize the intercom to speak to the Ghoul at any time.

- Bright Brotherhood Robe (3)
- Stealth Boy

Caution Expect almost constant Feral Ghoul attack throughout this Facility. Also note that this location has three floors; Lower, Upper, and Top.

2 3 (Lower) Restroom (Gentlemen and Ladies)

The drinkable water here is irradiated.

- First Aid Box (2)

4 (Lower) Cleaning Closet

- Scrap Metal (2)
- Carton of Cigarettes

5 (Lower) Pantry

There are scattered Bottle Caps on the ground, empty bottles, and Food in the fridge.

- Carton of Cigarettes

6 (Lower and Upper) Pool Room and Upstairs Dorms

There's a Vending Machine, and a partially collapsed ceiling, allowing access between the floors.

- Footlocker Items (2)
- Sleeping Quarters

B Door to REPCONN Test Site (Exterior)

7 (Lower) Northwest Entrance Corridor

Whether you entered via this main doors or the northwest entrance, you're given instructions over the intercom by a Ghoul, to head up to the top of the building. This allows a more Sneak-based approach.

8 (Upper) West Hallway

This widens to the north, and is a good thoroughfare to the north.

9 (Upper) Filing Room [Easy]

This is locked via either door. A skeleton is slumped near a Safe [Easy].

- Floor Safe Items [Easy]
- Microfusion Cell (20 x3)
- Hunting Revolver

10 (Upper) Reference Room and Storage

- First Aid Box

11 (Upper) East Hallway

This widens to the north, and has dead Robed Ghouls to search, and a break room to the east with Vending Machines and scattered Caps on the ground.

- Bright Brotherhood Robe (2)

12 (Lower and Upper) Basement Stairs

Accessible from the northeast warehouse and main east-west corridor, learn this location as you'll head down these steps numerous times during Side Quest: Come Fly With Me.

C (Lower) Door to REPCONN Basement [Easy]

You can enter this area independent of the Side Quest if you unlock the door.

13 (Upper) Locked Closet [Easy]

- First Aid Box
  Tool Cabinet Items

14 (Upper) Server Room

Portions of the east wall have collapsed, allowing access across. Above is a hole; which you can drop down from the top floor, after exiting the Research Labs (heading down only).

- Bright Brotherhood Robe

15 (Upper and Top) Office Cubicles

REPCONN Office cubicles sit around a collapsed ceiling section, allowing access up to a top story office, and access to the top corridor via a locked door in the south wall [Very Easy]. Employee terminals are still active, and all bring up the following first two menu options, while one near the Server Room has additional access, and two others on the Upper floor have information on Martin's retirement:

- > Public Kitchen: A clean kitchen is a happy kitchen.
- > Welcome to RobCo!: The RobCo takeover has been finalized.
- > AG%(V$*: A missive about "Stealth Boys."
- > Private Server Access
  - > RobCo Visit: Request for an experiment to go well.
  - > Re: RobCo Visit: Apparently, the test didn't go well.
  - > Re: RobCo Visit: Someone needs to be punished.
- > Martin's Retirement: This is a surprise. Hope there's cake.
- > Cake: Apparently, there is no cake. It is a lie.

16 (Upper and Top) Stairwell and Empty Office; and Dorms

Offices cleared due to downsizing after the RobCo takeover are on the upper floor, around a stairwell up to some dorm bunks, and access to the top floor.

- Footlocker Items (2)
- Sleeping Quarters

17 (Top) Top Corridor

There is an identical corridor below this one; but this is accessed via the stairwell or Office Cubicles, and is the only way to reach the Executive Office. The west end of this corridor is blocked, and cannot be accessed from this direction.

18 (Top) Executive Office

This lavish office has been ransacked, but the Administrator Terminal is still active:

- > Storage Room Terminal
- > Retirement: Cutting remarks from a man named Martin.

- Carton of Cigarettes
- Wall Safe Items [Average]

19 (Upper and Top) Rocket Construction Warehouse

Signs of battling between Nightkin and Ghouls are found on the ground. At the top of the chamber is a covered control area and another Intercom, allowing access into the Research Lab.

- Bright Brotherhood Robe

D Door to REPCONN Research Labs

H Door from REPCONN Research Labs

27 (Top) Top Office

This is only accessible via the Research Labs, and used as a way back down to the Server Room. The other areas (stairs and doorway to the top corridor) are blocked. One of the Employee Terminals near the hole you drop down to reach the Server Room has an additional message:

- > Visitor Policy: According to Steve, only you can prevent corporate espionage!

REPCONN Research Labs (Interior)

E Door to REPCONN Facility

20 (Floor 1) Entrance Corridor (East)

You're greeted by Chris Haversam here, during Side Quest: Come Fly With Me. This corridor winds south and west around the perimeter of this area.

21 (Floor 1) Entrance Corridor (South)

F (Floor 1) Door to REPCONN Test Site

This leads to a tiny observation window in the exterior of the building, where the culmination of Side Quest: Come Fly With Me occurs.

22 (Floor 1) Storage Room

You want your entire party to wear Party Hats, right? This is the place to go!

- Unique Item: Party Hat [79-88/95] (10)
- First Aid Box
- Scrap Metal

23 (Floor 1 and 2) Laboratory

Jason Bright may be wandering this area; the leader of the Brotherhood, and an integral part of Side Quest: Come Fly With Me. Note the two Workbenches (one on each floor), and an upstairs Employee Terminal with an extra message for Martin:

> Retirement: The research staff is sad to see him go under the circumstances.

- Workbench [34/41]
- First Aid Box
- Workbench [35/41]
- Scrap Metal

24 (Floor 2) Jason Bright's Bedroom

There's some Rad Chems to steal, and a place to sleep too.

- Rad-X (7)
- Footlocker Items
- RadAway (3)
- Sleeping Quarters
- Tool Cabinet Items

25 (Floor 1) Sleeping Area

- Sleeping Quarters

26 (Floor 1) Entrance Corridor (West)

This allows you to access the unexplored area of the REPCONN Facility, but it takes longer to reach the basement heading in this direction.

G Door to REPCONN Facility

REPCONN Basement

Warning! You are under almost constant threat of cloaked Nightkin attack during this exploration!

I Door to REPCONN Facility [Easy]

This can be unlocked as part of Side Quest: Come Fly With Me, or using your skill.

28 (Floor B1) Pressure Control Room

- Sleeping Quarters

29 (Floor B1 and B2) T-Junction Corridor

There are few Caps scattered at this junction and along this corridor, which allows access to all the main chambers in this area.

- Scrap Metal

30 (Floor B1) Server Room

31 (Floor B1) Projector Room

32 (Floor B1) Food Hall

There's Food in the Fridge, and more on the table.

- Stealth Boy

33 (Floor B1) Storage

- Tool Cabinet Items
- Scrap Metal (5)

34 (Floor B1) Davison's Room

The leader of the Nightkin, and his boss (a Brahmin skull named Antler) are here, and aren't hostile to you if you converse appropriately. You can help them both out as part of Side Quest: Come Fly With Me. Consult that Quest for all conversation topics. Davison's Key allows access to Harland's Shipping Warehouse room.

- Quest Item: Davison's Key
- Bumper Sword

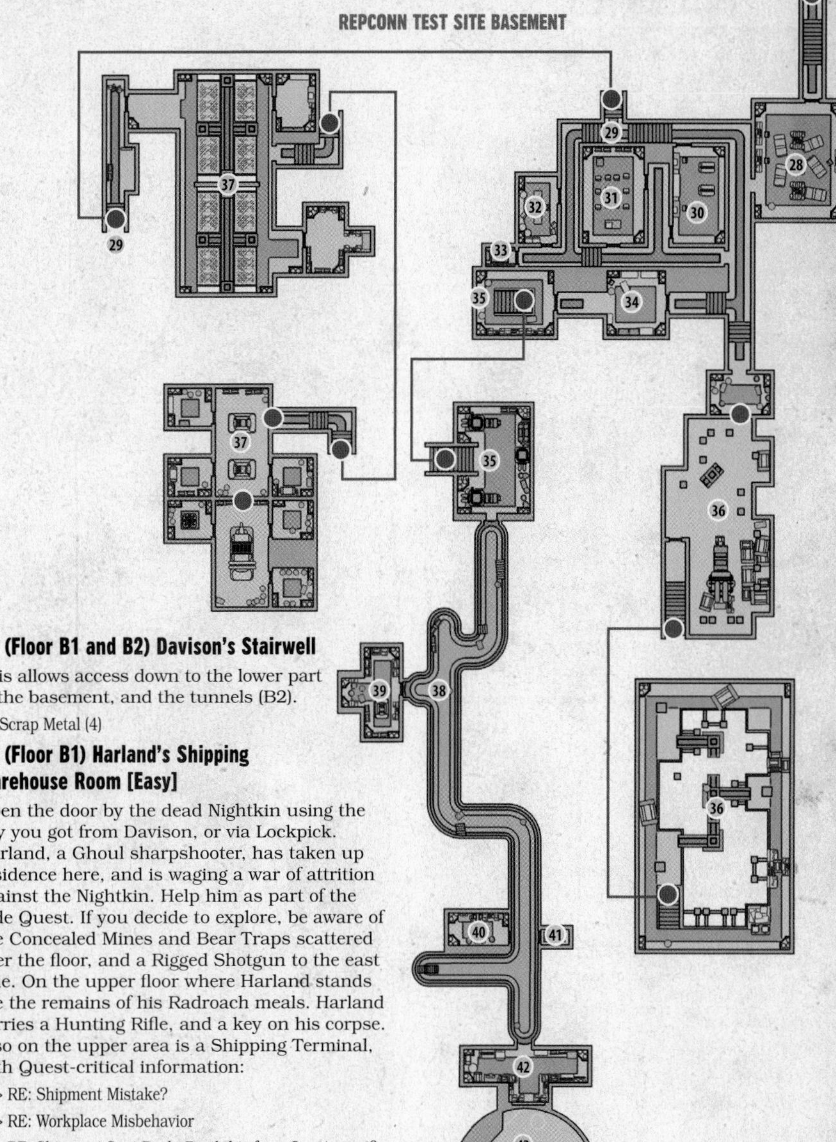

35 (Floor B1 and B2) Davison's Stairwell

This allows access down to the lower part of the basement, and the tunnels (B2).

- Scrap Metal (4)

36 (Floor B1) Harland's Shipping Warehouse Room [Easy]

Open the door by the dead Nightkin using the key you got from Davison, or via Lockpick. Harland, a Ghoul sharpshooter, has taken up residence here, and is waging a war of attrition against the Nightkin. Help him as part of the Side Quest. If you decide to explore, be aware of the Concealed Mines and Bear Traps scattered over the floor, and a Rigged Shotgun to the east side. On the upper floor where Harland stands are the remains of his Radroach meals. Harland carries a Hunting Rifle, and a key on his corpse. Also on the upper area is a Shipping Terminal, with Quest-critical information:

> RE: Shipment Mistake?

> RE: Workplace Misbehavior

> RE: Shipment Sent Back: Read this for a Quest-specific Note.

- Nailboard
- Harland's Key
- Frag Mine (9)
- Quest Item: Stealthboy Shipment Update
- Bear Trap (7)
- Hunting Rifle and Ammo

37 (Floor B1 and B2) Generator Rooms

Access this area via the corridor from the T-junction. Inside, cross the catwalks with the generators underneath. Among the Nightkin you encounter is a Jailer, who has a key to help during the Side Quest. On the upper floor is a southeast storage room, and an almost empty northeast storage room. Take the stairs to the east down to the Blast Door [Easy], which can be opened using the Jail Key.

- Quest Item: Jail Key
- Scrap Metal (3)
- Carton of Cigarettes

The first lower generator room has four small side chambers, each with some Scrap Metal. Head south through the connecting door (requiring the Jail Key to open) to a second generator room with three side chambers. One has a dead Ghoul Prisoner; a friend of Harland's.

- Bright Brotherhood Robe

38 (Floor B2) Sewer Tunnel

- Scrap Metal

39 (Floor B2) Tunnel Storage

- Scrap Metal

40 (Floor B2) Workshop and Storage

- Reloading Bench [30/36]

41 (Floor B2) Generator Alcove

- Footlocker Items

J Ladder to Mojave Wasteland

This leads up to the hatch on the surface that you can't initially reach from the outside.

42 (Floor B2) Rocket Viewing Chamber

Chris Haversam works here while Jason Bright readies his followers for their final trip into the stars. Consult the Side Quest for all conversation options. The hatch down to the Rocket Launch Pad cannot be accessed. You can also speak into the Intercom (which results in amusing conversation if you haven't entered the Research Lab yet). Finally, check the Unique items on the shelf, if you want to dress up as Captain Cosmos!

- Workbench [36/41]
- Stimpak
- Unique Item: Space Helmet [89/95]
- Unique Item: Space Suit [90/95]

43 Rocket Launch Pad [Inaccessible]

[5.18] Novac

- Main Quest: They Went That-A-Way
- Side Quest: Come Fly With Me
- Side Quest: For Auld Lang Syne
- Side Quest: One For My Baby
- Side Quest: Talent Pool
- Free Quest: Andy and Charlie
- Free Quest: Getting a Leg Up from Andy
- Free Quest: Old School Ghoul
- Free Quest: Straus Calls
- Free Quest: The Screams of Brahmin
- Free Quest: We Must Stop Meeting Like This, II
- Threat Level: ●●●●●
- Faction: Novac
  - Entity: Boone
  - Entity: Manny Vargas
  - Entity: Jeannie May Crawford
  - Entity: Cliff Briscoe
  - Entity: Ranger Andy
  - Entity: Daisy Whitman
  - Entity: Bruce Isaac
  - Entity: Doctor Straus
  - Entity: Victor
  - Entity: No-Bark Noonan
  - Entity: Alice McBride
  - Entity: Dusty McBride
- Fame/Infamy
- Services:
  - Caravan Player [13/15]
  - Caravan Player [14/15]
  - Healer/Dealer [30/31]
  - Trader [30/31]
- Crafting:
  - Reloading Bench [31/36]
  - Workbench [37/41]
  - Workbench [38/41]
  - Upgrades [10/10]
- Dangers:
  - Traps
  - Radiation
- Collectibles:
  - Caravan Cards [27/30]
  - Caravan Cards [28/30]
  - Skill Book [Medicine] [4/4] [5/6]
  - Sunset Sarsaparilla Star Cap [76/100]
  - Sunset Sarsaparilla Star Cap [77/100]
  - Unique Item [91/95]
  - Unique Weapon [32/42]

- Area Is Locked
- Follower
- Guns and Ammo
- Health, Chems, or Water
- Highly Visible
- Home Sweet Home
- Interior Exploration
- Lots O' Caps
- Main Trading Route
- Perk!
- Perk!
- Radio Signal [Black Mountain]
- Sleeping Quarters
- Wasteland Vegetation
- Quest Item

Before the war, this community was a small hamlet built as a refueling and restroom break along Highway 95, with extra tourists coaxed in to gaze at the settlement's main attraction: Dinky, a huge metal dinosaur biting "The World's (2nd) Largest Thermometer!" Some of the locals are friendly folk, though most are distrusting of outsiders. They appreciate the protection of the NCR, but are afraid of what's going on at the REPCONN Test Site to the west. The local law, Ranger Andy, is unable to investigate due to an injury, and periodic intrusions by Ghouls and the odd Viper from the hideout down the road.

NOVAC EXTERIOR

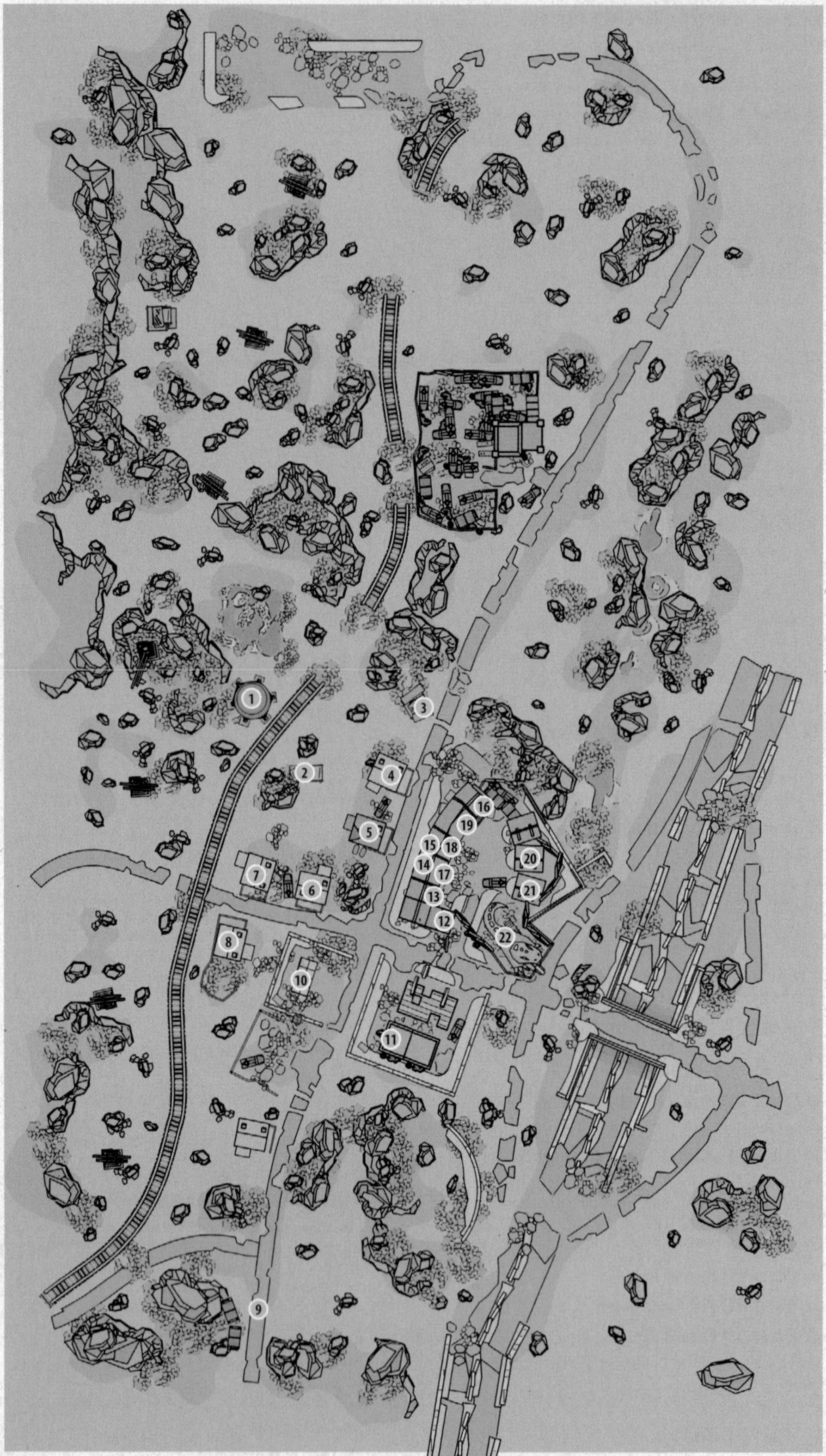

1 Water Tower

The water is unfortunately irradiated, but you can still sip it if you're desperate. To the west is the Tower Relay Alcove [5.S09]; useful if you're in need of a Shovel.

2 Lean-To Shack

- Workbench [37/41]
- Scrap Metal (5)

3 No-Bark's Shack

A mad old prospector lives here, along with his two "guards," and a Rigged Shotgun Trap without a trigger. Disarm it before speaking to the coot (who may be wandering around town, too). You can ask about his name, the men who tried to kill you (which progresses Main Quest: They Went That-A-Way), and interesting activities in the area. He regales you with stories about the chupacabra (Free Quest: The Screams of Brahmin) and Commie ghosts up at the REPCONN Test Site, which is one way to start Side Quest: Come Fly With Me. Finally, you can play Caravan with the man.

- Caravan Player: No-Bark Noonan [13/15]
- Caravan Cards [27/30]

4 Novac House #1

A group of Novac Settlers live here, and you can engage them in general chit-chat.

- Sunset Sarsaparilla Star Cap [76/100]
- Sleeping Quarters

5 Novac House (Burned)

- Grave Items (2)

6 Jeannie May Crawford's House

During the night, Jeannie leaves the Dino Dee-lite Motel and returns to her shack, where you can speak to her (see Location #12). Check the kitchen for a locked fridge [Average] with Food and some Caps to steal.

- Caps (100+)

7 Novac House #2

- Teddy Bear
- Footlocker Items [Average]
- 10mm Pistol and Ammo
- Sleeping Quarters

8 McBride House and Brahmin Corral

The decorative Brahmin skulls are a clue to the type of folks that live in this modest property; Alice and Dusty McBride ranch a few Brahmin in their back corral, and aside from the stranger that keeps killing their livestock (Free Quest: The Screams of Brahmin), they can also tell you about No-Bark, the people that live in Novac, and information pertaining to Side Quest: One for My Baby.

- First Aid Box [Easy]
- Gun Case Items [Average]
- Dino Toy

9 Burned-out Coach Liner

This marks the southern boundary of Novac, and is close to the hostile Highway 95 Viper's Encampment [5.24].

10 The Novac Eatery

Caravan Traders usually stop here for a bite to eat, although there's little to scavenge when you arrive.

11 Poseidon Gas Station

If you need Scrap Metal and other industrial parts for your tinkering, this is the place to get them. Sift through the metal shelves for a Reloading and Workbench.

- Reloading Bench [31/36]
- Scrap Metal
- Workbench [38/41]

12 DIno Dee-Lite Front Desk

Jeannie May Crawford heads up the front of house in the Motel, the broken sign of which is where the town takes its name. There are actually "Vacs" and for 100 Caps, you can lease a room right here, in the attached block, for as long as you like. Jeannie May is also a party of interest in Side Quest: One for My Baby. You can obtain a key to the floor safe behind the counter if you Pickpocket (or kill) her. There's a few other items in this room, too:

- Quest Item: Jeannie May's Safe Key
- Quest Item: Dino Dee-Lite Room Key
- First Aid Box
- Dinky the T-rex Souvenir (5)
- Cash Register Items
- Floor Safe Items [Easy]
- Quest Item: Bill of Sale
- Bottle Caps (150+)
- Home Sweet Home

13 (Upper) DIno Dee-Lite Rental Room #1

This is only accessible once you pay Jeannie May 100 Caps, and she gives you the Dino Dee-Lite Room Key. You can make yourself at home here, checking out the Drinks in the fridge, and Caps inside the footlocker. Return here as often as you like.

- First Aid Box
- Sleeping Quarters
- Teddy Bear
- Home Sweet Home
- Footlocker Items

14 (Upper) Dino Dee-Lite Room #2

- Carton of Cigarettes
- Sleeping Quarters
- First Aid Box

15 (Upper) DIno Dee-Lite Room #3

There's little of worth inside this room, aside from a man named Bruce Isaac, who cowers and asks if you work for Mr. Bishop. Talking to him reveals a crazy past for the singer in New Reno. This is all very entertaining, but it's only actually useful if you have Side Quest: Talent Pool active.

- First Aid Box
- Sleeping Quarters

16 (Upper) DIno Dee-Lite Room #4

An old dear named Daisy Whitman rents this room out, when she's not standing outside on the balcony. Speak to her, and she tells you she used to be a pilot. But the full revelations about her storied past aren't revealed until you're accompanied here by Arcade Gannon, as part of Side Quest: For Auld Lang Syne.

- First Aid Box
- Sunset Sarsaparilla Star Cap [77/100]
- Sleeping Quarters

17 (Lower) Manny Vargas' Room

The sniper in the mouth of Dinky the Dinosaur that watches over Novac during the day is Manny Vargas. This is his room, containing a number of mattresses, and a terminal. This has an interesting message from a Great Khan named McMurphy, which helps your progress during Main Quest: That Went That-A-Way.

> Message: Khan Hospitality

- First Aid Box
- Sleeping Quarters

18 (Lower) DIno Dee-Lite Room #6

An empty room.

- Teddy Bear
- Sleeping Quarters
- First Aid Box

19 (Lower) Craig Boone's Room

The sniper in the mouth of Dinky that watches Novac at nighttime is Boone. This is his room, and if he's in it, he tells you to get out, and meet him up in the mouth at 9 PM. Killing Boone gives you a selection of First Recon clothing, but little else, and isn't recommended. Search the room for the following:

- Frag Grenade
- Sleeping Quarters
- Ammo Box Ammunition

20 Ranger Andy's Bungalow

Andy was an exceptional Ranger, but after two nasty attacks that all but crippled him, he's stationed himself here to keep Novac protected. He has another ache; to reunite with his old Ranger buddies at Ranger Station Charlie [5.23], but he's infirm. Speak to him, and you can coax an Unarmed move out of him, and an investigation of the station. Free Quests: Getting a Leg Up from Andy, and Andy and Charlie. Make sure Raul the Ghoul is with you, as part of Free Quest: Old School Ghoul.

- FIrst Aid Box
- Skill Book: D.C. Journal of Internal Medicine [Medicine] [4/4] [5/6]
- Gun Case Items [Average]
- Sleeping Quarters

21 Cliff Briscoe's Bungalow

Call it a hunch, but Cliff Briscoe—the proprietor of the shop inside DInky's belly—may have over-ordered his shipment of Dinky toys. The rest of the room (including the tiny "finishing line" Tripwire you can disarm) has Food in the fridge, and a few other items of interest. Cliff is here during the night, and plays Caravan at any time.

- Pool Cue
- Gun Case Items
- Dinky the T-Rex Souvenir (27)
- Sleeping Quarters

22 Dinky the Dinosaur: Dino Bite Gift Shop

Up the steps, and into the stomach of Dinky, there's a gift shop run by Cliff Briscoe. He's attempting a not-so cunning ruse to get rid of his over-abundance of plastic trinkets. You can ignore them, and look through a wide variety of tradable goods. Cliff also enjoys Caravan, and you can ask him about the man in the checkered coat. It also becomes apparent that he has a job lot of souvenir rockets from the REPCONN Test Site [5.17], which are important for Side Quest: Come Fly With Me (buy at least five). In addition, there's stuff to steal, and the store closet to open [Very Easy]; which can also be accessed using the Storeroom Key on Cliff.

- Trader: Cliff Briscoe [30/33]
- Trader: Cliff Briscoe Upgrades [Energy Weapons, Guns] [10/10]
- Caravan Player: Cliff Briscoe [14/15]
- Caravan Cards [28/30]
- Dinky the T-rex Souvenir (1029)
- Magazines (Random; to purchase)
- Unique Weapon: That Gun [32/42]
- Dino Bite Storeroom Key
- First Aid Box
- Bobby Pins
- Rocket Souvenir (160)

Dinky the Dinosaur's Mouth

Depending on the time of day, you'll encounter Manny Vargas (days) or Boone (nights) at this location. The two used to be in the First Recon Snipers, but have fallen out. Talk to Manny about it, what he does, and about the man in the checkered coat. He also needs your help removing the population of Ghouls from the REPCONN Test Site (Side Quest: Come Fly With Me). Talk to Boone, and he gradually opens up about his wife, her abduction, and needs you to find out how she came to disappear. This begins Side Quest: One for My Baby. Upon satisfactory completion of that Quest, you can urge Boone to join you as a Follower, which gradually unlocks more of Side Quest: I Forgot to Remember to Forget.

- Follower: Boone
- Perk! Spotter
- Unique Item: 1st Recon Beret (Boone's Beret) [91/95]

Free Quest: Andy and Charlie

Another part of the conversation with Ranger Andy is to ask about his job; he's been contacting the folks down at Ranger Station Charlie [5.23], but hasn't received any recent updates. He thinks it's a prank, but he's worried. Ask him if he'd feel better if you checked on his friends, and he blusters that they're good enough soldiers without him not being able to let go. However, at the end of the conversation, he changes his mind. You receive a note.

- Quest Item: Check on Ranger Station Charlie

The Ranger Station is just southwest of Novac, along the railroad. Enter the concrete office, to a scene of devastation; bodies of the Rangers are strewn everywhere, and have even been booby-trapped with Frag Mines! Take extreme care where you step! Disarm and search the dead Rangers, before returning to Ranger Andy, who's sickened by your news, and tells you to look out for who did it.

Free Quest: Getting a Leg Up from Andy

A man wearing a Ranger uniform is usually found in his bungalow near Dinky. You can ask about his job (guarding the parts of town Manny and Boone don't), his past, and his bad leg, as well as information on the man in the checkered coat. Continue to ask about his battle damage, and when he mentions that he's useless, you can:

Tell him it's his body that's injured, and not his mind. He's flattered; to such an extent that he offers to teach you a New Unarmed Technique; a power attack while moving backward.

- Perk!: Unarmed Technique: Ranger Takedown

Free Quest: Straus Calls

Doctor Ada Straus is a wandering medical practitioner with two Mercenary guards, and your first encounter is likely to be in Novac. She offers cut-price medical treatment (50 Caps instead of the usual 100), but lacks the skill of better doctors. In fact, she's as much of a doctor as you are a Super Mutant. She has some items to trade, too.

- Healer: Dr. Ada Straus [30/31]

Free Quest: The Screams of Brahmin

During your conversations with the slightly deranged No-bark Noonan, he mentions "things of a disturbing nature" down at the McBride corral. Dead Brahmin have been turning up, and No-bark knows this is the work of the chupacabra, a livestock vampire (with an automatic weapon, after explaining away the bullet holes). He mentions the chupacabra was invisible, talking to a "more invisible" friend, and used a rotating gun. You'll get no more from this lunatic, so visit the McBrides. Speak to Dusty about him losing livestock. He tells you about the "crazy hollering and gunshots," but just one animal dead, left full of holes. You receive a note to remember this.

- Quest note: Midnight Ranch Attacks

Coming back at midnight is the key to success. Wait until around 11:55 PM, and then situate yourself to the west of the Brahmin paddock, near the railroad tracks. Something shimmers into view soon afterward; a Nightkin ranting to itself. It can't be reasoned with, but it can be attacked. You find a hefty Minigun and a Holodisk on the corpse, explaining the mental auguish the Nightkin was suffering from. Return to Dusty, and let him know the "chupacabra" is dead. He's thankful, doling out some Caps, and a fridge full of Brahmin Steaks.

- Minigun and Ammo
- Quest note: The Screams of Brahmin
- Caps (75)
- Brahmin Steak (10)
- Novac Fame Gained!

Free Quest: We Must Stop Meeting Like This, II

As you wander through town, and you haven't yet met Mr. House at the Lucky 38 Casino [2D.02], you may spot a Securitron rolling down Novac's crumbling streets. Who's that pretending not to follow you at a safe distance? It's Victor, the good-time cowpoke Securitron! If you spot him in Novac (which you might if you haven't spoken to him on The Strip yet), you can ask what he's doing, ask about the men who jumped you, or to stay out of your way. Although he might be tailing you, he's not prepared to become a Follower. You can shoot at him too, but he has no items to loot.

[5.19] Emergency Service Railyard

- Threat Level:
- Faction: None
  - Entity: None
- Crafting: Campfire [81/109]
- Collectibles:
  - Sunset Sarsaparilla Star Cap [78/100]
  - Sunset Sarsaparilla Star Cap [79/100]
- Health, Chems, or Water
- Highly Visible
- Sleeping Quarters

This railroad track is the edge between Zones 4 and 5, and this yard is on the cusp of them both. Use the crane to find it from a distance.

- Campfire [81/109]
- Sledgehammer
- First Aid Box
- Sunset Sarsaparilla Star Cap [78/100]
- Sunset Sarsaparilla Star Cap [79/100]
- Sleeping Quarters

[5.20] Primm Pass

- Threat Level:
- Faction: Abomination
  - Entity: Blind Deathclaw
- Collectibles: Hollowed-Out Rock [30/42]

If you're attempting to move from west to east (or as the name suggests, to Primm [4.17] from the east), this usually involves a lot of unnecessary hiking. However, just east of the Emergency Service Railyard is a gully across the mountain top, which offers excellent access to Harper's Shack [5.21], and the eastern map. There's scattered remains of a Prospector and Bright Follower here, as a Blind Deathclaw guards this pass. Sneaking or using a Stealth Boy is ineffective, you must fight, flee, run quickly past, or have a Companion lure the Blind Deathclaw away while you seek safety! Close to Brahmin bones, on the western end of the pass is a Hollowed-Out Rock.

- Hollowed-Out Rock [30/42]
- Bright Brotherhood Robe

[5.21] Harper's Shack

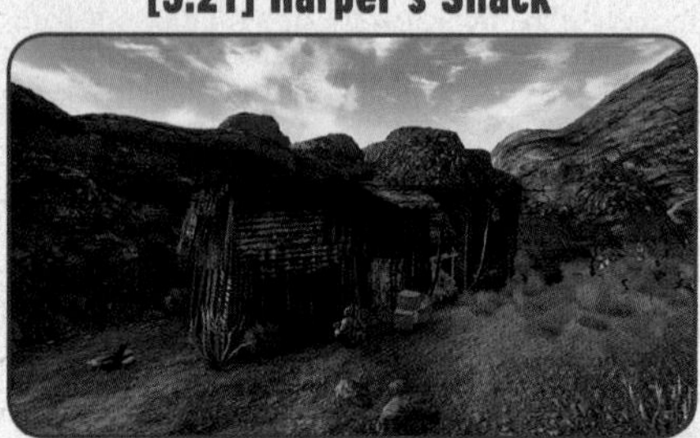

- Threat Level:
- Faction: None
  - Entity: None
- Crafting:
  - Campfire [82/109]
  - Reloading Bench [32/36]
  - Workbench [39/41]
- Collectibles: Sunset Sarsaparilla Star Cap [80/100]
- Guns and Ammo
- Interior Exploration
- Sleeping Quarters
- Wasteland Vegetation

A long shack nestled below the eastern end of Primm Pass has some Deathclaws up the ravine to the southwest near Dead Wind Cavern [5.22]. There's a Campfire around to the side of the building. Check the outside, then the inside for the following:

- Campfire [82/109]
- Reloading Bench [32/36]
- Workbench [39/41]
- Shovel
- Varmint Rifle
- Ammo Box Ammunition (3)
- Sunset Sarsaparilla Star Cap [80/100]
- Sleeping Quarters

[5.22] Dead Wind Cavern

- Threat Level:
- Faction: Abomination
  - Entity: Young Deathclaw
  - Entity: Deathclaw
  - Entity: Deathclaw Mother
  - Entity: Legendary Deathclaw
- Collectibles:
  - Hollowed-Out Rock [31/42]
  - Unique Weapon [33/42]
- Guns and Ammo
- Interior Exploration

Inside, the cavern lives up to its name; there are Deathclaws everywhere! Before you enter, check the rocks to your left, about 20 feet down from the cave mouth, for a Hollowed-Out Rock.

- Hollowed-Out Rock [31/42]

Ⓐ Exit to Mojave Wasteland

① Entrance Cave

② Large Tunnel (East)

Don't get trapped to the right, here!

③ Nursery

Take the left fork, and prepare for combat with the Deathclaw Mother; a feat only a few have even attempted, and far fewer have completed! Exercise extreme caution here!

④ Large Tunnel (West)

This takes you past the nursery, around another corner where more prowling beasts are ready to skewer and rip you apart. Don't forget the tunnel in the northeast wall!

⑤ Skeleton's Duffle Bag

- Duffle Bag Items

⑥ Lair of the Legendary Deathclaw

The final chamber features a beast so ferocious and tough that no one has faced it and lived; the Legendary Deathclaw! Tackle it, along with its lesser brethren, then inspect the body of a fallen Brotherhood of Steel Paladin for a prize almost worth the terror!

- Brotherhood T-45d Power Armor
- Brotherhood T-45d Power Helmet
- Unique Weapon: Mercy [33/42]

DEAD WIND CAVERN

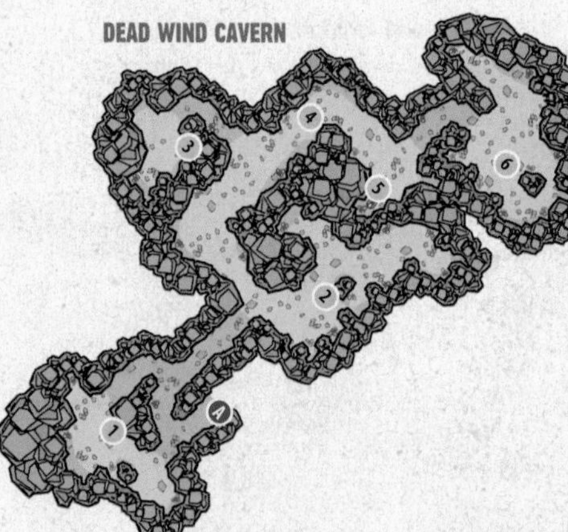

[5.23] Ranger Station Charlie 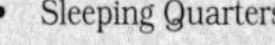

- Side Quest: Return to Sender
- Free Quest: Andy and Charlie
- Threat Level:
- Faction: NCR
  - Entity: Comm Officer Stepinac
- Highly Visible
- Interior Exploration
- Sleeping Quarters

Perhaps the most defendable station, this is certainly the least remote. The cluster of buildings around a ranch house have mattresses you're welcome to sleep on (Infamy permitting), as well as stand on the roof of, if you're sniping. There's some Sunglasses up here, too. Inside, Comm Officer Stepinac isn't very friendly, but you can ask him about their interact with Camp McCarran [2.19], the purpose of the station (to keep the road to Novac "civilized"), and the NCR Rangers, including the one in charge; Ranger Beaumont, who is off on patrol, and isn't available. There's little in here to steal, but there's more places to sleep.

- Sleeping Quarters

[5.24] Highway 95 Viper's Encampment

- Threat Level: ●●●○○
- Faction: Viper Gang
  - Entity: Viper Gunslinger
- Crafting: Campfire [83/109]
- Collectibles: Sunset Sarsaparilla Star Cap [81/100]
- Guns and Ammo
- Health, Chems, or Water
- Sleeping Quarters

By the Fancy Lads Billboard, at the southern slip-road to Novac, a group of Viper Gang Members have taken up residence, within view of Dinky the Dinosaur.

- Campfire [83/109]
- Ammo Box Ammunition (3)
- Healing Powder (2)
- Sunset Sarsaparilla Star Cap [81/100]
- Sleeping Quarters

[5.25] Wrecked Highwayman

- Threat Level: ●○○○○
- Faction: Mutated Animal
  - Entity: Bloatfly, Bighorner
- Collectibles: Sunset Sarsaparilla Star Cap [82/100]
- Guns and Ammo
- Health, Chems, or Water

Close to Clark Field [6.07] on the south side of the 95 where Bloatflies and Bighorners graze uneasily, there's the remains of an old perambulator: The open trunk has a number of stolen items (listed below), and usually a Power Fist inside the Footlocker.

- Stimpak and Chems
- Energy Weapons Ammo
- Sunset Sarsaparilla Star Cap [82/100]

[5.26] Coyote Den

- Threat Level: ●○○○○
- Faction: Mutated Animal
  - Entity: Coyote

Before the rock slide, near the abandoned pick-up is a dark alcove where a Coyote Den Mother and her young are playing with the bones of past meals. At the den entrance is a Lottery Ticket, and Inside the den is the body of a Bright Follower, far away from home base, over at the REPCONN Test Site.

- Bright Follower's Robe

[5.27] Hidden Supply Cave

- Side Quest: Wheel of Fortune
- Threat Level: ●○○○○
- Faction: Prospector
  - Entity: None
- Collectibles:
  - Skill Book [Melee Weapons] [3/4] [6/6]
  - Hollowed-Out Rock [32/42]
- Area Is Locked
- Health, Chems, or Water
- Interior Exploration
- Wasteland Vegetation
- Quest Item

A gully leading to a Hollowed-Out Rock and an unassuming door, which is locked [Average]. Pry open the door to enter a gloomy single chamber stacked with crates, and a footlocker with a Radiation Suit on top of it. The footlocker has other suits if the Side Quest is active. Check for other items before you leave:

- Hollowed-Out Rock [32/42]
- Skill Book: Grognak the Barbarian [Melee Weapons] [3/4] [6/6]
- Footlocker Items
- Radiation Suit
- Radiation Suit Package
- First Aid Box

[5.28] Walking Box Cavern

- Threat Level: ●●●○○
- Faction: Mutated Animal
  - Entity: Nightstalker
- Collectibles: Hollowed-Out Rock [33/42]
- Interior Exploration

Nightstalkers hiss in these parts. Note the Hollowed-Out Rock near the copse of trees, by the entrance.

- Hollowed-Out Rock [33/42]

A Exit to Mojave Wasteland

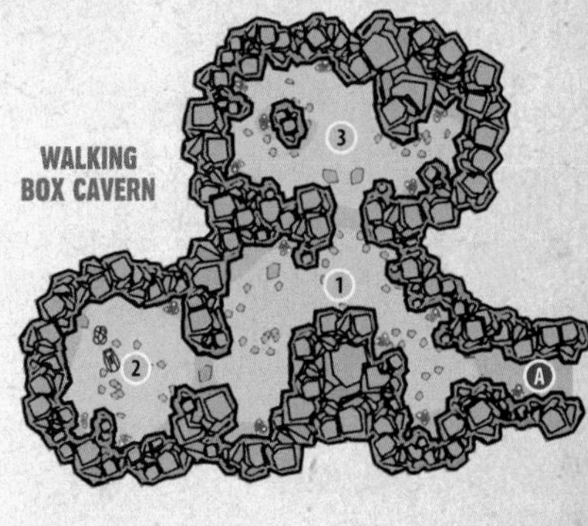

1 Connecting Passage

Inside is a glowing gloom of fungi and dank cave walls. The main curving chamber features a plle of bones, and two connecting chambers.

2 3 North and West Chambers

There's little here but a group of Nightstalkers, and a Duffle Bag plus Egg Clutch in the west chamber.

- Duffle Bag Items
- Egg Clutches

[5.29] Legion Raid Camp

- Side Quest: Booted
- Threat Level: ●●○○○
- Faction: Caesar's Legion
  - Entity: Legionary
  - Entity: Powder Ganger
- Crafting:
  - Campfire [84/109]
  - Campfire [85/109]
- Sleeping Quarters

While many of the Legion responsible for the razing of Nipton headed back to Cottonwood Cove, a few remained to pillage the area, and take prisoners. Two of them, Powder Gangers now tied up at the upper campfire, are ready to be rescued (if you want to incur the wrath of Recruit Decanus and his troops). The camp itself has bedrolls and footlockers in the red tents to loot, and a lower Campfire area too.

- Lottery Ticket (2)
- Campfire [84/109]
- Campfire [85/109]
- Sack Items (3)
- Sunset Sarsaparilla Crate Items
- Healing Powder (2)
- Footlocker Items (6)
- Sleeping Quarters

[5.30] Broc Flower Cave

- Threat Level: ●●●○○
- Faction: Prospector/ Mutated Animal
  - Entity: Rodent of Unusual Size
  - Entity: Giant Rat
- Dangers: Radiation
- Collectibles:
  - Magazine [Barter] [16/16] [5-9/10]
  - Magazine [Medicine] [22/23] [5-9/10]
  - Magazine [Science] [23/23] [5-9/10]

- Magazine [Science] [19/19] [5-9/10]
- Magazine [Survival] [28/30] [5-9/10]
- Hollowed-Out Rock [34/42]
- Unique Weapon [34/42]
- Guns and Ammo
- Health, Chems, or Water
- Interior Exploration
- Wasteland Vegetation

In the desolate rocky terrain east of the Legion Raid Camp, the largest rocky hillock around has an opening on its western side. Head up the narrow path near the Hollowed-Out Rock, passing a Prospector and the dotted Broc Flowers to reach the mine door.

- Hollowed-Out Rock [34/42]

A Exit to Mojave Wasteland

Watch out for Rodents of Unusual Size!

1 Entrance

As soon as you step into the cave, look down for a cluster of discarded objects, listed below.

- Knife
- Magazine: Salesman Weekly [Barter] [16/16] [5/10]

2 West Cave

Either path links to the main cavern, but the right path deposits you here first.

- Sunset Sarsaparilla Crate Items

3 Main Cavern

The main cavern is littered with radioactive barrels. Check the half-buried barrels for the following:

- Ammo Box Ammunition
- .357 Magnum Revolver
- Magazine: Lad's Life [Survival] [28/30] [6/10]

4 Main Cavern Ledge

This winds around to an old Prospector's hideout. There's little here on the ground to pick up except slight radiation.

5 Prospector's Hideout

Take a clockwise gander for the following items, including a Unique Varmint Rifle:

- Various Health and Chems
- Unique Weapon: Ratslayer [34/42]
- Magazine: Programmer's Digest [Science] [22/23] [7/10]
- Magazine: Programmer's Digest [Science] [23/23] [8/10]
- Magazine: Today's Physician [Medicine] [19/19] [9/10]
- Radiation Suit
- First Aid Box (2)
- Doctor's Bag
- Ammo Box Ammunition

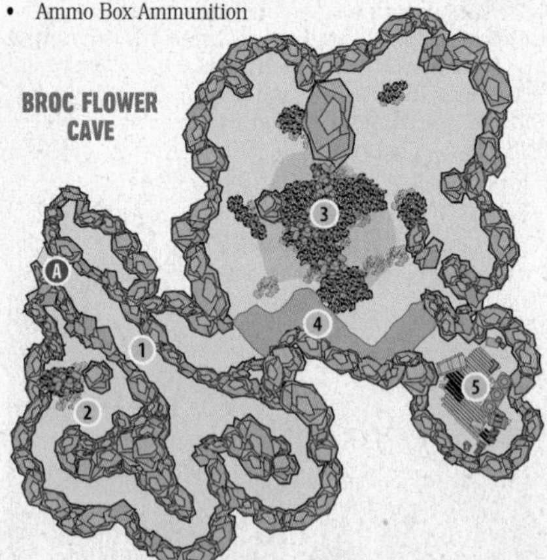

[5.31] Snyder Prospector Camp

- Threat Level: ●●●●●
- Faction: Prospector
  Entity: None
- Crafting: Campfire [86/109]
- Collectibles: Sunset Sarsaparilla Star Cap [83/100]
- Health, Chems, or Water
- Sleeping Quarters
- Wasteland Vegetation

This small shack is deserted, save for a Campfire and the following:

- Campfire [86/109]
- Sunset Sarsaparilla Star Cap [83/100]
- Healing Powder and Fruit
- Sleeping Quarters

ZONE 5: SECONDARY LOCATIONS

[5.S01] Fetid Pond

- Threat Level: ●●●●●
- Crafting: Campfire [87/109]
- Collectibles: Magazine [Survival] [29/30] [10/10]

The skeletal remains of a man who forgot to read Lad's Life, and the Magazine itself, still in reasonable shape. Check the bluff in the rocky foothills below for a Campfire.

- Magazine: Lad's Life [Survival] [29/30] [10/10]
- Campfire [87/109]

[5.S02] Boulder City Billboard Sign

- Threat Level: ●●●●●
- Highly Visible
- Main Trading Route
- Wasteland Vegetation

One of two either side of the 95 Highway, use this to situate yourself with the nearby roads and Primary Locations.

[5.S03] Savaged Brahmin

- Threat Level: ●●●●●
- Faction: Mutated Animal
  Entity: Giant Ant
- Main Trading Route

You can pick out a few provisions from the corpse.

[5.S04] Gore Bag

- Threat Level: ●●●●●
- Faction: Super Mutant
- Guns and Ammo

The sign of a Super Mutant offal-collection is here, accessed from over the hill to the north.

- Tire Iron
- Combat Helmet
- Hunting Revolver
- Cap (3)

[5.S05] Quarry Junction Cargo Platform

- Threat Level: ●●●●●
- Faction: Abomination
  Entity: Deathclaw
- Highly Visible
- Sleeping Quarters

The upright crane allows you to spot this station from afar. Be incredibly careful, as Deathclaws prowl here. The shack has some items to gather.

- Beer and Whiskey
- Scrap Metal (3)
- Sleeping Quarters

[5.S06] Pack of Wild Dogs

- Threat Level: ●●●●●
- Faction: Mutated Animal
  Entity: Wild Dog

A trio of Wild Dogs are guarding some collected bones and sinew.

[5.S07] Correctional Parking Lot

- Threat Level: ●●●●●
- Guns and Ammo
- Sleeping Quarters

Two rusting trailers remain on the outskirts of the NCR Correctional Facility, on the cracked tarmac of the parking lot.

- Explosives Crate Items
- Sleeping Quarters

[5.S08] Powder Ganger Alcove

- Threat Level: ●●●●●
- Faction: Powder Ganger
  Entity: Powder Ganger
- Crafting: Campfire [88/109]
- Health, Chems, or Water

A small alcove in the rocky hillside provides cover for a couple of Powder Gangers guarding the Facility perimeter.

- Campfire [88/109]
- Stimpak and Chems

[5.S09] Tower Relay Alcove

- Threat Level: ●●●●●
- Crafting: Campfire [89/109]
- Guns and Ammo
- Health, Chems, or Water
- Highly Visible
- Sleeping Quarters

The radio mast still upright, west of Novac, has a nearby alcove hewn into the mountain wall. Check it for the remains of a Wastelander, and the following:

- Campfire [89/109]
- Shovel
- First Aid Box
- Frag Grenade (2)
- Sleeping Quarters

[5.S10] Gibson's Shack

- Side Quest: I Could Make You Care
- Threat Level: ●●●●●
- Faction: Novac / Brotherhood of Steel
- Crafting: Campfire [90/109]
- Guns and Ammo
- Health, Chems, or Water
- Quest Item

Aside from a dangerous indoor Campfire, there's a Comm Station Terminal, which can't be opened unless Veronica is with you, and the Side Quest is active.

- Campfire [90/109]
- Whiskey, Mentats and Chems
- Machete

[5.S11] End of the Road

- Threat Level: ●●●●●

Use the truck as a defensive camping spot and try sniping Ants (or passing Caravaneers) for fun.

[5.S12] REPCONN Test Site Checkpoint

- Side Quest: Come Fly With Me
- Threat Level: ●●●●●
- Faction: Ghoul
  - Entity: Feral Ghoul
  - Entity: Glowing One
- Guns and Ammo
- Health, Chems, or Water
- Lots O' Caps
- Sleeping Quarters

This is the only road to and from the REPCONN Test Site, and is teeming with Ghouls. Be on your guard, and check the checkpoint for Chems on the small table, then ransack the Checkpoint under the bridge itself. Then run to the sandbag defenses at the far (southwest) end, under the bridge, to collect a number of items (don't forget to check any Ash Piles!). Finally, double-back up the north slope of the bridge to the top of the bridge itself, and claim further items. You could Sneak to this final point and snipe from up here.

- Chems and Med-X
- Ammo Box Ammunition (4)
- Grenade Box Ammunition [Easy]
- Energy Cell (20 x 11)
- Damaged Garden Gnome
- Footlocker Items
- Cap (31)
- First Aid Box
- Scrap Metal (3)
- Cowboy Repeater and Ammo
- Doctor's Bag
- Sleeping Quarters

[5.S13] Sealed Train Tunnel

- Threat Level: ●●●●●
- Faction: Viper Gang
  - Entity: Viper Gunslinger
- Crafting
  - Campfire [91/109]
- Wasteland Vegetation

Expect an attack by five or so Viper Gang Members if you venture to the end of the railroad line. The tunnel itself is sealed. Beware of Deathclaws to the west.

- Campfire [91/109]

[5.S14] Radioactive Barrels

- Threat Level: ●●●●●
- Dangers: Radiation

There are metal boxes to search, but little else.

[5.S15] Wrecked Biker

- Threat Level: ●●●●●

A motorcyclist took a wrong turn here. However, if you pry the skull off the helmet, you have a serviceable piece of headgear.

- Metal Helmet

[5.S16] Bright's Darkness

- Threat Level: ●●●●●
- Faction: Viper Gang

A mysterious cowled Ghoul lies against the rocks on the other side of the road to Novac.

- Bright Brotherhood Robe

[5.S17] Legion Camp

- Threat Level: ●●●●●
- Faction: Caesar's Legion
  - Entity: Recruit
  - Entity: Legionary
- Crafting: Campfire [92/109]
- Sleeping Quarters
- Wasteland Vegetation

The Legion scouts are already encroaching, and looking for weaknesses in the NCR defenses.

- Campfire [92/109]
- Sleeping Quarters

[5.S18] Mole Rat Burrow

- Threat Level: ●●●●●
- Faction: Mutated Animal
  - Entity: Mole Rat
- Wasteland Vegetation

This area offers good views of the area, and an inaccessible burrow.

[5.S19] Viper Gang Ambush

- Threat Level: ●●●●●
- Faction: Viper Gang
  - Entity: Viper Gunslinger
- Dangers: Mines
- Collectibles: Sunset Sarsaparilla Star Cap [84/100]
- Guns and Ammo

A classic ambush spot takes advantage of an old traffic accident on the gully road east of Nipton. Each side of the overturned big-rig is a traffic cone with a Frag Mine under it, and Viper Gunslingers behind rocks and on top of hills, ready to snipe and bludgeon. Wading in on the road is one plan, but a better one is to Sneak around the top of the hills and tag the foes using height to your advantage. Check the back of the big-rig container for items (including a Star Cap).

- Frag Mine (2)
- Sunset Sarsaparilla Crate Items
- Sunset Sarsaparilla Star Cap [84/100]
- Hydra and Gun Cabinet Items

[5.S20] Viper Gang Alcove

- Threat Level: ●●●●●
- Faction: Viper Gang
  - Entity: Viper Gunslinger
- Crafting: Campfire [93/109]
- Guns and Ammo
- Health, Chems, or Water
- Lots O' Caps
- Wasteland Vegetation

In the hills to the northwest of Wolfhorn Ranch is a rocky alcove where the Viper Gang (who are active in this area) have stored some provisions. Kill or Sneak by them to see what you can take.

- Campfire [93/109]
- Sack Items
- Explosive Crate Items
- Gun Case Items

[5.S21] Signpost 164

- Threat Level: ●○○○○

The remains of a freeway instructional signpost still give you advice on where Novac and Searchlight are.

[5.S22] Fancy Lads Billboard

- Threat Level: ●○○○○
- Faction: Caesar's Legion

Wandering far from home, a Bright Follower's remains lie at the foot of this billboard.

- Bright Brotherhood Robe

[5.S23] Astor's Recon Camp

- Side Quest: Eye for an Eye
- Side Quest: We Will All Go Together
- Threat Level: ●●●○○
- Faction: NCR
  - Entity: First Sergeant Astor
  - Entity: NCR Trooper
- Crafting: Campfire [94/109]
- Dangers: Radiation
- Guns and Ammo
- Health, Chems, or Water
- Wasteland Vegetation
- Quest Item

The devastating radiation attack by the Legion on Camp Searchlight has pushed the surviving NCR soldiers back to minimum safe distance. The fury and emotion is still raw, as First Sergeant Astor leads his men on patrol, and witnesses what his brothers in arms have turned into. You can help him in two Side Quests to put his men to rest, and even the score. Be sure to visit the modest camp and read First Sergeant Astor's Log; it reads as if the man blames himself, and is ready to drop.

- Campfire [94/109]
- Sunset Sarsaparilla Crate Items
- Explosives Crate Items [Average]
- Gun Case Items
- First Aid Box
- Note: First Sergeant Astor's Log
- Quest Item: NCR Bug

[5.S24] Highway 95: All Signs Point to Novac

- Threat Level: ●●○○○
- Highly Visible

The Highway 95 carves through the desert en route to 188 Trading Post to the north, and the signs here pinpoint where the road splits into two parallel lanes. The start of the Ghoul activity from Camp Searchlight begins here, too.

ZONE 6: EAST CLIFFS AND SOUTH RAD ZONE

Topographical Overview

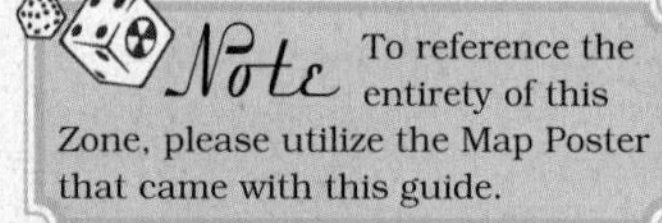

Note: To reference the entirety of this Zone, please utilize the Map Poster that came with this guide.

The final zone is a sliver of land that begins in the northwest at El Dorado Gas & Service [6.01], and continues south and east from this point, following the boundaries of the 95 Highway, and the Colorado River itself; which can be descended into, drunk from, and investigated as there are unmarked Secondary Locations on the Arizona banks to the east. Major warring settlements of Camp Forlorn Hope [6.02] and Nelson [6.06] offer constant target practice and Quest opportunities, and as you travel farther south, the terrain becomes even more rugged. Watch your footing as you search out lonely shacks for items. The southern edge of this zone (and the Mojave Wasteland) has a number of radioactive hot-spots, including an Old Nuclear Test Site [6.23], and the recently irradiated Camp Searchlight [6.16], where NCR soldiers now roam in a more Feral state. The empty Searchlight Airport [6.26] is just south of here, but the biggest concern for the NCR is Cottonwood Cove [6.20]; a staging ground for the Legion, and a place where you can travel up-river, into Caesar's Fortification Hill itself.

Highways and Byways

To the west is the winding Highway 95, and following it north to south allows you to easily gauge where the majority of this zone is. The zone ends abruptly to the east, with cliffs down to the Colorado River; another huge landmark allowing you to easily situate yourself. Aside from a main road running from the REPCONN Test Site [5.17], through Novac [5.18] and ending up in Nelson, the major east-west road is to the south; Trail 164 cuts across all the way from the Mojave Outpost [4.27], through the troubled town of Nipton [4.30], and across Camp Searchlight to end at Cottonwood Cove. Note the lack of railroad tracks in this zone.

Available Services, Crafting and Collectibles

Services: Caravan Players: [1/15]
Services: Gambling: [0/15]
Services: Healers/Dealers: [1/31]
Services: Repairers: [0/9]
Services: Traders: [3/33]
Crafting: Campfires: [15/109]
Crafting: Reloading Benches: [4/36]
Crafting: Workbenches: [2/41]
Crafting: Weapon Upgrades: [0/10]
Collectibles: Snow Globes: [0/7]
Collectibles: Caravan Cards: [2/30]
Collectibles: Hollowed-Out Rocks: [8/42]
Collectibles: Skill Books: [9/51]
Collectibles: Skill Magazines: [5/213]
Collectibles: Star Bottle Caps: [16/100]
Collectibles: Unique Items: [4/95]
Collectibles: Unique Weapons: [8/42]

Primary Locations

[6.01] El Dorado Gas & Service
[6.02] Camp Forlorn Hope ●
[6.03] Southern Nevada Wind Farm
[6.04] Abandoned BoS Bunker
[6.05] Toxic Dump Site
[6.06] Nelson ●
[6.07] Clark Field
[6.08] Techatticup Mine
[6.09] Lucky Jim Mine
[6.10] Ranger Station Echo ●
[6.11] Cliffside Prospector Camp
[6.12] Searchlight North Gold Mine
[6.13] Coyote Mines
[6.14] Wolfhorn Ranch
[6.15] Raided Farmstead
[6.16] Camp Searchlight
[6.17] Searchlight East Gold Mine
[6.18] Sniper's Nest
[6.19] Cottonwood Overlook
[6.20] Cottonwood Cove ●
[6.21] Bradley's Shack
[6.22] Caesar's Legion Safehouse
[6.23] Old Nuclear Test Site
[6.24] Crashed Vertibird
[6.25] Matthews Animal Husbandry Farm
[6.26] Searchlight Airport
[6.27] Fire Root Cavern
[6.28] Cottonwood Crater
[6.29] Smith Mesa Prospector Camp
[6.30] Blue Paradise Vacation Rentals

Secondary Locations

[6.S01] Camp Forlorn Hope Supply Shipment
[6.S02] Wrecked Commuter
[6.S03] Dry Bones
[6.S04] Road to Nelson
[6.S05] NCR Ranger Checkpoint
[6.S06] Minefield
[6.S07] Nelson Lookout
[6.S08] Knob Hill
[6.S09] Recon Legion Camp
[6.S10] Bootjack Cavern
[6.S11] Camp Searchlight Trailer Park
[6.S12] Highway 95 (South)
[6.S13] Little Rock Camp
[6.S14] Lakelurk Hideaway
[6.S15] Rusting Boat
[6.S16] Deathclaw Promontory
[6.S17] Fallen Hiker
[6.S18] River Bank Alcove

PRIMARY LOCATIONS

[6.01] El Dorado Gas & Service

- Threat Level:
- Faction: Prospector
  - Entity: Prospector
- Crafting: Campfire [95/109]
- Collectibles: Sunset Sarsaparilla Star Cap [85/100]
- Guns and Ammo
- Interior Exploration
- Radio Signal [Black Mountain]
- Sleeping Quarters

A reststop along Highway 95, this is close to both HELIOS One [5.13] and Boulder City [3.32]. Outside, there's usually a Prospector, and a lit Campfire, with scattered bedding. Inside, the gas station offers a ruined series of shelves mostly picked clean.

- Campfire [95/109]
- Sleeping Quarters
- Gun Cabinet Items
- Ammo Box Ammunition
- Sunset Sarsaparilla Star Cap [85/100]

[6.02] Camp Forlorn Hope ●

- Side Quest: Medical Mystery
- Side Quest: No, Not Much
- Side Quest: Restoring Hope
- Side Quest: Return to Sender
- Side Quest: We Are Legion
- Free Quest: An Ear to the Ground
- Free Quest: Tags of Our Fallen
- Threat Level:
- Faction: NCR
  - Entity: Major Polatli
  - Entity: Tech Sergeant Reyes
  - Entity: Quartermaster Mayes
  - Entity: Doctor Richards
  - Entity: Private Sexton
  - Entity: Private Stone
  - Entity: NCR Trooper
  - Entity: NCR Guard Dog
- Fame/Infamy
- Services:
  - Caravan Player [15/15]
  - Healer/Dealer [31/31]
  - Trader [31/33]
- Crafting:
  - Campfire [96/109]
  - Campfire [97/109]
  - Reloading Bench [33/36]
- Collectibles:
  - Caravan Cards [29/30]
  - Skill Book [Science] [4/4] [1/9]
  - Sunset Sarsaparilla Star Cap [86/100]
- Guns and Ammo
- Health, Chems, or Water
- Highly Visible
- Interior Exploration
- Quest Item

After NCR captured Hoover Dam, it took them a while to fully reinforce the river to the south. The first camp that was established was Camp Forlorn Hope; an improvised mess of tin shacks, salvaged rubble from Boulder City, tents, and lots of sandbags, it is the most pathetic-looking of all NCR's camps, but the one that sees the most action. It only exists at all because of the natural spring there (in fact the camp is named for the spring). Recently, Caesar's Legion captured NCR's logistical/planning forces in the ruins of the small, ruined town of Nelson, a disaster that has disrupted Forlorn's Hopes attempts to patrol the western coast of the river.

Camp Forlorn Hope: North of Stream

1 North Entrance

Spot the flag as you traverse the gully/Bighorner trail.

2 Graveyard of No Hope

A nickname some in the camp whisper about the collection of graves of the fallen, on a two-tiered promontory behind the shacks, overlooking the Colorado River. Shoot the Bloatflies in the area for sport. Due to the height disadvantage, attack from here only if you plan to be stealthy.

3 Northeast Guard Tower

Offering commanding views of the Colorado River.

4 Northwest Guard Tower

Jump up onto the sandbags, then onto the top of the roof for an even better, unobstructed view. This is one of the best views for making out landmarks.

5 Camp Forlorn Hope Medical Center

Doctor Richards has been up to his elbows in blood and guts recently, and would quite like some help, as well as a fine-looking fellow at his side. Talk to him about the Camp, and the Legion attacks, then agree to help him find out who's stealing supplies to begin Side Quest: Medical Mystery.

- Healer: Doctor Richards [31/31]

6 Tent #1 and #2

The adjacent tents are where the officers sleep during the night.

7 Tent #3

- Note: Forlorn Hope Letter 5

8 Camp Forlorn Hope Jail

9 Spring of Forlorn Hope

The water source from whence the camp takes its name allows you to drink non-irradiated water. The stream bisects the camp.

10 Camp Forlorn Hope Shack

- Duffle Bag Items

CAMP FORLORN HOPE EXTERIOR

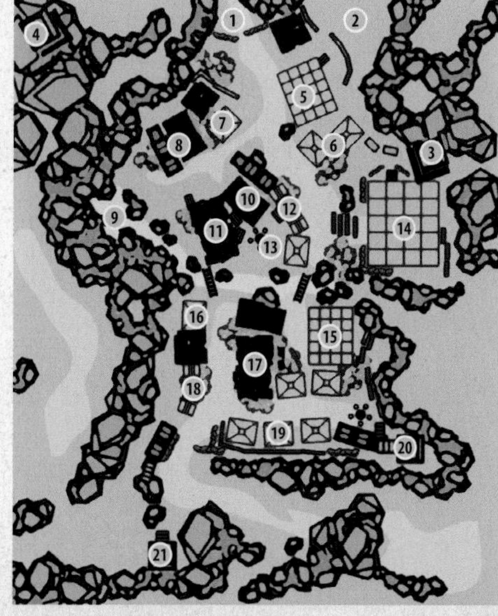

11 Camp Forlorn Hope Barracks

Private Stone, a party of interest during Side Quest: Medical Mystery, usually stands outside here. Let's just say his morale is at an all-time low. On the table in the adjoining room is a Note to steal; a letter about a brother writing his last letter to a sister. Private James Sexton is also here, and he's a little more chipper than Stone, although he is in charge of camp morale. He's having a competition; if you want in, begin Free Quest: An Ear to the Ground.

- Note: Forlorn Hope Letter 7
- Teddy Bear

12 Overflow Rest Stop

13 Tent #4 and Campfire

A small tent near the stream is adjacent to the settlement's central Campfire.

- Campfire [96/109]

14 Camp Forlorn Hope Command Center

Two key players in the camp work out of the main tent (with the flag); Tech Sergeant Reyes and Major Polatli. Both give you information on the NCR's living conditions and the Legion's threat. Speak to Reyes about the new radio codes for the Ranger Outposts to begin Side Quest: Return to Sender. Talk to Polatli, who is in charge of this camp to progress Side Quests: No, Not Much and Restoring Hope.

- Skill Book: Big Book of Science [Science] [4/4] [1/9]

Camp Forlorn Hope: South of Stream

15 Camp Forlorn Hope Quartermaster's Tent

Speak with Quartermaster Hayes, who's happy to tell you the dire situation regarding the camp's supplies. So much so, that he'll purchase anything you have; he only has some very small amount of ammunition. As a man with a sense of duty and honor, Hayes also asks whether you might conduct a small favor for him; Free Quest: Tags of Our Fallen.

- Caravan Player: Quartermaster Hayes [15/15]
- Trader: Quartermaster Hayes [31/33]
- Caravan Cards [29/30]

16 Tent #5 and Storage Shed

The tent is empty, but just east is a shack called the Storage Shed. Open the door [Very Hard] and steal the first aid inside if you want.

- First Aid Box Items (3)
- Reloading Bench [33/36]

17 Camp Forlorn Hope Mess Hall

A place to eat, although the Food is mostly squirrel-based.

- Sunset Sarsaparilla Star Cap [86/100]

18 Overflow Rest Stop

19 Southern Tents

A set of five tents provide respite from the hot Nevada sun. Check the duffle bag and the footlocker in two of the tents for a couple of poignant letters from the frontline troops.

- Note: Forlorn Hope Letter 2
- Note: Forlorn Hope Letter 3

20 Southeast Guard Tower

If you're attacking this camp, and your fighting isn't going well, flee up here, and then jump to the roofs of the tents and crouch for a brief respite, or snipe from this location.

- Campfire [97/109]

21 South Guard Tower

Technically outside the camp, this overlooks the no-man's land of the Minefield [6.S06], and the Legion-held Nelson to the south.

Free Quest: An Ear to the Ground

Private James Sexton may admit that Camp Forlorn Hope's morale is "lower than a feral Ghoul's IQ," but that's because no one has started his competition yet. Partly to complete a pun he's been working on, but mainly to improve morale, he'll pay (you a compliment) for every Legion's Ear you bring back to him. Agree to the task if you wish. For every Ear (whether on a Legionary or Caesar himself), you receive a small Fame gain.

- Legion's Ear
- NCR Fame Gained!
- Note: Sexton's Note

Free Quest: Tags of Our Fallen

Quartermaster Hayes wants to ensure the NCR commanders receive a full count of the casualties of the war with the Legion, and to honor the dead. To this end, he requests you locate any Dogtags you find from NCR soldiers found dead on your travels. For example, there are four inside the small hotel in Nipton [4.30]. Of course, if you have the Mister Sandman perk, you can murder NCR troops without a Reputation hit. However; the rewards may not be worth it.
For every Dogtag (not irradiated ones from the Ghouls at Camp Searchlight [6.16]), you receive a small Caps and Fame reward.

- NCR Dogtag
- NCR Fame Gained!
- Note: Mayes Request

[6.03] Southern Nevada Wind Farm

- Threat Level: ●●●●●
- Faction: Mutated Insect
  - Entity: Cazador
- Crafting: Workbench [40/41]
- Collectibles:
  - Skill Book [Repair] [3/4] [2/9]
  - Sunset Sarsaparilla Star Cap [87/100]
- Highly Visible
- Interior Exploration
- Radio Signal [Black Mountain]
- Wasteland Vegetation

A cluster of rusting windmills, still blowing their remaining propellers in the breeze. The place is derelict now, and Cazadors swarm about nearby. Enter the Wind Farm Maintenance Shack, and uncover a small workshop that's well worth a visit:

- Workbench [40/41]
- Skill Book: Dean's Electronics [3/4] [2/9]
- Sunset Sarsaparilla Star Cap [87/100]

[6.04] Abandoned BoS Bunker

- Threat Level: ●●●●●
- Faction: Brotherhood of Steel
  - Entity: None
- Crafting: Reloading Bench [34/36]
- Dangers: Mines
- Collectibles:
  - Skill Book [Repair] [4/4] [3/9]
  - Hollowed-Out Rock [35/42]
- Interior Exploration
- Sleeping Quarters

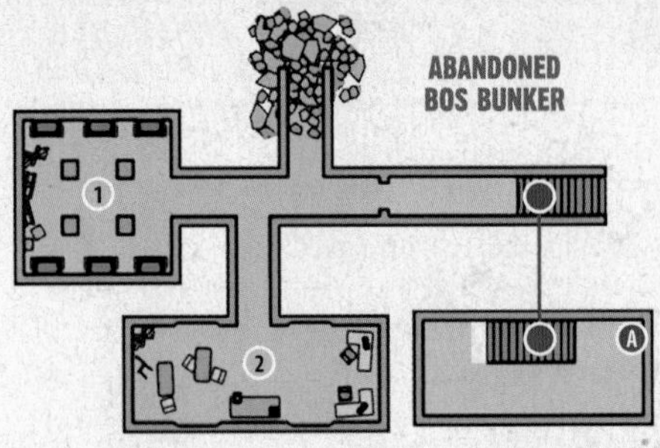

East of the Minefield [6.S06] where NCR Troopers are coming a cropper (so beware of Frag Mines as you explore this area), is a steep indent with a Hollowed-Out Rock and drainage grate; this leads to a long-abandoned Brotherhood of Steel bunker.

- Hollowed-Out Rock [35/42]

A Ladder to Mojave Wasteland

1 Western Dormitory

- Weapon Repair Kit
- Footlocker Items (4)
- Sleeping Quarters

2 Canteen and Workshop

- Reloading Bench [34/36]
- Skill Book: Dean's Electronics [4/4] [3/9]

[6.05] Toxic Dump Site

- Threat Level: ●●●●●
- Faction: Robot
  - Entity: Crazed Mister Handy
- Dangers: Radiation

Directly east of Novac [5.18] is a collection of dumped radioactive barrels, occasionally guarded by a Crazed Mister Handy. It doesn't take much to bring him down, but he will go down fighting! There's nothing else here except slight radiation poisoning.

[6.06] Nelson ●

- Side Quest: Back in Your Own Backyard
- Side Quest: Restoring Hope
- Side Quest: We Are Legion
- Side Quest: I Forgot to Remember to Forget
- Threat Level: ●●●●●
- Faction: Caesar's Legion
  - Entity: Legionary
  - Entity: Explorer
  - Entity: Mongrel
  - Entity: NCR Trooper
  - Entity: Dead Sea
- Fame/Infamy
- Crafting: Campfire [98/109]
- Dangers: Mines
- Collectibles:
  - Unique Item [92/95]
  - Unique Weapon [35/42]
- Guns and Ammo
- Health, Chems, or Water
- Interior Exploration
- Sleeping Quarters

Nelson was a second NCR outpost, as the Republic slowly gained ground along the Colorado River to stem the tide of the Legion's advancement across Arizona. But Caesar struck back, razing Nelson, and capturing any NCR troopers that weren't executed or shot, and crucified them as an example of barbarism; to crush the NCR morale.

Around the perimeter and on the thoroughfares are Legion Explorers who stop you and ask what you're doing. You can:

Offend them, and attack.

- Tell them you're passing through. You're asked to go before the Legion's Decanus in this camp; Dead Sea. You can:
  - Refuse and attack. Attacking Nelson, you should expect at least eight Legionaries, a couple of Mongrels, and Dead Sea himself. Slay him to claim his Unique Machete.
  - Or agree. Dead Sea is a little less eager to fight you; he knows you are free to wander this area (even before you've received the Mark of Caesar during the Main Quest). Or, you can team up with him, and start Side Quest: We Are Legion.

1 Road to Nelson

The main road from Novac to Nelson has an NCR Ranger Checkpoint [6.S05] where Ranger Milo is attempting to give the crucified Troopers in town a quick death. The road continues down (watch for Frag Mines) and around the perimeter, to the northeast Guard Tower.

2 The Fleeing Rocks

A good way to flee out of Nelson is to use the planks to the rocky ground and then to the road.

3 Northwest Guard Tower

Watch for Frag Mines on the path above town. This area, and the ridge along the western side of the settlement, are excellent hiding or sniping spots. The empty flagpole waits for the Bear to roar again!

4 Southwest Guard Tower

This marks the perimeter of the settlement, and where most troops move through.

5 Southwestern Nelson House

- Sleeping Quarters

6 Western Nelson House

- Carton of Cigarettes
- Sleeping Quarters

NELSON EXTERIOR

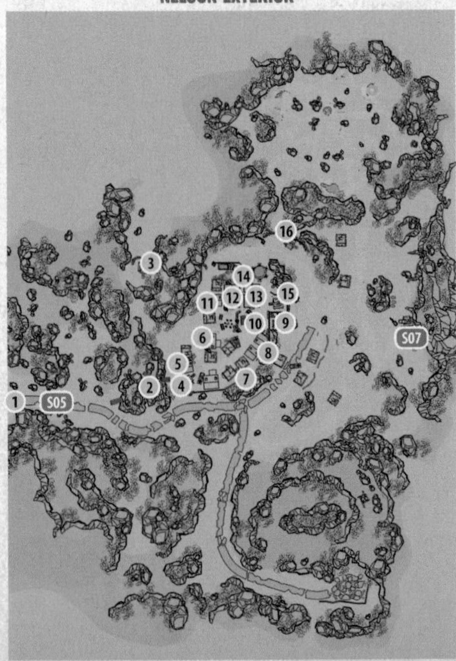

7 Portable Generator and Burned Houses

You can turn this off, and switch off the lights. This simply causes it to become slightly darker (including the nearby house interiors, sometimes). Note that all the burned-out shells of Nelson homes have no items of interest.

8 Nelson Row Houses (2)

Inside one you'll find a load of Food in the fridge and on shelving, while the other one has been turned into a storage room.

- Carton of Cigarettes
- Ammo
- Sleeping Quarters

9 Eastern Entrance

You approach this from lower ground, which isn't usually a great move (as you can see foes moving about), but is a good way to Sneak quickly to the crucified soldiers.

10 Crucified NCR Troopers

You can leave them to rot, or untie and free them, depending on your emotional state. Be sure you're engaged in a Side Quest first!

- Campfire [98/109]

11 Northwest Nelson House

- Unique Item: Nuka-Cola Victory [92/95]
- Sleeping Quarters

12 Center Barracks

The remains of the fallen NCR soldiers still litter this building.

- Sleeping Quarters

13 Northeast Barracks

The intact building nearest the water tower is where Dead Sea resides, along with his unique Machete.

- Unique Weapon: Liberator [35/40]
- First Aid Box
- Sleeping Quarters

14 Portable Generator

You can turn this generator between the two barracks to "off," and dim the lights, coaxing the enemy out of their barracks, and into your fire.

15 16 Northern Guard Towers (Outer and Inner)

The other two towers are at the north end of the settlement, which faces the NCR Camp Forlorn Hope through a mine-filled opening. Entering town from here is trickier, as you need to content with the hill, and lack of view of the enemy. To the west is the Nelson Lookout [6.S07], with views of the Colorado River.

[6.07] Clark Field

- Side Quest: Come Fly With Me
- Threat Level:
- Faction: Mutated Animal
    - Entity: Golden Gecko
- Dangers: Radiation
- Quest Item

Highway 95 winds around this place, as if to escape the death and stagnation: A small power plant and nuclear storage site bombed long ago, with containment reactors slowly leaking out radiation, Clark Field now sports broken concrete and dead corpses, succumbing to the poisoning or the pack of Golden Geckos that roams here. The facility itself has little to scavenge, although a fallen Pack Brahmin has spilled out a couple of Stimpaks. A skeleton near the south parking lot has some scattered Caps and ammo. But the main item of interest is on the Scavenger in the Radiation Suit on the road from Novac [5.18]. This is the late, great Mr. RADical; and his Igniting Agent fuels rockets to the stars! Check out his Journal to read the musings of a man a little too over-confident in the abilities of his suit.

- Stimpaks and Caps
- Radiation Suit
- Note: Mr. RADical's Journal
- Isotope-239 Igniting Agent

[6.08] Techatticup Mine

- Side Quest: Anywhere I Wander
- Threat Level:
- Faction: Caesar's Legion
    - Entity: Recruit Legionary
    - Entity: Legion Mongrel
    - Entity: Alexus
    - Entity: NCR Trooper
- Dangers: Radiation
- Collectibles:
    - Magazine [Explosives] [12/12] [1-3/5]
    - Magazine [Survival] [30/30] [1-3/5]
    - Magazine [Unarmed] [11/11] [1-3/5]
    - Hollowed-Out Rock [36/42]
- Guns and Ammo
- Interior Exploration
- Wasteland Vegetation
- Quest Item

Also known colloquially in the past as Knob Hill Mine, this hole in the ground is at the turnaround at the end of the road from Nelson, and seems to have been a dumping ground, or storage area for radioactive waste that the Legion now occasionally utilizes. Along the road, you may meet Private Renolds, talking about "that bastard" Alexus; a Legion commander who's taken his squad hostage. This begins Side Quest: Anywhere I Wander, but you can free (or ignore or kill) the NCR in here without running into Renolds. Check the Hollowed-Out Rock at the entrance before proceeding.

- Hollowed-Out Rock [36/42]

A Exit to Mojave Wasteland

1 Entrance Chamber

This junction chamber features scattered radioactive barrels.

2 Upper Cavern

With the remains of a wooden floor, this too is filled with radioactive barrels (and some scattered skeletons) as well as a Legion presence (around four soldiers and a mongrel). The two gates [Average] are locked, and each contains an NCR soldier. Picking the lock causes the Legion to turn hostile. Inside the gates are the following:

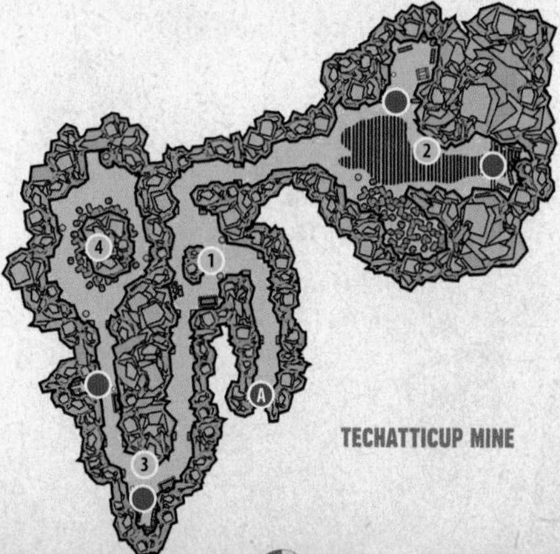

- Legion Explorer Armor
- Melee Weapons
- Magazine: Patriot's Cookbook [Explosives] [12/12] [1/5]
- Magazine: Lad's Life [Survival] [30/30] [2/5]
- Doctor's Bag
- Ammo Box Ammunition
- Food and Picked Plants

3 Storage Tunnel

There are two storages room to break into [Average] along the way, with the following goods inside:

- Doctor's Bag
- Food and Super Stimpak (2)
- Magazine: Boxing Times [Unarmed] [11/11] [3/5]
- Ammo Box Ammunition (2)
- Brass Knuckles (2)
- Frag Grenade (3)
- Frag Mine (2)
- Explorer Hood
- Legion Recruit Armor

4 Lower Cavern

This is the most spectacular of the caverns, now ruined by the piles of radioactive barrels. The Legion are here, too; there's around six soldiers, and their leader Alexus. You can speak to him, but he doesn't do much talking unless the Quest is active. You can steal (Pickpocket or from his corpse) his key though; this opens every storage gate.

- Techatticup Storage Key

[6.09] Lucky Jim Mine

- Threat Level:
- Faction: Mutated Animal
    - Entity: Fire Gecko
- Crafting: Workbench [41/41]
- Collectibles:
    - Skill Book [Speech] [4/4] [4/9]
    - Hollowed-Out Rock [37/42]
- Guns and Ammo
- Interior Exploration
- Sleeping Quarters
- Wasteland Vegetation

Before entering, check the side of the side where the lean-to is, for a Hollowed-Out Rock. You can also leap onto the shack roof and take pot-shots at Geckos without fear of retaliation. There isn't actually a mine here anymore, although Bootjack Cavern [6.S10] is on the other (western) side of the mountain ridge the Mine House sits on. Bootjack Cavern is easily accessed from Highway 95.

- Hollowed-Out Rock [37/42]
- Workbench [41/41]
- Sleeping Quarters
- Skill Book: Lying, Congressional Style [Speech] [4/4] [4/9]

[6.10] Ranger Station Echo

- Side Quest: Return to Sender
- Side Quest: We Will All Go Together
- Threat Level:
- Faction: NCR, Ghoul
    - Entity: Ranger Erasmus
    - Entity: Comm Officer Green
- Fame/Infamy
- Guns and Ammo
- Highly Visible
- Sleeping Quarters

This is arguably the most remote of the Ranger Stations. Look for the radio mast to guide you to the small encampment. The place is run by Ranger Erasmus, who watches the Legion's movement toward Cottonwood Cove [6.20]. The rest of the Rangers are Ghouls, as this particular camp is friendly to these type of folk. Comm Officer Green (the other Smoothskin) operates the radio, and you can quiz him about troop movements too.

- Binoculars
- Ammo Box Ammunition [Easy]
- Sleeping Quarters

[6.11] Cliffside Prospector Camp

- Threat Level: ●●●●●
- Faction: Caesar's Legion/ Mutated Animal
  - Entity: None
- Crafting: Campfire [99/109]
- Collectibles: Sunset Sarsaparilla Star Cap [88/100]
- Health, Chems, or Water

Offering some of the most spectacular views of the Colorado River, this is a lonely perch surrounded by rocky terrain.

- Campfire [99/109]
- Sunset Sarsaparilla Star Cap [88/100]
- Healing Powder (2)

[6.12] Searchlight North Gold Mine

- Threat Level: ●●●●●
- Faction: Ghoul
  - Entity: Feral Trooper Ghoul
  - Entity: Glowing Trooper Ghoul
- Dangers: Radiation
- Collectibles:
  - Hollowed-Out Rock [38/42]
  - Sunset Sarsaparilla Star Cap [89/100]
- Area Is Locked
- Guns and Ammo
- Health, Chems, or Water
- Interior Exploration

Just outside the irradiated perimeter of Camp Searchlight [6.16] and almost adjacent to the Coyote Mines is a hole in the ground, close to the water tower. Check the Hollowed-Out Rock just to the left and above the entrance.

- Hollowed-Out Rock [38/42]

1 Gold Mine Junction

Expect your first interior Ghoul fight at this point.

2 Storage Alcove

A Feral Trooper Ghoul is guarding this collection of bric-a-brac:

- Sunset Sarsaparilla Star Cap [89/100]
- Sunset Sarsaparilla Crate Items
- Purified Water
- Dynamite (3)

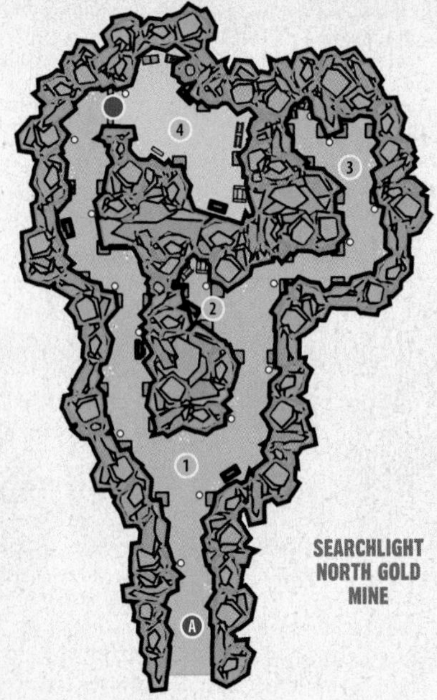

3 Dead-End

Glowing Ghoul Troopers guard this second storage area with a dead Prospector nearby.

- Searchlight North Mine Key
- Dynamite (7)

4 Locked Gate and Storage

At the end of the other corridor (and Ghoul fighting) is a locked Gate [Hard], also opened using the Searchlight North Mine Key.

- Ammo Box Ammunition

[6.13] Coyote Mines

- Threat Level: ●●●●●
- Faction: Prospector
  - Entity: Prospector
- Collectibles: Sunset Sarsaparilla Star Cap [90/100]
- Guns and Ammo
- Health, Chems, or Water
- Interior Exploration
- Sleeping Quarters
- Wasteland Vegetation

Among the Prickly Pears are the ruins of the old Coyote Mines. There are two places to investigate: the mine house and the shaft. Check the house for the following:

- Sunset Sarsaparilla Star Cap [90/100]
- First Aid Box (3)
- BB Gun and Ammo
- Sleeping Quarters

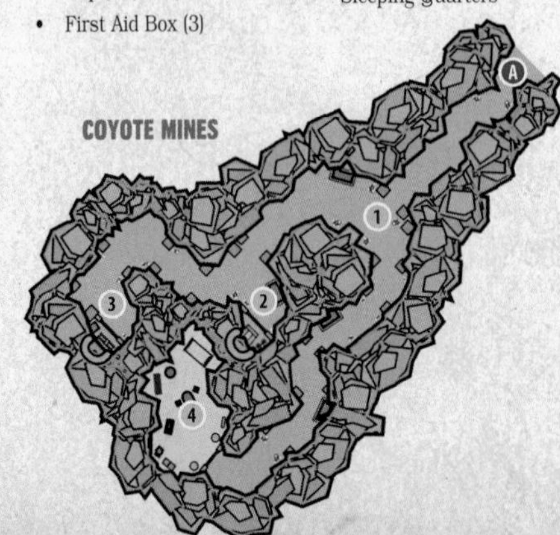

A Exit to Mojave Wasteland (under Shack)

1 Mine Entrance

On the other side of the rocky outcrop, under the mine house, is the entrance to the mine itself.

2 Storage Alcove

Open the unlocked gate to gather Dynamite.

- Dynamite (8)
- Sack Items (3)

3 Second Storage Alcove

- Dynamite (7)
- Frag Grenade (3)

4 Prospectors' Cavern

There's a couple of Prospectors, as well as the following items:

- Hydra Healing Powder (2)
- Sleeping Quarters

[6.14] Wolfhorn Ranch

- Threat Level: ●●●●●
- Faction: None
  - Entity: None
- Crafting: Campfire [100/109]
- Collectibles:
  - Skill Book [Lockpick] [4/4] [5/9]
  - Unique Weapon [36/42]
- Guns and Ammo
- Highly Visible
- Interior Exploration
- Sleeping Quarters
- Wasteland Vegetation

What was once a profitable Bighorner ranch has recently been abandoned, and its owner—a man named Ulysses—is nowhere to be found. Scour the place, especially the farmhouse itself (which has most of the items you want). Down at the bottom of the garden is a well and a tank with irradiated water (only sip if you're desperate), and an allotment with a few plants to pick.

- Campfire [100/109]
- Skill Book: Tumblers Today [4/4] [5/9]
- Unique Weapon: Chopper [36/42]
- Grave Items
- Ammo Box Ammunition (3)
- Sleeping Quarters

[6.15] Raided Farmstead

- Threat Level: ●●●●●
- Faction: Viper Gang
  - Entity: Viper Gunslinger
- Collectibles: Sunset Sarsaparilla Star Cap [91/100]
- Guns and Ammo
- Health, Chems, or Water
- Wasteland Vegetation

An old farmstead with Maize still in the patch of earth. The place has been picked clean, most likely by Viper Gang members, who usually turn up here to ambush you. There are some items to grab inside the caravan trailer, and the roof makes a good sniping or viewing platform.

- Healing Powder
- Ammo Box Ammunition
- Ammo Case Ammunition
- First Aid Box
- Sunset Sarsaparilla Star Cap [91/100]

[6.16] Camp Searchlight

- Side Quest: Come Fly With Me
- Side Quest: We Will All Go Together
- Side Quest: Wheel of Fortune
- Threat Level: ●●●●●
- Faction: Ghoul
  - Entity: Trooper Ghoul
  - Entity: Feral Trooper Ghoul
  - Entity: Glowing Trooper Ghoul
  - Entity: Private Edwards
  - Entity: Logan
  - EntityL Prospector
  - Entity: Golden Gecko
  - Entity: Radscorpion
  - Entity: Radscorpion Queen
- Crafting: Reloading Bench [35/36]
- Dangers: Radiation!
- Collectibles:
  - Skill Book [Sneak] [4/4] [6/9]
  - Magazines [Random]
  - Magazine [Speech] [12/12] [4/5]
  - Sunset Sarsaparilla Star Cap [92/100]
  - Unique Item [93/95]
  - Unique Item [94/95]
  - Unique Weapon [37/42]
  - Unique Weapon [38/42]
- Area Is Locked
- Guns and Ammo
- Health, Chems, or Water
- Highly Visible
- Interior Exploration
- Quest Item
- Wild Wasteland

As an unfortunate twist of fate would have it, a convoy of flatbed trucks transporting nuclear waste from San Onofre was passing through Searchlight when the Great War broke out. Local police directed the drivers to temporarily park their vehicles in the fire department, but no one ever came back to retrieve them. There they sat in their extremely sturdy solid steel spent fuel flasks for over 200 years. The NCR recently set up a sizable base here; but this was a major obstacle for Caesar's Legion due to its size and clear view of the surrounding desert. When it became obvious that a direct assault would not prove fruitful, Vulpes Inculta sent in some spies to learn more about the situation. After he learned about the radioactive waste being stored in the fire station, he ordered some unwitting legionaries to open the containers. Though the legionaries died almost instantly, the sacrifice produced a massive wave of death and ghoulification among NCR troops that effectively destroyed Camp Searchlight as a viable military base.

This location is also the most radioactive in the Mojave Wasteland, so stock up on Rad-X and RadAway, and obtain a Radioactive Suit (there's a free one in Clark Field [6.07]) to minimize sickness.

Automated Turret Defenses

Five sets of Mark III Turrets guard the north (Location #4), northeast (#5), east (#6), south (#10), and west (#8) perimeter roads of Camp Searchlight. Currently, all are dormant, as the NCR Ghoul Troopers don't have the semblance of brainpower needed to utilize them. But you do; you can optionally Sneak to, and then hack into each nearby terminal (one per set of turret defenses), and activate them. They now mow down all enemies; allowing you to coax foes into the firing line.

CAMP SEARCHLIGHT EXTERIOR

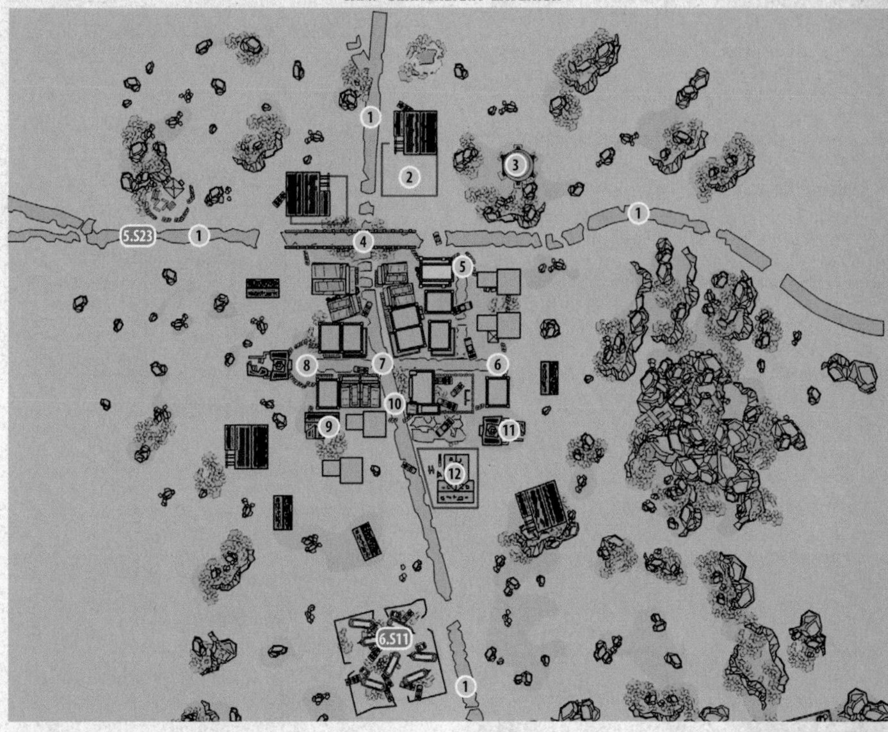

Camp Searchlight: Exterior

Note There are a number of bungalows, stores, and other structures in this town. Unless otherwise stated, these are sealed, and their surroundings have no items of any use.

1 Radioactive Perimeter (N, S, E, W)

No matter which direction you approach this settlement, as soon as you pass the radiation markers (in this case, traveling west to east), you begin to suffer Radiation poisoning.

2 Brahmin Paddocks

Flies are buzzing about the irradiated bodies of the Brahmin, killed in the attack. The bungalows are boarded up.

3 Water Tower

In the northeast outskirts, this has the benefit of being on higher ground, so you can snipe the Ghouls below from here, or (if you're not wearing a Radiation Suit) from the hill a few dozen feet northwest of the tower.

4 I-95 Overpass Bridge and North Turret Defenses [Easy]

This is a reasonably good location to attack from; allowing you to strike from above, back up if you're charged and overwhelmed by the Ghouls near the Police Station, and drop to the road below if you need to flee. Note the Turrets you can use to your advantage here.

5 Searchlight Police Station and Northeast Turret Defenses [Average]

This was the base of communications operations before the sabotage occurred. Currently it is sealed up, and the only known key resides with a Prospector called Logan; Side Quest: Wheel of Fortune. Expect a Ghoul and Radscorpion presence around this building. Note the turrets you can take advantage of.

6 Eastern Turret Defenses [Very Easy]

As this road ends at a bungalow, the turrets are easy to hack. There's Ghouls here too, and easy access over the cliff to the Searchlight East Gold Mine [6.17].

7 Main Street

The I-95 runs through from north to south, passing the Fire Station (with the NCR flag) and Elementary School along the way. This is a great place to back up and use your line of sight to attack enemies.

8 Searchlight Western Chapel and Turret Defenses [Average]

Beware of both Ghouls and Radscorpions in this area. The ruined chapel offers reasonable defensive areas (the walls and doorways) to attack from. At the back is a Cellar Door to Searchlight NCR Storage.

Enter the Cellar Door and root around in this root cellar, although three Prospectors (including Logan) have got there first. Logan's a real piece of work, but if you can stand him, you can team up and begin Side Quest: Wheel of Fortune. Or you can kill him for the keys to the two largest buildings in town. Check the NCR Storage Database Terminal [Average] (as part of the Side Quest) or open the Floor Safe [Average] using Bobby Pins. Search the room for the following:

- > Current Inventory
- > Log Entry #1836
- > Log Entry #2257
- Reloading Bench [35/36]
- Quest Item: Searchlight Fire Station Key
- Quest Item: Searchlight Police Station Key
- First Aid Box and Chems
- Doctor's Bag
- Scrap Metal
- Carton of Cigarettes (2)
- Ammo Box Ammunition
- Ranger Grey Hat
- Floor Safe Items [Average]

9 Searchlight Home

The only bungalow able to be entered is this one, which is home to Private Edward; the only (non-feral) survivor of the attack. Speaking to him at length is the crux of Side Quest: We Will All Go Together. He has a Dogtag on him, but the home is pretty spartan, aside from the Magazine on the bedroom dresser.

- Magazine: Meeting People [Speech] [12/12] [4/5]
- Quest Item: Irradiated Dogtag
- Dino Toy
- Knife

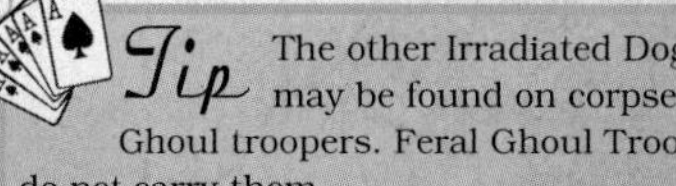

Tip The other Irradiated Dogtags may be found on corpses of Ghoul troopers. Feral Ghoul Troopers do not carry them.

10 Searchlight Fire Station and Southern Turret Defenses [Very Hard]

Activating the turrets here is difficult. This is the main defenses on the south side, adjacent to the Fire Station and School. Currently, the Fire Station is sealed up, and the only known key resides with a Prospector called Logan; Side Quest: Wheel of Fortune.

11 Eastern Church

The small church on the eastern side of town also has a cellar door and basement. The room is far less stocked, but features far more useful items than Location #8; expunge the Golden Geckos, and check the room out for three anointed grenades, some Mini-Nukes, and a Skill Book on the floor by the shelves.

- Skill Book: Chinese Army: Spec. Ops. Training Manual [Sneak] [4/4] [6/9]
- Unique Item: Mini-Nuke [93/95]
- Unique Item: Mini-Nuke [94/95]
- Unique Weapon: Holy Frag Grenade (3) [37/42]

12 Searchlight Elementary School

Golden Geckos are slobbering around here, so take care of them before conducting a thorough search.

- First Aid Box
- Teddy Bear
- Dino Toy (5)
- Rocket Souvenir (3)

Tip There's many more of these Rocket Souvenirs up at Novac; and they are needed as part of Side Quest: Come Fly With Me. You require five for a Quest Objective; so visit Novac for more.

Searchlight Police Station: Interior

Note NCR Equipment is stored in this location, which Logan needs as part of Side Quest: Wheel of Fortune. The equipment is NOT THERE if the Quest isn't active! If the Quest is active, here's where to find everything:

SEARCHLIGHT POLICE STATION

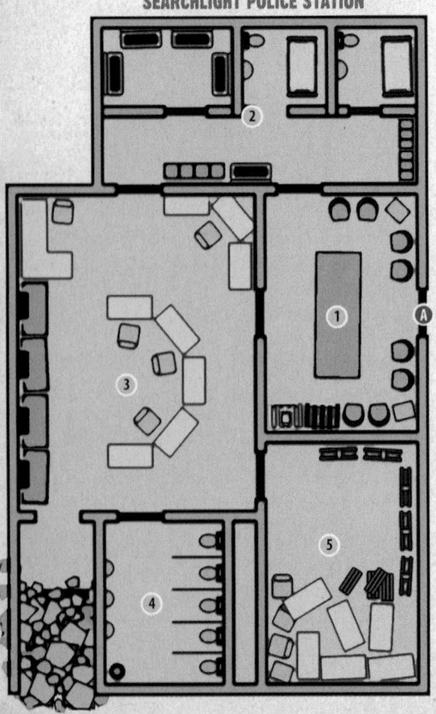

Room Description	Quest Item	Location
Southeast Storage Room	NCR Grenade Rifle	On the wooden crates
Southeast Storage Room	NCR Frag Grenade (3)	On the metal shelf
Communications Room	NCR 10mm Pistol	On a desk
Communications Room	NCR Computer Parts	Inside two separate desks
Communications Room	NCR Radio Parts	Inside two separate desks
Cell Row	NCR 9mm Submachine Gun	Inside right-side cell, below mattress

A Doors to Camp Searchlight

1 Entrance Room

Check the Vending Machines for items. Expect the NCR Troopers manning this communications building to be a lot more feral, and a lot less human.

2 Cell Row

- Rad-X
- Quest Item: NCR 9mm Submachine Gun

3 Central Communications Room

The main chamber in the Police Station has a Communications Terminal [Easy] to access, offering the following information snippets (including the final missive from Camp Searchlight as the radiation seepage was detected):

> Communications Status
> Communications Entry #842
> Communications Entry #923
> Communications Entry #937

- Quest Item: NCR 10mm Pistol
- Quest Item: NCR Computer Parts
- Quest Item: NCR Radio Parts

4 Bathrooms

- First Aid Box

5 Storage Room

- Ammo Box Ammunition (2)
- Scrap Metal
- Quest Item: NCR Grenade Rifle
- Quest Item: NCR Frag Grenade (3)

Searchlight Fire Station: Interior

Room Description	Quest Item	Location
Fire Officer's Southwest room	NCR 9mm Submachine Gun	On a wooden bookcase
Fire Officer's Southwest room	NCR Frag Grenade (2)	On a wooden bookcase
Eastern Barracks/ Mess Room	NCR Radio Parts (2)	On a small table
Eastern Barracks/ Mess Room	NCR Computer Parts (2)	Inside a Duffle Bag
Eastern Barracks/ Mess Room	NCR Computer Parts (2)	Inside a Duffle Bag

A Door to Camp Searchlight

1 Station Garage

A gigantic Radscorpion Queen dominates the ground floor, and is a fearsome foe. Beware her pincers, and smaller brethren! If you survive, there's bottles in the Vending Machine, and the following:

- Fire Axe (2)
- Fire Helmet (5)
- Radaway (2)

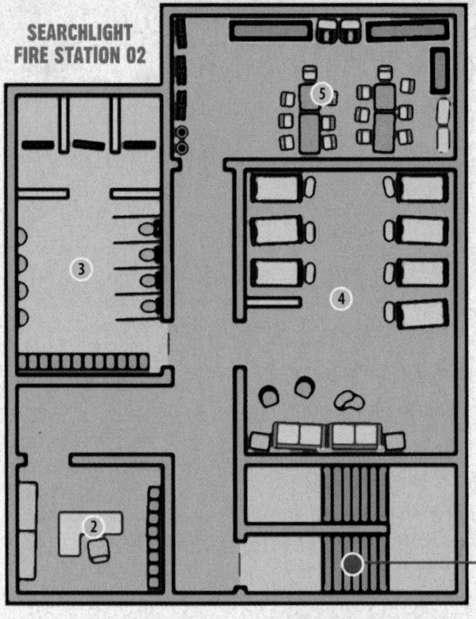

SEARCHLIGHT FIRE 01

2 (Upper) Fire Officer's Southwest Room

This chamber is empty of humans, but there's some information contained on the Chief Fire Officer's Terminal [Easy].

> Chief Fire Officer Report No. F1-218

- Fire Helmet
- Radaway
- Quest Item: NCR 9mm Submachine Gun
- Quest Item: NCR Frag Grenade (2)

3 (Upper) Restrooms

There's a skeleton of a long-dead fireman in one of the stalls, and an extra-special Fireaxe!

- Fire Helmet
- Radaway (2)
- Unique Weapon: Knock Knock [38/42]

4 Eastern Barracks/Mess Room

The beds can't be slept on (as you're in a Radiation hot-zone), but be sure to check all the duffle bags as one usually contains a number of Magazines.

- Trooper Helmet
- Magazines: [Random]
- Quest Item: NCR Radio Parts (2)
- Quest Item: NCR Computer Parts (4)

5 (Upper) Kitchen

The shelves of Food are irradiated, meaning you'll receive radiation if you consume it. Only the fridge Food is safe. Check the table with the bottle on it for a Star Cap.

- Sunset Sarsaparilla Star Cap [92/100]

[6.17] Searchlight East Gold Mine

- Threat Level: ●●●●●
- Faction: Viper Gang
  - Entity: Viper Gunslinger
  - Entity: Viper Leader
- Collectibles: Hollowed-Out Rock [39/42]
- Interior Exploration

Mesh reinforced paths and a small bridge over the side of the ravine lead to one of two gold mines close to town. Climb the shale pile southeast of the entrance to locate a well-hidden Hollowed-Out Rock.

- Hollowed-Out Rock [39/42]

Ⓐ Exit to Mojave Wasteland

① Big Cavern Viper Gang

The eastern mine is one huge cavern of still air and half-covered mine carts and tracks. Use the lanterns to situate yourself and follow the half-buried rails to the far end, where Viper Gang scavengers must be faced.

- Healing Powder (2)

② Viper Gang Ambush

When combat begins, four more Viper Gunslingers appear to ambush you from the entrance/exit.

[6.18] Sniper's Nest

- Threat Level: ●●●●●
- Faction: Caesar's Legion
  - Entity: Legion Sniper
- Crafting: Campfire [101/109]
- Collectibles:
  - Sunset Sarsaparilla Star Cap [93/100]
  - Unique Weapon [39/42]
- Guns and Ammo
- Health, Chems, or Water
- Sleeping Quarters

Usually with a Legion Sniper inside the lean-to, this cliff-top perch offers coverage of the valley down to the Cottonwood Cove [6.20] and the river, as well as an aiming platform facing Ranger Station Echo [6.10] to the north. Pry open the locked Gun Case [Very Hard] for a very special Sniper Rifle.

- Campfire [101/109]
- Sunset Sarsaparilla Star Cap [93/100]
- Unique Weapon: Gobi Campaign Scout Rifle [39/42]
- Ammo Box Ammunition (2)
- Healing Powder
- Sleeping Quarters

[6.19] Cottonwood Overlook

- Side Quest: Eye For An Eye
- Threat Level: ●●●●●
- Faction: Caesar's Legion
  - Entity: None
- Crafting: Campfire [102/109]
- Dangers: Radiation
- Quest Item

A popular scenic overlook is now an abandoned promontory offering a good view (and sniping position) of the Legion at Cottonwood Cove below. A precariously parked big-rig with its trailer cargo of highly radioactive barrels is teetering on the edge of the north cliff. You can release the barrels, killing everyone in the camp, but only if you wish to incur the fury of Caesar!

- Campfire [102/109]

[6.20] Cottonwood Cove ●

See map on the following page

- Main Quest: Render Unto Caesar
- Side Quest: Aba Daba Honeymoon
- Side Quest: Oh My Papa
- Side Quest: An Eye for an Eye
- Side Quest: I Forgot to Remember to Forget
- Side Quest: Left My Heart
- Free Quest: Arizona Scavenger
- Free Quest: Caching in at the Cove
- Threat Level: ●●●●●
- Faction: Caesar's Legion
  - Entity: Anders
  - Entity: Legionary Explorer
  - Entity: Legionary
  - Entity: Legion Mongrel
  - Entity: Decanus Severus
  - Entity: Canyon Runner
  - Entity: Mrs. Weathers
  - Entity: Kenny Weathers
  - Entity: Sammy Weathers
  - Entity: Cursor Lucullus
  - Entity: Aurelius of Phoenix
- Fame/Infamy
- Services: Trader [32/33]
- Crafting:
  - Campfire [103/109]
  - Reloading Bench [36/36]
- Dangers: Radiation
- Collectibles:
  - Hollowed-Out Rock [40/42]
  - Skill Book [Melee Weapons] [4/4] [7/9]
  - Magazine [Energy Weapons] [10/10] [5/5]
  - Magazine [Random]
  - Sunset Sarsaparilla Star Cap [94/100]
  - Unique Weapon [40/42]
- Area Is Locked
- Guns and Ammo
- Health, Chems, or Water
- Interior Exploration
- Lots O' Caps
- Wasteland Vegetation
- Quest Item
- Wild Wasteland

The largest encampment of Legion forces on the western side of the Colorado River, these Arizonian slavers have a foothold in Nevada, and use this position to bring in troops and supplies from Caesar's main base on Fortification Hill. As you approach, you can see a once-picturesque river camp, you're stopped by a Legionary explorer, who wants to know why you're here. You can:

Show him the Mark of Caesar, if you've received it from Vulpes Inculta at The Tops Casino [2D.04].

Reply that you're a trader passing through.

Tell him you're a friend of the Legion

Attack him, or get attacked if your Reputation is problematic enough.

Soon afterward, you can pass by some crucified Wastelanders, and all are beyond help. If Side Quest: Aba Daba Honeymoon or Oh My Papa are active, one of the slaves is a man named Anders who you can rescue as part of either Quest. Now enter the camp.

① Camp Cottonwood Entrance

Check the road between the sets of crucifixion poles for a special rock. Note the container truck perched on the low bluff to the south, on the edge of Cottonwood Overlook [6.19], which can be opened to kill this entire settlement.

- Hollowed-Out Rock [40/42]

② Ruined Chalets

These are boarded up and near an irradiated pond.

③ Legion Tents

The northern part of the camp has a set of red tents near a Campfire, and a larger tent where Decanus Severus and Canyon Runner reside. You can ask him questions about this place, and the battles with the NCR. Severus carries a slightly more damaging Machete, and a more feathery helmet, which you can loot from his corpse.

- Campfire [103/109]
- Personal Footlocker Items (2)
- Machete Gladius
- Legion Prime Armor
- Prime Decanus Helmet

④ Capture Pen and Canyon Runner

A family of three; Mrs. Weathers and her children Kenny and Sammy, are being held against their will in the Capture Pen. They have explosive collars around their necks, so unlocking the pen gate [Hard] and telling them to flee doesn't work that well. Speaking to any of them is an alternate way to begin Side Quest: Left My Heart. Canyon Runner "owns" these slaves; although they aren't "broken in" yet, so he calls them "captures." You can:

Talk to him about how the Legion set up this camp, and how he joined the Legion.

And also about the slaves themselves. At this point you can purchase or bargain Canyon Runner into selling them to you, as part of the Side Quest. You can Pickpocket or loot the Slave Key from him, too.

- Slaver (Canyon Runner): The Weathers Family
- Quest Item: Slave Key
- Machete Gladius

⑤ Cottonwood Storage Building

Behind the main building is a small concrete hut. Inside you'll find a lot of scattered ammo, a Reloading Bench, Sunset Sarsaparilla crates, and the following:

- Ammo
- Reloading Bench [36/36]
- Apple
- Police Baton

⑥ Headquarters

This is the prominent structure in the Cove, being two stories tall. Inside the ground floor is the Legion Radio (which needs to be bugged as part of Side Quest: An Eye for an Eye). There's a fair few items to steal, too:

- Binoculars
- Combat Knife
- Machete (3)
- Police Baton (2)
- Hunting Rifle and Ammo
- Gun Cabinet Items (2)
- Lots of Ammo

The building has the grammatically incorrect "Romanes Eunt Domus" ("Romanes' they go to the house" instead of "Romans go home") daubed on the side.

COTTONWOOD COVE

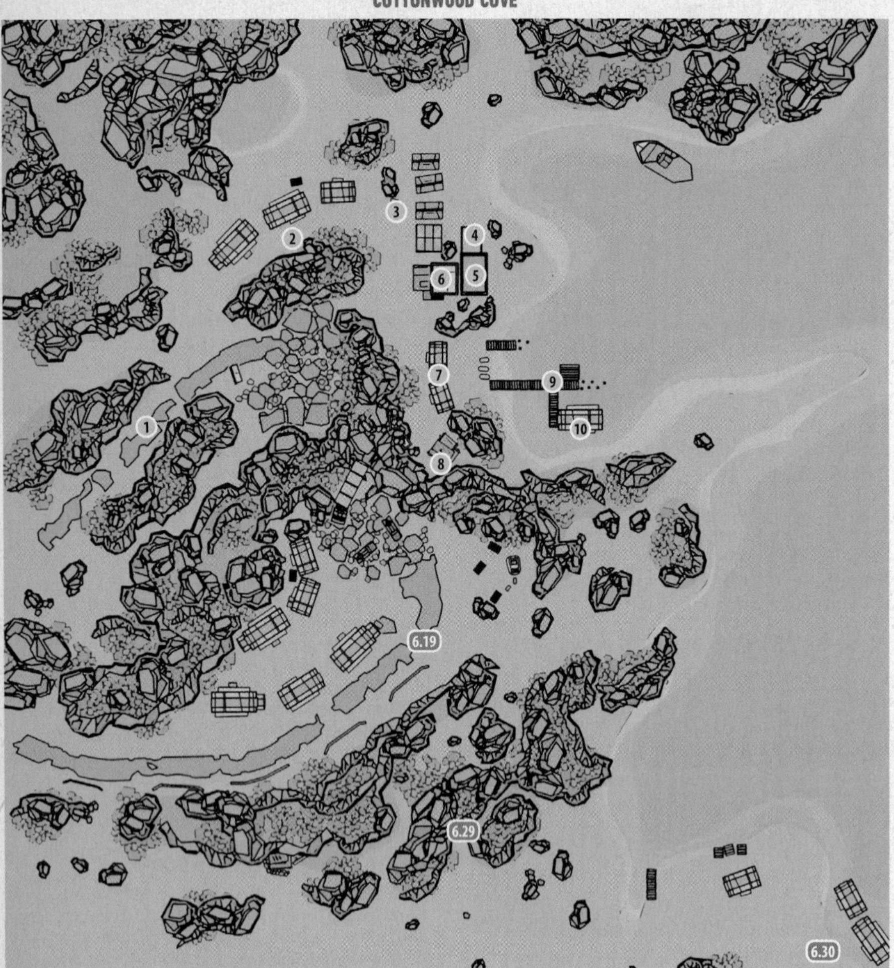

Upstairs, which is accessed from the exterior metal steps, is where the Camp's Centurion leader—Auelius of Phoenix—stands and surveys his camp, when he's not sleeping. When you've befriended him, you can begin Free Quest: Arizona Scavenger. Check inside the upper floor, to claim the following items, which includes Patrol Notes (vital for Side Quest: An Eye for an Eye), a possible Magazine inside his desk, and an impressive Unique Weapon made from Dogtags.

- Gun Cabinet Items (2)
- Skill Book: Grognak the Barbarian [Melee Weapons] [4/4] [7/9]
- Magazine: Lad's Life [Survival]
- Quest Item: Patrol Notes
- Unique Weapon: Recompense of the Fallen [40/42]
- Centurion Helmet
- Legion Centurion Armor
- Machete Gladius

7 Cove Restrooms

The two chalet structures aren't particularly sanitary, although the toilet (or urinal) water you can drink isn't irradiated.

- Magazine: Future Weapons Today [Energy Weapons] [10/10] [5/5]
- Sunset Sarsaparilla Star Cap [94/100]

8 Cove Shack

- Chems and Scrap Metal

9 Cottonwood Jetty

Out on the cove itself is a wooden jetty where Cursor Lucullus meets you, but only after you've met Vulpes Inculta after exiting The Tops Casino for the first time. It is here you can take a boat to The Fort [3.28] to meet Caesar himself.

10 Mess Hall

There is also a Mess Hall building attached to the jetty which is locked [Hard], and contains a lot of Maize, and food-preparation implements. It is usually empty.

- Maize

Free Quest: Arizona Scavenger

Speak with Aurelius of Phoenix at his headquarters, and after exchanging pleasantries, he lets you know about his killing prowess. At this point, you can ask him if he pays a bounty for NCR troops that you kill. He confirms this. You can:

Change the money reward to something more tangible; ammo and supplies. He tells you to speak to Denacus Severus, who sets up a trade for every Dogtag you bring him. The more Dogtags, the better the Food. Each ammo type requires one tag. Explosives require three.

Or agree to kill NCR troops in return for Caps.

- Trader: Decanus Severus [32/33]
- Dynamite [3 tags]
- Grenades [3 tags]

Or you can stick to Caps, and return to Aurelius, and you're rewarded 10 Caps per Dogtag.

The type of Dogtag is important; Irradiated Dogtags from the Ghouls in Camp Searchlight do not count. For the locations of Dogtags; simply head over to locations with a heavy NCR presence. You can Pickpocket Dogtags too, if you want to be sneaky.

- Quest Item: Legion Notes
- Caps
- Food
- Ammo and Explosives

Free Quest: Caching in at the Cove

If you're undertaking Quests on behalf of Caesar's Legion, and you have a mixed Reputation with them, or you're Liked, the Legion isn't above delivering some additional help so you sway over to their cause. Occurring randomly (and to trigger this, it is best to continue to improve your Fame with the Legion), you're stopped and told that supplies have been sent to Cottonwood Cove, and you can access them. This occurs every three days or so. Once you're told, head to the cove, and check the Supply Crate for the items, taking what you need.

- Supply Cache Items

[6.21] Bradley's Shack

- Threat Level: ●●●●●
- Faction: Jackal Gang
  - Entity: Jackal Gang Member
- Crafting: Campfire [104/109]
- Dangers: Traps
- Collectibles:
  - Hollowed-Out Rock [41/42]
  - Sunset Sarsaparilla Star Cap [95/100]
- Guns and Ammo
- Interior Exploration
- Sleeping Quarters

Bradley's Shack has members of the hapless Jackal to waste as you reach the Campfire, Hollowed-Out Rock on the opposite valley side, and patriotic shack exterior. Step inside, and immediately stop! There's a Rigged Shotgun to your right; disarm it. Now step inside and collect the following:

- Campfire [104/109]
- Hollowed-Out Rock [41/42]
- BB Gun and Ammo
- First Aid Box [Very Easy]
- Ammo Box Ammunition (2)
- Frag Grenade (3)
- Sunset Sarsaparilla Star Cap [95/100]
- Sleeping Quarters

[6.22] Caesar's Legion Safehouse

- Free Quest: A Trusted Aide
- Threat Level: ●●●●●
- Faction: Caesar's Legion
  - Entity: None
- Services: Trader [33/33]
- Crafting:
  - Campfire [105/109]
  - Campfire [106/109]
- Collectibles: Magazine [Random]
- Area Is Locked
- Health, Chems, or Water
- Home Sweet Home
- Interior Exploration
- Sleeping Quarters

A small, concrete chalet structure on the spine of a hilly ridge offers views northwest to Nipton [4.30] and northeast to Camp Searchlight. There's a Campfire outside the hut, and another over the small hill to the north, near a rock where Bighorners are grazing. This firmly sealed residence with a Campfire outside requires a key that is awarded, usually in The Fort.

- Campfire [105/109]
- Campfire [106/109]
- Sleeping Quarters

Much like other Safehouses across the Mojave, this offers a place of rest and healthy solace. The following benefits occur:

1. Any bed you sleep in at this location gives you a "Well Rested" bonus.
2. There is a water fountain here allowing you to sip purified water without Radiation.
3. If the location has a fridge, it is restocked with items once per day.
4. Aside from the fridge, there are containers you can store items without them disappearing. Choose a metal box, footlocker, or other chest type, place a low value item inside, then return after a day to ensure your items haven't been taken.
5. This location has a Veteran (Atticus), who visits every Tuesday and Friday. You can check the day of the week when you attempt to Wait or Sleep. Atticus hands over one set of the following, each time there is a visit (so you can choose items twice a week, assuming you're there when the Veteran is).

- Trader: Veteran Atticus [33/33]
- Skill Magazine (two random)
- Stealth Boy (2)
- Cateye (2)

[6.23] Old Nuclear Test Site

- Threat Level: ●●●●○
- Faction: Ghoul
  - Entity: Feral Ghoul
  - Entity: Glowing One
  - Entity: Radioactive Tumbleweed
  - Entity: Trash (Deceased)
- Dangers: Radiation
- Collectibles:
  - Sunset Sarsaparilla Star Cap [96/100]
  - Skill Book [Energy Weapons] [4/4] [8/9]
  - Unique Weapon [41/42]
- Guns and Ammo
- Health, Chems, or Water
- Interior Exploration

Venturing farther toward the parked truck and open gate proves detrimental to your health; it is wise to don a Radiation Suit and snipe Ghouls from a distance. Only one Nuclear Test Shack can be accessed. Inside there's scattered Chems, a Star Cap on the experiment table, and a Skill Book and special Shotgun that's well worth braving radiation sickness to reach. Finally, the corpse on the bed belongs to Trash; she recalls her attempts at enforced Ghoulification in the "Die-ary" Entries in the room (and on her person).

- Authority Glasses
- Skill Book: Nikola Tesla and You [4/4] [8/9]
- Sunset Sarsaparilla Star Cap [96/100]
- Unique Weapon: 12 Gauge Shotgun Dinner Bell [41/42]
- Note: Entry One in the Die-ary of Trash
- Note: Entry Two in the Die-ary of Trash
- Note: Entry Three in the Die-ary of Trash

[6.24] Crashed Vertibird

- Side Quest: For Auld Lang Syne
- Threat Level: ●●●○○
- Faction: Robot
  - Entity: Hardened Mister Gutsy
  - Entity: Hardened Sentry Bot
- Collectibles: Unique Weapon [42/42]
- Guns and Ammo

A deep scar that's hidden by the remoteness of the region reveals the remains of a Vertibird bearing strange insignia. The remnant of a past war, this craft is nevertheless well-guarded by Hardened Robots. The fracas is worth it; you find a powerful prototype cannon!

- Unique Weapon: Tesla-Beaton Prototype [42/42]

[6.25] Matthews Animal Husbandry Farm

- Threat Level: ●●○○○
- Faction: Prospector
  - Entity: None
- Collectibles:
  - Sunset Sarsaparilla Star Cap [97/100]
  - Skill Book [Survival] [4/4] [9/9]
- Guns and Ammo

The remains of two barns, a farmhouse, and two paddocks with Malnourished Bighorners and Brahmin are all that's left of this burned-out farmstead. Collect the Diary pages, which reveals the grim story of how the graves came to be, and the last days of Young Master Matthews; driven mad by his parents and livestock!

- Cattle Prod
- Diary Pages
- Skill Book: Wasteland Survival Guide [Survival] [4/4] [9/9]
- Sunset Sarsaparilla Star Cap [97/100]

[6.26] Searchlight Airport

- Threat Level: ●●○○○
- Faction: Mutated Animal
  - Entity: Radscorpion
- Lots O' Caps

The control tower of this mothballed airport can be seen as far away as Ranger Station Echo, and is just south of Camp Searchlight and its irradiated trailer park [6.S11]. The perimeter fence is still intact, forcing you to enter and exit via the road tunnel, and collapsed tarmac. The place is teeming with Radscorpions, and the terminal building is firmly sealed, although there's a couple of trunks near the rusting planes to loot for Caps.

- Caps (300+)

[6.27] Fire Root Cavern

- Threat Level: ●●●●●
- Faction: Mutated Animal
  - Entity: Fire Gecko
- Dangers: Radiation
- Collectibles: Hollowed-Out Rock [42/42]
- Interior Exploration
- Underground Connection

Fire Root Cavern links up to (and from) Cottonwood Crater [6.28].

In the extreme southeast corner of the Mojave Wasteland are treacherous and huge jagged cliffs, but there's also a couple of underground locales to explore too. One is accessed via a small, steep sloping entrance with a Hollowed-Out Rock, and leads to the Fire Root Cavern.

- Hollowed-Out Rock [42/42]

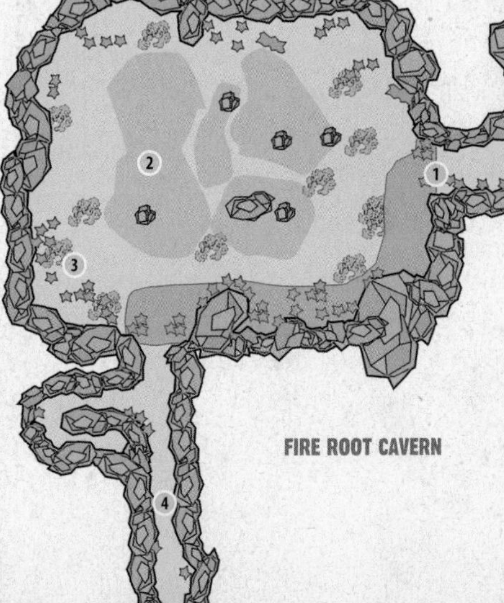

Ⓐ Exit to Mojave Wasteland

1 Fire Gecko Cavern: Northern Access

Said to be the genesis of the Fire Geckos, this cavern is filled with ferns and Fire Geckos too; head to the opening, and you can drop down. However, you can't return to the entrance unless you use the left ledge. Or, you can leap to the left ledge, working your way to location [3].

2 Fire Gecko Mire

The majority of this chamber is filled with ankle-deep radioactive water; a less pleasant location for fighting Fire Geckos.

3 Dead Prospector

- Duffle Bag Items

4 Fire Gecko Cavern: Southern Access

If you're entering from Cottonwood Crater, you can access either of the upper or lower tunnels. From the upper tunnel opening, you can nimbly leap to the ledge, and work your way round to location [1].

Ⓑ Exit to Cottonwood Crater

[6.28] Cottonwood Crater

- Threat Level: ●●●●●
- Faction: Mutated Animal
  Entity: Fire Gecko, Golden Gecko
- Dangers: Radiation
- Interior Exploration
- Underground Connection

Fire Root Cavern links down to (and from) Fire Root Cavern [6.27]. Consult that Primary Location for interior information. The site of a giant, radioactive pool on a massive cliff top, this place has a number of Golden Geckos and a Prospector (who's usually carrying a Fat Man or other big-ticket item). There's an entrance here to (and from) the Fire Root Cavern. Rock climbing up the exterior cliffs is both dangerous and tricky, so access here from the Fire Root Cavern. There's some incredible views of Cottonwood Cove and the Colorado River.

[6.29] Smith Mesa Prospector Camp

- Threat Level: ●●●●●
- Faction: Prospector
  Entity: Prospector's Dog
- Crafting: Campfire [107/109]
- Collectibles: Sunset Sarsaparilla Star Cap [98/100]
- Guns and Ammo
- Health, Chems, or Water
- Sleeping Quarters

Beware of Lakelurks and Fire Geckos as you traverse your way to an alcove in the mesa that Cottonwood Overlook sits on. Just outside the camp is a patient Prospector's Dog and a Campfire. Inside, check the concrete block for a Star Cap. There's other items, too:

- Campfire [107/109]
- Ammo Box Ammunition
  Sunset Sarsaparilla Star Cap [98/100]
  Sleeping Quarters

[6.30] Blue Paradise Vacation Rentals

- Threat Level: ●●●●●
- Faction: Abomination
  Entity: Lakelurk
- Dangers: Radiation
- Collectibles: Sunset Sarsaparilla Star Cap [99/100]
  Sunset Sarsaparilla Star Cap [100/100]
- Guns and Ammo
- Interior Exploration
- Wasteland Vegetation

As the Colorado River flood plain has risen, a small cluster of chalets has slowly sunk into the sand, and an old wharf (plus a boat) has vanished completely under water. The place is now overrun by around a dozen Lakelurks, so beware of their sonic attacks as you advance. Aside from the two sealed (and dry) Beach Houses, there are two waterlogged ones to inspect.

Sunset Sarsaparilla Star Cap [99/100]
Sunset Sarsaparilla Star Cap [100/100]
BB Gun and Ammo

ZONE 6: SECONDARY LOCATIONS

[6.S01] Camp Forlorn Hope Supply Shipment

- Side Quest: Restoring Hope
- Threat Level: ●●●●●
- Faction: NCR/Caesar's Legion
  Entity: Legionary
- Quest Item

Whether or not the Side Quest is active, you can stumble upon this chest, with its recently slain NCR Troopers (search them for Notes as well as Dogtags), but watch for a Legion ambush afterward!

- Quest Item: Camp Forlorn Hope Supply Shipment
- Note: Camp Forlorn Hope Letter 1
- Note: Camp Forlorn Hope Letter 8

[6.S02] Wrecked Commuter

- Threat Level: ●●●●●
- Main Trading Route

An ancient motorist came a cropper and his suitcase is still available to loot.

[6.S03] Dry Bones

- Threat Level: ●●●●●
- Health, Chems, or Water
- Main Trading Route

Two long-dead settlers provide some potentially scavenged items.

- Butter Knife
- Cap (12)
- Rad-X and Chems

[6.S04] Road to Nelson

- Threat Level: ●●●●●

It is important to learn where this road is (just to the east of Novac [5.18]), and the locations it accesses.

[6.S05] NCR Ranger Checkpoint

- Side Quest: Back in Your Own Backyard
- Threat Level: ●●●●●
- Faction: NCR
  Entity: Ranger Milo
  Entity: NCR Trooper
  Entity: Novac Settler
- Guns and Ammo
- Sleeping Quarters
- Quest Item

Ranger Milo valiantly defends the road to prevent the Legion from razing Novac, and his checkpoint is the last line of defense between here and the doomed settlement of Nelson [6.06]. Speak to Milo for a Side Quest, and don't forget to open the footlocker for some very handy items:

- C-4 Plastic Explosive (2)
- Detonator
- Sleeping Quarters

[6.S06] Minefield

- Threat Level: ●●●●●
- Faction: NCR
  Entity: NCR Trooper
- Dangers: Mines
- Guns and Ammo

Cutting off the attacks between Camp Forlorn Hope and Nelson, this Minefield (of Frag Mines thought to have been placed by the Brotherhood of Steel) is a no-man's land where careless NCR Troopers lie, waiting for death. Instead of stepping on Mines, you should either avoid the area, or collect them, along with any NCR Dogtags.

- Frag Mine (6)

[6.S07] Nelson Lookout

- Threat Level: ●●●●●
- Faction: Caesar's Legion
  Entity: Legionary
- Wasteland Vegetation

On the eastern cliffs overlooking the Colorado River, there's a lookout platform for Legionaries to communicate with forces on or across the gorge. Expect light resistance.

[6.S08] Knob Hill

- Threat Level: ●●●●●

This rarely tracked area offers exceptional views of the river. At this point there's a filled-in mine shaft that used to lead to Techatticup Mine [6.08].

[6.S09] Recon Legion Camp

- Threat Level: ●●●●●
- Faction: Caesar's Legion
  - Entity: Legionary
- Crafting
  - Campfire [108/109]
- Sleeping Quarters
- Wasteland Vegetation

Patrols of Legionaries in the area usually rest here (allowing you to murder them as they rest during the night), at this modest camp site of bedding and a fire.

- Campfire [108/109]
- Sleeping Quarters

[6.S10] Bootjack Cavern

- Side Quest: Debt Collector
- Threat Level: ●●●●●
- Faction: Mutated Animal
  - Entity: Fire Gecko
- Interior Exploration
- Quest Item

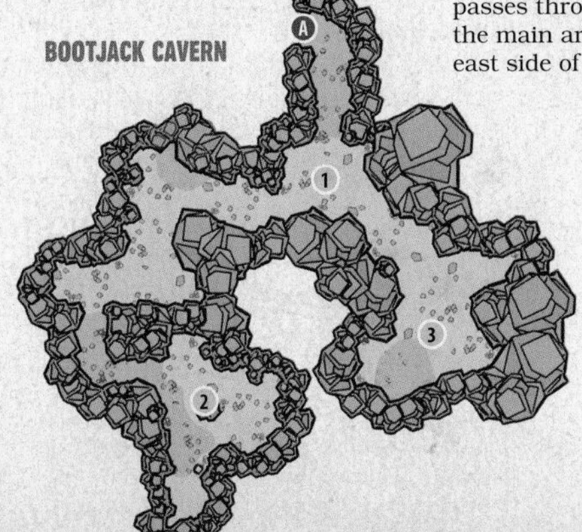

A small cave system in the hills to the east of Highway 95, this is a place you must visit during Side Quest: Debt Collector, and is filled with Fire Geckos.

Ⓐ Exit to Mojave Wasteland

① Entrance Junction

After the initial corridor, the tunnel widens considerably to this point.

② Southwest Cavern

There's a dead Prospector to search here.

③ Southeast Cavern

There's also a dead Prospector to search here. Each cavern has numerous Fire Geckos to deal with.

[6.S11] Camp Searchlight Trailer Park

- Threat Level: ●●●●●
- Faction: Mutated Animal
  - Entity: Golden Gecko
- Dangers: Radiation
- Health, Chems, or Water

On the southern perimeter of Camp Searchlight [6.16] is more evidence of mass irradiation by the Legion; a trailer park reduced to a radioactive graveyard of trailers. Golden Geckos now swarm the area, and it's useful to snipe them from a distance before searching the area.

- First Aid Box
- Footlocker Items
- Hydra and Rad-X (2)
- Sleeping Quarters

[6.S12] Highway 95 (South)

- Threat Level: ●●●●●
- Faction: Ghoul
- Dangers: Radiation
- Highly Visible

Although irradiated, the road that passes through Camp Searchlight is the main artery for travel along the east side of the Mojave Wasteland.

[6.S13] Little Rock Camp

- Threat Level: ●●●●●
- Wasteland Vegetation
- Crafting: Campfire [109/109]

Amid the scattered rocks is a burned-out car and a nearby Campfire.

- Campfire [109/109]

[6.S14] Lakelurk Hideaway

- Threat Level: ●●●●●
- Faction: Abomination
  - Entity: Lakelurk
- Guns and Ammo
- Wasteland Vegetation

If you're swimming the mighty Colorado River, beware of a gaggle of Lakelurks on the eastern side, near a small alcove within a larger inlet channel. There are 16 of these slimy beasts to take down. Then check the alcove for items on and around a dead Mercenary.

- Duffle Bag Items (2)

[6.S15] Rusting Boat

- Threat Level: ●●●●●

A vessel, less than seaworthy, has been aground near Cottonwood Cove for as long as anyone can remember.

[6.S16] Deathclaw Promontory

- Threat Level: ●●●●●
- Faction: Abomination
  - Entity: Deathclaw Mother
  - Entity: Deathclaw Alpha Male
  - Entity: Deathclaw
- Collectibles:
  - Caravan Cards [29/30]
  - Unique Item [95/95]
- Guns and Ammo
- Health, Chems, or Water
- Wasteland Vegetation

Many have attempted to purloin the riches of past victims (or the natural vegetation) in this terrifying and sprawling rocky promontory, but none have returned, due to the sizable Deathclaw population. This represents a real challenge, so prepare well before you explore here! To the southeast are two well-armed, but dead Prospectors. Sift through their corpses for some fine items:

- Caravan Cards [29/30]
- Unique Item: Remnants Power Armor [95/95]
- T-51b Power Armor
- T-51b Power Helmet
- Tri-Beam Laser Rifle
- Multiplas Rifle

[6.S17] Fallen Hiker

- Threat Level: ●●●●●
- Faction: Abomination
  - Entity: Lakelurk
- Collectibles:
  - Magazine [Random]
- Wasteland Vegetation

Check his duffle bag for a variety of items and a random Magazine.

- Duffle Bag Items
- Magazine

[6.S18] River Bank Alcove

- Threat Level: ●●●●●
- Faction: Abomination
  - Entity: Lakelurk
- Guns and Ammo

A small gaggle of Lakelurks guard this river rock alcove, which has Egg Clutches to rob.

- Lakelurk Egg (3)
- Explosive Crate Items (2)

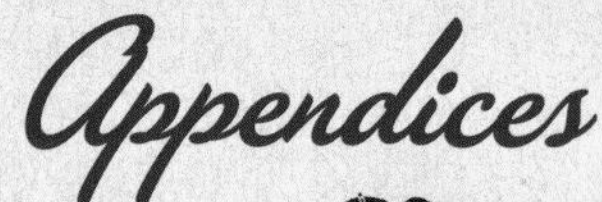

Appendices

Keeping track of your adventure is more difficult than wrangling Wind Brahmin. Therefore, the following Appendices are presented so you can keep track of your Endings, Achievements, Collectibles, and more.

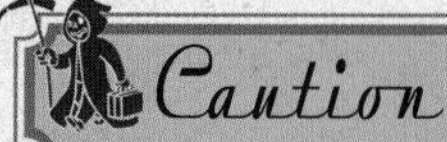

Caution: All of this information is horribly secretive, so avert your gaze unless you're wanting to know it all!

APPENDIX I: THIS IS THE END

Once the Battle for Hoover Dam (Act III) has concluded, a series of Ending slides is shown. However, the multitude of actions you accomplished during your adventure affects 27 different aspects of the Ending in a variety of ways. Here they all are:

Ending Part 1: Main Quest

1. Ally with Caesar's Legion, save Caesar's life during Main Quest: Et Tumor, Brute?, then complete Main Quest: Veni, Vidi, Vici.
2. Ally with Caesar's Legion, kill or fail to save Caesar during Main Quest: Et Tumor, Brute? then complete Main Quest: Veni, Vidi, Vici.
3. Ally with Mr. House and complete Main Quest: All or Nothing.
4. Ally with NCR and complete Main Quest: Eureka!
5. Opt for an independent New Vegas, upgrade the Securitron Army during Main Quest: You and What Army? then complete Main Quest: No Gods, No Masters.
6. Opt for an independent New Vegas, destroy or ignore the Securitron Army during Main Quest: You and What Army? then complete Main Quest: No Gods, No Masters.

Ending Part 2: Female Courier

1. Ally with Caesar's Legion and possess Good Karma when completing Main Quest: Veni, Vidi, Vici.
2. Ally with Caesar's Legion and possess Neutral Karma when completing Main Quest: Veni, Vidi, Vici.
3. Ally with Caesar's Legion and possess Bad Karma when completing Main Quest: Veni, Vidi, Vici.
4. Ally with Mr. House and possess Good Karma when completing Main Quest: All or Nothing.
5. Ally with Mr. House and possess Neutral Karma when completing Main Quest: All or Nothing.
6. Ally with Mr. House and possess Bad Karma when completing Main Quest: All or Nothing.
7. Ally with NCR and possess Good Karma when completing Main Quest: Eureka!
8. Ally with NCR and possess Neutral Karma when completing Main Quest: Eureka!
9. Ally with NCR and possess Bad Karma when completing Main Quest: Eureka!
10. Opt for an independent New Vegas and possess Good Karma when completing Main Quest: No Gods, No Masters.
11. Opt for an independent New Vegas and possess Neutral Karma when completing Main Quest: No Gods, No Masters.
12. Opt for an independent New Vegas and possess Bad Karma when completing Main Quest: No Gods, No Masters.

Ending Part 3: Male Courier

1. Ally with Caesar's Legion and possess Good Karma when completing Main Quest: Veni, Vidi, Vici.
2. Ally with Caesar's Legion and possess Neutral Karma when completing Main Quest: Veni, Vidi, Vici.
3. Ally with Caesar's Legion and possess Bad Karma when completing Main Quest: Veni, Vidi, Vici.
4. Ally with Mr. House and possess Good Karma when completing Main Quest: All or Nothing.
5. Ally with Mr. House and possess Neutral Karma when completing Main Quest: All or Nothing.
6. Ally with Mr. House and possess Bad Karma when completing Main Quest: All or Nothing.
7. Ally with NCR and possess Good Karma when completing Main Quest: Eureka!
8. Ally with NCR and possess Neutral Karma when completing Main Quest: Eureka!
9. Ally with NCR and possess Bad Karma when completing Main Quest: Eureka!
10. Opt for an independent New Vegas and possess Good Karma when completing Main Quest: No Gods, No Masters.
11. Opt for an independent New Vegas and possess Neutral Karma when completing Main Quest: No Gods, No Masters.
12. Opt for an independent New Vegas and possess Bad Karma when completing Main Quest: No Gods, No Masters.

Ending Part 4: Followers of the Apocalypse

1. Out of respect for his former people, Caesar allows the Followers of the Apocalypse safe passage out of the Mojave Wasteland following Main Quest: Veni, Vidi, Vici.
2. As a result of Caesar dying during Et Tumor, Brute? the Legate hunts down the Followers of the Apocalypse and destroys the Old Mormon Fort following Main Quest: Veni, Vidi, Vici.
3. By allying with the NCR and completing Main Quest: Eureka! the Followers of the Apocalypse are pushed out of the Old Mormon Fort in Freeside.
4. As a result of killing Julie Farkas and the Followers of the Apocalypse, the Old Mormon Fort is lost to local drug addicts and junkies.
5. After completing Main Quest: No Gods, No Masters, the Followers of the Apocalypse become overwhelmed by an increase in patients in an independent New Vegas.

Ending Part 5: Great Khans

1. By maintaining their alliance with Caesar's Legion, the Great Khans aid in the Second Battle of Hoover Dam during Main Quest: Veni, Vidi, Vici after which they are forcibly integrated into the Legion, resulting in the loss of their clan identity.
2. By severing their alliance with Caesar's Legion in Side Quest: Oh My Papa, the Great Khans support the NCR in the Second Battle of Hoover Dam during Main Quest: Veni, Vidi, Vici, resulting in their destruction in an assault on Red Rock Canyon by the Legion.
3. By severing their alliance with Caesar's Legion in Side Quest: Oh My Papa, the Great Khans support the NCR in the Second Battle of Hoover Dam during Main Quest: Eureka! and the clan is allowed to inhabit Red Rock Canyon for a short time before NCR expansion forces them out.
4. As a result of choices made in Side Quest: Oh My Papa, the Great Khans flee from the Mojave during the Second Battle of Hoover Dam and travel to Wyoming, joining with the Followers of the Apocalypse to rebuild their clan.
5. As a result of choices made in Side Quest: Oh My Papa, the Great Khans take on too many casualties during the Second Battle of Hoover Dam and are wiped out as a clan.
6. As a result of slaughtering members of the Great Khans, the clan is wiped out before the Second Battle of Hoover Dam ever takes place.

Ending Part 6: Goodsprings

1. As a result of allying with Caesar's Legion and completing Main Quest: Veni, Vidi, Vici, the population of Goodsprings declines as inhabitants flee out of fear of Caesar's rule.
2. As a result of allying with the NCR and completing Main Quest: Eureka! heavy taxation forces the town of Goodsprings into decline.
3. By allying with Mr. House and completing Main Quest: All or Nothing, the town of Goodsprings is kept safe by Mr. House's Securitron Army.
4. With New Vegas made independent in Main Quest: No Gods, No Masters Goodsprings thrives as a result of more travelers passing through the town on their way to New Vegas.
5. With its inhabitants massacred, Goodsprings is rendered a ghost town before the Second Battle of Hoover Dam even begins.

Ending Part 7: Jacobstown

1. After finding a cure for Stealth Boy schizophrenia in Side Quest: Guess Who I Saw Today, Jacobstown booms with an influx of Super Mutants looking for treatment.

2. As a result of Side Quest: Guess Who I Saw Today and killing Keene, the Nightkin abandoned Jacobstown because it took too long to find a cure for Stealth Boy-induced schizophrenia, and angry over their leader's demise they also scattered in to the wasteland.
3. As a result of Side Quest: Guess Who I Saw Today, the Nightkin follow Keene out of Jacobstown to the Mojave Wasteland because it took too long to find a cure for Stealth Boy-induced schizophrenia. With Keene, the Nightkin terrorized the Wasteland for years.
4. As a result of Side Quest: Guess Who I Saw Today, it took more time than expected to devise a cure for Stealth Boy-induced schizophrenia, but Keene invited Nightkin across the Mojave to journey to Jacobstown for treatment, leading the small resort to thrive.
5. As a result of Side Quest: Guess Who I Saw Today, no cure for Stealth Boy-induced schizophrenia is devised and the Nightkin departed from Jacobstown to terrorize the Mojave Wasteland.
6. As a result of killing Marcus, the Super Mutants and Nightkin of Jacobstown abandon the mountain resort.

Ending Part 8: The Kings

1. Having established a truce between the Kings and NCR in Side Quest: G.I. Blues, the Kings are ultimately destroyed by Caesar's Legion following Main Quest: Veni, Vidi, Vici for supporting the NCR.
2. Having maintained tensions between the Kings and NCR by ignoring Side Quest: G.I. Blues, the Kings are ultimately destroyed by Caesar's Legion following Main Quest: Veni, Vidi, Vici.
3. Having exacerbated tensions between the Kings and NCR in Side Quest: G.I. Blues, Caesar offers to assimilate the Kings following Main Quest: Veni, Vidi, Vici; however, the Kings refuse and are destroyed by the Legion.
4. Having established a truce between the Kings and NCR in Side Quest: G.I. Blues, the Kings work to make Freeside safer following Main Quest: Eureka!
5. Having maintained tensions between the Kings and NCR by ignoring Side Quest: G.I. Blues, the NCR attempts to secure Freeside following Main Quest: Eureka! but have difficulty defeating the Kings.
6. Having exacerbated tensions between the Kings and NCR in Side Quest: G.I. Blues, the Kings attack NCR citizens in Freeside during Main Quest: Eureka! which prompts the NCR to crack down on the Kings with an assault after the Second Battle of Hoover Dam.
7. Having established a truce between the Kings and NCR in Side Quest: G.I. Blues, the Kings are ultimately destroyed by Mr. House following Main Quest: All or Nothing for supporting the NCR.
8. Having maintained tensions between the Kings and NCR by ignoring Side Quest: G.I. Blues, Mr. House sends in his Securitron Army to wrestle control of Freeside from the Kings following Main Quest: All or Nothing, resulting in the destruction of the Kings.
9. Having exacerbated tensions between the Kings and NCR in Side Quest: G.I. Blues, the Kings attack NCR citizens in Freeside during Main Quest: All or Nothing and are rewarded by Mr. House by leaving them alone.
10. Having established a truce between the Kings and NCR in Side Quest: G.I. Blues, the Kings secure Freeside and make it one of the safest places in the independent New Vegas that arises from Main Quest: No Gods, No Masters.
11. Having maintained tensions between the Kings and NCR by ignoring Side Quest: G.I. Blues, the Kings maintain control over Freeside and merely tolerate NCR citizens in the independent New Vegas that arises from Main Quest: No Gods, No Masters.
12. Having exacerbated tensions between the Kings and NCR in Side Quest: G.I. Blues, the Kings maintain control over Freeside and active drive NCR citizens out of Freeside after the creation of an independent New Vegas in Main Quest: No Gods, No Masters.
13. With the King killed, the Kings as a group dissolve and Freeside is relinquished from their grip.

Ending Part 9: Lily

1. Encouraged to take medication to combat Stealth Boy-induced schizophrenia after a cure is found during Free Quest: Lily and Leo, Lily maintains sanity and lives a happy, productive life.
2. Encouraged to stop taking medication concocted during Free Quest: Lily and Leo, Lily succumbs to schizophrenia .
3. Not telling Lily to either diligently take or stop taking her medication for schizophrenia as devised during Free Quest: Lily and Leo, she decides only to take half her prescribed medication resulting in further mental instability; Lily ends up wandering the Wasteland in search of her grandchildren.
4. After succumbing to injuries during her time with the Courier, Lily dies.

Ending Part 10: The Misfits

1. Successfully training the Misfits during Side Quest: Flags of Our Foul-Ups leads the group to honored service in the Second Battle of Hoover Dam during Main Quest: Eureka!, All or Nothing, or No Gods, No Masters.
2. Failing to train the Misfits, opting to lie about their performance record, or ignoring them entirely during Side Quest: Flags of Our Foul-Ups, results in the soldiers being killed in the Second Battle of Hoover Dam or court marshaled for fleeing the battlefield after completing Main Quest: Eureka! as allied with the NCR, All or Nothing as allied with Mr. House, or No Gods, No Masters when opting for an independent New Vegas.
3. Successfully training the Misfits during Side Quest: Flags of Our Foul-Ups leads the group to honored service in the Second Battle of Hoover Dam, although allying with Caesar's Legion in Main Quest: Veni, Vidi, Vici results in Caesar's Legion victory and the Misfits's fall in the battle.
4. Encouraged to get hooked in Psycho during Side Quest: Flags of Our Foul-Ups the Misfits become crazed and terrorize innocent Wasteland travelers after completing Main Quest: Eureka! as allied with the NCR, All or Nothing as allied with Mr. House, or No Gods, No Masters when opting for an independent New Vegas.
5. The Misfits are outright slaughtered before the Second Battle of Hoover Dam even begins.

Ending Part 11: NCR Correctional Facility

1. Having allied with Caesar's Legion and completing Main Quest: Veni, Vidi, Vici, the Powder Gangers flee the NCR Correctional Facility out of fear of Caesar's heavy-handed rule.
2. Having allied with the NCR and completing Main Quest: Eureka! the NCR successfully recaptures the Correctional Facility, wiping out the Powder Gangers in the process.
3. After completing Main Quest: All or Nothing as allied with Mr. House or No Gods, No Masters when opting for an independent New Vegas, the NCR are unable to attempt a takeover of the Correctional Facility, which leaves it in the hands of the Powder Gangers.
4. After killing their leader and completing Main Quest: All or Nothing as allied with Mr. House or No Gods, No Masters when opting for an independent New Vegas, the Powder Gangers abandon the NCR Correctional Facility and leave it in ruins.

Ending Part 12: Novac

1. Allied with Caesar's Legion and completing Main Quest: Veni, Vidi, Vici, Novac is destroyed by the Legion; nobody comes to the town's rescue as a result of ignoring Side Quest: Come Fly With Me.
2. As a result of ensuring the success of Jason Bright's rocket launch in Side Quest: Come Fly With Me and completing Main Quest: Veni, Vidi, Vici as allied with Caesar's Legion, Bright and his followers come to Novac's aid in the rescue and evacuation of Novac's citizens as the Legion lay waste to the town.
3. As a result of ensuring the success of Jason Bright's rocket launch in Side Quest: Come Fly With Me and completing Main Quest: Eureka! as allied with the NCR, All or Nothing! as allied with Mr. House, or No Gods, No Masters supporting an Independent New Vegas, Bright and his followers return from their journey to help restore Novac's defenses, allowing them to keep their independence.
4. Ignoring Side Quest: Come Fly With Me and completing Main Quest: Eureka! as allied with the NCR, All or Nothing as allied with Mr. House, or No Gods, No Masters when opting for an independent New Vegas results in Novac being overwhelmed by Feral Ghoul attacks.
5. As a result of sabotaging the rockets at the RECONN site during Side Quest: Come Fly With Me, radioactive waste scars Novac and makes it uninhabitable.
6. The inhabitants of Novac are slaughtered, leaving the town empty well before the Second Battle of Hoover Dam.

Ending Part 13: Powder Gangers

1. By helping Samuel Cooke reach the sulfur deposits beneath Vault 19 in Side Quest: Why Can't We Be Friends, the Powder Gangers arm themselves with powerful explosives and harass Wasteland travelers.
2. By having leaders Philip Lem or Samuel Cooke lead the Powder Gangers to join the Greak Khans in Side Quest: Why Can't We Be Friends, any Powder Gangers who don't follow are left on their own in the Wasteland.

3. By surrendering to the NCR in Side Quest: Why Can't We Be Friends, the Vault 19 Powder Gangers are reincorporated in the corrections program.
4. By killing Cooke, the Powder Gangers at Vault 19 fall apart.

Ending Part 14: Primm

1. Allying with Caesar's Legion and completing Main Quest: Veni, Vidi, Vici, the NCR abandons Primm despite promising protection and Caesar maintains a firm grip on the town.
2. By selecting Meyers for sheriff in Side Quest: My Kind of Town and allying with Caesar's Legion for Main Quest: Veni, Vidi, Vici, Primm is prompted to fight against Legion occupation and ends up being trampled by Caesar's forces.
3. By selecting Primm Slim for sheriff in Side Quest: My Kind of Town and allying with Caesar's Legion for Main Quest: Veni, Vidi, Vici, Primm is prompted to fight against Legion occupation and ends up being enslaved by Caesar's forces.
4. Allying with the NCR and completing Main Quest: Eureka! leads to continued protection of Primm by the NCR, leading to greater merchant trade and prosperity.
5. Allying with Mr. House and completing Main Quest: All or Nothing leads to Securitron Army control over Primm and suffocating taxes for the town inhabitants.
6. Opting for an independent New Vegas in Main Quest: No Gods, No Masters results in Primm losing NCR protection and struggling to survive.
7. By selecting Meyers for sheriff in Side Quest: My Kind of Town, Primm thrives under the fair, though often rogue watch of Sheriff Meyers.
8. By selecting Primm Slim for sheriff in Side Quest: My Kind of Town, Primm thrives under the occasionally incompetent tenure of Sheriff Slim.
9. Killing the inhabitants of Primm results in the town falling into ruin.

Ending Part 15: Rangers

1. As a result of Side Quest: Return to Sender, Chief Hanlon's suspicions are confirmed as the NCR lose Hoover Dam to Caesar's Legion in Main Quest: Veni, Vidi, Vici.
2. As a result of Side Quest: Return to Sender and Chief Hanlon being killed during the Second Battle of Hoover Dam in Main Quest: Veni, Vidi, Vici, the NCR honors the Rangers as debate rages about who to blame for the loss.
3. As a result of Side Quest: Return to Sender and Chief Hanlon's sabotage plot playing out during Main Quest: Veni, Vidi, Vici, the NCR lose Hoover Dam and the Rangers fall into decline after Hanlon's plot is exposed.
4. As a result of Side Quest: Return to Sender and Chief Hanlon's sabotage plot being stopped during Main Quest: Veni, Vidi, Vici, the NCR still lose Hoover Dam despite help from the Rangers.
5. As a result of Side Quest: Return to Sender and Chief Hanlon's sabotage plot being stopped during Main Quest: Eureka! the NCR secure Hoover Dam with help from the Rangers.
6. As a result of Side Quest: Return to Sender, Chief Hanlon and the Rangers threw themselves against Caesar's Legion in the Second Battle of Hoover Dam during Main Quest: Eureka! and die in the process.
7. As a result of Side Quest: Return to Sender and Chief Hanlon's sabotage plot being stopped during Main Quest: Eureka! the NCR secure Hoover Dam.
8. Allowing Chief Hanlon's sabotage plot to play out, the NCR still manage victory during Main Quest: Eureka! and the Rangers are exposed for betrayal.
9. As a result of Side Quest: Return to Sender, the NCR are successful in battling Caesar's Legion, but cannot stave Mr. House in Main Quest: All or Nothing or pressure for an independent New Vegas in Main Quest: No Gods, No Monsters and are forced to evacuate to Mojave Outpost.
10. As a result of Side Quest: Return to Sender, the NCR are successful in battling Caesar's Legion, but cannot stave Mr. House in Main Quest: All or Nothing or pressure for an independent New Vegas in Main Quest: No Gods, No Monsters.
11. By murdering Chief Hanlon, the Rangers are fractured and take years to rebuild.

Ending Part 16: Raul

1. As a result of freeing him from Tabitha in Side Quest: Crazy, Crazy, Crazy, and completing Free Quest: Old School Ghoul, Raul decides to leave the Mojave Wasteland and take a new identity.
2. As a result of freeing him from Tabitha in Side Quest: Crazy, Crazy, Crazy and completing Free Quest: Old School Ghoul, Raul settles down in Outer Vegas as a machinist.
3. As a result of freeing him from Tabitha in Side Quest: Crazy, Crazy, Crazy, and completing Free Quest: Old School Ghoul, Raul sets out to find Raphaela.
4. After succumbing to injuries during his time with the Courier, Raul dies.

Ending Part 17: Enclave Remnants

1. By completing Side Quest: For Auld Lang Syne and supporting the NCR in Main Quest: Eureka! Mr. House in Main Quest: All or Nothing, or an independent New Vegas in Main Quest: No Gods, No Monsters, the Enclave Remnants fought in the Second Battle of Hoover Dam and were never heard from again.
2. By allying the Remnants with Caesar's Legion during Side Quest: For Auld Lang Syne, completing Main Quest Veni, Vidi, Vici, and saving Caesar's life during Main Quest Et Tumor, Brute?, Caesar's Legion declines to pursue the Enclave Remnants following the Second Battle of Hoover Dam.
3. By allying the Remnants with Caesar's Legion during Side Quest: For Auld Lang Syne, completing Main Quest: Veni, Vidi, Vici, and killing Caesar during Main Quest: Et Tumor, Brute?, Caesar's Legion opts to pursue the Enclave Remnants following the Second Battle of Hoover Dam.
4. Massacred, the aging Enclave Remnants are wiped from the Mojave Wasteland.

Ending Part 18: Rex

1. By transplanting Rey's brain into Rex during Side Quest: Nothin' But a Hound Dog, Rex survives.
2. By transplanting Lupa's brain into Rex during Side Quest: Nothin' But a Hound Dog, Rex survives.
3. By transplanting Violetta's brain into Rex during Side Quest: Nothin' But a Hound Dog, Rex survives.
4. As a result of being ignored, Rex dies from neurological degradation.
5. After succumbing to injuries during his time with the Courier, Rex dies.

Ending Part 19: Arcade Gannon

1. With Arcade enslaved to the Legion and Caesar's life saved in Main Quest: Et Tumor, Brute? Arcade finds himself as the personal physician to the dictator after completing Main Quest: Veni, Vidi, Vici.
2. With Arcade enslaved to the Legion and Caesar dead after Main Quest: Et Tumor, Brute? Arcade finds himself as the personal physician to Caesar's successor Legate Lanius; unfortunately, he doesn't take to Arcade's personality and has him crucified After Main Quest: Veni, Vidi, Vici.
3. Departing before the completion of Main Quest: Veni, Vidi, Vici, Arcade ends up a casualty in the Legion's victorious march on New Vegas.
4. As a result of the Courier's influence in Side Quest: For Auld Lang Syne, Arcade ends up surviving the aftermath of Caesar's Legion's assault on Hoover Dam in Main Quest: Eureka! and helps NCR citizens in Freeside before moving onwards to NCR territory.
5. As a result of the Courier's influence in Side Quest: For Auld Lang Syne, Arcade ends up surviving the aftermath of Caesar's Legion's assault on Hoover Dam in Main Quest: Veni, Vidi, Vici and administers medical aid to NCR citizens in Freeside before a Centurion murders him.
6. Following the victory of Mr. House in Main Quest: All or Nothing, Arcade is crushed and leaves Freeside to escape the watchful eye of Mr. House.
7. Upon assembling the Enclave Remnants in Side Quest: For Auld Lang Syne and fighting against Caesar's Legion in the Second Battle for Hoover Dam during Main Quest: All or Nothing, Arcade is crushed by Mr. House's ascent to power and leaves Freeside to escape the watchful eye of the Securitron Army.
8. Following the creation of an independent New Vegas in Main Quest: No Gods, No Masters, Arcade stays in Freeside to care for the unfortunate amid the chaos.
9. Upon assembling the Enclave Remnants in Side Quest: For Auld Lang Syne and fighting against Caesar's Legion in the Second Battle for Hoover Dam during Main Quest: No Gods, No Masters, Arcade stays in Freeside to care for the unfortunate amid the chaos of an independent New Vegas.
10. After succumbing to injuries during his time with the Courier, Arcade dies.

Ending Part 20: Black Mountain

1. By repairing Tabitha's robot pal Rhonda in Side Quest: Crazy, Crazy, Crazy, the pair wandered off into Legion territory for adventures.
2. By sneaking Raul away from Black Mountain in Side Quest: Crazy, Crazy, Crazy, Tabitha is enraged and heads off into the Wasteland with her Nightkin followers in tow.
3. As a result of ignoring Black Mountain, Tabitha's bizarre radio broadcasts continue and Raul faces execution, and is pardoned each day.
4. As a result of killing Tabitha in Side Quest: Crazy, Crazy, Crazy, many Super Mutants and Nightkin travel to Black Mountain, only to be met with little trace of existence.

Ending Part 21: Boomers

1. By gaining favor with the Boomers and dredging the old bomber in Side Quest: Volare for use in support of Caesar's Legion during Main Quest: Render Unto Caesar, the Legion was cautious of attacking their home at Nellis Airforce Base following the Second Battle of Hoover Dam resulting in the Boomers retaining their independence.
2. By gaining favor with the Boomers and dredging the old bomber in Side Quest: Volare for use in support of the NCR in Main Quest: For the Republic, Part 2 the Boomers guarantee NCR success in the Second Battle for Hoover Dam and establish trade with the NCR.
3. By gaining favor with the Boomers and dredging the old bomber in Side Quest: Volare for use in support of Mr. House in Main Quest: The House Always Wins II, Mr. House allows the group their independence as they open up to trade with the Wasteland.
4. By ignoring the Boomers and pursuing an independent New Vegas in Main Quest: Wild Card: Side Bets, the Boomers are left to defend themselves in the chaos that follows.
5. By gaining favor with the Boomers and dredging the old bomber in Side Quest: Volare for use in support of an independent New Vegas in Main Quest: Wild Card: Side Bets, the Boomers scare off potential rivals from assault Nellis Airforce Base in the aftermath of the Second Battle of Hoover Dam.
6. By massacring clan's leadership, the Boomers faded as a distinct group long before the Second Battle of Hoover Dam takes place.

Ending Part 22: Boone

1. As a result of completing Side Quest: I Forgot to Remember to Forget by getting Boone to make amends for Bitter Springs and allying with Caesar's Legion for Main Quest: Veni, Vidi, Vici, Boone takes it upon himself to hunt down members of the Legion.
2. As a result of completing Side Quest: I Forgot to Remember to Forget by getting Boone to become vengeful over Bitter Springs and allying with Caesar's Legion for Main Quest: Veni, Vidi, Vici, Boone is driven mad and launches a suicidal attack against the Legate Lanius.
3. As a result of failing to complete Side Quest: I Forgot to Remember to Forget, Boone leaves the Mojave Wasteland to hunt down the NCR officer responsible for the massacre at Bitter Springs.
4. As a result of completing Side Quest: I Forgot to Remember to Forget by getting Boone to make amends for Bitter Springs and allying with the NCR for Main Quest: Eureka!, Boone re-enlists with his old unit in the NCR.
5. As a result of completing Side Quest: I Forgot to Remember to Forget by getting Boone to make amends for Bitter Springs and allying with Mr. House for Main Quest: All or Nothing or siding for an Independent New Vegas for Main Quest: No Gods, No Masters, Boone remains in the Mojave Wasteland as a caravan security guard.
6. As a result of completing Side Quest: I Forgot to Remember to Forget by getting Boone to become vengeful over Bitter Springs and allying with Mr. House for Main Quest: All or Nothing or siding for an Independent New Vegas for Main Quest: No Gods, No Masters, Boone becomes a mercenary willing to take any job the Mojave Wasteland has to offer.
7. Left to wander the Wasteland, Boone ends up dead.

Ending Part 23: Brotherhood of Steel

1. By arranging a truce between the Brotherhood of Steel and NCR in Side Quest: Still in the Dark, then completing Main Quest: Eureka! both factions maintain a tense truce following the Second Battle of Hoover Dam.
2. As a result of Caesar's Legion and the NCR losing power in the Mojave Wasteland with the successful take over of Hoover Dam by Mr. House in Main Quest: All or Nothing or the creation of an independent New Vegas in Main Quest: No Gods, No Masters, the Brotherhood of Steel retake Helios One without opposition.
3. As a result of allying the Brotherhood and the NCR in Main Quest: For the Republic, Part II and completing Main Quest: No Gods, No Masters, the Brotherhood of Steel allow the NCR to leave the Mojave Wasteland without incident and continue to inhabit Hidden Valley.
4. By massacring the Brotherhood of Steel leadership and destroying their bunker, the group is wiped from the Mojave Wasteland.

Ending Part 24: Rose of Sharon Cassidy

1. As a result of never completing Side Quest: Heartache by the Number, Rose of Sharon Cassidy witnesses the victory of Caesar's Legion in the Second Battle of Hoover Dam following Main Quest: Veni, Vidi, Vici.
2. As a result of never completing Side Quest: Heartache by the Number, Rose of Sharon Cassidy witnesses the victory of the NCR in the Second Battle of Hoover Dam following Main Quest: Eureka!
3. As a result of never completing Side Quest: Heartache by the Number, Rose of Sharon Cassidy witnesses the victory of Mr. House in the Second Battle of Hoover Dam following Main Quest: All of Nothing.
4. As a result of never completing Side Quest: Heartache by the Number, Rose of Sharon Cassidy witnesses the creation of an independent New Vegas after the Second Battle of Hoover Dam concludes in Main Quest: No Gods, No Masters.
5. As a result of completing Side Quest: Heartache by the Number by political subterfuge, the NCR blackmailed the Van Graffs and Crimson Caravans following the destruction of Cassidy Caravans.
6. As a result of completing Side Quest: Heartache by the Number by destroying the Van Graffs and Crimson Caravan, the NCR are squeezed for supplies as other caravans withdraw support.
7. As a result of leaving the Mojave Wasteland and heading back West, Rose of Sharon Cassidy lives another 30 years before passing away in a small shack near Vault City.
8. Unable to cope with the dangers of the Wasteland, Rose of Sharon Cassidy dies and is buried in an unmarked grave.

Ending Part 25: ED-E

1. As a result of being repaired in Side Quest: ED-E My Love, ED-E accompanies the Courier across the Mojave Wasteland and helps the Followers of the Apocalypse recover valuable information relating to the Poseidon Energy Company to be used in improving the quality of life in New Vegas.
2. As a result of being repaired in Side Quest: ED-E My Love, ED-E accompanies you across the Mojave Wasteland and helps the Brotherhood of Steel build an advanced fighting force.
3. As a result of being repaired by the Followers of the Apocalypse in Side Quest: ED-E My Love, the Followers are able to recover valuable information relating to the Poseidon Energy Company to be used in improving the quality of life in New Vegas. After being dismissed by the Courier, ED-E is picked up by a wandering caravan who take him on as a protector.
4. As a result of being repaired by the Brotherhood of Steel in Side Quest: ED-E My Love, the Brotherhood are able to recover information vital for building an advance fighting force. After being dismissed by the Courier, ED-E is picked up by a wandering caravan who takes him on as a protector.
5. As a result of never completing Side Quest: ED-E My Love, ED-E accompanies the Courier across the Mojave Wasteland until one of its memory banks activates and causes it to journey to Navarro where it is never seen or heard from again.
6. As a result of never repairing it, ED-E lay in Johnson Nash's Primm workshop until repaired by another courier. Eventually ED-E is discovered by the Followers of the Apocalypse who uncover vast scientific knowledge from its data storage.
7. Unable to survive the harshness of the Mojave Wasteland, ED-E is destroyed.

Ending Part 26: Fiends

1. Having ignored Side Quest: Three-Card Bounty and allied with the NCR for Main Quest: Eureka! the Fiends attack Camp McCarran during the Second Battle of Hoover Dam, but are repelled by the victorious NCR forces.
2. Having completed Side Quest: Three-Card Bounty and allied with the NCR for Main Quest: Eureka! the weakened Fiends attack Camp McCarran during the Second Battle of Hoover Dam and are obliterated by victorious NCR forces.

3. Having ignored Side Quest: Three-Card Bounty and allied with Mr. House for Main Quest: All or Nothing, the Fiends launch an attack on Camp McCarran that proves successful; however, the Fiends's victory over the NCR is short-lived as Mr. House's Securitron Army quickly puts them down in an assault on the Camp.
4. Having weakened the Fiends in Side Quest: Three-Card Bounty and allied with Mr. House for Main Quest: All or Nothing, the Fiends launch an unsuccessful attack on Camp McCarran. Afterwards, Mr. House's Securitron Army enters outer Vegas and wipes out the Fiends completely.
5. Although the Fiends succeed in attacking the NCR stronghold at Camp McCarran, Caesar's Legion destroys the ragtag group following victory in the Second Battle of Hoover Dam in Main Quest: Veni, Vidi, Vici.
6. With Side Quest: Three-Card Bounty ignored, the Fiends launch a successful assault on Camp McCarran as an independent New Vegas is established during the Second Battle of Hoover Dam in Main Quest: No Gods, No Masters.
7. Weakened by the deaths of their leaders as a result of Side Quest: Three-Card Bounty, the Fiends still manage to secure Camp McCarran as an independent New Vegas is established during the Second Battle of Hoover Dam in Main Quest: No Gods, No Masters.
8. With the leaders of the Fiends murdered, the Fiends eventually disperse across the Mojave Wasteland.

Ending Part 27: Veronica

1. Upon completing Side Quest: Still in the Dark and allying the Brotherhood of Steel with the NCR, Veronica decides to leave the Brotherhood in Side Quest: I Could Make You Care.
2. Upon completing Side Quest: Still in the Dark and allying the Brotherhood of Steel with the NCR, Veronica decides to remains with the group at Hidden Valley in Side Quest: I Could Make You Care, despite her desire to see the Brotherhood take a more active role in the Wasteland.
3. Despite leaving the Brotherhood of Steel during Side Quest: I Could Make You Care, the destruction of Hidden Valley in Side Quest: Still in the Dark stuns Veronica.
4. Having decided to put her differences with the Elder aside, the destruction of the Brotherhood of Steel in Side Quest: Still in the Dark saddens Veronica; despite butting heads with the Elder, she is content with her decision to stick with the group in what proved to be their final days.
5. As a result of not finishing Side Quest: I Could Make You Care, Veronica's frustration with the Brotherhood's leadership leads to her banishment. She spends the rest of her life as a wandering tinkerer.
6. As a result of lifting the lockdown in Side Quest: Still in the Dark and Veronica deciding to stay with the Brotherhood of Steel in Side Quest: I Could Make You Care, Veronica hesitantly accepts the group's aggressive push on the Mojave Wasteland.
7. As a result of lifting the lockdown in Side Quest: Still in the Dark, Veronica dislikes the Elder's his aggressive approach and is content to leave the group in Side Quest: I Could Make You Care.
8. Succumbing to the trials and tribulations of the Mojave Wasteland, Veronica dies.

APPENDIX II: CHALLENGES

The following chart shows every single available Challenge, how to complete it, and what your rewards are.

TYPE	CLASS	TITLE	DESCRIPTION	(XP)	PERK	PERK NAME	ASSOCIATED ACHIEVEMENT OR TROPHY	UNLOCKED BY	REPEATABLE
Damage	Unarmed	...And Boy Are My Arms Tired	Do 100,000 damage unarmed	75					
Item	Water	...And Not a Drop to Drink	Drink 100 Water items	100	Water 15% better at removing Dehydration and healing	Camel of the Mojave			
Misc Stat	Misc Stat	...Maybe That's a Lie	Become Addicted 10 times	25					
Misc Stat	Explosives	...Or Are You just Happy to See Me?	25 Pants Exploded	50					
Misc Stat	Energy	...And Know Disintegrations	Disintegrate 32 enemies	75					
Kill	Unarmed	A Fistful of Hollars	Kill 42 enemies unarmed	50					
Damage	Damage	A Little Critical	Score 100 critical hits with 1H pistols`	50					
Damage	Limbs	A Matter of Heart	Cripple 100 Torsos	75				Limber Jack	Yes
Damage	Limbs	A Matter of Perception	Cripple 100 Heads	75				Limber Jack	Yes
Kill	Creature	Abominable	Kill 50 Abominations	50	3/6/10% damage increase	Abominable			Yes
Damage	Explosives	Aiming is Optional	Do 10,000 damage with launchers	50	Increase launcher damage by 10%			Kaboom-boom-pow	
Misc Stat	Modding	All Things in Modder Nation	Apply 20 Weapon Mods	50			Yes		Yes
Kill	Creature	Animal Control	Kill 50 Animals	50	3/6/10% damage increase	Animal Control			Yes
Misc Stat	Misc Stat	Apocalypse Ain't Got Nothin' On Me	Kill 1000 Creatures and NPCs	50				Lord Death of Murder Mountain	
Misc Stat	Challenge	Artful Pocketer	Pick 50 pockets	50			Yes		
Misc Stat	Misc Stat	At a Loss for Words	100 Speech Failures	75					
Damage	Energy	Beam Me Up	Do 25,000 damage with rifle grip laser weapons		+2/+4% crit chance with lasers	Set Lasers for Fun		More Energetic	
Damage	Challenge	Blaster Master	Do 10000 energy damage	50			Yes		
Kill	Creature	Bug Stomper	Kill 50 insects	50	3/6/10% damage increase	Bug Stomper			Yes
Misc	Challenge	Caravan Master	Win 27 games of Caravan	50			Yes	Know When to Hold 'Em	
Damage	Guns	Click	Do 20,000 damage with Submachine gun, light machine gun, or the minigun.	75				Shoot 'em Up Again	
Damage	Guns	Condition Critical	Get 100 critical hits with Guns	50					Yes
Misc Stat	Crafting	Crafty	Craft 20 items				Yes		
Misc Stat	Crafting	Crafty Veteran	Craft 100 items	75				Crafty	Yes

TYPE	CLASS	TITLE	DESCRIPTION	(XP)	PERK	PERK NAME	ASSOCIATED ACHIEVEMENT OR TROPHY	UNLOCKED BY	REPEATABLE
Damage	Energy	Critical Reaction	Get 128 critical hits with rifle-grip energy weapons	75				More Energetic	Yes
Misc Stat	Misc Stat	Day Tripper	25 Chems Taken	50	Chems last longer	Day Tripper			
Kill	Creature	Demise of the Machines	Kill 50 Robots	50	3/6/10% damage increase	Machine Head			Yes
Misc Stat	Challenge	Desert Survivalist	Heal 10,000 health with Food	100			Yes		
Damage	Unarmed	Destroy Something Not So Beautiful	Do 10,000 damage with Unarmed weapons		Reduce AP cost of specials by 10%	Beautiful Beatdown		A Fistful of Hollars	
Misc Stat	Misc Stat	Devourer of Nations	Eat 200 Corpses	100				Dine and Dash	
Misc Stat	Misc Stat	Dine and Dash	Eat 25 Corpses		NPC bodies have "food" on them	Dine and Dash		Cannibal Perk	
Misc Stat	Explosives	Disarming Personality	Disarm 25 mines	50					Yes
Misc Stat	Misc Stat	Doctor Wasteland, M.D.	Use 25 Doctor's Bags	75					Yes
Misc Stat	Challenge	Double Down	Play 10 games of Blackjack	100			Yes		
Kill	Energy	Energetic	Kill 64 Enemies with Energy Weapons	64					
Item	Turbo	Fast Times	Use Turbo 20 Times		Perk—increase turbo duration 50%	Fast Times			
Misc Stat	Challenge	Fixin' Things	Repair 30 items	50					
Kill	Unarmed	For a Few Hollars More	Kill 75 enemies with Unarmed weapons	100				A Fistful of Hollars	Yes
Item	Rad-Away	Free Radical	Use Rad-Away 20 times		Double the effectiveness of Rad-Away	Free Radical			
Damage	Unarmed	Full of Stars	Cripple 100 enemy heads with unarmed combat	50				Lethal Weapons	Yes
Damage	Unarmed	Go for the Eyes	Do 6,000 damage to enemy heads with unarmed weapons	75				A Fistful of Hollars	Yes
Damage	Explosives	Gotta Hand Grenade it To You	Do 10,000 damage with grenades and mines	100				Kaboom-boom-pow	
Damage	Unarmed	Gut Checker	Disable 100 enemy torsos with unarmed combat	50				Lethal Weapons	
Misc Stat	Misc Stat	H4x Supr3m3	25 Terminals Hacked	50				Healthy Glow	Yes
Misc Stat	Misc Stat	He Moves in Mysterious Ways	15 Mysterious Stranger Visits		Double the chance the VATS Helpers appear	Friendly Help		Mysterious Stranger Perk	
Misc Stat	Misc Stat	Healthy Glow	25 Terminals Hacked	50			Yes		
Damage	Limbs	I Am Not Left Handed	Cripple 100 Right Arms	100				Limber Jack	Yes
Damage	Melee	I Can Do It One Handed	Do 10,000 Damage with 1h Melee Weapons	50	1h Melee Attack Speed +10%	Melee Hacker		Up Closer	
Kill	Weapon	I Can Kill You With One Hand	Use 1 handed Guns to kill 250 Enemies	75					Yes
Misc Stat	Misc Stat	I Can Stop Any Time I Want	25 Chems Taken	75				Day Tripper	Yes
Misc Stat	Dismember	I Dismember You	Dismember 1000 limbs	50					
Damage	Guns	I've Got Shotgun	Do 20,000 damage with Shotguns	75				Shoot 'em Up	
Kill	Weapon	Just Point and Click	Use handle weapons to kill 250 enemies	75					Yes
Kill	Explosives	Kaboom	Kill 25 enemies with explosive weapons	50					
Kill	Explosives	Kaboom-boom-pow	Kill 50 enemies with explosive weapons	75				Kaboom	Yes
Damage	Knock	Knocked Up	Knock Down 100 Enemies	75					Yes
Misc	Challenge	Know When To Fold Em	Lose at Caravan.	50					
Misc	Challenge	Know when To Hold Em	Win 3 games of Caravan	100					
Damage	Challenge	Lead Dealer	Do 10000 Guns damage	50			Yes		
Damage	Unarmed	Lethal Weapons	Do 100 critical hits with unarmed weapons	50				A Fistful of Hollars	Yes
Damage	Energy	Let's Get Critical	64 critical hits with 1 handed energy weapons	75				More Energetic	Yes
Damage	Limbs	Limber Jack	Cripple 100 Limbs	50					Yes
Misc Stat	Challenge	Little Wheel	Play 10 games of Roulette	100			Yes		
Misc Stat	Misc Stat	Lord Death	Kill 200 Creatures and NPCs	100	1% damage bonus	Lord Death			
Misc Stat	Misc Stat	Lord Death of Murder Mountain	Kill 700 Creatures and NPCs	100	1% damage bonus	Lord Death		Lord Death	
Damage	Challenge	Love the Bomb	Do 10000 explosives weapon damage	50			Yes		
Misc Stat	Misc Stat	Low Tech Hacking	25 Locks Picked	50					
Misc Stat	Challenge	Master of the Mojave	Explore 75 locations				Yes	Walker of the Mojave	
Misc Stat	Misc Stat	Miss Fortunate Son (or Daughter)	15 Miss Fortune Appearances		Double the chance VATS Helpers Appear	Friendly Help		Miss Fortunate Perk	
Kill	Energy	More Energetic	Kill 64 Enemies with Energy Weapons	75				Energetic	Yes
Damage	Challenge	New Vegas Samurai	Do 10000 melee weapons damage	50			Yes		
Kill	Melee	Not So Up Close	Kill 25 enemies with Throwing Weapons	50				Up Close	Yes
Kill	Weapon	Nuke it From Orbit	Use shoulder mounted launchers to kill 250 enemies	75					
Damage	Challenge	Old Tyme Brawler	Do 10000 unarmed weapons damage	50			Yes		

TYPE	CLASS	TITLE	DESCRIPTION	(XP)	PERK	PERK NAME	ASSOCIATED ACHIEVEMENT OR TROPHY	UNLOCKED BY	REPEATABLE
Misc Stat	Challenge	One Armed Bandit	Play 10 games of Slots	100			Yes		
Misc Stat	Misc Stat	Questin' Mark	Complete 5 Quests	100					Yes
Item	Rad-X	Radical	Use Rad-X 20 times	75					
Damage	Energy	Set Lasers for Fun	Do 16,000 Damage with 1H Laser Weapons		+2/+4% crit chance with lasers	Set Lasers for Fun		Energetic	
Kill	Guns	Shoot 'em Up	Kill 75 enemies with Guns	75					
Kill	Guns	Shoot 'em Up Again	Kill 50 enemies with Guns	75				Shoot 'em Up	Yes
Misc Stat	Misc Stat	Sir Talks-a-lot	50 Speech Successes	50					
Misc Stat	Misc Stat	Stimp addict	Use 100 Stimpaks	50					Yes
Misc Stat	Challenge	Stim-ply Amazing	Heal 10,000 health with Stimpaks	100			Yes		
Kill	Creature	Super Mutant Massacre	Kill 50 Super Mutants or Nightkin	50	3/6/10% damage increase	Mutant Massacre			Yes
Damage	Guns	The Big Squeezy	Do 18,000 damage with Guns rifles	75				Shoot 'em Up Again	
Kill	Weapon	The Rifleman	Use 2 handed rifles to kill 250 enemies	75					Yes
Damage	Melee	This is Hacking	Get 100 one handed melee weapon critical hits	50				Up Closer	Yes
Misc Stat	Limbs	Tough Guy	Have 50 Limbs Crippled		Reduce Limb Damage	Tough Guy			
Damage	Melee	Two Hands are Better Than One	Do 10,000 Damage with 2h Melee Weapons	50	2h Melee attack speed boost 5% & 10%	Melee hacker		Up Closer	
Kill	Melee	Up Close	Kill 50 enemies with Melee Weapons	75					
Kill	Melee	Up Closer	Kill 75 Enemies with Melee Weapons	75				Up Close	Yes
Misc Stat	Challenge	Up to the Challenge	Complete 50 Challenges	100					Yes
Misc Stat	Challenge	Walker of the Mojave	Find 50 locations				Yes		
Damage	Melee	Were You Using That?	Disable 200 limbs with two handed melee weapons	50				Up Closer	Yes
Damage	Guns	You Missed the Apple	Damage 100 enemy heads with non-automatic guns rifles	75					Yes
Misc Stat	Barter	You Run Barter Town	Barter 10,000 caps worth of goods	100			Yes		
Damage	Energy	You'll Blind Somebody	Do 4096 damage to enemy heads with Energy Weapons	100				Energetic	Yes

APPENDIX III: ACHIEVEMENTS AND TROPHIES

Are you seeking points or trophies? Then check this chart, which shows what you have to do.

	NAME	DESCRIPTION	TYPE (PS3)	POINTS
		GENERAL		
	New Kid	Reach Level 10	Bronze	10
	Up and Comer	Reach Level 20	Silver	20
	The Boss	Reach Level 30	Silver	30
	Crafty	Craft 20 items	Bronze	15
	Mod Machine	Install 20 weapon mods	Bronze	15
	Walker of the Mojave	Discover 50 locations	Bronze	10
	Master of the Mojave	Discover 125 locations	Silver	25
	Globe Trotter	Discover all snow globes	Silver	25
	You Run Barter Town	Sell 10,000 caps worth of goods	Bronze	15
	Blast Mastery	Cause 10,000 damage with Energy Weapons	Bronze	15
	Love the Bomb	Cause 10,000 damage with Explosives	Bronze	15
	Lead Dealer	Cause 10,000 damage with Guns	Bronze	15
	No Tumbler Fumbler	Pick 25 locks	Bronze	15

	NAME	DESCRIPTION	TYPE (PS3)	POINTS
	Stim-ply Amazing	Heal 10,000 points of damage with Stimpaks	Bronze	15
	New Vegas Samurai	Cause 10,000 damage with Melee Weapons	Bronze	15
	Jury Rigger	Repair 30 items	Bronze	15
	Hack the Mojave	Hack 25 terminals	Bronze	15
	Artful Pocketer	Pick 50 pockets	Bronze	15
	Outstanding Orator	Make 50 Speech challenges	Bronze	15
	Desert Survivalist	Heal 10,000 points of damage with food	Bronze	15
	Old-Tyme Brawler	Cause 10,000 damage with Unarmed weapons	Bronze	15
	Know When to Fold Them	Win 3 games of Caravan	Bronze	10
	One Armed Bandit	Play 10 spins of Slots	Bronze	10
	Little Wheel	Play 10 spins of Roulette	Bronze	10
	Double Down	Play 10 hands of Blackjack	Bronze	10
	Caravan Master	Win 30 games of Caravan	Silver	30

	NAME	DESCRIPTION	TYPE (PS3)	POINTS
	The Courier Who Broke the Bank	Get banned from all the Strip's casinos	Silver	30
	MAIN AND SIDE QUESTS			
	Ain't That a Kick in the Head	Complete Ain't That a Kick in the Head	Bronze	10
	They Went That-a-Way	Complete They Went That-a-Way	Silver	25
	Ring-a-Ding-Ding	Complete Ring-a-Ding-Ding	Silver	25
	The House Always Wins	Complete The House Always Wins	Silver	30
	For the Republic	Complete For the Republic	Silver	30
	Render Unto Caesar	Complete Render Unto Caesar	Silver	30
	Wild Card	Complete Wild Card	Silver	30
	All or Nothing	Complete All or Nothing	Bronze	15
	Veni, Vidi, Vici	Complete Veni, Vidi, Vici	Bronze	15
	Eureka!	Complete Eureka!	Bronze	15
	No Gods, No Masters	Complete No Gods, No Masters	Bronze	15

	NAME	DESCRIPTION	TYPE (PS3)	POINTS
	Come Fly With Me	Complete Come Fly With Me	Bronze	20
	Talent Pool	Complete Talent Pool	Bronze	20
	Return to Sender	Complete Return to Sender	Bronze	20
	Arizona Killer	Complete Arizona Killer	Bronze	20
	You'll Know It When It Happens	Complete You'll Know It When It Happens	Bronze	20
	G.I. Blues	Complete G.I. Blues	Bronze	20
	That Lucky Old Sun	Complete That Lucky Old Sun	Bronze	20
	Volare!	Complete Volare!	Bronze	20
	The Legend of the Star	Complete The Legend of the Star	Bronze	20
	MAIN QUESTS: ALLIANCES			
	Hardcore	Play the game from start to finish in Hardcore mode	Gold	100
	COMPANIONS			
	Ol' Buddy Ol' Pal	Recruit any companion	Bronze	10
	The Whole Gang's Here	Recruit all companions	Silver	25

APPENDIX IV: VENDORS, WEAPON UPGRADES, & GAMBLING DENS

This shows the name and locations of every Caravan Player, Gambling Den, Healer, Repairer, Trader, and where Weapon Mod Upgrades can be bought.

Vendor Services

ZONE #	LOCATION NAME	HEALER/DEALER	REPAIRER [AND SKILL LEVEL]	TRADER
[1.04]	Followers Safehouse	Doctor Luria [1/31]		
[1.10]	Jacobstown		Calamity [60] [1/9]	Calamity [1/33]
[1.14]	Red Rock Drug Lab	Jack [2/31]		
[1.15]	Red Rock Canyon			Great Khan Armorer [2/33]
[2.02]	Miguel's Pawn Shop			Miguel [3/33]
[2.09]	Crimson Caravan Company			Blake [4/33]
[2.10]	New Vegas Medical Clinic	Doctor Usanagi [3/31]		
[2.14]	Gun Runners			Vendortron [5/33]
[2.19]	Camp McCarran	Doctor Kemp [4/31]		Sergeant Contreras [6/33]
		Corporal William Farber [5/31]		
[2.22]	Aerotech Office Park	Bert Gunnarsson [6/31]		
[2.32]	Grub n' Gulp Rest Stop			Fitz [7/33]
				Lupe [8/33]
[2A.02]	Westside Co-op			Clayton Etienne [9/33]
[2A.03]	Klamath Bob's Liquor Store			Klamath Bob [10/33]
[2.08]	Freeside's North Gate	Julie Farkas [7/31]		
		[2C.S02] Genaro's Fodder [8/31]		
		[2C.S08] Tapper [9/31]		
[2.15]	Freeside's East Gate	[2C.S14] Dixon [10/31]		
[2C.02]	Mick & Ralph's		Mick [75] [2/9]	Ralph [11/33]
				Mick [12/33]
[2C.07]	Silver Rush			Gloria Van Graff [13/33]

ZONE #	LOCATION NAME	HEALER/DEALER	REPAIRER [AND SKILL LEVEL]	TRADER
[2D.01]	Gomorrah	Brimstone Bartender [11/31]		
		Zoara Club Bartender [12/31]		
		Lower Brimstone Bartender [13/31]		
[2D.04]	The Tops Casino	Restaurant Bartender [14/31]		
		Aces Theater Bartender [15/31]		
[2D.05]	Ultra-Luxe Casino	Top Shelf Bartender [16/31]		
		Gourmand Food Supplier [17/31]		
		[2D.S04] Street Vendor [18/31]		
[2D.06]	Vault 21			Sarah Weintraub [14/33]
[2D.07]	NCR Embassy			[2D.S01] Mister Holdout [15/33]
[3.01]	Nellis Air Force Base	Doctor Argyll [19/31]		
[3.02]	Nellis Hangars	Boomer Chef [20/31]		Boomer Munitions Manager [16/33]
[3.06]	Brotherhood of Steel Safehouse		Paladin Sato [100] [3/9]	
[3.08]	Bitter Springs	Lieutenant Markland [21/31]		
[3.21]	Followers' Outpost	Doctor Alvarez [22/31]		
[3.23]	Camp Golf	Doc Sawbones [23/31]		
[3.28]	The Fort	Siri [24/31]	Dale Barton [30] [4/9]	Dale Barton [17/33]
[3.32]	Boulder City	Ike [25/31]		

ZONE #	LOCATION NAME	HEALER/DEALER	REPAIRER [AND SKILL LEVEL]	TRADER
[3.33]	Hoover Dam			Quartermaster Bardon [18/33]
[4.05]	Goodsprings	Trudy [26/31]		Chet [19/33]
		Doc Mitchell [27/31]		
[4.08]	Sloan	Jas Wilkins [28/31]		
[4.17]	Primm			Johnson Nash [20/33]
[4.27]	Mojave Outpost		Major Knight [100] [5/9]	Lacey [21/33]
[5.02]	188 Trading Post		Samuel Kerr [40] [6/9]	Michelle Kerr [22/33]
				Samuel Kerr [23/33]
				Arms Merchant [24/33]
				Alexander [25/33]
[5.03]	NCR Ranger Safehouse			Ranger Gomez [26/33]
[5.07]	Black Mountain		Raul Tejada [100] [7/9]	
[5.11]	Hidden Valley	Senior Scribe Schuler [29/31]	Knight Torres [100] [8/9]	Knight Torres [27/33]
[5.14]	Gibson Scrap Yard		Old Lady Gibson [65] [9/9]	Old Lady Gibson [28/33]
[5.15]	NCR Correctional Facility			Carter [29/33]
[5.18]	Novac	Doctor Ada Straus [30/31]		Cliff Briscoe [30/33]
[6.02]	Camp Forlorn Hope	Doctor Richards [31/31]		Quartermaster Mayes [31/33]
[6.20]	Cottonwood Cove			Decanus Severus [32/33]
[6.22]	Caesar's Legion Safehouse			Veteran Atticus [33/33]
TOTAL		31	9	33

Weapon Modification Upgrade Vendors

VENDOR NUMBER	VENDOR NAME	ZONE #	CLOSEST LOCATION	ENERGY WEAPONS	EXPLOSIVES	GUNS
1	Great Khan Armorer	[1.15]	Red Rock Canyon			✔
2	Blake	[2.09]	Crimson Caravan Company	✔		✔
3	Vendortron	[2.14]	Gun Runners	✔	✔	✔
4	Gloria Van Graff	[2C.07]	Silver Rush	✔		
5	Dale Barton	[3.28]	The Fort	✔		✔
6	Chet	[4.05]	Goodsprings			✔
7	Michelle	[5.02]	188 Trading Post			✔
8	Knight Torres	[5.11]	Hidden Valley		✔	✔
9	Old Lady Gibson	[5.14]	Gibson Scrap Yard	✔		
10	Cliff Briscoe	[5.18]	Novac	✔		✔

Gambling Dens

ZONE #	LOCATION NAME	BLACKJACK	ROULETTE	SLOTS
[2.17]	Sunset Sarsaparilla Headquarters	Lucky Horseshoes [1/15]		
[2C.06]	Atomic Wrangler	Yes [2/15]	Yes [3/15]	Yes [4/15]
[2D.01]	Gomorrah	Yes [5/15]	Yes [6/15]	Yes [7/15]
[2D.04]	The Tops Casino	Yes [8/15]	Yes [9/15]	Yes [10/15]
[2D.05]	Ultra-Luxe Casino	Yes [11/15]	Yes [12/15]	
[4.17]	Primm	Yes [13/15]	Yes [14/15]	Yes [15/15]
TOTAL		5 (+ Lucky Horseshoes)	5	4

APPENDIX V: CRAFTING LOCATIONS

This shows the locations of every Campfire, Reloading Bench, and Workbench.

Campfires

#	ZONE #	CLOSEST LOCATION	DESCRIPTION
1	[1.06]	Horowitz Farmstead	In the center of the middle derelict barn structure, by the mattresses, lit by the Viper Gang.
2	[1.07]	Charleston Cave	Inside the cave, at the first chamber (Entrance Camp), by the sleeping mattresses and skeletons.
3	[1.12]	Ranger Station Foxtrot	By the tent, with the bedrolls surrounding it, in the middle of the station camp.
4	[1.13]	Brewer's Beer Bootlegging	Inside the shack, in the middle of the floor.
5	[1.14]	Red Rock Drug Lab	Between Jack and Diane's recliners, surrounded by the trailers.
6	[1.15]	Red Rock Canyon	Inside Papa Khan's longhouse; the stone fireplace at the west end of the banquet room.
7	[1.15]	Red Rock Canyon	Near Regis' personal tent; the main Campfire roasting a Brahmin, near the cluster of four tents.
8	[1.15]	Red Rock Canyon	Inside Regis' personal tent, close to the two outhouses in the cluster of four tents near the main Campfire.
9	[1.15]	Red Rock Canyon	Edge of the cliffs at the northwest end, overlooking the training circle, outside the cluster of three tents.
10	[1.20]	Bonnie Springs	At the end of the road where the Viper Gang has camped, in front of the main ghost town building.
11	[1.22]	Whittaker Farmstead	Under the cooking Brahmin, just outside the farmstead shack, close to the car wreck and swings.
12	[1.S01]	Radioactive Road Block	Between the lanes of the 95 Freeway remains, southeast of the truck debris.
13	[1.S02]	Hovering Anomaly/Mercenary Camp	On the perimeter cliffs west of the Brooks Tumbleweed Ranch.
14	[1.S07]	Jackal Shack	In front (south) of the Jackal Shack, next to an abandoned house, south of the perimeter road.
15	[1.S18]	Westside Turnaround and Playground	By the large rock and picnic tables, close to the flying saucer climbing frame and old play area.
16	[2.09]	Crimson Caravan Company	Close to Alice's main office shack, outside in the northeast of the walled area, surrounded by picnic tables.
17	[2.16]	Durable Dunn's Sacked Caravan	Between the two bridges, by the scattered items and dead bodies.
18	[2.32]	Grub n' Gulp Rest Stop	Inside the Rest Stop camp, by the shack with the bedding surrounding it.
19	[2.S18]	Cook-Cook's Territory	Inside Cook-Cook's Territory, in the ruined building north of the entrance.
20	[2C.S10]	Signal Box Tower	Behind the railway station, in the northwest corner of Outer Freeside, by the Signal Box Tower.
21	[2C.S20]	Squatter Camp #2	Behind the barrels, east Squatter Camp on the far side of the ruined building, across from Mick & Ralph's [2C.02].
22	[2C.S20]	Squatter Camp #2	By the wall, east Squatter Camp on the far side of the ruined building, across from Mick & Ralph's [2C.02].
23	[2C.S27]	Squatter Camp #3 and Old Ben	One of two; small Squatter Camp to the right of the North Gate, southwest Inner Freeside [Zone 2C].
24	[2C.S27]	Squatter Camp #3 and Old Ben	One of two, small Squatter Camp to the right of the North Gate, southwest Inner Freeside [Zone 2C].
25	[2C.S28]	Squatter Camp #4	Small Squatter Camp to the left of the North Gate, southwest Inner Freeside [Zone 2C].
26	[2E.S01]	Sentry Post Mattress	Near a mattress close to the West Entrance, inside South Vegas Ruins.
27	[2E.S03]	Lean-to Shack	Outside the Lean-To Shack, north of the ruined warehouse building and Vault 3 entrance.
28	[3.01]	Nellis Air Force Base	In the irrigation farm, between the two runways, southwest of Nellis Array [3.03], between three small tents.
29	[3.07]	Bloodborne Cave	By the scattered skeletons, in the interior of the cave.
30	[3.08]	Bitter Springs	In the western part of the refugee shanty huts, half-surrounded by small A-frame tents and shacks.
31	[3.08]	Bitter Springs	In the eastern part of the refugee shanty huts, half-surrounded by small A-frame tents and shacks.

Campfires

#	ZONE #	CLOSEST LOCATION	DESCRIPTION
32	[3.08]	Bitter Springs	Inside the tent in the middle of the lower refugee camp, south of the largest shack.
33	[3.08]	Bitter Springs	At the north, upper end of the camp, in the middle of the NCR tent camp.
34	[3.11]	Cannibal Johnson's Cave	Inside the cave, in the center of the main cavern area.
35	[3.17]	Fisherman's Pride Shack	Nestled between the shack and the outside rock.
36	[3.20]	Guardian Peak	Near the tent, by the narrow rickety bridge, at the lookout point camp area.
37	[3.23]	Camp Golf	Southwest end, between the two sets of the tent rows, close to Lake Las Vegas [3.22].
38	[3.23]	Camp Golf	Inside the resort building; the kitchen fireplace to the left of the main entrance hall.
39	[3.24]	Mountain Shadows Campground	On the flat picnic area, close to the picnic table, bedding and small trailer.
40	[3.25]	Scavenger Platform	On the northeast floating shanty hut platform, on Lake Mead.
41	[3.28]	The Fort	The lower infantry camp, south of the rows of tents, between the two Centurion tents.
42	[3.28]	The Fort	The lower infantry camp, south of the rows of tents, close to the training dummies and weather station.
43	[3.30]	Ranger Station Alpha	In the middle of the camp, outside the middle tent.
44	[3.31]	Boulder Beach Campground	Surrounded by tires, on the upper grounds near a picnic table.
45	[3.34]	Legate's Camp	By the machete-sharpener by the tent, near the steps down to the training area.
46	[3.34]	Legate's Camp	By the drying Brahmin skins, northwest area of camp, west of the cluster of red tents.
47	[3.35]	Cazador Nest	On the rounded summit of the hill northwest of the nest, overlooking Boulder City.
48	[3.35]	Cazador Nest	Due west of the nest, on the rocky terrain southwest of the road to Boulder City.
49	[3.36]	Ranger Station Delta	Surrounded by sandbags, by the NCR flag, inside the camp.
50	[3.S01]	Power Transformer	Under the freeway support pillar, just outside the Fields' Shack [3.04].
51	[3.S02]	Chem Addicts' Camp	South of the railroad tracks, by the road between the mattresses; the Chem Addicts' Camp.
52	[3.S12]	Super Mutant Camp	Around the bedding, northeast of The One, in the small Super Mutant Camp close to the Devil's Throat [3.10].
53	[3.S17]	Lake Mead Scenic Overlook	East of the lake, on the Lake Mead shoreline near two picnic tables, at the Overlook close to Lake Las Vegas [3.22].
54	[3.S21]	Sunset Sarsaparilla Billboard	At the foot of the Sunset Sarsaparilla Billboard, next to the Lonesome Drifter.
55	[4.01]	Tribal Village	In the center of the small camp, surrounded by tents and dead bodies.
56	[4.02]	Makeshift Great Khan Camp	In the middle of the camp, close to the rock wall and rolled-up bedding.
57	[4.03]	Great Khan Encampment	By the bedding mats, close to the quarried rock wall.
58	[4.11]	Goodsprings Source	Among the rocks and scattered wood, where Sunny teaches you Recipes, near the other two Campfires.
59	[4.11]	Goodsprings Source	Among the rocks and scattered wood, below the rusting blue car and other two Campfires.
60	[4.11]	Goodsprings Source	Among the rocks and scattered wood, east of the small trailer and other two Campfires.
61	[4.13]	Powder Ganger Camp West	In the middle of the camp, by the small table.
62	[4.15]	Powder Ganger Camp South	At the end of the tipped red cargo carriage and low-lying rocks, close to the railroad track.
63	[4.17]	Primm	On a narrow flat promontory south of Lone Wolf Radio, overlooking Primm.
64	[4.17]	Primm	At the west end of the street of houses, adjacent to the freeway wall, south of the Casinos.
65	[4.17]	Primm	Inside the Bison Steve Casino, under a cooking Brahmin, in the main gambling hall.
66	[4.20]	The Prospector's Den	On the path to the east of the den, out in the open.
67	[4.21]	Mesquite Mountains Camp Site	On the camp site plateau, near the two tents and picnic tables.
68	[4.26]	Jack Rabbit Springs	East of the radioactive pools, on the higher ground; the Super Mutant Camp [4.S22].
69	[4.29]	Nipton Road Pit Stop	In the open ruin east of the northwest billboard, north side of the road, guarded by the Jackal Gang.
70	[4.30]	Nipton	Outside the long trailer parked in the southwestern corner of the trailer park south of the main drag.

Campfires

#	ZONE #	CLOSEST LOCATION	DESCRIPTION
71	[4.S09]	Deathclaw Trailer	Outside the small trailer with the two chairs and barbecue, across from the Whittaker Farmstead [1.22].
72	[4.S19]	California Sunset Drive-In	Under the Prospector's Lean-To [4.S19], west of the Primm NCR tents, north of California Sunset Drive-In [4.18].
73	[5.07]	Black Mountain	At the crater base camp, near the shack and lookout ruin, at the top of the mountain.
74	[5.07]	Black Mountain	In the middle of the up-turned radar dish base camp, at the top of the mountain.
75	[5.07]	Black Mountain	In a small, upturned satellite dish, in Tabitha's summit camp, near the radio mast and first building.
76	[5.10]	Powder Ganger Camp North	Under the shack, inside the Ganger camp.
77	[5.11]	Hidden Valley	By the sleeping mat, in the eastern dead-end bunker.
78	[5.11]	Hidden Valley	By the sleeping mat and radio, inside the southern dead-end bunker, where Ranger Dobson is camping.
79	[5.15]	NCR Correctional Facility	In the northwest corner of the interior courtyard, between two watch towers.
80	[5.16]	Powder Ganger Camp East	In the middle of the tiny camp, near the Ammo Boxes and assorted junk.
81	[5.19]	Emergency Service Railyard	On the east side of the rail tracks, just north of the main service building.
82	[5.21]	Harper's Shack	Around the side of the shack, outside by the southwest corner.
83	[5.24]	Highway 95 Viper's Encampment	Near the shack on the south side of the camp, adjacent to the road to Novac.
84	[5.29]	Legion Raid Camp	In the camp, where the Powder Gangers are tied up, on the upper ground by the main tent.
85	[5.29]	Legion Raid Camp	In the eastern lower ground, close to a red A-frame tent.
86	[5.31]	Synder Prospector Camp	In the rocky gravel just outside the shack structure.
87	[5.S01]	Fetid Pond	North of the substation, on a bluff in the rocky foothills below the Fetid Pond, overlooking the El Dorado Substation [5.04].
88	[5.S08]	Powder Ganger Alcove	In a small, refuse-strewn cave alcove outside the NCR Correctional Facility perimeter fence, in the northeast rocky bluffs.
89	[5.S09]	Tower Relay Alcove	Northwest of Novac, on a large rocky plateau with a radio mast, in the alcove.
90	[5.S10]	Gibson's Shack	Inside the shack, to the west of Gibson's Scrap Yard, near the Black Mountain foothills and southwest of HELIOS One [5.13].
91	[5.S12]	Sealed Train Tunnel	The Viper Gang camp, southeast of Harper's Shack [5.21], in front of the Sealed Train Tunnel.
92	[5.S17]	Legion Camp	West of the Wrecked Highwayman [5.25] in the rocky ground, the fire is near some bedding in a small Legion Camp.
93	[5.S20]	Viper Gang Alcove	In the Viper Gang Alcove, northwest of the Wolfhorn Ranch [6.14] and Highway 164.
94	[5.S23]	Astor's Recon Camp	Inside Astor's Recon Camp, west of Camp Searchlight.
95	[6.01]	El Dorado Gas & Service	Outside the gas station, surrounded by bedding.
96	[6.02]	Camp Forlorn Hope	In the middle of camp, surrounded by shacks, a blue rusting carriage shell, a tent, and the stream.
97	[6.02]	Camp Forlorn Hope	Southeast of camp, at the end of the tent alley, close to the watch tower.
98	[6.06]	Nelson	Between the picnic tables and crucifixion platform in the middle of the settlement.
99	[6.11]	Cliffside Prospector Camp	Among the rubble and junk at the edge of the lean-to.
100	[6.14]	Wolfhorn Ranch	By the grave, at Wolfhorn Point, on the northwest edge of the camp by the rickety bridge.
101	[6.18]	Sniper's Nest	Just outside the Sniper's Nest shack, overlooking Camp Cottonwood.
102	[6.19]	Cottonwood Overlook	Near the burned-out trailer and picnic tables, on the eastern overlook, close to the turnaround.
103	[6.20]	Cottonwood Cove	The north end of the Legion camp, near a large rock and three A-frame tents.
104	[6.21]	Bradley's Shack	In front of the shack, guarded by the Jackal Gang.
105	[6.22]	Caesar's Legion Safehouse	Just outside of the Safehouse shack.
106	[6.22]	Caesar's Legion Safehouse	Near a rock on the hilly summit, north of the safehouse, and south of the Viper Gang ambush [5.S19].
107	[6.29]	Smith Mesa Prospector Camp	Outside the camp, just to the right of the sandbag lean-to.
108	[6.S09]	Recon Legion Camp	Southeast of the road turnaround, near the bedding in the Recon Legion camp, below the entrance to Techatticup Mine.
109	[6.S13]	Little Rock Camp	Little Rock Camp; near the rock and burnt-out car, southeast of the Prospector Camp, in the sandy flats.
TOTAL	**109**		

Reloading Benches

#	ZONE #	CLOSEST LOCATION	DESCRIPTION
1	[1.06]	Horowitz Farmstead	Western farmstead cluster; behind the small, front shack, between the shack and the barn.
2	[1.10]	Jacobstown	Climb the curved stairs from the entrance hall; upper floor, first bedroom on the left after entering right balcony doorway.
3	[1.12]	Ranger Station Foxtrot	By the side of the tent, close to the crates, on the right (west) side of the camp.
4	[1.15]	Red Rock Canyon	In the Great Khan Armory. Against the wall opposite the cell doors, next to a Workbench.
5	[2.02]	Miguel's Pawn Shop	Inside the shop, on the left wall as you enter.
6	[2.12]	Monte Carlo Suites	In the Scorpion Gang suite, near a Workbench, far right (southwest) of the ground floor entrance.
7	[2.12]	Monte Carlo Suites	Also in the Scorpion Gang suite, near a Workbench, far right (southwest) of the ground floor entrance.
8	[2.14]	Gun Runners	At the Vendortron Store, in front of the building, on the roadside.
9	[2.14]	Gun Runners	Inside the mechanics' chamber, in the main Gun Runners' building. First of two in this room.
10	[2.14]	Gun Runners	Inside the mechanics' chamber, in the main Gun Runners' building. Second of two in this room.
11	[2.19]	Camp McCarran	In Sergeant Contreras' supply shack at the Concourse end, in an alcove with a Workbench right of the door.
12	[2B.01]	The Gray	Upper floor inside the hotel; through the room door on the opposite wall.
13	[2C.04]	Cerulean Robotics	On the wall in the Protectron Pod area, on the same wall as FISTO's Pod, near a Reloading Bench.
14	[3.02]	Nellis Hangars	At the far-left end next to a Reloading Bench, inside the curve-roofed workshop building.
15	[3.02]	Nellis Hangars	In the far left workshop area of the second (northern) hangar. Adjacent to a second bench near Worbenches.
16	[3.02]	Nellis Hangars	In the far left workshop area of the second (northern) hangar. Adjacent to a second bench near Workbenches.
17	[3.06]	Brotherhood of Steel Safehouse	In the bunker beneath the safehouse shack, inside the storage and sleeping area, by a Workbench.
18	[3.12]	Vault 34	In the alcove by the pool table, in the Armory Common room. Follow the sign after descending down.
19	[3.36]	Ranger Station Delta	In the cellar below the ruined homestead, to the right of the door at the bottom of the stairs.
20	[4.05]	Goodsprings	In the side alley between the General Store and the Prospector Saloon, near the AC unit.
21	[4.17]	Primm	Inside the sheriff's shack, to the right of the entrance, behind the counter.
22	[4.20]	The Prospector's Den	Inside the cave system, and subterranean den structure; in the tiny store room at the far end.
23	[4.23]	Nevada Highway Patrol Station	In the corner of the cell block, guarded by Jackal Gang members.
24	[4.30]	Nipton	Inside the Nipton House to the east of the Town Hall, in the small entrance hall.
25	[4.S05]	Abandoned Shack	Inside the Abandoned Shack to the northwest of the Yangtze Memorial [4.07], left of the door.
26	[5.02]	188 Trading Post	East side, behind the blue carriage shell store, on the other side of the picnic tables.
27	[5.03]	NCR Ranger Safehouse	In the first room on the right, once you enter the safehouse.
28	[5.07]	Black Mountain	On the summit, inside Tabitha's storage room, on the far wall below the stop sign.
29	[5.11]	Hidden Valley	In the research lab on the east side of Bunker L2, inside the base; in the far right dark corner.
30	[5.17]	REPCONN Test Sites	Off the main tunnel to the basement rocket laboratory, in the small storage room with the radiation symbol near the door.
31	[5.18]	Novac	Inside the Poseidon Gas garage building.
32	[5.21]	Harper's Shack	To the left of the entrance door, as you step inside, next to the Work Bench.
33	[6.02]	Camp Forlorn Hope	Inside the Storage Shed, near the stream and across from the Quartermaster's tent.
34	[6.04]	Abandoned BoS Bunker	In the bunker beneath the grating, inside the storage area.
35	[6.16]	Camp Searchlight	In the western chapel basement, where Logan is waiting, in the opposite corner to the terminal.
36	[6.20]	Cottonwood Cove	Inside the concrete storage structure, behind the Headquarters building.
TOTAL	36		

Workbenches

#	ZONE #	CLOSEST LOCATION	DESCRIPTION
1	[1.04]	Followers Safehouse	Opposite the entrance door, in the first room, far right corner.
2	[1.08]	Silver Peak Mine	In the back room of the shack, close to the entrance to the mine interior, on the left wall.
3	[1.15]	Red Rock Canyon	In the Great Khan Armory. Against the wall opposite the cell doors, next to a Reloading Bench.
4	[2.09]	Crimson Caravan Company	Inside the walled area, on the outside edge of the middle building, close to the road.
5	[2.12]	Monte Carlo Suites	In the Scorpion Gang suite, near two Reloading Benches, far right (southwest) of the ground floor entrance.
6	[2.14]	Gun Runners	Inside the mechanics' chamber, in the main Gun Runners' building. First of four in this room.
7	[2.14]	Gun Runners	Inside the mechanics' chamber, in the main Gun Runners' building. Second of four in this room.
8	[2.14]	Gun Runners	Inside the mechanics' chamber, in the main Gun Runners' building. Third of four in this room.
9	[2.14]	Gun Runners	Inside the mechanics' chamber, in the main Gun Runners' building. Fourth of four in this room.
10	[2.19]	Camp McCarran	In Sergeant Contreras' supply shack at the Concourse end, in an alcove with a Reloading Bench right of the door.
11	[2C.02]	Mick & Ralph's	Under the "sensitive electronics" sign inside the shop, far end of the ground floor, in Mick's workshop.
12	[2C.04]	Cerulean Robotics	On the wall in the Protectron Pod area, on the same wall as FISTO's Pod, near a Reloading Bench.
13	[2D.02]	Lucky 38 Casino	On the Presidential Suite level home, between the trunks, close to the door into the dining room with the long table.
14	[2D.07]	Michael Angelo's Workshop	On the upper gantry walkway above the ground, inside the main workshop warehouse. Northern end.
15	[2D.07]	Michael Angelo's Workshop	In the workshop room, north of the main workshop warehouse. First of three Workbenches.
16	[2D.07]	Michael Angelo's Workshop	In the workshop room, north of the main workshop warehouse. Second of three Workbenches.
17	[2D.07]	Michael Angelo's Workshop	In the workshop room, north of the main workshop warehouse. Three of three Workbenches.
18	[2D.07]	Michael Angelo's Workshop	On the upper gantry walkway above the ground, inside the main workshop warehouse. Eastern area.
19	[2E.01]	Zapp's Neon Signs	Against a wall in the main chamber, close to the metal steps, first of three adjacent Workbenches.
20	[2E.01]	Zapp's Neon Signs	Against a wall in the main chamber, close to the metal steps, second of three adjacent Workbenches.
21	[2E.01]	Zapp's Neon Signs	Against a wall in the main chamber, close to the metal steps, third of three adjacent Workbenches.
22	[3.01]	Nellis Air Force Base	At the far-left end next to a Reloading Bench, inside the curve-roofed workshop building.
23	[3.02]	Nellis Hangars	In the far left workshop area of the second (northern) hangar. Back-to-back with a table.
24	[3.05]	Raul's Shack	Inside the shack, on the right wall, across from the mattress.
25	[3.06]	Brotherhood of Steel Safehouse	In the bunker beneath the safehouse shack, inside the storage and sleeping area, by a Reloading Bench.
26	[4.05]	Goodsprings	In the side alley between the General Store and the Prospector Saloon, near the AC unit.
27	[4.08]	Sloan	Inside the Machine Shop, one of the shacks within Sloan's perimeter.
28	[4.30]	Nipton	In the main room inside one of the ranch houses with the Mister Gutsy Prototype, on the east side of town.
29	[5.07]	Black Mountain	Inside the inner room of Raul's "prison" building, at the summit of Black Mountain.
30	[5.07]	Black Mountain	Inside the outer room of Raul's "prison" building, at the summit of Black Mountain.
31	[5.11]	Hidden Valley	In the research lab on the east side of Bunker L2, inside the base; middle of the wall near the server.
32	[5.14]	Gibson Scrap Yard	Next to the bed, in the scrapyard interior; garage area.

Workbenches

#	ZONE #	CLOSEST LOCATION	DESCRIPTION
33	[5.15]	NCR Correctional Facility	In the prison yard, on the wall and just to the side of the exit door from the visitor center.
34	[5.17]	REPCONN Test Site	Inside the laboratory, in one corner of the very top floor of the research lab, close to the stairs.
35	[5.17]	REPCONN Test Site	Inside the laboratory, at the corner of an inner wall near two computer banks, on the main research lab floor.
36	[5.17]	REPCONN Test Site	Just right of the entrance door in the basement rocket laboratory, overlooking the launch chamber.

Workbenches

#	ZONE #	CLOSEST LOCATION	DESCRIPTION
37	[5.18]	Novac	In a small open shack, northwest of the motel, close to the water tower and railroad track.
38	[5.18]	Novac	Inside the Poseidon Gas garage building.
39	[5.21]	Harper's Shack	To the left of the entrance door, as you step inside, next to the Reloading Bench.
40	[6.03]	Southern Nevada Wind Farm	Inside the wind farm shack, right of the entrance.
41	[6.09]	Lucky Jim Mine	Inside the mine shack, in the corner, between the door and oven.
TOTAL	41		

APPENDIX VI: COLLECTIBLES: SNOW GLOBES

Where are all seven of Mr. House's favorite trinket? Here!

#	NAME	ZONE #	LOCATION	DESCRIPTION
1	"Mt. Charleston"	[1.10]	Jacobstown	On the large curved desk near the terminals, in the large reception lobby of the lodge.
2	"Mormon Fort"	[2C.01]	Old Mormon Fort	On top of the wooden bookcase, inside the tower where Julie Farkas has her office.
3	"Test Site"	[2D.02]	Lucky 38 Casino	Cocktail Lounge: Behind the cash register against the central curved sideboard opposite side the entrance.
4	"The Strip"	[2D.06]	Vault 21	Inside Sarah's locked bedroom, between the two beds, on a small circular vault table.
5	"Nellis AFB"	[3.01]	Nellis Air Force Base	On the corner table, under the mural, inside Pete's "museum" curve-roofed shack.
6	"Hoover Dam"	[3.33]	Hoover Dam	On one of the two large curved desks, near the terminal, inside the visitor center.
7	"Goodsprings"	[4.06]	Goodsprings Cemetery	At the foot of the small, rectangular gravestone and disturbed earth, close to the water tower.
TOTAL	7			

APPENDIX VII: COLLECTIBLES: CARAVAN CARDS & PLAYERS

Where can you find friendly folk to play Caravan against, and more Caravan Cards to build up your collection? In this Appendix.

PLAYER NUMBER	CARAVAN PLAYER NAME	ZONE #	LOCATION	DESCRIPTION
1	Blake	[2.09]	Crimson Caravan Company	Purchased from Blake the Trader.
2	Isaac	[2.14]	Gun Runners	On the Caravan Player: Outside, or in his house at night [2.S05].
3	Little Buster	[2.19]	Camp McCarran	On the Caravan Player: In the parking lot, near First Recon tents.
4	Keith	[2.22]	Aerotech Office Park	On the Caravan Player: Inside Aerotech Suite 200.
6	Jules	[2B.S03]	Jules, of North Vegas Square	On the Caravan Player: Inside the Square [2.07], near the Squatters.
7	Private Jake Erwin	[2D.07]	NCR Embassy	On the Caravan Player: Inside the Embassy.
8	Ambassador Dennis Crocker	[2D.07]	NCR Embassy	On the Caravan Player: Inside the Embassy.
9	Prospector Corpse	[U2.C]	Central Sewers	On the corpse, location "Prospector's Rest," inside the Sewer.
10	Poindexter	[3.23]	Camp Golf	On Poindexter the Misfit, who isn't a Caravan Player.
11	Dale Barton	[3.28]	The Fort	On the Caravan Player: Near the (inaccessible) Legate's Gate.
13	Ringo	[4.05]	Goodsprings	Given to you by this Caravan Player inside the Poseidon Gas Station.
14	Ringo	[4.05]	Goodsprings	On the Caravan Player: Inside the Poseidon Gas station.
15	Chet	[4.05]	Goodsprings	Purchased from Chet the proprietor of the General Store.
16	Johnson Nash	[4.17]	Primm	On the Caravan Player: Inside the Vikki & Vance Casino.
17	Prospector Corpse	[4.20]	Prospector's Den	On the corpse, just outside the cave entrance.
18	Prospector Corpse	[4.20]	Prospector's Den	On the corpse, scattered inside the cave area.
19	Prospector Corpse	[4.20]	Prospector's Den	On the corpse, scattered inside the cave area.
20	Prospector Corpse	[4.20]	Prospector's Den	On the corpse, scattered inside the cave area.
21	Prospector Corpse	[4.20]	Prospector's Den	On the corpse, inside the dorm room.
22	Prospector Corpse	[4.23]	Nevada Highway Patrol Station	On the corpse, inside the station's cells.
23	Lacey	[4.27]	Mojave Outpost	On the Caravan Player: Propping up the barracks bar.
24	Prospector Corpse	[5.12]	Scorpion Gulch	On the corpse, in the rocky ravine to the east, near the metal ramp.
25	Old Lady Gibson	[5.14]	Gibson Scrap Yard	Purchased from Old Lady Gibson, the Trader.
26	Carter	[5.15]	NCR Correctional Facility	Purchased from Carter the Trader, in Cell Block B.
27	No-Bark Noonan	[5.18]	Novac	On the Caravan Player: In his shack, or wandering the town.
28	Cliff Briscoe	[5.18]	Novac	On the Caravan Player: Inside the Dino Dee-Lite Gift Shop, inside Dinky.
29	Quartermaster Mayes	[6.02]	Camp Forlorn Hope	On the Caravan Player: Inside his tent, grumbling about provisions.
30	Prospector Corpse	[6.S16]	Deathclaw Promontory	On the corpse, near the second corpse, surrounded by Deathclaws.
TOTAL	30			

APPENDIX VIII: COLLECTIBLES: HOLLOWED-OUT ROCKS

Is the Sun killing you? Seek these out for some random items.

#	ZONE #	CLOSEST LOCATION	DESCRIPTION
1	[1.02]	Northern Passage	On the right (east) rock wall, near the grave, with "The Sun is Killing Me" graffiti.
2	[1.03]	Ruby Hill Mine	Part of the rock wall, just right of the entrance door.
3	[1.07]	Charleston Cave	Part of the rock wall, just right of the entrance door, with the heart graffiti.
4	[1.08]	Silver Peak Mine	Part of the rock wall, just right of the entrance shack.

#	ZONE #	CLOSEST LOCATION	DESCRIPTION
5	[1.09]	Vault 22	On the right (north) bank, across from the "Keep Out" sign, near the entrance.
6	[1.10]	Jacobstown	Just outside the perimeter, to the right of the main entrance, where the Super Mutants are guarding.
7	[1.11]	Remnants Bunker	About 10 feet to the right (north) of the bunker entrance, part of the rock wall.
8	[1.16]	Chance's Map	Adjacent to the dirt map, with "The Sun is Killing Me" graffiti.
9	[3.07]	Bloodborne Cave	Just to the right (east) of the cave entrance.
10	[3.11]	Cannibal Johnson's Cave	Just to the right (northeast) of the cave entrance.
11	[3.17]	Fisherman's Pride Shack	By the Campfire, just a few paces northwest of the shack itself.
12	[3.19]	Camp Guardian	Adjacent to the Camp Guardian Population sign, where the Coyotes prowl, at the base of the path up to Guardian Peak.
13	[3.21]	Follower's Outpost	Built into the steps of the signal box structure, with "The Sun is Killing Me" graffiti.
14	[3.31]	Boulder Beach Campground	By the side of the road, just northwest of the jetties, with "The Sun is Killing Me" graffiti.
15	[3.35]	Cazador Nest	Part of the rock wall, on the right (east) side of the Nest alcove, facing the alcove itself.
16	[4.01]	Tribal Village	At the start of the Ravine Path [1.S26], close to the corpses and tents.
17	[4.02]	Makeshift Great Khan Camp	Near the desert plants on the right (west) side of the camp.
18	[4.07]	Yangtze Memorial	On the rocky bluff at the base of the south steps, with the peace symbol graffiti.
19	[4.09]	Goodsprings Cave	Just to the right (south) of the cave entrance.
20	[4.17]	Primm	Attached to a larger rock, near the scattered Chems, near the rock perimeter above the concrete support wall.
21	[4.26]	Jack Rabbit Springs	South of the radiation pools, on the edge of the Dry Lake.
22	[4.28]	Morning Star Cavern	By the entrance to the cavern, with the bones and explosives crate at the base of it.
23	[4.32]	Crescent Canyon West	In the canyon, on the west exit slope, adjacent to a rusting car husk.
24	[4.33]	Crescent Canyon East	In the canyon, on the east exit slope just after the fallen rail bridge.
25	[5.05]	Vault 11	Just to the right (northeast) of the cave entrance.
26	[5.08]	Black Rock Cave	Just to the right (north) of the fallen radar dish and cave entrance.
27	[5.09]	El Dorado Dry Lake	Due west of the Savaged Brahmin [5.S03] on Highway 95, in the sands of the Dry Lake.
28	[5.11]	Hidden Valley	Just west of the eastern bunker, with the "no missile" and heart graffiti.
29	[5.16]	Powder Ganger Camp East	Next to a Honey Mesquite Tree, 20-30 feet south of the camp.
30	[5.20]	Primm Pass	Close to Brahmin bones, on the western end of the pass.
31	[5.22]	Dead Wind Cavern	On the left (south) rock wall slope, 20-30 feet from the entrance.
32	[5.27]	Hidden Supply Cave	To the left (south) of the cave entrance, with the "no missile" graffiti.
33	[5.28]	Walking Box Cavern	Around 20-30 feet away (east) of the cavern entrance.
34	[5.30]	Broc Flower Cave	At the foot of the entrance slope, with "The Sun is Killing Me" graffiti.
35	[6.04]	Abandoned BoS Bunker	With the small cluster of rocks and shale on the slope to the bunker grating.
36	[6.08]	Techatticup Mine	Just to the right of the entrance door, on the rock wall, with the white blocks graffiti.
37	[6.09]	Lucky Jim Mine	Slightly farther up and behind (southwest of) the shack, near the wooden cart.
38	[6.12]	Searchlight North Gold Mine	On the flat, raised rock bank to the left (south) of the entrance hole.
39	[6.17]	Searchlight East Gold Mine	On the rock and shale pile, left (southeast) of the entrance, slightly farther down the slope; climb on the pile to reach it.
40	[6.20]	Cottonwood Cove	On the road (before the entrance sign) between the two sets of crucifixion poles, with "The Sun is Killing Me" graffiti.
41	[6.21]	Bradley's Shack	On the opposite (west) side to the shack entrance, by the small valley landslide.
42	[6.27]	Fire Root Cavern	At the foot of the entrance slope on the left side.

APPENDIX IX: SKILL BOOKS

Adding permanent points to your skills is well worth the searching for these esteemed tomes.

#	ZONE #	CLOSEST LOCATION	DESCRIPTION
		TALES OF A JUNKTOWN JERKY VENDOR [BARTER]	
1	[1.09]	Vault 22	Pest Control; from the elevator head north up the steps, into the lab room. On the table with the bubbling vials.
2	[2.30]	Allied Technologies Offices	On the floor of the southwest corner of the large open-plan office room to the left (west) of the entrance room.
3	[3.14]	Cap Counterfeiting Shack	On the suitcase by the bed and near the sofa, in the smaller, back cellar room.
4	[4.17]	Primm	Inside the Bison Steve Casino; on the floor behind the counter of the gift shop.
		NIKOLA TESLA AND YOU [ENERGY WEAPONS]	
1	[2.35]	REPCONN Headquarters	Inside the locked shipping room with the collapsed ceiling and filing cabinets, on top of a safe on the floor, in the corner.
2	[2.35]	REPCONN Headquarters	On the second floor, in the northeast server room, on the table with the terminal in the far corner.
3	[5.11]	Hidden Valley	In the white plastic bin by the desk, inside Schuler's office; Bunker L1. West of the central hub corridor junction.
4	[6.23]	Old Nuclear Test Site	On the small table opposite the entrance, inside the irradiated shack.
		DUCK AND COVER! [EXPLOSIVES]	
1	[3.01]	Nellis Air Force Base	Among the neatly arranged books on the bookcase, on the interior corner inside Mother Pearl's Barracks.
2	[4.08]	Sloan	Inside the small barracks shack next to the trailer, on the left locker shelf, below the First Aid Box, near the bunk beds.
3	[4.27]	Mojave Outpost	Inside the bar and barracks building, on the bottom shelf, in the middle below the bar counter.
		GUNS AND BULLETS [GUNS]	
1	[2D.01]	Gomorrah	In the Zoara Club, on the first low bookshelf, on the left side of Big Sal's office (same side as the wall safe).
2	[3.05]	Raul's Shack	In the small wooden crate on the floor, at the foot of the metal shelves, left of the entrance.
3	[3.12]	Vault 34	On the small metal table between the sofas by the pool table, in the Armory Common room. Follow the sign after descending.
4	[4.23]	Nevada Highway Patrol Station	On the desk without the computer in the entrance open-plan office room, nearest the door leading to the cells.
		TUMBLERS TODAY [LOCKPICK]	
1	[1.08]	Silver Peak Mine	Inside the shack, behind the two small tables, on the ground lying in an open locker, to the right of the entrance.
2	[3.16]	Bitter Springs Recreation Area	Inside the office shack to the west, on the office desk in the smaller of the two rooms, left of the entrance.
3	[4.20]	The Prospector's Den	Inside the cave system, and subterranean Den structure; in the large barracks room, on the floor in the far right corner.
4	[6.14]	Wolfhorn Ranch	Inside the farmhouse, partially under the refrigerator without the door, right of the oven, to the right of the entrance.
		D.C. JOURNAL OF INTERNAL MEDICINE [MEDICINE]	
1	[1.04]	Followers Safehouse	On the bedside table shelf, by the bed on the right, in the second room.
2	[4.19]	Mesquite Mountains Crater	Inside Hell's Motel, below the globe with the hat on it, on the table with the Repair Kit and Radio, right of the entrance.
3	[5.13]	HELIOS One	On the bed with the pillow, in the room with the Holotape password; at the very top floor, accessed via the planks in the room with the holes in the floor.
4	[5.18]	Novac	In the middle of the queen-sized bed, inside Ranger Andy's motel bungalow.
		GROGNAK THE BARBARIAN [MELEE WEAPONS]	
1	[1.10]	Jacobstown	Lying on the floor next to the cooker, inside the eastern bungalow chalet, near the pond.
2	[3.11]	Cannibal Johnson's Cave	On the sleeping mattress near the ham radio, close to the cave campfire.
3	[5.27]	Hidden Supply Cave	Resting on one of the large metal crates, inside the cave.
4	[6.20]	Cottonwood Cove	Inside the Headquarters building, upper floor, on the shelf of the bedside table.

#	ZONE #	CLOSEST LOCATION	DESCRIPTION
			DEAN'S ELECTRONICS [REPAIR]
1	[3.01]	Nellis Air Force Base	Inside Loyal's workshop shed, on the long metal counter next to the ruined terminal.
2	[4.08]	Sloan	Inside the barracks, on the shelf between the Dino Toy and Radio, above the corner bed.
3	[6.03]	Southern Nevada Wind Farm	Inside the shack, on the table with the clipboard and Scrap Metal.
4	[6.04]	Abandoned BoS Bunker	On the metal sill, opposite the Reloading Bench, inside the area with the office area.
			BIG BOOK OF SCIENCE [SCIENCE]
1	[1.13]	Brewer's Beer Bootlegging	In the basement of the shack, on the table with the vial experiment, opposite the still.
2	[2.35]	REPCONN Headquarters	Inside the headquarters, on a shelf inside the Gift Shop storeroom, near the Rocket Souvenirs.
3	[4.30]	Nipton	On the mayor's desk, top floor of the Town Hall, next to the Programmer's Digest magazine.
4	[6.02]	Camp Forlorn Hope	Inside Major Polatli's tent, in the far right corner, on a desk.
			CHINESE ARMY: SPEC. OPS. TRAINING MANUAL [SNEAK]
1	[2.20]	NCR Sharecropper Farms	On some papers, by the corner desk inside the ranch house near the four fertilizer hoppers, northeast corner.
2	[2.24]	Vault 3	On the low bookcase, in the living quarters, inside the executive dorm.
3	[4.05]	Goodsprings	Under a book in the low bookcase, inside the ranch house just east of the schoolhouse.
4	[6.16]	Camp Searchlight	East chapel, inside the Gecko-filled basement, on the stone floor at the foot of the metal shelves.
			LYING, CONGRESSIONAL STYLE [SPEECH]
1	[1.01]	Brooks Tumbleweed Ranch	On an open locker shelf, in the upstairs room with the chessboard, inside the shack.
2	[2C.04]	Cerulean Robotics	On the floor among the office desks, inside the building.
3	[5.15]	NCR Correctional Facility	In the Administration Building, on the desk in the darkened room opposite Eddie's room.
4	[6.09]	Lucky Jim Mine	Inside the shack, on a metal shelf below the Varmint Rifle, right of the two empty fridges.
			WASTELAND SURVIVAL GUIDE [SURVIVAL]
1	[3.25]	Scavenger Platform	Among the books under the fallen metal bookshelf, on the northern platform section.
2	[4.14]	Lone Wolf Radio	Inside the radio trailer, near the Scrap Electronics and mattress.
3	[4.21]	Mesquite Mountains Camp Site	Inside the western tent, behind the rolled-up bedding.
4	[6.25]	Matthews Animal Husbandry Farm	Top balcony of the northern barn, near the barrel crate.
			PUGILISM ILLUSTRATED [UNARMED]
1	[2D.04]	The Tops Casino	On a small table near the pool tables, in the Presidential Suite.
2	[3.17]	Fisherman's Pride Shack	On the bedside table near the lamp and mattress, inside the shack.
3	[4.22]	Nipton Road Reststop	On one of the wooden bookcase shelves (close to the cash register), inside the store marked "Lester."
4	[5.05]	Vault 11	Inside the living quarters, in female dorm #1, by the fallen dresser.
TOTAL	**51**		

APPENDIX X: SKILL MAGAZINES

Needing a temporary boost to a skill? Then some required reading is needed, in order to find your required reading.

#	ZONE #	CLOSEST LOCATION	DESCRIPTION
			SALESMAN WEEKLY [BARTER SKILL]
1	[2.19]	Camp McCarran	Inside the small tent, just west of the Mess Hall tent, in the Tent City parking lot.
2	[2.22]	Aerotech Office Park	On the reception desk on top of the date planner, inside Aerotech Suite 300.
3	[2.32]	Grub n' Gulp Rest Stop	On one of the picnic tables, just to the side (north) of the shack.
4	[2A.01]	Casa Madrid Apartments	Underneath the copy of Locksmith's Reader, on the lobby table, left as you walk in.
5	[2A.02]	Westside Co-op	Inside the co-op, on the corner of the counter near Etienne.
6	[2D.01]	Gomorrah	In the Gomorrah Suites area, in Nero's suite, on the mezzanine area, top of the corner bookcase.
7	[2D.04]	The Tops Casino	On the 13th floor, room 1301 (first door on your left), on the dresser by the bed.
8	[2D.04]	The Tops Casino	On the 13th floor, Benny's room, on top of the low bookcase to the right of Benny's bed.
9	[3.08]	Bitter Springs	On the straw mattress bedding in the northeast shack, in the refugee camp.
10	[3.08]	Bitter Springs	Inside the small, eastern tent (Gille's tent), on a table.
11	[4.05]	Goodsprings	On the bottom shelf of the bookcase, on the left side of the General Store interior.
12	[4.05]	Goodsprings	On a wooden crate, on top of a copy of Meeting People, in Trudy's office, inside the Prospector Saloon.
13	[4.05]	Goodsprings	On the floor below the ransacked wooden shelves, inside the schoolhouse.
14	[4.17]	Primm	On a corner table, in the (partially ruined) lounge area between the bar and the bank of the Vikki & Vance Casino.
15	[4.30]	Nipton	On the corner of the counter in the ransacked General Store, where Boxcars resides.
16	[5.30]	Broc Flower Cave	On the ground, near some empty Whiskey Bottles, in the entrance tunnel.
			TRUE POLICE STORIES [CRITICAL CHANCE]
1	[1.17]	Poseidon Gas Station	Next to the duct tape, inside the police car parked beneath the garage roof.
2	[2.09]	Crimson Caravan Company	On the floor inside the first restroom stall, in the Main Office building.
3	[2.29]	The Basincreek Building	On the small corner table inside the entrance foyer.
4	[2.30]	Allied Technologies Offices	On the small corner table inside the entrance foyer.
5	[2.S04]	Ruined Building with Locked Cache	Inside the locked storage room, part of the cache inside the Ruined Building east of the Mole Rat Ranch [2.11].
6	[2D.01]	Gomorrah	In the Gomorrah Suites area, on the small table by the one of the round beds, upper floor of Clanden's suite.
7	[2D.02]	Lucky 38 Casino	On one of the small tables in the cocktail lounge, on the middle tiered section.
8	[2D.04]	The Tops Casino	On the small bedside table, in the bedroom of the Presidential Suite.
9	[3.12]	Vault 34	In the reactor level, inside the ruins of the security room, on the rubble near the Doctor's Bag.
10	[3.32]	Boulder City	Inside Boulder City Ruins, on the upper floor bookcase of the blown-out store building, across from Great Khans.
11	[4.18]	California Sunset Drive-in	On the picnic table in the playground, south of the Prospector's Lean-To [4.S19].
			FUTURE WEAPONS TODAY [ENERGY WEAPONS]
1	[1.22]	Whittaker Farmstead	On top of the low bookcase, in the kitchen, inside the farmstead.
2	[1.S22]	Violet and Violetta Trailer Compound	On a metal shelf, upper balcony of the "trailer tower," in the middle of Violet and Violetta's Trailer Compound.
3	[2.14]	Gun Runners	On the small table with the fan on it, in the restrooms, inside the building.
4	[2.19]	Camp McCarran	On a medical shelf tray, inside the large storage tent, in the Tent City parking lot.
5	[2D.02]	Lucky 38 Casino	In the dark corner, left of the television, in the game room of the Presidential Suite.
6	[2D.02]	Lucky 38 Casino	On one of the larger coffee tables in the cocktail lounge, by the windows, with the casino logo on the carpet below.
7	[3.23]	Camp Golf	Inside a small wooden crate, in the corner of the Misfit's tent.
8	[3.23]	Camp Golf	On top of a filing cabinet next to the terminal, at the dead-end hallway, upper floor of the House Resort.
9	[4.30]	Nipton	Inside the smashed cabinet behind the mayor's desk, top floor of the Town Hall.
10	[6.20]	Cottonwood Cove	In front of the middle urinal, inside the gentlemen's restroom building.
			THE PATRIOT'S COOKBOOK [EXPLOSIVES]
1	[1.S04]	Horowitz Farmstead	On the shelf of the bookcase, inside the Sharecroppers' Lament building remains [1.S04].
2	[2.14]	Gun Runners	On the floor of the corner stall, in the restrooms, inside the building.

#	ZONE #	CLOSEST LOCATION	DESCRIPTION
3	[2.26]	New Vegas Steel	On the desk, across from the vending machine, in the office overlooking the smelting chamber.
4	[2.S04]	Ruined Building with Locked Cache	Inside the locked storage room, part of the cache inside the Ruined Building with Locked Cache east of the Mole Rat Ranch [2.11].
5	[2D.01]	Gomorrah	In the Gomorrah Suites area, in Big Sal's suite, on the lower mezzanine area, side table.
6	[3.01]	Nellis Air Force Base	Under the Tæles of Chivalrie, on the book shelf, inside Pete's mural shed.
7	[3.01]	Nellis Air Force Base	On top of the bookshelf between two bunks, inside the L-shaped male barracks.
8	[3.12]	Vault 34	1st floor; by the Lead Pipe and Doctor's Bag, in the barricaded diner.
9	[3.12]	Vault 34	1st floor; inside Dorm Room #1 (Floor B1), in the corner on the small table.
10	[3.23]	Camp Golf	On the footlocker, next to one of the beds in the Misfit's tent.
11	[5.15]	NCR Correctional Facility	Inside Cellblock A, on a bed frame in the cell with the Ammo Boxes, far right corner.
12	[6.08]	Techatticup Mine	Next to the Lad's Life, on the metal shelf, in the locked storage room with the NCR Trooper.

MILSURP REVIEW [GUNS]

#	ZONE #	CLOSEST LOCATION	DESCRIPTION
1	[1.15]	Red Rock Canyon	On the bedroll, inside Regis' tent, near the campfire and four tents, around from the longhouse.
2	[2.19]	Camp McCarran	1st Recon Tent in the parking lot Tent City, under the bunkbed with the Sniper Rifle on it, with a copy of iLa Fantoma!
3	[2.19]	Camp McCarran	On the metal box on the tables, inside the large storage tent, in the Tent City parking lot.
4	[2.19]	Camp McCarran	Concourse building, on a seat cluster in the terminal area with the pool table and storage crates.
5	[2.24]	Vault 3	Recreation Area: Floating at the water's surface near the ceiling, in the western Submerged Storeroom.
6	[2D.01]	Gomorrah	In the Gomorrah Suites area, by the bedside table and round bed, top floor of Cachino's suite.
7	[3.12]	Vault 34	1st floor; inside Dorm Room #2 (Floor B1), in the corner on the small table.
8	[3.12]	Vault 34	Reactor: Security Room, on the table next to the terminal.
9	[3.36]	Ranger Station Delta	In the stone basement, in the pool room, on top of the generator under the table with the Radio and Cigarette Pack on it.
10	[4.17]	Primm	Outdoors, on the roof-less upper floor of the ruined building adjacent to the Mojave Express.
11	[4.30]	Nipton	On the top floor of the General Store where Boxcars is, in the middle of the large rug in the middle of the apartment.

LOCKSMITH'S READER [LOCKPICK]

#	ZONE #	CLOSEST LOCATION	DESCRIPTION
1	[2.19]	Camp McCarran	Concourse, large central pillar, on the floor near the seats and upturned Vending Machine.
2	[2.24]	Vault 3	With two other Magazines, on a metal bedside table in the living quarters, inside the executive dorm.
3	[2.24]	Vault 3	Recreation Area: On the pillow of the bed in South Dorm #1.
4	[2.24]	Vault 3	Recreation Area: Floating at the water's surface near the ceiling, in the eastern Submerged Storeroom.
5	[2.24]	Vault 3	Recreation Area: Floating at the water's surface near the ceiling, in the western Submerged Storeroom.
6	[2.24]	Vault 3	Maintenance Wing: Inside the locked storage room, on the table with the chessboard.
7	[2.S04]	Ruined Building with Locked Cache	On the bookcase near the mined front door of the Ruined Building with Locked Cache, east of the Mole Rat Ranch [2.11].
8	[2A.01]	Casa Madrid Apartments	Next to a copy of Salesman Weekly, on the lobby table, left as you walk in.
9	[2D.01]	Gomorrah	In the Gomorrah Suites area, on the table with the Mentats, on the upper mezzanine balcony of Nero's suite.
10	[2D.04]	The Tops Casino	On the 13th Floor, Benny's room, on the metal drill table, in the room with Yes Man.
11	[3.23]	Camp Golf	On the floor next to the Tæles of Chivalrie, first top-floor bedroom accessed via the right hallway, right wall.
12	[3.33]	Hoover Dam	Power Plant 01: On the upper north balcony desk.

TODAY'S PHYSICAN [MEDICINE]

#	ZONE #	CLOSEST LOCATION	DESCRIPTION
1	[1.07]	Charleston Cave	With two other Magazines, on a low shelf, inside the one-man vault with other items.
2	[1.14]	Red Rock Drug Lab	On the picnic table near the Programmer's Digest, inside the "cooking" trailer.
3	[1.21]	Vault 19	First floor, in the ruined clinic, on the red table with the wrecked monitor.
4	[2.10]	New Vegas Medical Clinic	On the side table near the sofa, in the reception/waiting room.
5	[2.14]	Gun Runners	On the floor of the near stall, in the restrooms, inside the building.
6	[2.19]	Camp McCarran	On a medical shelf tray, inside the large Storage Tent, in the Tent City parking lot.
7	[2.19]	Camp McCarran	On the desk with the terminal, inside the medical tent, east side of the parking lot Tent City.
8	[2.22]	Aerotech Office Park	In the reception room, on the side table next to the sofa to the right, inside Aerotech Suite 300.
9	[2.24]	Vault 3	Recreation Area: Inside the doctor's office, on the table near the terminal and glasses.
10	[2.24]	Vault 3	With two other Magazines, on a metal bedside table in the Living Quarters, inside the executive dorm.
11	[2C.01]	Old Mormon Fort	Next to the terminal, on the desk inside the tower where Julie Farkas has her office.
12	[2C.02]	Mick & Ralph's	Upper floor, in the middle of the large bed.
13	[2D.02]	Lucky 38 Casino	On the writing desk in the corner of the guest room with the curtained bathroom, in the Presidential Suite.
14	[2D.02]	Lucky 38 Casino	On the coffee table, in the large master bedroom of the Presidential Suite.
15	[3.01]	Nellis Air Force Base	On the side table with the lamp on it, next to the sofa in the Nellis Children's Barracks.
16	[3.24]	Mountain Shadows Campground	On the picnic table near the small trailer and rusting pickup truck.
17	[4.05]	Goodsprings	In Doc Mitchell's house, across from the bed you woke up on, near the gurney on the typewriter table with the glasses.
18	[4.12]	Jean Sky Diving	Northeast, up the road, and inside the small trailer at Powder Ganger Junction [4.S15].
19	[5.30]	Broc Flower Cave	On the table near the Radiation Suit, in the Prospector's hideout.

TÆLES OF CHIVALRIE [MELEE WEAPONS]

#	ZONE #	CLOSEST LOCATION	DESCRIPTION
1	[2.26]	New Vegas Steel	In one of two plastic bins by the smaller desk, in the office overlooking the smelting chamber.
2	[2.29]	The Basincreek Building	In the rubble-strewn, "help me!" locked office, on a low bookcase behind the desk.
3	[2.30]	Allied Technologies Offices	On one of the low bookcases, in the office and break room.
4	[2C.02]	Mick & Ralph's	On the upper floor, on the table in the middle of the room, by the galley kitchen.
5	[2D.04]	The Tops Casino	On a small table on the mezzanine balcony overlooking the main gambling hall.
6	[2D.04]	The Tops Casino	Presidential Suite: In the kitchen, on the long wooden sideboard, near the coffee maker.
7	[3.01]	Nellis Air Force Base	On top of the Patriot's Cookbook, on the book shelf, inside Pete's mural shed.
8	[3.23]	Camp Golf	On the floor next to the Locksmith's Reader, first top-floor bedroom accessed via the right hallway, right wall.
9	[5.15]	NCR Correctional Facility	On a low shelf on the wall of low bookcases, against the visitor center wall.

FIXIN' THINGS [REPAIR]

#	ZONE #	CLOSEST LOCATION	DESCRIPTION
1	[1.07]	Charleston Cave	With two other Magazines, on a low shelf, inside the one-man vault with other items.
2	[1.10]	Jacobstown	Inside Jacobstown Lodge, in the (Upper) Connecting Corridor Lounge #3, on the table with the Programmer's Digest.
3	[2.10]	New Vegas Medical Clinic	On the side table near the sofa, in the reception/waiting room.
4	[2.19]	Camp McCarran	In the small tent, on a footlocker one of two, center west tent in the parking lot Tent City.
5	[2.19]	Camp McCarran	In the small tent, on a footlocker two of two, center west tent in the parking lot Tent City.
6	[2.21]	East Pump Station	Inside the smaller east cistern, on a small metal table near the trash can.
7	[2.24]	Vault 3	Recreation Area: Inside the locked filing room, on a shelf.
8	[2.24]	Vault 3	Recreation Area: Floating at the water's surface near the ceiling, in the western Submerged Storeroom.
9	[2.24]	Vault 3	Maintenance Wing: Inside the locked storage room, on a metal shelf.
10	[2.26]	New Vegas Steel	In one of two plastic bins (with a Programmer's Digest) by the smaller desk, in the office overlooking the smelting chamber.
11	[2E.01]	Zapp's Neon Signs	On the side table with a copy of iLa Fantoma!, next to the sofa in the booby-trapped reception foyer.
12	[3.01]	Nellis Air Force Base	In a pile with a Boxing Times and Programmer's Digest, on the teacher's desk inside the schoolhouse.
13	[3.01]	Nellis Air Force Base	Inside the workshop, on the long metal table next to some Wonderglue.

#	ZONE #	CLOSEST LOCATION	DESCRIPTION
14	[3.08]	Bitter Springs	Inside the large north tent, on the table in front of the filing cabinets.
15	[3.09]	Ranger Station Bravo	Inside the container truck with the ammo boxes.
16	[3.12]	Vault 34	1st Floor Interior: On the upper mezzanine bridge, near a skeleton and tin cans, by the furniture defenses.
17	[3.12]	Vault 34	1st Floor Interior: Floor B1, in the Operations Room with the Ghouls, near the Submachine Gun and First Aid Box.
18	[3.12]	Vault 34	Reactor: On the computer bank wall, near the terminal that accesses the Reactor room.
19	[3.23]	Camp Golf	Inside House Resort, left upper corridor, on a dresser inside (Upper) Left Corridor Bedroom #1.
20	[3.23]	Camp Golf	Inside House Resort, in the (Upper) Connecting Corridor Lounge #2, on the table with the Programmer's Digest.
21	[3.33]	Hoover Dam	Hoover Dam Offices: on the ground at the corner of the corridor, just outside Colonel Moore's office, by the Scrap Metal and lamp.
22	[4.05]	Goodsprings	Prospector's Saloon; on the sideboard under the Dean Domino poster, in the pool room lounge, left wall.
23	[4.05]	Goodsprings	On a broken sink, in the ensuite bathroom of the ranch house southeast of Doc Mitchell's house.
24	[4.17]	Primm	Inside the Mojave Express building, on the bedside table, next to the Programmer's Digest magazine.
25	[4.17]	Primm	On a side table next to the sofa, in the (partially ruined) lounge area between the bar and the bank of the Vikki & Vance Casino.
26	[4.S21]	Mesquite Mountains Lean-To	On the motorcycle in front of the Mesquite Mountains Lean-To, close to the Mesquite Mountains Crater [4.19].
27	[5.13]	HELIOS One	Power Plant (Interior): Halfway down the southwest stairwell, on a metal table with a wrench and toolbox.

PROGRAMMER'S DIGEST [SCIENCE]

#	ZONE #	CLOSEST LOCATION	DESCRIPTION
1	[1.09]	Vault 22	Between two Pre-War Books, by the explorer's bedding, in the Entrance Hall near the vault "cog" door.
2	[1.10]	Jacobstown	Inside Jacobstown Lodge, in the (Upper) Connecting Corridor Lounge #3, on the table with the Fixin' Things.
3	[1.14]	Red Rock Drug Lab	On the picnic table near the Today's Physician, inside the "cooking" trailer.
4	[1.15]	Red Rock Canyon	Beneath the Lad's Life inside Regis' tent, near the campfire and four tents, around from the longhouse.
6	[1.17]	Poseidon Gas Station	On a metal shelf, upper balcony of the "trailer tower," in the middle of Violet and Violetta's Trailer Compound [1.S22].
5	[1.21]	Vault 19	Inside the blue sector dormitory, under the desk with the terminal on it; dorm #1.
7	[2.17]	Sunset Sarsaparilla Headquarters	On the coffee table by the sofa, near the vending machine, across from Festus, in the reception lobby.
8	[2.26]	New Vegas Steel	In one of two plastic bins (with a Fixin' Things) by the smaller desk, in the office overlooking the smelting chamber.
9	[2C.02]	Mick & Ralph's	On the upper floor, on the desk near the filing cabinet, across from the galley kitchen.
10	[2D.04]	The Tops Casino	On the 13th floor, room 1305 (second door on your right), on the small wooden writing desk.
11	[3.01]	Nellis Air Force Base	In a pile with a Boxing Times and Fixin' Things, on the teacher's desk inside the schoolhouse.
12	[3.23]	Camp Golf	Inside Sergeant McCredie's tent, on the far-right desk, in the corner of the tent.
13	[3.23]	Camp Golf	Inside House Resort, in the (Upper) Connecting Corridor Lounge #2, on the table with the Fixin' Things.
14	[3.33]	Hoover Dam	In the toilet stall, inside guard tower 02, the second one along the dam bridge, moving from west to east.
15	[3.33]	Hoover Dam	Hoover Dam Offices: Inside Colonel Moore's second, smaller office, on the table by the terminal and glasses.
16	[4.05]	Goodsprings	Inside the schoolhouse, on the long, battered side cabinet.
17	[4.05]	Goodsprings	Inside the schoolhouse, between the footlocker and tool box, near the terminal.
18	[4.17]	Primm	Inside the Mojave Express building, on the bedside table, next to the Fixin' Things magazine.
19	[4.30]	Nipton	On the mayor's desk, top floor of the Town Hall, next to the Big Book of Science.
20	[4.S21]	Mesquite Mountains Lean-To	In the pile of ruined books by the motorcycle, close to the Mesquite Mountains Crater [4.19].
21	[5.13]	HELIOS One	Power Plant (Interior): Near the blast door to the west, on a metal table with a ruined terminal.
22	[5.30]	Broc Flower Cave	On the table near the Radiation Suit, in the prospector's hideout.
23	[5.30]	Broc Flower Cave	On the science experiment table at the back of the prospector's hideout.

#	ZONE #	CLOSEST LOCATION	DESCRIPTION

¡LA FANTOMA! [SNEAK]

#	ZONE #	CLOSEST LOCATION	DESCRIPTION
1	[1.17]	Poseidon Gas Station	By the Fixer and Ammo Box inside a small trailer on the outer rim of Violet and Violetta's Trailer Compound [1.S22].
2	[2.06]	H&H Tools Factory	On top of the long bookcase, in the entrance Tool Company foyer area.
3	[2.09]	Crimson Caravan Company	On the desk by the Ham Radio, inside the barracks overlooking the Brahmin Pen, inside the compound.
4	[2.19]	Camp McCarran	First Recon tent in the parking lot Tent City, under the bunk bed with the Sniper Rifle on it, with a copy of Milsurp Review.
5	[2E.01]	Zapp's Neon Signs	On the side table with a copy of Fixin' Things, next to the sofa in the booby-trapped reception foyer.
6	[3.01]	Nellis Air Force Base	Fallen onto the bed from the book shelf, inside Pete's mural shed.
7	[3.16]	Bitter Springs Recreation Area	In the corner side table by the waiting room chairs, inside the shack.
8	[3.32]	Boulder City	Next to the Boxing Times, at the foot of the chute structure, in the old cement works by the train station.
9	[3.32]	Boulder City	Inside Boulder City Ruins, on the ground floor near a mattress, by the stairs of the blown-out store building, across from Great Khans.
10	[4.S17]	The Devil's Carbunkle	Southeast of the Powder Ganger Camp West, below the burned-out car, in the shallow irradiated pond known as The Devil's Carbunkle.

MEETING PEOPLE [SPEECH]

#	ZONE #	CLOSEST LOCATION	DESCRIPTION
1	[2.10]	New Vegas Medical Clinic	On the side table near the sofa to the left of the entrance door.
2	[2.17]	Sunset Sarsaparilla Headquarters	On the picnic table, just outside the building, on the western side, accessible from inside, or over the fallen fence section.
3	[2.19]	Camp McCarran	On the metal shelf with the fan, in the central tent of Tent City, in the parking lot.
4	[2.24]	Vault 3	With two other Magazines, on a metal bedside table in the living quarters, inside the executive dorm.
5	[2A.01]	Casa Madrid Apartments	On a table between the oven and fridge inside the third room from the entrance (clockwise).
6	[2D.01]	Gomorrah	In the Gomorrah Suites area, on the kitchen sideboard near the two cookers, below the mezzanine area of Nero's Suite
7	[2D.04]	The Tops Casino	Presidential Suite: In the large entrance lounge with the pool tables, on the small side table by the sofa, to the right of the entrance.
8	[3.23]	Camp Golf	House Resort: On the tiled floor by the bathtub, in the third left bedroom, accessed via the upper left corridor.
9	[4.05]	Goodsprings	On the floor below the broken metal shelves, inside the long trailer north of the Prospector Saloon.
10	[4.05]	Goodsprings	On a wooden crate, below a copy of Salesman Weekly, in Trudy's office, inside the Prospector Saloon.
11	[4.05]	Goodsprings	On the floor of the schoolhouse by the upturned school desk, near the long battered side cabinet.
12	[6.16]	Camp Searchlight	On the corner dresser by the bed, inside the ranch house where Private Edwards resides.

LAD'S LIFE [SURVIVAL]

#	ZONE #	CLOSEST LOCATION	DESCRIPTION
1	[1.07]	Charleston Cave	With two other Magazines, on a low shelf, inside the one-man vault with other items.
2	[1.10]	Jacobstown	Inside the lodge, on the bed inside (Upper) Right Corridor Bedroom #4, with the shelf fallen onto the bed.
3	[1.15]	Red Rock Canyon	On top of the Programmer's Digest, inside Regis' tent, near the Campfire and four tents, around from the longhouse.
4	[2.19]	Camp McCarran	In a small crate, inside the tent west of the mess hall, north end of Tent City.
5	[2.19]	Camp McCarran	On the desk with the terminal, inside the medical tent, east side of the parking lot Tent City.
6	[2.19]	Camp McCarran	On the food table (one of two Magazines), inside the mess hall, northeast tent in Tent City, in the parking lot.
7	[2.19]	Camp McCarran	On the food table (two of two Magazines), inside the mess hall, northeast tent in Tent City, in the parking lot.
8	[2.19]	Camp McCarran	Concourse building, on the floor near the middle seat cluster in the terminal area with the pool table and storage crates.
9	[2A.02]	Westside Co-op	Inside the Co-op, on the corner of the counter near Etienne.
10	[2D.04]	The Tops Casino	13th floor, inside the comped room (last door on the right wall), on the fireplace mantle. Awarded during Free Quest: Big Winner.
11	[2D.04]	The Tops Casino	On the 13th floor, Benny's room, on top of the fireplace mantle.
12	[2E.01]	Zapp's Neon Signs	By the copy of Boxing Times, on the bottom of the shelf near the Nuka-Cola Quartz, in the upper foreman's office.
13	[3.11]	Cannibal Johnson's Cave	On a rusting metal shelf near the Campfire, against the natural rock wall.
14	[3.18]	Callville Bay	On the bottom shelf of the middle bookcase (left side), inside Captain Dean's Boats & Bait shack.

#	ZONE #	CLOSEST LOCATION	DESCRIPTION
15	[3.23]	Camp Golf	Inside Sergeant McCredie's tent, on the right-side desk with the terminal on it.
16	[3.23]	Camp Golf	Inside the House Resort, on the bed inside (Upper) Right Corridor Bedroom #1 (first door on the left), with the shelf fallen onto the bed.
17	[3.24]	Mountain Shadows Campground	On the single picnic table on the eastern side of the campground overlook, away from the trailer and pick-up.
18	[3.27]	Lake Mead Cave	Underwater, in the main cavern, to the southwest between a group of suitcases, and glowing fungi.
19	[3.30]	Ranger Station Alpha	Inside the Comm Officer's tent, on the table next to the Ham Radio.
20	[3.36]	Ranger Station Delta	Inside the Comm Officer's tent, on the table next to the Ham Radio.
21	[3.S17]	Lake Mead Scenic Overlook	Inside the small trailer parked by the bank of the Lake Mead Scenic Overlook, close to Lake Las Vegas [3.22].
22	[4.05]	Goodsprings	On the top step of the metal stepladder, in the room with the metal shelves, in the ranch house northeast of Doc Mitchell's.
23	[4.05]	Goodsprings	On the floor near the strewn school desk, in front of the ransacked lockers, inside the schoolhouse.
24	[4.15]	Powder Ganger Camp South	In the small wooden crate with ruined books, below the "fight apathy, or don't" graffiti, below the metal ramp.
25	[4.03]	Great Khan Encampment	Other side of the quarry, among the small rocks, near the skeletal remains (and corpse), in Scorpion Gulch; The Dead Survivalist [4.S04].
26	[4.07]	Yangtze Memorial	On the metal floor in front of the toilet, inside the Abandoned Shack to the northwest [4.S05].
27	[4.S19]	Prospector's Lean-To	Under the Prospector's Lean-To, next to the Campfire west of the Primm NCR tents, just north of California Sunset Drive-In [4.18].
28	[5.30]	Broc Flower Cave	In the main caven area, near a pile of half-buried barrels and Ammo Box.
29	[5.S01]	Fetid Pond	Due north of the El Dorado Substation [5.04], on the top of the hill, next to a skeleton in the Fetid Pond.
30	[6.08]	Techatticup Mine	Next to the Patriot's Cookbook, on the metal shelf, in the locked storage room with the NCR Trooper.

BOXING TIMES [UNARMED]

#	ZONE #	CLOSEST LOCATION	DESCRIPTION
1	[1.10]	Jacobstown	Lodge: On the wooden sideboard with the Buffout, inside Connecting Corridor Bedroom #3.
2	[2.06]	H&H Tools Factory	On the large curved reception desk, in the entrance Tool Company foyer area.
3	[2C.05]	King's School of Impersonation	On a kidney-shaped table, near the King's massive bed, near the pool table in the King's Master Bedroom suite.
4	[2D.02]	Lucky 38 Casino	On the casino floor level, upper bar, in the frame behind the Golden Gloves Unique Weapon.
5	[2D.02]	Lucky 38 Casino	On one of the larger coffee tables in the cocktail lounge, by the windows, with the casino logo on the carpet below.
6	[2E.01]	Zapp's Neon Signs	By the copy of Lad's Life, on the bottom of the shelf near the Nuka-Cola Quartz, in the upper foreman's office.
7	[3.01]	Nellis Air Force Base	In a pile with a Fixin' Things and Programmer's Digest, on the teacher's desk inside the Schoolhouse.
8	[3.23]	Camp Golf	House Resort: On the wooden sideboard, inside Connecting Corridor Bedroom #2.
9	[3.32]	Boulder City	Next to the iLa Fantoma!, at the foot of the chute structure, in the old cement works by the train station.
10	[4.05]	Goodsprings	Poseidon Gas Station; on one of the store shelves, behind Ringo.
11	[6.08]	Techatticup Mine	Inside the locked storage room, halfway down the winding tunnel, as the tunnel bends around in a U-shape.
TOTAL	**213**		

APPENDIX XI: SUNSET SARSAPARILLA STAR BOTTLE CAPS

Many have died, or gone mad searching out these fabled blue Caps. Here's where they didn't look.

#	ZONE #	CLOSEST LOCATION	DESCRIPTION
1	[1.01]	Brooks Tumbleweed Ranch	Adjacent to the fire extinguisher, on the floor at the bottom of the shelving, in the ground floor corner storage room with the stove.
2	[1.06]	Horowitz Farmstead	On the left wooden crate, near the sack and two ammo boxes, on the ground, inside the skeletal barn, middle building cluster.
3	[1.08]	Silver Peak Mine	Between two bottles on the table in front and right of the entrance, inside the mine shack.
4	[1.10]	Jacobstown	Northern exterior chalet (adjacent to perimeter stakes): On the gaming table with the cards and empty Whiskey bottles.
5	[1.13]	Brewer's Beer Bootlegging	On top of the small bookcase with other caps and a key, just left of the door to the cellar.
6	[1.20]	Bonnie Springs	In the small wooden crate, one of two Star Caps, on the earth mound, south porch on the corner of the second building away from the Campfire.
7	[1.20]	Bonnie Springs	In the small wooden crate, two of two Star Caps, on the earth mound, south porch on the corner of the second building away from the Campfire.
8	[1.21]	Vault 19	Living Quarters, Blue Sector: Inside the second dorm on the desk with the terminal and chessboard.
9	[2.09]	Crimson Caravan Company	Main Office: On top of the Ham Radio amplifier, on the corner desk, right of the desk with the terminal, on the opposite wall to Alice McLafferty's desk.
10	[2.14]	Gun Runners	At the bottom of a small bottle crate on the floor by the metal table with the coffee machine on it, opposite the curved reception desk.
11	[2.18]	El Rey Motel	On the long bookcase next to the hat and fan, upper floor rental room (with fairy lights) above the eastern exterior steps.
12	[2.19]	Camp McCarran	In a small crate on one of the many metal shelves, close to a footlocker where Sergeant Contreras stands, in his Supply Shack.
13	[2.20]	NCR Sharecropper Farms	Northeast barracks, by the fertilizer silos, on the table with the bottle, by the larger radio, across from the bunk beds.
14	[2.22]	Aerotech Office Park	Aerotech Suite 300: On the kitchen sideboard counter near the Deviled Eggs, in the far-end kitchen room (last door on the left).
15	[2.24]	Vault 3	Recreation Area: On the metal table with three bottles and terminal, in (Upper) South Dorm #2.
16	[2.26]	New Vegas Steel	On the desk, across from the Vending Machine, near a Patriot's Cookbook Magazine, in the office overlooking the smelting chamber.
17	[2.30]	Allied Technologies Offices	One of two on the concrete cubicle desk with the other scattered Caps, in the filing room with the cabinets, to the right of the entrance.
18	[2.30]	Allied Technologies Offices	Two of two on the concrete cubicle desk with the other scattered Caps, in the filing room with the cabinets, to the right of the entrance.
19	[2.32]	Grub n' Gulp Rest Stop	On the plate, on the picnic table adjacent to (north side of) the shack.
20	[2.34]	Hunter's Farm	In the middle of the cluster of Caps, on the kitchen work surface with the crates and bottles.
21	[2.34]	Hunter's Farm	On the edge of the cluster of Caps, on the kitchen work surface with the crates and bottles.
22	[2.35]	REPCONN Headquarters	Ground floor: On the long cash register counter with the three bottles, in the gift shop.
23	[2.35]	REPCONN Headquarters	Ground floor: On the desk with the (inactive) terminal, next to two bottles, by the filing cabinets, in the Robot Recharge and Security Office.
24	[2.35]	REPCONN Headquarters	REPCONN Office 2nd floor, East Office: On the desk across from the one with the red keycard on it.
25	[2.35]	REPCONN Headquarters	REPCONN Office top floor: Leonard Steeple's Office: On the large wooden executive desk near two bottles and a terminal.
26	[2.35]	REPCONN Headquarters	REPCONN Office top floor: Piers Isley's Office: On the floor at the foot of the corner bookcase with the other scattered Caps and bottles.
27	[2.S05]	Hostetler House	West of the Caravan, inside the Hostetler House, on the small table with the bottle, between the two sofas, in the living room.
28	[2B.01]	The Gray	On the small table with a bottle on it, upper floor by the bed, "9 o'clock room."
29	[2C.04]	Cerulean Robotics	On the dining table next to the bottle, close to three open fridges.
30	[3.02]	Nellis Hangars	In the Mess Hall Hangar, on the closest table to the kitchens, left side (as you're looking into the hangar), with other Caps and a bottle. Adjacent to second Cap.
31	[3.02]	Nellis Hangars	In the Mess Hall Hangar, on the second closest table to the kitchens, left side (as you're looking into the hangar), with other Caps and a bottle. Adjacent to first Cap.
32	[3.04]	Fields' Shack	Next to the two bottles inside the open fridge, by the oven, on the right as you walk in.
33	[3.13]	Gypsum Train Yard	Inside the office building: Single Cap on the corner desk with the burned-out terminal, back room with the egg clutches.
34	[3.14]	Cap Counterfeiting Shack	One of three: On the table nearest the Vending Machines, right next to the lantern, near the Nuka-Cola and Sarsaparilla Caps and bottles.

#	ZONE #	CLOSEST LOCATION	DESCRIPTION
35	[3.14]	Cap Counterfeiting Shack	Two of three: On the table nearest the Vending Machines, right next to the lantern, near the Nuka-Cola and Sarsaparilla Caps and bottles.
36	[3.14]	Cap Counterfeiting Shack	Three of three: On the corner of the table nearest the Vending Machines, right next to the lantern, near the Nuka-Cola and Sarsaparilla Caps and bottles.
37	[3.16]	Bitter Springs Recreation Area	On the sideboard with the bottles, one of two near the Ham Radio and coffee maker, below the Poseidon Energy poster, right of the dead tree.
38	[3.16]	Bitter Springs Recreation Area	On the sideboard with the bottles, two of two near the Ham Radio and coffee maker, below the Poseidon Energy poster, right of the dead tree.
39	[3.17]	Fisherman's Pride Shack	With other scattered Caps on the table with the Toaster and Sailsbury Steak, left of the fridge.
40	[3.18]	Callville Bay	Captain Dean's Boat and Bait Shack: Near the three standing bottles on the smashed-up counter, fifth from the left wall.
41	[3.18]	Callville Bay	Captain Dean's Boat and Bait Shack: In the far-right corner, on the desk with the cash register, near the First Aid Box on the wall.
42	[3.20]	Guardian Peak	On the upturned crate, near the plate and empty whiskey bottle, by the Radio, close to the cave mouth.
43	[3.23]	Camp Golf	House Resort: (Upper) Right Corridor Bedroom #1, on the dresser with the bottles and Caps, one of three.
44	[3.23]	Camp Golf	House Resort: (Upper) Right Corridor Bedroom #1, on the dresser with the bottles and Caps, two of three.
45	[3.23]	Camp Golf	House Resort: (Upper) Right Corridor Bedroom #1, on the dresser with the bottles and Caps, three of three.
46	[3.24]	Mountain Shadows Campground	On the red picnic table with the bottle and plates, in the main camp area, next to the Campfire.
47	[3.25]	Scavenger Platform	On a metal shelf near another Cap, adjacent to the Ammo Box, above the Radio, northeast floating shack.
48	[3.32]	Boulder City	Big Horn Saloon: On the large, round table with the chessboard on it, in front and left as you walk in.
49	[3.S18]	Sunken Sarsaparilla Supplies	Warning! Don't disturb the debris! Across Lake Mead, on the southwest side. One of three underwater at the back end of the container.
50	[3.S18]	Sunken Sarsaparilla Supplies	Warning! Don't disturb the debris! Across Lake Mead, on the southwest side. Two of three underwater at the back end of the container.
51	[3.S18]	Sunken Sarsaparilla Supplies	Warning! Don't disturb the debris! Across Lake Mead, on the southwest side. Three of three underwater at the back end of the container.
52	[4.05]	Goodsprings	On the game table with the chessboard and bottles, in the master bedroom, in the ranch house northeast of Doc Mitchell's.
53	[4.05]	Goodsprings	Ranch house east of the schoolhouse: On the kitchen sideboard bar, near the two bottles and toaster, right next to an exit door.
54	[4.08]	Sloan	On the round table with the lantern and bottle, near the Vending Machine, in Jas Wilkins' Mess Hall.
55	[4.10]	The Devil's Gullet	Bottom of the Gullet, in the small wooden crate with two bottles, next to the skull and rusty Ammo Box.
56	[4.12]	Jean Sky Diving	Inside the shack, on the desk next to the Ham Radio, by the bottle and burned-out terminal.
57	[4.14]	Lone Wolf Radio	With the other scattered Caps, near the footlocker and mattress, inside the trailer.
58	[4.17]	Primm	Southeast ranch house on the street south of Mojave Express: On top of the bookcase with the radio on it, in the living room of the shack.
59	[4.17]	Primm	Bison Steve Hotel: On the side table with the bottle, by the sofa, in the large lobby room with the rug, same side as the gift shop.
60	[4.18]	California Sunset Drive-in	On the slab of concrete, by the ruined north concrete hut, right of the trash can, between two scattered bottles.
61	[4.18]	California Sunset Drive-in	Next to the fourth bottle (looking left to right), on the slab of concrete, by the ruined north concrete hut, right of the trash can.
62	[4.19]	Mesquite Mountains Crater	On the formica table next to the bottle, in the kitchen, inside Hell's Motel.
63	[4.20]	The Prospector's Den	In the den building, first room on the right, on the chessboard, resting on the sideboard bar with the radio on it, near the bed.
64	[4.21]	Mesquite Mountains Camp Site	On top of the metal box, inside the northwest tent near the sleeping mattress.
65	[4.22]	Nipton Road Reststop	On the cash register counter, with three other Caps.
66	[4.23]	Nevada Highway Patrol Station	By the body near the green cot in the cell room with the Mantis Nymphs.
67	[4.27]	Mojave Outpost	Barracks; on the long section of the bar counter as you walk in, by a bottle.
68	[4.30]	Nipton	Ranch house opposite the "Trading Post" General Store: On top of the ruined bookcase near the chessboard and bottle, in the master bedroom.
69	[4.S21]	Mesquite Mountains Lean-To	Inside the tipped wooden Sunset crate, between the mattress and half-buried Metal Box, near the Mesquite Mountains Crater [4.19].
70	[5.01]	Junction 15 Railway Station	On the corner of the green bench, left of the boarded-up door, on the platform.
71	[5.02]	188 Trading Post	On the wooden bar shelf, by the bottle and lantern, at the end of the blue shack bar.
72	[5.04]	El Dorado Substation	On the trash can, next to the Eat'o'tronic 3000, left corner as you step inside.
73	[5.07]	Black Mountain	Inside Tabitha's store shack, on the bottom shelf, between the two bottle crates, just behind and left of the Super Mutant dummy.
74	[5.14]	Gibson Scrap Yard	Corner of the low metal shelf with the tires and vehicle rims, in the main garage.
75	[5.15]	NCR Correctional Facility	Next to the bottle on the curved desk, in the vistor center.
76	[5.18]	Novac	On the small round table in the corner of the galley kitchen, in the ranch house one building south of No-Bark Noonan's Shack, northwest part of town.
77	[5.18]	Novac	Daisy Whitman's Dino Dee-Lite rental room, top floor above the far steps: On the table with the noodles and broken TV.
78	[5.19]	Emergency Service Railyard	On the mattress on the train platform, with other scattered Caps.
79	[5.19]	Emergency Service Railyard	On the mattress on the train platform, with other scattered Caps.
80	[5.21]	Harper's Shack	On the small table with the fan on it, near the small crate of bottles and a pressure cooker, across from the bunk bed, left room.
81	[5.24]	Highway 95 Viper's Encampment	Next to two other Caps on one of the two makeshift bedding rolls, northwestern lean-to.
82	[5.25]	Wrecked Highwayman	Among the debris and footlocker, in the open trunk of the crashed car.
83	[5.31]	Snyder Prospector Camp	On top of the two ruined books, next to the bedding and sandbags under the lean-to.
84	[5.S19]	Viper Gang Ambush	On the half-bured crate spilling out of the back of the container, east of Nipton, at the Viper Gang Ambush.
85	[6.01]	El Dorado Gas & Service	On the cash register counter, with two other Caps.
86	[6.02]	Camp Forlorn Hope	Mess Hall (south of stream): By the bottle the table with the coffee pot, close to the metal shelves, in front of the entrance (as you walk in).
87	[6.03]	Southern Nevada Wind Farm	On the metal work table with other Caps, near the copy of Dean's Electronics.
88	[6.11]	Cliffside Prospector Camp	On the chessboard with the bottle on it, on top of the damaged wooden crate.
89	[6.12]	Searchlight North Gold Mine	On the wooden crate, by the metal shelfing, across from the mine cart, in the rock alcove, halfway down the right tunnel.
90	[6.13]	Coyote Mines	On the middle table, lower area right of the stairs, just inside the large miner's shack.
91	[6.15]	Raided Farmstead	In the open fridge with the Cap and bottles, near the Ammo Box, inside the long trailer.
92	[6.16]	Camp Searchlight	Fire Station, upper floor, on a dining table with two bottles, in the kitchen area, far end of the corridor.
93	[6.18]	Sniper's Nest	On the long plank of wood next to the mattress, next to the .308 Ammo Box, inside the lean-to.
94	[6.20]	Cottonwood Cove	Inside the ladies restrooms building, on the lowest metal shelf with a bottle, right corner.
95	[6.21]	Bradley's Shack	Behind the sandbags, near the other scattered Caps, by the Ammo Box and mattress, under the wooden canopy.
96	[6.23]	Old Nuclear Test Site	Inside the shack, on the table with the science experiment and two bottles on it.
97	[6.25]	Matthews Animal Husbandry Farm	On a wooden crate with two bottles and a Cap, on the top balcony, in the western of the two ruined barns.
98	[6.29]	Smith Mesa Prospector Camp	On the concrete block, at the back of the rock alcove, behind the lean-to.
99	[6.30]	Blue Paradise Vacation Rentals	Floating above the sideboard near the mattress, with a Teddy Bear, bottles, and other Caps, in the submerged north bungalow.
100	[6.30]	Blue Paradise Vacation Rentals	Among the floating bottles and Caps near the open fridge, in the submerged middle rental bungalow.
	TOTAL	100	

APPENDIX XII: UNIQUE ITEMS

With the exception of one Party Hat, every ultra-rare or unique item has been found and cataloged.

#	NAME	TYPE [AND #]	ZONE #	CLOSEST LOCATION	DESCRIPTION
1	Remnants Power Helmet	Headgear	[1.08]	Silver Peak Mine	Behind the gate, on the upper ledge of the Mine Cavern.
2	Nuka-Cola Victory	Victory [1/8]	[1.10]	Jacobstown	Inside Jacobstown Bungalow #1 (South).
3	Gannon Family Tesla Armor	Armor	[1.11]	Remnants Bunker	Possible reward at the culmination of Side Quest: For Auld Lang Syne.
4	Gannon Family Tesla Helmet	Headgear	[1.11]	Remnants Bunker	Possible reward at the culmination of Side Quest: For Auld Lang Syne.
5	Papa Khan's Helmet	Headgear	[1.15]	Red Rock Canyon	Worn by Papa Khan
6	Adventurer's Pack		[1.19]	Nopah Cave	Next to a skeleton inside the southwest cavern.
7	Vance's Lucky Hat	Headgear	[1.S05]	Wins Hideout	Worn by Sammy Win.
8	Vikki's Bonnet	Headgear	[1.S05]	Wins Hideout	Worn by Pauline Win.
9	Nuka-Cola Quartz	Quartz [1/21]	[1.S22]	Violet and Violetta Trailer Compound	On one of the shelves in the central fortification.
10	Bounty Hunter Duster	Outfit [1/3]	[2.04]	The Thorn	Worn by Red Lucy
11	Nuka-Cola Victory	Victory [2/8]	[2.18]	El Rey Motel	Near the dead guy, inside Upper Floor Room #1.
12	NCR Emergency Radio		[2.19]	Camp McCarran	Usually awarded here; once your Reputation with the NCR has increased.
13	Nuka-Cola Victory	Victory [3/8]	[2.24]	Vault 3	Vault 3 Recreation Area, inside the storage room.
14	Nuka-Cola Quartz	Quartz [2/21]	[2.35]	REPCONN Headquarters	Inside the locked gift shop storeroom.
15	Nuka-Cola Quartz	Quartz [3/21]	[2.35]	REPCONN Headquarters	Inside the locked gift shop storeroom.
16	Nuka-Cola Victory	Victory [4/8]	[2.35]	REPCONN Headquarters	Inside the locked gift shop storeroom.
17	Nuka-Cola Victory	Victory [5/8]	[2.35]	REPCONN Headquarters	Inside the locked gift shop storeroom.
18	Explorer's Gear	Outfit	[2.S06]	Orion Moreno's House	Available from Orion Moreno south of Gun Runners.
19	Recipe: Cook-Cook's Fiend Stew	Recipe [1/3]	[2.S18]	Cook-Cook's Territory	On the metal shelving inside the ruined camp.
20	Schematic: .44 Magnum, Hand Load	Schematic [1/5]	[2B.S04]	Jules of North Vegas Square	After you complete Free Quest: Meeting an Equal.
21	Bounty Hunter Duster	Outfit [2/3]	[2C.01]	Old Mormon Fort	Worn by Beatrix Russell.
22	Followers Lab Coat	Outfit	[2C.01]	Old Mormon Fort	Worn by Julie Farkas
23	Naughty Nightwear	Outfit	[2C.02]	Mick & Ralph's	Found in Mick's hidden cache of weapons and items
24	Viva Las Vegas	Outfit	[2C.05]	King's School of Impersonation	Worn by the King.
25	Caleb McCaffery's Hat	Headgear	[2C.06]	Atomic Wrangler	Worn by Caleb McCaffery
26	Bounty Hunter Duster	Outfit [3/3]	[2C.06]	Atomic Wrangler	Worn by Caleb McCaffery
27	Nuka-Cola Victory	Victory [6/8]	[2C.06]	Atomic Wrangler	Inside Francine's Bedroom, top floor.
28	Van Graff Combat Armor	Armor	[2C.07]	Silver Rush	Rewarded during Side Quest: Birds of a Feather.
29	Destroyed Collar	Headgear	[2C.S18]	Dead Man	Found on a dead man in Freeside, near Mick & Ralph's [2C.02].
30	Nuka-Cola Quartz	Quartz [4/21]	[2D.04]	The Tops Casino	On the kichen shelves, inside The Tops Restaurant.
31	Nuka-Cola Quartz	Quartz [5/21]	[2D.04]	The Tops Casino	On the kichen shelves, inside The Tops Restaurant.
32	Nuka-Cola Quartz	Quartz [6/21]	[2D.04]	The Tops Casino	On the kichen shelves, inside The Tops Restaurant.
33	Nuka-Cola Quartz	Quartz [7/21]	[2D.04]	The Tops Casino	On the kichen shelves, inside The Tops Restaurant.
34	Nuka-Cola Quartz	Quartz [8/21]	[2D.04]	The Tops Casino	On the kichen shelves, inside The Tops Restaurant.
35	Benny's Suit	Outfit	[2D.04]	The Tops Casino	Worn by Benny.
36	Recipe: Brahmin Wellington	Recipe [2/3]	[2D.05]	Ultra-Luxe Casino	On a shelf, in the kitchens where Philippe prepares his food.
37	Ambassador Crocker's Suit	Outfit	[2D.07]	NCR Embassy	Worn by Ambassador Dennis Crocker.
38	Schematics: Billboard	Schematic [2/5]	[2D.08]	Michael Angelo's Workshop	In the north workshop. The Schmatics cannot be used.
39	Codac R9000	Camera	[2D.08]	Michael Angelo's Workshop	Given during Side Quest: Classic Inspiration.
40	Nuka-Cola Quartz	Quartz [9/21]	[2E.01]	Zapp's Neon Signs	Inside the upstairs foreman's office.
41	Nuka-Cola Quartz	Quartz [10/21]	[2E.01]	Zapp's Neon Signs	Inside the upstairs foreman's office.
42	Rebreather	Headgear	[3.02]	Nellis Hangars	Given to you by Loyal, the Boomer.
43	Schematic: Rock-It Launcher	Schematic [3/5]	[3.02]	Nellis Hangars	On the storage shelves in the southwest hangar.
44	Mini-Nuke	[1/11]	[3.02]	Nellis Hangars	In a small crate on the shelf with other ammo, near the Munitions Manager.
45	Mini-Nuke	[4/11]	[3.03]	Nellis Array	Among the large ammo storage, next to the ramp, lower interior floor.
46	Mini-Nuke	[5/11]	[3.03]	Nellis Array	Among the large ammo storage, next to the ramp, lower interior floor.
47	Schematic: Dog Tag Fist	Schematic [4/5]	[3.20]	Guardian Peak	Rewarded by Halford, during Free Quest: Help for Halford.
48	Nuka-Cola Quartz	Quartz [11/21]	[3.23]	Camp Golf	House Resort: Inside the mess hall.
49	Nuka-Cola Quartz	Quartz [12/21]	[3.23]	Camp Golf	House Resort: Inside the mess hall.
50	Nuka-Cola Quartz	Quartz [13/21]	[3.23]	Camp Golf	House Resort: Inside the mess hall.
51	Nuka-Cola Quartz	Quartz [14/21]	[3.23]	Camp Golf	House Resort: Inside the mess hall.
52	Nuka-Cola Quartz	Quartz [15/21]	[3.23]	Camp Golf	House Resort: Inside the mess hall.
53	Caesar's Armor	Armor	[3.28]	The Fort	Worn by Caesar.
54	Nuka-Cola Quartz	Quartz [16/21]	[3.32]	Boulder City	On the shelf, inside the Big Horn Saloon.
55	Nuka-Cola Quartz	Quartz [17/21]	[3.32]	Boulder City	On the shelf, inside the Big Horn Saloon.
56	Nuka-Cola Quartz	Quartz [18/21]	[3.32]	Boulder City	On the shelf, inside the Big Horn Saloon.
57	Jessup's Bandana	Headgear	[3.32]	Boulder City	Worn by Jessup.
58	President Kimball's Suit	Outfit	[3.33]	Hoover Dam	Worn by President Aaron Kimball.
59	Chinese Stealth Armor	Armor	[3.33]	Hoover Dam	In the Hoover Dam Offices area, inside the radioactive barrel storage.
60	General Oliver's Cap	Headgear	[3.33]	Hoover Dam	Worn by General Lee Oliver.
61	General Oliver's Outfit	Outfit	[3.33]	Hoover Dam	Worn by General Lee Oliver.
62	Legate's Helmet	Headgear	[3.34]	Legate's Camp	Worn by Legate Lanius.
63	Acoustic Guitar		[3.S21]	Sunset Sarsaparilla Billboard	Carried by the Lonesome Drifter.
64	Regulator's Duster	Outfit	[3.S21]	Sunset Sarsaparilla Billboard	Worn by the Lonesome Drifter.

#	NAME	TYPE [AND #]	ZONE #	CLOSEST LOCATION	DESCRIPTION
65	Mini-Nuke	[2/11]	[4.04]	Quarry Junction	In the silt pool right next to the Fat Man. Underwater.
66	Mini-Nuke	[3/11]	[4.04]	Quarry Junction	Among the eggs in the Deathclaw Nest.
67	Recipe: Rose's Wasteland Omelet	Recipe [3/3]	[4.08]	Sloan	Reward after completing Free Quest: You Gotta Break Out a Few Eggs.
68	Nuka-Cola Quartz	Quartz [19/21]	[4.27]	Mojave Outpost	On the shelves in Lacey's Bar, in the Outpost Barracks.
69	Nuka-Cola Quartz	Quartz [20/21]	[4.27]	Mojave Outpost	On the shelves in Lacey's Bar, in the Outpost Barracks.
70	Nuka-Cola Quartz	Quartz [21/21]	[4.27]	Mojave Outpost	On the shelves in Lacey's Bar, in the Outpost Barracks.
71	Nuka-Cola Victory	Victory [7/8]	[4.30]	Nipton	Inside the Mayor's Storage Room, top floor of the Town Hall.
72	Mini-Nuke	[6/11]	[5.05]	Vault 11	Living Quarters, inside the locked storage room.
73	Sheet Music Book		[5.07]	Black Mountain	Inside Tabitha's broadcast building.
74	Mini-Nuke	[7/11]	[5.11]	Hidden Valley	Inside the north bunker entrance (by fallen concrete).
75	Mini-Nuke	[8/11]	[5.11]	Hidden Valley	Inside the north bunker entrance (by fallen concrete).
76	Mini-Nuke	[9/11]	[5.11]	Hidden Valley	Inside the south bunker entrance (right side of fallen concrete dead-end)
77	Brotherhood Elder's Robe	Outfit	[5.11]	Hidden Valley	Worn by Elder McNamara
78	Schematic: Powder Charge	Schematic [5/5]	[5.15]	NCR Correctional Facility	Inside the locked prison cell, Cell Block B.
79	Party Hat	Headgear [1/10]	[5.17]	REPCONN Test Site	On a shelf, inside the top floor Research Labs storage room.
80	Party Hat	Headgear [2/10]	[5.17]	REPCONN Test Site	On a shelf, inside the top floor Research Labs storage room.
81	Party Hat	Headgear [3/10]	[5.17]	REPCONN Test Site	On a shelf, inside the top floor Research Labs storage room.
82	Party Hat	Headgear [4/10]	[5.17]	REPCONN Test Site	On a shelf, inside the top floor Research Labs storage room.
83	Party Hat	Headgear [5/10]	[5.17]	REPCONN Test Site	On a shelf, inside the top floor Research Labs storage room.
84	Party Hat	Headgear [6/10]	[5.17]	REPCONN Test Site	On a shelf, inside the top floor Research Labs storage room.
85	Party Hat	Headgear [7/10]	[5.17]	REPCONN Test Site	On a shelf, inside the top floor Research Labs storage room.
86	Party Hat	Headgear [8/10]	[5.17]	REPCONN Test Site	On a shelf, inside the top floor Research Labs storage room.
87	Party Hat	Headgear [9/10]	[5.17]	REPCONN Test Site	On a shelf, inside the top floor Research Labs storage room.
88	Party Hat	Headgear [10/10]	[5.17]	REPCONN Test Site	On a shelf, inside the top floor Research Labs storage room.
89	Space Helmet	Headgear	[5.17]	REPCONN Test Site	Inside the basement (B2) rocket viewing chamber.
90	Space Suit	Outfit	[5.17]	REPCONN Test Site	Inside the basement (B2) rocket viewing chamber.
91	Boone's Beret	Headgear	[5.18]	Novac	Given to you by Craig Boone.
92	Nuka-Cola Victory	Victory [8/8]	[6.06]	Nelson	Inside the northwest Nelson house.
93	Mini-Nuke	[10/11]	[6.16]	Camp Searchlight	On the table with the Holy Frag Grenades, basement of east chapel.
94	Mini-Nuke	[11/11]	[6.16]	Camp Searchlight	On the table with the Holy Frag Grenades, basement of east chapel.
95	Remnants Power Armor	Armor	[6.S16]	Deathclaw Promontory	On the corpse, near the second corpse, surrounded by Deathclaws.
	TOTAL	**95**			

APPENDIX XIII: UNIQUE WEAPONS

Want to know where all the most potent firearms and bludgeoning devices are? Then this is the Appendix for you.

#	NAME	TYPE	ZONE #	CLOSEST LOCATION	DESCRIPTION
1	Displacer Glove: Pushy	Unarmed	[1.03]	Ruby Hill Mine	On the body of a Jackal Gang member inside the Ruby Hill Mine.
2	Oh, Baby!	Melee Weapon	[1.07]	Charleston Cave	Found near a Chewed Stealth Boy in the deepest part of Charleston Cave.
3	Laser Rifle: AER14 Prototype	Energy Weapon	[1.09]	Vault 22	Found inside Vault 22 Common Area, on the blocked stairwell only accessible from the Food Production level.
4	Spiked Knuckles: Love and Hate	Unarmed	[1.20]	Bonnie Springs	Found on the Viper Gang Leader in Bonnie Springs.
5	Alien Blaster	Energy Weapon	[1.S02]	Hovering Anomaly	Found at Hovering Anomaly. Wild Wasteland trait must be taken.
6	Gauss Rifle: YCS/186	Energy Weapon	[1.S02]	Mercenary Camp	Found at the Mercenary Camp. Wild Wasteland trait must NOT be taken.
7	9mm Submachine Gun: Vance's Submachine Gun	Gun	[1.S05]	Wins Hideout	Inside the safe at Wins Hideout.
8	Laser Pistol: Pew Pew	Energy Weapon	[2.17]	Sunset Sarsaparilla Headquarters	Found on the body of Allen Marks, after Side Quest: The Legend of the Star is completed.
9	Bladed Gauntlet: Cram Opener	Unarmed	[2.19]	Camp McCarran	Owned by Little Buster, in Camp McCarran.
10	Cowboy Repeater: La Longue Carabine	Gun	[2.19]	Camp McCarran	Carried by Corporal Sterling, member of the First Recon, Camp McCarran.
11	This Machine	Gun	[2.19]	Camp McCarran	Rewarded by Contreras if you don't turn him in, at the end of Free Quest: Dealing with Contreras.
12	Plasma Rifle: Q-35 Matter Modulator	Energy Weapon	[2.35]	REPCONN Headquarters	Found in a pod casement, in the locked shipping room of the REPCONN Headquarters.
13	9 Iron: Nephi's Golf Driver	Melee Weapon	[2.28]	Samson Rock Crushing Plant	Carried by a Fiend named Driver Nephi, in his territory [2.S22].
14	Euclid's C-Finder	Energy Weapon	[2C.02]	Mick & Ralph's	Carried by Max, in and around Mick & Ralph's, on the Freeside streets [2C.S12].
15	Straight Razor: Figaro	Melee Weapon	[2C.05]	Kings School of Impersonation	Owned by Sergio, in the back of King's School of Impersonation.
16	Boxing Gloves: Golden Gloves	Unarmed	[2D.02]	Lucky 38 Casino	On the upper bar of the casino floor, inside the Lucky 38 Casino.
17	9mm Pistol: Maria	Gun	[2D.04]	The Tops Casino	On Benny, when you kill him.
18	Lead Pipe: The Humble Cudgel	Melee Weapon	[U2.?]	Sealed Sewers	Found near the Prospector corpse inside the Sealed Sewers.
19	Grenade Rifle: Thump-Thump	Explosive	[3.03]	Nellis Array	Lying on the floor, near the Ant Mound; Nellis Array.
20	BB Gun: Abilene Kid LE BB Gun	Gun	[3.04]	Fields' Shack	Found lying on a shelf inside the Fields' Shack.
21	Minigun: CZ57 Avenger	Gun	[3.10]	The Devil's Throat	Inside, at the back of the container trailer, by the dead body, in the Devil's Throat.
22	Marksman Carbine: All-American	Gun	[3.12]	Vault 34	On the floor, on an upturned table in the Armory Cache, Vault 34.
23	Pulse Gun	Energy Weapon	[3.12]	Vault 34	Found in the Armory Cache, Vault 34.
24	Bumper Sword: Blade of the East	Melee Weapon	[3.34]	Legate's Camp	Carried by Legate Lanius, in the Legate's Camp.

#	NAME	TYPE	ZONE #	CLOSEST LOCATION	DESCRIPTION
25	.44 Magnum Revolver: Mysterious Magnum	Gun	[3.S21]	Sunset Sarsaparilla Billboard	Owned by the Lonesome Drifter, Sunset Sarsaparilla Billboard close to the El Dorado Dry Lake.
26	Fat Man	Explosive	[4.04]	Quarry Junction	Near the skeleton by the southern silt pool. NOTE! This weapon may be found on Prospector corpses too, and has a Modification Upgrade.
27	.357 Magnum Revolver: Lucky	Gun	[4.17]	Primm	In the floor safe inside the cashier's area of the Vikki & Vance Casino, in Primm.
28	Combat Knife: Chance's Knife	Melee Weapon	[4.S01]	Chance's Grave	Found in Chance's Grave.
29	Missile Launcher: Annabelle	Explosive	[5.07]	Black Mountain	Carried by the Nightkin Sniper on Black Mountain summit: Black Mountain.
30	Zap Glove: Paladin Toaster	Unarmed	[5.08]	Black Rock Cave	Found near the body of the dead Prospector in Black Rock Cave.
31	Sawed-Off Shotgun: Big Boomer	Gun	[5.14]	Gibson Scrap Yard	Carried by Old Lady Gibson; in Gibson Scrap Yard.
32	That Gun	Gun	[5.18]	Novac	On a shelf in the locked storage room inside the Dino Bite Gift Shop, in Novac.
33	Grenade Machinegun: Mercy	Explosive	[5.22]	Dead Wind Cavern	On the floor of the cavern, near the body of a dead Brotherhood of Steel Paladin, Dead Wind Cavern.
34	Varmint Rifle: Ratslayer	Gun	[5.30]	Broc Flower Cave	Propped up against the desk, inside the Broc Flower Cave.
35	Machete: Liberator	Melee Weapon	[6.06]	Nelson	Carried by Dead Sea, in Nelson.
36	Cleaver: Chopper	Melee Weapon	[6.14]	Wolfhorn Ranch	Found on the stove of the Wolfhorn Ranch.
37	Frag Grenade: Holy Frag Grenade	Explosive	[6.16]	Camp Searchlight	Three available, in the basement of the eastern church, Camp Searchlight. Wild Wasteland trait must be taken.
38	Fire Axe: Knock Knock	Melee Weapon	[6.16]	Camp Searchlight	Found in the restrooms on the upper floor of the Fire Station, in Camp Searchlight.
39	Sniper Rifle: Gobi Campaign Scout Rifle	Gun	[6.18]	Sniper's Nest	In the footlocker of the Sniper's Nest [6.18], overlooking Cottonwood Cove.
40	DogTag Fist: Recompense of the Fallen	Unarmed	[6.20]	Cottonwood Cove	Found in Aurelius' desk, on the upper floor of the main building in Cottonwood Cove.
41	Hunting Shotgun: Dinner Bell	Gun	[6.23]	Old Nuclear Test Site	Inside the shack, at the Old Nuclear Test Site.
42	Tesla Cannon: Tesla-Beaton Prototype	Energy Weapon	[6.24]	Crashed Vertibird	On the ground near the Crashed Vertibird.
	TOTAL	42			

APPENDIX XIV: WILD WASTELAND ODDITIES

The Mojave Wasteland is a strange place, made all the more bizarre if you chose the Wild Wasteland perk. If you want to know what's in store, read on. Otherwise, avert your eyes now!

Hovering Anomaly

Occurrence: As you close in on the area just north of Horowitz Farmstead [1.06], what looked like a Mercenary Camp from a distance turns into an extra-terrestrial landing, complete with spacecraft, and three Aliens! Defeat the Captain to take his Unique Alien Blaster.

What Is It, Boy?

Occurrence: Speak to Rex while you're out in the Mojave Wasteland. At some point, Rex will answer with an "aroo!" You then divine that Little Jimmy may have fallen into a well, the location of which is unlocked on your Pip-Boy's world map.

Granny's Gang

Occurrence: A fearsome gang of old ladies are harassing townspeople and eluding the NCR. You may be randomly assaulted by this gang, especially when exiting the Cerulean Robotics building [2C.04] in Outer Freeside.

We Named the Dog Indiana

Occurrence: A battered fridge appears in the Mojave Wasteland; it looks like it has survived a devastating blast, but the occupant has not; the skeletal remains of an adventure are inside, along with his hat. No snakes, thankfully.

Getting Too Close

Occurrence: During Side Quest: I Put a Spell on You, if you unwittingly divulge to Captain Curtis that you know a mole is using the Control Tower during the night, and then stake it out, he ambushes you there. Right before the ambush occurs, Curtis says "You're getting too close, shamus!"

R.O.U.S.

Occurrence: You may not think they exist, but in certain underground locations, such as the New Vegas Sewers, the Broc Flower Cave, or Vaults with peeling election posters, are rats one-and-a-half to two-times bigger than normal. These are Rodents of Unusual Size.

Owen and Beru

Occurrence: Somewhere in the deserted part of the Mojave Wasteland are two corpses. One looks to be a male human, while the other is female, lying next to each other. They look like they've been charred. Alas, there's no power converter to loot.

Holy Hand Grenades

Occurrence: Somewhere, in a place where two spires once shot forth skyward, is a basement with a box of Holy Hand Grenades to utilize. There is a sign on the box that reads "Holy Hand Grenades. Pull pin, count to five (scratched out)... 3, and throw."

Romanes Eunt Domus

Occurrence: Scrawled on a concrete building in Cottonwood Cove, some upstart has scrawled the graffiti "Romanes Eunt Domus." Obviously, this is improper conjugation of a long-dead language, and whoever was responsible must be crucified.

Crusoe Sucks as an Investigator

Occurrence: During Side Quest: Beyond the Beef, a dead investigator is discovered inside an Ultra-Luxe hotel room. Further investigation of this crime-scene reveals his name to be "Crusoe," with a shock of red hair, sunglasses, and a business suit.

The Future of Law Enforcement

Occurrence: While listening to the Securitrons interact with the visitors to The Strip, you swore you heard one state "your move, creep." Should you frame Heck Gunderson during Side Quest: Beyond the Beef, the arresting Securitron may have no preference over Heck's life; he's still going with him.

Stay Classy, Mr. New Vegas

Occurrence: Mr. New Vegas sometimes introduces his music with: "You know, I tried to measure my charisma on a Vit-o-matic Vigor Tester once. The machine burst into flames." The sweet-talking doesn't end there either. He has a special news sign-off, and some home truths about the Mojave.

The Big One

Occurrence: Close to the Devil's Throat is a large, unexploded bomb known as The Big One. Amid the crackle of your radiation counter, you can open up the bomb, and scavenge some Energy Weapon ammunition, if you can stand the Glowing One and Super Mutant attacks.

Johnny Five-Aces

Occurrence: During Free Quest: Barton the Fink, you're instructed to investigate an overlook south of Goodsprings. There's a dead Prospector up here named Johnny, wearing glasses, with a glass pitcher next to him, and five aces on the table. On the cliff are four balls in a line.

Game Over Man, Game Over!

Occurrence: If you're listening to the NCR Emergency Radio during the final battle for Hoover Dam, among the chatter about positioning snipers and reinforcing positions, you swore you heard some Troopers getting attacked by enemies coming out of the dam walls.

Now take time to read the Credits.